INSURANCE

PRINCIPLES AND PRACTICE

(FOR GRADUATION AND PROFFESSIONAL COURSES)

S. CHAND & COMPANY LTD.
(An ISO 9001 : 2000 Company)
RAM NAGAR, NEW DELHI - 110 055

S. CHAND & COMPANY LTD.
(An ISO 9001 : 2000 Company)
***Head Office*: 7361, RAM NAGAR, NEW DELHI - 110 055**
Phone: 23672080-81-82, 9899107446, 9911310888
Fax: 91-11-23677446
Shop at: schandgroup.com; e-mail: info@schandgroup.com

***Branches*:**

AHMEDABAD	:	1st Floor, Heritage, Near Gujarat Vidhyapeeth, Ashram Road, **Ahmedabad** - 380 014, Ph: 27541965, 27542369, ahmedabad@schandgroup.com
BANGALORE	:	No. 6, Ahuja Chambers, 1st Cross, Kumara Krupa Road, **Bangalore** - 560 001, Ph: 22268048, 22354008, bangalore@schandgroup.com
BHOPAL	:	238-A, M.P. Nagar, Zone 1, **Bhopal** - 462 011, Ph: 4274723. bhopal@schandgroup.com
CHANDIGARH	:	S.C.O. 2419-20, First Floor, Sector - 22-C (Near Aroma Hotel), **Chandigarh** -160 022, Ph: 2725443, 2725446, chandigarh@schandgroup.com
CHENNAI	:	152, Anna Salai, **Chennai** - 600 002, Ph: 28460026, chennai@schandgroup.com
COIMBATORE	:	Plot No. 5, Rajalakshmi Nagar, Peelamedu, **Coimbatore** -641 004, (M) 09444228242, coimbatore@schandgroup.com
CUTTACK	:	1st Floor, Bhartia Tower, Badambadi, **Cuttack** - 753 009, Ph: 2332580; 2332581, cuttack@schandgroup.com
DEHRADUN	:	1st Floor, 20, New Road, Near Dwarka Store, **Dehradun** - 248 001, Ph: 2740889, 2740861, dehradun@schandgroup.com
GUWAHATI	:	Pan Bazar, **Guwahati** - 781 001, Ph: 2738811, 2735640 guwahati@schandgroup.com
HYDERABAD	:	Sultan Bazar, **Hyderabad** - 500 195, Ph: 24651135, 24744815, hyderabad@schandgroup.com
JAIPUR	:	A-14, Janta Store Shopping Complex, University Marg, Bapu Nagar, **Jaipur** - 302 015, Ph: 2719126, jaipur@schandgroup.com
JALANDHAR	:	Mai Hiran Gate, **Jalandhar** - 144 008, Ph: 2401630, 5000630, jalandhar@schandgroup.com
JAMMU	:	67/B, B-Block, Gandhi Nagar, **Jammu** - 180 004, (M) 09878651464
KOCHI	:	Kachapilly Square, Mullassery Canal Road, Ernakulam, **Kochi** - 682 011, Ph: 2378207, cochin@schandgroup.com
KOLKATA	:	285/J, Bipin Bihari Ganguli Street, **Kolkata** - 700 012, Ph: 22367459, 22373914, kolkata@schandgroup.com
LUCKNOW	:	Mahabeer Market, 25 Gwynne Road, Aminabad, **Lucknow** - 226 018, Ph: 2626801, 2284815, lucknow@schandgroup.com
MUMBAI	:	Blackie House, 103/5, Walchand Hirachand Marg, Opp. G.P.O., **Mumbai** - 400 001, Ph: 22690881, 22610885, mumbai@schandgroup.com
NAGPUR	:	Karnal Bag, Model Mill Chowk, Umrer Road, **Nagpur** - 440 032, Ph: 2723901, 2777666 nagpur@schandgroup.com
PATNA	:	104, Citicentre Ashok, Govind Mitra Road, **Patna** - 800 004, Ph: 2300489, 2302100, patna@schandgroup.com
PUNE	:	291/1, Ganesh Gayatri Complex, 1st Floor, Somwarpeth, Near Jain Mandir, **Pune** - 411 011, Ph: 64017298, pune@schandgroup.com
RAIPUR	:	Kailash Residency, Plot No. 4B, Bottle House Road, Shankar Nagar, **Raipur** - 492 007, Ph: 09981200834, raipur@schandgroup.com
RANCHI	:	Flat No. 104, Sri Draupadi Smriti Apartments, East of Jaipal Singh Stadium, Neel Ratan Street, Upper Bazar, **Ranchi** - 834 001, Ph: 2208761, ranchi@schandgroup.com
VISAKHAPATNAM	:	Plot No. 7, 1st Floor, Allipuram Extension, Opp. Radhakrishna Towers, Seethammadhara North Extn., **Visakhapatnam** - 530 013, (M) 09347580841, visakhapatnam@schandgroup.com

First Edition 1979
Subsequent Editions and Reprints 1982, 84, 86, 89, 93, 95, 97, 98, 99, 2001, 2002, 2003, 2004, 2005, 2006, 2007 (Twice), 2008
Thoroughly Revised Sixteenth Edition 2009

ISBN : 81-219-1021-8 **Code :** 07A 023

PRINTED IN INDIA
By Rajendra Ravindra Printers Pvt. Ltd., 7361, Ram Nagar, New Delhi -110 055 and published by S. Chand & Company Ltd., 7361, Ram Nagar, New Delhi -110 055.

To
My Respected Parents
Who were Loving me Lot

PREFACE TO THE SIXTEENTH EDITION

Insurance in India has taken galloping stage. It has shown maximum growth rate of 56.99 per cent in 2006 in world after Liechtenstein (61.58%). Recently De-tariffing since January 1, 2007 have facilitated the insurer to serve the society with quality and lowest cost in the competitive environment. Now insurance is not limited only to life and property risks; it has expanded its scope to insure all the uninsurable risks. It has innovated avenues to manage all the risks attached to business industry, agriculture, transport, banking and credit, health, catastrophe, liability, guarantee and surety bancassurance and corporate governance. It is expected that in future political parties would go for insurance of the risks involved in election. However, the present state of insurance has tried to insurance all the risks related to family, society, business, industry and other economic activities. Therefore, the present edition of the book has included all sorts of innovative insurance products.

Part six of the book has discussed the prospects of Insurance companies under Prospects of Insurance, Privatisation of Insurance Industry, Insurance Innovation, Risk Management, Health Insurance, Catastrophe Insurance, Liability Insurance, Credit Insurance and Surety, Corporate Governance, Bancassurance and International Insurance Scene. Part seven has included all the latest provisions of insurance legislation beginning from totally amended Insurance Act 1993 to IRDA (Protection of Policyholder Interest) Regulation 2002. The IRDA may conduct inspections like RBI does to banks on routine basis with terms of references to protect policyholders interests. We are highly thankful to IRDA officials, editors and friends who helped me lot for updating this book.

The book is comprehensively rewritten to educate the students of the latest development of insurance in India and abroad. It projects the prospects of insurance and also deals with the possibilities of managing the insurance sector. Though the book is written primarily for the students of graduate and post-graduate, it is becoming popular amongst the insurance personnel who are required to know the general knowledge of insurance as well as develop their specialities in a particular field of insurance. Progress of private insurers are given in the chapter of privatisation.

We are thankful to our family members who have been giving us sufficient time for rewriting the book. We hope that this book will be a guiding star for all the insurance minded people. We shall feel obliged if comments and suggestions are given for the improvements of the book.

4, Brahmanand Ext. I
Durgakund
Varanasi- 221005
Phone 0542 - 2313291
Ram Navami, Sambat- 2066

M.N. MISHRA
S. B. MISHRA

PREFACE TO THE FIRST EDITION

Insurance is as old as the civilization. It was present in the form of mutual help. Joint Stock Companies and Corporations are the recent forms of the insurance. The 'Yogakshena' has been the oldest term of insurance used in the Rigveda for some kind of insurance. Manu had emphasised that a special charge be made on goods carried from one town to another to ensure their safe carriage. Manusmriti says—

क्रयाविक्रयमध्वानं भक्तं च सपरिव्यम्।
योगक्षेमं च संप्रेक्ष्य वणिजों दापयेत्करान्।।

(Chap.7)

"The Trader should be made to pay taxes or duty taking into account the price of purchase, the price of sale, the length of the journey, incidental expenses and yogakshena *i.e.*, Risk and Safety". Ancient India was a prominent maritime power. Today, the nationalisation of life insurance business and general insurance business is expected to contribute maximum for the well-being and safety of the people by providing insurance services in every walk of life. The principles and practices of insurance have been changing from time to time according to needs.

The present book 'Insurance—Principles and Practices' has been written taking into consideration of the prevailing principles and practices in the different fields of insurance in India. The book has been written according to the Syllabi prescribed for the B.Com. and Honours examinations of Indian universities and of Federation of Insurance Institutes. Various authoritative works have been consulted so that all the required subject matter could be given in a concised and comprehensive form. The book has been divided into Five Parts. Introduction, Life, Marine, Fire and Miscellaneous. Each part includes all the required chapters on the subject in a brief and illustrative form. It is expected that the book will be interesting for the general readers as well.

I am highly obliged to the officials of the LIC and the GIC who supplied all the information and statistics required by me.

I shall be grateful to receive comments and criticism of this book for the further improvement of the book.

M.N. MISHRA

CONTENTS

PART ONE
INTRODUCTION

PART TWO
LIFE INSURANCE

PART THREE
MARINE INSURANCE

PART FOUR
FIRE – INSURANCE

PART FIVE
MISCELLANEOUS INSURANCE

PART SIX
PROSPECTS OF INSURANCE COMPANIES

PART SEVEN
INSURANCE LEGISLATION

PART ONE
INTRODUCTION

1

DEFINITION AND NATURE OF INSURANCE

Insurance is defined as a co-operative device to spread the loss caused by a particular risk over a number of persons who are exposed to it and who agree to ensure themselves against that risk. Risk is uncertainty of a financial loss. It should not be confused with the chance of loss which is the probable number of losses out of a given number of exposures. It should not be confused with peril which is defined as the cause of loss or with hazard which is a condition that may increase the chance of loss. Finally, risk must not be confused with loss itself which is the unintentional decline in or disappearance of value arising from a contingency. Wherever there is uncertainty with respect to a probable loss there is risk.

Every risk involves the loss of one or other kind. The function of insurance is to spread the loss over a large number of persons who are agreed to co-operate each other at the time of loss. The risk cannot be averted but loss occurring due to a certain risk can be distributed amongst the agreed persons. They are agreed to share the loss because the chances of loss, *i.e.,* the time, amount, to a person are not known. Anybody of them may suffer loss to a given risk, so, the rest of the persons who are agreed will share the loss. The larger the number of such persons, the easier the process of distribution of loss. In fact; the loss is shared by them by payment of premium which is calculated on the probability of loss. In olden time, the contribution by the persons was made at the time of loss. The insurance is also defined as a social device to accumulate funds to meet the uncertain losses arising through a certain risk to a person insured against the risk.

FUNCTIONS OF INSURANCE

The functions of insurance can be studied into two parts (*i*) Primary Functions, and (*ii*) Secondary Functions.

Primary Functions

(*i*) *Insurance provides certainty.* Insurance provides certainty of payment at the uncertainty of loss. The uncertainty of loss can be reduced by better planning and administration. But, the insurance relieves the person from such difficult task. Moreover, if the subject matters are not adequate, the self-provision may prove costlier. There are different types of uncertainty in a risk. The risk will occur or not, when will occur, how much loss will be there? In other words, there are uncertainty of happening of time and amount of loss. Insurance removes all these uncertainty and the assured is given certainty of payment of loss. The insurer charges premium for providing the said certainty.

(*ii*) *Insurance provides protection.* The main function of the insurance is to provide protection against the probable chances of loss. The time and amount of loss are uncertain and at the happening of risk, the person will suffer loss in absence of insurance. The insurance guarantees the payment of loss and thus protects the assured from sufferings. The insurance cannot check the happening of risk but can provide for losses at the happening of the risk.

(*iii*) *Risk-Sharing.* The risk is uncertain, and therefore, the loss arising from the risk is also uncertain. When risk takes place, the loss is shared by all the persons who are exposed to the risk. The risk-sharing in ancient time was done only at time of damage or death; but today, on the basis of probability of risk, the share is obtained from each and every insured in the shape of premium without which protection is not guaranteed by the insurer.

SECONDARY FUNCTIONS

Besides the above primary functions, the insurance works for the following functions:

(*i*) *Prevention of Loss.* The insurance joins hands with those institutions which are engaged in preventing the losses of the society because the reduction in loss causes lesser payment to the assured and so more saving is possible which will assist in reducing the premium. Lesser premium invites more business and more business causes lesser share to the assured. So again premium is reduced to, which will stimulate more business and more protection to the masses. Therefore, the insurance assist financially to the health organisation, fire brigade, educational institutions and other organisations which are engaged in preventing the losses of the masses from death or damage.

(*ii*) *It Provides Capital.* The insurance provides capital to the society. The accumulated funds are invested in productive channel. The dearth of capital of the society is minimised to a greater extent with the help of investment of insurance. The industry, the business and the individual are benefited by the investment and loans of the insurers.

(*iii*) It *Improves Efficiency.* The insurance eliminates worries and miseries of losses at death and destruction of property. The carefree person can devote his body and soul together for better achievement. It improves not only his efficiency, but the efficiencies of the masses are also advanced.

(*iv*) *It helps Economic Progress.* The insurance by protecting the society from huge losses of damage, destruction and death, provides an initiative to work hard for the betterment of the masses. The next factor of economic progress, the capital, is also immensely provided by the masses. The property, the valuable assets, the man, the machine and the society cannot lose much at the disaster.

DEFINITION OF INSURANCE

The definition of insurance can be made from two points: (*i*) Functional Definition and, (*ii*) Contractual Definition.

Functional Definition

Insurance is a co-operative device to spread the loss caused by a particular risk over a number of persons, who are exposed to it and who agree to insure themselves against the risk. Thus, the insurance is (*a*) a co-operative device to spread the risk; (*b*) the system to spread the risk over a number of persons who are insured against the risk; (*c*) the principle to share the loss of each member of the society on the basis of probability of loss to their risk; and (*d*) the method to provide security against losses to the insured.

Similarly another definition can be given. Insurance is a co-operative device of distributing losses, falling on an individual or his family over a large number of persons, each bearing a nominal expenditure and feeling secure against heavy loss.

Contractual Definition

Insurance has been defined to be that in which a sum of money as a premium is paid in consideration of the insurer's incurring the risk of paying a large sum upon a given contingency. The insurance, thus, is a contract whereby (*a*) certain sum, called premium, is charged in consideration, (*b*) against the said consideration, a large sum is guaranteed to be paid by the insurer who received the premium, (*c*) the payment will be made in a certain definite sum, *i.e.,* the loss or the policy amount whichever may be, and (*d*) the payment is made only upon a contingency. More specific definition can be given as follows—Insurance may be defined as a consisting one party (the insurer) agrees to pay to the other party (the insurer) or his beneficiary, a certain sum upon a given contingency (the risk) against which insurance is sought.

NATURE OF INSURANCE

The insurance has the following characteristics which are, generally, observed in case of life, marine, fire and general insurances.

1. Sharing of Risk

Insurance is a device to share the financial losses which might befall on an individual or his family on the happening of a specified event. The event may be death of a bread-winner to the family in the case of life insurance, marine-perils in marine insurance, fire in fire insurance and other certain events in general insurance, *e.g.,* theft in burglary insurance, accident in motor insurance, etc. The loss arising from these events if insured are shared by all the insured in the form of premium.

2. Co-operative Device

The most important feature of every insurance plan is the co-operation of large number of persons who, in effect, agree to share the financial loss arising due to a particular risk which is insured. Such a group of persons may be brought together voluntarily or through publicity or through solicitation of the agents. An insurer would be unable to compensate all the losses from his own capital. So, by insuring or underwriting a large number of persons, he is able to pay the amount of loss. Like all co-operative devices, there is no compulsion here on anybody to purchase the insurance policy.

3. Value of Risk

The risk is evaluated before insuring to charge the amount of share of an insured, herein called, consideration or premium. There are several methods of evaluation of risks. If there is expectation of more loss, higher premium may be charged. So, the probability of loss is calculated at the time of insurance.

4. Payment at Contingency

The payment is made at a certain contingency insured. If the contingency occurs, payment is made. Since the life insurance contract is a contract of certainty, because the contingency, the death or the expiry of term, will certainly occur, the payment is certain. In other insurance contracts, the contingencyis the fire or the marine perils etc., may or may not occur. So, if the contingency occurs, payment is made, otherwise no amount is given to the policy-holder. Similarly, in certain types of life policies, payment is not certain due to uncertainty of a particular contingency within a particular period. For example, in term-insurance the, payment is made only when death of the assured occurs within the specified term, may be one or two years. Similarly, in Pure Endowment payment is made only at the survival of the insured at the expiry of the period.

5. Amount of Payment

The amount of payment depends upon the value of loss occurred due to the particular insured risk provided insurance is there up to that amount. In life insurance, the purpose is not to make good the financial loss suffered. The insurer promises to pay a fixed sum on the happening of an event. If the event or the contingency takes place, the payment does fall due if the policy is valid and in force at the time of the event, like property insurance, the dependents will not be required to prove the occurring of loss and the amount of loss. It is immaterial in life insurance what was the amount of loss at the time of contingency. But in the property and general insurances, the amount of loss, as well as the happening of loss, are required to be proved.

6. Large Number of Insured Persons

To spread the loss immediately, smoothly and cheaply, large number of persons should be insured. The co-operation of a small number of persons may also be insurance but it will be limited to smaller area. The cost of insurance to each member may be higher. So, it may be unmarketable. Therefore, to make the insurance cheaper, it is essential to insure large number of persons or property because the lesser would be cost of insurance and so, the lower would be premium. In past years, tariff associations or mutual fire insurance associations were found to share the loss at cheaper rate. In order to function successfully, the insurance should be joined by a large number of persons.

7. Insurance is not a gambling

The insurance serves indirectly to increase the productivity of the community by eliminating worry and increasing initiative. The uncertainty is changed into certainty by insuring property and life because the insurer promises to pay a definite sum at damage or death. From a family and business point of view all lives possess an economic value which may at any time be snuffed out by death, and it is as reasonable to ensure against the loss of this value as it is to protect oneself against the loss of property. In the absence of insurance, the property owners could at best practice only some form of self-insurance, which may not give him absolute certainty. Similarly, in absence of life insurance, saving requires time; but death may occur at any time and the property, and family may remain unprotected. Thus, the family is protected against losses on death and damage with the help of insurance. From the company's point of view, the life insurance is essentially non-speculative, in fact, no other business operates with greater certainties. From the insured point of view, too, insurance is also the antithesis of gambling. Nothing is more uncertain than life and life insurance offers the only sure method of changing that uncertainty into certainty. Failure of insurance amounts gambling because the uncertainty of loss is always looming. In fact, the insurance is just the opposite of gambling. In gambling, by bidding the person exposes himself to risk of losing, in the insurance, the insured is always opposed to risk, and will suffer loss if he is not insured. By getting insured his life and property, he protects himself against the risk of loss. In fact, if he does not get his property or life insured he is gambling with his life on property.

8. Insurance is not Charity

Charity is given without consideration but insurance is not possible without premium. It provides security and safety to an individual and to the society although it is a kind of business because in consideration of premium it guarantees the payment of loss. It is a profession because it provides adequate sources at the time of disasters only by charging a nominal premium for the service.

PRINCIPLES OF INSURANCE

The insurance is based upon (*i*) Principles of Co-operation and, (*ii*) Principles of Probability.

(*i*) *Principles of Co-operation.* Insurance is a co-operation device. If one person is providing for his own losses, it cannot be strictly an insurance because in insurance, the loss is shared by a group of persons who are willing to co-operate. In ancient period, the persons of a group were willingly sharing the loss to a member of the group. They used to share the loss to a member of the group. They used to share the loss at the time of damage. They collected enough funds from the society and paid to the dependents of the deceased or the persons suffering property losses. The mutual co-operation was prevailing from the very beginning up to the era of Christ in most of the countries. Lately, the co-operation took another form where it was agreed between the individual or the society to pay a certain sum in advance to be a member of the society. The society by accumulating the funds, guarantees payment of certain amount at the time of loss to any member of the society. The accumulation of funds and charging of the share from the member in advance became the job of one institution called insurer. Now it became the duty and responsibility of the insurer to obtain adequate funds from the members of the society to pay them at the happening of the insured risk. Thus, the shares of loss took the form of premium. Today, all the insured give a premium to join the scheme of insurance. Thus, the insured are co-operating to share the loss of an individual by payment of a premium in advance.

(*ii*) *Principles and Theory of Probability.* The loss in the shape of premium can be distributed only on the basis of theory of probability. The chances of loss are estimated in advance to affix the amount of premium. Since the degree of loss depends upon various factors, the affecting factors are analysed before determining the amount of loss. With the help of this principle, the uncertainty of loss is converted into certainty. The insurer will have not to suffer loss as well have to gain windfall. Therefore, the insurer has to charge only so much of amount which is adequate to meet the losses. The probability tells what are the chances of losses and what will be the amount of losses.

The inertia of large number is applied while calculating the probability. The larger the number of exposed persons,, the better and the more practical would be the findings of the probability. Therefore, the law of large number is applied in the principle of probability. In each and every field of insurance the law of large number is essential. These principles keep in account that the past events will incur in the same inertia. The insurance, on the basis of past experience, present conditions and future prospects, fixes the amount of premium. Without premium, no co-operation is possible and the premium cannot be calculated without the help of theory of probability, and .consequently no insurance is possible. So these two principles are the two main legs of insurance.

QUESTIONS

1. What are the various functions of insurance?
2. State briefly a suitable definition of insurance.
3. Insurance is not to prevent risk, but to indemnify the losses arising from a certain risk'.—Comment.
4. What are the various principles of insurance?

2

EVOLUTION OF INSURANCE

The origin of insurance is lost in antiquity. The earliest traces of insurance in the ancient world are found in the form of marine trade loans or carriers' contracts which: included an element of insurance. Evidence is on record that arrangements embodying the idea of insurance were made in Babylonia and India at quite an early period. In Rigveda, the most sacred book of India, references were made to the concept 'Yogakshema' more or less akin to the well-being and security of the people. The codes of Hummurabi and of Manu had recognised the advisability of provision for sharing the future losses. However, there is no evidence that insurance in its present form was practised prior to the twelfth century.

1. Marine Insurance

The marine insurance is the oldest form of insurance. Under Bottomry bond, the system of credit and the law of interest were well-developed and were based on a clear appreciation of the hazard involved and the means of safeguarding against it. If the ship was lost, the loan and interest were forfeited. The contract of insurance was made a part of the contract of carriage, and Manu shows that Indians had even anticipated the doctrine of average and contribution. Freight was fixed according to season and was expected to be reasonable in the case of marine transport which was then very much at the mercy of winds and elements. Travellers by sea and land were very much exposed to the risk of loosing their vessels and merchandise because the piracy on the open seas and highway robbery of caravans were very common. Besides there were several risks. Many times, it might have been captured by the king's enemies or robbed by pirates or got sunk in the deep waters. The risk to owners of such ships were enormous and, therefore, to safeguard them the marine traders devised a method of spreading over them the financial loss which could not be conveniently borne by the unfortunate individual victims. The co-operative device was quite voluntary in the beginning, but now in modern it has been converted into modified shape of premium.

The marine policies of the present forms were sold in the beginning of fourteenth century by the Brugians. On the demand of the inhabitants of Burges, the Court of Flanders permitted in the year 1310, the establishment in this Town of a charter of Assurance, by means of which the merchants could insure their goods, exposed to the risks of the sea. The insurance development was not confined to the Lombards and to the Hansa merchants, it spread throughout Spain, Portugal, France, Holland and England. The marine form land lending prominence of Lombards merchants got a prominent section of the London City. They built homes there and took the name of Lombard Street. Later on, this street became famous in insurance history. The Lloyd's coffee-house gave an impetus to develop the marine insurance.

2. Fire Insurance

After marine insurance, fire insurance developed in present form. It had been observed in Anglo-Section Guild form for the first time where the victims of fire hazards were given personal assistance by providing necessaries of life. It had been originated in Germany in the beginning of sixteenth century. The fire insurance got momentum in England after the great fire in 1666 when the fire losses were tremendous. About 85 per cent of the houses were burnt to ashes and property worth of sterling ten crores were completely burnt off. Fire Insurance Office was established in 1681 in England. With colonial development of England, the fire insurance spread all over the world in present form 'Sun Fire Office' was successful fire insurance institution.

In India, the general insurer started working since 1850 with the establishment of the Triton Insurance, Calcutta. Again in 1861, the North British and Mercantile catered the requirements of insurance business. The general insurance in India could not progress much. The slow growth of joint-stock enterprise and mechanised production was another reason for the low level of general insurance business.

3. Life Insurance

Life insurance made its first appearance in England in sixteenth century, the first recorded evidence in England being the policy on life of William Gybbons on June 18, 1653. Even before this date annuities had become quite common in England, and marine insurance had, in fact, made its appearance three thousand years ago. The life insurance developed at 'Exchange Alley'. The first registered life office in England was the Hand-in-Hand Society established in 1696. The famous 'Amicable Society for a Perpetual Assurance Office started its operation since 1706. Life insurance did not prosper in the United States during the 18th century, because of serious fluctuations in death-rate, but soon after 1800 some active interest began to be shown in this enterprise because of the application of level premium plan which had by then been in operation in U.K. for more than a generation. In India, some Europeans started the first life insurance company in Bengal Presidency, viz., the Orient Life Assurance Company in 1818. The year 1870 was a year of a landmark in the history of Indian Insurance separating the early period of pioneering attempts at life insurance from the subsequent period of steady development at the establishment of Indian Life Office, viz., Bombay Mutual Life Assurance Society in 1871. The next important life office was Oriental Government Security Life Assurance Co., Ltd., which started its operation since 1874. Since then several offices developed in India.

4. Miscellaneous Insurance

The miscellaneous insurance took the present shape at the later part of nineteenth century with the industrial revolution in England. Accident insurance, fidelity insurance, liability insurance and theft insurance were the important form of insurance at that time. Lloyds's Association was the main functioning institution. Now, insurances such as cattle insurance, crop insurance, profit insurance, etc., are taking place. The scope of general insurance is increasing with the advancement of the society.

KINDS OF INSURANCE

The insurance can be divided from two angles: first, from the business point of view and the second, from the risk point of view.

Business Point of View

The insurance can be classified into three categories from business point of view: (*i*) Life Insurance, (*ii*) General Insurance, and (*iii*) Social Insurance.

(*i*) Life Insurance

Life Insurance is different from other insurance in the sense that, here, the subject matter of insurance is life of human being. The insurer will pay the fixed amount of insurance at the time of death or at the expiry of certain period. At present, life insurance enjoys maximum scope because the life is the most important property of the society or an individual. Each and every person requires the insurance. This insurance provides protection to the family at the premature death or gives adequate amount at the old age when earning capacities are reduced. Under personal insurance a payment is made at the accident. The insurance is not only a protection but is a sort of investment because a certain sum is returnable to the insured at the death or at the expiry of a period. The business of life insurance is wholly done by the Life Insurance Corporation of India.

(*ii*) General Insurance

The general insurance includes property insurance, liability insurance and other forms of insurance. Fire and marine insurances are strictly called property insurance. Motor, theft, fidelity and machine insurances include the extent of liability insurance to a certain extent. The strictest form of liability insurance is fidelity insurance, whereby the insurer compensates the loss to the insured when he is under the liability of payment to the third party.

(*iii*) Social Insurance

The social insurance is to provide protection to the weaker section of the society who are unable to pay the premium for adequate insurance. Pension plans, disability benefits, unemployment benefits, sickness insurance and industrial insurance are the various forms of social insurance. With the increase of the socialistic ideas, the social insurance is an obligatory duty of the nation. The Government of a country must provide social insurance to its masses.

Risk Point of View

Insurance is divided into property liability and other form from high point of view.

A. Property Insurance

Under the property insurance property of a person/persons are insured against a certain specified risk. The risk may be fire or marine perils, theft of property or goods, damage to property at accident.

(*a*) *Marine Insurance.* Marine insurance provides protection against loss of marine perils. The marine perils are collision with rock, or ship attacks by enemies, fire and capture by pirates, etc. These perils cause damage, destruction or disappearance of the ship and cargo and non-payment of freight. So, marine insurance insures ship (Hull), cargo and freight. Previously only certain nominal risks were insured but now the scope of marine insurance had been divided into two parts: (*i*) Ocean Marine Insurance and (*ii*) Inland Marine Insurance. The former insures only the marine perils while the latter covers inland peril which may arise with the delivery of cargo (goods) from the godown of the insured and may extend up to the receipt of the cargo by the buyer (importer) at his godown.

(*b*) *Fire Insurance.* Fire insurance covers risks of fire. In the absence of fire insurance, the fire waste will increase not only to the individual but to the society as well. With the help of fire insurance, the losses, arising due to fire are compensated and the society is not losing much. The individual is protected from such losses and his property or business or industry will remain approximately in the same position in which it was before the loss. The fire insurance does not protect only losses but it provides certain consequential losses also. War risk, turmoil, riots, etc., can be insured under this insurance, too.

(*c*) *Miscellaneous Insurance.* The Property, goods, machine, furniture, automobile, valuable articles, etc., can be insured against the damage or destruction due to accident or disappearance due to theft. There are different forms of insurances for each type of the said property whereby not only property insurance exists but liability insurance and personal injuries are also insured.

B. Liability Insurance

The general insurance also includes liability insurance whereby the insured is liable to pay the damage of property or to compensate the less of personal injury or death. This insurance is seen in the form of fidelity insurance, automobile insurance and machine insurance, etc.

C. Other Forms

Besides the property and liability insurances, there are certain other insurances which are included under general insurance. The examples of such insurances are export-credit insurances, State employees insurance, etc., whereby the insurer guarantees to pay certain amount at the certain events. This insurance is extending rapidly these days.

KINDS OF INSURANCE FROM RISK POINT OF VIEW

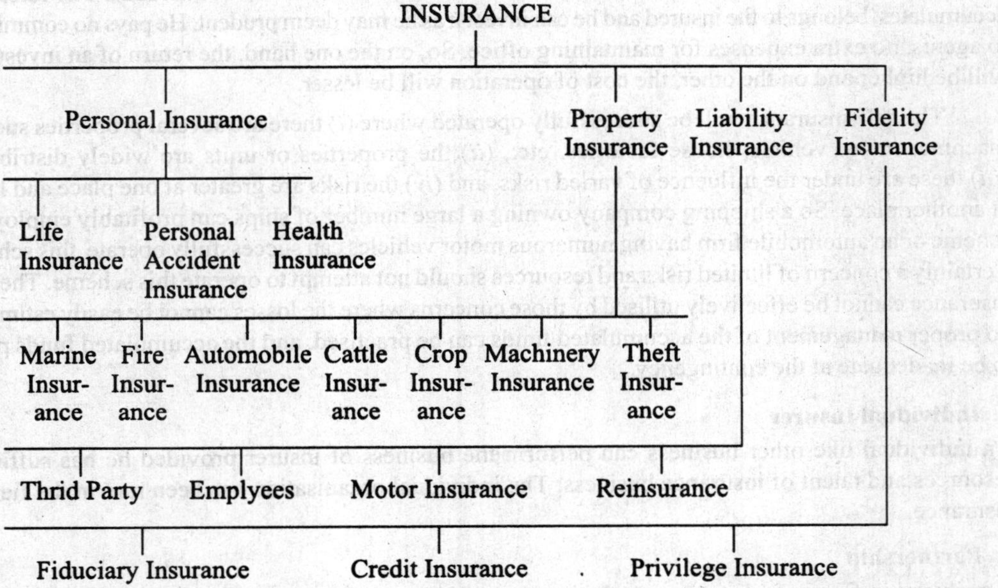

1. Personal Insurance

The personal insurance includes insurance of human life which may suffer loss due to death, accident and disease. Therefore, the personal insurance is further sub-classified into life insurance, personal accident insurance and health insurance.

2. Property Insurance

The property of an individual and of the society is insured against the loss of fire and marine perils, the crop is insured against unexpected decline in production, unexpected death of the animals engaged in business, break-down of machines and theft of the property and goods.

3. Liability Insurance

The liability insurance covers the risks of third party, compensation to employees, liability of the automobile owners and reinsurances.

4. Guarantee Insurance

The guarantee insurance covers the loss arising due to dishonesty, disappearance and disloyalty of the employers or second. The party must be a party of the contract. His failure causes loss to the first party. For example, in export insurance, the insurer will compensate the loss at the failure of the importers to pay the amount of debt.

TYPES OF INSURANCE ORGANISATIONS

The insurance organisation developed in different forms with the advancement of insurance practices. Some of the forms are discussed below.

1. Self-Insurance

The plan by which an individual or concern sets up a private fund out of which to pay losses is termed "Self-insurance". The person lays aside periodically certain sum to meet the losses of any contemplated risk. While it may be called "self-insurance", it is not, as a matter of fact, insurance at all because there is no hedge, no shifting or distributing of the burden of risk among larger persons. It is merely a provision for meeting the contingency. Here the insured becomes his own insurer for the particular risk. But, it can be successfully worked only when there is wide distribution of risks subject to the same hazard. It may be lesser expensive, provided the amount of loss is tremendous. The fund, as it accumulates, belongs to the insured and he can invest it as he may deem prudent. He pays no commission to agents, no extra expenses for maintaining office. So, on the one hand, the return of an investment will be higher and on the other, the cost of operation will be lesser.

The self-insurance will be successfully operated where (*i*) there are several properties such as, machine, motor vehicle, house factories, etc., (*ii*) the properties or units are widely distributed, (*iii*) these are under the influence of varied risks, and (*iv*) the risks are greater at one place and lesser at another place. So a shipping company owning a large number of ships can profitably employ this scheme or an automobile firm having numerous motor vehicles can successfully operate this scheme. Certainly a concern of limited risks and resources should not attempt to operate this scheme. The self-insurance cannot be effectively utilised by those concerns where the losses cannot be easily estimated, no proper management of the accumulated funds can be practised, and the accumulated funds prove to be inadequate at the contingency.

2. Individual Insurer

An individual like other business can perform the business of insurer provided he has sufficient resources and talent of insurance business. The individual organisation has been rare in the field of insurance.

3. Partnership

A partnership firm can also carry on the insurance business for the sake of profit. Since it is not an entity distinct from the persons composing it, the personal liability of partners in respect of the partnership debts is unlimited. In case of huge loss the partners have to pay from their own personal funds and it will not be profitable to them to start insurance business.

In the early period before the advent of joint stock companies many insurance undertakings were partnership or unicorporated companies. They were constituted by deed of partnerships which regulated the business. Before formation of joint stock companies, the crown had empowered to grant an application letters patent to such unincorporated companies to operate the business with limited liabilities. Sometimes, the policy-holders were permitted to share the management of the concern.

These forms of insurance had been completely disappeared with the advent of joint stock compahies.

4. Joint Stock Companies

The joint stock companies are those which are organised by the share-holders who subscribe the necessary capital to start the business, are formed for earning profits for the stock-holders who are the real owners of the companies. The management of a company is entrusted to a Board of Directors who are elected by the share-holders from among themselves. The company can operate insurance business and the policy-holders have nothing to do with the management of the concern. But, in life insurance, it is the practice to share certain portion of profit among the certain policy-holders. The participating policy-holders are getting the bonus. Before nationalisation, according to Insurance Act, 1938, the policy-holders had a right to elect their representatives to the Board of Directors to the extent of one-fourth of the total number of directors of the company. The provision enabled the policy-holders to have an effective voice in the management of the company. Most of the insurance businesses were done on joint stock basis before nationalisation. They were operating within the memorandum of association and articles of association framed by them. They used to distribute only 5 per cent of divisible profit to the share-holders and more than 95 per cent of the divisible profit was distributed amongst the policy-holders.

5. Mutual Companies

The mutual companies were co-operative associations formed for the purpose of effecting insurance on the property of its members. The policy-holders were themselves the share-holders of the companies, Each member was insurer as well as insured. They had power to participate in, management and in profit to the full extent. When ever the income was more than the expenses and claims, it was accumulated in the form of saving and was entitled in reducing the rate of premium. Since the insured were insurers also, they always tried to reduce the management expenses and to keep the business at sound level.

The theoretical base of the mutual companies, is issuing of participating policies, *i.e.*, the policy-holders had full power in management and profit, whereas the joint-stock companies, strictly were to issue non-participating policies. But, in practice, the joint-stock companies were also issuing participating policies. It made them mixed companies *i.e.*, where the features of joint stock companies and of mutual companies were present.

6. Co-operative Insurance Organisation

Co-operative insurance organisations are those concerns which are incorporated and registered under Indian Co-operative Societies Act. The concerns are also called 'Co-operative Insurance Societies'. These societies like mutual companies are non-profit organisation. The aim is to provide insurance protection to its members at the lowest reasonable, net cost. The Indian Insurance Act, 1938, has provided special provisions for the co-operative insurance societies, but after nationalisation the societies have been ceased. IRDA has also permitted cooperative insurance organisation in 2005

7. Lloyd's Association

Lloyd's Association is one of the greatest insurance institutions in the world. Taking its name from the Coffee House of Edward Lloyd, where underwriters assembled to transact business and pick-up news, the organisation traces its origin to the latter part of the seventeenth century. So, it is an oldest insurance organisation in existing form in the world. In 1871, Loyd's Act was passed incorporating the members of the association into a single corporate body with perpetual succession and a corporate seal. The powers of Lloyd's Corporation was extended from the business of marine insurance to other insurances and guarantee business. The Lloyd's association is an association of individual insurers known as 'underwriters'. They are also termed as 'Syndicates' or 'Names'. Any insurer who wants to become a member of such association has to deposit a certain fee as security for the regular payment of his liabilities. The association before enrolling the insurer as a member of the association will inquire about the financial position of the concern, business reputation and experience. On satisfactory proof the association admits him in the association. The business is effected by the insurers called underwriters, syndicates, or names. The association is merely a controlling and guiding body. Anybody desirous of taking insurance will approach to the 'underwriters' and not to the association. Each underwriter will be responsible for his business underwritten of a policy. Thus, a policy will be underwritten by several underwriters but their share or portion of business are fixed individually. When the policy becomes a claim, the insured realises money from all the underwriters who had underwritten the policy according to their respective shares. If an underwriter fails to pay his share of claim, the association will pay from his security which he had taken at time of enrolment of the underwriter. Never is one member or underwriter liable for the losses of other members either on a policy or in a syndicate. Underwriter assumes liability 'each for himself and not for another'.

Lloyd's as a corporation is never liable on a policy. It does supervise the conditions under which its members may issue policies; it undertakes to provide collective protection for the commercial and maritime interest of its members.

The Lloyd's has done commendable work not only in the field of marine insurance but in other insurances also. War risk election risk, export risk, aeroplane risk, etc., have been insured by the Lloyd's Association. The association also publishes, 'Lloyd's List' and 'Register of Shipping' for the information of insuring public and the insurers.

8. State Insurance

The Government of a nation sometimes owns the insurance and runs the business for the benefit of the public. The state insurance is defined as that insurance which is under public sector put; more specifically it can be stated that when governments have taken over the insurance business particularly life insurance. France had nationalised larger insurance companies in 1946. In Brazil, Japan and Mexico, the insurances are largely nationalised. Previously, the state undertook only those insurances which were regarded to be very vital for the public interest or where private companies were not able or willing to enter the field of insurance. Social security, unemployment, crop insurance, war risk insurance, export credit insurance, aeroplane insurance were generally under state insurance.

In India, the life insurance business was nationalised in 1956 and the general insurances were nationalised in 1971. Thus, the insurance business in India, today, is under the control and ownership of the Central Government although they are in different forms of insurances.

INSURANCE ORGANISATION IN INDIA

(*i*) *Departmental Organisation.* Departmental insurances are prevalent in different departments of the Central and State governments. The postal department of the country has its own system of insurances under which the employees of post-offices are insured, Similarly, the postal department as a carrier of goods has also provided insurance for the goods to be despatched. These insurances are not compulsory in India. The State Governments of different states have provided life insurance to their respective employees. Apart from this, the State Governments have also provided sickness maternity, disability, medical and pension insurances to respective employees.

(*ii*) *Corporations.* In India two corporations are established under separate Acts to deal with the insurance business.

(*A*) The Life Insurance Corporation of India Act, 1956, had provided for life insurance legislation for life insurance business conducted by the Life Insurance Corporation of India established under the said Act. It started its functions since Sept. 1, 1956. It owns all the life insurance business (including annuities) in India.

(*B*) The general Insurance Corporation of India established under the General Insurance Corporation of India Act, 1972 into four distinct companies which are (*i*) National Insurance Companies Ltd. (*ii*) New India Insurance Companies Ltd. (*iii*) Oriental Fire and General Insurance Companies Ltd. and (*iv*) United India Fire and General Insurance Companies Ltd. These companies would work separately maintaining their distinct features but they are controlled and guided by the General Insurance Corporation of India. This is a neo-techno scheme of nationalisation where the companies are also to work freely in the market. They will suffer and gain their own losses and profits. The monopoly on the concern, may be corporation, has gone in this new technique. These companies will be subsidiary to the G.I.C. (The General Insurance Corporation).

(C) Employees State Insurance Corporation

This corporation was established in 1948. This corporation provides social insurance to labourers of factories who are getting less than four hundred rupees per month., They are provided a definite assistance in sickness, maternity, disability, medical expenses and assistance to dependents.

(D) Deposit Insurance Corporation

This corporation was established in 1962. It provides protection to the depositors of a bank. In case the bank fails, the depositors can get returned their deposits up to rupees ten thousand.

(*iii*) *Government Companies.* Companies were established by the government according to the provision of Indian Companies Act. In 1957, export risks insurance corporation was established to insure the export risks. The name of this company was converted to Export Credit and Guarantee Corporation in 1964. Now all the general insurance businesses are conducted by the said four government companies.

QUESTIONS

1. Describe the main kinds of insurance and examine briefly the nature of risks protected by each kind of insurance.
2. Detail the different kinds of insurance oganisations and illustrate the merits demerits and of each organisation.
3. The latest and the oldest form of insurance is 'Lloyd's one'. Illustrate briefly.
4. Discuss the organisations of insurance business in India.

3

ROLE AND IMPORTANCE OF INSURANCE

The process of insurance has been evolved to safeguard the interests of people from uncertainty by providing certainty of payment at a given contingency. The insurance principle comes to be more and more used and useful in modern affairs. Not only does it serve the ends of individuals, or of special groups of individuals, it tends to pervade and to transform our modern social order, too. The role and importance of insurance, here, has been discussed in three phases: (*i*) uses to individual, (*ii*) uses to a special group of individuals, viz., to business or industry, and (*iii*) uses to the society.

USES TO AN INDIVIDUAL

1. Insurance provides Security and Safety

The insurance provides safety and security against the loss on a particular event. In case of life insurance payment is made when death occurs or the term of insurance is expired. The loss to the family at a premature death and payment in old age are adequately provided by insurance. In other words, security against premature death and old age sufferings are provided by life insurance. Similarly, the property of insured is secured against loss on a fire in fire insurance. In other insurance, too, this security is provided against the loss at a given contingency. The insurance provides safety and security against the loss of earning at death or in olden age, against the loss at fire, against the loss at damage, destruction or disappearance of property, goods, furniture and machines, etc.

2. Insurance affords Peace of Mind

The security wish is the prime motivating factor. This is the wish which tends to stimulate to more work, if this wish is unsatisfied, it will create a tension which manifests itself to the individual in the form of an unpleasant reaction causing reduction in work. The security banishes fear and uncertainty, fire, windstorm, auto-mobile accident, damage and death are almost beyond the control human agency and in occurrence of any of these events may frustrate or weaken the human mind. By means of insurance, however, much of the uncertainty that centres about the wish for security and its attainment may be eliminated.

3. Insurance protects Mortgaged Property

At the death of the owner of the mortgaged property, the property is taken over by the lender of money and the family will be deprived of the uses of the property. On the other hand, the mortgagee wishes to get the property insured because at the damage or destruction of the property he will lose his right to get the loan repayed. The insurance will provide adequate amount to the dependents at the early death of the property-owner to pay off the unpaid loans. Similarly, the mortgagee gets adequate amount at the destruction of the property.

4. Insurance eliminates dependency

At the death of the husband or father, the destruction of family need no elaboration. Similarly, at destruction of, property and goods, the family would suffer a lot. It brings reduced standards of living and the suffering may go to any extent of begging from the relatives, neighbours or friends. The economic independence of the family is reduced or, sometimes, lost totally. What can be more pitiable condition than this that the wife and children are looking others more benevolent than the husband and father, in absence of protection against such dependency. The insurance is here to assist them and provides adequate amount at the time of sufferings.

5. Life Insurance encourages saving

The elements of protection and investment are present only in case of life insurance. In property insurance, only protection element exists. In most of the life policies elements of saving predominates. These policies combine the programs of insurance and savings. The saving with insurance has certain extra advantages—(*i*) Systematic saving is possible because regular premiums are required to be compulsorily paid. The saving with a bank is voluntary and one can easily omit a month or two and then abandon the program entirely. (*ii*) In insurance the deposited premium cannot be withdrawn easily before the expiry of the term of the policy. As contrast to this, the saving which can be withdrawn at any moment will finish within no time. (*iii*) The insurance will pay the policy money irrespective of the premium deposited while in case of bank-deposit, only the deposited amount along with the interest is paid. The insurance, thus, provides the wished amount of insurance and the bank provides only the deposited amount. (*iv*) The compulsion or force to premium in insurance is so high that if the policy-holder fails to pay premiums within the days of grace, he subjects his policy to lapsation and may get back only a very nominal portion of the total premiums paid on the policy. For the preservation of the policy, he has to try his level best to pay the premium. After a certain period, it would be a part of necessary expenditure of the insured. In absence of such forceful compulsion elsewhere life insurance is the best media of saving.

6. Life Insurance provides profitable Investment

Individuals unwilling or unable to handle their own funds have been pleased to find an outlet for their investment in life insurance policies. Endowment policies, multipurpose policies, deferred annuities are certain better form of investment. The elements of investment *i.e.*, regular saving, capital formation, and return of the capital alongwith certain additional return are perfectly observed, in life insurance. In India the insurance policies carry a special exemption from income-tax, wealth tax, gift tax and estate duty. An individual from his own capacity cannot invest regularly with enough of security and profitability. The life insurance fulfils all these requirements with a lower cost. The beneficiary of the policy-holder can get a regular income from the life-insurer; if the insured amount is left with him.

7. Life Insurance fulfils the needs of a person

The needs of a person are divided into (*A*) Family needs, (*B*) Old-age needs, (*C*) Re-adjustment needs, (*D*) Special needs, (*E*) The clean-up needs.

(A) Family Needs

Death is certain, but the time is uncertain. So, there is uncertainty of the time when the sufferings and financial stringencies may be fall on the family. Moreover, every person is responsible to provide for the family. It would be a more pathetic sight in the world to see the wife and children of a man looking for some one more considerate arid benevolent than the husband or the father, who left them unprovided. Therefore, the provision for children up to their reaching earning period and for widow up to long life should he made. Any other provision except life insurance will not adequately meet this financial requirement of the family. Whole life policies are the better means of meeting such requirements.

(B) Old-age heeds

The provision for old-age is required where the person is surviving more than his earning period. The reduction of income in old-age is serious to the person and his family. If no other family member starts earning, they will be left with nothing and if there is no property, it would be more piteous state. The life insurance provides old age funds alongwith the protection of the family by issuing various policies.

(C) Re-adjustment Needs

At the time of reduction in income whether by loss of unemployment, disability, or death, adjustment in the standard of living of family is required. The family members will have to be satisfied with meagre income and they have to settle down to lower income and social obligations. Before coming down to the lower standard and to be satisfied with that, they require certain adjustment income so that the primary obstacles may be reduced to minimum. The life insurance helps to accumulate adequate funds. Endowment policy, anticipated endowment policy and guaranteed triple benefit policies are deemed to be a good substitute for old age needs.

(D) Special Needs

There are certain special requirement of the family which is fulfilled by the earning member of the family. If the member becomes disable to earn the income due to old age or death, those needs may remain unfulfilled and the family will suffer.

(*i*) *Need for Education.* There are certain insurance policies, and annuities which are useful for education of the children irrespective of the death or survival of the father or guardian.

(*ii*) *Marriage.* The daughter may remain unmarried in case of father's death or in case of inadequate provision for meeting the expenses of marriage. The insurance can provide funds for the marriage if policy is taken for the purpose.

(*iii*) *Insurance needs for settlement of children.* After education, settlement of children takes time and in absence of adequate funds, the children cannot be well placed and all the education go to waste.

(E) Clean-up funds

After death, ritual ceremonies, payment of wealth taxes and income taxes are certain requirements which decrease the amount of funds of the family member. Insurance comes to help for meeting these requirements. Multipurpose policy, education and marriage policies, capital redemption policies are the better policies for the special needs.

USES TO BUSINESS

The insurance has been useful to the business society also. Some of the uses are discussed below:

1. Uncertainty of business losses is reduced

In world of business, commerce and industry a huge number of properties are employed. With a slight slackness or negligence, the property may be turned into ashes. The accident may be fatal not only to the individual or property but to the third party also. New construction and new establishment are possible only with the help of insurance. In absence of it, uncertainty will be to the maximum level and nobody would like to invest a huge amount in the business or industry. A person may not be sure of his life and health and cannot continue the business up to longer period to support his dependents. By purchasing policy, he can be sure of his earning because the insurer will pay a fed amount at the time of death. Again, the owner of a business might foresee contingencies that would bring great loss. To meet such situations they might decide to set aside annually a reserve, but it could not be accumulated due to death. However, by making an annual payment, to secure immediately, insure policy can be taken.

2. Business-efficiency is increased with insurance

When the owner of a business is free from the botheration of losses, he will certainly devote much time to the business. The care free owner can work better for the maximisation of the profit. The new as well as old businessmen are guaranteed payment of certain amount with the insurance policies at the death of the person; at the damage, destruction or disappearance of the property or goods. The uncertainty of loss may affect the mind of the businessmen adversely. The insurance, removing the uncertainty, stimulates the businessmen to work hard.

3. Key Man Indemnification

Key man is that particular man whose capital, expertise, experience, energy, ability to control, goodwill and dutifulness make him the most valuable asset in the business and whose absence will reduce the income of the employer tremendously and up to that time when such employee is not substituted. The death or disability of such valuable lives will, in many instances, prove a more serious loss than that by fire or any hazard. The potential loss to be suffered and the compensation to the dependents of such employee require an adequate provision which is met by purchasing an adequate life-policies. The amount of loss may be up to the amount of reduced profit, expenses involved in appointing and training, of such persons and payment to the dependents of the key man. The Term Insurance Policy or Convertible Term Insurance Policy is more suitable in this case.

4. Enhancement of Credit

The business can obtain loan by pledging the policy as collateral for the loan. The insured persons are getting more loan due to certainty of payment at their deaths. The amount of loan that can be obtained with such pledging of policy, with interest thereon will not exceed the cash value of the policy. In case of death, this value can be utilised for setting of the loan alongwith the interest. If the borrower is unwilling to repay the loan and interest, the lender can surrender the policy and get the amount of loan and interest thereon repaid. The redeemable debentures can be issued on the collateral of capital redemption policies. The' insurance properties are the best collateral and adequate loans are granted by the lenders.

5. Business Continuation

In any business particularly partnership business may discontinue at the death of any partner although the surviving partners can restart the business, but in both the cases the business and the partners will suffer economically. The insurance policies provide adequate funds at the time of death. Each partner may be insured for the amount of his interest in the partnership and his dependents may get that amount at the death of the partner.

With the help of property insurance, the property of the business is protected against disasters and the chance of disclosure of the business due to the tremendous waste or loss.

6. Welfare of Employees

The welfare of employees is the responsibility of the employer. The former are working for the latter. Therefore, the latter has to look after the welfare of the former which can be provision for early death, provision for disability and provision for old age. These requirements are easily met by the life insurance, accident and sickness benefit, and pensions which are generally provided by group insurance. The premium for group insurance is generally paid by the employer. This plan is the cheapest form of insurance for employers to fulfill their responsibilities. The employees will devote their maximum capacities to complete their jobs when they are assured of the above benefits. The struggle and strife between employees and employer can be minimised easily with the help of such schemes.

USES OF SOCIETY

Some of the uses of insurance to society are discussed in the following sections.

1. Wealth of the society is protected

The loss of a particular wealth can be protected with the insurance. Life insurance provides loss of human wealth. The human material, if it is strong, educated and care-free, will generate more income. Similarly, the loss of damage of property at fire, accident, etc., can be well indemnified by the property insurance; cattle, crop, profit and machines are also protected against their accidental and economic losses. With the advancement of the society, the wealth or the property of the society attracts more hazardous and, so new types of insurance are also invented to protect them against the possible losses. Each and every member will have financial security against old age, death, damage, destruction and disappearance of his wealth including the life wealth. Through prevention of economic losses, instance protects the society against degradation. Through stabilization and expansion of business and industry, the economic security is maximised. The present, future and potential human and property resources are well-protected. The children are getting expertised education, working classes are free from botherations and older people are guiding at ease. The happiness and prosperity are observed everywhere with the help of insurance.

2. Economic Growth of the Country

For the economic growth of the country, insurance provides strong hand and mind, protection against loss of property and adequate capital to produce more wealth. The agriculture will experience protection against losses of cattle, machines, tools and crop. This sort of protection stimulates more production in agriculture, in industry, the factory premises, machines, boilers and profit insurances provide more confidence to start and operate the industry welfare of employees create a conducive atmosphere to work: Adequate capital from insurers accelerate the production cycle. Similarly in business, too, the property and human material are protected against certain losses, capital and credit are expanded with the help of insurance. Thus, the insurance meets all the requirements of the economic growth of a country.

3. Reduction in Inflation

The insurance reduces the inflationary resource in two ways. First, by extracting money in supply to the amount of premium collected and secondly, by providing sufficient funds for production narrow down the inflationary gap. With reference to Indian context it has been observed that about 5.0 per cent of the money in supply was collected in form of premium. The share of premium contributed to the total investment of the country was about 10.0 per cent. The two main causes of inflation, namely, increased money in supply and decreased production are properly controlled by insurance business. Insurance Need and Selling.

QUESTIONS

1. Describe in detail the importance of insurance. What are its uses to the business community and society as a whole?
2. 'Insurance is able to curtail inflation, so it should be made compulsory'. Comment.

4

INSURANCE CONTRACT

Insurance may be defined as a contract between two parties of whereby one party called insurer undertakes, in exchange for a fixed sum called premiums, to pay the other party called insured a fixed amount of money on the happening of a certain event. Since insurance is a contract, certain sections of Indian Contract Act are applicable. Section 10 of this Act says, "All agreements are contract if they are made by free consent of the parties, competent to contract, for a lawful consideration and with a lawful object and which are not hereby declared to be void". The insurance contract involves—(A) the elements of general contract, and (B) the element of special contract relating to insurance.

The special contract of insurance involves principles :(1) Insurable Interest, (2) Utmost Good Faith, (3) Indemnity, (4) Subrogation, (5) Warranties, (6) Proximate Cause, (7) Assignment and Nomination, (8) Return of Premium. So, in total, there are eight elements of insurance contract which are discussed below:

1. GENERAL CONTRACT

The valid contract, according to Section 10 of Indian Contract Act 1872, must have the following essentialities.

I. Agreement (offer and acceptance).

II. Legal consideration.

III. Competent to make contract.

IV. Free consent.

V. Legal object.

I. Offer and Acceptance

The offer for entering into contract may generally come from the insured. The insurer may also propose to make the contract. Whether the offer is from the side of insurer or from the side of insured, the main fact is acceptance. Any act that precedes it is offer or a counter-offer. All that precede the offer or counter-offer is an invitation to offer. In insurance, the publication of prospectus, the canvassing of the agents are invitations to offer. When the prospect (the potential policy-holder) proposes to enter the contract it is an offer and if there is any alteration in the offer that would be a counter-offer. If this alteration or change (counter–offer) ill accepted by the proposer, it would be an acceptance. In absence of counter-offer, the acceptance of offer will be an acceptance by the insurer. At the moment, the notice of acceptance is given to other party, it would be a valid acceptance.

II. Legal Consideration

The promiser to pay a fixed sum at a given contingency is the insurer who must have some return or his promise. It need not be money only but it must be valuable. It may be sums, right, interest, profit, or benefit. Premium being the valuable consideration must be given for starting the insurance contract. The amount of premium is not important to begin the contract. The fact is that without payment of premium, the insurance contract cannot start.

III. Competent to make contract

Every person is competent to contract (*a*) who is of the age of majority according to the law, (*b*) who is of sound mind, and (*c*) who is not disqualified from contracting by any law to which he is subject. A minor is not competent to contract. A contract by a minor is void excepting contracts for necessaries. A minor cannot sign a contract. A person is said to be of sound mind for the purpose of making a contract if at the time when he makes it, he is capable of understanding it and of forming a rational judgment as to its effect upon his interests. A person who is usually of unsound mind, but, occasionally of sound mind may make a contract when he is of sound mind. An alien enemy, an undischarged insolvent and criminals cannot enter into contract. Contract made by incompetent party/parties will be void.

IV. Free Consent

Parties entering into the contract should enter into it by their free consent. The consent will be free when it is not caused by—(1) coercion, (2) undue influence, (3) fraud, or (4) misrepresentation, or (5) mistake. When there is no free consent except fraud the contract becomes voidable at the option of the party whose consent was so caused. In case of fraud the contract would be void. The proposal for free consent must sign a declaration to this effect, the person explaining the subject matter of the proposal to the proposer must also accordingly make a written declaration on the proposal.

V. Legal Object

In order to make a valid contract, the object of the agreement should be lawful. An object that is (*i*) not forbidden by law, or (*ii*) is not immoral, or (*iii*) opposed to public policy, or (*v*) which does not defeat the provisions of any law, is lawful. In proposal from the object of insurance is asked which should ,be legal and the object should not be concealed. If the object of an insurance, like the consideration, is found to be unlawful, the policy is void.

2. INSURABLE INTEREST

For an insurance contract to be valid, the insured must possess an insurable interest in the subject matter of insurance. The insurable interest is the pecuniary interest whereby the policy-holder is benefitd by the existense of the subject-matter and is prejudiced death or damage of the subject-matter. The essentials of a valid insurable interest are the folowing:

(*i*) There must be a subject-matter to be insured.

(*ii*) The policy-holder should have monetary relationship with the subject-matter.

(*iii*) The relationship between the policy-holders and the subject-matter should be recognised by law. In other words, there should not be any illegal relationship between the policy-holder and the subject-matter to be insured.

(*iv*) The financial relationship between the policy-holder and subject-matter should be such that the policy-holder is economically benefited by the survival or existence of the subject-matter and or will suffer economic loss at the death or existence of the subject-matter.

The subject-matter is life in the life insurance, property and goods in property insurance, liability and adventure in general insurance. Insurable interest is essentially a pecuniary interest, *i.e.*, the loss caused by the happening of the insured risk must be capable of financial valuation. No emotional or sentimental loss, as an expectation or an anxiety, would be the ground of the insurable interest. The event insured should be one that if it happens the party suffers financially and if it does not happen, the party is benefited by the existence. But a mere hope or expectation, which may be frustrated by the happening of some extent, is not an insurable interest.

3. UTMOST GOOD FAITH

The doctrine of disclosing all material facts is embodied in the important principle 'utmost good faith' which applies to all forms of insurance. Both parties of the insuranre contract must be of the same mind (ad idem) at the time of contract. There should not be any mispepresentation, non-disclosure or fraud concerning the material. In case of insurance contract the legal maxim 'Caveat Emptor' (let the buyer beware) does not prevail, where it is regard of the buyer to satisfy himself of the genuineness of the subject-matter and the seller is under no obligation to supply information about it. But in insurance contract, the seller, *i.e.*, the insurer will also have to disclose all the material facts. An insurance contract is a contract of *uberrimae fidei*, *i.e.*, of absolute good faith both parties of the contract must disclose all the material facts and fully.

1aterial Facts

A material fact is one which affect the judgment or decision of both parties in entering to the contract. Facts which count materially are those which knowledge influence a party in deciding whether or not to offer or to accept such risk and if the risk, is acceptable, on what terms and conditions the risk should be accepted. These facts have a direct bearning on the degree of risk in relation to the subject of insurance. In case of life insurance, the material facts or factors affecting the risk will be age, residence, occupation, health, income, etc., and in case of property insurance, it would be use, design, owner and situation of the property.

Full and True Disclosure

The utmost Good Faith says that all the material facts should be disclosed in true and full form. It means that the facts should be disclosed in that form in which they really exist. There should be no concealment, misrepresentation, mistake or fraud about the material facts. There should be no false statement and no half truth nor nay silence on the material facts.

Duty of Both the Parties

The duty to disclose the material facts lies on both the parties the insured as well as the insurer, but in practice the assured has to be more particular, about the observance of this principle because he is usually in full knowledge of facts relating to the subject-matter which, despite all effective inspections of the insurer, wouid not be disclosed.

Facts need not be disclosed by the insured

The following facts, however, are not required to be disclosed by the insured:

(*i*) Facts which tend to lessen the risk.

(*ii*) Facts of public knowledge.

(*iii*) Facts which could be inferred from the information disclosed.

(*iv*) Facts waived by the insurer.

(*v*) Facts governed by the conditions of the policy.

4. PRINCIPLE OF INDEMNITY

As a rule all insurance contracts except personal insurance are contracts of indemnity. According to this principle, the insurer undertakes to put the insured, in the event of loss, in the same position that he occupied immediately before the happening of the event insured against. In certain form of insurance, the principle of indemnity is modified to apply. For example, in marine or fire insurance, sometimes, certain profit margin which would have earned in absence of the event, is also included in the loss. In true sense of the indemnity, the insured is not entitled to make a profit of his loss.

Uses

(*i*) To discourse over insurance the principle of indemnity it an essential feature of an insuran contract, in absence whereof this industry would have the hue of gambling and the insured wou to effect over-insurance and then intentionally cause a loss to occur so that a financial gai achieved. So, to avoid this international loss, only the actual loss becomes payable and not sum (which is higher in over-insurance). If the property is under-insured, *i.e.*, the insured amount is less than the actual value of the property insured, the insured is generally regarded his own insurer for the amount if under insurance and in case of loss one shall share the loss himself.

(*ii*) To avoid an Anti-social Act

If the assured is allowed to gain more than the actual loss, which is against the principle of indemnity, he will be tempted to gain by destruction of his own property after getting it insured against a risk. He will be under constant temptation to destroy the property. Thus, the whole society will be doing only anti-social act, *i.e.*, the persons would be interested in gaining after destruction of the property. So, the principle of indemnity has been applied where only the cash-value of his loss and nothing more than this, though he might have insured for a greater amount, will be compensated.

(*iii*) To maintain the Premium at Low-level

If the principle of indemnity is not applied, larger amount will be paid for a smaller loss and this will increase the cost of insurance and the premium of insurance will have to be raised. If premium is raised two things may happen—first, persons may not be inclined to insure and second, unscrupulous persons would get insurance to destroy the property to gain from such act. Both things would defeat thc purpose of insurance. So, principle of indemnity is here to help them because such temptation is eliminated when only actual loss and not more than the actual financial loss is compensated provided there is insurance up to that amount.

Conditions for Indemnity Principle

The following conditions should be fulfilled in full application of principle of indemnity.

(*i*) The insured has to prove that he will suffer loss on the insured matter at the time of happening the event and the loss is actual monetary loss.

(*ii*) The amount of compensation will be the amount of insurance. Indemnification cannot be more than the amount insured.

(*iii*) If the insured gets more amount than the actual loss, the insurer has right to get the extra-amount back.

(*iv*) If the insured gets some amount from third party after being fully indemnified by insurer, the insurer will have right to receive all the amount paid by the third party.

(*v*) The principle of indemnity does not apply to personal insurance because the amount of loss is not easily calculable there.

5. DOCTRINE OF SUBROGATION

The doctrine of subrogation refers to the right of the insurer to stand in the place of the insured, after settlement of a claim, in so far as the insured's right of recovery from an alternative source is involved. If the insured is in a position to recover the loss in full or in part from a third party due to whose negligence the loss may have been precipitated, his right of recovery is subrogated to the insurer on settlement of the claim. The insurers, thereafter, recover the claim from the thrid party. The right of subrogation may be exercised by the insurer before payment of loss.

Essentials of Doctrine of Subrogation

(*i*) *Corollary to the Principle of Indemnity.* The doctrine of subrogation is the supplementary principle of indemnity. The latter doctrine says that only the actual value of the loss of the property is compensated, so the formen follows that if the damaged property has any value left, or any right against a third party the insurer can subrogate the left property or right of the property because if the insurered is allowed to retain, he shall have realised more than the actual loss, which is contrary to principle of indemnity.

(*ii*) *Subrogation is the Substitution.* The insurer, according to this principle, becomes entitled to all the rights of insured subject matter after payment because he has paid the actual loss of the property. He is substituted in place of other persons who act on the right and claim of the property insured.

(*iii*) *Subrogation only up to the amount of payment.* The insurer is subrogated all the rights, claims, remedies and securities of the damaged insured property after indemnification, but he is entitled to get these benefits only to the extent of his payment. The insurer is, thus, subrogated to the alternative rights and remedies of the insured, only up to the amount of his payment to the insured. In the same way if the insured is compensated for his loss from another party after he has been indemnified by his insurer he is liable to part with the compensation up to the extent that the insurer is entitled to. In one U.S. case it was made clear "If the insurer, having paid the claim to the insured, recovers from the defaulting third party in excess of the amount paid under the policy, he has to pay this excess to the insured though he may charge the insured his share of reasonable expenses incurred in collecting.

(*iv*) *The Subrogation may be applied before Payment.* If the assured got certain compensation from third party before being fully indemnified by the insurer, the insurer can pay only the balance of the loss.

(*v*) *Personal Insurance.* The doctrine of subrogation does not apply to personal insurance because the doctrine of indemnity is not applicable to such insurance. The insurers have no right of action against the third party in respect of the damage. For example, if an insured dies due to the negligence of a third party his dependent has right to recover the amount of the loss from the third party along with the policy amount. No amount of the policy would be subrogated by the insurer.

6. WARRANTIES

There are certain conditions and promises in the insurance contract which are called warranties. According to Marine Insurance Act, "A warranty is that by which the assured undertakes that some particular thing shall or shall not be done, or that some conditions shall be fulfilled, or whereby he affirms or negatives the existence of a particular state of facts." Warranties which are mentioned in the policy are called express warranties. There are certain waranties which are not mentioned in the policy. These warranties are called implied warranties. Warranties which are answers to the question are called affirmative warranties. The warranties fulfilling certain conditions or promises are called promissory warranties.

Warranty is the very important condition in the insurance contract which is to be fulfilled by the insured. On breach of warranty the insurer becomes free from his liability. Therefore insured must have to fulfill the conditions and promises during the insurance contract whether it is important or not in connection with the risk. The contract can continue only when warranties are fulfilled. If warranties are not followed, the contract may be cancelled by the other party whether risk has occurred or not or the loss has occurred due to other reason than the waiving of warranties. However, when the warranty is declared illegal and there is no reverse effect on the contract, the warranty can be waived.

7. PROXIMATE CAUSE

The rule is that immediate and not the remote cause is to be regarded. The maxim is *sed causa proxima non-remota spectature*, *i.e.*; see the proximate cause and not the distant cause. The real cause must be seen while payment of the loss. If the real cause of loss is insured, the insurer is liable to compensate the loss; otherwise the insurer may not be responsible for loss. But, proximate cause is not a device to avoid the trouble of discovering the real cause or the common sense cause. Proximate cause means the active efficient cause that sets in motion a train of events which brings about a result, without intervention of any force started and working actively from a new and independent source.

The determination of real cause depends upon the working and practice of insurance and circumstances to losses. A loss may not be occasioned merely by one event. There may be concurrent causes or chain of causes. They may occur in a sequence or in broken chain. Sometimes, certain causes are excepted by the insurance contract and the insurer is not liable for the accepted peril.

The efficient cause of a loss is called the proximate cause of the loss. For the policy to cover the loss must have an insured peril as the proximate cause of the loss or also the insured peril must occur in the chain of causation that links the proximate cause with the loss. The proximate cause is not necessarily, the cause that was nearest to the damage either in time or in place, but is rather the cause that was actually responsible for loss.

Determination of Proximate Cause

(*i*) If there is a single cause of the loss, the cause will be the proximate cause and further if the peril (cause of loss) was insured,insurer will have to indemnify the loss.

(*ii*) If there are concurrent causes, the insured perils and excepted perils have to be segregated. The coneurrent causes may be first, separable and second, inseparable. Separable causes are those which can be separated from each other. The loss occurred due to a particular cause may be distinguishly known. In such a case if any cause, is excepted peril, insurer will have to pay up to the extent of loss which occurred due to insured perils. If the circumstances are such that the perils are inseparable, then the insurers are not liable at all when there exists any excepted peril.

(*iii*) If the causes occurred in form of chain, they have to be observed seriously.

(A) If there is unbroken chain the excepted and insured perilfi have to be separated. If an excepted peril precedes the operation of the insured peril so that the loss caused by the latter is the direct and natural consequences of the excepted peril, there is no liability. If the insured peril is followed by an excepted peril there is valid liability.

(B) If there is a broken chain of events with no excepted peril involved, it is possible to separate the losses. The insurer is liable only for that loss which caused by an insured peril; where there is an excepted peril, the subsequent loss caused by an insured peril will be a new and indirect cause because of the interruption in the chain of events. The insurer will be liable for the loss caused of insured peril which can be easily segregated. Similarly, if the loss occurs by an insured peril and there is, susbsequently loss by an excepted peril, the insurer will be liable for loss occurred due to the insured peril.

In brief, if the happening of an excepted peril is followed by the occurrence of an insured peril, as a new and independent cause there is a valid claim. If an insured peril is followed by the happening of an excepted peril, as a new and independent cause, there is a claim excluding loss or damage, caused by the excepted peril.

8. ASSIGNMENT OR TRANSFER OF INTEREST

It is necessary to distinguish between assignment of (*a*) the subject-matter of insurance, (*b*) the policy, and (*c*) the policy money when payable.

Marine and life policies can be freely assigned but assignment under fire and accident policies, are not valid,without the prior consent of the insurers—except changes of interest by will or operation of law. Moreover, assignments under fire and accident policies must be made before the insured parts with his, interest. Once he has lost the interest the policy is void and cannot be assigned.

The life policies can, be assigned whether the assignee has an insurable interest or not. Life policies are frequently charged, assigned or otherwise dealt with, for they are valuable securities. A marine policy is freely assignable unless it contains terms expressly prohibiting assignment. It assigned either before or after loss. A marine policy may be assigned by endorsement thereon or in other customary manner. In practice, a marine cargo policy is frequently endorsed in blank and becomes in effect a quasi-negotiable instrument. Thus, it will be appreciated, adds considerably to the convenience of mercantile transactions as the policy can be negotiated through a bank along with other documents of title.

Assignment in fire insurance cannot be recognised without prior consent of the insurer, change of interest in fire policies (unless by will or operation of law) are not valid unless and until the consent of the insurer has been given. The fire policies are not in the nature of assignment nor intended to be assigned from one person to another without the consent of the insurer. Assignment in fire insurance constitutes a new contract.

9. RETURN OF PREMIUM

Ordinarily the premium once paid cannot be refunded. However, in the following cases the refund is allowed.

(*i*) By Agreement in the Policy

The assured may pay full premium while effecting the insurance but it may be agreed to return it wholly or partly in the happening of certain events. For example, special packing may reduce the risk.

(*ii*) For Reasons of Equity

(*i*) *Non-attachment of risk.* Where the subject-matter insured or part thereof, has never been imperilled for example, term insurance with returnable premium where premium is returned to the policy-holder if death does not occur during period of insurance.

(*ii*) *Undeclared balace of on open policy.* The policy may be cancelled and premium may be returned for short interest allowed provided there was no further interest in the policy.

(*iii*) *Payment of Premium is apportionable.* The apportioned part of the consideration is refundable when a part of policy interest is not involved. For example, insurance may be taken for a voyage in stages, each stage being rated separately. In such a case if some stages are not completed the premium relating to incomplete stage is returnable.

(*iv*) Where the assured has no insurable interest throughout the currency of the risk, the premium is returnable provided the policy was not attached by way of wagering.

(*v*) Unreasonable delay in commencing the voyage may also entitle the insurer to cancel the insurance by returning the premium.

(*vi*) Where the assured has over-insured under an unvalued policy a proportionate part of the premium is returnable.

3. Over-insurance by Double Insurance

If there is over-insurance by double insurance, a proportionate part of the several premium is returnable provided that if the policies are taken at different times and any earlier policy has at any time born the entire risk or if a claim has been paid. On the policy in respect of the full insured thereby, no premium is returnable in respect of that policy and when double insurance is effected knowingly by the assured no premium is returnable.

DIFFERENCE BETWEEN DIFFERENT TYPES OF INSURANCE CONTRACT

1. Forms

The insurance contract may be divided into two forms—first life insurance contract and second contract of indemnity.

2. Occurring of Event

The event, the death, in life insurance is certain, but the only uncertainty is the time when the death will occur. In indemnity insurance (in fire and marine insurances) the even may not take place at all or may take place in part. Therefore, in life insurance, ordinarily every place will become a claim sooner or later but it is not certain in indemnity insurance.

3. Subject-Matter

The subject-matter in life insurance is life. The chances of death would increase along with the advance in age whatever precautionary measures may be taken for improvement of health whereas the property in other insurance can be repaired and replaced and may remain usually in good condition.

4. Variance in Premium

In life insurance premium is not much variable whereas in other insurance premium is variable in numerous forms.

5. Classification of Risk

The classification of risks is generally more simple in life insurance than in other types of insurance contract. In life contract it would be standard, sub-standard and uninsurable but in other insurance it may be several.

6. Period of Insurance

Generally the life insurance is taken for longer period. Whereas the other forms of insurance are taken for not more than one two years.

7. Protection and Investment

The life insurance contract provides protection against loss early death and investment to meet the old age requirements. Other forms of insurance do not provide investment because the premium paid is not returnable if the contingencies (hazards) do not occur within the period. Other forms of insurance provide only protection against loss on damage of the property against the insured perils.

8. Premium Payment

The mode of premium payment in life insurance is generally level premium whereas in other forms of insurances, it is single premium.

9. Insurable Interest

Insurable interest must be at the time of proposal in insurance but in property insurance it must be present at the time of loss.

DIFFERENCE BETWEEN FIRE INSURANCE AND LIFE INSURANCE

1. Type of Contract

The fire insurance is a contract of indemnity, where payment of loss will be made only when fire occurred, but the life insurance contract is a contract of certainty, wherein payment is certainly made.

2. Occurring of Event

The fire may or not occur in fire insurance but in life insurance the death will certainly occur.

3. Classification of risk

There are numerous types of risk in fire insurance whereas the risks in life insurance are divided into three classes—the standard risk sub-standard risk and uninsurable risk.

4. Period of Insurance

The term of insurance in fire insurance does not exceed generally more than one year but in life insurance it lasts for a very long period.

5. Protection and Investment

Fire insurance includes only the element of protection whereas the life insurance includes the element of protection and investment because the premium paid or sum assured is returnable in the latter case whereas no premium or amount is returnable in fire insurance.

6. Insurable Interest

In fire insurance, the insurable interest must exist from the date of the proposal to the date of completion of the contract whether by death or by expiry of term. In life insurances insurable interest must exist at the time of proposal. This is the reason that the insured property, insurance policy, or policy amount-cannot be assigned to others in fire insurance whereas it is freely assignable in life insurance.

7. Moral Hazard

The degree of moral hazard in fire insurance is maximum whereas it is very nominal in case of life insurance.

DIFFERENCE BETWEEN FIRE INSURANCE AND MARINE INSURANCE

Fire and marine insurance contracts are similar in most of the cases because both these contracts are indemnity contracts. But, the following differences are observed in both the contracts.

(*i*) Moral Hazard

In marine insurances, the chances of moral hazard do not exist so much as are in the fire insurance.

(*ii*) Insurable Interest

The insurable interest must exist both the time, at the inception and at the completion of the contract. This is the reason fire insurance policies cannot be freely assignable. The insurable interest in marine insurance must exist at the time of loss. So, the marine policies are freely assignable.

(*iii*) Profit

Marine policies generally allow certain margin of profit to be charged at the time of indemnification of loss, but the fire policies do not allow it ordinarily.

(*iv*) Valued Policies

Marine insurance policies are generally valued policies and the market fluctuation is avoided; but the fire polices strictly adher to the doctrine of indemnity and only the market value of the property at the time of loss (valuable amount) is compensated.

INSURANCE AND GAMBLING

Insurance and gambling was considered alike because there are uncertainty of events and payment is made when the event occurs. Like gambles the insured is unaware of the time and amount of loss. If the event occurs, the insured like the gambler gains, otherwise they are experiencing the loss. But there are certain differences between the insurance contract and gambling.

(*i*) Nature of risk

In insurance, risks are existing, they may occur at any time. For example, death, old age, fire, marine perils, accident, etc., may occur any time. If there is no insurance, the person will suffer at the occurrence of these perils, but if insurance is taken against these risks, the insurer will provide a fixed amount or indemnify the amount of loss occurred due to the insured perils. Thus, insurance is protection against these risks.

In case of gambling, the risk does not exist, it is being created for game or amusement while one will suffer and another will gain. In absence of such game, nobody will suffer. In absence of insurance the property owner will suffer while due to insurance, no party will suffer.

(*ii*) Insurable Interest

In insurance contract, insurable interest is essential. Without insurable interest, it would be wagering contract. Thus, this principle clearly distinguishes the insurance contract from the gambling.

QUESTIONS

1. What are the various essentials of insurance contract?
2. Explain fully insurable interest, utmost good faith, principle of indemnity doctrine of subrogation and warranties in insurance contracts.
3. Differentiate the types of insurance contract.
4. 'Proximate cause is not very essential in case of life insurance contract'. Explain in detail.

PART TWO
LIFE INSURANCE

5

NATURE OF LIFE INSURANCE CONTRACT

Life insurance contract may be defined as the contract, whereby the insurer in consideration of a premium undertakes to pay a certain sum of money either on the death of the insured or on the expiry of a fixed period. The definition of the life insurance contract is enlarged by Section 2 (*ii*) of the Insurance Act 1938 by including annuity business. Since, the life insurance contract is not an indemnity contract, the undertaking on the part of the insurer is an absolute one to pay a definite sum on maturity of policy at the death or an amount in instalment for a fixed period or during the life.

Features of Life Insurance Contract

(*i*) Nature of General Contract.

(*ii*) Insurable Interest.

(*iii*) Utmost Good Faith.

(*iv*) Warranties.

(*v*) Proximate Cause.

(*vi*) Assignment and Nomination.

(*vii*) Return of Premium.

(*viii*) Other Features.

In life insurance contract the first three features are very important while the rest of them are of complementary nature.

1. NATURE OF GENERAL CONTRACT

Since the life insurance contract is a sort of contract it is approved by the Indian Contract Act. According to Section 2 (H) and Section 10 of Indian Contract Act, the valid contracts must have the following essentialities:

(*i*) Agreement (offer and acceptance).

(*ii*) Competency of the parties.

(*iii*) Free consent of the parties, *i.e.*, the parties must be *ad. idem*.

(*iv*) Legal consideration.

(*v*) Legal objective.

1. Offer and Acceptance

An offer or proposal is an intimation to another of one's intention to do or to abstain from doing anything with a view to obtaining the assent of that other person to such an act or abstinence. When the person to whom the proposal or offer is made signifies his assent to it, the offer is said to be accepted. The offer and acceptance in life insurance is of typical nature. The proposal form is completed by the proposer and along with the proposal form first premium is paid. The same may be accepted at normal rates and terms. The Agents' canvassing or publication of prospects and of uses of insurance constitute invitation to offer because the public in general and individual in particular are invited to make proposal for insurance. Submission of proposal along with the premium is an offer and the despatch of acceptance-letter is the acceptance. The risk will commence as soon as the acceptance letter is despatched by the insurer. When proposal is not accompanied with the first premium, it would be an invitation to offer by the prospect and the letter of insurer (generally acceptance letter with modification is sent) asking the proposer to pay the first premium without any alteration is an offer and the payment of first premium by the prospect is acceptance. As soon as premium is despatched, acceptance is made provided there was no alteration in the terms and conditions.

Another case may be when the insurer desires to accept the proposal only on certain modifications. The letter (generally the acceptance letter) sent to the prospect about the desire of change in terms and conditions is an offer if the first premium was not sent along with the proposal. But if the first premium was sent along with the proposal, it would be a counter-offer. If the prospect accepts the terms and conditions and sends the first premium if the premium was not already sent, it would be an acceptance. Thus, the acceptance letter sent by the insurer is not always acceptance. It would be acceptance only when the first premium was accompanied with the proposal and the proposal is acceptable on normal rates and terms. In other cases it would be an offer or counter-offer.

2. Competency of the Parties

The essential element of a valid contract is that the parties to, it must be legally competent to contract. Every person is competent to contract who is of the age of majority according to the law, (2) who is of sound mind, and (3) who is not disqualified from contracting by any law.

The insurer will be competent to contract if he has got the licence to carry on insurance business. The insurer is working within the Article of Association and Memorandum of Association or the Deeds of Partnership. In India, the Life Insurance Corporation is solely authorised to carry on life insurance business.

Majority

Majority is attained when a person completes the age of 18 years. A minor is not competent to contract. A contract by a minor is void excepting contracts for necessaries. The minor can repudiate the contract at any time during his minority. If the life insurance policy is issued to a minor, the insurer cannot repudiate it but the minor can repudiate it during his minority. At the attainment of majority, he has to exercise the option, within a reasonable time, whether he would continue to carry on the policy or not. Generally, insurer accepts the proposal forms completed by the guardians of the minors. So, the incompetency of contract does not arise.

Person of Sound Mind

Persons of sound mind can enter into a contract. A person is said to be of sound mind for the purpose of making a contract if at the time when he makes it, he is capable of understanding it and of forming a rational judgment as to its effect upon his interests. A person who is usually of unsound mind, but occasionally of sound mind may make a contract when he is of sound mind. A person usually of sound mind, but occasionally of unsound mind, may not make a contract when he is of unsound mind. So, an intoxicated person cannot enter into a contract. The contract may be voidable at his option, but in order to be avoided, it must be repudiated by the insured within a reasonable time of his becoming sober. Similarly, when an originally valid contract has been entered into, it will not be affected by one of the parties becoming lunatic afterwards.

Other Disqualification

A contract with an alien enemy is void. An alien enemy is disqualified from, and is incapable of, entering into contract or enforcing it. When an alien with whom an insurance contract has been entered into becomes an enemy afterwards, the contract is either suspended or terminated as from the declaration of war.

3. Free Consent of the Parties

Both parties must be of the same mind at the time of contract. If the two parties do not meet in this respect, there is no perfect agreement between them. It is necessary to call it free consent of parties that the contract is not made (consent is not obtained) through coercion, undue influence, fraud, misrepresentation or mistake. In life insurance, both parties must know the exact nature of the risk to be underwritten. If the consent is not free, the contract is generally voidable at the option of the party whose consent was not freely given. According to Section 13 two persons are said to consent freely when they agree upon the same thing in the same sense.

4. Legal Consideration

The presence of a lawful consideration is essential for a legal contract. The insurer must have some consideration in return of his promise to pay a fixed sum at maturity or death whichever may be the case. The consideration need not be money only. It should be anything valuable or to which value may be assigned. It may be interest, right, dividend, etc. In Raj Narain vs. Hindustan Co-operative Insurance the insurance was accepted and the premium was paid but the policy was not issued by the insurers. The insured died and could get the policy amount in allegiance of policy because at the payment of premiums contract was complete. The first premium is consideration and subsequent premiums are merely conditions to contract.

5. Legal Objective

The contract would be legal only when the object is legal. The object of a legal life insurance contract is to protect oneself or one's family against financial losses at the death of the insured. The contract is, sometimes, to provide for financial emergencies that may occur in old age. In brief the contract will be lawful only when the objective is legal. The objective will be legal only when there is insurable interest. Without having this interest, the object of the contract would not be legal. It would be wager contract and against public policy.

2. INSURABLE INTEREST

Insurable interest is the pecuniary interest. The insured must have an insurable interest in the life to be insured for a valid contract. Insurable interest arises out of the pecuniary relationship that exists between the policy-holder and the life assured so that the former stands to loose by the death of the latter and/or continues to gain by his survival. If such relationship exists, then the former has insurable interest in the life of the latter. The loss should be monetary or financial. Mere emotion and expectation do not constitute insurable interest in the life of his friend or father merely because he gets valuable advices from them.

Insurable interest in life insurance may be divided into *two* categories: (1) insurable interest in own life, and (2) insurable interest in other's life. The latter can be sub-divided into *two* classes: (*a*) where proof is not required, and (*b*) where proof is required. Again this insurable interest, (*b*) can be divided into two classes: (*i*) insurable interest arising due to business relationship, and (*ii*) insurable interest in family relation.

Insurable Interest in Own's Life

An individual always has an insurable interest in his own life. Its presence is not required to be proved. Bunyon says, "Every man is presumed to possess an insurable interest in his estate for the loss of his future gains or savings which might be the result of his premature death." According to the definition of insurable interest it is also evident that the person will continue to gain financially while he is surviving and will suffer loss if he is dead because he will be unable to earn or protect the property.

The insurable interest in own life is unlimited because the loss to the insured or his dependents cannot be measured in terms of money and, therefore, no limit can be placed to the amount of insurance that one may take on one's own life. Thus, theoretically, a person can take a policy to any unlimited amount on his own's life; but in practice no insurer will issue a policy for an amount larger than amount seems suitable to the circumstances and means of the applicant. Generally, it is mentioned that one cannot purchase policy usually more than ten times of his one year's income. The premium can be paid by third party provided there was no intention to speculation. If there is possibility of wager contract it would be void.

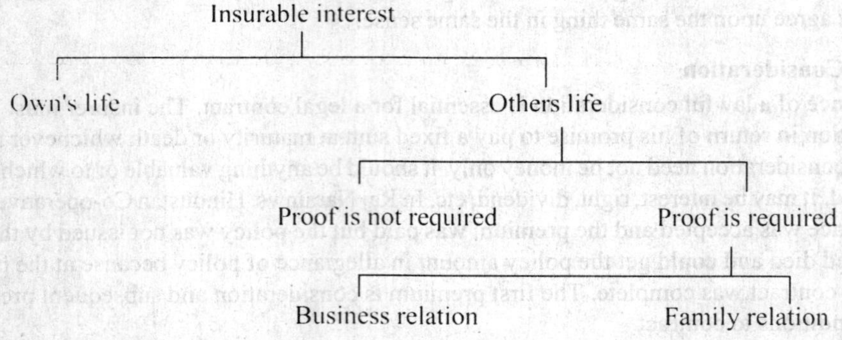

Insurable Interest in Other's Life

Life insurance can be effected on the lives of third parties provided the proposer has insurable interest in the third party. There are two types of insurable interest in other's life. First where proof is not required and second, where proof is required.

A. Proof not required

There are only two such cases where the presence of insurable interest is legally presumed and therefore need not be proved.

1. Wife has insurable interest in the life of her husband

It is presumed and decided by *Reed* vs. *Royal Exchange* (1795) that wife is presumed to have insurable interest in the life of her husband because husband is legally bound to support his wife. The wife will suffer financially if the husband is dead and will continue to gain if the husband is surviving. Since, the extent of loss or gain cannot be measured in this case, the wife has insurable interest in the husband's life up to an unlimited extent.

2. Husband has insurable interest in the life of his wife

The insurable interest is presumed to exist here and no proof is required. It was decided in *Griffith* vs. *Fleming* (1909) that the husband has insurable interest in his wife's life because of domestic services performed by the wife. If the wife is dead husband has to employ other person to render the domestic services and certain other financial expenditures will involve at her death which are not calculable. The husband is benefited at the survival of his wife, so it is self-proved that husband has insurable interest in his wife's life. Since the monetary loss at her death or monetary gain at his survival cannot be measured, there is unlimited insurable interest in the life of wife.

B. Proof is required

Insurable interest has to be proved in the following cases:

1. *Business Relationship.* The policy-holder may have insurable interest in the life of assured due to business or contractual relationship. In this case, the amount of insurable corresponds with the amount of risk involved. Some of such examples are narrated below:

(*a*) *A creditor has in the life or his debtor.* The creditor may lose money if the debtor dies before the loan is repaid. The continuance of debtor's life is financially meaningful to the creditor because the latter will get all his money repaid at the former's survival. The maximum amount of loss to a creditor may be the amount of outstanding loan plus interest thereon and the amount of premium paid. So, the maximum amount of insurable interest is limited to the outstanding loan, plus interest and amount of premium expected to be paid. The interest is calculated on the estimation of duration of debt to be paid. The maximum amount of interest does not say about the payment of policy amount, it, merely, determines the chances of speculation. The full amount of policy is payable irrespective of the payment of loan and interest. Since it is life insurance, the full policy amount is paid.

(*b*) *A trustee has insurable interest in respect of the interest of which he is trustee* because at the survival of the other person the trustee is benefited and at his death he will suffer.

(*c*) *A surety has insurable interest in the life of his principal.* If the principal (the debtor) is dead, the surety is responsible for payment of outstanding loan, or obligated amount. At the survival of principal, he will not suffer this loss. The insurable interest is limited up to the amount of outstanding loan, interest and premium paid.

(*d*) *A partner has insurable interest in life of each partner.* At the death of a partner, the partnership will be dissolved and the surviving partner will lose financially. Even if the firm continues at the death of the partner, the firm has to pay deceased partner's share to his dependents. This will involve a huge financial loss to the partnership. Therefore, the firm collectively can purchase insurance policies in the life of each partner of the firm. Since the firm part of money up to the extent of deceased partner goodwill, capital, share of profit and reserve, the firm has insurable interest up to the extent in each partner. Similarly all the partners have insurable interest in life of each partner because they will financially suffer at a death.

(*e*) *An employer has in the life of a key-man.* A key-man is the person whose presence, capital, capacity cause profit to the business. If the key-man is dead, the business will reduce profit up to a certain extent. The business suffers reduced profit, expenses involved in appointing and training new persons and the amount to be given to the dependents of key-man at his death. So the business has insurance interest up to such extent in the key-man's life.

(*f*) *An insurer has in the life assured.* The insurer suffers at the death of life assured and, therefore, he can get reinsurance of the assured persons by him. The insurable interest is limited up to the policy amount.

2. Family Relationship

The insurable interest may arise due to family relationship if pecuniary interest exists between the policy-holders and life assured because mere relationship or ties of blood and of affection does not constitute insurable interest, the proposer must have a reasonable expectation of financial benefit from the continuance of the life of the person to be insured or of financial loss from his death. The interest must be based on value and not on mere sentiments. Similarly, mere moral obligation is not sufficient to warrant existence of insurable interest although legal obligation to get support will form insurable interest of the person who is supported in life of the person who is supporting. Thus, a son can insure his father's life only when he is dependent on him and the father can take insurance policy on his son's life only when he is dependent on his son.

GENERAL RULE OF INSURABLE INTEREST IN LIFE INSURANCE

1. Time of Insurable Interest

The insurable interest must exist at the time of proposal. Policy, without insurable interest, will be wager. It is not essential that the insurable interest must be present at the time of claim.

2. Services

Except the services of wife, services of other relatives will not essentially form insurable interest. There must be financial relationship between the proposer and the life assured. In other words, the services performed by the son without dependence of his father, will not constitute insurable interest of the father in the life of his soil. Vice-versa is not essential for forming insurable interest.

3. Insurable Interest must be valuable

In business relationship the value or extent of the insurable must be determined to avoid wager contract of the additional insurance. Insurance is limited only up to the amount of insurable interest.

4. Insurable interest should be valid

Insurable interest should not be against public policy and it should be recognised by law. Therefore, the consent of life assured is very essential before the policy can be issued.

5. The legal responsibility may be basis of insurable interest

Since the person will suffer financially up to the extent of responsibility, the proposal has insurable interest to that extent. For instance, a person will be under legal responsibility to expense at the funeral of his wife and children, he can purchase insurance in their lives up to that extent.

6. Insurable Interest must be definite

The insurable interest must be present definitely at the time of proposal. Mere expectation of gain or support will not constitute insurable interest.

7. Legal Consequence

The insurable interest must be there to form legal and valid insurance contract. Without insurable interest, it would be null and void.

3. UTMOST GOOD FAITH

The life insurance requires that the principle of utmost good faith should be preserved by both the parties. The utmost good faith says that both the parties, proposer (insured) and insurer, must be of the same mind at the time of contract because only then the risk may be correctly ascertained. They must make full and true disclosure of the facts material to the risk.

Material Facts

In life insurance material facts are age, income, occupation, health, habits, residence, family history and plan of insurance. Material facts are determined not on the basis of opinion, therefore, the proposer should disclose not only those matters which the proposer may feel are material but all facts which are material.

Duty of both parties

It is not only the proposer but the insurer also who is responsible to disclose all the material facts which are going to influence the decision of the proposer, whether apply or not to apply for insurance. Since the decision is taken mostly on the basis of subject-matter, the life to be insured in life insurance, and the material facts relating to the subject-matter are known or is expected to be known by the proposer; it is much more responsibility of the proposer to disclose the material facts.

Full and True Disclosure

Utmost good faith says that there should be full and true disclosure of all the material facts. Full and true means that there should be no concealment, misrepresentation, half disclosure and fraud of the subject matter to be insured.

Extent of the Duty

The duty of disclosure finishes at the moment when the proposal form has been fully and correctly fulfilled provided there is no such facts which he considers or expected to be considered material and have not been disclosed. The proposer cannot defened on the ground that he had omitted to disclose it by carelessness or by mistake or that he did not regard it material to the contract.

Legal Consequence

In the absence of utmost good faith the contract will be voidable at the option of the person who suffered loss due to non-disclosure. The intentional non-disclosure counts fraud and is void *ab initio* and the unintentional non-disclosure is voidable at the option of the party not at fault.

Once the voidable contract has been validated by the party not at fault, the contract cannot be avoided by him later on. For instance, if the insurer has continued to accept the premium when certain non-disclosure, say mis-statement of age, has been disclosed the insurer cannot invalid the contract and cannot refute to pay the amount of claim. If the party not at fault does not exercise its option, the contract will remain valid.

Indusputability of Policy

The doctrine of utmost good faith works as a great hardship for a long period on the plea of mis-statement at the time of proposal. In such cases, it would be very difficult to prove or disprove whether a particular statement made at the time of policy was true. Therefore, to remove this hardship, certain sections in the concerned Act are provided. In India, Section 45 of the Insurance Act 1938 deals with such dispute. It is called *indisputable clause*, "... No policy of life insurance, after expiry of two years from the date on which it was effected, be called into question by an insurer on the ground that a statement made in the proposal for insurance or in any report of a medical officer or referee or friend of the insured or in any other document leading to the issue of the policy was inaccurate or false, unless the insurer shows that such statement was on a material matter or suppressed facts which it was material to disclose and that it was fraudulently made by the policy-holder and that the policy-holder knew at the time of making it that the statement was false or that it suppressed facts which it was material to disclose. Provided that nothing in this section shall prevent the insurer from calling for proof of age at any time if he is entitled to do so.

FACTS NOT REQUIRED TO BE DISCLOSED

The following facts are not required to be disclosed:

(*i*) Circumstances which are diminishing the risk.

(*ii*) Facts which are known or reasonably should be known to the insurer in his ordinary course of business.

(*iii*) Facts which the insurer should infer from the information given.

(*iv*) Facts which are waived by the insurer.

(*v*) Facts which are superfluous to disclose by reason of a condition or warranty.

(*vi*) Facts of public knowledge.

4. WARRANTIES

Representation

For understanding warranties 'Representations' are to be thoroughly understood because in life insurance those representations which are embodied in the policy and expressly or impliedly forming part of the basis of the contract, are called *warranties*. Every information given by a proposer for insurance to the insurer during the negotiations is a representation. The representations may be material or non-material. The material representations are the basis of insurance contract as has been clear in the utmost good faith under material facts. If the proposer's representation is false or untrue, the contract may be voidable at the option of the insurer. The representations made during the negotiations do not form an integral part of the contract.

Warranties

Warranties are an integral part of the contract, *i.e.*, these are the bases of the contract between the proposer and insurer and if any statement, whether material or non-material, is untrue the contract shall be null and void and the premium paid by him may be forfeited by the insurer. The policy issued will contain that the proposal and personal statement shall form part of the policy and be the basis of the contract. So that representation will be warranty. As has been disclosed already that the warranties may be (*i*) informative, and (*ii*) promissory.

(*i*) *Informative Warranties.* In life insurance the informative warranties are more important. The proposer is expected to disclose all the material facts to the best of his knowledge and belief.

(*ii*) *Promissory Warranties.* Warranties relating to the future may only be statements about his expectation or intention, for instance, the proposer promises that he will not take up any hazardous occupation and will inform the insurer if he will take the hazardous occupation.

Breach of Warranty

If there is breach of warranty, the insurer is not bound to perform his part of the contract unless he chooses to ignore the breach. The effect of a breach of warranty is to render the contract voidable at the option of the other party provided there is no element of fraud. In case of fraudulent representation or promise, the contract will be void *ab initio*.

5. PROXIMATE CAUSE

The efficient or effective cause which causes the loss is called *proximate cause*. It is the real and actual cause of loss. If the cause of loss (peril) is insured, the insurer will pay; otherwise the insurer will not compensate. In life insurance the doctrine of *Causa Proxima* (Proximate Cause) is not applied because the insurer is bound to pay the amount of insurance whatever may be the reason of death. It may be natural or unnatural. So, this principle is not of much practical importance in connection with life assurance, but in the following cases the proximate causes are observed in the life insurance, too.

(*i*) *War-risk.* Where policy is issued on exclusion of war and aviation risks, the proximate cause of death is important because the insurer waives its liability if death occurred, in this case, while the insured was in field or is engaged in operation of war and aviation. Only premium paid or surrender value whichever is higher is payable and the total policy amount is not payable.

(*ii*) *Suicide.* If suicide occurs within one year of the policy, or there was intention to commit suicide and the payment of policy would be restricted, only up to the interest of the third party in the policy provided the interest was expressed at least one month before the suicide.

(*iii*) *Accident Benefit.* A problem arises when an insured under an accident policy is killed or suffers an injury which has an immediate cause and also a remote cause. In accident benefit policy, double of the policy amount is paid. So, the cause of death in this policy is of paramount importance.

6. ASSIGNMENT AND NOMINATION

The policy in life insurance can be assigned freely for a legal consideration or love and affection. The assignment shall be complete and effectual only on the execution of such endorsement either on the policy itself or by a separate deed. Notice for this purpose must be given to the insurer who will acknowledge the assignment. Once the assignment is completed, it cannot be revoked by the assignor because he ceases to be the owner of the policy unless reassignment is made by the assignee in favour of the assignor. An assignee may be the owner of the policy both on survival of the life assured, or on his death according to the terms of transfer. The life policies are the only policies which can be assigned whether the assignee has an insurable interest or not. Life policies are frequently charged, assigned or otherwise dealt with for they are valuable securities because a fixed sum is certainly paid, in life policies excepting a few, say, pure endowment and temporary polices.

Nomination

The holder of a policy of life insurance on his own life may either at the time of affecting policy or at any subsequent time before the policy matures, nominate the person or persons to whom the money secured by the policy shall be paid in the event of his death. A nomination can be cancelled before maturity, but unless notice is given of any such cancellation to the insurer, the insurer will not be liable for any bona fide payment to a nominee registered in the records. When the policy matures, or if the nominee dies, the sum shall be paid to the policy-holder or his legal representatives.

7. RETURN OF PREMIUM

Ordinarily, the premium once paid cannot be refunded. However in the following cases the premiums paid are returnable.

1. For reason of Equity

Equity implies a condition that the insurer shall not receive the price of running a risk he runs. Thus, there the contract does not come into effect or it is held to be void *ab initio*. For example, on account of misrepresentation or breach of warranty, the insured, in the absence of any express condition to the contrary, can claim the return of any premiums paid. But if the policy runs for a time and becomes void later on, the insured is not entitled to the return of any part of the premium.

Where the insured is guilty of fraud in obtaining a policy, he will fail in his claim to the sum assured. He cannot also ask for a return of the premiums because he will have to allege his own fraud to succeed in his claim and no court will assist such person.

8. OTHER FEATURES

Life insurance policies have the following additional features:

Life insurance contract is (*i*) an Aleatory contract, (*ii*) a unilateral contract, (*iii*) a conditional contract, (*iv*) a contract of Adhesion, and (*v*) not a contract of indemnity.

(*i*) *Aleatory Contract.* Aleatory contract means contract depends on chance. In ordinary contract approximately equal value is exchanged by both parties; but in life insurance contract, the full sum assured may be payable even if all premiums are not paid. Thus, on the chance of death, higher amount is payable. It should be clear, here, that, this does not make the contract of wager because of insurable interest.

(*ii*) *Unilateral Contract.* Life insurance contract is unilateral contract because, here, only the insurer makes an enforceable promise. The proposer had already performed his duty of payment of premiums. If the first premium is paid, the insurer is bound to accept subsequent premium and to pay the amount claim when it arises except on the ground of fraud.

(*iii*) *Conditional Contract.* Life insurance contract is conditional contract because the insurer shall pay the assured sum only when the contract is continuing by payment of premium. In addition, the insurer's promise to pay the sum assured is also conditional upon the furnishing of satisfactory proof of death and other conditions mentioned in the policy.

(*iv*) *Contract of Adhesion.* Contract of adhesion means that the terms of the contract are not arrived by mutual negotiations between the parties as in the case of ordinary contracts. The proposer is not in a position to bargain about the terms of contract because these terms are already determined. The only course open to the proposer is whether to accept or not a particular policy.

(*v*) *Indemnity contract is not applied.* In life insurance the indemnity contract is not applicable because the value of loss at death cannot be ascertained. It is not possible to ascertain the time up to which the insured would have survived and it is also difficult to ascertain the amount of money to be earned by him during life-time. So, the doctrine of subrogation is also not applicable. In life insurance a fixed sum is paid which may be the sum assured and bonus if the policy is participating one.

QUESTIONS

1. Describe the essential features of life insurance contract.
2. Explain in detail how insurable interest, utmost good faith, warranties and proximate cause are applicable in life insurance.
3. 'The policies are freely assignable in case of life insurance.' Discuss.

6

CLASSIFICATION OF POLICIES

The life insurance contract provides elements of protection and investment. After getting insurance, the policy-holder feels a sense of protection because he shall be paid a definite sum at the death or maturity. Since a definite sum must be paid, the element of investment is also present. In other words, life insurance provides against pre-mature death and a fixed sum at the maturity of policy. The two elements of protection and investment exist in various degrees in different types of policies. Not only this, but these elements will vary according to the different times in the same policy. The older the policy, the lesser the element of protection and higher the element of investment and vice-versa is also true.

Having different elements in different policies, the policy-holders are free to choose the best policies according to their requirements. It would be known that no one policy is the best policy for all the policy-holders due to variance in cost, elements of investments and protection, requirements of the policy-holders and availability of the policy.

The life insurance policies can be divided on the basis of (*a*) Duration of policy, (*b*) Method of Premium payments, (*c*) Participation in profit, (*d*) Number of lives covered, (*e*) Method of payment of claim amounts and (*f*) Non-conventional Policies.

A. POLICIES ACCORDING TO DURATION OF POLICIES

The life insurance policies according to the duration may be (*i*) whole-life, (*ii*) term insurance, (*iii*) endowment insurance and (*iv*) survivorship policy.

(*i*) *Whole-life policies.* Whole-life policies are issued for life. It means that the policy amount will be paid at the death of the life assured. The life assured, thus, cannot get the policy amount during his life time; only his dependents will get the advantages of this policy. The whole life policies can be effected either by payment of (*i*) single premium, (*ii*) continuous premium, payment or (*iii*) limited premium. The single premium payment is not very common whereas the limited premium payment is the most popular form of whole-life policies because, it is convenient to the policy-holder to arrange the payment of premium during his income-earning period. In continuous premium payment, this benefit is not available because premium is payable up to the life of the policy-holder. This is losing its importance because only the dependents of life assured are getting the benefit. Also, in extreme cases, he pays, more by way of premium than the benefits relievable under the policy and that too when earning capacity of the assured is reduced. This plan is cheaper and suits to an young man with limited resources and whose requirements for protection is maximum. It is, also beneficial to pay estate duty. If payment of premiums, ceases after at least, 3 years' premiums have been paid, a free paid up policy for such reduced sum, as can be allowed according to the rules, will be automatically secured provided the reduced sum assured is not less than Rs. 250.

(*ii*) *Limited Payment Whole-Lite Policies.* The payment of premium is limited to certain period, although the amount secured under this plan is payable on the death of the policy-holder. Premium under this plan is higher than the premium payable under a whole life plan. The amount of premium depends upon the number of annual premiums stipulated since premiums are payable for a selected period of years or until death if it occurs within this period, the life assured is satisfied to know the amount of maximum premium payable. If the life assured survives the premium paying period, the policy continues in full force, provided all premiums have been paid, but no further premiums are required to be paid. With profits limited payment policies do not cease to participate in profits after completion of the premium-paying period but continue to share in the periodical bonus distribution.

This plan is suitable for persons in whose case the need for money would arise only on the happening of the death, but who either on account of personal and family history are not eligible for a whole life plan or do not want to extend the premium-paying period beyond their earning years. The minimum amount for which a policy will be issued under this plan is Rs. 1,000.

(*iii*) *Convertible Whole-Life Policy.* This is a whole-life policy which gives its holder an option to get it converted at the end of five years, into an endowment policy. If this option is exercised, the policy no longer remains a whole-life policy, if it is not exercised the policy continues to be, a whole-life policy. The policy is designed to meet the needs of the young man who is on the threshold of his career and has prospect for increase in income after a short period. The object is to provide maximum insurance protection at a minimum cost and at the same time to offer a flexible contract which can be allowed to an endowment policy, at the end of five years of the policy. If the option is not exercised, the policy continues as a whole life assurance with premiums ceasing at age 70. If the policy is converted into endowment, the premium is suitably increased. However, no difference in premiums for the previous five years, and interest thereon, will be charged and he is not required to go under fresh medical examination. The vested bonus additions would be altered to an amount which the policy would have earned had it been effected from the commencement as an endowment policy and further, the policy would thereafter be entitled to bonus at the rate applicable to endowment assurance. The minimum sum assured for which a policy will be issued under this plan is Rs. 5,000 and the maximum age at entry shall be 45 years.

TERM INSURANCE POLICIES

Term insurance is far a short period of years ranging from 3 months to seven years. Sum assured is payable only in the event of death of the life assured occurring during the period; but the assurance comes to an end, should the life assured survive. The selected term premiums are usually payable throughout the term of the policy or till the prior death of the life assured. Term insurance policies are the cheapest policies. Without profit term insurance issued at age 35 requires a single premium of Rs. 13.62 for a Rs. 1,000/- whereas the single premium rate far whole life without profit policies issued at corresponding age is Rs. 519.69. Term insurance policies are always 'without profits'.

The term insurance policies are useful to those (*i*) who need extra-protection far a short duration or (*ii*) who need protection for long duration but are unable to purchase for the time-being due to ill-health or lesser income, (*iii*) a young businessman can take the policy to save the business-disaster during initial stage of the business, (*iv*) key-men's insurances are generally on term insurance basis, (*v*) a mortgagor of the property may be benefited by this scheme, (*vi*) a father can take this policy during the period of education of his child, and (*vii*) any such persons who are willing to provide insurance far a shorter period.

Term insurances are of the following types in India.

(*i*) *Straight-Term (Temporary) Insurance.* The corporation issues term-insurance for two years, which is also called as two-years temporary assurance policy. The sum assured will be payable only in the event of the life assured's death occurring within two years from the commencement of the policy. A single premium is required to be paid at the outset. The policies are issued only under, the without profits plan. The proposes is required to pay the medical examination fee. The policy is not entitled to any surrender value and no loan can be granted on the security thereof because, it is not of accumulative nature and payment is not always certain. This plan cannot be converted into other plans.

This policy is beneficial to the dependents who are required to pay Estate Duty and to those persons who are given charity or donation of fixed property.

(*ii*) *Renewable Term Policies.* These policies are renewable at the expiry of term for an additional period without medical examination; but the premium rate will be altered according to the age attained at the time of renewal. This policy is beneficial to those whose health are deteriorating and will be uninsurable at an advanced age. With the help of this policy, they continue to enjoy the insurance benefit without going under fresh medical examination. However, the premium rate will be increasing according to the attained age. The policy-holder can renew it many times provided the attained age has not crossed 55 years.

(*iii*) *Convertible Term Policy.* Under this policy, option to convert it into whole life or endowment policy is available. In corporation, the life assured under this plan has an option to convert the policy, provided it is in full force, into either a limited payment life policy or an endowment assurance policy, without having to undergo fresh medical examination, at any time during the specified term except the last two years. If the option of conversion is exercised, a new policy under the limited payment life-plan or endowment assurance plan will be issued as the case may be subject to the rates of premium and terms and conditions prevailing on the date of conversion. In other words, the premium rates ,will be increased according to the age attained.

This policy is issued only to first class lives. Persons aged over 40 years nearer birthday at entry and those following hazardous occupation including persons in the Armed Forces will not be eligible for assurance under this plan. Proposals on the lives of ladies are also not considered under this plan. Proposals for policies under this scheme will be entertained only from persons in government or quasi-government service, or in the service of reputed commercial firms. The cost of medical, examination will have to be borne by the proposer. The minimum sum assured is Rs. 5,000 and the term is 5, 6, or 7 years. Admission of age before issuing of policy is essential. Premium may be single, yearly or half-yearly instalments only. No surrender values loan, paid-up values, no rebate in premium whether for large sum or for mode of payment of premium are allowed under this policy.

This plan is of much use to those who are initially unable to pay the larger premium required for a whole life or endowment policy. This is useful to those who desire to leave the final decision of permanent insurance at later date. The premium rate is considerably lower in this case. It is specially suitable to a young man with large family just entering in life who, due to his low, income, is unable to afford high premium required to give him adequate protection under a permanent policy.

ENDOWMENT POLICIES

The endowment policies can be several, of which important endowment policies are discussed below:

1. Pure Endowment Policy

The sum assured is payable on the life assured's surviving the endowment term. In the event of his death within the term (endowment), premiums may be returnable or not. In corporation, all premiums paid, without any deduction, will be refunded to. Thus the pure endowment policy is opposite of the term policy, because the insured is paid if he survives in pure endowment and if dies with, in the term in term policy. Actually, these two policies, *i.e.*, pure endowment and term policies, are the bases of all other policies. Pure endowment is for the benefit of the policy-holder and term policy is for the benefit of others. So, the pure endowment policy has the element of investment and the term policy has the element of protection. Pure endowment grants protection against 'living long' while the term policy grants protection against living too short. The former is old-age protection while the latter is family protection.

This policy can be issued in the life of adult as well as in the life of child. In the case of a policy effected on the life of a child payment of premiums does not case on the death of the proposer but must be continued during the whole currency of the policy. Paid-up and surrender values are allowed on this policy. The mode of payment of premium under this plan is only yearly or half-yearly.

This policy is useful to the person who does not care to present himself for medical examination. This is also beneficial to those who, for reasons of health, would be unacceptable for life insurance on standard premium. It is a sort of compulsory saving for old age.

2. Ordinary Endowment Policy

This is the policy which actually represents the life insurance in true sense. It provides an ideal combination of both the family protection and the investment. It is taken out for a specified term of years, the sum assured being payable either on the life assured's death during the period or on his survival to the end of the period. Premiums are payable throughout the term of the policy or to a limited period or till the prior death of the life assured. Ordinary endowment policy is the combination of term insurance and of pure endowment. So, the net premium rate for an ordinary endowment policy is equal to the net premiums of term and pure endowment policies issued at the same age, for the same period of time.

This provides solutions to various problems of life whether living too long or too short. In other words, the old age provision and the family protection is possible by purchasing only this single policy. Moreover, compulsory saving is possible due to this policy which is not present in other types of savings. It is a means of hedging against the possibility of saving period being cut short by death. The next advantage of this policy is to meet the marriage; education or other requirements of the family.

3. Joint Life Endowment Policy

This policy covers more than one life under a single policy. Under this plan, the sum assured is payable on the expiry of the term or on the death of one of the assured lives during the endowment period. Premiums are payable throughout the endowment period or till the prior-death of anyone of the lives assured. The premium is calculated with certain modification according to the age of all insured partners. Paid-up and surrender values are payable on the policy.

This policy is suitable to partners of a firm because firm will not discontinue on the tremendous outflow of the funds at the death of a partner. This policy is also beneficial to a couple. The practice of granting insurance to husband and wife under this plan was withdrawn in 1960; but it has again been reinstated. The ceiling on the sum to be assured will be determined by the earned income on the wife or the husband whichever is less and also taking into account the previous insurance held on that life.

4. Double Endowment Policy

Under this policy, if the life assured dies during the endowment period, the basic sum assured is payable and if he survives to the end of the term, double of the sum assured is paid. Premiums are payable throughout the endowment term or till the prior death of the life insured. The premiums, are generally quoted according to the endowment period, irrespective of the age at entry subject to the provision that maturity age is not beyond 65. The term of policy is ranging from 10 years to 40 years but no policy is insured to mature at an age exceeding 65 years. This policy is combination of an endowment insurance and a pure endowment (without return of premiums) for the same period and for the same amount.

This plan is beneficial to the person who by reason of some physical disability is not eligible for acceptance at the tabular rates under any of the other classes of insurance. This is also to benefit to those who are confident of living long but would like to have some cover in the event of his early death. The investment element is higher than the protection element in this plan.

5. Fixed Term (Marriage) Endowment Policy

Under this plan, the sum assured is payable only at the end of a stipulated period, but the premium ceases if death of the policy-holder occurs earlier. In such an event the policy will remain fully paid until the maturity date but the beneficiary may discount the policy before maturity. This plan is issued on without profit basis, paid-up values are paid under this policy. This policy is designed to meet the needs of a family man who wants to make available a certain sum for marriage of a female dependents.

6. Educational Annuity Policy

Like marriage endowment policy, this policy is also taken out on the life of the father or guardian who undergoes medical examination, The child for whose benefit (education) policy is taken is called beneficiary. The difference is that the sum assured is not payable in, a lump sum but is payable, in equal instalments over a period of five years. It is payable in half-yearly instalments for five years.

7. Triple Benefit Policy

This policy is a combination of a whole life limited payment and a pure endowment (without return of premium) with a guaranteed annual bonus payable on death during the endowment term. This policy is granted for a fixed terms of 15, 20 or 25 years. Premiums are payable throughout the term or till prior death of the life assured.

The special feature of the plan is that there is a guaranteed and steadily increasing family provision during the selected period along with the old age benefit. The provision for the family does not terminate when the old age benefit is paid at the end of the period and no further premiums are payable thereafter; but a sum equal to the original sum assured still remains to be paid on the death of the life assured thereafter.

The following benefits are guaranteed provided the policy remains in force for the original sum assured.

A. If death occurs within the stipulated period

The benefits payable to the dependents, in this case, are:

(*i*) The basic sum assured, and

(*ii*) A guaranteed bonus per annum equal to Rs. 25/- per - 1,000/- sum assured for each full year's premium paid excluding the first year's premium.

This is a non-participating scheme where under the sum assured increases by fixed amounts during the term. The amount of guaranteed bonus is fixed and does not defend on the profits of the insurer.

B. On survival to the Selected Term

The following amounts are paid at the survival of the life assured at the selected term:

(*i*) The basic sum assured in cash, and

(*ii*) Actually paid-up whole life assurance for a like amount payable at death thereafter.

However, the life assured is given the following options in lieu of these two benefits:

An increased cash payment

OR

fully 'paid-up whole life policy for an increased sum assumed.

The alternative benefit of an increased paid-up assurance will be allowed without medical examination subject to the exercise of this option not less than three years before expiry of the selected term. Paid-up values are also given in this case. The benefits available under the policy on maturity will also be reduced in the same proportion. The policy so reduced will thereafter be free from all liability for payment of premiums but shall loose all rights to the guaranteed additions assured in the event of death subsequent to the date of the conversion into a reduced paid-up value. Guaranteed surrender value is applicable to this policy.

The plan is useful to a person who, in addition to providing cover for his family, wants to make some provision for his old age. It overcomes the main drawback of the whole life policy, *i.e.*, the assured is permitted to get the policy amount. The other advantage is that the insurance element is greater than in an ordinary endowment assurance policy.

8. Anticipated Endowment Policy

This policy is similar to endowment assurance except that a part of the sum assured is paid at certain interval before death within maturity of the policy and the balance of the sum assured is payable at maturity. In the event of death at any time during the term of the policy, *i.e.*, before the maturity date, full sum assured is payable without any deduction of installments paid earlier. The policy may be issued both under with and without profit plan. The term may be 15, 20 or 25 years.

The payment of policy amount by the corporation is as below:

1. 1/5 of the sum assured becomes payable on the life assured's surviving 5, 10 or 15 years according as the selected term of insurance is 15, 20 or 25 Years;
2. Another 1/5 of the sum assured on his surviving 10, 15 or 20 years according as the selected form of assurance is 15, 20 or 25 years; and
3. The balance 3/5th of the sum assured on his surviving the selected term of years.

But in the event of death at any time within the selected term the full sum assured is payable without any deduction or adjustment for amount that may have been paid earlier by way of survivance benefit. The LIC has discontinued this policy.

The money back policy is useful for those who, besides desiring to provide for their own old age and family, feel the need for lump sum benefits at periodical intervals. Under this scheme, the following benefits are payable:

(*i*) For a policy with a term of 12 years, 1/5th of the sum assured becomes payable on the life assured's surviving 4 years, a further 1/5th of the sum assured becomes payable on his surviving 5 years and the balance 3/5th of the sum assured on his surviving to the end of the term of 12 years.

(*ii*) For a policy with a term of 15 years, 1/4th of the sum assured becomes payable on the life assured's surviving 5 years, a further 1/4th of the sum assured becomes payable on his surviving 10 years and the balance 1/2 of the sum assured becomes payable on his surviving to the end of the term of 15 years.

(*iii*) For a policy with a term of 20 years, 1/5th of the sum assured becomes payable on the life assured's surviving 5 years, a further 1/5th of the sum assured becomes payable on his surviving 10 years, a further 1/5th of the sum assured becomes payable on his surviving 10 years, a further 1/5th of the sum assured becomes payable on his surviving 15 years and the balance 2/5th of the sum assured becomes payable on his surviving to the end of the term of 20 years.

(*iv*) For a policy with a term of 25 years, 1/5th of the sum assured becomes payable on the life assured's surviving 10 years, a further 1/5th of the sum assured becomes payable on his surviving 15 years, a further 1/5th of the sum assured becomes payable on his surviving 20 years and the balance 2/5th of the sum assured becomes payable on his surviving to the end of the term of 25 years.

However in the event of death at any time within the selected term the full sum assured is payable without any deduction or adjustment for the amount that may have been paid earlier by way of survivance benefit. The bonus additions to the policy will be reckoned of the full sum assured and are payable at the end of the selected term of years or at the life assured's death, if previous.

In the event of cessation of payment of the premiums under this policy, a paid up assurance, payable at the end of the selected term of years or at the life assured's death if previous, is automatically secured provided premiums have been paid under the policy for not less than three years and a minium paid up assurance of Rs. 250 exclusive of any attached bonus is secured. All bonuses declared and attaching to the policy at the date of cessation of payment of premiums remain attached to the reduced paid up policy but the policy is not entitled to participate in the profits declared thereafter. No loan will be granted under this policy. The minimum amount for which a policy will be issued under this plan is Rs. 5,000. Further, policies will be issued for terms of 12, 15, 20 and 25 years only.

10. Progressive Protection Policy with Profits

This policy is very useful for those who want to provide additional insurance benefits for additional responsibilities. Only first class lives will be accepted under this plan. For' the purpose of Non-Medical (Special) Scheme, this policy will be deemed to be for double the sum assured. The sum assured increases automatically by half the initial sum assured at the end of five years and again by half the initial sum assured at the end of ten years, irrespective of the state of health of the policy-holder at that time. In other words, medical evidence of health will not be required on the occasion of subsequent increase in the sum assured under the policy. After ten years the benefits under the policy will be double the initial sum assured, payable on survival at the end of the selected term or on death within the term.

For the first five years, premiums will be for the initial sum assured. At the end of five years, and again at the end of ten years, the premiums will increase with the increase in the sum assured. Bonus will be paid at the end of the selected term or at the death of the life assured, whichever is earlier, and will be calculated on the initial sum assured for the first five years. After the increase in the sum assured, bonus will be calculated on the increased sum assured from the date of increase. Loans will be available within the surrender value of the policy. If, after at least three full years premiums have been paid in respect of this policy, any subsequent premium be not duly paid, this policy shall not be wholly void, but the sum assured by it shall be reduced to such a sum as can be allowed according to the rules of the Corporation. The policy so reduced shall not be entitled to participate in future profits. The existing vested bonus additions, if, any, will remain attached to the reduced paid up policy. The maximum age at entry is 45 years and maximum maturity age is 65 years. The policy is offered for 20, 25, 30 and 35 years. The minimum sum assured for which it policy will be issued under this plan is Re. 5,000/- and the maximum will be Rs. 1,00,000. All policies taken under, this plan will be taken into account while arriving at the maximum sum assured.

11. Anticipated Whole Life Policy With Profits

This policy provides two distinct types of benefits in one policy—the benefit of Whole Life Limited Payment Policy and anticipated payments at five yearly intervals. It provides complete long-range insurance protection or the family and in addition helps meet various short-term needs through periodical payments. The following benefits are available under this policy:

(*i*) For a policy with a term of 20 years, 1/8th of the sum assured becomes payable on the life assured's surviving 5 years, a further 1/8th of the sum assured becomes payable on his surviving 15 years and a final 1/8th of the sum assured becomes payable on his surviving to the end of the term of 20 years.

(*ii*) For a policy with term of 25 years, 1/10th of the sum assured becomes payable on the life assured's surviving 5 years, a further 1/10th of the sum assured becomes payable on his surviving 10 years, a further 1/10th of the sum assured becomes payable on his surviving 20 years and a final 1/10th of the sum assured becomes payable on his surviving to the end of the term of 25 years.

However, in the event of death at any time, the full sum assured is payable without any deduction or adjustment for the amount that may have been paid earlier by way of survivance benefit. Premiums are payable for 20 or 25 years depending upon the premium paying term selected or till death if it occurs within the period. The bonus will be reckoned on the full sum assured and will be payable at the life assured death. The policy will not cease to participate in profits after completion of premium paying period but will continue to share in the periodical bonus distribution for full sum assured until the death of the life assured.

No loan is payable under the policy during the premium paying period, but after the policy becomes fully paid up, loan will be available within the surrender value of the policy for such amounts and on such terms and conditions as may be prescribed from time to time. The minimum amount for which a policy will be issued under this plan is Rs. 5,000. The maximum age at entry is 50 years for a policy with premium paying term of 20 years and 45 years for a policy with premium paying term of 25 years.

12. New Jana Raksha Policy

This policy has been designed taking into account the problem of non-payment of premiums in time. A special facility whereby the policy continues to provide full cover for three years on payment of an initial extra single premium has been incorporated under this policy. The benefits under this policy are, the same as those applicable for all Endowment Assurance Policy with Profits.

The policy will be issued to male lives only. Policies will issued with, maximum age at entry of 40 years. The minimum age at entry will be 18 years completed. Policies will be issued for terms 12, 15 and 40 year only. The minimum sum assured for which policy will be under this plan is Rs. 5,000 and tile maximum sum assured will Rs. 16,000. The sum assured will be issued in the denomination or Rs. 5000, Rs. 10,000 and Rs. 15,000.

In the event of non-payment of premiums within the days of grace, after the payment of premium for the first two years, the policy will be kept in force for the full sum assured for a period of three years on payment of a single extra premium along with the first premium at a rate of Rs. 10.50 per thousand, for ages at entry 29 years and below and at a rate of Rs. 15.00 per thousand for ages at, entry 30 years and above. No commission is payable on this additional premium. If any portion of this extra premium is not utilised for the risk cover, this unutilised portion will be refunded without interest at the time of claim arising by maturity or by death or at the time of surrender. After atleast two years' premiums have been paid, if default occurs in the payment of premium, full death cover is continued for a period of three years from the first unpaid premium due date. At any time during the first 36 months from the date of first unpaid premium, the policy-holder can pay the arrears of premium in full with interest or arrears of first two unpaid premiums with interest or arrears of first unpaid premium with interest. No evidence of health will be required. In ease the arrears of premiums are paid in full, the facility of temporary assurance cover for further three years can be availed of at a future date, during the term of the policy. If the arrears of the premium are paid in part only, the amount will be utilised towards the adjustment of premium starting from the first unpaid premium due date onwards; but no gaps in the adjustment of premium will be allowed.

The policy can be revived by payment of full arrears of premiums with interest, if the period elapsed from the first unpaid premium due date is more than 36 months but not more than 60 months. For revival after three years' default in payment of premiums, a Declaration of Good Health is necessary. After revival, the facility of temporary assurance cover for a further period of three years will be available.

13. Mortgage Redemption Assurance Policy

This policy meets the requirements of institutions and individual borrowers to ensure that the outstanding loan is automatically extinguished in the event of the borrower's death. The benefits under the plan at any time during the currency of the policy would be the amount of outstanding loan at the beginning of the year as envisaged at the beginning of the transaction, and would become payable in the event of death of the borrower. A schedule showing the amounts of outstanding loan at the beginning of each year would be drawn up at the outset on the basis of predetermined rate of interest. The benefits payable would be fixed as shown in the schedule and only these amounts will be paid under the policy irrespective of the actual loan payments. The policies would normally be issued only to male lives aged upto 50 years at entry subject to the condition that the insurance cover would in no case extend beyond 65 years. It means the loans should be liquidated by the time the borrower attained age of 65. The policy may be taken either by single premium or annual premiums. Policies on which premiums are payable annually or monthly will not carry any surrender value. The minimum sum assured, under the above plan shall be Rs. 10,000 except ill the case of large institutional lenders *e.g.* a Co-operative House Mortgage Society and the minimum sum assured for individual will be Rs. 5,000.

14. Children's Deferred Endowment Assurance

Sometimes a parent or guardian or near relative of a child wishes to take an insurance policy on the lift of the child under which the premium is paid by the proposer during the first few years and by the life assured (*i.e.* by the child) thereafter. This can be done by taking the children's deferred endowment assurance. The low premium rate under this plan is a great attraction. A parent can help to his children to take a policy at a rate which is considerably lower than that what they would be called upon to pay at the attaining of majority. The second advantage of this policy is that the habit of thrift is developed among the child and from the very beginning tries to save some money. The third advantage is that the cash value if the policy is discontinued before or at majority, can be available for meeting specific expenses of education and marriage. The policy is taken on the life of child and not on the life of parent. The parent is merely a proposer and is contracting on behalf of the child. The policy can be issued on whole life basis, too; but the corporation issues it on endowment basis.

Commencement of Risk

The risk does not commence immediately at the issue of policy but only on the policy anniversary, following completion of 18 or 21 years. The policy envisages two stages, one covering the period from the date of commencement of policy to the deferred date, *i.e.*, the date of commencement of risk on the child's life, called deferment period, and the other covering the period from the deferred date to the date on which the policy emerges as a claim by the death of the child or its survival to a stipulated date. A combined policy is issued to cover both the aforesaid periods. Policies under this scheme are issued on the lives of children, both male and female who have completed one year of age but have not completed 18 year. No medicinal examination is required where the deferment period is 10 years or more. Policies under this scheme will not be issued for deferment period less than 4 years. The risk may commence on the life of child since 18 or 21 years of his age, as desired by the proposer.

The provisions of this policy make it obligatory on the life assured to adopt the policy in writing at any time after attaining majority but before the deferred date. This provision is necessary to ensure that the life assured will be a major on the deferred date, *i.e.*, will be of age 18 years. On such adoption by the life assured, the policy will be deemed to be a contract between the corporation and the life assured as the absolute owner of the policy and the proposer or his estate shall not thereafter have any right or interest in the policy. The person entitled to the policy money will have the option of taking a cash payment in entire cancellation of the policy contract before the deferred date.

In the event of the life assured, death (the child's death) before the deferred date, *i.e.*, the date of commencement of risk, the policy shall stand cancelled and all premimums paid.

15. Children Anticipated Policy with Profits

This policy can be taken by parent or legal guardian or any near relative on the life of a child on whose life risk will commence at the age of 18 completed, or 21 years as required by the proponent. The policy will automatically vest in the child at the end of the deferment period and half of the premiums paid during this period will be paid to him in lump sum. Risk will commence at the Deferred Date and full sum assured will be payable on survival of the life assured to the date of maturity or on his death, if earlier. The policy will attach bonus from the Deferred Date at the Endowment Assurance Rate. This policy is issued on the lives of children both males and females upto the age of 14 years. Like Children's Endowment Policy, medical examination is not required where the deferment period is 10 years or more. Where it is less than 10 years, medical examination of the child is required. Policies are issued for maturity ages 35, 40, 45, 50, 55 and 60 years. Policies under this plan will not be issued for deferment periods less than four years. The proposals on the lives of minor girls will be entertained only when the father and other insurable members of the family are of adequately insured and the social, cultural, and educational back-round of the family is good. An extra-premium on account of sex will be payable from the Deferred Date. If the premiums due prior to the Deferred Date have been paid, an amount equal to 90 per cent of the total amount of premiums paid excluding the premiums for the first year is payable as a cash option.

The policy will be cancelled in case the life assured dies before the Deferred Date. A sum of money equal to the premiums paid will become payable to the person entitled to the policy moneys in such event provided the policy is in full force. The payment of premiums does not cease on death of the proposer during the deferment period.

No loan will be granted on this policy during the deferment period. Disability benefit unless specifically excluded will be available on this policy with effect from such date.

PLANS WITHDRAWN BY LIC

1. Anticipated Endowment Assurance
2. Convertible Whole Life with Profits
3. Centenary Policy
4. Grihalakshmi Policy
5. Cash and Cover Policy

Premium rates have been reduced in certain policies and some of the policies have been modified. Jana Raksha Policy has been introduced in June 1981.

16. 'Jeevan Saathi'

'Jeevan Saathi' is the new Joint Life Plan with a difference. The Plan is designed to gift a total protection to families; particularly for the working couple.

Row 'Jeevan Saathi' is different from the existing Joint Life Plan!

Under the existing Joint Life Plan two persons' lives can be jointly covered and the Sum Assured becomes payable either on the first death or on the expiry of the selected term.

Under the Jeevan Saathi Plan, only the lives of husband and wife are jointly covered. The basic S.A., together with vested bonuses are payable in event of survival to maturity of either or both of the partners. In the event of the first death of anyone of the lives assured, the survivor gets the basic Sum Assured. Again basic Sum Assured with bonuses is payable to the nominee, in the event of the premature death of the second partner.

Another important feature of this plan is that the premium under the policy ceases on the first death and the surviving partner need not have to pay any more premiums. But inspite of non-payment of premium after the first death, the policy will continue to participate the bonuses will accrue till the final settlement.

From the benefits available it could be seen that a family that is used to certain economic comforts, gets a lump sum immediately, if one of the partners dies, to maintain a certain level of economic stability. Once again the basic Sum Assumed is paid to the surviving partner on, maturity or in the event of other early death, to the nominee. Thus this plan gives a total and complete insurance protection to the whole family.

What are the eligibility condition for purchasing life insurance, under this plan?

Policies under this plan will be issued on the lives of husband and wife, provided the latter belongs to Category-I.

The plan is available for specified Terms of 15, 20 and 25 years only· The age of the older life at maturity should not be more than 65 years.

The minimum basic Sum Assured, under this plan, is Rs. 5,000/- and the maximum is Rs. 1,00,000/- under one or more Policies.

The premium should be minimum Rs. 3 per thousand. S.A. over the premium under Endowment Assurance on older life for the same term. The minimum difference between the Double Joint Life Endowment Assurance premium and Endowment Assurance premium, as calculated in the aforesaid manner, is Rs. 3 per thousand S. A. only against Rs. 5 per thousand S. A. applicable to existing Joint Life Endowment Assurance plan.

17. Married Women's Property Act Policy

A married man can effect a policy on his own life, wife and/or children and shall be deemed to be a trust for their benefits and shall not, so long as any object of the trust remains, be subject to the control of the husband or his creditors, or form part of his estate. The policy effected under Sect. 6 of the Married Women's Property Act 1874 for the above purpose, shall not be aggregated with his other property provided the trust is absolute. The term 'children' means sons and daughters only and excludes an adopted son by Hindus. Grih Lakshmi Policy issued in December, 1975, is an important instance of Married Women's Property Act Policy.

18. Survivorship, Reversionary or Centingent Assurance

There are two persons in this policy, first a named insured and another named person. The sum assured is payable if the life assured dies before another specified person (named person) or counter life. If the counter life dies first, nothing is payable and the contract ceases. These assurances usually arise in connection with reversionary transactions. Suppose in terms of a trust or will A will be entitled to certain property at the death of B provided A is then living, Here A possesses a contingent interest in that property and his interest has a market value. But the purchaser of the interest will receive nothing if A precedes B and, therefore, he effects a contingent assurance for the amount of capital. The purchaser is thus fully protected because (*a*) the purchaser is thus fully protected, as he receives the capital from trust or will if A is living at B's death, (*b*) he receives the policy money if A dies before B.

The rate of premium depends upon the age of the insured, of named person. When the life assured is young and the counter life is old the risk and premium, therefore, would be possible equal to that of a short period temporary insurance. If the ages are equal to or the counter life is younger the premium is roughly that of a whole life assurance. This policy is not widely written.

B. POLICIES ACCORDING TO PREMIUM PAYMENT

The policies according to the premium payment may be of the following types:

1. Single Premium Policy

In this policy, the whole premium is paid at the beginning of the policy. As compared to the annual premium payable, it is costlier; but as compared to aggregate of all annual premiums payable, it is much smaller because all the premiums are received in advance and the insurer can earn additional amount on the premiums received.

This type of policy can be afforded by those who got a windfall income and are expected not to continue such return in subsequent years. The single premium policy is not useful to other persons because of chances of death whereafter the subsequent premiums are not required to be paid.

2. Level Premium Policy

Under this policy regular and equal premiums are paid at a definite interval. This premium is lesser than the single premium and is convenient to make premium at a regular period. This may take the shape of an expense and can be constantly paid. The equal installments may be paid monthly, tri-monthly (quarterly), half yearly and yearly. So, it suits the requirements of different types of the policy-holders. Since, originally the premium is calculated and charged on annual basis, the unpaid premiums for the year are required to be paid at the time of payment of claims due to death. The amount of each monthly, quarterly and half-yearly is not just the one twelfth. One-fourth and one-half of the annual premium because the insurer is involved in more expenses while collecting more frequent premiums and is at loss of the interest for the balance of the annual premium. For monthly installments an additional charge of 5 per cent on the annual premium is made to cover loss of interest and additional cost of collection. The additional charge of 5 per cent of the premium shall be waived if the premiums are paid through a co-operative society or by trustees of a staff provident or super-annuation fund or are collected by deduction from salary and remitted by or under the supervision of the Corporation. If premiums are payable yearly or half-yearly reduction of Re. 0.75 and Re. 0.50 per thousand of sum assured is ordinarily deductible from the annual premium. There is no deduction or reduction in quarterly premium. The level premium policy may be either a continuous level premium or a limited level premium policy.

C. POLICIES ACCORDING TO PARTICIPATION IN PROFITS

Policies according to participation in profits may be (*i*) without profit policies, and (*ii*) with profit policies.

(*i*) *Without Profit Policies or Non-participating Policies.* The holders of without profit policies are not entitled to share the profits of the insurer. These policy-holders get only the sum assured and no bonus is given to them.

(*ii*) *With Profit Policies or Participating Policies.* The holders of the with profit policies are entitled to share the profit of the insurer. Since the policy-holders can share the profit and not the loss, they can not be treated as co-owner of the insurance business. If there is loss, the policy-holders cannot get bonus, *i.e.*, the share in profit. They are entitled to get the share of profit, *i.e.*, the bonus only when there is profit. The amount of bonus depends on the profit after deducting provision for taxes, contingency, etc. In participating policy there is no guarantee that the insured will get something by way of profit every year. The only law is that the corporation has to distribute 95 per cent of its profits among the policy-holders. Thus, if there is no profit in a year, no amount can be distributed to the participating policy-holders. However, the Corporation has decided that at least bonus rate of previous years should not decrease while declaring bonus in the present year.

The Corporation issues both types of policies, *i.e.*, participating and non-participating. Since the participating policies share profit the premium rate is higher in this case. The difference between the premiums of participating policies and of non-participating polices is called 'bonus loading' because the additional premium in participating policies is charged for allowing bonus. The amount of insurance to be paid is certain in non-participating policies but it is not certain in participating policies due to accrual of bonus, the rate of which is not constant.

D. POLICIES ACCORDING TO THE NUMBER OF PERSONS INSURED

On the basis of number of persons insured in a policy, the policy may be (*i*) single life policies, and (*ii*) multiple life policy.

(*i*) *Single Life Policies.* Under single life policies, only one individual is insured. It is not necessary that the policy should be issued in one's own life, it may be in other's life; but the fact is that this policy insures only one life. The policy amount is payable only when the assured event occurs.

(*ii*) *Multiple Life Policies.* In this policy more than one life is insured. It may be (*a*) Joint Life policy, and (*b*) Last Survivor Policy.

(*a*) *Joint Life Policy.* This policy covers two or more lives and the policy amount is payable on the first death. This is beneficial to the partners of a firm and to a couple.

(*b*) *Last Survivorship Policy.* The policy amount is payable at the last death. So long as any one of the insured is alive, no payment is made.

E. POLICIES ACCORDING TO THE METHOD OF PAYMENT OF POLICY AMOUNT

The policy amount may be paid in (*i*) Lump sum policies or (*ii*) installments.

(*i*) *Lump Sum Policies.* Where the sum assured is paid in lump sum at the events insured against.

(*ii*) *Installment or Annuity Policies.* Under this policy, the policy amount is payable in installments. It is beneficial to those whose earning capacities are reduced to minimum in old age. At that time, this policy may be more helpful. He may continue to get up to a fixed period or up to death or both.

Non-Conventional Policies

The Life Insurance Corporation of India has introduced several non-conventional policies to meet the requirements of the population. The conventional policies have the main attributes of protection at early death or living too long; but majority of the population, is interested mainly in investment. The LIC has designed several new policies from time to time to meet these requirements. Some of the important new policies are described here.

1. Policies under LIC Mutual Fund
2. Jeevan Akshay
3. Jeevan Dhara.
4. Jeevan Kishor
5. Jeevan Chhaya

The LIC is conducting market research to find suitable policies to meet the requirements of the people. Every year, some policies are issued to benefit the population.

1. POLICIES UNDER LIC MUTUAL FUND

LIC launched its Mutual Fund with a promise to the investors to provide high returns alongwith safety and security of investment. LIC Mutual Fund entered the Indian capital market on 19th June 1989. During the first year of operation LIC Mutual Fund came up with 5 schemes which provide distinct benefits to various cross sections of investors. Out of the 6 schemes, 3 are close ended schemes viz., Dhanashree 1989, Dhan 80 CC (I) and Dhanvarsha while the other two schemes viz.,. Dhanaraksha 1989 and Dhanavridhi 1989 are open ended schemes. Dhan 80 CC B (I) has been introduced since Feb. 11, 1991. The salient features of Dhanasahayog and Dhan 80 CC B (1) are given to illustrate the LIC Mutual Fund Policies.

I. Dhanasahayog

Introduction. LIC Mutual Fund was set up as a separate Trust by Life Insurance Corporation of India. The basic objectives of LIC Mutual Fund are mopping up the savings of people, especially from rural and semi-urban areas and providing good returns, liquidity and security to the investors through investment in the capital market for productive purposes.

LIC Mutual Fund mobilised nearly Rs.375 crores in the very first year of operations from $1\frac{1}{2}$ lakh investors. Other schemes launched by the Mutual Fund are also having very good response from investors.

LIC Mutual Fund has declared a handsome income distribution (dividend) for 1989-90 which is higher than that promised under various schemes. For example, a rate of 12% was promised under Dhanashree 1989 but the dividend declared is 13.50% p.a. under this scheme.

LIC Mutual Fund has already launched seven schemes which are primarily income and growth oriented. However, several requests have come from investing public to launch an income and growth oriented scheme which is to be available on tap. The investors can invest in this scheme depending upon their liquid position and convenience.

The details of Dhanasahayog are as follows:

1. Who can apply for Dhanasahayog units?

(*a*) Resident citizens of India who are (*i*) Adult individual or individuals not exceeding three in number jointly or on either/anyone or survivor(s) basis, (*ii*) Minors through their parents/step-parents/guardians (No joint ownership is permitted with minors), (*iii*) Hindu Undivided Family (by the Karta acting on behalf of H.U.F.).

(*b*) Companies registered in India, Bodies Corporate, Trusts, Societies, Co-operative Societies, Schools, Colleges, Universities, Clubs created under the applicable laws and authorised to invest in the units of the Mutual Fund.

(*c*) Non-Residents of Indian Nationality/Origin on non-repatriation basis.

Exploration: A person shall be deemed to be of Indian origin if (*i*) he/she, at any time, held an Indian passport, or (*ii*) he/she, or either of his/her parents or any of his/her grandparents was an Indian and a permanent resident of undivided India at any time.

However, Pakistani and Bangladeshi nationals, even though they satisfy the definition of Indian Origin shall not be eligible to apply for the units.

The wife of a citizen of India or a person of Indian Origin shall also be deemed to be of Indian Origin even though she may be of non-Indian parentage.

Note: Partnership firms and others not mentioned, above are not eligible to apply.

2. How much one can Invest?

There is no upper limit, on investment. The face value of the units will be Rs. 10/- each. Minimum investment for individual investor is 100 units and in multiples of 50 units thereafter. In case of Trusts, Societies, Companies. etc., the minimum investment will be 1000 units and thereafter in multiples of 100 units. The amount payable will be calculated on the basis of the prevailing selling price per unit of Dhanasahayog scheme.

3. Where can you submit your application with subscription?

(*a*) At any designated branch of Central Bank of India (CBI). The branches of CBI authorised to collect subscriptions under the earlier schemes of LIC Mutual Fund are the designated branches for this purpose. The application alongwith the bank draft for the amount of investment less the bank draft commission may be sent to any designated branch of CBI. The facility of deduction of bank charges is available only in places where there is no designated branch of CBI .

(*b*) Non-Residents of Indian Nationality/Origin should remit their application money to authorised dealers of CBI branches as mentioned in the instructions on the back of the application form.

4. Selling and Repurchase price of the units

The scheme is open for subscription from 1st January 1991 and the units will be sold at Rs. 10/- to the investors in this scheme upto September 1991. Thereafter the selling price of the units will be fixed every month. On and after 1st January 1992, units can be sold back to LIC Mutual Fund at the rate fixed by LIC Mutual Fund.

5. Incentive for early subscription

Incentive for the period upto 31st March 1991 will be payable as follows:

Period of Collection	Incentive amount
01.1.1991 to 15.1.1991	3.0%
16.1.1991 to 31.1.1991	2.5%
01.2.1991 to 15.2.1991	2.0%
16.2.1991 to 28.2.1991	1.5%
01.3.1991 to 15.3.1981	1.0%
16.3.1981 to 31.3.1991	0.5%

6. Plans of Investment

The investor has a choice between the following two plans:

Plan A: Under this plan, dividend declared after the close of each accounting year will be remitted to the investor.

Plan B: Under this plan dividend declared after the close of each accounting year will be reinvested under the scheme the prevailing selling price.

The investor will indicate his/her choice between the above plans in the application form. In case where the applicant does not tick the relevant plan column, it will be considered that he/she has opted for Plan B. The investor is free to switch from Plan A to Plan B or vice versa after payment or accrual of two annual dividends from the date of earlier option. Any dividend declared will be treated as per the option exercised and recorded last.

7. Benefits

Safety: The investment will be safe as the risk is distributed among a huge number of investors and the funds are invested in varied securities and spread over a wide range of sector wise industries.

Regular Income: The investment will be so managed as to ensure a flow of regular income consistent with safety.

Growth: Growth in income and capital will be achieved through investment planning and constant monitoring to resort to profitable switching operations.

8. Tax benefits

The following tax benefits will be available to the sole/first individual applicant only.

(*i*) **Benefits under Section SOL of Income. Tax Act, 1961:** Permissible maximum deduction of Rs. 10,000/- from the taxable income under Sec. 80L of Income Tax Act, 1961 as follows:

(*a*) Income on Dhanasahayog together with other income from specified securities/deposits etc., shall be eligibly for deduction from total income upto a maximum of Rs. 7,000/- [Sec. 80L (1) (Va)].

(*b*) A further deduction from total income upto a maximum of Rs. 3,000/- is also available on income from Dhanasahayog along with income from certain other specified categories [proviso to sec. SOL (I)].

The dividend certificates will be issued under Plan B for claiming tax relief under the Section.

(*ii*) **Wealth Tax Exemption:** Investment in Dhanasahayog would be treated at par with investments entitled to exemption within the overall limit of Rs. 5,00,000/- referred to in Sec. 5 (1) (XXIVa) of Wealth Tax Act, 1957.

(*iii*) **Long Term Capital Gains:** If the investor holds Dhanasahayog Units for a minimum period of three years, he/She is eligible to the following Capital Gains Relief, along with gains from other assets, under Sec. 48 (2) of Income Tax Act, 1961. (*a*) Total exemption of capital gains upto Rs. 10,000/,- (*b*) A deduction of 60% of the capital gains in excess of Rs. 10,000/-. If the investor is a company, the deduction rate is 30%.

(*iv*) **No deduction of tax at source:** There shall be no deduction of tax at source.

9. Liquidity

Loan facility: Dhanasahayog certificate holders can avail of loan facility from Central Bank of India as per their terms and the instructions/guidelines issued to them by Reserve Bank of India.

II. Dhan 80 CCB (1)

Introduction: LIC Mutual Fund was set up as a separate Trust by Life Insurance Corporation of India. The basic objectives, of LIC Mutual Fund are mopping up the savings of people especially from rural and semi-urban areas and providing good returns, liquidity and security to the investors through investment in the capital market for productive purposes.

LIC Mutual Fund mobilised nearly Rs. 375 crores in the very first year of operations from about $1\frac{1}{2}$ lakh investors. Various schemes launched by LIC Mutual Fund are receiving very good response from investors.

All the close of first Accounting year LIC Mutual Fund has declared a handsome income distribution (dividend) for 1989-90 which is higher than that promised under various schemes. For example, a rate of 12% was promised under Dhanashree-1989 but the dividend declared is 13,5% p.a. under this scheme.

LIC Mutual Fund has already successfully launched eight schemes of various types. Out of these, there have been as many as three open ended schemes. One tax savings scheme viz. Dhan 80CC (I) was also introduced by the Mutual Fund in the year 1990. LIC Mutual Fund has been in forefront in catering to the diverse needs of investors. Keeping this in view, LIC Mutual Fund has seen to it that Dhan 80CCB (I) scheme is launched at the earliest to enable its investors to take advantage of the tax concessions. The scheme is formulated under the Equity Linked Savings Scheme, 1991.

1. Who can apply for Dhan 80CCB (1) Units

(*a*) **Resident Citizens of India who are:** (*i*) Adult individual or individuals not exceeding three in number jointly or on either/anyone or survivor basis (*ii*) Minors through, their Parents/Step-parents (No joint ownership is permitted with minors) (*iii*) Hindu Undivided Family (by the Karta acting on behalf of H.U.F.).

(*b*) **An association of persons** or body of individuals consisting, in either case, only of husband and wife governed by the system of community of property in force in the State of Goa and the Union Territories of Dadra and Nagar Haveli and Daman and Diu.

2. Minimum Investment

Units of face value of Rs. 10/- each will be issued at par. Investment can be made in a **minimum of 50 units and in multiples of 50 units thereafter**. These units will be called 'Capital Units'. There is, no upper limit on Investment. Investment can be made maximum four times in a financial year. Each investment will be subject to the minimum specified above.

3. Where can you submit your application with subscription?

At any designated branch of central Bank of India. The branches of Central Bank of India authorised to collect subscriptions under the earlier schemes of LIC Mutual Fund are the designated branches for this purpose.

4. Scheme Period and Issue Period

The scheme would be terminated at the close of the 10th financial year from the financial year of subscription. The scheme will be open for subscription from 11th February, 1991 to 30th March, 1991 only. However, LIC Mutual Fund reserves its right to close the issue earlier after giving due public notice, but in any case not before 15th March, 1991.

5. Selling and Repurchase Price of the Units

The Selling and Repurchase prices Mutual Fund periodically after one year from the date of allotment of the Units.

6. Incentive for early subscription

Incentive on subscription amount will be payable as follows while issuing the unit certificates. The unit certificates will be issued before 31st July, 1991.

Period oj Collection	Incentive amount
11.02.1991 to 15.02.1991	2.0%
16.02.1991 to 28.02.1991	1.5%
01.03.1991 to 15.03.1991	1.0%
16.03.1981 to 30.03.1991	0.5%

7. Plan of Investment

The investor has a choice out of the following plans:

Plan A—Annual Income

Under this plan, dividend declared after the close of each accounting year will be remitted to the investor.

Plan B—Accumulation with 8OL Benefits

Under this plan, dividend declared after the close of each accounting year will be reinvested under the scheme at the prevaling selling price. The certificate, as to the quantum of dividend declared and reinvested, will be issued to the investor to enable him to claim tax benefits under Sec. 80L of Income Tax Act, 1961. The units issued against the dividend declared will be called 'Dividend Units'.

Plan C—Growth with Capital Gains Benefits

Under this plan, units equivalent to dividend in value will be allocated to the investor at the prevailing selling price, but no certificate for claim under Sec. 80L of Income Tax Act,. 1961 will be issued. Units thus allocated will be called 'Dividend Units'. On encashment of such units, the investor will be liable to pay Capital Gains Tax.

The investor will indicate his/her choice out of the above plans. In case where the applicant does not tick the relevant plan box, it will be considered that he/she has opted for Plan A. The investor is free to switch from Plan A to B or vice versa after payment or accrual of 2 annual dividends from the date of earlier option. Any dividends declared will be treated as per the option exercised and recorded last. The Plan option C, once exercised cannot be interchanged with Plan option Aor B.

Benefits

Safety: The investment will be safe as the risk is distributed among a large number of investors and the funds are spread over a wide range of sector-wise industries.

Regular Income: The investment will be so managed as to ensure a flow of regular income consistent with safety and capital appreciation.

Growth: Growth in income and capital will be achieved through investment planning and constant monitoring to resort to profitable switching operations.

9. Tax Benefits

The following tax benefits will be available to the sole/first individual applicant only.

(*i*) **Benefits under Section 80 CCB of Income Tax Act, 1961:** A deduction in computation of income under Sec. 80 CCB of the Income Tax Act, 1961, of so much of the amount, invested as does not exceed the amount of Rs. 10,000/- will be allowed. Provided however, any amount invested by the assessee in the capital units in respect of which a deduction has been allowed is returned in whole or in part either by way of repurchase of such units or on the termination of the Scheme by the Mutual Fund, as the case may be, it shall be deemed to be the income of the assessee and charged to tax.

Provided further, where a partition has taken place among the members of a Hindu Undivided Family (H.U.F.) or where an association of persons has been dissolved after a deduction has been allowed, the person in receipt of income referred in the provided herein before shall have to pay tax.

(*ii*) **Benefits under Section SOL of Income Tax Act. 1961:** Permissible maximum deduction of Rs. 10.000/- from the taxable income under Section 80L of Income Tax Act, 1961 as follows will be available under Plans A and B.

(*a*) Income on Dhan 80 CCB (1) together with other income from specified securities/deposits etc. shall be eligible for deduction from total income upto a maximum of Rs. 7.000/- [Sec, 80L (1) (Va)],

(*b*) A further deduction from total income upto a maximum of Rs. 3,000/- is also available on income from Dhan 80 CCB (1) along with income from certain other specified categories [proviso to Sec. 80L (1)].

(*iii*) **Wealth Tax Exemption:** Investment in Dhan 80CCB (1) would be treated at par with investments entitled to exemption within the overall limit of Rs. 5,00,000/- referred to in Section 5 (1) (XXIVa) of Wealth Tax Act, 1957.

(*iv*) **Long Term Capital Gains:** Under Plan C the investor will be eligible to the following Capital Gains Relief, along with gains from other assets, under Section 48 (2) of Income Tax Act, 1961.

1. Total exemption of Capital Gains upto Rs. 10,000/-.
2. A deduction of 80% of the Capital Gains in excess of Rs. 10,000/-.

(*iv*) **Tax Deduction:** There shall be no deduction of tax at source on the Dividend declared under Plans A and B. However, when the units are encashed in whole or in part other by way of repurchase of these units or on termination of the scheme by the trustees as the case may be, the amount invested by the assessee in 'Capital Units' shall be deemed to be the income of the assessee as per the provisions of Section 80 CCB of Income Tax Act, 1961 and tax at the standard rate of 20% as per Section 194F of Income Tax Act, 1961 will be deducted. The Mutual Fund shall issue certificate of tax so deducted at source.

10. Termination of the Scheme

The scheme will be terminated at the end of the Scheme Period. The Scheme may also be terminated after 90% of the investors withdraw from the scheme, If so decided by the Trustees. The Scheme's assets will be realised and distributed among the Unit holders on books at that time in proportion to their total investment in Capital and Dividend Units. Thus there would be 100% participation in Capital Growth.

11. Liquidity

The Units issued under the Scheme can, be encashed at any time after the initial locks in period of three years is over from the date of allotment at the applicable repurchase price. No partial encashment of the Unit Certificate would however be allowed.

In the event of the death of sole/first applicant, the units can be encashed at any time after the completion of one year from the date of allotment of the units.

The Units Issued under the Scheme, save as provided in Sub-section (3), of Section 89 CCB of Income Tax Act, 1961, **cannot be transferred assigned or pledged.**

2. JEEVAN AKSHAY

In return for purchase price paid by the purchaser a monthly pension will be paid during the lifetime or the purchaser of the pension.

The last payment would be falling due prior to the date of death of the pensioner. No medical examination is necessary to get the policy.

Post-dated monthly cheques are sent in advance for the whole year. No existence certificate is required for receipt of the pension.

Pension cheques are payable at par on all branches of the Central Bank of India and such other nationalised bank which LIC may notify.

On the death of the pensioner, the original amount invested by the employee along with an additional bonus will be returned to the nominee or his legal heirs.

The minimum amount to be invested (premium) is Rs. 10,000 and in multiples of Rs. 100 thereafter. There is no maximum limit.

For every Rs. 10,000 purchase price, pension payable would be Rs. 100 per month.

Minimum age at entry is 50 years. There is no restriction as regards maximum age at entry. Only persons aged 50 or more can avail of pension benefits on their own lives.

Since the pension is payable monthly, the gross annual return works out to nearly 12.7 per cent—an excellent return by any standard on a safe, long-term investment. The plan guarantees the return for the lifetime of the pensioner which can be as long as 50 years or more. No other investment guarantees such a high rate of return for such a long period. The rate of return is guaranteed even when the rate of interest falls in the future.

The Jeevan Akshay policies also enjoy various tax benefits:

3. JEEVAN DHARA

The payment of annuities in respect of policies under Jeevan Dhara has to start one month after the completion of the deferment period. In order to enable the annuitant to get the payment on the due date, the annuity cheque has to be posted at least two weeks earlier. Since Jeevan Akshay/Jeevan Dhara payments are centralised at Zonal Offices, it means that the input forms for building master records for payment of annuities have to reach the Zonal Machine Department well in advance to enable them to process it and despatch the cheques to the annuitant about two weeks before the date of vesting.

However, in the case of policies under SSS, the payment of final installment premium will be received only after the date of vesting, making it impossible to build the master record in time. The delay in building of master record will be much more when there are gaps, in premium payment. This is one of the reasons behind discontinuing issue of Jeevan Dhara policies under Salary Savings Scheme.

The problems involved in building the master record in time are being faced, to a lesser extent, in the case of policies under are half-yearly mode of payment also.

In order to obviate these difficulties, wherever the mode is other than single premium, it has been decided to limit the premium paying term under Jeevan Dhara Plan to one year less than the deferment period. That is, if the deferment period under a policy is 20 years, the premium paying term will be limited to 19 years. (The amount of annual premium shown against term 20 in the Premium Table will be payable for 19 years). If the deferment period is 15 years, the premium paying term will be limited to 14 years. Policies with deferment period of 2 years will be issued only as single premium policies.

Revival of Jeevan Dhara Policy which has been in a lapsed condition will not be permissible in the last year of the policy term because of the problems involved in preparation of cheques in time.

The revised rates of annual premium for Jeevan Dhara Policies is enclosed herewith (Annexure I).

Mode of payment of premium: The premium can be paid yearly or half-yearly or Salary Savings Scheme only.

Jeevan Dhara Policies under SSS: Effective from 1st December, 1990, Jeevan Dhara policies can be issued under Salary Savings Scheme.

Rebate for mode of payment of premium: A rebate of 1.5% of the Tabular Premium is allowed if the mode of payment of premium is yearly. No rebate is allowed for other modes of payment.

Rebate for large premium: The allowed in case of large premiums:

Mode	Rebate	Eligible Amount
Yearly	1.5%	Portion of the instalment premium in excess of Rs. 5,000/-.
Half-yearly	1.5%	Portion of the instalment premium in excess of Rs. 2,500/-.
Monthly (SSS only)	1.5%	Portion of the instalment premium in excess of Rs. 417/-.

4. JEEVAN KISHOR

The salient features of the plan are as follows:

Who are eligible?

Children, both male and female, between the ages of 1 (last birthday) and 12 (last birthday) are eligible to be proposed for , insurance under this Plan.

Who can propose?

(*a*) If both parents are alive, generally the father should propose. However, if the mother has an income of her own, she can be, the proposer.

(*b*) If father is not alive, mother can propose.

(*c*) If both parents are not alive, then the legal guardian can propose.

Commencement of risk

The risk will commence either-two years after the date of commencement of the policy or from the policy anniversary falling immediately after the completion of 7 years of age, whichever is later. However, the date of commencement of risk will not, in any case, go beyond the policy anniversary falling immediately after the completion of 12 years of age.

The following table will further clarify the point:

Age (last birthday at entry)		Risk to commence from
(*i*)	1 to 4	Policy anniversary falling immediately after completion of 7 years of age.
(*ii*)	5 to 10	Second policy anniversary from the date of commencement of policy.
(*iii*)	11	First policy anniversary from the date of commencement of policy.
(*iv*)	12	From the date of commencement.

Waiting Period

The period starting from the date of commencement of the policy to the date of commencement of risk will be known as the 'Waiting Period'.

Bonus

The policy is eligible for bonus even during the waiting period. However, the bonus for the waiting period will vest only on the policy anniversary from which the risk is covered or at the end of five years from the commencement of the policy, whichever is later, provided the policy is then in force for full sum assured.

Vesting of the Policy

The policy shall automatically vest in the Life Assured on the policy anniversary falling on or immediately following his/her attaining majority.

Benefits

The Sum Assured alongwith vested bonus and final additional bonus, if any, will be payable on maturity or on death if earlier, provided the death occurs on or after the date of commencement of risk.

In case of death of the child before the date of commencement of risk, the premiums paid (excluding the premiums for premium waiver benefit) will be refunded.

Substitution of child will not be permitted.

Premium Waiver Benefit

There is also the provision for waiving of premium under the policy till the child attains majority, in the event of death of the proposer. This premium waiver benefit is available subject to payment of a small, additional premium and medical examination of the proposer.

Medical Examination of the child

No medical examination will be necessary if the age of the child as on the date of proposal is less than 10 years (last birthday). Otherwise, medical examination will be necessary. Only Standard Lives will be eligible for Insurance under this plan.

Other Conditions

(*a*)	Minimum Term	:	15 years
(*b*)	Maximum Term	:	35 years
(*c*)	Maximum Sum Assured	:	Rs. 5,00,000/-, if the age (last birthday) as on the date of proposal is less than 10. In all other cases, it will be Rs. 10,00,000/-
(*d*)	Minimum Sum Assured	:	Rs. 10,000/-
(*e*)	Mode of Payment of Premium	:	Only Yearly

5. JEEVAN CHHAYA

"*Jeevan Chhaya*" introduced in March 1991, can be considered to be a combination of '*Jeevan Mitra*' and '*Money Back*' plans.

Couples having a child (not an adopted one), of age less than one year can avail of this plan, in order to ensure that an adequate financial provision is made for the higher education of the child. The child should not have completed one year of the date of registration of the proposal. Either father age or mother or each one of them individually can take policies or under this plan.

Premium payment

The premiums under this plan payable during the life time of the life assured and shall cease on the death of the life assured or on the expiry of the term of the policy, whichever is earlier.

Benefits

The benefits under the '*Jeevan Chhaya*' plan are:

Fixed Benefits

The following benefits (on all inforce policies) are payable whether or not the life assured survives the term of the policy:

(*i*) One fourth of the sum assured each at the end of ($n-3$), ($n-2$), ($n-1$) and nth year (where n is the term of the policy).

(*ii*) Bonus for the full term on the full sum assured on the date of maturity.

For example, if the term of the policy is 20 years, one-fourth the sum assured will be payable at the end of the 17th, 18th, 19th and 20th year. The bonus on full sum assured for the full term of the policy along with final additional bonus, if any, will be payable at the end of 20 years.

Death Benefit

In addition to the above fixed benefits, one additional sum assured will be payable on the death of the policy-holder at any time during the term of the policy. (Future premiums, falling due from the policy anniversary following the date of death will stand waived.)

For example, if the term of the policy is 21 years, one-fourth the sum assured is payable at the end of 18th, 19th, 20th and 21st year. If death occurs during the 19th year, full sum assured (without bonus) will be payable immediately. One instalment of one fourth the sum assured would have already been paid at the end of the 18th year. The balance three instalments of one fourth sum assured, each due at the end of the 19th, 20th and 21st year, and the bonus on full sum assured (for the full term) due at the end of the 21st year shall be paid to the person eligible to receive the policy moneys.

Restrictions

(*i*) The term can be 20, 21, 22, 23, 24 or 25.

(*ii*) Minimum sum assured	Rs. 10,000
Maximum sum assured	Rs. 1,00,000
(*iii*) Minimnm age at entry	20 (nearer birthday)
Maximum age at entry	40 (nearer birthday).

The maximum age at entry can be raised to 45 if the original or attested *xerox copy* of birth certificate or school certificate is submitted as age proof.

(*iv*) Maximum maturity age	65 (nearer birthday)

Underwriting

Proposals under this plan can be entertained under non-medical (general) scheme, both in respect of male and female lives upto Rupees one lakh sum assured. However, if anything adverse is indicated at the time of underwriting and the case cannot be accepted under non-medical, then the regular underwriting procedures like calling for full medical report, special reports (if need be) are to be followed.

In the case of female lives, the following three restrictions will apply:

(*i*) Only category-I and category-II female lives will be eligible for insurance under this plan.

(*ii*) No proposal will be entertained within 3 months of the date of delivery.

(*iii*) In case the female life had undergone a caesarian operation, a single extra premium of Rs. 5 per thousand sum assured is to be charged.

The father and, mother should, jointly sign a declaration regarding the date of birth of the child.

Similarly Jeevan Suraksha has ,been introduced on Aug. 15, 1996 to meet the requirements of all categories of people.

6. JEEVAN KISHORE

Jeevan Kishore— With Profit Plan further curtails the age from which the risk on child's life is covered. As previsions of this policy, risk commences either two years from third the date of commencement or from the policy anniversary following immediately after the completion of 7 years of age, whichever is later. Contrary to participation in bonus from the deferred date, or the risk date or vesting date, this policy allows participation in bonuses from the very date of commencement of policy. However, vesting of the bonus was allowed either from the risk date 5 years from the commencement of the policy, whichever is later.

7. JEEVAN SUKANYA

Jeevan Sukanya—With Profit is designed exclusively for female children. The premiums under this plan are payable for a limited period only. The premium ceases from the policy anniversary following on or immediately after completion of 20 years of age by the life assured. The policy matures on the policy anniversary following or immediately after completion of 50 years by the child. The policy provides following benefits:

Death Benefits

(*a*) Before the commencement of risk, the premiums paid, excluding premiums for premium waiver benefit are refunded.

(*b*) Fun sum assured alongwith vested bonuses after commencement of risk but before maturity of the policy.

(*c*) After marriage of the life assured and commencement of the risk cover on the life of the husband but before the date of maturity full sum assured without bonus in case husband predeceases the wife.

Survival Benefits

(*a*) Full sum assured on the life assured's surviving till the end of the end of the premium-paying term.

(*b*) The vested bonuses are paid on the life assured's surviving up to the age of maturity (bonuses continue to vest upto the end of the policy term).

8. CHILDREN'S MONEY BACK PLAN

Children's Money Back Plan—Yet another innovative plan has been introduced by LIC with effect from 16th January 1995. The plan envisages full and complete growth of the child. The plan provides for educational as well as start in life expenses—a series of financial benefits at the time when the child needs them most. Under a policy of Rs. 5 lakhs sum assured, Rs. 1 lakh is paid as survival benefit on the policy anniversary immediately after the child completes 18 years of age. A similar amount is paid on the policy anniversary two years hence. The amount is increased to Rs. 1.5 lakhs as survival benefit payable on the policy anniversary immediately after completion of 22 years of age. A similar amount is paid on the policy anniversary two years hence. The guaranteed additions at the rate of Rs. 80/- per thousand sum assured are payable on the maturity date *i.e.*, the policy anniversary immediately after commencement. The sum of the guaranteed and loyalty additions would be as under:

	Age at entry at last birthday		
	0	***5***	***10***
Total Guaranteed Additions	10,40,000	8,40,000	6,40,000
Loyalty Addition, if Policy is			
Annual Premium Policy	3,00,000	1,75,000	1,25,000
Net, Annual premium payable	26,525	39,815	67,995

All the premiums are paid by the parents. They can claim tax concession under Section 88 of Income Tax Act 1961. The single premium policy under the above plan can be gifted to the child for his advancement by close relations. The policy can be taken even for a new born child upto 10 years of age last birthday—the age on the commencement of the policy.

"any sum received under a life insurance policy,
including the sum allocated by way of bonus on such
policy".

The benefits payable under the policy are exempt in terms of section 10(10D) of Income Tax Act 1961. The provisions are reproduced for ready reference:

The maturity proceeds in the form of guaranteed and loyality additions will stand in good stead when the child takes up his career.

Another attractive feature of the plan is an option available to the proposer to obtain insurance in the form of term rider on his life to the extent of 20% of the sum assured under the policy not exceeding Rs. 50,000/-. The cover being in the form of term rider, the cost is nominal as granting of it does not involve administrative expenses.

This is the first time that the Corporation is granting a covery in the form of term rider. The insurance protection to the family will provide additional assistance in the event of unfortunate death of the bread-winner.

1994 happened to be the Year of the Family, the intention of the plan is to cover up two of the family members together.

The payment of survival benefits does not in any way reduce the insurance protection. In case of death of the life assured after commencement of the risk, the full sum assured together with guaranteed additions is payable without any deduction for the amount that may have been paid earlier by way of survival instalment. Loyalty addition is another novel feature which will depend upon Corporation's experience with regard to three factors viz. Mortality Expenses and Interest. In case the Corporation's experience is maintained at the current level without any further improvement, a good percentage of sum assured will accrue as Loyalty Addition.

LIC has taken interest for introducing different new policy schemes to cater the needs of customers of different segments—Asha Deep, Bima Kiran, Jeevan Shree, Jeevan Adhar, Bima Sandesh, Bhavishya Jeevan, Jeevan Surabhi, Jeevan Mitra, Jeevan Sathi, Jeevan Sarita, Jeevan Balya and Jeevan Griha have been introduced by LIC.

9. JEEVAN SURAKSHA

Jeevan Suraksha plan was introduced on 15th August, 1996. It enables individuals to provide for retirement income from a chosen date. The Policy is with life cover but can be taken without life cover under certain conditions. The Policy holder taking policy with life cover provides minimum of 50% of the target pension to spouse on death during the deferment period. Spouse's pension is not provided under without life cover plan. On vesting, the policy holder, has the option to receive 25% of the notional cash option in lumpsum and balance in annuity.

10. JEEWAN SNEHA

Jeevan Sneha introduced on 16th June 1997 is specially designed for women. The plan is without profits money back type plan with the added feature of guaranteed additions.

Loyalty addition, encashment of survival benefit, as and when required, flexibility to pay premium in advance, in-built accident cover. Free insurance cover for a period of 3 years from the date of first unpaid premium provided at least 2 full years' premiums have been paid and option to receive pension in lieu of maturity benefits.

Comments on New Policy

Remember when Jeevan Shree Plan (112) was launched in 1994/95 almost everyone felt that it will not sell as it was minimum 5 lakhs policy. During those days the high sum assured cases were very rare and the average size of LIC policy was Rs. 25,000/- only. A rebate of Re. 1 for sum assured more than Rs. 25,000/- and Rs. 2/- for sum assured more than Rs. 50,000/- was offered. That meant even a policy of Rs. 25,000/- was high sum assured then.

One more interesting fact; most of our policies will be sold in the size of Rs. 25,000/-, Rs. 50,000/- and Rs. 1,00,000/-. Because when the primary salesperson *i.e.*, agent discusses a policy he may begin with Rs. 1 lakh sum assured if he is little courages but on further negotiation and discussions, he will directly come down to Rs. 50,000/ - in 99% of the cases as the "Ready Reckoner" with him gives the premium rates for Rs. 50,000/- instantly. The agent normally will not talk of sum assured of Rs. 75,000/- or Rs. 90;000/- even though the customer could have gone for that sum. This may be called Ready Reckoner yndrome.

Now imagine the scenario today. Agents all across the country are selling high sum assured policies. The Jeevan Shree was withdrawn last year in January 2002 but has made a big contribution that our average agents also started talking and selling Rs. 5 lakhs policy. Had Jeevan Shree not been there perhaps even today selling Rs. 5 lakhs or more policy would have been difficult for most of us.

After Jeevan Shree (112), New Jeevan Shree (151) has arrived on the scene. The sales have been very moderate so far. Let us examine what are the myths and mindsets that are coming in our way in selling some of our newly launched plans.

(A) New Jeevan Shree: Misconception about the Plan is minimum sum assured and premium is high

Fact: (i) Jeevan Shree (112) with minimum sum assured of Rs. 5 lakhs was sold in large numbers (26387 in Mumbai D.O. III) last year based on high yield. It means people will buy even high sum assured policies if product is attractive yield-wise or benefitwise.

(*ii*) The guaranteed additions @ Rs. 70/- per thousand sum assured per year with accident benefit and term assurance of Rs. 15 lakhs each makes this plan attractive. Even with the higher premium the yield is upto 7%. We should always see the benefits and not the cost. Cost is only relative to benefit.

Selling Points

- Ideal for executives, professionals, businessmen, artists having limited span of active earning life/career and wish to provide for later part of life.
- Suitable for Key Man Insurance. Short term is suitable as Keyman may keep changing his job.
- Transferability between employers under Key Man Insurance.
- Limited premium paying term and single premium option.
- Loan is permissible after 2 years.
- Ideal for gift under single premium.

(B) Jeevan Rekha-Misconception about the plan is money back is after every 5 years which is long survival gap compared to plan life Mahalife of Tata AIG.

Fact: (*i*) It is true that money is returned after every 5 years on survival. However what need to be analysed is that money back is quicker *i.e.,* after just 5 years from DOC and at higher rate *i.e.*, 10% of sum assured-thereby offering good liquidity whereas Mahalife has long initial waiting period of 12 years. For example a 13 years person will get his full sum assured back under survival benefits by 63 years of age. Further the life cover with bonuses continue till death. Longer the life, higher the benefit under Jeevan Rekha. As there is choice of premium payment terms an even single premium, life long unlimited Survival Benefited security and savings can be

Selling Points:

- Regular–life long money back @ 10% sum assured every five years.
- Life long cover for full S.A. irrespective of S.B. paid.
- Bonus and sum assured payable to dependants, as a parting gift.
- As a birthday or anniversary gift every 5th year.
- Single and Limited premium payment terms as per one's convenience 5, 10, 15,20,25 and for life.
- As a provision of foreign tour or holiday every 5th year.
- Most suitable for short career profession as like sports persons/singer artists who can take 5 Single Premium or 5 years' term policies for, successive 5 years and get regular tax free income every year until life. This is all the while necessary in view of increased average longevity.

(C) New Jeevan Dhara-I, New Jeevan Akshay-l, New Jeevan Suraksha-l: Misconception about the plan is:

(*i*) No guaranteed pension or annuity

Fact: (*i*) The pension schemes available in the Insurance market are almost on LIC's pattern, No company can afford to guarantee a pension that too after 20-25 years at the current interest rates. The interest rates are very volatile and are changing fast. There is lot of risk interest rates and increased longevity. Therefore almost all insurance companies or pension funds are going for "defined contribution" from "defined benefit" type of annuities.

(*ii*) The annuities are low

It has been specified that annuity rates for New Jeevan Surakhsa-l/ New Jeevan Dhara-I will be same as that of New Jeevan Akshay-I current at the time of vesting. Today, New Jeevan Akshay-I, an immediate annuity plan offers life long guaranteed pension @ 6.66% p.a. to 8.11 % p.a. with return of purchase price depending on age of annuitant being 40 or 79 years.

By all counts in today's scenario this yield which is guaranteed and safe should be considered excellent. We need to market "New Jeevan Akshay-I" not only as immediate annuity plan but also as scheme which can give you a regular income with safety of your capital.

***(iii)* No bonus indicated in New Jeevan Surakhsa-I/New Jeevan Dhara-I**

Fact: By now all of us know that bonus depends on surplus fund generated by LIC. However we offer more bonus to long term and high premium policies as they give higher reserve for surplus. Traditionally we have been selling policies like endowment and money back by presuming a bonus rate however, same is not being done in New Jeevan Suraksha-I. While computing in the latest valuation should be added to NCO while computing annuity rates.

Selling Points:

New Jeevan Suraksha-I

- Single Premium payment availability.
- The most flexible deferment period 2–35 years in New Jeevan Suraksha- I.
- Income tax exemption upto Rs. 10,000/- p.a. u/s. 80 CC (I)
- Tax free commutation of 25% of NCO + Bonuses.
- 5 different options to receive annuity.
- Tax rebate available for persons with more than Rs. 5 lakhs of income also.

New Jeevan Akshay-I

- Available from 40 years to 79 years of age. Suitable for middle aged and short careerists also.
- Minimum of purchase price Rs. 25,000/- only.
- 5 convenient pension options.

LIC has got very powerful products – each one of them having its own distinctive and specific features which we need to highlight. Our need based ideal product range include some of the plans where sales are low as we have not understood fully the entire spectrum of benefit of the plan in totality. I will recommend Plan 5, 89,91, 103, 109, 121, 150, 151, 143, 149, 152, 159 in particular apart from our usual 'bread and butter' plans 14 & 75.

Given below are the highlights of some of the other favourite plans:

Plan 89: Jeevan Sathi

- A superb plan.
- Two lives are covered at little over half the cost of separate Endowment Plans.
- P.W.B. offered free after 1st death + Free risk cover for another life till maturity.
- Both lives get accident benefit if death of both lives take place in the same policy year by accident.

Plan 91: New Jana Raksha:

- Ideal Endowment policy for persons with irregular or uncertain income and even salaried class working in companies/factories facing job security syndrome.
- After the premiums are paid for 2 years, free risk cover in case of non-payment of premiums upto 3 years from F.D.P.
- Easy revival terms.

Plan 103: Jeevan Chhaya

- Ideal for annual educational expenses of children.
- Free term assurance on proposer's death during term.
- Free P.W.B. after death of life assured.

- **Guaranteed Policy benefits:** Education provision guaranteed during life time or even in the contingency of premature death of Life Insured.

Plan 121: Asha Deep

- A policy combining benefits of health and life Insurance.
- Four critical illnesses covered.
- Free P.W.B.
- Immediate contingent benefit equal to 50% of sum assured in case of policy holder suffers from critical illness.
- Balance 50% Sum Assured repaid in 10 equal instalments.
- Full risk cover in case of death.

Plan 153: Bima Nivesh Triple Cover

- Ideal for younger people — VRS at middle age or retirees from Army.
- Guaranteed returns and thrice sum assured risk cover.
- Convenient single premium.

Every product has distinct segment, only and eagle's eye will pave the way to enlarge the compass of clientile.

JEEVAN PRAMUKH

BENEFITS

Guaranteed Additions

Guaranteed Additions @ Rs. 50/- per thousand Sum Assured for each completed year, for the first five years.

Participation in profits: The policy shall participate in profits of the Corporation from the 6th year onwards and shall be entitled to receive bonuses declared as per the experience of the Corporation.

Maturity benefit: Sum Assured together with accrued Guaranteed Additions and accrued Simple Reversionary Bonuses and Final Additional Bonus, if any, will be paid to the Policy-holder on surviving the term of the policy provided the policy is in full force for full sum assured.

Death benefit: On death of the Life Assured during the term of the policy an amount equal to the Sum Assured along with accrued Guaranteed Additions and accrued Simple Reversionary Bonuses and Final Additional Bonus, if any, will be paid provided the policy is in full force for full Sum Assured.

Grace period: A grace period of 30 days will be available for payment of yearly, half-yearly or quarterly premiums and 15 days for monthly premiums.

15-day cooling-off period: If you are not satisfied with the 'Terms and Conditions' of the policy you may return the policy to us within 15 days.

Paid-up value: The policy will acquire paid-up value after more than one year's premiums have been paid subject to Terms-and Conditions.

Guaranteed surrender value: The policy can be surrendered for cash after more than one year's premiums have been paid. The Guaranteed Surrender Value allowable under the policy will be equal to 30% of the total amount of premiums paid excluding the premiums for the first year and the extra premiums, if any.

The cash value of any existing vested Guaranteed Additions and vested simple reversionary bonuses, if any, will also be payable after completion of 3 years.

Revival: The policy-holder can revive his lapsed policy by paying arrears of premium together with interest within a period of five years from the date of first unpaid premium subject to satisfactory evidence of health and continued insurability of the Life Assured. The rate of interest will be as determined by the Corporation from time to time. Currently, the rate of interest is 9% p.a.

Loan: Subject to Terms and Conditions loan is permissible after the policy has acquired paid-up value. The rate of interest charged on such loan amount would be determined from time to time. The present rate is 10.5% p.a. payable half-yearly.

Payment of premium: Premium under this policy are payable over a period of 3, 4 or 5 years. The following modes of payment of premium are allowed – Yearly. Half-yearly. Quarterly or Monthly.

Policy Term: 5, 10, 15, 20 or 25 years.

Eligibility conditions and other restrictions:

(*a*) Minimum Age at entry - 18 years completed
(*b*) Maximum Age at entry - 65 years (age nearer birthday)
(*c*) Maximum Maturity age - 75 years (age nearer birthday)
(*d*) Policy Term - 5, 10, 12, 20 or 25 years
(*e*) Sum Assured - Minimum Rs. 10 lakhs. Thereafter in multiples of Rs. 1,00,000

Rebate for mode of premium payment:

yearly - 2% of tabular premium
Half-yearly - 1 % of tabular premium
Quarterly - Nil
Monthly - 5% extra of tabular premium

Sum assured rebate:

Up to and including Rs. 50 lakhs : Nil
Above Rs. 50 lakhs : Rs. 0.50 per thousand Sum Assured

Exclusions: This policy will be void if the Life Assured commits suicide within one year from the date of commencement of risk under the policy.

SPECIMEN PREMIUM RATES

Premium Paying Term 3 years

Age	*Policy Term*				
	5	*10*	*15*	*20*	*25*
20	362.70	306.00	256.40	213.85	177.85
25	362.75	306.05	256.55	214.10	178.40
30	362.75	306.10	256.75	214.65	179.55
35	362.85	306.35	257.35	215.95	181.85
40	363.10	306.90	258.60	218.30	185.80
45	363.50	307.85	260.65	222.05	191.95
50	364.30	309.55	264.00	228.00	201.55
55	365.55	312.05	269.00	236.95	000.00
60	367.25	315.75	276.75	000.00	000.00
65	370.35	322.30	000.00	000.00	000.00

Premium Paying Term 4 years

Age	*Policy Term*				
	5	***10***	***15***	***20***	***25***
20	277.60	234.20	196.25	163.65	136.15
25	277.65	234.25	196.35	163.90	136.55
30	277.65	234.30	196.50	164.30	137.45
35	277.75	234.50	197.00	165.30	139.25
40	278.05	235.00	198.00	167.15	142.25
45	278.50	235.85	199.70	170.15	147.10
50	279.40	237.40	202.50	174.90	154.60
55	280.80	239.70	20.65	182.05	000.00
60	282.75	243.05	213.05	000.00	000.00
65	286.20	249.05	000.00	000.00	000.00

Premium Paying Term 4 years

Age	*Policy Term*				
	5	***10***	***15***	***20***	***25***
20	239.95	202.45	169.65	141.50	117.70
25	240.00	202.50	169.75	141.70	118.70
30	240.00	202.55	169.90	142.05	118.85
35	240.15	202.75	170.35	142.95	120.40
40	240.50	203.30	171.30	144.60	123.10
45	241.05	204.15	172.85	147.25	127.30
50	242.10	205.70	175.45	151.55	134.00
55	243.75	208.05	179.35	158.00	000.00
60	246.05	211.55	185.45	000.00	000.00
65	250.20	217.70	000.00	000.00	000.00

Benefit Illustration

Statutory Warning

Some benefits are guaranteed and some benefits are variable with returns based on the future performance of your Insurer carrying on life insurance business. If your policy offers guaranteed returns then these will be clearly marked 'guaranteed' in this illustration table on this page. If your policy offer variable returns then the illustrations on this page will show two different rates of assumed future investment returns, These assumed rates of return are not guaranteed and they are not the upper or lower limits of what you might get back, as the value of your policy is dependent on a number of factors including future investment performance".

Age at Entry	*35 years*	*Yearly Premium (Rs.)*	*178213*
Term	*25 years*	*Sum Assured*	*1000000*
ppt	*3 years*		

End of Yrs.	*Total Premium paid (Rs.)*	*Guaranteed*	*Death Benefit/Maturity Benefit (Rs.) payable at end of year* *Variable*		*Toral*	
			Scenario 1	*Scenario 2*	*Scenario 1*	*Scenario 2*
1	178213	1000000	0	0	1000000	1000000
2	356426	1050000	0	0	1050000	1050000
3	534639	1100000	0	0	1100000	1100000
4	534639	1150000	0	0	1150000	1150000
5	534639	1200000	0	0	1200000	1200000
6	534639	1250000	22000	104000	1272000	1354000
7	534639	1250000	44000	208000	1294000	1458000
8	534639	1250000	66000	312000	1316000	1562000
9	534639	1250000	88000	416000	1338000	1666000
10	534639	1250000	110000	520000	1360000	1770000
15	534639	1250000	220000	1040000	1470000	2290000
20	534639	1250000	440000	2080000	1690000	3330000
25	534639	1250000	586000	2773000	1836000	4023000

(i) This illustration is applicable to a non-smoker male/female standard (from medical, life style and occupation point of view) life.

(ii) The non-guaranteed benefits (1) and (2) in above illustration are calculated so that they are consistent with the protected Investment Rate of Return assumption of 6% p.a. (Scenario 1) and 10% p.o. (Scenario 2) respectively. In other words, in preparing this benefits illustration, it is assumed that the Projected Investment Rate of Return that LICI will be able to earn ***throughout the term of the policy will be*** *6% p.a. or 10% p.a., as the case may be. The Projected Investment Rate of Return is* ***not guaranteed.***

(iii) The main objective of the illustration is that the client is able to appreciate the features of the product and the flow of benefits in different circumstance with some level on quantification.

(iv) Future bonus will depend on future profits and as such is not guaranteed. However, ones bonus is declared in any year and added to the policy, the bonus so added is guaranteed.

(v) The Maturity Benefit is the amount shown at the end of the policy term.

Section 41 of Insurance Act 1938

(1) No person shall allow or offer to allow, either directly or indirectly as an inducement to any person take out or renew of continue an insurance in respect of any kind of risk relating to lives or property in India, any rebate of the whole or part of the commission payable or any rebate of the premium shown on the policy, nor shall any person taking out or renewing or continuing a policy accept any rebate except such rebates as may be allowed in accordance with the published prospectuses or tables of the insurers provided that acceptance by an insurance agent of commission in connection with a policy of life insurance taking out by himself on his own life shall not be deemed to be acceptance of the rebate of premium within the meaning of this sub-section if at the time of such acceptance the insurance agent satisfies the prescribed conditions establishing that he is a bona fide insurance agent employed by the insurer.

(2) Any person making default in complying with the provisions of this Section shall be punishable with a fine, which extend to 500 rupees.

LIC'S JEEVAN NIDHI

SALIENT FEATURES

(*a*) **Guaranteed Additions:** Guaranteed Additions @ Rs. 50/- per thousand Sum assured for each completed year, for the first five years.

(*b*) **Participation in profits:** The policy shall participate in profits of the Corporation from the 6th year onwards and shall be entitled to receive bonuses declared as per the experience of the Corporation.

(*c*) **Benefits on Vesting:**

1. *Option to commute* up to 1/3rd of the amount available on vesting, which shall include the Sum Assured under the Basic Plan together with accrued Guaranteed Additions, simple Reversionary Bonuses and Terminal Bonus, if any.
2. *Annuity as per the option selected:* Annuity on the balance amount if commutation is exercised, otherwise annuity of the fun amount.

(*d*) **Death Benefit on death before annuity vests:** One the death of the Life Assured during the deferment period of the policy, *i.e.,* before the annuity vests, an amount equal to the Sum Assured under the Basic plan along with the occurred: Guaranteed Additions, simple Reversionary Bonuses and Terminal Bonus, if any, will be paid in a lump sum to the appointed nominee, provided the policy is in force for full Sum Assured. Nominee will also have the option to purchase an annuity with this amount.

(*e*) **Annuity Options:** On vesting, the annuity instalment, mode of annuity payment and type of annuity which shall be made available to the Life Assured (Annuitant/Nominee will depend upon the then prevailing Immediate Annuity plan of the Life Insurance Corporation of India and its terms and conditions.

Currently the following options are available under LICs Immediate Annuities:

1. **Annuity for life:** The annuity is paid to the life assured as long as he/she is alive.
2. **Annuity Guaranteed for certain periods:** The annuity is paid to the life assured for periods of 5 or 10 or 15 or 20 years as chosen by him/her, whether or not he/she survives that period. After the chosen period, the annuity is paid to the life assured as long as he/she is alive.
3. **Annuity with return of purchase price on death:** The annuity is paid to the life assured as long as he/she is alive. On the death of the life assured, the purchase price of the annuity is paid as death benefit. The purchase price includes the Sum Assured under the Basic Plan, the accrued Guaranteed Additions and any accrued bonuses, excluding the commuted value, if any.
4. **Increasing annuity:** The annuity is paid of the life assured as long as he/she in alive. The amount of annuity increases every year at a simple rate of 3% per annum.
5. **Guaranteed Surrender Value:** Before the annuity vests, the policy can be surrendered at any time after the completion of 3 policy years. For a regular premium policy, the Guaranteed Surrender value is available provided 3 years premiums are paid, and it is 30% of the premiums paid excluding premiums paid in the first year. For a Single Premium policy, the Guaranteed Surrender Value available after completion of 3 policy years is 90% of the Single Premium: Any extra premiums and premiums for Term Assurance Rider Option, Critical Illness Rider option and Accident Benefits, if any will be excluded.

The cash value of any existing vested Guaranteed Additions and vested Simple Reversionary Bonuses. If any, will be allowed in the surrender value.

(*g*) **Grace Period:** A grace period of 30 days will be available for payment of yearly, half-yearly or quarterly premiums and 15 days for monthly premiums.

(*h*) **15 – day Cooling-off period:** If policy-holder is not satisfied with the 'Terms and Conditions" of the policy, he/she may return the policy to us within 15 days.

(*i*) **Paid-up Value:** The policy will acquired paid-up value after at least 3 full year's premiums have been paid.

(*j*) **Revival:** The policy-holder can revive his lapsed policy by paying arrears or premium together with interest within a period of five years from the date of first unpaid premium subject to satisfactory evidence of health. The rate of interest for this purpose will be decided by the Corporation from time to time. The present rate of interest in 9% p.a.

(*k*) **Options:** 1. *Accidental Death and Disability Benefits:* In case of death accident (within 180 days) an additional amount equal to the Accident Benefit Sum assured will be payable. In case of Total and Permanent disability arising due to accident an amount equal to accident benefit sum assured will be able over a period of 10 years in monthly instalments. However, the payment of accident benefits will be subject to an overall limit of Rs, 25 lakh under all policies of the Life Assured with the Corporation taken together.

The disability due to accident should be total and such that the Life Assured is unable to carry out any work to earn a living. Following disabilities due to accident are also covered.

(*a*) irrevocable loss of the entire sight of both eyes or

(*b*) amputation of both hands at or above the wrists of

(*c*) amputation of both feet at or above ankles, or

(*d*) amputation of the hand at or above the wrist and one foot at or above the ankle.

Not benefit will be paid in case of accidental death or disability due to accident in case of:

(*a*) international self-injury, attempted suicide, insanity or immorality or the Life Assured is under the influence of intoxicating liquor, drug of narcotic,

(*b*) engagement is aviation or aeronautics other than that a passenger in any air craft

(*c*) injuries resulting from riots, civil commotion, rebellion, war, invasion, hunting, mountaineering, steeple chasing or racing of any kind

(*d*) accident resulted from committing any breach of law

(*e*) accident arising from employment in armed forces or military services of police organisation.

2. **Term Assurance Rider Option:** Term Assurance as optional rider will be available under this plan. Premiums for this option are payable during the premium paying term and an amount equal to Term Assurance Sum Assured will be payable on death during the policy term. The maximum cover for this rider will be Rs. 25 lakh under all policies of the Life Assured with the Corporation taken together.

3. **Critical Illness Rider Option:** An amount equal to the Critical Illness Rider Sum Assured as optional rider will be payable in case of diagnosis of defined categories of Critical Illness subject to certain terms and conditions. The maximum cover for this rider will be Rs. 5 lakh under all policies of the Life Assured with the Corporation taken together.

ELIGIBILITY CONDITIONS AND OTHER RESTRICTIONS UNDER THIS PLAN

For Basic Benefit

(*a*) Minimum age at entry:	18 years (completed)
(*b*) Maximum age at entry:	65 years

(*c*) Minimum age at vesting:	40 years
(*d*) Maximum age at vesting:	75 years
(*e*) Policy terms:	6 to 35 years under Single Premium policies and 5 to 35 years under Regular Premium policies
(*f*) Modes of premium payment:	Yearly, Half-yearly, Quarterly, SSS & Single Premium
(*g*) Sums Assured allowed:	Rs. 50,000/- and in multiples of Rs. 5,000/- thereafter, with no upper limit
(*h*) Minimum Annual Premium:	Rs.3,000/-
(*i*) Minimum Single Premium:	Rs. 10,000/-

For Term Assurance Rider Option:

(*a*) Minimum age at entry:	18 years (completed)
(*b*) Maximum age at entry:	50 years
(*c*) Maximum age at vesting:	60 years
(*d*) Policy terms:	6 to 36 years under Single Premium mode and 10 to 35 years under regular
(*e*) Minimum Sum Assured:	Rs. 1,00,000/-
(*f*) Maximum Sum Assured:	An amount equal to the Sum Assured under the Basic plan subject to a limit to Rs. 25,00,000/- taking all Term Assurance Rider Sum Assured under all policies of a life assured
(*g*) Multiples of Sum Assured:	Rs. 25,000/-

For Term Assurance Rider Option:

(*a*) Minimum age at entry:	20 years (completed)
(*b*) Maximum age at entry:	50 years

A BLEND OF HAPPINESS AND SECURITY JEEVAN ANAND

Table No. 149

A two-in-one policy that gives the advantage of both whole life & Endowment schemes.

- **Survival Benefit:** Sum Assured + Bonus at the end of the selected term and risk cover continues.
- **Death Benefit:** Sum Assured + Bonus if death takes place during the selected term and policy comes to an end. However, if death takes place after the selected term, then the Sum Assured alone is payable to the nominee/legal heirs.
- **Accident and Disability Benefit:** Exclusive in-built accident and disability benefit up to Rs. 5,00,000.
- **Minimum Sum Assured:** Rs. 1,00,000.
- **Loan facility:** Available

The LIC has introduced five new policies during 2005-2006. These are LIC's Golden Jubilee Policy—Bima Gold, LIC's Jeevan Plus, LIC's Bima Bachat, LIC's Amulya Jeevan and LIC's Jeevan Tarang. Similarly, LIC's Jeevan Akshay III was repriced and replaced as LIC's Jeevan Akshay IV. New Bima Gold (Table 179) having regular premium money back plan with return of total premium in instalments at prescribed intervals with loyalty additions, if any, at maturity and extended free risk cover was introduced in 2008.

SOCIAL SECURITY SCHEMES

Janashree Bima Yojana : The object of this scheme is to provide insurance protection to the rural and urban poor below the poverty line or marginally above it. 50% of the premium is subsidised from the Social Security Fund maintained by LIC and the remaining 50% is contributed by members / Nodal Agency / State Government. Persons aged between 18 and 59 years are covered for an amount of Rs. 30,000/- each under this scheme. In case of death or total disability (including loss of 2 eyes / 2 limits of use) due to accident, a sum of Rs. 75,000 and in case of partial permanent disability (loss of 1 eye / 1 limit of 1 use) due to accident, a sum of Rs. 37,500/- is payable to the nominee / beneficiary.

QUESTIONS

1. What are the various kinds of life insurance policies?
2. 'Multi-purpose policy is fulfilling almost all types of human needs'. Comment.
3. "These days Children's Deferred Endowment Policies are gaining ground." Discuss in detail.
4. Describe the different types of endowment and term policies.
5. "Life insurance is insurance against dying too soon and endowment insurance is insurance against living too long." Explain.
6. Explain the distinctive features of (*a*) Anticipated Policies. (*b*) Double endowment policies and, (*c*) Simple benefit policies.
7. Explain the salient features of Jeevan Chhaya.
8. Describe the terms and conditions of "Jeevan Pramukh" what is LIC's Jeevan Nidhi? Explain with advantages.

7

ANNUITIES

An annuity is a periodical level payment made in exchange at the purchase money for the remainder of the life time of a person or for a specified period. The recipient is usually as an annuitant. In annuity contract, the insurer undertakes to pay certain level sums periodically up to death or expiry of the term. Since at the early death, the insurer does not suffer loss, no medical examination is necessary. However, evidence of age is essential at the time of proposal.

The annuity is beneficial to those who do not want to leave amount for others but want to use their money during their life-time. During the life-time, they may make maximum use of the money by purchasing annuity which is not possible otherwise. In bank, he may leave certain amount at early, death or may suffer loss in living long due to stoppage of the money after a certain period. The payment of annuity generally continues up to the life. So the premium rate is determined according to longevity. The amount premium is higher at younger age and lower at advanced age.

Difference between Annuity Contracts and Life Insurance Policies

Annuity contract is just opposite of the insurance contract.

(*i*) The annuity contract liquidates gradually the accumulated funds whereas the life insurance contract provides gradual accumulation of funds.

(*ii*) The annuity contract is taken for one's own benefit but the life assurance is generally for benefits of the dependents.

(*iii*) In annuity contract generally the payment stops at death whereas in life insurance the payment is usually given at death.

(*iv*) The premium in annuity contract is calculated on the basis of longevity of the annuitant but the premium in life insurance is based on the mortality of the policy-holder.

(*v*) Annuity is protection against living too long whereas the life insurance contract is protection against living too short.

Both of these contracts complete the economic programme of an individual from beginning to an end. When life insurance stops to serve the annuity contract starts to help the individual up to his survival.

Classification of Annudeties

The annuities can be defined according to (*i*) commencement of income, (*ii*) number of lives covered, (*iii*) mode of payment of premium, (*iv*) disposition of proceeds, and (*v*) special combination of annuities.

Annuities According to Commencement of Income

1. Immediate Annuity

The immediate annuity commences immediately after the end of the first income period. For instance, if the annuity is to be paid annually, then the first instalment will be paid at the expiry of one year. Similarly, in half-yearly annuity, the payment will begin at the end of six months. The annuity can be paid either yearly, half-yearly, quarterly or monthly. The purchase money (or consideration) is in single amount. Evidence of age is always asked for at the time of entry. The advantage of this is that with this help, it is possible to obtain a larger income than can be secured from the yield of investments. The form of contract is of special interest to persons without dependents and it provides maximum possible consistent income.

2. Annuity Due

Under this annuity, the payment of instalment starts from the time of contract. The first payment is made as soon as the contract is finalised. The premium is generally paid in single amount; but can be paid in instalments as is discussed in deferred annuity.

The difference between the annuity due and immediate annuity is that the payment for each period is paid in its beginning under the annuity due contract while at the end of the period in immediate annuity contract. The annuity due contract is beneficial for acturial valuation.

3. Deferred Annuity

In this annuity contract, the payment of annuity starts after a deferment period or at the attainment by the annuitant of a specified age. The premium may be paid as a single premium or in instalments. Generally the deferred annuity is sold on level premium. The payment of premium continues until the stated date for commencement of the instalments or until prior death of the annuitant. At the death, the premium may be returned without interest. The deferred annuity can be surrendered for a cash amount (or cash option) at the end of or before the deferment period. The surrender value is normally 950 per cent of the premiums paid excluding first premium before deferment period. No surrender value is payable after the deferment period.

The deferred annuity can be issued to male or female lives. The female lives are generally able to avail lesser amount due to their higher longevity as compared to male lives after certain age. The corporation does not require any medical examination but only proof of age is required. The corporation also issues this annuity provided the amount of annuity is not less than Rs. 100 per annum or the instalment of annuity is not less than Rs. 25 per month or the cash option is not less than Rs. 1,000.

This annuity is useful to those who desire to provide a regular income for themselves and their dependents after the expiry of specified period.

CLASSIFICATION OF ANNUITY ACCORDING TO THE NUMBER OF LIVES

1. Single Life Annuity

Under this annuity one single person following is contractor. This annuity is most beneficial to those who have no dependent and want to use all this saving during his life-time.

2. Multiple Life Annuity

In this annuity more than one life is contracted. The annuity is also of *two* types: (*a*) Joint Life Annuity where payment of annuity stops at the first death, and (*b*) Last survivor annuity where payment continues up to the death of the last person of the group.

Classification of Annuities according to Mode of Premium

The annuities according to payment of premium can be level single premium annuities.

1. Level Premium Annuities

For availing the annuity, the annuitant can deposit some amounts periodically so that, at the end, he can get sufficient amount of annuity in equal instalments. During the accomolation period, *i.e.*, before commencement of the payment of annuity, he is given option to get the surrender value in cash or to get the paid up values reduced in proportion to the premium paid to the premium payable. At the death of the depositor, the beneficiary can get the surrender values or premiums paid whichever is higher.

2. Single Premium Annuities

The annuity in this case is purchased by payment of a single premium. Generally, the life insurance amount is utilised for purchasing this annuity.

Classification according to the disposition of Proceeds

The annuities according to this classification may be (*i*) Life Annuity; (*ii*) Guaranteed Minimum Annuities; and (*iii*) Temporary Annuities.

1. Life Annuity

This annuity offers a regular income to the annuitant throughout his life-time. No payment is made after his death. This is beneficial not in every case. When the annuity dies before receiving all the amounts of the purchase price he is at loss. But, if he survives for a longer period than expected, he is benefited by this annuity. When we talk of annuity we mean such types of annuity. In other words, annuity means annual payment up to life. But this annuity will be treated as fair-weather friend and the dependents may be at loss because the father who had accumulated a large amount could not use the funds at early death.

2. Guaranteed Minimum Annuity

Annuity payment up to a period is guaranteed by the insurer. If the annuitant dies before the specified period, annuity will continue up to the unexpired period. This annuity may be of two types, (*i*) Immediate Annuity with guaranteed payment, and (*ii*) Deferred annuity with guaranteed payment.

(*i*) *Immediate Annuity with Guaranteed Payment.* To safe-guard the loss in case of early death of the annurant, this annuity is issued where payment for a fixed number of years will continue, irrespective of death. Sometimes, instead of continuing the annuity payments after the death of the policy-holder, the difference of the purchase money and annuity instalments already paid is returned as a lump sum to the legal representative of the annuitant. This annuity may be of *two* types: first, where payment is continued up to the fixed period and second, where payment continues up to the fixed period and up to life thereafter. The corporation issues the second type of annuity where payments are guaranteed for 5, 10, 15 or 20 years and thereafter up to life. It means that payment certainly be made up to this period whether the annuitant is alive or dead within this period and if the annuitant survives after period, he is paid the annuity up to this survival.

(*ii*) *Deferred Annuity with Guaranteed Payment.* During the deferment period, there is no difference between this annuity and ordinary deferred annuity. After deferment period, the payment under this policy will continue for a fixed period, say 5, 10, 15 or 20 years and up to life, thereafter. This policy also guarantees refund of cash value of the balance of annuity where the insurer promises to pay a lump sum to the beneficiary or to the annuitant's estate, the difference, if any, between the total of annuities received before the annuitant's death and the purchase price.

3. Temporary Life Annuity

Under this plan, annuity payments cease at the end of a specified period or at the death whichever is earlier. The corporation does not issue such annuity.

4. Retirement Annuity Policy

This annuity is useful employees at the time of retirement. This annuity is issued under the following conditions: (*i*) The main object of the annuity contract must be the provision of life annuity to the individual in old age; (*ii*) During the life of the individual no sum other than the annuity to the individual shall be payable under the contract; (*iii*) All annuities must be payable in India only; (*iv*) The annuity must commence between the ages of 58 and 68; (*v*) The annuity payable shall not be capable of surrender, commutation or assignment; (*vi*) The annuity will ordinarily be payable for the life of the annuitant but if so desired provision can be made for annuity to continue for a specified period notwithstanding the death of the annuitant within the term on condition that such period of guarantee for payment of the annuity does not exceed ten years. This Annuity Policy will not be issued for an annuity of less than Rs. 600 per annum or where the annuity instalments are payable for a monthly instalment of less than Rs. 50.

8

SELECTION OF RISK

The selection of a risk is a process whereby inferior lives are "weeded out". The function of the selection process is to determine whether the degree of risk presented by applicant for insurance is commensurate with the premium established for persons in his category or some additional premium should be charged or the applicant should be rejected the insurance.

Purpose of Selections

(*i*) The first and the foremost purpose of the selection of risk is to determine whether the proposal should be accepted or not.

(*ii*) The second objective of the selection is to determine the rate of premium to be charged from the assured. The premium depends upon the amount of risk. Higher is the risk the more will be amount of premium. Each and every proposal should be evaluated to determine the amount of risk for calculation of premium. The evaluation of risk is also known as the *selection of risk*.

(*iii*) Since there are various degrees of risk to a person and so theoretically at least, all the persons should be charged different premiums, but it is not practicable to charge so many premiums as many applicants are. Therefore for practical purpose the risks are classified and premiums are determined accordingly. This is discussed in the next section of this chapter.

Insurance risk may be classified into standard or sub-standard on the basis of selection. It is possible to determine what risks are to be accepted at normal rate of premium and what at extra premium what not to be accepted at all.

(*iv*) The fourth aim of selection is to avoid any discrimination on the part of the lives assured. Since the degree of risk is not the same to all the persons, different premiums should be charged from different groups. If one premium is charged from all the proposers, it would be unjustified. For instance, it would be wrong to charge the same premium from the persons who are engaged in the hazardous occupation and from the persons who are enjoying robust health and conducive occupation.

(*v*) The selection of risk is also essential to avoid adverse-selection: Selection of risk is very essential to check the anti-selection or adverse-selection which means selection of the persons for insurance who are not insurable and charging of lesser premium for those who are to be charged higher premium. The persons in adversity of insurance, *i.e.*, the person who are imminent to death may try to purchase insurance at any cost to gain. If it is permitted not only the insurer will be losing, but the honest insured would be required to pay more premium to meet the total loss of the insurer. If they accept the higher premium they are purchasing insurance at higher cost, and if they are not going to purchase the policy, the insurer will be losing sounding business and would be again at loss. Therefore, it is very essential to select standard risk at standard cost and sub-standard risk at extra premium to avoid inequality of cost and unfavourable selection of risk.

FACTORS AFFECTING RISK

In life insurance, the factors which may affect the risk are usually those factors which are affecting the mortality; they are also called *factors affecting longevity of a person*. The mortality is not the only risk but the capacity and willingness of a person also influence the insurance decision. These factors are discussed in following paragraphs:

1. Age

The age of the life to be assured is the most important factor to affect mortality. Except for a few years of the childhood, the premium is determined at every year of the completion of age. The corporation asks for the age nearer to birthdays. The person below six months and the person above six months older of the age will be treated of the same age. For instance, a person of 22 years 7 months and another person of 23 years 5 months will be treated the age of 23 years.

The age proof is very essential for calculating premium rate. So, unless age is proved payment of claim is not made if the age was not admitted at the time of proposal. Now it has been the common practice that the age should be admitted at the time of proposal to avoid dispute. On the basis of age, in future, if a misstatement is discovered after the policy has become a claim, the amount of the claim is adjusted in accordance with the rectification of age. Age proof is essential at the proposal if the policy is term insurance, non-medical policies and immediate annuity or the insurance is taken at advance age or for a child because they are maximum and minimum limits of age.

Minimum and Maximum limit of age

The maximum age limit is fixed to avoid adverse selection. At advance age, the need for insurance is a doubtful proposition, *i.e.*, the chances of moral hazard is higher. The third reason for fixing maximum limit is the medical examination will disapprove most of the proposal at that stage. Mortality is certainly increased at that age. The minimum age limit is meant to avoid risk of infant mortality.

2. Build

Build refers to physique of the proposed life and includes height, weight, the distribution of weight and chest expansion. There are standards of weight according to maximum weight reveal the indication of certain hidden diseases. Therefore this sign is not favourable. The relationship between height, weight, girth and expansion of chest are the basic determinants of mortality expectations.

Overweight is dangerous in advanced age and underweight is similarly not desirable at younger age, say, below 35 years. The corporation, for example, has fixed the minimum weight, and maximum weight at a specified height. If the assured life is not within the standard the proposal may not be accepted at the time of proposal and it may be postponed or may be accepted at extra-premium or may be rejected at all.

3. Physical Condition

The physical condition of the age life proposed has a direct bearing on the mortality of the life. Insurers are, therefore, very particular about the conditions of an applicants' sight, hearing, heart, arteries, lungs, tonsils, teeth, kidneys, nervous system, etc. The experts in the field can assess the longevity or mortality of a person due to impairment of certain organs. The questions are also designed to elicit information on the physical status of the applicant in the proposal form. The information is confirmed and supplemented by a medical examination. The primary purpose of the medical examination is to detect any malfunctioning of the vital organs of the body.

4. Personal History

The personal history of the life proposed would reveal the possibility of death to him. The history may be connected with the (*i*) health record, (*ii*) past habit, (*iii*) previous occupation, (*iv*) insurance history.

(*i*) *Health Record*. The past health record is the most important factor under personal history because it affects the longevity or mortality of a person to a greater extent. It includes any operations of the life proposed. The medical examination may reveal these facts. These information is also given by the applicant. Particular emphasis is placed on the recent injuries and illness. It is customary to consult attending physicians. It has been the practice not to accept the proposal form of the applicants who are suffering from illness. If the applicant has suffered from certain serious disease or operation during the past 5 years, he may be under the possibility of getting it again.

(*ii*) *Past Habits*. The insurers want to know the past habit the life proposed, for drugs or alcohol because the cure may be only temporary. The past history is usually expected to be repeated. Therefore, past history is very cautiously examined.

(*iii*) *History of Occupation*. If the proponent was employed in hazardous or unhealthy occupation, there is a possibility that he may still retain ill-effects therefrom or may revert to such occupation. An intimate association within a person suffering from a contagious disease may influence the health of the life proposed. The past hazardous occupations generally affects, health slowly occupational diseases are contacted. Inorganic dust may create silicosis.

(*iv*) *Insurance History*. The previous amount of insurance may disclose the degree of risk of the applicant. If he was refused insurance, it might be a suspicious factor of his insurability. If it was found that the applicant was already insured for adequate amount this request for more insurance is regarded with suspicions.

5. Family History

Like the personal history, family history also requires information of habit, health, occupation and insurance of other family members, particularly of the parents, brother and sisters. The children's history of health is also required. The certain diseases, like tuberculosis and insanity, etc., and longevity of the parents will be relevant factors for determining the degree of risk of the proponents. The favourable family history, however, is not considered for offsetting the adverse effect of the personal history. The family history is considered significant to know the transmission of certain, characteristics by heredity. Heart, lungs, build, etc., follow family.

6. Occupation

Occupation is an important factor to affect the risk. It affects the occupation in various ways. Firstly, the nature of work may be hazardous because he may suffer an accident at any time while at work. Secondly, the morale of the workers may go down. They may be tempted to indulge in intoxicating or liquor or other forms of immoral living. Thirdly, the chemical effect may be poisonous. For instance, the workers may contact poison while engaged in match or chemical factories. Fourthly, the dusty or unventilated house, unhealthy or insanitary environments may deteriorate the health of the workers. Fifthly, in certain occupation, the occupational diseases are common. Sixthly, excessive mental and nervous strain may cause financial worries, and lastly, the lesser income may affect the health of the worker.

7. Residence

The residence also affects the risk. The risk will be lesser in a good climate area and more in a bad climate although the difference is narrowed down because of better medical and sanitary facilities. Information about the previous residence is equally important. The geographical location, atmosphere, political stability, climate, construction of house, travel, etc., are important factor which may affect the risk.

8. Present Habits

The general mode of living of the proposer affects the risk. Drunkards and non-temperate persons cause increase in mortality. Similarly, temperate habits tend to increase longevity of a person. Excessive and careless smoking tends to shorten the life due to development of nicotine poisoning. The past habits are also considered important. The intoxication affects the health of a person and consequently his mortality. The general mode of living is also considered in habits.

9. Morals

It has been observed that the departure from the commonly accepted standards of ethical and moral conduct involve extra mortality. Infidelity and departure from the code of sex behaviour are seriously regarded because these may affect the health. Unethical conduct is considered to be another form of moral hazard. Insurance is not generally given to bankrupt and reputed dishonest persons.

Consideration, of morals is essential to determine the moral hazard. There are two types of hazards—(l) Moral and Physical hazards—we have discussed factors affecting physical hazards in the other sections. Moral hazard will be discussed only under this heading.

The moral hazard occurs due to intention of the insured whereas the physical hazard is beyond his approach. The former is present where the policy is taken not with a view to protect one-self against losses but to obtain gain through crooked means. The moral hazard is judged by the reputation and fairness in dealings. The moral hazard is expected to present where insurance is taken at advanced age, where person is suffering from serious disease, proposal is on other's life and the proponent is engaged in hazardous occupation.

10. Race and Nationality

The mortality rate differs from race to race and nation to nation. In India, persons of high, race or caste are expected to live longer than the scheduled castes or tribes. Similarly, countries near to equator have more mortality. The climate and way of life of a country affect the health conditions of the people.

11. Sex

Mortality among female sex is, generally, higher than that of male sex because the physical hazard of maternity is present in the former case. Moreover, the ladies are physically more handicapped. The lesser education, conservatism and non-employment of the ladies also affect the mortality. The absence of proper examination of the ladies also count more hazard. The chances of moral hazard are also present in the female insurance. So, unless woman has good financial reasons for insurance, her proposal is not generally conceded.

12. Economic Status

It is essential to examine that the family and business circumstances of the proponents are such as to justify the amount of insurance applied for. This investigation also reveals whether the income of the applicants bears a reasonable relationship to the amount of insurance which he proposes to carry. The higher economic status generally provides a better field for insurance due to various reasons. Educational, financial and professional consciousness make the proponent insurance minded. The chances of death is also lower in higher strata of the society.

13. Defence Services

Though there has been much improvement in defence technology, yet flying or gliding, etc., is still considered hazardous one. Sometimes, certain restrictive clauses are imposed for insuring persons engaged in such services. In some other works, extra premiums are required. In commercial flying, no occupational extra is required. The war clause is added to avoid the occupation risk in defence, say, navy, air force and military.

14. Plan of Insurance

Certain plans involve more responsibility to the insurer at death and so these plans are restricted to only first class lives, Similarly, some plans have lesser risk and, therefore, can be issued without any extra investigations. For example, the multi-purpose policy is issued only to first class lives and the pure endowment policy can be issued to any one irrespective of health.

SOURCES OF RISK INFORMATION

Information on the factors affecting risk is collected before it can be evaluated to determine the degree of risk. It is collected from various sources because it is not possible to get all information from one source. Moreover, information from various sources on a particular item will provide an effective check.

1. The Proposal Form

The first and the important source of risk information is application form. The proposer is required to disclose all the material facts truly and fully. If any information is not asked by the insurer, the proponent should reveal the information if he thinks it to be material. Usually, the agent asks all the questions which are written in the proposal form.

The proposal form is divided into *two* parts:

1. Application form; and
2. Personal Statement.

The application includes questions pertaining to home, address, term of insurance, sum to be assured, mode of premium payment, date of birth, object of insurance, name of the nominee, previous insurance history, acceptance or rejection of the proposal, engagement in navy, air force and military services or the intention to be engaged in these services. Double accident benefit is sought or not. There are some additional questions to be answered by formal proposers, which are about education, their income, income occupation and insurance of husband. There is declaration in the end of the form which form the basis of contracts between the insured and the insurer.

Part II of the proposal form is called *personal statement* which is filled by (*i*) either the life to be assured, or (*ii*) the agent or the development officer, writing at the dictation of the life to be assured. This statement mentions name of the life to be assured, family history of father, mother, brothers and sisters in connection with their health and illness and cause of death. Questions about the bodily impairments, serious disease, habits, operation, accident or injury. There are special questions for such as observing of predate, conceptions, miscarriages and abortion for female proposers. Declaration of the proposer is also essential.

In non-medical proposals some detail information is also required. Name and address of family physicians, absent on ground of ill-health, height, weight, name and address of present and previous employers and declaration.

The proposal form gives all the required information of risk. Different types of proposal forms are used for different policies.

2. Medical Examiner's Report

The medical examiner has to identify the applicant to avoid the case of impersonation. The knowledge of medical examiner to the assured is also required. General appearance is an important question where proposal's apparent age, general health, habit, vaccination, deformity are asked. Measurement of height, weight, conditions of teeth, gums, ears, chest, heart, digestive tract, gentito-urinary system, nervous system operations and other details, etc. are inquired by physical test of the life to be assured. There are special questions for female proposers. Opinions of the medical examiner for the longevity, suspected health, first class lives, etc., are required. He has to declare that the findings are true and correct.

The information given by medical examiner is deemed to be correct and it is expected that the medical examiners would give true and fair picture; but certain cases in India have revealed that the reports of medical examiner are not hundred per cent reliable. Therefore, the underwriting officers at divisional or zonal office are required to go into details of suspected cases because once proposal has been accepted it cannot be repudiated on the ground of wrong medical reports.

3. Agent's Report

Although agents has to pursue or canvass a lot for getting proposal, yet he is required to state whether the life to be assured, is insurable or not. He has to furnish information of sum assured, name, acquaintances with the proposer, time and place of first introduction, identity of the life, medical examiners, name and address, monthly income and occupation of the proposer, general state of health, relationship with the agent, etc. The agent has also to disclose the financial and social position of the proposer. The agent is required to disclose all the unfavourable information of the life proposed. The agent's report can be of great value to the underwriting department because he has personal acquaintances with the life proposed and can give a full and correct information of all the factors affecting the risk.

Insurers do not place too much reliance on the agent's certificate because, he, in his zeal to increase his commission, might tend to colour his judgement. The comparision of agent's reports with information of other sources may reveal the fair or unfair reports of the agent. In case of wrong information of material facts, his licence may be cancelled.

4. The Inspection Report

The insurers generally verify the information obtained by an independent agency. Sometimes this investigation is conducted without the knowledge of the applicant. Today, the insurers have their own inspection staff who are generally known as inspectors or field officers or development officers. When the amount of insurance is not large, the inspectors make a general inquiry but when the amount is substantial, a deep and thorough inquiry of habits, character, social condition, occupation and health is required. In this case, the inspector interviews the applicant's neighbours, employers, bankers, business associates and other who have had special information pertaining to business, personal ethics, temperate habit, social behaviour and health.

The main advantage of this source is that the inspectors provide fair and frank information because they have no interest in the outcome of the case.

5. Private Friends Reports

The information from private friends is not generally required. But for some checking purposes, confidential reports of the friends of the proposer are considered. They are requested to reply those questions which are generally asked in agents report. Since friends are fully aware of the personal and private life of the proposer, they can give better information than the agents. But naturally the real friend does not want to harm his friend. So friends report may not always be correct.

6. Attending Physicians

The attending or family physicians can give better records of health, history of the proposed life and his family. It has been revealed that the family physicians have given true and fair reports of the required information by the insurers. The family physicians give the information only after charging a certain amount of fees.

7. Medical Information Bureau

The organisation commonly known as 'MIB' is an effective bureau for furnishing confidential medical reports. This bureau is common in U.S.A, but in India such bureau has not started. The insurers are members of this bureau and pay a certain fees annually. Sometimes they are required to pay commission for furnishing information. The MIB has recorded sufficient information of reputed and distinguished persons so the bureau is competent enough to report adequate and fair information.

8. Neighbours and Business Associates

Confidential reports about the applicant can be easily obtained from the neighbours and business associates although it may be prejudice to the extent of friendship or enemity with the proposer. The obtained information can be tallied with other information.

9. Commercial Credit Investigation Bureau

The bureau assembles financial and social information of businessmen. The credit worthiness is decided by the Bureau. The information given by the Bureau is treated confidential. These reports are expected to be correct and fair to a greater extent.

INSURANCE OF LADIES AND MINORS

Proposals on the lives of minor boys and girls who have not completed 15 years of age will be considered only under Children's Deferred Endowment Assurance and Children's Anticipated Plans. The proposals on the lives of minor boys and girls who have completed 15 years of age will be entertained only under Limited Payment Life Endowment Assurance, Double Endowment, Guaranteed Triple Benefit, Anticipated Whole Life, Convertible Whole Life Assurance, Children's Deferred Endowment. Assurance and Children's Anticipated Plans. Proposals under Progressive Protection Plan will be considered on the lives of minor boys and not girls provided they have completed 16 years of age. All such proposals will be entertained subject to medical examination except under Children's Deferred Endowment Assurance and Children's Anticipated Plans where the deferment term is 10 years or more.

The minor girls can get the benefits of insurance coverage subject to the condition that she should be studying in the school/college, the maximum limit of Rs. 1 lakh on total sum assured, usual extra-premium for sex if applicable, the amount of insurance would depend, *inter alia* on the financial status of the family and amount of insurance on the lives of parents, brothers and sisters.

The proposal form must be signed by the father/mother. In absence of both the parents, it will have to be signed by the legal guardian of the minor. A policy issued on the life of a minor under a plan of insurance, except the Plan Endowment, Children's Deferred Assurance or Children's Anticipated Plan will automatically vest in the life assured on his attaining the age of majority, provided no application for surrendering the policy is received before the date on which the life assured attains majority. A policy under Children's Deferred Assurance or Children's Anticipated Plan will vest in the life assured on the Deferred Date as per Special Provisions applicable to the policy and it is in no event assignable by the proposer before the Deferred Date. Such policy is not assignable by the proposer to any person other than the life assured. If the policy issued on the life of minor has vested in the life assured, the life assured may appoint a nominee/s or create an assignment thereof.

Precautions and Conditions. The treatment of proposals on the lives of ladies and minors should be made at extra precautions because physical and moral hazards are very high in such cases. The proposed lives should have a genuine need for life insurance, adequate income and employment, educational standard, marital status, social background etc. If the merit of proposal is unwarranted for acceptance on above grounds, the proposals may be rejected. The terms and conditions laid down for treatment of such proposals should be maintained.

The following rating is done for female lives under Endowment Assurance and Whole Life Plans.

Category of lives	*Rating*	*Amount of Maximum Insurance*
1. Woman with earned income	Same as in the case of men	Same as in the case of men.
2. Women with unearned income attracting income	— do —	Equal to 5 times her own average assessed income for the last 3 years but not exceeding the insurance

Category of lives	*Rating*	*Amount of Maximum Insurance*
tax or with sizeable personal properties likely to attract Estate Duty.		cover on husband's life or Rs. 5,00,000 whichever is lower. For Estate Duty purposes, upto the amount of estimated Estate Duty.
3. Women not covered by 1 and 2	Extra 3%	(*a*) *Single Woman*—On consideration of insurance needs, subject to maximum of Rs. 1,00,000; the actual amount would depend on the financial status etc., of the family and the father and other insurable members of the family being sufficiently insured. (*b*) *Married Women*—Not exceeding 3/4th of husband's insurance in force for full sum assured with a maximum of Rs. 2.50 lakhs. (*c*) *Widows*—On consideration of insurance needs.

No policy is issued under Convertible Term Assurance Plan to ladies.

Restrictions and Conditions. (1) Proposals for assurance on the lives of ladies who have not undergone a normal full time confinement are accepted with the first pregnancy clause. This clause may be removed on payment of a single-extra-premium of Rs. 5 per thousand. This clause may be waived in the case of ladies who may be expected to go to qualified doctors for delivery.

2. Proposals for assurance on the lives of ladies after a child birth are considered only six months after delivery. Where menstruation has not been re-established even after six months from the date of delivery the acceptance of proposals in such cases are subject to the one year pregnancy clause.
3. Proposals on the lives of ladies who are pregnant at the time of proposals are not enter-tained.
4. Proposals are not entertained on the lives of ladies who observe *purdah* whether full or partial.
5. Proposals are not entertained on the lives of ladies who have had many miscarriages.
6. Proposals are not entertained on the lives of those married ladies who, though not divorced, live separately from husbands as a matter of precaution against contracting an infectious disease from which the husband is suffering or for any other reason which raises reasonable doubts as to moral hazard.

JEEVAN BHARATI (TABLE NO. 160)

On International Women's Day, Life Insurance Corporation of India as a tribute to Indian women has launched an exclusive policy Jeevan Bharati. LIC has chosen the best way to honour women on this very special day by devising this very plan for them because LIC cares and understands the Indian Women.

Women excel everywhere—as anchor at home, achiever at work. They give life and LIC protects theirs. The woman takes care of so many lives that she is hardly ever left with time for her own. LIC's Jeevan Bharati Policy protects and nurtures her life.

All female lives including physically handicapped with certain conditions are covered. This policy is most suited for entrepreneurs and professionals like software engineers, doctors, managers, officials, self-employed, artists, salaried class, home-makers, students in the age group of about 18 to 50 years.

What is so exclusive about this plan?

1. Female Critical Illness (FCI) Cover

For the first time ever, FCI cover's for the women will be available under the umbrella of this plan. No other Indian Insurer has a product having such a unique inbuilt feature. It is indeed a brave step taken by LIC in corning out with Jeevan Bharati with additional benefits. In today's world, the most prevalent cancer among women is Breast and Ovarian Cancer, which are covered under this plan. FCI benefit offers 100% of Sum Assured (maximum Rs. 2 lakh) on diagnosis of such critical illness.

2. Congenital Disability Benefit (CDB) Cover

Some unfortunate women have to endure the pain of bringing up children born with congenital disabilities. To alleviate their hardships and to reimburse to a certain extent the expenses of treatment for rectifying the disability and the cost of bringing up such disabled child, CDB Cover offers 50% of Sum Assured (maximum Rs. 1 lack—upto 2 children).

The payment of FCI benefit or CDB does not restrict the original benefit *i.e.*, basic risk cover throughout the term and maturity benefit as well.

The plan provides for payment of 20% of Sum Assured at the end of 5 years and 10 years in case of 15 years' policy and at the end of 5, 10 and 15 years in respect of 20 years' policy. Balance Sum assured along with guaranteed addition at the rate of Rs. 50 per thousands Sum Assured for the first five years and thereafter, reversionary bonuses is payable on maturity of the policy. The policy provides an option to the female policyholder to retain survival benefit with LIC and withdraw it after its due date subsequently depending upon her need. This provision will take care of unforeseen contingencies like covering of medical expenses of family members, celebrating certain occasions like wedding, engagement, etc. of their beloved ones. The policyholders also exercise this option to plan for payment of fees of her child's education.

3. Another feature of this plan is option to receive maturity Proceeds in the form of an Annuity. People at advanced stage find it difficult to manage investment of lumpsum amount and at times there is an apprehension that the lumpsum amount may be spent on luxury items etc. Instead they prefer safety of investment with regular income. This option takes care of such women who may desire to have regular income for routine family maintenance without spending the capital amount.
4. Free risk cover for basic Sum Assured for three years in case of default of premiums after payment of the premiums for at least two years is another unique feature of this plan. The provision especially takes care of housewives and women with irregular income who may find it difficult to pay premium in unavoidable circumstances.
5. As the mode of payment of premium is yearly only, for the of convenience who may not be able to pay the premium in lumpsum, a provision to deposit premium in advance in maximum three instalments is also available under the plan.
6. In case of death of the policyholders during the term of the policy, basic Sum Assured along with guaranteed additions and reversionary bonuses, if any, is payable irrespective of survival benefits paid earlier.

The plan also provides for accident benefit and disability benefit upto an overall limit of Rs. 25 lakh Sum Assured.

Other Details

- Diseases covered under Critical Illness are Breast Cancer, Ovarian/Fallopian Tube Cancer, Cervical Cancer/Uterine Cancer/Vaginal/Vulval cancer.
- The Congenital Disabilities on the life of new born child include Downs Syndrome, Spina Bifida, Tetralogy of fallot, Oesophageal Atresia & Tracheoesophageal Fistula, Anal Atresia, Imperforate anus, Cleft Palate with or without Cleft Lip.
- Minimum and Maximum Sum Assured is Rs. 50,000 and Rs. 25 lakh (in multiples of Rs. 5,000) respectively.

- The plan is granted under Medical Scheme only.
- Being a money back plan, policy loan is not available.

(An attempt is made to give as much details as possible. For waiting period and exclusions, original circular/plan brochure please be referred).

Specimen Premium Calculation Under Jeevan Bharati (Table No. 160)

(I) Policy Particular

(*i*) Age of the Life Assured	:	30 years (last birthday)
(*ii*) Term	:	20 years
(*iii*) Sum Assured	:	Rs. 2,00,000
(*iv*) Mode	:	Yearly

Premium Calculation: (Rs.)

Tabular Premium for Basic Plan (Table 1)	:	71.45 × 200	=	14,290
Tabular Premium for Special Benefits of FCI Table (2)	:	1.35 × 200	=	270
Tabular Premium for Special Benefits of CDB (Table 3)	:	2.75 × 200	=	550
Total Tabular Premium	:			15,110
Less: Sum Assured Rebate for full Sum Assured	:			– 400
Total Instalment Premium	:			14,710

(II) Policy Particulars:

(*i*) Age of the Life Assured	:	30 years (last birthday)
(*ii*) Term	:	20 years
(*iii*) Sum Assured	:	Rs. 5,00,000
(*iv*) Mode:		Yearly

Premium Calculation:

Tabular Premium for Basic Plan (Table 1)	:	71.45 × 500	=	35,725
Tabular Premium for Special Benefits of FCI (Table 2)	:	1.35 × 200*	=	270
Tabular Premium for Special Benefits of CDB (Table 3)	:	2.75 × 200*	=	550
Total Tabular Premium	:			36,555
Less: Sum Assured Rebate for full Sum Assured	:			– 1,000
Total Instalment Premium				35,545

(*The maximum benefit available under FCI and CDB is Rs. 2,00,000/-).

Note:

1. The total instalment premium is to be rounded off to the nearest rupee.
2. CDB premium is payable upto age 40 years and hence the total instalment premium reduces by CDB premium from age 41 (e.g. in case (II) premium of Rs. 35,545 reduces by Rs. 550 from age 41).
3. Method in Case (II) is applicable for Sum Assured above Rs. 2 lacs.

NON-MEDICAL BUSINESS

Some lives are insured without undergoing medical examinations. It has been observed that medical examination may be clearly dispensed within insuring certain standard lives. There are *two* types of non-medical business: (1) Non-medical General Scheme, and (2) Non-Medical Special Scheme.

1. *Non-medical General Scheme.* Under Non-medical General Scheme, a special report is completed. The special report replaces the medical report and is prepared by those officers and agents who are related to the proponents.

Classes of lives acceptable. Male lives not more than 40 years nearer birthday are accepted for non-medical general schemes; but minors are not issued policies under this scheme. Illiterate male lives must have earned income for getting the benefits of this scheme and must be below 40 years.

Maximum Sum Assured. The maximum sum assured under this scheme is Rs. 7,500.

Types of Policies. Only Endowment, Double Endowment, Marriage Endowment, Educational Annuity, Limited Payment Endowment and Money Back Policies are issued under this scheme. The illiterate lives are insured with minimum lien of 50% during first 6 months and 25% during next six months. If lien is not desired Medical Examination will be necessary.

Maximum Age. The maximum age at maturity is 60 nearer birthday. The Maximum Policy Term is 25 years.

2. *Non-medical (Special) Scheme.* The Non-medical (Special) Scheme is available to males who are literate, not more than 45 years nearer birthday and are employed in special types of employment such as Government offices, Quasi-Government offices e.g., Municipalities, Distt. Boards, Local Boards: etc.; Schools, Hospitals etc. run by Government offices and Quasi-Government offices; State Corporations, Government Industrial Undertakings; Reputed Commercial Firms who keep accurate leave records and non-Government Industrial Undertakings on merit.

Types of Policies. The Non-medical (Special) Scheme covers only Limited Payment Life, Endowment, Double Endowment, Marriage Endowment, Educational Annuity, Guaranteed Triple Benefits Convertible whole Life, Money Back, Progressive Protection and Anticipated Whole Life Policies.

Maximum Sum. The maximum sum assured under this scheme is Rs. 20,000. The special condition for this scheme is that the employee should not be less than one year.

Non-Medical (Special) Scheme to Commissioned Officers in Armed Forces. This scheme is available to Commissioned Officers in Armed Forces who are not more than 45 years.

The types of policies as mentioned above are also available in this scheme. The maximum sum assured is Rs. 40,000. The Officer should not be put in lower category during the two years prior to the date of the proposal.

The existing non-medical limits are based on the total sum assured under all plans taken together and once the limits are exhausted there is no further scope for taking policies under non-medical. The current basis as also the limits were reviewed and it has been decided to make the following revisions:

Basis for non-medical limits

The maximum limits are now based on sum under consideration *i.e.*, rated up sum assured during current and last calendar year (on the basis of date of commencement). Any insurance taken under non-medical business prior to the latest two calender years is not to be considered while deciding the eligibility under non-medical business.

Limits

The upper limits under non-medical business are revised upwards as shown below:

Non-medical (Special) Business

1. To Personal employed with length of service not less than one year in
   (*i*) Government and Quasi-Government Offices.
   (*ii*) Schools, Hospitals etc. run by Government/Quasi Government.
   (*iii*) State Corporations, Industrial Undertakings, Private schools, Colleges, etc.

Classes of Lives	Maximum Sum Assured (based on SUC only)
(i) Literate major males and SSC passed major females not aged over 45 years	Rs. 8 lakhs Maximum aggregate basic sum assured under table nos. 88, 89, 103, 106, 107, 108, 121, and 150—Rs. 2 lakhs.
(ii) Literate males and SSC passed females aged between 46 and 50 years	Rs. 2 lakhs Maximum aggregate basic sum assured under table nos. 88, 89, 103, 106, 107, 108, 121 and 15—Rs. 1 lakh. Maximum sum assured under Table-91—Rs. 1 lakhs

2. Commissioned Officers in Armed Forces

(i) Length of service not less than one year.

(ii) Not below medical category A-1.

(iii) Not been placed in a lower category during the 2 years period prior to the date of proposal.

Classes of Lives	Maximum Sum Assured (based on SUC only)
(i) Commissioned Officer in armed forces not aged over 45 years	Rs. 10 lakhs Maximum aggregate basic sum assured under table nos. 88, 89, 103, 106, 107, 108, 121, and 150—Rs. 2 lakhs. Maximum sum assured under Table 91—Rs. 2 lakhs
(ii) Commissioned Officer in armed forces aged between 46 and 50 years	Rs. 4 lakhs Maximum aggregate basic sum assured under table nos. 88, 89, 103, 106, 107, 108, 121, and 150—Rs. 1 lakhs. Maximum sum assured under Table 91—Rs. 1 lakhs

Non-medical (General) business

1. Self-employed professionals

Chartered Accountants, Cost Accountants, Engineers, Architects, Management/Computer consultants, Doctors, Lawyers, Teachers, LIC Agents, etc.

Classes of Lives	Maximum Sum Assured (based on SUC only)
(i) Professionals not aged over 45 years	Rs. 6 lakhs Table allowed are 5, 8, 14, 27, 48, 75, 90, 91, 93, 95, 152, 154, 155, 156, 157 Maximum sum assured under Table 91—Rs. 1 lakhs
(ii) Professionals aged between 46-50 years	Rs. 3 lakhs Tables allowed are 5, 8, 14, 27, 48, 75, 90, 91, 93, 95, 152, 154, 155, 156, 157 Maximum sum assured under T 91—Rs. 50,000/-

2. Others

(i) Major males and literate females with own income (earned or (unearned) not\aged over 40 years	Rs. 2 lakhs Tables allowed are 14, 48, 75, 90, 91, 93, 95, 154, 155, 156, 157 Maximum SA under T91—Rs. 50,000/- Maximum maturity age for non-standard age proof: —65 years for endowment type —60 years for money back type Maximum term—25 years

(*ii*) Males and literate females with own income (earned or unearned) not aged between 40 and 45 years with standard age proof	Rs. 1 lakhs Tables allowed are 14, 48, 75, 90, 91, 93, 95, 154, 155, 156, 157 Maximum SA under T91—Rs. 50,000/- (Provisions of Circular Ref: Act 1/1775/4 dated 2nd January 2002 regarding self-declaration will remain unaltered)
(*iii*) Males and literate females with own income (earned or unearned) not aged between 46 and 50 years with standard age proof	Rs. 40,000/- Tables allowed are 14, 48, 75, 90, 91, 93, 95, 154, 155, 156, 157

Non-medical (Express) business

Maximum sum under consideration—Rs. 10 lakhs

Special Reports

Only sum under consideration (not modified SUC) will be the basis for calling for special reports. Where SUC is such that it falls within the limits of non-medical business, no special reports are to be called for.

Plans not allowed under non-medical business

Table Nos. 2, 43, 52, 58, 131, 133, 143, 153, 160.

All other existing rules in respect of non-medical schemes remain unaltered.

P.S.: All ages mentioned above are Nearer Birth Day.

CLASSES OF RISK

The various life risks cannot be treated individually, so they are put under a few broad categories based on the degree of each risk. There are *two* main classes of risk:

(*i*) Uninsurable Risks; and

(*ii*) Insurable Risks.

(*i*) *Uninsurable Risks*. If the insurance can be purchased at higher premium, there should not be any uninsurable risk. Theoretically, after investigating all the factors affecting a risk, the life insurance company should be able to give each due consideration and determining the premium charge for the insurance. Practically, however, there are a number of reasons why some persons are not insurable. The premium would be much high for these persons which will be against the insurance principle because higher premium will stimulate only to those who are at death bed. If they are allowed it would be a case of speculation because after payment of a few premiums he will be gaining. It would be unfair to other healthy policyholders. The second reason is that unknown risk cannot be insured to avoid the existing policyholders. So, in order to protect existing policy-holders, the insurance company must accept those risks against which it can assess adequate and fair premiums to provide for claims.

(*ii*) *Insurable Risks*. The insurable risks are those which after the selection process can be carried out by an insurer although there can be different terms and conditions for different policy-holders. There is a standard of risk, if the risk is not too great (*i.e.*, uninsurable) it can be insured as sub-standard risks even if he does not meet the requirement of a standard risk. The risk of death among sub-standard lives varies, but in all cases it is higher than that of standard lives. Insurable risks are divided into *three* broad classes—standard, sub-standard and super-standard. Every insurer, however, does not use all these classifications. Generally distinction between standard and super-standard is not made.

(a) *Standard Risk.* The standard risk is related with the normal life where there is no much or no less risk. There is certain criteria on which the risks are judged as normal life. It does not refer to ideal or first class life but it is rather a mix of good and bad lives. This group does not contain only those persons who are free from all impairments nor those persons who are under serious illness. It is the group where majority of the persons can be included and who may be either more or less than the average.

(b) *Sub-Standard Risk.* Sub-standard risks are those risks which are higher though insurable than the standard risk. Thus, the sub-standard risks are above the standard risk and below the uninsurable risk. If the life proposed crosses the maximum limit of sub-standard risk, that will be treated as uninsurable. The sub-standard risk is insured after payment of additional premium. This has been discussed in detail in chapter on Treatment of sub-standard risk.

(iii) *Super-Standard Risk.* The super-standard risk is present where there is lesser risk than the standard risk. This is also called a *preferred risk.* An insurer does not prefer to issue preferred risk policies because it increases the premium on other standard risk which may cause reduction in loss of business.

METHODS OF RISK CLASSIFICATION

There are two methods of classification of risk. First, the judgment method and second, the numerical rating system.

1. The Judgment Method

Under this method the individual decisions of experienced persons, in the medical, actuarial, underwriting and other departments are combined. These persons are qualified and permitted to take decision. Unlike the other method, no rigid rules and scales are prescribed and followed. Personal judgment, therefore, plays vital part in the whole system of underwriting. Under this system the routine cases are processed with a minimum of consideration by assistants trained in the review of applications and doubtful or significant cases or border line cases are resolved by experts who take the decision on their experience and general impressions. This method is still used in India by the Life Insurance Corporation.

The judgment method is generally used where a single factor is to be considered or where the decision for acceptance or rejection is to be taken. The second use of this method is that where numerical rating fails to decide, this method comes to much assistance because the merit of each and every factor is personally considered. The personal decision of the officers and experts may be quick and significant. The various difference in the reports, thorough inquiries is made and personal judgment is substituted by the other method.

The disadvantage of this method is that the personal direction may be biased by the whims and negligence of the officers. Inexperienced decision may harm the insurance business. The second criticism is that it is not very much scientific. There is no basis except the personal experience, for taking correct decision.

To avoid the weaknesses of the judgment method, a method known as the numerical rating system was devised and is commonly used by the insurers.

2. Numerical Rating System

This system is based upon the principle that a large number of factors enter into the composition of a risk and that the impact of each of these factors on the longevity of the risk can be determined by a statistical study of lives possessing that factor. It assumes that a standard risk has a rating of 100. Each factor has 100 if they are standard and no marks will be assigned. Information for each factor one by one is considered. Favourable factors are assigned negative values called *credits* while unfavourable factors are assigned positive values called *debits*. The particular percentages to be added or deducted for each factor will depend upon the degree of its variation from the situation assumed for the normal risk and the experience of each insurer. The algebraic summation of the debits and credits added to the per value of 100 represents the numerical value of risk. In practice, value are generally assigned to the important factors such as build, physical condition, personal history, family history, occupation, residence, habits, moral and plan. The value assigned to the various factors are on the basis of mortality. For example, if the mortality experience of a group of insured lives with a particular medical history reflected a certain degree of overweight has been found to be 135 per cent of that among all standard risk, a debit (+) of 35 marks will be assigned to such medical history. Similarly, the degree of risk on the basis of each factor is evaluated in terms of percentage. If it is more than 100, *i.e.*, if the risk is more than the standard the extra percentage will be debited (+) and if the degree of risk expressed in percentage is less than the 100, the lesser percentage will be credited (–) up to the difference.

One example of numerical rating system will make it clear. A married man having two children of the age 3.2 has good physical condition. He is over-weight by 60 per cent. His expanded chest measurement is one inch less than the girth of his abdomen. He has no indication of adverse effect on longevity. His family was from tuberculosis, insanity etc. He was working as blacksmith. His habits and morals are good. He lives in a posh house in good surrounding. The plan of insurance is twenty-year endowment. According to following table, he is given 60 marks in debit (+) side for overweight. The unfavourable build (girth greater than chest expanded) is a basis of an additional debit of 10 marks. The family history is favourable which has been given him 15 marks in credit side. The plan of insurance 20-year's endowment would call for an additional credit of 10 marks. The residence, habits, good behaviour, occupation and physical conditions have no credit marks, only debit marks are assigned to these.

Table 8.1

Factory	*Debit* (+)	*Credit* (–)
1. Build (Overweight)	60	—
2. Physical condition (Favourable)	—	—
3. Build unfavourable (Chest in lesser the girth)	10	—
4. Family History (Superior)	—	15
5. Occupation: favourable	—	—
6. Residence: normal	—	—
7. Habits and morals: favourable	—	—
8. Plan of insurance 20 year's endowment	—	10
	70	25

Net rating = 70 – 25 = 45

So, Total Rating 100 + 45 = 145

Extra Premium	Rs. per thousand of sum assured.
1. For unfavourable occupation	2/-
2. For Higher Rating	2/-

145 – 125 = 20

Age and occupation are separately valued, so they are excluded from the rating table.

The rating, thus, makes it easier to classify the risk.

Super-standard/	Standard/sub-Standard/	Uninsurable
75	125	500

If the rating is below 75, it is generally treated as super-standard and if the rating is between 75 and 125, it is standard risk, if the rating is more than 125 and below 500, it is sub-standard and the rating of more than 500 is uninsurable. The degree of rating for classification may vary from insurer to insurer.

The numerical rating system follows the same procedures as that is followed by those who judge a risk with only difference of allotting marks. The same factors are considered and the final decision is based upon the relationship of the various favourable and unfavourable features of the risk. The numerous method is objective standards which assist in the final valuation of risk and makes for greater consistence of decision. The method expedites the handling of cases and holding done the expense of the selection process. It enables to make decision on the medico-acturial investigation and reduces the operation of the subjective factor in the under-writing of risks to a minimum. The basic ratings are continuously reviewed in the height of up-to-date trends in insurance.

Various criticisms have been levied on the system. The system is thought to be too arbitrarian. There are many impairments concerning which knowledge is too limited to permit the assignment of numerical values. The interrelated factors are non-additive. Too many minor debits and credits are taken into account in evaluating risk. Ratings have often to be modified by taking into account the interaction of various aspect of the risk and in particular, the probable influence on the risk of occupation, habits, mode of living, socio-economic status, moral hazard, etc.

Supporters of the system recognise its flaws but fell that it is still superior to any other method. The numerical ratings arrived at can only be regarded as a guide; and the selection of risk depends to a considerable extent on the individual judgment and skill of the medical examiner, actuaries and underwriting officers of the life insurance business.

QUESTIONS

1. What is risk and how risk is determined in life insurance?
2. Critically examine the various factors affecting risk. From where these information of risk is obtained ?
3. Examine the 'Judgments Method' and Numerical rating system of evaluating risk.
4. What are the various classes of life insurance risk?
5. Explain in detail (*a*) Proposal form, (*b*) Medical Examination, (*c*) Proof of age, and (*d*) Insurance of female lives.

9

MEASUREMENT OF RISK AND MORTALITY TABLE

The risks are measured or evaluated for fixation of premium be charged by the insurer. There are *two* methods of calculation of Premium: (*i*) Value of Service, (*ii*) Cost of Service.

(*i*) *Value of Service*. The value of service determines the rate of premium according to the utility of insurance to each proponent. Since, the value or utility to each person differs, the premium rate will also vary. The *value* of *service* principle cannot be used in insurance because its utility to each individual cannot be determined. Moreover, the value is higher to the proper section of society and to the head of large family; but they cannot be charged higher premium than the premium charged by richer class of the society. Moreover, the higher premium will not attract business from them. The value of service cannot be used due to its impracticability.

(*ii*) *Cost of Service*. In fact, the premium should be charged according to cost to the insurer. In insurance demand side does not play important role. Therefore, it is called that the insurer is no bought, but it is sold. So, the insurer must fix the cost or premium to be charged on a particular risk or policy. Insurance business may carry on only when the cost of insurance is met. The cost includes all expenses of the business plus small profit margin. Above the profit margin, insurer is not expected to gain. This is the reason that insurance business is expected to run on 'no loss, no gain', basis. The most important cost to insurer is cost of claim. Therefore, the insurer must charge at least so much of premium that can be used to pay the full amount of claim. Technically, the premium charged to meet the amount of claim, is called *net premium*. Another cost to insurer is cost of administration. It includes all expenses of management and other amount for provisions of contingency. The cost of administration may be of *two* types, (*i*) fixed cost, and (*ii*) recurring cost. The fixed cost is spread over the policy-life but the recurring expenses do not involve much problem of allocation. The method of distribution of the expenses is called loading which, is discussed in detail in a separate chapter. With the help of loading net premium is enhanced to charge a fixed amount regularly from the policy-holders, which is called gross premium or office premium. So, the first problem before the insurer is to calculate the cost of claims.

Cost of Claims

The claims may arise at the death of the life assured or at the of the policy. In annuity contract the payment shall continue to death therefore, the expectation of survival will be the basis of the cost. In life insurance, in most cases, payment of claims depends upon the death. The death is certain but when it will take place is not certain.

Therefore, the main problem before the insurer is to decide when the death will take place. The forecasting of death is very important factor to decide the period and amount of claim. If the period and amount of claims have been decided, the premium can be easily calculated. The forecasting of death can be done on (*i*) experience of medical science, and (*ii*) On the experience of past records. If the medical science of insurance has been sufficiently advanced and its knowledge could be perfectly used, the same, then, might have projected the time of death of each applicant. The medical science can be useful to modify the past experience according to the present mortality prospects. The insurer bases the calculating of time of death on the basis of experience of past death with certain modification in special cases. The insurer has to rely upon the past experience which is treated as a basis for germinating future mortality. It has been assumed that there is law of mortality on the basis of which deaths have been taking place in future. Evidently, the death of one life cannot be forecasted; but the expectation of a number of deaths from a group of persons of the same age can be forecasted on the basis of (*i*) Theory of probability and (*ii*) The law of large numbers.

Theory of Probability

The theory of probability reveals the possibility of occurring a certain event or not occurring a certain event out of the given events. Thus, in insurance, the theory of probability reveals the chances of death of a person out of a group of persons. The theory of probability can be of three types: (*i*) certainty, (*ii*) simple probability and (*iii*) compound probability.

1. Certainty

The probability of certainty is expressed as one. It means the chance of happening a certain event, say death, is 100 per cent. It sure that the death will occur in this expression. Naturally factor, *i.e.*, certainty is taken as the, basis of comparison. In other words, the chance of death is related with the unity or one or certainty.

2. Simple Probability

When the events are mutually exclusive or when only event is present, the probability will be known as simple probability. For example; if at the age of 40, 2 persons die out of 10,000 the probability of death of a person, who is of 40 years, can be expressed as:

$$\frac{2}{10,000} = .02 \text{ per cent or} = 0.0002 \text{ of units.}$$

Generally, the probability is expressed in term of unity or one, *i.e.*, the probability is related with one which can be expressed in the decimals. Similarly, if there are more than one person and the death rate of each person is to be calculated separately, the simple probability is applied. For example, if there are two persons of ages 40 and 42 years the causes of death of one person only can be expressed as probability of death of first person plus probability of death of second person.

3. Compound Probability

Multiplication is a applied when the probability of the combined happening of two or more independent events, if the probabilities their separate happening are known when two or more events occur together, their joints occurrence is called compound event. For example; if the probability of death of *A* at the age of 40 is 0.002 and the probability of death of *B* at the age of 42 is 0.0003, the compound probability shall be calculated when we are required to know the probability of death of any of the persons. Thus, the probability of death of any of the, persons, will be 0.0002 × 0.0003 = 0000006. In insurance, the simple probability is generally used to calculate death rate of one person.

Estimation of Probability

The probability can be estimated whether (*i*) Priori basis and or (*ii*) Posteriori basis.

(*i*) *Priori Basis.* In this case, the probability is estimated merely on the basis of knowledge. It is not derived after experiment or practice. It is also called deductive reasoning where estimation is based on from general to particular. Although it is not exirically tested, but it is useful to correct the defects of experimental probability where the probability not expected to give hundred per cent correct results. It is well known fact that the death rate after 50 years, will not decline but it will go on increasing year after year. If in any year there is fluctuation in mortality which has been calculated on the basis of experiment that is corrected with the help of interpolation or graphical method. Thus, the apriori, probability is of much use in such circumstances.

(*ii*) *Posteriori Probability.* The probability in this case is calculated on the basis of experiment. It is also called as Inductive method because in this case, estimation is based from particular to general. The posterioi probability can give correct result only when the experiment involves a large number of units and the data are correct. In mortability estimation we cannot depend merely on the posteriori probability because cent per cent accuracy and universal experiment are not possible.

Hundred per cent correct results. It is well known fact that the death after 30 years will not decline but it will go on increasing year after year. If in any year there is fluctuation in mortality which has been calculated on the basis of experiment that is correct.

Law of Large Numbers

The accuracy of probability depends on two factors:

(*i*) Accuracy of data;

(*ii*) The large number of units.

The important fact to be considered is that the probable experience should be nearest to the actual experience. If there is difference between the actual and probable experience, the probability will be of no use. To avoid this deviation or difference, the data of estimation should be accurate enough and the experiment should base on a large number. It has been observed that the larger the number, the lesser the deviation between actual and probable estimation. So far calculating death rate or mortality rate a large number of persons should be selected and their age should be correctly recorded.

MORTALITY TABLE

Definition

Mortality table is such data which records the past mortality and is put in such form as can be used in estimating the course of future data. Thus the mortality table is to predict future mortality. It is also described as the picture of a generation of individuals passing through time. A large number of persons are selected and served for death and survival rated till all of them is dead.

Features

***(i)* Observation of Generation**

In preparation of mortality table persons of a generation (*i.e.*, persons of a single age) are selected and they are observed up to death. No new entries or withdrawals are assumed at any stage of the study.

***(ii)* Start from a point**

The mortality table starts from a point, which depends on the requirement of the insurer, and will continue up to the point all of them has been dead.

***(iii)* Yearly Estimation**

The mortality table records the yearly death or survival rate. Each and every year is considered for calculating the rates.

***(iv)* Mortality and Survival Rates**

The mortality and survival rates of the generation who are selected at a particular age are considered each and every year. Any table giving mortality rates only is not mortality, table unless mortality rate of a generation is calculated every year. Each year's number, living is the previous year's number of living minus previous year's number dying and, therefore, as persons go on dying year after year the number of living goes on shrinking till it is reduced to zero and modality table ends there.

CONSTRUCTION OF MORTALITY TABLE

The best method of construction of mortality table will be to select a large number of persons at attained age. Attained age means age nearer to birth date. For example, persons of 19 years 6 months to 20 years 5 months and 29 days will be treated as the age of 20 years. The attained age will be selected at which policy is to begin. The selected persons of the attained age will be observed and the number of deaths will be recorded during a year till the persons selected are dead. Theoretically speaking this type mortality table will be the actual mortality table. The number of death in a year is deducted from the number of living at the beginning of year to get the number of living in the begining of the ne year.

Criticism

(*i*) Preparation of such table is difficult because a large number of persons or an attained age is impracticable to get.

(*ii*) Constant, watch on them is not possible.

(*iii*) It will require a long-period to construct the table and for which a permanent officer, say for about 100 years, is required.

(*iv*) A lot of money and time will be wasted to record number of deaths every time.

(*v*) However, if such impossibilities are dared to do the mortality table will be quite obsolete because it had been constructed at least within 100 years during, which a lot of changes might have occurred.

Age	*Number of Living*	*Number of Death*	*Death Rate*	*Survivers Rate*
20	10,00,000	2,000	0.002	0.998
21	9,98,000	3,000	0.003	0.997
22	9,95,000	4,000	0.004	0.996

CONSTRUCTION OF DEATH RATE ON YEARLY BASIS

To avoid the above difficulties, death rate is calculated on yearly basis. The death rate is calculated for every age. Separate sample is taken for each age. The number of living in each age is observed and number of death during the age is recorded. By dividing number of death by number of living in each age, the death rate for the age is calculated. A year is selected because a year constitute various types of weather and, therefore, low, high and normal mortalities are averaged in the year. Secondly, rates of premium in insurance are quoted on an yearly basis and so the cost depending on mortality showed also be based on yearly basis.

SOURCES OF MORTALITY INFORMATION

For construction of mortality table, number of living of the beginning of each age and the number of deaths during the age are required. The mortality table should be constructed to represent the past experience as accurately as possible. So the figures of mortality construction should be as accurate as possible and based on a large number of persons. The sources of mortality construction can be obtained either from (*i*) population statistics, and (*ii*) records of life insurers.

Population Statistics

The insurer gets number of living at each age from the census records and the number of deaths from municipal and other death records. The population statistics will reveal how many persons have died at what age. So, with the radix of total number of persons at the beginning, it can be calculated how many died in a particularly age. The calculation of mortality table on this basis is not very easy and correct.

Criticism

The population statistics is not very much useful to insurers. It was applied only when there was no insurance experience in this field.

(*i*) The accuracy of population statistics is doubtful in absence of age-proof. There has been over-estimation or under-estimation in several cases. Sometimes, members of a certain section of society are unaware of ages.

(*ii*) It has been also noticed that some deaths are unrecorded. It is difficult to know exactly how many deaths are unrecorded and similarly. It is also difficult to know exactly how many deaths occurred a particular age.

(*iii*) Census figures are available only after 10 years and therefore, it would not be very recent figure. A particular census figure may be biased with the abnormality of the year.

(*iv*) Interpolation and extrapolation are involved and correct figures are generally not known.

(*v*) The population statistics will give statistics of all types persons without any separation while the insurer requires mortality of only insurable lives. Mortality for standard and substandard lives are required separately.

2. Records of Insurers

The records of insurer give a correct figure because the death rates can be correctly recorded. No death will go unrecorded, correct number of persons living and dead for each age can be known. Collection of figures is done from the records of as many insurers as possible in large numbers but is not more than 10 years covering, favourable and favourable years. Generally 10-year period may be quite sufficient. The abnormal years are excluded from the sample. Separate mortality tables may be prepared for standard lives, sub-standard lives, female and male lives. Sub-classification according to sex, marital status, occupation, geographical area, class may be made and tables are constructed separately.

The counting of persons is done very cautiously, withdraw and lapsation are excluded. Persons included for calculation caused exposed to risk. If the calculation starts at the withdrawal from this number is excluded.

Yearwise aggregation of number of deaths and number of loving persons is done from the information of all insurers. Mortality rate at every age will be counted by dividing the number of expired lives by number of exposed lives.

CONSTRUCTION OF MORTALITY TABLE

An example is taken for construction of mortality table. For example 10,000 persons are taken at age 20,2,000 persons at age 21,5,000 persons at age 22 and so on. The number of deaths observed at these ages are 20, 80 and 15 respectively. Therefore the death rate will be 0.002, 0.004 and 0.003 respectively at this stage and the death rate is calculated by the formula.

$$\text{Death rate} = \frac{\text{Number of deaths during the year}}{\text{Number of living at the begining of the year}}$$

Table 9.1 Yearly Death

Age	*Number of Living*	*Number of Death*	*Death Rate*	*Survivers Rate*
20	10,000	20	0.002	0.002
21	20,000	80	0.004	0.003
22	5,000	15	0.003	0.004
23	10,000	60	0.006	0.005
24	20,000	100	0.005	0.006

Crude and Graduated Mortality Rates

It has been observed on the basis of the theoretical analysis that the death rate normally decreases gradually from 1 to 10 years age. It increases thereafter and fastly increases after the age of 50. The yearly death rate may not be given the same phenomena because (*i*) the generation of an age is not observed. Different persons at different ages are observed, (*ii*) there may not be a large numbers for observation, and (*iii*) the date may be cent per cent correct. Therefore, there may be fluctuation in the death rate. Therefore, the death rates calculated on yearly basis having fluctuations are called Crude Death Rate. This death rate is not used for calculation of premium due to absence of a certain trend.

The graduated Mortality Rates are those which are obtained by smoothing the fluctuations of crudes rate. The smoothing or graduation is done with the help of interpolation or graphical methods. The above crude death rate is graduated by the graphical methods as below:

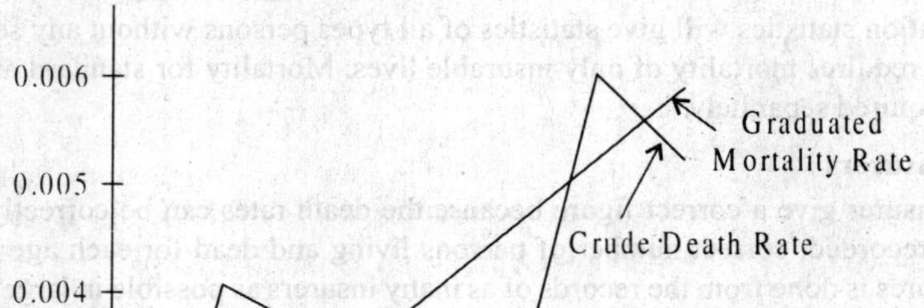

The graduated mortality rate is used for construction of mortality table. Assumption of a large number of persons at the radix is made.

Table 9.2 Mortality Table

Age	*Number of Living*	*Number of Death*	*Mortality Rate*	*Survival Rate*
x	l_x	*dx*	*qx*	*px* = 1 – *qx*
20	10,00,000	2,000	0.002	0.998
21	9,98,000	2,994	0.003	0.997
22	9,95,006	3,980	0.004	0.996
23	9,91,026	4,955	0.005	0.995
24	9,86,065	5,716	0.006	0.994

The number of death at a particular age is calculated by multiplying number of living at the age with the, mortality rate. Thus, $dx = 1x \times qx$. Here at age 20 the $d_{20} = 1_{20} \times q_{20} = 10,00,000 \times 0.002 = 2,000$. Similarly the number of living persons to the net age is calculated by deducting number of death s from the number of living persons during the age.

$1_{21} = 1_{20} - d_{20} = 10,00,000 - 2,000 = 9,98,000$

The graduated mortality rate is not sufficient to calculate or the death rate or survival rate after a certain period, so the number of living and number of deaths at every age are calculated. This makes possible to calculate the death or survival rate, after a certain period. For example, the death rate of a person aged 20 after 3 years cart be calculated as—

$$q_{x+3} = \frac{lx - lx+3}{lx}$$

$$q_{20+3} = \frac{l_{20} - l_{20+3}}{l_{20}}$$

$$q_{20+3} = \frac{10,00,000 - 9,19,026}{10,00,000}$$

$$= 0.008974$$

The Annuity Tables are also constructed besides the life table as discussed above. The only difference is that the Annuity Table will last 5 or 10 years longer to the Life Mortality Table which is commonly known as *Mortality Table.*

A Complete Mortality Table

Apart from the ordinary mortality table, the insurer uses complete mortality table. All the components of complete mortality table are discussed in the following mortality table.

***H^m* Maikaham Graduation Mortality Table**

Age	*No. of Living at x*	*No. of Deaths between x and x + 1*	*Death Rate*	*Survival Rate*	*Force of Mortality at age x*	*No. of Survival at min age lx and lx + 1*	*Total Survival No.*	*Complete Expectation of life at age x*	*Age*
Age	*No. of*	*No. of*	*Death*	*Survival*	*Force of*	*No. of*	*Total*	*Complete*	*Age*
x	l_x	dx	$q_x = \frac{dx}{l_x}$	$p_x = 1 - q_x$	U_x	$Lx = ½ (l_x + l_{x+1})$	$T_x = \Sigma L_x$	$°e_x = \frac{T_x}{L_x}$	x
20	96061	548	0.00572	0.99428	0.00550	95787	4044238	42.101	20
21	95513	582	0.00608	0.99392	0.00592	95222	3948451	41.339	21
22	94931	609	0.00643	0.99357	0.00629	94626	3853229	40.590	22
23	94322	631	0.00668	0.99332	0.00659	94007	3758603	39.849	23
24	93691	647	0.00691	0.99309	0.00682	96367	3664596	39.114	24

1. ***Column* (x).** Column x denotes the age of the prospect. The mortality table can start from any age and continue to 100 to 120 years, as required by the insurer.
2. ***Column* (l_x).** This column indicates the number of living persons at the beginning of each year. If the table starts from age 0, the number in the l_x column against this age that is to say l_0 is any convenient number like 9,000,000 or even an arbitrary number and represents the number of persons of age 0 *i.e.,* the number of persons just born. Having fixed the starting number l_0, any other number l_x in the column appearing against age x gives the number of persons living, out of the l_o persons born, who reach age x. All mortality tables may not start with age 0. If the table starts with, say age 30, any number can be assumed, for the starting value of the l_x column *i.e.,* for l_{30}. The figures in the l_x column have a meaning in relation to the starting value like l_0, l_{30} etc. and it is wrong to describe l_x as the number of persons living who are of age x in a given population.

3. Column (dx). Number of persons dying between x and $x + 1$ are given under this column. The difference $l_x - l_x + 1$ is the number of persons who die between ages x and $x + 1$. Thus, $dx = l_x - l_x + 1$.

So, we get $l_x + 1 = l_x - dx$. The next value of the l_x column *i.e.*, $l_x + 1$ can be obtained by subtracting dx, from l_x. This process continues until all the living number are dead or the mortality table is completed. Thus, the sum of all the deaths on and after age x to the extreme age w is equal to the number living at that age.

4. Column (q_x). This column indicates the probability of death. It gives for successive values of x the probability that a person aged x dies within one year *i.e.*, before reaching age $x + 1$. Thus, the death rate or mortality at age x is equal to number of deaths at age x divided by the number of living at age x or $q_x = \frac{dx}{l_x} = \frac{l_x - l_{x+1}}{l_x}$. So, $dx = l_x + q_x$; the values of dx can be found from the corresponding l_x by multiplying l_x by the rate of mortality q_x. Except at the very young rates, the rate of mortality (q_x) increases as age (x) advances. At the extreme age (w) the mortality will be equal to 1 as $q_{w-1} = \frac{l_{w-1} - l_w}{l_{w-1}} = 1$ as $l_w = 0$.

5. Column (p_x). The column (p_x) indicates the rate of survival. It gives for successive ages the probability that a life aged x survives to age $x + 1$. Thus, the probability of survival (p_x) is equal to number of survivors to age $x + 1$ divided by total number living at age x. Hence, $p_x = \frac{l_{x+1}}{l_x}$.

Except at very young ages, the value of p_x decreases as x increases *i.e.*, probability of survival decreases as age advances.

So,
$$q_x = \frac{dx}{l_x} = \frac{l_x - l_{x+1}}{l_x}$$
$$= 1 - \frac{l_{x+1}}{l_x} = 1 - p_x$$

It is also known as
$$p_x = 1 - q_x$$

The mortality table can be used for calculating the various probabilities of survival and death.

(*a*) np_x. The probability that a person aged x survivers n years is denoted by np_x. So, this probability is equal to the number of persons living at age $x + n$ divided by number of persons living at age x. *i.e.*, $np_x = \frac{l_{x+n}}{l_x}$.

(*b*) m/q_x. The probability that a person aged x dies within the next m years is denoted by mq_x. This probability is equal to number of death within m years out of persons now aged x divided by number of persons living at age x *i.e.*, $\frac{l_x - l_{x+m}}{l_x} = 1 - \frac{l_{x+m}}{l_x} = 1 - mp_x$.

(*c*) m/q_x. It is the probability that a person aged x dies in the year of age $x + m$ to $x + m + 1$. This is equal to $m/q_x = \frac{dx + m}{l_x}$.

It is different from $\frac{d_{x+m}}{l_{x+m}}$ *i.e.*, q_{x+m}

It can be expressed as:

$$m/q_x = \frac{d_{x+m}}{l_x} = \frac{l_{x+m}}{l_x} \cdot \frac{d_{x+m}}{l_{x+m}}$$

$$= mp_x \cdot q_{x+m}$$

6. Force of Mortality (U_x). The force of mortality at age x is denoted by U_x. The force of mortality at age x can thus be defined as the limiting value of the nominal yearly rate of mortality at age x, over a small interval of time d_t as the length of interval d_t, tends to zero. In practice the smallest interval we can consider is one day *i.e.*, $d_t = 1/365$ days of a year. The deaths between age x and $x + \frac{1}{365}$ are $(l_x - l_{x+1/365})$ and the rate of mortality at age x per day is $\frac{l_x - l_{(x+1/365)}}{l_x}$

and the corresponding yearly rate is

$$\frac{l_x - l_{(x+1/365)}}{\frac{1}{365} l_x} = \frac{365\,(l_x - l_{x+1/365})}{l_x}$$

7. No. of survival at mid age x and $x + 1$ (L_x). The number of persons in the population between ages x to $x + 1$ is denoted by L_x. Thus,

$$L_x = \tfrac{1}{2}\,(l_x + l_{x+1}) = l_{x+1/2}$$

Also, $l_{x+1} = l_x - d_x$ and hence, $L_x = \tfrac{1}{2}\,(l_x + l_x - d_x) = l_x - \tfrac{1}{2}\,d_x$

8. Total Number of Survival (T_x). The total number of survival at any age is equal to summation of number of persons living between mid age x to the end of the table. Thus,

$$T_x = L_x + L_{x+1} + L_{x+2} \ldots L_{w-1}$$

In particular, T_0 represents the whole population at all ages and is given by:

$$T_0 = L_0 + L_1 + L_2 \ldots\ldots$$

$$= \frac{1}{2}[(l_0 + l_1) + (l_1 + l_2) + \ldots\ldots]$$

$$= \frac{1}{2} l_0 + (l_1 + l_2 + l_3 + \ldots\ldots)$$

$$= \frac{1}{2} l_0 + N'_0$$

where $N'_0 = \quad = l_2 + l_2 + l_2 \ldots\ldots\ldots\ldots l_w$

9. Complete Expectation of Life at age x ($°e_x$). This column is known as the complete expectation of life denoted by the symbol $°e_x$. The expectation of life (e_x) is the average number of complete years of life lived by each person aged x, after reaching age x. It is an average obtained by dividing by l_x, the total number of future years of life lived by the l_x persons. The total number of completed years lived by l_x persons after reaching age x is given by $(l_{x+1} + l_{z+2} \ldots\ldots)$ which is denoted by N'_x. The expectation of life will be obtained by dividing this quantity N'_x by l_x. Thus

$$e_x = N'_x / l_x$$

This expectation of life is called the curtate expectation of life as it takes into account only complete years of life lived and ignores fraction of the year lived in the year of death. If fractions are taken into account we get the complete expectation of life denoted by $°e_x$. The additional number of years of life to be included in respect of the fractional years lived is equal to $\frac{1}{2}(d_x + d_{x+1} ....) = \frac{1}{2} l_x$.

Therefore, the total number of years lived by the l_x persons, taking fractions of a year into account is:

$$N'_x + \frac{1}{2} l_x$$

The complete expectation of life at age x *i.e.*, $°e_x$ is obtained dividing this quantity by l_x. Thus,

$$°e_x = \frac{N'_m + \frac{1}{2} l_x}{l_x} = \frac{T_x}{l_x}$$

Types of Mortality Tables

There are three types of mortality tables: (*i*) Aggregate Table. (*ii*) Select Table, and (*iii*) Ultimate Table.

(*i*) *Aggregate Table.* A table constructed without distinguishing the select, and ultimate lives is called an Aggregate Mortality Table. The lives from which the mortality rates of the aggregate lives are derived being a mixture of the 'Select' lives and Utimate lives, the aggregate rates lie between the select and ultimate rates for the same age attained, that is to say, they are lighter than ultimate rates but heavier than the select rates. This is also called Mix or General Mortality Tables. In this table persons of same age irrespective of the consideration whether they were insured at age 30 or some years before the age 30. The above table is the example of aggregate table.

This table is used where no selection is required, or non-medical policies are issued. This table is also used in Group Insurance.

2. *The Select Table.* Mortality table giving rate depending on both age and duration elapsed since entry are called, select mortaility tables. Thus, persons taking policies at different ages ,are separate from each other for the purpose of the calculation, even though they all may be of the same age now. This is done because mortality rate among them will not be the same despite the same attained age. It will vary according to the duration of insurance because at the initial stage, all the policy-holders are selected after a thorough inquiry of health. The method to select, only insurable live is called 'Selection'. It has been observed that the effect of this selection wears out quickly and that two groups of persons so seleeted at different times will not experience the same mortality though they are of the same age. The group which has been selected first now is found to experience lighter mortality than another of the age at present but selected some time ago. The effect of selection may be eliminated altogether after a certain pariod *i.e.*, 5 years.

Table 9.3 Mortality Rate per 1000 (d_x)*

Age	*Years of insurance*						*Age*
	1	*2*	*3*	*4*	*5*	*6 years & over*	*attained*
20	2.73	3.59	3.80	3.96	4.13	4.31	25
21	2.78	3.66	3.86	4.01	4.18	4.35	26
22	2.83	3.72	3.91	4.07	4.21	4.38	27
23	2.86	3.76	3.06	4.08	4.24	4:41	28

* Life Insurance by O.S. Gupta Page, 139

The above table shows that the mortality, rate is 2.86 per, thousand at age 23 during 1 year after selection, 3.72 per thousand at 22 during 2 years after selection, 3.86 per thousand at age 21 during 3 years after selection and 3.96 per thousand at age 20 during 4 years after selection. Thus, it reveals that as the selection period passes the mortality rate increases although they are of the same age at present. The effect of selection is removed after 5 years and the mortality rate will be approximately equal if there are not approximately the same, there will be a case of spurious selection, *i.e.*, where effect of selection is not required.

Form a Select Table

It should be noted that in the select table the values of number of living at each are not related. Thus, $l_{(x)}, l_{(x+1)}, l_{(x+2)}$...... will not be interlinked as bas been observed earlier, but $l_{(x)+1}, l_{(x)+2}$ will be linked together.

Table 9.4 Select Mortality Table

Age	*Number of living*	*Number of Death*	*Death Rate per thousand*
X	l_z	l_x	*l*
35	1,00,000	316	3.16
35 + 1	99,684	428	4.29
35 + 2	99,256	454	4.57
35 + 3	99,802	474	4.80
36	1,00,000	323	3.23
36 + 1	99,677	411	4.42

Select table is useful where lowest and accurate death rates required. It has been used for calculating short-term and participating policies.

3. *Ultimate Morlality table.* A mortality table in which the rates in the select period are omitted and only the ultimate rates are tabulated is called an ultimate mortality tables. In other words, figures for policies that still have the effects of selection are not included. In the above example, the mortality rates for the years will not be included for preparing an ultimate mortality table.

Table 9.5 Ultimate Mortality Table

Age at entry	*6 and over*	*Age attained*
20	4.31	25
21	4.35	26
22	4.38	27
23	4.41	28

But, generally both the 'Select' and 'Ultimate' Mortality tables are shown together. In the Table No. 9.3 the select table was up the 5 years of the selection (6) and over with attained age was ultimate table.

The ultimate table is used for valuation purposes. Where insurer wants to have a reasonable safety margin and where policies are participating ones, the ultimate table is used. It gives maximum possible rate of death.

INTEREST FACTOR

The second factor after death rate is interest factor for calculating net premium because the premium is obtained in advance and claim is paid subsequently. So, during this period the insurer can earn certain rate of interest. Since the insurer can earn additional amount on the premium collected, its benefit should be given to the policy-holders. The insurer, therefore, is required to assume a rate of return that may be earned taking into consideration various factors that would affect such earnings. Insurers are generally conservative in assuming such rate of return. Since the premium is determined in advance the present value or pre sent net worth should be calculated so that this value at an assumed compound rate of interest must be adequate to pay the amount of claim. The present value is calculated by the following formula:

$$P = \frac{S}{(l+i)}$$

where P stands for present value of the given sum.

S stands far the given sum of which present value is to be calculated.

i stands far assumed rate of interest.

n stands for the number of years before which present value is to be calculated.

There is the third factor called loading which is discussed in detail in the next Chapter.

QUESTIONS

1. 'The risk can be measured by the mortality rate in life insurance'— Explain.
2. 'The martolity rate can be ascertained by the mortality table'—comment.
3. Explain how mortailty table is constructed.
4. The information of insurers' is one of the several sources of constructing the mortality table'—critically examine the various sources of information of construction of mortality tabes.
5. What are the different types of mortality table? State the fundamental principles on which mortality tables are constructed.
6. Fill up the banks in the following portion of a life table:

Age	*Living Numbers*	*No. of Deaths*	*Probability of Death*	*Probability of Survival*
x	l_x	d_x	q_x	p_x
20	10,00,000	—	0.0050	—
21	—	—	0.0045	—
22	—	—	—	0.9960
23	—	—	—	0.9965
24	—	—	—	0.9970
25	—	—	0.0025	—

7. From the following information find the number living at age 43 and l_{x+4}.

Age	*Living Numbers*	*No. Dying*	*Probability of Death*	*Probability of Survival*
x	l_x	d_x	q_x	p_x
40	—	400	0.006	—
41	—	—	0.007	—
42	—		0.008	—
43	—	300	—	—

8. From the table given below, evaluate $3p_{(21)+1}$ and $1/2q_{20}$.

Select Table

Age at Entry x	$l_{(x)}$	$l_{(x)+1}$	$l_{(x)+2}$	*Attained Age*
20	4,95,393	4,94,534	4,93,633	22
21	4,94,480	4,93,620	4,92,716	23
22	4,93,566	4,92,702	4,91,795	24
23	4,92,647	4,91,781	4,90,868	25

9. From the select mortality table (period of selection 2 years given below; find out $2p_{(30)+1}$; / $2q_{(31)+1}$; $I/q_{(32)}$.

Age at entry	$l_{(x)}$	$l_{(x)+1}$	$l_{(x)+2}$	*Attained Age* $x + 2$
30	4,86,024	4,85,094	4,84,096	32
31	4,85,028	4,85,080	4,83,305	22
32	4,84,012	4,83,042	4,81,994	34
33	4,83,000	4,82,000	4,81,000	35

10. Fill up the blanks in the following portion of a life table.

Age x	*Living Numbers* l_x	*No. of Deaths* d_x	*Probability of Death* q_x	*Probability of Survival* p_x
20	10,00,000	—	0.00409	—
21	—	—	0.00370	—
22	—	—	—	0.99653
23	—	—	—	0.99658
24	—	—	0.00342	—
25	—	—	0.00335	—

10

CALCULATION OF PREMIUM

The premium is of two types: (1) Net Premium and (2) Gross Premium. The two premiums are further sub-divided into two parts: (*i*) single premium, and (*ii*) level premium. The net premium: is based on the mortality and interest rates whereas the gross premium depends upon the mortality rate, the assumed interest rate, the expenses and the bonus loading. Single premium is paid in one lump sum while the level premium is paid periodically in instalments. The level premium may be yearly, half-yearly, quarterly and monthly. Firstly, net single premium is calculated and other premiums are based on this calculation.

Net Single Premium

Net single premium is that premium which is received by the insurer in a lump sum and is exactly adequate, along with the return earned thereon, to pay the amount of claim wherever it arises whether at death or at maturity or even at surrender. It does not provide for expenses of management and for contingencies.

Steps for Calculation

1. Determine what constitutes a claim (*a*) death, (*b*) survival or (*c*) both.
2. Determine when claims are paid (*a*) at the beginning, (*b*) at the end, or (*c*) during the year.
3. Determine the number of insured.
4. Determine the duration of the policy.
5. Determine the probable number of claims per year.
6. Determine the value of claims per year.
7. Determine the number of years of interest involved and find the present value of a rupee.
8. Determine the present value of the claim for each year.
9. Determine the present value of all future claims.
10. Determine the net single premium, (*i.e.*, present value of future claims) divided by number assumed for buying policy.

The step of premium calculation vary according to the nature of the policy which will be clear later on. When premium is calculated several questions emerged simultaneously.

Assumptions underlying Rate Computations

There are certain variables which are to be assumed at a level for calculation and alterations in premium calculation are made at later stage according to the change in the variable. The following factors are assumed while calculating the net single premium.

(*i*) As many policies of the given type are being issued as are the number of persons.

(*ii*) Premiums are collected in advance or in the beginning of the period.

(*iii*) All collections are immediately invested and will remain invested until money is needed for the payment of claims.

(*iv*) The insurer will receive an assumed rate of interest. The assumed rate should be conservative to avoid future decline in interest rate.

(*v*) The interest or dividend or any return of the invested funds is immediately invested for re-earning.

(*vi*) Mortality rate will be the same as given in the mortality table and will he uniformly distributed throughout the year.

(*vii*) All policies are of the same amount, say, Rs. 1,000.

(*viii*) Claims will be paid only at the end of the period.

These assumptions may not be totally practicable, but they are taken as for making calculation easy. The changes in assumption can be adjusted accordingly.

Calculation of Net Single Premium

The calculation of net single premium is discussed in different types of policies.

Term Insurance

This is the simplest type of contract whereby, payment is made only when the life assured dies within the term specified. Nothing will be paid if death does not occur during the designated term. This is also called temporary insurance. The premium is received in advance and it will not be returned if life assured survives. The premium is paid only once in a single sum at the inception of the policy. Death claims will be paid at the end of the year in which they occur and not at the end of the term. Thus the probability of death in each year along with the present value, of the claim for each year will be calculated because the death may occur at any moment and the insurer may be required to pay. The term may be one, two, five or seven years. Here we assume that the period of term insurance is 5 years. Before we start we assume that the (1) rate of return on investment is 3 per cent and the mortality experience will be like the one shown in the oriental 1953-54 Experience Life Table. The person is proposing at the age of 40 for the period of 5 years.

Table 10.1 Oriental 1953-54 Experience Life Table, Ultimate Table

Age	*Number of Persons living*	*Number of deaths*	*Mortality Rate per 1,000*
40	96,463	273	2.83
41	96,190	302	3.14
42	95,888	336	3.50
43	95,552	375	3.92
44	95,177	418	4.39
45	94,759	467	4.03

The number of details can be known from the above table we assume that each person dead will be paid Rs. 1,000. The next factor of calculation is that the insurer will earn a fixed return on the investment, therefore, only the present value of the claim should be taken as a premium. Thus, the net single premium for each year will be calculated:

Number of deaths × Amount of claims × Present value of Re. 1 = Present value of claims.

Table 10.2 Net Single Premium for 5 years Term Policy

Year of Insurance	*Age attained*	*Number of living*	*Number of death*	*Amount of claims per death*	*Present value of Re. 1.0*	*Present value of 4 × 5 × 6*
1	2	3	4	5	6	7
1	40	96,463	273	1000	0.971	2,65,083
2	41	96,190	302	1000	0.943	2,84,786
3	42	95,888	336	1000	0.915	3,07,440
4	43	95,552	375	1000	0.888	3,33,000
5	44	95,177	418	1000	0.863	3,60,734

Present value of all claims = Rs 15,51,043

Total premium to be charged on all 96,463 policies = Rs. 15,51,043.

Therefore, premium per policy = Rs. 15,51,043/96,463 = Rs. 16.18.

The present value of the first year will be calculated for one year in the first year of insurance because of death occurs during the first year, the insurer can earn interest at least for one year. Similarly, in the second year of insurance, the present value of Re. 1 is calculated for two years at 3.0 per cent per annum. The formula for calculating present value is $P = \frac{S}{(1+i)^n}$. In this case:

$$P = \frac{1}{(1+0.03)^2} = P = \frac{1}{(1.03 \times 1.03)} = 0.943$$

where P stands for the present value, S for the amount of which present value is to be calculated and i for the rate of interest and n for number of years for which present value is to be calculated.

Thus, the present value of claim for the first year will be 273 × 100 × 0..971 = 265083 because the number of deaths are 273 and the total amount of claim, so, would be 2,73,000. If multiplied by factor of present value it gives present value of claim. The formula can be used for the calculation

$$NSP = \frac{Vd_x + V^2 d_{x+1} + ...V^2 d_{x+n}}{l_x}$$

where V represent present value of Re.1.0.

d_x represent deaths

l_x = numbers of living in the beginning.

Another Method of Calculation of Premium on a Single Policy

The probability of death is taken into account while the premium for one policy is to be calculated:

Table 10.3

Year of Insurance	*Age*	*Probability of Deaths expression in units*	*Amount of policy of*	*Present value of Re. 1.0*	*Net single Premium*
1	40	0.00283	1000	0.971	2.74793
2	41	0.00314	1000	9.943	2.96102
3	42	0.00350	1000	0.915	3.20250

Year of Insurance	*Age*	*Probability of Deaths expression in units*	*Amount of policy of*	*Present value of Re. 1.0*	*= Net single Premium*
4	43	0.00392	1000	0.888	3.48096
5	44	0.00439	1000	0.863	3.78857
					Rs. = 16.8098
					Rs. 16.18

Thus the net single premium will be the same whether it has to be calculated on the basis of group policy or on the basis of single policy; The probability method is generally used for calculation of premium.

Net Single Premium in Whole Life Policies

A whole life policy continues for the whole of life and promises to pay the sum assured upon the death of the insured to his beneficiary. This policy is like the term insurance policy with only difference that instead of being limited to a definite number of years, it continues for the largest possible length of life and will certainly be paid at some time. It has been assumed in most of the mortality table that the life will continue up to 100 years. Therefore, the calculation of premium will start from the date of commencement of risk to the 100th year. If a person has taken policy at age 45, the calculation will continue until 100th year.

The chances of death in each separate year will be multiplied by the face value of the policy and this amount is discounted by the present value for the period.

Table 10.4 Calculation or Net Single Premium on the basis or CSO Mortality Table

Age	*Probability of Death*	×	*Policy amount*	×	*Present value of Re. 1.0 @ 2.5%*	=	*Present value of the claim*
45	$\frac{7340}{852554}$	×	1000	×	0.975610	=	8.399441
46	$\frac{7801}{852554}$	×	1000	×	0.951814	=	9.039243
99	$\frac{125}{852554}$	×	1000	×	0.257151	=	10.037703
			Net Single Premium				= Rs. 551.372587

The amount Rs. 551.37 is the present value of all the death claims payable from age 45 until the mortality table ends, which will be the single premium amount which can purchase policy of Rs. 1,000. The sum assured is payable upon the insured's death when ever it may take place. Therefore, the chance of death in each year is taken into account. The present value in the 99 years was the lowest because the chance of survival at this stage is very nominal. Second, the sum deposited at the inception of the contract to hedge this possibility would earn interest for 55 years. Therefore, very nominal amount 0.25751 is charged for making it Re 1.0 at the end of 99th year.

Actuarially the net single premium in a whole life policy will be-:

$$NSP = \frac{V_{dx} + V^2{}_{dx+2} + V^3{}_{dx+3} \text{.... for the end of the mortality table}}{I_x}$$

The expression of the symbols has been made in the previous section of the chapter.

Net Single Premium in Pure Endowment Policy

In this policy, insurer promises to pay the insured value in case the holder survives a certain fixed period. Thus the holder of 5 years pure endowment will be paid only when he survives at the end of 5 years. The insured ,cannot get possession of the money invested in a pure endowment before the expiration of the endowment period. If the insured dies during this period, all the premium paid is fourfeited.

Table 10.5 Single Premium Pure Endowment

Actually form of calculation is	*Probability of Survival*	×	*Policy Amount*	×	*Present value of Re. 1.0 for the endowment period*	=	*Net single premium*
$NSP = \frac{V^n l_{x+n}}{l_x}$							
$= \frac{94689}{93463}$	= 0.981	×	1000	×	0.863	=	846.603

Thus, the net single premium of Rs 1000/ for 5 years pure endowment will be Rs. 846.60.3

Net Single Premium in Ordinary Endowment Policy

Under this policy payment of claim amount is made at the survival of the term or at the death of the life assured whichever is earlier. Payment in this case is certain. Since payment is based on the death and survival, the net premium is calculated on death and survival rate. The net single premium on the basis of death has been discussed in case of term insurance and on the basis of survival in case of pure endowment assurance. For example, we have to complete net single premium of ordinary endowment policy of 5 years, we can easily base our calculation on death and survival rates.

1. Net single premium on the basis of death for 5 years = Rs. 16.18
2. Net single premium survival at the end of 5 year = Rs 846.60

Rs. 862.78

Net single premium on the basis of death and survival rate = Rs. 862.78

Thus,

The net single premium in ordinary endowment policy of Rs. 1,000 for 5 years is Rs. 862.78.

Actually the formula for calculating net single premium in ordinary endowment is:

$$NSP = \frac{Vd_x + V^2 d_{x+1} \ldots V^n{}_{dx+n-1}}{l_x} + \frac{V^n l_{x+n}}{l_x}.$$

Net Single Premium in Double Endowment

Under this policy, double of the amount is paid if the life assured survives at the end of the term of policy and only single amount will be paid if the death occurs within the term. Thus, it is first like ordinary endowment policy with only difference that double of the policy amount is paid if life assured survives up to the term. Since the double of the policy amount is paid at the survival, one more premium on the basis of pure endowment is added to the premium of ordinary endowment policy. For example, double endowment policy is to be calculated of Rs. 1,000 for 5 years.

The Net Single Premium of Ordinary Endowment + Net single premium of Pure Endowment Policies for 5 years issued at same age.

= policy for 5 years issued at the same age.

= Rs. 862.78 + 846.60 = 1709.38.

Thus, the net single premium of double endowment policy of Rs. 1,000 for 5 years will be Rs. 1.709.38. If death occurs within the term, he is paid merely Rs. 1,000 and Rs. 709.38 will be a loss to him; but if he survives up to the period, he is paid Rs. 2,006 only on payment of Rs. 1,709.38.

Actuarial expression of net single premium in this case will bc:

$$NSP = \frac{(Vd_x + V^2 d_{x+1} + V^2 d_{x+2} ... V^n d_{x+n-1} + 2V^2 l_{x+n}}{l_x}$$

Net Single Premium for a Joint Life Policy

Under this policy payment of claim will bc made at the first death of the assured lives who may be two or more. Here, the process of calculation will be the same as has been discussed in term insurance with only difference that the probability of death is compound one. The compound probability of death is calculated by addition of the probability of deaths of one other and all of the envy aged.

For example:

Compound Probability of any one of the two lives assured will be

(*a*) Probability of death of the younger person

+

(*b*) Probability of death of the older person

+

(*c*) Probability of death of both the persons.

It is calculated by multiplying the probability of death of each person. The compound probability may also be calculated by the following method.

$$= 1 - \left(\frac{\text{Probability of Survival of}}{\text{younger life}} \times \frac{\text{Probability of Survival}}{\text{of older life}} \right).$$

Net Single Premium for Last Survival Policy

The policy amount is payable, under this policy, only when all lives covered by the policy expire. The compound probability of all policy-holders is calculated. The calculation will continue up to the youngest life's reaching to the highest age of the mortality table, it will not stop at the first death. Thus, the compound probability will be

= Probability of death of one person × Probability of death of other person.

When the youngest son is supposed to be dead, calculation stops.

NET SINGLE PREMIUM IN ANNUITIES

An annuity may be defined as a contract whereby for a cash consideration, (called premium) one party (the insurer) agrees to pay the other (the annuitant) a stipulated sum (the annuity), throughout life, or during the life within a fixed term, either annually, semiannually quarterly or monthly. The purpose of the annuity, is to protect a hazard–the outliving of one's income. It is just opposite of insurance contract. The annuity protects against the absence of income in old age. A periodical amount is given by the insurance to the insured up to his life or up to a fixed period life thereafter.

Under this annuity the payment of annuity starts from the date of first annuity period. For example, if annuity is to be paid six monthly and contract of annuity, *i.e.*, payment of purchase price is made on 1st Jan., 1976, the first annuity will be paid on 1st June, 1976. Therefore, up to this period, the insurer can enjoy the premium paid six months ago. If he survives to next period of instalment, the insurer has to pay the second instalment of annuity. The immediate annuity may be (1) Life Annuity, and (2) Term Annuity.

(1) *Net Single Premium in Life Annuity.* In this case, the payment of annuity shall continue up to the life of the annuitant. No annuities are paid after his death nor is any part of the consideration refunded to his beneficiaries. The cost of annuity depends upon his survival, therefore, the calculation is based upon the probability of survival.

Suppose, net single premium for an immediate annuity of Rs. 1,000 to be paid annually issued at the age 105 is to be calculated. Assuming a rate of 3 per cent of interest and 1937 Standard Annuity. Mortality Table, the calculation will be as below:

Age	*Probability of Survival*	×	*Amount of Annuity*	×	*Present value of Re. 1,00*	=	*Present value of Annuity*
106	97/249	×	1000	×	0.971	=	94187/249
107	30/249	×	1000	×	0.943	=	28290/249
108	6/249	×	1000	×	0.915	=	5490/249
109	1/249	×	1000	×	0.888	=	888/249
110	0/249	×	1000	×	0.863	=	0/249
							= Rs. 128855/249

Present value of total amount = Rs. 517.

(2) *Net Single Premium for Temporary (Term) Annuity.* The process of calculation is the same as discussed above with only difference that the calculation continues only up to a fixed period. It does not, like annuity, continue up to the completion of Annuity Mortality Table. For example, an annuity of Rs. 1,000 to be paid annually is taken at the age of 70 and continues up to 5 years. The net single premium will be as below if rate of interest is $2\frac{1}{2}$ p.a.

Age	*Probability of Survival*	×	*Amount of Annuity*	×	*Present value of Re. 1.0*	=	*Present value of Annuity*
71	$\frac{553332}{577445}$	×	1000	×	0.975610	=	934.87
72	$\frac{5238443}{577445}$	×	1000	×	0.951814	=	871.04
73	$\frac{502843}{577445}$	×	1000	×	0.928599	=	808.63
74	$\frac{476611}{577445}$	×	1000	×	0.905951	=	747.75
75	$\frac{449841}{577445}$	×	1000	×	0.883854	=	688.54

Present value of total amount Rs. 4,050.79.

Actuarial Expression of Immediate Annuity:

(*i*) *Life Annuity:*

$$NSP = \frac{Vl_{x+1} + V^2 l_{x+2} + V^2 l_{x+3} \text{....life}}{l_x}$$

(*ii*) Temporary Annuity:

$$NSP = \frac{Vl_{x+1} + V^2 l_{x+2} + V^2 l_{x+2} \text{(if it is for 3 years)}}{l_x}$$

DEFERRED ANNUITIES

In this case payment of annuity starts after a fixed period called deferred period or deferment period. Since the premium has been received at the time of contract and payment shall start only at the end of the deferment period, the present value will defer with the deferment period. The survival rate will also be calculated after the deferment period.

For Example:

Age	*Probability of Survival of 100,000 persons*	×	*Amount of Annuity*	×	*Present value of Re. 1.0*	=	*Present value of Annuity*
40	Year of Contract		—		After 30 years		—
70 deferred date	$\frac{2000}{100000}$	×	1000	×	0.477	=	9.540
71	$\frac{1000}{10000}$	×	1000	×	0.465	=	4.650
72	$\frac{500}{100000}$	×	1000	×	0.454	=	2.270
							Rs. 16.46

$$NSP = \frac{V^{i+1} l_{x+i+1} + V^{i+2} l_{x+i+2} + ...}{x}$$

Net Single Premium for Minimum Payment Annuity

(*i*) Under this contract a minimum specified number of annuity payments have to be made on each contract irrespective of the death of the annuitant.

(*ii*) Thereafter annuity is paid so long as annuitant lives.

(*iii*) The probability of survival up to the fixed period will be treated as one because payment of annuity is certain up to this period and thereafter the actual probability of survival at that age will be taken into consideration.

(*iv*) It is a combination of Annuity certain and life Annuity. Therefore, for payments guaranteed for a certain period, the amount of annuity is certainly paid irrespective of death and survival rate is not required.

Net Single Premium for Annuity Due

Under this, annuity payment begins from the start of the period and not at the end of the period. For example, if annuity is taken, on annual basis on 1st July, 1975, the first payment will be made at that time and second payment will be made on 1st July 1976, while in other annuity contract, it is the first payment. Since first payment is certain it is not based on survival rate. In other words, for the first payment the survival rate is treated to one.

Actuarial expression is:

$$NSP = \frac{l_x + Vl_{x+1} \quad V^2 l_{x+2} \ldots life}{l_x}$$

Calculating of Net Level Premium

The net level premium is collected periodically while, the net single premium is charged only once in the beginning of the contract. The net level premium cannot be calculated first by dividing net single premium by the number of premiums payable in instalments because in net single premium whole of the premium is received in advance and will remain invested until is paid as a claim whereas the net level premium will be invested. The second reason is that the net single premium will be paid by all the policy-holders whereas the level premiums could be paid only by the surviving policy-holders.

The net single premium is the present value of all claims and the present value of all net level premiums is also equal to the total of present values of all claims. It means the present value of all net level premiums is equal to the net single premium. So, if the present value of a unit level premium is known, the net single premium can be converted into level premium.

CALCULATION OF LEVEL PREMIUMS

The single premium of a given policy can be easily converted into level premium by establishing ratio between net level premium and net single premium. The ratio will differ according to the age at the beginning, nature and duration of the policy. This calculation of the ratio is illustrated in the following table. The single premium in 5 years Term policy is to be converted into level premium on annual basis for 5 years. Assuming that the net level premium for the policy is Rs. 1.0 per thousand of sum assured, the calculation of the present value of all the level premium is given as below.

Using Oriental 1953-54 Experience Life Table–

Ultimate and 3 per cent rate of interest.

Year of Insurance	*Age*	*Number of persons living*	*No. of premium received*	*Amount of premium received*	*Present value of Re.1*	*Present value of Premium received*
1	40	96,463	96,463	96,463	1,000	96,463
2	41	96,190	96,190	96,190	0.971	93,400
3	42	95,880	95,880	95,880	0.943	90.415
4	43	95,552	95,552	95,552	0.915	87,430
5	44	95,177	95,177	95,177	0.888	84,517

Total Present value = Rs. 4,52,225.

The present, value of all level premiums to be received during the five years is Rs. 4,52,225 on all policies which comes to Rs. 4,52,225/96,463 per policy. Since, the present value per policy of all the net level premiums is equal to the net single premium of all the policy, the ratio between level premium and net single premium is 1:45E25/96463. Thus, the ratio for converting net single premium of term policy for 5 years is, established as

I. : 452225/96463

On this ratio the net single premium of Rs. 16.18 $= \frac{1555l043}{96463}$ can be converted into several premium policy.

Since, For N.S.P. of Rs. $\frac{452225}{96463}$ the NLP is = Re. 1.0

$\therefore$ For N.S.P. of Rs. 1 the NLP $\frac{1 \times 96463}{452225}$

$\therefore$ For N.S.P. of Rs $\frac{1551043}{96463}$ the NLP $\frac{96463 \times 1551043}{452225 \times 96463}$

= Rs. 3.43 p.a.

This ratio was easily calculated in this policy of 5 years, but it is very difficult in the case of whole life and endowment policies because, the calculation is made for a very large number of years.

Annuity Due Principle

The second method of calculating the net level premium is on the basis of annuity due principle because the annuity due for the same period and issued at the same age is just like level premium. In the life insurance for the same period and issued at the same age is just like level premium. In both the cases, the payments are made in the beginning of the period and so long as the assured is alive. It may be limited to a particular period also like term and endowment policies. For purchasing life insurance single premium is given and for purchasing annuity due purchase price of the annuity due is given. In exchange if the purchase price of the annuity due, periodical annuity is paid constantly up to the life or up to the fixed period as the case may be similarly in exchange of the single premium, the issued is not required to pay the level premium. Since net purchase price of annuity due issued at the particular age for a particular period or up to life is equal to the net single premium of the life insurance issued at the same age for the same period. Therefore, if the payment of periodical annuity due is known, the level premium for the same period can be easily known.

Thus, the expression can be made as :

Net level premium (*Px*) : Net single premium (*Ax*) :Annuity· due amount: Purchase price to the annuity due contract (*ax*)

or,

$$\text{Net level Premium (Px)} = \frac{\text{Net Single Premium } (Ax) \times \text{Annuity Due}}{\text{Purchase price of Annuity Due } (ax)}$$

Here we assume that Annuity due io Re 1.0 per annum.

$$P_x = \frac{(Ax)(1)}{ax}$$

If the purchase price of Annuity due of Re. 1.0 and net single premium are known, the net level premium can be easily converted into net level premium.

CALCULATION OF GROSS PREMIUM

The gross premium is that premium which is charged by the insured to meet the amount of claims and expenses. Thus, the gross premium includes the net premium and loading. Loading is the process to add the expenses to net premium. The loading may add a certain amount to meet the bonus charges on participating policies. The policy-holders are required to pay this gross premium and they even do not know the net premium. Therefore the gross premium is also know as 'Office Premium'. The policy-holder are, thus, required to pay amount to meet the cost or claim, expenses of business, and loading for bonus if the policy is participating one.

Allocation of Expenses

.As has been made it clear that the expenses of business are allocated amongst the net premiums. So, in allocation, the insurer faces two problems (*i*) Allocation of expenses over various policies and (*ii*) Allocation of expenses over duration of the policy.

(*i*) *Allocation of Expenses over Various Policies*. The allocation of expenses over various policies should be equitable. It means that every policy should be allotted the due share of its expenses, some policies involve higher expenses than others and should, therefore, bear higher loading. The policies involving lesser expenses should be lesser share of the total expenses. The total expenses are, therefore, classified so that equitable distribution can be easily done.

CLASSIFICATION OF EXPENSES ON THE BASIS OF VARIATION

There are three classifications on the basis:

1. Those expenses that vary with the size of the premium, for example, first year or renewal commissions.
2. Those expenses that vary with the amount of policy, for example, stamp fee, and medical examiner's fee.
3. Those expenses that are independent of both, being either the same per policy or the expenses are incurred for the business as a whole for example, salaries, and establishment charges.

These expenses would be equitably distributed only the relationship between the premium, policies or fixed is determined. For example,

Loading = A fixed percentage of net premium
+ A fixed amount per 1,000 of sum assured
+ A fixed amount per policy.

The insurer will have to establish what expenses are varying at what degree with premium, policy or policy amount. Therefore, he has to analyses the expenses and to determine the percentage.

(*i*) Analysis of Expenses

All the expenses incurred during a particular period are classified into (*i*) those expenses which are related to the premium, (*ii*) those expenses which are related with the policy, and (*iii*) those expenses which are independent of these two.

(*ii*) Determination of Percentage

After classifying the expenses it is essential to determine the percentage according to the premium or policy or with other factor. The percentage is determined on the basis of past, experience. If it has been known that Rs. 10,000 will be expended in connection with premium of Rs. 10,00,000, it can be established that the expenses varying with the premium will be 1 per cent of the premium collected. Similar percentage in relation to policy amount and to policy number can be easily established. Thus the net premium can be easily loaded with these percentage or fixed amount per policy.

The expenses should be allocated according to policies amount, premium amount and per policy although various methods have been derived for allocation of expenses.

Methods of Loading

The expenses can be allocated by any of the following methods:

1. Constant Addition Loading

Under this method a fixed amount per thousand of sum assured is loaded to the net premium. This method is not scientific because it assumes that all expenses vary according to the amount of the policy which is not correct. Some expenses vary according to variation in the rate of premium.

2. Percentage Addition Loading

According to this method a fixed percentage of net premium is added to the net premium. It assumes that all expenses vary according to the premium amount. But there are certain expenses which vary according to the policy amount or per policy.

3. Modified Percentage Method

Under the method, the loading is divided into two parts: (*i*) expenses varying according to net level premium of the given, policies and (*ii*) expenses varying according to net level premium, of the whole life policy issued at the given age. This method is modification of the above two methods; but it does not relate the expenses according to their variations.

4. Constant and Percentage Addition Method

Under this method, the loading is done under two parts (*a*) a constant amount per thousand of the sum assured and (*b*) a fixed percentage related to the net premium of the policy. The percentages are determined on the basis of past experience. This method assumes that the expenses vary either with the net premium or the sum assured, but the expenses also vary with the amount per policy which is not taken into account. However, this method is more scientific than the methods discussed above.

B. DISTRIBUTION OF EXPENSES OVER THE PERIOD OF POLICY

There are certain expenses which are incurred in the inception of the policy, certain expenses incur every year of the policy and certain expenses incur only in the end of the policy. The allocation of expenses requires that equal amount should be distributed every year. Therefore, firstly, the nature of expense according to occurrence and secondly, equal distribution of the expenses every year are to be done for equitable distribution of loading.

1. Classification of expenses

The expenses for the above purpose are distributed into four categories :

(*a*) *The Initial Expenses.* The initial expenses are those expenses which incurred at first before or at the time of issuing the policy. The expenses, for example, may be medical examiner's fees, inspection of risk of agents' commission, expenses involved for preparation of the policy and correspondence expenses and so on.

(*b*) *The Recurring Expenses.* The recurring expenses are those expenses which are incurred every year for the policy. Some of them may be limited only up to the period of premium collection The expenses may be expenses for issue of premium notices, premium receipts, keeping accounts and payment of renewal commissions to agents.

(*c*) *The Final Expenses.* The final expenses are incurred at the time of payment of claims or of surrender values. They are expenses for approving the claims, cost of paying surrender values and cost of correspondence, etc.

(*d*) *The General Expenses.* These expenses are fixed and incurred for the business as a whole. The important general expenses are accounting expenses actuarial and legal expenses, maintenance and establishment charges. They are not related to a particular policy or point of time.

The recurring and final expenses, normally, vary with the policy amounts, premium amount or per policy. But the general expenses may not vary in the above manner.

Equal Distribution of the Expenses

All the above expenses should be equally distributed over the policy year. The main problem of distributions of initial expenses is that a heavy expense is involved in the beginning of the policy but it has to be distributed over the life of the policy, *i.e.*, over the period of premium payment.

Dr. Sprague's Formula for Loading

Dr. Sprague's formula can be discussed as below:

(*a*) A single percentage of sum discussed to cover the initial expenses.

(*b*) A percentage of net premium to cover recurring renewal expenses.

(*c*) A fixed amount to cover general office expenses.

The inital expenses are equally spread over the period of premium payment by dividing it by the present value of Annuity due, of Re. 1.0 over the given period.

Thus,

Office Premium = Per cent of sum Assured + Per cent of

$$\text{Net level Premium} + \frac{\text{Initial Expenses}}{\text{Present value of Annuities Due of Re. 1.0 for the period}}.$$

Actually, the gross premium is calculated as below:

$$P = P + I / a + \frac{r}{100} P + c$$

where P is gross premium, P is net premium, I is the initial expenses, is the present value of annuity due of Re. 1.0, r is the renewal expenses as a percentage of Office Premium and c constant addition, for fixed renewal expenses. The above formula can be refined as below:

$$P = P + I / a + c \div \left(1 - \frac{r}{100}\right)$$

QUESTIONS

1. What are the various assumptions underlying the calculation or premium.
2. What are the various factors affecting the calculation of premium.
3. Net Single Premium and loading compute gross premium—explain in detail.
4. Illustrate the methods of computing premiums in different types of policies and annuities.
5. What are the various methods of Loading?
6. Loading of expenses and Bonus are done in two parts—(*a*) Distribution according to time and (*b*) distribution according to policies.
7. From the following mortality table, calculate net level premiums in Term Insurance for five years, Endowment Insurance for five years, Pure Endowment for five years and Double Endowment for five years, assuming 5 per cent rate of interest and Rs. 1,000 policy amount in each policy.

x	25	26	27	28	29	30
lx	100000	99500	98900	98200	97400	96500
dx	500	600	700	800	900	1000

8. Calculate the value of an anticipated endowment assurance for a person aged 25 with the following benefits.
   (*i*) a sum of Rs. 100 at the end of 2nd year.
   (*ii*) a sum of Rs. 200 at the end of 3rd year.
   (*iii*) a sum of Rs. 300 at the end of 5th year if the life assured is alive at the end of respective years.
   (*iv*) a sum of Rs. 600 whenever the dies during the 5 years period.

   Use the data given above with 5 per cent rate of interest.
9. Calculate on the basis of mortality table given below, net annual premium at 5% rate of interest for a 5 year Term Insurance for Rs. 1,000 effective at the age of 60 years.

Age	*Number Living*	*Number Dying*
60	1000	20
61	980	22
62	958	25
63	933	33
64	900	40
65	860	45

10. Calculate the net annual level premium for a Double Endowment Assurance of Rs. 100 for a person aged 60 years, the assured benefit being Rs. 100 in the case of his death before attaining age 63 and Rs. 200 if he survives to age 63. Use the above mortality table and rate of interest.
11. Using the above mortality table and rates of interest, calculate level premium for the Anticipated Endowment Policy of Rs. 1000 where Rs. 200 is paid in the case of death in the second year, Rs. 200 is paid in the case of death in the third year, Rs. 600 in case of death in the fourth year and Rs. 1000 in case of survival upto five years.
12. If the annual premium for an endowment assurance of Rs. 1000 for a person aged 40 years for a term of 20 years is Rs. 30.00, calculate the office premium, making the following provisions:
    (*a*) Initial Expenses at Rs. 40 per 1000 S.A.
    (*b*) Renewal Expenses at 10% of office premium.
    (*c*) A constant expenditure of Rs. 2.50 per thousand sum assured.
    Given a_w : 19 = Rs. 16.00
13. The net premium for an endowment assurance of Rs. 1000 for a person aged 30 for a term of 25 years is Rs. 30.97. Calculate the office premium, making the following provisions:
    (*a*) Initial Expenses at Rs. 40 per 1000 B.A.
    (*b*) Renewal Expenses at 8% of office premium.
    (*c*) A constant expenditure of Rs. 2.50 per thousand sum assured.
    Given a_w : 29 = Rs. 15.640
14. The following particulars are given:

x	25	26	27	28	29	30
l_x	97380	97088	96794	96496	96124	95887
dx	292	294	298	302	307	313

Calculate, using a rate of interest of 3% p.a.
    (*a*) The value of a Temporary Assurance of Rs. 1000 for 2 years for a person aged 25.
    (*b*) The value of Endowment Assurance benefit of Rs. 1000 for 4 years to a person aged 25.
    (*c*) The value of a pure Endowment of Rs 600 for a person aged 27, receivable on attaining age 30.
15. Find the value of a Pure Endowment Benefit of Rs. 600 for a person aged 40, payable on his surviving to age 60 at 4% p.a. compound interest; given:
    a_{40} : 20 = 13.060 and
    a_{40} : 19 = 12.691 at 3% p.a. compound interest.
16. Calculate the net annual premium for an Endowment Assurance of Rs. 2500 for a period of 5 years for a person aged 25 using mortality table in question no. 7 at 3% rate of interest.
17. Find the office annual premium at 3% rate of interest for a whole life assurance on the life of a person, aged, 36 years. Make provision for expenses at 80% of office premium for first year and 7% for all premiums, including that for, the first year.
    Given a_{35} = 18.182.

11

TREATMENT OF SUB-STANDARD RISKS

We have discussed how some of the accepted risks are considered as 'standard' and others a 'sub-standard'. The standard risks are accepted at standard or normal premium rates. In this chapter, we shall discuss what treatment may be given to sub-standard risks so that equity is maintained as between standard risks and sub-standard risks. Equity can be maintained only when the extra-risk in sub-standard risk is given special treatment or additional premium is charged.

Types of Sub-standard Risks

The sub-standard risks are divided into three categories according to the incidence and intensity of extra-risk.

(*a*) Increasing Extra-Risk

In this category, the extra mortality increases as the life assured grows older. For example, patients of diabetes, occupational diseases, overweight, etc. The effect of extra-risk in these cases tend to rise with the passage of time and on the lives assured becoming order.

(*b*) Decreasing Extra-Risk

In this category, the extra hazard decreases with increase in age. The extra mortality, consequently, would be experienced more in the early years and would be going down as time passes. In some cases, the extra-mortality tends to decrease until the extra risk might, have disappeared. For example, persons of defective past history.

(*c*) Constant Extra-Risks

Here, the extra hazard remains at the same level throughout the life-time of the assured. There cannot be any risk which are strictly constant. They may decrease or increase to some extent. However, there are certain cases when risks are approximately constant. For example, blindness, or loss of limb, deafness, etc.

Such a classification permits the company to assess premiums according to the incidence of the extra deaths, that is, assuming the company expects the same number of extra-deaths to occur in two groups more will have to be collected for the extra-risk in a group where the deaths occur early (decreasing risk) than where the deaths occur later (increasing risk), because the effect of reserves have to be estimated. In level premium plan the reserve increases year after year and so, the amount at risk decreases along with the increase in reserve. The rate at which reserves are accumulated is also very important. For meeting decreasing risk, higher reserve should be made in the beginning and for increasing risk, the rate of reserve should constantly increase as the time passes. The rate of reserve in constant risk may remain at par.

METHODS OF TREATING SUB-STANDARD RISKS

The Sub-standard risks may be treated in five ways:

1. Increase in premium,
2. decrease in death, benefits,

3. change in class and period of assurance,
4. any combination of the above-mentioned methods, and
5. postponement of risk.

1. Increase in Premium

The premium can be increased in any of the following manners:

(*a*) Rating up of Age

Under this method, the life assured is assumed to be a number of years older than his real age. The premium rate is calculated according to the assumed higher age. So, the cash value, loan, paid up and surrender values are also increased according to the increased premium. The extra number of years to be added is determined according to the extra risk involved with the life assured. The policies issued under this plan will be similar to those issued at standard premium. The only difference is that the premium is increased according to the assumed higher rate. Once the premium determined, cannot be decreased. So, this method is not suitable in decreasing risk. The rated up plan is best adopted to the increasing type of extra-risk although it does not deal equitably with all risks of this type.

The plan has certain advantages. It is easy for the insured to understand; it appeals him because of the increased surrender values and loans. It is simple for insurer to handle. There are certain disadvantages, too. The insured may take advantage of higher surrender values and can get back a substantial part of the premium paid by surrendering the policy.

(*b*) Flat Extra Premium

Under this method a flat annual extra premium of so many rupees per thousand sum assured per year is charged. Thus, a Constant additional premium is added to standard premium; but unlike the rated up age, the extra premium is not taken into accounting for surrender and paid up values. The extra-premium is constantly charged up to the life of policy or up to the existence of the extra-risk. In practice, however, it is usual to charge a level extra premium when the extra risk is constant or decreasing one (as in the case of hazardous occupations or even in the case of decreasing extra risk such as a young under-weight). Extra premium is also charged for certain defects and deformity like imputed arms and legs, partial or total blindness, deafness, etc., or in the case of standard imprepairments. Under numerical rating system, the extra-hazard risk is treated by charging that extra according to the degree of extra-hazards.

The extra premium should not be flat or constant when there is heavy and immediate risk in the inception. Otherwise as soon as the period of heavy extra passed, there will be a tendency to drop the policy. In such cases, therefore, if extra is to be charged, a heavier extra should be charged for initial period of so many years when the risk is considered to be very heavy and the extra is removed there-after.

The Life Insurance Corporation of India charges flat extra premium for a Scheduled Occupation. This extra rating mostly vary from Rs. 2/- to Rs. 6/- per thousand of sum assured per annum. Heavy extra flat is also charged from commissioned officers in submarines.

(*c*) Extra Percentage Plan

There are certain classes of sub-standard risks which are determined by numerical rating system. For each class of extra risk, a certain percentage of the standard premium is charged. This extra percentage is added to the standard premium and is charged along with the standard premium. The classes of sub-standard risks are divided on the basis of incidence of extra risk on the mortality. Once the extra premium is determined on the standard premium, it would not vary later on and will be charged according to that extra premium. The difference has in the fact that the amount of extra percentage premium will vary according to the standard premium. Thus, it will be higher when standard premiums are higher. But, in case of flat extra, the same extra premium is charged irrespective of the age or standard premium. Thus, the rate of extra premium as compared to standard premium is higher in the early age and lower in the advanced age. The extra percentage may be used in increasing risks also while the flat extra premium will not be suitable to increasing risks.

2. Decrease in Death Benefits

The death benefits may be reduced in two ways:-

(*a*) Lien Method; and

(*b*) Restrictive Clause.

(*a*) Lien Method

The amount payable under this method would be the sum assured less the outstanding lien at the particular time of the policy. The lien is for a fixed number of years. If the life assured dies within this period, the amount of lien is deducted from the policy amount and rest is paid to the beneficiary but if the life assured survives the period of lien, the whole of the policy amount is paid at the claim.

The amount of lien goes on decreasing in most of the cases, as time passes until whole of the lien is finished. Thus, the amount of claim will go on increasing as time expires because lesser amount of lien is to be deducted at later age. The premium charged is the standard one but only policy amount is reduced. Thus, the effective premium per thousand of the sum payable will be higher in the beginning and lower at the later stage and consequently, in the end, when the lien is terminated, it will be equal to the standard premium.

For example, a reducing lien of Rs. 500 per Rs. 1,000 sum assured for l0 years would mean that the sum payable would be reduced by Rs. 500 if death occurs in the first year, by Rs. 450 if in the second year, and Rs. 400 if in the third year and so on, so that the full sum assured will he paid if death occurs only after the expiry of 10 years. The lien may be constant, and decreasing for the first few years. The type, amount and term of lien would always depend on the nature and extent of extra-risk.

This method is most appropriate when the extra-risk is of decreasing type. As the risk decreases, the amount of lien decreases. For example, an underweight young man with family history of tuberculosis is subject to an extra risk of death during the early years but as age advances, the effect of this extra risk reduces. In this case the lien would be most suitable because other treatments may not provide sufficient fund at the early death. The insured may also be willing to purchase the policy at standard premium only. Thus, the insurer is not at loss if death occurs during the first few years of the policy because he can deduct a certain sum before payment. The insured is also assured of getting the policy amount after the lien period without payment of extra-premium. The plan is simple in operation and is readily understood.

The method is not useful for increasing extra-risk. A small degree of extra mortality may ripe out a substantial amount of claim at the early death. The method appears to be arbitrary in its working as the extra-risk operates fully on one day and then suddenly on the next day, the assured becomes a first class life. The next disadvantage is that a lien reduces the protection substantially during the early years when the need for it is the greatest.

The corporation, therefore, uses this method in special cases. For example, lien is allowed when the life assured is underweight and the life is aged below 33 and there is specific request from the proposer. The lien is used to factory workers, low income people, persons from mofussil centres with inadequate or no income, no arrangements for medical examination, personal or family history of tuberculosis or plurisy and suspicion of moral hazard.

(*b*) Restrictive Clause

Under this clause, the extra hazard is accepted with a restrictive clause which limits death benefit under certain circumstances. Such a clause usually states that the amount payable under this policy will be on a reduced basis which any be surrender value or return of premiums paid, in case death occurs due to the specified extra hazard, For example, the first pregnancy clause which excludes the risk of death arising from causes connected with first pregnancy is often applied to lives of ladies who have not undergone a normal full-time confinement and who do not wish to pay extra premium to cover the extra-hazard. Similarly, in aviation clause, the amount of claim is restricted to surrender value or premiums paid if death occurred while the life assured was engaged in flight.

This method can be used satisfactorily where the cause of death can be distinctly known. In India this method is used in certain life assured "with certain types of policies".

3. Change in the Class and Period of Assurance

The life assured is not given all types of insurance and for a longer period. There is neither a lien on the policy nor any extra premium by way of flat nor rating up to ages. The policy is given at standard premium but all types of policies are not issued. The types of policies to which the choice is restricted are those which carry a higher rate of premium such as ordinary endowment policy. Whole life, multipurpose or triple benefit policies are not given because in these cases the degree of risk is higher as compared to accumulation of reserves. This plan is useful where the extra-risk is expected to occure later in life, such as the case of an over-weight, unfavourable family history. Special dividend plans may be issued to those who are expected to give share of dividend or bonus with higher mortality. By declaring lower bonus rates the insurer is in a position to charge an extra amount for the extra risk assumed. This plan can be used only for the participating policies.

The period of assurance in all types of insurance is limited. The age at the inception or maximum maturity ages for policies are fixed in various types of policies.

4. Any Combination of the above-mentioned Methods

For certain proponents, any of the above methods can he used, which depends on the practical experience of the insurer. For example, a proposal for a multipurpose plan may be accepted under an endowment Assurance Plan with a lien, if the proponent is young and underweight.

5. Postponement

Consideration of proposal is postponed for a period, when the initial risk is so heavy that there is little hope of offering insurance immediately and the proposal is postponed. In future when health will improve, the proposal can be accepted. Postponement in different type of risk are different. It has been observed that the postponement vary from 3 months to 3 years.

The extra premium or line etc. may be removed later on when the extra-risk is improved and the extra-mortality was nominal discreet and no chance of recurrence. In practice the extra are removed in special cases when there are agreement for this.

QUESTIONS

1. What do you understand by sub-standard risks! How far it is distinguished from standard risks?
2. What are the various methods of treating sub-standard risks?
3. "Classification of increasing, decreasing and constant sub-standard risks are very crucial while treating them." Comment.
4. 'Is the sub-standard risk the same as is uninsurable risk?' Distinguish them.

12

THE RESERVE

Nature

The reserve in life insurance is different from the reserve in other business. It is not an accumulation of profit. In Insurance, it is a liability which is to be met by the insurer at and when it arises. It represents a liability which must be adequately met.

Definitior

The reserve is that fund, which, together with future premiums and interest, will be sufficient to pay the future claims. This is called prospective definition because here the future amounts are considered. Another definition of the reserve is the retrospective definition under which the reserve is considered as the accumlation at interest of the difference between the net premiums received in the past and the claims paid out.

The reserve has nothing to do with an insurer's actual past experience. It is always calculated on the assumption that experience has been in accordance with the mortality table selected and interest rate assumed. However, the assumptions as to future interest and mortality are made on a safe basis. It is, thus, clear that on each policy a certain sum must be accumulated every year to be increased at an interest to form fund to meet the future liability of the policy. This accumulated is called the Reserve on the Policy.

Origin of Reserve

The reserve in any group of policies originates in the excess of premium receipts over payment of claims. The premium receipts are more than the payments in the beginning and less after a point. The excess receipts are accumulated at the assumed rate of interest and build up the 'Reserve' up to a point of time, the 'reserve' grows, particularly, because of such receipts. It is to be noted again here that the reserve is accumulated on the assumed mortality and interest. The reserve based on this assumptions is compared to the funds based on the actual experience. The difference may create 'surplus', or deficit. As has been noted that the reserve accumulates at a point and starts declining thereafter because of heavy mortality and receipts of premium at the advanced age.

Sources of Reserve

1. The first and the foremost source of reserve is premium. It should be noted that reserve is accumulated in level premium plan because the premium is more the actual cost of insurance in the beginning. In other two methods of premium, reserve cannot be accumulated. This is discussed as below:

(*a*) Assessment Premium Plan

The members of a group would, under this plan, contribute to a fund which could be utilised in rendering assistance at the time of death to the deceased's dependents. The payment is made by contribution only at the time of death. Therefore, there is no need to accumulate amount for payment of the claim.

(*b*) Natural Premium Plan

Under this plan, the rate of premium will increase as the insured grows older. It is based on the risk. Since risk increases as time passes, the premium charged from the policyholder also increases. The premium increases year after year with the increase in mortality rate and, so it is also called yearly renewable premium plan. The reserve is not accumulated in this case, because premium increases as cost of insurance increases.

(*c*) Level Premium Plan

Here, the premiums to be paid are levelled so that usually the same premiums are paid every year. The premiums in the early years are greater than the actual cost (determined by the mortality rate) with the result that the excess payments of premium in the earlier years are accumulated as reserve which makes up any deficiency out of lower premium in later years.

2. The second source of reserve is interest because the accumulated fund is not remaining idle, it is invested. While calculating premium it was assumed that the insurer will earn a certain rate of interest, so to earn at least that much of amount, the accumulated funds have to be invested. The assumed rate of interest is the source of reserve.

3. Nature of Policy

The reserve can be calculated only in those policies where payment is not certain, reserve is generally not requiring. Thus the amount of reserve depends upon the duration of the policy and nature of the policy.

Need for Reserves

The reserves in life insurance is required for the following reasons:

I. To Meet the Amount of Claims

The reserve is required to meet the amount of claim whenever the given event takes place. The incurring of this liability does not bother the insurer at all if in any given period it receives by way of consideration from the policyholders concerned an amount which is equal to the amount it has to pay during this period. The insurer must have sufficient amount to meet the claims. Therefore, the reserve is essential to meet these claims.

II. To Build up Funds

Besides being essential for meeting future cost of claims, the 'reserve' is also useful to build up funds that can be invested for long period to earn at least assumed rate of return. The invested funds help not only to the insurer to obtain a required amount of return but are also helpful for the economic development of the country. The insurers are in a position to accumulate a huge fund and, therefore, can contribute a significant amount for country's advancement.

III. Policyholders are Benefited

The accumulated fund or the reserve belongs to policyholders. This fund is safely and profitably invested by the insurer who are in a position to do that.

The main purpose of creating reserve is to meet the obligation of payment of claims whenever it arises. How should the reserve be created is the main problem of the insurer. The assumed rates of mortality and interest are mainly taken into consideration while calculating reserve for a particular policy, assumed mortality rate, assumed rate of interest, nature of policy, period of premium payments and duration of policy.

METHODS OF CALCULATING RESERVE

The reserve can be calculated by applying retrospective method or by prospective method. The reserve calculated by either of these methods will give the same result provided the mortality rates and interest rates remain the same in both the methods. Reserve can be calculated either on all the policies or on a single policy. This can be expressed by the following illustration–

I. Present value of all premiums	=	Present value of all benefits
II. Accumulated value of past premium + discounted value of future premiums	=	Accumulated value of past benefits + discounted value of future benefits
III. Accumulated value of past premiums–Accumulated Value of past benefits	=	Discounted value of future benefits + Discontinuity value of future premium.
IV. Retrospective Reserve	=	Prospective Reserve

RESERVE

- Retrospective Method
  - Group policies
  - Single policy
- Prospective Method
  - Group policies
  - Single policy

RETROSPECTIVE METHOD

Under this method, the reserve is derived entirely by reference to past experience. The reserve represents the net premiums collected by the insurer for a particular class of policies plus interest at an assumed rate, less the death claims paid out. We calculate for each year how much would have been received by way of premiums on the basis of assumed mortality figures, how much interest would have been earned on the basis of assumed interest rate and how much would have been paid by way of claims on the basis of assumed mortality figures.

Group Approach

The calculation begins with the first year when the total net premium has been received for the first time. We, then, determine the amount of interest that this total of net premium receipts will earn for one full year at the assumed rate of interest. For the total of these two claims paid for the first year are deducted to get the reserve. Again in the second year, we carry forward the reserve.

The net premium received from the surviving policyholders is added to the reserve of past year which is taken together and is called initial reserve of the second year. This process continues until all the policyholders are dead or policy period expires. Per policy reserve can be calculated by dividing the total reserve by the number of policies. It can be illustrated with the following formula.

For example, there are 10 policyholders insured for Rs. 10,000 each for the period of 10 years. They are required to pay net premium of Rs. 1,000 each. The rate of interest is 10 per cent per annum.

First Year

Net premiums of 10 policyholders		
@Rs. 1000/–each		10000
Add interest @ 10%		1000
Total amount		11000
Less		
Claims paid out (no claims)		——
Terminal reserve	Rs.	11000

Second Year

Net premium of 10 policyholders @ Rs. 1000/–each		1000
Add Terminal reserve of last year		11000
Initial Reserve		21000
Add Interest @ Rs. 10 per cent		2100
		23100
Less claims paid out (one death)		10000
Terminal Reserve	Rs.	13100

The process of calculating reserve continues till the 10th year. In the third year, the net premium will be paid by only 9 policy-holders because one person is dead during second year.

Reserve in a Particular Year

The reserve at a particular time can be calculated by the following formula–

Reserve = Reserve at the close of the previous year (if any)
+ Premium of the Year.
+ Interest thereon at the assumed rate for one year
– Claims for the year

With this help reserve can be calculated at any moment provided the initial reserve is known.

Another Method on Accumulation Basis

The accumulated value of premiums over the accumulated value of claims will be the retrospective reserve.

Reserve = Accumulated value of Past Premiums
– Accumulated value of Past Claims

The accumulated value is calculated on the basis of assumed death rate per year and assumed rate of interest. The accumulation factors can be known from the interest table. Thus, the calculation is simple in this method.

Individual Approach

The retrospective reserve may also be calculated on every policy. The method of calculation is the same as discussed above with only difference that the reserve will be calculated on the basis of cost of insurance instead of claims paid on. The 'cost of insurance' reveals how much amounts will have to be shared by the policyholders in payment of claims of other policy-holders. Technically, the po-rate share of death claims in any particular year is called the 'cost of insurance'. It is the amount which must be paid for the protection. The cost of insurance is arrived by multiplying amount at the risk with the probability of death to him. The amount at risk is the amount which is obtained by deducting the initial reserve of the policy-holders from the policy amount.

In brief-

Cost of Insurance =Amount at risk × Probability of Death.
= (Policy Amount-Initial Reserve) × Probability of death.

The individual reserve can be explained by an illustration. For example, a policyholder takes policy of Rs. 10,000 (for ten years) and pays Rs. 1,000 an annual premium, the rate of interest being 10 per cent. The probability of death in the first year is 0.002 and in the second year 0.003. We have to calculate reserve for two years.

First Year

	Rs.
Net Premium	1,000
Add interest @ 10%	100
	1,100
	Rs.
Less: 'Cost of Insurance'	
= Amount of risk × probability of death	
= Policy amount – Reserve × Prob. of Death.	
= 10,000 – 0 × 0.002	20
	1,080

Second Year

Net Premium	1,000
Add Reserve of Previous Years	1,080
Initial Reserve	Rs. 2,080
Add Interest @ 10%	208
Total:	2,288
Less: Cost of Insurance (10,000 – 1,080) × 0.003 = 8920 × 0.003	26 approx.
Terminal Reserve	Rs. 2,262

At a Particular Year

Thus, Individual Reserve can also be calculated at a particular year =

Reserve = Initial Reserve + Interest at assured rate – Cost of Insurance.

The accumulation method can also be used for the calculation of Reserve = Accumulated Value of Premiums paid – Accumulated Value of Cost of Insurance.

Difference between Group Reserve and Individual Reserve

1. The group reserve increases up to a point of time and decreases thereafter until it is finished completely. The individual reserve increases each year and in the end it becomes equal to the policy amount.
2. The group reserve will be zero when payments of claims of all the policy-holders are made whereas the individual reserve must be equal to the face value of the policy at the maturity.

PROSPECTIVE METHOD

The second method of calculating reserve is prospective method. Under this method we determine how much is required to be paid in future and how much premium will be received in future. So, how much the insurer should arrange for payment. The present values of future claims and of future premiums are calculated. In other words, the reserve is the difference between the present value of future benefits and the present value of premiums. At the beginning of the contract the present value of future claims or benefits (PVFB) is exactly equal to the present value of the future premiums. Thus, PVFB =PVFP at the inception of the policy. But as soon as one premium is paid, the present value of future benefit exceeds the present value of future premiums. This is because less premiums remain to be paid and the present value of future benefits increases as the policy is nearer to the claim.

The difference will go on increasing up to the point when the present value of future benefit equals the policy amount and the present value of future claims goes on decreasing until it becomes zero. The difference between these two must be held by the insurer. This difference is reserve because so much of amount must be with the insurer to pay the amount of claim.

Reserve = PVFB – PVFP

Since, the net single premium of a policy is equal to the present value of future benefits, the PVFB can be replaced by NSP (net single premium).

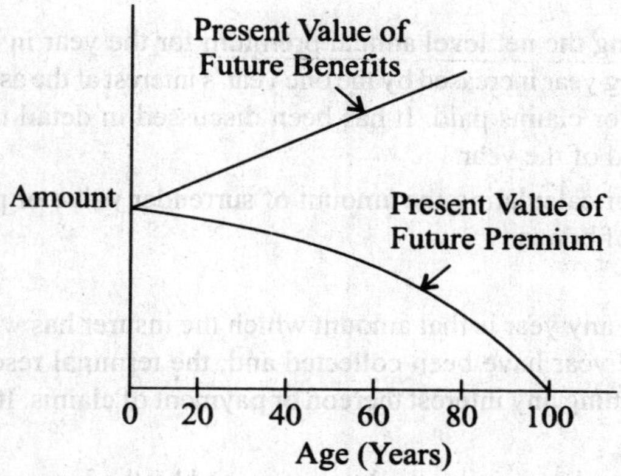

Fig. 12.1

Present Value

$$\frac{1}{(1+i)}$$

The present value, which invested to a given rate over a number of years, will amount to Re. 1.0. The Re. 1.0 is called the accumulated value. The calculation is reverse of accumulation value. To find the accumulated value (A) of Re. 1.0 it was multiplied by one plus the rate of interest (i) raised to the power equal to the number of time units (n) in the period of calculation. Thus,

$$\text{Accumulated } (A) = ix\,(1+i)^n$$

To find the present value of 1.0 it is to be divided by one plus the rate of interest raised to the power equal to the number of time units in the period, or

$$\text{(Present value) PV} = \frac{1}{(1+i)^n}$$

Thus the present value of any amount can be calculated by multiplying it by =

Now,

Prospective Reserve = NSP – PVFP

The present value of future premium must necessarily be equal to the net level premium (NLP) for the contract under consideration multiplied by the present value of a life annuity due (PV AD) of Re. 1.0 for the remaining premium paying period. Now the equation will be—

Reserve = NSP – (NLP × PVAD of Re. 1.0).

The reserve can be calculated at any time during the policy period. The NSP will vary according to the time. The PVAD will be calculated for the remaining period of premium payment. NLP is the same as was at issue of policy. Thus,

Reserve (age of valuation)	= NSP (age of valuation)	– NLP (age of issue)	× PVAD of Re 1.0 (remaining premium paying period).

The method of calculation of NSP, NLP and PVAD have been discussed in the previous chapter. They are easily calculated on the basis of tables.

Terminal, Initial and Mean Reserves

1. Terminal Reserve

It is obtained by adding the net level annual premium for the year in question to the terminal reserve of the preceding year increased by the one year's interest at the assumed rate and deducted the cost of insurance or claims paid. It has been discussed in detail in previous section. It is obtained out at the end of the year.

The reserve is used for calculating the amount of surrender value or paid up values. It is also used for distribution of bonus.

2. Initial Reserve

The initial reserve for any year is that amount which the insurer has with him in the beginning after premium for the year have been collected and, the terminal reserve of the last year has been added before earning any interest thereon or payment of claims. It has also been discussed already.

This reserve is used for determining the interest earned by the insurer.

3. Mean Reserve

The mean reserve is the arithematic average of initial reserve and terminal reserve during a year. This is used in connection with the Annual statements. Mean reserve is used for valuation purposes.

QUESTIONS

1. How is reserve created and for what is it created?
2. Discuss the two methods of calculating reserves.
3. What are the uses of Terminal Initial and Mean Reserves?
4. 'Reserve is to determine solvency' discuss in the light of insurance fund.
5. Calculate the retrospective policy value at 2% interest at the end of 3 years for a Temporary Assurance of Rs. 1000 for a period of 6 years on the life of a person aged 40. Use the following mortality table on the basis of which a net annual premium of Rs. 3.89 per thousand has been charged.

Age (x)	40	41	42	43	44
l_x	475	474	472	470	465

6. A person aged 28 is insured for Rs. 1000 for a term of 6 years with the following benefits.
   (*a*) Rs. 200 on survival to age 30
   (*b*) Rs. 300 on survival to age 32
   (*c*) Rs. 500 on survival to age 34
   (*d*) Rs. 1000 at the end of year of death before 34.

   If the net annual premium is Rs. 150.61, find the retrospective policy value at 3% interest at the end of 3 years. Given the following mortality table.

Age (x)	28	29	30	31	32	33	34
l_x	966	962	958	953	950	946	940

7. Find the prospective policy value in the following cases :

$a_{31}:\overline{31} = 2.801;\ a_{31}:\overline{21} = 1.90;\ a_{31}:\overline{11} = 0.966$

8. Find the prospective policy value using the data given in Q. 6.
9. 8969 persons aged 30 insure under 1 year temporary assurance for sum assured of Rs. 1000 each at a single premium of Rs. 29.20. Sum assured is payable at the end of the year of death. Premium is based on 3% interest, ignoring expenses. Number of survivors year after year are.

$l_{30} = 9987$	$l_{36} = 8533$
$l_{31} = 8899$	$l_{37} = 8458$
$l_{32} = 8829$	$l_{38} = 8367$
$l_{33} = 8759$	$l_{39} = 8272$
$l_{34} = 8688$	$l_{40} = 8125$
$l_{35} = 8613$	

Calculate the balance of accumulated funds at the end of 4th year after meeting all the claims.

10. A man now aged 40 effected 5 years ago a Whole Life Assurance for Rs. 1000, the number of annual premiums being limited to a maximum of 20. He now desires to alter it to an Endowment Assurance maturing at age 55. Find the amount of the Whole Life Assurance at present.
11. On the basis of above information of survivals and the 3% rate of interest, calculate the value of an Endowment Assurance Policy for Rs. 5000 granted 5 years ago to a person now aged 40 at an annual premium of Rs. 250.
12. An insurer is having the following Children Differed Assurances on its books as on 31-12-85.

Years of issue	*No. of Policies*	*Total Sum Assured*	*Total office Annual Premium*
1974	6	30,000	900
1978	4	25,000	1000
1982	10	40,000	1080

Assume that policies were issued on 31st Dec. in the year of issue, that the premium due on 31-12-85 has been paid and that all the policies are running in the deferment period. If policy conditions provide return of 90% office-premium with 2% interest in case of death of child during deferment period, find the minimum amount the insurer has to keep in reserve to meet his obligations as above.

13

INVESTMENT OF FUNDS

While calculating premium, it has been assumed that the accumulated premiums are invested. The funds are invested to earn at least assumed rate of interest. The needs of investment of funds are given here in brief.

NEEDS OF INVESTMENT

1. Payment of Claims

The first and most important obligation of the insurer is to pay the amount of claims whenever they arise. For this, insurer is getting a substantial amount in form of premiums and has to preserve them for payment later on. To keep such amounts idle will be a failure on the part of the insurer who is expected to invest them on behalf of the policy-holders.

2. To Avoid Financial Deficit

If funds are not invested, the total income of the insurer will fall short of its requirements for meeting its commitments because a particular rate of interest on its investments has been assumed while calculating the rate of premium. Again, if funds are not invested and interest not earned, it would be an under-estimation of its future liability which may prove disastrous at the time of higher mortality.

3. National Interest

A huge fund of the society is taken by the insurers in form of premiums. Therefore, it is essential for the insurers to invest the funds for the economic development of the nation.

SOURCES OF FUNDS

The funds with the insurers are accumulated from the various sources, some of which are given below:

(*i*) Premiums

The main source of funds is the premiums collected by the insurer. The premiums may be single premium, level premiums or annuity considerations. The excess of these premiums over the needed premiums for meeting claims and expenses is the source of funds.

(*ii*) Interest

The second source of funds is the excess interest earned over the assumed rate of interest. The assumed rates are lesser than the actual rate in most of the cases. In reverse, the funds will decline.

(*iii*) Capital Gain

Funds obtained from the sale of share capital and debentures are included under capital gains.

(*iv*) Savings in Expenses

Savings in expense loadings, bonus loadings or mortality savings are also contributing to the funds of the insurers.

(v) Non-Payment of Claims

In pure endowment or term insurance, the claims may not arise, therefore, the premiums paid for such benefits are saved. Sometimes, in certain cases, the claimants do not come for payment at all. Thus, the saved money also form a part of the funds of insurers.

PROBLEMS OF INVESTMENT

While investing the funds, the insurer will have to face various problems, some of which are given in the following sections:

1. The main problem of investment is to preserve the interest of the policy-holders. The insurer keeps the money of the policy-holders as a trust money. To maintain the trusteeship it is essential that the fund must be invested in such securities which are safe and secured.
2. The payment of the claim amount is the second problem of the life insurer. The insurer must have sufficient funds to pay the claims. So, the interest earned from the investment must be adequate enough.
3. The assets of the insurer should be protected from any elements of fluctuations. Therefore, the insurer must earn sufficient amount to pay its expenses. Moreover, the earning should be constant and the market price of the securities must not fall considerably.
4. There should be complete good faith of the public in the insurer's management of funds. In case of doubtful investment the purpose of public may be defeated. The insurer, therefore, may be loosing its business in future.
5. A great care has to be taken while selecting suitable channels of investment. The principles of investment should be followed to a considerable extent. Investment should be such that profit thereon should be maximum without hampering safety and marketability.

THE PRINCIPLES OF INVESTMENT

The canons of investment are safety, profitability, liquidity, diversification and increasing of life business.

1. Safety

The securities in which the funds of insurer is to be invested should never at any time fall in their face values, otherwise the liability will be more than its corresponding assets. The primary purpose of investment is not to earn maximum profit but to maintain a complete security. Therefore, speculative investments involving possibilities of large profits of large losses are not suitable for life insurance funds. On account of trusteeship status, the insurer should invest the funds only in sound channels. Security of principal amount is more important consideration. Therefore, in India, the investment regulations are made whereby the life insurer is required to invest at least 50 per cent of his controlled funds in Government Securities.

Safety includes safety of principal amount and interest, thereon. It means that the principal and interest must not fall, below the expected level at any time. This principle is the keystone of investment.

2. Profitability

The insurer must earn at least the assumed rate of interest otherwise he will suffer loss. The investment, so, should be made in such securities which yield the highest return consistent with the principle of safety. The insurer can reduce his future premiums by earning higher interest and thus will be able to increase his business. It has been realized that the safety and the profitability principles are opposite to each other. The most safe securities earn little profit and vice-versa is also true. Therefore, the investment department has to establish a proper balance between safety and profitably. However, there are certain securities where the safety and the profitability principles are fully observed. Gilt-Edge-Securities, National-Defence Securities are some of the examples of such securities.

A very large portion of funds may be invested in safe-securities which might yield at least assumed rate of interest while the other small portion may be invested in profitable securities guaranteeing at least safety of principal amounts. In addition, an investment fluctuation funds may also be created to meet any possible losses on account of fluctuations in return. In profitability reasonable rate of return with regularity and stability of income is essential. The second factor to be considered is no fluctuation in capital and lesser expenses of investments. The third factor *i.e.*, taxation is also important because unfavorable taxation may reduce the net income of the insurer.

3. Liquidity

It represents convertibility of investments into cash without undue loss of capital. The principle is essential because of immediate requirement of money for payment of claims. However, there is no higher chance of maximum outflow at any time because the maturity, unlike the bank withdrawal, may not fall within a short period. The claims are, generally, following a set-trend on the maturity and death experience. A rough estimation can be made of the payments of claims, surrender values, policy loans and regular expenses 'Funds' should be invested according to the requirements of the insurers, *i.e.*, investments are so made that the maturities will occur at intervals adjusted to meet the needs of maturity obligations.

For meeting the daily outflow of funds, it is not essential to keep maximum amount in cash or in readily convertible securities because a vast inflow of cash is observed in form of premium return on investment and sale of securities. For the established and financially stronger insurers, the liquidity is not much essential. Moreover, the insurer can insert a clause of delay in payment for a specific period.

The principle of liquidity is against the principle of profitability because the idle cash will earn nothing and invested cash will have no liquidity.

4. Diversification

Diversification of investment may mean spreading investment over different channels. The spreading may take place in the following manners.

(*a*) Diversification on the basis of geographical distribution.

(*b*) Distribution of the protfolio over the different economic enterprises of the country, political changes and time.

(*c*) Diversification may be according to number of investment in a security, maturity of security and duration of security.

(*d*) The distribution of funds according to industries, firms and sectors.

The diversification provides maximum security with high yield and better liquidity provided the diversification was done taking into account of all these factors. Do not invest all the funds at one place in an industry, in a security and for a period of maturity. Investments should spread over the widest possible range to minimise unfavourable consideration and to gain favourable advantages. Under diversification, the law of average reduces the losses to minimum.

5. Increasing of Life Business

Investments should also be made in those sectors which are going to benefit the business in the return. Naturally, the social objective principle helps in increasing the business. For example, the life funds, if utilised to finance the schemes of housing, sanitation, medical and education, it will go a greater way to lower the mortality and to increase the standard of people. Decreased mortality and increased income cause more business to insurer because the lower mortality tends to reduce the rate of premium which increases the business. Higher income induces person to get more policies.

Principles of Investment as laid down by Mr. A. H. Bailey

Mr. A. H. Bailey was actuary of the London Assurance Corporation. He contributed a paper in 1862, which was published in Journal of Institute of Actuaries, Vol. X. The principles are commonly known as 'Bailey's Canons' which remain as much applicable to insurance business today as they were in 1862. However, their mode of application can be changed with the changing conditions. His principles of investment are summarised as below:

(*i*) That the first consideration should invariably be the security of the capital.

(*ii*) That the highest practicable rote of interest be obtained, but that this principle should always be subordinate to the previous one, *i.e.,* the security of capital.

(*iii*) That a small proportion of the total funds (the amount varying according to the individual circumstances of each case) should be held in readily convertible securities for the payment of current claims.

(*iv*) That the remaining and much larger proportion may be safely invested in securities that are not readily convertible.

(*v*) That as far as possible the capital should be employed to aid the life insurance business.

COMMENTS ON THE PRINCIPLES

1. The presentation of the principles shows that Mr. Bailey was fully aware of the safety, profitability and liquidity principles but he presented in an exemplary way which did not reveal all scheme of a picture. He would have presented it in a simple way.
2. He was extra cautious with the negative relationship between the safety and profitability. But there are certain securities where the safety and profitability principles are fully applicable simultaneously. In gift-edge securities and postal certificates or national defence bonds may achieve both security of capital and maximum return. Moreover, Investment Fluctuation Fund may be created for meeting losses on investments.
3. He put undue stress on liquidity. Liquidity, at least for established concerns, are not very essential because a vast fund inflows daily to the business in form of premium, return on investment and other sales proceeds.
4. He discussed the principle of diversification in his second, third and fourth principles which can be given only under one principle of diversification because the diversification may also be according to profitability and liquidating besides according to class, character and geographical locations.

USEFULNESS OF MR. BAILEY'S PRINCIPLES

Mr. Bailey's principles are as much useful today as were in his time.

1. Security of Capital

As he thought, security of capital is very useful today also, because of fiduciary relationship of the insurer and insured. Therefore, he pointed out first principle of security in his canons.

2. Profitability

He suggested the second principle only after the first one because he was aware of the negative correlationship between high security and high profitability. It is correct in most of the cases even today. He tried to establish happy balance between the first and second principles. Therefore, he suggested that a fund should be invested in safe security first and in profitable securities, later on. At least the assumed rate of interest must be earned to avoid losses.

3. Liquidity

The negative correlationship between liquidity and profitability was fully known to him. Therefore, he suggested that a larger portion of funds should be invested in non-liquid securities and a smaller part in the liquid securities, *i.e.,* which can be easily converted into cash.

4. Social Objective

His fifth rule to increase life insurance business is now gaining more importance because of awareness of the government towards Social objectives. He suggested that life insurer should make investment in social institutions such as municipal boards, hospitals, housing societies, health centres and schools because these will help in reducing mortality which will tend to reduce premium rates. The life business will increase, consequently.

SUITABILITY OF VARIOUS TYPES OF INVESTMENTS

There are various types of investments having their own advantages and disadvantages. Skill and sound judgment may influence the result. The suitability of some of the investments is discussed here.

1. Government Securities

Government Securities are deemed to be the safest securities in the senses theat there are no substantial fluctuations in their values. Securities of Central Government are safer than that of State Governments. The return on these securities may not be higher. The foreign government securities are not much favourable due to fluctuation and political conditions. The social objective principle is also fulfilled by these securities because the stronger government can look after better its masses.

2. Industrial Securities

The shares and debentures of business and industrial units are included in this category. The rate of return on these securities is comparatively higher than the return on government securities but the safety principle is not so much applicable as in latter case. They are also desirable investments for fulfilling socio-economic purposes. Maximum diversification of investments industry-wise, nature-wise and sector-wise etc. is very much possible.

Relative Importance of Shares and Debentures

Debentures and bonds offer a greater amount of security. The preference shares are more secure than the equity shares. The returns on debentures and preference share being fixed are not more profitable than the return on equity shares. But, the return is more stable in the former case. However, the rate of return depends largely on the normal rate of the concerns, size and nature of business and management of the unit. For example return on shares of a well managed and sound concern will be better than that of financially unsound concerns. Moreover, the equity shares will be more secured in the former case than the debentures of the lattern concern. The investment department of the insurer must have constant vigilance over the prices of such securities, and securities of only those concerns should be selected which promise constant and regular income and lesser or no fluctuations in their price. From return point of view the equity shares of sound concerns are better investment. Some experts are of the opinion that the equity shares do not form proper investment because it tempts to secure full control of the business units, which is beyond the purview of insurance business. The government has also laid down various regulations of investment in shares. The investment of a very large proportion of the funds of a life insurance is undoubtedly objectionable, but it is not necessary to prohibit such investments altogether.

Preference shares give lower yield but the return is more assured while ordinary stocks involve more speculation about the return. Debentures rank high in order of security and are placed next to government securities. Debenture-holders are creditors and as such have prior right to both interest as well as capital over shareholders of a particular unit.

3. Mortgages

Loans are, generally, granted on the mortgage of buildings and land. Usually loans are given to a lower amount than the value of property to provide sufficient margin for safety. Adequate rate of return is observed on such loans and there are sufficient scopes of diversification. Moreover, these loans are relatively expensive to initiate and to service. The marketability of such loans is also doubtful. But a mortgage loan carrying a provision of amortization whereby the loan is entirely paid off in a particular period, are perfectly satisfactory. Mortgages are a specified form of investment and, as such, need skill and experience in their managements.

4. Real Estate

The purchase of land and buildings is included under investment in real estate. This is not a proper investment for insurer because there are a huge fluctuations in the prices of real estate. Moreover, he real estate does not guarantee a constant and higher income apart from the lesser marketability. Therefore, the insurer has only as much real estate as is needed for his own requirements, *i.e.*, for opening offices. Investment in real estate requires specialised knowledge. Hence, the insurer has a special department for its management.

5. Policy Loans

Policy loans are given to the policy-holders against the security of the surrender value of the policy. The amount of loan and interest thereon will not be more than the surrender value of the policy. The loan, if not paid, can be taken over from the amount of surrender. The liquidity factor is not bright because the unpaid loans cannot be treated as unpaid until the duration of the policy. The rate of expenses in handling such loans are very high. However, this is an important investment as it improves business and customer relationship and provides facilities to the policy-holders.

6. Other Assets

The funds of the life insurer may be invested in the business it self in the shape of cash, machine, furniture and properties etc. These investments are as essential as other forms of investment because they assist in smooth running of the business.

Bases for Formulation of Investment Policy by a Life Insurer

1. Basic Principles

The safety, profitability, liquidity diversification and aid to business are guiding principle for formulating the investment policies. These principles vary according to the nature and size of business. However basically, these principles have to be, applied for proper investment policy.

2. The Outlook of Management

Apart from the basic principles, the investment portfolio is affected with the attitude of the management of the concern. If the management wishes to earn maximum profit, investment will be made in high-yielding securities rather than in safe securities. The sound and effective management will always try to invest in safe and constant earning securities.

3. The Present Composition of Investment Portfolio

Where the present composition of investment portfolio shows heavy concentration on government securities, fresh investment may be made in industrial securities. An effective investment policy will have to establish a proper balance between all types of investment channels.

4. Present Position of the Insurer

Investment of the insurer is affected mostly with the size, age, capital and progress rate of the business. For example, new insurer must see safety to the maximum level while the established concern may invest in high-yielding security.

5. Availability of Suitable Securities

When the most suitable securities are not available, investment will have to be confined to the next suitable investment. The requirement of time may also bound the investment portfolio, e.g., during war period, government securities are considerably used.

6. Adequacy of Funds

If there is adequate fund with the insurer investment may be made in high-yielding securities and if funds are insufficient, safety principle is the most considerable factor.

7. Socio-Economic Needs

Bailey had also suggested that investment must be made according to the social and economic requirement of the society. It has been discussed earlier that for meeting social objectives, investment, sometimes, is made even in low yielding securities.

Environment of the Country

Political and economical environment of the country also affect the investment portfolio. International and national relationship are also taken into account while investing the funds.

9. Limitation of Investment

Investment of funds is subject to two limitation:—

(*a*) Legal; and
(*b*) Self-imposed.

(*a*) Legal Limitations

It can be of two types:—

(*i*) Quantitative; and
(*ii*) Qualitative

(*i*) Quantitative Limitation

The quantitative aspects of investment regulations stem from the specification of eligible types of investment and the minimum quality criteria for individual investments within the eligible categories.

(*ii*) Quantitative

Limitations may be imposed on the amounts that can by placed in eligible investments. For example, in India at least 50 per cent of the controlled funds should be invested in government securities.

(*b*) Self-Imposed Limitations

Life insurers also place limitation on their investments which is determined by the tradition and outlook of management. These limitations may be change from time to time.

INVESTMENT REGULATIONS FOR LIFE INSURERS

The Insurance Regulatory and Development Authority (IRDA) Formulated Investment Regulations in August, 2000 and subsequently amended them in May 2001. The latest regulations which are applicable are as per Regulation (3).

S.No.	*Type of Investment*	*Percentage*
(*i*)	Government Securities	25%
(*ii*)	Government Securities or other approved Securities (including (*i*) above)	Not less then 50%

Contd...

(*iii*)	Approved Investments as Specified in Schedule	
(*a*)	Infrastructure and Social Sector Explanation: For the purpose of this requirement, Infrastructure and Social Sector Shall have the meaning as given in relation 2(h) of Insurance Regulatory and Development Authority (Registration of Indian Insurance Companies) Regulations, 2000 and as defined in the Insurance Regulatory and Development Authority (Obligations of Insurers to Rural and Social Sector) Regulations, 2000 respectively.	Not less than 15%
(*b*)	Other to be governed by Exposure norms as specified in regulations 5. Investments in "other than approved Investment in "other than approved Investments" can in no case exceed 15% of the fund.	Not exceeding 35%

Regulation 3. "1. Life Business: In terms of explanation is Section 27A of the Act, the Authority has determined that assets relating to Pension business, Annuity business and Linked Life Insurance business shall not form part of the Controlled Fund for the purpose of that section.

Without prejudice to Section 27 or Section 27A of the Act, Every insurer carrying on the business of life-insurance shall *invest and at all times keep invested* his controlled fund (other than funds relating to pension and general annuity business and unit linked life insurance business) in the following manner.

2. **'Pension and General Annuity Business':** Every insurer *shall invest and at all times keep invested* funds belonging to his Pension Business, General Annuity Business in the following manner:

Sr. No.	*Type of Investment*	*Percentage*
(*i*)	Government Securities, being not less than	20%
(*ii*)	Government Securities of other approved Securities (inclusive (I) above, being not less than)	40%
(*iii*)	Balance to be invested in Approved Investments as specified in Schedule 1 and to be governed by Exposure/Prudential Norms specified in Regulation 5	Not exceeding 60%

Note: for the purposes of this sub-regulation no unapproved investments shall be made.

3. 'Unit Linked Life Insurance Business': Every insurer shall invest and at all times keep invested his segregated fund of unit linked life insurance business as per investment offered to and approved by the policy-holders. Uni Linked policies may only be offered here the units are linked to categorie of assets which are both marketable and easily realizable. However, the total investment in other than approved category of investments shall at no time exceed 25% of the fund.

An attempt has been made to discuss the issues arising out of the investment regulations pertaining to life business.

- The inclusion of infrastructure appears to aim for channeling insurance funds into infrastructure projects which need long term funds in significant amounts. Further in the changed economic scenario, the funds could be invested in Corporate Sector for implementing he infrastructure projects.
- Earlier also the mandated investments were directed towards social sector. However the definition of social sector under IRDA regulations is more rigorous and basically these investments are meant for the development of economically backward segments in both urban and rural sectors.
- Even though the objectives are laudable, given the slow pace of progress in the implementation of infrastructue projects thereby slowing the off take of funds coupled with the rigorous definition

of social sector the insurers, more so the existing players may find it difficult to deploy the funds in the social Sector on accretion basis, as per the Regulations.

- The regulator may consider under the definition infrastructure Oil and Gas Pipelines, CNG, LNG Terminals, which also need huge sums of money. Further, it may also consider investments in funds exclusively devoted for infrastructure sectors as investments under infrastructure.
- Many Infrastructure projects have foreign collaborations. The companies, for implementing these projects, are being incorporated as Private Limited Companies. On doing so, apparently, the foreign partners in these Companies enjoy certain tax benefits. But the insurance Act, 1938 as amended, explicitly states that an insurer shall not out of his controlled fund invest or keep invested any sum in the shares or debentures of a private limited company. The act therefore effectively bars any investment in a private limited company. This provision may act as an impediment for flow of funds into private limited companies implementing infrastructure projects. This issue therefore needs to be re-examined.
- In addition, the definition of rural and social sector is quite rigorous. It is indeed quite challenging for the insurance companies to evolve norms for granting loans in the social sector, wherein mostly the loanees are individuals with little or no security.
- The insurance companies, as they are not equipped to identify the beneficiaries/genuine credit needs, may have to involve village level panchayats, NGOs, Co-operative Societies and other government agencies to lend for the social sector. Even by lending through these organisations, the issue of monitoring will still be left unanswered, in view of the lack of administrative mechanisms available with insurers. The regulator may have to look into these practical aspects and review this regulation. Alternatively, the insurance companies may be directed to lend to government rural organisations/nodal agencies either directly or by way of refinancing and such investments may be treated as investments under social sector.
- The regulation does not specify any definite percentage of investments separately for infrastructure and social sectors. However, in a recent amendment proposed, it explicitly mentions that every insurer shall endeavor to maintain a proper balance between the investments made in infrastructure and social sectors thus inhibiting insurers from investing in one sector completely and complying with the regulation.
- The compliance with this regulation may not be easy for existing life insurer *i.e.*, LIC, as it has a huge controlled fund approximating to Rs. 200,000 Cr. 15% of this will amount to Rs. 30,000 Cr. If one has to strike balance in the investments between infrastructure and social sector, the investment figures are mind boggling and to deploy that kind of money in the social sector may not be very easy. Even on accretion basis, wherein the yearly accretions are in the range of Rs. 28,000 to 30,000 Crs. compliance with this regulation will be difficult as the numbers involved are about Rs. 4200-Rs. 4500 Cr. If a balance has to be struck between the investments in infrastructure and social sector, at least an amount of Rs. 1000-1500 Cr. may have to be invested in the social sector. Therefore to comply with the regulation on year to year accretion basis, let along on total control fund, would be very difficult.
- These investments, notwithstanding the issues mentioned above, have to comply with the norms as specified in Schedule-1. The recent amendments to Schedule-1 say that bonds issued for development of infrastructure and social sectors, duly guaranteed by government or otherwise rated AA by an independent rating agency, issued by others would qualify as approved investment.
- Most of the infrastructure projects are implemented under new companies without any track record. General view among the rating agencies is that project bonds/debentures will not get a rating of more than A+ on their own accord. As these projects involve substantial investments, the guarantees from parent companies may not be forthcoming. Therefore in practice bonds

may not qualify as approved investment. It is assumed that "others" means other than Government.

- The IRDA, under Section 27A, amended the following clause:

"All secured loans, secured debentures, secured bonds, other secured debt instruments, shares and preference shares and debt instruments issued by all India Financial Institutions recognised as such by RBI-investments to be made in terms of investment policy guidelines, benchmarks and exposure norms/limits approved by the Board of Directors of the Insurer".

The Notes 2 to 4 under regulations 3 & 4 mention that all investment in assets/instruments which are capable of being rated as per market practice be rated and should carry a minimum rating of AA. If sufficient investments of this grade are not available, Investment Committee may approve investments in instruments rated A+.

Going by the workings of the clause, one may infer that all the project loans/debentures etc., which are generally secured by a first charge on the assets of the company and are not rated as per market practice may qualify as approved investments.

Another significant issue is point 7 in the notes which states "investments in equity shares listed on a recognised stock exchange should be made in actively traded and liquid instruments viz., its trading volume does not fall below 10,000 in any trading session during the last 12 months or trading value of which exceeds Rs. 10 lacs in any trading session during last 12 months".

It is presumed that it pertains to only secondary market operations. By virtue of this note, it is assumed that the insurer is not prohibited from investing in IPOs, project equities and other privately placed equities in companies which may not be listed immediately. In fact many infrastructure project companies seek equity investments as part of project finance and these companies generally propose to get listed only after the project is commissioned and start earning profits. Further, many infrastructure related funds are being floated for initial project development and these funds need equity Investments.

- The regulations mention that other approved investments shall be governed by Exposure Norms. Hence it may be inferred that Exposure Norms may not apply for Infrastructure and Social Sector Investments.
- The regulator has included Commercial Paper with "very strong" or more rating, inter alia, in the approved investments. In view of the developing market for Securitisation, the regulator may also consider including "Pass Through Certificates" issued with "very strong rating" as approved investments. In recent times, PTCs have slowly started coming into the market and will provide a good investment opportunity for insurers as these are generally backed by cash flows and also asset cover in the case of mortgage backed securities and suitable credit enhancement facilities. In recent times, all PTC issued were rated as "AAA (so)". It may be noted that in the domestic market, none of the securitised deals has experienced default as of today.

SEBI in its latest move has banned the carry forward trading and introduced options on individual equities w.e.f. 2nd July. The Index futures have already started trading. Options and futures, world over, are used by insurance companies as portfolio hedging instruments. As per the reporting formats prescribed by the IRDA, it appears there is no bar on insurance companies to deal in derivative instruments. However, detailed guidelines may be necessary in view of the varied risk profile of derivatives depending upon the purpose for which they are traded in/held. For example if an insurance company holds derivative instruments purely for hedging its portfolio, which will enable it to reduce the investment risk on the portfolio, it may be considered as an approved investment.

- As already mentioned above, many infrastructure projects are being implemented as Private Ltd. companies. Besides, many of these projects are coming up with structured products such as Take Out Finance etc. These instruments may be considered as part of the financing instruments for the projects along with the traditional instruments.

EXPOSURE NORMS

The IRDA Regulations also provide norms regarding investment exposure to individual companies.

The Exposure Norms briefly are as follows:

- The Capital Employed is defined as total of ordinary and preference shares, debentures, long/medium/short term loans (excluding public deposits), free reserves but excluding revaluation reserves of the investee company as shown in the last audited balance sheet.
- The regulator would have done well by giving a definition of each of the terms used in the regulations as there is wide scope for different interpretations of definitions such as capital employed, free reserves etc.
- The investments in equity (ordinary, preference and convertible portion of debentures) should not exceed 50% of the above mentioned exposure norms. In effect in the case of individual Investee Company, insurance companies and existing insurers should not exceed 5% and 10% of the capital employed respectively. Further, the regulator restricts investment in the promoters' groups of the life insurance Company to 5% of the controlled fund.
- The norms are uniform for all insurers in principle, limiting exposure to individual company, group and industry sector and to promoters' groups reduces the risk of concentration and excessive self-investments.

Type of Investment (1)	*Limit for Investee Company* (2)	*Limit for the entire group to which the Investee company belongs* (3)	*Limit for the industry sector to which the Company belongs* (4)
Equity/Preference Shares/Convertible portion of Debenture at face value Debenture—(face) value) including Private place	As on any date Not exceeding 20% of the total Capital Employed	As on any date Not exceeding 15% of the total Capital Employed of group companies	As on any date Not exceeding 15% of the total Capital Employed in all such companies.
NCDs and Non-Convertible portion of Convertible Debentures Short/Medium/ Long Term Loans and "any other financial assistance	During the year not exceeding 5% of estimated annual accretion of funds	During the year not exceeding 10% of estimated annual accretion of funds	

PRUDENTIAL NORMS

- The regulator has earlier specified various prudential norms for investments in NCDs and Terms Loans. However, in the latest amendment, the Regulator has left prudential norms to the discretion of the board thus removing a major impediment. This provides leeway as the board, keeping in view the availability of skills for appropriate risk assessment of an investment with the company, may evolve the norms such that the policyholders funds enjoy highest amount of safety.

- The discussion in the foregoing paragraphs clearly indicate that the regulations are prescriptive in nature, with an objective to protect the funds of the policyholders and as in the case of any prescription impose constraints on the flexibility and innovative ability of the insurer in investing the funds. By no means these restrictions are undesirable, given the nascent development of Indian financial markets, inability of various regulators to prevent market manipulations, inadequate and lack of prompt punitive system and slow and complicated legal systems.

Some Concluding Remarks

- If we compare the Indian regulations with those prevailing in U.K., the developed insurance market, there are no restrictions on the investment pattern in U.K. The value of assets has to be maintained at more than the value of liabilities. However, for valuation, which is based on market value of assets, the admissible of asses and caps on investments in particular assets have been specified. However, these rules do not preclude insurers from holding assets, which are not admissible, as long as they demonstrate solvency. The insurer has to disclose all his investments completely so that policyholders are aware of the investment pattern and its performance.
- On the other hand, the regulations in US are again prescriptive with quantitative qualitative restrictions on the investments of insurers even though the markets are well developed and efficient. India over a period of time, as its gains experience may gradually progress towards the US pattern and from there to UK pattern, if our markets and legal systems are fully developed and equipped to deal with any eventuality efficiently.

(*The views in the article are those of the author. The article is an obridged version of a presentation made by the author at National Insurance Academy, Pune*)

INVESTMENT PATTERN OF LIC AND OVERVIEW OF INVESTMENTS AS ON 31ST MARCH, 2002

The investment of LIC are governed by Section 27A of the Insurance Act, 1938 and the (Investment) Regulations as prescribed by the Insurance Regulatory and Development Authority (IRDA). LIC follows a very prudent and sound systems of investment. The decision for investments are taken by a high level committee comprising Chairman of LIC, Managing Director and some members of the Board of the corporation, and an investment is made only if the decision to do so is taken with unanimity. In all its investments LIC follows the exposure and prudential norms prescribed by the Investment Committee and the IRDA. In our investment decisions the emphasis is on obtaining the highest yield commensurate with the total security of our funds. The pattern of Investments as prescribed for LIC is as under:

Investment Norms for LIC: Life Business

Sr.No	*Type of Investment*	*IRDA Norm*
1.	Govt. Securities	Not less than 25%
2.	Govt. Securities of other Approved Securities. (including item no. 1)	Not less than 50%
3.	Approved investments	
	(*a*) Infrastructure and Social Sector	Not less than 15%
	(*b*) Others	Not exceeding 35%

Investment Norms for LIC: Pensions and Group Schemes Business Not less than 15%

Sr.No	*Type of Investment*	*IRDA Norm*
1.	Govt. Securities	Not less than 20%
2.	Govt. Securities of other Approved Securities including 1 above	Not less than 40%
3.	Balance in Approved Investment	Not exceeding 60%

The Break-up of investment are as under:

LIC's Investments (Rs. Cr.) As on 31st March

Sr.No	*Type of Investment*	*2001-02*	*2003-2004*	*2006-2007*
1.	Govt. Securities and Govt. Guaranteed Bonds	126752	99256	272498
2.	Other approved securities	2982	2630	64285
3.	Investments in Infrastructure and Social Sector	4492	11747	73746
	(*i*) Others to be governed by exposure norms Specified in Regulation 5.			
	(*ii*) Out of the above 35% percentage of investment in Other than Approved Investments not to exceed 15%	60874	15198	
	Total Investments	195100	128831	410529

INVESTMENTS IN THE INFRASTRUCTURE AND SOCIAL SECTOR

LIC has been investing in Infrastructure and Social sector in a major way. As per IRDA norms, LIC is required to invest 15% of the accretion to the controlled fund in Infrastructure and Social Sector. The major investments in social sector are as under:

Total Investments And Outstanding Position In The Social Sector As on 31st March

Sector	*Total investment*	*(Rs. in Crore)*
	2002	*2007*
Housing	4817.28	22451
Power	135.16.44	37881
Road Railways, Port & Bridges	892.84	1516
Irrigation / Water Supply & Severage	3950.28	7500
Others	3404.70	4398
Total	26581.54	73746

LIC'S INVESTMENTS ARE WELL DIVERSIFIED AND SECURE

LIC has a very strong and robust base of investment and is one the largest financial institutions in the country. The Asset bases of LIC stands at Rs. 2,45,387 Crore as on 31st March 2002 which includes investments of Rs. 2,15,392 Crore. LIC's investment activities are well distributed in all categories of

Sectoral Investment by Life Insurers as at March 31, 2006

Insurer	Life Fund (Rs. Crores)										Pension and General annuity			
	Central Govt Securities		State Govt Securities and other approved Securities Including central Govt Securities		Infrastructure / Social Sector		Investment Subject to Exposure Norms (INCL. OTAI)		Other than Approved Investments (OTAI)		Total (Life fund)		Central Govt Securities		State Govt Securities and other approved securities including central Govt Securities	
Public Sector	31/3/05	31/3/06	31/3/05	31/3/06	31/3/05	31/3/06	31/3/05	31/3/06	31/3/05	31/3/06	31/3/05	31/3/06	31/3/05	31/3/06	31/3/05	31/3/06
LIC	1,67,718.86	1,97,419.39	206,906.87	2,41,103.52	44,660.40	48,182.22	1,09,861.60	1,00,161.78	26.111.98	26,286.06	3,61,428.87	3,89,447.52	5,650.77	18,987.86	9,083.36	28,881.26
Total (A)	1,67,718.86	1,97,419.39	2,06,906.87	2,41,103.52	44,66.40	48,182.22	1,09,861.60	1,00,161.78	26,111.98	26,286.06	3,61,428.87	3,89,447.52	5,650.77	18,987.86	9,083.36	28,881.26
Private Sector																
HDFC STD	286.29	463.82	286.29	463.82	85.80	213.28	108.67	233.43	19.58	14.82	480.77	910.53	117.37	215.39	117.37	215.39
MAX NYI	109.02	505..97	315.67	505.6	89.08	130.90	11.62	57.06	15.06	29.80	436.37	693.90	281	14.79	12.90	14.79
ICICI PRU	552.82	683.64	552.82	683.64	159.04	226.11	258.77	404.34	75.82	67.37	970.63	1314.09	121.87	184.53	121.87	184.53
Birla Sun	84.73	141.95	110.75	141.95	3174	41.97	27.58	68.72	9.56	7.25	170.06	252.64	0.06	0.15	0.06	0.15
Tata-Aig life	311.91	511.43	311.91	511.43	64.66	121.50	16.19	91.37	1.33	4.69	392.76	724.30	58.25	72.93	58.75	72.93
Om Kotak	103.11	128.97	113.10	180.53	66.92	59.99	40.64	##	0.73	1.98	200.52	338.54	8.23	##		
SBI life	587.78	758.38	792.78	780.18	155.26	264.96	212.86	500.76	88.48	167.70	960.89	1545.91	55.36	90.85		
Allianz Bajaj	235.67	403.04	235.67	403.04	74.02	141.91	72.79	178.15	20.89	30.94	382.28	723.10	7.13	18.12	7.13	18.12
Metlife	101.51	127.20	101.51	127.20	30.05	43.87	25.63	37.40	13.34	17.69	157.18	208.67	0.21	0.36	0.21	0.36
Reliance life	63.54	95.80	65.30	95.80	22.94	34.34	22.47	33.81	6.58	6.00	110.71	163.98	27.87	50.38	27.87	50.38
ING Vysya	132.91	196.16	132.91	196.16	46.63	75.93	61.69	99.4	14.30	49.01	241.22	371.73	0.00	37.85	0.00	37.85
Vysya Life	79.70	128.91	79.70	128.91	30.21	38.15	35.04	51.24	0.00	4.94	144.95	218.29	0.00	0.00	0.00	0.00
Ahara Life	60.47	48.42	102.90	90.52	24.27	28.37	15.32	26.00	0.01	2.71	142.48	145.69	0.06	0.32	0.06	0.32
Hriram life		65.25		65.25		34,95		29.55		7.59		129.75		0.00		0.00
Total (B)	2,714.53	4,258.93	3,001.31	4,374.41	860.61	1,456.23	929.07	1,910.49	265.75	412.50	4,790.98	7,741.13	399.22	694.79	414.32	723.18
Total (A+B)	1,70,433.39	2,01,678.32	2,09,908.18	2,45,477.93	45,521.01	49,638.45	1,10,790.66	1,02,072.27	26,377.73	26,698.56	3,66,219.85	3,97,188.65	6,049.99	19,682.65	9,492.68	29,604.44

Note: The figures are based on provisional Returns filed with IRDA

Fund (Rs. Crores)				Group excluding froup Pension and Annuity Fund (Rs. Crores)								Unit Linke fund (Rs. Crores)						—	
Estatement Subject to Posure norms		Total (Pension Fund)		Central Govt Securities		State Govt Securities and other approved Securities Including central Govt Securities		Investment Subject to Exposure Norms		Total (Group Fund)		'Other Approved Investments		Other than Approved Investments		Total (Unit Linked fund)		Total (All Funds) (Rs. Crores)	
31/3/05	31/3/06	31/03/05	31/3/06	31/3/05	31/3/06	31/3/05	31/3/06	31/3/05	31/3/06	31/3/05	31/3/06	31/3/05	31/3/06	31/3/05	31/3/06	31/3/05	31/3/06	31/3/05	31/3/06
2,378.66	7,276,38	11,462.03	36,157.64	25,039.54	16,665.46	33,297.31	21,231.45	9,342.11	5,506.08	42,639.42	26,737.53	2,547.87	10,269.86	210.80	1,158.59	2,758.67	11,428.45	4,18,288.99	4,63,771.14
2,378.66	7,276.38	11,462.03	36,157.64	25,039.54	16,665.46	33,297.31	21,231.45	9,342.11	5,506.08	42,639.42	26,737.53	2,547.87	10,269.86	210.80	1,158.59	2,758.67	11,428.45	4,18,288.99	4,63,771.14
34.56	57.24	151.91	262.63	0.00	0.00	0.00	0.00	0.00	0.00	0.00	0.00	280.17	1,396.26	10.49	21.86	290.67	1,418.13	921.39	286.79
1.13	1.06	14.03	15.83	1.45	3.76	6.81	3.76	0.44	0.16	7.25	4.92	20.11	142.33	0.33	28.85	20.44	121.18	478.09	885.85
44.77	60.02	166.64	244.55	0.00	0.00	0.00	0.00	0.00	0.00	0.00	0.00	1,896.27	5,270.23	440.89	656.63	2337.16	5,926.86	3,474.43	485.50
0.00	0.00	0.06	0.16	0.00	0.00	0.00	0.00	0.00	0.00	0.00	0.00	1,047.34	1,862.92	78.38	235.13	1,125.72	2,098.05	1,295.85	2,350.85
18.53	23.69	76.78	96.62	14.70	40.69	14.70	40.69	0.00	0.00	14.70	40.69	76.00	325.79	4.81	34.95	80.81	360.74	565.05	1,222.35
5.13	9.56	13.36	20.68	205	3.52	2.05	3.52	0.00	0.49	2.05	4.00	304.75	750.35	3.57	10.26	308.33	760.61	524.40	1,123.82
18.60	160.49	78.97	277.75	420	0.00	4.20	0.00	6.57	0.00	10.77	0.00	3.46	193.27	0.08	18.06	3.54	211.33	1,054.17	2,034.98
2.15	0.00	9.28	18.12	127	8.00	1.27	8.00	0.00	5.82	1.27	13.82	336.14	2,325.67	33.10	243.65	369.24	2,569.32	762.07	3,324.36
0.00	0.08	0.21	0.44	252	5.76	2.52	5.76	0.00	0.53	2.52	6.29	1.62	50.52	0.12	0.00	1.74	50.52	161.66	265.92
22.58	39.21	50.45	89.58	0.00	0.00	0.00	0.00	0.00	0.00	0.00	0.00	21.40	93.25	0.00	6.09	21.40	99.34	182.56	352.90
0.00	37.11	0.00	74.96	0.00	0.00	0.00	0.00	0.00	0.00	0.00	0.00	73.70	214.12	4.91	31.56	78.61	245.68	319.83	692.36
0.00	0.00	0.00	0.00	0.76	0.76	2.06	1.54	0.80	0.77	2.85	2.32	122.95	490.87	8.18	41.27	131.13	532.15	278.93	725.76
0.00	0.00	0.06	0.32	0.02	0.06	0.02	0.06	0.00	0.00	0.02	0.06	0.00	15.57	0.00	0.21	0.00	15.79	142.56	161.86
	0.00		0.00		0.00		0.00		0.00		0.00		0.00		0.00		0.00		129.75
147.43	383.46	561.75	1,106.65	26.97	62.55	33.63	63.33	7.81	8.77	41.43	72.09	4,183.91	13,131.15	584.86	1,328.53	4,768.77	14,459.68	10,162.94	23,379.55
2,526.09	7,659.84	12,023.78	37,264.29	25,066.52	16,728.01	33,330.93	21,294.78	9,349.92	5,514.85	42,680.85	26,809.62	6,731.78	23,401.01	795.66	2,487.12	7,527.45	25,888.13	4,28,451.93	4,87,150.69

investments such as Treasury Bills, Government Securities, State Government Securities, Equity, Projects Financing, Infrastructure, Social Sector etc. LIC is one of the largest investors in Government Securities and social sector and infrastructure investment thereby contributing in a significant way to the economic growth of the nation.

Sectoral Investment by Life Insurers as at March 31, 2006

QUESTIONS

1. What is fund and why the fund is invested?
2. Give the various solutions of the problems of investment.
3. Critically examine the connons of investment.
4. How far is Bailey's principle of investment suitable to modern life insurance? Comment in the light of socialistic goal of a country.

14

SURRENDER VALUE

Nature and Meaning

It has been revealed in previous chapter that the premiums received by the insurer are accumulated with a certain rate of interest, which form the shape of reserve. When the insured wishes to surrender his policy or fails to pay his premium, reserve is no longer accumulated and the insured, generally, is given a surrender value. The surrender value will not be equal to the accumulated reserve because certain expenses or losses are involved in payment of surrender values. Now, the definition of surrender value can be as that amount of premiums paid which is returned to the policy-holder at the time of surrendering the policy. Normally no surrender value is paid if the policy lapses within two or three years of its issue because huge expenditures are involved during the inception of the policy. It has been realised that the insurer may return the excess of receipts over expenditure only after two years of the policy. In India, the policy can be surrendered for cash after the premiums have been paid for at least two years or to the extent of one-tenth of the total number, stipulated for in the policy, provided such one-tenth exceeds one full year's premium.

BASES OF CALCULATING SURRENDER VALUES

There are two bases of calculating surrender values:–

I. Accumulation Approach and

II. Saving Approach.

I. The Accumulation Approach

Under this approach, surrender value is the accumulation of overcharges in the net premium, which upon the surrender of the policy is no longer required to pay the amount of claims, therefore, theoretically he should pay all the accumulated reserve but if it is allowed, the insurer will be left a vary small amount for meeting other obligations because a huge expenses are involved at the time of surrender.

The accumulation approach is very scientific because it allows surrender values to all types of policies, whereas, in practice surrender values on the term policies and pure endowment policies are not allowed because there the question of payment may or may not arise. Had the surrender values allowed on these policies, the insurer may be losing when claims would not arise on the policies.

The accumulation approach regards reserve for policy as the basis of distribution of surrender values. The reserve is calculated in this case on gross premium. So the expenses are also deducted from the premium received. Thus, the reserve would be equal to all the premiums paid and interest earned thereon minus shares of death claims and of over all expenses of the insurer. The surrender value can be the largest amount which the insurer can pay without going into loss. The full amount of reserve to a particular policies cannot be given as a surrender value because there are certain expenses and loss because of surrendering the policies. Thus,

Surrender Value = Full Reserve–Surrender Charges

Surrender Charges

The surrender charges are those expenses and losses which occurred on account of a surrender or lapsation of policy. The surrender charges are discussed below:

(*i*) Initial Expenses

In the beginning of the contract, certain expenses are involved for processing the proposals, payment of commission to agents and medial officer, correspondence and issuing of policy. The initial expenses are so high that the first year's premium is unable to meet all the expenses. These expenses, actually, are recouped after several years' continuation of the policy. Moreover, the initial expenses involved are equally distributed throughout the premium paying period. If policy is lapsed or surrendered before maturity, a part of the initial expenses are left unpaid. So, it is a justified matter to charge the unpaid initial expenses from the reserve of the policy which is surrendered. If it is not done, it would be a great injustice to remaining policy-holders who are willing to continue the policy. The surrender values are lesser in the beginning and higher at later stage because initial expenses to be recouped in the beginning are more than at later age.

(*ii*) Adverse Financial Selection

During the period of business depression, the surrendering of policies weaken the financial standing of the insurer because at that time most of the policy-holders will rush for surrender values and the insurer's funds will be reduced to minimum. In such cases the policyholders should not be allowed to receive surrender values more than the realized values of the invested funds. The insurer has to liquidate some assets at depressed prices. The demand of surrender values necessitates some liquid assets with the insurer, which means the insurer is unable to earn sufficient amount on the liquid assets.

(*iii*) Adverse Mortality Selection

It is well-known fact that the persons in extremely poor health are not likely to surrender their policies. They will beg, borrow or steal to maintain the protection. Those who do surrender are expecting longer lives than those who do not surrender. Consequently at every surrender, the average or actual mortality tends to increase more than the assumed mortality. Thus, the increased mortality should be adjusted while surrender value is permitted.

(*iv*) Contribution to Contingency Reserve

While calculating gross premium a small amount for contribution to contingency reserve is charged from the policyholders to meet the sudden and accidental rise in claims due to wars and epidemics. If the policy is surrendered in the beginning, the contribution is left unrealised.

(*v*) Contribution to Profits

The policy is expected to contribute a fund towards the profit. If the policy surrendered, the expectation is lost. So this contribution should also be treated as surrender charges while permitting surrender of policy.

(*vi*) Cost of Surrender

The insurer will incur a certain amount of expenses in processing the surrender of policies. Sometimes, the cost of surrender is like other expenses, spread over the premium paying period. In early surrender, the cost is left unrealised and a deduction from the reserve is permitted.

These expenses and losses are estimated by the actuary. He tries to allow maximum surrender values keeping all the above factors.

II. Saving Approach

An insurer is responsible for payment of claims whenever it may arise; but if a policy is surrendered, the insurer is relieved of its obligation for payment of the assured sum. He is in a position to save something due to non-payment of claims. Thus, where the insurers is relieved of the responsibility of payment of claims, he is in a position to return some amounts to the insured. But where he may not be required to pay the claims, he is not relieved of the responsibility and no surrender value can be given to the policyholders. For example, in Term Insurance and Pure Endowment policies, the insurer may or may not be required to pay the claims. So the insurer is not bound to pay the amount of surrender. The insurer may certainly agree to pay a cash surrender value to the policy-holder in lieu of paying the sum assured at maturity or death.

The saving approach is more scientific because it reveals the reason of payment of surrender value. Thus, it forbids payment of surrender values on term and pure endowment policies and agrees to pay the surrender amount on whole life and endowment policies.

Under this method, the surrender value is paid in lieu of the claim amount. Here it is to be understood that the amount of saving in non-payment of claim can be calculated only after considering various transactions from the inception of the policy up to its surrender and from the date of surrender up to the maturity or deaths. Had, instead of surrendering the policy, the insurance continued, the insurer would have received the level premiums on the policy and have earned interest on invested amounts and would have occupied certain expenses. Thus, at the surrender of the policy, the insurer does not get certain income and has not to occur future expenses in relation to the policy. The incomes or expenses will continue up to the policy life. Therefore, the life expectancy is to be known while determining the saving in expenses or loss of income. So, at the time of surrender of the policy, it is expected that the policy would have continued up to the maturity or till the end of mortality table. The surrender value on a policy can be calculated as below:

Surrender Value = (Sum assured + Accumulated value of future expenses + Future reversionally bonus, if participating policy) – (Accumulated value of all future premiums + expenses incurred in processing the surrender value).

On the basis of above formula, at the time of maturity or death, the surrender, value is calculated; but it does not mean that the surrender value is paid only at that time. A provisional sum, called minimum surrender allowance, is paid at the time of surrender and then, at the time of maturity or death the surrender value is adjusted. The adjusted amount will be the full surrender value minus the accumulated value of the minimum surrender allowance.

FORMS OF PAYMENT OF SURRENDER VALUES

The policyholder can get the surrender values in any of the following forms:

1. Cash Surrender Value

The policyholder can get the value of surrender in cash. When the policyholder gets the cash, the contract comes to an end and the insurer has no further obligation to pay on that particular policy. Since all the amounts surrendered is given at the time of surrender, the cash benefit is generally less than the other benefits. However, the cash surrender value gives immediate relief to the policyholders; so it is generally preferred by them.

2. Reduced Paid up Insurance

In this case, the surrender value is not paid immediately, but the original amount of policy is reduced in certain proportion and the reduced amount is paid according to the term of Policy . Thus, if, after at least two full years' premiums have been paid in respect of the policy, any subsequent premium be not duly paid, the policy shall not be wholly void, but the sum assured by it shall be reduced to such a sum as shall bear the same ratio to the full sum assured as the number of premiums actually paid shall bear to the total number premiums payable as originally stipulated for in the policy provided such reduced sum together any attached bonus in the case of a policy for a sum assured of Rs. 1,000 or over be not less than Rs. 100 and in the case of a policy for or a sum assured of less than Rs. 1,000 be not less than Rs. 50.

Since, January 1, 1976 the provision for non-forfeiture clause has been altered as below.

1. If the premium under the policies have been paid for a period of five years or 1/4 of the original premium paying period of the policy whichever is less but subject to the condition that minimum 3 years' premiums are paid.
2. The paid up value under the policy is not less than Rs. 250 excluding of attached bonuses for policies where under original sum assured is Rs. 1,000 or more and Rs. 100 exclusive of attached bonus where the original sum assured is less than Rs. 1,000.

The above non-forfeiture condition would apply to proposals completed on and after 1-1-1976.

3. Extended Term Insurance

The net cash value arisen at the time of surrender of a policy can be used for payment of as single premium for purchase of term insurance, where the sum assured will be paid only when death of the life assured occurs within the term of the policy. The main disadvantage of this scheme is that if the life assured does not die within the specified time, the premium paid is forfeited by the insurer. Thus, the surrender value would be lost with no use to the insured. However, in case of death during the term, the policy-holder would be benefited for a higher amount with only a small sum of surrender value. Moreover, the term insurance under this scheme is given without medical examination.

4. Automatic Premium Loan

Under this scheme, the surrender value is used for payment of future premium. Thus, the policy will continue up to the period the surrender value is adequate enough to meet the amount of further premiums. Each premium is paid automatically as it comes due by creation of a loan which with interest becomes a lien upon the face of the policy amount until paid. The premiums continue to be paid until the surrender value is completely exhausted. After this period the policy stands cancelled and no amount is paid to the policy-holder because all the surrender value has been used for payment of premiums.

The advantage of this scheme is that if the policyholder dies after surrender but before expiry of the surrender value, full policy amount minus the loan and interest thereon is paid. The policy does not lapse but remains in full force subject to the lien. The insured is permitted to regain his original status without furnishing an evidence of insurability by simply repaying the amount which he owes to the insurer.

The rate of interest on loan is now 9 per cent p.a. with effect from Feb. 1974. The loan can be granted only up to 90 per cent of surrender value if policy was in force.

5. Purchase of Annuity

The policyholder, with the surrender value, can purchase an annuity. Thus instead of taking surrender value in cash, the annuity is purchased from the available surrender value. The amount of annuity depends upon the amount of net cash value, the attained age of the policyholders and the type of annuity required. The option of an annuity is better alternative to those who require to use all their savings during their life-times.

QUESTIONS

1. Discuss the method of calculating Surrender Value.
2. What are the various forms of payment of Surrender Values?

15

VALUATION AND SURPLUS

Valuation is a process to value the net liabilities of a life insurer as on a particular date. It determines the total amount of reserve that an insurer must have to meet his obligations. It means that the valuation, firstly, determines the total net liabilities of the insurer and secondly, compares his liabilities with the available funds. Ultimately, it can be revealed whether the insurer has sufficient funds to meet his obligations or not.

Purpose of Valuation

There are two main objectives of the valuation (*i*) to determine the solvency of the insurer and (*ii*) to determine the distributable surplus amongst the participating policyholders.

(*i*) ***To determine the Solvency.*** The life insurer must find out whether he has sufficient funds to meet the current obligations or not. In case of insolvency, he has to curtail his expenses and increase the income. He has to raise the premium rates and has to stop bonus distribution. Extra-precaution has to be applied in restraining the outflow of funds.

(*ii*) ***To determine the divisible Surplus.*** The excess of receipts over expenditures of a period cannot be regarded as profit of the year because unless all the claims are paid out, insurer cannot know the actual amount of profit. Since the insurer transacts a continuing business, he cannot know the exact amount of profit at a point. The valuation comes to help the insurer at this stage. The net profit or net loss is estimated through the comparison of net liability at a particular point of time with the available funds at that time. If the funds are more than the net liability, a part of the excess can be distributed as a bonus or as a dividend to shareholders. How much will be distributed depends upon the amount of surplus at that time.

THE CALCULATION PROCESS

The valuation involves calculation of net liabilities apart from this main process, the valuation also includes comparison of insurance funds with the net liabilities during a particular period. The comparison will reveal the surplus or deficiency which is treated accordingly. If the fund is more than the net liabilities (reserves), it would be a case of surplus. Similarly, deficiency will occur where the insurance fund is less than the net liabilities.

1. Calculation of Net Liabilities

The Net liabilities may be calculated with prospective method or retrospective method. Whatsoever method may be applied, the result will be the same provided the past assumptions are also applicable to future estimations. In other words, if deaths occurred as anticipated, interest earned is also as expected and expenses are also incurred according to assumptions, there will be no difference between the value accumulated (retrospective reserve) and the present value required (prospective reserve) to meet the obligations. This brings out the fact that policy value would be the same whether obtained retrospectively from past experience or prospectively on future anticipation. But in practice, the assumed rate of mortality has been observed more than the anticipated mortality. Similarly, the assumed rate of interest has been lesser than the future rate of interest. Thus, the retrospective value has been more than the prospective values.

It has been made clear while explaining the relative merits of these methods that the valuation is made on the gross premium. In the chapter of reserve we have dealt with the calculation of reserve on the basis of net premium. But, so far determination of solvency is concerned, reserve or value is calculated on gross premium where we take into account not only mortality and interest but expenses also.

(*a*) **Prospective Value**

The excess of present value of future claims over the present value of the future premiums is called net liability. There will always be excess because the net liability is calculated after some time of the commencement of the policies. The calculation has been explained in detail in the chapter of reserve. There is only difference of gross and net premium. Here the value is calculated on the basis of gross premium. The method reveals the net liabilities up to which the Insurer must have sufficient funds.

VALUATION BALANCE SHEET AS ON 31ST MARCH 1983

Liabilities	*Rs.*		*Assets* *Rs.*
Net Liabilities	90,17,20,00,000	Life Insurance Fund	98,00,38,00,000
	783,18,00,000		
	9800,38,00, 000		9800,38,00,000

The above balance sheet reveals that the Life Insurance Fund is Rs. 783.18 crores more than the net liabilities.

(*b*) **Retrospective Method**

Under this method, the premium is accumulated every year with certain rate of interest after meeting the claims. The accumulated excess is called life values (reserves). The actual accumulated funds should always be more than the assumed reserves. But if the insurer has experienced heavier mortality than what he expected, earned less interest, or incurred greater expenses, the excess of his income over outgo would be less than what it ought to be. If it were so, the insurer's position is not solvent because if this state of affairs were left to continue, he would not be able to meet his future obligations. Similarly, if his experience had been favourable, he would have accumulated more than what he ought to have accumulated and this difference is therefore the 'Surplus'.

1. Bases of Valuation of Net Liabilities

While calculating rates of premium, the insurer bases his calculation on mortality rates, interest, expenses and bonus loading on past experience. But, at the time of valuation of net liabilities, assumptions would have been changed completely and the estimation of 'net liabilities' would be erroneous. Therefore, it is very essential to calculate the 'net liabilities' only on the future estimation which are expected to occur because the net liabilities do not represent past; it reveals the future responsibilities. These bases of calculation of net liabilities are discussed in the following sections.

(*i*) **The Mortality Rate**

The morality rate is assumed that which is likely to be experienced in future during the policy. The past mortality which is revealed recently is modified in the light of present conditions and future prospects of the mortality rates.

(*ii*) **Rate of Interest**

Like mortality rates we are not depending upon the past assumed rate; but we should base our valuation on such rates which may reasonably be anticipated. The expectation of future earnings is well regarded although some conservative rates are used for valuation.

(*iii*) **Rate of Expenses**

The appropriate expenses should be assumed. Past expenditure ratios may not be the correct figure of valuation. The future expense may be unduly heavy, if businesses are expanding or viceversa is also true. All the classes of expenses are well anticipated for purpose of valuation.

(*iv*) **Bonus Rate**

Premiums on the participating policies are loaded with bonus extras. In exchange of the bonus loading, the participating policyholders are getting bonus. At last, past years' bonus should be distributed. So the bonus loading must assume at least previous loading.

2. Calculation of Life Insurance Fund

The Life Fund is obtained from the revenue account of the insurer. The previous fund is shown in the credit side of the revenue account in respect of life insurance. During the period, all incomes including premiums, interest, rents, etc., are credited to the revenue account and all payments, like policy claims, annuities, management expenses etc., are debited to the account. The difference of the two sides will disclose the Life Insurance Funds available to insurer at the end of the period. The excess of the incomes over the expenditures during the year will disclose the life insurance fund of the year. Thus, the Life Insurance Fund at a particular date is the accumulation of previous excesses of actual total income to total expenditures in respect of life insurance business. Here, it should be noticed that the Life Insurance Fund is different from Life Insurance Reserve. The Fund reveals the actual amount with the insurer whereas the Reserve discloses the net liabilities of the insurer. Reserve ensures what amount should be with the insurer to pay the claims and Fund replies what amount is with the insurer.

3. Comparison of Net Labilities with Life Insurance Fund

The valuation in India is done in every alternate year because the process of valuation of 'net liabilities' is very different and it cannot be estimated every year. The insurance Act has provided that the valuation should be done once in a period of 3 years. However, the Life Insurance Corporation of India has taken a liberal attitude and makes the valuation once within 2 years. The last valuation was done on 31st March, 1977 and the next valuation will be on 31st March, 1979:

The comparison of net liabilities with Life Insurance Fund will disclose surplus or deficiency. If the former is less than the latter one, surplus is created and when the former is more than the latter one, deficiency is arrived.

Treatment of Deficiency

When deficiency arises, the insurer has to apply some drastic actions such as the expenses are curtailed, profitable investments are sought and bonus is not declared. The premium rates are increased. But increase in premium rates causes reduction in business.

Treatment of Surplus

The surplus arrived on can be distributed among the policyholders and shareholders only after certain provisions. The provisions may be General Contingency Fund, Dividend Equalisation Fund, Bonus Equalisation Fund, and Taxation Fund. As is clear from their names, these funds are provided for meeting certain objectives, *e.g.*, constant rate of bonus to the policyholders or dividend to shareholders.

SOURCES OF SURPLUS

1. Excess Interest

While calculating the net liabilities, a certain rate of interest is assumed; but if the insurer gets more than this rate, the surplus is originated. In other words, the excess of actual interest over the assumed one gives rise to surplus. Sale of securities at more than the book value also contributes the surplus.

2. Savings from Mortality

If the actual rate of mortality is lesser than the assumed rate of mortality, surplus is created by the excess amount. It has been observed that the mortality rate assumed in calculation of policy value has always been lesser than the actual death-rate. Had the former been higher than the latter one, there would be a deficiency, but the insurer, to avoid the deficiency, assumes a very conservative rate of interest.

The savings from mortality act in three ways to induce surplus. Firstly, lesser death causes higher amount of premium which shall be received from the persons more than the expected one. Secondly, lesser payment of claims on account of lesser death causes Surplus to a great extent. Thirdly, the extra-premium will not be required due to death less than the expected one.

3. Savings from Loading

A certain amount is added to the net premium to obtain the office premium for meeting the expenses of the insurance-business. If this assumed loading is more than the actual expenses, surplus will arise.

4. Lapses and Surrenders

Early termination of policy during policy-life may give rise to surplus, if the surrender value given is less than the reserve accumulated or amount of surrender to be given. Actually, this is not surplus because the excess amount will be required to meet the losses on account of surrender.

5. Bonus Loading

On participating policies, bonus loading is added to declare at least a certain minimum rate of bonus. The unutilised portion of it along with interest thereon is added to surplus.

Miscellaneous Sources

Saving in various types of annuity contract may give rise to surplus. Similarly in pure-endowment or Term insurance, some amount may remain unpaid, which will be taken as a surplus.

DIFFERENCE BETWEEN SURPLUS AND PROFIT

As the surplus is a cash sum, being the excess of the funds over the net liabilities brought out by the valuation, the surplus is not the same thing as profits. After having sent some of the surplus to these various funds, what the insurer is left with may be called 'profit'. Thus, to estimate profit, surplus is calculated. The difference between the two arises on account of provisions for various funds.

Divisible Profit

After setting aside certain portion of surplus to various funds, the profit is to be distributed. The supreme consideration for this distribution is legal requirements. For example, Section 28 of the LIC Act, 1956 requires that not less than 95 per cent of the surplus of the Corporation shall be allocated to or reserved for the policy-holders of the Corporation.

BASES OF ALLOTMENT OF PROFIT

The losses of allotment of profit are simplicity, equity, suitability, popularity and flexibility.

1. Simplicity

It is desirable from the expense point of view and from understanding point of view.

2. Equity

The most important principle is 'Equity'. Due weightage should be given to each policyholder according to his contribution to surplus. But in practice, this cannot be rigidly adhered to. So, a broad equity or rough justice in distribution of divisible surplus is taken into account.

3. Suitability

A system of distribution of surplus should be suitable according to the nature, size and age of the insurance business.

4. Popularity

The system should not be confirmed merely to the acturial undersanding but it should be popularly known to the policyholders.

5. Flexibility

The better system of divisible profit will be that which can be changed or altered according to the requirement.

In practice hundered per cent equity is not possible. So the flexibility, simplicity and popularity are generally practised.

METHODS OF DISTRIBUTION OF SURPLUS

The divisible profit is to be distributed amongst the policyholders and shareholders. The main problem is distribution of profit to policyholders. Two methods (*i*) Uniform Bonus Plan and (*ii*) Contributory Plan are assured while distributing the profit to policyholders.

1. Uniform Bonus Plan

Under this method, a uniform bonus rate is given to all policyholders of a particular type. The bonus rate is based on the policy amount. For example, Rs. 25 per thousand on whole life policies have been declared as bonus. Thus, the only equity with this plan is the amount of policy. Higher the policy amount, higher will be the bonus amount to a policy. The bonus rate is determined simply by calculating the total amount of divisible profit and multiplying it with the amount of insurance of Rs. 1,000 and again dividing the whole sum by the amount of insurance under participating policies, at the time of valuation. Thus the bonus per thousand can easily be calculated for a particular period. Thus, this system is popular, simple and flexible, but it is not very much equitous or it makes no distinction between policies on the basis of their contribution to the surplus. However, some persons argued that taking the long term duration, it would be equitous because in the early period of the policy when his contribution is smaller, he is getting higher amount and at the later stage when his contribution will be higher he will be getting lesser amount of bonus. Thus taking the total duration of policy, he is getting equal share of his contribution.

2. Contribution Method

The essential principle of this method is that the divisible surplus should be allotted to the various policies in proportion to the individual contribution of each policy to the surplus. The higher the contribution of a policy, the higher should be the amount of bonus declared on it. Since there are several sources of surplus, contribution of each source should be analysed. For this purpose two things have to be taken into account.

1. The contribution of a particular type of policy to the total surplus.
2. Contribution of each source of surplus of a particular policy to the total surplus is to be determined. Then, on the basis of the contribution of each policy, the surplus is allocated. The calculation has been made simple by taking only three sources of surplus viz. Mortality, Interest arid Expenses savings. This is called 'Three Factor Contribution Plan' . Sometimes, mortality saving is ignored and only two factors viz. excess interest and loading saving are taken into consideration for determining the amount of contribution of each policy.

This method observes mostly the equity principle. But in practice, the calculation is very hard and complicated. Therefore, it is not popular.

CLASSIFICATION OF BONUS

The bonus can be classified on the bases of calculation, resting of bonus and results of calculation.

1. Bonus on the Basis of Calculation

There are two methods of calculation of bonus. Therefore, the bonus may be either uniform bonus or contributory bonus. Where the rate of bonus varies according to the policy amount, that is known uniform bonus and where the contribution method is applied the bonus is known as contributory bonus.

2. Bonus on the Basis of Vesting

The bonus may vest as soon it is declared or after a period when the declared bonus is payable soon as it is declared, it is known as the immediate bonus and when the bonus does not become a liability of the insurer as soon as it is declared, it is called as deferred bonus. In the latter case bonus is payable only when particular conditions are fulfilled. The bonus having already been declared is only in the nature of one of contingent liabilities. The bonus remains with the insurer and ultimately is shared by those policy-holders who satisfy the given condition.

3. Bonus on the Basis of Results

Under this category, bonus is determined on the basis of actual results or fixed on an adhoc basis. When the actual valuation has taken place, the bonus declared is known Final Bonus, and the bonus declared before the acturial valuation is known as Interim Bonus. It is a rough estimation of bonus that will take place in future. It is required where the policy matures before the valuation takes place on the basis of guess the bonus for the interim period is declared.

BONUS OPTIONS

1. Cash Bonus

Under this plan, the bonus when declared is paid to the assured in cash and the original sum assured alone is payable at claim. However, the cash bonus can be converted into other options of bonus.

2. Reversionary Bonus

The bonus is allotted as a uniform percentage addition to the sum assured or sum assured plus existing bonus addition and is payable along with the sum assured according to the terms of the policy. The former case is known as 'Simple Reversionary Bonus' and the latter is known as 'Compound Reversionary Bonus'. The former is simple popular and flexible as every time a bonus is distributed some addition is made to the policy amount. The compound reversionary becomes more equitable but is hard to calculate. So, the simple reversionary bonus is practically used today.

3. Reduction in Premium Bonus

When the bonus is not added to the assured sum but is utilised for permanent reduction in the future premium payable, it is called 'Reduction in Premium Bonus'. As soon as the yearly bonus will be equal to the yearly premiums payable, the policy becomes paid up and no future premiums are required. After this point, the additional increase in bonus may be added to the policy amount.

4. Accumulation at Interest Bonus

The bonus on the policy is kept in deposit with the insurer. The insurer gives a fixed rate of interest on the deposited amount and the insured at any time can withdraw the accumulated bonus or can use it for payment of future premiums.

5. Endowment Option

Under this option, the bonus is accumulated with a certain rate of interest and when the accumulated value of the policy becomes equal to the policy amount, the policy amount is paid in full before maturity. The accumulated value of the policy will increase with the amount of bonus reserves and interest thereon. Thus, before maturity at any time the accumulated value of the policy will be equal to the policy amount.

In India, the Corporation declares simple reversionary bonus at the interval of one year. The bonus can also be used for payment of future premiums.

QUESTIONS

1. What are the factors of valuation? How is valuation done?
2. What do you-mean by profit in L.I.C. and how it is estimated and distributed?
3. What are the various option of Bonus?

16

POLICY CONDITION

The policy conditions are studied in five forms:

1. Conditions relating to commencement of risk,
2. Conditions of Premium,
3. Conditions relating to continuation of policies,
4. Lapse-conditions, and
5. Claims conditions.

CONDITIONS RELATING TO COMMENCEMENT OF RISK

1. Commencement of Risk

The letter of acceptance is not a cover note, it only intimates that the risk will commence when the first premium is offered to and accepted by the insurer. If premium was paid along with the proposal form, the date of letter of acceptance will be the date of commencement of risk. After acceptance of risk, policy is issued. The policy contains terms and conditions of the insurance and is a document which can be used as a proof of insurance.

2. Proof of Age

The proof of age must be produced at the time of proposal or immediately after the proposal because the rate of premium depends upon the age of the life assured. The insurer does not withhold the issue of the policy for want of proof of age, but does not admit any claim unless the age is proved to the satisfaction of the insurer. However, if it is subsequently found that the age at entry was mentioned lower than the correct age, the assured sum is reduced to such amount as would have been purchased at the true age.

If the actual age comes out to be lower than the stated age, the difference is either refunded or adjusted towards future premium or policy amount. The proof of age is very essential at the time of proposal in the term policies. Multi-purpose policy, children's Defered Endowment Assurance, Immediate Annuity and defered annuity, where the life assured has not completed 20 years or where the life to be assured has completed 50 years of age or the proposal is under the Salary Saving Scheme.

CONDITIONS OF PREMIUMS

1. Payment of Premiums

The premium rate is calculated annually, but for the convenience of the assured, it can be paid half-yearly, quarterly or even monthly. It should be remembered that these premiums are not just the portion of yearly premium because the insurer losses interest on the unpaid premium of a year and expenses are involved for frequent calculation of premium. When premiums are not annual but fractional and if death takes place before all the premiums have fallen due for the current policy year, the corporation deducts the unpaid instalments from policy year, the corporation deducts the unpaid instilments from the assured sum at the time of settling the claim.

2. Days of Grace

Premium is paid at or before the due date. But for convenience of the policyholders, certain additional period called days of grace, is allowed to pay, the premium. The insured can pay the premium within the days of grace and the policy would not lapse up to the days of grace. However, the policy will lapse if the due premium is not paid even within the days of grace.

One calendar month but not less than 30 days of grace is allowed for payment of yearly, half-yearly and quarterly premiums, and fifteen days for payment of monthly premiums. The days of grace are to be counted excluding the due date of the premium. When the days of grace expire on a Sunday or a holiday observed by the office of the insurer where premiums are payable, the premium must be paid on the following working day to keep the policy in force. The insurer is not responsible for any delay in remittance caused through the post office or otherwise.

3. Premium Notice

In order that the policyholder may not forfeit the benefit of his policy, notice of premiums falling due will be regularly sent to him except in the case of policies under which the mode of payment of premium is monthly where no such notice is required, the insurer is not bound to give any such notice and the want of it cannot be admitted as an excuse for not paying the due premium in time.

CONDITIONS RELATING TO THE CONTINUE POLICIES

1. Indisputable Clause

In order to protect the interests of the assured, indisputable clause is added which provides that the policies shall be indisputable after a state period, viz., two years from the date of issue except for non-payment of premiums or for fraud. Section 45 of the insurance Act has provided that the policy will not be disputed on ground of unintentional misstatement, misrepresentation or non-disclosure of a material fact after two years of the issue of the policy. However, on ground of fraud it can be disputed at any time during the currency of the policy.

2. Alterations in Policies

The insurer permits certain alterations in terms and conditions of the policies at the request of the policyholders. The insurer reserves the right to decline such requests without assigning any reason. Alteration may be change: in class or term, reduction in sum assured, increase in sum assured, change in mode of premium payment, splitting up of a policy into two or more policies and so on. The insurer, generally, does not permit alterations which increase the amount of risk to the insurer.

3. Exclusion

Ordinarily, the insurer does not assure the hazardous occupation. If any insured person has taken up or intends to take up hazardous occupation, he has to pay extra-premium. The hazardous occupations have been listed, by the Corporation in India. The policies issued at standard rates are free from all restrictions to change in occupation. However, the policies issued to students are on the term of hazardous occupation because a student's occupation is not determined till he completes his education and hence the degree of risk is not known. Standard premium rates are not sufficient to cover the risk of war mortality, therefore, war clause is included in such policies where it is mentioned that if the death will occur due to war the liability of the insurer is limited to the premium paid or surrender value whichever is higher. The total sum assured will not be paid in this case.

4. Lost Policy

The insured must inform to the insurer whenever the policy is lost or destroyed. On the satisfactory evidence of loss or destruction, the insurer will issue a duplicate copy after advertising the fact and will charge the assured the fee for issuing the duplicate copy.

5. Loans

The insurer may grant loan on the security of the surrender value of the policies. In India, loans are granted on unencumbered policies up to 90 per cent of the surrender value in case of policies which are in force for full sum assured and 85 per cent of the surrender value in the case of policies which are paid up being in force for reduced sum assured. In case, policies are due to mature within three years a larger percentage may be granted. The minimum amount for which a loan can be granted is Rs. 150 and the rate of interest is 7½ per cent per annum payable half-yearly. Loans are not granted on certain type of policies where surrender values are not accumulated.

6. Nomination

According to Section 39 of the Insurance Act, 1938, the holder of a policy of life insurance on his own life may, when effecting the policy or at any time before the policy matures for payment, nominate a person or persons to whom the policy money secured by the policy shall be paid in the event of his death. Nominee is the person named by the policyholder to whom the policy amount may be paid if the policy amount is payable on death and the nominee is alive when the life assured expires. In absence of any of these, the nominee does not acquire a right in the policy. If policy matures by expiry of time, the policy amount is payable to the insured himself and not to the nominee.

Notice of Nomination

When such nomination is made for the first time, the corporation will register it even if no notice is served, provided the nomination is in order. But for all cancellation, changes and for all nominations subsequent to the first, the Corporation insists on a notice of nomination in the light of Sec. 39 of the Ins. Act, 1938, otherwise it will not be liable for any payment.

7. Assignment

A transfer or assignment of a policy of life insurance, whether with or without consideration, may be made only by an endorsement upon the policy itself or by a separate instrument, signed in either case by the transferor or by the assignor or has duly authorised agent and attested at least by one witness, specifically setting forth the fact of transfer or assignment. The transfer or assignment shall be complete and effectual upon the execution of such endorsement or instrument only attested until a notice in writing of the transfer or assignment and either the said endorsement or instrument itself or a copy thereof have been delivered to the insurer. The priority of claims will go by the date on which the notice of assignment is served on the Corporation. The insurer has to record the fact of the transfer or assignment and has to give a written acknowledgment of receipt of such notice. As a result of the assignment, all the rights and liabilities under the policy will be transferred to the assignee subject to any condition contained in the assignment.

The assignment can be of two kinds

l. Absolute and 2. Condition. An absolute assignment is an assignment where all rights, title and interest of assignor in the policy pass to assignee without reversion to the former or his estate in any event. Under such an assignment, the policy rests absolutely in the assignee and forms part of his estate on his death. A conditional assignment provides that on the happening of a specified event which does not depend on the will of the owner, the assignment shall be either wholly or partially inoperative. An example of the conditional assignment is one which reverts to the assured in the event of his surviving the date of maturity or in the event of his being alive on the death of the assignee.

8. Suicide

In the event of suicide committed by the assured within one year from the date of commencement, whether insured or not, at the time, the liability of the Corporation shall be limited to the extent of the beneficial interest which any person shall prove to the satisfaction of the. Corporation to have been acquired in the policy bona fide and for valuable consideration, of which notice in writing shall, at least one calendar months previous to death, have been given to the, within mentioned, divisional office of the Corporation and save and except to that extent, this policy shall be void and all claims to any benefit, advantage or interest in the funds of the Corporation by virtue of this policy shall cease.

9. Double Accident Benefit

This provides for payment of double of the sum assured on death by accident. If the life assured sustain any bodily injury resulting solely and directly from accident caused by outward violent and visible means and if such injury within 90 days of its occurrence, solely directly and independently of all other intervening causes results in the death of the life assured, double of the sum assured will become payabie. The benefit is available only to limited proposals. The aggregate limit of assurance under this policy is Rs. 1,00,000.

10. Disability Benefit

This benefit will be granted to all lives assured under all plans except pure endowment, term assurances, children's Differed Endowment, Deferred and Retirement Annuities. Life assured disabled by accident from earning his livelihood, will be exempted from paying premiums on his policy, falling due after the date of disablement. This benefit is granted on the first Rs. 20,000 of assurance. The example of permanent disablement are loss of sight of both eyes or amputation of both hands at or above the wrists or amputation of both feet and hands.

11. Extented Disability Benefit

It provides for waiver of premiums and also for payment of an amount equal to the sum assured on permanent total disability as a result of an accident. The example of permanent total disability is given above. This benefit is available by paying extra premium of Rs. 2/- per thousand of sum assured.

LAPSE CONDITIONS

1. Lapse of Policies

The insurer shall remain liable for the payment of the claim so far the assured continues to pay the premiums when they fall due. If the policyholder fails to pay any of the due premiums within the days of grace, the insurance liability ordinarily ceases under the policy and the contract comes to an end. Thus the policy is lapsed and all the benefits related to the policy are terminated. The insurer, however, provides certain alternatives to help the insured at the time of lapsation.

2. Revival of Lapsed Policies

If a policy lapses by non-payment of premium within the days of grace, it may be revived to the full policy amount at any time during the life time of the life assured, but within a period of five years from the due date of the first unpaid premium and before the date of maturity. The revival is possible within six months from the due date of the first unpaid premium without evidence of health on payment of the premiums in arrears with interest at the rate of 7 ½ per cent per annum compounded half yearly. The revival after the first six months from the due date of the first unpaid premium but before five years from the due date of the first unpaid premium will be effective only on satisfactory production of evidence of health and habits of the life assured and no adverse change in personal or Family History or occupation.

3. Special Revival Scheme

Many policyholders find it difficult to pay the arrears of premiums with interest to revive their policies. For them the special revival scheme is beneficial to gain the cover of insurance. Under this scheme, the date of commencement of policy will be fixed by dating back the policy. The period for which the policy will be dated back depends upon the amount of premium paid. The plan and period of insurance will be the same as those under the original policy. The revival will be effected ordinarily by issue of a fresh policy.

The special revival is possible only when all of the following conditions are fulfilled.

1. The policy must not have acquired surrender value.
2. Period from the date of lapse must not be less than 6 months and not over two years.
3. Such a revival is not allowed more than once under the same policy.

4. Surrender Value

When the assured is unable to revive his policy, he can surrender his policy and can get cash surrender value. With this payment, the contract comes to an end and the assured will get the cash value without any liability to pay further premiums. In India, the Corporation has guaranteed surrender value if the premiums have been paid for at least two years or to the extent of one-tenth of the total number of premiums stipulated for in the policy provided such one-tenth exceeds one full year's premium. The minimum surrender value allowable under this policy is equal to 30 per cent of the total amount of the, within mentioned, premium paid excluding the premiums for the first year and all extra premium. The percentage increases along with the increase in duration of premium payment because the amount of the surrender on any policy depends on its reserve value. Thus, on such policies which do not have any reserve, no surrender value is allowed.

Since January 1st, 1976, the provision for non-forfeiture clause has been amended.

1. If the premiums under the policy have been paid for a period of five years or 1/4 of the original premium paying period of the policy, whichever is less but subject to the condition that minimum 3 years' premiums are paid.
2. The paid up value under the policy is not less than Rs. 250 (excluding of attached bonuses) for policies whereunder original sum assured is Rs. 1,000 or more and Rs. 100 exclusive of attached bonus where the original sum assured is less than Rs. 1,000.

The above non-forfeiture conditions would apply to proposals completed on and after 1-1-1976.

Since April, 1980, the above conditions have been changed. Surrender value is secured only when the policy was continued for three years.

5. Extended Term Insurance

If a premium remains unpaid at the end of the days of grace and the policy has been in force for at least three years, the insurance will continue as paid up for the full sum assured up to a period called term.

The term depends upon the amount of premium paid. During this period, if the life assured dies payment will made up to the full amount. But, if the assured survives the period, no payment is made. Actually, the amount of premium paid before the lapsation is utilised as a single premium or purchasing term insurance and the duration of the term insurance upon the amount of premium paid for meeting as single premium.

6. Automatic Premium Loan

The assured may use the option of automatic premium loan before the maturity of the policy. In this case, if the assured is unable to pay the premiums the insurer will not allow the policy to lapse but will automatically pay the premiums out of the net surrender value. The assured can repay the unpaid premiums with interest at any time while the policy is so kept in force without furnishing evidence of insurability. If the whole of surrender value is exhausted by advances on account of payment of premium, the policy will lapse and can be revived only after payment of all the premiums unpaid and interest thereon at the rate of 7½ per cent per annum compounded half yearly. This option can be exercised only when premiums of consecutive three years have been paid.

In this case one benefit is also available that if after at least three years, premiums have been paid, the assured dies without payment of the premium within six months from the due date of the first unpaid premium, the policy amount will be paid subject to deduction of unpaid premiums with interest thereon up to the date of death.

7. Reduced Paid-up Insurance

When the policyholder is unable to pay further premiums and does not want cash immediately he can paid up the policy. The sum assured under the policy is reduced in the same proportion as the amount of premiums paid bears to the total premiums payable. The reduced sum assured is payable according to the original term of the policy. Where uniform premiums are payable, as in the case of endowment or whole life limited payment assurances, this proportion is easily ascertained. The paid up value of whole life policy is calculated as per the formula $1-\frac{dx}{d(x+n)}$ sum assured, where dx is the premium for the age when the policy was affected, and $d(x+n)$ is the premium for the present age of the life assured when policy is surrendered.

CLAIMS CONDITIONS

1. Settlement of Claims

The policy amount becomes payable either on the assured's death during the term of insurance or on his surviving till the end of the term, *i.e.,* on maturity. In case of death claims proof of death, proof of title and age proof are essential. In case of maturity proof of title and age proof are required. The age proof is required only when the age was not admitted before to the claims. In maturity claim, the policyholder is generally advised well before the actual date of maturity in order that the necessary papers may be completed. The proof of death may be certificate from the doctor who attended the deceased in his last illness, or certificate of Registration of the Death by the Official Registrar of Deaths, or Certificate from employer identifying the deceased or if the deceased was not in service a certificate of identity from a responsible person acquainted with the deceased. In case of assignment and nomination, or assured having the policy right, no proof of title is required. In other cases, proof of title is essential, the probate of Will or succession certificate or Administration General's Certificate may be used as a proof of title.

2. Settlement Options

The claim amount may be paid in cash or in instalment. The instalment payment may be of different types payment of interest annually for a particular period or up to survived and the sum assured at a time may be paid. Annuity may be purchased for life or for a particular period and life thereafter.

QUESTIONS

1. What are the various conditions relating to commencement of risk, payment of premium and continuation of policies?
2. Discuss in detail the conditions of lapsation and claims.

17

LIFE INSURANCE FOR THE UNDER—PRIVILEGED

Under-privileged persons are those persons whose incomes are too low to purchase life insurance policies, who have no adequate provision for old age and family security and who become incapable to earn adequate income due to accident injury or disease. For them, four alternatives are generally provided in life insurance, which are *(i)* Industrial Life Insurance, *(ii)* Group Life Insurance Policies, *(iii)* Disability Benefit Policies, and *(iv)* Pension Plans.

INDUSTRIAL LIFE INSURANCE

Industrial Life Insurance is a form of life insurance specially designed to meet the requirements of wage earning population of industry. It may also apply to low income classes of business or even of the population. It may be issued without medical examination. The premiums may be collected by agents on weekly or monthly basis. Industrial insurance should not be confused with social insurance, which means workmen's compensation, employers, liability, etc.

Purpose

The main purpose of industrial life insurance is to provide at least clean up funds to meet lest expenses of the assured. Since, the amount of industrial life insurance is not much, family protection is not always possible. The second aim is to educate the habit of saving amongst the low income group to meet their contingencies. Weekly premium can be easily saved and it may provide funds to create property.

COMPARISON OF INDUSTRIAL AND OTHER FORMS OF LIFE INSURANCE

Industrial insurance is a form of life insurance, therefore, most of the characteristics of life insurance are present in this insurance apart from the following dissimilarities:

(i) The premiums in industrial insurance are payable weekly and monthly whereas in ordinarily life insurance, they are payable annually, semi-annually, quarterly and monthly.

(ii) The premiums, instead of being payable at the office of the insurer are collected in most of the cases at the houses of the assured persons by insurance agents.

(iii) The amount of a policy in industrial insurance is generally not more than Rs. 1,000 whereas in other forms of insurance it is usually more than Rs. 1,000.

(iv) In Industrial insurance, medical examination is not essential, but in other forms of life insurance, medical examination is required in most of the cases.

(v) Industrial insurance is extended to every member of the family. Thus, it covers more areas than the other forms of insurance.

Types of Contracts. The policies issued under this form of the insurance are generally limited payment life or endowment plans because saving element in these plans are maximum.

Cash Values

The Industrial Policy should be in force for a longer period for getting cash or paid up values. It may be from 3 years to 5 years. Extended term assurance is available after payment of premiums for at least six weeks.

Loan Values

Since the servicing cost of the loan is higher and the protection element is elapsed in granting loan, the policy does not bear the provision for loan.

Assignment

Assignment of the Industrial Policy is prohibited because the amount secured may not be useful to the assured in case of assignment.

Indisputable Clause

The industrial policy becomes indisputable after one year of the issue whereas the ordinary life insurance policies become indisputable after two years on any ground except that of fraud and age admission.

Suicide

The suicide waiver clause does not apply to this policy.

Reinstatement

Industrial policies that have been in force more than 5 years and are not more than six months in arrears may usually be reinstated without medical examination.

Conversion of Plan

The industrial policy can be converted into ordinary endowment policy or whole life policy.

Beneficiaries

The beneficiaries of the policy may be usually those persons who got the insurable interest in the life of assured.

Premium Rates

The premium rates in industrial life policies are generally higher than that of ordinary life insurance policies because of higher mortality cost, higher cost of administration and higher lapse rates.

In India, the form of Industrial Insurance Policy is Janata policy which is issued generally to comparatively poorer sections of the society. The maximum amount under this policy is Rs. 1,000, the minimum sum assured is Rs. 250 and the maximum sum assured to a policyholder is Rs. 3,000. The maximum age at entry is limited to 45 years. No medical examination is required up to 35 years. A lapsed policy can be revived during a period of 3 years from the due date without medical examinations. No loans or other benefits are granted on this policy.

Janata Personal Accident Policy

This scheme would benefit industrial workers, domestic servants, road transport operators and the like who are engaged in hazardous jobs.

The scheme is truly a Janata Scheme for anybody between the ages of 16 to 60 can join it. The annual premium is Rs. 12 or one rupee per month. Risk cover is for Rs. 10,000. The scheme is designed to give insurance protection of Rs. 10,000 to the family of any person in case the subscriber is fatally injured and Rs. 200 as cash help for hospital expenses. According to Chairman, G. V. Kapadia of GIC, it is meant for the worker, the office goer, truck operator, rickshaw-puller, students or just anybody. Such a scheme would be a great help to the people, it covers apart from death and hospitalisation, loss of limbs and eyes and disablement.

2. Group Life Insurance

Under this plan a large number of persons are insured by a single policy without medical examination at a low cost. The group consists employees of a common employer, debtors of the same creditor or members of the same trade union. The policy is issued to the employer, creditor or the trade union although the number and information of all the assured lives are mentioned, in the policy.

Minimum Number of Persons Insured

The minimum number to be insured is fixed according to the nature of business, number of employees and methods of contribution. The contributory plan is that where employees are also liable to pay a portion of the premium. In non-contributory plan, only employer pays the whole amount of premium. In non-contributory plan, all the employees should be included under this plan whereas in the contributory plan all employees may not be insisted for contribution. However, 75 per cent of the employees must be covered by this scheme.

Eligibility

Only regular and permanent employees are included under this scheme. Seasonal and part time employees are excluded from this scheme.

Termination of Employment

The employee who is terminated may elect within thirty-one days and without medical examination to take an ordinary policy in his own name.

Group Term Insurance Scheme by Corporation

This scheme is a form of renewable term insurance. In the event of death of life assured while in service, the sum assured is paid to the dependents of the deceased persons. A policy is issued to the employer and each member included in this scheme is given a certificate thereto. The sum assured cannot be assigned or mortgaged.

The scheme is applicable to all the permanent employees of an employer. The amount of insurance to each employee is determined by mutual understanding of the employer and the Corporation. In case of non-contributory scheme all existing permanent employees must join the scheme. The amount of insurance is generally fixed for all employees of a given class. There may be different amounts for a different classes of employees.

Group Insurance for U.P. Government Employees

The U.P. Government has enforced the scheme of group insurance for their gazetted and non-gazetted government servants since March 1, 1976. The scheme will, however, not apply to those State Police Personnel who had already been provided with group insurance cover separately. The members of the teaching community and legal profession in the State had also been brought within the ambit of group insurance scheme earlier.

Under the scheme, each Government servant would be required to subscribe Rs. 10 per month in lieu of which the Life Insurance Corporation of India will pay Rs. 12,000 to the family of the Government servants who die in harness. Otherwise, the employee concerned will, on retirement, be paid his share of money deposited. The employee concern will, on retirement, be paid his share of money deposited by him along with compound interest at the rate of six per cent per annum.

3. Disability Benefit

This benefit is granted to all the lives assured excepting a few policies such as Pure Endowment, the Temporary Assurance, Mortgage Redemption Assurance, Convertible Term Assurance, the deferred Annuity, Retirement Annuity and Restrictive Policies. The benefit is offered free of cost and no premium is charged for the purpose.

The Nature and Extent

If a life assured is disabled by accident from earning, he will be exempted from paying premiums on his policy falling due after the date of disablement. This benefit will be granted only on the first Rs. 20,000 of assurance on a life.

The policy must be in force for the full sum assured at the time the disability occurs. The disability must be result of an accident and must be total and permanent and such that there is no scope to do any work, occupation, or profession. Satisfactory proof of the disability must be furnished to the Corporation within 90 days.

Extended Disability Benefit

The extended disability benefit provides for waiver of premiums and also for payment of an amount equal to the sum assured on permanent total disability as a result of an accident. The accident must occur before the age 60 during the continuation of the policy.

Benefits

1. Payment in monthly instalments spread over 10 years an additional sum equal to the sum assured by the policy, the first instalment becoming payable one month after the date of disablement. However, if the policy becomes a claim before the expiry of the said period, the disability benefit instalments which have not become due will be paid along with the claim.
2. Waiver of payment of future premiums up to an assurance of Rs. 1,00,000.

The annual premium for this benefit is Rs. 2 per thousand.

Conditions

The disability of the Life Assured shall not

1. be caused by intentional self-injury, attempted suicide, insanity or immorality or while the Life Assured is under the influence of intoxicating liquor, drug or narcotic; or
2. taken place as a result of accident while the Life Assured is engaged in aviation or aeronautics in any capacity other than that of fare-paying, part or non-paying passenger; or
3. be caused by injuries resulting from riots, civil commotion, rebellion, war, invasion, hunting, mountaineering, steeple chasing or racing of every kind; or
4. be result from the Life Assured committing any breach of law; or
5. arise from employment of the Life Assured in the armed forces or military service of any country at war.

The disability must be disability which is the result of an accident and must be total and permanent and such that there is neither than nor at any time thereafter any work, occupation or profession that the Life Assured can never sufficiently do or follow to earn or obtain any wages, compensation or profit.

4. Pension Plans

Today several schemes, providing regular pensions to the employees after their retirement, which may continue even after his death, may be for a specified time or during the life time of his wife as was chosen.

Deferred Annuity Plan is the effective method to provide for the pension. The pension plan can be purchased through the employer or it can be purchased individually. In case of non-contributory plan, participation by all the eligible employees in specified categories is compulsory. The existing employees in other categories may be given the option of joining the scheme.

Benefit on Death During Service

If the member dies while in service, all contributions with interest thereon at a rate ascertained by the Corporation are returned to him.

Insurance of Weaker Section of Society

The Government of India has provided insurance to the weaker section of the society to the tune of Rs. 5,000 at the death. Other people may get benefit of this insurance provided they pay Rs. 75 per annum premium to the LIC. Half of the premium will be met by the State Government and Central Government as provided in the budget 1995-96. The amount of insurance has increased to Rs. 10,000 w.e.f. 15-8-96. It has been extended to all types of people who were unable to purchase policies on their lives.

QUESTIONS

1. Discuss the main proviso of Industrial Life Insurance.
2. 'Group Life Insurance is becoming more popular', discuss its appealing feature.
3. 'Disability and Pension Plans are useful to under-privileged,'—comment it.

18

PROGRESS OF LIFE BUSINESS OF LIC

The life insurance was carried on by the private insurances before 1956; but since January 19, 1956, the Life business came under the control and ownership of government. In June 1956, a Bill was passed for establishing Life Insurance Corporation of India, which started functioning since September 1, 1956. The Corporation is a body corporate having perpetual succession and a common seal with powers to acquire, hold and dispose of property and may be its name sue and be sued. There will be not more than 15 members including a Chairman thereof. The Corporation is charged with the main duty to carry on life insurance business. It has one Central Office, 7 Zonal Offices and several Divisional and Branch offices.

Table 18.1 A New Business (1957-1994)

1. New Business **(inclusive of Group Insurance Business)**

(Amount in crores of Rs.)

Business in India			*Business Outside India*	*Total Business*
December 31,	1957	277.67	5.40	283.07
31st March	1963	734.72	11.24	745.96
31st March	1970	1,025.80	10.28	1,036.08
31st March	1974	2,575.01	11.32	3,112.43
31st March	1975	3,100.70	11.73	3,112.43
31st March	1976	5,373.02	12.32	5,385.34
31st March	1980	7,998.16	11.22	8,009.38
31st March	1981	8,787.26	14.41	9,801.67
31st March	1984	11,917.20	18.30	11,945.50
31st March	1985	13,033.38	22.64	13,056.02
31st March	1989	33,473.96	45.74	33,519.70
31st March	1990	43,490.34	100.00	43,590.34
31st March	1994	80,560.88	19.07	80,759.95
31st March	2001	2,03,049.39	179.01	2,03,228.40
31st March	2002	2,88,503.80	212.69	2,88,716.49

Note: *The statutes are now given as per IRDA rules as is attached in the end of this chapter.*

The new business of individual insurance (excluding annuities) has increased from 86.54 lakhs policies in 1990-91 to Rs. 108.88 lakhs policies in 1994-95 and 140-07 policies in 1995-96; amounting to Rs. 2,824 crores, Rs. 55,46,882 crores and Rs. 68,039.16 crores in the respective years. It indicates that the LIC is trying hard to increase its new business at a very rapid speed that is, more than 2 times during the period of five years. The business out of India, increased to Rs. 240.32 crores in 1994-95 under 13 thousand policies. The total individual business touched the minimum of Rs. 1,24,950.63 crores in 2001 and Rs. 1,92,784.96 in 2002.

Table 18.1B New Business Individual Insurance (Excluding Annuities)
(No. of policies in lakhs; sum assured in crores of Rs.)

	In India		*Out of India*		*Total*	
Year	*No. of*	*Sum*	*No. of*	*Sum*	*No. of*	*Sum*
1990-91	86.45	28139.07	0.09	100.03	86.54	28239.10
1991-92	92.38	32064.44	0.10	131.86	92.48	32196.30
1992-93	99.58	35956.82	0.10	158.98	99.68	36115.80
1993-94	107.26	41813.83	0.12	199.07	107.38	42012.90
1994-95	108.75	55228.50	0.13	240.32	108.88	55468.82
1995-96	110.21	51815.54	0.13	255.99	110.34	52071.53
1996-97	122.68	56740.50	0.12	253.44	122.81	56993.94
1997-98	133.11	63617.69	0.14	310.14	133.25	63927.83
1998-99	148.44	75316.28	0.13	289.98	148.57	75606.26
1999-2000	169.77	91214.25	0.13	276.69	169.89	91490.94
2000-2001	196.57	124771.62	0.08	179.01	196.65	124950.63
2001-2002	224.91	192572.27	0.08	212.69	225.00	192784.96
2002-2003	242.68	179.51	0.10	298.95	242.79	179.81

Table 18.1C
New Business Progress under Group Insurance (Including Group Gratuity and GSLI) Scheme

	New Schemes			*New Business under existing Schemes*		*Existing Members*		*Total*	
Year	*No. of schemes*	*No. of Member (in lakhs)*	*Sum Assured Rs. in crores*	*No. (in lakhs)*	*Sum Assured Rs. in crores*	*No. in lakhs*	*Increases in Sum Assured Rs. in crores*	*Renewable of Term Insurance Rs. in crores*	*Total Sum Assured Rs. in crores*
1990-91	11548	17.08	3392.05	11.61	1,257.56	112.89	1,844.90	19,417.57	25,912.08
1991-92	12293	34.83	3837.23	4.97	1,221.66	116.71	2,443.32	21,439.57	28,941.78
1992-93	6465	26.49	2923.43	11.63	1,841.13	139.63	3,682.25	31,459.84	39,906.65
1993-94	6529	9.94	2382.77	9.58	835.58	188.60	1,123.11	34,687.42	38,723.88
1994-95	6772	10.49	2773.06	4.85	468.30	195.47	1,346.29	46,064.20	50,651.85
1995-96	9078	11.77	2657.22	8.18	923.32	207.29	2,769.95	56,368.01	62,718.50
1996-97	8381	18.89	3237.59	12.08	718.03	192.81	2,154.11	56,582.15	62,691.88
1997-98	8640	15.80	3692.24	9.43	867.18	201.95	2,601.54	67,987.26	75,148.22
1998-99	8832	15.84	3793.93	5.31	541.21	195.56	1,895.53	63,327.47	69,558.14
1999-2000	9266	17.59	3571.12	4.95	632.78	212.39	1,927.38	60,488.15	66,619.43
2000-2001	8492	14.91	4563.20	3.95	739.15	195.94	2,217.45	70,614.86	78,134.66
2001-2002	5957	21.57	6703.08	3.73	752.62	221.88	3,296.55	77,749.49	88,501.74

The, renewable term insurance, under group insurance, has, gone up from Rs. 19,417.57 crores in 1990-91 to Rs. 46,064.20 crores in 1994-95, whereas the sum assured has increased from Rs. 25,912.08 crores in 1990-91 to Rs. 50,651.85 crores in 1994-95. During 1994-95 many new schemes of group insurance have been added to the extent of 6772 amounting to Rs. 2773-06 crores, covering 10-49 lakhs people. The total business under the schemes increased to the maximum of Rs. 78,134.66 crores in 2001 and Rs. 88,50l.74 crores in 2002.

Table 18.1D New Business Progress under Group Superannuation Schemes

Year	New Schemes		New Members		Existing Members		Total	
	No. of Schemes	No. of Members	Annuities per annum	Number	Annuity per annum	Number	Increase in amounts	Annuities per annum
1990-91	275	12165	5.49	5036	2.28	176317	2.54	10.31
1991-92	306	15028	6.78	7559	3.42	215263	2.10	12.30
1992-93	249	28411	9.10	6298	3.01	234662	2.31	14.42
1993-94	273	31695	11.65	10487	3.85	271480	2.67	18.17
1994-95	328	31299	14.85	9407	4.46	313662	4.93	24.24
1995-96	353	75692	49.34	12384	4.52	330906	5.47	59.33
1996-97	373	125272	78.42	9676	5.53	419156	8.92	92.87
1997-98	393	33143	122.45	9401	8.63	530000	13.92	145.00
1998-99	369	51592	80.92	10902	17.10	691101	34.40	132.42
1999-2000	323	64004	82.62	11762	20.24	733123	36.06	138.92
2000-2001	408	93695	84.35	4908	23.96	785168	37.80	146.11
2001-2002	427	59814	92.14	2135	26.69	918341	44.21	163.35

The number of existing members under group super-annuation schemes has increased from 176317 in 1990-91 to 313662 in 1994-95 *i.e.*, by more than 15 times, but the amount of total annuity increased only by more than 2 times from Rs. 10.31 crores in 1990-91 to Rs. 24.24 crores in 1994-95. It shows that the Corporation is trying to increase the number of assured people under this scheme. It has increased to Rs. 146.11 crores in 2001 and Rs. 163.35 crores in 2002.

Business in India

The new business in India has tremendously increased during the period of 25 years. It has gone up from Rs. 277.67 crores in 1957, to Rs. 734.72 crore in 1963 and to Rs. 1,025.80 crores in 1970 and again to Rs. 8,787.26 crores in 1980-81 and Rs. 43,490.34 crores in 1989-90 and Rs. 80,560.88 crores in 1993-94. Thus, it had shown a satisfactory progress so far new business was concerned upto 31 March 1990 from Rs. 13,033.38 crores in 1985. It has gone to Rs. 2,88,503.80 crore in 2002.

Business outside India

The new business outside did not rise satisfactorily. It has gone up from Rs. 5.40 crores in 1957. Rs. 11.73 crores in 1975 and to Rs. 14.41 crores in 1981, and Rs. 28.30 crores in 1984. The cause of the lesser rate of increase was that the Corporation has to compete with other concerns outside India whereas in India it is a monopolistic concern. However, it improved in 1989-90 when it rose to Rs. 100.00 crores and Rs. 199.07 crores in 1993-94 and Rs. 212.69 crore in 2002.

Total Business

The total new business had also gone up significantly from Rs. 283.07 crores in 1957 to Rs. 745.96 crores in 1963 to Rs. 2,586.33 crores in 1974 and further to Rs. 3,112.43 crores in 1975 and to Rs. 5,385.34 crores in 1976; but it declined to Rs. 5,119.23 crores in 1977 and increased to Rs. 8,009.38 crores in 1980, Rs. 9,801.67 crores in 1981 and Rs. 13,056.02 crores in 1985. It touched the highest of Rs. 43,590.34 crores in 1989-90 and Rs. 80,759.95 crores in 1993-94 and Rs. 2,03,228.40 crores in 2001 and Rs. 2,88,716.49 crore in 2002.

2. Average amount per policy

The average amount per policy has also been rising constantly in India and outside India. The average policies has increased from Rs. 3,425 in 1957 to Rs. 7,345 in 1970 and further to Rs. 9,807 in 1975, Rs. 13,041 in 1980, Rs. 14,789 in 1981. Rs. 1,99,134 in 1985, Rs. 39,125 in 1994 and Rs. 50,945 in 1995. Thus, the average sum assured has risen by about 12.3 times during the period of last 30 years. The growth in average sum per policy was not as fast as the sum assured had risen. The rise in the average sum outside India was higher than the rise in India. The total average sum assured has also risen more than 12.4 times during this period. The sum assured per policy went upto Rs. 63,539 in 2001 and Rs. 85,682 in 2002.

Table 18.2 Average sum Assured per Policy (New Business) Individual

	India	*Outside*	*Total*
1963	4179	11834	4220
1970	7345	22055	7394
1974	9344	24518	9378
1975	9807	27985	9848
1976	10502	30750	10581
1980	13041	40129	13077
1981	14789	39020	14835
1984	18541	57439	18622
1985	19913	43256	19959
1989	28804	59457	28843
1990	31411	117523	31510
1994	38986	160851	39125
1995	50786	180637	50945
1996	47015	196915	47192
1997	46250	211200	46408
1998	47793	221528	47975
1999	50738	223061	50889
2000	53728	212838	53853
2001	63474	223762	63539
2002	85622	265862	85682

3. New Business in Rural Areas

One of the main purposes of nationalisation was to spread the life insurance business to rural areas where population was less than one lakh. The amount of rural business in absolute term is rising whereas the percentage share of rural business to total business is going down. The definition of Rural/Social Sector has been redefined by the Insurance Regulatory and Development Authority (IRDA) Insurance legislation in India under Section V.

Table 18.3 Rural Business as compared to Individual Business of LIC

	Policies		*Business*	
	Lakhs of Policies	*% to total Policies*	*Rs. in crores*	*% to Total Business*
1969–1970	4.61	33.0	251.76	24.5
1973–1974	6.43	31.3	498.17	19.2
1974–1975	5.72	35.7	464.27	14.9
1975–1976	6.50	32.5	563.53	26.8
1979–1980	5.91	28.16	603.77	22.0
1983–1984	8.30	35.00	1260.24	28.54
1984–1985	9.52	35.20	1569.62	29.07

Contd...

	Policies		Business	
	Lakhs of Policies	*% to total Policies*	*Rs. in crores*	*% to Total Business*
1969–1970	4.61	33.0	251.76	24.5
1988–1989	24.12	40.29	5818.22	33.69
1989–1990	30.48	41.19	8086.35	34.68
1992–1994	48.56	45.3	16680.41	39.9
1994–1995	49.02	45.1	21571.00	39.1
1995–1996	52.57	47.7	21263.59	41.0
1996–1997	60.33	49.2	24278.73	42.8
1997–1998	68.40	51.4	27550.69	43.3
1998–1999	81.23	54.7	35372.94	47.0
1999–2000	97.04	57.5	44168.19	48.7
2000–2001	35.34	18.2	17955.88	14.6
2001–2002	37.01	13.7	25461.94	16.9
2002–2003	45.23	18.9	23547.69	13.37
2003–2004	62.19	17.85	35651.99	17.85
2004–2005	55.03	22.97	46037.01	25.18
2005–2006	74.66	23.65	60971.85	21.21
2006–2007	88.50	23.16	68497.21	22.60

Note: This decline is as per the definition of rural/social sector as stated by the Insurance Regulatory and Development Authority.

The share or rural business to total business has been continuously declining from 31.8 per cent in 1961 to 24.5 per cent in 1970 and further to 14.9 percent in 1975. It improved from 22.0 per cent in 1980 to 34.68 per cent in 1975. It improved from 22.0 per cent in 1980 to 34.68 per cent in 1990. Not only this but the percentage of policies issued in rural areas to total policies has also been decreasing from 38.5 percent in 1962-63 to 31.3 per cent in 1974 although it has a slight improvement in 1975. This, evidently, reveals that the percentage of rural business to total new business, instead of going up, is going down which is very discouraging sign. The figure of 1981 has revealed that the percentage Share of rural business in total number of policies and in total amount of business has been improved slightly in 1985. It has improved in 1990 and touched the highest figure in 1994. It decline to 13.7 per cent to total policies and 16.9 per cent of total sum assured.

The most discouraging sign is that the number of policies and amount of insurance in rural areas had been fluctuating. Thus the Corporation could not achieve its main objective of expansion of rural insurance.

4. Annuities

The amount of annuities has been declining with fluctuations. The deferred annuities in India has gone down from Rs. 14.05 crores in 1966 to Rs. 12.68 crores in 1970 and further to Rs. 9.67 crores in 1975. However, there has been a slight improvement so far immediate annuities are concerned. It has gone up from Rs. 1.90 crores in 1966 to Rs. 2.07 crores in 1975. Thus, the immediate annuities was gaining popularity. Moreover, the Group Super Annuation Scheme has given a significant rise, it has gone up from Rs. 106.20 lakhs per annum. During 1979-80, 681 Immediate Life Annuity amounted to Rs. 30.78 lakhs per annum and 141 Deferred Life Annuity amounted to Rs. 6.98 lakhs per annum. It declined in 1985 to the level of 28 Immediate Life Annuity Policies of Rs. 1.27 lakhs and 88 Deferred Life Annuity Policies of Rs. 4.10 lakhs per annum. The number of annuities has been Rs. 1.85 lakhs to the extent of Rs. 1261.19 crores in 1989-90. Immediate annuities of Rs. 2.50 crores and Deferred Life Annuities of Rs. 7.11 crores were sold during 1994-95 which were Rs. 6.54 crores and Rs. 6.48 crores respectively in 1998-99.

Non-Medical Schemes

The increase in non-medical insurance is a sign of rapid progress of the insurance business. The amount of non-medical business has increased from Rs. 155.67 crores in 1963 to Rs. 223.65 crores in 1970, to Rs. 447.26 crores in 1974 and further to Rs. 375.0 crores in 1975 and Rs. 422.86 crores in 1977, although the percentage share to total business has declined from 21.2 per cent in 1963, to 21.8 per cent in 1970, 17.3 per cent in 1974 and further to 12.0 per cent in 1975 and increased to 20.0% in 1977. The number of policies issued under this scheme has also gone up from 7.12 Lakhs in 1963 crores Rs. 8.42 lakhs in 1975 although it touched the highest number of 6 lakhs in 1977. New Business under the Non-Medical Scheme amounted to Rs. 519.3 lakhs under 8.35 lakhs policies in 1980 and Rs. 1,508.94 crore under 13.63 lakhs policies in 1985. New business under the Non-Medical schemes increased to Rs. 10,234.94 crores under 40.37 lakhs in 1989-90.

New Schemes

The Group Insurance Scheme has been extended to groups other than those of employees working for a single employer. Deposit Linked Insurance and Cooperative Housing Financial Societies schemes have been formulated in 1970. Centenary Policy Unit Link Insurance Plan, Group Insurance Schemes for handloom weavers, for Government employees, for teachers of Primary and Junior High Schools has also been extended to the employees of Military, Navy and Air Force departments in 1975. The Corporation is, thus making every effort to popularise the insurance benefits among the masses. Money Back, Cash and Cover Plan and Progressive Protection Policies had been introduced during 1976-77. With effect from 1st April 1980, Grihalakshmi Policies, Anticipated Endowment Assurance, Cash and Cover, Centenary Policy and Convertible Whole Life Policies have been withdrawn. Jeevan Sathi and modified New Jana Raksha Policies were introduced in 1985. Jeevan Chhaya has been introduced in March 1991 and Jeevan Shree in 1995. Bima Kiran Plan and Jeevan Shree Plan were introduced in 1996. The sum assured under Bima Nivesh was Rs. 3,594.85 crore under 357665 policies in 2002-2003. Jan Shree was Rs. 3,285 crore under 636116 policies in 2002-2003.

BUSINESS IN FORCE

A. Individual Business

The life insurance business in Force in India has been continuously from Rs. 1,473 crores in 1957 to Rs. 3,168 crores in 1963; to Rs. 6,425 crores in 1970; and further to Rs. 11,852 crores in 1975 and Rs. 19,114 crores in 1980; and Rs. 94408 crores in 1990. Thus the business, in force, has been increased by more than 4 times during the period of last 10 years. The total business in force has increased to Rs. 19,243 crores in 1980 and Rs. 30,426 crores in 1984, Rs. 94,823 crores in 1990, Rs. 2,08,619 crores in 1994 and Rs. 2,54,572 crores in 1995 and Rs. 645042 crores in 2001 and Rs. 8,11,017 crore in 2002.

Table 18.4 Total Business in Force Individual Insurance

	Indian	*Non-Indian*	*Total Business*
Dec. 31st			
1951	793	80	873
1955	1128	92	1220
1960	2176	109	2285
March 31st			
1966	4282	112	3878
1969	5606	119	5725
1974	10725	124	10849

Contd....

	Indian	Non-Indian	Total Business
1975	11725	124	11852
1976	13248	124	13372
1980	19114	129	19243
1981	20923	134	21067
1984	30266	160	30426
1985	3785	166	33951
1989	74129	300	74429
1990	94408	415	94823
1994	207601	1018	208619
1995	253333	1239	254572
1996	294336	1422	295758
1997	343018	1601	344619
1998	398959	1789	400748
1999	457435	1766	459201
2000	534589	1862	536451
2001	643241	1801	645042
2002	809170	1847	811017

The business in-force of Group Insurance Schemes has rapidly been increasing from Rs. 39.0 crores in 1967 to Rs. 6137.46 crores in 1980 and Rs. 1021856 crores in 1985, Rs. 23049.64 crores in 1990, Rs. 46,742.75 crores in 1994 and Rs. 51,034.71 crores in 1995. The business-in-force of Group Superannuation Schemes has increased from Rs. 1.79 crores of annuities in 1967 to Rs. 61.02 crores of annuities in 1980 and Rs. 146.51 crores in 1985 and further to Rs. 245.11 crores in 1990 and Rs. 403.51 crores in 1994 and Rs. 422.66 crores in 1995. This reveals that the Group Insurance has been constantly and rapidly rising in India. It is a very good indicator of the popular form of life insurance which can be adopted to benefit the masses, individually as well as a group. The group insurance scheme amounted Rs. 89,326.19 crores under 84,203 schemes and group Superannuation Scheme 5753 giving Rs. 1,137.72 crores in 2001, and Rs. 1,271.94 crore in 2002.

Table 18.4a Business in Force

(Rs. in Crores)
(Sum Assound and Bonus)

Individual Insurance:	2002-2003	2003-2004	2004-2005	2005-2006
Assurance	956675.20	11114198.37	1288468.80	1535439.60
Annuities	1449.53	1406.02	1189.80	1296.16
Jeevan Suraksha	8899.81	8611.92	3136.27	3208.08
			(No. of Policies in Lakh)	
Assurance	1388.77	1541.88	1649.35	1835.77
Annuities	9.84	9.98	9.31	9.79
Jeevan Suraksha	13.02	15.95	19.38	19.44
			(Sum Assured in Crore Rs.)	
Group Schemes:				
Group insurance	124312.26	1541.88	1649.35	1835.77

Contd....

Annuities for annum	1488.98	1705.50	1916.64	2189.28
			(No. of schemes)	
Group insurance	95325	10005.50	106912	109995
Group Superannuation	6461	7232	7321	6135
			(No. of Lives in lakhs)	
Group insurance	240.99	253.46	306.50	302.71
Group Superannuation	10.86	12.34	12.73	12.52

Table 18.5 Group Insurance and Superannuation Schemes Business-in-Force

(Business in crores)

As on March 31	***Group Insurance Schemes***		***Group Superannuation Schemes***	
	Number of Scheme	*Sum assured (in Crores of Rupees)*	*Number of Schemes*	*Amount of Annuities (in Crores of Rupees)*
1967	259	39.00	Included in Group Insurance Schemes	1.79
1970	385	77.00		3.12
1975	2062	1457.07	366	6.59
1980	7442	6137.46	639	61.02
1981	8537	6960.32	783	69.90
1984	10624	9251.33	1287	118.67
1985	14521	10218.56	1391	146.51
1989	30028	20052.48	2095	213.95
1990	37089	23049.64	2405	245.11
1994	64426	46742.95	3314	403.51
1995	71726	51034.71	3642	427.66
1996	72592	64651.54	3977	483.05
1997	78372	64606.60	4349	545.59
1998	78600	4798.75	4719	682.84
1999	80785	77918.65	4963	815.96
2000	83254	76384.53	5246	971.15
2001	84203	89326.19	5753	1137.72
2002	93836	100597.64	6109	1271.94

The lapsation of policy is harmful for the insurers as well as insured because the goodwill and reputation of the former decline whereas the benefits of insurance are not available to the latter one. Therefore, attempts should be made to reduce the lapse-per-centage. It is a very encouraging sign that the percentage of net lapses to mean life insurance-business-in-force has declined from the highest of 8.1 per cent in 1963 to 3.8 percent in 1980 and 5.6 percent in 1990. Even this percentage is very high and Corporation should try to minimise the lapse-ratio. But it could not improve the problems of lapses as the lapse-ratio. But it could not improve the problems of lapses as the lapse-ratio increased to 4.5 per cent in 1984 but declined to 4.2 per cent in 1985 and again increased to 5.8 per cent in 1990 and 6.3 per cent in 1994 and 6.1 per cent in 1995 and 5.0 per cent in 2003.

Table 18.6 Percentages of Net Lapses to Mean Life Insurance Business-in-force

Year	*Percentage*
Dec.31, 1957	6.4
Dec.31, 1960	6.6
March 31, 1963	8.1
" " 1970	5.9
" " 1975	5.4
" " 1976	5.4
" " 1980	3.8
" " 1981	3.8
" " 1984	4.5
" " 1985	4.2
" " 1989	5.0
" " 1990	5.6
" " 1994	6.3
" " 1995	6.1
" " 1996	6.4
" " 1997	5.1
" " 1998	5.0
" " 1999	4.9
" " 2000	5.1
" " 2001	4.9
" " 2002	5.5
" " 2003	5.0

Working Results

The working results of LIC can be evaluated by various indicators such as Life Insurance Fund, Premium-Income, Total Income, Expenses, Interest Rates, Investment, Claims-settlements, Number of offices, Productivity of Agents and so on.

(i) *Life Insurance Fund.* An increasing trend of life insurance found is a clear indication of progressive business. If the rate of increase of life insurance fund is progressive, it is undoubtedly a significant increase in life insurance business.

The, life insurance fund has been increasing at a faster rate bring the period of 33 years. It is a very encouraging sign that the life insurance fund has increased from Rs. 410.47 crores on Dec. 31, 1957 to Rs. 5,818.09 crores on March 31, 1980 by more than 13 times. It increased to Rs. 9,800.38 crores in 1984 by more than 24 times and again to Rs. 11,191.09 crores in 1985. It has gone up to Rs. 9,568.79 crores in 1989, Rs. 23,471.84 crores in 1990. Rs. 8,667.53 1994 and Rs. 10,313.08 crores in 1995.

Table 18.7 Total Income, Outgo and Funds

(In crores of Rs.)

An on	*Total Income*	*Total Outgo*	*Total Funds*
Dec. 31, 1957	101.98	58.91	410.41
Dec. 31, 1960	117.90	62.28	560.38
Mar. 31, 1963	186.25	96.03	120.10
" " 1970	346.35	169.11	1611.04
" " 1915	690.02	360.65	3033.19
" " 1916	190.84	383.66	3440.91
" " 1980	1291.18	596.01	5818.09
" " 1981	1461.25	631.94	6641.44
" " 1984	2113.22	1004.56	9800.88
" " 1985	2519.99	1194.56	11191.09
" " 1989	5310.41	2426.22	19568.79
" " 1990	6835.04	2931.99	23471.84
" " 1994	15212.31	6544.18	8661.53
" " 1995	18102.32	1189.24	10313.08
" " 1996	22046.16	9245.60	12801.16
" " 1991	25933.09	10841.58	14919.90
" " 1998	30132.60	12659.61	18012.93
" " 1999	36352.59	14196.42	21556.11
" " 2000	44129.61	18101.93	26621.61
" " 2001	53968.46	21981.45	31981.02
" " 2002	12169.91	28283.50	44486.41
" " 2003	80981.82	40886.08	40101.14
" " 2004	93088.91	44106.11	48382.14
" " 2005	112346.24	48460.10	63885.54
" " 2006	139146.88	52251.57	
" " 2007	173527.08	77938.52	

(*ii*) *Total Income.* Total income has also increased from Rs. 107.98 crores in 1957 to Rs. 2,519.99 crores in 1985 by more than 23 times during the period. It has increased to Rs. 6,835.04 crores in 1990. Rs. 15,212.31 crores in 1994, Rs. 18102.32 crores in 1995 and Rs. 53,968.46 crores in 2001 and Rs. 72,769.91 crore in 2002.

(*iii*) *Total Outgo.* Total outgo includes payment to policy-holders, expenses of management, commission to agents, salaries and other benefits to employees. Other outgo such as other expenses, taxes, reserves etc. It has increased from Rs. 58.97 crores in 1957 to Rs. 1,194.56 crores in 1985 by more than 19 times. Thus, the income has increased at a faster late than the increase in III outgo. The outgo has gone upto Rs. 2,931.99 crores in 1990 and Rs. 6,544.78 crores in 1994 and Rs. 7,789.24 crores in 1995 and Rs. 21,987.45 crores in 2001 and Rs. 28,283.50 crore in 2002.

(*iv*) *Premium Income.* Increase in premium income has been considerably high as it has increased in absolute as well as in relative term. The percentage increase per annum has been rising year after year. The percentage change over previous year was the highest 15.06 per cent in 1976 and the lowest 7.90 per cent in 1963.

The Premium income has increased from Rs. 88.6,5 crores in 1957 to Rs. 875.37 crores in 1980 by about 10 times and to Rs. 1,355.10 crores in 1984 by more than 15 times and again to Rs. 1,559.33 crores in 1985. It has touched the highest level of Rs. 4,489.39 crores in 1990 and Rs. 9,735.34 crores in 1994, Rs. 11,527.80 crores in 1995 and Rs. 34,207,78 crores in 2001 and Rs. 48,963.60 crores in 2002.

Table 18.8 Premium Income

	Premium income crores of Rs.	*Percentage increase over previous year*
Dec. 31, 1957	88.65	
Dec. 31, 1960	97.55	12.68
March 31,1963	151.05	7.90
" " 1970	260.41	10.92
" " 1975	511.24	12.39
" " 1976	588.25	15.06
" " 1980	875.37	12.95
" " 1981	964.88	10.22
" " 1984	1355.10	11.86
" " 1985	1559.33	15.07
" " 1989	3432.72	28.48
" " 1990	4489.39	30.78
" " 1994	9735.32	21.88
" " 1995	11527.80	18.41
" " 1996	14181.77	23.02
" " 1997	16351.39	15.30
" " 1998	19252.07	18.55
" " 1999	22805.80	18.46
" " 2000	27461.71	20.42
" " 2001	34207.78	24.56
" " 2002	48963.60	43.14
" " 2003	54602.37	9.63
" " 2004	62130.26	15.63
" " 2005	75083.37	18.25
" " 2006	90759.20	20.88
" " 2007	127782.26	

(v) *Expenses.* The expenses as a percentage to total premium should not increase. The overall expense-ratio and renewal. Expense Ratio are the important expense ratio. The overall expense ratio had touched the highest figure of 30.48 per cent in 1975 and declined to 24.52 percent in 1980 and further to 22.37 per cent in 1984. It increased to 23.84 per cent in 1990 and declined to 21.39 per cent in 1995. The Renewal Expense ratio has also gone down from 18.97 per cent in 1975 to 13.01 per cent in 1980 and again to 13.92 per cent in 1985. It was merely 3.04 per cent in 1990. Rs. 4.95 percent in 1995,6.32 per cent in 1995 and 2.43 per cent in 2001 and 4.20 per cent in 2002.

Table 18.9 Expenses as a Percentage to Total Premium

Year ending on	*Overall Expense Ratio*	*Renewal Expenses Ratio*
Dec. 31, 1957	27.20	15.89
Dec. 31, 1960	28.45	12.90
Mar. 31, 1963	29.31	14.13
Mar. 31, 1970	27.69	16.15
" " 1975	30.48	18.97
" " 1976	29.66	18.14
" " 1980	24.52	13.01
" " 1981	24.24	12.62
" " 1984	22.37	11.16
" " 1985	24.68	13.92
" " 1989	25.52	6.89
" " 1990	23.84	3.04
" " 1994	21.83	4.95
" " 1995	21.39	6.32
" " 1996	20.79	7.00
" " 1997	21.43	7.09
" " 1998	20.53	6.09
" " 1919	20.48	5.38
" " 2000	21.16	5.63
" " 2001	19.89	2.43
" " 2002	17.72	–4.20%
" " 2003	17.62	2.40
" " 2004	17.30	2.73
" " 2005	16.57	2.30
" " 2006	14.47	2.69
" " 2007	12.72	2.35

(*vi*) *Interest Rate.* The interest rate reveals the profitability of the concern. The rising rate of interest is a promising sign. In LIC, the gross interest rate has increased from 4.58 per cent in 1957 to 7.89 per cent in 1980 and the net interest rate has increased from 3.74 per cent in 1957 to 7.44 percent in 1980 and 9.76 per cent in 1985. It has increased to 11.13 per cent in 1990, 12.21 per cent in 1995 and 11.60 per cent in 2001. Thus, it is clear that the profitability position of LIC has been improving gradually.

Table 18.10 Interest-Rate earned on Mean Life Insurance Fund

Year ending on	*Gross Interest Rate*
Dec. 31, 1957	4.68
" 1960	4.58
Mar. 31, 1963	4.76
" 1970	6.06
" 1975	6.93
" 1976	7.13

Contd....

" 1980	7.89
" 1981	8.21
" 1984	9.19
" 1985	9.46
" 1986	10.95
" 1990	11.13
" 1994	12.43
" 1995	12.21
" 1996	12.29
" 1997	12.39
" 1998	12.37
" 1999	11.96
" 2000	12.08
" 2001	11.60
" 2002	11.59
" 2003	10.40
" 2004	9.57
" 2005	9.93
" 2006	8.72
" 2007	8.21

Table 18.11a Amount of Investment

As on	*Investment in crores of Rs.*
Dec. 31, 1957	329.75
" 1960	457.43
Mar. 31, 1963	678.81
" 1970	1528.66
" 1975	2803.20
" 1976	3134.64
" 1980	5747.51
" 1981	6534.32
" 1984	9613.74
" 1985	10804.03
" 1986	17342.70
" 1990	20503.74
" 1994	46560.63
" 1995	56182.44
" 1996	68275.60
" 1997	82665.17
" 1998	98947.77
" 1999	120445.40
" 2000	139032.15
" 2001	175491.18
" 2002	221697.50
" 2006	613266.58

(*vii*) *Investment.* The amount of investment has been constantly increasing from Rs. 329.75 crores in 1957 to Rs. 5747.51 crores in 1980 by more than 18 times and Rs. 10804.03 crores in 1985 by 30 times. It had gone upto Rs. 20503.74 crores in 1990, Rs. 46560.63 crores in 1994 and Rs. 56182.44 crores in 1995 and Rs. 221697.50 crore in 2002. The investment has contributed significantly in the development of the nation.

The percentage distribution of LIC investment reveals that LIC has favoured public sector as more than 79 per cent of total investment was made in public sector. The investment in cooperative sector has also been rising but in 1980 it declined to 9.7 per cent and increased to 10.2 per cent in 1984 and came down to 6.5 per cent in 1990. Investment in private sector had gone down from 22.7 per cent in 1957 to 11.6 per cent in 1977 but it improved to 12.5 per cent in 1980, 13.7 per cent in 1990, 13.8 per cent in 1995 and 86.5 per cent 2002. LIC investment has been directed towards socially oriented securities. It is a great achievement that LIC has tried to develop electricity, health, drinking facilities, water and sewerage schemes, small-scale industries, fertilisers, housing and other infrastructures.

Table 18.11b Percentage Distribution of LIC Investment in Different

As on	*Public Sector*	*Cooperative Sector*	*Private Sector*
Dec. 31, 1957	77.3	—	22.7
" 1960	78.7	—	21.3
Mar. 31, 1963	76.8	3.3	19.4
" 1970	73.6	9.5	16.5
" 1975	75.4	12.0	12.6
" 1976	76.3	11.8	11.9
" 1980	63.4	9.7	12.5
" 1984	79.3	10.2	10.5
" 1985	79.6	8.4	10.6
" 1989	80.9	7.2	11.9
" 1990	79.8	6.5	13.7
" 1994	82.1	3.9	14.0
" 1995	82.9	3.3	13.8
Mar. 31, 1996	84.63	2.90	12.47
" 1997	84.58	2.49	12.93
" 1998	84.66	2.17	13.17
" 1999	84.49	1.84	13.67
" 2000	84.2	1.5	14.3
" 2001	84.6	1.3	14.1
" 2002	86.5	1.0	12.5

Note — Joint Sector is included under private sector.

(*viii*) *Claims-Settlement.* The claims settlement is an indicator of the efficiency of the LIC in meeting claims-obligation. The percentage of outstanding claims to claims intimated should decline. It has been observed that percentage of outstanding claims to total claims intimated has decreased from 60.52 per cent in 1957 to 14.14 per cent in 1977. It was a tremendous achievement in the field of claim-settlements; but it has again deteriorated and percentage of claims outstanding to total claims intimated has increased to 17.08 per cent in 1980. It decreased to 11.23 per cent in 1995 and 5.96 per cent in 1990 and 4.86 per cent in 1994 and increased to 5.26 per cent in 1995 and 3.70 per cent in 2001 and declined to 1.85 per cent in 2002.

Table 18.12 Claims—Settlement

(In crores of Rs.)

As on	*Claims intimated*	*Claims outstanding*	*Percentage of claims outstanding to claims intimated*
Dec. 31, 1957	28.70	13.03	60.53
" 1960	30.60	13.47	43.89
Mar. 3 1. 1963	43.95	13.55	38.45
" 1970	81.44	24.29	29.83
" 1975	148.32	31.72	21.39
" 1976	162.73	28.60	17.58
" 1980	283.00	48.35	17.08
" 1981	314.20	67.05	21.34
" 1984	517.28	73.62	14.23
" 1985	638.29	73.23	11.53
" 1989	1211.08	84.71	6.61
" 1990	1425.14	90.56	5.96
" 1994	3845.45	171.50	4.86
" 1995	4130.80	226.23	5.26
" 1996	4594.69	288.70	6.28
" 1997	6722.38	319.59	5.58
" 1998	6673.07	315.62	4.73
" 1999	7615.78	348.22	4.57
" 2000	9266.25	403.17	4.35
" 2001	11666.82	432.01	3.70
" 2002	14358.55	273.34	1.85
" 2003	—	213.98	0.23
" 2004	—	—	1.11
" 2006	—	—	0.82
" 2007	—	—	0.68

Number of Offices. The number of offices has not increased satisfactorily. As compared to the bank-branches, the expansion in LIC offices has been almost negligible. The total offices of LIC have increased from 735 in 1963 to 888 in 1980 and 1160 in 1985 and 1603 in 1990. The number of branch offices has been growing from 340 in 1963 to 738 in 1980 and 1023 in 1984 and 1528 in 1990. The number of sub-offices increased to 179 in 1963 and declined to only 4 sub-offices in 1980. The number of development centres has also been decreasing from 175 in 1963 to 100 in 1980 and further to only 5 in 1985. The total number of LIC offices in 1995 was 2128, out of which 2021 were branch offices.

The total number of LIC offices increased to 2155 in 2001 but of which 2048 were branch offices.

Table 18.13 Number of Offices

As on	Zonal offices	Divisional offices	Branch offices	Sub offices	Development centres	Total offices
Dec. 31, 1957	5	33	105	45	—	278
Mar. 31, 1963	5	36	340	179	175	735
" 1970	5	36	424	115	123	703
" 1975	5	41	651	29	105	831
" 1976	5	41	659	23	110	838
" 1980	5	41	738	4	100	888
" 1981	5	42	826	—	63	936
" 1984	5	43	1023	—	12	1083
" 1985	5	43	1107	—	5	1160
" 1989	5	64	1427	—	—	1496
" 1990	6	69	1528	—	—	1603
" 1994	7	100	2008	—	—	2115
" 1995	7	100	2021	—	—	2128
Mar 31, 19967	100	2021	—	—	2128	
" 1997	7	100	2023	—	—	2130
" 1998	7	100	2046	—	—	2153
" 1999	7	100	2048	—	—	2155
" 2000	7	100	2048	—	—	2155
" 2001	7	100	2048	—	—	2155
" 2002	7	100	2048	—	—	2155
" 2003	7	100	2048	—	—	2156
" 2004	7	101	2048	—	—	2156
" 2005	7	101	2048	—	—	2156

(*x*) *Productivity of Agents*. The productivity or Active Agents has been constantly increasing from Rs. 31,000 in 1957 to Rs. 2,47.641 in 1980 by about 8 times and Rs. 3,63,772 in 1985 by 11 times. The productivity of agent has been Rs. 6,66,605 in 1990, Rs. 7,97,324 in 1994, 1063101 in 1995 and Rs. 12,59,013 in 1999 and Rs. 7,44,003 in 2002.

Table 18.14 Productivity of Agents

As on	Number of Active Agents	Business Per Active Agents in Rs.	
Dec. 31, 1957		8900	31,000
1960	1,01,600	47,900	
Mar. 31, 1963	1,41,000	52,070	
" 1970	1,32,790	77,241	
" 1975	1,46,103	1,20,518	
" 1976	1,44,385	1,45,722	

Contd....

As on	Number of Active Agents	Business Per Active Agents in Rs.
" 1980	1,10,366	2,47,641
" 1984	1,32,947	3,29,980
" 1985	1,47,783	3.63.722
" 1989	2,96,713	5,80,455
" 1990	3,48,325	6,66,605
" 1994	5,24,427	7,97,324
" 1995	5,19,504	10,63,101
Mar. 31, 1996	5,13,897	10,08,286
" 1997	5,33,133	10,64,284
" 1998	5,58,517	11,39,047
" 1999	5,98,217	12,59,013
" 2000	6,83,190	13,28,292
" 2001	7,43,064	16,56,370
" 2002	7,44,083	23,55,697
" 2003	9,02,199	19,51,767
" 2004	10,03,241	21,97,675
" 2005	10,41,737	—

Valuation

The valuation of life assets and liabilities is very important process to assess the solvency of the concern. Prior to nationalisation the insurers were required to make an acturial valuation at least once in three years. In terms of the Life Insurance Corporation Act 1956, the Corporation has to conduct valuation of its assets and liabilities at least once in two years. The rate of reversionary bonus has increased very slowly from Rs. 16.00 per thousand in 1957 to Rs. 31.00 per thousand in 1981 in case of Whole Life Policy and form.

Table 18.15 Valuation of Life Assets

As on	Policyholders share, excluding interim bonus (in crores of Rs)	Government's share (in crores of Rs)	Rewrsionary Endowment	Bonus Declared per thousand Rs. Whole-life
Dec. 31, 1957	27.56	1.45	12.80	16.00
" 1959	24.48	1.28	12.80	16.00
" 1961	32.73	1.27	12.80	16.00
Mar. 31, 1963	25.03	1.32	14.00	17.50
" 1965	58.93	3.10	16.00	20.00
" 1967	68.67	3.61	16.00	20.00
" 1969	90.30	4.75	17.60	22.00
" 1971	110.18	5.80	17.60	22.00
" 1973	144.34	7.60	17.60	22.00

Contd....

As on		Policyholders share, excluding interim bonus (in crores of Rs)	Government's share (in crores of Rs)	Rewrsionary Bonus Declared per thousand Rs.	
				Endowment	Whole-life
"	1975	172.43	9.07	17.60	22.00
"	1977	241.04	12.69	20.00	25.00
"	1979	354.30	18.65	24.80	31.00
"	1981	495.83	26.10	28.00	35.00
"	1983	743.98	39.16	34.00	42.50
"	1985	997.17	52.48	44.00	55.00
"	1989	905.02	47.63	62.00	77.50
"	1990	1128.58	58.40	64.00	80.00
"	1993	2368.10	118.43	75.00	96.00
"	1995	2803.00	140.15	75.00	96.00
"	1996	3362.31	171.69	78.00	95.00
"	1997	2768.65	198.35	80.00	97.00
"	1998	4439.36	233.64	85.00	102.00
"	1999	5635.00	265.0	87.00	104.00
"	2000	5035.48	265.02	89.00	106.00
"	2001	6016.26	316.65	89.00	106.00
"	2002	7232.60	380.66	89.00	106.00
"	2003	9767.00	488.13	89.00	106.00
"	2004	10087.60	548.13	89.00	106.00
"	2005	13951.69	696.60	—	—
"	2006	12463.0	621.71		
"	2007	15156.0	757.81		

Rs. 12.80 per thousand to Rs. 24.80 per thousand in case of endowment policy. The bonus per thousand has been 64.0 in case of endowment and 80.00 in whole life in 1990 which increased to 75.00 and 96.00 respectively in 1993. The Reversionary bonus in 1995 per thousand for was Rs. 75 whole life which increased to 106 per thousand and 89 per thousand in 2002.

Organisation Scheme of the LIC

As per the suggestions of Era-Sezhiyan Committee, the LIC has adopted reorganisation schemes of its divisional and branch offices. At present the reorganisation work has been completed in all the divisions and branches.

Reorganised Divisions: The reorganised divisions have nine departments. The marketing department, planning and review department and divisional management committee are important departments of the divisions. There are discussed in the following sections:

1. Marketing Department

It is responsible for branch performance and is the single point of contact for supervising them. The department is responsible for judging the quality of work done in branches through its sections sales, policy-holders' service section, sales training section and branch support section.

(*a*) *Sales Section.* It is responsible for carrying out supervisory functions relating to sales and the field-force and customer-satisfaction.

The major task of the sales managers in charge of the sales section is the supervision of the sales functions at the branches and the performances of the field-personnel. This section is also responsible for spreading awareness among the general public about the benefits of life insurance and the nature of cover that LIC's policies provide and how section assesses the quality of business of the various branches and effectiveness of their plans in penetrating the respective territories and markets assigned.

(*b*) *Policyholders' Service Section.* It is responsible for supervising the policyholder servicing function including claims and the operational function of early settlement of claims. It handles matters referred to divisional office by branches in respect to all policyholder's service functions. It may undertake the training of branch staff and carry out timeliners and the quality of the service rendered by the branches to the policyholders. This section has also to deal with the individual cases referred to by branches. All old claims have to be got investigated and settled by this section.

(*c*) *Sales Training Section.* This section is entrusted with responsibility for training in product, in selling and sales planning in the field personnel. It arranges and conducts training of field-personnel, such as ABM(D), development officers and agents.

(*d*) *Branch Support Section.* It is responsible for providing secretarial support to the various sections in marketing department. It provides administrative support to the sections under the Marketing Manager. This section is responsible for analysis of budget proposals and monthly review of data. They analyses the performance data, raise special issues concerning the performance of branches and generally help the various sections in the marketing department to process work and perform liaison work with other departments and take up routine functions as assigned to them. They have to undertake general follow up of routine matters with the branches and with other departments of the Divisional Office.

The marketing department controls the entire sales and service functions in the Divisional area and also services as a single point contract between the branches and the departments of the divisional office.

2. New Business and Acturial Department

New Business and Acturial Department is responsible as specialists to decide on the proposal referred to the divisional office in respect to all individual, SSS and GSD proposals, cheque, Delined Life Index Cards and undertake supervisory, inspection tasks, vis-a-vis branches. They also have the responsibility to train new business incumbents in branches according to their judgment of their capabilities and of their needs. This department is responsible for supervision of branch functions from under-writing to issue of policy, appointment and control of medical examiners etc. It underwrites proposals of higher sum assured, which are beyond the powers of the branches and conducts acturial valuation and undertakes acturial research.

3. Accounts Department

The Accounts Departments is responsible for supervision of accounts in the branches, collection of branch accounts and all the accounting functions in the division, also training of staff and test-checking how well the work in branches is being done. Accounts department has two sections: (*a*) Branch Accounts Section has responsibility for supervision of branch accounts, expenses and training of staff. They analyses the trial-balances from branches and recommend suitable action to divisional management, (*b*) General Accounts Section which has three units: (*i*) Cash and Banking Section; (*ii*) Salary and Provident Fund Section; and (*iii*) Final Accounts Section.

4. Legal and Mortgage Department

The legal and mortgage department has the responsibility for all legal and mortgage loan work in the division, They advise branches when required for mortgage loans and legal matters.

5. Office Management Department

The office management department consists of two divisions; (*a*) Purchase Section which has responsibility for purchases, inventory and materials utilisation and (*b*) Service Section that consists of security despatch, duplicating and office services, transportation etc.

6. Machine Department

It is responsible for data processing and offers service to user-departments in the Divisional office and to branches that do not have machine support. It has two sections (*a*) System Section which is responsible to oversee the systems and programmes of data processing machines in branches and division; (*b*) Operations Section that is responsible for providing machine support to branches that do not have an in-house system, as also to the divisional office.

7. Personnel Department

It consists of three sections:

(*a*) *Management Development Section.* This section is responsible for management forecast, management development and career planning of staff. It has responsibility to ensure that branches implement the policies laid down in letter and spirit. They carry out periodic personnel audit to ensure that the corporate plans and policies are implemented satisfactorily.

(*b*) *Industrial Relations Section.* It is responsible to develop relations with trade unions and to carry out negotiations in matters that relate to the division as a whole.

(*c*) *Training Section.* It is responsible for organising programme for supervisors and middle management personnel within the division. This section is also responsible to organise functional programmes according to the needs of various departments in the divisional office.

8. Planning and Review Department

The planning and review department has responsibilities in two main areas. One is the operation section with responsibility for locality data suitable for planning, education and developing among concerned people, the understanding of the concepts and their applications, review of performance budget proposals and review of monthly, quarterly or six monthly performance reports. The other is the Special Studies Section with responsibility for undertaking studies that the performance data may indicate or the divisional management may consider necessary.

REORGANISED BRANCH OFFICE

The reorganised branch offices of the LIC have the following sections:

1. Sales Section

This section is responsible for supervision of development officers agents and for building up the agency force in its jurisdiction. It has to plan and review business performance and take remedial action where necessary. It registers new proposals, settles commission and make all payments to agents and development officers.

2: New Business Section

This section is responsible for underwriting all new business and issue of new policies. It sends recommendations and obtains approval for business beyond its permmissible limits, from higher authority.

3. Policy holders' Servicing Section, Including Claims

This section is responsible for total servicing of policies, including loans and claims and to obtain approval from higher authority for matters beyond their sanctioned powers. A separate section for claims and salary saving scheme is created, if the volume of work justifies.

It is responsible for providing the required support to all departments. An in-house machine will be provided only where size justifies it. In other cases, such support will come from the divisional office.

5. Office Service Section

It is responsible for establishment and personnel matters in the Branch.

6. Accounts Section

This section is responsible for Cash and Banking, preparation of trial balance of the branch, reconciliation of various accounts and issue and control of premium, receipts.

7. Branch Management Committee

This committee consists of the Branch Manager and all the heads of sections and has higher financial powers. The members of the Branch Management Committee are Section Heads, Higher Grade Assistants, Superintendents, Assistant Administrative officers or Administrative officers. The Committee has also been vested with a financial authority beyond the power of the officer in charge of the branch in matters relating to underwriting and policy-services. The decisions of the Management Committee on all matters have to be unanimous and in case of differences in the committee the matters have to be referred to the Divisional office.

The basic function of the Committee is to review the performance of the branch, discuss its work-status and evolve methods to overcome problems facing the branch. The review of the performance of the branch has to be made in relation to some standards. The performance budget for the branch, agreed between the Division and the Branch provides the yardstick for this comparison.

This review would be meaningful if the planning and budgeting itself is done after a thorough discussion at the Management Committee, so that all members of the Committee have a sense of commitment and identity with the plan. The review of the performance at the Branch Management Committee provide feedback for future planning and enables suitable measures to be taken speedily wherever necessary to bring performance in line with plans, by a careful analysis of the reasons for its deviation.

The performance plan and budget evolved, after discussions in the Management Committee provides common goals for the branch to reach and the involvement of individual departmental heads in evolving these goals. It brings in them a sense of commitment so that when reviews are made individual departmental heads become prepared to sacrifice narrow departmental interests, Whenever required, in the interest of the branch attaining the common objectives. The review of performance and analysis of the problems faced which the Committee does enable emergence of a problem-solving culture. It leads to a realisation that operational problems can be solved primarily by putting heads together, identifying the causes and tackling the issues that provide the cause and not by referring to higher officers and awaiting their advice or directions. Only those matters are referred to higher authority, which are beyond the powers and levels of expertise available at the branch.

CUSTOMERS RELATIONS MANAGEMENT

In order to provide individual attention to the policyholders and to monitor continuously the quality of service delivery, the LIC has introduced the CRM initiatives during 2001-2002. As a part of the initiatives Managers (CRM) at the Divisional Office are positioned. Customer Relations Executives (CRE) and Customer Relations Group (CRG) have been constituted at branch level Helplines Letters etc. Standing committees on customer Relations have been Constituted.

INSURANCE OMBUDSMAN

The office of Insurance ombudsman was created in the year 1998 for arbitration between the customers and the insurance companies. These are 12 insurance ombudsmen in the country. There is no cost involved in taking the grievance to the ombudsman and generally the decisions are more expeditions. The ombudsmen are empowered to receive and consider disputes arising of repudiation of claims by an insurer premiums paid or payable in terms of the policy, legal construction of the policies relating to claims, delay in settlement of claims, non-issue of any insurance document to customers after receipt of premium.

UPGRADING OF INFORMATION TECHNOLOGY

The LIC is one of the largest users of Information Technology in terms of hardware and in house developed application software. The "Green Channel" is for on the spot policy completion and the "Single Window" provides all policy servicing at one single point. The "CRM" module shows all the relevant details of a customer displaying his individual interest in particular plans and giving marketing leads to meet his future needs.

The LIC has Wide and Metro Area Network Connect 90 centres covering 101 division and 2037 branches.

Through the LIC's website www.licindia.com, people get information about the Corporation's products services, subsidies, and addresses of branches and about the premium payment through the internet. The LIC has installed **Information**. Kiosles at prominent places in India.

LIC (INTERNATION) LTD.

The branches at Fiji and Mauritius have shown very good business growth. Similarly LIC (Int.) Behrain, LIC (Nepal) Ltd., LIC (Lanka) Ltd. The branch at UK in progress-process. Botswana, Tanzania, Maldives and New Zealand are getting LIC services.

INFORMATION RELATING TO PRIVATE INSURANCE (LIFE)

Bank of Punjab (BoP), announced its tie up with the state-owned life insurance major LICI for distributing the latter's insurance products.

The Indian Cricket Board will launch a unique insurance policy offered by LICI for its players wherein their returns would rise by 43 per cent annually compared to an existing benevolent fund.

All the life insurance companies in India have decided to jointly work out a standardised individual pension product. The N.K. Shinkar Committee which was appointed by the IRDA has submitted its report on the same.

Vijaya Bank, Punjab National Bank (PNB), the Principal Financial Group of the US and a leading tyre company have signed a memorandum of understanding (MoU) and have applied to IRDA for a license for a life insurance venture.

Private insurance players are targeting Non-resident Indians (NRIs) as the premiums coming from this segment of society are huge. Birla Sun Life Insurance Company and SBI Life Insurance are coming up with special insurance-cum-investment products targeted at NRIs.

LIC is toying with the idea of launching a credit-cum-debit card in a tie up with one of the largest financial companies-Capital One Financial of the US, a Fortune 500 company with a customer base of 46.4 million.

The Supreme Court has ruled that an insurance company which has issued a Third Party (TP) liability policy has to pay compensation to the victims of a road accident even if the driver of the vehicle which meets with an accident had a fake driving licence.

LIC is looking at extending insurance cover to HIV–infected women under the Jeevan Bharati plan. The life insurance company will need national level data on AIDS/HIV infection and relevant statistical information to take any decision on extending insurance cover to women affected by this disease.

IRDA has granted in-principle permission to the Sahara Group to enter the life insurance business, subject to the latter fulfilling some regulatory requirements.

In the context of declining interest rates, Senior citizens ate awaiting for the launch of LIC's pension scheme, guaranteeing an annual return of 9%, in the form of monthly pension scheme.

Reliance General Insurance has been slapped with a penalty of Rs. Two lakh by IRDA for failing to meet the insurance regulator's rural business target for the fiscal 2001-02 .

RECENT PROGRESS OF LIC

1. LIC Plans Micro-risk Products for Rural Poor

The Life Insurance Corporation of India (LIC) is planning to forge an alliance with the four state-owned general insurance companies to jointly develop micro-insurance products affordable for the rural poor. The new Insurance Reguatory and Development Authority (Irda) regulations permit life insurance companies for offer non-life micro-insurance products, provided the life insurer has a tie-up with a non-life insurance company. Similarly, nonlife insurance companies can also offer life products if they have a tie-up with a life insurer.

"LIC would perfer to have an arrangement, preferable with all the government owened general insurance companies, but a final decision would depend on Irda's views." T.S. Vijayan, managing director of LIC, told reporters on the sidelines of a seminar on corporate governance organised by the Indian Merchant's Chamber.

LIC would be able to distribute micro-insurance policies through its existing agent network and will also appoint agents only to hawk micro-insurance products. Besides servicing policies, the micro-insurance agents would also collect premium.

Vijayan said LIC would have to rework its organisational network to make the business of micro-insurance cost-effective and also make it serve the target customer segment.

The minimum and maximum cover for accident, health and endowment policies would range between Rs. 5,000 to Rs. 50,000 per policy.

The remuneration or commission to agents would be a maximum of 10 per cent for single premium life product and 20 per cent for other products. For non-life products, the commission to micro-insurance agents would be upto 15 per cent of the premium.

2. LIC to Add Corporate Agencies

The 10 lakh plus army of individual agents has been one of the core strengths of the Life Insurance Corporation but now the life insurer is looking at corporate agencies to complement this channel, "We are looking at tying up with as many banks as possible to reach out to more customers. As of now the banking channel accounts for a small per cent of our business but in the next five-l0 years this will go to about 20-25%", S. Viswanathan, executive director (marketing-bancassurance and alternate channels) said.

The bancassurance channel currently brings in premium of Rs. 200 crore out of a total Rs. 12,000 crore for LIC. LIC has tied up 38 bancassurance deals with the latest being the MoU with Bank of maharashtra which was signed in pune on Wednesday. Ashok Kumar Dugade, ED, Bank of Maharashtra said bancassurance would be introduced in 200 select branches and gradually rolled out across its network of 1 ,300 branches. In the first year the bank is looking at an income of Rs. 10 crore through selling of life insurance. Mr. Viswanathan said LIC had, tied up with nine PSU banks and 21 cooperatives banks and it had and it had a good equation with PSU banks. "Two PSU banks come to us after they severed ties with private insurance companies and some more will come in the near future. He said "Apart from the alternate channels, LIC is currently working on its foray into micro-insurance products for the rural markets and low-income groups through NGOs, SHGs and banks," he said.

3. LIC to Hire Consultant for Credit Card biz

The country's largest life insure. Life Insurance Corporation Ltd. (LIC) will appoint a consultant soon for weighing the credit card business options. Many banks are approaching LIC for tying up offers. LIC has decided to appoint a consultant before diversifying into such ventures. Speaking to FE, TS Vijayan, managing director, LIC said, "Lot of banks are approaching us for entering into the business. We, are in the process of appointing a consultant in January for this purpose. The report would be expected in another six months.

The consultant would provide views on two issues: one, what are the value addition LIC's customer would get from such a product and second, what are the stand-alone profitability and break even points from the business, "We would like to see that by a venturing into this new business what are the value addition we would be able to provide for our customer for example, if the customer could pay the premium through the card and other aspects.

In addition, the consultant will also measure the stand alone profitability of the new entity and the break even point," Mr. Vijayan added. If LIC, finally, launches such card, it would be the first insurance firm in India to enter the plastic money business. The industry expects that the insurance gant can change the rules of the game by offering lower interest as compared to the existing card issuers.

4. LIC Plans to Foray Into New Zealand

Plans composite company in Riyadh

The Life Insurance Corporation of India plans to start a composite company in Riyadh, the capital of Saudi Arabia soon and also make a foray into the insurance sector in New Zealand.

Talking to reporters here recently, its Managing Director, K, Sridhar, said the LIC was working out a strategy to establish itself in New Zealand. The decision on whether to establish a subsidiary or a branch or take up joint venture would hinge upon the result of the ongoing survey, he said. The LIC owned subsidiaries in Bahrain, Sri Lanka and Nepal and had overseas branches in Fiji, Mauritius and London. The Zonal Manager, G. Prabhakara, said till November-end, the Southern Zone achieved 41.43 per cent of annual target in selling policies and 51.06 per cent in premium income mobilisation and stood number two in the country in performance.

5. BOM, LIC Tie up for Bancassurance

The giant insurer, Life Insurance Corporation of India has signed Memorandum of Understanding (MOU) with Bank of Maharashtra (BoM). Putting its plan into action, the insurance products will be initially made available at selected 200 branches, which will move to 500 branches later on. The expansion levels are aimed to be achieved within a span of two years.

This is the 35th tie up of bancassurance for LIC, It had earlier tied up with a couple of public and private sector banks. It has also apped in 22 cooperative banks for its bancassurance venture. Other options like NGOs are also being considered. For non insurance products, BoM will approach United India Insurance Company.

NEW BUSINESS (INDIVIDUAL)

	In India			*Out of India*			*Total*		
Year	*No. of Policies*	*Sum Assured/ NCO/APA Rs. in crores*	*Annual Premium Receivable (Rs. in crores)*	*No. of policies*	*Sum Assured/ NCO/APA Rs. in crores*	*Annual Premium Receivable (Rs. in crores)*	*No. of Policies*	*Sum Assured/ NCO/APA Rs. in crores*	*Annual Premium Receivable (Rs. in crores)*
Individual Assurance									
2001-02	22490852	192569.11	16009.13	8695	212.68	12.57	22499547	192781.79	16021.70
2002-03	24267282	179504.34	12504.19	10359	298.95	18.85	24277641	179803.29	12523.04
2003-04	2646320	198707.12	12540.82	11562	341.40	23.27	26467882	199048.52	12564.09

2004-05	21817967	179481.39	11224.19	13807	409.27	26.50	21831774	179886.66	11.250.69
2005-06	129284800	283763.74	15157.76	13370	416.10	25.24	29298170	284179.84	15183.00
2006-07	20910041	201620.74	11672.72	12059	403.71	24.94	20922100	202042.45	11697.66
General Annuity									
2001-02	515948	740.38	125.08	14	0.15	0.03	515962	740.53	125.11
2002-03	6394	17.36	8.34	0	0	0	6394	17.36	8.34
2003-04	6777	31.93	10.78	0	0	0	6777	31.93	10.78
2004-05	4577	15.43	1.26	0	0	0	4577	15.43	1.26
2005-06	4678	26.73	0.75	—	—	—	4678	26.73	0.75
2006-07	5903	132.16	0.65	—	—	—	5903	132.16	0.65
Pension									
2001-02	259515	6596.37	255.99	0	0	0	259515	6596.37	255.99
2002-03	234390	2165.03	243.39	9	0.05	0.01	234399	2156.08	243.40
2003-04	318761	2826.63	342.87	23	0.16	0.04	318784	2826.79	342.91
2004-05	413441	3590.40	320.15	11	0.06	00	413452	2590.46	320.15
2005-06	40842	270.07	35.78	—	—	—	40842	270.07	35.78
2006-07	16288	207.63	18.86	—	—	—	16288	207.63	18.86
Unit Linked									
2001-02	452	3.15	0.32	0	0	0	452	3.15	0.32
2002-03	1134	7.89	1.19	0	0	0	11341	7.89	1.19
2003-04	170061	990.90	19.12	0	0	0	70061	990.90	19.12
2004-05	7190.85	3378.88	122.51	0	0	0	719085	3378.88	122.51
2005-06	35692	153.53	8.07	—	—	—	35692	153.53	8.07
2006-07	—	—	—	—	—	—	—	—	—
Future Plus started in 2004-05									
2004-05	1004633	260.961	166.52	0	0	0	1004633	260.96	166.52
2005-06	1902505	279.41	133.62	—	—	—	1902505	279.41	133.62
2006-07	1273443	71.44	86.23	—	—	—	1273443	71.44	86.23
Jeevan Plus started in 2005-06									
2005-06	304030	3612.97	273.37	—	—	—	304030	3612.97	273.37
2006-07	228570	2846.11	314.78	—	—	—	228570	2846.11	314.78
Market Plus Started in 2006-07									
2006-07	4993655	699.14	1419.55	—	—	—	4993655	699.14	1419.55
Market Plus									
2006-07	4975762	681.75	1409.23	—	—	—	4975762	681.75	1404.23

NEW BUSINESS (GROUP)

Year	*No. of Schemes*	*No. of Members (in lakh)*	*Sum Assured/Annuity annum (Rs. in crore)*
Group Insurance (incl. Social Security)			
2001-2002	15957	22.33	88501.74
2002-2003	15329	25.20	110763.34
2003-2004	15797	44.48	128047.85
2004-2005	18189	81.00	117662.56
2005-2006	18160	114.68	177317.32
2006-2007	20434	140.38	152864.52
Group Superannuation			
2001-2002	427	0.62	163.35
2002-2003	305	1.08	186.87
2003-2004	344	1.72	214.90
2004-2005	231	0.43	82.50
2005-2006	127	0.71	91.10
2006-2007	263	1.12	212.09
Linked Business G-plus			
2006-2007	20	0.14	97.68

NEW BUSINESS (INDIVIDUAL)

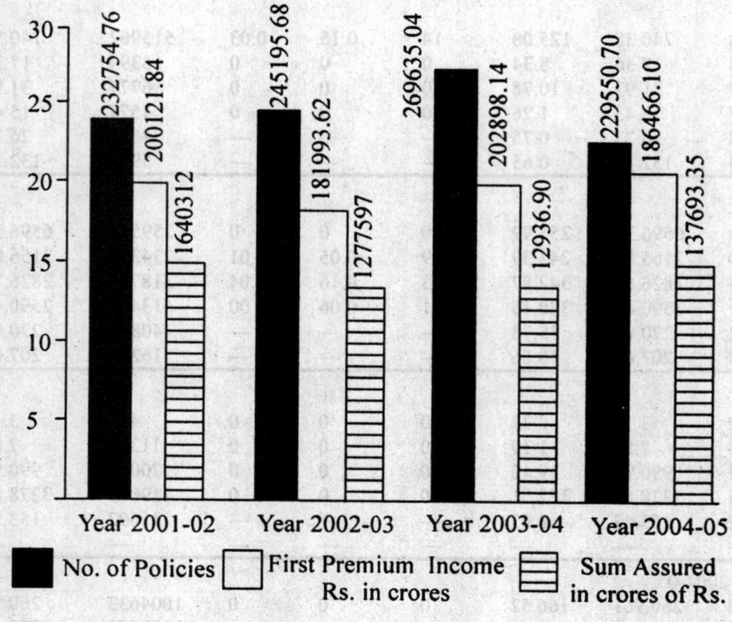

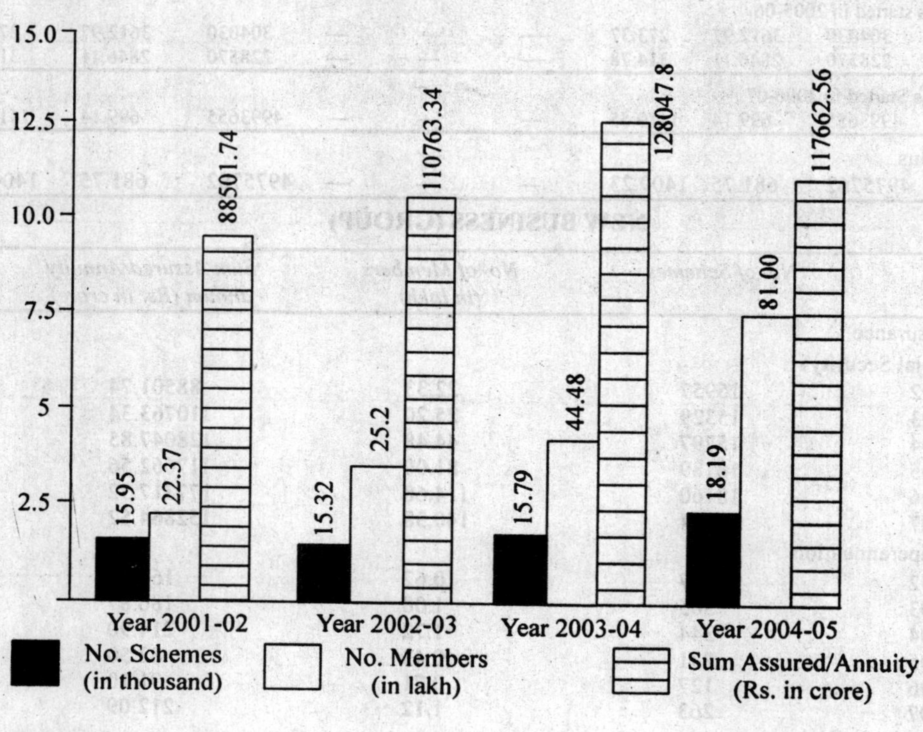

NEW BUSINESS (GROUP INSURANCE)

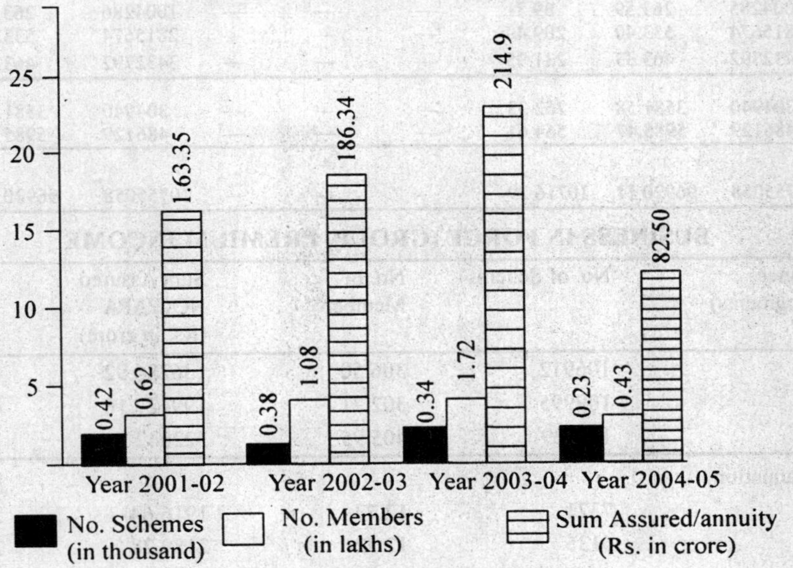

BUSINESS IN FORCE

	Business in-force in India			*Business in-Force out of India*			*Total Business in force*		
Year	*No. of Policies*	*Sum Assured/ NCO/APA Rs. in crores*	*Annual Premium Receivable (Rs. in crores)*	*No. of policies*	*Sum Assured/ NCO/APA Rs. in crores*	*Annual Premium Receivable (Rs. in crores)*	*No. of Policies*	*Sum Assured/ NCO/APA Rs. in crores*	*Annual Premium Receivable (Rs. in crores)*
Individual Assurance									
2001-02	125786529	668113.76	44656.63	87181	1476.66	79.01	125873680	669590.42	44735.64
2002-03	138784878	790176.65	53994.12	89544	1746.66	107.82	138874422	792463.31	54101.94
2003-04	153921144	925033.33	62333.71	93853	2038.97	131.42	154014997	927072.30	62465.13
2004-05	162950920	1029839.55	68700.99	100007	2213.18	137.16	163050927	1032053.03	68838.15
2005-06	179563850	1280159.24	77303.43	98912	2308.64	145.00	179662768	1282467.87	77448.43
2006-07	189417301	1397468.14	81382.12	100197	2587.77	139.81	189517498	1400055.91	81521.93
General Annuity									
2001-02	985274	1453.89	2323.01	169	1.18	0.16	985443	1455.07	2323.17
2002-03	984066	1449.53	1892.90	2	0	0.15	984068	1449.53	1893.05
2003-04	998001	1406.20	1877.51	2	0	0	998003	1406.02	1877.51
2004-05	930568	1189.80	89.01	2	0	0	930570	1189.80	89.01
2005-06	979264	1296.16	107.32	2	—	—	979266	1296.16	107.32
2006-07	1001537	1322.55	100.96	2	—	—	1001539	1322.55	100.96
Pension									
2001-02	1077963	9005.45	842.24	0	0	0	1077963	9005.45	842.24
2002-03	1301630	8898.55	1056.88	174	1.26	0	1301804	8899.81	1056.88
2003-04	1594946	8610.57	1454.48	194	1.35	0	1595140	8611.92	1454.48
2004-05	1937632	3135.07	1617.05	198	1.20	0	1937830	3130.27	1617.05
2005-06	1943639	3206.79	1398.45	178	1.29	—	1943819	3208.08	1398.45
2006-07	1906309	3196.78	1322.37	164	1.11	—	1906473	3197.89	1322.37
Unit Linked									
2001-02	2308	17.47	0.30	0	0	0	2308	17.47	0.30
2002-03	3066	21.70	2.41	0	0	0	3066	21.70	1.41
2003-04	172693	1009.69	19.56	0	0	0	172693	1009.69	19.56
2004-05	880452	4163.75	187.88	0	0	0	880452	4163.75	187.88
2005-06	793548	3206.39	173.84	—	—	—	793548	3206.39	173.84
2006-07	590447	2330.86	148.93	—	—	—	590447	2330.86	148.93

Future Plus started in 2004-05									
2004-05	1004285	263.59	69.31	—	—	—	1004286	263.59	69.31
2005-06	2815674	533.40	209.40	—	—	—	2815674	533.40	209.40
2006-07	3432792	463.33	231.95	—	—	—	3432792	463.33	231.95
Jeewan Plus									
2005-06	304940	3581.58	262.33	—	—	—	304940	3581.58	262.33
2006-07	486129	5985.47	564.61	—	—	—	486129	5985.47	564.61
Money Plus									
2006-07	10755058	96920.11	10716.29	—	—	—	10755058	96920.11	10916.29

BUSINESS IN FORCE (GROUP) PREMIUM INCOME

Group Insurance (inc. social segments)	No. of Schems	No. of Member	Sum Assured NOC/APA (Rs, in crore)	
2004-2005	106912	306.50	136286.92	4019.57
2005-2006	109995	302.71	199427.16	4669.76
2006-2007	111729	405.95	322042	11462.91
Group Superanuation				
2004-2005	7321	12.73	1916.64	3723.75
2005-2006	6135	12.52	2189.28	2946.11
2006-2007	6180	12.93	2575.98	4051.36
Linked Business G=Plus				
2006-2007	20	0.14	97.68	1737

As per IRDA, life Insurers are required to publish their new business and business in force under Individual Insurance General Annuity, Pension and Unit Linked. The LIC is experiencing increasing trends in all respects.

MARKET INTELIGENCE

LIC to Introduce Rima Nivesh 2005

LIC's Bima Nivesh 2005, a single-premium product, will offer a return of 5.5% for a 10-year policy and 5.3% for a 5-year cover. Bima Nivesh 2004 offers 5% on a 10-year policy and 4.8% on a 5-year cover. Since 2000, when the original single premium policy, Bima Nivesh, came into being, the assured rate or return on this plan has been slipping from a height of 10.5% for a 10-year cover. This is the first time the return will go up.

Bima Nivesh 2005 is awaiting approval from the insurance Regulatory and Development Authority, IRDA, and is expected to be launched before the close of the financial year. With market interest rates rising, the 50 basis point increase is in line with the growth in returns. LIC is also awaiting approval for its unit-linked pension plan filed earlier this years. Despite the removal of tax exemption on this plan, on account of its being a single-premium product, LIC has seen a growth rate of 474% in sales of this product this years.

Between April 2004 and January 2005, LIC mopped up Rs. 2,071 crore (Rs. 20.71 billion). from the sale of single-premium products, a large portion accounted for by Bima Nivesh 2004. LIC sold single-premium plans worth Rs. 360 crore (Rs. 3.6 billion) in the corresponding 10-months period last year. With Bima Nivesh 2005, that is expected to be introduced before the end of 2004-2005, LIC hopes to push this growth rate further. Despite the removal of the tax exemption under Section 88 for single-premium plans, policyholders of Bima Nivesh enjoy tax-free returns at end of the policy period under Section 10 (10D). Thus, many individuals who are not in the tax bracket tend to put large sums of this plan.

LIC to Have Separate Investment Units

LIC has decided to carve out the investment activity of group business into a separate division. From April the investment activities of group and pension business will be conducted separately. Until now the corporation had a common investment department for both individual as well as group business.

The group business, which currently accounts for an investment portfolio of around Rs. 30,000 crore (Rs. 300 billion) has a different investment outlook compared to long-term life insurance policies.

Last year, the corporation had decided to create separate strategic business units for pension and group business, international operation and real estate. The SBUs have also been given a separate actuary.

LIC to Recruit Lakh Agents

The Life Insurance Corporation of India plans to recruit around one lakh agents mainly from areas that have not contributed much towards premium income.

The corporation, apart from increasing the number of agents also plans to work out ways to increase the productivity of the existing agent work force. It plans to cross Rs. 3.11 crore new policies by March 2005 an increase of about 15%.

Life Insurers Ready to Share Network With MFs

The life insurance industry has indicated a desire to work in collaboration with the mutual funds, offering them its distribution strength. The move comes ill the wake of mutual funds complaining to the Securities and Exchanges Board of India (SEBI) of life insurers encroaching into mutual funds territory with unit-linked plans. Life insurance companies feel that by working together, both the insurers and the asset management companies can increase their share of the savings pie, which they feel is under threat from increased spending of FMCG, White goods and automobiles. They feel that with over 40% of domestic savings in banks, insurance companies (14.5% share) and mutual funds (1.1%) can grow without hurting each other's prospects.

Unlike traditional products where investment details and various charges are kept under wraps, ULIPs project all this information up-front. But at the same time the investor also takes upon himself the investment risk.

PNB Plans Life Insurance Foray

Punjab, National Bank (PNB), the country's second largest public sector banks, is now planning to diversity into life insurance business. PNB has already applied to the Reserve Bank of India (RBI) in this regard. The company will set up the life insurance business in a joint venture with the Principal Finance Group of the US, Vijay Bank and Berger Paints with equity participation of 24%, 12% and 34% respectively. The PNB will have 30% stake. The joint venture will be the country's first agent-less life insurance office. The proposed joint venture, which will start operations in the next six months has a model distinct from the other 14 life insurance ventures in the country and is being planned to be the country's first agent-less life insurance office.

Principal Group has plans only to sell group and corporate life insurance policies and would not venture into retail insurance products. It would prefer to sell through bancassurance tie-ups.

IRDA May Allow NGOs to Sell All Insurance Products

The Insurance Regulatory and Development Authority may allow Non-Governmental Organisation (NGOs) and self-help groups (SHGs) to act as agencies for life and non-life insurance companies under the new micro-insurance scheme. Until now NGOs and SHGs were allowed to sell health insurance products only. However, they are now likely to be allowed to distribute other life and non-life products as well.

Non-governmental organisation and self-help groups are not required to have the mandatory capital base of Rs. 100 crore, as applicable to insurance companies. The scheme will be unveiled soon. It is expected to help in better distribution of products in rural areas. The comprehensive scheme will cater to the poorer section of society. The IRDA has decided to relax its norms in a bid to offer insurance products for a minimum assured sum of Rs. 10,000.

IRDA Irked with Inconsistent Pricing

Unhappy with the present pricing, the IRDA has asked insurance companies to be consistent in pricing critical illness products by sticking to one standard data. With no reliable data available at present to base the rates on life insurance companies are modifying the critical illness rates provided by reinsurer based on the experience abroad.

The insurance regulator has asked the Actuarial Society of India (ASI) to suggest reference tables that can be the basis till a morbidity table in drawn up. Once that happens, insurance companies will have to follow the said data for pricing products.

Life Insurers Want to Keep Tabs on Mortality Trends

Life insurers are coming together to unravel the mystery of mortality. With some serious number crunching on mortality trends and sickness incidence, life insurers aim to get a clear view to design their products and work out premium. At present, all life insurance payers depend on the data on mortality of the Life Insurance Corporation of India. The move, proposed by the Life Insurance Council; is to set up a Mortality and Morbidity Investigation Bureau in collaboration with the Actuarial Society of India. The exercise will be funded by the life insurance industry and technical support will be provided by ASI. It will be a joint venture entity.

The whole exercise would be based on decoding statistical data on death rate in every age group. The mortality rates are improving in the country with access to better healthcare facilities. On the other hand, there is a rise in sickness level and there is no data available correlating age, nature and extent of sickness.

Eligibility of UCB's lowered to Rs. 50 crore

Urban co-operative banks toying with the idea of taking a plunge into insurance as a corporate agent can now be a happier lot. For, the Reserve Bank of India (RBI) has brought down the minimum eligibility to Rs. 50 crore from Rs. 1000 crore. Urban cooperative banks UCBs will now be able to undertake risk business on a referral basis without RBI approval.

The apex bank had earlier laid down stringent rules to ensure that only those UCBs that are financially strong participated in the insurance business. But, with the relaxation allowed. It has said that no restrictive practice should be adopted by UCBs and that customers should be allowed to exercise their own choice. Also it has said that the UCB's agreement with an insurance company should be for a period not exceeding three years.

Insurance Costs to Increase Post April 1, 2007

Insurance policies will become dearer from April 1. This means that a policyholder will have to sell out 1.2-1.2% addition premium in the coming financial years, depending on the type of product chosen, and the composition of savings and risk elements within the cover. The less the savings element, the higher the additional premium a policyholder will have to bear as the service tax is being loaded on the risk portion of the cover. Following the government's decision to load a 10% service tax on the risk portion of insurance premium plus the 2% education cess, policyholders will have to bear the tax, which has till now been absorbed by the insurance companies.

In a meeting of the life insurance council, which has representation of all the 14 life payers, it was decided that insurance companies would pass on the tax liability to policyholders with respect to unit-linked plans, pure term insurance covers and group plans. In case of a pure term insurance plan, the tax will be levied at the rate of 10.2%. On traditional plans, it was decided that individual companies would decide whether they would bear the burden and absorb the costs, or pass it on to the policyholders

There is a divergence among private players when it comes to passing on the tax to customers in the case of traditional policies. LIC is bearing the entire cost of the service tax. As it is not possible to segregate the risk and savings portion on existing policies, the corporation will absorb the tax liability. It has yet to take a final view on the road ahead when the percentage of service tax rises.

S. No	*Life Insurance Company*	*Market Share in% Premium Share*				*No. of Policies Sold in%*			
		2001-02	2004-05	2005-06	2006-07	2001-02	2004-05	2005-06	2006-07
1	LIC	92.03	78.10	72.30	60.65	96.70	90.41	87.67	82.83
2	ICICI Prudential	2.96	6.51	7.20	6.97	0.96	2.63	2.78	4.24
3	Birla Sunlife	1.21	2.85	1.80	1.17	0.26	0.84	0.84	0.92
4	HDFC Standard	1.08	1.91	2.97	2.15	0.49	0.91	1.23	1.13
5	MAX New York	0.62	0.26	1.38	1.22	0.29	0.19	1.57	1.20
6	SBI Life	0.59	2.35	1.85	3.31	0.07	0.48	0.75	0.98
7	TATA-AIG	0.48	1.51	1.60	0.85	0.36	1.11	1.12	0.89
8	Bajaj Allianz	0.44	2.70	7.29	5.66	0.46	1.11	2.17	4.51
9	Om Kotak	0.25	0.79	0.76	0.82	0.13	0.26	0.30	0.36
10	Ing Vysya	0.14	0.55	0.75	0.62	0.11	0.48	0.40	0.50
11	Aviva	0.10	0.87	1.12	0.96	0.07	0.38	0.52	0.64
12	Met Life	0.05	—	0.43	0.46	0.04		0.35	1.46
13	Amp Sanmar	0.04	—	—	—	0.06		—	—
14	Reliance Life	—	—	05.9	1.22			0.23	0.53
15	Sahara Life	—	—	0.06	0.06			0.08	1.46
16	Bharti Axa Life	—	—	—	0.01				0.01
17	Shriram Life	—	—	—	0.24				0.21

Life Insurance Corporation of India Report on relief measures by LIC or India to Tsunami affected (As on 17th February, 2005) No. of Claims Settled)

INDIVIDUAL

Division	*No.*	*Amount*	*Division*	*No.*	*Amount*
Tamil Nadu (South Zone)					
Vellore	35	3129160	Vellore	16	800000
Tirunelveli	39	3337779	Tirunelveli	18	900000
Thanjavur	159	10374061			
Chennai I	12	1148084	Chennai-I	1	105034
Madurai	28	3717670	Madurai	2	139995
Chennai II	17	3272496			
Coimbatore	2	342233			
Salem	2	278577			
Kerala (South Zone)					
Trivandrum	5	338000			
Kottayam	5	269986			
Emakulam	8	1148707			
Andhra Pradesh (SC Zone)					
Machilipatnam	3	869350			
Nellore	3	699230			
Visakhapatham	2	187900			

Andaman (Eastern Zone)					
Andaman	6	1045298			
Total	326	30158531	**Total**	37	1945029

NO. OF CLAIMS REPORTED

Individual	341	(Settled: 326, Pending: 15)
Group	44	(Settled: 37, Pending: 7)

Insurance Indications

Premium Volume USD (Millions)

	Total			*Life*			*Non-Life*			*Population (millions)*		*GDP (USD billion)*	
	2004	*2005*	*2006*	*2004*	*2005*	*2006*	*2004*	*2005*	*2006*	*2005*	*2006*	*2005*	*2006*
1. South Korea	68623	85097	101179	48680	60683	72298	19944	24414	28881	48.1	48.8	685	911
2. China	52171	60144	70805	35407	39604	45092	16765	20540	25713	1299.0	1323.6	1599	2613
3. Taiwan	43236	48984	51562	33851	38788	41245	9385	10169	10318	22.7	22.9	309	355
4. South Africa	30682	34773	40731	24381	27596	33106	6301	7177	7624	43.9	47.6	213	255
5. India	21249	27410	43032	16919	22587	37220	4330	4823	5812	1077.0	1119.5	595	901
6. Brazil	18042	23947	30930	8199	10553	13699	9843	13394	16691	178.5	188.9	600	1067
7. Russia	16352	17336	21904	3544	894	571	12809	16442	20932	142.9	142.5	566	929

Source: Sigma R 5/2005 and 4/2007

Global Market Share of Insurances

Ranks		*Home Market*	*Premium in USD in 2004*	*Global Market Share 2004/1998*	
1.	AIG	USA	66837	3.6%	1.8%
2.	Metropolitan Life	USA	58732	3.2%	2.4%
3.	AXA	France	58422	3.2%	3.3%
4.	Allianz	Germany	56178	3.0%	1.8%
5.	ING	Netherlands	45978	2.5%	1.5%
9.	Aviva	U.K.	37612	2.0%	0.9%
13.	Prudential (US)	U.S.A.	27751	1.5%	1.3%
23.	Standard Life	U.K.	18719	1.0%	0.6%
28.	Sun Life	Canada	15406	0.8%	0.6%
30.	LIC	India	13746	0.7%	0.4%

Source: signs 1 /2006

F.No. 300 (Rev. '74)

Office use only
Date of Receipt ....
....
Inward No. Initials
Is licience in force? .... Initials ....

LIFE INSURANCE CORPORATION OF INDIA

(Established by the Life Insurance Corporation Act, 1956)

PROPOSAL FOR INSURANCE ON OWN LIFE

(Not to be used for Insurance on the Lives of Minors)

Divisional Office: .... **Branch Office:** .... **Proposal No.** ....

Agent's Name .... **Licence No.** .... **Date of Expy.** .... **Agent's D.O's. Code Nos.** ....

(All answers to be filled in legibly. Answers must be given in words. Strckes of the pen or date of dashes will not be accepted as replies)

Specimen

1. (*a*) Name in full ....
(IN BLOCK LETTERS) ....
(*b*) Short Name ....
(*c*) Nationality ....
(*d*) Address which will be incorporated in the Policy and at which notices will be sent ....
....
(*e*) Permanent Residential Address ....
....
(*f*) Father's Name in full ....
....
(*g*) Present Occupation ....
(*h*) Nature of Duties ....
(*i*) Name of present employer ....
(*j*) Length of service with him ....
(*k*) Name of previous employer ....

2. Table and Term of Assurance | Sum to be Assured Rs. | State if premiums are payable Yearly Half-Yearly, Quarterly or Monthly. | Amount of the deposit | If policy is to be dated back, state date.

3. Date of Birth	Age Nearer Birthday	Nature of Age Proof	Place of Birth	If Age proof is service record, what proof was submitted to employer?	

4. Do you desire to secure Double Accident Benefit and Extended Permanent. Disability Benefit? ....

N.B.: *The maximum Double Accident Benefit or Combined Double Accident Benefit and Extended Permanent Disability Benfit allowed on any one life under one or more policies of the Corporation or of the insurers whose business has been taken over by the Corporation, shall be limited to Rs. 1,00,000.*

Contd....

5. What is the object of this assurance? ....

N.B. —If the policy is to be effected (a) under the Married Women's Property Act, 1987, or (b) for the purpose of paying Estate Duty, or (c) for the Marriage of a dependent female relation, please state so. If the object is as per (d) please complete the relevant addendum.

6. A. If you wish to nominate under Section 39 of the Insurance Act, 1983, a person to whom the moneys secured by the policy applied for are to be paid in the event of your death, please state:

Full Name of Nominee .... Relationship to Yourself .... Age ....
(IN BLOCK LETTERS)

Full Address ....

B. If the nominee is a minor, please state the name of the person whom you wish to appoint to receive the policy money in the event of the claim arising during the minority of the nominee. The appointee must sign below to show his/her consent to the appointment.

Full Name of the Appointee ....
(IN BLOCK LETTERS)

Full Address ....

Signature of the Appointee .... Relationship to the Nominee .... Age ....

Specimen

7. N.B. — For non-medical cases only (*a*) What is your height (without shoes)? .... (*a*) ....
(*b*) What is your exact weight (with thin clothes)? .... (*d*) ....

8. If you are already employed in the Armed Forces, please state:

(*a*) The wing to which you belong	(*b*) Your rank therein	(*c*) The date of your last Medical Examination	(*d*) Your medical category after Medical Examination	(*e*) Were you below A-I category? If so, when?

9. Have you any prospect or intention of engaging in Aviation or of enterior Naval or Millitary Service or taking up any other hazardous occupation or pursuit? If so give details. ....

10. Is your life now being proposed for another assurance to, or is any other perposal, or an application for revival of a policy, on your life, under consideration of this or any other Office of the Corporation? If so, which is the Office and give details. ....

Contd...

11. State below details of all your previous Policies under. *(*A*) Medical basis, +(*B*) Non-Medical Basis:

Name of the Divl. Office of the Corp. or of the Insurer	Policy Number	Sum Assured	lan of Absence	Year of issue of Policy	Whether accepted as proposed at ordinary rates	With or Without Accident Benefit	Whether in force, for the full sum Assured?	*If not, give due date of last premium paid and mode of payment
*A								
+B								

*N.B.: Corporation does not entertain any fresh proposal for Insurance where previous policy has lapsed or converted into paid up policy within last three years.

12. Has a proposal on your life on an application for revival of a policy on your life made to this or any other Office of the Corporation or any Insurer ever been.

(*a*) withdrawn or dropped? .... (*c*) accepted with an extra premium or lien? ....

(*b*) deferred or declined? .... (*d*) accepted or terms otherwise than those proposed? ....

If so, give details ....

Additional questions to be Answered by Female Proposers (Qns. 13 and 14)

13. (*a*) Your educational qualification, if any .... (*b*) Your average monthly income, if any ....

(*c*) State Sources of income .... (*d*) Whether you pay Income-tax ....

14. If you are married, please state:

(*a*) Husband's full name ....

(*b*) His occupation .... (*c*) His average monthly Income Rs. ....

(*d*) The following details of his life insurance:

Contd....

Office of the Corporation	Policy Number	Sum Assured	Table and Term	Present condition

15. Family History

	LIVING		DEAD			
	Age	State of Health (if not good, give full details)	Year of Death	Age of Death	Duration of last illness	Cause of death
Father ...	...					
Mother ...	...					
Brothers ... Total Living ... Total Dead ...	No.					
Sisters ... Total Living ... Total Dead ...	No.					
Wife/Husband ...	No.					
Children ... Total Living ... Total Dead ...						

Specimen

16. Has any of your relations, living or dead, suffered from any hereditary or infectious disease like diabetes, insanity, epliepsy, gout, asthma, tuberculosis, cancer, leprosy, etc.? ... .

Contd....

17. (*a*) What has been your usual state of health? ...... (*a*) ....

(*b*) Have you any bodily defect or deformity? If so, give details. ...... (*b*) ....

(*c*) Have you had (*i*) Small Pox or (*ii*) Successful vaccination ...... (*c*) (*i*) .... (*ii*) ....

(*d*) (*i*) Are you suffering from Pyorrhea? ...... (*d*) (*i*) ....

(*ii*) State number of missing teeth, if any ...... (*ii*) ....

(*iii*) For how many missing teech a denture is worn? ...... (*iii*) ....

18. Have you ever suffered from or are you suffering from:	Answers "Yes" or	If 'yes' describe fully each ailment giving its nature the number of attacks, dates, duration, seycrity, treatment taken, result and names and address of doctors consulted, giving reference to Question No. for questions 18 to 22.
(*a*) Presistent cough, asthma, bronchitis, pneumonic pleurisy, spitting of blood, tuberculosis or any other disease of lungs?	(*a*)....................	Details of Q. No. ....
(*b*) High or low blood pressures, rhenumatic fever, pain chest, breathlessness, palpitation, infraction, or any disease of the heart of arteries?	(*b*)....................	
(*c*) Peptic ulcer, colitis, jaundice, anaemia, piles, dysentery or any disease of the stomach, liver, spreen, gall bladdeer or, pancreas?	(*c*)....................	
(*d*) Any disease of kidney, prostate, or urinary system?	(*d*)....................	
(*e*) Paralysis, insanity, epilepsy, fits of any kind or nervous breakdown or any other disease of the brain or the nervovs system?	(*e*)....................	
(*f*) Hernis, hydrocele, varicocele, fistula, varicose venis, skin eruption, filariasis, goitre, gonorrhea, syphilis or any other venereal disease?	(*f*)....................	
(*g*) Cancer, leprosy, rheumatism, gout, enlarged glands or tumours?	(*g*)....................	
(*h*) Any disease of the ear, nose, throat or eyes, including defective sight or hearing and discharge from the ears?	(*h*)....................	

Contd....

19. Have you been suspected of diabetes or are you suffering from diabetes or have ever passes sugar, albumen, pus or blood in urine?	....	
20. Have you consulted a raodical practitioner, within the last five years for any ailments requiring treatment for more than a week?	....	
21. Have your remained absent from place of your work on ground of health during the last 5 years?	....	
22. (*a*) Did you ever have any operation, accident or injury?	(*a*)	
(*b*) Have you ever had, an electrocardiogram, X-ray or screening, blood, urine or stood examination?	(*b*)	
(*c*) Have you ever been in any hospital, asylum, or panatorium for check-up, observation, treatment or any operation?	(*c*)	
23. Do you use or have you ever used alcoholic drinks, narcotics or any other drugs? If so, what? Also state quantity consumed per day.	....	

Specimen

For Females only

24. (*a*) Do you observe purdah? (*a*) ....

(*b*) Have the menstrual periods always been regular and painless? (*b*) ....

(*c*) State the date of last menstruation. (*c*) ....

(*d*) Are you pregnant now? (*d*) ....

(*e*) State the date of the last delivery. (*e*) ....

(*f*) Have you had any abortions or miscarriages? (*f*) ....

(*g*) Did you have any complications related to pregnancy? (*g*) ....

(*h*) Have you any weakness or injury resulting from child bearing or miscarriage? (*h*) ....

(*i*) Have you suffered or are you suffering from any disease of breast, ovaries or uterus? (*i*) ....

Contd....

DECLARATION BY THE PROPOSER

I ....the person whose life is hereinbefore proposed to be assured, do hereby declare that the foregoing statements and answers have been given by me after fully understanding the questions and the same are true, and complete in every particular and that I have not withheld any information and I do hereby agree and declare that these statements and this declaration shall be the contract of assurance between me and the Life Insurance Corporation of India and that if any untrue averment be contained therein the said contract shall be absolutely null and void and all moneys which shall have been paid in respect thereof shall stand forfeited to the Corporation.

SPECIMEN SIGNATURE ....

Notwithstanding the provisions of any law, usage, custom or convention for the time being in force prohibiting any doctor, hospital, and/or employer from divulging any knowledge or information about me concening my health or employment, on the grounds os secrecy, I, my heirs, executors, administrators and assigns or any person or persons, having interest of any kind whatsoever in the policy contract issued to me hereby agree, that such autbority having such knowledge or information, shall be at liberty to divulge any such knowledge or information to the Corperation.

And I further agree that if after the date of submission of the Proposal but before the issue of First premium Receipt (*i*) any change in my ccupation or any adverse circuumstance connected with my financial position or the general health of myself or that of any member of my family, occurs or (*ii*) if a Proposal for assurance or an application for evival of a policy on my life made to any Office of the Corporation hasbeen withdrawn on dropped, deferred or declined, or accepted at an increased premium or subject to a lien or on terms other than as proposed I shallforthwith intimate the same to the Corportion in writing to reconsider the terms of acceptance of assurance. Any omission on my part to do so shall render this Assurance invalid and all moneys which shall have been paid in respect thereof forfeited to the Corporation.

Dated at..on the .... day of 197

Signature of Witness ....

Occupation & Address ....

....

.... Signature or thumb impression of the Proposer.

If in this form the answers to the questions and/or signature of the Proposer is/are in vernaoular then he should declare in his own handwriting above his signature that all questions were explained to him and that his replies were given after fully and properly understanding the same.

1. This declaration should be made by the person filling in the form

Address of the declarant ....

(I) I hereby declare that I have fully explained the above questions to the Proposer and I have truthfully recorded the answers given by the Proposer.

....

Signature

2. The thumb impression of the proposer should be attested by a person of standing whose identity can easily be established, but unconnected with the Corporation and this declargtion should be to the questions has affixed his thumb impression to the proposal

Address of the declarant ....

(I) I hereby declare that I have explained the contents of the proposal form to the proposer in .... (language) and that I have read out to the Proposer the answers made by from after fully understanding the contects thereof.

....

Signature

Extracts from Section 41 of the Insurance Act, 1938

1. No person shall allow or offer to allow, either directly or indirectly, as an inducement to any person to take out or renew or continue an insurance in respect of any kind of risk relating to lives or property in India, any rebate of the whole or part of the commission payable or any rebate of the premium shown on the Policy, nor shall any person taking out or renewsing or continuing a Policy accept any rebate, except such rebate as may be allowed in accordance with the published prospectuses or tables of the Insurer.
2. Any person making defaut in complying with the provisions of this section shall be prunishable with fine which may extend to five hundred rupees.

THE CORPORATION ALLOWS THE FOLLOWING REDUCING IN THE ANNUAL PREMIUM

Reduced Premiums for Policies of Large Amounts:

In respect of Policies for Rs. 5,000/- and upwards, there will be allowed a reduction in the Annual Premium per thousand Sum Addured of (*i*) Re. 0.50 for each policy for Rs. 5,000/- and upwards, but less than Rs. 10,000/- (*ii*) Re. 0.75 for each policy for Rs. 10,000/- and upwards but less than Rs. 20,000/- and (*iii*) Rupee one for each policy for Rs. 20,000/- and upwards. These reductions are not applicable to Single Premium Policies or to policies effected under the (*i*) Pure Endowment,

Contd....

(*ii*) Multi-purpose, (*iii*) Children's Deferred Assurance, (*iv*) Convertible Term Assurance, (*v*) Immediate Annuity and (*vi*) Deferred Annuity Plans. However, under the Multi-purpose Plan, a reduction of Re. 0.50 per thousand basic sum assured would be allowed in the Annual Premium in respect of Policies for Rs. 5,000/- and upwards. In the case of the Educational Annuity Policy, the above reduction will be calculated on the nominal sum assured.

Reducted Premium where the Mode of Payment is Yearly or Half-Yearly:

If the premiums are payable yearly or half-yearly, a reduction of Re. 0.75 and Re. 0.50-respectively will be allowed in the Annual Premium per thousand sum assured under all classes of assurance except under the Pure Endowment, Children's Deferred Assurance and Deferred Annuity Policies where the reductive will be the rate of Rs. 0.37 and Re. 0.25 respectively. These reductions are not applicable to (*i*) the Immediate Annuity Policy, (*ii*) the Convertible Term Assurance Policy, (*iii*) the additional premium payable to secure the Premium Waiver Benefits under the Children's Deference Assurance Policy, (*iv*) the additional premium payable to secure the Supplementary Benefis under the Multi-purpose Policy and (*v*) the Janata Policy. In the case of the Deferred Annuity Policy the above reduction will be calculated on the cash option, while under the Educational Annuity Policy the said reduction will be calculated on the nominal sum assured.

Croup and Superannuation Scheme:

Special rates will apply to policies issued under these Schemes.

FOR MEDICAL CASE ONLY

Specimen

"I certify that the Proposer has signed/put his/her thumb impression in my presence after admitting that all the answer to Question Nos. 15 & onwards of this from have been correctly recorded.

....

Signature or thumb impression of the Life Proposal

N.B.: Signature or thumb impression should be affixed in presence of Medical Examiner.

....

(Signature of the Medical Examiner)

To be completed by the Agent

Branch No. ....

Agent's Name ....

Dev. Off. Name ....

Proposal No ....

Policy No. ....

LIFE INSURANCE CORPORATION OF INDIA

(Established by the Life Insurance Corporation Act, 1956)

MEDICAL EXAMINER'S CONFIDENTIAL REPORT

(*i*) Please satisfy yourself about the identify of the Life Proposed to guard against impersonation.

(*ii*) Give full detials of ailment or impairment detected. Ascertain & give details such as dates & duration etc.

(*iii*) If this is a new proposal, obtain proposal form completed as per instractions therein & attach it with this.

(*iv*) The Life Proposed and the person introducing him/her to you should sign in your presence. Do not use the form signed in advance.

Full Name of the Life to be examined .... **Age** .... **Years**

Father's Name .... **Occupation of the Life Proposal**....................

Introduced by .... **His designation** .... **His signature** ....

Specimen

1. Identification

(*a*) Is the examinee known to you (*i*) personally ~~or (*ii*)~~ professionally? (*a*) (*i*) .... (*ii*) ....

(*b*) Give identification marks .... (*b*) ....

2. Appearance

(*a*) (*i*) What is his/her apparent age? (*a*) (*i*) ....

(*ii*) Does he/she look older than the stated age? (*ii*) ....

Contd....

(*b*) Is the general appearance healthy?	(*b*)	
(c) Does the person appear to be of sober and temperate habits?	(*c*)	
(*a*) Are there marks of (*i*) small pox or (*ii*) successful vaccination? ...	(*d*) (*i*) .... (*ii*)	
(*e*) Is those any defect or deformity, swellings of joints, enlarge ment of thyroid or lymphatic glands or any cicatrices?	(*e*)	
(*f*) Is there any evidence of filariasis, varicose veins or skin disease?	(*f*)	
(*g*) Is there any evidence of pesent or past malignancy?	(g)	
3. Measurements and Weight		OFFICE REMARKS
(*a*) Chest (over nipples) on (*i*) complete expiration	(*a*) (*i*) .... cms.	....
(*ii*) full inspiration	(*ii*) .... cms.	....
(*b*) Abdomen (over naval)	(*b*) .... cms.	....
(*c*) Height (without shoes)	(*c*) .... cms.	....
(*d*) Height (with thin clothes)	(*d*) .... cms.	....
4. Mouth, Eyes, Ears and Throat		
(*a*) Are the gums, teeth and tongue healthy	(*a*)	
(*b*) Is there any pyorshea? If so, is it moderate or marked?	(*b*)	
(*c*) (*i*) Are there any missing teeth? If so, how many? ..	(*c*) (*i*)	
(*ii*) For how many missing teeth a denture is worn? ..	(*ii*)	

Specimen

Contd....

(*d*) Is there any evidence of past or present disease of the eyes, ears nose or throat? (If the visioner hearing is affected, degree should be stated. Ascertain and mention the power of glasses.)	(*d*) ....
5. Respiratory System	
(*a*) Is the chest symmetrical and well formed?	(*a*) ....
(*b*) Are there any symptoms or signs suggesting abnormality of disease of the repiratory system?	(*b*) ....
6. Cardiovascular System	
(*a*) Is the heart normal in size, position and impulse? Are the heart sounds normal?	(*a*) ....
(*b*) (*i*) State pluse rate (*ii*) Describe abnormalities, if any.	(*b*) (*i*)..................(*ii*)..................
(*c*) Is the condition of blodd vessels healthy?	(*c*) ....
(*d*) Blood Pressure : (in supine position with a mercury manometer)	(*d*) Ist reading systolic..........mm.Hg.......... „ Diastolic..........mm.Hg.......... 2nd reading Systolic..........mm.Hg.......... „ Diastolic..........mm.Hg..........

N.B. If the Systolic reading is 140 or over, or Diastolic reading is 90 or ocer, a second reading should be 90 or over, a second reading should be taken in supine position after 10 minutes rest.

7. Abdomen	
(*a*) Is there any evidence of disease or of enlargement of liver or spleen? If so, its degree.	(*a*) ....
(*b*) Is there any evidence of gastric or duodenal ulcer? ..	(*b*) ....

Contd....

(*c*) Is there any lump or tenderness or free fluid in the abdomen?	(*c*) ....
(*d*) Is there any evidence of piles or fistula?	(*d*) ....
8. Genito-Urinary System	
(*a*) Urine: (The sample of urine must be passed under such circums-	(*a*) (*i*) Sugar.................... (*ii*) Sp. Gravity....................
	(*iii*) Albumen.................... (*iv*) Other Abnormalities....................
(*b*) Is there any evidence of past or present venereal disease?	(*b*) ....
(*c*) Is hernia present? If so, state side, type, size reducible or not whether a properly fitting truss is worn & history of strang lation	(*c*) ....
(*d*) Are the testis normal in location, size and consistency? ..	(*d*) ....
(*e*) Is hydrocele present? Is so, give the maximum horizontal circumference of the whole scrotum.	(*e*) ....
9. Nervous System	
(*a*) Is there any evidence or nervous disease, such as, paralysis, epilepsy, wasting, tremors, involuntary movements, etc.?	(*a*) ....
(*b*) Are the kenee-jerks and pupil reflexes normal?	(*b*) ....
10. Operation and other details	
(*a*) Is there any evidence of any operation, accident or injury? State the degree of impairment if any. Give the location, size and condition of scar.	(*a*) ....

Contd....

(*b*) Has the person ever undergone any ECG, X-Ray, Screening, Blood, urine or stool examinatiens? If so, ascertain nature of test, date, reason and result.	(*b*) ....
11. For Female Applicants only	
(*a*) Is there any disease of teh breasts?	(*a*) ....
(*b*) Is there any evidence of pregnancy?	(*b*) ....
(*c*) Do you suspect any disease of uterus, cervix or overies? ..	(*c*) ....
(*d*) Is there any weakness or injury resulting from childbearing or miscarriage?	(*d*) ....
12. (*a*) Have you carried out ECG or any other special examination give such as heart report etc. alongwith this examination? If so, details.	(*a*) ....
(*b*) Are there any other circumstances or findings which might affect the longevity?	(b) ....
(*c*) Do you suspect any adverse features of past history or habits or existence of any other disease or any other complaint not noted above.	(*c*) ....
(*d*) Do you consider the life to be first class? If not, state the reason.	(*d*) ....

Space for Additional Remarks:

Dated at .... on the .... day on .... 97, at .... a.m. / p.m

Contd....

I hereby certify that I have this day examined the above Life to be assured personally, in private and have recorded in my own hand the true and correct findings. I declare I am not related to the party.

Signature of the Life Prosposed Signed in my presence	Signature of the Medical Examiner
Signature of the Medical Examiner	Qualification .... Code No. ....

Name & Address ....

....

F.No. 300 (Rev. '75)

Office use only
Name of Agent..
Agency No..
Prosposal No..

LIFE INSURANCE CORPORATION OF INDIA

(Established by the Life Insurance Corporation Act, 1956)

AGENT'S CONFIDENTIAL REPORT

N.B—Agent should complete this report only after medical examination is arranged.

Full name of the Proposer..Age........................years.

Full Name of the Life to be Assured..Age........................years.

Residence .... **ccupation**..

.... **Sum Proposed**..

1.	(*a*) How long you have known the life to be assured?	(*a*) ....
	(*b*) Are you related to him? If so, how?	(*b*) ....
2.	(*a*) Give (*i*) name of medical examiner and (*ii*) date of medical examination.	(*a*) (*i*)............ (*ii*)............
	(*b*) State if any special reports were done and if so, give date, doctors' name and nature of reports.	(*b*) ....
3.	(*a*) Does he look older than the stated age? If so, by how many years?	(*a*) ....
	(*b*) What is the educational qualification of the Life to be Assured?	(*b*) ....
4.	What is his monthly income and state the sources: (*i*) Employment (*ii*) Business or Profession (*iii*) Other sources (to be specified) (*iv*) H. U.F., if any N.B.—*State also income of life to be assured, if he is different from proposer*	.... (*i*) .... (*ii*)............ (*iii*) .... (*iv*)............ ....
5.	(*a*) What is general state of health of the Life to be assured? ..	(*a*) ....
	(*b*) Is there anything unhealthy about his appearance, such as being very thin and emaciated, anaemic etc.? ..	(*b*) ....

Specimen

Contd....

(*c*) Has he any deformity, impaired sight or hearing, amputation? ..	(*c*) ....
(*d*) Is he (*i*) tall or short (*ii*) underweight or overweight? ..	(*d*) (*i*) ....(*ii*)..................
(*e*) Have you any knowledge of his having suffered from any	(*e*) ....

6. Have you verified the particulars relating to the previous policies? If so, give following particulars.

(*a*) Policy No.	Date of last Premium Receipt	Policy No.	Date of last Premium Receipt

(*b*) State whether the policy document shows that the age is admitted? ....

(*c*) Verify/ascertain what proff of age was submitted under previous policy..

7. (*a*) Give mark of identification. .. (*a*) ....

(*b*) Does he bear marks of (*i*) successful vaccination (*iii*) small-pox? .. (*b*) (*i*)..................(*ii*)..................

(*c*) Give below weight and physical measurements; (Please see not below)(*c*)

(*i*) Exact Height (*ii*) Exact Weight .. (*i*) ....cms.(*ii*)..................kgs.

(*iii*) Girth of abdomen at level of navel .. (*iii*) ....cms.

Girth or chest at nipple (*iv*) on expiration (*v*) on inspiration .. (*iv*) ....cms. (*v*)..................cms.

N.B.— Height and girths of chest and abdomen should be found by measurement. Places where weighing machines are available actual weight should be given. Places where a weighing machines is not available, weight should be estimated and the word 'Estimated' should be added after the estimated figure of weight.

8. Are you aware of anything in the occuptaios, financial or social position of the life to be assured, his personal habits or any other circumstances which might be likely to add to the risk?	

Contd....

9. Do you recommend the acceptance of the proposal?

I hereby declare that the foregoing statements are true and correct to the best of my knowledge and belief.

Dated at ....on the ....day of..19.

____

Signature of the Agent.

The agent should type here or write in block letters his name and address so that the acceptance advice may be sent to him without any delay.

....

....

....

From No. 460-A(Revised)

LIFE INSURANCE CORPORATION OF INDIA

(Established by the Life Insurance Corporation Act, 1956)

PERSONAL STATEMENT REGARDING HEALTH

Divisional Office..Branch Office...Proposal/Policy No..years.

Agent's Name...Agent's Code No...................................

(All answers to be filled in legibly. Answers must be given in words. Srokes of the pen or dots or dashes will not be accepted as replies).

Instruction:— Please fill this form

(*i*) When specifically requested, if you apply for the issue of a new policy

(*ii*) When more than 6 months have passed since the date of lapse; if you apply for the revival of a lapsed policy. (when this form is used in respect of . assurances under Non-medical Schemes, detect room the first line of Question 3 hereunder the words "Your last medical examination for ")

Specimen

1. Name in full (in BLOCK LETTERS)........................	
Full address	
2. Is this application for:	If the answer is 'Yes' please give the Proposal Number or the Policy Number.
(*a*) Issue of a new Policy?	(*a*) .... Proposal No........................
(*b*) Rvival of a lapsed Policy?	(*b*) .... Policy No........................
3. Since the date of your last Medical Examination for the above mentioned proposal or Policy:	
(*a*) Have you suffered from any physical or mental illness, injury or disability? If so, give details.	(*a*) ....
(*b*) Have you been required to take medical treatment? If so, give details (Such as date and duration of illness, effect of treatment etc. as also name and address of the doctor who treated you).	(*b*) ....

Contd....

(*c*) What deaths or illness have there been in your family (parents, wife/husband, brothers, sisters or children)? Give age at death, date of death and duration of illness.	(*c*) ....
(*d*) Has there been any change in your mode of life habits and occupation? If so, give details	(*d*) ....
(*e*) Has a proposal on your life or an application for revival of a policy on your life made to this or any other office of the Corporation or any. Insurer ever been withdrawn or dropped, deferred or declined, accepted with an extra premium or lien or on terms otherwise than those proposed? If So, give details.	(*e*) ....
4. Are you at present in sound health?	
5. Have you paid any deposit or arrears of premiums? If so, give details.	(*i*) Amount: Rs. .... (*ii*) Dates: .... (*iii*) How paid: ....
6. Since the date of your last Medical Examination for the abovementioned Proposal or Policy:	
(*a*) Have you been menstruating regularly?	(*a*) ....
(*b*) Have you had any miscarriages?	(*b*) ....
7. Please give the date of :	
(*a*) Last menstruation.	(*a*) ....
(*b*) Last delivery	(*b*) ....
8. Are you pregnant now?	

Contd....

I,.. do hereby declare that the foregoing statements and answers are true in every particular and agree and declare that these statements and this declaration along with my Proposal for Insurance shall be the basis of the contract of *assurance/revival of the lapsed policy, between me and the Life Insurance Corporation of India and that if any untrue averment be contained therein the said contract shall be absolutely null and void and all moneys which shall have been paid in respect thereof shall stand forfeited to the Corporation.

(* Delete words not applicable)

**And I further declare that if the Corporation revives the policy on the original terms or otherwise and (*i*) if any change in my occupation or any adverse circumstance connected with my financial position or the general health of myself of that of my family, however unimportant I may consider the same, occurs or (*ii*) if a Proposal for assurance or any application for revival of a policy on my life made to any office of the Corporation is pending or has been withdrawn or dropped, deferred or declined or accepted at an increased premium or subject to a lien or on terms other than as proposed or (*iii*) if I have been selected for service in any of the branches of Military, Naval or Air Force Services between the date of this declaration and the date of revival of the policy, the Revival shall be absolutely null and void and all moneys which shall have been paid in respect thereof forfeited, unless intimation of such event be made in writing to the Corporation and the revival be reapproved by the Corporation.

(** Delete this paragraph in case of application for the issue of a new policy.)

Dated at.. on the.. day of.. 197

Signature of Witness..

Occupation..

Address..

Signature of Thumb Impression of the Proposer/Life Assured.

Specimen

If the answers to the question in this form are given in vernacular or if the answers to the questions are given in English but the Proposer/Life Assured signs in vernacular then the Proposer/Life Assured should declare in his own handwriting above his own signature that all questions were explained to him and that his replies were given after fully and properly understanding the same.

In case the Proposer/Life Assured is illiterate:

1. This declaration should be made by the person filling in the form.

   Address of Declarant..

   ....

I hereby declare that I have fully explained the above questions to the Proposer/Life Assured and I have truthfully recorded the answers given by the Proposer/Life Assured.

.... (*Signature*)

2. The thumb impression of the Proposer/Life Assured Should be attested by a person of standing whose identity can easily be established, but unconnected with the Corporation, and this declaration should be made by him.

Address of Declarant..

....

I hereby declare that I have explained the contents of the statement to the Proposer/ Life Assured in (language) .... and that I have read out to the Proposer/Life Assured the answers to the questions dictated by the proposer/ Life Assured and that the Proposer/Life Assured has a fixed his thumb impression to the statement after fully understanding the contents thereof.

..............................(*Signature*)

If the life assured/to be assured is different from the proposer, the questions are to be answered in respect of the life assured/to be assured.

Contd....

LIFE INSURANCE CORPORATION OF INDIA

SHORT MEDICAL REPORT

Instructions: (*i*) Please have this report completed by an authorised medical examiner of the Corporation.

(*ii*) The fee of Rs. 8/- for this report is to be paid to the medical examiner by the policyholder/proposer.

On the life of Shri/smt./Ku. ....

who was introduced by Shri/smt./Ku. ....

1. (*a*) Is the person to be examined known to you (*i*) personally or (*ii*) professionally? .. .. (*a*) ....
   (*b*) Are you satisfied about his identity? .. .. (*b*) ....
   (*c*) Describe personal marks or peculiarities by which we may be identified. .. .. (*c*) ....
   (*d*) Is the general appearance of the applicant healthy? .. (*d*) ....
   (*e*) Are there any physical defects or deformities? .. (*e*) ....

2. Are the breath sounds normal over whole of the chest?

3. (*a*) State the character of heart's action. .. .. (*a*) ....
   (*b*) Are its sounds and rhythm regular and normal? .. (*b*) ....
   (*c*) Are there any indications of disease of heart or blood Vessels? .. .. (*c*) ....

4. Do you find any evidence of the past or present disease of the following:
   (Give details where necessary)
   (*a*) Brain or the nervous system? .. .. .. (*a*) ....
   (*b*) Respiratory System? .. .. .. (*b*) ....
   (*c*) Digestive organs, missing teeth or Pyorrhea? .. (*c*) ....
   (*d*) Genito-urinary tract, syphilis, gonorrhea or stricture? (*d*) ....

Contd....

(*e*)	Hernia or Hydrocele?	(*e*) ....
(*f*)	Eye, ear or throat?	(*f*) ....

5. Height...............................cms. 6. Wt...................................Kgs.

7. Chest (over nipples) stripped 8. Abdomen...........................cms.

On complete expiration.........................cms.

On full inspiration...............................cms.

N.B: If the systolic reading is. 140 mm. Hg. or over, or the 5th phase diastolic reading is 90 mm. Hg. or over, a second reading should be taken in a supine position after 10 minutes.

11. For Female Applicants.

(*a*) Is there any evidence of pregnancy? .. .. (*a*)..

(*b*) Does your examination show any disease of the breast or of the uterus? .. .. (*b*)..

12. Do you consider the life to be first Class? If not state reasons for your opinion .. ..

I hereby certify that I have this day examined the above life to be Assured personally, in private and have recorded in my own hand the true and correct findings. I declare I am no related to the party.

Dated.......................................on the..................................day of.......................................197

....

Signature of the Life Assured/Life to be Assured. *Signature of the Life Assured/Life to be Assured.*

(*N.B.* –The Medical Examiner should see that the applicant signs in his presence).

PARTICULARS OF THE MEDICAL EXAMINER

Appointed by the Corporation or not... Medical Degree and name of the University..

....

Medical Examiner's Code No.................................... Year in which degree obtained...

(allotted by the Corporation)

Name and Address (IN BLOCK LETTERS)..

....

....

PART THREE

MARINE INSURANCE

19

NATURE OF MARINE INSURANCE CONTRACT

Definition

Marine insurance has been defined as a contract between insurer and insured whereby the insurer undertakes to indemnify the insured in a manner and to the interest thereby agreed, against marine losses incident to marine adventure.

Section 2(13)A of the Insurance Act 1938 defines marine insurance as follows:

"Marine insurance business" means the business of effecting contracts of insurance upon vessels of any description, including cargoes, freights and other interests which may be legally insured in or in relation to such vessels, cargoes and freights, goods, wares, merchandise and property of whatever description insured for any transit by land or water or both, and whether or not including warehouse risks or similar risks in addition or as incidental to such transit and includes any other risks customarily included among the risks insured against in marine insurance policies.

The above definition clearly lays down the following classification of the marine insurance.

1. Hull Insurance

Insurance of vessel and its equipments are included under hull insurance. There are a number of classification of vessels such as ocean steamers, sailing vessels, builders, risks, fleet policies and so on.

2. Cargo Insurance

It may be written under a single risk policy or floating policies. The cargo may be of any description, for example, wares, merchandise, property, goods and so on.

3. Freight Insurance

Freight is to be payable for the carriage of cargoes or if the vessel is chartered, the money to be paid for the use of the vessel. The carrier is unable to earn freight if the goods or property (called cargoes) are not safely transported.

4. Liability Insurance

The marine insurance policy may include liability hazards such as collision or running down. Insurance can also be taken for the expenses involved in non-compliance of rules and regulations without any intention to deceive. It should be clear here that marine perils insurance covers not only the "ocean but also the inland perils." The perils to be included in the policy are clearly defined and the insurer will be liable only for the insured perils.

PROCEDURE TO EFFECT MARINE INSURANCE

The proposer may approach to the insurer directly or through an agent or broker. Generally, the proposal is made through brokers because they are well known of the insurance practices. The broker prepares a slip where material informations are recorded. This slip is presented to the insurer who will signify his acceptance by initialling the slip and indicating the sum they are prepared to· accept. The risk may commence from the date of acceptance or from at any other date which is mutually agreed.

Sometimes, the insurer asks additional information from the broker. When the additional information called closing slip has been accepted by the insurer he may issue policy. Before issuing the policy, open cover is issued to the insured, which becomes inoperative as soon as policy is issued. The document containing the term of the contract is called policy. The assured cannot lagally make any claim over the underwriter if the loss occurs before a final policy is issued. The 'open cover' or 'slip' is not legally binding on the insurers. In practice, however, the insurer pays the amount of claims even before the issue of policies. Insurers in marine insurance generally called 'underwriters'.

ELEMENTS OF MARINE INSURANCE CONTRACT

The marine insurance has the following essential features which are also called fundamental principles of marine insurance, (1) Features of General Contract, (2) Insurable Interest, (3) Utmost Good Faith, (4) Doctrine of Indemnity, (5) Subrogation, (6) Warranties, (7) Proximate cause, (8) Assignment and nomination of the policy. (9) Return of premium.

1. FEATURES OF GENERAL CONTRACT

(*a*) Proposal

The broker will prepare a slip upon receipt of instructions to insure from shipowner, merchant or other proposers. Proposal forms, so common in other branches of insurances, are unknown in the marine insurance and only the 'slip' so called 'the original slip' is used for the proposal. The original slip is accompanied with other material information which the broker deems necessary for the purpose. The brokers are expert and well versed in marine insurance law and practice. The various kinds of marine proposals are altogether too diverse, so elaborate rating schedules are not possible and the proposals are considered on individual merits.

(*b*) Acceptance

The original slip is presented to the Lloyd's Underwriters or other insurers or to the Lead of the insures, who initial the slip and the proposal is formally accepted. But the contract can not be legally enforced until a policy is issued. The slip is an evidence that the underwriter has accepted an insurance and that he has agreed subsequently to sign a policy on the terms and conditions indicated on the slip. If the underwriter should refuse to issue or sign a policy, he could not legally be forced to do so.

(*c*) Consideration

The premium is determined on assessment of the proposal and is paid at the time of the contract. The premium is called consideration to the contract.

(*d*) Issue of Policy

Having effected the insurance, the broker will now send his client a cover note advising the terms and conditions, on which the· insurance has been placed. The broker's cover note is merely an insurance memorandum and naturally has no value in enforcing the contract with the underwrites. The policy is prepared, stamped and signed without delay and it will be the legal evidence of the contract. However, after issue of the policy the court has power to order the rectification of the policy to express the intention of the parties to the contract as evidenced by the terms of the slip.

2. INSURABLE INTEREST

An insured person will have insurable interest in the subject matter where he stands in any legal or equitable relation to the subject matter in such a way that he may benefit by the safety or due arrival of insurable property or may be prejudiced by its loss, or by damage thereto or by the detention thereof or may incur liability in respect thereof. Since marine insurance is frequently effected before the commercial transactions to which they apply are formally completed it is not essential for the assured to have an insurable interest at the time of effecting insurance, though he should have an expectation of acquiring such an interest. If he fails to acquire insurable interest in due course, he does not become entitled to indemnification. Since the ownership and other interest of the subject matter often change from hands to hands, the requirement of the insurable interest to be present only at the time of loss makes a marine insurance policy freely assignable.

Exceptions

There are two exceptions of the rule in marine insurance.

1. Lost or Not Lost

A person can also purchase policy in the subject-matter in which it was known whether the matters were lost not lost. In such cues the assured and the underwriter are ignorant about the safety or otherwise of the goods and complete reliance was placed on the principle of Good Faith. The policy terminated if anyone of the two parties was aware of the fact of loss. In this case, therefore, the insurable interest may not be present at the time of contract because the subject-matter would have been lost.

2. P.P.I. Policies

The subject mater can be insured in the usual manner by P.P.I. (Policy Proof of Interest), *i.e.*, interest proof policies. It means that in the event of claim underwriters may dispense with all proof of insurable interest. In this case if the underwriter does not pay the claims, it cannot be enforced in any court of law because P.P.I. policies are equally void and unenforceable. But the underwriters are generally adhering on the terms and pay the amount of claim.

The insurable interest in marine insurance can be of the following forms:

I. According to Ownership

The owner has insurable interest up to the full value of the subject-matter. The owners are of different types according to the subject-matter.

(*a*) In Case of Ships

The ship-owner or any person who has purchased it on charter-basis can insure the ship up to its full price.

(*b*) In Case of Cargo

The cargo-owner can purchase policy up to the full price of the cargo. If he has paid the freight in advance, he can take the policy for the full price of the goods plus amount of freight plus the expense of insurance.

(*c*) In Case of Freight

The receiver of the freight can insure up to the amount of freight to be received by him.

II. Insurable Interest in Re-insurance

The underwriter under a contract of marine insurance has an insurable interest in his risk, and may re-insure in respect of it.

III. Insurable Interest in other Cases

In this case all those underwriters are included who have insurable interest in the salary and own liabilities. For example, the master or any member of the crew of a ship has insurable interest in respect of his wages. The lender of money on bottomry or respondentia has insurable interest in respect of the loan.

3. UTMOST GOOD FAITH

The doctrine of caveat emptor (let the buyer beware) applies to commercial contracts, but insurance contracts are based upon the legal principle of uberrimae fides (utmost good faith). If this is not observed by either of the parties, the contract can be avoided by the other party.

The duty of the utmost good faith applies also to the insurer. He may not urge the proposer to effect an insurance which he knows is not legal or has run off safely. But the duty of disclosure of material facts rests highly on the insured because he is aware of the material common in other branches of insurance are not used in the marine insurance. Ships and cargoes proposed for insurance may be thousands of miles away, and surveys on underwriters' behalf are usually impracticable. The assured, therefore, must disclose all the material information which may influence the decision of the contract. Any non-disclosure of a material fact enables the underwriter to avoid the contract, irrespective of whether the non-disclosure was intentional or inadvertent. The assured is expected to know every circumstance which in the ordinary course of business ought to be known by him. He cannot rely on his own inefficiency or neglect.

The duty of the disclosure of all material facts falls even more heavily on the broker. He must disclose every material fact which the assured ought to disclose and also every material fact which he knows. The broker is expected to know or inquire from the assured all the material facts. Failure in this respect entitles the underwriter to avoid the policy and if negligence can be held against the broker, he may be liable for damages to his client for breach of contract. The contract shall be *ab initio* if the element of fraud exists.

Exception

In the following circumstances, the doctrine of good faith may not be adhered to:

(*i*) Facts of common knowledge.

(*ii*) Facts which are known should be known to the insurer.

(*iii*) Facts which are not required by the insurers.

(*iv*) Facts which the insurer ought reasonably to have in ferred from the details given to him.

(*v*) Facts of public knowledge.

4. DOCTRINE OF INDEMNITY

The contract of marine insurance is of indemnity. Under no circumstances an insured is allowed to make a profit out of a claim. In the absence of the principle of indemnity it was possible to make a profit. The insurer agrees to indemnify the assured only in the manner and only to the extent agreed upon. Marine insurance fails to provide complete indemnity due to large and varied nature of the marine voyage. The basis of indemnity is always a cash basis as underwriter cannot replace the lost ship and cargoes and the basis of indemnification is the value of the subject matter. This value may be either the insured or insurable value. If the value of the subject matter is determined at the time of taking the policy, it is called 'Insured Value'. When loss arises the indemnity will be measured in the proportion that the assured sum bears to the insured value. In fixing the insured value, the cost of transportation and anticipated profits are added to original value so that in case of loss the insured can recover not only the cost of goods or properties but a certain percentage of profit also. The insured value is called agreed value because it has been agreed between the insurer and the insured at the time of contract and is regarded as sacrosanct and binding on both parties to the contract. In marine insurance, it has been customary for the insurer and the assured to agree on the value of the insured subject-matter at the time of proposal. Having, agreed of the value or basis of valuation, neither party to the contract can raise objection after loss on the ground that the value is too high or too low unless it appears that a fraudulent evaluation has been imposed on either party. Insured value is not justified in fire insurance due to moral hazard as the property remains within the approach of the assured, while the subject-matter is movable from one place to another in case of marine insurance and the assured value is fully justified there. Moreover, in marine insurance, the assured value removes all complications of valuation at the time of loss.

Technically speaking the doctrine of indemnity applies where the value of subject-matter is determined at the time of loss. In other words, where the market price of the loss is paid, this doctrine has been precisely applied. Where the value for the goods has not been fixed in the beginning but is left to be determined ai the time of loss, the measurement is based on the insurable value of the goods. However, in marine insurance insurable value is not common because no profit is allowed in estimating the insurable value. Again if the insurable value happens to be more than the assured sum, the assured would be proportionately uninsured. On the other hand, if it is lower than the assured sum, the underwriter would be liable for a return of premium of the difference.

Exceptions

There are two exceptions of the doctrine of indemnity in marine insurance.

1. Profits Allowed

Actually the doctrine says that the market price of the loss should be indemnified and no profit should be permitted, but in marine insurance a certain profit margin is also permitted.

2. Insured Value

The doctrine of indemnity is based on the insurable value whereas the marine insurance is mostly based on insured value. The purpose of the valuation is to predetermine the worth of insured.

5. DOCTRINE OF SUBROGATION

The aim of doctrine of subrogation is that the insured should not get more than the actual loss or damage. After payment of the loss, the insurer gets the light to receive compensation or any sum from the third party from whom the assured is legally liable to get the amount of compensation. The main characteristics of subrogation are as follows:

1. The insurer subrogates all the remedies rights and liabilities of the insured alter payment of the compensation.
2. The insurer has right to pay the amount of loss after reducing the sum received by the insured from the third party. But in marine insurance the right of subrogation arises only after payment has been made, and it is not customary as in fire and accident insurance, to alter this by means of a condition to provide for the exercise of subrogation rights before payment of a claim. At the same time the right of subrogation must be distinguished from abandonment. If property is abandoned to a marine insurer, he is entitled to whatever remains to the property irrespective of value of subrogation.
3. After indemnification, the insurer gets all the rights of the insured on the third parties, but insurer cannot file suit in his own name. Therefore, the insured must assist the insurer for receiving money from the third party. If the insured is revoking from filing suit against the third party, the insurer can receive the amount of compensation from the insured.

6. WARRANTIES

A warranty is that by which the assured undertakes that some particular thing shall or shall not be done, or that some conditions shall be fulfilled or whereby he affirms or negatives the existence of a particular state of facts. Warranties are the statement according to which insured person promises to do or not to do a particular thing or to fulfil or not to fulfil a certain condition. It is not merely a condition but statement of fact. Warranties are more vigorously insisted upon than the conditions because the contract comes to an end if a warranty is broken whether the warranty was material or not.

In case of condition or representation the contract comes to end only when these were material or important. Warranties are of two types:

(1) Express Warranties, and (2) Implied Warranties.

1. Express Warranties

Express warranties are those warranties which are expressly included or incorporated in the policy by reference.

2. Implied Warranties

These are not mentioned in the policy at all but are tacitly understood by the parties to the contract and are as fully binding as express warranties.

Warranties can also be classified as (1) Affirmative, and (2) Promissory. Affirmative warranty is the promise which insured gives to exist or not to exist certain facts. Promissory warranty is the promise in which insured promises that he will do or not do a certain thing up to the period of policy.

In marine insurance, implied warranties are very important. These are:

1. Seaworthiness of Ship.
2. Legality of venture.
3. Non-deviation.

All these warranties must be literally, complied with as otherwise the underwriter may avoid all liabilities as from the date of the breach. However, there are two exceptions to this rule when a breach of warranty does not affect the underwriter's liability: (1) Where owing to a change of circumstances the warranty is no longer applicable. (2) Where compliance would be unlawful owing to the enactment of subsequent law.

1. Seaworthiness of ship

The warranty implies that the ship should be seaworthy at the commencement of the voyage, or if the voyage is carried out in stages at the commencement of each stage. This warranty implies only to voyage policies, though such policies may be of ship, cargo, freight or any other interest. There is no implied warranty of seaworthiness in time policies. A ship is seaworthy when the ship is suitably constructed, properly equipped, officered and manned, sufficiently fuelled and provisioned, documented and capable of withstanding the ordinary strain and stress of the voyage.

The seaworthiness will be more clear from the following points:

1. The standard to judge the seaworthiness is not fixed. It is a relative term and may vary with any particular vessel at different periods of the same voyage. A ship may be perfectly seaworthy for Trans-ocean voyage. A ship may be suitable for summer but may not be suitable for winter. There may be different standard for different ocean, for different cargo, for different destination and so on.
2. Seaworthiness does not depend merely on the condition of the ship, but it includes the suitability and adequacy of her equipment, adequacy and experience of the officers and crew.
3. At the commencement of journey, the ship must be capable of withstanding the ordinary strain and stress of the sea.
4. Seaworthiness also includes "Cargo-Worthiness". It means the ship must be reasonably fit and suitable to carry the kind of cargo insured. It should be noted that the warranty of seaworthiness does not apply to cargo. It applies to the vessel only. There is no warranty that the cargo should be seaworthy. It cannot be expected from the cargo-owner to be well-versed in the matter of shipping and overseas trade. So, it is admitted in seaworthiness clause that the cargo would be seaworthy of the vessel and would not be raised as defence to any claim for loss by insured perils.

It should be noted that the ship should be seaworthy at the port of commencement of voyage or at the different stages if voyage is to be completed in stages.

2. Legality of Venture

This warranty implies that the adventure insured shall be lawful and that so far as the assured can control the matter it shall be carried out in a lawful manner of the country. Violation of foreign laws does not necessarily involve breach of the warranty. There is no implied warranty as to the nationality of a ship. The implied warranty of legality applies total policies, voyage or time. Marine policies cannot be applied to protect illegal voyages or adventure. The assured can have no right to claim a loss if the venture was illegal. The example of illegal venture may be trading with an enemy, violating national laws, smuggling, breach of blockade and similar ventures prohibited by law.

Illegality must not be confused with the illegal conduct of the third party *e.g.*, barratry, theft, pirates, rovers. The waiver of this warranty is not permitted as it is against public policy.

3. Other Implied Warranties

There are other warranties which must be complied in marine insurance.

(*a*) No Change in Voyage

When the destination of voyage is changed intentionally after the beginning of the risk, this is called change in voyage. In absence of any warranty contrary to this one, the insurer quits his responsibility at the time of change in voyage. The time of change of voyage is determined when there is determination or intention to change the voyage.

(*b*) No Delay in Voyage

This warranty applies only to voyage policies. There should not be delay in starting of voyage and laziness or delay during the course of journey. This is implied condition that venture must start within the reasonable time. Moreover, the insured venture must be despatched within the reasonable time. If this warranty is not complied, the insurer may avoid the contract in absence of any legal reason.

(*c*) Non deviation

The liability of the insurer ends in deviation of journey. Deviation means removal from the common route or given path. When the ship deviates from the fixed passage without any legal reason, the insurer quits his responsibility. This would be immaterial that the ship returned to her original route before loss. The insurer can quit his responsibility only when there is actual deviation and not mere intention to deviation.

Exceptions

There are following exceptions of delay and deviation warranties:

1. Deviation or delay is authorised according to a particular warranty of the policy.
2. When the delay or deviation was beyond the reasonable approach of the master or crew.
3. The deviation or delay is exempted for the safety of ship or insured matter or human lives.
4. Deviation or delay was due to barratry.

7. PROXIMATE CAUSE

According to Marine Insurance Act, 'Subject to the provisions of the Act and unless the policy otherwise provides the insurer is liable for any loss proximately caused by a peril insured against, but subject to as aforesaid he is not liable for any loss which is not proximately caused by a peril insured against.'

1. The insurer is not liable for any loss attributable to the wilful misconduct of the assured, but, unless the policy otherwise provides, he is liable for any loss proximately caused by a peril insured against.
2. The insurer will not be liable for any loss caused by delay unless otherwise provided.
3. The insurer is not liable for ordinary wear and tear, ordinary leakage and breakage, inherent vice or nature of subject matter insured, or for any loss proximately caused by rats or vermin, or for any injury to machinery not proximately caused by maritime perils.

Dover says .... "The causa proxima of a loss is the cause of the loss, proximate to the loss, not necessarily in time, but in efficiency. While remote causes may be disregarded in determining the cause of a loss, the doctrine must be interpreted with good sense." So as to uphold and not defeat the intention of the parties to the contract. Thus the proximate cause is the actual cause of the loss. There must be direct and non-intervening cause. The insurer will be liable for any loss proximately caused by peril insured against.

8. ASSIGNMENT

A marine policy is assignable unless it contains terms expressly prohibiting assignment. It may be assigned either before or after loss. A marine policy may be assigned by indorsement thereon or on other customary manner.

The feature of return of premium has been already discussed in the portion of life insurance.

QUESTIONS

1. What are the subject matters which are insured by Marine Insurance?
2. Discuss how are the Insurable Interest, Utmost Good Faith and Indemnity applicable to Marine Insurance?
3. What do you mean by warranties? What are the important warranties in Marine Insurance?

20

MARINE INSURANCE POLICIES

The marine insurance policy is issued only when the contract has been finalised and it would be legal documents of evidence of the contract. The form of marine insurance policies has been taken from pretty old times. There has been a slight change in the wordings of the policies. For example, 'Be it known that' is substituted for the words 'In the name of God, Amen'. The old form of policy has been practised today due to its practicabilities which took after a numerous legal decisions during the past centuries. It has also been practised that only form of policy is standarised and different clauses are added for applying to various types of policies. The standard policy generally contains the following information:

(*i*) Name of insured or his agent.

(*ii*) Subject matter insured. It may be ship (hull) cargo and freight.

(*iii*) Risks insured against.

(*iv*) Name of vessel and officers.

(*v*) Description of voyage or period of insurance.

(*vi*) Amount and term of insurance.

(*vii*) Premium.

There are various clauses which are suitably inserted according to the nature and type of policies. Hull, cargo and freight policies have different standard clauses. In case of hull insurance, the clauses provide that if the insured vessel at the expiration of the policy is at sea, or at a port of refuge. Generally the ship may be covered until arrival at port of destination. In case of cargo policies—with Average, Free of particular Average, or All Risks are generally used. There are standard clauses which are invariably used in marine insurance. Firstly, policies are constructed in plain, ordinary and popular sense, and, later on, specific clauses are added to them according to terms and conditions of the contract. Clauses attached to the policy would override the printed wording in the policy.

CLASSES OF POLICIES

Different classes of policies are used in marine insurance.

1. Voyage Policies

The policy is issued to cover a particular voyage from one port to another and from one place to another. The policy mentions the port of departure and the port of destination, between which the risks are generally underwritten. This policy is not suitable for hull insurance as a ship usually does not operate over a particular route only. However, this policy may include time factor also as from Bombay to London for one year. In this case the risk may be covered from one place to another covering a period of one year.

The policy is used mostly in case of cargo insurance. The goods remain covered even when the ship halts at intermediate ports. The risks at the port of departure and at the port of destination may be covered by incorporating suitable, clauses in the policy. The liability of the insurer continues during landing and re-shipping of the goods.

2. Time Policies

Under this policy, the subject-matter is insured for a definite period of time, *e.g.*, from 6 a.m. of 1st January, 1976 to 6 a.m. of 1st January, 1977. The policy is generally taken for one year although it may be for less than one year. This policy is commonly more used for hull insurance than for the cargo insurance. The policy may cover, while navigating the vessel or while under construction. Risks covered under construction are for more than 12 months. There are standard clauses in relation to freight, premium, interests, etc., which are added to this policy. The time policy may be taken in case of goods and other movable vessels.

3. Voyage and Time Policy or mixed Policies

In this policy, the elements of voyage policy and of time policy are combined in under this policy. The reference is made certain period after completion of voyage. For example, 24 hours after arrival. It may be beneficial to hull as well as to cargo insurance.

4. Valued Policies

Under this policy the value of loss to be compensated is fixed and remains constant throughout the risk except where there is fraud and excessive over-valuation. The value of the subject-matter is agreed between the insurer and the assured at the time of taking the insurance. It is also called insured value or agreed value. It forms the measure of indemnity at the time of loss. The insured value is not necessarily the actual value. It may be total of invoice, *e.g.*, cost of goods, freight; shipping charges, insurance and a certain percentage of margin (generally 10 per cent) to cover anticipated profits.

5. Unvalued Policies

When the value of policy is not determined at the time of commencement of risk but is left to be valued when the loss takes place. The value thus left to be decided later on is called the insurable value or unvalued or valuable policy. In deciding the value, the invoice cost, freight, shipping and insurance charges are included and no margin for anticipated profit is added. Usually unvalued policies are not common in marine insurance because evaluation of loss at the time of damage poses a difficult problem. It is extremely difficult when consignment goes nearer the port of destination.

In hull insurance, the insurable value is determined taking into account the value of the ship at the commencement of risk including provision and, stores for officers and crew plus the charges of insurance. In insurance on freight whether paid in advance or otherwise, the insurable value is the gross amount of freight plus the charges of insurance. Similarly, in cargo insurance it would be the cost of goods plus expenses and insurance charges.

A limitation of insurable value is desirable not only to fix the measure of indemnity under an unvalued policy, but also to provide an approximate basis for the calculation of value in a valued policy.

6. Floating Policies

This policy describes the general terms and leaves the amount of each shipment and other particulars to be declared later on. The declaration is made in order of despatch of shipment. The policy is taken for a round large sum which is specified at each declaration and is attached to each shipment. With each declaration the amount will be reduced till it is exhausted when the insured sum is said to be 'closed' and the policy is 'fully declared' or, 'run off'.

The most popular form of contract is 'Open Cover'. It is an agreement between the insured and the insurer by which the assured on his part agrees to declare, and the insurer on his part agrees to accept all the shipments falling within the scope of the 'open cover' which is merely an original ship'. It is not a legal contract of marine insurance and suffers from the same legal disability as the 'original 'ship'. However the insured and the insurers are honour bound. To give 'Open Cover' a legal form, a policy is issued for the purpose. Separate policies are not issued in case of each shipment but only one policy is issued at the time of entering into contract. All declarations are written on the back of the policy. A classification clause is usually inserted in 'open cover' to provide the agreed rates of premium. Similarly, valuation clauses are also inserted to provide the basis for valuation in the event of loss taking place.

This policy is suitable for a cargo-owner who makes regular shipments of cargoes. All his shipments are automatically covered as soon as the declarations are made. The floating policies are mostly used in the age of gigantic trade.

7. Blanket Policies

The policy is taken to cover losses within the particular time and place. The policy is taken for a certain amount and premium is paid on the whole of it in the beginning of the policy and is re-adjusted at the end of the policy according to the actual amount at risk. If the actual coverage of risk is less than the total amount of insurance, the premium related to the excess amount is returned to the insured. On the other hand, if the amount of shipments are greater than the insured sum, additional premium is charged over the excess protection.

8. Named Policies

Under this policy, the name of the ship and the amount of insured cargo are mentioned. These policies are specific policies.

9. Single Vessel and Fleet Policies

A ship or a fleet of ships is insured in a single policy. When one policy is assured, it is called single vessel policy and when a fleet of ship is insured in single policy, it is called fleet insurance policy. The advantages of the fleet policies are that even old and weak ships are also insured. This insurance facilitates easy and smooth functioning of insurance benefits.

10. Block Policies

This policy insures incidental inland risks, too, along with the marine perils. For example, cotton is insured from the time of processing to the time when it was delivered at the point of destination.

11. Currency Policies

Policies issued in foreign currency is called currency policy, where the sum assured is stated in foreign currency, This policy avoids the fluctuation in foreign currencies because the claim amount is determined in the foreign currency and the fluctuations in the exchange rates of the inland and foreign currencies up to the period of the policy are meaningless.

12. P.P.I. Policies

The policy is issued to avoid the complication of the principle of insurable interest. This is called 'Policy Proof of Interest' and are honoured by the insurer even in absence of insurable interest. This policy is based on mutual understanding, so, it is called honoured policies. This is also called wagering policies because insurable interest is not required; consequently, it cannot be legally enforceable.

QUESTIONS

1. What are the various kinds of Marine Insurance Policies?
2. Discuss the feature of marine insurance policies.

21

POLICY CONDITIONS

The old form of policy is even used today. In order to make the standard policy suitable for the different types of contracts, suitable conditions are added to the policy. The conditions are inserted in the policy in the form of clauses. The clauses took the standard form with special meanings. They may be pertaining to Hull, Cargo and Freight.

1. Hull Clauses

These clauses are mainly framed with the insurances on vessels and are incorporated in hull policies. The clauses may be pertaining to losses resulting from collision, standing, general average, etc. 'All risks policy' may be issued or certain risks may be excluded from the policy by inserting suitable clauses. 'Inland or Port Risk Clauses' may be incorporated in the policy to determine the extent of loss. These clauses are known as 'Institute Time Clauses'.

2. Cargo Clauses

These clauses are used in the insurance of goods and are incorporated in cargo policies. The clauses describe the nature, extent; and scope of the insurance and define comprehensive conditions and restrictions. The additional marine perils against which cover may be sought or which are excluded from the policies are inserted through special clauses. Terms and conditions of Cargo insurance are specially incorporated in the policies. 'With Average (W.A.) or With Particular Average, (W.P.A.),' 'Exposed during transit', etc., are the important clauses of cargo insurance. The underwriting of cargo-risks depends upon the nature of goods, the susceptibility of the goods, intentions of the insurer and insured and willingness of the assured to pay extra premium. This clause is known as 'Institute Cargo Clause'.

3. Freight Clauses

The clauses are framed in connection with the loss of freight due to maritime perils which may be insured for a period or for a voyage. A person which paid the freight in advance and the person who will receive the freight on completion of voyage are interested in covering the risk. The General Average (G.A.), Particular Average (P.A.) etc. are used in the freight clauses. The clauses are known as 'Institute Freight Clauses'.

The clauses to be incorporated in the policy are generally taken from Lloyd's Association.

LLOYD'S FORM OF POLICY

BE IT KNOWN THAT ..... as well in....... own name as for and in the name and names of all and every other person or persons to whom the same doth, may or shall appertain, in part or in all doth make assurance and cause, and them, and every of them, to be insured lost or not lost, at and from.

Upon any kind of goods and merchandise, and also upon the body, tackle, appeared, ordinances munition, artillery, boat, and other furniture, of and in the good ship or vessel called the.

Whereof is master under God, for this present voyage or whosoever else shall go for master in the said ship, or by whatsoever other name or names the said ship, or the master thereof, is or shall be named or called, beginning the adventure upon the said goods and merchandises from the loading thereof abroad the said ship.

Upon the said ship and so, shall continue and endure, during her abroad there.

Upon the said ship, & c. And further, until the said ship, with all her ordinance, tackle, apparel, and goods and merchandises whatsoever shall be arrived at.

Upon the said ship, & c, until she hath moored at anchor twenty-four hours in good safety; and upon the goods and merchandises, until the same be there discharged and safely landed. And it shall be lawful for the said ship, & c, in this voyage, to proceed and said to and touch and stay at any ports or places whatsoever without prejudice to this insurance. The said ship, & c., goods and merchandises, & c., for so much as concerns, the assured by agreement between, the assured and assurers in this policy, are and shall be valued at.

Touching the adventures and perils which we the assurers are contented to bear and do take upon us in this voyage. They are of the seas, men of war ...

... And it is agreed by us the insurers, that this writing or a policy of assurance shall be of as much force and effect as the surest writing or policies of assurance heretofore made is Lombard Street, or in the Royal Exchange, or elsewhere in London.

DESCRIPTION OF THE CLAUSES

The usual clauses which are or may be incorporated in a marine policy are:

(*i*) Assignment clause,

(*ii*) Lost or not lost,

(*iii*) At and from clause,

(*iv*) Warehouse to warehouse clause,

(*v*) Deviation, touch and stay clause,

(*vi*) Inchmaree clause,

(*vii*) Running down clause,

(*viii*) Sue and Labour clause,

(*ix*) Reinsurance clause,

(*x*) Memorandum clause,

(*xi*) Continuation clause.

1. Assignment Clause

The clause of assignment is as below .... as well as in his/their own name as for and in the name and names of all and every other person or persons to whom the same doth may or shall appertain, in part or in all doth make assurance ... and cause ... and them and every of them, to be insured ....

This clause makes it clear that the marine policy is freely assignable unless this is expressly prohibited. The policy can be assigned to anyone who may acquire an insurable interest in the subject-matter as soon as the assured parts with his interest. Cargo policy is freely assignable and no notice, thereof is essential to be given to the underwriter. But, in case of hull insurance the policy cannot be assigned freely and the consent of underwriter is essential because the degree of risk of the subject-matter is materially changed when the management and ownership of the vessel is changed. Since the owner of cargo has no control over the cargo in transit, blank endorsement may be permitted. But in hull insurance, specific endorsement of an assignment is essential.

It is interesting to note that marine policy can be assigned even after it takes place, but the assignee does not get a better title than the assignor. However, where the assured has parted with his interest in the subject, matter insured and has not, before or at time of so doing, expressly or impliedly agreed to assign the policy and subsequent assignment of the policy is inoperative.

2. Lost or Not Lost Clause

The clause is as ..... to be insured, lost or not lost. The policy was taken in good faith. The meaning of the clause is that the insurer insures the subject-matter irrespective of the fact that it has already been lost or not lost before the issue of the policy. It is taken in such a case where a merchant receives information of the shipment of his cargo very late after the sailing of the steamer and, therefore, when he submits the risk to the underwriter and effects insurance it was not known whether the subject-matter to be insured was lost or was not lost. So, to provide full protection to shipment, the words, 'Lost or not Lost' are inserted. It means that the insurer undertakes to indemnify the insured whether the subject matter before the date of issue of the policy was already lost or not. In this case, it is assumed that the assured and the underwriters are ignorant about the safety or otherwise of the subject-matter. The policy terminates if it is proved later on that one of the two parties was aware of the subject-matter at the time of loss. The introduction of this clause has a retrospective effect to provide for any loss which have occurred during the period from the date of shipment to the date of issue of policy. This clause was mostly prevalent in olden times when the media of communication were not developed so much. Now, the clause has lost much of its importance.

3. At and From Clause

This clause is applicable in voyage policies insuring hull, and freight. It determines the time when the actual risk commences. As soon as the ship will arrive at the port, the risk will commence. It means that the policy covers the subject-matters while it is lying at the port of departure and from the time the ship sails when the policy contains From only instead of 'At and Form.' From means the risk commences from the time of departure of the ship and not previous to that.

In case of cargo policy this clause is amended as the risk may commence boom the 'time the cargo is loaded on the vessel. In voyage policy, if the ship is not at that place when the contract is concluded, the risk commences as soon as the ship arrives there in good safety. If the place of departure is specified by the policy, and the ship sails from other place than the specified one, the risk does not attach.

Termination of Risk

The wordings of policy in this case are as follows:

"And upon the goods and merchandises until the same be there discharged and safely landed."

When the ship arrives the port of destination, the goods must be landed within a reasonable time and if they are not landed the risk ceases. The risk of landing within the reasonable time is permitted in most of the cases. But, where it is allowed with standard policy, clauses such as craft, lighters, etc., are inserted to the policy.

4. Warehouse to Warehouse Clause

Generally, underwriters are responsible for the risk commencing from the time of loading to the time of unloading the cargo. But, in certain cases the risks are beyond these two limits, *i.e.*, departing and destination. So, in order to cover the inland risks from the original place of departure to the port of sailing and from the port of discharge to the place of final destination are insured under 'Warehouse to warehouse clause'. Under this policy, the risk commences from the specified place and continues to the specified place of destination named in the policy. Thus, the risk of land, craft transport and transhipment are also covered under a single marine insurance policy. Sometimes, time-limit is also inserted in the policy and extra cost is required from the insured to cover the remaining voyage. But, where goods are wilfully detained, the underwriter shall cease his liability.

The clause as appeared in the Institute Cargo clause is as follows:

"The risks covered by this policy attach from the time the goods leave the Warehouse and/or Store at the place named in the policy for the commencement of the transit and continue during the ordinary course of transit, including customary transhipment, if any, until the goods are discharged overside from the overseas vessel at the final port. Thereafter the risks covered are continued whilst the goods are in transit and/or awaiting transit until delivered to final warehouse at the destination named in the policy or until the expiry of 15 days (30 days if the destination to which the goods are insured is outside the limits of the port) whichever shall first occur. The time limit referred to above to be from midnight of the day on which the discharge overside of the goods hereby insured from the overseas vessel is completed. Transhipment, if any other than as above, and/or delay in excess of the above time limits arising from circumstances beyond the control of the assured, held covered at a premium to be arranged.

5. Deviation Touch and Clauses

The ship should not deviate from the course of the voyage described in the policy or where the course is not a specifically designated one, from the customary course. Any departure from the specified course or a customary course amounts to deviation. A deviation is different from change of voyage. In the latter case, the destination agreed upon is changed, while in the former case the destination is the same as agreed, but the course thereto is deviated from. In the change of voyage the underwriter's liability comes to an end from the time the intention or decision to change the voyage is taken, but in deviation mere intention to deviation is not material; there should be an actual deviation to avoid the policy. Once deviation has taken, place the risk ceases to attach for the rest of the voyage even though loss has occurred after the vessel had reverted to the proper course.

Where the ship deviates without lawful excuse the underwriters are relieved of the liability as from the time of deviation. The fact that deviation did not increase the risk or that the ship regained her route before any loss occurred, would not amount to non-deviation. This clause applies only to voyage policies. In time policies, this clause does not apply.

Deviation is excused under certain circumstances but it should be noted that the ship must resume her course and prosecute the voyage with reasonable despatch. Deviation or delay is excused in the following cases:

1. Where authorised by any special term in the policy. The special term must be incorporated in the policy. Underwriters are usually willing to extend the protection of the policies after charging additional premium.
2. Where deviation is caused by circumstances beyond the control of the master and his employer.
3. Where deviation or delay is necessary to comply with an express or implied warranty.
4. The deviation or delay is necessary for the safety of the ship or subject-matter insured.
5. For the purpose of saving human life or aiding a ship in distress where human life may be in danger. For, and for obtaining medical or surgical aid, deviation or delay is required.
6. Where deviation is caused by the barratrous conduct of the master or crew, if the barretry be one of the perils insured against.

Touch And Stay

It accords liberty to the vessel to touch and stay at any port, or place whatsoever. In absence of the clause, the liberty to touch and stay at any port or place whatsoever does not authorise the ship to depart from the course of her voyage from the port of departure to the port of destination. Where several ports are specified, the ship may touch or stay at all or any of them. In the absence of any usage or sufficient cause to the contrary the ship must proceed to the designated ports. Following wordings are incorporated in the standard policy.

"And it shall be lawful for the said ship, etc., in the voyage to proceed and sail to and touch and stay at any ports or places whatsoever without prejudice to this insurance."

It means that the vessel in course of the voyage must touch and stay at such ports and in such order as are mentioned in the policy or if no course is mentioned in the policy, the ports must be in the ordinary course of the voyage.

6. Inchmaree Clause

The clause protects the shipowners against losses to be included in claims by the assured. This clause is taken from an illustration of a steamer called 'Inchmaree'. The donkey pump of the steamer was damaged due to salt. Claim was covered under the "and all other perils, losses, and misfortunes clause". The court decided that due to negligent such losses were outside the scope of the insurance and should not be covered by it. So, now to provide indemnity for the insured for damage to the hull or machinery resulting from the negligence of the master or crew, at well as from explosion or latent defects, a clause was introduced into hull policies which is commonly known as 'Inchmaree clause'. This clause is also incorporated in cargo policies.

Hague Rules

A Maritime Law Committee of the International Law Association sat at The Hague in 1921 and framed a set of rules regarding the rights and liabilities of cargo-owners and shipowners in connection with Bills of Lading so that no complication may arise in settlement of claims.

7. Running Down Clauses (R.D.C.)

This clause is also called collision clause and is included in hull policies. It provides that the underwriter agrees to take upon the liability of the owner of the ship for damage done by his vessel to another vessel on collision to the extent of three-fourths of such liability. The underwriter will be responsible only when this clause is added in the policy. The assured himself has to bear one-fourth of the loss so that he may exercise greater care in the navigation of the vessel. The full protection can be given by deleting the words 'Three-fourths' from the clause. In case the ship sinks in a collision and is held liable for the damage done to the other vessel, the underwriter may have to pay a total loss and a heavy claim under the R.D.C. The amount of damage extends to include damage done to other ship, her cargo and compensation for loss of employment in consequence of the collision.

8. Sue and Labour Clause

This clause reads as follows: "And in case of loss of misfortune it shall be lawful to the assured, their factors, servants and assigns to sue, labour and travel for in and about the defence, safeguards, and recovery of the said goods and merchandises, and ship, ete., or part thereof, without prejudice to this insurance, to the charges whereof we, the assurers, will contribute each one according to the rate and quantity of his sum herein assured".

Thus, it is the duty of the assured and his agents to act in such a way that they are uninsured and to take such measures as may be reasonable for the purpose of averting or minimising loss or damage. This clause requires underwriters to pay any expenses properly incurred by the assured or his agents in preventing or minimising loss or damage to the subject-matter. The reasonable expenditure is payable even though it may be, in addition, to total loss.

The essential features of Sue and Labour Charges are:

(*i*) The expenses must be incurred for the benefit of the subject-matter insured. If occurred for the common benefit they may become a part of general average which is not recoverable under this clause.

(*ii*) They must be reasonable.

(*iii*) They may be incurred by 'the assured, his factors, his servants or assigns'. The clause excludes salvage charges.

(*iv*) The expenses are incurred to avert or minimise a loss from a peril covered by the policy. Expenses incurred for purpose of averting or diminishing any loss not covered by the policy are not recoverable under this clause.

9. Reinsurance Clause

The reinsurance clause .... "being a reinsurance and subject to the same clauses and conditions as the original policy, and to pay as may be paid thereon." .... is generally added to the original policies. The reinsurer is liable only for claims for which the original underwriter is liable. If the reassured has paid a claim for which he is not legally liable under his policy, the reinsurer is under no obligation to reimburse him. The cost incurred by the original insurer in contesting liability under the original policy, need not be paid by the reinsurer. The reinsurance policy is closely linked with the original insurance and any alteration in the original policy must be agreed with the reinsurer.

10. Memorandum Clause

The memorandum clause reads as under:

"Corn, fish, salt, fruit, flour and seed are warranted free from average, unless general, or the ship be stranded—sugar, tobacco,... are warranted free from average, ... and all other goods, also the ship and freight, are warranted free from average, ..."

This clause is meant to provide a minimum limit to be underwriter's liability regarding claims for particular average by exempting him from such claims.

11. Continuation Clause

This clause refers that the vessel shall continue to be covered even after completion of voyage under the policy at a *pro rato* premium to her port of destination provided previous notice was not given.

QUESTIONS

1. What are the various clauses of marine insurance policies?
2. Discuss in detail Touch and Stay, Running Down Clause, At and From, Sue and Labour Clause.

22

PREMIUM CALCULATION

Premium can be ascertained either by numerical rating system or by judgment method. The numerical rating system evaluates each and every item and marks are assigned to them according to their merits and degrees of influencing risk. Since the marine perils are varied, the only numerical rating system cannot be successfully utilised. However, tabulation of statistical experience on many risks can serve the purpose as a basis of supplementary factors for underwriter's judgment. Marine insurance grants protection against a large number of perils which are viewed in relation to (*i*) the inherent character of a large variety of subject-matter of insurance (*ii*) the effects of season, adverse physical forces and trade customs, (*iii*) the policy conditions.

Individual insurance account is used for personal valuation by a leading underwriter who enter into the making of marine insurance rates very materially. The judgment and personal evaluation is very vital in rate making. There are various factors to influence the risk. The management and ownership are very important factors while risks are evaluated for the purpose of rate making.

RATE-MAKING IN MARINE INSURANCE

Hull Insurance

1. Management

One management may be efficient in the upkeep of the vessel and the appointment of officers and crew. Other management, through negligence, indifference and undue economy, may show a bad record. To treat these managements alike would be an injustice to the better managed concerns. It would penalize efficiency and carefulness and put a premium on inefficiency and carelessness.

2. Natural Forces and Topography

The underwriters consider the character of the route, the construction, type and the nationality of the vessel and conditions of the contract. Some natural hazards are permanent while others are of seasonal dangers. References are made to storms, submerged shoals, shifting sand bars, shallow water, narrow channels, ice, currents, tides and seaquakes while calculating the premiums to a particular route. Dangers from an underwriting point of view are associated with the ports of departure, call or destination. Some ports are known for insufficient depth, absence of good anchorage ground, lack of protection against tides or tidal waves.

3. Construction, Type and Nationality of the Vessel

The quality and fitness of the vessel to serve as a carrier on the particular route is naturally of the utmost importance. The underwriter wants to know the vessel with respect to its builder and owner, structural plan, material used in construction, type of propulsion, structural strength to resist stresses and strains, adaptability to carry various kinds of cargo and its age and physical condition. In foreign countries, certain societies are formulated to promulgate rules for the construction of vessels, supervising such construction and assigning a class to each vessel. The Lloyd's Register contains information to numerous vessels of other countries, name and nationality of the vessel, materials of construction, details of the decks, the engine and boiler equipment of the vessel. Periodical changes are noted down there. Nationality of the vessel is important to insurer because it discloses the dependence of the nations upon the ocean trade. The nationality reveals the acumanship or skilfulness of the masters and crew. The rates may vary greatly as to the standard or commercial honour in trade, high standard and commercial ethics.

4. Policy Conditions

Innumerable clauses are used to limit or increase the underwriter's liability. Some policies may cover against total loss. Some may cover partial losses. Others may relate only to general average or particular average.

Cargo Rates

The premium on cargo depends upon the following factors:

1. Ownership

It may happen that two separate ownerships of the same kind of cargo, carried on the same ship and to the same place will command different rates. Proper packing, profitable accounts and previous refusal of insurance may determine the rate.

2. Character of the Cargo

The difference in hazard between various kinds of commodities, different forms of the same commodity, different shipments, different types of packing and durability of the commodity may influence the premium rates.

3. Hazards and Customs

The natural forces and topography considered in the case of ship are also considered in the case of cargo. The effect of seasons has important bearing upon commodities that are seriously affected by cold or heat. The season or climate at the port of destination may influence the risk. In certain season the port is busy with a particular cargo. Varying trade customs associated with the different commercial routes will influence cargo rates materially. The moral hazard is greater on certain routes.

4. Quality and Suitability of the Vessel used as Carrier

The underwriters take into account the fitness of the vessel to carry the particular cargo. The premiums are higher in the case of ship of slower speed due to longer exposure of the cargo. In case of highly perishable goods, moving in large quantities, special types of vessels have been designed to carry such commodities.

5. Duration of Voyage and Policy Conditions

Insurers take into account the length of time. Sometimes, loading of the goods aboard the vessels and protection of the goods while on the dock are considered in calculation of premium.

6. Miscellaneous Factors

The operating efficiency or proved experience of ship may affect the risk on cargo. The methods of handling and stowing cargo, the regularity of the service, etc., are the various factors to influence the premium rate.

RETURN OF PREMIUM

Circumstances may happen when the proposed shipment of goods may not take place or only a reduced quantities may be shipped. In the following circumstances the premium is returnable.

1. By agreement in the Policy

The assured may pay full premium while effecting the insurance. The insurer may agree to return it wholly or partly at the happening of a certain event. The premium is returnable by agreement in the following circumstances:

(*i*) Improvement in the character of insurance. For example, change of ship to safer routes, use of first class liner, good packing etc.

(*ii*) The insurer may encourage to return a part of the premium if claims do not arise.

(*iii*) Cancellation of policy due to change in the ownership of hull.

(*iv*) Mutual cancellation of the policy.

2. For Reasons of Equity

The premium is returnable for reasons of equity.

(*i*) *Non-attachment of risk:* Where the subject-matter has never been under the risk, or the risk has not been started. For example, the voyage might not have been made or the goods might be short shipped.

(*ii*) Undeclared balance of an open policy is entitled for return of premium. The premium shall be returned only when there has no further interest to declare within the scope of the policy.

(*iii*) Where there is a total failure of an apportionable part of the consideration, the apportionate part of the premium is returnable to the assured provided where is no fraud or illegality on the part of the assured or his agents. Where voyage was to be completed in stages and each stage is being rated separately. If some stages are not completed, the premiums relating to uncompleted stages are returnable.

(*iv*) When the assured has no insurable interest throughout the life of the policy the premium is returnable provided the policy does not amount to fraud.

(*v*) The insurer can cancel the voyage when there is unreasonable delay in commencing the voyage.

(*vi*) In ease of over-insurance, a proportionate part of the premium is returnable. Where two or more policies are effected by or on behalf of the assured on the same adventure and interest or any part thereof, and the sums insured exceed the indemnity allowed, the assured is said to be over-insurance by double insurance. In this case, a proportionate part of the several premiums is returnable, provided that if the policies are taken at different times, and any earlier policy has at any time borne the entire risk, or if a claim has been paid on the policy in respect of the full sum insured, no premium is returnable in respect of that policy.

QUESTIONS

1. What are the factors to effect premium calculation?
2. When is premium of marine insurance returnable?

23

MARINE LOSSES

Losses in marine insurance business are result of the various perils. Marine insurance policy does not necessarily cover all the risks. All insurer is liable to indemnify an insured in respect of only losses which result from perils insured against. When the loss occurred is beyond the insured peril, the insured himself shall have to bear.

Marine Perils

The perils insured against are mentioned in the policy and the underwriter shall be liable for damages caused by the insured perils.

"Marine Perils means the perils consequent on", or incidental to the navigation of the sea, that is to say, perils of the seas, fire, war perils (enemies), pirates, rovers, thieves, captures, seizures, restraints and detainment of princes and peoples, jettisons, barratry and other perils, either of the like kind or which may be designated by the policy."

1. Perils of Sea

Under perils of sea, ordinary action of the winds and waves, ordinary wear and tear to the vessel, inherent risk of the cargo are not included. The underwriter may be liable for losses caused by Perils of the sea, he is not necessarily liable for perils on sea. Pertils of the sea refers to fortuitous accidents or casualties of the sea. If the loss arising out of any of the perils of the sea insured is attributable to the fraud or wilful misconduct of the assured, the underwriter is acquitted from the liability under the policy.

2. Fire

In olden times fire was the biggest maritime perils, but recently it has been under control to a greater extent. Damage resulting from fire and smoke is included under fire-peril. The water used for extinguishing fire may cause damage to the insured goods. So, this peril is also insurable. The damage due to spontaneous combustion may be maritime peril and be insured against. Damage done due to lightning, explosion and fire originating from negligence of the crew is recoverable from underwriters. The losses which are not included in the standard policy can be covered by having special clauses and paying extra-premium.

3. Man-of-War

This is the vessel which is authorised by nations for the purpose of defence or attack in the event of hostilities. Any damage to the goods or ships arising out of collision against a man-of-war is insurable.

4. Enemies

The ships belonging to the foe (enemy) may cause loss to the insured and is re-underwritten by the marine policy. This policy extends to all the persons of the enemy country and to their hostile acts provided such acts form part of the enemy actions.

5. Pirates, Rovers, Thieves

The perils on account of pirates, rovers and thieves were common in olden times, but it has been reduced considerably these days. These acts are generally committed for the pursuit of individual gain by the persons beyond the jurisdiction of a state. The term 'thieves' does not mean clandestine theft or a theft committed by any one of the crew or officers or passengers.

Jettison

Jettison means voluntary throwing away of the cargo or part of a vessel's equipment for the lightening or relieving the ship for common safety. The aim of the intentional throwing away of the goods or property is to relieve the vessel from some imminent peril. Accidental falling of things does not constitute jettison. The own inherent-vice of cargo is also not included in the jettison.

Barratry

Barratry includes every wrongful act wilfully committed by the master or crew the prejudice of the owner. The act of barratry must be committed without the knowledge of the owner. The theft, the setting fire to ship, fraudulent selling of vessel and cargo without the connivance of the ship-owner are the various examples of the barratry. The insurer, if barratry insured, is liable for losses arising out of barratry.

Restraints and Detainments

The prevention to free use of a port by the government of the country is called restraints. It may cause interruption and possible loss of voyages involving such ports and sacrifice of cargo. The term 'detainments' covers losses resulting from the detention of a vessel and its cargo by blockage or possibly quarantine regulation or other interference by the police power of a nation while a vessel is in port. It does not cover losses which are the result merely of delay or interruption of the voyage, or loss of market or some other remote result.

The Free of Capture and Seizure Clause (F.C. & S. Clause)

The policy generally covers war perils. But, to include perils of sudden declaration of war, the war clause or free of capture and seizure clause is added to relieve war perils. By deletion of this clause, the policy is automatically restored to its original condition and adequate premiums are charged for the purpose.

Explosion

The risk of explosion has greatly increased. The explosion on board of a vessel damaging hull or cargo or both could be constructed as a peril on the sea. An explosion on shore might damage a ship or its cargo. Marine cargo policies were amended to include the risk of explosions not clearly caused by war perils. The explosion, in case of hull policies, 'on shipboard or elsewhere' is covered in the amended "Inchmaree or Negligence clause".

Strikes, Riots and Civil Commotion Clause

The marine insurance on cargo is extended to cover from warehouse to warehouse or otherwise insures the goods on shore prior to shipment and after discharge, the danger of underwriters being held liable for losses, resulting from the unlawful acts of strikers from riots or civil commotions is materially enhanced. The insurers are unwilling to assume liability for losses due to unlawful acts.

All Other Perils

Loss occurred by salt water of the sea, action of worms on timber, cattle dying due to want of fodder as a result of lengthy voyage constitute sea perils. There may be other damages due to oil, sweat, heat, which are insured under other perils.

MARINE LOSSES

If the loss takes place on account of any of the perils insured against with the insurer, the insurer will be liable for it and shall have to make good the losses to the assured. If the peril is insured, the insurer will indemnify the assured, otherwise not. The doctrine of causa proxima is to be applied while calculating the amount of loss. It means for payment of losses, the real or proximate cause is to be taken into account. If the proximate cause is insured, the insurer will pay, otherwise not. It has been discussed in a previous chapter.

TOTAL LOSS

Losses are deemed to be total or complete when the subject-matter is fully destroyed or lost or ceases to be a thing of its kind. It should be distinguished from partial loss where only part of the property insured is lost or destroyed. In case of total loss, the insured stands to lose to the extent of the value of the property provided the policy amount was to that limit.

1. Actual Total Loss

Actual total loss is a material and physical loss of the subject-matter insured. Where the subject-matter insured is destroyed or so damaged as to cease to be a thing of the kind insured, or where the insured is irretrievably deprived thereof, there is an actual total loss. When a vessel is foundered or when merchandise is so damaged as to be valueless or when ship is missing it will be an actual total loss.

The actual total loss occurs in the following cases:

1. The subject-matter is destroyed, *e.g.*, a ship is entirely destroyed by fire.
2. The subject-matter is so damaged as to cease to be a thing of the kind insured. Here, the subject-matter is not totally destroyed but damaged to such an extent as the result of the mishap, it is no longer of the same specie as originally insured. The examples of such losses are—food-stuff badly damaged by sea water became unfit for human consumption, hides became valueless as hides due to admission of water. These damaged food-stuffs or hides may be used as manure. Since the characters of the subject-matters are changed and have lost their shapes, they are all actual total loss.
3. The insured is irretrievably deprived of the ownership of goods even they are in physical existence as in the case of capture by enemy, stealth by thief or fraudulent disposal by the captain or crew.
4. The subject-matter is lost. For example, where a ship is missing for a very longtime and no news of her is received after the lapse of a reasonable time. An actual total loss is presumed unless there is some other proof to show against it.

In case of actual total loss, notice of abandonment of property need not be given. In such total losses, the insurer is entitled to all rights and remedies in respect of damaged properties. In no case, amount over the insured value or insurable value is recoverable in a total loss form the insurers. If the property is under-insured, the insured can recover only up to the amount of insurance. If it is over-insured he is not over-benefited but only the actual loss will be indemnified.

Where the subject-matter had ceased to be of the kind insured, the assured will be given the full amount of total loss provided there was insurance up to that amount, and the insurer will subrogate all rights and remedies in respect of property. Any amount realised by the sale of the material will go to the insurer.

2. Constructive Total Loss

Where the subject-matter is not actually lost in the above manner, but is reasonably abandoned when its actual total loss is unavoidable or when it cannot be preserved from total loss without involving expenditure which would exceed the value of the subject-matter. For example, the cost of repair and replacement was estimated to be Rs. 50,000 whereas the ship was estimated to be Rs. 40,000. The ship may be abandoned and will be taken as constructive total loss. But if the value of ship was more than Rs. 50,000 it would not be constructive total loss. Here it is assumed that retention of the subject-matter would involve financial loss to the insured.

The constructive total loss will be where—

(*a*) the subject-matter insured is reasonably abandoned on account of its actual total loss appearing to be unavoidable;

(*b*) the subject-matter could not be preserved from actual total loss without an expenditure which would exceed its repaired and recovered value.

The insured is not compelled to abandon his interest, where the goods are abandoned, the insurer will have to pay the full insured value. Where there is constructive total loss, the assured may either treat the loss as a partial loss or abandon the subject-matter insured to the insurer and treat the loss as if it was an actual total loss.

Notice of Abandonment

The notice of abandonment is essentially given to the insurer to claim the loss as constructive total loss. If he fails to do so, the loss can only be treated as a partial loss. The notice can be given orally or in writing. The notice should be unconditional and absolute. The insurer may either elect to accept or decline the proposal. But, when the insurer elects to object the notice, the insured should at once commence legal action against the insurer to claim 'the loss' under constructive total loss. In brief, the notice of abandonment involves the following:

1. Subject to the contrary provision, where the insurer elects to abandon the subject-matter insured to the insurer, he must give notice of abandonment. If the insured fails to furnish the notice, the loss can be treated as a partial loss.
2. The notice can be given in writing or orally. It may be given in any terms which indicate the intention of the assured to abandon his insured interest in the subject-matter insured unconditionally to the insurer.
3. Notice of abandonment must be given with reasonable diligence after the receipt of reliable information of loss, but where the information is of a doubtful character, the insured is liable to furnish the required information.
4. If notice of abandonment is properly given, the rights of the assured are not prejudiced by the fact that the insurer refuses to accept the abandonment.
5. The acceptançe of an abandonment may be either express or implied from the conduct of the insurer. The mere silence of the insurer is not an acceptance.
6. Where notice of abandonment is accepted the abandonment is irrevocable.
7. Notice of abandonment is unnecessary where there is no possibility of benefit to the insurer if notice was given to him.
8. Notice of abandonment may be waived by the insurer.

Effect of Abandonment

1. In case of valid abandonment the insurer is entitled to take over the interest of the assured in whatever may remain of the subject matter insured.
2. At the time of abandonment of ship, the insurer is entitled of any freight in course of being earned.

In case of constructive total loss, the insurer have a right, after the settlement of the claim in full, to take over the property or whatever may remain of it. Where the insurers elect to take over the remainders of the wreck, the cost of removing the wreck is borne by the insurers. But, in case insurers elect not to take over the destroyed party, it becomes the liability of the ship-owners to remove the wreck and incur necessary expenditure for the same. The constructive total loss in the case of vessels is distinguished from the constructive total loss in cargo or freight. In case of cargo, the constructive total loss will be there where the assured is deprived of the goods by insured perils. In case of damage to the goods there is a constructive total loss where the cost of reconditioning the goods and forwarding the goods to the destination would exceed their value an arrival. Hull policy covers total and partial losses and partial losses are paid in full irrespective of the insured amount, the insured amount merely serves as the maximum limit.

Difference between Actual and Constructive Total Loss

Actual total loss is related with the physical impossibility and the constructive total loss is related with the commercial impossibility. For example, if the hides are so damaged that it is impossible to prevent the hides from the destruction and it may become a mass of putrefied matter, the case is of an actual total lass. But if it was possible to restore the hides to their original condition, though the cost of so doing would exceed their value at destination, the damaged hides can be claimed as constructive total loss because the completion of the adventure has became commercially impossible.

Salvage Loss

Where actual total loss occurred, and the subject-matter is so damaged as to cease to be a thing of the kind insured or when they have been sold before reaching the destination, there is a constructive total loss. The usual form of settlement is that the net sale proceeds will be paid to the assured. The net sale proceeds is calculated by deducting expenses of the sale from the amount realised by the sale. The insured will recover from the insurer the total loss less the net amount of sale. This amount received from the insurer is called a 'Salvage Loss'.

PARTIAL LOSS

Partial loss is there where only part of the property insured is lost or destroyed or damaged. Partial losses, in contradiction from total losses, include (*a*) Particular Average Losses, *i.e.*, damage, or total loss of a part, (*b*) General Average Losses (General Average) *i.e.*, the sacrifice expenditure, etc., done for common safety of subject-matter insured, (*c*) Particular or special charges, *i.e.*, expenses incurred in special circumstances, and (*d*) salvage charges.

Particular Average Loss

Particular Average loss is defined as 'a partial loss' of the subject-matter insured caused by a peril insured and is not a general average loss. The general average loss or expense is voluntarily done for the common safety of all the parties insured. But, the particular average loss is fortuitous or accidental. It cannot be partially shifted to others but will be borne by the persons directly affected. The particular average loss must fulfil the following conditions:

1. Particular Average Loss is a partial loss or damage to any particular interest caused to that interest only by a peril insured against.
2. The loss should be accidental and not intentional.
3. The loss should be of the particular subject-matter only.
4. It should be the loss of a part of the subject-matter or damage thereto or both. The distinguishing feature in this matter is that where the properties insured are all of the same description, kind and quality and they are valued as a whole in the policy, the total loss of a part of this whole is a particular loss, but where the properties insured are not all of the same description, kind and quality and they are separately valued in the policy, the loss of an apportionable part of the interest is a total loss.

In case of total loss of a part of recoverable either as a total loss or as a particular average loss, the basis of settlement will be on the total loss of the whole lot and the insurer will be liable to pay in proportion according to the insured or insurable value of the whole interest.

Particular Average on Cargo

The particular average loss may be either the damage and depreciation of a particular interest or a total loss of its part. If the property is insured under one value for the whole and is all the same kind, quality or description, a total loss of part will be recovered as a particular average loss. In case where goods are delivered in a damaged condition or where the value is depreciated, the resulting particular average loss will be adjusted upon the basis of comparison between the gross sound value and damaged value. The process of valuation is as follows:

1. The gross sound value of the goods damaged is found out. This is the value for which the goods would have been sold if the goods had reached the port of destination in sound condition.
2. After calculating the above value, the gross damaged value of the goods damaged or depreciated is found out on the basis of market price at that time.
3. Deduct the gross damaged value from the gross sound value. The difference is the measure of the actual damage or depreciation.
4. The ratio of the damage or depreciation is calculated by dividing the amount of damage or depreciation by the gross sound value.
5. Apply the above ratio to the value (insured or insurable value as the case may be) of the damaged or depreciated goods which will give the amount of particular average loss.
6. Of the amount thus arrived at, the insurer is liable for that proportion which his sum insured bears to the value (insured or insurable).

ILLUSTRATION

For example, the cargo was of Rs. 20,000. Half of the goods are damagcd which realised Rs. 4,000 at destination. If the damaged goods would have realised (*a*) Rs. 8,000, (*b*) Rs. 16,000 had they reached undamaged.

(*a*) Gross sound value on arrival		Rs. 8,000
Gross realised value on arrival		Rs. 4,000
	Damage	Rs. 4,000

Damage is Rs. 4,000 which is 1/2 of gross sound value. Therefore, the claim on policy is 1/2 of Rs. 10,000 (20,0002)-Rs: 5,000.

(*b*) Gross sound value on arrival		Rs. 16,000
Gross realised value on arrival		Rs. 4,000
	Damage	Rs. 12,000

Damage is Rs. 12,000 which is 3/4 of gross sound value. Therefore, the claim on policy is 3/4 of Rs. 10,000 = Rs. 7,500. The main reason for the above computation was to keep the underwriter free from the liability or otherwise of the rise or fall in the price of the damaged goods.

Valuation by Services

The valuation by services removes the defects of memorandum clause which is used to free certain commodities from particular average and in the case of other commodities the damage has to amount to at least 5 per cent to become recoverable. Specifically, the provisions are:

1. Corn, fish, salt, fruit, flour and seed, etc., are warranted free from particular average unless the ship be stranded.
2. Sugar, tobacco, hemp, flax, hides and skins, etc., are warranted free from particular average unless the ship be stranded or unless amounting to 5%.
3. All the other goods are warranted free from particular average unless the ship be stranded or unless amounting to 3%.

The stranding of the ship vitiates the Memorandum and renders insurers liable for any particular average which has occurred on the voyage irrespective of the franchises mentioned. Percentage has to be taken into consideration in ascertaining whether the franchise is reached, but when attained the damage is paid in full. If the particular average reaches the stated percentage, the insurer becomes liable in respect of the whole loss and not merely for the excess over the franchise or exemption limit.

As has been mentioned above, the particular average loss can be claimed only when it exceeds 'certain fixed percentage' of the total value of the goods. But this limit or percentage may account a huge amount when a very large amount has been insured. In such a case, it will work as a great hardship to the assured as he will have to suffer this partial loss himself. In order to lessen the rigours of memorandum clause, the subject matter is divided in sections known as 'series' and the franchise *i.e.*, the exemption limit will be considered for each series separately for the purpose of calculating particular average loss. The subject-matter may vary according to the type of interest, packing, original localities. The last series which does not fulfil the required limit or amount is called tail series. A tail series is dealt as a complete series. The assured is free to recover particular average in respect of each series separately.

Particular Average on Ship

In case of partial loss of ship the following factors are considered:

1. Where the ship has been repaired, the assured is entitled to the reasonable cost of the repairs less the customary deductions. The amount of repair shall not be more than the sum insured.
2. Where the ship has been only partially repaired; the assured is entitled to the reasonable cost of such repairs, reasonable depreciation.
3. If the ship has not been repaired and has not been sold in her damaged state during the risk, the assured is entitled to be indemnified for the reasonable, depreciation arising form ,the unrepaired damage.

The measure of indemnity for particular average is the reasonable cost of repairing the damage less the customary deductions 'new for old'. If the damaged parts of the ship are old then the insurers is obliged to indemnify the insured only to the extent of the value of the old parts. But when new parts are added, the difference between the value of the new parts and the value of the old parts are made. Insurers are liable for the cost of repairing particular average damage to the ship irrespective of the insured or actual value of the ship where temporary repairs are necessary the insurers are liable for such repairs in addition to the permanent repairs. Where a ship cannot be repaired at the port of refuge, cost of removal to another port is regarded as part of the cost of repairs. Extra expenses involved in 'over time' working are not allowed.

Particular Average in Case of Freight

Where there is a partial loss of freight, the measure of indemnity is such proportion of the sum fixed by the policy in the case of a valued policy, or of the insurable value in the case of an unvalued policy as the proportion of freight lost by the assured bears to the whole freight at the risk of assured under the policy.

General Average

The general average loss will be there where the loss is caused by an extraordinary sacrifice or expenditure voluntarily and reasonably made or incurred in time of peril for the purpose of preserving the property imperilled in common adventure. The following elements are involved in general average.

1. The loss must be extra-ordinary in nature. The sacrifice or expenditure must not be related to the performance of routine work. A state of affairs may compel the master to do something beyond his ordinary duty for the preservation of the subject-matter.

2. The whole adventure must be imperilled. The peril should be something more than the ordinary perils of the sea. It should be imminent and real.
3. The general average act must be voluntary and intentional accidental loss or damage is excluded.
4. The loss, expenses or sacrifice must be incurred or made reasonably and prudently. The master of the ship is proper person to decide the reasonableness of a particular circumstance.
5. The sacrifice, loss or expenditure should be made for the preservation of the whole adventure. It should be made for the common safety.
6. If the sacrifice proved abortive, it will be allowed as the total loss. Therefore, to call it general average, it must be successful at least in part.
7. In absence of contrary provision, the insurer is not liable for any general average loss or contribution where the loss was not incurred for the purpose of avoiding, or in connection with the avoidance of a peril insured against.
8. The loss must be direct result of a general average act. Indirect losses such as demurrage and market losses are not allowed as general average.
9. General average must not be due to some default on the part of the person whose interest has been sacrificed.

Difference Between General Average Loss and Particular Average Loss

1. General average is incurred for the benefit of all interests but the particular average is in connection with any of the interests.
2. General average is always voluntary and intentional but the particular average is an accidental or fortuitous.
3. General average is shared by all those who is benefited by the general average act. Particular average is paid by the insurer.
4. General average may include expenditure and sacrifice along with loss whereas the particular average results from a loss or damage.

TYPES OF GENERAL AVERAGE LOSS

The general average losses are divided into two classes.

1. General Average Sacrifices

The general average sacrifices are made for common safety. For example 'jettison' which means throwing away of the cargo in order to lighten the ship. Similarly, the use of cargo as fuel, cutting away of a spare and sails.

2. General Average Expenditure

The general average act involves expenditure. In this case extra expenditures are involved for common safety. Here, additional charges are incurred at the port ship is repaired, expenses may be involved for lightening and re-loading of the cargo.

GENERAL AVERAGE CONTRIBUTION

The general average loss is rateable contributed by the parties interested. In contribution of general average loss the contributory interest, amount to be made good and contributory values are considered.

1. Contributing Interests

The interests saved by the general average act are liable to contribute rateably to make good the sacrifices or expenses. There are certain articles which are not required to contribute towards general average loss. For example, postal articles, parcel, crews, effects and the personal effects of passengers not shipped under a bill of lading. There are three main contributing interests—ship, freight and cargo. When a general average loss occurred among different interests, it is of vital importance that the interest which has been sacrificed must also rateably contribute to the loss, otherwise it would be in a better position than the interests saved by general average act.

2. Amounts to be Made Good

The amount to be made good in general average differs from adventure to adventure.

(*a*) *Ship.* The amount to be made good in general average in respect of a ship is measured by reasonable cost of repairs less the actual deduction (if any) new for old. The costs of repairs are taken into account as they have been actually effected either at a port of refuge or at destination.

(*b*) *Cargo.* The amount of general average in case of goods is their net value. The net value is calculated taking into account the value of goods sacrificed at their safe arrival and from this the expenses (*i.e.,* freight unpaid, duty and landing charges) which would have been incurred had the goods arrived safely, are deducted. Thus, the net value of goods is obtained. The remaining cargo arrives damaged from causes which would have actually affected the sacrificed goods. The amount to be made good for general average purposes is their net value based on what the goods sacrificed would have realised, had they reached the destination damaged to some extent as the other cargo. For goods arriving damaged owing to general average sacrifice, the allowance is the difference between their net value in sound condition and net value in damaged state.

(*c*) *Freight.* Where the freight is to be paid at destination in respect of a cargo which is used for general average act, the shipowner will lose it and it would be made good in general average. The shipowner is entitled for the gross freight which he would have earned, had the goods not been sacrificed less the charges which he would have incurred to earn such freight during the remainder of the voyage, but which he has not incurred as a result of the sacrifice.

(*d*) *Expenses.* All the extra-ordinary expenses properly incurred by the shipowner in time of peril for the common safety of all the interests are also made under the general average contribution.

3. Contributory Values

The third process is to determine what are the bases to contribute to general average. The interest contributes on their net value at the place where the voyage ends, *i.e.*, at destination or at intermediate port if the voyage be abandoned there. The values are contributory values. It may be of three types.

(*i*) *Ship.* The shipowner will contribute on the ship's value as saved by the sacrifice. The value is the amount for which the shipowner as a reasonable man would be willing to sell her on arrival at her destination. Any amount that may have been contributed in respect of general average damages is added to this value to arrive at contributory value.

(*ii*) *Cargo.* The cargo owner will contribute on the market value of goods saved at the place where the voyage ends. To arrive at the value the expenses incidental to the safe arrival of the cargo is deducted from the selling price of the cargo.

(*iii*) *Freight.* If the freight has been paid in advance, it would have been included in the value of separate interest. The goods arrived safely at destination will have to contribute on the basis of the net value of freight saved if the freight was not paid in advance. The contribution of freight will arrive at by ascertaining the actual sum of freight received at port of destination less the expenses of earning it from the date of general average act.

Application of General Average to Insurance

In absence of contrary to the contract, the general average losses and contributions are recoverable from the respective marine insurers insuring ship, freight and cargo if the general average has been incurred for the purpose of avoiding a peril insured against. The extent of insurers, liability for general average contribution is the full amount of the contribution provided the contributory value does not exceed the insured value.

The York-Antwerp Rules 1950

The York-Antwerp rule was formulated in 1877. The rule was again revised and extended at a meeting of the International Law Association held at Stockholm in Sept. 1924. The rule was again amended in 1950. Now, the rule is called the York-Antwerp Rules 1950. It has been formulated in two forms (1) Lettered Rules and (2) Numbered Rules.

Lettered Rules

There shall be a general average act when and only when any extra-ordinary sacrifice or expenditure is intentionally and reasonably made or incurred for the common safety for the purpose of preserving from peril. The general average sacrifices and expenses shall be borne .by the different contributing interests. Only such losses, damages, or expenses which are the direct consequence of the general average act shall be allowed as general average. The lettered rules are described from A to G.

Numbered Rules

The numbered rules I to XIX specify the various losses and expenses that are considered to be general average sacrifices. The last three rules XX, XXI and XXII govern the banking arrangements in connection with the adjustment. It is provided that cash deposits paid to the adjusters as security for the final general assessment shall be treated as a fiduciary funds and placed in a special bank account.

Jettison of Cargo, Fire

No Jettison of cargo shall be made good as general average unless such cargo is carried in accordance with the Rule I and II.

Rule III

Extinguishing fire on shipboard done to a ship and cargo or either of them by water or otherwise will be included in general average.

Rule IV and V

Cutting Away wreck, stranding: Where a vessel has been partially wrecked by a sea peril and portion of the spares remain, the cutting away of these remnants is not allowed for in general average. The place of stranding should be voluntarily selected by the master. Loss or damage incurred in refloating such stranded ship shall be allowed as general average.

Rule VI and VII

Damage or loss caused to soils and spares and machinery shall be allowed in general average if it was due to general average act.

Rule VIII to XII

Expenses involved from lightening a ship to the reloading or discharge of cargo are involved in general average ships' materials and stores build for fuel are also taken as general average. Wages ana maintenance of crew and other expenses at a port of refuge are taken into general average if these are involved for general average act.

Rule XIII

In adjusting claims for general average repairs to be allowed in general average shall be subject to deductions in respect of "new for old" according to the rules. Temporary repairs made for the common safety shall be admitted as general average (Rule XIV).

Rule XVII

This rule mentioned that the contribution to a general average shall be made upon the actual net value of the property at the termination of the adventure to which values shall be added the amount made good as general average for property sacrificed.

Rule XV, XVI, XVII, XVIII

These deal with the loss of freight, amount to be made good for large and damage to ship.

Rule XIX

This rule deals with the undeclared value of goods without the knowledge of the shipowner or his agent or to goods wilfully misdescribed of the shipowner or his agent or to goods wilfully misdescribed at the time of shipment shall not be allowed to general average but such goods shall remain liable to contribute.

Rules XX, XXI and XXII deal with the banking provision of the general average.

EXPENSES

The expenses are (*i*) Particular charges and (*ii*) Salvage charges.

1. 0Particular Charges

Where the policy contains a "Sue and Labour" clause, the engagement thereby entered into is deemed to be supplementary to the contract of insurance and the assured may recover from the insurer any expenses properly incurred pursuant to the clause. The clause requires the insurers to pay any expenses properly incurred by the assured or his agents in preventing or minimising loss or damage to the subject matter by an insured peril. The essential features of the clause are as below:

1. The expenses must be incurred for the benefit of the subject matter insured. The expenses incurred for the common benefit will be a part of general average.
2. The expenses must be reasonable and be incurred by "the assured, his factors, his servants or assigns" and this provision effectively excludes salvage charges.
3. They are recoverable only when incurred to avert or minimise a loss from a peril covered by the policy.

QUESTIONS

1. What are the procedures of adjusting marine insurance losses?
2. What do you mean by the following terms:

   Particular Average Loss, General Average Loss, Constructive and Total Losses.

24

PAYMENT OF CLAIMS

When the policy has been issued the risk for the peril insured against is covered. The contingency against which protection is given or not materialised when the loss insured against actually occurs, the insured has got to make a claim on the insurer for in-demnification of loss. If loss does not occur, no payment would be made to the insured.

Evidence

Before admitting a claim, relevant evidence in connection with the policy is required. In marine insurance the policy is generally issued on mutual understanding and Good Faith of both the parties. But, at the time of claim, the insurer should satisfy himself on the information furnished by the insured. Value of subject matter, nature of the subject matter; warranties, insurable interest etc. are some of the matters to be considered at the time when the claim arises. For these purposes, the production of certain documents becomes necessary.

Notice of Claim

A prompt notice of claim by the insured is required. The receipt of notice or approval of the course of action taken by the insured does not mean that the liability of any loss is acknowledged. The damage notice must be given prior to survey by insurer's representative and the survey report signed by him.

The compliance with the rules of notice is necessary to enforce the right of recovery of the loss by the insured. After the notice, the insured must take delivery of the damaged goods at once or otherwise deal with the damage because the insurer is not responsible for further and continued depreciation of the interest damaged. In case of any theft or pilferage, the insured must give notice to the insurer within 10 days from the date on which the risk expired. If ship-owner is also liable for any loss or damage, he or his agent is also entitled to a written notice. The notice is generally given at the time of taking delivery of goods. But if loss could not be determined or detected before such delivery, the notice is to reach the ship-owner or his representative within 3 days of the delivery. The notice is an important factor in the matter of claim.

DOCUMENTS REQUIRED FOR CLAIM

The following documents are required at the time of claim.

(*i*) Policy or certificate of insurance.

(*ii*) **Bill of lading.** It determines the scope of the contract of carriage.

(*iii*) **Invoice or bill** stating terms and conditions of sale.

(*iv*) **Copy of protest.** In the event of stranding of or accident to the vessel, the master of the ship notes 'protest' before a counsel or notary public. The protest states that everything was done to bring to safety the ship and cargo and loss or damage was not due to lack of diligence on the part of the master or crew.

(*v*) **Certificate of Survey.** This is necessary to find out whether the necessary franchise is reached or not in case of particular average.

(*vi*) **Account sales or Bill of sale.** Similar documents where goods have been sold. The difference between gross sound value and proceeds as per account sales might be accepted as amount of loss.

(*vii*) **Letter of subrogation.** It gives the underwriters to sue and recover compensation from third parties where the same is due.

DOCUMENTS IN DIFFERENT TYPES OF CLAIMS

Total Loss

(*i*) **Insurance policy.** It furnishes an evidence of the terms and contract of insurance.

(*ii*) **Bill of lading.** It is the correspondence of the insurance contract with the voyage and vessel.

(*iii*) **Copy of the invoice.** A copy of the Invoice relating to the goods insured should be sent. It will help in estimating the correct value of the goods.

(*iv*) ***Protest.*** A copy of protest is required when the total loss is due to the loss of the vessel or other accident.

(*v*) **Letter of subrogation.** A letter of subrogation is sent if anything remains of the subject matter insured after the total loss or if there are rights or remedies regarding the interest or against third parties.

(*vi*) **Notice of Abandonment.** If there is a constructive total loss, the notice of abandonment is given in the manner described in previous chapter.

Partial Loss

In case of partial average loss:

(*i*) the policy or the certificate,

(*ii*) the invoice for the whole shipment,

(*iii*) the bill of lading should be sent to the underwriters and

(*iv*) the copy of the Master's protest or an extract from logbook of the ship is to be presented with the policy if the particular average is recoverable in certain circumstances according to the terms of the policy, *e.g.*, standing of the vessel, accident, heavy weather, etc.

(*v*) **A Surveyor's Report.** A surveyor's report prepared by some recognised surveyor should be appended to the above documents when evidence is necessary to show that the settled franchise has reached.

(*vi*) **Bill of Sale.** When there is a sale of the damaged goods the bill of sale is required by the measures.

(*vii*) **Letter of Subrogation.** The letter of subrogation should be duly furnished by the insured if required by the insurers.

(*viii*) **Cost of Protection.** On the proof, the cost of protection is paid by the underwriters apart from the particular average if there was a successful claim. In unsuccessful claims, insurers are not liable to pay these charges.

Particular Charge

When claim is made under those heads, shipping and insurance documents with evidence for the amount of the particular charges are required. When the case is taken up by an Average Adjuster, his report or the appropriate extract will have to be furnished to the underwriters.

General Average

While making a claim for general average loss, all the documents required for claims in total losses or in particular average losses if partial sacrifices are required to be represented to the underwriter. The Average Adjuster's Statement or the appropriate extract from it will have to be presented when claims for General Average Contribution are made. When the Average is claimed for General Average Deposits, the insurers will require the deposit receipt to enable them to recover any refund that may be due to them.

Salvage Charges

The documents in support of a salvage claim and the procedure to be followed are almost identical to those for a General Average Claim.

EXTENT OF LIABILITY

The insured can recover from the underwriter a loss to the extent of the insurable value of the property insured if it was an unvalued policy. In case of a valued policy, the assured can recover the loss to the full extent of the value fixed by the policy. Subject to the average-clause, where there are two or more underwriters, they shall bear the loss in the proportion of their subscription.

Successive Losses

The underwriters are generally not liable for more than the insured value; but they may be liable for successive losses which may in the aggregate exceed the insured value, by payment of extra premium and stamp duty. This provision is made by 'reinstatement clause'. Where there is partial loss which has not been repaired or otherwise made good is followed by a total loss, the assured can recover only the total loss. For example, where a damaged ship in an unrepaired state is lost, the insurers are liable only for total loss and not for unrepaired damage.

Other Charges

The amount of claim cannot include survey fees, cost of certificates and professional average adjuster's fees. Once the claim is proved to be recoverable, these charges can be recovered in full from the underwriters. The 'Sue and Labour' clause defines the procedure of payment of the expenses. Expenses incurred by or on behalf of the assured for the safety or preservation of the subject matter insured, other than general average and salvage charges, are called particular charges. The underwriter is liable for particular charges and other expenses properly incurred pur sant to the provision of the suing and labouring clause in order to avert a loss insured against.

Effect of Over-Insurance and Under-Insurance

If two or more policies are effected by or on behalf of the assured on the same adventure and interest or in respect of any part thereof, and the sums insured exceed the minimum amount allowable as indemnity, the assured is said to be over-insured. Where the assured is insured for an amount less than the insurable value, he is said to be under-insured. In this case, he is deemed to be his own insurer in respect of the uninsured balance. Where the assured is over-insured, each insurer is bound as between himself and the other insurers to contribute rateably to the loss in proportion to the amount for which he is liable under his contract.

Subrogation

Where the insurer pays for a total loss, either of the whole, or in the case of goods, of any apportionable part, of the subject-matter insured, he thereupon becomes entitled to take over the interest of the assured in whatever may remain of the subject matter so paid for, and he is thereby subrogated to all the rights and remedies of the assured in and in respect of that subject matter. Subject to the foregoing provisions where the insurer pays for a partial loss, he acquires no title to the subject matter insured, or such part of it as may remain, but he is thereupon subrogated to all rights and remedies of the assured in and in respect of the subject matter insured as from the time of the casualty causing the loss, in so far as the assured has been indemnified. The right of subrogation ensures that the assured should not make a profit out of the contract.

Salvage

The salvage is the remuneration or reward payable according to maritime laws to salvors who voluntarily and independently of contract render services to maritime property at sea. Salvage charges insured in preventing a loss by perils insured against may be recovered as a loss by those perils. The salvage awarded to salvors is apportioned over the values saved. This charge is not recoverable from marine underwriters.

Claims and 'Causa Proxima'

In determining the amount of the loss, the rule of Causa Proxima Non Remota Spectature is applied. It means that when there are more than one cause for the loss or damage the proximate cause and not the remote cause is regarded. The underwriter will pay the amount of loss only when the real or the proximate cause is insured. The peril insured against must be the proximate cause of the loss and it must not be due to the fault or misconduct of the insured.

The insurer is not liable for any loss attributable to the wilful misconduct of the assured, but unless the policy otherwise provides, he is liable for any loss proximately caused by a peril insured against, even though the loss would not have happened but for the misconduct or negligence of the master or crew. Unless the policy otherwise provides, the insurer on ship of goods is not liable for any loss proximately caused by delay although the delay be caused by a peril insured against. Unless the policy otherwise provides, the insurer is no liable for ordinary wear and tear, or dinary leakage and breakage, inherent vice or nature of the subject matter insured or for any loss proximately caused by rate or vermin or for any injury to machinery not proximately caused by maritime perils.

QUESTIONS

1. Discuss the procedures of settlement of claims.
2. How is the extent of liability determined by the insurer?

25

PROGRESS OF MARINE INSURANCE BUSINESS IN INDIA

The marine insurance business was nationalised, along with other general insurance by the General Insurance (Emergency Provisions) Ordinance 1971, which was subsequently replaced by the General Insurance (Emergency Provisions) Act, 1971. The management of the insurers carrying on General Insurance Business in India was taken over by the Central Government with effect from 13th May, 1971. The General Insurance Corporation of India was formed on 22nd Nov. 1972, under the General Insurance Business (Nationalisation) Act 1972 and by virtue of the same Act, 55 Indian General insurance companies became subsidiaries of the General Insurance Corporation of India and the undertakings of the other erstwhile insurers were merged in one or the other of four selected ultimate companies which were to operate in the nationalised set-up, viz., National Insurance Company Ltd., New India Assurance Company Limited, Oriental Fire & General Insurance Company Ltd. and United India Fire & General Insurance Company Limited. On 1st January, 1974, the 55 Indian insurance companies were also merged into the four ultimate companies by schemes merger. The setting up of a new organisational set-up for the four ultimate companies is still in the process of being completed. Thus the period from 13th May, 1971 to 31st Dec. 1974 has been a period of transition. The progress of marine insurance has been analysed under progress before nationalisation and progress after nationalisation.

Business of Indian Insurers Progress Before Nationalisation

The Gross Premium of Indian Insurers has increased from Rs. 21.06 crores in 1969, *i.e.*, 76.6 per cent of the gross premium received by the marine insurers, to Rs. 31.61 crores, *i.e.*, 79.4 per cent of the gross premium in 1972. Thus, the gross premium has increased not only in absolute term but it has increased in relation of total gross premium. The business of non-Indian insurers has decreased from 23.4 per cent of total gross premium in 1969 to 20.6 per cent or gross premium in 1972. The non-Indias insurers were unable to increase their share in total business. The total gross premium income of nationalised insurers have increased from Rs. 70.83 crores in 1975 to Rs. 98.32 crores in 1978.

Not only the share of gross premium to Indian Insurers, but, the share of net premium to Indian Insurers has also increased from 75.2 per cent of net premium to 78.2 per cent of net premium in 1972. The share of non-Indian insurers has decreased from 24.8 per cent of total net premium to 21.8 per cent of total net premium in 1972. The total net premium has been constantly rising from Rs. 17.96 crores in 1969 to Rs. 27.79 crores in 1972.

As compared to general total general insurance business, the Indian insurers have booked less business in the form in marine insurance business as the share of Indian insurers to total general insurance business in 1969 was 80.2 per cent of total net received by all general insurers which increased to 81.7 per cent in 1971 and 82.8 per cent in 1972 while the corresponding percentage in case of marine insurance was 25.2, 76.9 and 78.2 per cent respectively. Thus, the share of marine insurance of Indian insurers was not so high as was total business in case of general insurances.

Table 25.1 Marine Insurance Business in India, (1969-1981)

(All Insurers) **Rs. in Crores**

Year	*Gross Premium*					*(Net Premium)*					*Total General Insurances (Net Premium)*				
	Indian Insurers		*Non-Indian Insurers*		*Total*	*Indian Insurers*		*Non-Indian Insurers*		*Total*	*Indian Insurers*		*Non-Indian Insurers*		*Total*
	Rs.	*% to total*	*Rs.*	*% to total*	*Rs.*	*Rs.*	*% to total*	*Rs.*	*%to total*	*Rs.*	*Rs.*	*% to total*	*Rs.*	*to% total*	*Rs.*
1969	21.06	76.6	6.44	23.4	27.5	13.50	75.2	4.46	24.8	17.96	73.22	80.2	18.12	19.8	91.35
1970	24.31	77.8	6.95	22.2	31.26	14.45	74.5	4.94	25.5	19.38	84.41	81.5	19.13	18.5	103.57
1971	30.22	79.4	7.85	20.6	38.07	18.48	76.9	5.56	23.1	24.04	93.76	81.7	20.94	18.3	114.70
1972	31.61	79.4	8.22	20.6	39.84	21.73	78.2	6.06	21.8	27.79	119.11	82.8	23.46	17.2	136.57
*1975					70.83					39.32					247.07
1977					95					85					326
*1978					102					92					370
1979					115					103					398
*1980					137					117					481
1981					168					146					599

*Figure relate subsidiary companies of GIC.

The net premium in marine has also increased from Rs. 17.96 crores in 1969 to Rs. 24.04 crores in 1971 and Rs. 27.79 crores in 1972 and Rs. 48.71 crores in 1977. The net premium of all insurances has also increased from Rs. 91.35 crores in 1969 to Rs. 114.70 crores in 1971 and further to 136.57 crores in 1972.

Table 25.2 Analysis of Ratio to Net Premium (%) (1970-1981)

Year	*Indian Insurers*						*Non-Indian Insurers*					
	Net claim Payable	*Net Comm-ssion*	*Expen-ses of Mang.*	*Incerease in Reserve*	*Misc. Income*	*Balance of Income*	*Net claim Payable*	*Net Commis-sion*	*Expen-ses of Mang.*	*Increase in Reserve*	*Misc. Income*	*Balance of Income*
1970	65.7	2.4	19.5	2.7	0.6	4.8	62.8	–1.5	32.4	4.8	0.1	1.4
1971	59.7	1.2	17.1	10.5	5.5	16.6	68.0	–0.4	32.9	5.6	0.7	–6.2
1972	61.3	2.2	17.3	5.1	6.7	20.6	68.4	–0.3	35.2	4.1	2.8	–5.1
1975	49.9	18.9	0.6	16.5		14.1						
1977	41.1	18.0	0.9	2.8	—	37.2						
1978	54.3	17.2	1.0	10.6	—	16.9						
1980	68.5	17.9	0.8	20.9		8.1						
1981	61.3	18.2	0.8	18.9	—	0.8						

Note: Figure of 1975, 1977 and 1978 are related with the nationalised business.

—(Not Applicable)

Indian Insurers

The percentage of net claim to net premium has declined from 65.7 in 1970 to 59.7 percent in 1971 and increased to 61.3 per cent in 1972 while non-Indian insurers have experienced correspondingly a higher percentage viz. 62.8, 68.00 and 68.9 per cent. It reveals that the Indian insurers were rational in payment of claims and were gaining on ground of payment claims. But so far payment of commission was concerned Indian insurers were not saving as compared to that of non-Indian insurers. Indian insurers paid net commission as high as 24 per cent of net premium in 1970. But the Indian insurers were controlling their management expenses more effectively than that of non-Indian insurers who experienced 32.4 per cent of net premium at the minimum while the Indian-insurers experienced the expenses of 19.5 per cent of the net premium at the rnaximum. More-over, the expenses ratio was declining. This shows that the Indian-insurers were more efficiently managing their business and were gaining much more than the non-Indian insurers. The non-Indian insurers suffered loss to the tune of 6.2 per cent of net premium whereas the Indian insurers got the balance of income as low as 14.8 per cent of net premium which has increased to 16.6 per cent in 1971 and 30.6 per cent in 1972 and 16.9 per cent in 1978. Thus the Indian Insurers were more benefited at every level so far as ratios to net premiums were concerned.

Table 25.3 Analysis of Ratio to Gross Premium (%) (1958-1972)

Year	*Indian Insurers*						*Non-Indian Insurers*					
	Gross claim payable	*Direct Commission*	*Expenses of Mang.*	*Increase in Reserve*	*Misc. Income*	*Balance of Income*	*Gross claim payable*	*Direct Commission*	*Expenses of Mang.*	*Increase in Reserve*	*Misc. Income*	*Balance of Income*
1958	56.7	7.4	19.2	—	—	16.4	49.5	8.6	27.0	—	—	14.9
1970	49.8	2.6	14.2	6.6	2.6	29.4	63.2	4.4	23.0	3.6	0.1	5.8
1971	41.7	2.4	13.5	9.8	2.7	35.1	57.6	4.5	23.3	5.1	0.5	8.9
1972	50.7	2.7	14.8	0.9	3.1	33.9	64.2	4.4	25.9	2.2	2.1	5.0

Indian Iusurers

The percentage of gross claims payable to gross premium has been constantly declining from 56.7 per cent in 1958 to 46.8 per cent in 1970 to 41.7 per cent in 1971 and further to 50.7 per cent in 1972. As compared to that of non-Indian insurers, it has been about two-thirds of their ratios. Thus the Indian insurers were saving much in shape of payment claim. Similarly, the Indian-insurers were also curtailing their expenses in the form of payment of direct commission which has been as low as 2.4 per cent of the gross premium in 1971 whereas it was 4.5 per cent in the case of non-Indian-insurers. The expenses of management were also curtailed more effectively by the Indian insurers as were done by the non-Indian insurers. The Indian insurers had expended only 19.2 per cent of their gross premium at the maximum in 1958 whereas it was 23.3 in 1971 of Non-Indian insurers. The Indian insurers were experiencing declining ratios of management expenses to gross premium. The increase in reserve to the Indian insurers were more than the increase in reserve of the non-Indian insurers. The balance of income to Indian insurers was rising rapidly from 16.4 per cent of gross premium in 1958 to 35:1 per cent in 1971 whereas the non-Indian insurers were grossing the share of balance of income to gross premium. Conclusively, it can be stated that the Indian insurers were improving their business and were doing business more effectively than that of non-Indian insurers.

Table 25.4 Indian Insurers, Ratio to Gross Direct Premium Income Outside India (%) (1970-1972)

	1970	*1971*	*1972*
1. Gross claims Payable	64.3	91.9	64.0
2. Direct Commission	10.8	11.8	12.6
3. Expenses of Managing	16.6	14.2	15.0
4. Increase in Reserve	–8.2	1.8	2.8
5. Misc. Income	5.1	5.4	8.3
6. Balance of Income	17.2	–18.6	17.9

The Indian insurers were losing their business outside India as the balance of income has decreased from 17.2 per cent of gross premium in 1970 to — 18.8 per cent of gross premium. Similarly, the percentage of gross claims payable to Gross Direct Premium has increased from 64.3 per cent in 1970 to 91.9 per cent in 1971 and declined to 64.0 per cent in 1972. The direct commission has also increased from 10.8 per cent in 1970 to 11.8 per cent in 1971. However the management expenses has declined from 16.6 per cent in 1970 to 14.2 per cent in 1971 and increased to 15.0 per cent in 1972.

Table 25.5 Net Premium Income Marine Insurance (1975-1981)

(In crores of Rs.)

	1975	*1977*
In India	39.32	48.91
Outside India	14.28	17.75
Total	53.60	66.66

Total Insurance

	1975	*1977*	*1978*	*1979*	*1980*	*1981*
In India	166.12	254	287	323	385	486
Outside India	63.75	72	83	75	96	113
Total	229.87	326	370	398	481	599

The net premium income of marine insurance out of India has increased from Rs. 14.28 crores in 1975 to Rs. 17.75 crores in 1977. The net premium income in case of total General Insurance out of India has also increased from Rs. 63.75 crores in 1975 to Rs. 71.46 crores in 1977.

1. Gross Direct Premium Income

The gross direct premium has been analysed under the GIC and the four subsidiary companies. They are National Insurance Company Ltd., New India Assurance Company Ltd., Oriental Insurance Company Ltd. and United India Insurance Company Ltd.

Table 25.6 Gross Direct I remium Income in Marine in Insurance (*In Crores of Rs.*)

	GIC	*National*	*New India*	*Oriental India*	*United*	*Total*
1975	—					70.83
1980	—	28.02	32.49	37.34	34.76	132.61
1981	—	35.26	49.58	48.77	51.13	185.04
1982	—	40.18	60.70	53.65	55.09	209.62
1984	—	49.15	67.70	58.97	71.58	247.40
1985	—	57.31	79.85	64.12	73.91	275.19
1986	—	62.40	86.52	69.96	85.02	303.90
1987	—	68.27	93.56	78.59	97.19	337.61
1988-89*	—	92.78	129.01	108.08	135.03	464.90
1989-90*	—	88.30	129.01	97.01	125.44	439.77
1994-95	—	165.30	230.16	170.56	260.83	826.85
1997-98	—	209.76	312.64	217.14	286.13	1025.67

*Note: 1988-89 has 15 months period.

The gross direct premium income has increased from Rs. 70.83 crores in 1975 to Rs. 132.61 crores in 1980, Rs. 275.19 crores in 1985, Rs. 464.90 crores in 1988-89 and Rs. 826.85 crores in 1994-95. The rate of increase has been higher in the later period. It shows that the general insurance industry has been very particular to extend its benefits to a larger population of the country. United India has increased its premium income from Rs. 34.76 crores in 1980 to Rs. 135.03 crores in 1988-89 and Rs. 260.83 crores in 1994-95. New India has also tried to increase its business from Rs. 32.49 crores in 1980 to Rs. 129.01 crores in 1988-89 and Rs. 230.16 crores in 1994-95. They have regular and constant progress. On the other hand, Oriental has increased its business very slowly from Rs. 37.34 crores in 1980 to Rs. 108.08 crores in 1988-89 and Rs. 170.56 crores in 1994- 95. National has the least amount of business. It increased its business from Rs. 28.02 crores in 1980 to Rs. 92.78 crores in 1988-89 and Rs. 165.30 crores in 1994-95.

2. Net Premium Income

Net premium income has been observed in the GIC because it does accept reinsurance functions although it does not work directly for marine and fire insurance. The amount of net premium of the GIC has increased from Rs. 38.11 crores in 1982 to Rs. 102.81 crores in 1988-89 and Rs. 187.43 crores in 1994-95. It has maximum business than those of subsidiaries. The total net premium income in marine insurance has increased from Rs. 48.00 crores in 1973 to Rs. 156.38 crores in 1982 by more than three times. This premium could not increase at faster rate at later part of the period. It increased to Rs. 260.36 crores in 1985, Rs. 433.01 crores in 1988-89 and Rs. 734.33 crores in 1994-95. United India has shown satisfactory progress from Rs. 34.88 crores in 1982 to Rs. 93.27 crores in 1988-89 and Rs. 133.85 crores in 1994-95. New India has shown rapid progress from Rs. 31.05 crores in 1982 to Rs. 96.56 crores in 1988-89 and Rs. 179.84 crores in 1994-95. Oriental has been at the last place for promoting its business from Rs. 30.10 crores in 1982 to Rs. 70.66 crores in 1988-89 and Rs. 113.07 crores in 1994-95. National insurance has improved its position from the lowest to the second lowest position.

Table 25.7 Net Premium Income in Marine Insurance

(In crores of Rs.)

	GIC	*National*	*New India*	*Oriental India*	*United*	*Total*
1973						48.00
1975						68.00
1980						117.00
1982	38.11	22.24	31.05	30.10	34.88	156.38
1983	44.35	27.53	40.66	34.37	42.70	189.61
1984	61.75	33.29	45.10	38.25	82.48	227.21
1985	72.59	37.95	53.35	40.78	55.69	260.36
1986	71.93	44.79	61.87	45.64	62.79	287.02
1987	77.69	51.53	68.34	50.23	74.41	322.20
1988-89	102.81	69.77	96.56	70.66	93.27	433.01
1989-90	95.47	64.37	95.90	65.48	85.33	311.08
1994-95	187.43	120.14	179.84	113.07	133.85	734.33
1997-98	221.90	136.36	188.74	124.07	151.41	822.48

*Note : The GIC transacts mainly reinsurance business.

3. Underwriting Experiences in Marine Insurance

The underwriting profit/loss experience of marine insurance has decreased from Rs. 6.86 crores in 1982 to Rs. 5.88 crores in 1985 but increased to Rs. 37.81 crores in 1988-89 and Rs. 56.61 crores in 1994-95. It shows that the underwriting profit has increased rapidly at later part of the analysis. But as percentage to net premium, it has increased from 4.3 percent in 1982 to 12.70 per cent in 1988-89 and declined to 7.0 per cent in 1994-95. National and New India have shown losses in 1994-95. National, Oriental and United India have experienced losses in some years, whereas United India has the highest underwriting profit. National and New India have shown higher rate of claims. Oriental have the lowest claim-ratio. United India and Oriental have higher expense-ratio than those of New India.

Table 25.8 Underwriting Experience in Marine Insurance

		% to Net Premium						
	Net Premium Rs. crores	*Net Claims payable %*	*Net commission %*	*Expenses to Management %*	*Miscellaneous Outgo %*	*Unexpired Risks Reserve %*	*Underwriting Profit/Loss (–) %*	*Underwriting Profit/Loss (–) Rs. Crores*
1985								
GIC	72.59	61.5	17.4	–0.9	—	14.9	5.3	3.88
National	37.95	70.6	–7.6	25.3	0.3	12.3	–0.3	–0.13
New India	53.35	64.0	–6.9	21.3	–0.6	16.5	6.7	3.55
Oriental	40.78	82.7	–9.8	26.1	–0.4	6.2	–4.8	–1.96
United India	55.69	69.4	–3.5	20.8	—	12.3	1.0	0.54
Total	260.36	68.4	—	16.8	–0.2	12.7	2.3	5.88
1989-90								
GIC	95.47	47.5	18.9	1.26	–0.02	13.8	18.5	17.64
National	64.37	64.5		19.6		13.3	22.6	1.67
New India	95.90	51.6		18.9		19.4	10.1	9.67
Oriental	65.48	57.7		21.5		13.7	7.1	4.65
United India	85.33	63.0		19.5		12.6	4.9	4.18
Total	311.08	56.9		18.4		14.6	12.6	37.81
1994-95								
GIC	187.43	53.5	17.6	1.0	–0.6	7.5	21.0	39.50
National	120.14	97.7	–5.0	23.50	0.30	–5.80	–9.70	–11.60
New India	179.85	86.0	–2.1	17.9	—	–1.2	–0.6	–1.13
Oriental	113.07	70.0	–7.6	23.90	—	1.0	12.7	14.39
United India	133.85	80.5	–11.5	25.00	—	–5.6	11.6	15.53
Total	734.34	77.34	–1.72	18.26	—	–0.82	7.0	56.61

Contd...

	% to Net Premium							
	Net Premium Rs. crores	*Net Claims payable %*	*Net commission %*	*Expenses to Management %*	*Miscellaneous Outgo %*	*Unexpired Risks Reserve %*	*Underwriting Profit/Loss (–) %*	*Underwriting Profit/Loss (–) Rs. Crores*
997-98								
IC	221.90	45.5	18.1	0.9	0.00	3.6	31.9*	70.82
ational	136.36	75.63	–9.46	24.33 (*b*)	0.08	6.51	3.07	4.19
ew India	188.74	54.39	–9.37	25.49	–@	–9.03	38.52	72.70
riental	124.07	74.3	—	28.3	–11.1	–0.1	8.6	10.67
nited India	151.41	70.3	–13.5	30.9	16.3	7.9	5.4	8.15
otal	822.48	320.12	–14.23	109.92	5.28	7.97	87.49	166.53

Note: @ includes commission also (*b*) includes miscellaneous outgo

Progress of Marine Insurance after Privatisation

(*In crores of Rs.*)

ear	*National*	*New India*	*Oriental India*	*United*	*Total*
998-1999	199.2	297.7	208.9	291.9	997.7
999-2000	198.0	310.4	209.8	276.8	995.0
000-2001	203.8	313.8	187.9	279.6	985.1
001-2002	207.1	339.3	205.6	255.2	1003.7

Gross Direct Premium Outside India

'ear	*National*	*New India*	*Oriental India*	*United*	*Total*
998-1999	3.5	16.8	6.8	0	27.1
999-2000	3.4	18.2	7.7	0	29.3
:000-2001	3.7	19.2	7.2	0	30.1
:001-2002	4.0	23.4	8.9	0	—

Total Gross Direct Premium

Year	*National*	*New India*	*Oriental India*	*United*	*Total*
1998-1999	202.7	314.5	215.7	291.9	1024.8
1999-2000	201.4	328.6	217.5	276.8	1024.3
2000-2001	207.5	333.6	195.1	279.6	1015.2
2001-2002	211.2	362.7	214.6	255.2	

Financial Highlights of Marine Insurance

(Rs. in crores)

Year	Net Premium		Net Incurred Claim		Commission		Expenses of Managment		Other income (–) outgo (+)		Increase in Reserve for Unexpired Risks		Investment Income		Under Working Profit Less +	
	Rs.	% to GP	Rs.	% to NP	Rs.	%	Rs.	%	Rs.	%	Rs.	%	Rs.	%	Rs.	%
General Insurance Corporation																
1998-1999	221		108.2	47	40.8	18	–	–	–	–	7.4	3	–	–	72.9	32
1999-2000	233.3		130.0	55.7	39.8	17.1	2.08	0.9	0.25	0.10	3.98	1.7	–	–	57.21	24.5
2000-2001	296.8		89.0	39.6	36.0	15.9	2.03	0.9	52.6	0.2	–6.53	–2.9	64.2	27.5	105.01	46.3
2001-2002	207.6		131.0	57.8	43.0	19.0	1.7	0.8	00.3	–0.1			56.5	24.9	51.2	22.6
National Insurance Co. Ltd.																
1998-1999	14.3	71	126.8	88	27.3	19					6.9	5			–17.7	–12
1999-2000	139.3		110.13	79	–6.8	–4.9	37.24	26.74	–0.62	–0.01	–3.9	–2.9	344.4		2.65	1.90
2000-2001	149.1		56.9	38	–9.11	–6.1	35.05	23.50	0.13	0.08	9.8	6.6	381.8		56.26	37.7
2001-2002	132.8		78.0	58.8	–6.51	–4.9	38.3	288	–0.07	–0.05	–16.31	–12.3	30.4	22.9	69.7	52.5
The New India Assurance Co. Ltd.																
1998-1999	190.3	61	96.8	51	14.5	8					1.6	1			77.4	40
1999-2000	192.1		122.4	63.7	–17.64	9.18	50.88	26.48			1.78	0.93			34.69	18.06
2000-2001	188.12		141.8	75.4	–17.22	–9.2	54.19	28.80			–4.00	–2.13	50.71	24.14	13.40	7.12
2001-2002	220.69		131.33	62.51	10.34		51.64	24.5	80.09		21.97	10.46	35.22	37.41	15.49	7.33

(Rs. in crores)

Year	Net Premium		Net Incurred Claim		Commission		Expenses of Managment		Other income (–) Management Risks		Increase in Reserve for outgo (+)		Investment Income Unexpired		Under Writing Profit Less +	
	Rs.	%	Rs.	%	Rs.	%	Rs.	%	Rs.	%	Rs.	%	Rs.	%	Rs.	%
The Oriental Insurance Company Ltd.																
1998-1999	132.1	61	85.9	65	22.4	17									15.7	12
1999-2000	132.08	60.7	97.01	73.4	40.41	30.6	–9.40	–7.1			0.04	0.01	367.53		4.11	3.1
2000-2001	121.71	62.4	91.35	75.1	33.48	27.5	–6.95	–5.7			–10.37	8.5	396.23		14.20	11.7
2001-2002	139.11	64.0	74.27	53.3	41.18	29.6	–4.66	–3.3			–40.10	28.8	–24.21	–17.4	94.30	67.8
United India Insurance Company Ltd.																
1998-1999	145.8	50	92.6	64	26.3	18					–5.6	–4			32.5	2.2
1999-2000	149.51		99.80	66.8	–25.34	–16.95	41.10	27.49			3.74	2.50			30.21	20.21
2000-2001	142.77		118.85	83.2	–18.99	–13.3	44.45	31.37			–6.73	4.71			4.85	3.40
2001-2002	126.60		81.64		–15.24		41.36		–6.56		–16.18		39.33		67.84	
Indian Market Total																
1998-1999	840.8	82	510.3	61	131.3	16					18.4	2			180.5	21
1999-2000	846.3	83	559.3	66	152.6	18					5.5	1			128.9	15
2000-2001	828.4	82	498.7	60	153.0	18					–17.8	2			194.5	24
2001-2002																

PART FOUR

FIRE-INSURANCE

26

NATURE AND USE OF FIRE INSURANCE

Fire insurance has not a long history. The real establishment of fire insurance came only after the Great Fire of London in 1066. This fire lasted for four days and nights burning over 436 acres of ground and destroying over 13,000 buildings was the most disastrous fire in history and forcibly awakened the people to the necessity for a form of protection against such calamities. The main cause of its late development was slow progress of trade and commerce. After a certain period when the business and commerce ran high, fire insurance received a real fillip. Previously there was no basis on which the premimium could be based. There were a few concerns which made a remarkable progress. Gradually as they gained experience the data went on accumulating and the premium rates became more equitable and scientific. The decisions of law court also brought the principles of fire insurance to a standard form. With increasing competition and experience, the fire insurance is evolved in its present scientific form. However, the progress in fire insurance was not so tremendous and categorical as was in the case of life insurance.

Definition and Nature

Fire insurance is a device to compensate for the loss consequent upon destruction by fire. Thus the fire insurer shifts the burden of fire losses from their actual victims over to all the members of the society. It is a cooperative device to share the loss. It relieves the insured from the horror of the fire losses to which he is exposed.

Functions

It is a well-known fact that the fire causes huge losses every year. The individual owner by taking fire insurance can prevent the fire waste to some extent. The insurer acts as a middle man between all the members of the society who are exposed to the fire risk on the one hand and the members who will be the actual victims of the fire losses on the other. The insurer charges the premium from all the insured members and makes good the losses when they occur to any of them.

The system of fire insurance cannot save the society from the economic loss to the community to the extent of the property lost by fire, but it compensates someone and this saves him from a ruinous loss, at the cost of group of some others.

Causes of Fire

Fire waste is the result of two types of hazard viz., 'physical' and 'moral'.

1. **Physical Hazard:** It refers to the inherent risk of fire in the property which may occur due to inflammable nature, construction, artificial lighting and heating, lack of extinguishing apparatus use of the property etc.
2. **Moral Hazard:** The moral hazard depends upon the man as physical hazard depends on the property. The property may be set on fire by the owner or by any person with his willingness, carelessness and lack of sense of duty may also increase the fire waste. Sometimes, when market price is going down the owner can willingly set fire on the property and gain from the payment of insurance money. Thus, where the property was destroyed with the willingness of the property owner, moral hazard exists.

Prevention of Less

Insurance is meant for indemnification of loss and not for prevention of loss although every reasonable step can be taken to eliminate it or minimise it through the agencies engaged in prevention of loss. Thus, insurance may help in two ways 1. Indemnification and 2. Preventive efforts.

1. **Indemnification or curative efforts:** According to doctrine of indemnification, the financial loss suffered by the perils insured against will be compensated in full, not more than this and not less than this. The insurance provides protection by indemnifying the financial loss suffered by insured person which occurred beyond the control of insured and insurer.
2. **Preventive efforts:** The loss cannot be prevented by insurance. But, the insures help those who are engaged in the preventive efforts by granting financial and other assistance. This will benefit insurers as well because if the loss of society is reduced, they can charge lesser premium which will stimulate the public for purchasing more insurance policies because of cheaper rate of insurance. Fire insurers stimulate the installation of protective devices and better types of construction through granting credit. They help in installation of fire-fighting apparatus, water supply and engineering services.

   Preventive efforts are divided into two parts (*i*) private activities and (*ii*) public activities.

(*i*) Private Activities

Private activities are those which include those activities which the property owner may engage in for the purpose of preventing fire loss. Insurers given sincere advice of financial help to property owner on the following factors.

(*a*) **Construction:** In construction of building, fire resistive materials, fire proof construction, greatest care in exercising selection of the type and planning of the construction, availability of fire extinguisher, water supply, proper passage in emergency are various activities which reduce the chance of fire. For these activities, the insurers provide advice and assistance.

(*b*) **Fire Services:** The important thing is to extinguish fire before it reaches large proportions. The owner should consider equipping his building with an automatic sprinkler system. Similar fire fighting equipment may be established. Such services can be provided by insurers with the help of fire fighting associations.

(*c*) **Occupation:** There are considerable hazard in certain occupation e.g. in oil or coke or chemical industry. Insurance in these concerns is available at higher rate. Insurers help by stimulation and charging lesser premium in fire fencing occupation.

(*d*) **Management:** Good management of property may reduce the chances of fire. Carelessness and indifference cannot be over-emphasized because these increase the chance of fire.

(*e*) **Exposure:** Fire insurance rates are determined on the basis of possibility of exposure. Fire-proof services may reduce the chances of exposure to a greater extent.

(*ii*) Public Fire Prevention Activities

Fire insurers have performed numerous important services to reduce the fire waste with the help of public institutions which are engaged in fire fighting activities.

(*a*) **Community Surveys:** Engineering survey of the cities and localities is made. As a result of its investigation many have improved their fire departments, water supplies and other facilities involved in the protection against fire.

(*b*) **Standard schedule for grading cities:** Under this schedule a number of cities, town, or mohallas are divided, according to fire preventive devices. The deficiencies in each part is sorted out and attempts are made to remove them.

(*c*) **Underwriters' laboratories:** The laboratories are to find out the possible causes of fire losses. Every time research or investigation is made to find out the possible attempts to prevent fire losses.

(*d*) **Equipment:** Fire can be properly checked only through the possession and maintenance of adequate equipment, personnel fire alarm system and water supply. Fire fighting apparatus and equipment for any city or town can be determined by the Fire Protection Association.

(*e*) **Salvage Corps and salvage works by fire deparments:** The chief aim of the corps is to protect property from unnecessary smoke and water damage. The protective benefits are extended to all those who suffer fire damages. The protective benefits are extended to all those who suffer fire damages regardless of whether they are insured or not. Training school and colleges are, sometimes, engaged in giving general education to all and particular education to few students to train them in fire fighting methods and fire preventive methods.

(*f*) **Legislation and Regulation:** National Board of fire underwriters' fire brigade and other such associations are engaged in fire preventive and protective efforts under a certain law. The property owner and the fire protection engineer must keep in mind the numerous legal requirements relating to the various phases of fire prevention.

(*iii*) General Devices

Apart from the above contribution to prevention protection, the following devices are utilised for preventing the losses.

(*i*) The insurer compensates loss at a reasonable cost.

(*ii*) Serious hazards are to be cooperatively reinsured.

(*iii*) Loans are provided for better construction and building.

(*iv*) Fire insurers stimulate the installation of protective devices to reduce losses.

(*v*) Fire fighting methods are organised with public utility concerns.

(*vi*) Insurers investigate the causes of loss and attempts are made to reduce the causes.

(*vii*) Insurers study various devices for fire proof, protection and problems of special processes.

(*viii*) Periodical examination of insured property is made and instructions are issued for the purpose of investigation.

QUESTIONS

1. What do you understand by the fire insur.nce?
2. What are the uses of the Fire Insurance?

27

FIRE INSURANCE CONTRACT

Fire insurance contract may be defined as "an agreement whereby one party in return for a consideration undertakes to indemnify the other party against financial loss which the latter may sustain by reason of certain defined subject-matter being damaged or destroyed by fire or other defined perils up to an agreed amount." The party responsible to indemnify the loss is called the insurer, the party who is to be indemnified is called the insured, the consideration for the contract is termed 'the premium', the defined subject matter is termed 'the property insured" the sum set forth in the contract is called the assured sum, and the document containing the terms and conditions of the contract is known as 'the policy.'

The contract of insurance involves all the elements of an ordinary contract and insurance contracts. The elements of contract are discussed in following paragraphs.

Before discussing the elements of the fire insurance contract, the special meaning of the 'Fire' must be understood.

Fire

Fire, in order to make the insurer liable under the contract, must satisfy two conditions. First, there should be actual fire or ignition, and second, the fire must be fortuitons in its nature.

Ignition

The expression in the policy we have to construct is loss or damage occasioned by fire. This means that loss or damage must be either by ignition of the article or property or premises or part thereof. In other words, the damage should be occasioned by fire. Loss or damage caused by excessive fire heat cannot be included in 'loss or damage by fire'. If should be proved here, that the loss should be caused by fire. The cause of fire is not important. The fire even if caused by the negligence of the servant or himself may come under the definition of fire. There should be no fraud or wilful misconduct by the assured. There should be actual ignition but a process resembling fire may not be fire. For example, the damage done due to smoke due to faulting chimney, or overheated iron are not the example of fire. Similarly chemical actions, explosion, lighting etc. are not occasioned or example of fire.

Fire should be accidental and not intentional

Any loss caused by fire lighted purposively is not a loss by fire if it was intentional. However the property burned accidentally in an ordinary fire, such as domestic fire, the loss is covered even if the fire remains under control. When a fire was purposively lighted but became out of control at a later stage is taken under the definition of fire. The object of fire insurance is to indemnify the insured against accidental loss by fire.

ELEMENTS OF FIRE INSURANCE CONTRACT

1. Features of General Contract. All the features of general contract are also applicable to the fire insurance contract.

(*a*) **Proposal:** The proposal for fire insurance can be made either verbally or in writing. The proposer gives the necessary description of the property to be insured. In practice the printed proposal form is used for the purpose. Introduction, type of properties, value of properties, construction, occupation, etc., are the various information which are required by the insurer. The answers to these questions must be completely correct. The assured must disclose all the material facts and should observe utmost good faith. The description of the subject matter of insurance is the basis of contract for assessing the risk and fixing the premium.

(*b*) **Acceptance:** On receipt of the proposal form, the insurer will assess the risk. Sometimes, when the contents and subject-matters are not of very high amount, the insurer may accept on the basis of proposal forms only. When the subject-matters is of larger magnitude and where the hazard involved is of a variable or unknown nature, the insurer may send his surveyor to survey the property. The surveyors being expert in the field of insurance evaluation will consider the proposal in the light of this report. The unknown proposers are required to submit an evidence of respectability. The insured is required to submit a certificate from some known and respectable person about honesty and integrity. As soon as the proposal is accepted, the assured is informed about the decision.

(*c*) **Commencement of risk:** The risk commences as soon as the contract is completed provided there is no specific time for the purpose. As soon as the proposal is accepted, risk will commence irrespective of the fact that no policy was issued and no premium was paid. Where risks are unknown and tremendous, the payment of premium will be the basis of the completion of the contract. The risk will commence only when the premium has been paid and not before that when the policy has been issued, payment of premium will not be the basis of commencement of risk.

(*i*) **Cover note:** The insurer issues a 'Cover Note' or 'Interim Protection Note' when the risk was accepted provisionally or subject to the condition of payment of premium. This note will cover the property so far the final policy has not been issued. If loss occurs before issue of policy the cover note will be sufficient to prove insurance. The cover note, however, is not taken at par to the policy.

Policy

The insurer issues a duly stamped policy which will bear all the terms and conditions of the contract. Any contract of fire insurance, comes within the meaning of the word 'policy'. It is a statutory and formal document of insurance contract. There are different forms of policies for different types of policies. However, a standard form is also used. The policy contains the name and address of the insured, the subject-matter of insurance, the sum insured, the term and the premium. There are various clauses governing the conditions of insurance contract. The terms and conditions of the policy can be changed.

Period of Fire Insurance Policies

Usually fire policies are issued for one year and are called 'Annual Insurance.' Policies issued for a period shorter than one year are known as 'Short-Term Policies' and those issued for a period more than one year are called 'Long-Term Polices'. But in practice only annual policies are common. 'Short-term' and 'Long-term' policies are rarely used. Long-term policies are generally issued in case of building. Alteration in the policy will be made according to the change in building and terms of insurance. The premium rate is determined according to the nature, location, construction of the property.

Moreover, the period of insurance is also taken into account for computing premiums.

More Than One Fire During a Period

When there is more than one fire in respect of the same subject matter insured, the insurer is not bound to pay more than the sum assured. During the policy-life, payment of each loss, automatically, reduces the amount of the policy by the amount so paid. When, after payment of certain losses, the property insured is totally destroyed, the insurer will pay loss not more than the balance of insured amount remaining after compensation of the previous losses.

However, if the insured is willing to get payment of full loss, he can reinstate the assured sum to the original amount by paying a fresh premium on a pro-rata basis to the date of expiry.

More Than One Policy

If the same subject-matter is insured with more than one insurer, he cannot realize more than the actual loss from all the insurers. Each insurer will pay his ratable proportion of loss to the property insured against fire. If there is average clause, then the insurers will pay accordingly.

2. Insurable Interest. Insurable interest is the general principle of insurance without which an insurance cannot lawfully be enforced for an insurance unsupported by an insurable interest would be a gambling transaction. Insurable interest will be there where the subject-matter should be in such a position that the insured may suffer loss at the time of damage and may gain by its protection. The insurable interest in fire insurance must be present at the time of contract and at the time of loss. Insurance contract will be invalid if the property is sold to another party. Similarly if there is no insurable interest at the time of insurance, the contract will be invalid.

The following conditions must be fulfilled to constitute an insurable interest.

(*i*) There should be a physical object capable of being damaged or destroyed by fire.

(*ii*) The object must be the subject matter of insurance.

(*iii*) The insured must stand in such relationship as recognized by law where the insured is benefited by the safety of the subject-matter or be prejudiced by its loss.

The insurable interest is the 'pecuniary interest'. The fire insurance is a personal contract between the insured and the insurer. So, the transfer of interest would invalidate the contract.

The following persons have insurable interest in the subject-matter concerned.

1. The owner of the property or asset whether fixed or current has as insurable interest whether he is the legal owner or the equitable owner. The owner may be a single or joint, holder. ' Partial owner can take policy for full value as trustee of all the property. A Life tenant entitled to the use of the property during his life time only has an insurable interest.
2. An agent has insurable interest in the property of his principal.
3. A partner has an equitable interest in the firm's property.
4. A creditor has an insurable interest in property on which he has a lien for the debt.
5. An insurer has it in respect of risks underwritten by him for the purpose of reinsurance.
6. Where the subject-matter is mortgaged, the mortgagor has an insurable interest in the full value thereof and the mortgagee has an insurable interest in respect of any sum due to become due under the mortgage.
7. A bailee can insure any article or property bailed. He may be a gratuitous bailee or bailee for reward.
8. A trustee has insurable, interest in the property put on trusteeship.

3. Principle of Good Faith. The contract of fire insurance is one in which the observance of the utmost good faith-uberrima fides-by both the parties are of vital significant. The utmost good faith in fix insurance has two aspects-first, disclosure of material facts and second, preservation of the property insured.

The insurer and the insured must furnish detailed information regarding the subject-matter to be insured. The insured, since he has more, information about the subject-matter, must disclose all the information asked truly and fully. The, assured is also required to disclose all the material information which are known to him although it was not asked by the insurer; material fact is one which influences the decisions of the insurance. The decision may be pertaining to the acceptance or declination or determination of the premium. In case of fire insurance the examples of material facts are construction of buildings. If the assured has not observed good faith, the contract can be avoided by other party. It was immaterial to plead that the insured was unaware of the fact and could not disclose. In a given circumstance, it is expected from the insured to-know all the material facts. The insurer has also to disclose such material facts as are within his knowledge.

The second phase of good faith is preservation of property. Thus, the observance of good faith is necessary not only during the negotiations of the contract but throughout the term of the policy and in making claims. Any change after commencement of risk must be communicated to the insurer. The insured or his agents as well as the insurer must take all such steps as may be reasonable for averting or minimising loss. Since the insured is near to the property, he must act to prevent the fire and if fire occurred, he must do his utmost to extinguish it. In such cases he must act as if he was not insured.

Exceptions

In the following circumstances, the insured is not required to disclose information.

1. All those circumstances which diminish the risk.
2. All those facts which are known or reasonably presumed to be known to the insurer.
3. Information which are of common knowledge.
4. Those facts which the insurer in the ordinary course of his business ought to know or which the insurer ought reasonably to have inferred from the details given.
5. Those facts which are superfluous to disclose by reason of a condition or warranty.

4. Principle of indemnity. The doctrine of indemnity aims to compensate the insured for a loss sustained, and the compensation should be such as to place him as nearly as possible in the same pecuniary position after the loss as he occupied immediately before the occurrence. The insured cannot claim anything in excess of the amount required to recoup the actual loss sustained. The insurers undertake to make good the insured's loss by monetary payment or by reinstatement or replacement so that the insured shall be fully indemnified, but this is subject to the sum insured. The law does not sanction any insurance which would enable the insured to profit by the destruction of the thing destroyed. It will check the temptation to destroy the property insured thereby to secure the money.

The assured amount is not the measure of indemnity but it sets an upper limit up to which the loss can be indemnified. The actual amount of indemnity will be the market value of the subject-matter destroyed or damaged by fire at the time and place of the occurrence of fire. It will never exceed the assured amount. When the actual loss is more than the assured amount then only the insured sum will be paid and nothing more is paid. But, this principle does not hold good when the policy is valued policy. Here, the basis of indemnity will not be the actual cash value of the property at the time of loss but the insured value which is named in the policy when it was taken. In a valued policy, no consideration is given to the actual loss. Thus, the amount of claim may be greater or less than the actual loss at the time of fire in case of valued policies.

Interpretation of Indemnity

The insured is entitled to perfect indemnity subject to the sum assured being sufficient. But, in practice such perfection may be difficult to attain. Previously, the meaning of the word 'indemnity' was understood in the sense of material indemnity only, *i.e.,* tangible and material property only. The intangible loss, *i.e.*, loss of profit, rent, etc., was not compensated. It worked as a great hardship to the honest insured persons. Now, the insurance is extended to cover not only the material loss of property insured but also to cover the 'consequential loss'. When a business property is burnt, not only the material loss on account of the destruction of building, plant and stock are covered but the consequential loss of profits on account of cessation of sales, salaries, taxes, rent, rates, etc., are also indemnified. Now-a-days tangible and intangible losses are insured and the consequential loss is also within the meaning of indemnity.

Consequences of Indemnity

The consequences of the doctrine of indemnity are as below:

1. The insured may claim only the amount of the loss sustained.
2. In case of partial damage, the insured may claim compensation only for the amount of damage done.
3. The insured must transfer to the insurer any rights which he may possess against a third party in respect of the loss.
4. If the insured have effected more than one policy, he is precluded from obtaining more than one complete indemnity.

Measure of indemnity varies with the type of property. For damaged buildings, the measure of indemnity is the cost of repairing or reinstating the buildings to their pre-loss condition. Similarly, for machinery, the measure of indemnity is the market value which is arrived at after taking into account wear and tear and depreciation. For stock in trade, the measure is the net cost to the insured. The indemnification may be in the form of cash, repair, replacement and reinstatement.

5. Doctrine of Subrogation. Subrogation means the right of one person to stand in the place of another and to avail himself of the latter's rights and remedies. The principle of subrogation is just a corollary to the principle of indemnity. The insured can realise only the actual value of the loss or damage to the property according to the principle of indemnity and it follows that if the damaged property has any value left or the assured can recover the lost property or has any right against a third party regarding that property. These must pass on to the insurer. If the assured is allowed to retain them, he shall have realised more than the actual loss which is contrary to the indemnity principle. The assured can proceed against the third party, if he so, desires, and if he recovers damages the insurer is relieved of liability. If the insured has received the full amount of his loss any sums obtained from the third party belong to the insurer up to the amount of their disbursement.

The right of subrogation is exercisable at common law after the insurer has paid the claim made against him.

6. Warranties. The contents of proposal form are expressly incorporated in the policy, which form warranty. Warranty is that by which the assured undertakes that some particular thing shall or shall not be done, or that some conditions shall be fulfilled or whereby he affirms or negatives the existence of a particular state of facts. Warranties which are mentioned in the policy are called express warranties and those warranties which are not mentioned in the policy are called implied warranties.

Warranties must be complied with literally and the effect of a breach of warranty is to render void the relevant item of the policy, even if no increase in risk is involved. Every warranty to which the property insured or any item thereof is, or may be, made subject, shall from the time the warranty attaches apply and continue to be in force during the whole currency of the policies, and non-compliance with any such warranty, whether it increases the risk or not, shall be a bar to any claim in respect of such property or item. The condition states that every warranty is attached during the whole currency of the policy and if during this period a warranty has not been complied with, the insured will not entertain any claim in respect of the property or item affected. However, if the policy is renewed and there was breach of a warranty before the renewal date and not after it and a loss occurs after the renewal is effected, in such a case the claim can be made. Non-compliance with a warranty prior to the current renewal period of a policy is not a bar to a claim. The non-compliance with a warranty avoids a cover only during the period of insurance in which the breach occurred.

7. Proximate Cause. The rule is that the immediate and not the remote cause is to be regarded–causa proxima non-remota spectature. Proximate cause is very important in fire insurance. The principle of proximate cause has already been discussed in detail. The insurer always takes the proximate cause while paying the claim. If the property insured is burned but the fire was preceded and brought into operation by an excepted peril, the legal position depends upon whether the excepted peril was the proximate. The remote cause is when an incendiary bomb damaged the property, the proximate cause is enemy action.

QUESTIONS

1. Discuss the features of Fire Insurance Contract.
2. 'Assignment is set possible in fire insurance' Comment.

28

KINDS OF POLICIES

The policies can be of various types which are discussed in the following paragraphs.

1. Valued Policy. The value of the property to be insured is determined at the inception of the policy. In this case, the insurer pays the total admitted value irrespective of the then market value of the properties. The measure of indemnity is, in consequence, not value at the time of fire, but a value agreed at the inception of the policy. The insurer pays the insured a fixed sum following the destruction of the insured property. The amount fixed may be greater or less than the actual market value of the property destroyed by fire at the time of loss. In this policy, the measure of indemnity is based on the value of properties rather than on the market values of the property destroyed. This policy is used for insuring specially pictures, sculptures, works of art, jewellery, rare things, articles of everyday use. Since the value of damage of these articles cannot be easily determined at the time of loss, the valued policies are commonly used. Strictly speaking the valued policies are betrayal from the principle of indemnity because the market price is not paid in this case.

The valued policy is beneficial to the insured because he is relieved of proving the value of property at the time of loss by searching of invoices and receipts. The disadvantages is that the new purchases and replacement cannot be added to the valued policy. The valuation, therefore, is revised at frequent intervals. The insurer will have to pay more than the actual loss if the market price of the property has gone down. It may increase the moral hazard. There may be difficulty in settling the partial losses. The valued policies can be disputed on grounds of fraud.

2. Valuable Policy. Valuable policy is that policy where claim amount is to be determined at the market price of the damaged property. The amount of loss is not determined at the time of commencement of risk but is determined at the time and place of loss. This policy is truly representing the doctrine of indemnity.

3. Specific Policy. Where a specific sum is insured upon a specified property in case of a specified period, the whole of the actual loss is payable provided it does not exceed the insured amount. Here the value of property insured has no relevance in arriving at the measure of indemnity in a specified policy and the insured sum sets a limit upto which the loss can be made good.

4. Floating Policy. The floating policy is the policy taken to cover one or more kinds of goods at one time under one sum assured for one premium and in relation to the same owner. This policy is useful to cover fluctuating stocks in different localities. Since the properties are spread over various localities and in different forms, the physical and moral hazards are also varying and, therefore, it makes difficult to determine premium rates. In India, the premium rate is approximately the same in such case except the case of most hazardous risk. Such policies are specially taken by big manufacturers or traders whose merchandise might be lying in parts at warehouse, godown, port, or railway station. In such cases, it is very difficult for the owner of such goods to take specified policy for each good because the quantities of the goods deposited in each will fluctuate from day to day, place to place, according to sales or consumption or consequent removal and replacement. The average rate of premium is ascertained by taking into account the total premium payable had the property been insured by specific policies. The floating policy contains the 'average' and 'marine' clauses.

5. Average Policy. Policy containing 'average clause' is called an Average Policy. The amount of indemnity is determined with reference to the value of the property insured. If the policy holder has taken policy for lesser amount than the actual value of the property, the insured will be deemed to be his own insurer for the amount of under-insurance. The insurer will pay only such proportion of the actual loss as his insurance amount bears to the actual value of the property at the time of loss. For example, the property worth Rs. 30,000 is insured for Rs. 20,000 is damaged up to Rs. 12,000, the insurer will pay only Rs. 8,000 as is evident from the following:

Claim = Insured amount / value of property × actual loss

= 20,000 / 30,000 × 12,000 = Rs. 8,000

The insured, thus, will suffer himself up to Rs. 4,000 and the insurer will pay only Rs. 8,000 out of Rs. 12,000. In this case, if the insurance was taken up to the full value of the property, the assured would have been paid all the financial loss, *i.e.*, Rs. 12,000. Since the insurance was taken for lesser than the actual value of property, the assured is compensated the loss in that proportion.

The average clause is operative only in case of an under-insurance. This clause is ineffective when the property is insured for the full value as in that case the insured is protected to the extent of his total loss. The under-insurance penalises the assured by inserting 'average clause' to the policy because he is supposed to insure himself for the amount by which he under-insures his property and, therefore, is supposed to contribute in that ratio to the loss sustained. The average clause is accompanied, sometimes, with the co-insurance clause which is discussed in the next chapter.

6. Excess Policy. Sometimes, the stock of a businessman may fluctuate from time to time and he may be unable to take one policy or specific policy. If he takes policy for a higher amount, he has to pay a higher premium. On the other hand, if he takes insurance for lower amount, he will have to bear the proportionate amount of loss. The insured in this case can purchase two policies, one 'First Loss Policy" and second, 'excess policy.' The 'First Loss Policy' will cover that stock below which the stock never goes. The minimum level of stock can be found out from the past experience and for the other portion of stock which exceeds the minimum limit, he can purchase another policy called 'excess policy'. The actual value of the excess stock is declared every month. The amount of premium is calculated on the average monthly excess amount. Since the chances of payment on the excess amount are very remote, the rate of premium is also very nominal. Thus, the insured will pay very nominal premium as compared to the premium payable on the total amount had the policy been specific one. The average .clause also applies to this policy.

7. Declaration Policy. The excess policy contributes to only a rateable proportion of the loss because if the amount of excess stock exceeds the sum set in the excess policy the businessman will not have a full cover owing to average condition. Moreover, if the First Loss Policy was also subject to average condition the assured will be at a loss. The declaration policy will give a better protection in such cases where the stock fluctuates from time to time. Under the declaration policy, the insured takes out an insurance for the maximum amount that he considers would be at risk during the period of the policy. On a fixed date of every month or a specific period, the insured furnishes a declaration of the amount. The premium is provisionally paid to 75% of the annual premium amount. Practically, the annual premium is determined on the average of these declarations. If the premium is higher than the provisional premium already paid, the insured has to pay the difference to the insurer. On the other hand if the premium so calculated is lesser than the premium already paid, the excess is returned to the policy holder. The declaration must be made on a specified day or within the next 14 days, otherwise the sum insured will be deemed to be the declaration value.

The great advantage of this policy is that the premium is limited to the actual amount at risk irrespective of the sum insured. Unlike the excess policy, the premium is not unnecessarily paid. Moreover, the insurer may pay up to the full sum insured throughout the period of the policy because the premium amount can be adjusted accordingly. The policy is very advantageous to those businessmen whose stocks fluctuate from time to time. The amount of the declaration offers scope for fraud because the insured may pay lesser premium by undervaluing the stock. Therefore, this policy is issued only to reputed concerns.

8. Adjustable Policy. The above disadvantage is removed by adjustable policy. This policy is nothing but an ordinary policy on the stock of the businessman with liberty to the insured to vary at his opinion, the premium is adjustable pro-rata according to the variation of the stock. In case of declaration policy, since the excess premium is refundable at the end of the year, the insured may put fire to the property. This danger is avoidable in an 'Adjustable Policy'. This is issued for a definite term on the existing stock. The premium is calculated in the ordinary manner and is paid in full at the inception of the policy. Whenever, there is variation in the stock, the insured informs the insurer. As soon as the information of variation is received, the policy is suitably endorsed and ,the premium is adjusted on a pro-rata basis. The policy amount will, thus, be changeable from time to time. The premium is also settled accordingly.

Difference between Declaration and Adjustable Policies

In case of declaration policy, the insurer's liability is the insured amount but in the case of adjustable policy, the insurer's liability is the value of the last declaration made. The periodical declarations have no direct bearing on the measurement of indemnity in case of declaration policy but these have been the basis of measurement of indemnity. The advantage of the declaration policy over the adjustable policy is that in the former a margin of safety is present because the maximum amount insured is always at the risk, but in the latter case the cover is always for the declared value. The declaration in the case of declaration policy is meant only for the purpose of ascertaining the average of the actual cover given throughout the year to arrive at the figure to which the actual premium will be calculated, but in case of adjustable policy the declaration is the basis of policy amount adjusted by endorsement. The drawback of this policy is that the insured will have to deposit 75 per cent of the premium fixed for the maximum cover in the beginning although a portion of it if found in excess of the actual premium required for the full coverage will be returned at the end of the year. In case of adjustable policy, the premium is adjusted from time to time according to the variation of the risk and the liability of the insurer.

9. Maximum Value with Discount Policy. Under this policy no declaration or adjustment of policy is required, but the policy is taken for a maximum amount and full premium is paid thereon. At the end of the year, in case of no loss, one-third of the premium paid is returned to the policy-holder. This policy is similar to the declaration policy where the botheration of checking and recording declarations is avoided. It serves as a rough and ready method of coverage for maximum amount. This policy is not issued on all types of commodities and is confined only to selected commodities.

10. Reinstatement Policy. This policy is issued to avoid the confict of indemnity. In other types of policies only the market value of the damage or loss is indemnified but, this policy under takes to reinstate the insured property lost by fire to new condition irrespective of its value at the time of loss.

In other types of policies, in case of building or machinery, the actual loss is arrived at by deducting the regular depreciation from the original cost of it. The amount of indemnity will be lesser than the amount to be spent in reinstating the property destroyed or damaged. In order to provide full coverage 'reinstatement or replacement' policies are issued. Under this policy, the basis of settlement in the event of destruction is the cost of rebuilding the premises or in case of plant and machinery, the placement is done by similar machinery. The reinstatement of the damaged property indicates the meaning of repair of the damages. The restoration of the damaged portion of the property to a condition substantially the same is but not better or more extensive than its condition, at the time of its renovation. The cost of the property when partially destroyed will not be more than the cost which would have been insured if such a property has been totally destroyed. The payment of the actual expenditure on replacement will not be made until the expenditure has actually been incurred. This policy is also called 'New for Old' policy because the old property is replaced by new properties. However, such policies are issued only on building, plant and machinery. This policy is not issued on stock, merchandise or materials. Each item of the insured property is subject to average. The policy provides the definite amount in case of purchase of new property in place of the old property destroyed.

11. Comprehensive Policy. This policy undertakes full protection not only against the risk of fire but combining within the risk against burglary, riot, civil commotion, theft, damage from pest, lightning. The policy is also termed as 'All in policies'. Here the 'Comprehensive' does not mean that every type of risk is covered. There may be many exclusions and limitations. This policy is beneficial to the insured and the insurer. The insurer can get higher premium and the assured is protected against losses due to several specified perils.

12. Consequential Loss Policy. The fire insurance is originally purchased to indemnify the material loss only. The intangible interest was not indemnified. This provided a check on the insured to exercise a greater care with respect to the property. However, the settlement of a loss covering material damage only was not sufficient. The consequential loss was also to be provided. Thus, the consequential loss policy includes the loss of tangible and intangible properties.

Thus, this policy provides an indemnity to the insured for loss of net profits, payment of standing charges and expenditure in respect of increased cost of working. As a consequence of fire, there is a reduction in the volume of business which in its turn leads to a reduction in the net profit which the lost business would have ordinarily contributed and to an increase in the proportion of the standing charges such as rents, rates, salaries and others to the total business done. Thus, the policy is to indemnify the insured against financial loss which he may sustain due to the interruption of his business following a fire. Previously the measure of indemnity was a specified percentage of the amount payable under an ordinary fire policy in respect of a material loss. The insurer, thus, used to pay the amount of loss and a specified percentage of the loss. However, now, the measure of indemnity is changed because the specified percentage cannot be the true estimation of the intangible loss. So, the resultant loss is calculated by estimating figures of loss of profits based on a reduction in turnover or output and secondly, increased cost of working in maintaining the business on its pre-fire level.

13. Sprinkler Leakage Policies. This policy insures destruction of or damage to by water accidentally discharged or leaking from automatic sprinkler installation in the insured premises. However, the discharge or leakage of water due to heat caused by fire, repair or alteration of building or sprinkler installation, earthquake, war, explosion are not covered by this policy.

QUESTIONS

1. What do you mean by the following policies—Valued Policies, Reinstatement Policies and Adjustable Policies?
2. Discuss the essential features of fire insurance policies.

29

POLICY CONDITIONS

The fire insurance may be defined as a contract by which the insurer agrees to make good any loss suffered by the insured through damage or destruction of properties by fire up to the sum assured in consideration of payment called premium. The contract of fire insurance is expressed in a document described as a policy. It provides for the payment of a sum of money as representing the pecuniary loss incurred by the insured through the damage or destruction by fire of the property described in the policy or alternatively the restoration or replacement of what has been damaged or destroyed.

Standard Form of Policy

The conditions in fire insurance may be of varied nature, but the standard form of policy includes several conditions which are common to most of the fire policies. The fire insurance contract, principle and practice are governed by the conditions contained in the policy. The standard form of policy at present is the outcome of several vicissitudes in the past. In the beginning, the conditions were very few but with the advancement of the fire insurance several conditions were introduced. Now the conditions became very complex and varied. Now, therefore, several conditions are deleted from the policy and sometimes, the policy is called 'conditionless policy' although no policy can be conditionless at a time.

Needs have arisen about the common conditions of the policy. The leading insurers agreed on a code of essential conditions which are embodied in the standard form of policy. The standard form of policy is now commonly used by the fire insurers. According to standard form the condition of fire-policies are divided into two parts: (*i*) informative and (*ii*) proper conditions. The informative conditions are also divided into two parts: (*i*) Preamble and (*ii*) Perils insured.

Preamble of the Policy

The preamble of the policy sets forth the agreement between the insurers and the insured subject to the conditions of the policy. Payment of premium is an essential consideration of the contract. The insurer, therefore, undertakes to pay to the insured the value of loss to the property at the time of its destruction or the amount of the damage done or to reinstate or replace the property or any part thereof. The agreement clause sets forth that the insurer's liability shall not exceed the sum set opposite each item.

The second clause of the preamble provides for the conditions and terms of the renewal of the policy which limits the liability of the insurer to any term in respect of which the insured shall have paid and the insurer shall have accepted the premium in renewal of the policy.

The third part contains the schedule where the name of the insured, the property insured, sum assured, the total sum assured, period of insurance and premium amount are mentioned.

Perils Insured

The next important part of the policy is description of the perils insured. The perils insured under the standard form of policy are described below.

1. Fire

Fire (whether resulting from explosion or otherwise) is not occasioned by or happening through:

(*a*) its own spontaneous fermentation or heating or its undergoing any process involving the application of heat,

(*b*) earthquakes, subterranean fire, riot, civil commotion, war, invasion, act of foreign enemy, hostilities (whether war be declared or not), civil war, rebellion, revolution, insurrection or military or insured power.

To constitute fire within the meaning of contract of fire insurance two essentials must be present, viz., (1) there must be ignition and (2) the fire, so far as the insured is concerned, must be fortuitous in origin. The 'fire' must be understood in its popular sense, it does not include chemical actions which result in no ignition. The term 'fire' does not include a fire lighted for a specific purpose while confined to its limits. Fire used for cooking, warming or manufacturing is not a fire within the meaning of the contract because there is nothing fortuitous about it. Any loss occasioned by such a fire, whether by burning of any property in the fire itself, or by the scorching or cracking of any property adjacent to it owing to its intense heat, if unaccompanied by origin, is not covered by the contract since the cause of the loss cannot be regarded as a peril insured against. However, if the fire causes ignition by throwing out sparks or otherwise, outside its proper limits it will be fire in the sense of fire insurance. The fire thus occurred, being fortuitous in its origin, is a fire within the meaning of the contract and any loss occasioned thereby, whether by direct building, or by scorching or cracking, or by smoke is within the meaning of fire insurance. The assured must show that he has sustained a loss by fire within the meaning of the fire insurance. The fire caused deliberately by insured or at his convenience will not be included in the meaning of 'fire'. However, the fire caused by incendiarism without the knowledge or connivance of the insured will be included under fire insurance.

The following forms of loss or also indemnified provided they are proximately caused by fire since.

(*i*) damage caused during or immediately following fire by smoke, scorching and falling walls or part of the building in which fire takes place,

(*ii*) damage caused by firemen and others in the discharge of their duties by using water or other extinguishing agent, demolition of buildings to prevent spreading of fire, and damaging property so as to gain access to fire,

(*iii*) damage to property immediately after removal from burning building caused by exposure to weather, provided the removal was justified.

2. Lightning

The lightning may be a form of fire, but loss occasioned by lightning without ignition is not a loss by fire; where the lightning results in ignition, a loss occasioned by such ignition is a loss by fire. However, in practice any damage caused by lightning whether ignition results or not is covered under fire insurance.

3. Explosion

The explosion of gas used for illuminating and domestic purposes in a building in which gas is not generated and which does not form part of gas works will be insured under fire insurance.

POLICY CONDITIONS

The policy conditions may be precedent to the contract conditions subsequent to the contract and conditions precedent to liability. The conditions must be fully complied with to make the insurer liable under the contract. The conditions may be implied or express. Conditions which are set out in the policy are known as express conditions which may be either of general nature and, therefore, printed on the policy or conditions specially designed with reference to a particular contract and are incorporated in the policy. The implied conditions are not mentioned on the policies but are deemed to be present with reference to the policy.

A. Implied Conditions

The following conditions are implied conditions in fire insurance.

(*a*) **Existence of property:** The subject-matter of insurance should exist when the policy is effected.

(*b*) **Insured property:** When the fire occurs the property damaged should be the property insured for obtaining claim on the property.

(*c*) **Insurable interest:** The insured must have insurable interest from the time of the commencement of risk up to the completion of the contract.

(*d*) **Good Faith:** The insured must observe good faith towards the insurer. He must disclose all the material facts truly and fully, and should try to prevent the fire and extinguish the fire, if it occurred, with a reasonable care.

(*e*) **Identity:** The subject-matter of insurance should be described in the policy as to identify it clearly and so define the risk which insurers have undertaken.

B. Express Conditions

The express conditions in fire insurance are discussed in the following paragraphs.

1. Misdescription

The policy shall be voidable in the event of misdescription, misrepresentation or non-disclosure of any material facts. If there is any material misdescription of any of the property insured, the insurer shall not be liable upon this policy so far as it relates to property affected by any such misdescription, misrepresentation or omission. This condition is a reiteration of the implied condition of utmost good faith. Therefore, if the assured fails to disclose all material facts or be guilty of misrepresentation or misdescription in any way, the policy shall be voidable at the insurer's option. Under Common Law, a breach of utmost good faith goes to the root of the whole contract. By virtue of this condition, insurer will limit the avoidance of the contract to that part only of the property affected if risk is divisible into distinct parts. If the misrepresentation, under good faith, relates to a part of the policy only, it will render the whole contract voidable, for a breach of good faith cuts at the root of the whole contract. According to the condition of misdescription, any misrepresentation, misdescription or omission must be material. Usually all the questions asked in the proposal forms are material. Therefore, they should he answered correctly and fully. The insurer should be protected in the manner described in this condition should it be subsequently discovered that the insurance has been obtained through an inaccurate statement on the part of the insured.

2. Alteration

The insurance contract may be avoided if there is any alteration after the commencement of this insurance. The alteration may be of the following types.

(*a*) **Removal:** The removal of the insured property without the consent of the insurer makes the contract voidable. If without the consent of the insurer, the property is removed from one place to another, the insurer will no longer be responsible for any loss arising in relation to the property removed. For example, if the furniture insured has been removed from dewelling house to factory, the risk has increased. In this case, the insured is responsible to inform the insurer who may accept or refuse to cover the furniture in the new place because risk has increased. Nevertheless the insured is always responsible for informing the insurer whether the risk has increased or not by removal.

(*b*) **Increase in risk:** The alteration may take place where the risk of the insured property has increased. The insurer can avoid the policy in respect of the item altered. However, if the insurer is agreed to continue the contract the charging extra-premium on the increased risk, after getting information of alteration, he can do so. If the assured has not informed the insurer, the insurer can waive the contract. The insurer usually accommodates the insured either by waiving his right or by charging extra premium depending on the circumstances.

(*c*) **Change of interest:** Without the consent of the insurer the interest on the insured property cannot be changed. If the interest has been changed, the insurer will cease his responsibility. The assignment, or transfer of property, interest thereon and policy will be valid only when it has been made after the express consent of the insurer. Except the case of change to hazardous or more risky assignment, the insurer generally accepts the proposal of assignment. Without the consent of the insurer, the assignment or transfer will be invalid.

The insurer can accept the assignment or transfer and the interest of the vendor and of the purchaser may remain intact. Now-a-days, by inserting 'optional memorandum', the property can be transferred under good faith and the interests of both the parties are protected.

Exception

The change in interest is ceaseable in the case where the property changes on account of will or operation of law. The insurer in this case will be liable though the consent has not been obtained.

3. Exclusions

The risks which are excluded from the fire policies are called exceptions or exclusions. The exclusions are explained below:

(*i*) Destruction or damage by explosion (whether the explosion be occasioned by fire or otherwise) except as stated on the face of the policy.

(*ii*) Goods held in trust or on commission, money, securities, stamps, documents, manuscripts, business books, patterns, models, moulds, plans, designs, explosives unless specially insured by the policy.

(*iii*) Destruction of or damage to property which at the time of the happening of such destruction or damage is insured by any Marine Policy.

The above exceptions can be covered or modified by payment of extra premium. The meaning of certain words should be clarified. Damage by explosion is not covered but damage by fire consequent on explosion is covered. Goods held in trust can be insured by the trustee provided he has an insurable interest in them. The trustee must have some legal liability or reputation at stake for the loss of the goods to create an insurable interest for which he can insure. Money, securities, documents and business books are practically uninsurable under an ordinary policy for the very nature of them, except that money can be covered up to a certain small amount under a comprehensive policy. Documents and business books can be insured for the cost of their reinstatement. Some classes of goods when in stock are liable to spontaneous fermentation or heat on account of the internal temperature engendered by compression. There are many heating processes regularly used in trade and in many business. Such cases are underwritten only on payment of additional premium. Stamps, manuscripts, plants, designs are highly perishable articles, and it is very difficult to assess their values. However, they can be covered by payment of a special rate. Earthquake, riot, civil commotion, foreign enemy, etc., can be covered by payment of a special rate of premium and under special conditions. The burden of proof that the fire occurred due to excepted perils lies on the insurer.

4. Fraud

Fraud always invalidates a contract and the following provision is made in the standard policy.

"If the claim be in any respect fraudulent or if any fraudulent means of devices be used by the insured or anyone acting on his behalf to obtain any benefit under this policy or if any destruction or damage be occasioned by the wilful act or with the connivance of the insured of benefit under this policy shall be forfeited."

The clause clarifies that the fraud would forfeit all the benefits under the policy. It contemplates three eventualities—presentation of a fraudulent claim, use of fraudulent means and acts of wilful destruction like arson, etc. Fraudulent does not necessarily include improper or excessive claims. Fraud cannot necessarily be in case of price. However, it may be in respect of quantities. Excepted property if included under insured properties would amount fraud. False valuation of insured properties comes under fraud. incendiarism or arson committed by the insured or by anyone else with his connivance will be fraud and will avoid the policy.

5. Claim

The claim clause runs as below—

"On the happening of any destruction or damage the insured shall forthwith give notice thereof in writing to the insurer and shall within fifteen days after such destruction or damage, or such further time as the insurer may in writing allow, containing as particular on account as may be reasonably practicable of the several articles or portions of property destroyed or damaged and of the amount of destruction or damage thereto respectively having regard to their value at the time of the destruction or damage together with details of any other insurances on any property hereby insured. The insured shall also give to the insurer all proofs and information with respect to the claim as may reasonably be required together with (if demanded) or statutory declaration of the truth of the claim and of any matters connected therewith. No claim under this policy shall be payable unless the terms of this conditions have been complied with."

From the Above clause, it appears that the notice of loss is to be given forthwith after its occurrence though details can be given thereafter. The expenses of claim will be borne by the insured. The insured has to disclose other inferances in respect of the property for the purpose of determining the contribution that may be payable by other insurer. The insured must give immediate written notice of any destruction or damage and should be followed with a written notice within 15 days of the claim. The time may be extended by the insurer where there is a reasonable case for it. The insured must furnish all reasonable proofs and information required together with a statutory declarations as to the truth of the claim or any matters connected there with.

6. Reinstatement Clause

The insurer has the option to discharge his liability by reinstating or replacing the damaged property. The cash payment of actual loss is not made under this clause. It needs as below:—

If the company elects to reinstate or replace any property, the insured shall, at his own expense, furnish the company with such plans, specifications, measurements, quantities and such other particulars as the company may require and no acts done or caused to be done by the company with a view to reinstatement or replacement shall be deemed an election by the company to reinstate or replace.

The insurer shall not be bound to reinstate exactly or completely, but only as circumstances permit and in reasonably sufficient manner, and in no case shall the insurer be bound to expend more in reinstatement than it would have cost to reinstate such property, as it was at the time of the occurrence of such loss or damage, nor more than the sum insured by the insurer thereon. If in any case the insurer is unable to reinstate or repair the property thereby insured, because of certain regulations, the insurer may be liable to pay such sum as would be requisite to reinstate or repair such property if the same could lawfully be reinstated to its former condition.

The clause removes the dispute between insured and insurer because the insurer can replace the goods by similar ones without submitting to the stated value given to them by the insured. The reinstatement is optional with the insurer and not with the insured, but once the former has elected to reinstate or replace he has no right to reverse his decision.

7. Insurer's Rights After A Fire

On the happening of any loss or damage to any of the property insured by this policy, the company may:

(*a*) enter and take and keep possession of the building or premises where the loss or damage has happened;

(*b*) take possession of or require to the delivered to it any property of the insured in the building or on the premises at the time of the loss or damage;

(*c*) keep possession of any such property and examine, sort, arrange, remove or otherwise deal with the same; and

(*d*) sell any such property or dispose of the same for account of whom it may concern.

The powers conferred by this condition shall be exercisable by the company at any time until notice in writing is given by the insured that he makes no claim under the policy or, if any claim is made until such claim is finally determined or withdrawn, and the company shall not by any act done in the exercise or purported exercise of its powers hereunder, incur any liability to the insured or diminish their right to rely upon any of the conditions of this policy in answer to any claim. If the insured or any person on his behalf shall not comply with the requirements of the company or shall hinder or obstruct the company in the exercise of its powers hereunder, all benefit under this policy shall be forfeited.

8. Subrogation

The clause subrogation reads as below:—

Any claimant under this policy shall at the request and at the expenses of the company do and concur in doing and permitting to be done all such acts and things as may be necessary or reasonably required by the company for the purpose of enforcing any rights and remedies, or of obtaining relief or indemnity from other parties to which the company shall be or would become entitled or subrogated upon its paying for or making good any destruction or damage under this policy, whether such acts and things shall be or become necessary or required before or after his indemnification by the company.

The clause is corollary to the doctrine of indemnity. It makes clear that the insured is precluded from obtaining more than the actual loss. When the insurer has indemnified the insured against a loss the insured must transfer all the rights regarding the property damaged. The insured cannot recover from the third party as well as from the insurer more than the actual loss. However, both the parties can indemenify only up to the amount of loss. The insured is entitled to receive payment from the third party, by reason of negligence of law or agreement. The insurer cannot recover from third party more than the sum paid by him. The excess amount can be retained by the insurer only as the trustee of the insured.

The insurer is entitled to the advantage of every right of the insured whether such right consists in contract, fulfilled or unfulfilled or in remedy for tort capable of being insisted on or already insisted on or in any other right whether by way of condition or otherwise. The insured is bound to give all necessary facilities to the insurer which the latter may require in enforcing his rights against third parties. The steps taken in such field are in the name of the insured. The cost will be borne by the insurer. Amounts recovered by the insurer become his property subject to the right of the insured to be fully indemnified.

9. Warranties

The warranties clause is as follows:—

Every warranty to which the property insured or any item thereof is or may be made subject shall from the time the warranty attaches apply and continue to be in force during the whole currency of this policy, and non-compliance with any such warranty, whether it increases the risk or not, shall be a bar, to any claim in respect of such property or item, provided that if this policy is renewed a claim in respect of loss or damage occurring during the renewal period shall not be barred by reason of warranty not having been complied with at any time before the commencement of such period.

The compliance of warranties is very essential Non-compliance with any of the warranty or even substantial compliance is fatal to the contract whether the risk thereby has increased or not. According to the clause the warranties of the previous policies or policy may not essentially be applied to renewed policies.

10. Arbitration

The arbitration clause in the policy is mentioned as below:

"If any difference arises as to the amount of any loss or damage such difference shall independently of all other questions be referred to the decision of an Arbitrator, to be appointed in writing by the parties in difference, or if they cannot agree upon a single Arbitrator, to the decision of two disinterested persons as arbitrators, of whom one shall be appointed in writing by each of the parties within two calendar months after having been required so to do in writing by the other party. In case either party shall refuse or fail to appoint an arbitrator within two calendar months after receipt of notice in writing requiring an appointment, the other party shall be at liberty to appoint a sole arbitrator, and in case of disagreement between the arbitrators, the difference shall be referred to the decision of an umpire who shall have been appointed by them in writing before entering on the reference and who shall sit with the arbitrators and preside at their meetings."

The above clause is meant to avoid undue litigation and settle the dispute by arbitration. It is a very simple, cheap and expeditious method of settling disputes.

11. Purchaser's Interest Clause

Sometimes a further memorandum in the following terms is also added to the policies:

If at the time of destruction or damage to any building hereby insured, shall have contracted to sell his interest in such building and the purchase shall not have been but shall be thereafter completed, the purchaser on the completion of the purchase, if and so far as the property is not otherwise insured by or on behalf of the purchaser against such destruction or damages, shall be entitled to the benefit of this policy so far as it relates to such destruction or damage without prejudice to the rights and liabilities of the insured or the company under this policy up to the date of completion.

The above clause is useful to the vendor and purchaser up to the date of completion of the sale for their respective interests. If the purchaser elects to continue the insurance in his own name, in that case the purchase price will include the value of the unexpired insurance.

12. Loss Procedure

It is the responsibility of the insured to inform about the loss as soon as the loss occurs. The insurer will send a claim form to the insured. In this form a detailed information about the loss, the place and the circumstances under which it occurred and the description of the property insured are given. The insurer will examine the claim form and if find it reasonable, claim is paid at once. If the loss is serious and disputable the insurer may appoint an assessor called adjuster. The assessor or the adjuster will examine the cause of fire, the amount of loss and the amount of salvage. The details of the examination are sent to the insured and the insurer. The completed claim form and the consent of the insured are also sent to the insurer. The insurer will see whether warranties are complied with or not. If the insurer is satisfied and the insurer is agreed, the amount of claim is paid. In case of dispute, the arbitrators and umpire may settle the dispute as has been described above.

In case the property was insured for more than one insurer, the leading office may pay the amount of the claim.

Ex-Gratia Payment

When the insurer pays certain portion of the claim before final settlement, it is called ex-gratia payment. It is an act of grace. It is paid to avoid the hardship to the insured and also to keep the reputation of the insurer.

13. Contribution and Average

The contribution and average clauses are as below:

If at the time of any loss or damage happening to any property hereby insured there be any other subsisting insurance or insurances, whether effected by the insured or by any other person or persons, covering the same property, this company shall not be liable to pay or contribute more than its rateable proportion of such loss or damage.

If the property hereby insured shall, at the breaking out of any fire, be collectively of greater value than the sum insured thereon, then the insured shall be considered as being his own insurer for the difference and shall bear rateable proportion of the loss accordingly. Every item, if more than one, of the Policy shall be separately subject to this condition.

The contribution clause clarifies that if there is more than one insurance, all the insurers will indemnify according to their proportion to the total insurance. So, the liabilities of the insurers are limited to their rateable proportions of the loss. One alternative is also available that the insured can recover the whole of the loss from any one insurer leaving him to collect the proper contributions from the other insurers. The contribution clause simplifies the claim settlement. The rateable proportion of each insurer is arrived at by dividing the sum insured under his policy by the total insured sum of all policies on the risk.

The following conditions must be fulfilled for this clause:

(*i*) The subject matter of insurance must be common to all the policies.

(*ii*) The peril which is insured again must be common to all of them.

(*iii*) The same insured must be interested in all the policies.

(*iv*) All the policies must be in force at the time of the loss.

The average clause in fire insurance penalises as under-insurance by a corresponding under-payment of loss. The clause reveals that the loss will be paid in proportion to the insured amount and total amount of property. For example

$$\text{Loss} \times \frac{\text{Amount of Insurance}}{\text{Amount of the Property}}$$

The pro-rata condition of average is applicable to all policies issued by tariff offices in India.

QUESTIONS

1. What do you mean by policies conditions?
2. What are the important conditions of policies?
3. Discuss Contribution and Average Clause.

30

RATE FIXATION IN FIRE INSURANCE

The rate fixation in fire insurance is not so scientific as in life insurance. The physical hazard can be estimated satisfactorily but the moral hazard, being varied and unknown, cannot be ascertained so correctly. While calculating the premium, various relevant factors of both the hazards are properly estimated and evaluated. The premium must be adequate enough to provide for full payment of claims including catastrophic losses, expenses of management and a margin of profit. The tariff offices follow the collective system of tariff rating. After nationalisation of general insurance businesses, the tariff rating is applied.

SYSTEM OF RATE FIXATION

The actual process of rating consists of three steps: 1. Classification, 2. Discrimination and 3. Fixing rates or schedule rating.

1. Classification

Properties to be insured are of various nature and risk. Since the premium is fixed in relation to the class of risk, the properties are classified accordingly. Properties are generally divided into three main classes, viz., (*i*) common or ordinary, (*ii*) hazardous and (*iii*) doubly hazardous. Different premium rates are fixed for each class. These classifications do not hold good for a long time because of varied nature of risk. Now the risks are classified into various classes according to factors affecting fire risk.

(*i*) **Construction or Structure:** The construction of the building has always been of great importance in rating. Building made of brick will be more sound than the building made of wood. Today, the construction of building is divided into two types of structure. First fire-proof building and second, building without fireproof. The height of the building, the area, the number of unprotected floor openings, construction of walls, floors, roof, etc., are considered in calculating the fire hazard.

(*ii*) **Occupancy:** The risk considerably varies according to the nature of occupancy, *i.e.,* the use to which the building is devoted. One building may be used as a dry goods store or hardware store, or furniture-store or for residential purposes. The building may have different risks because of the different substances and processes which they contain and the different uses to which they are put. There is inherent connection between the building and its contents. It is essential for companies to change their rates to meet changing business conditions. Rate making in fire insurance does not present constant factors. Justice demands that the insurer should recognise the important changes. A building occupied as a residence or an office is a better risk than a retail shop. A storeroom used for the storage of highly combustible goods is more hazardous from a fire insurance viewpoint than a grocery shop. The process of manufacture, the nature of raw materials used, the type of machinery are important factors to influence the physical hazard.

(*iii*) **Nature of Flooring:** The nature of flooring influences the risk to a greater extent. Existence of wooden floors in the building introduces an additional physical hazard. Wooden floor becomes a fuel in the event of fire. It may collapse easily causing damage to property.

(*iv*) **Height:** The height adds difficulty in fighting a fire on the upper floors. There may be risk of water damage to property on the lower floors when water is used to extinguish a fire on the upper floors. The floors involve heavy risk of collapse of the upper floors.

(*v*) **Floor and wall opening:** Openings in the floor for lifts and belts constitute higher physical hazard. It may cause greater chances of ignition of fire and difficulty of extinguishing the fire.

(*vi*) **Exposure:** The chances of risk may differ from property to property according to the degree of exposure. A building or property may be situated in a congested conflagration locality involving greater danger to the property. Exposure stands second as a cause of fire and is more than the occupancy hazard.

(*vii*) **Lighting, Heating and Power:** The fire may occur due to short-circuit. Combustion can also arise from faulty installation and dampness. The lighting system *e.g.* by gas or oil, leakage of fuel and naked flames cause more hazard to property.

(*viii*) **Place or Situation:** The location of the property, nature of adjoining premises, the distance from a fire brigade station or the source of water supply, the degree of congestion in the area are some of the important factors to influence the degree of risk.

(*ix*) **Protection:** The availability of protection against fire influences the degree of risk. The protection facilities may be public or private. When protection facilities are available the fire may be extinguished in its incipiency. The fire extinguishing apparatus, water supply, police system etc. can reduce the degree of risk. Smaller premium is charged where modern devices for preventing and extinguishing fires are present. It would be injustice to charge the same rate for all types of risk.

(*x*) **Time:** The time of loss must be kept into consideration. The annual loss ratio is by no means uniform every year. So, the rate fixation must account for good or bad years to determine approximately the real loss. Therefore, a long period of time is taken into consideration while calculating the premium.

2. Discrimination

The differentiation of the rates for individual risks in a particular class is known as discrimination. Each additional feature of risk is charged extra premium. The better types of risks are encouraged and attracted by the insurer. Lesser premium is charged where fire extinguishing appliances or fire-resisting construction are present. The tariff system is based on the law of average and graded schedule is formulated where different rates are ascertained for the different types of risks. Thus, the different risks are put in a specified class, and are differentiated from each other according to the merits and demerits of the individual risk. It aims at a more equitable basis of rating. For example, dwelling house is a class and, therefore, all the dwelling houses are put in the same class. Since the dwelling houses are of different type, the class may be sub-divided into several classes according to the degree of hazard. An appropriate discount could be given for those houses which have fire extinguishing appliances, nearness to fire brigade station and absence of exposure in the vicinity.

3. Schedule Rating

It is a plan by which hazards with respect to any particular risk are measured. It is defined as, ".......... an empirical standard for the measurement of relative quantity of fire hazard. Schedule rating takes into consideration the various items influencing the peril of fire. It is based on the theory that the aggregate fire hazard of any risk is capable of ultimate analysis into its component factors to each of which could be assigned an appropriate charge. A standard or average premium is determined as a base for calculating the premium. The average premium rate for a class of risk is determined taking into account the total loss and the sums assured during a period of year. The period should be such that the experience of good as well as bad years may be taken into account. A large number of items, as far as possible, are taken so that the law of average may apply. Larger the number, the more representative will be the rate of premium.

Thus the average fire rate is calculated as follows:

$$L/V \times 100$$

Where L represents the losses, and V represents the values of insured amount.

The rate arrived at will be net premium which is just sufficient to meet all the losses in that particular risk. This basic or net premium is loaded with expenses of management, commission, rents and a margin for profit to arrive at the gross premium or office premium.

The rate so calculated is called 'normal rate' or average rate for the particular group. In each group, risks may differ from one another and in order to maintain equity between different types of risk and between the insurer and the insured, it is necessary to apply the principle of discrimination, *i.e.,* differentiation, of individual risks in a group taking into account their particular features. Extra rates are provided for bad features, *i.e.,* for inferior construction, timber flooring, height, situation in a congested area and discounts are granted for good features, *i.e.,* for fire extinguishing appliances, automatic sprinklers ets. The rebate will be allowed taking into account the efficacy of the means adopted.

PRINCIPLES OF RATE FIXATION

The fire insurance rates are determined by three ways: 1. Personal judgement, 2. Tabulated experience and 3 by schedule.

1. Personal Judgement Rating

This method was the first to be generally used. Under this method, the rates so made indicate the opinion or judgement of the rate makers. The judgement is the result of the experience and observation of many years. The rate made were equitable. No attempt was made to take account of minor differences. All the good features and all the defective features were put together and the rate was calculated by differentiating from the average premium.

Since the personal judgements differ greatly, different rates may be determined to the same risk. With the increasing complexities of modern properties, the short-comings of this system became more and more apparent. This method may create dissatisfaction amongst the policyholders because of different premiums to the same type of properties. Now less reliance is placed upon personal judgement in making rates.

2. Experience Rating

The method is not essentially based upon judgement. The combined judgement of a large number of individuals is taken into account. It is based on the experience of several years and of several persons. Therefore, it reflects a reasonably accurate treatment of the various elements to measure the fire hazard. Under this method, the risks are classified according to their loss experiences.

This system may not be practical as so many classes of risks would be necessary. The experience collected in the past will be of no great value in the future. However, rates made on this basis may more correctly be utilised as compared to that of other systems.

3. Schedule Rating

Under this method, fire hazard is separated into various elements and each element is assigned a particular value. The schedule describes a property as 'Standard'. For each standard risk, a standard premium is assigned. To this basic rate or standard premium, a certain stipulated charges are made for defects in construction and arrangement of property and certain deductions are made for unusually good features as compared with the standard.

The advantages of the schedule rating system are that it provides more equitable treatment of all insured. Due to the systematic treatment of the risk, the premium rates come approximately the same. The second advantage is that it reduces friction between the company and the insured because the insured is able to understand how his rate is made in every case. The third advantage is that it tends to reduce the Fire Waste because it encourages proper construction of buildings by intelligently charging for deficiencies from standards and recognizing exceptionally good construction by deductions. The fourth advantage is that it secures more thorough inspection and rating.

TARIFF RATES

Fire insurance business is governed by the tariffs formulated by the Tariff Advisory Committee which is a statutory body established under the provisions of the Insurance (Amendment) Act 1968 "to control and regulate the rates, advantages, terms and conditions that may be offered by insurers in respect of general insurance business. The Tariffs provide rates of premium for almost all classes of risks as also rules and regulations governing the business and standard form of wordings for the contract and its extensions. The Tariff Advisory Committee has constituted four Regional Committees at Delhi, Calcutta, Madras and Bombay.

Delhi: The States of Jammu and Kashmir, Punjab, Haryana, Rajasthan, Uttar Pradesh, Himachal Pradesh and the Union Territories of Delhi.

Calcutta: The States of Assam, Bihar, Orissa, West Bengal and the Union Territories of Andaman and Nicobar Islands, Manipur and Tripura.

Madras: The States of Andhra Pradesh, Kerala, Tamil Nadu and Karnataka and the Union Territories of Laccadiv, Minicoy and Amindive Islands.

Bombay: The States of Gujarat, Maharashtra and Madhya Pradesh.

Each region has its own Tariff providing for rates, warranties and other regulations applicable to risks situated in its territorial jurisdiction. The Tariffs applicable to each of the regions are similar in broad outline but differ in matters of detail such as actual rates which reflect local hazards and past experience of the area. These Tariffs are formulated by applying the principles of fire insurance rating discussed earlier. Risks are classified into principal groups and rates are provided for each group on the basis of loss experience of each such group. After classification, discrimination is another feature of the tariff system of rating. In the same group of risks, there will be differences in the circumstances of individual risks. The differences are dealt with by charging extra premium for unfavorable feature and granting discount for favourable features.

The following three broad principles are adopted by the Tariff :

Occupancy: Risks are classified according to the occupation of premises. Goods stored are classified into hazardous or non-hazardous. Under this factor manufacturing process heating, lighting and power, the nature of goods, combustion and damage by smoke and water, etc.

Construction: Buildings are classified into 3 or 4 categories according to materials used in the construction of external walls and roof. Fire resisting materials, fire extinguishers, etc., are considered.

Situation: Risks are estimated according to the situation of the property, big cities, smaller towns, narrow streets, fire brigade facilities, water supplies, survey facilities, etc.

The tariff provides:

1. Definition of the class of risks.
2. A minimum basic rate for a normal risk in a class.
3. Extra rates for specified, common and special hazards of a particular risk, *e.g.*, situation in the mofussil, conflagration area, height, night work, etc.

4. Discount in the premium for improvements in the risk, *e.g.*, sprinkler installation, fire extinguishing appliances.
5. General rules and regulations governing the business.
6. Standard wording for the policy forms, clauses and warranties.

THE TARIFF SYSTEM IN PRACTICE

The Tariffs have prescribed the order in which the various additional rates and discounts are to be applied to the final rate.

1. Tariff rates as mentioned against the relevant item in the tariff.
2. Extra rate mentioned in the item itself.
3. Extra for inferior reconstruction.
4. Conflagration extra.
5. Artificial light extra.
6. Extra for the use of mobile goods handling appliances.
7. Mofussil or classified towns extra.
8. Extra for electrical installation not in accordance with the Tariff regulations.
9. Night work extra.

QUESTIONS

1. Discuss the methods of Rate Fixation in Fire Insurance Policies.
2. What are the principles of rate fixation in fire insurance?

Application of Average Clause in Payment of Claim

When insurance is subject to the ordinary, or Pro-Rata condition of Average, *i.e.*, under-insurance, the liability of the insurers is restricted to that proportion of the loss that the sum insured bears to the value of the property at the time of the destruction or damage. The insurer's liability in the event of a claim under a policy subject to average, the loss is assessed in the ordinary manner, but the amount payable is determined after a comparison of the sum insured and the value of the property. Where under-insurance exists, the liability of the insurers is limited.

The Pro-Rata Condition of Average

"Whenever a sum insured is declared to be subject to average, if the property covered thereby shall at the breaking out of any fire or at the commencement of any destruction of or damage to such property by any other peril hereby insured against the collectively of greater value than such sum insured, then the insured shall be considered as being his own insurer for the difference and shall bear a rateable share of the loss accordingly."

The operation of the condition can be shown as below

	Rs.
Sum assured	1,500
Loss	300
Value of the property at the time of fire	1,800

The insurer's liability is $\dfrac{\text{sum asured}}{\text{value of property}} \times \text{loss}$

$$= \frac{1500 \times 300}{1800} = \text{Rs. } 250$$

Thus the insured will bear Rs. 50 and the insurer will pay Rs. 250.

The insurers cannot be called upon to pay the full sum insured. If the property is totally destroyed, there will be a total loss under the policy.

Special Condition of Average

"Whenever a sum insured is declared to be subject to the special condition of Average, then, if such sum shall at the breaking out of any fire or at the commencement of any destruction of or damage to the property by any other peril hereby insured against, be less than three-fourths of the value of the property insured in that amount the insured shall be considered as being his own insurer for the difference between the sum insured and the full value of the property insured at the time of such fire or at the commencement of such destruction or damage and shall bear a rateable share of the loss accordingly."

This condition shall operate only if the sum assured is less than the three-fourths of the value of the property. If the sum assured exceeds this proportion of the value at risk, the insured recovers, the full amount of his loss up to the sum insured.

The assessor in the fire insurance deals with some typical tasks which are described in the following paragraphs. The assessor is also called 'Adjuster'.

Task of Adjuster

The adjuster has to examine and collect the following information:

(*i*) What policies and agreement covered the property at the time of loss.

(*ii*) Whether the property described in the policy is really located and placed at the described place. Whether property had been removed at the safer place at the time of loss.

(*iii*) The nature and extent of the insurer's interest in the property.

(*iv*) Loss occurred after the commencement and before the expiration of the contract.

(*v*) Whether loss was the direct result of fire or other insured perils.

(*vi*) Whether any part of the loss was caused directly or indirectly by enemy attack, military offence, etc.

(*vii*) Whether the loss occurred while the hazard was increased by any means within the control or knowledge of the insured.

(*viii*) Whether before or after the loss the insured wilfully concealed or misrepresented any material facts.

The adjuster must do the following:

(*i*) Fix by agreement with the insured or by appraisal, the actual cash value of the property at the time of loss and the amount of loss thereto.

(*ii*) Exclude from the claim, uninsurable property or excepted property.

(*iii*) Determine the extent of the application of the insurance and the contribution to be made by the insurer to the loss.

(*iv*) If there are two or more policies covering the property, apportion the loss among these policies.

(*v*) See that the requirements in case of loss that are necessary to produce informative essentals to establish the status of liabilities under the policy or the value or loss of the property are complied with.

(*vi*) Consider the interest of any mortgagee named as payee in the policy and the action that should be taken by the insurers.

(*vii*) Investigate any disputed cancellation of the policy.

(*viii*) Exercise the option to take all or any part of the property at the agreed or appraised value.

(*ix*) Preserve any right of recovery from third parties to the loss.

PAYMENT AND DISCHARGE BY ADJUSTER

The adjuster should:

(*i*) Meet the insured or the person who will act for him in the adjustment, discuss the loss with him and make any necessary examination of records.

(*ii*) Examine his policy if it cannot easily be produced, the record of insurer's agents or broker's record should be searched.

(*iii*) Inspect the scheme of the loss and examine any of the property still in evidence.

(*iv*) Examine available records or reports covering the occurrence of the loss, those of fire department, peril or salvage corps, police, etc.

(*v*) Examine records or documents deeds or mortgages, contracts of sale, leases, etc.

(*vi*) Consider whether any insurance held by others should bear the loss or any part of it.

(*vii*) Withdraw if the insurance is not liable for the loss from contract with the insured and report to the insurer or have nonwaiver agreement.

(*viii*) Estimate the situation and the probable results of adjustments.

(*ix*) Choose the method of adjustment used.

(*x*) Make any necessary preparation for conducting the adjustment according to the method chosen.

(*xi*) Negotiate an agreement with the insured as to value and loss, submit the disagreement.

(*xii*) Check any claim for possible errors and omissions also for improper inclusion, of property.

(*xiii*) Apply contract conditions and determine the sum for which any policy or contract is liable.

(*xiv*) Forward to insurer with final report and supporting papers.

(*xv*) Account the salvage and its proceeds with the final report.

WAIVER AND ESTOPPEL

Waiver

Waiver is defined as the voluntary relinquishment of a known right. The waiver may be (*i*) expressed or (*ii*) implied. An insurer is informed that a policy under which claim is made is void because the person insured had no insurance interest in the property; but still, the insurer is going to pay it as a waiver.

Estoppel

Estoppel is the legal bar raised by a person's own action against asserting a right that he once possessed or making a choice that once was open to him. An insurer may be estopped from exercising its option to take all or any part of the property at the agreed or appraised value if it delays its notice to the insured that it intends to do so.

QUESTIONS

1. Discuss the procedure of settlement of fire insurance claims.
2. Explain—Estoppel, Adjuster, Waiver and Estoppel.

32

REINSURANCE

Reinsurance is an arrangement whereby an original insurer who has insured a risk insures a part of that risk again with another insurer, that is to say, reinsures a part of the risk in order to diminish his own liability. The difference between the retention and the total amount of acceptance is reinsured. The limiting or retention and effecting of reinsurance brings about a wider distribution of the risks and secures to the insurer the full advantages of the law of average.

Insurance is a contract between the insurer and the original insured. Reinsurance is a contract between the reinsured (the insurer) and the reinsurer.

Therefore, the original insured is not a party to the contract of reinsurance. Now, if insurer goes into liquidation can the original insured sue the reinsurer for recovery of loss under the policy?

This question involves the protection of the rights of the reinsured's policyholders. In America, a special provision is made in the reinsurance contracts to safeguard the interests of the reinsured's policyholder, that is the original insured. A specific clause called 'loss assumption clause' is incorporated in the body of the reinsurance contract whereby the original insured can recover his loss on the policy from the reinsurers, if the reinsured goes into liquidation.

Limits

It is usual to fix a limit up to which the insurer is prepared to lose on risks in a specified class. The limit depends upon the following circumstances:

1. The financial status and premium income of the insurer. A new insurer with small premium income cannot afford to sustain a loss which might be borne with ease by established insurer with ample reserve.
2. The experienced in a particular class of risk:
   (*i*) The degree of the fire hazard present.
   (*ii*) The extent of the damage likely to be sustained.
   (*iii*) The fire extinguishing facilities available.
3. The limit will vary according to the nature and size of the concerns proposing for insurance.
4. Location and other factors affecting the risk are also taken into account while calculating the amount of limit.

Retention

After deciding the limit, retention can be easily fixed. Retention is the amount of maximum liability which the insurer can assume on a particular risk. The retention is determined according to the class to which it belongs and to its merit and demerits. The retention is also decided upon the total amount of insurance in force, the average size of its policies and the amount of surplus fund available with it. It also depends upon the size of company, age of issue, the type of policy and the class of risk.

Reinsurance

Reinsurance is the transfer of insurance business from one insurer to another. The insurer transferring the business is called the 'principal' or ceding or original office and the office to which the business is transferred is called for 'reinsurer or guaranteeing office'. It is also a contract of indemnity. The original company must disclose all the material facts to the reinsurer. At the time of loss the reinsurer indemnifies the loss up to the amount of reinsurance. The reinsurance amount is obtained by deducting retention amount from the original policy amount.

Advantages of Reinsurance

1. The original insurer can accept the risk to the extent of his limit. In absence of reinsurance, a person desiring a large amount of insurance will have to take a number of policies from several insurers. This reinsurance contract makes it possible to purchase only one policy from an insurer.
2. Reinsurance makes it possible to accept each risk for the very amount desired by the proposer and to transfer the excess above the 'retention limit' to another insurer.
3. The reinsurance gives the benefit of the greater stability resulting from a widespread of business. By accepting many risks and scaling down, by reinsurance, all those that are larger than the normal carrying capacity of the insurer justifies, certainty in business is substituted for uncertainty through the better application of the law of average.
4. The reinsurance makes stability in underwriting and consistency in underwriting results over a period.
5. It provides a safeguard against serious effects of conflagration.
6. The reinsurance has the effect of stabilizing income and losses over a period of years.

METHODS OF REINSURANCE

1. Shopping or 'Street' Reinsurance

Under this method, there is no standing agreement regarding re-insuring of risk of one company by the other. Each policy is treated on an individual basis. The reinsurer is sought only when the need of reinsurance on a policy arises. The reinsurer serutinises each case on its merits and may accept the risk on any terms and conditions or may decline it. Since the ceding company is not certain about the availability of reinsurance and a term, it will exercise a greater care in selecing the risk.

2. Facultative Reinsurance

The essential feature of this method is that each individual risk is submitted by the ceding office to the reinsurer who can accept or decline whatever sum they consider appropriate subject to the amount of their acceptance being approved by the ceding office. The reinsurer is offered the particulars of original contract. The reinsurer will see the plan and report on the risk offered for reinsurance. The reinsurer may qualify the acceptance subject to plan and report. The ceding office may retain certain amount on the insurance. The agreement does not make it binding upon the re-insuring company to provide reinsurance on a particular risk. The ceding office is under no obligation to submit all its business to the insurer.

This method differs from the 'Shopping' in the sense that the two companies are agreed in advance as to the form in which risks, premium, terms and other details are to be submitted. Thus, many expenses connected with 'shopping' are reduced. Under this method also, the ceding office may have to wait before accepting the original risk till it is accepted for insurance. When the underwriting rules of the two companies are similar and the plan of insurance seems to be fairly satisfactory, it can be assumed with reasonable safety that the required reinsurance will be available.

The ceding office knowing that the risk may also be declined for reinsurance will be more careful in accepting the original risk and may avoid the higher risk. It may receive valuable advice from the reinsurer.

Facultative reinsurance policies

As mentioned earlier, a reinsurance policy is essentially different from a reinsurance contract. A reinsurance policy is in respect of risk which is already written and the reinsurance is required for limits in excess of net retention limits and other reinsurance capacities. It is not obligatory for the reinsured to effect facultative reinsurances and the reinsurers have option open to accept or reject a risk. Facultative reinsurances are of two types, viz., Pro-rata or Contributing Facultative Reinsurance and Facultative Excess of Loss Reinsurance. Reinsurance policies are contracts for risks already written and not for future risks to be written.

A reinsurance policy is issued under Facultative reinsurance and such a policy contains detailed description of the risk, its location, its period of coverage, perils covered, exclusions if any, territorial scope, premium rate, limits of liability, reinsurance commission etc. Such policy is for each individual risk reinsured. Generally, there is a convention of not providing profit commission on such reinsurances. Premium and losses are accounted separately as provided therein.

Reinsurance Treaties and Reinsurance policies are not synonymous; reinsurance treaties are contracts for insurance and reinsurance policies or cessions are contracts of insurance.

Facultative reinsurance is not for creation of capacity but it is for risks already underwritten, where limits are beyond the capacity of the insurer. It is a contract of insurance by way of a reinsurance policy for current single risk.

Under Reinsurance Treaty method, the reinsurance contract is for creation of capacity for future portfolio of risk to be underwritten and declared therein.

Again, under Quota Share treaty and Excess of Loss treaty the risk accepted by the ceding office of insurer are automatically reinsured according to the terms of the treaty. But under Surplus treaties, a risk is reinsured once it crosses the retained limit of liability. Thus under Surplus treaties the reinsured has to declare a risk by an entry on bordereau.

Open covers or Automatic Facultative covers or Facultative obligatory covers are agreements to make future reinsurance where the reinsured has got an option to declare a risk but, once declared, the reinsurer has to accept it as on obligation under the contract. Thus such reinsurance is 'Facultative' for reinsured but 'Obligatory' for the reinsurer.

3. Automatic or Treaty Reinsurance

Under this method, there is an agreement between the ceding office and reinsurer office that the amount of insurance on a policy above the retention of the ceding office shall be submitted by it for reinsurance and the same shall be accepted by the reinsuring company. As soon as the original contract is completed the excess above retention amount becomes automatically reinsured under the agreement. The ceding office need not even inform the reinsuring office immediately that a risk has been accepted by it. The terms and conditions of the reinsurance contract are the same as of the original insurance contract. The maximum reinsurance amount acceptable to the reinsurer bears a definite relationship with the retention limit of a ceding company.

TREATIES ARE OF THREE TYPES

(*i*) Quota Share Treaty

Under this method, the ceding insurer is bound to cede and the reinsurer is bound to accept a fixed share of every risk coming within the scope of the treaty. This treaty is used where the direct insurer is new in the field with little or no past experience or has had adverse experience in the past. This method is favourable to the reinsurers. The liability of the reinsurer attaches as soon as the ceding office assumes the risk. Then the ceding office furnishes the accepting office with full particulars of each cession, copies of proposal papers. It does not give the reinsurer an option of acceptance or rejection. It enables the reinsurer to consider any marked divergence of underwriting standards and if persistent to its disadvantage, it may indicate the need for revision or cancellation of the treaty in respect of new business.

***(ii)* The Surplus Treaty**

The purpose of this treaty is to reinsure the surplus of a risk beyond the amount of the ceding insurer's retention. Up to what extent the surplus can be reinsured is determined by the size of the treaty measured in terms of lines—not retention, There may be second surplus treaty to absorb the amounts which are beyond the capacity of the first surplus treaty.

The scope of treaty is defined with the scope of geographical area, class of business, etc. The liability of the insurer commences obligatorily and simultaneously with that of the ceding insurer as soon as retention of the ceding insurer is exceeded. The ceding insurer has the right to demand immediate payment from the reinsurer of the latter's share of any loss exceeding an agreed value.

There may be two problems under this method

(*a*) There may be selection against the reinsurer as the ceding insurer will retain more of the better type of business with type result that the bulk of the business under a treaty will be of an inferior nature.

(*b*) There may be problem of accumulation of acceptances.

***(iii)* Excess of Loss Treaty**

This method provides against catastrophic loss. The excess of loss reinsurance comes into operation when the total net loss suffered by the insured due to one event exceeds the figure agreed in the treaty. Such excess of the amount or a proportion of it, being paid by the reinsurer subject to a maximum limit. The net loss means the loss computed after taking into account recoveries from facultative and treaty reinsurers. If the total net loss exceeds the maximum limit provided in the treaty the excess amount is paid by the reinsurer. The premium depends upon the nature and extent of reinsurance.

ADVANTAGES OF TREATY-METHOD OVER FACULTATIVE

1. The Treaty-method provides obligatory and automatic nature of reinsurance acceptances. The reinsurer cannot decline to accept any cession coming within its scope.
2. The risk commences simultaneously with that of the ceding insurer. Under the facultative method, the reinsurance cover operates only from the time the reinsurer accepts the risk.
3. The treaty method involves much less clerical work and costs as compared to the costs involves in the facultative reinsurance.
4. The rights and obligations of each party are clearly defined in the treaty agreement whereas in facultative, it has not been so easy.
5. The treaty-method ensure a constant and regular flow of business.

4. "Pool or Syndicate Method"

Under this method, a number of insurer agrees to pool together all their business to a leading office and the payment is made by this leading office. The profit of this association is distributed amongst the insurers according to their shares to the business.

Reinsurance Treaty Contracts

A reinsurance treaty is a contract for reinsurances. A set of terms and conditions for a given class of business is provided and the reinsurance capacity is created for the reinsured to underwrite any risk which will be written in future. As opposed to facultative reinsurance it is meant to create capacity and it gives a reinsurance facility to cede risks after retentions. All future writing of risks has got an automatic, simultaneous and continuous reinsurance cover.

A reinsurance treaty is an agreement for twelve months between the reinsured on one part and the reinsurer on the other whereby the reinsured agrees to cede and the reinsurer agrees to accept the reinsurance business, pursuant to the provisions.

Treaty reinsurance is a contract for future reinsurance. It is offered before its inception and main terms of the treaty are specified on a SLIP. The prospective reinsurer goes through the slip and decides his acceptance. After its acceptance, the reinsurer signs one copy of the slip and returns it to the reinsured. Such signed slip is called a Binder, when a broker is given an order for placement of a treaty. When he completes his order he issues a Cover Note to the reinsured giving list of participating reinsurers along with slip terms of the treaty. The reinsured then issues full contract wording called Treaty Document or Treaty Wording to each reinsurer. There should not be any discrepancy between the slip terms and the terms in the contract. Any such discrepancy is to be cleared off before executing the Treaty Document.

In the event of any discrepancy between the slip and the treaty document discovered subsequent to signing, in strict legal sense, document supercedes the slip.

Reinsurance treaties are placed before the inception of the treaty year on the basis of a slip which summarises 'main' terms and conditions of the treaty arrangement, Generally, it contains name of the company, type of treaty, class of business, perils covered, territorial scope, retention, limits of reinsurance cession, commission percentage, profit comission formula and percentage, portfolio provision or reserve provision, if any with interest (less tax) on reserves, cash loss limits, frequency of accounts rendering and underwriting information with mention of specific exclusions essential for the reinsurer's acceptance. Once the treaty is placed on the basis of the slip, the broker prepares a cover note with names and shares of reinsurers. Such cover note serves the basis of reinsurance agreement and later on treaty wording is preparted. The treaty wording is to be corrected if there is any error in the main terms as compared to the slip.

If the slip is wrong and wording is correct, the ceding company must give satisfactory explanation and obtain agreement of the leader to be followed by other reinsurers.

Treaty wordings have a number of variations in form and structure but standardised London market clauses are common in use. American market treatise contain American market standard clauses. Every market has its own peculiar provisions of law and the wordings may vary. Again, wordings will vary according to type of treaties as shown in the following chart :

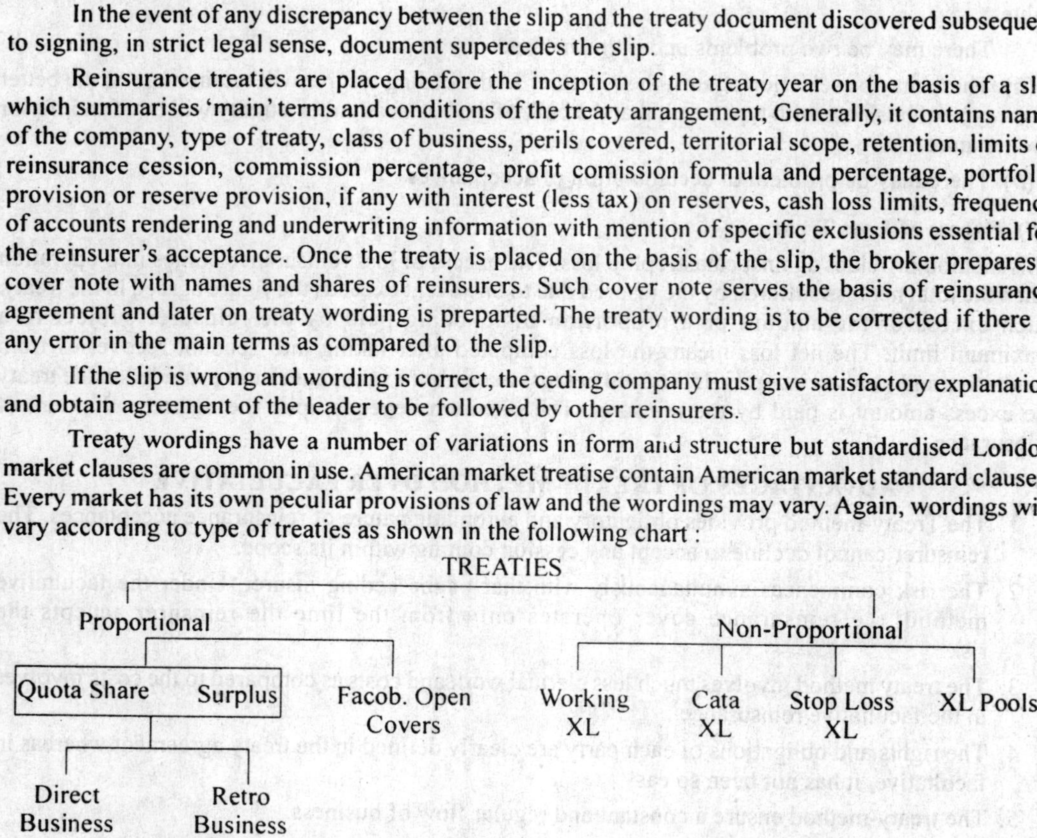

Again, from class to class there will be variation of clauses in treaty wordings. Therefore, the best way, according to me, is to generalise common pattern of treaty wording and then add special clauses peculiar to the type of treaty or particular class of business.

The Reinsurance Officers Association has made valuable contribution to standardise Treaty Wording in late seventies and eighties. With computerisation and standardization, Treaty Clauses are drafted and are available in a CD.

After WTC attack losses, leading global reinsurers like Munich Re/ Swiss Re have drafted Terrorism Exclusion Clauses, Political Risks Exclusion Clauses and introduced Treaty Slip formats with attached main clauses to avoid any misgiving. Such Treaty Slips are standardised by them and run into 100 pages instead of earlier slips of 3 or 4 pages.

Some Legal Conventions

Follow the Fortune Clause means Reinsurers follow Legal and Technical Fortune of the Reinsured in respect of claims settlements.

Reinsurers do not follow Ex-gratia payment of claims.

Claims Co-Operation Clauses provide that Reinsured must seek Reinsurer's advices before entering into litigation in respect of a disputed claim.

Claims payable by Reinsurers **can be more than TSI** to the extent of legal expenses, court awards, punitive damages etc.

Proportional Treaty Contract Clauses

- Time Clause
- Territorial Scope Clause
- Covered Perils Clause
- Exclusion Clause
- Operative Clause
- Premium Clause
- Commission Clause
- Claims Settlement Clause
- Borderaux Clause
- Accounts Clause
- Profit Commission Clause
- Inspection of Records Clause
- Error, Omissions and Alternation Clause
- Portfolio Adjustment Clause
- Reserves Clause
- Cash Loss Clause
- Arbitration Clause
- Intermediary Clause
- Insolvency Clause
- Currency Conversion Clause
- Cut-Through Clause
- Special Termination Clause like Sun-Set Clause

Changes by Way of Addendum

XL Treaties : Some clauses in addition to common clauses between proportional Treaties and XL Treaties.

- Definition of Loss Occurrence
- Ultimate Net Loss Clause
- Net Retained Lines Clause
- Definition of GNPI Clause
- Reinstatement Clause
- Extended Expiration Clause
- Notification of Claims and Loss Settlement Clause

QUESTIONS

1. Discuss the methods of reinsurance.
2. What are the principles of reinsurance?

33

PROGRESS OF FIRE INSURANCE

The fire insurance has not a long history. The real establishment of fire insurance came only after the Great Fire which took place in London in 1666. This fire lasted for four days and destroyed over 13,000 buildings, which awakened the people to the necessity for a form of protection against such calamities. The insurance received a real fillip only after the growth of commerce. There were a few companies which tried to be more scientific even in some cases, their rates remain standard even now. The decisions of law courts brought the principles of fire insurance to a standard form.

In India, the fire insurance business is not so developed as in foreign countries. With nationalisation of General Insurance Business, it is expected to have a new turn in annals of fire insurance. Before nationalisation the fire insurance had got the following position.

The Gross Premium to Fire Insurers had increased from Rs. 42.83 crores in 1969 to Rs. 51.52 crores in 1971 and further to Rs. 55.29 crores in 1972 and Rs. 117.64 crores in 1978. The share of Indian insurers to the gross premium has increased from 72.72 per cent in 1969 to 74.0 per cent in 1970 which declined to 73.6 per cent in 1971 and increased to 78.0 per cent in 1972. Thus, the Indian insurers were not experiencing established business and were not well off as compared to non-Indian insurers. The percentage of net premium received by Indian fire insurers to the total net premium had increased from 76.2 per cent in 1969 to 78.8 per cent in 1970 which declined slightly to 78.1 per cent in 1971 and increased to 78.9 per cent in 1972. The non-Indian insurers were losing their business up to 1970 and got a slight improvement in 1971. The net premium has increased from Rs. 33.59 crores in 1969 to Rs. 42.12 crores in 1971 and further to Rs. 50.98 crores in 1972 and Rs. 98.61 crores in 1977. The Indian insurers were far away in the field of fire insurance as compared to total general insurance. The share of Indian insurers to the net premium of total general insurance has increased from 80.2 per cent in 1969 to 81.7 per cent in 1971 and further to 82.8 per cent in 1972. The total net premium has increased from Rs. 91.34 crores in 1969 to Rs. 114.70 crores in 1971 and further to Rs. 136.57 crores in 1972 and Rs. 268.43 crores in 1977. It reveals that the Indian fire insurers were not doing more effective business than that of non-Indian insurers.

Indian Insurers

The percentage of net claims payable to net premium has declined to 36.3 per cent in 1970 to 33.5 per cent in 1971 and increased to 35.6 per cent in 1972 giving an increase in balance of income which has gone up from 29.1 per cent of net premium in 1970 to 36.0 per cent in 1971 and increased to 30.4 per cent in 1972. However, the net commission has increased from 8.8 per cent of net premium in 1970 to 9.0 per cent in 1971 and further to 13.0 per cent in 1972. It was a satisfactory state of affairs that the expenses of management had gone down from 21.6 per cent of net premium in 1970 to 20.1 per cent in 1971 and further to 19.5 per cent in 1972. But the percentage of reserve has declined from 5.5 per cent in 1970 to 3.8 per cent in 1971 and increased to 4.7 per cent in 1972. The Indian insurers were experiencing higher proportion of the net claims as compared to that of non-Indian insurers which declined from 29.7 per cent of net premium in 1970 to 22.6 per cent of net premium in 1971. The expenses of commission were missing in case of non-Indian insurers whereas the Indian insurers

Table 33.1 Premium: Fire Insurance Business (1969-1981)

Year	Gross Pemium					Net Premium					All Types of General Insurance (Net Premium)				
	Indian Insurers		Non-Indian Insurers		Total	Indian Insurers		Non-Indian Insurers		Total	Indian Insurers		Non-Indian Insurers		Total
	Rs.	%to total	Rs.	%to total	Rs.	Rs.	%to total	Rs.	%to total	Rs.	Rs.	%to total	Rs.	%to total	Rs.
1969	31.13	72.7	11.71	27.3	42.83	25.59	76.2	8.00	23.8	33.59	73.22	80.2	18.12	19.8	91.34
1970	35.17	74.0	12.35	26.0	47.52	30.72	78.8	8.25	21.2	38.97	84.44	81.5	19.13	18.5	103.57
1971	37.93	73.6	13.60	26.4	51.53	32.92	78.1	9.20	21.9	42.12	93.76	81.7	20.94	18.3	114.70
1972	43.11	78.0	12.18	22.0	55.29	40.21	78.9	10.76	21.1	50.98	113.11	82.8	23.45	17.2	136.57
1975					91.90					87.02					229.87
1977					110					117					326
1978					121					130					370
1979					124					130					398
1980					148					157					481
1981					180					189					599

Table 33.2 Ratio to Net Premium Income (1970-1981)

Year	Indian Insurers						Non-Indian Insurers			(In Percentage)		
	Net Claims Payable	*Net Commis-sion*	*Expenses of Mange-ment*	*Increase in Reserves*	*Misc. Income*	*Balance of Income*	*Net claims Payable*	*Net Commis-sion*	*Expenses of Manage-ment*	*Increase in Reserves*	*Misc Income*	*Balance of Income*
1970	36.5	8.8	21.6	5.5	2.1	29.1	29.7	9.2	42.1	1.2	0.2	36.3
1971	33.5	9.0	20.1	3.8	2.6	36.0	22.6	–12.1	42.2	4.2	0.6	43.4
1972	35.6	13.0	19.5	4.7	3.5	30.4	23.0	–4.2	37.0	5.8	—	38.3
1975	23.2	36.6	1.2	8.9	—	30.1						
1977	28.6	38.7	2.0	–0.7	—	31.4						
1978	26.8	38.5	2.1	6.0	—	26.6						
1980	30.5	36.1	1.9	7.4	—	24.1						
1981	32.8	35.7	1.6	10.0	—	19.9						

Table 33.3 Percentages of Gross Direct Premium (1970-1972)

Year	Indian Insurers						Non-Indian Insurers					
	Gross Claims Payable	*Direct Commis-sion*	*Expenses of Mange-ment*	*Increase in Reserves*	*Misc. Income*	*Balance of Income*	*Gross claims Payable*	*Direct Commis-sion*	*Expenses of Manage-ment*	*Increase in Reserves*	*Misc. Income*	*Balance of Income*
1970	25.1	4.2	24.1	4.5	1.6	43.5	24.8	4.4	28.9	2.1	0.2	40.7
1971	22.3	4.2	23.8	2.9	1.6	48.3	19.6	4.6	28.5	3.7	0.4	43.8
1972	23.6	4.3	24.1	2.9	2.0	47.0	19.8	5.1	32.6	4.6	—	47.0

were controlling their expenses of management. The non-Indian insurers were benefited by higher balance of income as compared to that of Indian Insurers.

The share of gross claims payable to gross direct premium has declined from 25.1 per cent in 1970 to 22.3 per cent in 1971 and increased to 23.6 per cent in 1972. The payment of direct commission remarked at the same level while the expenses of management have declined from 24.1 per cent of gross direct premium in 1970 to 23.8 per cent in 1971 but increased to 24.1 per cent in 1972. The proportion of miscellaneous income remained at the same level. Thus, the balance of income has increased from 43.5 per cent in 1970 to 48.3 per cent in 1971 and declined to 47.0 per cent in 1972.

The non-Indian insurers have saved more in the shape of gross claims payable. It has declined from 24.8 per cent in 1970 to 19.6 per cent of gross direct premium in 1971.

Direct commission in case of non-Indian insurers has increased. So, the balance of income has not increased so much in the case as had increased in the case of Indian insurers.

Table 33.4 Indian Insurers Business written outside India (1970-1972)

	1970	*1971*	*1972*
1. Gross Claims Payable	42.6	26.9	69.0
2. Direct Commission	28.8	28.0	29.1
3. Expenses and Management	25.4	26.4	23.4
4. Increase in reserve	–1.5	–1.8	0.9
5. Miscellaneous Income	3.2	6.8	13.3
6. Balance of Income	0.8	25.3	10.4

The gross claims payable outside India has declined from 42.6 per cent of gross direct premium in 1970 to 26.9 per cent in 1971 and increased to 69.0 per cent in 1972. It reveals that the Indian Insurers were able to save in payment of claims outside India. However, the expenses of management has increased from 25.4 per cent of gross direct premium in 1970 to 26.4 per cent in 1971 and decreased to 23.4 per cent in 1972. Miscellanenous Income has also increased. The balance of income has increased tremendously from 0.8 per cent in 1970 to 25.3 per cent of gross premium in 1971 but became negative in 1972.

Table 33.5 Net Premium Income (1975-1977)

Fire Insurance (*In crores Rs.*)

	1975	1977
In India	63.47	70.36
Outside India	23.55	28.25
Total	87.02	98.61

Total Insurance

	1975	1977
In India	166.12	196.97
Outside India	63.75	71.46
Total	229.87	268.43

The net premium income in case of fire insurance outside India has revealed that the business out of India has been increasing. The total net premium income in case of fire insurance has gone upto Rs. 98.61 crores in 1977.

PROGRESS AFTER NATIONALISATION

The progress of fire insurance after nationalisation has been analysed under 1. gross direct premium 2. net premium and 3. underwriting experiences.

1. Gross Direct Premium in Fire Insurance

The gross direct premium in fire insurance has increased from Rs. 96.00 crores in 1975 to Rs. 142.28 crores in 1980, Rs. 318.94 crores in 1985, Rs. 581.91 crores in 1988-89 and Rs. 1248.18 crores in 1994-95. New India has been the first company to procure maximum fire insurance business. It has increased its business from Rs. 38.79 crores in 1980 to Rs. 179.67 croress in 1988-89 by 463.19 per cent. Its gross premium was Rs. 415.44 crores in 1994-95. The business of United India increased by 405.99 per cent from Rs. 38.72 crores in 1980 to Rs. 157.20 crores in 1988-89 and its business was Rs. 327.19 crores in 1994-95. These companies have shown a higher rate of increase, as well as a higher amount of business. Oriental has been at the third place and increased its business from Rs. 34.27 crores in 1980 to Rs. 128.41crores in 1988-89 by 374.70 per cent. Its gross premium was Rs. 262.21 crores in 1994-95. National has increased its business from Rs. 30.50 crores in 1980 to Rs. 116.63 crores in 1988-89 by 382.39 per cent and Rs. 243.34 crores in 1994-95. New India has been at the top for increasing its gross direct premium with the help of a larger number of offices. National has been at the lowest ladder in all types of general insurance. It has the smallest number of offices and the lowest figure of employees. New India has the maximum number of employees. It has higher productivity also. The fire insurance business in India increased fastly after nationalisation.

Table 33.6 Gross Direct Premium in Fire Insurance

	GIC	*National*	*New India*	*Oriental*	*United India*	*Total*
1975	—	—	—	—	—	96.00
1980	—	30.50	38.79	34.27	38.72	142.28
1981	—	40.52	62.12	48.08	56.43	207.15
1982	—	47.63	72.44	57.81	63.22	241.10
1984	—	56.40	85.41	64.00	71.24	277.05
1985	—	66.29	95.29	72.48	84.88	318.94
1986	—	76.24	115.18	86.13	100.29	377.84
1987	—	86.68	129.75	94.43	115.93	426.79
1988-89*	—	116.63	179.67	128.41	157.20	581.91
1989-90*	—	118.44	187.17	128.33	155.04	588.98
1994-95	—	243.34	415.44	262.21	327.19	1248.18
1997-98	—	390.58	624.17	401.13	500.22	1916.10

2. Net Premium

Net premium of fire insurance has increased from Rs. 85 crores in 1973 to Rs. 106 crores in 1975, Rs. 157 crores in 1980, Rs. 354.02 crores in 1985, Rs. 493.88 crores in 1988-89 and Rs. 1333.21crores in 1994-95. New India has increased its net premium from Rs. 53.01 crores in 1982 to Rs. 142.20 crores in 1988-89 by 268.20 per cent whereas the net premium of Oriental increased from Rs. 38.21 crores in 1982 to Rs. 102.20 crores in 1988-89 by 267.47 per cent. United India increased its business from Rs. 48.44 crores in 1982 to Rs. 129.24 crores in 1988-89 by 266.80 per cent. National increased its net premium from Rs. 35.93 crores in 1982 to Rs. 108.40 crores in 1988-89 by 301.70 per cent. Thus, the National Company having the lowest amount of net premium has shown the highest rate of growth. New India has shown the second highest growth with the maximum amount of net premium. This company has been more efficient in expanding its fire insurance business than those of other companies. GIC has increased its reinsurance business from Rs. 38.27 crores in 1982 to Rs. 118.40

crores in 1988-89 by 309.38 per cent which stood at Rs. 277.26 crores in 1994-1995. The nationalised companies have shown satisfactory progress. Before nationalisation, the fire insurance was not popular in India. These four companies have taken special initiatives to increase fire insurance coverage to a larger market and have shown a higher amount of net premium in 1994-95, *i.e.,* Rs. 349.33 crores by New India, Rs. 269.79 crores by United India, Rs. 216.08 crores by Oriental and Rs. 220.75 crores by National Insurance.

Table 33.7 Net Premium in Fire Insurance

	GIC	*National*	*New India*	*Oriental*	*United India*	*Total*
1973						85
1975						106
1980						157
1982	38.27	35.93	53.01	38.21	48.44	213.86
1983	50.27	43.55	68.73	48.48	61.67	272.70
1984	65.80	50.90	71.29	54.32	67.14	309.45
1985	77.52	58.96	82.84	56.21	78.49	354.02
1986	78.76	67.15	95.88	67.65	81.65	391.09
1987	88.54	78.38	108.31	76.40	95.66	447.29
1988-89	118.40	108.40	142.20	102.20	129.24	493.88
1989-90	105.34	102.76	156.25	102.83	123.87	380.36
1994-95	277.26	220.75	349.33	216.08	269.79	1333.21
1997-98	377.80	320.81	504.59	323.68	392.08	1919.02

3. Underwriting Experiences

The underwriting profit of all the companies have increased from Rs. 63.69 crores in 1982 to Rs. 95.40 crores in 1988-89 by 149.79 per cent which raised to Rs. 1217.49 crores in 1994-95. The maximum amount of underwriting profit was Rs. 79.13 crores in United India in 1994-95. It is quite a satisfactory profit amount, as its underwriting profit to net premium has also been the highest in that year. National had the lowest amount of profit in 1982, 1988-89 and in 1994-95. Claims-ratio has been 44.7 per cent in 1982, 51.8 per cent in 1985, 50.3 per cent in 1988-89 and 63.3 per cent in 1994-95 in case of New India. It shows that the maximum claims-ratio has taken away a larger position of net income. Oriental had the least claims-ratio and the highest expense-ratio in 1988-89. New India and National faced higher claims-ratio. New India and Oriental has higher expenses-ratio also. The higher claims-ratios have been associated with the gross direct premium. Highest rate of profit in United India is attributed to lower claim and expenses-ratios in 1994-95.

Table 33.8 Underwriting Experience in Fire Insurance

	Net Premium Rs. Crores	*% to Net Premium* Net Claims Payable	*Net Commission*	*Expenses to Management*	*Miscellaneous Outgo*	*Unexpired Risks Reserve*	*Underwriting Profit/ Loss(–)*	*Underwriting Profit/ Loss (–) Rs. Crores*
1985								
GIC	77.52	46.8	34.4	1.7	–	7.6	9.5	7.37

Contd...

National	58.96	53.6	–3.0	29.9	0.4	6.8	13.1	7.71
New India	82.84	51.8	–1.2	28.4	–1.3	7.0	15.3	
Oriental	56.21	46.8	–6.7	35.5	–0.8	1.7	23.5	13.24
United India	78.49	57.5	–0.1	27.0	0.1	7.2	8.1	6.32
Total	354.02	51.5	5.7	23.6	–0.5	6.3	13.4	47.31
1989-90								
GIC	105.34	35.4	34.8	3.18	–	5.0	21.8	22.94
National	102.76	50.4	–	34.4	–	7.8	7.4	7.63
New India	156.25	36.0	–	28.3	–	13.6	21.2	33.12
Oriental	102.83	43.0	–	32.7	–	10.2	14.1	14.46
United India	132.83	40.2	–	26.7	–	8.3	24.8	30.80
Total	380.36	41.2	–	37.74	–	8.98	19.6	108.85
1994-95								
GIC	277.26	47.4	35.0	2.0	–0.4	6.0	10.0	28.02
National	220.75	61.49	–0.85	31.66	0.67	–1.45	5.59	12.34
New India	349.33	63.3	–14.8	31.9	–	4.5	15.1	52.74
Oriental	216.08	48.3	–7.2	33.9	–	4.0	21.0	45.26
United India	269.79	46.4	–8.3	29.0	–	3.6	29.3	79.13
Total	1333.21	58.38	+0.77	25.69	–	3.91	16.20	1217.49
1997-98								
GIC	377.86	37.1	34.6	1.8	–0.20	3.8	22.90	86.43
National	320.81	43.13	–5.0	32.2	–0.25	1.84	27.77	89.09
New India	504.59	41.04	–8.87	33.12	–8.5	–4.35	30.36	153.17
Oriental	323.68	38.7	–	34.2	27.9	4.1	31.4	101.63
United India	392.08	39.3	–8.0	35.7	+3.9	7.9	28.9	113.28

Progress of Fire Insurance After Privatisation Gross Premium Income of Fire Insurance

	National	*New India*	*Oriental India*	*United*	*Total*
In India					
1998-1999	423.10	681.80	434.8	548.20	2087.9
1999-2000	460.87	760.29	485.03	606.03	2312.22
2000-2001	408.09	654.24	471.28	526.11	2059.72
2001-2002	491.83	859.88	521.67	635.89	2504.97
Out of India					
1998-1999	2.9	84.7	6.30	1.00	94.9
1999-2000	3.07	87.04	6.66	1.02	97.8
2000-2001	4.21	125.15	8.94	1.11	139.1
2001-2002	4.32	246.81	9.36	1.09	261.58
Total of India					
1998-1999	426.00	766.5	441.10	549.20	2182.8
1999-2000	463.94	847.33	491.69	607.05	2409.9
2000-2001	412.30	779.39	480.22	527.22	2199.1
2001-2002	496.16	1106.70	531.03	636.98	2766.55

Financial Highlights of Fire Insurance

Year	Net Premium		Net Claim		Commission		Expenses of Management		Other Outgo		Increased in unexpired Risks reserve		Investment Income		Under writing Profit	
	Rs.	%	Rs.	%	Rs.	%	Rs.	%	Rs.	%	Rs.	%	Rs.	%	Rs.	%
General Insurance Corporation																
1998-1999	402.0		157.10	39	143.4	36	–	–	–	–	12.1	3.0			89.4	22
1999-2000	451.09		169.61	37.6	156.10	34.6	8.90	2.0	0.32	0.1	24.54	5.4			91.62	20.3
2000-2001	379.16		230.76	60.9	129.32	34.1	7.24	1.9	0.34	0.1	–35.96	–9.5			47.46	12.5
2001-2002	634.99		356.23	70.25	212.05	41.8	7.66	1.51	–1.61	–0.32			65.88	13.0	–67.25	–13.26
National																
1998-1999	354.7	83	163.10	46.0	113.5	32					17.0	5.0			61.1	17
1999-2000	395.51	85	163.18	41.3	–20.11	–5.08	141.35	35.7	0.29	0.07	20.38	5.15			90.42	22.86
2000-2001	365.51	89	179.03	49.0	–11.99	–3.28	121.03	33.1	0.35	0.09	–15.00	4.10			92.08	25.19
2001-2002	367.6		192.36	52.3	–17.66	–4.80	126.47	34.0	0.37	0.10	1.04	0.3	44.55	12.11	109.57	29.80
New India																
1998-1999	526.7	69	210.9	40.0	139.0	26.0					11.1	3.0			165.7	31.0
1999-2000	655.72	77	297.30	45.3	–48.95	–7.47	208.56	31.81			64.52	9.84			134.29	20.48
2000-2001	599.64	77	392.69	65.5	–1.25	–0.21	200.11	33.37			–28.04	–4.68	73.40		36.13	6.03
2001-2002	758.84		371.77	49.0	8.50	1.12	211.47	27.87			79.60	10.5	73.50		87.5	11.53

Financial Highlights of Fire Insurance

Year	Net Premium		Net Claim		Commission		Expenses of Management		Other Income		Increased in unexpired Risksin reserve		Investment Income		Under writing Profit	
	Rs.	%	Rs.	%	Rs.	%	Rs.	%	Rs.	%	Rs.	%	Rs.	%	Rs.	%
Oriental																
1998-1999	335.3	76.0	148.9	45.0	92.2	27					5.8	2.0			88.4	26.0
1999-2000	412.72	83.94	173.17	42.0	–3.98	–1.0	152.67	37.0	82.3		38.72	9.4	367.53		52.13	12.6
2000-2001	393.43	81.93	266.28	67.7	–19.55	–5.0	133.49	33.9	45.5		–9.64	–2.5	396.23		22.86	5.8
2001-2002	392.22	73.86	192.75	49.1	–186.4	–4.7	145.41	37.1			–0.61	–0.2	–3.36	0.80	125.29	31.9
United India																
1998-1999	426.0	78	169.1	40	105.3	25					17.0	4			134.6	31.0
1999-2000	487.65	80	159.32	32.7	–38.93	–7.98	163.80	33.59	–17.42		30.81	6.32	444.46		172.65	35.40
2000-2001	487.33	78	288.19	69.9	–38.34	–9.30	136.63	33.14	–55.80		–37.66	–9.13	484.29		63.51	15.40
2001-2002	480.28		175.60	36.6	–37.45		148.74		–11.48		33.98		63.93		211.86	
Indian Market Total																
1998-1999	2044.7	94	849.1	42.0	593.4	29					63.0	3			539.2	26
1999-2000	2402.7	100	962.6	40.6	720.0	30					178.9	–			541.2	23
2000-2001	215.4	98	1357.1	63.6	657.3	31					–126.3	6			262.0	10
2001-2002	2998.94			46.6												

Agency.. **FIRE INSURANCE PROPOSAL-FORM** C/Note No. ....

Code No.. Policy No. ....

THE ORIENTAL FIRE AND GENERAL INSURANCE COMPANY LIMITED

Specimen

1. Name of Proposer in full ....
(In case of mortgage or other interests the names of all parties should be given)

2. Address in full ....

3. Business or Profession ....

4. Period of Insurance: From .... 19 to 19

Please insure as follows:

5. **Sums Insured:**

(*a*) On the Building(s).. } Rs. ....

(*b*) On household goods, furniture, fixtures, fittings and personal effects .... Rs. ....

(*c*) On Merchandise and stock-in-trade consisting of (in shop or godown) .... Rs. ....

(*d*) On furniture, fixtures and fittings in trade .... Rs. ....

(*e*) On Machinery/Accessories .... Rs. ....

(*f*) On stock and stock-in-process .... Rs. ....

(*g*) On Electrical Installations .... Rs. ....

Contd....

(*h*) Any other items (to be specified) .... Rs. ....

Total Rs. ____________

Note:–(*i*) Unless otherwise stated in the Policy this Insurance does not cover Securities, Bond or Paper money or Claques, Obligations or Documents of any kind, Stamps or Stamp Collections, Coin Collections, Books of Accounts or Manuscripts or other business Books, Computer system records. Any curiosity or work of Art for an amount exceeding Rs. 250/-

(*ii*) It is desirable that the property is insured for its full value as only a proportionate amount will be recoverable in the event of under insurance.

(*iii*) If more than one building is to be Insured se ate particulars and Sum Insured must be given.

The above property is situated at:

(*a*) Name of Building and other means of identification ....

(*b*) Street No. and Name/Municipal No. .... (*c*) Town .... (*d*) District....................

6. Construction:

The said building consists of ground floor and .... upper floors.

The wall are built of ....<u>Cement</u> / <u>Set in lime mortar.</u> / mud The roof of ....<u>Rcc</u> laid over <u>steel</u> frame / timber

The walls are built of ....on ground floor and of .... on upper floors.

How are the premises lighted and heated ....
(i.e. electric light, oil, lanterns, etc.)

The said building belongs to .... of ....

7. Adjacent Buildings:

Is the building detached? If so, the distance from the nearest building

Contd....

If any of the adjacent buildings are within 50 feet, state the construction

	CONSTRUCTION Of Walls	Of Roof	How occupied
(*a*) Building to the North?	(*a*)		
(*b*) Building to the south?	(*b*)		
(*c*) Building to the East?	(*c*)		
(*d*) Building to the West?	(*d*)		

8. Use of Building

(*a*) Are you the sole occupier of the building? .. (*a*)

(*b*) Give full particulars of how each .. (*b*)

(*c*) If any goods are stored, state nature of such goods (*c*)

(Distinguish between hazardous and non-hazardous goods as per list overleaf)

(*d*) If any trade or process of manufacture is carried on, give full particulars. .. (*d*)

(*e*) If the proposed insurance applied to business premises state how long have you carried on business in the supremacies, and if in other premises, where and how long? (*e*)

Also state:

(*a*) How frequently stock is taken? .. (*a*)

(*b*) Whether a proper set of Account Books is kept? .. (*b*)

(*c*) Whether the Account Books are liked up in a fireproof Safe, or removed to another Building at all times when the Premises are not open for business purposes? (*c*)

Riot and Strike Yes/No

Contd....

9. Additional Perils:

Do you wish to insure against any additional perils given opposite? If so, please indicate Yes/No. ..

N.B.—An additional premium will be charged for covering these perils.

Malicious Damage	Yes/No
Earthquake, Fire and Shock	Yes/No
Flood & Inundation	Yes/No
Storm and Tempest	Yes/No
Aircraft Damage	Yes/No
Explosion	Yes/No.

10. Existing/Previous Insurance:

Has the property been previously insured or are there any existing insurances with this or any other Company of the same property? If so, state

Name of Company	Amount Insured	Premium	Period of Insurance From to

11. Previous Experience:

Has any Company—

(*a*) declined to insure this or any other property belonging to you? .. (*a*)

(*b*) Cancelled any of your Insurance Policy .. (*b*)

(*c*) refused to renew any Policy? If so, give details .. (*c*)

12. Have you over sustained loss by Fire, or any other Perils now proposed for insurance..? If so, state full particulars.

Name of the Co.	Sum Insured	Date of Fire	Amount of Loss

13. Do you wish the Insurances on buildings/machinery to be on the basis of Reinstatement Value? ..

Contd....

INDIAN INSURANCE ACT 1938

Section-3 " This proposal is only acceptable on the terms and conditions lodged with the Controller of Insurance."

DECLARATION

I/We hereby declare that the above statements are true and that I/We have withheld no information which might influence the acceptance of this Proposal. I/We further declare that the Sum proposed for Insurance represents and will be maintained at no less than full value of the property. I/We agree that this proposal shall be the basis of the Contract between me/us and the Company and deemed to be incorporated in the Policy.

Date.. *Signature of proposer:* ....

No Insurance in force until the Proposal has been accepted by the Company and the premium paid.

HAERRDOUS GOODS

The following is a list of goods deemed hazardous, but as other goods may be equally hazardous, this list is not necessarily a complete one. In case of doubt, reference may be made to the company.

Acetylene (liquid)
Acids of all kinds except Acetic (but not Glacial Acetic), Boric Citric and Tartaric
Aluminium Carbide, Bust, Powder and Resinate
Aniline
Areca Nuts (unshelled)
Asphalt
Bomboo Mats
Benzyl Acetate
Bichromate of potash
Biri Leaves

Blacks of all kinds [except as Provided in N.B 1(e)]
Calcium Carbide
Calcium Cyanamide, unless certified to contain not more than 0.3% of Carbide and packed in air-tight metal containers
Camphene
Camphor
Candles
Caustic Potash and Caustic Soda
"Celluloid" and "Xylonite" and other similar substances

Sopra, copra Cake and Copra neal
Carcass Sisal (loose and/or in bags)
Cotton (whether is fully pressed bales is otherwise)
Creosote
Diethyl Pthalare
Disinfectant Liquids and Liquid Insecticides with flash point Below 65.5°C (250°F)
Explosives of all kinds [including

Fish Guano and Fish Manure
Ganja
Ghee [other than Vegetable ghee in tins not exceeding 4.5 Kg. (10 1b.) in weight and/or in bottles]
Glycerine [except as provided in N. B. 1 (b)]
Grasses of all kinds and straw
Grass Mats (other than in fully-) Pressed bales)
Gunnies and/or Hessians (other

Contd....

Bi-Sulphide of Carbon
Bitumen (other than emulsified Bitumen containing not less than 45 per cent of water and packed in metal drums)
Inflammable Liquids
Inks, Printing
Jute (in fully-pressed bales or) otherwise)
Leaves, dried, of all kinds except tobacco)
Lime (Unslaked)
Liquefied petroleum Gas oil and other mineral products
Matches of all kinds
Matting, used
Metallic Potassium
Mungo
Nephthalene
Nitrates of all kinds

Charcoal
Chlorates of all kinds
Codilla
Coir Yarn, Coir matting and Coir rope
Nitro-cellulose plastics
Oils of all kinds [other than vegetable oils in tins not exceeding 4.5 kg. (10 lbs.) in weight and/or in bottles]
Oil Seed Cake (including Cotton Seed Cake)
Oil Seed meal
ble base
Paper, Waxed, Asphalted and Oiled
Perchlorate or Potash and Perchlorate of Soda
Permanganate of Potash and Permanganate Soda
Peroxide of Potash and Peroxide of Soda
Phosphorus
Pitch

Ammunition and Percussion caps) (except as provided in N. B. 1 (d)]
Films, non-safety
Fireworks of all kinds
Poisons, if stored on the same floor as or on floors above foodstuffs
Rags
Rayon fibres and rayon waste
Resins, natural
Rubber (unmanufactured) if stored with other goods
Rubber, Foam
Rubber Goods, Foam
Rubber, Waste and Reclaimed
Sawdist
Shoddy
Spirits of all kinds except potable Spirit in bottles and/or jars
Staple (man-made Fibre)
Stearine

than in fully pressed bales) (except as provided in N. B.) 1 (C))
Herbs, dried, of all kinds
Hyool
Sulfides, metallic, generally
Sulphur
Sulphur dyes or colour [excluding those packed in air tight metal vessels, labelled with a Certificate by the manufacturers that the dyes (or colours) contain at least 10 per cent inert inorganic salts]
Tallow (manufactured or unmanufactured)
Tar and/or its liquid products (other than in bottles)
Tarred Cloth, Felth, Rope, String and Twine
Varnish
Vegetable fibres of all kinds
Waste of all kinds (excluding silk and tea waste)
Wax of all kinds

N.B.1 The Following articles may be treated as non-hazardous if stored in the manner indicated:

(*a*) "Ruberoid" and/or "Pioneer" roofing material and/or small quantities of "Carbo lastic" and "Sealtite" in air-tight kegs.

(*c*) Loose Gunnies for packing purposes provided the quantity will never be largely in excess of that required for imediate packing purposes.

Contd....

(*b*) Glycerine in tins, cases, steel drums or other large packages subject to the following warranty: glyceriene will not be stored with or within 6 metres (20 feet) of permanganate of soda or potash nitrates, metallic sulfides, strong acids, fibres or fibrous goods or blacks such as lamp black."

(*d*) Loaded cartridges not exceeding in all 5% of total value of stockes.

(*e*) Gas Carbon Block if stored in a separate buidling.

(*f*) Betel Nuts (Unshelled).

(*g*) Rubber goods other than foam rubber goods.

(*h*) Titanium dioxide (Powder).

THE ORIENTAL FIRE AND GENERAL INSURANCE COMPANY LIMITED

(Incorporated in India)

Subsidiary to General Insurance Corporation of India

Refistered Office:

Jeevan Udyog, Asaf Ali Road, New Delhi

Issuing Officer:

PROHIBITION OF REBATING

Section 41 of the Insurance Act 1933 as amended provides as follows:-

1. No person shall allow or offer to allow, either directly or indirectly, as an induscement to any person to take out or renew or continue an insurance in respect of any kind of risk relating to lives or property in India, any rebate of the whole or part of the commission payable or any rebate of the premium shown on the Policy, nor shall any person taking out or renewing or continuing a Policy accept any rebate except such rebate as may be allowed in accordance with the published prospectuses or tables of the insurer.
2. Any person making default in complying with the provisions of this section shall be punishable with fine which may extend to five hundred rupess.

Specimen

FIRE INSURANCE

The Oriental Fire and General Insurance Company Limited

THE ORIENTAL FIRE AND GENERAL INSURANCE COMPANY LIMITED

Classes of Business Transacted

FIRE* MARINE * AVIATION

LOSS OF PROFITS

MOTOR CAR

WORKMENS COMPENSATION

BURGLARY

PERSONAL ACCIDENT

FIDELITY GUARANTEE

MONEY IN TRANSIT

ETC., ETC.

TheCompany's policies are liberal contracts free from restrictive conditions and the premiums charged are strictly moderate consistent with absolute security.

Quotations on Application to the company or its Agents

PART FIVE

MISCELLANEOUS INSURANCE

34

MOTOR INSURANCE BURGLARY AND PERSONAL ACCIDENT INSURANCE

Motor insurance got recently a great momentum. In the older times, persons, who were injured or killed through the negligence of the motorists, could not get financial redress either to them or to their legal heirs because no scheme of insurance was present at that time. To mitigate the financial hardship caused to the persons, the Motor Vehicles Act, 1939, as amended from time to time, has made it compulsory for the motorists to insure against the risk of liability to third parties.

The rate of premium is standardised because the business is tariff. No insurer can charge lower rates than the tariff rates and no insurer can grant benefits exceeding than those prescribed by the tariff.

Vehicles for the purpose of insurance are classified as below:

(*i*) Private Cars (not used for carrying passengers for hire or reward).

(*ii*) Commercial vehicles such as goods carrying vehicles, passenger vehicles, tractors and others.

(*iii*) Motor cycles, scooters and autocycles.

KINDS OF POLICIES

The policies under motor insurance are as follows:

(*i*) Act Liability only.

(*ii*) Third Party only.

(*iii*) Comprehensive Policy.

1. Act Policies

This policy is designed to meet the requirements of Motor Vehicles Act, 1939, which provides for compulsory insurance in regard to liabilities arising out of use of motor vehicles in a public place. This kind of policy is limited to bodily injury or death of the third parties. Section 95(2) of the Motor Vehicles Act lays down that a policy of insurance shall cover any liability incurred in respect of anyone accident up to the following limits:

(*i*) *Goods Vehicle.* Rs. 50,000 in all including the liabilities if arising under the W.C. Act, 1923, in respect of death of or bodily injury to employees (other than the driver) not exceeding six in number being carried in the vehicle. This means that liabilities if any towards driver and employees (above six) being carried in the vehicle under W.C. Act in addition to Rs. 50,000.

(*ii*) *Passenger Vehicles.* Vehicles in which passengers are carried:

(*a*) For hire or reward.

(*b*) By reason of or in pursuance of contract of employment.

(1) in respect of persons other than passengers carried for hire or reward—Rs. 50,000 in all.

(2) in respect of passengers.

Rs. 50,000 in all where the vehicle is registered to carry not more than 30 passenger;

Rs. 75,000 in all where the vehicle is registered to carry not less than 30 but not more than 60 passengers;

Rs. 1,00,000 in all where the vehicles are registered to carry more than 60 passengers; and

Subject to the limit aforesaid, Rs. 10,000 for each individual passenger where the vehicle is a motor car (used to carry not more than 6 passengers excluding the driver) and Rs. 5,000 for each individual passenger in any other case.

(*iii*) *Other Vehicles.* The amount of liability incurred except as provided otherwise.

The Act Policy besides the cover as required under the Motor Vehicles Act provides for indemnification of the claimants costs and expenses which the insured shall become legally liable to pay as also costs and expenses incurred with the written consent of the insurer. The policy may extend to indemnify any driver who is driving the motor vehicles on the Insured's order or with his permission provided, he is not entitled to indemnify under any other policy.

2. Third Party Policy

This policy cover the liabilities of the third parties who suffered less in connection with the damage of property and personal injury or death. Thus, this policy indemnifies the insured against his legal liability in respect of damage to property of third parties over and above 2000. The limit of liability is as follows:

(*a*) Private Car—Unlimited.

(*b*) Commercial Vehicle.

(*i*) Goods or passenger-carrying vehicles—Rs. 20,000.

(*ii*) Other miscellaneous or special type of vehicles—Rs. 50,000. Motor cycle—Unlimited.

The policy may be extended to include:

(*a*) fire,

(*b*) theft risks,

(*c*) legal liabilities to persons employed in connection with the operation and/or maintenance and/or loading and/or unloading of motor vehicles.

The private car policy extends to indemnify the insured (individual only) against legal liabilities incurred by him subject to limitations of indemnity whilst personally driving a private motor car. Private car policy covers legal liability of the insured to passengers (not for hire or reward) in the car although under the passengers (not for hire or reward) in the car although under the Motor Vehicles Act, it is not required to be covered. Liabilities arising while the motor cat is being used in private places is covered. The policy covers bodily injury or death, property damage and medical expenses. Due to the amendment to the Motor Vehicles Act, 1994, liability on third party claims has gone up as 'No fault' liability compensation has been enhanced and Structured Compensation has been introduced.

3. Comprehensive Policy

The comprehensive policy covers the following risks

1. Damage to car parts or body.
2. Removal charges for repairs.
3. Third Party Liabilities.
4. Costs and Expenses incurred with risk.
5. Repair Charges.
6. Medical expenses.

At the payment of extra premiums, the following risks are also insured:

(*i*) Death or injury to family members who are above 16 years and below 65 years.

(*ii*) Riots, strikes, thefts, larceny, etc.

(*iii*) Loss of Rugs.

Jald Rahat Yojna (Pre-litigation Settlements) has been introduced to help claimants to get payment of compensations without approaching courts. Structured Compensation formula has been used for quick settlements of claims.

PROCEDURES OF INSURANCE

The proposal form is completed for making proposal for motor insurance. The form is divided into three parts:

(*i*) *identification of vehicles*—registered number, horse-power shape and size, model, etc.

(*ii*) *Risk-information*—past insurance, type of policy got previously, equipments, vehicles.

(*iii*) *Declaration*—The declaration of true and full statement of the questions is made at the end of the policy.

Rating the Motor Insurance

Since the motor insurance is subject to tariff, basic premium is determined by the tariff association. Additional premium is added to the basic premium on the basis of shape, size, horse power, use, value of the motor car, etc. The higher the risk, the more will be the amount of premium. Rebate in premium is allowed if the insured has more than one car, is a member of Automobile Association and there was no loss in the previous years. The car was under the personal use and care of the owner.

Issue of Policy

As soon as the proposal form is accepted, cover note is issued. The cover note is a certificate of insurance although it cannot be used as a proof of insurance in a court of law. As soon as the policy is issued the cover note is cancelled.

Term of Insurance

The motor insurance policy is issued generally for one year. However, the policy can be issued for less than one year but the premium rate will be higher, *e.g.*, the premium rate is three-fourths of annual premium of the policy issued for six months.

Additions of Benefits

During the currency of policy, after payment of extra-premium additional benefits can be added to the original policy. Thus additional risks can be included to the original policy.

Change of Vehicle

The insured vehicles can be disposed of along with the policy. The term of policy will remain the same. The policy will continue up to the unexpired period with the purchaser of the car. Similarly the insured can replace another car under the same policy.

Furlough Concessions

When risk is reduced, the proportionate share of premium is returned or the period of coverage is extended by the excess premium. This is called 'furlough concessions'.

Settlement of Claims

As soon as the damage occurs, notice of that is given to the insurer. The evidence or eye-witness should be placed to the insurer. When the insurer is satisfied with the notice and evidence, he can issue claim form which is returned to the insured after completing it in all respects. Personal injury is also made in connection with the personal injury, damage to property, defence and prosecution.

Negligence of the Parties

The insurer will pay the amount of liability only when the insured is at negligence. In other words, the insurer shall pay only when the insured not legally liable for indemnification to third party.

Knock for Knock Agreement

This clause says that the liability of the insurers will be limited only to the liability to the insured. In this case the third party liabilities do not arise.

Halving Agreement

Under this agreement the loss of both partners (insured) and third party and is equally divided amongst the insurer.

Private Car

Cover is granted against the loss of or damage to motor car and its accessories whilst thereon, anywhere in India, caused by any of the following perils:

1. Accidental, external means
2. Fire
3. External explosion
4. Self-ignition.
5. Lighting
6. Frost
7. Burglary, house breaking or theft, and
8. Malicious act.

The cover is also operative whilst the car is in transit by road, rail, in land, waterway, lift or elevator.

The following are excluded:

(*i*) Consequential loss;
(*ii*) Depreciation;
(*iii*) Wear and tear; and
(*iv*) Mechanical or electrical breakdowns, failures or breakages.

Damage to tyres is ordinarily not payable. If, however, the insured car is also damaged at the same time, the damage to tyres is payable but the amount payable in that event is limited to 50% of the cost of replacement of the tyres. The exclusion applies to damage to tyres and, therefore, losses of tyres due to theft is payable.

If the motor car is disabled as a result of damage covered by the Policy, the insurers bear a reasonable cost of protecting the car and removing it to the nearest repairs, as also of redelivery to the insured. The amount so borne by the insurers is limited to Rs. 150 in respect of any one accident.

Normally, repairs arising out of damage covered by the policy can be carried out only after they are authorised by the insurers. In terms of this section of comprehensive policy, the insured may authorise the repair to the car provided that:

(*a*) the estimated cost of such repair does not exceed Rs. 300;
(*b*) the insurers are furnished forthwith a detailed estimate of the cost; and
(*c*) the insured gives the insurers every assistance to ensure that such repair is necessary and that the charge is reasonable.

Section II

It provides for the cover in respect of liability to the third parties.

Section III

If any bodily injury is caused to the insured or to any occupant of the motor car by violent accidental, external and visible means, as the direct result of an accident to the motor car, and if the insured incur medical expenses for the treatment of such injury, the medical expenses reasonably incurred by the insured in this behalf are reimbursed to him, subject to a limit of Rs. 350 in respect of any accident. A notable feature of this provision is that insured car must meet an accident in order to attract the benefit.

General Exceptions

The insurer is not liable under the policy in respect of:

(*i*) any accident, loss, damage and liability caused, sustained or incurred outside the Geographical Area specified in the schedule of the policy, *i.e.*, India. On request it can be extended to Nepal, Sikkim and Bhutan.

(*ii*) Any claim arising out of any contractual liability. If, however, the liability arises independent of the contract, the claim is payable.

(*iii*) Any claim arising whilst the vehicle is being:

(*a*) used otherwise than in accordance with the limitations as to use specified in the schedule of the policy; or

(*b*) driven by any person other than a driver described in the schedule of the policy.

(*iv*) Any claim arising after any variation in or termination of the insured's interest in the vehicles.

(*v*) Any claim directly or indirectly arising from:

(*a*) Ionising, radiations or contamination by radio-activity from any nuclear waste from the combustion of nuclear fuel.

(*b*) Nuclear weapons material.

(*c*) Flood, typhoon, hurricane, volcanic eruption, earthquakes or other convulsions of nature.

(*d*) war, invasion, act of foreign enemies, hostilities or war-like operations, civil war, strike, riot, civil commotion, invasion, rebellion, military or usurped power.

(*e*) Driving of the car under the influence of intoxicating liquor or drugs.

(*vi*) This does not cover use for hire or reward or gaining, pace-making, reliability trial, speed testing, the carriage of goods (other than samples) in connection with any trade or business or use for any purpose in connection with motor trade.

Extra Benefits

The policy may be extended to cover the following extra-benefits. On payment of additional premium:

(*i*) Accidents to insured or any named person (not less than 16 not more than 65 years of age) other than a paid driver or cleaner. This provide for specified scale of benefits in the nature of personal accident cover.

(*ii*) Accidents to insured and wife. Benefits and limits are similar to (*i*) above. In the event of both the insured and his wife being in the same car at the time of an accident the benefits will apply to insured and his wife to the extent of 50% only.

(*iii*) Accidents to unnamed passenger other than insured and his paid driver or cleaner. The benefits and age limits are similar to (*i*) above.

(*iv*) The legal liabilities to employees of the insured who may be travelling in or driving the employer's car (other than paid drivers).

(v) Business use by fellow employers. The policy extends to include use by persons other than insured for the business of the insured's employer and to indemnify such person. The additional premium depends upon whether use of one named person or use by unnamed is desired.

(vi) Accident to soldiers/sailors/airmen employed as by officers in their private capacity.

(vii) Trailers. Trailers may not be insured separately and the cover on the trailers must correspond to the cover on the car.

(viii) Riot and strikes.

(ix) Earthquake (fire and damage).

(x) Flood, inundation, typhoon and hurricane.

(xi) Rugs, coats and luggage.

(xii) Legal liability of passengers for acts of negligence; and

(xiii) Reliability trials and rallies.

Commercial Vehicles

The following points of difference between this policy and private car policy comprehensive policy should be noted:

(a) Loss of or damage to the vehicle and its accessories whilst thereon is not covered.

  (i) against the risk of frost.

  (ii) if loss or damage is due to overloading or strain or by explosion of the boiler or the motor vehicle.

(b) Loss or damage to accessories whilst on the vehicle is covered against the risk of burglary, house-breaking or theft only if the vehicle is stolen at the same time.

(c) The insured can authorise repairs if estimated cost of repairs does not exceed Rs. 150 (against Rs. 300 in the case of Private Car).

(d) There is a compulsory excess for each and every claim in respect of goods carrying vehicles, taxis or private car type vehicles plying for public hire and public passenger service vehicles, buses and motorised rickshaws.

(e) Loss of or damage to tyre, lamps, bumpers, mudguards and Painting of vehicles is not covered except in case of total loss.

Application of Limit of Indemnity

It is provided that if out of an accident indemnity is available to more than one person the limit of-indemnity prescribed by the policy applied to the total of the amounts payable to all eligible persons and if the limit is less than the total of the amounts due, the insured will have priority, in indemnification. For example, if an indemnity of Rs. 40,000 is due to the insured and of Rs. 20,000 to some other person against a limit of Rs. 50,000 under the policy, the insured will be paid Rs. 40,000 first and only the balance of Rs. 10.000 will be paid to the other person.

Motor Cycle

Under this policy following points should be noted:

(i) The cost of removal, etc., in one event of an accident is limited to Rs. 50;

(ii) The amount up to which the insured is authorised to repair is specified at Rs. 50; and

(iii) The polices covering motor scooters are made subject to an excess of Rs. 50 for each and every claim.

The liability in respect of death or bodily injury to any person being conveyed in or on the motor cycle is excluded. Such liability is, however, covered if the said person is being conveyed by reason of or in pursuance of a contract of employment in terms, and subject to, limitation of indemnity.

Under this section the insured individual is indemnified whilst personally driving a motor cycle not belonging to him and not hired to him under a Hire Purchase System. The extension, however, is not available for policies issued in respect of auto-cycles or mechanically assisted pedal cycles.

Extra Benefits

The following extra benefits may be granted on payment of additional premium:

(*a*) increase in the limit of indemnity for liability to public risks can be effected;

(*b*) full liability under Workmen's Compensation Act, 1923, Indian Fatal Accidents Act or at Common Law for accidents to paid driver, cleaner or conductor can be covered on payment of extra annual premium per head of Rs. 5; and

(*c*) in the case of vehicles plying for hire—(*i*) legal liability for loss or damage to goods caused by accident whilst being conveyed on the insured vehicle can be covered; (*ii*) Fire risk whilst vehicle is garage can be covered.

Underwriting Considerations

Relating to the insured and driver. The insured himself persents a great hazard in Motor insurance; he is likely to be the principal driver, particularly in private cars. Besides he will have a good deal of influence in the selection of other drivers. If the insured is a firm, the underwriter may have to examine the policy of the proposed firm in the matter of selection of drivers.

The business or profession of the insured is another important consideration, because this would show how, where and to what extent the vehicle will be used.

The nationality of the proposer is an underwriting consideration because:

(*i*) Foreigners are not accustomed to the local road and traffic conditions;

(*ii*) It is not always possible to ascertain their (insurer) history and driving experience;

(*iii*) In the event of an accident, they may not be available when they are required as witnesses for their own defence; and

(*iv*) Language difficulties may make them unsatisfactory witnesses.

Age of the driver is also important as very young persons are prone to accident as well as very old persons. The physical condition of the driver should also be considered when underwriting the risk. All convictions for driving offences are also material facts and must be reported to the insurers. The underwriter may ignore a series of convictions for minor offences but may take serious note of a single conviction for a major and dangerous offence. Drunken drivers have always been posing a serious problems to the under writers.

After examining the proposal and assessing the risk, the underwriter will decide on anyone or more of the following lines:

(*i*) accept the risk at normal terms,

(*ii*) increase the premium,

(*iii*) impose a compulsory excess in respect of each and every loss, under one or more sections of the policy,

(*iv*) restrict the cover to third party, fire and theft risk only,

(*v*) restrict the cover to third party risk only,

(*vi*) restrict the cover to act liability only, and

(*vii*) decline the risk. The declinature is, however, resorted to in exceptional circumstances only.

Table 34.1 Progress of Motor Insurance

(In Crores Rs.)

	Motor				*Miscellaneous*			
	Premium Less Reinsure-ance	*Expenses of Manage-ment*	*Incurred Claims*	*Working Results Profit/ Loss(–)*	*Premium Less Reinsurs-ance*	*Expenses of Manage-ment*	*Incurred Claims*	*Working Results Profit/ Loss(–)*
1991-92								
GIC*					368.08	4.42	294.71	–41.71
National*					302.02	77.49	224.58	–25.84
New India	334.07	71.74	293.48	–57.00	193.85	51.09	123.85	13.48
Oriental	219.11	86.46	184.36	–17.84	117.25	–	68.46	–
United India	230.97	50.90	213.33	–55.05	146.27	31.25	104.23	–0.11
Total	784.15	209.10	691.17	–129.89	1127.47	164.25	815.83	41.82
1994-95								
GIC*					553.61	5.30	585.12	–198.94
National*					428.04	107.25	452.22	–155.56
New India	510.28	96.32	633.71	–268.64	293.99	77.87	815.65	39.60
Oriental	314.25	122.70	439.49	–190.44	178.50	–	106.92	–
United India	321.70	57.44	452.29	–209.87	211.52	43.79	157.75	4.29
Total	1146.23	276.46	1525.49	–668.95	1665.66	234.21	2117.66	–310.61

* Includes Motor Insurance and Miscellaneous Insurances.

Motor insurance business in India has suffered loss to the extent of Rs. 668.95 crores in 1994-95 whereas other insurance has experienced loss of Rs. 310.61 crores.

The Motor Third Party business of Rs. 2114 crore is 11 per cent of the total market. It grew by Rs. 34 crore only in 2004-2005.

Table 34.2 Progress of Motor Insurance After IRDA

(Rs. in Crore)

	Company Performance All General Insurance		*Motor Business*		*Motor TP Business*		*Motor OD Business*	
	2003-04	*2004-05*	*2003-04*	*2004-05*	*2003-04*	*2004-05*	*2003-04*	*2004-05*
Earned Premium	1972	2122	916	1035	292	342	624	693
Net Incurred claims	1587 (80%)	1908 (90%)	981 (107%)	1238 (120%)	694 (238%)	832 (243%)	287 (46%)	406 (59%)
Net O/S claims	2552	2859	1984	2256	1825	2066	159	190

Source — IRDA Journal.

Table 34.3 Place of Motor Insurance in General Insurance

	Total Premium	*Motor Premium*	*Motor OD Premium*	*Motor TP Premium*
2003-04	16550	6460 (39%)	4377 (27%)	2080 (12%)
2004-05	18860	7500 (40%)	5384 (29%)	2114 (11%)

Motor insurance constitutes about 40% of total general insurance. Motor OD premium higher than motor TP premium whereas claims of TP insurance are very high *i.e.*, 243%.

Burglary Insurance

Burglary Insurance is one of the major classes of business underwritten in the miscellaneous department and accounts for a sizeable portion of the department's premium income. For the business house Burglary insurance is as essential as Fire insurance, as it enables them to recoup the losses suffered by them consequent on burglary or house breaking. In addition to the burglary policy, other types of policies giving wider covers have also been devised by the burglary department.

The main types of policies are as follows:

(*i*) Business Premises Policy,
(*ii*) Private Dwelling Policy,
(*iii*) Jewellary and Valuable Policy,
(*iv*) All Risk Policy, and
(*v*) Money in Transit Policy

Definitions

Burglary

The criminal law of the country does not speak of an offence called burglary. Hence it becomes necessary for the insurers to lay down in the policy the definition of the term. As normally understood burglary is:

(*a*) Theft of property from the premises following upon felonious entry of the said premises by violent and forcible means, or

(*b*) Theft by a person in the premises who subsequently breaks out by violent and forcible means provided there shall be visible marks made upon the premises at the place of such entry or exit by tools, explosives, electricity or chemicals. Use of force may be against property and person.

Theft

Indian Penal Code in Section 378 defines theft as follows: "whoever intending to take dishonestly any movable property out of the possession of any person without the consent of that person or of any person having for that purpose authority, moves that property in order to such taking is said to commit theft."

House-breaking

The word in practice is equal to 'Burglary'. Section 445 of the Indian Penal Code has laid down a definition of the term. A person is said to commit housebreaking who commits house trespass if he effects his entrance into the house (or any part of it), or if being in the house (or any part of it) for the purpose of committing an offence, or having committed an offence therein he quits the house, such entrance or exit being made by use of force in one of the six ways as described in the Indian Penal Code.

Robbery

Section 390 of the Indian Penal Code laid down, "If in order to the commission of or in committing of the theft or in carrying away property obtained by theft, the offender, for that end, voluntarily causes (or attempts to cause) to any person death or hurt or wrongful restraint or fear of instant death or hurt or wrongful restraint or fear of instant death or hurt or wrongful restraint".

Dacoity

Section 391 of the Indian Penal Code states dacoity as "where five or more persons conjointly commit or attempt to commit a robbery or are present and aid such commission or attempt, every one of them is said to commit dacoity"

Coverage

Business premises are generally covered against burglary and house breaking only. Mere theft without the use of force and violence is not covered, robbery and dacoity being aggravated forms of theft. It also covers risk of holdup. Burglary and house breaking fall within the scope of this cover. Under policies issued for private dwellings, the contents are covered against burglary, house-breaking and theft risks. Similarly Jewellery and valuables are also insured in the same manner.

Money in Transit

Policies, as a matter of rule, cover robbery, hold-up and dacoity in addition to burglary, house-breaking and theft.

Business Premises Insurance Policies

Policies issued to business premises cover stock-in-trade, goods in trust or on commission, fixtures and fittings, tools of trade such as typewriters, calculators and other similar property and cash and currency notes in locked safe against the risk of burglary and house-breaking. Loss or damage to contents or to any part of the building caused by burglary or any attempt therefore is also covered. In regard to stock-in-trade and other goods the policy may be issued on full value basis or on "first loss" basis.

A "*First Loss*" 'Policy insures the property up to a specified amount only which is calculated to be the maximum likely loss on any one occasion. This type of policy is taken where a total loss is a physical impossibility. First loss policies are usually taken for bulk commodities. The amount insured is always specified as a certain percentage of the full value, say, 10% or 12.5% of the full value.

The amount of premium-loss reinsurance was Rs. 16.60 crores by New India in 1994-95. It has got profit of Rs. 12.12 crores in that year.

Cash-in-Safe Insurance

The cover includes only when the cash is secured in a safe and is granted only if the safe is burglar proof and is of an approved make and design. Safe which is permanently installed in the premises is a better risk than a safe which can be shifted. The cover is granted subject to the following two clauses.

(*a*) The loss of cash obstructed from the safe following the use of the key to the said safe or any duplicate these of belonging to the insured is not covered unless such key has been obtained by violence or through means of force. The use of force need not necessarily be against the person or an individual. It can be against property as well. Thus cupboard is removed after forcing open the cupboard, the loss is covered by the policy.

(*b*) A complete list of the amount of cash in safe should be kept secure in some places other than the safe and the liability of the insurer is limited to the amount actually shown by such records.

All Risks (Jewellery and Valuables) Insurance

Policies under this form of insurance cover risks in respect of jewellery, plate, watches, personal ornaments and other valuables. Loss or damage by any accident or misfortune including fire, theft, robbery from the person, defective settings or fastening and accidental damage are thus covered. The policies do not, however, cover loss or damage:

(*i*) occasioned by or in consequence of war, invasion, act of foreign enemy, hostilities, civil war, nuting, rebellion, revolution, insurrection, military or usurped power, riot, civil commotion, earth-quake or other convulsions of nature;

(*ii*) caused by or arising from any process of repairing, restoring or renovating any property insured;

(*iii*) due to moth, wildew, wear or other deterioration or inherent defect in any property insured. The insurance is applicable in all places within the geographical limits provided for in the policy.

Exclusions

The exceptions peçuliar to a burglary (business premises) policy are:

(*i*) loss or damage where any member of the insured's household or his business staff is concerned as principal or accessory or resulting from any act committed by any other person lawfully on the premises wherein the property may happen to be;

(*ii*) loss or damage which can be insured against by a fire or a plat glass or a motor insurance policy;

(*iii*) loss of or damage to deeds, bonds, bills of exchange, promissory notes, cash, treasury, bank notes, cheques, securities for money, stamps, stamp collections, books of accounts, manuscripts, documents of any kind and medals and coins, unless specially mentioned and agreed to be covered.

Extension Under the Policy

An extension of the policy frequently sought is in respect of riot and strike damage which is a common exclusion in all policies. Riot as included in the policy is deemed to mean riot as defined in the Indian Penal Code.

Insurance of Money in Transit

This is a modified version of Burglary Insurance covering money or securities in transit between the insured's premises and bank or post office or other specified place or between the insured's (main) premises and branch premises. The cover is granted only to commercial and industrial establishments.

The coverage of money in transit policy is as below:

(*a*) Wages in transit from bank to insured's premises.

(*b*) Cash in transit from insured's premises to post office for purchase of postal orders, money orders and postage or Revenue Stamps.

(*c*) Postal orders, money orders and postage or revenue stamps in transit from Post Office to insured premises.

(*d*) Wages in transit from the insured's (main) premises to insured branch premises.

(*e*) Cash other than wages in transit from Bank to insured's premises from insured's's to bank and between insured's premises and the insured's branch premises.

(*f*) Cheques, bills of exchange, money orders and postal orders in transit from the insured's premises to bank.

(*g*) Cash collected by employees from the time of collection during rounds and until delivered at the insured's premises or bank on the day of collection.

(*h*) Cash (other than wages) secured in locked safe when the insured's premises or closed.

(*i*) Cash (other than wages) contained in the insured's premises whilst occupied for business purposes.

In a money-in-transit policy, two sums are significant:

(*i*) Limit of the insurer's liability for anyone loss; and

(*ii*) Estimated amount in transit during the year.

Extension (Infidelity of Employees)

The normal policy does not cover loss to the insured arising through the acts of dishonesty by the employees entrusted with the carrying of the money. The policy is extended at additional premium to cover any loss to the insured of the property insured by any act of fraud or dishonesty committed by the employees or employees carrying the property. This is known as 'Infidelity Extension'.

UNDERWRITING

Underwriting of burglary insurance includes the following steps:

1. Nature of Insured property

The value of the property and the weight and/or volume of the property are two aspects of risk considerations. Small volume/weight having high value are attached more risks of burglary.

2. Premises in which the insured property is housed

The class of construction of the premises situation of the premises etc. are considered for risk evaluation premises situated in densely populated areas are less risk prone than those situated in lonely areas.

3. Occupancies

It is noted how many hours the premises are occupied. The hours for which the premises are unoccupied are noted.

4. Safety Measures

Safety measures if adequately taken will give less risk.

5. History

History of post claim and insurance policies are considered for risk evaluation.

6. Moral Hazard

Underwriters take into consideration moral hazard of the proposer. Survey of heavy sum assured and special attributes thereof are taken into consideration.

7. Books of Accounts

Books of accounts enable underwriter to assets correctly amount of liability. Information relating to stock taking and airdib is useful for the purpose.

8. Identification

Correct description of goods are given for proper identification.

9. Conditions

Whether sum insured have been given separately against the insured's own stock, similar goods held in trust or on commission, furniture etc., cash or valuables in safe.

Survey Report

Acceptance and the terms of cover of are based on the report given by the surveyors for the following particulars:

(*i*) Proposer's name, address and business
(*ii*) Exact description of the property proposed for insurance
(*iii*) Highest value of a single article
(*iv*) Whether the stock books are properly maintained and whether the exact amount of loss can be ascertained
(*v*) Maximum possible loss
(*vi*) Whether the proposer resides on the premises
(*vii*) Hours and time the premises are left unoccupied
(*viii*) History of burglary in the locality and steps taken to present them
(*ix*) Number of doors, windows, skylights and other openings

(*x*) Whether there is special precautions like alarms, collapsible gates, warning clock etc.

(*xi*) Points of entry, exit, guards etc.

Rating

Rating is done as per standard percent of the sum assured. The rate varies according to type of goods location and construction of premises, security measures such as close circuit T.V., armed guard, locked Bars, electronic alarms.

Claim Procedures

Immediate notice is given to the insurer about the circumstance of loss, happening or event giving rise or likely to give rise to a claim under the policy. Within 7 days of the notice, the insured has to lodge with the insurer a detail statement in writing of the loss or damage with an estimate of the intrinsic value of each article lost and the amount of damage sustained.

Prevention and Minimisation of Loss

The insured is required to exercise reasonable steps to safeguard the property insured and to secure all doors windows and upper openings.

The insured has to give immediate notice to the police. He will take all reasonable steps to apprehend the guilty and to recover property lost. If insurer requires the insured has to take steps for the prosecution and conviction of the guilty persons to recover the property. The expenses will be borne by the insurer.

Indemnification of Loss

The insurer may reinstate replace, repair the property or premises, as the case may be instead of paying the amount of the loss or damage. The doctrine of subrogation applies after payment is made.

The insurer will pay only pro rata of the loss or damage. Where the property insured at the time of loss or damage shall be greater value than the sum insured thereon.

BURGLARLY (PRIVATE DWELLINGS) INSURANCE

Similar to Burglarly (Business Premises) Insurance Burglarly insurance is also applicable to property of private dwellings. The policy does not pay more than the value of any particular article. The private dwellings insurance may be All Risk Insurances and Baggage Insurance.

All Risks Insurance Policy

The policy seeks to cover loss or damage by fire or burglary or theft or any other accidental or fortuitous circumstances.

The policy is suitable for Jeweller, valuables, antiques, paintings, watches, clocks, works of art cameras, trumpets, and other similar articles. The insured values in respect of these items are decided on an agreed value basis. For Jewellery, gold and silver plates, the values are fixed in consultation with a professional Jewellery appraiser.

Full description of jewellery, number of precious stones, amount of gold, type of ornament and valuation made by reliable recognised jeweller.

Baggage Insurance Policy

This policy provides indemnity to the insured to the extent of the insurisic value of the accompanied personal baggage of the insured or member of his family while the insured is travelling on tour and/or holiday.

Exclusions:

The specific exclusions are loss or damage

(*i*) Occurring during routine travel

(*ii*) Articles which do not form part of the baggage when the journey commenced, unless declared and accepted by the insurer.

(*iii*) Articles of consumable and perishable nature.

(*iv*) Loss of articles l:ke sticks, umbrellas etc. properly in use on the voyage or journey, articles or clothes whilst being worn or carried out.

(*v*) Loss arising from leakage, spilling of liquids, oils etc.

(*vi*) Damage caused by repairing or renovating.

(*vii*) Loss or damage arising through delay detention or confiscation by customs or by other authorities.

Conditions

1. Baggage must be insured for its full value condition of average will apply.
2. The cover inscripts from the time travel begins and cover continues during the stay also at intermediate places and destination and ends at the original place, expires the policy-period.
3. The value is specifically declared when the article is fragile and high value in nature. Premium increases if the value is very high.
4. Notice has to be sent to the nearest office of the company during the journey. Secondly, a written notice on Railway Authorities, Shipping Co. Airline or Hotel may be necessary where the loss has taken place.
5. Notice to police in the case of theft is required to investigate into the matter.

Underwriting

The baggage insurance policy covers accompanied baggage (not dealer's stock or traveller's samples) during specified journey. Which includes air, sea, rail or road travel undertaken by the insured.

Proposal form fully describes the content and value of each package. All descriptions and individual values should be given for jewellery.

It is necessary to have a full inventory and individual valuation of each item. It is essential to have adequate valuation at the time when the policy is effected. Separate valuations are insisted for each item such as cameras, watches, jewellery etc.

Claims:

The following steps are involved for claims settlement

(*i*) an immediate written notice of the occurrence must be given for claim.

(*ii*) It is necessary to take all possible steps to discover the guilty person and to recover the stolen property.

(*iii*) It is necessary to furnish such evidence of the loss as the insurers may require.

(*iv*) It is to furnish to the insurers the claims form duly completed by him.

(*v*) It is to cooperate fully with the insurers and with the claims survey/inspection who many be appointed by insurer.

(*vi*) It is to abstain form fraud or intentional exaggeration in the particulars of the claims.

(*vii*) Claim form includes.

(*a*) The description and value of the property stolen.

(*b*) Allowance has to be made for depreciation and wear and tear to arrive at the amount of the claim.

(*c*) Details are required in respect of date and time of loss.

(*viii*) The claim is processed on the basis of the claim form, survey report, the policies report and the various vouchers, proof of ownership and other evidence submitted by the insured to substantiate the loss.

(*ix*) There must be evidence of a broken lock, broken window, broken roof etc. to substantiate the claim. These would be violent and forcible entry.

PERSONAL ACCIDENT INSURANCE

Introduction

Personal accident insurance is one of the popular classes of accident insurance and as a supplement to life insurance, it provides an ideal protection against death or disability. Though the majority of the policies still issued are to individuals, it has found favour with employers who offer personal accident insurance benefits as a part of the service benefits to their employees.

Due to rapid industrialisation, and more and more use of complex machinery, industrial accidents are more frequent. To cater to the varying and increasing needs, different forms of cover are available. Individuals are granted this cover under an individual personal accident insurance' policy. For a group of individuals, the insures have devised a group personal accident insurance policy.

Coverage

Personal accident policy provides for specific benefits of insured person suffering injury, resulting in death or disablement arising solely and directly from an accident caused by violent external and visible means. The bodily injury within twelve calendar months (period varies) from occurrence thereof shall solely and directly cause or result in—

1. Death,

2. Loss by Physical Separation at or above the wrist or ankle of:

(*i*) both hands or feet or one hand and one foot (known as loss of limbs).

(*ii*) complete and irrecoverable loss of sight in both eyes.

(*iii*) loss of one limb and complete and irrecoverable loss of sight in one eye.

In these above cases capital sum insured is given.

(*iv*) loss of one limb or complete and recoverable loss of sight of one eye—in this regard 50% of capital sum insured.

3. Temporary total disablement—in this respect 33% of capital sum insured, maximum Rs. 500 per week.

Features of the Policy

1. The maximum liability of the insurer is the capital sum insured.
2. The amount of the claim is payable to the insured person or his legal representative in case of death. Appointment of nominee is desirable.
3. No weekly compensation shall become payable, until total amount shall have been ascertained and agreed.
4. Personal accidents cover (other than coupon insurance) with another insurer must be within the knowledge and written permission of the insurer or else policy becomes void.
5. Age limits between 16 and 25 years. The upper age limit may be relaxed in certain cases on merit.

Rating

The rate of premium to be charged depends mainly on the type of cover desired and the insured person's occupation. This is a non-tariff business. The rates or premium charged by the various insurers for the same risk may, therefore, vary. The proposal and the policy forms used by the various insurers also differ widely. The rates are usually charged per mile of the capital sum insured by the policy.

Extensions of Policy (Motor cycling)

In most parts of India, motor cycling and scooter riding have become so common that if accidents arising out using them are not covered, the policy is hardly of any practical significance. Most of the insurers are, therefore, willing to grant cover against these risks with or without additional premium.

Exceptions

1. War and kindered risk, riot, strike and civil commotion or intentional self-injury whether criminal or not.
2. Injury sustained whilst the insured person is under influence of intoxicants or is suffering from insanity.
3. Injury occasioned by or contributed to by venereal disease or pregnancy.
4. Flying for the purpose of any trade of technical operation or as a member or an aircrew or any other aerial activities.
5. Hunting, stable-chasing, racing of any kind (other than one foot), rugby, football, polo, motor cycling or winter sports, underwater pastime or pot-holding except in so far as the company have by endorsement agreed to extend the insurance.

Classification of Occupations

Profession or occupation is an important factor to guide the underwriter as regards assessment of risk in each case and consequently it stands to serve as the basis of rating. A representative classification is given as under:

Class I—Accountants, Bankers, Member of Legal and Medical Profession, teachers, consulting engineers, mercantile assistants and those engaged in executive, administrative, etc., duties.

Class II —Architects, engineers (Superintendents) only, Planters, Salesmen and master tradesmen who supervise but do not do manual work.

Class III—Engineer (superintending and working), engineering contractors engaged in manual work not involving unusual hazards.

Class IV—Any occupation involving unusual hazards.

It is not possible to give an exhaustive list and the classification given above is only indicative of the considerations involved.

Personal Accident and Specified Diseases Insurance

In addition to the death and disablement arising out of accidental bodily injury, insurance may also provide for benefits for disablement arising out of specified diseases. This is provided by issuing personal accident and specified diseases insurance policies. These policies contain the usual personal accident.

Extensions

Certain diseases like malaria, influenza, etc., which are not included in the list of diseases specified in the policy, can be included within the scope of the cover afforded by the policy, on payment of additional premium. The additional premium is usually charged @ 0.1 % of the capitalism insured for each additional disease included.

Underwriting Consideration

Underwriting involves the selection of risks for insurance. Based on the information collected, the underwriter has to decide to accept, particular risk and if he decides to accept, at what premium and on what terms. In fulfilling this task in respect of personal accident insurance the underwriter is guided broadly by the following considerations:

(*i*) age of the insured person;

(*ii*) health and physical build of the insured person;

(*iii*) occupation of the insured person;

(*iv*) other pursuits of the insured person; and

(*v*) medical history and family history in case cover is extended to diseases.

Medical Benefits and Hospitalisation Schemes

As part of their service benefits, many employers reimburse to their employees the expenses incurred by their employees for medical treatment. Insurers have, therefore, devised medical benefits and hospitalization schemes which they offer to the employers. There is a tendency on the part of many employers to buy such insurance schemes rather than electing to reimburse the employees from their funds, because such scheme reduce the cost of providing medical facilities for the employees and cut out clerical work for them.

35

MISCELLANEOUS FORM OF INSURANCE

EMPLOYERS' LIABILITY INSURANCE

Introduction

The genesis of employers' liability insurance can be traced to the industrial development. It was, however, thought the employer had no more than ordinary duty of care to his employees. Hence an employee injured as a result of negligent on the part of his employer had just the same right of action against the employer for damage as any other citizen had. The employer's duty of care to his employees was to provide:

(*a*) a safe place of work;

(*b*) proper plant, tools, machinery and working implements and for their maintenance in good working order,

(*c*) a safe system of work with adequate warning to the employee of any danger of which he might not be aware; and

(*d*) competent and sober fellow employees.

It would appear that the duties of an employer were wide enough to encompass all situations in which an employee might be placed that would give him automatically a right of action against the employer and enable him to obtain damages.

The underwriting by insurers of employers' liability arising under the status or in common law is a comparatively later development. In India most employers' liability policies are issued in respect of their liability under the Fatal Accidents Act 1955, the Workmen's Compensation Act 1923 and common law. In India these are referred to as workmen's compensation policies.

The Fatal Accident Act was nevertheless an inadequate measure, as it made no provision for the employees who were not killed but were maimed and totally or partially disabled. The Workmen's Compensation Act 1923 filled the gap and also made employers' liability more neigous. Though the liability of employer under the Act for accidental injuries sustained by his workmen arising out of and in the course of employment is absolute, in certain circumstances employer is not liable. Section 3 of the Workmen's Compensation Act 1923 provides that the employer is not liable to pay compensation in respect of any injury not resulting in death caused by an accident which is directly attributable to—

1. the workmen having been at the time of injury under the influence of drink or drugs,
2. the wilful disobedience of the workmen to an order expressly given or a rule expressly framed, for the purpose of securing the safety of the workmen, or,
3. the wilful removal or disregard by the workman of any safetyguard or other device which he knew to have been provided for the purpose of securing the safety of the workman.

An employment injury which may be personal injury sustained or an occupational disease specified in the Workmen's Compensation Act contracted by a workman in the course of fulfilling his duties to his employer. An occupational disease peculiar to an employment which a person exposed to the vigours of that employment contracts.

Classification of Risk and Coverage

In India the business of Workmen's Compensation Insurance is governed and regulated as to underwriting coverage, proposal and policy forms and endorsements by the Workmen's Compensation Tariff. The tariff is administered by the tariff advisory committee, which is a statutory body set up under Section 54 of the Insurance Act 1938. The tariff applies to all policies issued to employees to provide reimbursements of compensation to their employees in respect of accidents and occupational diseases. The tariff provides three forms of insurance, viz.—

Table 'A'

Table 'B'

Table 'C'

Whatever may be the form of cover issued, no policy is to be issued to cover liability in excess of that provided by the tariff forms of policies and endorsements unless specifically authorised and no policy is to be issued which does not include all employees (other than individuals employed on monthly wages exceeding Rs. 500) in the Insured's Service. The premium to be paid has to be calculated on the total wages of the employees, since the actual wages may not be available in advance, a provisional premium calculated on the estimate of the total wages is paid and at the expiry of the policy the actual premium is calculated on the actual total wages and the difference between the provisional and the actual premium is made good a further payment by the insured or a refund by the insurers as the case may be.

Policy Form

The Policy form is prescribed by the tariff and all insurers have to use the form. The wording is the same for all the three **tables A, B and C except that when a table 'A' policy is to be issued**, the laws in respect of which the policy is issued are to be mentioned in the schedule in the space provided therefore viz. the Workmen's Compensation Act, 1923 and subsequent amendments to the said Act prior to the date of the issue of the policy and the Fatal Accident Act 1855.

Extensions to the Policy

The extensions granted are as follows:

(*i*) The tariff permits the inclusion of the risk of the insured in respect of the empolyees of contractors at a premium calculated at the tariff rate for the work contracted for;

(*ii*) Where the insured are themselves contractors to a certain Principal, policy may be extended to include the vicarious/liability of the principal.

(*iii*) Occasional domestic labour may be covered for common law (tortious) liability at an additional premium of 25% of the premium charged for the permanent servants. When no permanent servants the charge for occasional domestic labour must be a minimum of Rs. 6.25 to cover legal liability only.

(*iv*) Table 'A' and 'C' policies may be extended on the following scale and provide for the payment of medical, surgical or hospital expenses (including cost of transport to hospitals) incurred by the insured.

Limit (Per case)	Additional Premium
Rs. 50/	12½%
Rs. 75/	15%
Rs. 100/	17½%
Rs. 250/	20%
Rs. 500/	25%

The Proposal Form

An employer desirous of insuring nimself against his liability arising under the Workmen's Compensation Act, 1923, the Employer's Liability Act 1938, the Common Law and Fatal Accident Act, 1855, has to approach the insurer for this purpose. He has to fill in and submit a proposal form to the insurer. The particulars required in this form are the proposer's name, proposer's business, address, proposer's trade or occupation, particular hours work, description of employees, estimated number of employees, estimated annual wages, salaries and other earnings, insurance cover required and other particulars regarding the nature of the work done in the employer's premises. The proposer has also to state whether any proposal or renewal of insurance of his liability was never declined or (withdrawn). Finally he has to sign the declaration to the effect that every information supplied in the proposal form is correct. Any concealment or misstatement of material facts will render the policy void.

Duration

The tariff makes it compulsory for all policies to be issued for 12 months. The exceptions are:

1. Policies which may be issued for a period in excess of 12 months where an additional odd period is required to make a policy renewable on a particular date to meet the convenience of the insured.
2. Policies which may be issued for a period less than 12 months in cases of specific contracts or work which will be completed in less than 12 months provided the policies are written for the full period involved.

Employees State Insurance Act, 1948

The scheme envisaged under the Act applies compulsorily to all persons working in factories using power and employing twenty or more persons but seasonal factories are excluded; so also the dependents of workers in perennial factories. The scheme is applicable only to Industrial workers and excludes agricultural labourers. The scheme provide for five-fold benefits, namely, medical, sickness, maternity, disablement and dependents. Medical treatment is provided free of charges to the sick insured persons; and this medical cost is provided through the panel system of the doctors. Under this system, panel of approved doctors is drawn up and the insured person is given the choice to select his own doctor from among the list. The insured is qualified to receive benefit during the benefit period if he has paid at least a minimum number of twelve weekly payments in the course of sixteen weeks or two-thirds of the number of week in the 'Contribution period'. The amount of cash sickness benefit is about half the daily wage of the insured person. He can claim it for a maximum of fifty-six days in any period of 365 days.

For the administration of Employees State Insurance Scheme, a statutory corporation known as the Employees State Insurance Corporation has been established. The scheme is contributory, the contributions to be paid by both the employcr and employees. The amounts of compensation are on a scale more liberal than those payable under the Workmen's Compensation Act. The Employees State Insurance Act comes into force at the very region where it is interested to extend by a notification by the Government of India.

In the case of risk coming under the purview of the Employees' State Insurance Act 1948 it is permissible under the tariff to issue separate table 'B' or 'C' 'Workmen's Compensation Policies covering those members of staff who are not 'employees' within the meaning of the Act provided all, such employees (other than individuals employed on monthly wages exceeding Rs. 500) in the insured's service are included hereunder.

Fidelity Guarantee Insurance

Fidelity Guarantee is one of the main classes of insurance written in the accident department. As a handmade of business and commerce, it is an essential insurance protection, for it seeks to indemnify the employer against direct pecuniary loss that he may sustain through acts of fraud or dishonesty by an employee in the course his employment. The basis for a fidelity guarantee originates from an employer and employee or a fiduciary relationship where confidence or trust reposed plays a crucial part.

Broadly, fidelity guarantee business can be divided into the following sections:

(*i*) Commercial Fidelity Guarantees,
(*ii*) Court Bonds, and
(*iii*) Government Bonds.

Types of Policy

The following types of policy are in general demand:

(*a*) Individual Policy

This type of policy is used where only one individual is to be guaranteed.

(*b*) Collective Policy

Where the entire staff or a number of selected individuals are to be covered, a collective policy is issued.

(c) Floating Policy or Floater

This is an extension to the collective form of contract in which the names and duties of the individuals to be covered are inserted in schedule but instead of individuals amounts of guarantee a specified sum of guarantee is floated on the whole group.

(*d*) Positions Policy

This is similar to a collective policy with the difference that instead of using names, the position is guaranteed for a specified amount so that a change in the person holding the position does not affect the cover. It is noted to be that the liability of the insurers in respect of each position remains limited to the amount guaranteed for the irrespective of the number of persons acting in that position.

(*e*) Blanket Policy

This policy covers the entire staff without showing names or positions. No enquiries about the employees are made by the insurers. Such policies are only suitable for an employer with a large staff and the organisation to make adequate enquiries into the anticidents of employees.

(*f*) Excess Floating Policy

This is a combination of collective policy and a floating policy.

Proposal Form (Employer's Form)

Several different types of proposal form are in use for the various classes of fidelity guarantee. For commercial guarantees the employer has to complete an employer's statement. This statement may be likened to the proposal form as it forms the basis of the contract between employer and the insurers.

Commercial Fidelity Guarantee

Application Form

The application (the person to be guaranteed) has to fill in an application form which requires in addition to his name, age and address the name, address and business activities of the employer, the position to be covered by the guarantee, the salary or other remuneration to be received, details of past guarantees also details the applicant's status (single or married) and dependents, if any. The extent of debts, private income, whether or not the applicant has ever been bankrupt or insolvent, details of past employment, whether he is house-holder and owns furniture and details of his life assurance are also required.

Private Referee's form

At one time great significance was attached to private referees' forms. This is a form which may be sent to persons whose names and addresses have been supplied by the applicant.

Previous Employers' form

A reference for the applicant from all the employers for the previous five years in an important underwriting tool to the insurers. This form is only for the proof of applicants integrity and honesty.

Collective Proposals

For collective floating and blanket policies, individual applicants' forms are dispensed with. The employer has to set out in a statement all such particulars relating to the employees to be covered as are required for individual policies.

Underwriting Considerations

The main considerations are employers' style of establishment, methods of selection of employees, working conditions generally emoluments and benefits in relation to responsibilities and other organisation and how far the system of check and control measures are effective and what supervision is exercised over the employees. To improve the risk, the insurers may make suggestions to the employer for tightening up the system of check. But where the system is fundamentally unsatisfactory no piece-meal improvement is of any avail. An entirely new system may have to be agreed upon.

Risk Covered

The perils covered are variously described under different insurers, but the risk of pecuniary loss to the employer by reason of breach of trust misuse of office is uniform. The normal wording runs as follows:

The employee shall in the course of the duties, specially commit any act or acts of forgery or of embezzlement, laxency and fraudulent conversion of moneys or goods of the insured the insurer will make good to the Insured any loss which the insured shall thereby directly sustain up to an amount not exceeding the amount Insured.

Following points should be noted in connection of Risk:

(*i*) The cover granted is against a direct pecuniary loss and not a consequential one;

(*ii*) the pecuniary loss should be sustained by the insured in respect of the moneys or goods; and

(*iii*) the act should be committed in the course of the duties specified.

Period of Discovery

Unlike other classes of business, fidelity guarantee policies stipulate time limit for discovery of losses. This is also because the loss can occur over a long period without discovery. Investigation of such losses would be troublesome and recoveries may become legally and practically difficult. The customary time limit provided is that the act or acts insured against should be discovered not later than six months after the resignation, dismissal, retirement or death of the employees or not later than three months after the termination of the policy. Whichever be the earlier the time limit may be increased up to 12 months, if the insurers agree to it.

Some of the important conditions are considered here viz.—Application of control measures, notice of claim, prosecution condition, subrogation and contribution.

Hazardous Risks

Not all risks proposed for insurance are accepted at normal terms; certain risks are considered not good for insurance because of the very high degree of hazard associated therewith and the high incidence of claims. A representative list of such risks is given below:

(*i*) Collection agents whose financial limits are disproportionately high compared to their remuneration and the security deposit given by them;

(*ii*) Jewellery Travellers;

(*iii*) Cashiers in eating houses, cinema houses and other places of entertainment;

(*iv*) Estate Agents;

(*v*) Treasurers of friendly societies of Associations;

(*vi*) Employees of Bullion merchants, antiques, furs and other valuables.

Service Security Policies

Another offshoot of the fidelity guarantee business is guaranteeing a minimum period of service an employee has agreed to render an employer in return for the training imparted to him by the employer in enabling the employee to acquire qualifications. In the event of failure by the employee to honour his commitment, the policy has to pay the amount guaranteed. Here again it is doubtful, whether this type of policy falls within the province of fidelity guarantee though some insurers are inclined to treat breach of minimum service conditions a default and write the business in the fidelity guarantee department.

Rating of Fidelity

Guarantee Business premium under individual and collective policies is charged as a rate per cent of the amount guaranteed subject to a minimum premium. The rate per cent varies from risk to risk depending upon the merits of each case. Generally speaking it ranges from 0.25% to 1.50%. The premium for a floating policy comprises a percentage charge and a per capita charge. The percentage charge is applied on the amount guaranteed and the per capita charge on the number of employees to be guaranteed. For example, if a floating policy has to be issued covering 200 employees for an amount of Rs; 2,00,000 and the percentage charge is, say, 1%, and per capita charge of Rs. 5, the premium payable would be Rs. 3,000 arrived at as shown below:

Percentage charge @ 1% of Rs. 2,00,000	Rs. 2,000
Per capita charge @ Rs. 5 for 200 persons	
(200 × 5)	Rs. 1,000
Total	Rs. 3,000

A minimum premium is always insisted upon because the expenses accruing of proposal, issue of policy, stationery, cost etc., would be the same whether the cover is for Rs. 1,000 or Rs. 1,00,000.

Extensions under Fidelity Guarantee Policies

It is not unusual for employers to ask for extending the conventional Policy to cover negligence or lack of care on the part of the employee, government departments, the Posts and Telegraphs Directorate Railways and many. Public Sector institutions, as a rule, demand such extension. Since the terms of negligence and lack of care do not admit of precise definitions it is not a safe underwriting proposition to cover them. Nevertheless, some insurers do cover such risks.

Administration Bonds

The appointment of the administrator is made by the Court by the grant of letters of administration spelling out the duties and obligations of the administrator.

The amount of bond is stipulated by the court making the appointment and it depends upon the value of both the real and the personal estate of the deceased. The administrator may be an individual or a corporate body but whoever he is, he would be thoroughly screened by the court before making the appointment. All the same insured who have to be satisfied about the bona fides of the applicant for the bond have to make exhaustive enquiries before accepting the proposal.

Unlike a commercial Fidelity Guarantee Policy, an administration bond is a specially contract to be executed under seal and it attracts stamp duty higher than the ordinary policy. The stamp duty varies from state to state depending on the rules framed under the Stamp Act. An administration bond provides for payment up to the amount guaranteed as a Penalty on demand and hence considerations of utmost good faith, disclosure of material facts etc. would not arise. Only in the event of fraud, the insurers can raise a plea of no liability before the court, but the onus of proof that the bond was obtained fraudulently rests on the insurers.

Difference Between Commercial Guarantee & Court Bonds

1. Commercial guarantees are simple contracts, whereas court bonds are specially contracts executed under seal.
2. The proposal made by the employer is the basis of a commercial guarantee and it is deemed to be incorporated in the policy and hence any misrepresentation or inaccuracy in the proposal will make the policy void or voidable. In the court bonds the proposer does not form part of the contract and hence the contract is not affected even if the proposal contains materially inaccurate particulars.
3. The commercial guarantee is subject to conditions the breach of which may render the policy void or voidable, but no such conditions are incorporated in court bond.
4. Commercial guarantees are normal annual contracts which the insurers may renew at their option. But court bonds are automatically renewable, unless the insurers give sufficient notice to the court of their intention not to renew the bond.
5. In a court bond the person guaranteed is a party to the contract, whereas in commercial guarantee he is not.
6. In order to obtain a payment under a commercial guarantee the insured has to prove to the satisfaction of the insurers that he has suffered a pecuniary loss arising out of the insured contigencies. In a court bond a demand from the appropriate authority of the amount guaranteed for a failure in the discharge of duties or obligations by the person guaranteed is sufficient.
7. Commercial guarantees are stamped with an ordinary insurance stamps, while court bonds have to be stamped in accordance with the stamp duty.
8. The cover under a commercial guarantee is restricted in scope as compared with that under a court bond.
9. Commercial guarantees prescribe time limits within which the insured has to intimate defaults to the insurers. Court bonds are not subject to this restriction of time limit.

Government Bonds

Government bonds are like court bonds. They can be classified into parts viz. custom bonds and excise bonds.

Custom bonds are to be executed by importers in favour of the controller of imports and exports agreeing, inter alia, to perform the conditions stipulated in the import trade control regulations. Excise bonds are to be executed by manufacturer in the country in respect of finished products assembled or produced in the company which are dutiable. The excise is to be paid to the Excise Department in lieu of which a bond may be executed. Manufacturers of alcohol, sugar, textiles automobiles etc. are the categories of persons are required to execute the bond.

Liquidator's and Recovership Bond

Estates which are under dispute and referred to the court for adjudication are temporarily placed under the care of a receiver during the pendency of the case. The receiver has to administer the estate and render proper accounting of the estate when under his care to the court. A receiver may also be appointed to administer the estate of a minor who is placed under the court of wards till he attains majority or of a person who is pronounced mentally incapable.

Liquidators are appointed by the court to deal with the estates of persons who filled insolvency petitions before the court or are declared insolvent by the courts. Unlike the receivers, the liquidators have to meet the claims of the insolvent's creditors and realise amounts due to the insolvent's estate from his debtors. The liquidator has to produce a bond guaranteeing his honest and faithful accounting of the estate.

Other Classes of Accident Insurance

Accident department also deals with some other types of insurance:

PEDAL CYCLES INSURANCE

The cover is generally granted in respect of:

(*a*) Loss of or damage to the Pedal Cycle described in the schedule of the Policy by fire, lightning, explosion, burglary, housebreaking, theft or accidental external means. The loss or damage to the Pedal Cycle by accidental external means is subject to an excess of Rs. 10 in respect of each claim.

(*b*) Insured's legal liability for bodily injury to the public and for damage to the property of the public limit of Rs. 15,000 in all limit may be increased.

The premium rates depend on the cover desired by the insurance (*i.e.*, whether comprehensive or third party liability only) and the limit of indemnity selected by the insured in respect of third party cover. Some insurers grant a discount of say, 10% if more than two cycles are insured under a single policy.

PEDAL CYCLE INSURANCE

The policy provides cover against the breakage of the plate glasses by an to display windows or show cases of commercial establishments by any reason whatever, except those that are specifically excluded by the policy. Breakage normally excluded from the policy are by reason of:

(*i*) Fire and explosion,

(*ii*) Typhoon, flood, hurricane, volcanic eruption, earthquake or other convulsions of nature; and

(*iii*) Fight, strikes, war and kindred risks (riot and strike risks may be covered on payment of additional premium).

Unless specifically stated in the Schedule of the Policy, glass means plain glass and does not include any embossing, silvering, lettering or ornamental work. Damage to frames and the cost of removal or replacement of any fittings or fixtures necessitated for replacing the broken glass are not paid for under the policy.

The rate of premium depends on the type of glass, situation, previous experience and neighbourhood. The rate ranges from 5% to 10% of the value of the glass.

Missing Documents Indemnity

Documents like share certificates, bank deposit receipts, life insurance policies, etc., sometimes get lost or misplaced and consequently the owners of these documents may have to apply for the issue of duplicate documents. Since there is no guarantee that the original documents have perished or they have not fallen into wrong hands who may misuse them, there is element of risk in the issue of duplicate documents. The authorities concerned, therefore, ask for an indemnity from an insurance company before they issue duplicate documents. The indemnity issued by insurers seeks to indemnify the authority issuing the duplicate documents or paying any sums under the missing documents against any loss that it might sustain as a result of its having issued a duplicate document or having made any payment under the missing document. Insurers, while granting such an indemnity, almost always obtain a counter-indemnity in order to safeguard their interests.

There are no standard premium rates for this indemnity, because the risk varies from case to case.

AVIATION INSURANCE

This class of insurance has been mainly because of the steep increase in the values of aircraft and the consequent phenomenal increase in the limits of indemnity under third party and other legal liability covers. It may be interesting to note here that the Jumbo Jets which are being operated by Air India are covered for a sum of Rs. 18,75,00,000 each and the third party legal liability and passenger legal liability that may be incurred by Air India out of the operation of this aircraft are covered for a combined limit of Rs. 75,00,00,000. Gross direct premium collected by General Insurance Corporation of India amounted to Rs. 119.51 crores during 1994-95. The overall operations have given a profit of Rs. 8.99 crores in that year.

Flights operated on scheduled routes by recognised airlines as also chartered flights are covered. The rate of premium for chartered flights is higher because of the greater hazard involved.

Aircraft Comprehensive Policy

The policy is divided into three sections, viz.—

(*i*) loss of or damage to aircraft;

(*ii*) third party legal liability; and

(*iii*) legal liability to passengers.

(*i*) Loss of or damage to Aircraft

The indemnity is provided for loss of or damage to the aircraft (also known as aircraft hull, *i.e.*, the body of the aircraft and its component parts) by any cause whatever except those that are specifically excluded by the policy. The cover is also granted in respect of standard component parts (of the aircraft) temporarily detached in connection with overhaul or repair while in the custody or control of the insured. The cover is operative whilst the aircraft is in flight or is taxing or is on the ground or is moored.

Wear and tear and gradual deterioration are excluded. The losses or damage arising from mechanical, structural or electrical breakdown or failure is excluded, but if the loss or damage is caused by fire, explosion or impact of the aircraft with an external object, the said loss or damage is payable even though the fire, explosion or impact might have been caused by the breakdown or failure referred to above.

In addition to the actual cost of repairs, the following are also payable in the event of valid claim:

(*a*) The reasonable expenses incurred by the insured with the written consent of the insurers in respect of:

(i) maintenance of watch on the damaged aircraft and safeguarding it from further loss or damage;

(ii) transportation of the necessary materials, parts and/or technical personnel to the site of the accident;

(iii) transportation of aircraft from the site of the accident to the repairers.

(b) Such proportion of the cost of obtaining a new certificate of Airworthiness as shall apply to the period from the date of accident to the date of expiry of the current certificate of Airworthiness.

The rate of the premium varies with the value of the aircraft, and has a bearing on the type of aircraft. The premium, in respect of low valued aircraft like 'Pushpak' which are valued around Rs. 20,000 is charged at a high rate as 15%. The rate of premium charged for Jumbo Jets of Air India which are insured for as high as Rs. 18,75,00,000 is about 2.5% only.

(ii) Third Party Legal Liability

Insurers indemnify the insured or any member of the operative crew of the aircraft acting in the course of their duties with the insured, against all sums which they may become legally liable to in respect of death, sickness or disease, and bodily injury sustained by any person and caused by an accident arising out of the ownership, maintenance or use of the aircraft. There are ordinarily two limits under third party liability: a limit per accident and a limit per policy year. Under this section of the aircraft comprehensive policy, however, limit per accident is the only limit that is specified. In other words, the liability of the insurers per policy year is unlimited. The limit of indemnity depends on the type of aircraft to be covered and the route over which it is to be flown.

The following are not treated as third parties for the purpose of this section of the policy:

(i) any member of the insured's household or family;

(ii) any sub-contractor whilst such person is engaged in his duties as such or any other person claiming by virtue of any contract the insured;

(iii) any passenger whilst entering into, being carried in or alighting from the aircraft; and

(iv) any member of the crew of the aircraft or any person working in or about the aircraft.

(iii) Passenger Legal Liability

Insurers indemnify the insured or any member of the operative crew of the aircraft acting in the course of his duties with insured in respect of all sums which insured or any such, member of crew, shall become legally liable to pay as compensation in respect of:

1. death, personal injury, sickness or diseases caused to any passenger by an occurrence arising out of the ownership, maintenance or use of such aircraft whilst such passenger is entering into, being carried in or alighting from the aircraft;
2. loss of or damage to passenger's baggage and personal effects whether registered or personally retained by the passengers whilst in the course of carriage by the insured.

The insurers are not liable in respect of death, personal injury, sickness or disease, damage or loss caused to or sustained by any member of the insured's household or family, any sub-contractor of the insured or any agent or servant of the insured or of any such subcontractor whilst such person is engaged in his duties as such.

General Exceptions

The policy will not pay under both the sections, hull and liability, in respect of bodily injury, disease, loss, damage or liability under the following contingencies:

(i) Whilst the aircraft is being used for any illegal purpose or for the purpose other than that stated in the policy or whilst outside the geographical limit specified in the policy.

(*ii*) Whilst the aircraft is being piloted by a person other than the one specified in the policy.

(*iii*) Whilst the aircraft is being flown at night (*i.e.*, one hour after sunset and one hour before sunrise) unless due to force carriage.

(*iv*) Whilst the aircraft is being transported.

(*v*) Whilst the aircraft is using unlicensed landing areas unless due to force major use.

(*vi*) Due to or arising out of the use of the aircraft for racing speed trials, acrobatics, etc.

(*vii*) Contractual liability other than that assumed by the insured under an approved contract of carriage.

(*viii*) War and allied risks including hijacking and riot, strikes and civil commotion.

(*ix*) Whilst the total number of passengers carried exceeds the seating capacity.

The exception relating to night flying is normally removed without charging extra-premium since most of the modern aircraft are filled night-flying equipment.

Freight Liability Policy

In addition to the passengers and the crew, an aircraft carries passengers' baggage, cargo and mail. The airline operating the aircraft is, therefore, liable if the baggage, cargo or mail is lost or damaged. The liability for the passengers' baggage is dealt with under the aircraft comprehensive policy. The freight liability policy deals with the cargo carried on the aircraft. In terms of the provisions of this policy, the insurers indemnify the insured against all sums which the insured may become legally liable to pay to the owners of cargo as a result of loss or damage to cargo or delay in delivery of the cargo or the mishandling of the cargo. The limits of indemnity that appears in the freight liability policy range from Rs. 1 lakh to Rs. 25 lakhs for any one accident.

Airmail Liability Policy

This is similar to freight liability policy, except that this policy provides cover per liability in respect of mail carried on the aircraft. The limits of the liability that appear in the airmail liability policy range from Rs. 1 lakh to Rs. 5 lakhs.

Personal Accident Policy for Crew Members

The crew members can be granted personal accident insurance cover under this policy. Pilots, flight navigators, radio officers, air-hostesses, etc., are covered. The benefits are more or less similar to those granted under the personal accident insurance policies.

LIVESTOCK INSURANCE

Livestock insurance refers mainly to the insurance of horses and cattle. Since cattle insurance is discussed later in this section, we shall confine our discussion here to the insurance of horses alone.

A proposal form together with a report from a qualified veterinary surgeon on the form drawn up by the insurers is always insisted upon to minimise the difficulty of identification; each horse must be adequately described giving colour, all natural markings and age. All horses of a particular type owned by the proposer must be insured, so as to eliminate the possibility of the proposer making a selection against the insurers. The policy provides indemnity against the lose of a horse by death resulting either from accident or a disease specified in the policy, including the destruction of the animal on human grounds arising from an accident or disease.

Exclusions

Death of the animal, arising out of the following, are excluded:

1. War and allied risks, strikes, riot and civil commotion;
2. Slaughter of the animal without prior consent of the insurers;

3. Fire, lighting, seagoing transit, surgical operations, breeding and loss occasioned by the animal becoming unfit or incapable of fulfilling the functions for which it is kept or employed.

CATTLE INSURANCE

This insurance provides cover against death of animals, like bulls, buffaloes, cows and heifers, arising as a result of accident, disease, parturition or pregnant condition, as the case may be. The insurance is arranged on a sort of the excess basis, and provides for payment of an amount in excess of a certain other amount which is known as first loss. The Policy excludes, inter alia, destruction in compliance with any statute or orders of any government or local authority, or because of unfitness or incapacity from fulfilling duties for which the animal is kept. Any death arising out of castration or other surgical operation is also excluded. The number of animals covered by cattle insurance in India has increased from 2.10 lakhs in 1976 to 43.72 lakhs in 1 980, 160.79 lakhs in 1985 and 256.22 lakhs in 1988-89.

CROP INSURANCE

Crop insurance on a restricted scale is being underwritten in the Fire department where damage by fire to standing sugarcane crops is insured. Insurance of all crops against all risks of loss or damage has not found a beginning in our country so far. One of the chief reasons why crop insurance has not gained currency in the country is the inadequate data available on the position of loss. Since our country is dependant to a large extent on agriculture, such non-availability of data acts as a damper on undertaking the job. The climate conditions in the country vary from extreme heat to extreme cold and from swamping rains to severe drought. All the same, a beginning has been made and some crops have been insured on input basis, *i.e.*, the indemnity comprises the cost of all inputs like seeds, pesticides, weedicides, fertilizers, manure; labour; water; crop spraying, etc. The crop insured are crops like cotton where controlled conditions of cultivation can be applied. The experiment too is still rudimentary and may be extended to other crops like rubber, coffee and tea. GIC has taken up insurance of cotton grown by small and marginal farmers through adoption of Nursery Technology in Gujarat and Maharashtra.

Table 35.1 Progress of Cattle Insurance in India

	Number Covered (in Thousand)	*Premium (In Rs. Lacs)*
1974	30	25.84
1975	63	48.45
1976	210	132.93
1977	589	247.18
1978	1410	472.02
1979	3230	948.16
1980	4372	1333.78
1981	5676	1908.98
1982	8235	2633.03
1983	10578	3389.58
1984	14267	4596.45
1985	16079	5135.90
1986	18969	5935.00
1987	18536	69.45
1988-89	25622	10188.00
1989-90	19921	8604.00

Crop insurance scheme introduced by the Government of India commenced from kharif 1985-86. The corporation has been entrusted with the task of administering the scheme on behalf of the

Government. The insurance charges and claims in respect of crops insured in any State is showed between the Central Crop Insurance Fund and Crop Insurance Fund set up by the State Government concerned in the ratio of 2: 1. The number of farmers covered has been 4226 thousands for Kharif 1989 and 661 thousands for Rabi 1989-90. The claims have been Rs. 28085 lakhe and Rs. 622 lakhs respectively. However the number of farmers covered and premium income declined in 1994-95 to the tune of 4072 thousand for kharif and 545 thousand for rabi while premium-income declined to Rs. 21.90 crores and Rs. 3.35 crores respectively.

Contract guarantee also known as solvency guarantee comes under the classification of insurance of interest, when contracts for works or for supply of materials are awarded the awarders are required to guarantee that the contract awarded will be executed within the time stipulated or within such extension of time as may be allowed and in accordance with the terms of the contract and the specifications stipulated therein. The amount of guarantee varies with the nature of contract. Generally, it ranges from 1% to 10% of the contract. The purpose of a contract guarantee is two-fold. Firstly, by the deterrent of calling in the insurance guarantee for payment the contractor is discouraged from slowing down or the making down the quality of the work. Secondly, the requirement of a guarantee may dissuade all and sundry from rushing in to secure the award of the contract.

The risk under a contract guarantee is the skill, ability and intention of the person who is guaranteed. Hence, like fidelity guarantee it covers on intangible. The insurer who underwrites this class needs specialised knowledge and wide experience. Apart from the natures of contract, the important considerations are the financial status and reputation of the contractor, the experience he has in executing work similar to that contract, or the manpower, equipment and capital base he has and the skill and ability he has as may be judged from his completed contracts or as reflected in his existing contracts. A pitfall that has to be avoided as a tendency on the part of contractors to overtrade, that is, contractors trying to take more contracts on hand than he could successfully execute.

Contract guarantee takes on three distinct forms as stated below:

1. *Performance Bonds:* The bond undertakes to indemnify the principles against any failure on the part of the contractor to execute the contract works in accordance with the specifications and terms of the contract and within the time stipulated in the contract or in case of supply contracts if the materials, goods or products supplied by the contractor fall short of the standards set by the principals.
2. *Earnest Money (Bid) Bonds*: The bond is issued in lieu of the earnest money which every intending contractor has to pay to a principal while submitting his tender or bid. The bond provides for payment of the amount guaranteed if the contractor fails to enter into a contract with the principal after they have accepted his tender or bid.
3. *Security Depositor Retention Money Bond*: Before the commencement of this contract works, the contractor is required to provide as security deposit a certan percentage of the contract value for due performance of the contract. A security deposit bond issued in lieu of the security deposit undertakes to pay the amount guaranteed should there be any failure on the part of the contractor to perform the contract. Instead of a security deposit, the principals may deduct from each running bill of the contractor a fixed percentage as security for the due performance of the contract. This is known as retention money. A bond issued in lieu of the retention money is known as retention money bond.

Credit Guarantee

Credit guarantee is also an insurance of interest. It has for its risk the credit of any buyer or borrower to a supplier or financier. The term credit as used here means commercial credit and it connects the trust reposed and time allowed in making a payment or repayment. The trust is not only in relation to the integrity and honesty of the person who has to make the payment but also in the business ability of the person for his conducting the entire business and making a profit enough to repay one "debt". The subject-matter of insurance in credit guarantee is also called as finance guarantee. Like contract guarantee for credit guarantee also a very elaborate proposal is required to be submitted. In addition all the other particulars as called for in a contract guarantee are required to be provided. As no contracts are involved here, the proposer need not furnish details about his past or present contracts. Also a cash flow statement detailing as to how funds would be generated for repayment of the debt is required to be given. Full details of the purpose for which the loan is obtained and any security given to the financier have to be furnished.

Credit guarantee takes on many forms. A few are explained briefly below:

1. Hire Purchase Guarantee

Bank and other financial institutions may advance money to transport operators or fleet owners to enable them purchase motor cars or truck chassis. The advances with interest are repayable within a certain period by installments. This transaction is known as hire purchases. The banks or financiers who advance as the money invariably requires an insurance guarantee as security. The guarantee covers only up to 75% or 80% of the total purchase price of vehicle including sales taxes and other local taxes. The balance of 25% or 20% has to be paid in cash by the person buying the vehicle or has to be borne by the bank or financier, as the case may be. In respect of second hand vehicle, it may even be as low as 40% of the total purchase price. In the event of any failure on the part of the hire purchaser to pay any amount, the vehicle in question may be seized and disposed of.

2. Deferred Payment Guarantee

Various industrialists (Large Scale and Small Scale) need credit from banks for the purchase of machinery or capital goods both from foreign supplier and indigenous suppliers. The credit may not be necessarily monetary credit. It may be in the form of guarantee and payment on behalf of the clients from the bank to the suppliers of machinery or capital goods. In the case of foreign suppliers the opening of a letter of credit is with the supplier's bank. The payment of the purchase price may be spread over a period of vears and for payment of each instalment a date may be stipulated in the purchase agreement. The deferred payment guarantee provides for payment of any loss arising from any default committed by the purchaser in the payment of the instalments.

3. Cash Credit or Overdraft Guarantee

Businessmen frequently resort to overdraft or cash credit facilities with bank for obtaining working capital. The guarantee undertakes to indemnify the bank against any loss arising out of the failure of the borrower in repaying the amount advanced or the interest thereon .

4. Bills Discounting Guarantee

It is an established practice in business circles to discount bills of exchange banks. The banks which discount the bills proceed to collect the amount due thereon from the makers or acceptors thereof only on the dates of payment under those bills which may be dishonoured on their due dates. Banks, therefore, insist or insurance guarantee indemnifying them against such losses.

Period of Guarantee

The period of guarantee has to be concurrent with the period of the original agreements which they cover. In some cases they may even overstretch the period of the original agreements by a month or more. This is done to facilitate the principal parties to process their claims, if they have any under the insurance guarantees.

Counter-Guarantees and Tangible Security

A counter-guarantee is a document executed in favour of the insurers by the party who is guaranteed by the insurers. The counter guarantee may be from the guaranteed party only or it may be joined co-guarantors. When insurers pay a loss under an insurance the guarantee insurers lose. Insurers as a rule make it obligatory for the guaranteed party to execute a counter-guarantee.

In addition to counter-guarantee, insurers may also obtain some tangible security where they feel it is warranted. The tangible security may be by way of an equitable mortgage of the immovable assets or it may be assignment of life insurance policies or even a negative lien over the assets of the guaranteed party or pledge of share scripts, banks lodgement receipts, etc. Guarantees and counter-guarantees are specially contracts. Hence they have to be executed under the seal.

Engineering Insurance

Engineering insurance is one of the most technical branches of accident insurance. It comprises the following three broad types:

1. Boiler Explosion Insurance.
2. Machinery Breakdown Insurance.
3. Erection All Risks Insurance.

Boiler Explosion Insurance

The boiler explosion policy covers boilers and pressure vessels and seeks to indemnify the insured against—

(*a*) damage, other than by fire to the boilers and other pressure plants and to surrounding property of the insured.

(*b*) legal liability of the insured on account of bodily injury, fatal and non-fatal to the person or damge to the property of third parties.

The word 'boiler' as used in the policy means any fired closed vessel or a combined container piping system in which steam is generated under pressure. "Pressure Plant" means any unfixed closed container under steam, gas or fluid pressure.

"Explosion" means the sudden and violent rending or tearing apart of the permanent structure of a boiler or pressure plant or any parts thereof by force of internal steam, gas or fluid pressure causeing, bodily displacement of the said structure and accompanied by the forcible ejectment of its contents.

Strikes is not normally covered. But on payment of extra premium these risks can be covered.

It is very necessary that the boilers and pressure plant insured are inspected annually by inspectors appointed by the appropriate statutory authority and that they are operated by attendants holding a valid certificate of competency.

Machinery Breakdown Insurance

The fire policy covers loss of or damage to machinery only if the loss or damage is attributable to fire or any of the extraneous perils covered by the fire policy. But where loss or damage has originated from breakdown, fire policy is of no avail. This gap is made good by the machinery breakdown policy which provides indemnity against any unforeseen and sudden damage to the machinery by causes such as short circuit, action of the centrifugal forces, shortage of water in boilers, faulty design, bad workmanship, erection faults, lack of skill, carelessness, malicious, damage etc.

Erection All Risks Insurance

The erection all risks insurance policy covers plant and machinery under erection. The cover normally commences from the arrival at site of erection of the materials and it operates during storage of the materials, erection and test run of the plant and terminates on the commissioning of the plant.

Civil engineering work, provided they are incidental to the erection of plant of machinery, are also covered. Third party liability arising out of the insured's activities with the erection work is also covered. The erection policy is issued for the entire period of erection including trial run.

Excess

It is customary for excess to be applied under machinery break down and erection policies. Boiler explosion policy is, however, not subject to excess. The purpose of excess is two-fold: first, to eliminate small claims thereby reducing clerical work for the insurance and second, to make the insured more conscious of his responsibility to take adequate precautions and to observe all safety regulations and statutory rules.

Loss of Profits Insurance

As in the fire department the interruption risk arising out of machinery breakdown can be covered under a loss of profits insurance policy taken in conjunction with a basic machinery breakdown policy. The cover is similar to what is granted in the fire department excepting that the period of indemnity is restricted to 9 months ordinarily and 12 months in special cases.

Insurance Against Deterioration of Stocks

Agricultural commodities like potatoes, fruits, etc., preserved in cold storage are likely to be damaged if the refrigeration machinery breaks down or stops because of any failure of power supply. Such loss or damage to the commodities stored can be covered under a policy taken in conjunction with a basic machinery breakdown policy in respect of refrigeration machinery.

Contractor's All Risks Insurance

Civil works like buildings and marine works like bridges, dams, sea walls, etc., can be insured under a contractor's all risks policy against loss or damage during construction. The cover granted is quite comprehensive and includes most of the natural calamities. Third party liability arising out of the constitutional activities can also be insured under the policy. It is also usual to insure the plant and machinery used for construction as well as temporary structures set up for aiding the construction. The policy covers the entire period of construction which may be spread over a number of years. The policy is always subject to excess and it also provides for adjustment of the premium after expiry on basis of the completed cost.

Social Security Coverage In India:

Most Social security system in developed countries are linked to wage employment. In India, situation is entirely different. The key differences are:

1. We do not have existing universal social security system.
2. We do not face the problem of exit rate from the workplace. Rather on the contrary, lack of employment opportunities is the key concern.
3. 92 % of the workforce is in the informal sector which is largely unrecorded and the system of pay roll deduction is difficult to apply.

New Initiatives In Social Security :

Janashree Bima Yojana: The objective of this scheme is to provide life insurance protection to the rural and urban persons living below poverty line and marginally above poverty line. The main features are:

Eligibility: Person between 18 years and 59 years is benefited under the scheme. The member should normally be the head of the family.

Benefits:
Natural Death Rs. 30,000/-
Accident Death/
Permanent total Disability Rs. 75,000/-
Partial disability due to
accident Rs. 37500/-

Aam Admi Bima Yojana: This scheme provides coverage to Rural Landless Households.

Eligibility: Person between 18 years and 59 years. The member should normally be the head of the family.

Benefits: As per Janashree Bima Yojana.
This scheme is fully subsidized by Central and State Government.
Janashree Bima Yojana for Women SHG's Credit Linked to Banks
Target for F.Y. 2008 - 09 covering 2.5 lacs SHG group

Other Social Security Schemes Implemented Through LIC of India:

	Schemes	Commencement	Coverage (31/3/2008)
1.	Khadi Karigar Janashree Bima Yojana	15/8/2003	2,34,436
2.	Bima Yojana for Handicraft Artisan	July, 2003	97,636
3.	Mahatma Gandhi Bunkar Bima Yojana	02.10.2005	4,66,484
4.	Aanganwadi Karyakartri Janashree Bima Yojana	01.04.2004	15,26,970
5.	Kendriya Bhed Palak Bima Yojana	01.01.2008	3,435

Government of India has created Social Security Fund with LIC of India to provide subsidy to all the Social Security Schemes.

36

RURAL INSURANCE AND PROSPECTS OF AGRICULTURE INSURANCE IN INDIA

SCOPE OF RURAL INSURANCE

The scope of rural insurance is very high although it is poorly realised. Rural areas having 70 per cent of total population, livelihood to two-third of the total population, supply of raw materials to industrial production and other economic activities have compelled the insurance educators to make the insurance companies enter in the rural population. The agriculture is full of vagaries and natural calamities. which impede the sustainable growth of the country by sustaining agricultural development. The natural risks and disasters have pulled back the rural development. Therefore, there is dire needs of insurance of rural risks. Crop insurance, cattle insurance, life and property insurance, general insurance etc. have abundant scope of development.

CROP INSURANCE

Crop insurance is the main rural insurance wherein the product, price and income risks are insured. If the farmers do not get a standard amount of product, required price and income from the farms; they are compensated by insurance companies under crop insurance. In past insurance companies did not approach for the crop insurance because of non availability of records of land-ownership yield per acre, inputs used and expected outputs. The scattered and fragmented land holdings posed another problems. Large varieties of crops, simultaneous harvesting, small premiums and non-availability of records of labour, cost and input costs have discourged the insurer to insure the crop risk.

The General Insurance Corporation of India had prepared are approach of crop insurance in 1979. The area yield for each to tehsil and block have be standardised and was compared with the actual yield to find out the indemnity amount. It has paved the way for Comprehensive Crop Insurance Scheme (CCIS) in 1985 which was later on modified as National Agricultural Insurance Scheme (NAIS). At present NAIS has covered 30 million hectares of cropped area for 18 million farmers throughout the country.

Area Based Insurance

The natural hazards differ from state to state and district to district in one state. Weather indices have been prepared to decide the indemnity amount. The catastrophic income losses have been estimated for each year. Area based crop insurance covers the risks of drought, flood etc. in the respective districts and tehsils. The crop insurance covers these, the value of protection desired for meeting the cost of cultivation and value of production etc. Farmers in the same region will receive the same rate of payment of claims in the area. The area based rainfall data is used for deciding the premium amount and claims to be paid in the area.

Rainfall Index

The rainfall index of the last 30 years are used to demonstrate the rainfall index. It is decided weekly for 30 years to know the capped rainfall. The average of the week of the month in each year is taken for 30 years. Thus the average arrived at is modified with 2 standard deviation to find out the copped rainfall of the week of the month. If the rainfall in less than capped rainfall, the payment is made proportionately.

Similarly multiple weather parameter such as rainfall, temperature, frost, humidity, wind speed etc., are decided for fruits and vegetable insurance.

Revenue Insurance Products

Besides products, price is another factor of loss to farmers. For example, despite normal production, farmers often fail to maintain their level of income due to price fluctuations. Government has introduced Farm Income Insurance Scheme (FIIS) during Rabi 2003-2004 season. It encourages crop diversification for cash and ready income.

Individual farmers are also assessed for payment. Plant risks have been the significant example of such insurance. The resource poor farmers can get the insurance protection at the behest of the governments premium. The banking institutions and other financial institutions can ask for crop insurance so that their dues can be paid in time.

REGULATIONS OF IRDA

The IRDA has imposed social obligations on life and non life insurance companies. The rural obligation is one important social obligations for the insurers. It applied to all insurers separately covering five thousand lives in the first financial year, seven thousand lives in the second year, ten thousand lives in the third year, fifteen thousand lives in the fourth year and 20 thousand lives in each year. The Rural sector obligations in respect of a life insurer is defined as terms of total policies underwritten – 7% in first year, 9% in the second year, 12% in the third year, 14% in the fourth year 16% in the subsequent each year. Such obligations in respect of general insurers are in terms of total gross premium income underwritten each year: 2% in the first year, 3% in second year and 5% thereafter. Non fulfillment of these obligations invites penalties from the regulator.

Imposing such obligations would help the companies discover the appropriate paradigm. The rural obligations are meant to tap commercial as well as semi-commercial segments of rural areas. Social obligations are meant to extend insurance to the subsistence sector which are not pragcitable. Now every insurer has a separate cell/unit for rural and social obligations. The insurance products are sold with the help of NGOs and development agencies. Some insurance companies have taken rural and social obligations in a positive spirit and they have done more than the prescribed limits in rural areas and social sector.

MICRO INSURANCE

IRDA has come out with microinsurance and has paved the principles of role defining of agents with small and segmented insurance products. It is interested to develop insurance awareness in the remote corner of the country. It has adopted traditional techniques of motivations and joining hands with State governments. Postal Life Insurance (PLI) is very effective form of microinsurance. IRDA has approached postal authority to extend its insurance facilities to general public also. Cooperative societies should come forward to start insurance business for the benefits of the masses. Gujarat, Maharashtra and Karnataka have started such micro insurance. IFFCO has started insurance with the joint venture of Tok. Thus IFFO—Tokio has started micro insurance. Self Help Groups, Mahila Mandals, Panchayats etc. are motivated to extend insurance in rural areas.

The GIC and the four subsidiaries viz., National Insurance Co. Ltd., The New Assurance Co. Ltd., The Oriental Insurance Co. Ltd., and United India Insurance Co. Ltd., hereby known as National, New India, Oriental and United India have taken the responsibilities of insuring the rural masses against the growing risks in the areas of personal, property, livestock and packages. Their brief descriptions will highlight how far the General insurance industry has been successful to harness the existing opportunities in rural areas. Now private non-life insurance have taken the responsibility of rural insurance.

1. Personal Insurance

The personal insurance to rural people is granted in the form of Janata Personal Accident—Individual and Group and Gramin Personal Accident—Individual and Group.

(*i*) *Janata Personal Accident (Individual).* Persons between age group of 10 to 65 years are covered under Janata Personal Accident (Individual) policy whereby Rs. 15,000 is paid at the death or permanent total disablement due to accident. Rs. 7,500 is paid at the loss of one eye or one limb due to accident.

Sterilisation risks and claims arising out of racing on wheels, big game hunting, mountaineering whilst engaged in winter sports skiing or ice hockey are also covered. The premium is Rs. 12 per annum. The nominee should submit death certificate, original policy and claim form at the death of the assured due to accident.

(*ii*) *Janta Personal Accident (Group).* Persons between the age group of 10 to 65 years are entitled for Janata Personal Accident (Group). The benefits are Rs: 15,000 at the time of death or permanent disablement due to accident. At the loss of one eye or one limb in an accident is paid Rs. 7,500. The premium is Rs. 12 per annum:

The Janata Personal Accident Insurance has increased from Rs. 129.00 lakhs in 1982 to Rs. 440.24 lakhs in the form of direct insurance premium. During the period of five years, it became just double. In the form of number of persons covered; it has increased from 20.16 lakhs in 1982 to 42.26 lakhs in 1987. It shows that this non-traditional policies can be more popular if efforts are made systematically to increase the business. The growth rate has been not satisfactory as the premium income increased at faster rate in the beginning. The growth rate was 44.8 per cent in 1983 but there was also decline by 9.5 per cent in 1986. The persons covered has declined in 1986 by 6.8 per cent.

Table 36.1 Janata Personal Accident Insurance

(Rs. in Lakhs)

	Premium Income		*Number of persons covered*	
	Rs.	*% increase over previous year*	*Lakhs*	*% increase over previous year*
1980				
1981				
1982	219.00	—	20.16	—
1983	317.00	44.8	30.75	52.5
1984	361.00	13.9	35.10	14.2
1985	458.00	27.1	43.44	23.8
1986	414.97	–9.5	40.50	–6.8
1987	440.24	6.1	42.26	+4.4

(*iii*) *Gramin Personal Accident (Individual).* This policy is applicable to persons between the age group of 10 to 65 years living in rural areas. The benefits are Rs. 6,000 at death or permanent disablement due to accident or Rs. 3,000 at the loss of two eyes or two limbs or one eye and one limb due to accident. Sterilisation risks and claims arising out of racing on wheels, big game hunting, mountaineering whilst engaged in winter sports, skiing or ice hockey. The premium amount is Rs. 6 per annum. The nominee is required to submit death certificate, original policy and claim form at the death claims and medical certificate and bills in other cases.

(*iv*) *Gamin Personal Accident (Group).* This policy is issued to a large number of persons insured under one policy. The benefits are the same as discussed earlier in the case of Gramin Personal Accident (Individual). Basic premium for one year is Rs. 500 for 100 persons in two instalments. The discount is available if the number of persons have been higher.

Table 36.2 Gramin Personal Accident Policy

	Premium Income		Persons covered	
	Rs. in Lakhs	*% increase over previous year*	*Lakhs*	*% increase over previous year*
1982	6.47	—	1.30	—
1983	9.05	39.9	1.74	33.8
1984	18.27	101.9	3.04	74.7
1985	37.75	106.6	7.52	144.1
1986	39.67	9.1	7.06	6.1
1987	40.96	3.3	7.62	7.9

The premium income under Gramin Personal Accident Policy increased from Rs. 6.47 lakhs in 1982 to Rs. 40.96 lakhs in 1987. The persons covered has also increased from 1.30 lakhs to 7.62 lakhs in the respected years. The number of persons covered increased by more than 4 times. The premium income has increased by the same fold. The traditional policies during this period has increased by not more than twofold. It reveals that the non-traditional policies are becoming more popular in India.

2. Property Insurance

(*i*) *Agricultural Pumpset.* Agricultural pumpsets insurance policy indemnifies the insured against unforeseen and sudden physical damage to the pumpsets caused by/or solely due to mechanical/electrical breakdown, fire and lightning, theft and burglary. The minimum premium is Rs. 50 for electric pumpset and Rs. 70 for diesel pumpset. No claim discount is applicable on renewable premium at the rate of 10 per cent if no claim arises for one year. 15 per cent if no claim arises for two consecutive years and 20 per cent if no claim arises for three consecutive years. Long Term Discount is also available at the rate of 15 per cent if taken for 2 years and 25 per cent if taken for three years. Group discount is also applicable if a number of pumpsets are insured together. Annual premium depends on horse power types of pumpset and deductible franchise. The deductible franchise will be first borne by the Insured, out of each and every machinery breakdown claim where more than one item is lost or damaged in one and the same occurrence. The insured shall not be called upon to bear more than the highest deductible franchise applicable to any one such item.

Table 36.3 Agricultural Pumpset Insurance

	Premium Income		Number of Pumpsets	
	In Lakhs of Rs.	*% Increase over previous year*	*In Lakhs*	*% increase over previous year*
1982	105.30	—	1.35	—
1983	125.50	19.2	1.68	24.4
1984	170.00	35.8	2.36	40.5
1985	258.00	51.4	2.96	25.4
1986	373.82	44.9	3.66	23.7
1987	481.38	28.8	4.44	21.3

The number of pumpsets insured increased from 1.35 lakhs in 1982 to 4.44 lakhs in 1987. The premium income has also increased from Rs. 105.30 lakhs in 1982 to Rs. 481.38 lakhs in 1987. The premium became more than fourfold during the period 1982 to 1987. The growth rate has been maximum in 1985. The traditional business had risen only to twofold during this period. Considering the growning demand of pumpsets for the economic development of rural areas; the insurance opportunities are expanding every year. The subsidiary companies have to effort maximum to exploit the growing opportunities in rural insurance.

(*ii*) *Animal Driven Carts Insurance.* The Animal Driven Cart Insurance cover risks against death or permanent total disablement of the animals driving the cart. Gramin accident cover for driver while driving the cart at no extra premium. Damage to the cart/tonga and its accessories by accident, external means like fire, lightning, flood, cyclone and other allied perils while in transit by road, rail and inland waterways. Third party liability upto Rs. 5,000 per accident and maximum Rs. 10,000 for all accidents in a policy year. Insured will bear first Rs. 100 of each cart and Rs. 200 of each tonga claim. The age group of animals covered is 3 to 12 years for bullocks, male buffaloes, 2 to 6 years for horses and mules, 1 to 5 years for donkey and 5 to 15 years for camels. The sums assured will be the market value of cart tonga and animal. Premium rate is 2.00 per cent of the insured value. The insured value is decided on the basis of market value after deducting reasonable amount of depreciation for the number of years for which the cart has been in use. If diseases cover required, the premium applicable in respect of the animal covered will be charged. The scope of cover is loss or damage to the animal driven cart, death or permanent disablement of animal, liability to third parties and passengers and personal accident cover to person driving the cart.

Loss or damage due to any accident is subject to an excess of Rs. 100 per policy excluding wear and tear. In case of vehicles fitted with preumatic or hard rubber tyres only 50 per cent of value of the tyre is payable. Death or permanent disability of the animal used for pulling the cart provided that death/disablement arises out of and during the course of accident to insured cart and provided the animals are insured under the policy. Liability arising out of the accident to the insured cart resulting into injury, fatal or non-fatal and damage to the properties of the third party upto Rs. 5,000 in any accident and Rs.10,000 for all the accidents in a year. Personal injury or death of passengers is also covered within this limit. The liability is covered even when the vehicle is being loaded or unloaded. It is not extended to cover damage to the goods carried. The policy will not make any distinction between the use of the cart for private and professional purposes and for hire or reward. Personal accident cover to person driving the cart is upto Rs. 5,000 which becomes payable to the cart driver who whilst driving the cart meets with death following accident to the cart and or for loss of two entire feet, or two arms or complete loss of sight of two eyes and or loss of one entire foot and or arm and loss of sight of one eye. No information about the progress of insurance for animal driven cart is available.

(*iii*) *Hut Insurance.* Hut insurance policy indemnifies the insured against all accidental losses or damages due to fire, earthquake, inundation, storm, tempest, impact damage, riot, strike, malicious damage and aircraft damage subject to the exclusions of war, invasion, act of foreign enemy, hostilities, civil war, rebellion, revolution, insurrection, mutiny, military or usurped power. The maximum sum insured is Rs. 6,000. The maximum 200 huts situated in on contiguous area. In case the number of huts is more than 50 in contiguous area the insurer will accept the risk after inspection. The premium rate is Rs. 3 per mille per annum. 50 per cent of the premium is shared by Government. In practice, Government pay the premium in full in advance and recover 50 per cent of the premium from hut owner. Insurer shall pay compensation on the basis of a certificate issued by the Tehsildar regarding occurrence of the fire loss where compensation is less than Rs. 10,000. However, where the amount of loss involved is more than Rs. 10,000 or number of huts is more than 5, the Tehsildar shall report the occurrence to the company immediately who will depute their officer for inspection and assessment of the loss. The payment of compensation is made within a month of the occurrence.

A scheme to provide fire insurance cover for huts and belongings of landless labourers, small farmers, artisans and other poor families in rural areas which was introduced from May 1, 1988 was in operation in 406 districts of the country as on 31.3.1989. The scheme provides compensation not exceeding Rs. 1,000 for a hut and Rs. 500 for belongings therein the entire premium cost is being borne by the Central Government. Continuous efforts are on to propagate the benefits of the scheme among the poor families in rural areas. About 11,000 claims amounting to Rs. 1.24 crores have been settled upto the end of March 1989. National Insurance settled 18455 Hut Insurance claims, New India settled 457 claims, amounting Rs. 6.85 lakhs; 52.01 lakhs settled by Oriental and Rs. 242.56 lakhs by United India during 1994-95.

(iv) Gobar Gas Insurance. The Gobar Gas Insurance is applicable to all Khadi and Village Industries workers/artisans, IRDP beneficiaries, schedule castes, schedule tribes and such other identifiable groups. The risks covered are fire, lightning, explosion, riot, strike malicious damage, impact by rail/road vehicles or animals, aircraft and other aerial/devices, storm, cyclone, typhoon, tempest, hurricane, tornado, flood, landslide, earthquake and shock. The sum assured is inclusive of digester, gas holder and cost of construction depending on type and cubic capacity. Master policy agreement is preferable in respect of this insurance in view of the concessional rate of premium and to reduce overall administrative expenses. The rate of premium is Re. 1 per mille for widest cover subject to minimum premium of Rs. 15.

(v) New Well Insurance. The new well insurance is applicable to dugwells or borewells which are being newly installed. It does not apply to existing well. The cover is given to financing banks or individuals. The sum insured shall be limited to a maximum of Rs. 12,000 per well. The 75 per cent of sum insured is settled for complete failure and 50 per cent is paid for partial, failure. 500 imperial gallons of water per hour pumped intermittently for six hours by 2 to 3 horse power submersible pump and yield measured in contained of known capacity of at least 200 litres. If yield is between 300 to 500 gallons, the well shall be derived partially failed and compensation will be paid at 50 per cent of sum insured. Natural calamities like flood, earthquake, riot and strike are excluded from this insurance.

3. Cattle and Livestock

The cattle and livestock insurance was demanded since independence. No worth mentioning progress was made till 1972 when the general insurance was nationalised. Recently some progress has been made and figure of the progress is available since 1982. Cattle and livestock insurance have included cattle, sheep and goat, horse/pony/mule, pig, camel, duck, rabbit, elephant and dog.

(i) Cattle Insurance Schemes. The cattle insurance policy under market agreement covers milch cows, and buffaloes, calves/heifers, stud bulls, bullocks and castrated male buffaloes whether idigeneous or exotic or cross-bred. Exotic animal means an animal whose both parents are of foreign breed. This policy provides indemnity in event of death of insured cattle due to accident inclusive of fire, lightning, flood, cyclone, famine, surgical operation, strike, riot, civil commotion, diseases inclusive of anthrax, blackquarter foot and mouth disease haemorrhagic septicaemia, rinderpest and theileriasis; contracted or occurring during the period of policy and shall be subject to exclusions of theft and clandestine sale of the insured animal, partial disability of any type, whether permanent or temporary; permanent total disability, which, in case of milch cattle result in permanent and total incapacity to conceive or yield milk in the case of stud bulls, war, invasion, hosilities, civil war and military.

The age group of animals to be covered are 2 years to 10 years for milch cows, 3 years to 12 years for milch buffaloes, 3 years to 8 years for stud bulls, 3 years to 12 years for bullocks. The market value of cattle will be the amount of sum insured which varies from breed to breed, from area to area and from time to time. In the case of permanent total disablement, insurers, liability is limited to 75 per cent of sum insured. The premium rates are governed by market agreement varying from 2.75 per cent to 4.00 per cent. The premium rate is 3 per cent for milch cattle. The premium for cattle

Rural Insurance
No. of Policy Issued Lacs

GIC	*National*	*New India*	*Oriental*	*United India*
1999-2000	36.83		75.53	—
2000-2001	36.97		79.34	—
2001-2002	34.04		44.39	—
			Number crossed in lacs	
1999-2000	73.65		226.6	—
2000-2001	73.94		238.02	—
2001-2002	68.07		133.17	—
			Premium Received Rs. in crores	
1999-2000	76.92		45.32	50.78
2000-2001	86.25		47.60	78.41
2001-2002	75.50		26.63	58.04
			Incurred Claim in Rs. crores	
1999-2000	66.25		4.40	3.00
2000-2001	67.82		14.69	9.09
2001-2002	58.03		20.03	30.84
			Incurred Claim Ratio % (Claim to Premium)	
1999-2000	86.13		9.72	5.91
2000-2001	78.63		30.87	11.60
2001-2002	77.00		75.20	53.13

owned by individuals/institutions and bank financed oattle which do not provide regular and efficient veterinary attention is per cent. Cattle owned by well organised government, cooperative/private dairies/apex bodies providing regular and efficient veterinary attention are charged premium at the rate of 4.00 per cent if there are less than 50 animals, 3.95 per cent of number of animals insured is 50 to 250 and 3.90 per cent if number of animals insured is over 250. The market agreement helps decide the premium rates in other cases. The bullocks and male buffaloes are charged premium at the rate of 2.75 per cent. There are extra premium of 2 per cent for exotic milch cattle and stud bulls and 1 per cent for covering permanent total disablement. The minimum premium rate is Rs. 25/- per annum per animal and Rs. 20/- per annum per bullock. All the insured animals are suitably identified by one or more of the following methods: (*i*) ear tag made of aluminium or any other metal (*ii*) branding with hot iron and tattooing. The natural identification marks are clearly noted in the proposal form and veterinarian's report.

Cattle insurance schemes are also available under IRDP Project for cattle subsidised under SPDA/MFAL/DPAP/IRDP/TADP, Antyodaya projects. Milch cows, milch buffaloes and stud bulls of indigeneous or cross-bred variety between age group of 2 to 12 years are insurable for the sum assured agreed upon provided it does not exceed market value. The permanent total disability shall be covered at extra premium of 0.85 per cent. The premium rate is 2.25 per cent of sum insured per annum to be subsidised by the Project Authorities and financing bank. The risks covered are as mentioned in market agreement plan. The common exclusions are malicious or wilful injury or neglect overloading, unskilfully treatment or use of animal for purpose other than stated in the policy without the consent of the insurer, accident occurring and/or diseases contracted prior to commencement of risk, intentional slaughter of the animal except in cases where destruction is necessary to terminate incurable suffering on humane consideration on the basis of certificates insured by qualified veterinarian or in cases where destruction is resorted to by the order of lawfully constituted authority; theft and clandestine sale of the insured animal; war invasion, act of foreign enemy, hostilities, civil war, rebellion, revolution, insurrection, mutiny tumult military or usurped power, any accident, loss, destruction, damage or legal liability directly or indireclty caused by or contributed to by or arising from nuclear weapon and consequential losses.

(*ii*) *Sheep and Goat Insurance.* The sheep and goat insurance provides indemnity in the event of death of insured animals due to disease or accident contracted during the period of risk in the age group 4 months to, 7 years of the sheeps. Ramsused for breeding and aged more than 75 per cent of its market value. Goats are covered between age group of 6 months to 5 years. The sum assured will be restricted to 80 per cent of market value as certified by veterinary surgeon or 100 per cent bank advance whichever is higher. The premium rates are 8 per cent of sum assured in case of sheep and 10 per cent in case of goat of indigeneous breed for private insureds. This premium is 10 per cent for exotic breed. The premium rate for bank financed and IRDP project is 2.75 per cent in both the cases of sheep and goat. The foot rot is excluded for sheep under this category. The policy shall provide indemnity against death of sheep and goats due to accident including fire, lightning, flood, cyclone, famine, strike, riot and civil commotion or diseases contracted or occurring during the period of insurance.

(*iii*) *Horse/Pony/Mule Insurance.* The policy for horse/pony/mule insurance includes draught horses, half draught horses, ponies, mules against death due to accidents and/or specified diseases contacted during the period of insurance and subject to usual terms, conditions and exclusions of the policy. The age group for such animals to be insured are 2 years to 8 years. Indigeneous, cross-bred and exotic are insured. The sum assured is 100 per cent market value or bank loan which is higher. The non-scheme animals are charged premium at the rate of 4 per cent of sum assured whereas the scheme animals are charged at 2.75 per cent per annum.

(*iv*) *Pig insurance.* Pig insurance policy covers death risk due to accident or disease. The minimum number of animals covered is 10. Swire fever disease is excluded. The age group insurable is one month to 5 years. All indigeneous cross-bred and exotic pigs are insured. The maximum sum insured per pig is Rs. 500. The premium rate is 6 per cent per annum but pigs under SFDA/IRDP scheme are charged at 3.5 per cent per annum. The sum assured will be linked to 100 per cent of market value for organised breeding farms whereas in other cases it is 80 per cent of market value.

(*v*) *Camel Insurance.* The camel insurance policy is applicable to all male and female camels in India including camel subsidised by SFDA/DPAP/MFAL between age group of 3 years to 10 years. The sum assumed will be 80 per cent of market value or bank finance. The maximum sum insured is Rs. 3000 in case of bank finance SFDA/DPAP/MFAL. In case of PTD claim, 75 per cent of sum assured is payable. The premium rate is 4 per cent per annum for non-IRDP scheme camels and 2.25 per cent (net) for IRDP scheme camels. 'Surra' disease is excluded. The minimum premium is Rs. 25 per annum per animal. The policy provides indemnity only for death due to accident at inclusive of flood, cyclone, famine or disease inclusive of Rinderpest, Blackquarter, Haemorrhagic Septicaemia/ Anthrax contracted or occurring during the period of policy or strike, riot and civil common risks. The exclusions are common exclusions and specific exclusions.

Common exclusions are applicable to all types of cattle insurance. They are malicious or wilful injury or neglect over-loading, unskilful treatment or use of animal for purpose other than stated in the policy without the consent of the insurer in writing. Accident occurring and/or diseases contracted period to commencement of risk. Intentional slaughter of the animals except in cases where destruction is necessary to terminate incurable suffering on humane consideration on the basis of certificates issued by qualified veterinarian or in cases where destruction is resorted to by the order of lawfully constituted authority. Theft and clandestine sale of the insured animal, war, invasion, act of foreign enemy, hostilities whether war be declared or not, civil war rebellion, revolution, insurrection, mutiny, tumult, military or usurped power or any consequences thereof or attempt threat. Any accident, loss, destruction, damage or legal liability directly or indirectly caused by or contributed to by or arising from nuclear weapons. Consequential loss of whatsoever nature. Specific exclusion are transport by air and sea, partial disability of any type. Death of camel due to disease Surra. Diseases contracted prior to and within 15 days of commencement of risk.

(vi) Rabbit Insurance. The rabbit insurance policy is applicable to all breeds of Rabbits in India, in the age group of 1 day to 4 years, but death of rabbits due to disease till they complete the age of 30 days is not covered. The risks covered, death of rabbits due to accident and/or disease contracted during the period of insurance. The exclusions have common exclusions as described in camel insurance and specific exclusions of transport by air and sea, permanent and partial disablement of any nature pasteurellosis, culling, cannibalism and intentional slaughter, undergrowth, myxomatosis and coocidissis. The insured is compensed only 70 per cent of the sum assured, the rate of premium is 7 per cent of sum assured.

(vii) Elephant Insurance. The elephant insurance policy indemnifies the owner for death due to accident or disease contracted or occurring during the period of insurance subject to certain exclusions stipulated. The insurable age group is one year to 60 years. The policy is applicable to the elephants including those owned by temple, circus companies and individuals. The sum assured is 80 per cent of market value. The value of sum assured does not exceed Rs. 50,000. The premium rate is 5 per cent per annum. The common exclusions clause as mentioned under Cattle Market Agreement is also applicable in this case. Specific exclusions are surgical operations, disability, breeding and calving and certain specific diseases such as tuberculosis, foot, and mouth diseases etc.

(viii) Dog Insurance. The dog insurance policy insures the risks against death due to accident and/or disease contracted during the period of insurance subject to usual theory and conditions. The insurable age group is 8 weeks to 8 years. Dogs of indigeneous cross-bred and exotic breeds are insured under this policy. The minimum value of any breed should not be less than Rs. 200 and maximum value of any dog should not exceed Rs. 2,000 each dog. The premium rate is 5 per cent per annum. In the event of death of the insured dog, any amount received or receivable by the insured from third parties and the value of the salvage recovered if any would be deducted from the claim amount.

(ix) Livestock Insurance Master Policy. An open policy is issued without specifying the sum insured. This will be stamped document stating the type of cover grantee, perils covered, conditions exclusions etc. When loans are granted by the branch of the bank, the animals purchased will be covered under the insurance scheme. The insurance cover will commence from the time the animals are purchased by the beneficiaries and will be valid for one year. The declaration forms are supplied to bank's branches by the insurance company. As and when animals are financed, the branch will send to the insurance company the declaration giving details of the borrowers financed alongwith the certificate of veterinary doctor. Under the livestock insurance scheme livestock as milch cows, buffaloes, calves/heifers, stud bulls and bullocks castrated bulls and male buffaloes whether indigeneous cross-bred or exotic, sheep, goats and pigs are insured. This policy covers death of livestock due to any accident inclusive of fire, lightning, flood, inundation, storm, hurricane, earthquake, cyclone, tornado, tempest, famine snakebite etc., diseases inclusive of rinderpest, blackquarter, haemorrhagic septicaemia anthrax, foot and mouth diseases, surgical operation strike, riot and civil commotion.

The cattle and livestock insurance has shown an increase of Rs. 75.58 crores during 1982 to 1988-89 from Rs. 26.3 crores to Rs. 101.88 crores. It is about four-fold increase which far more above those of traditional increase. The percentage increase over previous year was maximum at 35.6 per cent in 1984 whereas it was the lowest in 1986. So for cattle number is concerned, it has in creased from 82.4 lakhs in 1982 to 256.22 lakhs in 1988-89 giving about three-fold increase. The growth rate as compared to previous year was maximum at 34.9 per cent in 1984 and the decline at 2.3 per cent in 1987. It shows that the year 1984 and 1985 have been very promising for non-traditional business. The subsidiaries of GIC have to expand their business through pragmatic strategies.

Table 36.4

	Premium Income		Number Insured	
	In Crores of Rs.	*% Increase over previous year*	*In Lakhs*	*% increase over previous year*
1982	26.3	37.9	82.4	45.1
1983	33.9	28.7	105.8	28.4
1984	45.96	35.6	143.0	34.9
1985	51.36	11.8	161.0	12.7
1986	59.35	15.6	189.69	18.0
1987	69.45	17.0	185.36	–2.3
1988-89	101.88	17.0	256.22	10.6
1989-90	86.04	—	199.21	—

4. Poultry Insurance

The general insurance companies have taken another big to insurance poultry, duck and other birds.

(*i*) *Poultry Insurance.* The poultry insurance policy cover poultry farms consisting of 100 or more pure and hybrid chicks, hens and cocks. All birds in a farm should be covered. The policy covers death of birds due to accident or disease contracted or occurring during the period of insurance subject to certain exclusions. Birds are covered from 0 to 72 weeks. The cover is for epidemics *i.e.* Ranikhet disease, Fowl Pox and Gamhoro. The sum assured is as per poultry market agreement. The sum insured is as per valuation table. The premium rate is Rs. 1.20 per bird where SFDA and other subsides are applied, the premium is Re. 0.90 per bird. Extra premium will be charged in case of addition of fresh birds. Each proposal is rated according to flock strength mortality and management of farm. The compulsory inspection of the risk by Company's Veterinary surgeon before assumption of risk, besides periodical routine inspection at intervals.

(*ii*) *Poultry Insurance Master Policy (IRDP).* Poultry Insurance Master Policy as Cattle Master Policy is issued to benefits the benefactors of IRDP.

(*iii*) *Duck Insurance.* The duck insurance policy provides indemnity against death of ducks due to accident including fire, lightning, flood, cyclone, famine, strike, riot, civil commotion or diseases contracted or occurring during the period of insurance subject to specific exclusions. This policy is applicable to all types of migratory and non-migratory birds in India, ducks farms consisting of minimum 100 ducks for non-IRDP and 50 ducks for IRDP and other subsidised schemes. The insurable age is first week to 52 weeks. The premium is Re. 1.00 per bird and Re. 0.90 per bird for IRDP and other scheme birds. Common exclusions are as mentioned under Cattle Market Agreement. Specific exclusions are improper management cannibalism, sun stroke virus, transit diseases such as Coli Aspirgillosis etc.

Table 36.5 Poultry Insurance

	Premium Income		Number of Birds	
	In Lakhs of Rs.	*% Increase previous year*	*In Lakhs*	*% increase over previous year*
1984	42.68	—	40.48	—
1985	68.63	60.8	63.49	56.8
1986	84.51	23.1	65.07	2.5
1987	111.74	32.2	85.71	31.7

The premium income under poultry insurance has, increased from Rs. 42 68 lakhs in 1984 to Rs. 111.74 lakhs in 1987 giving about two-fold increase. The growth rate has been declining from 60.8 per cent to 32.2 per cent. The number of birds insured increased from 40.48 lakhs in 1984 to 85.71 lakhs giving two-fold rise during 1987.

5. Insurance of Species

The general insurance industry has started insuring other species such as brackish water prawn, inland fish, silkworms and honey bees.

(*i*) *Brackish Water Prawn Insurance.* The brackish water prawn insurance policy cover risks against total loss of prawn, nursed seeds in hatcheries owned by State Government; FFDAS, State Fisheries Corporations, MPEDA or such other organisations. It is issued to provide insurance cover to the engaged in brackish water prawn farming against total loss of seedlings/Juveniles/prawns of all species raised in brackish waters after being transferred to the farm. It also provides cover to financial institutions to protect their interests and recover loans advanced for such brackish water prawn farming in the event of loss. The policy covers either the input cost or fixed value of the produce. The period of cover is from the stage prawn seeds being sown in hatcheries for rearing till the post larvae/ removed from the hatcheries. The period of cover for farms is from the stage of transferring of post larvae to the brackish-water till actual harvesting. The premium rate is 4 per cent of mean value declared for insurance for each crop period. The insurance covers total loss or destruction of prawns due to accident and disease such as summer kill, pollution, posioning riot and strikes, malicious acts of third parties, earthquakes, explosion, storms, tempest, cyclone, typhoon, hurricane, tornado, flood, inundation, volcanic eruption and other comulsions of nature, aircraft and other aerial devices or articles dropped therefrom, impact with any road vehicle, horses and cattle, shell disease, vibriosis aeromanas celiades and other viral form of opidemics and parasitical attacks. Wilful destruction losses due to natural mortality, overcrowding, loss due to negligence and error, theft, dacoity, war invasion, hostilities etc. arc excluded from this policy.

(*ii*) *Fish Insurance Policy.* The fish insurance policy indemnifies the insured against total loss due to accident or disease of Fry/Fingerlings/Fish in ponds, lakes and other still fresh water. This policy covers death or loss of fish due to disease of any kind, epidemic, parasitic infestation, poisoning, malicious act by third parties, pollution, summer kill, riot and strike, explosion, fire, aircraft damage and aerial devices, impact by any vehicle, storm, tempest, flood, innudation. The exclusions are loss due to improper management and bad handling, loss due to neglect and carelessness, loss due to malicious act, wilful injury, error or omission, partial loss of any kind, losses sue to dangerous insects, predators, competitions etc. losses due to variation in pH factor, physical, chemical status of the water and soils, asphyxia, losses due to natural mortality, burglary, house breaking, theft infidelity of any person, land and air accident loss, destruction damage or legal liability directly or indirectly caused by contributed to by or arising from nuclear weapons material. 80 per cent of fish as per valuation is indemnified. The premium rate is 2.5 per cent per annum on average value of fish.

(*iii*) *Silk Worms Insurance.* The silk worms insurance policy is applicable to mulberry silkworms only of Univoltine, Bivoltine or Multivoltine Breed. The disease free layings purchased from licensed seed preparers/Graineurs or Government Grainages are covered. Silkworms from egg stage to cocoon stage are insured. This policy covers death of silkworm due to accident or disease contracted during the period of insurance subject to the usual terms and conditions. The cover is in respect or total loss only. The malicious wilful act of insured his family member/person/worker; theft, clandestine sale, missing of the worms and non supply of adequate quality suitable quality of mulberry leaves. The valuation is done by Sericulture officer. The insured will send monthly declaration statement to the insurer based upon which premium is collected or adjusted. The premium is 5 per cent per annum of the sum assured on the market value of cocoon at the 5th stage.

(*iv*) *Honey Bee Insurance.* The honey bee insurance policy indeminfies the insured against all accidental losses or damages to the Hive and/or Bee Colony subject to the exclusion of loss of production, malicious or wilful act or neglect or improper management; theft, clandestine sale or missing of worms, war invasion, act of foreign enemy, hoslilities, civil war, rebellion, revolution, insurrection, mutiny, military or usurped power or any consequences thereof or attempt thereat; accident loss, destruction, damage or legal liability directly or indirectly, caused by or contributed to by or arising from nuclear weaks material. The rate or premium is 3 per cent of total insured value. Risk of theft can be covered on payment, of additional premium of 2 per cent.

The form subsidiary companies have underwritten small volume of business under pondfish insurance, silkworm insurance, agriculture insurance and animal driven cart insurance.

6. Package Insurance

The General Insurance Corporation and its four subsidiaries have evolved insurance policy known as package insurance with a view to offer complete, all round protection to the weaker sections of societies in respect of their dwelling premises and belongings from various hazards. They are composite package and farmers' package.

(*i*) *Composite Package Insurance.* The composite package insurance has been evolved to protect the weaker sections and tribes. The properties covered under this scheme are huts, dwelling, cottage industry sheds, contents including belongings personal accident and hospitalisation. The risks covered under this policy are fire, lightning, riots and strikes, malicious damage, aircraft damage, flood, inundations, cyclone, storm, tempest, typhoon, tornado, hurricane. The sum assured under Hut coverage is Rs. 2,000 and premium rate is 3 per cent annum. The contents are for Rs. 1,000 at 3 per cent premium. Personal accident covers Rs. 10,000 at the premium of Rs. 10. Hospitabsation for accidents and major diseases are for Rs. 4,000 at the premium of Rs. 40.00. Thus, the total premium Rs. 59 for covering all the above risks under one policy.

(*ii*) *Farmers' Package Insurance.* The farmers' package insurance policy has been issued to provide insurance coverage to the farmers for dwelling hut/houses, agricultural implements, seeds, fertilisers, pesticides against the risks of fire, lightning, cyclone, earthquake, flood upto Rs. 5000; cattle insurance against death due to accident and discase, permanent total disablement and breeding and calving risks upto Rs. 4000; agricultural pumpsets against fire, theft/burglary and machinery breakdown upto their market price, bullock cart against death/permanent disabilities to animal due to accident upto Rs. 2000, loss/damage to cart due to accident upto Rs. 1000, third party liability personal accident to cart driver and Gramin Personal Accident against death/permanent total disablement upto Rs. 6000 under single policy known as farmers' package insurance.

The premium is decided as per separate insurance policy.

7. Crop Insurance

The countrywide comprehensive crop insurance scheme introduced by the Government of India commenced from kharif 1985-86. The GIC has been entrusted with the task of administering the scheme on behalf of the Government. The insurance charges and claims in respect of crops insured in any state is shared between the Central Crop Insurance Fund and Crop Insurance Fund set up by the State Government concerned in the ratio of 2 : 1. GIC maintains close and constant liaison with State Governments, RBI, NABARD, State Cooperative Banks, Commercial Banks, Regional Rural Banks, and other agencies involved for smooth implementations of the scheme.

The number of farmers covered under crop insurance has increased from 26.30 lakhs in 1985 (Kharif) to 29.64 lakhs in 1988. The premium income has declined from Rs. 9.42 lakhs to Rs. 8.82 lakhs under Kharif. The number of farmers covered has declined from 12.13 lakhs in 1985-86 to 8.71 lakhs in 1988-89. The premium has also declind from Rs 4.48 crores to Rs. 3.12 crores. This shows that the crop insurance is not being properly managed by the GIC and its four subsidiaries.

Table 36.6
Crop Insurance

		Kharif							Rabi						
		1985	1986	1987	1988	1989	1997-98	2001	1985-86	1986-87	1987-88	1988-89	1989-90	1997-98	2001-02
1 No of farmers covered (in Lakhs)		26.31	40.66	46.31	29.64	42.26	51.35	85.69	12.13	11.28	21.28	8.79	6.61	6.82	20
2. Sum Insured	Rs.	542.73	856.20	1140.15	547.89	873.86	2230.74	7300.9	238.41	242.37	475.44	163.87	148.76	322.37	1600
3. Premium	Rs.	9.42	14.99	19.09	8.82	14.44	34.32	256.96	4.48	4.57	8.55	3.12	2.72	5.72	
4 Incurred claims	Rs.	83.00	159.54	277.38	27.84	28.05	—	508.10	2.96	7.80	12.07	3.10	—	—	

Table 36.7

Statement of New Business Under Janashree Bima Yojana & Krishi Shramik Samajik Suraksha Yojana-2001 as at 31-03-2003 by the LIC

ZONE	*JANASHREE BIMA YOJANA*						*KRISHI SHRAMIK SAMAJIK SURAKSHA YOJANA 2001*			*TOTAL FOR THE YEAR 2002-03*		
	GROWTH RATE (MARCH 2003)			*FOR THE YEAR 2002-03*			*FOR THE YEAR 2002-03*					
	SCH	*LIVES*	*PREMIUM*	*SCH*	*LIVES*	*PREMIUM*	*SCH*	*LIVES*	*PREMIUM*	*SCH*	*LIVES*	*PREMIUM*
NORTHERN	–56	82	82	292	36914	3691400	164	7909	1735600	456	44823	5427000
CENTRAL	–66	88	88	372	71523	7152300	43	8333	1001595	415	79856	8153895
NORTH CENTRAL	19	–1	–1	398	78525	7852500	137	2674	240660	535	81199	8093160
EASTERN	115	48	48	370	33290	3329000	435	26283	4590839	805	59573	7919839
SOUTHERN	337	848	848	387	62376	6237600	688	22372	4212165	1075	84748	10449765
SOUTH CENTRAL	–35	1055	1055	516	122597	12259700	429	8694	3010575	945	131291	15270275
WESTERN	43	109	109	950	230891	23089100	890	33748	5364610	1840	264639	28453710
CORPORATION	–7	199	199	3285	636116	63611600	2786	110013	20156044	6071	746129	83767544

*Budget 2002-03 include targets of Krishi Shramik Suraksha Yojana.

Since Government finding is involved, the scheme lacks smooth management. The triangular decisions and processes *i.e.*, GIC, Central Government and states have caused less efficiencies in crop insurance. The GIC may be given certain regular premium by the Central government who may get reimbursed from respective states for its proper management. The crop insurance in India needs thorough revision and systematic management.

The Government of India introduced National Agricultural Insurance Scheme (NAIS) replacing the Comphrehensive Crop Insurance Scheme (CCIS) with effect from Rabi 1999-2000 season. The scheme cover all farmers-loance and non-loance. Sugarcane, Potato and cotton. Onion Ginger, Gonlic and termeric are also covered. Similarly Jute, Tapioca Banana and Pineapple are introduced and covered.

Oriental Insurance has introduced Rice Insurance Policy. Khalihan Bima Policy, Jan Arogya Bima and Agricultural tractor Policies got much appreciation by villagers.

8. Rural Insurance Business

The overall performance, under Rural Insurance Business for 1994-95 has shown good progress. The premium income received was Rs. 31.26 crores by National Insurance. The Solatium Final Schemes were operative in all the insurance companies. United India paid death claim amounting to Rs. 23.95 lakhs and Rs. 1.45 lakhs injury to victims in "Hit and Run" accident cases during 1994-95. Under Personal Accident Social Security Insurance Scheme out of Claims amounting 2063 claims of Rs. 61.88 were settled by New India, Rs. 24.69 lakhs by Oriental Insurance and Rs. 218.86 lakhs by United India during 1994-95. All the companies have procured Rs. 336 crores during 1997-98.

PROSPECTS OF AGRICULTURE INSURANCE IN INDIA

Agriculture is the oldest occupation and is primary sector of the economy. Industrialisation and technological upgrading has increased the degree of risks in agriculture. The risks to be scaled up continuously to bring the much needed prosperity in the rural economy. The risks in agriculture are classified under production risk, pest risks, market risk, investment and credit risk, institutional risk, technology risks and personal risks. Production risks include rainfall, temperature variation, frost, solar radiation, wind and vapour pressure pest risks include soil, its fertility, PH texture, physiology, phenology and morphology, farmyard manners, pest management and irrigation.

Agriculture Insurance Company of India Limited (AIC)

The Government and the Agriculture Insurance Company of India Limited (AIC) have passed through the leaning curve in all areas of crop insurance and are looking to make crop insurance reachable and affordable to a majority of cultivators. Based on the data supplied by Indian Agriculture Research Institute (IARI), AIC is able to offer products on climate variation and locational differences in around 250 locations spread over around 50 districts of the country. AIC has been experimenting with unique insurance models in the management of crop insurance. AIC has kept management costs below a level of 2% and intermediary costs of low level. It has used the large banking network numbering 1.5 lakhs branches of commercial banks. Cooperative Banks and Rural Banks and Primary Agricultural Cooperative societies AIC has collaborator with the various Boards and Authories in the agriculture sector such as the Coffee, Rubber, Coconut, Spices Boards, Floriculture and all types of plantations.

Index based weather insurance is rapidly gaining interest in India. More than 5,00,000 Indian farmers have taken weather insurance policies through schemes provided by AIC and private sector insurance companies including ICICI Lombard and IFFCO Tokio, Swiss Reinsuring the schemes of micro-finance. AIC is actively promoting crop insurance, strengthening marketing, education and awareness of the benefits of insurance.

CROP INSURANCE

Crop insurance is a part of agriculture insurance. It has included the risks of weather, yield and so on.

Weather Insurance : Weather insurance is part of crop insurance which started since Kharif 2003 season through BASIX, a micro-finance institution. Agriculture Insurance Company of India Limited (AIC), a government entity is created to ensure agriculture risks. ICICI Lombard General Insurance Company and IFFCO. Tokio General Insurance Company have been piloting weather based crop insurance. Farmers have not responded positively because of unaffordable premium rates and lack of subsidies from the Government, technical challenges, unrealistic expectations, poor communication and lack of clarity AIC has been running a pilot weather insurance scheme since Kharif 2004. It has started weather based crop insurance scheme during Kharif 2007 in Karnataka. AIC designed the weather indices using weather parameters us unseasonal rains, frost heat relative humidity and technical inputs from the apex scientific institutions in designing the customised insurance product for Rabi 2007-08 season. Weather insurance seems to score better when it causes to data accuracy. transparency and quick settlement of payouts. Weather based crop insurance program and the challenges are designing a proxy weather index with predictive capability to realistically measure crop losses and is closer to the indemnity principle and the basis risk. A good insurance product should be able ensure either no claim if the crop is good or high claim of the crop is poor.

Role of Weather Insurance

Weather insurance has a role to play, particularly, as complimentary to the existing area yield crop insurance weather insurance is the solution for the areas where yield data are not available. Weather index is used to make early payments under area yield crop insurance. It is also used to design double trigger insurance products. Triggers are weather index and area yield estimate. Weather insurance is designed for micro level insurance products. It is an ideal tool for protecting a large port- folio at District/Regional/State level against droughts or floods. Weather, insurance produce design is to taken to minimise to basis risk creating realistic and appropriate communication, adopting reliable and sustainable pricing and product servicing.

Yield Insurance : Yield insurance covers the loss of Hurricane, Tornado, Flood, Inundation and Landslide, Drought, Dry Spells, Pests and diseases. Yield based crop insurance covers Food Crops, Cereals, Millets and Pulses, Oilseeds and Animal Crops, Commercial Crops and Horticultural Crops. It operates on 'Area Approach'. Individual assessment of losses is also being implemented on experimental basis. The size of area is Block/Mandal/ Nyaya Panchayat/Gram Panchayat. Village may be area for selected crops.

Sum Assured : The amount of crop loan is the minimum sum assured which is on compulsory basis. Additional coverage upto 150% value of average yield by paying premium at acturial rate. For the non-loanee farmers, the coverage is available at normal flat rates of premium for the value of normal coverage of yield. The value of sum assured is arrived at by multiplying the thresh hold yield/ average yield with the latest available Minimum Support Price (MSP) announced by the Government or the market price is MSP is not announced.

Premium : The premium at acturial rate as (AIC) communicated by Agriculture Insurance Company of India Ltd. (AIC) is generally 3.5% of Sum Insured for bagra and oilseeds, 2.5% for other food crops, 1.5% for wheat and 2% for other food crops. The premium for small and marginal farmers is subsidised to the extent of 10% which is shared by the State Government and Government of India.

Settlement of claims : Claim is a Notified Area, automatically payable if these is a shortfall in (NFA) become yield, i.e., current season's yield is less than the guaranteed yield. The shortfall is converter into claims by multiplying the percentage shortfall with sum insured. The guaranted yield or Threshold Yield (TY) for a crop in an insurance unit based on moving average of the preceding 3/

5 years multiplied by the idemenity level, i.e., 90% or 80% or 60% depending upon the variability in the yield of the crop.

Coverage : The summary of coverage under National Agricultural Insurance Scheme (Rabi 1999-2000 to 2006-07 season) is given in the table

Table 36.8

Coverage of Crop Insurance

Total number of farmers covered	9,70,73,736
Total Area covered (Hectares)	15,62,10,772
Total Sum Insured (Rs. crore)	97,180
Total Insurance changes (Rs. crore)	2943
Total claim (Rs. crore)	9763
Claim Ratio	1:3

International Agriculture Insurance

Agriculture Insurance in world in gaining ground. The Private Insurance are taking interest in agricultural insurance

Table 36.9

	Premium	USD (Million)	Private Insurer
Asia of which	428		
India		141	Low
South Korea		69	Medium
China		94	Medium
Latin America of which	309		
Argentina		92	High
Brazil		111	Low
Clule		3	Moderate
Mexico		30	Moderate
Eastern Europe of which	230		
Russia		15	Moderate
Poland		20	Moderate
Czech Republic		30	Moderate
Turkies		36	Moderate
Africa of which	103		
South Africa		60	High
Nigeria		1	Low
Mauritius		19	Low
Total	**1070**		

QUESTIONS

1. How far rural masses have been benefited by the rural insurance schemes?
2. What is cattle insurance? How many livestock are insured under cattle insurance?
3. 'Crop insurance in India is not very popular'. Discuss it.

37

URBAN NON-TRADITIONAL INSURANCE

The non-traditional insurance applicable in urban areas may be personal insurance, property insurance, liability insurance and package insurance.

1. Personal Insurance

Personal insurance covers personal accident insurance, medi-claim hospitalisation, overseas medi-claim policy, students, safety insurance, urban child welfare insurance and cancer medical expenses policy.

(*i*) *Personal Accident Insurance.* Personal accident insurance covers death, total or partial disablement due to accident. The insurable age is 12 to 70 years. The capital sum-insured is generally Rs. 10,000 wherein the sum assured is payable at death or at loss of two limbs, two eyes or one limb and one eye. Rs. 5,000 is paid at loss of one limb or one eye, Rs. 10,000 is paid at the permanent total disablement from injuries other than those named above. Medical expenses arising out of an accident upto 10 per cent of the capital sum insured or 25 per cent of the admissible claim whichever is lower at additional premium at the rate of 10 per cent of basic premium. The normal premium is Rs. 6.00 for Rs. 10,000 sum assured to be paid at death. Rs. 12.50 is charged for the benefits of death loss of two limbs, two eyes or one limb and one eye or loss of one limb or one eye permanent total disablement and permanent partial disablement. The normal risks and heavy risks are required to pay Rs. 6.00 and Rs. 9.00 respectively for death and Rs. 12.50 and Rs. 19.00 respectively for death and other benefits as given above. Heavy risks include persons working in underground mines, explosives, magazines, jockeys circus personnel, big game hunting mountaineering, winter sports, skiing or ice hockey, ballooning or polo and persons engaged in occupation of similar nature, due to the very nature of their profession. The cover is worldwide. Normal risks are others than those given in heavy risks.

(*ii*) *Personal Accident Insurance* (*family*). The family package cover is granted on the following pattern. The personal accident insurance family package incorporates all the conditions as mentioned in the personal accident insurance (individual). The cover for earning member (person insured) and spouse if earning will be 100 per cent of the capital sum insured for each *i.e.,* Rs. 10,000 (base figure). The cover is 50 per cent of the capital sum insured or Rs. 1 lakh whichever is lower if spouse is not earning member. 25 per cent of the capital sum insured or Rs. 50,000 whichever is lower per child, will be insured for children between age of 5 years and 19 years. For children the cover shall be limited to Death and Permanent Disablement (total and partial) only and premium payable will be at table II benefits and corresponding rates. Premium payable for husband and wife will be on the total Sum Insured at table III benefits and corresponding rates. A discount of 5 per cent may be granted on the gross premium under the Family Package Cover. It is applicable for the proposal exceeding Rs. 1,00,000 also.

(*iii*) *Medi-claim Hospitalisation and Domiciliary Hospitalisation Insurance.* The policy insures payment of 80 per cent of medical expenses actually and necessarily incurred in India by or on behalf of insured person. The age of insurable person is 12 to 70 years. Hospitalisation cover starts after 30 days for diseases from the commencement of the policy. It is not applicable to renewal policy. The categories of expenses to be reimbursed are mentioned in the table of benefits which are generally room, board and nursing expenses, surgeon and anaesthetist fees, oxygen and blood expenses, X-ray, medicines end drugs. The annual premium rates vary with the benefits required and categories of insurance. Personal accident insurance can also be sought alongwith this policy wherein the insured amount is paid at death or at loss of two limbs, loss of sight of two eyes or loss of one limb and loss of sight of one eye or loss of one limb or loss of sight of one eye or permanent total disablement from injuries other than the insured diseases. Mediclaim policy to persons above the age of 70 years subject to reduced limits of liability is being introduced. For the benefits of Mediclaim policyholder, tie up arrangements have been finalised with two hospitals in Bombay, and one each in Calcutta, Madras, Hyderabad and Pune. The subsidiary companies are negotiating such tie up arrangements in other centres also.

(*iv*) *Overseas Medi-claim, Policy.* Overseas medi-claim policy insures reimbursement of medical expenses incurred in connection with sickness/accident/disease/death outside India subject to applicable deductible. The persons eligible for this policy are persons undertaking bonagide trips abroad for business, official, professional purposes including training assignment officially sponsored; for holiday either in groups or as an individual and accompanying spouse and children of persons eligible as above. The maximum cover is 180 days for business tour, 60 days for plan A and 30 days under plan B for holiday travel. The proposals in excess of this are to be referred to GIC with medical reports. Plan A is worldwide excluding USA and Canada and plan B is worldwide including USA and Canada. The sum assured is $ 50,000 under Plan A and $ 1,00,000 under Plan B. The adults are insurable upto 70 years and children are insurable above 5 years. Claims are settled in foreign currency through authorised agents of G.I.C.

(*v*) *Student's Safety Insurance.* The student's safety insurance is intended to be issued to the schools/colleges or any other educational institution for the benefit of the student studying therein. The students are covered against death, total loss of two limbs, two eyes or one limb and one eye, total loss of one limb or one eye and permanent total or partial disablement. The benefits per student are Rs. 10,000 at death, Rs. 10,000 at loss of two limbs, two eyes or one limb and one eye or at permanent total disablement from injuries other than those mentioned above and Rs. 5,000 at the loss of one limb or one eye. There are other compensations verify from one per cent at the loss of more than one toe to 50 per cent at the loss of two ears. In addition to the above, the policy will provide for reimbursement of medical expenses subject to limb of Rs. 500. Claims are payable to parent or guardian of the student as mentioned in the school register. The premium is Rs. 6.00 per thousand of sum assured if students are 500 and Rs. 1.50 per thousand if students are 5000. The premium rates vary from Rs. 1.50 per thousand to Rs. 6.00 per thousand as per number of students included under this policies.

(*vi*) *Unborn Child Welfare Insurance.* The unborn child welfare insurance policy is applicable for expectant mothers in the age group of 18 to 40 years with pregnancy up to 3 months. The scheme provides for reimbursement of medical expenses for treating a child born with congenital anomalies and for its maintenance if the anomalies are certified as permanent total disablement. For permanent partial disablement, a proportion of the sum insured is payable as the percentage of disability certified by the doctor. Medical expenses are reimbursed upto 50 per cent of the capital sum insured as per table of benefits in case of congenital anomalies which are curable. Medical expenses are reimbursed as per Table of Benefits besides a certain percentage of the balance (unspent) amount will be paid as deposit in a bank or Unit Trust in case of congenital anomalies which are certified by a qualified doctor as 'Permanent Partial Disability'. Medical expenses are reimbursed and the balance unspent amount is put in a Bank or Unit Trust in case of congenital anomalies which are certified as 'Permanent

Total Disability'. On the death of the insured, the monthly benefits will be paid to the legally appointed guardian or failing that to the legally appointed guardian under whose care the child is placed. The premium rate is 2 per cent for capital sum insured and so on upto Rs. 75,000 sum assured. Claims under this policy is payable in Indian currency. All medical treatment for the purpose of this insurance will have to be taken in India only. The limit of liability in respect of hospitalisation is as for table of Hospitalisation and Domiciliary Hospitalisation Benefits.

(vii) Cancer Medical Expenses Policy. The cancer medical expenses policy covers medical expenses due to cancer for insured person or spouse. The sum assured is Rs. 50,000 at the premium of Rs. 100. The period covers treatment expenses started during the policy period till the sum assured is exhausted. Cover starts after 30 days of the issue of the policy. It is not applicable for renewals. Cumulative bonus at the rate of 5 per cent on continuous claim free medical renewal subject to maximum sum insured of Rs. 75,000. This cumulative bonus is not applicable to group policy. The group discounting applicable at the rate of 15 per cent if persons insured are below 100 and above 25. This discount is 66.7 per cent if persons covered increased 25,000. The Indian Cancer Society allows the above group discount on the membership fees for the number of persons covered by the Group. The group policy is issued to the member of the Indian Cancer Society. The members of Indian Cancer Society, Ratan Tata Medical and Research Centre, Bombay are benefited one free check up at Cancer Society, Detection Centre. The members are required to pay Rs. 200 per annum. The premium is paid by the Indian Cancer Society for its members under group insurance.

2. Property Insurance

The general insurance industry insures property of people, under boiler and pressure plant insurance, cold storage insurance domestic pumpset insurance, machinery insurance policy, pedal cycle insurance and baggage insurance.

(i) Boiler and Pressure Plant Insurance: The boiler and pressure plant insurance policy is taken for Boiler or Pressure Vessel against the risks of due explosion due to steam pressure. The explosion is causing damage to the boiler or pressure vessel and also the machines surrounding the boilers as well as personnel working in the boiler house. It will also damage the property of neigh bouring industry involving third party liability. Collapse of pressure vessels due to vacuum conditions to created due to lack of steam pressure or condensation of steam is also covered. Explosion shall mean the sudden and violent rending or tearing apart of the permanent structure of a boiler plant or any part or parts thereof by force or internal steam pressure causing bodily displacement of the said structure and accompanied by the forcible ejectment of its contents. Collapse shall mean the sudden and dangerous distortion of any part of a boiler plant by bending or crushing caused by steam pressure whether attended by rupture or not. It shall not mean any slowly developing deformation due to any cause. The premium rate is decided as per Tariff rate.

(ii) Cold Storage Insurance: The cold storage insurance covers potatoes and frozen food. It cover deterioration of stocks stores due to rise in temperature in the storage chamber on account of mechanical or electrical breakdown of machinery insured under concurrent machinery breakdown policy. The cause of machinery breakdown should be sudden and unforeseen damage to machinery insured by the concurrent machinery breakdown policy from any accidental cause, escape of refrigerant in the refrigerated chamber as a result of breakdown of the machines insured under concurrent machinery breakdown policy. The average price of stocks will be sum insured. The premium rate, terms and conditions are decided as per Tariff rate.

(iii) Domestic Pumpset Insurance. The domestic pumpset insurance policy covers domestic pumpset against the risks of loss due to short circuit, single phasing, faulty design, lack of skill, fluctuations in power supply, theft, burglary, fire and lightning. The premium is based on horse power. For example upto 3 H.P. premium is Rs. 50 and upto 10 H.P., the premium is Rs. 100 per

annum.

(*iv*) *Machinery Insurance.* The machinery insurance policy covers machinery like compressors, pumps, turbines etc. as also electrical machines such as transformers, electrical motors etc. The cover may be accident caused by faulty materials, action of centrifugal forces contributing to disruption of the rotating parts, malfunctioning or failure of safety devices, failure of lubrication due to malfunctioning of the lubricating oil pump or its own breakdown, electrical short-circuit including electrical fire originating from failure of insulation and/or over-voltage or under- voltage conditions, about and sudden stoppage of other connected machinery, entry of foreign bodies into a running machine and inexperienced operators causing damage due to error of judgement. The replacement value is considered for deciding the sum assured. The premium is decided as per Tariff-rate and inspection by the engineer of the insurer.

(*v*) *Pedal Cycle Insurance*: The pedal cycle insurance policy covers pedal cycle against the risks of loss or damage of pedal cycle by accident, fire, external explosion, malicious damage, theft and liability to third parties. Death of or bodily injury to any person damage to the property. Maximum limit is Rs. 10,000. The premium rate is 5 per cent of the sum insured.

(*vi*) *Baggage Insurance.* The baggage insurance policy covers baggage of travelling person except costly item like jewellery. It covers risks of loss, destroyed or damage at any time while travelling by accident, fire or theft. The premium rate per thousand is Rs. 4 upto 15 days, Rs. 6 upto 3 weeks, Rs. 8 for 1 month and Rs. 30 upto 12 months. The minimum premium is Rs.30.

3. Liability Insurance

Liability insurance includes doctors, composite package insurance, lift insurance, public and product liability.

(*i*) *Doctors' Composite Package Insurance.* The doctors' composite package insurance policy is devised to meet the insurance requirements of the doctors through a single composite package policy. There are seven coverage under this policy viz., fire and allied perils including burglary, house breaking, theft; fidelity guarantee insurance for cashier/compounder/any other authorised employee; money-in-transit by self/cashier/compounder/any other authorised employee; loss or damage to doctor's kit by fire, theft accident during visits within municipal city limits; all risks for ECG and other electronic machines and such other equipment pertaining to doctor's profession; signboard and doctor's professional indemnity, The coverage of fire and burglary is compulsory. More than two covers will entitle the proposer to a special discount of 15 per cent maximum.

(*ii*) *Lift Insurance.* The lift insurance is liability insurance against for compensation of any accidental death or bodily injury sustained by any person whilst in the lift. The premium is Rs. 200 for Rs. 1,00,000 and Rs. 700 for Rs. 5,00,000.

(*iii*) *Product and Public Liability.* A market agreement on product and public liability with standardised terms and conditions and scientific premium rating structure has been brought into force from January 1, 1988.

4. Package Insurance

Package insurance include a number of risks under one policy. There are certain insurances which are included under package in the beginning of the policy or during the currency of policy. The householders' insurance, shopkeepers' insurance all risks cover and social security scheme.

(*i*) *Householders' Insurance.* The householders' insurance policy is designed to cater to the requirements of the householder by combining under a single policy a number of contingencies which are otherwise covered separately. The policy covers are building of class 'A' construction; burglary, housebreaking, larcency or theft; all risks; plate glass; breakdown of domestic appliances; T.V. set; pedal cycles; baggage insurance, personal accident and public liability. The policy does not cover inter-alia loss or damage by war, civil war and the like, depreciation, wear and tear, consequential loss etc. The damage to building against fire, lightning explosion of gas in domestic appliances, bursting and overflowing of water tanks, apparatus or pipes, aircraft or articles dropped therefrom, riot and strike, earthquake, malicious act, flood, inundation, storm, cyclone, subsidence and landslide damage and impact damage are covered by this policy. Jewellery and valuables against loss or damage by accident or misfortune. Legal liability upto Rs. 25,000 and damage to insured's own property due to collapse of antenna upto Rs. 3000 under T.V. set insurance. Public liability is pertaining to insured's legal liability for bodily injury or loss of or damage to property of third party limited to amount specified in the schedule and workmen's compensation liability to domestic servants.

(*ii*) *Shopkeeper's Insurance.* The shopkeeper's insurance policy includes fire and allied perils, burglary and housebreaking, money, insurance, pedal cycle, plate glass neon and glow sign, baggage insurance, personal accident, fidelity guarantee, public, liability and workmen's compensation liability. The premium rate per thousand varies from the minimum of Rs. 0.50 for public liability to Rs. 20.00 per thousand for pedal cycle. The Premium rate varies contentwise.

(*iii*) *All Risks Cover Insurance.* Personal jewellery and valuable articles are insured against loss, damage or destruction by accident or misfortune. The premium rate varies from 1.00 per cent to 1.5 per cent of sum assured.

(*iv*) *Social Security Scheme.* A composite policy specifically designed for tribals had been introduced in 1985 to provide insurance cover in respect of huts, cottage industry, dwellings sheds, contents including belongings personal accident and hospitalisation. Composite package insurance policy was also introduced for beneficiaries under District Rural Development Agency Scheme. This policy is designed to provide all round protection to weaker sections of the society covering their residences and personal belongings from various hazards. Among the items covered by the policy are pedal cycles, electrical mechanical appliances, carts, milch cows and working animals, fishing boats, agricultural implements etc. Comprehensive insurance for artisans, village and cottage industries, tiny industries etc., against the fire and other perils for the plants and equipment not exceeding Rs. 10 lakhs. From 15th August 1985, the Government of India introduced a scheme for providing social security through an insurance cover in the event of accidental death of earning members of poor families. The scheme covers all earning members at the age group of 18 to 60 years and provides compensation of Rs. 3,000 to the dependents in the event of accidental death of any of the earning members.

Table 37.1 Social Security Scheme

	Districts Covered	*Claims Settled*
1985	91	—
1986	192	53
1987	214	155
1988-89	415	341
1989-90	417	482

The social security scheme under personal accident insurance increased from 192 districts in 1986 to 415 districts in 1988-89, settling the claims from Rs. 53 lakhs to Rs. 341 lakhs in the respective years.

India International Insurance

The general insurance industry has extended its activities in foreign countries besides the traditional and non-traditional insurance in rural and urban areas. The international insurance is considered under this scheme. India International Insurtence PTE Ltd. has been established as on 3rd Dec., 1987, The principal activities of the company are to undertake the business of insurance and reinsurance of all classes of the general insurance and to perform investment functions incidental thereto. There have been no significant changes in the nature of these activities. The total gross premium earned by this company for 1988 and 1989 respectively were $ 6.641 and 6.0051 million for fire, $16 .628 million and $ 18.466 million for marine, $ 21.675 million and $ 23.853 million for miscellaneous and $ 44.944 million and $ 48.370 million for the total general insurance. It has earned profit of $ 796 thousand and $ 58 thousand for fire, $ 1600 thousand and $ 425 thousand for marine and loss $ 3065 thousand and $ 2285 thousand for miscellaneous. It is expected that this company will earn profit in coming years. The profit before tax was $ 9.68 million and profit retained was $ 5.68 million in 1994-95.

QUESTIONS

1. Why is there non-traditional insurance in urban India?
2. What are the salient features of boiler and pressure plant insurance ?
3. Discuss the future of India International Insurance PTE Ltd.

38

PROGRESS OF MISCELLANEOUS GENERAL INSURANCE

The General Insurance Corporation of India was formed on 22nd Nov. 1972 under the General Insurance Business (Nationalisation) Act, 1972 and by virtue of the same Act, 55 Indian general insurance companies became subsidiaries of the General Insurance Corporation of India and the undertaking of other erstwhile insurance were merged in undertakings of one or other four selected ultimate companies which were to operate in the nationalised set-up, viz., National Insurance Co. Ltd., New India Assurance Co. Ltd., Oriental Fire and General Insurance Co. Ltd., and United India Fire and General Insurance Co. Ltd.

The progress of miscellaneous insurances before nationalisation has been analysed in the following paragraphs:

The gross premium of Indian Insurers has increased from Rs. 39.78 crores in 1969 to Rs. 45.90 crores in 1970 and Rs. 50.65 crores in 1971 and further to Rs. 57.28 crores in 1972. The gross premium received by the Indian insurers has increased from 85.5 per cent of total gross premium in 1969 to 87.4 per cent in 1971 and further to 88.5 per cent in 1972. This shows that the Indian insurers are getting increasing business. Consequently, the shares of non-Indian insurers were also declining from 14.5 per cent in 1969 to 11.5 per cent in 1972. Thus, the total gross premium of miscellaneous insurance a had increased from Rs. 46.55 crores in 1969 to Rs. 57.93 crores in 1971 and further to Rs. 64.70 crores in 1972.

As compared to total insurances, the share of Indian insurers to miscellaneous insurance had been higher. It was 82.6 per cent in case of total insurances and 88.5 per cent in ease of miscellaneous insurances. Thus the miscellaneous insurances of Indian insurers have been at higher level. Consequently the share of non-Indian insurer has been decreasing. The total gross premium has increased from Rs. 116.88 crores in 1969 to Rs. 131.62 crores in 1970 and further to Rs. 147.53 crores in 1971 and again to Rs. 195.83 of ores in 1972. In both the cases, the share of Indian insurers to gross premium has increased from Rs. 116.88 crores in 1969 to Rs. 131.62 crores in 1970 and further to Rs. 147.53 crores in 1971 and again to Rs. 195.83 crores in 1972. In both the cases, the share of Indian insurers to gross premium was rising.

Table 38.1 Gross Premium

Year	*Miscellaneous Insurances*					*Total Insurances*				
	Indian Insurers		*Non-Indian Insurers*		*Total*	*Indian Insurers*		*Non-Indian Insurers*		*Total*
	Rs.	*%to total*	*Rs.*	*% to total*		*Rs.*	*%to total*	*Rs.*	*% to total*	
1969 ..	39.78	85.5	6.76	14.5	46.55	91.96	78.7	24.91	21.3	116.88
1970 ..	45.90	86.9	6.94	13.1	62.83	105.38	80.1	26.24	19.9	131.62

Contd...

1971 ..	50.65	87.4	7.28	12.6	67.93	118.80	80.5	28.73	19.5	147.53
1972 ..	57.25	88.5	7.42	11.5	64.10	132.00	82.6	27.83	17.4	159.83
1975					84.34					247.07
1977					103.88					299.23
1978					123.09					339.05
1977					133					338
1978					155					378
1979					176					415
1980					218					503
1981					275					623

Table 38.2 Percentage Ratio to Net Premium

	Indian Insurances						*Non-Indian insurers*					
Year	*Net claim payable*	*Net commission*	*Exp. of management*	*Increase in Reserve*	*Misc. Income*	*Balance of Income*	*Net claim payable*	*Net commission*	*Exp. of maney*	*Increase in Reserve*	*Misc. income*	*Balance of Income*
1970 ..	56.8	11.4	21.3	4.6	3.0	8.5	50.1	6.3	32.7	1.9	1.1	8.5
1971 ..	57.2	11.8	19.4	3.7	3.5	11.2	43.5	5.7	33.3	1.5	0.6	15.5
1972 ..	57.0	12.5	19.2	4.4	3.7	10.3	46.9	6.2	34.3	2.8	0.6	9.8
1975 ..	58.5	26.6	0.8	9.7	—	42						
1977 ..	54.3	26.3	1.2	4.3	—	14.0						
1978 ..	60.9	25.7	1.3	7.1	—	5.3						
1980 ..	72.2	28.3	1.1	8.5	—	−10.2						
1981 ..	70.1	28.2	0.9	11.6	—	−10.6						

The share of net claims payable to net premium hall increased from 56.8 per cent in 1970 to 57.20 per cent in 1972. It means the amount of claim has been Increasing m case of miscellaneous Insurances. The net commission has also increased from 11.4 per cent of net premium in 1970 to 11.8 per cent in 1971 and further to 12.5 per cent in 1972. However, the percentage of management expenses has also been declining. The reserve has decreased but the balance of Income has increased from 8.5 per cent of net premium in 1970 to 11.2 per cent in 1971 and declined to 10.3 per cent in 1972.

The non-Indian Insurers have paid lesser amount in the shape of claims whereas the Indian insurers have paid more amount as compared to net premium. Expenses of management in case of non Indian insurers are also increasing. It had increased from 32.7 per cent of net premium to 34.3 per cent in 1972. The balance of income bass increased from 8.5 per cent in 1970 to 15.5 per cent in 1971, but declined to 9.8 per cent in 1972. Thus. The non-Indian insurers were increasing their balances at higher speed.

The gross claims payable has been 40.7 per cent of gross premium in 1958. 64.9 per cent of gross premium in 1970 and again 51.8 per cent in 1972. Thus, the share of gross claims payable has been decreased in 1971. The percentage of direct commission has been constantly decreasing. The percentage of management expenses has been declining from 32.6 per cent in 1958 to. 20.7 per cent in 1970 and further to 19.2 per cent in 1971 but increased to 20.1 per cent in 1972. The miscellaneous income has been increasing in both the cases. Similarly the balance of income in case of Indian insurers has increased from 13.5 per cent of gross premium in 1958 to 22.0 per cent of gross premium in 1971 and declined to 21.2 per cent in 1972. The Non-Indian insurers have lesser balance of income than the Indian insurers had.

Table 38.3 Gross Direct business written outside India by Indian Insurers

Ratio to Gross Direct Premium income	*1958*	*1970*	*1971*	*1972*
1. Gross claims Payable	..	68.2	70.8	53.8
2. Direct Commission	..	27.5	27.6	27.8
3. Expenses of Management	..	15.2	15.0	14.0
4. Increase in Reserve	..	–1.2	0.8	6.6
5. Miscellaneous Income	..	2.2	4.3	5.5
6. Balance of Income	..	–8.7	–11.7	2.1

The Indian insurers have experienced increasing loss in case of miscellaneous insurance. The loss has gone up from 8.7 per cent in 1970 to 11.7 per cent in 1971. It was most probably due to increasing amount of claims payable and direct commission.

From the analysis of progress of different types of insurance it has been revealed that the Indian insurers were doing well more in marine insurance than in other types of general insurances.

Table 38.4

Net Premium Income
Miscellaneous Insurance

	1975	1977
In India	63.33	77.70
Outside India	25.92	25.46
Total	89.25	103.16

Total Insurance

	1975	1977	1978	1979	1980	1981
In India	166.12	196.97	287	323	385	486
Outside India	63.75	71.46	83	75	96	113
Total	229.87	268.43	370	398	481	599

The net premium income of Miscellaneous insurance outside India has declined from Rs. 25.92 crores in 1975 to Rs. 25.46 crores in 1977. Thus, the miscellaneous insurance has lesser scope outside India.

Table 38.5 Percentage to Gross Premium

	Indian insurers						*Non-Indian Insurers*					
Year	*Gross claims payable*	*Direct commission*	*Expenses of Management*	*Increase in Reserve*	*Misc. Income*	*Balances of Income*	*Gross claims payable*	*Direct commission*	*Expenses of Management*	*Increase in Reserve*	*Misc. Income*	*Balance of Income*
1985 ..	40.7	13.1	32.6	..	..	13.6	48.9	12.6	27.9	–	..	10.6
1970 ..	64.9	7.7	20.7	4.5	2.1	4.2	49.6	8.9	28.0	1.0	0.5	12.0
1971 ..	50.4	6.9	19.2	3.8	2.4	22.0	40.8	8.6	28.3	1.9	0.5	20.0
1972 ..	51.8	7.7	20.1	1.3	2.3	2.12	46.2	8.9	30.7	0.8	0.5	13.4

Table 38.6 General Insurance: Income and, Outgo in respect of General Insurance excluding L.I.C

(Rs. in crores)

	1958	*1970*	*1971*	*1972*
1. Premium less reinsurance: In India	12.96	75.84	86.45	10.3.13
Out India	12.02	35.26	41.24	44.74
2. Net Interest Div. and Rents	0.37	3.21	4.18	5.16
3. Other Incomes	0.21	0.13	0.27	1.34
Total Incomes	25.56	132.14	132.14	154.37
1. Claims loss reinsurance	12.56	57.04	62.80	73.58
2. Net Commission	3.33	12.51	14.89	18.72
3. Expenses of Management	6.77	23.38	24.45	28.78
4. Misc. Outgo	0.24	0.60	0.37	0.41
Outgo	22.90	93.53	102.51	121.49
Excess of Income over Outgo	2.66	20.91	29.63	32.88
Increase in Reserve	1:57	7.31	12.61	9.40

The execess of income over outgo has been increasing from Rs. 2.66 crores in 1958 to Rs. 20.91 crores in 1970 and further to Rs. 32.88 crores in 1972. Thus, the reserve has also been increasing from Rs. 1.57 crores in 1958 to Rs. 7.31 crores in 1970 and further to Rs. 9.40 crores in 1972. The premium income in India has been constantly increasing from Rs. 12.96 crores in 1958 to Rs. 75.84 crores in 1970 and further to Rs. 86.45 crores in 1971 and again to Rs. 103.13 crores in 1972. The total income has increased from Rs. 25.56 crores in 1958 to Rs. 132.14 crores in 1971, and further to 154.37 crores in 1973, but the increase in total outgo was lesser than this, so the excess of income over outgo and increase in reserve has been rapidly rising.

The general insurance could not increase rapidly as industrial production did up to 1967. The general insurance would have risen at least parallel to the development of industries. If the general insurance is rising at a faster speed than the industria production does, it is a clear indication of satisfactory development or general insurance. The Index of general insurance reveals that it had gone up to 137.5 in 1967 and 158.9 in 1968 whereas the index of industrial production has gone up 143.2 in 1967 and 152.9 in 1968. Thus the general insurance started rising more rapidly after 1967 and touched the maximum of 22.5 in 1971 while the index of industrial production has gone only up to 173.6 in 1971 making a gap of 27.4 in 1971 which was maximum up to 1970. The index number of general insurance was 202.8 whereas the index number of industrial production was 182.6 in 1972. It reveals that the general insurance business was satisfactorily progressing.

Table 38.7 Profit & Loss of All General Insurance Business

In Lakhs of Rs.

	1975	*1978*	*1980*	*1981*
1. Interest Dividends & Rents	869.02	1484.36	2286.23	2658.20
2. Profit of				
Fire Insurance	560.97	548.60		

Contd...

Murine	210.32	2341.21	622.20	642.01
Miscellanoolls	74.15	131.08	—	27.55
3. Profits on sale of Investments	4.69	5.77	3.05	2.82
4. Capital gains	0.13	0.07	0.18	0.26
5. Miscellaneous	0.05	4.03	5.35	6.25
Total	1719.33	2515.12	2917.01	3337.02
1. Interest Payable	0·93	0·54	0.53	5.72
2. Preliminary Expenses	1.14	1.13	1.14	1.14
3. Other Amounts written off		0.23	610.10	514.89
4. Transferred to share Capitate Redemption	190.00	360.00	350.00	–
5. Provision for relation	937.00	1030.00	603.00	805.00
6. Balance	590.26	1133.20	1339.74	2002.45
Total	1719.33	2515.12	2917.01	3337.08

Progress of Miscellaneous Insurance After Nationalisation

The progress of miscellaneous insurance after nationalisation has been analysed under (*i*) gross premium, (*ii*) net premium and (*iii*) underwriting experiences.

1. Gross Premium in Miscellaneous Insurance

The gross direct premium has increased from Rs. 114.00 crores in 1980 to Rs. 218.00 crores in 1980 and again to Rs. 610.18 crores in 1985 and Rs. 1302.16 crores in 1988-89. The miscellaneous insurance increased by 590.32 per cent during 1980 to 1988-89. The maximum amount of miscellaneous insurance has been Rs. 75.00 crores in 1980 and Rs. 424.86 crores in 1988-89 in New India. It has increase by 744.06 per cent. The United India has increased its business from Rs. 47.60 crores in 1980 to Rs. 318.82 crores by 669.79 per cent. Oriental has increased its business by 701.56 per cent from Rs. 39.13 crores in 1980 to Rs. 274.52 crores in 1988-89. National has increased its business from Rs. 39.92 crores in 1982 to Rs. 234.41 crores in

Table 38.8 Gross Direct Premium in Miscellaneous Insurance

	GIC	National	New India	Oriental	United India	Total
1975						114.00
1980	34.25	39.92	57.10	39.13	47.60	218.00
1982	17.84	66.78	120.62	74.44	89.52	362.20
1983	22.73	80.40	141.23	91.07	108.94	444.37
1984	24.32	93.71	162.69	104.15	125.16	510.03
1985	33.31	115.65	195.07	121.67	144.48	610.18
1986	41.51	139.32	232.12	150.15	178.29	741.39
1987	49.80	162.13	279.32	181.21	215.32	887.78
1988-89	40.55	243.41	424.86	274.52	318.82	1302.16
1989-90	21.11	236.28	406.55	275.15	316.16	1234.16
1994-95	119.51	536.72	878.89	641.58	707.70	1367.69

1988-89 by 609.74 per cent. It shows that New India having maximum amount of gross direct premium has increased its business at the highest rate followed by Oriental, United India and National. The higher amount of miscellaneous Insurance in New India and United India has been attributed to several non-traditional policies issued by them. They have tried to attain the socio-economic objectives of the nationalisation. Oriental and National have been lagging behind. The GIC has no fixed trend. It deals only in aviation insurance which depends on the flights frequencies. It has to compete with foreign companies. The gross direct premium amounted to Rs. 1367.69 crores in 1994-95; out of which the contribution of all companies was Rs. 119.51 crores by GIC, Rs. 536.72 crores by National, Rs. 878.89 crores by New India by India, Rs. 641.58 crores by Oriental and Rs. 707.70 crores by United India.

2. Net Premium

The net premium of miscellaneous insurance has increases from Rs. 89.00 in 1973 to Rs. 207.90 crores in 1980 and again to Rs. 576.12 crores in 1980 and Rs. 1221.74 crores in 1988-89. It shows the rising trend of insurance business. The net premium increased by 344.31 per cent from Rs. 354.84 crores in 1982 to Rs. 1221.74 crores in 1988-89. The net premium of GIC increased from Rs. 66.55 crores in 1982 to Rs. 239.77 crores in 1988-89 by 360.29 per cent. National Insurance has increased its net premium from Rs. 52.26 crores in 1982 to Rs. 188.26 crores in 1988-89 by 360.24 per cent. New India increased from Rs. 103.60 crores to Rs. 337.99 crores by 326.25 per cent during 1982 to 1988-89. Oriental increased its net premium by 368.11 per cent from Rs. 57.55 crores in the corresponding period. United India has increased from Rs. 74.88 crores to Rs. 243.87 crores by 325.68 per cent during the period. Oriental increased its business at faster rate followed by National, New India and United India. The net amount has been the highest in New India followed by United India, Oriental and National. The net premium was Rs. 2811.89 crores in 1994-95. The highest net premium was Rs. 804.27 crores by New India and the lowest was Rs. 428.04 crores by National.

Table 38.9 Net Premium in Miscellaneous Insurance

In crores of Rupees

	GIC	*National*	*New India*	*Oriental*	*United India*	*Total*
1973						89.00
1975						107.00
1980	66.55	52.26	103.60	57.55	74.88	354.84
1983	82.07	61.66	116.21	69.67	89.35	418.96
1984	96.60	75.54	137.09	81.76	102.92	493.91
1985	112.12	89.56	160.79	94.40	119.25	576.12
1986	136.63	108.06	183.92	114.70	144.92	688.23
1987	155.56	125.14	221.98	139.26	168.36	810.32
1988-89	239.77	188.26	337.99	211.85	243.87	1221.74
1989-90	233.42	181.33	317.51	212.35	243.55	1188.16
1994-95	553.62	428.04	804.27	492.74	533.22	2811.89
1997-98	910.40	806.07	1251.67	788.09	859.24	4615.47

3. Underwriting Progress Experiences

The underwriting experiences has shown negative result. The underwriting loss has increased from Rs. 4.33 crores, in 1982 to Rs. 40.77 Crores in 1985 and Rs. 296.12 crores in 1988-89. The underwriting loss to net premium has gone up from 1.2 per cent in 1982 to 7.1 per cent in 1985 and again to 24.4 per cent. The maximum loss ratio has been in the case of United India *i.e.,* 26.4 per cent in 1988-89, 11.6 per cent in 1985 and 2.2 per cent in 1982. The reason has been the highest claims ratio ranging from 69.4 per cent to 96.7 per cent. However, the expense-ratio has been the lowest of all the companies in 1988-89. Oriental has the second largest loss followed by New India and National. The underwriting experience has shown that National and New India have experienced less loss-ratio because of less claims ratio. Underwriting experience in 1994-95 has revealed loss of Rs. 209.91 crores. All companies have incurred loss in 1994-95.

Table 38.10 Financial Highlights of Miscellaneous Insurance

	GIC	*National*	*New India*	*Oriental*	*United India*	*Total*
			In India			
1998-1999	55.7	1199.1	1750.0	1287.1	1381.2	5617.4
1999-2000	76.6	1334.5	1908.8	1429.3	1465.7	6138.3
2000-2001	280.1	1506.0	2073.1	1540.5	1635.4	6755.0
2001-2002		1666.7	2313.15	1719.16	1763.86	
			Out of India			
1998-1999	00	25.7	186.6	26.0	38.5	276.8
1999-2000	00	42.3	221.8	28.0	41.0	333.1
2000-2001	00	101.9	307.5	31.3	81.8	522.5
2001-2002		65.58	415.50	33.84	125.43	
			Total of India			
1998-1999	55.7	1224.8	1936.6	1313.1	1419.7	5949.9
1999-2000	76.6	1376.8	2130.6	1457.3	1506.7	6548.0
2000-2001	280.1	1607.9	2380.6	1571.8	1717.2	7557.6
2001-2002	311.57	1732.05	2728.65	1753.00	1889.29	—

Table 38.11 Miscellaneous Insurance

Year	*Net Premium*		*Net Claims*		*Commission*		*Expenses of Management*		*Other outgo*		*Increase in Reserve*		*Investment Income*		*Under writing*	
	Rs.	*%*	*Rs.*	*%*	*Rs.*	*%*	*Rs.*	*%*	*Rs.*	*%*	*Rs.*	*%*	*Rs.*	*%*	*Rs.*	*%*
								General Insurance Corporation								
1998-1999	1079.0		987.0	91	271.7	25					84.3	8			–264.0	–24
1999-2000	1201.94		1216.02	101.2	290.56	24.2	12.34	1.0	–0.12	0.0	61.49	5.1			–378.35	31.5
2000-2001	1580.63		1531.20	96.9	330.72	20.9	14.33	0.9	2.40	0.1	189.34	12.0	381.1	27.39	–487.36	30.8
2001-2002	1828.65		1807.83	106.05	381.24	22.36	15.77	0.93	1.17	0.07	–		446.92	26.22	–501.37	–29.41
								National								
1998-1999	968.0	79	861.0	89	282.3	29					81.0	8			–256.3	–26
1999-2000	1079.84		1029.43	95.32	1.49	–0.47	325.27	30.12	–0.72	0.07	55.98	5.18			–.324.98	–30.09
2000-2001	1289.92		1225.66	95.01	19.28	–1.49	336.22	26.06	–2.52	–0.19	104.99	8.13			393.71	30.52
2001-2002	1312.71		1454.66	110.81	14.03	1.06	399.58	30.43	–2.63	–2.0	11.39	0.86	245.00	18.66	–319.32	–24.32
								New India								
1998-1999	1469.9		1253.8	85	3368	23					109.1	7			229.8	–15
1999-2000	1629.61		1486.54	91.22	–5.06	–0.31	415.23	25.48			79.86	4.9			–346.96	–21.29
2000-2001	1883.72		1745.20	92.65	23.27	1.24	484.43	25.72			127.06	6.75	312.96		496.33	26.35
2001-2002	2099.30		2052.04	97.75	81.66	3.89	490.40	23.36			107.79	5.13	336.51		–632.59	–30.13

Year	Net Premium		Net Claims		Commission		Expenses of Management		Other outgo		Increase in Reserve		Investment Income		Under writing	
	Rs.	%	Rs.	%	Rs.	%	Rs.	%	Rs.	%	Rs.	%	Rs.	%	Rs.	%
Oriental																
1998-1999	956.3	73	998.2	104	235.4	25					84.1	9			–361.4	–38
1999-2000	1087.23	74.6	1061.99	97.7	26.98	–2.5	341.52	31.4			65.44	6.0			–354.74	–32.6
2000-2001	1210.21	77.0	1144.43	94.6	–19.07	–1.6	336.01	27.8			61.49	5.1			–312.66	–25.8
2001-2002	1287.17	73.43	1560.90	121.3	23	0.0	422.44	32.81			–38.48	3.0	–16.71	1.3	–476.32	–37.0
United India																
1998-1999	1043.8	74	1000.9	96	245.7	23					92.3	9			–295.1	–28
1999-2000	1115.84		1269.79	113.79	–20.99	–1.88	310.51	27.83			36.02	3.23			–479.49	–42.97
2000-2001	1329.27		1369.89	103.06	1.14	0.09	340.22	25.59			106.71	8.03			–488.69	–36.76
2001-2002	1438.18		1523.58		35.21		387.78		–58.60		54.46	106.71	373.35		–248.10	
Indian Market Total																
1998-1999	5517.0	93	5100.9	92	1371.9	25					45.08	8.0			–1406.6	–25
1999-2000	6114.4	93	6063.7	99	163.65	27					298.8	5.0			–1884.6	3.1
2000-2001	7293.27	97	7016.4	96	1866.5	26					589.5	8.0			–2178.7	–30
2001-2002																

Table 38.12 Underwriting Experience in Miscellaneous Insurance

	Net Premium In Rs. Crores	Net Claims Payable	Net Commission	Expenses Management	Miscellaneous Outgo	Undereriting Risks Reserve	Underwriting Profi/Loss(–)	Underwriting Profit/Loss(–) Rs. Crores
1985								
National	112.12	69.5	27.8	1.2	–0.9	6.9	–4.5	–5.04
New India	89.56	70.4	–2.3	28.8	–	7.8	–4.7	–4.26
Oriental	160.79	76.4	1.6	21.8	0.4	7.4	–6.8	–10.91
United India	94.40	76.2	–2.0	26.6	–0.3	6.7	–7.2	–6.77
Total	119.25	82.9	–0.5	22.3	0.1	6.8	–11.6	–13.79
1989-90	576.12	75.4	5.1	19.8	–0.3	7.1	–7.1	–40.77
GIC	233.42	79.4	21.0	1.7	–0.6	8.9	16.4	–38.31
National	181.33	89.4	–	29.3	–	8.5	–27.2	–49.36
New India	317.51	89.9	–	25.4	–	7.4	–22.7	–72.87
Oriental	212.35	86.9	–	25.9	–	10.1	–22.9	–48.62
United India	243.55	88.9	–	24.8	–	10.0	–23.7	51.61
Total	1188.16	86.9	–	25.5	–	8.98	22.58	266.77
1994-95								
GIC	553.62	105.8	23.3	1.0	–0.9	6.8	–36.0	–198.94
National	428.04	105.6	–2.5	27.5	0.1	5.6	–36.3	155.56
New India	804.27	101.9	–0.8	20.8	–	6.6	–28.5	–299.04
Oriental	492.74	110.9	–3.3	24.9	–	6.2	–38.7	–190.44
United India	533.22	114.4	–3.2	22.2	–	5.2	–38.6	–205.58
Total	2811.89	107.7	–2.7	9.28	–	6.1	35.62	–209.91
1997-98								
GIC	910.40	94.1	24.0	0.9	–0.1	5.3	–24.3	–220.78
National	806.07	92.93	–0.86	–26.09	0.13	5.05	–23.09	–186.09
New India	1251.67	86.25	–1.95	–24.74	–	4.04	–13.48	168.74
Orintal	788.09	94.1	24.0	–0.1	–	5.9	–28.5	224.99
United India	859.24	104.0	–31.2	28.6	20.9	5.2	–34.2	293.76

39

PROGRESS OF TOTAL GENERAL INSURANCE

The progress of total general insurance has been analysed under gross direct premium, net premium, underwriting experiences, return on total assets, number of employees and number of offices.

1. Gross Direct Premium

The gross direct premium of all general insurance has increased from Rs. 208 crores in 1973 to Rs. 284 crores in 1975 and again to Rs. 503 crores in 1980, Rs. 1204.31 crores in 1985 and Rs. 2348.92 crores in 1988-89. Thus, the total insurance has been increasing at a faster rate after nationalisation. It has increased by 466.98 per cent during 1982 to 1988-89. United India increased its business by 504.67 percent from Rs. 121.08 crores in 1980 to Rs. 611.05 crores in 1988-89. The gross direct premium of New India has increased from Rs. 128.03 crores in 1980 to Rs. 733.54 crores in 1988-89 by 572.94 per cent. The insurance business of Oriental has from Rs. 111.26 crores in 1980 to Rs. 511.01 crores in 1988-89, by 459.29 per cent. National has increased its business from Rs. 98.59 crores in 1980 to Rs. 452.82 crores 1988-89 be 459.30 per cent. The maximum growth rate in business has been. New India followed by United India, National and Oriental. The maximum amount of business has been done by New India followed by United India, Oriented and National. GIC has only aviation insurance which fluctuating as per flights frequency. New India and United India took lead in this field. They have maximum number of employees and offices. They did commendable task in expansion of insurance business although they did at the cost of lower underwriting profit. Their investment income has been comparatively higher. The lower business of Oriental and National has not affected underwriting profit. Their profits have been comparatively higher because they manag, risks and selected only few business working with profits. The total amount of gross premium was Rs. 4959.43 crores in 1994-95.

Table 39.1 Gross Direct Premium in All Types of Insurance

	GIC	*National*	*New India*	*Oriental*	*United India*	*Total*
1973						208
1980	44.04	98.59	128.03	111.26	121.08	503.00
1981	17.84	142.56	232.32	171.29	197.38	761.39
1983	22.73	168.21	274.37	202.53	227.25	895.09
1984	24.32	199.26	315.80	227.12	267.98	1034.48
1985	33.31	239.25	370.11	258.27	303.27	1204.31
1987	41.51	277.96	433.82	306.24	363.60	1423.13
1988	49.80	317.08	502.63	354.23	428.44	1652.18
1988-89	40.50	452.82	733.54	511.01	611.05	2348.92
1994-90	21.11	443.02	717.40	500.49	596.64	2278.66
1994-95	119.51	945.36	1524.49	1074.35	1295.72	4959.43
1997-98	88.38	1604.82	2433.73	1677.95	1930.64	7735.52

2. Net Premium

The net premium has increased from Rs. 222.0 crores in 1973 to Rs. 281.0 crores in 1975 and again to Rs. 481.0 crores in 1980, Rs. 1190.50 crores in 1985 and again to Rs. 2255.24 crores during 1982 to 1988-89. New India in 1988-89. The rate of increased has been 311.03 per cent has increased its business from Rs. 187.66 crores in 1982 to Rs. 576.76 crores in 1988-89 by 307.34 per cent. The business of United India has increased from Rs. 158.20 crores in 1982 to Rs. 466.38 crores by 294.80 per cent. The net premium of Oriental has increased from Rs. 125.86 crores in 1982 to Rs. 384.71 crores in 1988-89 by 305.67 per cent. National increased its business from Rs. 110.43 crores in 1982 to Rs. 366.42 crores in 1988-89 by 331.81 per cent. GIC has increased its business from Rs. 142.93 crores in 1982 to Rs. 460.98 crores in 1988-89 by 322.52 per cent. The net premium of New India has been maximum whereas of National has been the lowest. Although growth rate of business in National has been the maximum followed by GIC has been higher than the direct premium because it deals with reinsurance business also. The total amount of net premium was Rs. 4879.43 crores in 1994-95. National Insurance has given the lowest amount of premium.

Table 39.2 Net Premium in All Types of Insurance

	GIC	*National*	*New India*	*Oriental*	*United India*	*Total*
1973						222.00
1975						281.00
1980						481.00
1982	142.93	110.43	187.66	125.86	158.20	725.08
1983	176.69	132.74	225.60	152.52	193.72	881.27
1984	224.15	159.73	253.48	174.33	218.88	1030.57
1985	262.23	186.47	296.98	191.39	253.43	1190.50
1986	287.32	220.00	341.67	227.99	289.36	1366.34
1987	321.79	255.07	398.63	265.89	338.43	1579.81
1988-89	460.98	366.42	576.75	384.71	466.38	2255.24
1989-90	434.23	348.46	569.66	380.66	452.75	2085.76
1994-95	1018.31	768.93	1333.44	821.89	936.86	4879.43
1997-98	1510.16	1263.24	1945.00	1235.84	1402.73	5846.8

3. Underwriting Experiences

The total underwriting experiences has been very unfavorable. The profit of Rs. 66.04 crores in 1982 declined to Rs. 12.42 crores in 1985 and became loss of Rs. 145.72 crores in 1988-89. All the companies have faced loss in 1988-89 because of higher claim ratio which was between 70.7 per cent to 79.4 per cent. The expense ratio has varied from 25.6 per cent in New India to 29.00 per cent in National. The unexpired risks reserve could not increased as per their previous years figure. The maximum loss suffered was by United India which experienced loss-ratio of 7.7 per cent. GIC has different pattern of aviation insurance. Its loss is not comparable with those of other companies. The lowest loss-ratio was 5.2 per cent in New India because of comparatively lower expense-ratio. New India and United India has higher claims-ratio and National and Oriental have higher expense ratio. The underwriting experience has shown loss of Rs. 141.18 crores in 1994-95 by the companies and gone down to 35 crores in 2001.

4. Investment Income

The investment income of general insurance industry has increased industry has increased from Rs. 130.99 in 1982 to Rs. 244.09 crores in 1982 to Rs. 244.99 crores in 1985, Rs. 487.39 crores In 1988-89 and Rs. 1206.83 crores in 1994-95. As percentage to total assets, it has increased from 7.57 per cent to 8.27 per cent and again to 10.33 per cent in the respective years; but it declined to 8.58 per cent in 1994-95. It shows that the investment income has an increasing trend. On the other hand, the underwriting profit has declined from Rs. 66.04 crores to Rs. 39.60 crores, Rs. –145.72 crores and Rs. –110.92 crores in the respective years. They have also gone down as percentage to total asset from 3.82 per cent to 1.34 per cent, –3.09 per cent and –5.02 per cent in the corresponding years. The loss experience is mainly on account of losses faced under miscellaneous insurance, particularly nontraditional insurance. The other income has given loss for 1982 to 1988-89 and in 1994-95. Consequently the profitability before taxes has declined from 11.00 per cent in 1982 to 8.35 per cent is 1985,7.17 per cent in 1988-89 and 3.67 per cent in 1994-95, although the profit amount has increased from Rs. 190.40 crores in 1982 to Rs. 247.43 crores in 1985 and again to Rs. 338.43 crores in 1988-89 Rs. 502.51 crores in 1994-95 and Rs. 2057.75 crores in 2000-2001. The amount of profit increased mainly due to increase in investment income. The profitability of investment income has also increased. Had there not been this trend, the insurance industry would have faced loss. The investment income is shock absorber of the underwriting loss. They should try to increase investment income at faster rate to serve the society better by providing more insurance coverages because coverage of higher insurance will essentially have loss-bearing subject-matter.

Table 39.3 Total General Insurance Business
Gross Direct Premium

	GIC	*National*	*New India*	*Oriental*	*United India*	*Total*
			In India			
1998-1999		1821.4	2729.5	1930.8	2221.3	8703.0
1999-2000		1993.32	2979.53	2124.17	2348.57	9445.4
2000-2001		2117.88	3041.17	2199.67	2441.09	9799.8
2001-2002		2365.47	3512.33	2446.48	2654.96	9042.04
			Out of India			
1998-1999		32.10	288.1	39.1	39.5	398.8
1999-2000		48.79	327.00	42.38	42.01	460.2
2000-2001		109.85	451.88	47.43	82.91	692.0
2001-2002		73.94	685.73	52.15	126.52	938.34
			Total of India			
1998-1999	55.7	1853.5	3017.6	1969.9	2260.8	9157.5
1999-2000	76.60	2042.11	3306.53	2166.55	2390.58	9982.2
2000-2001	280.08	222.73	3493.05	2247.10	2524.00	10771.9
2001-2002	311.57	2439.41	4198.06	2498.63	2781.48	9980.38

Table 39.4 Underwriting Experience in Total Insurance

Underwriting Profi/Loss(–)	Net Premium Profit/Loss(–)	Net Claims In Rs. Crores Rs. Crores	Net Payable	% to Net Premium Expenses Commission	Other Management	Undereriting Outgo	Underwriting Risks Reserve	
1985								
GIC	262.23	60.6	26.9	1.2	–0.4	9.3	2.4	6.21
National	186.47	65.1	–3.6	28.5	–0.2	8.4	1.8	3.32
New India	296.98	67.3	–0.7	23.5	–0.6	8.7	1.8	5.31
Oriental	191.39	68.8	–5.0	29.1	–0.5	5.1	2.4	4.51
United India	253.43	72.1	–1.1	23.4	0.1	8.2	–2.7	–6.93
Total	1190.50	66.8	4.1	20.3	–0.3	8.1	1.0	12.42
1989-90								
GIC	434.23	61.7	27.1	1.9	–0.3	9.1	0.5	2.27
National	348.46	73.3	–	29.0	–	9.2	–11.5	–40.06
New India	569,66	68.9	–	21.1	–	11.1	–5.1	–29.29
Oriental	380.66	70.0	–	27.0	–	10.7	–7.7	–29.51
United India	452.75	70.7	–	24.3	–	10.0	–5.0	–22.63
Total	2185.76	68.9	–	26.02	–	10.02	5.7	24.75
1994-95								
GIC	1018.31	80.2	25.4	1.3	–0.7	6.7	–12.9	131.42
National	768.93	91.6	2.44	28.6	0.3	2.6	–20.1	155.56
New India	1333.45	89.6	–4.6	23.3	–	5.0	–13.3	177.43
Oriental	821.80	88.8	–4.9	27.1	–	4.9	–15.9	130.79
United India	936.86	90.0	–5.0	24.5	–	3.2	–11.8	110.92
Total	4879.43	88.0	–1.5	21.0	–	4.5	–15.0	141.18
1997-98								
GIC	1510.16	72.7	25.8	1.1	–0.1	4.7	–4.2	63.53
National	1263.24	78.42	–2.84	27.4	–0.3	4.39	–7.35	–92.81
New India	1945.00	71.43	–4.47	26.99	–	3.11	2.94	57.13
Orintal	1235.84	80.2	–	29.5	–5.4	4.8	–9.1	–112.09
United India	1402.7	82.3	5.9	30.8	22.0	5.1	–12.3	–172.33

Table 39.5 Underwriting Experience in Total Insurance

Year	Net Premium		Net Claims		Commission		Expenses of Management		Other outgo		Increase in unexpired Risks Reserve		Investment Income		Under writing profit	
	Rs.	%	Rs.	%	Rs.	%	Rs.	%	Rs.	%	Rs.	%	Rs.	%	Rs.	%
General Insurance Corporation																
1998-1999	1710.3		1252.3	73	455.9	27					103.8	6	592.1		–101.7	–6
1999-2000	1886.31		1515.63	80.4	486.42	25.8	23.32	1.2	0.45	0.0	90.02	4.8	635.2		–229.53	–12.2
2000-2001	2186.54		1851.83	84.7	496.10	22.7	23.51	1.1	3.14	0.1	146.85	6.7	652.6	25.24	–334.89	–15.3
2001-2002	2617.23		2295.08	94.12	636.34	26.10	24.45						569.33	233.5	–517.40	–21.22
National																
1998-1999	1466.0	79	1150.9	79	423.1	29					104.9		296.3		–212.9	–15
1999-2000	1614.72	79	1302.74	80.7	–31.91	–1.98	503.86	3120	–0.45	0.03	72.39	4.48	332.3		–231.91	–14.36
2000-2001	1804.55	81	1461.63	81.0	–1.82	–0.10	492.30	27.28	–2.04	0.11	99.84	5.53	17.64		–245.37	–13.60
2001-2002	1813.12		1725.11	95.14	–10.14	–0.55	564.34	31.12	–2.33	0.21	–3.88	0.21	319.96		–140.02	–7.72
New India																
1998-1999	2186.9	72	1561.5	71	490.3	22					121.8	6	551.4		133	
1999-2000	2477.45	75	1906.25	76.94	–71.65	2.89	674.67	27.23			146.16	5.90			–177.98	7.18
2000-2001	2671.48	76	2279.74	85.34	4.80	0.18	737.96	27.62			95.02	3.56	423.37		–446.04	–16.70
2001-2002	3068.23		2555.14	83.28	790.82	2.60	753.51	24.56			209.36	6.82	445.22		–529.60	–17.26

Contd...

Year	Net Premium		Net Claims		Commission		Expenses of Management		Other outgo		Increase in unexpired Risks Reserve		Investment Income		Under writing profit	
	Rs.	%	Rs.	%	Rs.	%	Rs.	%	Rs.	%	Rs.	%	Rs.	%	Rs.	%
Oriental																
1998-1999	1423.7	72	1233.0	87	350.0	25					98.0	7	324.4		–257.3	–19
1999-2000	1632.0	375.33	1332.17	81.6	–40.36	2.5	534.60	32.8			104.12	6.4	359.3		–298.50	–18.3
2000-2001	1725.35	76.78	1502.06	87.1	–45.57	–2.6	502.98	29.2			41.48	2.4	–314.68	–17.3	–275.60	–16.0
2001-2002	1818.50	72.78	1827.92	100.5	–23.07	–1.3	609.03	33.5			–223.0	0.1	21.74	1.2	–256.73	–.14.1
United Indian																
1998-19991	1615.6	71	1262.6	78	377.3	23					103.7	6	389.4		–128.0	–7
1999-2000	1753.00	73	1528.9	87.21	–85.26	–4.80	515.41	29.40			70.57	4.03	427.0	–276.63	–15.78	
2000-2001	1884.37	75	1776.93	94.30	–56.19	2.98	521.64	27.68			62.32	3.31	428.5		–420.33	–22.31
2001-2002	12045.06		1780.82		–17.53		577.88		–76.64		72.26		476.61		31.60	
Indian Market Total																
1998-1999	8402.5	92	6460.3	77	2096.6	25					532.21	6	21536		–686.6	–8
1999-2000	9363.4	94	7585.6	81	2509.1	27					483.2	5	2367.1		4214.5	–13
2000-2001	10272.1	45	8872.1	80	2670.0	25					445.4	2	2454.1		1722.2	–7

The profitability has been the lowest in United India as the percentage of profit-before tax to total assets has been 9.26 per cent in 1982, 9.52 per cent in 1985 and 4.91 per cent in 1988-89 and 3.86 per cent in 1994-95. The investment income-ratio has been the second lowest and the underwriting profits has given the highest loss-ratio. The company should increase its investment income ratio, to set off the losses of underwriting. The highest profitability has been 7.51 per cent in 1988-89 in New India, wherein the investment income-ratio has been the maximum and the underwriting loss ratio has been the lowest consequently the profitability has been the highest. Oriental have experienced maximum profitability in 1982 wherein the percentage of profit before tax to total assets has been 13.56 per cent. The highest investment income ratio and underwriting profit have given more profitability. The maximum underwriting profitability has been 6.40 per cent in 1982 in Oriental whereas the maximum investment income ratio has been 14.27 per cent in 1988-89 in GIC. It shows that the insurance companies should try to increase investment income as well as the underwriting profit. The profitability in case of insurance business is not very certain in insurance because of high uncertainty of risks. The general insurance can not predict correctly the claims because the accidents and other eventual factors are mostly unpredictable. However, the profitability of insurance companies in India is higher than those of USA, Japan, West Germany, France and Switzerland wherein the profitability in 1985 has been respectively 0.6 per cent, 1.3 per cent, 2.1 per cent 1.0 per cent and 1.2 per cent.

5. Number of Employees

The total number of employees in general insurance industry has been increasing from 41582 in 1982 to 50.559 in 1985 and again to 70940 in 1988-89 and 84561 in 1994-95. The number of employees has been maximum in New India followed by United India, Oriental and National. In the beginning National has the second lowest number of employees which be came the lowest in 1988-89. Thus, National did not attempt to increase number of employees tried to increase their business and the productivity per employee in National and Oriental.

6. Number of Offices

The number of offices of insurance industry has increased from 1550 in 1982 to 2731 in 1985, Rs. 3739 in 1988-89 and Rs. 4202 in 1994-95. It has also increased its branch offices from 1075, 2003, 2706 and 2997 in the respective years. The branch offices have been the main factors to procure business from the field. The productivity per branch office has been increasing constantly. The lowest number offices has been in National whereas United India has been the maximum. The productivity per office has been the highest in New India followed by United India, Oriental and National.

7. Overall Performances

The general insurance industry is progressive in India. At the companies particularly New India and United India have increased general insurance business rapidly. They have increased their productivity, claims per employee and investment income. They have tried to achieve the social subjectively of the nationalisation. The progress of non-traditional business given an impetus to general insurance industry to serve the society fully well.

Table 39.6 Investment Income and Underwriting profits in Companies

	Major Heads of Income						*Profit Before Tax*		
	Investment Income		*Underwriting Profit*		*Other Income*				
	Rs.	*% to Total Asset*	*Rs*	*% to Total Assets*	*Rs.*	*% to Total Assets*	*Rs.*	*Total Assets*	*Total Assets*
1985									
GIC	72.26	11.79	–39.01	–6.37	0.50	–0.08	23.35	3.81	612.80
National	33.08	10.32	10.18	3.17	–0.41	–0.13	36.82	11.48	320.63
New India	60.36	7.29	26.10	3.15	–0.42	–0.05	76.87	9.28	828.51
Oriental	40.50	7.93	23.89	4.68	–0.96	–0.19	57.80	11.32	510.75
United India	38.79	7.03	18.44	3.34	-0.69	–0.12	52.59	9.52	552.14
Total	244.99	8.27	39.60	1.34	-1.60	–0.05	247.43	8.35	2961.69
1989-90									
GIC	137.24	14.27	–38.88	–4.04	–1.15	–0.12	97.21	10.10	962.06
National	66.58	9.37	–20.27	–2.86	0.33	0.05	46.60	6.57	709.81
New India	129.51	9.77	–30.05	–2.27	0.02	0.02	99.98	7.51	1325.34
Oriental	74.04	8.78	–20.78	–2.47	–1.28	–0.15	51.48	6.17	842.76
United India	80.06	9.11	–35.74	–4.07	–1.16	–0.13	43.16	4.91	878.69
Total	487.39	10.33	–145.72	–3.09	–3.24	–0.07	338.43	7.17	4718.86
1994-95									
GIC	304.95	9.88	–131.42	–4.26	0.23	0.01	173.53	5.62	3085.85
National	169.17	8.94	–154.84	–8.18	2.47	0.13	16.80	0.89	1892.14
New India	342.19	8.05	–177.43	–4.18	3.51	0.08	168.27	3.96	4248.14
Oriental	178.51	7.95	–130.79	–5.82	–4.01	0.18	43.71	1.95	2245.51
United India	212.01	8.16	–110.92	–4.27	–0.89	0.03	100.26	3.86	2598.35
Total	1206.83	8.58	–705.49	5.02	1.31	0.01	502.51	3.67	14059.98
1997-98									
GIC	522.06	10.81	–63.53	–1.31	–4.28	–0.09	440.31	9.12	4829.38
National	284.69	8.76	–92.81	–2.86	–6.03	–0.19	185.85	5.72	3249.60
New India	573.90	9.45	57.13	0.94	–10.37	–0.17	67.66	11.05	6071.67
Oriental	312.23	9.24	–112.69	–3.34	–15.86	–0.47	183.68	5.44	3378.03
United India	364.69	9.04	–172.33	–4.27	+0.52	+0.01	192.88	4.78	4033.34
Total	2057.57	9.54	–348.55	–1.61	–36.02	–0.16	1673.38	7.76	21562.02

Table 39.7 Number of Employees

	Employees in Each Category				
	Officer	*Development Officers*	*Supervisory & Clerical Staff*	*Subordinate Staff*	*Total*
1982					
GIC	90	—	157	33	280
National	1219	2440	5135	1202	9996
New India	1467	2817	6102	670	11056
Oriental	1599	2476	4762	926	9727
United India	1474	2628	5361	1040	10523
Total	5849	10381	21418	3871	41582
1985					
GIC	145	—	209	16	400
National	1726	2042	5782	1299	11894
New India	1820	3393	7048	1269	13536
Oriental	2030	2972	5586	1190	1175
United India	2117	2958	6720	1200	12995
Total	7845	12365	25345	5004	50559
1988-89					
GIC	266	—	379	107	752
National	2684	3342	7616	2043	15685
New India	3425	3974	10272	2447	20118
Oriental	3065	3614	7861	2148	16695
United India	3297	3586	8838	1969	17690
Total	12737	14516	34973	8714	70940
1990-90					
GIC	282	—	380	105	767
National	3062	2328	8265	2514	7169
New India	3647	3923	10976	2790	21336
Oriental	3098	3488	8307	2622	17516
United India	3605	3463	9503	2063	18634
Total	13694	14202	37431	10095	75422
1994-95					
GIC	224	—	365	135	724
National	3470	3070	9987	2542	19069
New India	4072	3533	12681	3358	23644
Oriental	3643	3291	10325	2475	19734
United India	3918	3274	11487	2711	21390

Contd...

Total	15327	13168	44845	11221	84561
2000-2001					
GIC	224	—	346	113	683
National	3588	3004	10156	2419	19167
New India	4219	3579	13305	2942	24045
Oriental	3600	3185	10449	2499	11793
United India	3974	3210	11622	2699	21505
Total	15665	12978	45878	10672	85193
GIC	327	—	254	116	697
National	4055	2662	9800	2366	18883
New India	5229	3720	11700	2635	23284
Oriental	4397	2821	9271	2380	18869
United India	4684	2844	10907	2481	20916
Total	18692	12047	41932	20916	82649

Table 39.8 Non-Life Insurers Investment Statistics for The period Ended March 2005 and March 2006

Name of the Insurer	*Central Govt Securities*		*State govt Securities and Other approved Securities including Central Govt securities*		*Loans to Housing and Fire Fighting Equipments*	
	31-Mar-05	*31-Mar-06*	*31-Mar-05*	*31-Mar-06*	*31-Mar-05*	*31-Mar-06*
GIC of India	2,744	2,789	3,849	3,973	927	1,012
New India	2,398	2,826	3,658	4,166	495	617
National	1,083	1,346	1,596	1,942	385	486
United India	1,585	1,654	2,645	2,856	321	392
Oriental Insurance Co	1,395	1,692	1,977	2,214	308	280
Public Sector (A)	9,205	10,307	13,725	15,151	2,435	2,787
Reliance	97	75	97	75	13	15
Royal Sundaram	89	132	99	147	36	45
Iffco Tokio	128	245	128	245	21	41
Tata Aig General	207	198	207	238	26	41
Bajaj Allianz	257	294	257	294	55	79
ICICI Lombardy	160	210	227	382	30	64
Cholamandalam	140	133	140	133	16	26
HDFC Chubb	80	75	80	75	15	15
Private Sector (B)	1,158	1,364	1,235	1,590	212	320
Total (A+B)	10,362	11,670	14,960	16,740	2,647	3,107

Note: 1. Investments of Agricultural Insurance Corporation of India have not been included

2. The above figures are based on provisional returns filed with IRDA.

Table 39.9

Infrastructure and Social Sector		*Investment Subject to Exposure Norms (Incl.Otal)*		*Other Than Approved Investments (OTAL)*		*Total Investments*	
31-Mar-05	*31-Mar-06*	*31-Mar-05*	*31-Mar-06*	*31-Mar-05*	*31-Mar-06*	*31-Mar-05*	*31-Mar-06*
1,199	1,275	4,905	6,269	1,456	1,584	10,880	12,530
1,050	1,206	3,201	3,415	771	611	8,404	9,404
600	720	1,725	1,537	460	410	4,306	4685
691	685	2,556	2,720	706	734	6,211	65,52
460	527	2,312	2,228	540	592	5,056	5,249
4,001	4,413	14,695	16,169	3,932	3930	34,857	38,520
26	30	56	99	12	35	193	219
67	110	70	79	17	14	217	381
45	77	117	245	0	0	310	607
41	60	38	94	1	3	312	433
78	87	223	342	35	26	613	797
79	136	133	377	11	49	469	959
27	41	16	16	10	5	198	216
26	26	55	70	6	16	177	187
387	567	709	1,323	92	148	2,542	3,799
4,388	4,980	15,404	17,492	4,024	4,079	37,399	42,319

Table 39.10 Gross Direct Premium in India (Rs. in crores)

Insurer	*2003-04*	*Market shares*	*2004-05*	*Market shares*	*2006-07*	*Market shares %*	*Previous Growth over year in*	
							2005	*2007*
Royal sundram	211.33	1.61	270.00	1.83	600.03	2.40	27.76	30.63
Tata A/G	300.49	2.20	386.38	2.59	741.56	2.97	28.58	21.09
Reliance General	145.22	1.00	146.64	0.89	912.23	3.65	0.98	461.96
IFFCO Tokio	–265.32	1.84	403.78	2.80	1150.32	4.60	52.18	28.37
ICICI Lombard	403.63	3.16	752.14	4.89	3003.45	12.0	86.35	88.66
Bajaj Allianz	385.02	2.97	701.62	4.71	1804.60	7.22	82.23	40.48
HDFC	83.93	0.70	142.98	0.98	190.16	0.76	70.34	–7.59
Chclamandalam	76.45	0.60	145.05	0.94	314.59	1.26	89.74	41.57
New India	3229.49	25.23	–	23.25	5024.15	20.01	–	4.86
National	2839.11	21.31	–	21.14	3810.88	15.24	–	8.15
United India	2564.20	18.94	2473.62	16.31	3509.95	14.04	–3.53	11.26
Oriental	2368.64	17.66	2565.03	16.79	3940.53	15.76	8.29	11.26
ECGL	355.01	2.78	414.15	2.86	618.05	2.47	16.66	6.84
Total	13227.86	–	8401.38	–	25002.45	2.45	–	22.37

Table 39.11 Office of Subsidiary Companies

Offioce	*Nationa*						*New India*						*Oriental*						*United India*						*Total*					
	1982	1985	1989 –90	1994 –95	1997 –98	2001 –01	1982	1985	1989 –90	1994 –95	1997 –98	2001 –02	1982	1985	1989 –90	1994 –95	1997 –98	2001 –02	1982	1985	1989 –90	1994 –95	1997 –98	2001 –02	1982	1985	1989 –90	1994 –95	1997 –98	2001 –02
Regional	6	11	16	17	19	20	10	13	18	21	21	26	8	11	16	18	18	21	7	12	20	21	22	25	31	47	70	77	80	92
Divisional	94	149	223	248	254	286	115	185	285	315	352	397	113	157	229	251	274	309	222	190	293	311	322	368	444	681	1030	1128	1202	1362
Branch	222	462	642	677	681	662	327	555	793	827	788	688	243	474	686	701	680	626	283	512	804	792	777	723	1075	2003	2925	2997	2926	269
Total	322	622	881	942	954		425	753	1096	1163		1161	364	642	931	973	972	412	714	117	1124		1124	1	1550	2731	4025	4202		4208

THE ORIENTAL FIRE AND GENERAL INSURANCE COMPANY LIMITED

INCORPORATED IN INDIA

Regd. Office : Jeevan Udyog,
Asaf Ali Road, New Delhi

Issuing Office

PROHIBITION OF REBATE

Section 41 of the Insurance Act 1938 as amended provides as follows:

1. No person shall allow or offer to allow, either directly or indirectly, as an inducement to any person to take out or renew or continue an insurance in respect of any kind of risk relating to lives or property in India, any rebate of the whole or part of the commission payable or any rebate of the premium shown on the Policy nor shall any person taking out or renewing or continuing Policy accept any rebate except such rebate as may be allowed in accordance with the published prospectuses or tables of the insurer.
2. Any person making default in complying with the provisions of this section shall be punishable with fine which may extend to five hundred rupees.

Specimen

COMBINED HOUSEHOLD INSURANCE

For your Jewellery and other valuables particularly those worn or taken out of your residence, the best Insurance is an "ALL Risk" Policy from The Oriental Fire & General Insurance Company Ltd.

The Oriental
Fire & General Insurance
Company Limited

THE ORIENTAL FIRE AND GENERAL INSURANCE COMPANY LIMITED

Incorporated in India

Subsldiary to General Insurance Corporation of India

Registered Office:

Jeevan Udyog, Asaf Ali Road, NEW DELHI-1

For the Contents of
Privaate Dwelling houses and Flats

(*as detailed on the Proposal Form*)
The Sum Insured must represent the full value of property covered)

COVER

A. Loss or Damage caused by any of the undermentional perils:

(*i*) FIRE
(*ii*) LIGHTING
(*iii*) EXPLOSION
(*iv*) AIRCRAFT OR ARTICLES DROPPED THEREFROM (excluding enemy aircraft)
(*v*) BURSTING OR OVERFLOW OF WATER TANKS, APPARATUS OR PIPES (excluding damage caused thereto)
(*vi*) BURGLARY OR HOUSEBREAKING or any attempt thereat.
(*vii*) LARCENY OR THEFT excluding (*a*) Larceny or Theft of Cash, Currency Notes, Bank Notes or Stamps and (*b*) Larceny or Theft whilst the dwelling house or any part thereof is lent, let or sublet in whole or in part.

Extensions

If and so far as said Contents are not otherwise insured the Policy extends except as regards property removed for sale or exhibition or to Furniture Depositories and subject in every case to the exclusion and limitations specified to cover the same whilst temporarily removed and contained in any private dwelling house, club, hotal, boarding or lodging house but remaining in India, against all the said perils except Laceny and Theft.

The amount recoverable under these extensions shall be limited to 15% (fifteen per cent) of the declared full value of the contents.

B. Damage to the Buildings and/or Landlord's Fixtures and Fittings

Damages (other than by fire) but only for which the Insured is liable as Tenant and not as Owner directly caused by

(*i*) Bursting or Overflow of Water Tanks, Apparatus or Pipes:

(*ii*) Burglary, House breaking or any attempt thereat, except while the Dwelling is left unfurnished, Excluding in the case of (*i*) the first Rs. 100 of each and every loss and not exceeding in aggregate 10% of the declared full value of the contents.

C. Liability to the Public or Householders:

As occupier of the Premises only, not arising under any contract, in respect of accidents happening in or about the Insured's Private Dwelling house. Domestic Offices, Garages or Out Buildings covering:

(*i*) Bodily Injury (excluding the Insured's family household or servant).

(*ii*) Damage to property (excluding Property of the insured a family household or servants).

Limited to Rs. 2,00,000 in respect of any one one occurrence and in additions costs and expenses incurred with the Company's consent, Excluding liability for injury or damage arising out of or incidental to the Insured's Profession or Business or the use of lifts of Vehilcles.

D. Compensation for Death of the Insured or the wife or the husband the Insured:

By violence in his private dwelling house, caused by Byrglan or House-breakers or Fire, if death occurs within three months or injury (limited to 50% of the declared full value of the contents or Rs. 10,000/- whichever is the less).

Special Note

Policies do not cover any contingency occasionaed by or happening through:

(*a*) Earthquake, volcanic eruption or other convlusions of nature.

(*b*) Typhoon, hurricane, tornado, cyclone or other atmospheric disturbance.

(*c*) War, invasion, act of foreign enemy, hostilities or warlike operations (whether war be declared or not), civil war.

(*d*) Mutiny, riot, strike, military or popular rising, insurrection, reballion, revolution, military or usurped power, material law or state of siege or any of the events or causes which determine the proclamation or maintenance of material law or state of stage.

(*e*) Redioactive contamination.

EXTRA RISKS

The following additional covers are obtainable or request:

PERSONAL PUBLIC LIABILITY

The liabilities of the Insured and of members of his family reding with him in respect of claims by Third Parties for bodily injury or damage to property arising from accidents happening in the insure of private personal activities, but EXCLUDING accidents arising from the ownership or use of any mechanically propelled vehicle, aircraft vessel or craft (other than hand-propelled craft); the ownership or occupation of land or buildings, the carrying on of any trade, business or profession.

Proposer and un-named members of his family residing with him — Annual Premium Rs. 7.50

Limit of Indemnity Rs. 2,00,000/-

ACCIDENTS TO SERVANTS

The Liability of the Insured under the Workmen's Compensation Acts and at Common Law for accidents to Servants, Rate:

Indoor Servants	— Rs. 4 per capita	Syces	— Rs. 12 per capita
Mails	— Rs. 6 ,, ,,	Drivers	— Rs. 23 ,, ,,

N.B.: A separate Proposal Form must be completed for this cover.

PROPOSAL FORM **AGENCY** ....

1. Proposer's Name (in full) ....

Address .. ..

.. ..

Occupation .. ..

2. Property to be Insured

Situation ....

Household Goods and Personal Effects (except as specifically excluded below*) belonging to the Insured (or for which he is responsible) or permanently resident member of his family and fixtures and fittings the Insurerd's own (or for which he is responsible).

Sum to be Insured .... Rs. .... If the value of Jewellery, Good and Silver articles exceeds one-third of the Sum to be Insured please state their total value Rs. ....

The sum proposed must represent the full value of the property * Exclusions

(*i*) This Proposal does not apply to property more specifically insured, nor, unless specifically mentioned, to Deeds, Bonds, Bills of Exchange, Promissory Notes, Cheques, Securities for money, Documents of any kind, Manuscripts, Medals and Coins, Motor Vehicles and Accessories whilst thereon or Livestock, and,

(*ii*) No one Article, Curio, Picture or other work of art, stmap Collection or article of Gold, Silver or other Precious metal, Jewellery or Fur shall be deemed to be of greater value than 5% of the sum to be Insured, unless specifically insured under a separate item.

(*iii*) Cash, Currency Notes, Bank Notes and Stamps not forming part of or Stamp Collection are included up to 5% of the Sum to be Insured not exceeding Rs. 300/-. Loss by Larceny or Theft in respect of such property is not covered.

3. Dwelling

(*a*) Is it built of brick, stone or concrete, with state tiles, metal or concrete, with state tiles, metal or concrete root? ....

If not, please give full particulars ....

(*b*) Is it a private house? ....

If not, is it a self-contained flat with separate entrance? ....

(*c*) Is it exclusively occupied by yourself and family? ....

(*d*) State type of lockl securing door .... (*i*) Front ....

(*ii*) Stack ....

(*e*) Does it communicate with or is it over any trade risk or is any trade or business carried or is any trade or business carried on in the building? ....

(*f*) Except for shopping and the life, for what periods is it left without an occupant? ....

4. (*a*) Is the building in a good state of repair and will it be so maintained? ... .

(*b*) State approximate age of the building ....

5. In respect of any of the contingencies specified in the proposal have you ever

(*a*) been proviously insured? ... .

If so, with which Company? ... .

(*b*) sustained a loos? ... .

If so, please give particulars. ... .

6. Have you ever had:

(*a*) a proposal for insurance or renewal of a Policy declined? ... .

(*b*) a Policy canclled? ... .

(*c*) special conditions or rates imposed? ... .

If so, please give full particulars. ... .

7. Do you wish to effect these insurances?

(*a*) Personal Public Liability ....

(*b*) Accidents to Serants ... .

(see previous pages for details.)

DECLARATION TO BE SIGNED BY THE PROPOSER

I hereby declared that the above statements are true and that I have withheld no information that might influence the acceptance of this Proposal and I further declare that the sum proposed for insurance represents and will be maintained at no loss than the full value of the property and I agree that this Proposal shall be the Contract between me and The Oriental fire & General Insurance Company Limited and shall be deemed to be incorporated therein.

Dated .... Signature of Proposer ....

No insurance is in force until the Premium has been paid and the Proposal has been accepted by the Company.

Agency .... Policy No. ....

THE ORIENTAL FIRE AND GENERAL INSURANCE COMPANY LIMITED

(INCORPORATED IN INDIA)

Registered Office:

Telegrams: Oriential Buildings, Mahatma Gandhi Road,

"ORIENTFIRE" BOMBAY **BOMBAY-400001** **Telephone No. : 253911**

PROPOSAL FOR MACHINERY BREAKDOWN INSURANCE

Name : ....

Postal Address : ....

Nature of Business : ....

Works Address : ....

1. Give list of Machinery to be insured on the reverse bearing in rained the guiding notes.	
2. Do the items listed represene the whole of the machinery? If not, state items not included and reasons why they are not proposed for insurance.	
3. Is all or any of the machinery subject to periodical inspection? Is so, which by whom and at what intervals?	
4. Are you at present insured? Or have you ever made a proposal for machinery breakdown insurance? If so, has any such proposal (or renewal) been:	

(*a*) declined by any Insurance Co.? If so, give details. (*b*) subject to increased premium or special conditions?	
5. Have you ever suffered loss due to machinery breakdown? If so, give particulars of each breakdown (apart from small damages) during the past three years, giving the cause of the damage and the total cost of repairs in each case.	
6. State the time and date when the insurance is to commence:	

Date : .... Month : .... 19 Period of Insurance will be till noon of the same date and month the following year.

I/We hereby warrant that the answers stated above are true, that I/we have withheld no information which might influence the acceptance of this proposal, and that the warrantly hereby given shall be the basis of the Contract between me/us and the Company. I/we undertake to exercise all reasonable and ordinary precautions for the safety of the said machinery, and I/we agree to accept the conditions of Company's Policy, which I/we have read and understood.

Date : .... Signature : ....

Section 41 of the Indian Insurance Act, 1938, which is in force from the 1st July, 1939 reads as follows:

(1) No person shall allow or offer to allow, either directly or indirectly as an inducement to any person to take out or renew or conditions an Insurance in respect of any kind of risk relating to lives or property in India, any rebate of the whole or part of the commission payable or any rebate of the premium shown on the policy, nor shall any person taking out or renewing or continuing a policy accept any rebate, except such rebate, as may be allowed in accordance with the published prospectuses or tables of the insurer.

(2) Any person making default in complying with the provisions of this section shall be punishable with fine which may extend to five hundred rupees.

THE OTHER, PAYMENT OR ACCEPTANCE OF A REBATE OF THE PREMIUM HEREUNDER IS THEREFORE A BREACH OF THE LAW

SCHEDULE OF MACHINERY TO BE INSURED

Guiding notes for the completion of the Schedule of Machinery

1. Each machine should be entered separately with necessary identification particulars from the name plate stating the market's name, number, size, power, capacity, speed. Additional particulars for electrical equipments such as voltage, amperage, cycles & for steam equipments, pressure and temperature should be given.
2. If (*a*) foundation and/or masonry and brickwork: (*b*) oil in transformers and/or switchgear, are to be included separate entry and valuatin should be given.
3. All protable machines must be so designated. All outside items must be so described separately.
4. To avoid under insurance the sum insured on each machine must be on the basis of its present-day new replacement value including provision for Packing, Freight, Erection and customers and other duties.
5. If any of machines are "standby" or only intermittently inuse, this fact should be mentioned and the extent of use should be specified.

Situation of Machinery: ....

Serial No. (1)	Number of (2)	Description (3)	Year of make (4)	Sum Insured (5)	Excess (6)

Propeser' Signature ....

THE ORIENTAL FIRE AND GENERAL INSURANCE COMPANY LIMITED

(INCORPORATED IN INDIA)

Subsidiary to General Insurance
Corporation of India
Registered Office :
Jeevan Udyog, Asaf Ali Road, New Delhi

Issuing Office

PROHIBITION OF REBATE

Section 41 of the Insurance Act 1938 as amended provides as follows:

1. No person shall allow or offer to allow, either directly or indirectly, as an inducement to any person to take out or renew or continue an insurance in respect of any kind of risk relating to lives or property in India, any rebate of the whole or part of the commission payable or any rebate of the premium shown on the Policy, nor shall any person taking out or renewing or continuing Policy accept any rebate except such rebate as may be allowed in accordance with the published prospectuses or tables of the insurer.
2. Any person making default in complying with the provisions of this section shall be punishable with fine which may extend to five hundred rupees.

FIDELITY

Gurantee

(Individual or Collective)

The Oriential

Fire & General Insurance

Company Limited

The Oriental Fire and General Insurance Company Limited

FIDELITY

GURANTEE

Present -day loss experience in Fidelity Gurantee emphasies the importance of this type of insurance, and various types of Fidelity Policies issued provide Insurance against loss of cash and stock occasioned by the fraud or dishonesty of employees.

All monies or funds standing to the credit of a defaulting Employee are deducted from the loss and not from the amount of the Guarantee.

Policies are issued to meet every need whether a single Employees, or an entire Staff and workpeople, in the latter case without the name of Employees being submitted.

Quotations are available to meet all requirement.

THE ORIENTAL FIRE & GENERAL INSURANCE CO. LTD.

(Incorporated in India)

Subsidiary of General Insurance Corporation of India

Registered Office: Jeevan Udyog, Asaf Ali Road, New Delhi

FORM OF PROPOSAL FOR INDIVIDUAL OR COLLECTIVE FIDELITY GUARANTEE

Agency : .... Policy No.

1. Full name of Employer .... Business

   ....

   Address ....

2. Has any application for Fidelity Insurance been made to any other Company or Underwriters? If so, state date, name of Company or Underwriters, and the result? .. .. ..

3. Give particulars of any Losses suffered during the last five years through the dishonesty of your Employees and the steps taken to prevent a recurrance. .. ..

4. (*a*) Has any Employee power to operate on your Banking Account? .. .. (*a*)

   (*b*) State maximum amount of any one cheque:

   (*i*) on his signature alone. .. .. .. (*b*) (*i*)

   (*ii*) jointly with another Employee. .. .. (*ii*)

5. What system do you use to prevent inclusion of fictitious names in the Pay Roll? .. ..

6. How soon after receipt of money are Employees required to amount for same? .. ..

7. Are they required to bank collections in full to your credit at once or remit to you forthwith?

8. How often and by whom are:

(*a*) Employees Receipt Book Counterfoils checked against collections their reported collections?	(*a*)	by
(*b*) Accounts prepared and rendered direct to customers, and also the subsequent procedure to clear outstanding accounts?	(*b*)	by
(*c*) Cash Book entire checked with Pass Book Recepit Counter-foils and Vouchers?	(*c*)	by
(*d*) Petty Cash payments similary checked and the capability of the Employees to produce the balance tested?	(*d*)	by
(*e*) Your books balanced?	(*e*)	by
(*f*) Your professional audit arrangement carried out? ..	(*f*)	by
(*g*) Traveller's Stocks physically checked?	(*g*)	by
(*h*) Other Stocks Physically checked?	(*h*)	by
(*i*) Physical surprise and spot checks operated?	(*i*)	by

FULL NAMES AND PARTICULARS OF EMPLOYEES FOR WHOM GURANTEES ARE REQUIRED

Note: **Porposal Forms are required to be completed by each Employees named unless he has been in your service for three years or more when he may be included without completing an Application Form**

Surame	Christian Name(s)	Capacity	Amount of	Address	No. of Years in Employ-yer's Service	Salary and Commission (if any)

I/We hereby Declare that the particulars and statements in this Proposal Form are true and that this and any other written statement made by me/us or on my/our behalf for the purpose of the proposed Guarantee shall be the basis of and incorporated in the Contract between me/us and The Oriental Fire & General Insurance Co. Ltd., not only in respect of the persons named herein but also in respect of any other person or persons who may hereafter be included in the said Guarantee and I/we also declare that the conduct and accounts of the said persons have always been satisfactory.

Date .... Signature of Employer ....

This insurance will not be in force until the Proposal has been accepted by the Company and the Premium paid.

FULL NAMES AND PARTICULARS OF EMPLOYEES FOR WHOM GURANTEES ARE REQUIRED

Surame	Christian Name(s)	Capacity	Amount of	Address	No. of Years in Employer's Service	Salary and Commission (if any)

THE ORIENTAL FIRE AND GENERAL INSURANCE COMPANY LIMITED

(INCORPORATED IN INDIA)

Subsidiary to General Insurance Corporation of India
Registered Office :
Jeevan Udyog, Asaf Ali Road, New Delhi

Issuing Office

PROHIBITION OF REBATE

Section 41 of the Insurance Act 1938 as amended provides as follows:

1. No person shall allow or offer to allow, either directly or indirectly, as an inducement to any person to take out or renew or continue an insurance in respect of any kind of risk relating to lives or property in India, any rebate of the whole or part of the commission payable or any rebate of the premium shown on the Policy, nor shall any person taking out or renewing or continuing Policy accept any rebate except such rebate as may be allowed in accordance with the published prospectuses or tables of the insurer.
2. Any person making default in complying with the provisions of this section shall be punishable with fine which may extend to five hundred rupees.

CASH INSURANCE

The Oriential Fire & General Insurance Company Limited

CO. LTD

(INCORPORATION IN INDIA)

Subsidiary to General Insurance Corporation of India
Registered Office :
Jeevan Udyog, Asaf Ali Road, New Delhi

INSURANCE AGAINST LOSS OF CASH

The Company issues policies providing indemnity in respect of loss of Cash in the circumstances or situation as described in the Schedule overleaf subject to the followig exceptions:

(*a*) Shortage due to error or omission.

(*b*) Loss of cash entrusted to any person other than the Insured or an employee of the Insured.

(*c*) Loss due to the fraud or dishonesty of any employee of the Insured unless such loss is discovered within 48 hours of its occurance.

(*d*) Loss for which at the time of its occurrence indemnity is provided by or would but for the existence of this Policy by provided by any other existing Poliy or Policies except in respect of any excess beyond the amount which would have been payable under such other Policy or Policieis had this insurance not been effected.

(*e*) Less occasioned by riot or civil commotion.

(*f*) Any consequence of war invasion act, of foreign enemy hostilities (whether war be declared or not) civil war rebellion revolution insurrection or military or usured power.

Rates will be quoted on receipt of completed Proposal. An annual premium based on the sum insured is charged for Cash on the premises vide Item 4 of the Schedule overleaf, but in respect of Cash insured under Items 1, 2 and 3 is adjustable according to the total amount actually in transit per annum.

LOCAL REPRESENTATIVE

THE ORIENTAL FIRE & GENERAL INSURANCE CO. LTD.

(Incorporated in India)

Subsidiary of General Insurance Corporation of India

Registered Office: Jeevan Udyog, Asaf Ali Road, New Delhi

Branch : ....

Policy No. ....

Agency : ....

PROPOSAL FOR CASH INSURANCE

Definition:— For the purpose of this Insurance the terms "Cash" means current coin, bank and currency notes, cheques, postal ordersm, money orders and current postage stamps.

1. Name in Full .... Business

....

2. Address ....

3. Trade or Business ....

4. (*a*) Description of premises e.g., Shop, Office, Warehouse, Factory, etc ....

   (*b*) Are the whole of the premises occupied by you? If not, give particulars of other tenent. ....

   (*c*) Are the premises occupied at night? ....

   (*d*) ....

5. Are the employees engaged in the Handing of Wages and/or Cash guaratned under a Fidelity Policy? ....

6. Description of Cash to be insured: (If no insurance required for any items inser 'Nil")

Item No.	CIRCUMSTANCE OR SITUATION	Limit any one loss	Estimated total amount of cash (other than crosed cheques) in transit during onsuring twelve months
1.	Cash for the payment of wages, salaries and other earnings or for petty cash in the direct transit from the bank to the Insured's premises from the time the cash is received at the bank by the Insured or authoried employees of the Insured until delivered at the premises or other place of disbursement an whilst there until paid out provided that out of business hours Cash shall be secured in locked safe or locked strong room on the premises. Cheques drawn by the Insurance to provide for such Cash are covered in transit from the premises to the bank.		
2.	Cash (other than described in Item 1) in the personal custory of the Insured or the authorised employees of the Insured whilst in transit between the premises and the bank or post office or in night safe at the bank.		
3.	Cash (other than described in Item 1 and 2) collected by and in the personal custody of the Insured or the authorised employees of the Insured whilst in transit to the premises or bank within a period not exceeding forty-eight hours from the time of collection.		
4.	Cash (other than described in Item 1) whilst on the premises during business hours or whilst secured in locked safe or locked strong room on the Insured's premises out of business hours.		

ESTIMATED TOTAL AMOUNT OF CASH IN TRANSIT per annum

7. Approximate distance between Bank and Proposer's premises. ....

8. (*a*) Is there any transit to or form branches, outlying contract or elsewhere? ....

(*b*) Is so, give particulars, includind addresses. ....

(*c*) How is the Cash conveyed and how many employees have change of it? ....

9. State estimated maximum amount of wages salaries and petty cash retaied in sate or strong room overnight ....

10. (*a*) State following particulars of safe and/or strong room in which cash will be kept out of business hours : ....

Maker's Name	Weight	Dimensions	Identification Number

(*b*) Where and on which floor is the safe situated? ....

(*c*) Is it fixed to the walls or floor, If so, how? ....

(*d*) By whom are the keys of the safe and/or strong room held? ....

(*e*) Are all such keys removed from the premises after business hours? ....

11. (*a*) Are you now, or have you been insured in respect of loss of Cash? If so, state name of Insurer ....

(*b*) Has any Insurer in respect of an insurance against loss of Cash

(*i*) Declined your proposal or renewal? ....

(*ii*) Terminated your Insurance? ....

(*iii*) Required an increased premium? ....

or imposed special conditions? ....

12. Have you ever sustained any loss of Cash? If so, give particulars. ....

I/We desire to effect an insurance with THE ORIENTAL FIRE & GENERAL INSURANCE COMPANY LIMITED, as set forth above. I/We warrant that the above statements are true and complete and that nothing materially afterting the risk has been conceled by me/us. I/We undertake to keep the records necessary for the due adjustment of the premium and to rendeer at the end of each period of insurance a statement in the form required by the Company of the total amount of Cash in transit which is the subject of this proposal and I/we agree that this Proposal and Declaration shall be held to be promissory and shall form the basis of the contract between me/us and The oriental fire & general insurance company limited.

Date .... 19 ....

Signature of Proposer ....

No insurance is in force until a premium or Deposit has been paid and no acknowledgement of any premium or depoist is valid unless upon the Official Printed Form of the Company.

PART SIX

PROSPECTS OF INSURANCE COMPANIES

40

PROSPECTS OF INSURANCE

Prospects of insurance during second millennium have been forecasted as very bright because people accept it as essential cover of life. Privatisation of insurance brings additional technique of business. It has been assessed in the present chapter and succeeding chapter, 'Privatisation of Insurance'. The prospects of life insurance and general insurance have been analyzed based on their performances during last decade, *i.e.,* 1991-2000.

LIFE INSURANCE

Life insurance business is analyzed under new business individual insurance, rural new business, development of new products, new business projects under group insurance, new business projects under group superannuation schemes, business in force, individual and group schemes, lapsation of policies, valuation, working results, investment operations, number of active agents and their business, and social responsibilities.

New Business Individual Insurance

New business of the Life Insurance Corporation of India has increased rapidly after decentralisation of its functions in 1985-86. The impact has been clearly observed in 1990-91 when the total number of life policies has crossed 80 lakh of policies assuring more than Rs. 25,000 crores. During five years (1990-91 to 1994-95) The new business has additional increment of about 20 lakh policies of Rs. 25,000 crores. It reveals that the end of the century will witness total new business of Rs. 80,000 crores under 150 lakh of policies. LIC should reach to the level of Rs. 1,01,000 crore new business under 176 lakh of policies in 2004-2005. With the presence of foreign insurance business in India, it has to compete hard. The existing normal servicing has to be improved to get its outstanding place in insurance business. Business outside India has increased slowly. It is not very satisfactory as the number of policies per year has not increased more than 9 thousand. Sum assured increased by about Rs. 30 crores only per annum.

It is to be seen how much insurance business outside India would increase after entry of foreign insurers. LIC has to strike outside India as foreign insurers plan to achieve maximum business which was untapped by LIC. Challenges before LIC would be greater in the coming years. It is expected that life insurance business would take new turn during the years as people would be fully aware of insurance as a result of massive advertising practices of foreign insurers who believe in offensive advertising and sophisticated services. Many consumer goods have increased their market share as foreign companies have resorted to massive advertising. Coming years would be more materialistic and full of uncertainties. Science and technology would reach to common man. They would not spare any opportunities untapped. If income and uncertainties have increased, insurance desire would convert into insurance-craze.

Rural New Business

Rural LIC business has increased from Rs. 10,294.55 crores under 36.15 lakh policies in 1990-91 which increased to Rs. 21,263.59 crore under 52.47 lakh policies. The percentage share of policies to total new policies increased from 42.5 lakh to 49.2 lakh during the period. It is expected that the sum assured would increase upto Rs. 30,000 crore under 72 lakh policies in 1999-2000, and Rs. 45,000 crore under 85 lakh policies in 2004-2005. The percentage share of rural business in the total business would not change. The LIC would not devote much time and energy for procuring new business in rural areas, as it has to compete with foreign insurers who would devote only in urban areas. Profit motive is the basic object of foreign insurers. They would devote for enhancing business. Rural business would be ignored by the LIC and foreign insurers.

Table 40.1A New Business Individual Insurance (Excluding Annuities)

Mo. of Policies in Lakhs
Sum Assured in crores of Rs.

Year	*New Business in India*		*Out of India*		*Total New Business*	
	No. of Policies	*Sum Assured*	*No. of Policies*	*Sum Assured*	*No. of Policies*	*Sum Assured*
1990-91	86.45	28,139.07	.086	100.03	86.54	.28,239.10
1991-92	92.38	32,064.44	.096	131.86	92.48	32,196.30
1992-93	99.58	35,956.82	0.102	158.98	99.68	36,115.80
1993-94	107.26	41,913.83	0.124	199.07	107.38	42,012.90
1994-95	108.75	55,228.50	0.133	240.32	108.88	55,468.82
1995-96	110.21	51,815,54	0.133	255.99	110.34	52,071.53
1996-97	122.68	56,740.50	0.123	253.44	122.81	56,993.94
1998-99	148.43	75,316.28	0.170	283.72	148.60	75,600.00*
1999-2001*	150.00	80,000.00	0.250	300.00	150.25	80,300.00*
2004-2005*	175.00	100,000.00	1.00	1000.00	176.00	101,000.00*

*Expected as per crude estimate.

Table 40.1B New Business Individual Insurance of LIC

No. of Policies in Lakhs
Sum Assured in Crores of Rs.

Year	*New Business in India*		*Out of India*		*Total New Business*	
	No. of Policies	*Sum Assured*	*No. of Policies*	*Sum Assured*	*No. of Policies*	*Sum Assured*
1998-99	148.43	75316.28	0.14	289.98	14857	75606.26
1999-2000	169.77	91214.25	0.12	276.69	169.89	91490.94
2000-2001	196.56	124771.62	0.08	179.01	196.64	124950.63
2001-2002	224.91	192572.27	0.09	212.69	225.00	192784.96
2002-2003	242.67	179504.34	0.10	298.95	242.78	179803.27
2003-2004	264.56	198707.12	0.11	341.40	264.68	199048.52
2004-2005	218.18	179481.39	0.14	405.27	218.32	179886.66

The new business of LIC has increased to the level of Rs. 179886.66 Crore under 218.32 Lakh policies in 2004-2005 after touching the highest figure of Rs. 199048.52 Crore under 264.68 Lakh policies in 2003-2004. It is expected to enhance further in 2005-2006. It reveals that the life insurance new business has increased more than the forecasted at straight line fitting methods *i.e.*, Rs. 101000.00 crore under 176.00 Lakh policies in 2004-2005. Thus the prospects of life insurance is very light in India.

Table 40.2A Rural New Business

Year	*Rural New Business*		*Percentage share of Rural New Business in total new business*	
	No. of Policies (in Lakhs)	*Sum Assured (Rs. in crore)*	*Policies*	*Sum Assured*
1990-91	36.75	10,294.55	42.50	36.60
1991-92	41.27	12,439.93	44.70	38.80
1992-93	44.39	14,085.03	44.30	39.20
1993-94	48.56	16,680.03	45.30	39.90
1994-95	49.02	21,571.00	45.10	39.10
1995-96	52.57	21,263.59	47.70	41.00
1996-97	60.33	24,278.73	49.20	42.80
*1998-99	70.00	28,000,00	47.16	37.18
*1999-2000	72.00	30,000.00	48.00	37.50
*2004-2005	85.00	45,000.00	48.57	45.00

* Expected

Table 40.2B Rural New Business

Year	*Rural New Business*		*Percentage share of Rural New Business in total new business*	
	No. of Policies (in Lakhs)	*Sum Assured (Rs. in crore)*	*Policies*	*Sum Assured*
1997-98	68.40	27550.69	51.4	43.3
1998-99	81.23	3537294	54.7	47.0
1999-2000	97.04	44168.19	57.5	48.7
2000-2001	35.33	17955.88	55.53	47.78
2001-2002	37.01	25461.94	16.94	13.65
2002-2003	45.23	23547.69	18.90	13.37
2003-2004	62.19	35651.99	22.97	17.85
2004-2005	55.03	46037.01	22.97	25.18
2005-2006				

The figures since 2000-2001 are as per the definitions of rural/social set as approved by IRDA.

The rural new business of LIC has increased to the level of 25.18 per cent under 22.97 per cent policies in 2004-2005. It is more than expected in 2000-2001 the traditional definition has revealed 47.78 per cent of sum assured and 55.53% of policies as compared to 14.59 per cent and 18.18 per cent respectively based on latest definition of IRDA.

The role of LIC in enhancing rural business would socially be essential but commercially, it would be loss-making endure because LIC's urban share would be snatched by foreign and domestic insurers. The inertia of large-number applies in insurance. The mortality is comparatively lower in urban people than that of rural-people. Çream-people would be insured by private insurers, whereas the inferior stuff would be left to the LIC. It would cause deterioration in rural business. The spirit would not enhance for social-upliftment because profit is the index of achievement for which every insurer would aspire their functions and policies.

Development of New Product

People are not attracted with the traditional insurance products (policies) like whole-life, endowment and pure endowment. During 1996-1997, Jeevan Suraksha, Jeevan Sneha, and Jeevan Sanchaya were introduced. Under Jeevan Suraksha plan, retirement income is provided from a chosen date. The policy is with life cover but can be taken without life cover under certain conditions. The policyholder taking policy with life cover provides minimum of 50 per cent of the target pension to spouse on death during the deferment period. On vesting date, the policyholder has the option to receive 25% of the notional cash options in lumps urn and balance in annuity.

Jeeuan Sneha: This plan is a without profits money back type plan with the added features of guaranteed addition. Loyalty addition, encashment of survival benefit as and when required. Flexibility to pay premium in advance, in-built accident cover, free insurance cover: for a period of 3 years from the date of first unpaid premium provided at least 2 full years premium have been paid and option to receive pension in lieu of maturity benefits.

Jeeven Sanchaya: This is a without profits money back type plan with provision of loyalty addition and guaranteed addition. Accident benefit will also be granted under the plan with an upper limit of Rs. 5,00,000 in addition to existing limit of Rs. 5,00,000 under other plans.

New Business under Group Insurance

Group insurance provides insurance cover to those persons who are unable to purchase their own policies. It is purchased mainly by different institutions for the benefit of its employees. Many new organisations are approached by the LIC to insure their employees' life under group insurance and superannuation schemes.

New Group Insurance: The number of new members insured under new group insurance has been highest *i.e.,* 34.83 lakhs in 1991-92 when a large number of institutions was attached to this scheme. Since 1993-94, the number of new members under new schemes has been constantly increasing. The annuity amount (sum assured) was Rs. 3837.23 crore in 1991-92. There was no definite trend in the business of group insurance, but it is expected to increase to Rs. 4000.0 crore under 20 lakh policies in 1999-2000 and Rs. 4200.0 crore under 21 lakh policies in 2004-2005.

New Group Superannuation Scheme: The popularity of pension schemes are increasing rapidly. LIC has take some of its efforts in this direction, but it is negligible. The new members covered under group superannuation scheme has been less than a lakh during 1990-91-1995-96. It has increased slightly to 1.25 lakhs in 1996-97 and is expected go upto 2.00 lakh by 2005. It is not encouraging sign. LIC has to effort hard in this direction. The minimum expected annuity of Rs. 200.00 crore has to be crossed by 2005. However, considering the late entry of LIC in this field, the progress is comparable with other private insurers.

Table 40.3A New Business Under Group Scheme

Year	*New Group Insurance*		*Group Superannuation Scheme*	
	No.of Members (in Lakhs)	*Sum Assured (Rs. in Crore)*	*No. of Members (in Lakh)*	*Sum Assured (Rs. in Crore)*
1990-91	17.08	3392.05	0.12	5.49
1991-92	34.83	3837.23	0.15	6.78
1992-93	26.4	2923.43	0.28	9.10
1993-94	9.94	2382.77	0.32	11.65
1994-95	10.49	2773.06	0.31	14.85
1995-96	11.77	2657.22	0.75	49.34
1996-97	18.89	3237.59	1.25	78.42
*1999-2000	20.00	4000.00	1.70	150.00
2004-2005	21.00	4200.00	2.00·	200.00

*Expected

Table 40.3B New Business Under Group Scheme

Year	New Group Insurance		Group Superannuation Scheme	
	No.of Members (in Lakhs)	Sum Assured (Rs. in Crore)	No. of Members (in Lakh)	Sum Assured (Rs. in Crore)
1996-97	18.89	3237.59	1.25	78.42
1997-98	15.80	3692.24	0.33	122.45
1998-99	15.84	3793.93	0.51	80.92
1999-2000	17.59	3571.12	0.64	82.62
2000-2001	14.91	4563.20	0.94	84.35
2001-2002	21.57	6703.08	0.62	92.45
2002-2003	24.91	16707.57	1.09	110.94
2003-2004	44.48	128047.85	1.72	214.90
2004-2005	81.00	117662.56	0.43	82.50
2005-2006				

The new group insurance has increased to Rs. 117662.56 crore covering 81.00 lakh members in 2004-2005. It is more than the expected of Rs. 4200.00 crore covering 21.00 lakh. Similarly Group Insurance has reached to the level of Rs. 214.90 crore as compared to expected of Rs. 50.00 crore although it has declined to Rs 82.50 crore in 2004-2005.

The group business of LIC has increased faster than the expected. It reveals that the prospects of insurance is very high in India.

Table 40.4A Business in Force (Individual Assurance)

Year	In India		Out of India		Total	
	No. of Policies (in lakhs)	Sum Assured & Bonus (Rs. in crore)	No. of Policies (in lakhs)	Sum Assured & Bonus (Rs. in crore)	No. of Policies (in lakhs)	Sum Assured & Bonus (Rs. in crore)
1990-91	455.08	1,18,651	0.60	528	455.68	1,19,179
1991-92	508.63	1,45,929	0.63	748	509.26	1,46,677
1992-93	566.12	1,77,268	0.67	852	566.79	1,78,120
1993-94	608.00	2,07,601	0.73	1,018	608.73	2,08,619
1994-95	654.52	2,53,333	0.77	1,239	655.29	2,54,572
1995-96	708.78	2,94,336	0.82	1,422	709.60	2,95,758
1996-97	776.60	3,43,018	0.84	1,601	777.50	3,44,619
1999-2000	950.00	4,50,000	1.10	2,200	951.10	4,52,200
2004-2005	1200.00	700,000	4.00	6,000	1204.00	7,06,000

*Expected

Table 40.4B Business in force (Individual Assurance)

Year	In India		Out of India		Total	
	No. of Policies (in lakhs)	Sum Assured & Bonus (Rs. in crore)	No. of Policies (in lakhs)	Sum Assured & Bonus (Rs. in crore)	No. of Policies (in lakhs)	Sum Assured & Bonus (Rs. in crore)
1996-97	776.60	3,43,018	0.84	1,601	777.50	3,44,619
1997-98	849.15	398959	0.88	1889	850.03	400748
1998-99	916.37	457435	0.89	1766	917.26	459201
1999-2000	1012.99	534589	0.90	1862	1013.89	536451
2000-2001	2230.24	643241	0.87	1801	1131.11	645042
2001-2002	1257.89	809170	0.87	1847	1258.76	811017
2002-2003	1387.88	954501	0.90	2174	1388.77	956675
2003-2004	1539.21	925033	0.93	2039	1540.15	927072
2004-2005	1629.51	1029839	1.00	2213	1630.51	1032053
2005-2006						

The individual business in force has increased to Rs. 1032053 crore under 1630.51 policies in 2004-2005 whereas the expected business was Rs. 706000 under 1204.00 policies in the same year. It is realised that the real business have always been higher than the expected business the prospects of insurance business is very high.

Table 40.5A Business in Force (Group Insurance)

Year	New Group Insurance		Group Superannuation Scheme	
	No.of Members (in Lakhs)	Sum Assured (Rs. in crore)	No. of Members (in lakh)	Amount of Annuities per Annum (Rs. in crore)
1990-91	169.57	30,501.57	2.43	253.12
1991-92	189.53	32,973.46	2.54	301.77
1992-93	212.54	43,086.83	2.69	358.93
1993-94	227.31	46,742.95	3.14	403.51
1994-95	241.88	51,034.1	3.54	427.66
1995-96	246.49	64,651.54	4.19	483.05
1996-97	238.97	64,606.60	5.54	545.59
*1999-2000	270.00	81,000.00	7.00	700.00
*2004-2005	250.00	1,18,000.00	14.70	1,470.00

* Expected

Table 40.5B Business in Force (Group Insurance)

Year	New Group Insurance		Group Superannuation Scheme	
	No.of Members (in Lakhs)	Sum Assured (Rs. in crore)	No. of Members (in lakh)	Amount of Annuities per Annum (Rs. in crore)
1996-97	238.97	64606.60	5.54	545.59
1997-98	245.22	74798.75	6.71	682.84
1998-99	234.85	77918.65	7.54	815.96

(Contd.)

1999-2000	234.93	76384.53	8.09	971.15
2000-2001	236.68	89326.19	8.84	1137.72
2001-2002	247.19	100597.64	9.80	1271.94
2002-2003	240.99	124312.26	10.86	1488.98
2003-2004	252.46	143398.20	12.34	1705.05
2004-2005	306.50	136286.92	12.73	1916.64
2005-2006				

The group insurance business in force was Rs. 136286.92 crore for 306.50 Lakhs members in 2004-2005, and superannuation was Rs. 1916.64 crore covering 12.73 lakh members on the other hand the expected business was Rs. 118.000.00 crore for 250.00 lakhs members of group insurance and Rs. 1470.0 crore for 14.70 lakhs members of group superannuation scheme. It is very clear that the real business has been enhaving faster than the expected. It was also correct in 1999-2000.

Business-in-Force

Business-in-force has been constantly increasing alongwith bonus amount. It has been analysed under individual assurance and group insurance during last decade of 20th century.

Individual Assurance: Business-in-force (individual assurances) has increased from Rs. 1,19,179 crore in 1990-91 to Rs. 3,44,619 crore in 1996-97. It is expected that the sum assured and bonus would be Rs. 4,50,000 crore in 1999-2000 and Rs. 7,00,000 in 2004-2005 under 950 lakh policies and 1200 lakh policies respectively in India. Business outside India is not very encouraging. Number of policies would be expected to go up to 4.00 lakh for Rs. 6000 crore sum assured in 2004-2005. Thus, the total business in force has increased to Rs. 706000 crore. It is the minimum amount expected to be achieved in the beginning of 21st century. If LIC is unable to achieve the expected amount of business in business, its effectiveness is not praiseworthy.

Group Insurance: Business-in-force (group insurance) has increased from Rs. 30,501.57 crore in 1990-91 to Rs. 64,66.60 crore in 1996-97. Number of members increased from 169.51 lakh to 238.97 lakh during the period, which is expected to be 350.00 lakh in 2005. It is the minimum expected business that Rs. 1,18,000 crore would be in 2005. If LIC is unable to achieve that much, it would be a failure in this field. Group insurance is the cheapest form of insurance available to people. It is based on term insurance.

Group Superannuation Scheme: The amount of annuities has increased from Rs. 253.12 in 1990-91 to Rs. 545,59 in 199.6-97 and is expected to go upto Rs. 1470 crore in 2005. Similarly the number of members is expected to upto 14.70 lakh in 2005 although it was 2.43 lakh in 1990-91. LIC must increase its business at faster rate as there is enough scope of superannuation business in India.

Table 40.6A Lapsation of Policies

Year of New Business	*Percentage of Net Lapses to Mean Life Insurance Business in Force*	*New Lapse Ratio at Mean Duration of New Business*				
		0	1	2	3	Total
1990-91	6.0	0.5	13.5	8.0	3.4	25.4
1991-92	6.1	0.9	14.5	8.9	3.5	27.8
1992-93	5.9	1.0	15.6	8.9	3.8	29.3
1993-94	6.3	0.6	17.0	8.5	2.6	28.7
1994-95	6.1	0.6	17.0	8.0		
1995-96	6.4	0.9	15.6			
1996-97	5.1	1.1				
1999-2004	5.5					25.0
2004-2005	4.0					20.00

Note: Mean duration is year of lapse minus year of New business.

Table 40.6B Lapsation of Policies

Year of New Business	Percentage of Net Lapses to Mean Life Insurance Business in Force	New Lapse Ratio at Mean Duration of New Business				
		0	1	2	3	Total
1996-97	5.1	1.1	16.3	9.4	2.4	29.2
1997-98	5.0	0.8	16.4	9.8	2.3	29.3
1998-99	4.9	0.1	17.9	11.2	2.0	31.2
1999-2000	5.1	0.7	16.2	7.2	2.4	26.5
2000-2001	4.9	0.8	16.0	8.7		
2001-2002	5.5	0.7	16.0	8.7		
2002-2003	5.5	0.7	15.3			
2003-2004						
2004-2005						
2005-2006						

The reposition of policies has shown dismall results as the total lapses for three years in 1998-99 had louched the English figure of 31.2 per cent of new business. It was 26.5 per cent of new business in 1999-2000 although the expected was 25.5 per cent. The per cent of Net lapses to mean life insurance in force has not been declining. It remain constantal 5.5 per cen.

Table 40.7A Valuation Results

(In crores of Rs.)

Year	*Valuation Surplus*	*Shares of Central Govt.*	*Taxes Paid to Govt.*	*Reversionary Bonus on Sum Assured*	
				Whole-life	*Endowment*
1990-91	1800	90.00	254.90	80	64
1991-92	2108	105.41	326.60	96	75
1992-93	2368	118.42	407.15	96	75
1993-94	2803	140.15	431.92	96	75
1994-95	3219	160.94	508.98	96	75
1995-96	3434	171.69	582.28	95	78
1996-97	3967	198.35	585.06	95	78
1999-2000	5000	250.00	750.00	100	90
2004-2005	7000	350.00	1050.00	125	100

* Expected

Table 40.7B Valuation Results

Year	*Valuation surplus Rs.*	*Shares of central Govt. Rs.*	*Taxes Paid to Govt. Rs.*
1996-97	3967	198.35	585.06
1997-98	4673	233.64	563.06
1998-99	5300	265.00	726.96
1999-2000	6333	316.55	758.62
2000-2001	7613	380.66	709.65
2001-2002	8667	433.25	868.17
2002-2003	9767	488.10	1258.62

Contd...

2003-2004	10987	548.13	1506.28
2004-2005	13952	696.60	5365.16
2005-2006			

The total surplus has increased to Rs. 13952 crore in 2004-2005 as Rs 7000 expected. It is much more than the expected figure. Similarly the share of central government and taxes paid to government have been much higher than expected. It shows that LIC has worked hard for the development of insurance business.

Lapsation of Policies

The new business increased fastly but some of them did not continue for the stipulated period. They are known as lapsed policies. It should be analysed systematically. It reveals that the percentage of net lapses to mean Life Insurance Business in force has gone down from 6.0 in 1990-91 to 5.1 in 1996-97 and is expected to go down to 5.5. in 1999-2000 and 4.0 in 2004-2005. The net lapse ratio at mean duration has gone to 17.0 percent of new business during one year of new business. The total amount of percentage of percentage to new business has been 25.4. percent in 1990-91 which has gone upto 29.3 percent in 1992-93. It reveals that more than one fourth of new business did not continue for its term. It is failure of LIC and increase discredit and loss of expenses of business. If it is not very serious of its business loss the private insurers would procure higher amount of business. However, it is not correct to believe that private insurers would not face lapsation problems. In any case, it is great drawback of LIC's business.

Valuation of Results

The valuation surplus of LIC has increased from Rs. 1800 crore in 1990-91 to Rs. 3967 crore in 1996-97 and is expected to go upto Rs. 3000 crore in 2004-2005. The share of government is 5 percent of surplus. Thus, it should be Rs. 350 crore in 2005 and tax amount would be Rs. 1050 crores in that year. Reversionary bonus is expected to increase to 125 per thousand sum assured on whole life policies, and 100 per thousand sum assured on endowment policies. The LIC must meet the expectation of people at higher rate because the sum assured is highly hit with inflation. A person insured for 10 lakh will not get Rs. 10 lakh in real term after 20 years. Although long term activities/ investment/agreement is bound to be hit of inflation, LIC has to be very careful and the bonus rate is to be increased for the benefit of policy and compete with banking deposits:

Working Results

Working results is calculated by finding the life insurance fund which is equal to total income minus total outgo. Total income includes premium income, income from investments and miscellaneous. Premium income is denoted by first year premium and renewal premium as well as single premium. Total outgo includes commission etc., to agents, salary and other benefits to employees and other expenses. The transfer to reserve and surplus share paid to Government are also included under outgo. The comparison of real work-up results with the expected in 1999-200 and 2004-2005 has revealed the outstanding performance of LIC.

Table 40.8 Working Results

(In crores of Rs.)

Year	*Total Income over*	*Total Outgo*	*Excess of Income over outgo*	*Fund at the end*	*Fund % increase over Previous year*
1990-91	8,517.98	3,588.85	4,929.13	28,400.91	21.00
1991-92	10,690.69	4,400.27	6,290.42	34,691.39	22.15
1992-93	12,244.23	5,937.33	6,306.90	40,998.29	18.18
1993-94	15,212.31	6,544.78	8,667.53	49,665.82	21.14
1994-95	18,102.32	7,789.24	10,313.08	59,978.90	20.76
1995-96	22,046.76	9,24,5.60	12,801.16	72,780.06	21.34

Contd...

1996-97	25,933.09	10,841.54	14,979.90	87,759.96	20.58
1999-2000	44729.6	18101.93	26,627.67	1,54,043.73	20.92%
2004-2005	48460.70	63885.54	3,85,639.07	1,12,346.24	19.86%

Table 40.9 Expense Ratio, Interest and Claims Ratio

Year	*Expense Ratio Overall Expense Ratio*	*Renewal Ratio*	*Interest Earned Rate of interest Realised on Mean Life insurance Fund*	*Ratio of outstanding claims to claims Payable*
	%	%	%	%
1990-91	23.24	3.52	11.44	5.51
1991-92	22.27	3.49	11.95	5.50
1992-93	22.89	5.37	11.56	5.27
1993-94	21.83	4.95	12.43	4.86
1994-95	21.39	6.32	12.21	5.26
1995-96	20.79	7.00	12.29	5.99
1996-97	21.43	7.09	12.39	5.32
1999-2000	21.16	5.63	12.08	4.10
2004-2005	16.57		9.93	0.80

The excess of income over outgo has been Rs. 4,929.13 crores in 1990-91 and Rs. 14,979.90 crore in 1996-97 which re expected to go upto Rs. 30,000 crore in 2004-2005. From the total funds every year, claims amount are also deducted. The total fund at the end of 1996-97 was Rs. 87,759.96 crore which is expected to go upto Rs. 1,75,000 crore in 2004-2005. The corporation has to accumulate that amount by 2005 for investment. The LIC investment is made in social and economic projects.

Expense Ratio: Overall expense ratio has gone down from 23.24% of total premium income in 1990-91 to 21.43% in 1996-97 and expected to go down to 20.00% in 2000. Renewal ratio is increasing from 3.52% in 1990-91 to 7.00% in 1996-97 and expected to go upto 10.0% in 2005. It reveals that LIC is unable to restrain renewal rates, while some improvements are expected in overall expense ratio. But real experience showed at LIC has curtailed its expanses.

Rate of Interest Realised: The rate of interest increased from 11.44% in 1990-91 to 12.39% in 1996-97 and expected to go upto 13.5% in 2004-2005. It reveals that LIC is able to earn more interest. The rate in 2004-2005 is outcome or market positive.

Ratio of Outstanding Claims: The percentage of outstanding claims to claims payable has been rounding from the lowest 4.86% to 5.99%. It is expected to be at 5.00% in 2000 and 4.50% in 2005. Thus the outstanding claims have not been improved and could not go down to 4.00 per cent. It has improved to the label of 6.80 per cent on 2004-2005.

Investment Operations

The total Investment has increased from Rs. 24,899.65 crore in 1990-91 to Rs. 77,935.19 crore in 1996-97 and is expected to go upto Rs. 1,25,000.00 crore in 2005. It shows that LIC has taken serious step for socio-economic development of the country. The investment has gone to 84.58 percent in 1996-97 in Public Sector, whereas investment in private sector has declined from 14.00% to 12.93% in 1990-91 and 1996-97 respectively. It reveals that investment in public sector is given more importance. Public Sector enterprises are engaged in socio-economic development of India. Many infrastructure development projects have been taken up by public sector. The investment in private sector is expected to increase as a result of private insurers. The trend of investment would reverse in next century *i.e.,* private investment would increase as compared to investment in public sector. The real investment has increased to Rs. 4,13,800.00 crores in 2004-2005 as against the expected investment of Rs. 115.00. It reveals that the LIC profound excellently.

Table 40.10 Investment Operations

Year	Public Rs. in Crore	Sector % to Total	Cooperative Rs. in Crore	Sector % to Total	Private Rs. in Crore	Sector % to Total	Total Rs. in Crore
1990-91	19,979.76	80.2	1,444.47	5.80	3,475.12	14.0	24,899.65
1991-92	24,457.27	80.4	1,562.63	5.10	4,382.51	14.5	34,402.41
1992-93	28,983.24	79.8	1,657	56 4.60	5,681.31	15.6	36,322.11
1993-94	36,246.48	82.10	17,106.06	3.90	6,199.01	14.00	44,161.55
1994-95	44,318.93	82.87	1,793.05	3.35	7,367.49	13.78	53,479.47
1995-96	54,245.63	84.63	1,857.63	2.90	7,996.52	12.47	64,099.78
1996-97	65,917.41	84.58	1,938.98	2.49	10,078.80	12.93	77,935.19
1999-2000	1,17,058.95	84.20	2,129.31	1.53	19,843.89	14.27	1,39,032.15
2004-2005							4,13,200.45

Table 40.11 Productivity

Year As on 31st March	*Number of Active Agents*	*Average Business (Rs) per Agent*
1991	4,14,820	6,78,344
1992	4,64,505	6,90,293
1993	4,95,745	7,25,309
1994	5,24,427	7,97,324
1995	5,19,504	10,63,101
1996	5,13,897	10,08,286
1997	5,33,133	10,64,284
2000	6,83,190	13,28,292
2005	10,41,737	16,97,997

Productivity of Agents

Productivity of agents is calculated dividing total new business (individuals) by number of active agents. The average business per agent has increased from Rs. 6,78,344 in 1990-91 to Rs. 10,84,284 in 1996-97 and is expected to touch Rs. 15,00,000 in 2005 as the number of active agents is expected to go up to 7,00,000. The technological improvements will enhance their productivity. It is, therefore, more than the expected new businesses.

Computerisation has facilitated many branch offices of LIC to upgrade the services. Many agents have modernised their activities through application of computer. The agents have modernised their activities through application of computer. The agents' productivity is expected to increase in coming years. The productively of insurance agent has been Rs. 16,97,997 as compared to expected Rs. 15,00,000 in 2004-2005. It discloses the increased producing by of LIC. Business is expected to increase in future.

Table 40.12 Social Responsibilities

(In crores of Rs.)

Year	*Socially Oriented Investment (Rs.)*	*New Lives Insured under Social Security Group Schemes*	*Loans to Housing Schemes (Rs)*
1990-91	2,705.78	4,21,113	323.13
1991-92	3,189.58	19,42,913	456.52
1992-93	3,196.82	15,17,466	636.14
1993-94	8,19,9.00	7,01,207	548.30
1994-95	7,927.40	2,94,090	536.90
1995-96	9,535.59	3,96,326	733.00
1996-97	11,794.95	9,91,327	940.50
*1999-2000	26,026.56	49,49,987	1,651.10
*2004-2005	67,209.00	81,43,000	7,424.00

Social Responsibilities

The social responsibilities have been analysed under investment in social schemes, new lives insured under social security group schemes and loans to housing schemes.

Socially Oriented Investment: The socially oriented investment has increased from Rs. 2,705.78 crore in 1990-91 to Rs. 11,794.95 crore in 1996-97 and is expected to increase to Rs. 30,000 crore by 2005. These investments help to improve the quality of life of the people at large through improvement of basic amenities like potable water, drainage, housing, electrification and transport. In 2004-2005, it has been more than expected.

New Lives Insured under Social Security Group Schemes: New lives insured under social security group schemes has increased from 4,21,113 in 1990-91 to 9,91,327 in 1996-97 and expected to go up 28,00,000 by 2005. LIC made considerable efforts for creating greater awareness and benefits provided under Landless Agricultural Labourers (LALG- 1) and IRDP Group Insurance Scheme. The accidental death cover has been increased and Disability benefits have been included under Social Security Group Insurance with effect from 16th-October, 1995. In case of death or total permanent disability due to accident (including loss of two limbs of use) an amount of Rs. 25.00 is payable and in case of loss of limb of use, due to an accident, a sum of Rs. 12,500 is payable under these schemes irrespective of basic sum assured. These additional benefits have been provided from Social Security Fund without charging any additional premium. The performance of LIC in 2004-2005 have been for table than expected.

GENERAL INSURANCE

General insurance business in India came into hands of public sector under the caption of General Insurance Corporation of India and its four subsidiaries viz., National Insurance Company Ltd., New India Assurance Company Ltd., Oriental Insurance Company Ltd. and United India Insurance Company Ltd. in 1972. The prospects of General Insurance business is analysed under Gross Direct Premium Income, Investment Income, Profit After Tax, underwriting experience, Crop Insurance, Rural Insurance and foreign business.

Gross Direct Premium Income

The gross direct premium income has been analysed under fire insurance, marine insurance, miscellaneous insurance and total.

Fire Insurance: The amount of gross direct premium income in fire insurance has increased from Rs. 683 crore in 1990-91 to Rs. 1,997 crore in 1997-98 and is expected to go upto Rs. 3,500 crore in 2005. The business of fire insurance is comparatively better than marine insurance but better than miscellaneous insurance.

Marine Insurance: The gross direct premium income of marine insurance has increased from Rs. 524 crore in 1990-91 to Rs. 1,055 crore in 1997-98 and is expected to increase upto Rs. 1,550 crore in 2004-2005. It is very slow progress of marine insurance.

Miscellaneous Insurance: The gross direct premium income of miscellaneous insurance has increased from Rs. 1,706 crore in 1990-91 to Rs. 5,034 crore in. 1997-98 and is expected to rise up to Rs. 9,000 crore in 2004-2005. The insurance of motor vehicles and other accident insurance have become compulsory. So the miscellaneous insurance has increased faster than those of fire insurance and marine insurance. The general insurance in India is not progressing as expected.

Total Insurance: The gross direct premium income of all the insurance has increased form Rs. 2,913 crore in 1990-91 to Rs. 8,086 crore in 1997-98 and is expected to increase to Rs. 14,050 crore in 2004-2005. The increase of gross direct premium has increased by more than three times which would increase by more than five times during 1990-2005. The gross direct premium of General Insurance has been significantly higher than the expected ones.

Table 40.13 Gross Direct Premium Income.

(In crores of Rupees)

Year	*Fire Insurance*	*Marine Insurance*	*Miscellaneous Insurance*	*Total*
1990-91	683	524	1,706	2,913
1991-92	839	659	2,005	3,503
1992-93	988	803	2,279	4,070
1993-94	1.164	875	2,727	4,766
1994-95	1,323	852	3,096	5,271
1995-96	1,578	999	3,800	6,377
1996-97	1,800	1,021	4,527	7,348
1997-98	1,997	1,055	5,034	8,086
*1999-2000	2,300	1,250	6,000	9,550
*2004-2005	3,500	1,550	9,000	14,050
2004-2005				51,554.50
2005-2006				57,846.49

*Expected

Table 40.14 Investment Income and Profit After Tax

(Rupees in crores)

	Investment Income (Gross)	*Profit After Tax*
1990-91	566	334
1991-92	752	428
1992-93	859	503
1993-94	957	670
1994-95	1,150	377
1995-96	1,475	551
1996-97	1,687	719
1997-98	1,978	1,255
1999-2000	2,400	1,500
2004-2005	3,500	2,300

The gross direct premium is indication of the insurance business, but it does not increase so fastly as expected by public.

Investment Income

Investment income of General Insurance Business has increased from Rs. 566 crore in 1990-91 to Rs. 1978 crore in 1979-98 and is expected to go upto Rs. 3500 crore in 2004-2005. It shows that general insurance business has increased its investment income by more than two times during 1990-91 to 1997-98 and by about six times during 1990-91 to 2004-2006. It reveals that the investment income has increased faster than the gross direct premium income.

Table 40.15 Underwriting Experience

(Income of Rs.)

	Net Premium	*Net incurred claims*	*Expenses commission and other outgo*	*Increased in unexpired risk reserves*	*Underwriting Profit (+) Loss (–)*
1990-91	2,742	1,898 (69.2%)	652 (23.8%)	310 (11.3%)	–118 (4.3%)
1991-92	3,450	2,303 (66.8%)	802 (23.2%)	422 (6.2%)	– 77 (2.2%)
1992-93	3,868	2,839 (73.4%)	908 (23.5%)	240 (12.2%)	–119 (3.1%)
1993-94	4,427	3,050 (68.9%)	983 (22.2%)	312 (70%)	+ 82 (1.9%)
1994-95	4,879	4,289 (87.9%)	1,070 (21.9%)	225 (4.6 %)	–705 (14.4%)
1995-96	5,956	4,427 (74.3%)	1,567 (26.3%)	608 (10.2%)	– 646 (10.8%)
1996-97	6,731	5,105 (75.8%)	1,900 (28.2%)	357 (5.3%)	– 628 (7.3%)
1997-98	7,357	5,625 (76.5%)	1,799 (24.4%)	317 (4.3%)	–384 (5.2)
1998-99					–200 (4.0%)
1999-2000					–100 (2.0%)
2004-2005					

Profit After Tax

The profit after tax increased from Rs. 334 crore in 1990-91 to Rs. 1,255 crore in 1997-98 and is expected to increase to Rs. 2,300 crore by 2004-2005. Thus, the profit has increased faster than the investment income and gross direct premium income. The profit is expected to increase by more than six times to 2004-2005.

Underwriting Experience

Net premium of general insurance business has increased from Rs. 2,742 crore in 199-91 to Rs. 7,357 crore in 1997-98. Expenses of management have also increased from Rs. 652 crore in 1990-91 to Rs. 1,799 crore in 1997-98. Although unexpired risk reserves have also increased but in a slow rate. The underwriting loss has gone upto Rs. 705 crore in 1994-95 after getting profit of Rs. 82 crore in 1993-94.

All the performances of general insurance business have been discouraging. With the entry of private insurers, the performances of GIC and its 'subsidiaries are expected to go up because of competition and availability of measurement parameter. If private insurers enter for profit, why not GIC and its subsidiaries should earn profit. The causes of profit and the diagnose of losses reveal the points of modifications.

Crop Insurance

Crop insurance scheme was implemented in India since 1985. State Government is required to share the premium and claim in the ratio of 2 : 1. At present, the scheme is implemented in 15 states and 2 union territories. It is available for crop loans in selected areas for selected crops. During 1997-98 51.35 lakh farmers and 6.82 lakh farmers were covered for a sum insured of Rs. 2,230.74 crore and Rs. 322.37 crore in kharif 1997 season and Rabi 1997-98 season, respectively. The premium income for the period was Rs. 34.32 crore and, Rs. 5.72 crore for Kharif and Rabi season, respectively.

During 1997-98 season, Experimental Crop Insurance Scheme for non-loa nee small and marginal farmers was implemented in selected 24 districts of 8 states. The premium is totally subsidised for small and marginal, farmers and premium and claims are shared between Centre and State Government in the ratio of 4 : 1. Under this scheme, 4.78 lakh farmers are covered for a sum insured of Rs. 172 crore in 14 district of 5 states.

Rural Insurance

During 1997-98, new schemes have been devised such as Foetus Insurance Scheme and the Calf Heifer Rearing Insurance Scheme as recommended by the Task Force Committee on Cattle Insurance constituted by the Government of India. Farmers Package Policy was introduced to cover all the assets of the farmers under one policy. Aquaculture Insurance Scheme is also introduced for the benefit of rural population.

Foreign Business

GIC and its subsidiaries operate foreign business. During 1997-98, direct overseas operations of the four subsidiary companies produced a gross premium income of Rs. 382.95 crore as against Rs. 367.05 crore in 1996-97. Net claims amounted Rs. 245.41 crore during 1997-98. Foreign business of GIC and its subsidiaries is expected to increase as a result of foreign insurers.

GROWING ECONOMY AND INSURANCE

With the introduction of globalisation and privatisation, insurance industry in India is grooving more than 15% per annum. It is second highest after IT industry. The GDP in expected to grow by 10.00 per cent agriculture by 4 per cent and industry by 12.00. The insurance industry is developing in number, quality and class fication. The population and per capita income have been instrument for the growth of the industry. The quality life of people demands distills free lining. Insurance has increased several quality products to meet their requirement the different classes of prospects have started demanding deferent types of products. The company which is expert in diversification of its products and CRM can develop leap and found. The insurance intermediation has become a full time qualified profession. Professionally qualified agents of insurance can earn more than a doctor, engineer, CA and other professional expects.

Now, people are approaching insurance agents for their financial advises rater than business. Insurance in started to be bought by the people rater than previous thinking of bold. People are seeking now best publication for their lives, health, property, business and economic activities. IT and IRDA have asked agents to serve people better. The policyholders are getting more satisfaction today as compared to past year-experiences. Telecommunication has helped people to develop themselves through insurance. The business of insurance is expected to grow more than 18 per cent annum in future.

41

PRIVATISATION OF INSURANCE INDUSTRY

Public Enterprises in any country cannot perform all the economic and business activities efficiently. Even in a socialist country, public enterprises in all the fields cannot discharge their full responsibilities. Complete governmentalisation or nationalisation will lead towards serfdom or anarchism. In absence of free will personal interests; the economic activities will not provide adequate and qualitative production. This is the reason that some troubles have started in some parts of the USSR and China. In Indian conditions where we have adopted mixed economy, expecting too much from public enterprises will distort the economy and ultimately will lead towards wastage of precious resources. Supporting and subsidising by the Government indirectly punish the tax-payers and the country-men. Therefore, it is the high time to recast our Industrial Policy and should consider the productivity and efficiency as criteria to continue a particular unit whether public enterprises or private enterprises. The public enterprises cannot be sustained as sacred cow without milk. Similarly, the unscrupulous private enterprises declaring themselves sick cannot be put on ambulance for a longer time. It is a matter of satisfaction that the Government has started taking pragmatic approaches to revive the productivity and efficiency base criteria for the development of an enterprise. The restrictions on utilisation of full capacity by private enterprises are being removed gradually to increase production and productivity of the economy. The public enterprises will have to come at the compative of the private enterprises. If the formers are loosing in the efficiency and productivity criteria, they should be closed down and the private enterprises having more efficiency and productivity should be encouraged to increase production of the economy. The industrial policy that public enterprises provide more employment opportunities although production is nominal should be changed to bring them under productivity criterion. Providing employment for the sake of employment is adding fuel to the fire of inflation any trend in the economy because the productivity is very low. The Government decision to denationalise certain production undertaking is welcome step because they remain idle without production or very small production. Other political parties should realise the gravity of productivity and discard the public enterprises for the sake of political system.

The Government cannot perform all the functions with equal efficiency. The regulatory role, promotional role, entrepreneurial role and planing role have not been fully discharged by Government. Barring few enterprises as envisaged in the Industrial Policy 1956, rest of the public enterprises should be returned back to the private institutions if their productivities are not improved to the level of a private enterprise. The government should concentrate more on regulatory, and planning roles. The entrepreneurial role should be confined only to those areas where the private entrepreneurs are hesitant and cannot discharge their functions satisfactorily at national level. Non-profitable business activities, defence, transport, education, communication and such types of public activities should be undertaken by the Government. W.A. Levis observed: "The nationalisation of industry is not essential to planning, a government can do nearly anything it wants to do by way of controlling industry without resorting to nationalisation". Neither state monopoly nor private monopoly is desirable in the economy. The competition, being the backbone of the productivity should be encouraged to promote the economy. The competition may be between and amongst the public and private enterprises. The productivity and efficiency are the important criteria to permit the continuation of an enterprise. The public enterprises in some areas performed better than the private enterprises and, therefore, should be permitted to continue to accelerate the growth of the economy. On the other hand, many public enterprises are wasting public money because of continuous loss and less production. Such enterprises should be handed over to the competent private companies. On the reverse, some private enterprises are at loss and declaring themselves sick. They should be taken over by the Government companies of the area or by the private houses as the circumstances and nature of the business may be prevailing at that time. The privatisation may be done after analysing the efficiency of the organisation and their role in the economy. The problem of public enterprises, inefficiency of public enterprises and efficiency of private enterprises, are considered under privatisation and efficiency.

Problems of Public Enterprises

A large number of public enterprises and their size and variety have given complex problem. Some of them are on account of procedural defects and too much rigidity in their operation, but many problems are inherent due to the basic tenets of the public enterprises. They lack flexibility, effectiveness and efficiency of private enterprises. Over the last decades, the experiences of public enterprises particularly of departmental undertakings have been very discouraging. The control over performance and routine operations have been too rigid or too timid to yield higher productivity. The functioning of government companies have been better than those of other forms of public enterprises but they could not excel the private enterprises. It was considered that the public corporations could perform better than, other public enterprises but many corporations did not comply the expectations. The political parties and government hindered routine functioning of many public enterprises. Frequent changes of top management and alterations of policies and procedures have adversely affected their operations. The sense of belongingness which is the soul and spirit of success of any business is absent at top, middle and lower level of management in public enterprises. The workers of public enterprises are more reckless than those of private enterprises. The sense of belongingness is not common in many of the socialist countries, whereas the Japanese organisations have excelled on this pattern as the result of ringi (family) system of employment. The work-culture of Japan is being imitated by the U.S.A. The public enterprises are least suitable in the political upheavals. Many organisations are facing interferences by the Government. Overlapping and absence of power and authority are served at several levels.

The Government has modified the appointment policy recently. Instead of appointing politically supported bureaucrats, business experts are appointed at the top. The productivity improved consequently. Many committees have recommended that the Board of Directors should consist technical skill, representatives of labour and personnel management, financial talent and management experts. But, the Government has not paid full attention towards such suggestions. The appointment of Members of Parliament and civil servants are considered unhealthy and full of political backing which creates groupism in the organisation. It is also suggested that full time managing director should be appointed to manage that concern effectively and efficiently.

Decentralisation of power should be implemented to avoid the problems of overlapping and fraud. Recently, postal saving accounts have experienced a large number of fraud, corruption and red tapism because of too much centralisation and dual functioning of the operation. The branch as well as head post offices are maintaining account-books without entrusting responsibility to any one. On the other hand, banking operation because of decentralisation of power, authority and responsibility are functioning properly. The postal saving accounts should be transferred to banking systems to avoid the problems of public and retain the goodwill of post offices. The suggestions of Administrative Reform Commissions have not been fully complied to regulate and manage the public enterprises.

During the last three decades many public enterprises are running at loss and wasting public money in several forms. These organisations should be handed over to the private houses. The Government can exercise control on them. The regulatory and administrative functions of the Government should be strengthened to control the business activities. The Government should not take up entrepreneurial operations where it cannot function profitably and economically. Giving the picture of inefficiency and inactiveness, it cannot control the business to improve efficiency and effectiveness. The inefficiency and failure at business-front reflects the efficiency of the Government at large. It is in the interest of the nation and the public individually to denationalise sick government organisations.

The appointment policy of many public enterprises are defective. Redundant staff and scarcity are observed in many cases. Proper planning and recruitment is absent in these organisations. Labour relations in several public enterprises are not congenial inspite of maximum amenities and facilities to the labour. The productivity of labour in public enterprises is lower than their counterpart in private enterprise, whereas the salaries and amenities are higher in the former case than that in the latter case. The public enterprises in the name of socialistic approach adopting no profit no loss have resorted the practices of concealing low productivity. Many organisations fix their prices arbitrarily and at the instructions of the Government. It is observed that their pricing policies are no cheaper than those of private enterprises. The depending on competition and pricing systems help promote rational allocation of scarce resources, optimal utilisation of resources and accelerate the growth of economy. The retained earnings should be encouraged to strengthen the enterprisi but in absence of adequate profit, these organisations are depending on Government for financial strain and expansion. In any case the productivity cannot be at the altar of the socialistic pattern of the society. If any concern has not reached even the level of break even after 10 years of establishment, it should be handed over to competent business houses. The cost of production in several public enterprises is very high because of improper use of resources and absence of competition. The enterprises are left free at the cost-front. They are not personally liable for the higher cost of production. The Parliamentarians can be satisfied on this or that pretext if the performances of the public enterprises are below the standard. Comparing the performances of public enterprises with those of private enterprises is considered traditional approach as well as pre-capitalism. But this is the only criteria whereby the public enterprises performance can be judged to reveal their efficiencies and inefficiencies. Monopolistic protection either to public enterprises or private enterprises will lead only towards wastage of public money and exploitation of their dire needs. Therefore, the private enterprises should be left free to utilise their full capacity and public enterprises should be accountable if they do not come up to the standard. The techniques of financial control should be exercised by the public enterprises. The financial manager should be given the power of using the funds on business-exigencies rather than on the bureaucratic system. The problems of too much unnecessary reporting and auditing have obstructed the proper functioning of public enterprises. The government should realise that public enterprises should not be allowed to function for the sake of political motto. The national funds should be used economically and effectively. These enterprises should be given the autonomy of using the business principles to prove themselves worthy of continuation in the society. If a public enterprise after 5-10 years has not achieved the break-even-level, it should be handed over to some private organisation with the condition that they will bring them at profitable stage within specified time.

Insurance industry along with other financial institutions has been constantly under pressure of privatisation without going into the grass-root of the problems and its potential consequences. Many committees and government agencies have been arguing for privatisation, denationalisation and permitting foreign institutions to conduct insurance business in India. Insurance industry was nationalised at the behest and considerate thoughts of devoted and honest leaders. They have observed the increasing ills of private insurers and scope of socio-economic development with the help of insurance institutions.

In 1956, the then Finance Minister, Mr. Deshmukh had stated, "the misuse of power, position and privilege that we have reason to believe occurs under existing conditions in one of the most compelling reasons that have influenced us in deciding to nationalise life insurance". Thus, they have foreseen the misuse of power by the private insurers. The motives of private insurers have not changed today and will not change in future too because they work for self interest and maximisation of wealth. While putting arguments for privatisation at present, one should see whether the objectives of nationalisation have been fulfilled. If it is not fulfilled, arguments for privatisation may be accepted with the assumption that the privatisation would remedy all the problems and help succeed the nation to achieve its socio-economic development. One should not forget that insurance is not purely commercial industry, it is socialinstitution, too. Government should provide social security, safety and welfare to people of India. It is not possible for a government to achieve all these objectives at a time while carrying the responsibility of governance; it should entrust these responsibilities to an institution of national character. Basic duty of a Government is to protect its people from any sort of disturbances and invasion. If the social security and welfare is left to a national institution which can survive and grow on its own while providing social security and welfare to people; it would be an appropriate proposition for the government rather than leaving it to private hands who care for profits and appropriation of funds.

The government while having a nationalised insurance institution serves both the purposes at a time, *i.e.*, governance and social welfare an security to people. The arguments for privatisation can be judged on the basis of achievements of nationalised insurance institutions, critical analysis of the reports given for liberalisation and privatisation of insurance industry and past practices of private insurers.

Whether Objectives are Fulfilled?

The objectives of nationalisation have been incorporated in the form of corporate objectives of LIC. If the objectives of nationalisation are not fulfilled, whether the private insurers can fulfil those objectives, what can be the next step if both institutions, *i.e.*, the nationalised and private insurers have not achieved the objectives of insurance? These questions are dispassionately analysed.

1. *Rural Insurance*: The nationalisation of life insurance business in 1956 had aimed to spread the gospel of life insurance business in the remote corners of the country. In the word of the then Finance Minister: "The purpose of nationalisation was to see that the gospel of insurance is stored as far and wide as possible so that we reach out beyond the more advanced urban areas well into the hitherto neglected rural areas. Millions of lives in rural areas were left uninsured because the private insurers did not like to carry their business there. Now question arises whether private insurers including foreign companies would like to conduct their business in rural areas. The answer is certainly not because they would not be getting profit there. No private insurer would like to do business on loss. If the government is not agreeing to this logic, then why private airlines are not operating their business in non-remunerative areas. The nationalised institutions are doing satisfactory business in rural areas. They have national mission and performing the business in urban as well as rural areas. The insurance principles, inertia of large number is being followed by LIC and GIC. No private insurer can work longer on national mission to help peoples 'progress and security because they have the main motives of profit-making.' The Life Insurance Corporation has developed corporate objectives. "Spread life insurance much more widely and in particular to the rural areas reaching all insurable persons in the country and providing them adequate financial cover against death at a reasonable cost"

Table 41.1 New Business of LIP

(in crores of Rupees)

Year	*Individual New Business*	*Group Insurance*	*Rural Business*
1955	260.84	—	—
1962-63	745.96	18.33 (1966–67)	233.45 (31.8%)
1984-85	7,088.45	8,409.90	1,569.62 (29.7%)
1994-95	55,468.82	50,651.85	21,571.00 (39.0%)
1997-98	63,617.69(P)	76,619.21	

(P) = Provisional

The rural business was unheard before 1955. After nationalisation, it has increased to Rs. 21,570 crore which was 39.0 percent of individual new business. Rural business of LIC in 1995-96 was 49 lakh policies out of the total 110 lakh policies issued in that year giving rural business to the extent of 45% of total new policies issued. Can anyone think of such achievement by private insurer? Logics are hurled that nonbanking institutions are fetching maximum business from rural areas. It should be analysed from safety and security point of view. The business procured by them are not safe and secure because many non-banking institutions are getting business pressurising the rural people. It should be known that many non-banking institutions are eloping with the money of people. They open an office for some months and then close the office forever after extracting money from the people.

One finds it difficult to understand whether the government is unaware or unable to prevent such nefarious activities. If the government is unable to govern, it should not talk of privatisation or denationalisation of insurance industry. LIC and GIC are national institutions which are working for the nation and people. The LIC has covered a large number of people by insuring them under group insurance otherwise they would have been uninsured on account of low premium paying capacity. The new business under group insurance increased from Rs. 18.33 crore in 1966-67 to Rs. 50,651.43 crore in 1994-95.

Table 41.2 Business of General Insurance

(In crores ot Rupees)

Year	*Gross Direct Premium*	*Net Premium*
1971	147.53	127.69
1980	503.00	481.00
1985	1,204.31	1,190.50
1994-95	4,959.43	4,879.43
1997-98	8,086.00	7,357.00

All the four subsidiaries of General Insurance Corporation have tried to procure maximum business for the benefit of people at large. General insurance in rural areas have increased considerably under Personal Accident Social Security amounting more than Rs. 300 crores and Hut Insurance Scheme amounting about Rs. 300 crore. Hit and Run schemes have benefited a large number of beneficiaries.

Life Insurance Corporation of India has formulated corporate objective "Meet the various life insurance needs of the community that would arise in the changing social and economic environment.

The total payment under social security group/schemes amounted more than Rs. 240 crore in 1991-92 and Rs. 550 crore in 1995-96. The LIC and GIC have been working hard to benefit rural people through its branches which have been respectively 2024 and 2997 as, on March 1996.

The second objective of nationalisation of life insurance business was to conduct business with utmost economy as the Finance Minister said, "The business must be conducted with utmost economy and with the full realisation that money belongs to the policyholders. The premium must be no higher than is 'warranted by strict actuarial consideration". The LIC has accepted the corporate objectives. "Act as trustees of the insured public in their individual and collective capacities. Conduct business with utmost economy and with the fuu realisation that money belongs to the policyholders". The trusteeship principle has been carried by the LIC as it has tried to reduce the expense-ratio.

Table 41.3 Expense Ratios of LIC

Year	*Total Premium Income (in crores of Rs.)*	*Overall Expense Ratio*	*Renewal Expense Ratio*
1957	88.65	27.20%	15.89%
1984-85	1,559.33	24.68%	13.92%
1994-95	11,527.80	21.39%	6.32%
1997-98	19,252.07	20.54%	6.00%

The expense ratio which were very high before nationalisation were brought to a lower level in 1995. The overall expense ratio declined from 27.20% In 1957 to 21.35% in 1995 and the renewal expense ratio have come down from 15.89% to 6.32% in the respective years. The corporation would have reduced the expense ratio further had there been complete computerisation. General Insurance Corporation along with its subsidiaries has attempted to reduce the expenses considerably. The benefits of reduced expenses have been given to the policyholders in the form of enhanced bonus and reduced premium. The bonus of life policy per thousand sum assured has increased from Rs. 16 in 1956 to Rs. 86 varying to Rs. 95 in 1996 on whole life policies and Rs. 12.80 in 1952 to Rs. 69 varying to Rs. 78 on endowment policies. The lapse ratio to mean life insurance business in force has gone down from 7.6 per cent in 1955 to 3.1 per cent in 1991-92. With increase life fund from Rs. 410.40 crores in 1956 to Rs. 72,780.06 crore-in 1996; the LIC has achieved its corporate objective, *i.e.,* maximise mobilisation of people's savings by making insurance linked savings adequately attractive. The life insurance carrying capacity that is the ratio of business in force to national income has increased from 7.95% in 1951 to 30.30 per cent in 1995-96. The LIC has provided adequate financial cover to the people of India. It is also evident from the Table 41.4.

Table 41.4 Comparative Progress of LIC

Year	*% of business force to National Income*	*% of Premium Income to National Income*	*% of Annual Life Fund to National Income*
1951	7.95	0.38	0.2
1962-63	20.62	0.82	0.6
1984-85	25.42	0.90	0.7
1995-96	30.39	1.50	0.9

The rising rate of business in force has clearly shown that the, LIC has attempted to provide adequate financial cover to the people of India. The premium income as compared to national income has revealed the capacity of LIC for enhancement of business.

The third objective of nationalisation of life insurance business was to develop national economy as put in the words of the then Finance Minister, "Help development of National Economy in the right perspective for the benefits of the societies as a whole." Based on the objective, the corporate objective of LIC has been, "Bear in mind, in the investment of funds, the primary obligation to its policyholders whose money it holds in trust, without losing sight of the interest of the community as a whole". The LIC is performing this job through decentralised investment. The percentage of LIC investment, to national income has increased from 3.4 percent in 1956 to 6.26 percent in 1996. It had contributed to Rs. 184 crores during the Second Plan and Rs. 40303 crore during four years of Eighth Plan. No private sector enterprise can sacrifice so much for nation. It is illogical and anti-national to think to hand over the most contributing financial sector to private entrepreneurs including foreign companies. The money procured in the form of premium is helping reduced inflationary pressure because so much of money is withdrawn from circulation and is channelised for productive sector. The inflationary gap caused by the difference of money supply and production has been reduced at both the fronts, *i.e.*, reducing money supply through premium collection and increasing production through investment. The investment of LIC has increased from Rs. 372 crore in 1956 to Rs. 65057 crore in 1996, whereas the premium has increased from Rs. 88.65 crore to Rs. 14182 crore which were 0.2 percent and 2.4 percent respectively of the money in circulation, in the respective years.

The diversified investment policy of LIC has served almost all the industries, all the states and infrastructure from the drinking water facilities to development of hardcore industries, LIC has invested for their growth. The corporate objectives of LIC says. "Meet the various life insurance needs of the Community that would arise in the changing social and economic environment".

Table 41.5 Infrastructure Development through LIC Investment

(In crores of Rs.)

Year	*Housing*	*Transport*	*Water Supply*	*Electricity*
1967	121	30 (1980)	16	61
1995-96	8,731	477	1,881	7,580

The objectives of nationalisation was also to discourage greater concentration of economic power which have been achieved through diversified investment policy of LIC. The public sector has got a lion's share in the total investment of LIC.

Table 41.6 LIC Investment

	% of total investment in			
Year	*Public Sector*	*Other*	*Private Sector*	*Total (In crores of Rupees)*
1955	—	—	—	318.90
1962-63	76.8	3.8	19.4	623.64
1984-85	79.6	2.3	8.10	9,954.20
1995-96	82.87	3.35	13.78	53,479.47

The LIC investment in public sector has been approximately 80 percent of its total investment. Similarly, the general insurance companies have invested about 65 percent of its total investment in public sector. It has been varying from 6.3 percent to 73 percent in different subsidiary companies.

The Life Insurance Corporation of India has been contributing in the socio-economic development through its payment to government.

Table 41.7 Payment to Government

Year	*Surplus*	*Income Tax*	*Total*
1957	1.45	0.30	1.75
1961	1.28	0.09	1.37
1990-91	90.00	254.90	344.90
1995-96	160.94	582.28	743.22

Government has invested only Rs. 5 crore as capital of LIC but has received Rs. 160.94 crore as dividend in 1995-96. It is unthinkable ratio of dividend which is 32 times of capital employed. The tax money given to government is very high amount *i.e.,* more than Rs. 500 crore. Can any private insurer pay so much taxes to government and government may receive so much high of dividend rate? Certainly not. Therefore, the logic of government to denationalise the LIC is irrational and full of unwise step. Similarly, General Insurance Industry has given more than Rs. 100 crore as income tax and more than Rs. 800 crore as dividend. Taking the total funds received by life insurance and general insurance industry together, the government has received more tan Rs. 1,600 crore in 1995-96. If government is going to part with this revenue by throwing the insurance industry to private entrepreneurs doubts may arise on the rational functioning of the government. It may be on account of some concrete reasons *e.g.*, government is being run by irrational people, government does not care for the welfare of society, government is thinking to borrow money from international agencies rather than mobilising domestic savings. The scope of domestic saving is considerably high in India. There is need of honest and sincere attempt to mobilise people's saving for people's welfare. Government should not adhere on some of the reports on insurance because they have been prepared on government's liking and people's mood. The reports cannot be relied on considering the broader and wider interest of the country.

It has been anticipated that the funds required for Ninth Five-Year Plan can be met by insurance industry alone if the industry is given freehand for operation and investment. There will not be any need for inviting foreign investment and incurring socio-economic and political risks. Privatisation of insurance industry is totally out of context, irrational and antinational decision.

Life insurance business was nationalised with the objective of rendering prompt and efficient services to policyholders. Consequently, corporative objective, "Involve all people working in the Corporation to the best of their capability in furthering the interests of the insured public by providing efficient service with courtesy.

Table 41.8 Business per Active Agent in LIC

Year	*No.*	*New Business per Agent (Rs.)*
1955	8,900	31,000
1985	1,47,783	3,63,772
1995	5,19,504	10,63,101

The business per active agent has increased to Rs. 10,63,101 in 1995 from the lowest level of Rs. 31,000 in 1955. The LIC has fulfilled the responsibility of claims payment of which amounted to Rs. 4,532.22 crore on 42 lakh policies in 1995-96 from the lowest figure of Rs. 28.7 crore in 1956.. Outstanding claim which was 50% in 1956 came down to the level of 5.99 % in 1995-96. This shows that LIC has attempted hard to render prompt and efficient services to take policyholders.

Table 41.9 Production of Employees in LIC

Year	*No. of Employees*	*Average Business per Employee (Productivity) In terms of*			
		New Business Policy No.	*Business in force Policy No.*	*Premium Income (Rs.)*	*Claims Payment (Rs.)*
1957	30,768	26	185	28,810	10.940
1962-63	48,080	37	198	31,420	10,270
1984-85	62.977	43	422	2,68,210	1,18,420
1994-95	1,21,410	89	569	9,49,000	1,85,100

The business of LIC has been constantly increasing. The productivity in terms of new business has increased from 26 policies in 1957 to 89 policies in 1994-95. An employee who was required to serve 185 policies in 1957 is serving 539 policies in force in 1994-95. No one can argue that employees productivity has declined as has been in other public sector enterprises. The case of LIC is totally different from other public sector units which are running on losses and have been under constant pressure of government. LIC and GIC having the benefits of corporate character under statutory act of 1956 and 1972 are demonstrating its efficiency. They improve further if political interference whatever is there is eliminated from the horizon of the business. Statutory corporations having their autonomy and management techniques can perform better than any private entrepreneurs or government organisation. Departmental undertakings are always on the mercy and methods of government. The Indian Government has vididly demonstrated its corrupt practices during the last five years and cannot be relied upon for better management of nation and industry. But statutory corporations being free from direct involvement of government and performing efficiency in India and helping the society at large which is not possible by individual entrepreneurs who are always profit minded and least bothered to public welfare and nation-building. Many sick units are the glaring examples of unscrupulous motives of private entrepreneurs.

SUCCESS OF MULTI-PRODUCT DISTRIBUTION OF LIC

Customer loyalty depends on satisfaction of his multiple needs. They know them only when they are told about those needs. The Life Insurance Corporation of India has devised several life policies to satisfy these diversified needs of the customers. The research cell has explored these policies which are put in circulation. The outcome of each new product is tested generally for two-three years. On the basis of their acceptability by public, they are launched permanently in the field. Multi-product distribution has become a success for LIC, but it has failed on multi-channel. Only life insurance offices are sellers of the product. If the distribution channel is increased; people may purchase more diversified products from Financial Institutions, educational houses, hospital, health centres, village community centres, commercial and regional rural banks, public enterprises and big business houses may be appointed as distribution channel of life insurance policies. The LIC has not thought on this front but the researches conducted by me under exploring insurance avenues have revealed glaring avenues of insurance. The paper analyses the success of multi-product distribution of Life Insurance Corporation of India.

Analysis of Multi-Product

The multi-product distribution of Life Insurance Corporation of India (LIC) has been analysed under four periods:

1. Period of early growth (1956–1970)
2. Period of Fluctuation Business (1970–71 to 1979–80)

3. Period of Reorganisation (1980–81 to 1989–90)
4. Period of Product Diversification (1990–91 to 1997–98).

The period division has been done on the basis of product introduction. Early growth has shown introduction of the traditional policies and product diversification has demonstrated multiple policies to meet the requirements of policyholders.

1. Period of Early Growth (1956–1970)

The life insurance business in India increased rapidly during 1956–70 after nationalisation of life insurance business in January 1956; the private insurers were not taking serious interest in insurance particularly in rural areas. The average growth rate of business was about 5.00 percent per annum during this period.

New Schemes

During the period of early growth salary saving scheme and non-medial schemes and anticipated endowment insurance were introduced.

Table 41.10 Salary Saving Scheme as Compared to New Business

(Rs. in crores)

Year	*Salary Saving Scheme*		*Individual Insurance*		*% of Salary Saving Scheme to individual Insurance*	
	Policy Number in Lakhs	*Rs.*	*Policy Number In Lakhs*	*Rs.*	*% of Total Policies*	*% of Total sum assured*
1957	—	—	8.16	283.07	—	—
1970-71	4.86	252.06	16.16	1,224.14	30.07	20.58
1980-81	5.58	551.67	19.58	2,896.95	28.50	19.04
1985-86	9.25	1,535.62	32.94	7,088.45	28.08	21.66
1990-91	19.62	5,870.62	86.54	2,239.10	22.67	20.72
1991-92	21.29	7,071.16	92.48	32,196.30	23.83	21.96
1992-93	22.35	7,904.96	99.68	36,115.80	22.42	21.89
1993-94	22.58	8,468.11	107.38	42,012.90	21.03	20.16
1994-95	21.88	10,768.25	108.88	55,468.82	20.00	19.41
1995-96	38.06	16,750.22	110.34	52,071.53	34.49	32.16
1996-97	23.22	10,578.83	122.81	56,993.94	18.91	18.55

Salary Saving Scheme: The salary saving scheme was introduced to help salaried employees in paying their premium regularly. The employer is required to deduct premium from salaries and remit them to the Corporation (LIC). It waves the usual monthly extra and gives rebate on the tabular premium. It was introduced in 1958 booking only Rs. 13.93 crore during the year. The number of new policies under Salary Saving Scheme has been constantly increasing from 4.86 lakh in 1970-71 to 23.22 lakh in 1996-97. Similarly, the sum assured has also increased from Rs. 252.06 crore in 1970-71 to Rs. 10578.83 crore in 1996-97 under this scheme. The percentage share of salary saving scheme in the total individual insurance has not been less than 18 per cent in any year. It reveals that the LIC is relying on salary saving scheme for its business. If it is compared with the different segments of policyholders, it has major role in insuring a large number of people under salaried class. The different segments of potential policyholders are businessmen, labourers, advocates, farmers, people in small scale industries, traders and transporters.

Table 41.11 Contribution of Different Sectors to Net Domestic Product in India in 1997

Primary Sector	35.67%	Agriculture 31.55, Forestry 1.70, Fishing 0.91, Mining 1.51
Secondary Sector	24.19%	Manufacturing 17.07, Construction 6.17, Electricity, etc. 0.95
Transport, Communication Munication and Trade	19.87%	Transport, Storage and Communication 6.50, Trade, Hotel and Restaurant 13.17
Finance and Real Estate	7.98%	Banking and insurance 5.13, Real Estate, Ownership, Dwelling, Business services 2.85
Community and Personnel services	12.29%	Public Administration and Defence 5.75, Other Services 6.54
Total	100.00	

The salary saving scheme is mainly confined to community and personal services which account only 12.29 percent of total national income. There is enough scope of expansion of this scheme to other sectors, too, such as manufacturing, construction, electricity, transport, communication, trade, hotels, restaurants, etc.

Table 41.12 Number of People Employed in 1997 (in thousands)

	Public Sector	*Private Sector*	*Total*
1. Agricultural, etc.	551	876	1427
2. Mining and Quarrying	963	100	1063
3. Manufacturing	1856	4374	6230
4. Electricity, gas and water	862	41	903
5. Consumption	1188	63	1251
6. Wholesale and retail trade	144	285	429
7. Transport, storage, communication	3020	51	3071
8. Financing, insurance, real estate	1108	241	1349
9. Community, Social and Personnel service	8792	1426	10218
Total	18,484	2,457	25,941

The number of employees ranges from 14 lakh in agriculture to 102 lakh in community, social and personnel services, wnereas the total number of employees have been 259 lakh in all sectors. The number of policies issued under salary saving schemes have not been more than 38 lakh in any year. The self-employed are not included under this schemes. Thus, there is enough scope of expansion of salary saving scheme.

The salary saving scheme is very traditional in its procedure. There is need of its renovation, use of computers have started. If the LIC links its computer with those of employees associated with salary saving scheme, will be immediately credited in the account of LIC. Thus, crores of rupees lying unsettled with the employers will come in use with LIC. The return of premium saved would increase tremendously.

Non-Medical Scheme: Non-medical scheme was introduced in 1960 with a view to reduce premium rates in respect of lives, where medical examination is not likely to produce any tangible results. Many employees of government, armed forces and public sector enterprises have been insured under this scheme.

Table 41.13 Progress of Non-medical Scheme

(Policy in lakh/Rs. in crore)

Year	*Non-Medical Policy*	*Scheme Rs Sum assured*	*Total Policy*	*New Business to total Rs. Sum assured*	*% of Non-Medical Policy (%)*	*Sum assured*
1970-71	18.25	3,240.50	16.16	1,224.14	51.05	26.47
1980-81	8.20	552.87	19.58	2,896.95	41.88	19.08
1985-86	16.02	2,006.61	32.94	7,088.45	48.63	28.31
1990-91	47.08	12,436.87	86.54	28,239.10	55.10	44.04
1991-92	55.96	15,987.01	92.48	32,196.30	60.51	49.65
1992-93	85.34	19,381.87	99.68	38,115.80	85.55	53.87
1993-94*	68.72	22,048.25	107.38	42,012.90	64.00	52.48

*No information is available thereafter.

Many employees of government sector, public enterprises, educational institutions, defence forces and so on are insured under non-medical schemes. More than 50 percent of total individual insurance is coming under medical examinations in certain categories of people. The conditions of non-medical examination have been laid down to safeguard any loss to the LIC.

Anticipated Endowment Policy: Anticipated endowment policy increased due to inherent merits of periodical payment. It was introduced in 1962-63. The importance of anticipated endowment policy increased upto 1975-76. It was popular because of three reasons *viz.*; (*i*) policy holders prefer endowment policy where a part of the sum assured is returned in instalment earlier than the normal maturity date while enjoying the benefits of insurance protection during the currency of policy. (*ii*) Income Tax relief continues to be available for the full term of the policy even though part of the sum assured· is received earlier. (*iii*) Policyholders continue to receive bonus of the full sum assured although 40 per cent of the sum assured is returned to the policyholders before maturity. Anticipated endowment insurance declined from 9.93 per cent in 1962-63 to 0.92 per cent of the total individual insurance in 1980-81. It has been closed and now children's anticipated policy is in vogue which amount to Rs. 9.80 crore in 1996-97. Whole life and without profit schemes were declined as policyholders were not interested in them because of their long term agreement.

2. Period of Fluctuating Business (1970-71 to 1979-80)

Life insurance business during 1970-71 to 1979-80 experienced a wide ups and downs. Indian business declined in some years very drastically due to natural calamities and economic distress. The average rate of growth was below 4.00 per cent per annum. Industrial relations were not very much favourable during this period. Financial institutions posed problems of competition. People prefer bank deposits and postal saving certificates. In the later year of the period discipline and work culture improved. Consequently business increased in the later part of the period.

New Schemes

1. *Money Back Policy*: It was introduced in 1976-77 and got good response from public as the sum assured was 36.18 per cent and the policy was 28.15 percent of total individual business in 1980-81. People are interested in those policies which provide more benefits to policyholders during the currency of policy. From the detailed analysis of policy-planes, it has been revealed that people like such types of policies which provide money during policyholder's life for meeting different types of needs of life. They do not prefer those policies which provide money only at the end of certain period whether maturity or death. People prefer saving to protection. The percentage of sum assured under money back policy was 36.18 per cent to total individual insurance in 1980-81.

Table 41.14 Progress of Money Back Policy

Year	*Money Back Policy*		*Individual Insurance*		*% of Money Back to*	
	No. of Policy in Lakhs	*Sum Assured in Rs. crores*	*No. of Policy in lakhs*	*Sum Assured in crores*	*Total Individual Insurance Policy*	*Sum Assured in Rs. lakhs*
1980-81	—	—	—	—	28.15	36.18
1990-91	34.29	12,979.08	86.54	28239.10	39.62	45.96
1991-92	35.13	13,567.94	92.54	23196.30	37.99	42.14
1992-93	41.15	16,401.67	99.68	36115.80	41.28	45.41
1993-94	42.71	17,025.18	107.38	42012.90	39.77	40.52
1994-95	34.43	1,588.69	108.88	55468.82	31.62	28.10
1995-96	36.38	16,396.08	110.34	5271.53	32.97	31.49

The number of policies issued under Money Back Policy have been varying from the lowest number of 34.29 lakh in 1990-91 to the highest number of 42.41 lakh in 1996-97. Similarly sum assured has increased from Rs. 12,979.08 crore to Rs. 19,426.77 crore in the corresponding years. Their percentage to total individual insurance has been 31.61 percent in 1994-95 and 41.28 percent in 1992-93 in case of policy number and 31.49 percent in 1995-96 and 45.96 percent in 1990-91 in case of sum assured. It reveals that more than one third of individual business came from money back policy.

3. Period of Re-organisation (1980-81 to 1989-90)

The new business of LIC has increased by more than 7 percent per annum. The branch offices were given more authority. Decentralisation has yielded more business. New policies were introduced. Group insurance business increased during this period. The Group Insurance Scheme have several advantages over individual insurance. It has low cost and higher benefits. Many underprivileged persons also get the benefits of insurance. LIC laid considerable stress on development of Group and Superannuation Schemes because it is only through the group approach that rapid progress of insurance and protection of life insurance cover to society is possible. Employers can give the benefits of insurance through this scheme.

Group Insurance Schemes: Group Insurance Schemes were extended to various groups such as teachers of primary and junior high schools, employees of State Electricity Boards of several states, employees of central and state governments, employees of three defence services, employees of big business houses, employees of cooperative societies in Gujarat, Maharashtra, Tamil Nadu, Uttar Pradesh and Orissa. There are renewable term insurance issued to a particular group. If death does not take place within the contract period, the insured is refunded the amount of premium along with the prevailing rate of interest. Persons who cannot get the policy on medical ground can get insurance coverage under this scheme. Persons who cannot save adequate amount for payment of premium can also get the benefits of insurance if their employers agree to pay the premium amount.

Superannuation Scheme: The scheme provides pension (annual maturity) benefits to retired employees when they are old and not able to earn for their maintenance. The number of beneficiaries and schemes have increased fastly during this period. The superannuation is becoming more popular because of people's preference to investment.

Janashree Bima Yojana

On 10th August 2000, the Janashree Bima Yojana, a group insurance scheme was launched in order to extend the benefit of Social security and life insurance cover to poorer segments of the population. This scheme is being implemented with the help of non-governmental organisations and self-help groups who will help in identifying the groups of persons to be covered. In addition to persons below the poverty line, persons marginally above the poverty line also can be covered under the scheme, which provides cover and cover against accidental death and disability. During 2000-2001, 3,35,052 new lives were covered under the 40 approved occupations pertaining to the Social Security Schemes and the Janashree Bima Yojana. The First Premium Income under these schemes during the year 2000-2001 registered a significant increase of 192% and grew to Rs. 2.33 crore. During the year 778 new group schemes were brought into the book. The number of new lives covered was 98,603 under various Group Superannuation and Annuity Schemes which were for a sum of assured of Rs. 70,614.80 crore during 2000-2001.

Table 41.15 Group Insurance Business and All Business in Force

	Individual (All)		*Group Insurance including Superannuation*		*Total Business Policy No.*	*% of Group Insurance to Total Business*	
Year	*Policy Rs. in Lakhs*	*Rs.*	*Member covered*	*Rs.*	*in Lakhs*	*Policy Member*	*Sum Assured*
1957	56.83	1473	—	—	56.83	—	—
1970-71	147.85	7067	—	123	147.85		1.71
1980-81	228.12	21,057	64.45	6,980	292.57	22.03	24.49
1985-86	280.47	40,617	92.65	11,799	373.12	24.83	22.51
1990-91	455.68	1,19,179	172.00	30,755	627.68	27.40	20.51
1995-96	709.90	2,95,758	250.68	64,135	960.28	26.10	17.82
1996-97	777.50	3,44,619	244.48	65,152	1021.98	23.92	15.90

The business under group insurance and superannuation schemes has been constantly increasing. The policy number and members covered under group insurance and superannuation have increased to the level of 244.48 lakh in 1996-97. The share of group insurance and superannuation scheme have been 21.40 percent of the total policy and members. The assessed sum under this scheme was 24.49 percent of the total insurance in 1980-81. It accounts about one fifth of the total business of Life Insurance Corporation of India. The people are made aware of this scheme.

4. Period of Product Diversification (1990-91 to 1997-98)

The Life Insurance Corporation of India realised the importance of product diversification. Business increased by selling different types of policies. Product diversification is essential to meet the varying needs, changing preferences and rising aspirations of the customers.

The importance of whole life policies and endowment assurances are reducing gradually, that total sum assured under these policies are increasing although in relation to total individual business, they are not increasing.

Money back policies have increased to the level of 20,000 crore. It is prominent assurance policy because of its advantages of investment. The amount of children's anticipated endowment is reducing year after year. It has come down to nearly 10 crore.

Jeevan Raksha Policy has yielded insurance to the tune of Rs. 1,600 crore in 1996-97. It is rapidly increasing. Similarly Jeevan Mitra has crossed the level of Rs. 1,900 crore. Jeevan Sathi is also becoming popular. The sum assured was Rs. 566.70 crore in 1996-97. The marriage Endowment and Educational amenities have increased considerably to meet the requirements of marriage and education of children. Convertible whole life has gone down to the level of Rs. 165.74 crore in 1996-97. Jeevan Balya/Jeeven Kishore have been popular as they crossed the level of Rs. 800 crore. Similarly, Jeevan Chhaya has been gradually increasing although Bima Sandesh declined to Rs. 51.78 crore in 1996-97.

Those policies are becoming popular, which have features of investment and periodical payment alongwith coverage of risk.

Table 41.16 Progress of Insurance Plans in India

Sum assured in crores

S.No.	*Name of Plans*	*1985-86*	*1990-91*	*1995-96*	*1996-97*	*2001-02*
1.	Whole Life Policies	41.22	130.03	113.33	281.14	643.78
2.	Endowment Assurance	2900.77	9538.92	10699.36	12314.79	34702.84
3.	Money Back	2628.83	12979.08	16396.08	19426.77	23202.67
4.	Children's Anticipated Endowment	87.33	82.08	9.96	9.80	—
5.	Jeevan Raksha Policy (All)	35.11	525.22	1375.39	1666.05	8781.73
6.	Jeevan Mitra	751.25	1885.55	1769.17	1927.46	3725.19
7.	Jeevan Sathi	59.47	544.36	554.64	566.74	1108.37
8.	Marriage/Educational Endowment/Annuity	—	271.90	637.12	647.70	3547.43
9.	Convertible Whole Life	273.92	473.62	198.16	165.74	291.20
10.	Jeevan Balya Kiran	—	1090.65	834.96	865.67	
11.	Jeevan Chhaya	—	84.40	363.54	357.90	1728.85
12.	Bima Sandesh	—	205.01	64.69	51.78	

Product Development

The Life Insurance Corporation of India has diversified insurance products. Under this scheme, Asha Deep with some novel features was introduced in 1993-94. This plan besides providing death and maturity payment, provides benefits in case the life assured suffering from any of four major ailments, *viz.*, cancer, paralytic stroke leading to permanent disability, renal failure of both kidneys and coronary artery diseases, where bypass surgery has been done.

1. *Asha Deep–I:* Asha Deep-I increased from 7th September 1993 to 30th November, 1993. The total business under Asha Deep-I was Rs. 4,573 70 crore under 6.42 lakh policies in 1993-94. Asha Deep-I did not continue later on.

Table 41.17 Progress of New Insurance Plans Policies

Sum assured in crores of Rs.

	1990-91	*1991-92*	*1992-93*	*1993-94*	*1994-95*	*1995-1996*	*1996-97*	*2001-02*
Bhavisya Jeevan	1.58	1.46	1.33	1.13	0.84	0.39	45.60	3.55
Jeevan Swathi	—	—	1157.07	1003.83	2084.62	3360.78	4858.71	1108.37
Jeevan Sukanya	—	—	151.90	102.67	42.66	30.37	17.69	34.39
Asha Deep-I	—	—	—	4573.70	—	—	—	
Asha Deep-II	—	—	—	—	—	1362.341	886.11	
Jeevan Sarita	—	17.32	17.62	11.61	5.92	10.12	8.30	0.82
Jeevan Griha	—	55.66	132.54	169.85	141.07	129.89	136.58	299.07
Bima Kiran	—	—	—		19366.71	10944.84	9441.15	
Jeevan Shree	—	—	—		411.76	1320.34	1396.07	60212.66
Jeevan Adhar	—	—	—	—		21.12	19.52	15.15
Jeevan Sanjay	—	—	—	—	—		287.39	7267.5
Jeevan Sneha	—	—	—	—	—		251.07	3352.67
Children's Money	—	—	—	—	935.31	1583.50	1253.88	7040.89

2. *Asha Deep-II:* The Asha Deep Plan was first introduced in September 1993 on an experimental basis for a period of 3 months. In response to public demand the plan was reintroduced as Asha Deep-II in the month of November, 1995. This plan besides death and maturity payment, provides for benefits in case the life assured is affliated by any of four major ailments *viz.*, cancer, paralytic stroke leading to permanent disability, renal failure of both kidneys and coronary artery diseases where bypass surgery has been done. The amount of sum assured under this scheme was Rs. 1,362.34 crore in 1995-96 and Rs. 886.11 crore in 1996-97.

3. *Jeevan Aadhar:* Jeeven Aadhar introduced in January 1996 is specially designed for the benefit of handicapped dependents. Contributions under this Plan are eligible for income tax relief under Section 88 DDA of the Income Tax Act. This plan is basically a limited payment whole life assurance on the life of the proposer with provision for Guaranteed Additions and Terminal Addition to the basic sum assured. The claim amount will be payable partly in lumpsum and partly in the form of annuity to the handicapped dependents. The sum assured under Jeevan Aadhar was Rs. 21.12 crore in 1995-96 and Rs. 19.52 crore in 1996-97.

4. *Jeevan Suraksha:* Jeeven Suraksha was introduced on 15th August, 1996. It enables individuals to provide for retirement income from a selected date. The policy is with life cover but can be taken without life cover under certain conditions. The policyholder taking policy with life cover provides minimum of 50% of the target pension to spouse on death during the deferment period. Spouse's pension is not provided under without life cover plan. On vesting the policyholder has the option to receive 25 per cent of the notional case plan in lump sum and balance in annuity. The amount of Jeevan Suraksha was Rs. 102.65 crore in 1997-98.

5. *Jeevan Sneha:* Jeevan Sneha was introduced on 16th January, 1997 for women. It is a without profit money back type plan with the added features of guaranteed additions *viz.*, encasement of survival benefit as and when required. Flexibility to pay premium in advance, inbuilt accident cover, for insurance cover for a period of 3 years from the date of first unpaid premium provided atleast 2 full years premium have been paid and option to receive pension in lieu of maturity benefits. The sum assured under this scheme was Rs. 251.07 crore in 1996-97.

6. *Jeevan Sanchaya:* Similar to Jeevan Sneha, this plan was introduced on 16th January, 1997. It is without profits money back type of plan with provision of loyalty addition and guaranteed addition. Accident benefit is also granted under this plan with an upper limit of Rs. 5 lakhs in addition to existing limit of Rs. 5 lakhs under other plan.
7. *Children's Money Back:* Children's Money Back has assured Rs. 935.31 crore in 1994-95, Rs. 1,583.50 crore in 1995-96 and Rs. 1,253.88 crore in 1996-97. It is becoming popular because of inherent advantages to children. People want insurance for their children.

Impact of Product Diversification on Insurance Business

Product diversification of life insurance business yielded considerable results. People are attracted to purchase new policies of insurance which met their demands of children's education, marriage of daughter, their risk coverage, pension benefit to spouse and self, periodical monetary requirements and risk coverage. Different policies as discussed above have added more business as is clear from the foregoing tables. Had these policies not been issued, the insurance business would not have expanded so high. Being encouraged with the result of new schemes of life insurance, the LIC has introduced a very important scheme known as Jeevan Suraksha in 1998 and many other schemes are in pipe-lines. Jeevan Suraksha is available in three types to suit individual needs of person with life cover, pension without life cover and pension with endowment type.

Table 41.18 Impact of Product Diversification on Insurance Business

Policy Number in Lakh/
Sum Assured in Rupees Crore

	Individual Business		*Group Insurance*		*Superannuation*		*Total*	
Year	*Policy*	*Sum Assured*	*Members*	*Sum Assured*	*Members*	*Sum Assured*	*Policy Members*	*Sum Assured*
1957	45.18	1374	—	—		—	54.18	1374
1970-71	146.93	6952	3.10	119	—	4	150.00	7075
1980-81	227.58	20923	64.45	6960	—	20	292.03	27903
1985-86	279.89	40404	79.83	11764	—	35	359.72	52203
1990-91	455.08	118651	169.57	30502	2.43	253	627.08	149076
1991-92	508.63	145929	189.53	32973	2.54	302	700.70	179204
1992-93	566.12	177268	212.54	43087	2.69	359	781.35	220714
1993-94	608.00	207601	227.31	46743	3.14	404	838.45	254748
1994-95	654.52	253333	241.88	51035	3.54	428	899.94	304796
1995-96	708.78	294336	246.49	64652	4.19	483	961.48	359471
1996-97	776.66	343018	238.97	64607	5.54	546	1021.17	408171

The sum assured increased upto the level of Rs. 4,08,171 crore in 1996-97 under 1021.47 lakh policy/member. The business increased very fastly after 1985-86 on account of diversified business.

The percentage of population covered increased from 1.35 percent in 1957 to 8.30 percent in 1996-97 under individual business and from 1.35 percent to 10.91 percent under total insurance business. The percentage of policy number to total population was merely 4.79 percent in 1985–86 which rose to 7.47 per cent in 1990-91 due to product diversification scheme introduced in 1990. The role of group insurance and superannuation schemes was not very significant in expanding business per population as the percentage of the member number reanged between 2.68 to 1.06 during 1985-86 to 1996-97. Similarly, superannuation did not increase significantly. It is only individual business which contribute to insurance expansion. Only individual business has introduced new schemes of insurance. Group insurance and superannuation insurance continued on traditional scheme. Then the contribution to new insurance product is significant in business expansion.

Table 41.19 Percentage of Population Covered with Life insurance Schemes

Policy/Members in lakhs

Year	*Individual Policy*	*Group Member*	*Supernal nuation Member*	*Total policy/ Members*	*Population*	*Percentage of Policy Member Number to the total population*			
						Individual	*Group*	*Supern-nuation*	*Total*
1957	54.18	—	—	54.18	40.00	1.35	—	—	135
1970-71	146.93	3.10	—	150.00	53.70	2.73	0.06	—	2.79
1980-81	227.58	6445	—	292.03	68.38	3.33	0.94	—	4.27
1985-86	279.89	79.83	—	359.72	75.00	3.73	1.04	—	4.79
1990-91	455.08	169.57	2.43	627.08	83.90	5.48	2.02	0.02	7.47
1991-92	508.83	189.53	2.54	700.70	85.61	5.94	2.21	0.03	8.18
1992-93	566.12	212.54	2.69	781.35	87.20	6.44	2.44	0.11	8.96
1993-94	608.00	227.31	3.14	838.45	88.80	6.84	2.58	0.04	9.44
1994-95	654.52	241.88	3.54	899.94	90.40	7.24	2.68	0.03	9.95
1995-96	708.78	256.49	4.19	961.46	92.00	7.70	2.68	0.07	10.45
1996-97	776.66	238.97	5.54	1021.17	93.60	8.30	2.56	0.06	10.91

*It is assumed that every policy-holder/member has one policy.

Table 41.20 Life Insurance Carrying Capacity in India

Rs. in crores

Year	*Total Insurance Business in Force in India*	*Net National Production in India (at current prices)*	*% of Total Insurance Business Force to NNP*
1957	1374	11390	12.06
1970-71	7075	34476	20.52
1980-81	27903	104201	28.78
1985-86	52203	185333	18.25
1990-91	149078	416495	35.79
1991-92	179204	477868	37.50
1992-93	220714	684935	39.06
1993-94	254748	638979	39.87
1994-95	304796	759597	40.13
1995-96	359471	881216	40.79
1996-97	408171	996022	40.98

The Life Insurance carrying capacity is increased as the percentage share of insurance business in force to net national product increased. The life insurance carrying capacity in India increased from 12.06 in 1957 to 40.98 in 1996-97. The insurance carrying capacity was 18.25 in 1985-86 which rose to 35.79 in 1990-91 due to introduction of several new insurance schemes in 1990. Since then the life insurance carrying capacity is gradally increasing. It is on account of diversification of individual insurance business. Group insurance and Superannuation have not been diversified. The per capita insurance increased rapidly in context to individual insurance from Rs. 33.68 in 1957 to Rs. 538.72 in 1985-86 and again to Rs. 3,664.72 in 1998-97. Thus population in India is insured on an average of Rs. 3,664.72 in 1996-97 although there are a large number of uninsured population still left out. Only 8.30 percent of the population is insured if policy number is taken only one by a policyholder. But policyholder has more than one policy. It is established fact that not more than 8.00 percent is insured in India. If group insurance and superannuation are taken together, it has not crossed 10 percent. The 10 percent of population who are insured have given average insurance of Rs. 4,360.80 under all schemes. The government of India has insured all the weaker sections of the society to the range of Rs. 5000 to Rs. 10,000 to provide social benefits. It is free of cost in the sense that the beneficiaries are not required to pay the premium. The government bears the premium amount. It is unique scheme in India which is not present probably in other countries.

Table 41.21 Per Capita Insurance in India

Year	*Individual Insurance*	*Total Insurance*	*Policy No. per ten thousand of population*	
	(Rs.)	*(Rs.)*	*Individual*	*Total*
1957	33.68	33.68	133	133
1970-71	129.46	131.75	274	279
1980-81	305.98	408.06	333	427
1985-86	538.72	696.04	373	497
1990-91	1,414.19	1,776.82	548	747
1991-92	1,704.58	2,093.26	594	818
1992-93	2,032.89	2,531.72	649	896
1993-94	2,337.84	2,868.78	684	944
1994-95	2,802.36	3,371.64	724	995
1995-96	3,199.30	3,907.29	770	1045
1996-97	3,664.72	4,360.80	830	1091
2000-01	6,432.41	15,489.32	1,130	1,131

The Role of Private Sector in Agriculture Insurance

With the opening up of insurance sector in 2000, the scenario of insurance industry has taken a dramatic turn. There exists a vast potential in rural and semi urban, particularly in agriculture where benefit of insurance is highly-solicited but not reached. It is to be mentioned that despite regulatory requirements, companies are not taking much initiatives to spread their reach in rural sector. Most of their initiatives are just to fulfill the regulatory requirements of IRDA. One of the prominent features of rural sector is that of strong saving habits, and hence providing a huge potential to various industries including insurance. But lack of cost effective service delivery model and perception of huge investments in the sector deters them to exploit the opportunities.

Role of private sector in agriculture insurance had been limited to certain index based weather schemes. It started in year 2003 when ICICI Lombard, a private general insurance company, started its pilot program on rainfall insurance to protect the farmers of specified crop against deviation in rainfall. Since it was a pilot approach, the numbers were limited. Following the path, during Kharif 2004, IFFCO-Tokio General Insurance, another private general insurance company, launched its own variant of index based rainfall insurance program during karif season, initially in four states and as on date in ten states. Having learnt valuable lessons from such enterprises, pilots are now being done on protection from weather vagaries occurring during Rabi crops.

Private weather insurance products have been gaining momentum in agricultural market. Some of the prominent features of these products are :

- Point of sale policy insurance - receipt cum policy,
- Policy and promotion in vernacular language,
- Revision of policy every year based on past data / experiences,
- Local IMD weather station to be considered as reference stations.

Issues with private weather insurance schemes which curtail expansion in wider geographical areas are as :

- Service and claims issues,
- Price not affordable,
- Farmers perceiving insurance as investment with sure returns instead of risk mitigation tool,
- Absence of relevant weather data,
- Absence of government infrastructure in setting up weather stations to be used as reference weather stations,
- Misappropriate data correlation with risk occurrence,
- Small Holding size and wide variety of agricultural practices,
- Moral hazards.

Growth of life insurance in the post liberalization era:

With the advent of liberalization, privatization and globalization popularly known as IPG, productivity has enhanced. New products are marketed with greater innovation and utilization of technology has become a necessity not only to reduce the cost of production but also the cost of distribution as well. Liberalization creates a conducive climate for faster economic growth, allows up-gradation of technology, provides economy of scale and market expansion, domestically and internationally. The wave of LPG has influenced the insurance market globally. As of now, almost all the countries in the world have opened their insurance sector for the global players. The greatest advantage of allowing foreign partners is the inflow of direct foreign capital. Expertise of the foreign partner in the highly competitive insurance market in the other countries would definitely be leveraged by Indian partners. It leads to management efficiency and product innovation. Increased competition, technology-lead services, wide range of products and cost effective operations would finally benefit the customers. In the recent year there has been a slow growth of insurance market in the developed countries. The Insurance Market in the developed countries is almost saturated. During 2003 global life insurance witnessed a decline of 8% while the life insurance business in emerging markets grew by 6.6%. In the years to come the foreign insurance companies in the developed countries would therefore like to spread their wings to the emerging markets. Among emerging economies, India is one of the high growth countries with huge untapped potential, with the rise of middle class, increase in per capita income, rise in literacy rate and growth of service sector, there is certainly a huge scope of insurance penetration in India.

Role of IRDA :

The Insurance Regulatory and Development Authority has a very important role to play when more players join the market. Its primary function is to regulate the insurance sector allowing healthy growth but without compromising on consumer interest. This means ensuring proper disclosures, keeping affordable prices and making sure that the claims are paid by the insurers. Further ensuring the solvency of insurance companies is a very important function of the regulatory authority. It has to be ensured that not only regulatory authority. It has to be ensured that not only at the end of the financial year but also at all times an insurance company should be solvent. Consumer education is also one of the important functions that the regulator has to perform.

IRDA has issued guidelines on all aspects of insurance business like product pricing, itermediary, social responsibility, rural business, investment, solvency margin etc. As on 31/3/2008, 18 life insurance companies are operating in India and the composition of new business of these companies is below:-

Sr. No.	Insurer	Premium March, 2008 (Rs. in Crs.)
1.	Bajaj Allianz	6491.72
2.	ING Vysya	704.67
3.	Reliance Life	2752.76
4.	SBI Life	4792.86
5.	Tata AIG	967.78
6.	HDFC Standard	2679.61
7.	ICICI Prudential	8305.84
8.	Birla Sunlife	1965.01
9.	Aviva	1059.08
10.	Kotak Mahindra Old Mutual	1106.62
11.	Max New York	1594.21
12.	Met Life	826.79
13.	Sahara Life	122.17
14.	Shriram Life	309.87
15.	Bharati AXA Life	113.11
16.	Future Generali Life	2.50
17.	IDBI Future Life	11.90
18.	LIC	59182.20
	Grand Total	**92988.70**

Challenges

With the financial services becoming market driven and with unforeseen fluctuations in the interest rates, Life Insurance Companies have to exercise utmost care in product pricing. When the interest rates started moving southward in 200001, without-profit policies which gave some sort of interest guarantee were withdrawn by LIC. In respect of insurance, what is important is not the return on capital but the return of capital. Hence if the rates of interest fall below the assumed rate of interest on investment when the product was designed, it is always advisable to withdraw the product and limit the liability. Even the Unit Linked Products need to be reviewed at appropriate intervals.

The greatest challenge before the new entrants in the insurance sector is to establish their presence in the minds of the public. The most popular three letter word is said to be 'LIC'. LIC's presence is seen even in small villages with a population of 1000 or 2000 where a policyholder of LIC or an agent of LIC is seen. Insurance is always sold and never bought. To convince prospects who are comparatively not well informed about the intangible benefits of the life insurance is indeed an onerous task. On the top of it, to establish brand equity of a new name in a new field is also a great challenge. The second most important challenge faced by the new entrants is going to be setting up an infrastructure and reaching out to the geographically well spread areas of the country. Life insurance is based on probability of numbers and wider the spread, greater is the probability of business sustainence.

Pension Administration

All over the world life insurance companies manage two types of risks: (*i*) the risk of dying too early and (*ii*) the risk off living too long. Although commonly insurance is attributed to the first risk i.e. the risk of dying too early, the insurance companies have an important and significant port folio of pensions. The annuity (pension) business is developing very fast with improvement in health conditions has led to increase in longevity. Annuity business is a more risky business than life insurance business. Designing products that attract the changing needs of the people and managing the funds in the volatile interest rate scenario are two important challenges that need to be faced by all players in insurance industry in the days to come.

Product Innovation

Since the sector opened up, all the insurance companies started promoting Unit Linked Insurance Plans (ULIP). During that period the stock market was also booming. Since the NAVs were going up, it was easy to convince clients of benefits of the Unit Linked Insurance Plans and handsome growth we reported by most of the insurance compaines by marketing Unit Linked Insurance Plans. It was said that these products were for the benefit of the customers, but they were basically designed to suit the insurers. Insurance Companies undertake three major risks viz.

The risk of death is passed on to the reinsurer to a great extent. In case of Unit Linked Plans, even the risk of return and the risk of investment is passed on to the customers. Thereby the insurance companies retain a very small portion of mortality risk with them. The lesser the risk retained, the lesser is the requirement for solvency margin. Since solvency margin is to be provided by the owners, they always feel happy to do business at lower capital requirements. As it is, capital is scarce and with every sale effected, insurance companies require additional capital to be pumped in. Although insurance sector has shown extraordinary growth in new business due to sale of Unit Linked Products, the stability of the company may get affected once the sensex starts moving southwards.

This is precisely what has happened since 18th Jan., 2008. The sensex which had crossed 21,000 mark was stated to cross 25,000 by 31/3/2008. However, the sensex started melting down and has reached a three year low of less than 8,000. The consumers who have invested in Ulip products have lost heavily. The insurance companies are having a tough time in convincing the existing customers to continue their policies despite reduction in NAV. It is even more difficult to promote new customers to induce them to put their money in Unit Linked Products.

Every company has now started promoting conventional products which are not linked to equity market. In this type of non-unit linked products, surplus is valued at the end of the year and distributed to customers as 'Bonus'. Private Insurance Companies may take a long period to declare bonus on par with LIC. The insurance companies are thus caught between the grave and the great sea. On one hand they find it difficult to market Unit Linked Products due to slump in equity market and on the other, they are finding it difficult to market conventional products as the return on these products will be pretty low as compared to LIC. With the global recession faced by financial sector all over the world, bringing more inflow of capital is going to be a big question mark. Since more capital will be required for every increases in sale, whether to reduce operations in order to obviate the capital requirements is going to be a great challenge for the new insurance companies.

Future scenario

In India only 10% of the market share has been tapped by LIC and the balance 90% remains to be tapped. This vast population can be tapped only by a large number of insurers to serve the population of more than 100 Crs. Indian Insurance Market offers tremendous opportunities to the new insurance companies. Every financial company would like to be a financial conglomerate marketing banking, Mutual Fund, Credit Card and Insurance as well, through their sister companies, Mergers and acquisition seem to be inevitable. AMP Sanmar, an Australian Insurance Company decided to close its operations in India due to lack off interest shown by the Indian partner. The company was taken over by Reliance Capital and is now Reliance Life. Hostile takeovers can also not be ruled out. The insurance regulator has a great challenge to ensure ethical practices. LIC will have to come out with new products and advancement of technology in insurance market will need to be tackled. LIC will have to ensure that the trust of the people is not jeopardized and that it continues to be the insurer of choice.

The Regulator has to play an important role and should be strong enough to check the wrong practices of the new insurance companies. If properly regulated, the future of insurance industry looks bright.

SUMMARY

The research study has revealed that the life insurance business in India increased mainly on account of product diversification. The LIC authorities realised that different types of products are needed to meet diverse requirements of the people. Many new insurance schemes were launched to meet the investment and protection needs of the public. People are more concerned with the Children's welfare. So many policies such as Jeevan Balya/Jeevan Kishore, Children's Anticipated Endowment and Children's Money Back were introduced which became very popular. Similarly people are much concerned with old age regular income. Superannuation plans under ground insurance became very popular. Individual pension plans be came more useful for them. They purchased Asha Deep, Bima Kiran, Jeevan Shree, Jeeven Sanchay and Jeevan Sneha. The Life Insurance Corporation of India has rightly realised different needs of people and procured adequate amount of business on account of new policies. Restructuring of plans has been a continued exercise as the market rates of interest and yields available on securities have been changing from time to time. Accordingly Jeevan Dhara, jeevan Akshay and Jeevan Suraksha have been revised and have been put in the market as New Jeevan Dhara, New Jeevan Akshay and Jeevan Suraksha (revised). One can well appreciate the business in force figure which has been increasing from Rs. 1,473 crore in 1957 to Rs. 7,190 crore in 1970-71 and again to Rs. 1,49,934 crore in 1990-91. The business increased very rapidly after 1990-91, when many new schemes were launched. The total figure of business in force as on 31st March, 1997 was Rs. 4,09,771 crore which is a big jump in the area of insurance business. Not only the absolute figure, but life insurance increased as compared to net national product and other economic indicators. The per capita insurance in India was more than Rs. 2000 as on 1997 which was merely Rs. 34 in 1957. The number of persons insured have been more than 10 crore. All these progressive results are on account of introduction of new insurance schemes. It is concluded that the multiproduct diversification has captured more market and more insurable people in India.

Table 41.22 Business of Life Insures Individual Non-Single Premium

Insures	In crores to Rs. Premium V/w			In Lakhs No.of Policies/Schemes			In Lakhs Group Schemes No.			Market Share % Premium			Policies/Schemes			Group Schemes		
	2003-04	2004-05	2005-06	2003-04	2004-05	2005-06	2003-04	2004-05	2005-06	2003-04	2004-05	2005-06	2003-04	2004-05	2005-06	2003-04	2004-05	2005-06
1. Bajaj Allianz	156.29	401.23	1184.84	1.82	2.46	6.53	1.01	3.62	3.95		3.39	7.29		1.10	2.17		3.31	
2. ING Vysya	70.84	266.26	243.41	0.79	1.03	1.24	0.14	0.47	0.54		1.11	0.75		0.42	0.40		0.49	
3. Relince Life	—	23.26	64.55	—	0.27	0.62	—	0.95	1.29		—	0.59		—	0.23			
4. SBI Life	53.09	98.30	309.37	0.78	1.18	2.63	7.00	7.03	8.57		1.91	1.85		0.49	0.75		8.84	
5. Tata Aig	123.87	250.21	380.50	1.62	2.29	2.96	0.94	2.34	4.18		1.18	1.60		0.87	1.12		2.89	
6. HDFC Standard	209.33	353.23	774.77	1.64	2.107	2.55	—	0.49	0.22		1.92	2.97		0.79	1.23		1.89	
7. ICICI Prudential	622.11	1344.39	2101.03	4.26	6.07	7.86	0.07	0.56	2.07		6.25	7.20		2.34	2.78		1.00	
8. Birla Sunlife	267.41	507.80	562.95	1.27	1.48	1.97	1.95	0.77	0.48		2.45	1.80		0.76	0.84		0.75	
9. Aviva	71.54	179.63	391.31	0.70	0.81	1.62	0.89	2.96	1.90		0.76	1.12		0.32	0.52		2.71	
10. Kotak Mahindra Old Mixture	92.73	174.50	348.84	0.50	0.61	0.90	0.53	0.94	1.32		1.48	0.76		0.24	0.30		0.86	
11. Max New York	125.60	216.02	439.36	1.45	2.16	4.23	1.18	0.70	0.67		0.89	1.38		0.83	1.57		0.63	
12. Met Life	22.36	48.55	127.47	0.24	0.46	0.94	0.41	1.59	3.32		0.22	0.43		0.18	0.35		1.45	
13. Schara Life	—	1.65	4.49	—	0.10	0.19	—	0.02	0.00		0.01	0.06		0.04	0.08		0.02	
14. Sri Ram Life	—		10.31			2.08		0	0									
15. LIC	11195.69	11380.70	12945.82	266.34	223.34	292.98	—	00	00		78.07	72.30		91.50	87.67		74.31	
Total	18669.40	15245.83	19889.04	286.27	244.35	327.44	62.53	22.45	28.51		100.00	100.00		100.00	100.00		100.00	

Table 41.23 First Year Premium of Life Insurers for the Period Ended January, 2009

	Insurer	Premium u/w (Rs. in Crores)			No. of Policies/Schemes			No. of lives covered under Group Schemes		
		January, 09	Up to January, 09	Up to January, 08	January, 09	Up to January, 09	Up to January, 08	January, 09	Up to January, 09	Up to January, 08
1	**Bajaj Allianz**									
	Individual Single Premium	55.75	324.82	509.08	11544	80807	70066			
	Individual Non. Single Premium	267.72	2920.36	3903.45	194141	1932899	2648502			
	Group Single Premium	0.92	3.93	8.30	3	5	0	2274	4542	6177
	Group Non-Single Premium	19.02	97.26	41.47	86	558	246	718946	5558528	870858
2	**ING Vysya**									
	Individual Single Premium	0.93	20.55	19.08	121	2524	1862			
	Individual Non-Single Premium	46.57	477.46	449.59	30780	270112	256120			
	Group Single Premium'	0.56	12.04	3.05	0	1	1	335	5008	627
	Group Non-Single Premium	0.32	17.82	251	5	95	18	3613	56564	91908
3	**Reliance Life**									
	Individual Single Premium	30.08	306.90	197.97	6132	73885	44431			
	Individual Non-Single Premium	288.73	2215.85	1283.32	266143	1553224	660922			
	Group Single Premium'	2.13	79.66	205.72	0	20	47	151	46586	69553
	Group Non-Single Premium	3.27	24.79	21.06	32	277	217	37080	585417	317412
4	**SBI Life**									
	Individual Single Premium	38.44	421.30	916.89	7421	74079	126514			
	Individual Non-Single Premium	203.70	2042.20	1532.75	70138	601345	465952			
	Group Single Premium'	22.43	219.20	177.12	0	5	0	35321	157575	89362
	Group Non-Single Premium	47.23	1319.46	247.70	6	95	48	685993	4828926	527163
5	**Tata AIG**									
	Individual Single Premium	1.86	32.68	32.04	428	6782	5448			
	Individual Non-Single Premium	75.22	666.37	555.34	64578	537318	354040			
	Group Single Premium'	1.87	27.96	51.69	0	7	4	2913	77704	307813
	Group Non-Single Premium	31.92	86.91	50.49	8	63	60	27111	282081	182428
6	**HDFC Standard**									
	Individual Single Premium	27.83	119.57	103.83	1982	38202	210775			
	Individual Non-Single Premium	137.16	1798.75	1591.61	83229	690246	529952			
	Group Single Premium'	21.12	86.14	75.61	15	121	108	22944	176900	141062
	Group Non-Single Premium	1.78	23.13	51.68	1	9	40	192	15810	33467

7	**ICICI Prdential**									
	Individual Single Premium	18.98	174.37	300.37	2605	30145	47359			
	Individual Non-Single Premium	472.19	4102.91	4800.95	274016	2128522	2087810			
	Group Single Premium'	2.44	181.91	216.93	4	188	136	44857	567361	409902
	Group Non-Single Premium	133.31	844.30	474.17	10	319	291	17185	537534	377126
8	**Birla Sunlife**									
	Individual Single Premium	3.12	28.86	20.02	14941	129952	72526			
	Individual Non-Single Premium	196.27	1799.78	1147.20	98764	795382	346737			
	Group Single Premium'	0.97	16.22	4.47	0	1	3	2265	41633	5131
	Group Non-Single Premium	14.23	158.44	87.53	8	154	102	12535	214617	131962
9	**Aviva**									
	Individual Single Premium	1.01	34.40	17.11	179	4106	2588			
	Individual Non-Single Premium	50.93	510.11	697.24	28390	281560	268683			
	Group Single Premium'	0.00	0.05	1.73	0	0	0	1	66	984
	Group Non-Single Premium	0.82	15.62	22.33	4	60	93	90995	901109	536146
10	**Kotak Mahindra Old Mutual**									
	Individual Single Premium	0.89	15.87	22.94	142	2017	3066			
	Individual Non-Single Premium	76.93	863.38	582.28	25892	417595	199657			
	Group Single Premium	2.15	29.02	20.09	2	10	2	9669	110784	149333
	Group Non-Single Premium	8.77	52.69	50.54	37	319	206	39354	441562	381628
11	**Max New York**									
	Individual Single Premium	10.00	195.80	208.95	647	13398	13683			
	Individual Non. Single Premium	88.30	1254.27	885.50	68284	955234	595231			
	Group Single Premium	0.14	7.61	0.00	0	10	0	–38	206659	0
	Group Non-Single Premium	0.91	15.77	36.01	7	296	263	8784	204846	457349
12	**Met Life**									
	Individual Single Premium	0.65	5.39	17.37	119	1786	2726			
	Individual Non. Single Premium	92.83	754.95	475.35	30860	220216	157974			
	Group Single Premium	6.59	31.86	9.75	28	129	53	29184	268187	152744
	Group Non-Single Premium	0.00	0.00	0.00	0	0	0	0	0	0

13	**Sahara Life**									
	Individual Single Premium	5.07	37.62	30.22	1647	10304	7819			
	Individual Non. Single Premium	7.52	57.87	48.44	9197	68109	67279			
	Group Single Premium	0.00	0.00	0.00	0	0	0	0	0	0
	Group Non-Single Premium	0.00	0.02	0.00	0	9	6	0	770	271
14	**Shriram Life**									
	Individual Single Premium	1.25	126.15	135.21	246	20015	24466			
	Individual Non. Single Premium	4.46	142.04	90.93	3478	75618	56495			
	Group Single Premium	0.00	0.00	0.04	0	0	2	0	0	4633
	Group Non-Single Premium	0.02	0.40	0.00	0	3	2	2196	25744	623
15	**Bharti Axa Life**									
	Individual Single Premium	0.31	4.53	2.36	41	985	367			
	Individual Non. Single Premium	25.83	207.67	63.88	17778	142718	50222			
	Group Single Premium	0.73	6.13	0.69	1	2	1	1076	27699	371
	Group Non-Single Premium	0.00	0.00	0.00	0	0	0	0	0	0
16	**Future Generali Life**									
	Individual Single Premium	0.74	2.90	0.00	165	606	0			
	Individual Non. Single Premium	18.01	43.93	0.12	14046	41396	6			
	Group Single Premium	0.02	0.07	0.00	0	1	0	64	420	0
	Group Non-Single Premium	3.17	11.61	1.79	13	54	6	19737	242460	66213
17	**IDBI Fortis Life**									
	Individual Single Premium	9.34	84.48		1673	13472				
	Individual Non. Single Premium	12.20	112.88		4319	39028				
	Group Single Premium	0.00	0.00		0	0		0	0	
	Group Non-Single Premium	0.00	0.02		0	1		2955	16308	
18	**Canara HSBC OBC Life**									
	Individual Single Premium	1.83	4.07		147	285				
	Individual Non. Single Premium	34.68	180.01		4216	19862				
	Group Single Premium	0.00	0.00		0	0		0	0	
	Group Non-Single Premium	0.00	0.00		0	0		0	0	

19	**Aegon Religare**									
	Individual Single Premium	0.93	1.63		109	203				
	Individual Non. Single Premium	7.15	15.67		3041	14166				
	Group Single Premium	0.00	0.00		0	0		0	0	
	Group Non-Single Premium	0.00	0.00		0	0		0	0	
20	**DLF Pramerica #**									
	Individual Single Premium	0.00	0.00		0	0				
	Individual Non. Single Premium	0.31	0.79		467	1068				
	Group Single Premium	0.00	0.00		0	0		0	0	
	Group Non-Single Premium	0.00	0.00		0	0		0	0	
	Private Total									
	Individual Single Premium	209.03	1941.89	2533.46	50289	503553	633696			
	Individual Non. Single Premium	2106.70	20167.25	18107.95	1291757	10785618	8745582			
	Group Single Premium	62.08	701.80	775.18	53	500	357	151016	1691124	1337692
	Group Non-Single Premium	264.77	2668.26	1087.28	217	2312	1598	1666676	13912276	3974554
21	**LIC**									
	Individual Single Premium	8189.60	18608.49	15965.85	1648611	4538003	4330794			
	Individual Non. Single Premium	1607.29	12631.80	18076.25	2713141	20370473	22061778			
	Group Single Premium	604.24	8617.97	6581.94	1669	15564	17675	5033985	26200359	17548930
	Group Non-Single Premium	0.00	0.00	0.00	0	0	0	0	0	0
	Grand Total									
	Individual Single Premium	8398.63	20550.38	18499.31	1698900	5041556	4964490			
	Individual Non. Single Premium	3714.00	32799.06	36184.20	4004898	31156091	30807360			
	Group Single Premium	666.32	9319.78	7357.13	1722	16064	18032	5185001	27891483	18886622
	Group Non-Single Premium	264.77	2668.26	1087.28	217	2312	1598	1666676	13912276	3974554

Note. 1. Cumulative premium / No. of policies upto the month is net of cancellations which may occur during the free look period.
2. Compiled on the basis of data submitted by the Insurance companies
3. # Started operations in September, 2008

Source : IRDA Journal

Table 41.24

GROSS PREMIUM UNDERWRITTEN BY NON-LIFE INSURERS WITHIN INDIA (SEGMENT WISE):

Sl. No.	Insurer	Fire	Marine	Marine Cargo	Marine Hull	Engineering	Motor
1	**Royal Sundaram**	**45.51**	**15.05**	**15.05**	**0.00**	**28.54**	**375.36**
	Previous year	55.19	12.35	12.35	0.00	29.73	285.77
2	**TATA-AIG**	**132.01**	**90.47**	**90.47**	**0.00**	**28.49**	**171.75**
	Previous year	105.73	72.48	72.48	0.00	22.68	182.37
3	**Reliance**	**104.95**	**55.19**	**25.69**	**29.50**	**88.37**	**870.02**
	Previous year	112.87	32.14	25.14	7.00	74.95	982.71
4	**IFFCO Tokio**	**157.14**	**91.16**	**63.95**	**27.21**	**60.05**	**506.90**
	Previous year	190.70	49.34	41.62	7.73	67.19	320.62
5	**ICICI Lombard**	**257.22**	**193.99**	**72.04**	**121.96**	**160.05**	**982.99**
	Previous year	401.54	178.02	48.16	129.86	144.58	955.49
6	**Bajaj Allianz**	**184.53**	**69.22**	**56.95**	**12.28**	**95.13**	**1,162.77**
	Previous year	221.33	62.47	56.34	6.13	107.12	954.66
7	**HDFC ERGO**	**30.46**	**5.72**	**4.03**	**1.69**	7.83	**105.55**
	Previous year	6.23	2.20	2.20	0.00	4.54	102.17
8	**Cholamandalam**	**48.76**	**29.86**	**28.68**	**1.17**	**19.35**	**238.19**
	Previous year	58.39	25.64	24.16	1.48	22.98	153.71
9	**Future Generali $**	**11.69**	**4.22**	**4.22**	**0.00**	**8.97**	**57.63**
	Previous year	0.23	0.52	0.52	0.00	0.18	0.11
10	**Universal Sompo***	**2.46**	**0.29**	**0.29**	**0.00**	**0.03**	**1.04**
	Previous year	0.00	0.00	0.00	0.00	0.00	0.00
11	**Shriram**	**0.14**	**0.00**	**0.00**	**0.00**	**0.22**	**56.88**
	Previous year	0.00	0.00	0.00	0.00	0.00	0.00
11	**Bharti Axa**	**1.02**	**1.18**	**0.18**	**0.00**	**1.43**	**4.93**
	Previous year	0.00	0.00	0.00	0.00	0.00	0.00
11	**New India**	**577.55**	**356.15**	**139.51**	**216.64**	**193.16**	**1,457.63**
	Previous year	603.14	307.27	130.32	176.94	161.37	1,487.00
12	**National**	**300.27**	**157.88**	**102.92**	**54.97**	**107.77**	**1,623.86**
	Previous year sign	287.43	131.60	90.55	41.05	100.17	1,561.37
13	**United India**	**429.11**	**251.92**	**146.14**	**105.78**	**177.18**	**1,138.01**
	Previous year #	412.10	223.36	125.58	97.78	153.07	1,022.59
14	**Oriental**	**361.27**	**253.01**	**127.45**	**125.56**	**188.57**	**1,107.09**
	Previous year	402.92	262.49	121.70	140.80	162.90	1,196.26
	Grand Total	**2,644.09**	**1,574.32**	**877.56**	**696.76**	**1,165.13**	**8,860.60**
	Previous year	2,857.80	1,259.90	751.13	608.77	1,051.48	9,204.83
	SPECIALISED INSTITUTIONS						
15	**ECGC**						
	Previous year						
16	**Star Health & Allied Insurance**						
	Previous year						
17	**Apollo DKV $**						
	Previous years						

Note: In case of public sector insurance companies, the segment-wise data submitted may vary from the flash Nos filed with the Authority. As such, the industry totals may vary from the flash figures published for the month of September-2008.
$ Commenced operations in November, 2007.
* Commenced operations in February, 2008.
# There is variation between Segment-wise figures and Monthly Business figures for December, 2008.
Compiled on the basis of data submitted by the Insurance companies

Table 41.25 FOR THE PERIOD APRIL-DECEMBER-2008 (PROVISIONAL & UNAUDITED)

(Rs. Crores)

Motor OD	Motor TP	Health	Aviation	Liability	Personal Accident	All Others	Grand Total
299.45	75.91	**88.95**	**0.00**	**6.49**	**21.39**	**11.23**	**592.51**
231.48	54.30	80.10	0.00	4.08	22.62	6.05	495.90
146.95	**24.80**	**60.16**	**0.00**	**89.44**	**90.88**	**7.68**	**670.87**
152.01	30.35	52.07	0.00	73.90	78.20	2.04	589.48
622.51	**247.51**	**259.75**	**9.67**	**21.86**	**48.25**	**37.13**	**1,495.20**
713.26	269.45	221.10	5.99	11.86	36.56	46.27	1,524.47
351.91	**154.99**	**94.05**	**9.48**	**27.54**	**20.60**	**74.53**	**1,041.46**
219.86	100.77	66.99	4.03	20.14	15.17	65.96	800.13
657.01	**325.98**	**819.54**	**46.21**	**67.98**	**97.82**	**96.08**	**2,721.87**
679.74	275.75	674.41	30.07	67.71	94.33	78.52	2,624.67
813.70	**349.07**	**214.58**	**17.91**	**52.90**	**40.96**	**159.35**	**1,997.34**
695.48	259.17	181.57	9.81	35.92	29.02	111.00	1,712.89
87.17	**18.38**	**38.76**	**0.59**	**27.72**	**4.77**	**12.97**	**234.36**
90.53	11.65	25.69	0.00	17.41	4.46	5.81	168.51
181.50	**56.69**	**127.89**	**0.00**	**11.00**	**19.15**	**31.73**	**525.93**
123.68	30.03	82.59	-0.15	11.63	9.09	23.64	387.52
43.59	**14.04**	**27.01**	**0.00**	**3.45**	**7.71**	**3.15**	**123.83**
0.10	0.02	0.00	0.00	0.00	0.00	0.00	1.04
1.04	**0.00**	**0.41**	**0.00**	**0.01**	**0.87**	**1.94**	**7.06**
0.00	0.00	0.00	0.00	0.00	0.00	1.94	1.94
29.13	**27.75**	**0.00**	**0.00**	**0.07**	**0.00**	**0.00**	**57.31**
0.00	0.00	0.00	0.00	0.00	0.00	0.00	0.00
4.08	**0.85**	**0.00**	**0.00**	**0.18**	**0.04**	**0.06**	**7.83**
0.00	0.00	0.00	0.00	0.00	0.00	0.00	0.00
798.29	**659.34**	**1,042.37**	**45.53**	**79.85**	**64.93**	**296.30**	**4,113.48**
811.44	675.56	856.74	51.26	66.03	62.78	315.31	3,910.90
1,027.23	**596.63**	**628.63**	**45.56**	**36.60**	**53.71**	**244.21**	**3,198.40**
981.45	579.92	466.74	38.24	29.93	47.41	259.22	2,922.10
648.26	**489.75**	**631.01**	**13.05**	**57.52**	**53.49**	**392.11**	**3,143.40**
613.79	408.79	448.33	20.59	50.34	64.33	370.24	2,764.96
645.67	**461.42**	**525.79**	**66.16**	**60.57**	**68.02**	**335.22**	**2,965.71**
737.55	458.71	402.52	58.94	51.58	67.47	289.81	2,894.90
6,357.49	**3,503.11**	**4,558.90**	**254.06**	**543.18**	**592.60**	**1,703.68**	**22,896.56**
6,050.36	3,154.47	3,558.84	218.79	440.53	531.42	1,575.81	20,799.41
						537.39	**537.39**
						473.96	473.96
		363.24			**15.15**	**3.22**	**381.62**
		136.00			**14.87**	**2.63**	153.50
		31.02					**31.02**
		0.00					0.00

Table 41.26 General Insurance

Insure	*Gross Crors Premune*	*Premium In Rs.*	*Underwritten crores*	*Market*	*Shares in %*	
	2003-04	*2004-05*	*2005-06*	*2003-04*	*2004-05*	*2005-06*
1. Royal Sundaram	258.02	303.71	453.57	1.61	1.83	
2. Tata AIG	353.31	468.87	612.38	2.20	2.59	
3. Reliance General	161.05	161.68	162.33	1.00	0.89	
4. IFFOO-Tokio	295.64	501.28	896.11	1.84	2.80	
5. ICICI Landlord	506.72	885.16	1592.00	3.16	4.89	
6. Bajaj Allianz	476.31	856.07	1287.68	2.97	4.71	
7. HDFC CHUBB	3111.67	183.84	202.37	0.70	0.98	
8. Cholanandalam	96.68	170.10	220.42	0.60	0.94	
9. New India	4045.69	4210.81	4762.12	25.23	23.25	
10. Nitional	3417.00	3799.91	3524.00	21.3	21.14	
11. Until India	3038.05	2944.59	3146.98	18.94	16.37	
12. Oriental	2832.11	3017.78	3518.64	17.66	16.79	
Print Total		3557.72	5426.87			
Public Total		13973.10	14951.74			
Grand Total	1665.53	17530.81	20378.61	100.00	100.00	
Specialised Instance						
FCGC	445.12	515.54	578.46	2.78	2.86	

Table 41.27 Gross Premium Underwritten For and upto the Month of January 2009

Insurer	**January 2008-09**	**January 2007-08**	**April - January 2008-09**	**April - January 2007-08**	**Growth over the Corresponding period of previous year**
Royal Sundaram	70.52	70.30	663.03	566.20	17.10
Tata-AIG	76.19	82.81	749.72	672.28	11.52
Reliance General	140.70	149.17	1635.90	1673.64	–2.26
IFFCO-Tokio	120.07	127.34	1161.53	927.47	25.24
ICICI-lombard	317.80	278.43	3039.67	2903.10	4.70
Bajaj Allianz	217.09	212.57	2214.43	1925.46	15.01
HDFC ERGO General	33.62	17.46	267.97	185.98	44.09
Cholamandalam	62.04	48.00	587.97	435.52	35.01
Future Generali $	26.38	4.42	150.14	5.43	2662.80
Universal Sompo #	4.99	0.00	12.05	0.00	
Shriram General @	24.63	0.00	81.94	0.00	
Bharti AXA General @	6.47	0.00	14.30	0.00	
New India	456.58	451.30	4569.98	4359.75	4.82
National	360.55	373.96	3558.95	3296.06	7.98
United India	351.33	316.13	3491.07	3081.08	13.31
Oriental	338.93	328.68	3304.64	3223.58	2.51
Private Total	**1100.48**	**990.50**	**10578.65**	**9295.08**	**13.81**
Public Total	**1507.39**	**1470.07**	**14924.64**	**13960.47**	**6.91**
Grand Total	**2607.87**	**2460.57**	**25503.29**	**23255.55**	**9.67**
Specialised Institutions :					
1. Credit Insurance ECGC	62.15	56.99	599.53	530.95	12.92
2. Health Insurance					
Star Health & Allied Insurance	102.76	4.29	484.38	157.79	206.98
Apollo DKV	4.71	0.49	38.01	0.61	6167.24
Health Total	**107.47**	**4.78**	**522.39**	**158.39**	**229.80**
3. Agriculture Insurance AIC	71.54	126.57	653.12	700.16	–6.72

Note : Compiled on the basis of data submitted by the Insurance companies
$ Commenced operations in November, 2007 # Commenced operations in February 2008
@ Commenced operations in July, 2008 * Figures revised by insurance companies

Table 41.24 Progress of General Insurance

Year Ended March, 2007 (Provisional & Unaudited)

(Rs. in Crores)

S. No.	Insurer	Fire	Marine	Marine Cargo	Marine Hull	Engineering	Motor	Motor OD	Motor TP	Health	Aviation	Liability	Personal Accident	All Others	Grand Total
1.	Royal Sundaram (March 2007)	102.47	18.32	17.73	0.59	37.73	303.39	261.46	41.93	97.45	0.00	8.45	25.08	7.14	600.03
	Previous year (March 2006)	92.39	18.30	17.72	0.58	28.07	233.09	209.78	23.31	50.59	0.00	6.73	24.47	5.71	459.35
2.	TATA-AIG	130.25	71.31	71.31	0.00	26.29	288.09	262.21	25.88	45.35	0.25	73.47	79.40	27.15	741.56
	Previous year	119.00	49.11	49.11	0.00	21.71	259.34	239.56	19.78	30.62	0.02	57.61	58.48	16.50	612.39
3.	Reliance	146.15	24.92	16.45	8.47	93.68	454.99	408.60	46.39	67.69	7.23	10.03	16.47	91.07	912.23
	Previous year	46.68	20.75	10.18	10.57	23.73	26.41	26.19	0.32	8.61	7.00	4.95	5.98	18.12	162.33
4.	IFFCO Tokio	294.76	129.96	52.24	77.73	90.91	448.90	348.63	100.27	71.89	4.74	12.70	17.44	79.03	1,150.32
	Previous year	226.43	46.24	36.11	10.13	65.82	379.69	318.73	60.96	51.97	0.73	10.09	16.65	98.51	896.11
5.	ICICI Lombard	403.05	155.25	56.23	99.02	177.54	1,143.34	956.73	186.60	735.85	32.07	84.02	113.74	158.59	3,003.45
	Previous year	311.87	85.71	42.14	43.57	85.98	458.80	404.05	54.75	274.46	16.60	60.90	76.25	221.43	1,592.00
6.	Bajaj Allianz	383.67	72.99	60.43	12.56	154.77	843.87	668.39	175.48	158.26	7.94	29.73	24.31	129.07	1,804.60
	Previous year	360.79	55.73	41.42	14.31	99.88	536.61	357.76	178.85	97.69	4.75	23.59	15.50	90.02	1,284.57
7.	HDFC Chubb	7.65	2.37	2.37	0.00	5.98	132.36	123.83	8.53	10.18	0.00	4.76	7.69	19.17	190.16
	Previous year	5.82	1.72	1.72	0.00	3.52	158.03	149.85	8.18	4.55	0.00	2.81	11.77	17.56	205.77
8.	Cholamandalam	80.54	26.56	25.66	0.90	23.72	97.16	80.53	16.63	38.60	0.40	14.70	7.63	25.27	314.59
	Previous year	73.07	17.00	16.67	0.33	20.71	52.35	47.86	4.49	21.11	0.94	13.08	12.57	11.37	222.21
9.	New India	909.98	321.03	158.72	162.31	210.31	2,034.73	1,233.71	801.02	765.29	115.27	60.65	79.39	518.07	5,014.71
	Previous year	839.63	299.78	149.34	150.45	144.70	2,174.50	1,394.35	780.16	669.28	116.85	64.34	95.78	386.63	4,791.50
10.	National	491.21	196.97	120.29	76.68	134.95	1,980.16	1,310.14	670.03	333.12	84.49	36.42	55.24	498.30	3,810.88
	Previous year	482.01	172.29	126.84	45.45	109.11	1,853.29	1,289.60	563.69	294.25	71.26	35.68	66.87	438.91	3,523.67
11.	United India	674.77	264.35	135.31	129.05	203.96	1,219.18	767.30	451.88	434.64	45.36	67.79	95.31	504.59	3,509.95
	Previous year	645.48	203.96	125.01	78.95	184.96	1,138.16	703.26	434.90	359.26	37.07	59.14	98.98	427.76	3,154.78
12.	Oriental	538.50	349.78	168.76	181.02	214.27	1,732.26	1,158.88	573.39	440.53	119.54	61.61	85.69	398.35	3,940.53
	Previous year	546.89	325.12	166.92	158.20	187.01	1,495.36	981.27	514.10	359.72	149.65	58.17	97.05	308.16	3,527.13
	Grand Total	4,163.00	1,633.81	885.49	748.32	1,374.09	10,678.43	7,580.41	3,098.02	3,198.83	417.29	464.32	607.42	2,455.81	24,993.01
	Previous year	3,750.06	1,295.71	783.17	512.54	975.22	8,765.75	6,122.26	2,643.49	2,222.09	404.86	397.06	580.35	2,040.68	20,431.80
	Specialised Institutions														
13.	ECGC*													618.05	618.05
	Previous year (March 2006)													578.46	578.46
14.	Star Health & Allied Insurance**									11.05		11.38			22.42
	Previous year (March 2006)									0.00		0.00			0.00

Note : In case of public sector insurance companies, the segment wise data submitted may very from the flash Nos filed with the Authority. As such a industry totals may vary from the flash figures published for the month of March, 2007.

Life Insurers

S.No	Name of the Company	Name of Principal Officer	Name of Appointed Actuary	Telephone No. Fax No./E-male Web Address
1.	Bajaj Allianz Life Insurance Company Limited GE Plaza, Airport Road, yerawada Pune 411 006	Mr. Sam Ghosh	Mr. Andrew Wakeling	Tel: 020-4026666 Fax: 020-4026789
2.	Birla Sun Life Insurance Co. Ltd 6th Floor, Vaman Centre, Makhwana Road, off Andheri-Kurla Road Andheri(E), Mumbai-400 059.	Nani B Javeri	Mr. Kedar Mulgund	Tel: 022 56783333 Fax. 022 56783232
3.	HDFC Standard Life Insurance Co. Ltd "Trade Star" 2nd floor, 'A' Wing, Kondivita Road Junction Andheri-Kurla Road Andheri (East) Mumbai 400 059.	Mr. D.M. Satwalekar	Mr. Nick Taket	Tel: 022-8222234/ 5551 6551 Fax: 022-2822-8844
4.	ICICI Prudential Life Insurance Co. Ltd ICICI Prulite Towers, 1089, Appasaheb Marathe Marg, Prabhadevi, Mumbai 400 025	Ms. Shikha Sharma	Mr.V. Rajagopalan	Tel: 022-56621996 Fax: 022-5622031
5.	ING Vysya Life Insurance Company Pvt. Ltd. ING Vysya Home, 5th Floor, # 22 Mahatma Gandhi Road Bangalore-560 001.	Mr. Kshitij Jain	Ms. Hemamalini Ramakrishnan	Tel: 080-2532800 Fax:080-25559764
6.	Life Insurance Corporation of India Yougakshema, Jeeva Bima Marg, Post Box No. 19953 Mumbai 400 021	Shri TS. Vijayan	Mr. Gorakh Nath Agarwal	Tel: 56598701: 56598702 Fax: 22824386 E-mail: chairman@licindia.com
7.	Max New York LIfe Insurance Co. Ltd. 11th Floor, DLF square, Jacaranda Marg, DLF City, Phase-II, Gurgaon 122 002.	Mr. Gary R. Benett	MR. John Charles Poole	Tel: 0124-2561717 Fax:0124-2561764
8.	Met Life India Insurance company Pvt. Ltd. Brigade Seshamahal, No. 5, Vani Vilas Road Basavanagudi, Bangalore -560 004.	Mr. Venktesh Mysore	Mr. K. P. Sarma	Tel: 080-26438638 Fax:080-26521970 Toll Free No. 1-600-44-6969

9.	Kotak Mahindra Old Mutual Life Insurance Limited 6th Floor Penisula Chambers, Penisula Corporate Park, Lower parel, Mumbai-400 013.	Mr. Gaurang Shah	Mr. A. Venkatasubramanian	Tel: 022-56635000 Fax: 022-56635111
10.	SBI Life Insurance Co. Ltd. Turner morrison Building 2nd Floor, 16 Bank Street, Fort Mumbai-400 023.	Mr. S. Krishna Murthy	Mr. I Sambasiva Rao	Tel: 022-56392000 Fax:022-56621471
11.	Tata AIG Life Insurance Co. Ltd. 5th 7 6th Floor, Peninsula Tower, Peninsula corporate Park Ganpatrao kadam Marg, Lower Parel, Mumbai 400 013.	Mr. Trevor Bull	Mr. Heerak Basu	Tel: 022-56516000 Fax:022-56550711
12.	Reliance Life Insurance Company Limited "The Trapezium" 39, First Floor, Nelson Manickam Road Chennai- 600 029	Mr. P Nandagopal	Ms. Pournima Gupte	Tel: 044-30588200 Fax:044-30588220
13.	Aviva Life Insurance Co. India Pvt. Ltd. 5th floor, JMD Regent Square, Mehrauli road, Gurgaon - 122001	Mr. Stuart Purdy	Mr. KK Wadhwa	Tel: 0124-2804141 Fax:0124-2804151
14.	Sahara India Life Insurance Co. Ltd. Sahara India Bhawan, Kopoorthala Complex, Lucknow 226024	Mr. N. C. Sharma	Mr. K K Dharni	Tel: 0522-2337777 Fax:0522-2378200
15.	Shriram Life Insurance Co. Ltd. Regd. Office : 3-6-478, 3rd Floor, Anand Estate, Liberty Road, Himayat Nagar, Hyderabad - 500029	Mr R Duruvasan	Mr N S Sastry	Tel: 040-23434466-72 Fax: 040-23434488
16.	Bharti AXA Life Insurance Company Ltd. 61/62, Kalpataru Synergy, Vakola, Opp. Grand Hyatt Hotel, Santacruz (E) Mumbai-400 055	Mr. Nitin Chopra	Mr. K. S. Gopalakrishnan	Tel: 022-40306300/6301 Fax: 022-40306347

Non-Life Insurance

	Name of the Company	*Name of the Principal Officer*	*Name of the Appointed actuary*	*Telephone No. Fax. No./Email. & Web Address*
1.	Bajaj allianz General Insurance Co. Ltd. GE Plaza, Airport Road, Yerawada, Pune 411 006.	Mr. Kamesh Goyal	Ms. Asha J. Joshi	Tel: 020-6602 666 Fax: 020-6602 666
2.	ICICI Lombard General Insurance Co. Ltd. Zenith House, Keshavrao Khade Marg, Mahalaxmi Mumbai-400 034	Mr. Sandeep Bakshi	Mr. Liyaquat Khan	Tel: 022-2490699 Fax: 022-2492762
3.	IFFCO Toko General Insurance Co. Ltd 4 and 5th Floors, IFFCO Tower, Plot No. 3, Sector 29, Gurgaon-122001 (Haryana)	Mr. Ajit Narain	Mr. A. Peetambaram	Tel: 0124-285010 Fax: 0124-257792
4.	National Insurance Co. Ltd. 3, Middleton Street, P.B. No. 9229, Kolkata 700 071.	Mr. V. Ramasaamy	Mr. Bhudeb Chatterjee	Tel: 033-2283170 Fax: 033-2283171
5.	The New India Assurance Co. Ltd. New India Assurance Bldg. 87, M. G. Road, Fort, Mumbai 400 011.	Mr. B. Chakrabarthi	Mr. A. R. Prabhu	Tel: 022-2267461 Fax: 022-2265281
6.	The Oriental Insurance Co. Ltd. A-25/27, Asaf Ali Road New Delhi 110 002.	Mr. M. Ramadoss	Mr. P. C. Gupta	Tel: 011-23279221 Direct: 23265024 Fax: 23287192,232 23283971
7.	Reliance General Insurance Co. Ltd. 19 Reliance Centre Walchand Hirachand Marg, Ballard Estate, Mumbai-400 038	Mr. K.A. Somasekaran	Mr. Gopalakrishna Pai	Tel: 022-3023750 Fax: 022-3027123
8.	Royal Sundaram Alliance Insurance Co. Ltd. "Sundaram Towars" 45-46, Whites Road, Royapetah Chennai-600 014.	Mr. Antony Jacob	Mr. O. Lakshminarayana	Tel: 044-4222737 Fax: 044-28517370 Email: customer.services@
9.	Tata AIG General Insurance Co. Ltd.	Mr. Dalip Verma	Mr. K. Hanumanth Rao	Tel: 022-6669969

	Peninsula corporate Park, Nicholas Piramal Tower, 9th Floor Ganpatrao Kadam Marg Lower parel Mumbai 400 013			Fax: 044:2851737
10.	United India Insurance Co. Ltd. 24, Whites Road Chennai - 600 014.	Mr. M. K. Garg	Mr. S. Krishnan	Tel: 044-2852016 Fax: 044-2852382
11.	Cholamandalam MS General Insurance Co. Ltd. "Dare House" 2nd Floor New No. 2 (Old No. 234) N. S. C. Bose Road, Chennai-600 001	Mr. M. Anandan	Mr. Venkatesan	Tel: 044-4216600 Fax: 044-4216600
12.	HDFC-Chubb General Insurance Co. Ltd. 5th Floor, Express Towers, Nariman Point, Mumbai 400021	Mr. Shrirang V Samant	Mr. Narayannan Laksmanan	Tel: 022-6638 36 Fax: 022-6638 36
13.	Export Credit Guarantee Corporation Ltd. 10th Floor, Express Towers, Nariman Point, Mumbai-400021	Shri Christy Fernandez, IAS		Tel: 022-56590512-515 Fax: 022-5659051 022-5659053
14.	Agriculture Insurance Co. of India Ltd. 13th Floor, 14 K. G Marg Connaught Place, New Delhi -110001	Mr. M. Parshad	Mr. Nalin Kapadia	Tel : 011-4108199 Fax: 011-4108199 Email: aicho@aicofi
15.	Star Health and Allied Insurance Company Limited No.1, New Tank Street, Vlluvarkottam High Road, Nungambakkam, Chennai-600 034	Mr. V. Jagannathan	Mr. R. Soundararajan	Tel: 044-2826005 Fax: 044-2826006

मरीन कार्गो विभाग/ MARINE CARGO DEPARTMENT

एम ए/MA3

प्रति/ To,

युनाइटेड इंडिया इन्श्योरेन्स कम्पनी लिमिटेड
पंजीकृत व प्रधान कार्यालय :
24, व्हाइट्स रोड चेन्नै - 6000 01

United India Insurance Co. Ltd.
Redg. & Head Office:
24, Whites Road Chennai - 600 014

कृपया आप द्वारा जारी ओपेन पॉलिसी क्रमांक .... के अन्तर्गत निम्नलिखित माल की किश्त भुगतान के आधार पर बीमित करें :-

Please Insure the following goods under Open Policy No. .... Issued by you on account of

रेल/लारी द्वारा रे.र./प्र.स. .... के अन्तर्गत दिनांक .... को प्रेषित

Despatch by Rail/Lorry, under R.R./c. No. .... dated ....

पोत एस.एस. ".. ल.बि.सं. .... दिनांकत ....

Vesel S.S. ".." B/L No. .... dated ....

डेक के अन्तर्गत या पर .... से .... तक .... प्रेषित

Shipped on or under deck .... from .... to ....

आवरित किया जाने वाले जोखिम ....

Risk to be cover ....

मार्क और सं. **Marks or Nos.**	माल का विवरण **Description of Goods**	बीमित की जाने वाली राशि/मात्रा **Amount to be Insured**

केवल कार्यालय के प्रयोगार्थ/For Office Use Only

घोषणा सं. .... के अन्तर्गत बीमित/Insured under Declaration No.

ओपन पॉलिसी सं............. / Open Policy No.

दिनांक .... को अभिलेखित / Record on Date

प्रीमियम रू./ Premium Rs.......................................

हस्ताक्षर/ Singnature

आद्याक्षर / Initials

स्थान / Place

दिनांक / Date

Tata AIG General Insurance Company Limited
Marine Insurance Application Form

TATA AIG INSURANCE
WITH YOU ALWAYS

1. Name and Address of the applicant/Bank, if any*
2. Phone & Fax nos. & e-mail address
3. Merchandise/Goods to be insured*
4. Nature of Packing*
5. Marks & Nos.
6. Conveyance* ☐ Sea ☐ Air ☐ Closed Rail wagons Covered Trucks ☐ Courier ☐ Post ☐ Others
7. Name of the Vessel
8. B/L, AWB, RR/CN no. and date
9. Voyage/Transit* From To
10. Transshipment &/or storage if any (specify place and period)
11. Basis of Valuation*
12. Value declared for insurance*
    In foreign currency
    In Indian Rupees
13. Terms of cover required* ☐ All Risks ☐ Basic
14. Specify LC wordings, if any, to be incorporated:
15. Any other details about the risk:
16. Producer Name & Code, if applicable: *

Specimen

Declaration by Applicant

I/We here by declare that the statement made by me/us herein and in attachments here to are true to the best of my/our knowledge and belief and I/We hereby agree that this Proposal shall form the basis of the insurance contract between me/us and Tata AIG General Insurance Company Ltd. (referred to as the Company). I/We further confirm that if any additions or alterations are carried out in the risk proposed for insurance herein after the submission of this Proposal then particulars of such shall be forthwith conveyed to the Company. I/We further agree that the submission of this Proposal to the Company and its receipt thereof shall not constitute an acceptance of the risk by the Company.

Place		Signature of Applicant	
Date		Name & Designation	
Time		Cheque no. and Date	
Amount of Cheque			

ATTACHMENTS

Invoice/Packing List/LC wordings/BL or contract of affreightment/if other, specify.

(IMPORTANT) Prohibition of Rebates (Section 41 of the Insurance Act 1938)

1. No person shall allow or offer to allow either directly or indirectly as inducement to any Person to take out renew or continue an Insurance in respect of any kind of risk relating to lives or property in India any rebate of the whole or part of the commission payable or any rebate of the premium shown on the Policy, nor shall any person taking out or renewing or continuing a Policy accept such rebate except such rebate as may be allowed in accordance with the published prospectuses or tables of the insurer.
2. Any person making default in complying with the provision of this section shall be punishable with fine which may extend to five hundred rupees only.

NOTE.

1. Premium cheque to be drawn in favour of Tata AIG General Insurance Company Limited.
2. Policies proposed and taken after commencement of transit shall be deemed to be null and void.
3. Non-disclosure or misrepresentation in application form will render the contract null and void.
4. For Sea shipments-Institute Classification Clause (extended for Vessels upto 20 years).
   Vessels < 20 years > 25 years additional premium @ 0.125%. VESSELS NOT TO EXCEED 25 YEARS
5. Insurance policy taken should run concurrent to your sale terms and not exceeding the same.
6. This application shall form part of the policy and in case of a dispute referred to as base document.
7. Fields marked in* are Mandatory fields.
8. Please ask for copy of the Clauses in case you require it alongwith the Policy document
9. Shipment details to be furnished within 7 days of sailing

FOR OFFICE USE

- Ordinary leakage, ordinary loss in weight or volume, ordinary wear and tear and inherent flaws in the cargo insured;
- Delay
- Insolvency and financial distress of the carriers;
- Un-seaworthiness of vessel
- Strike, riot, civil commotion, war and nuclear risks

In appropriate cases, however, loss or damage to cargo insured due to strike, riot, civil commotion and/or war can be covered upon payment of additional premium.

Premium Payable

Sum insured for cargo for insurance purposes would be on the following basis:

Cost of cargo + Insurance + Freight (CIF) + 10% of CIF towards incidental charges.

Sum insured for Customs Duty shall be the actual duty payable.

The Company will determine the premium payable for the Policy from time to time depending on:

(*i*) Nature cargo
(*ii*) Mode of conveyance
(*iii*) Nature of packing
(*iv*) Risks to be covered
(*v*) Destination
(*vi*) Past experience with respect to claims, if any, under any Policy/Policies
(*vii*) Any other matters connected with or incidental to the risks to be covered

About us

Reliance General Insurance is one of the fastest growing general insurance companies in India with innovative product offerings and customer service standards that are benchmarked to the best in the world. The company aims to increase its presence in the retail and corportate sectors with a focus on customer centric products, multiple distribution channels and technology.

Reliance General Insurance is a 100% subsidiary of Reliance Capital Limited. Reliance Capital is a part of the Reliance Anil Dhirubhai Ambani group.

Some of our other product:

■ Reliance HealthWise Policy ■ Reliance Shopkeeper's Package Policy ■ Reliance HomeProtect Policy ■ Reliance Office Package Policy ■ Reliance Industry Care Policy ■ Reliance SME care Policy ■ Reliance Standard Fire & Special Perils Insurance Policy ■ Reliance Burglary & Housebreaking Insurance Policy

This product brochure gives the salient features of the plan only. For further details on all the conditions and exclusions related to Reliance Marine Cargo Policy, please contact us.

1800 3002 8282 (toll free)
3989 8282 (local charges apply)

sms 'protect' to 55454
www.reliancegeneral.co.in

RELIANCE General Insurance
Anil Dhirubhai Ambani Group
A Reliance Company

Reliance General Insurance Company Limited
Registered office Reliance Centre, 19, Walchand Hirachand Marg, Ballard Estate, Mumbai 400 001.
Insurance is the subject matter of solicitation. MC-01

Reliance Marine Cargo Policy

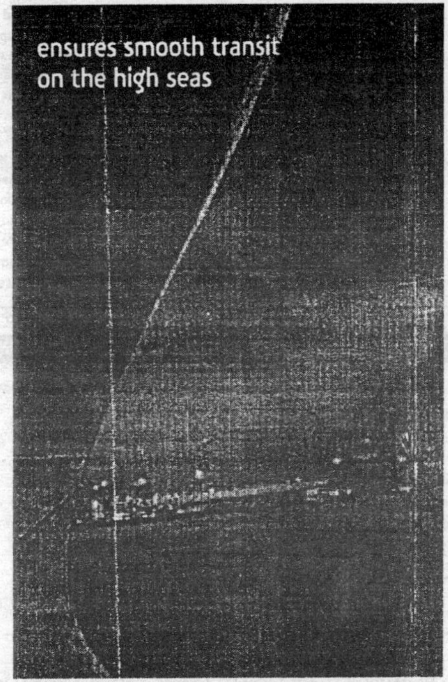

RELIANCE General Insurance
Anil Dhirubhai Ambani Group
A Reliance Company

Welcome to Reliance General Insurance

The term safety is strongly associated with transport and cargo business. However, sometimes even despite the best effort, an uncontrollable factor can cause an untoward event. This always leads to a considerable loss of valued goods, money and time. At such times, what you need is a Policy that offers you financial protection and saves you mental agony. Reliance General Insurance is pleased to offer you such a Policy, which ensures seamless coverage whether you cargo is on land, at sea, in the air or in the hands of any postal service.

Key Advantages

- Comprehensive coverage for your cargo during transit from ne place to another
- Provides cover for cargo sent by all modes of transport-be it Rail/Road/or Air
- World class service standards to facilitate prompt and quick claims settlement

Types of Policies

Specific Policy:

Covers specific transit of a cargo between specified locations.

Open Policy:

Covers a series of transits of cargo during a specific period of insurance.

Open Cover:

Similar to Open Policy but limited to covering imports.

Scope of Cover

Provides cover against loss or damage to cargo during transit from one place to another by any one or more modes of transport on 'strict liability basis', that is to say, whether or not fault or negligence on the part of the carrier is proved.

Coverage provided under Marine Cargo policies ranges from a restricted form of cover to the widest available form of cover, namely, All Risks as opted by the client.

Transit	Clauses available
Inland Transit	Inland Transit (Rail/Road) Clauses C (Basic cover) Inland Transit (Rail/Road) Clauses B (Restricted cover) Inland Transit (Rail/Road) Clauses A (All Risk cover)
Overseas Transit (by Sea)	Institute Cargo Clauses C Institute Cargo Clauses B Institute Cargo Clauses A Institute Commodity Trade Clauses
Transit by Air	Institute Cargo Clauses (Air)

Institute Cargo Clauses

Coverage available under the Institute Cargo Clauses are given here.

Institute Cargo Clauses A	Institute Cargo Clauses B	Institute Cargo Clauses C
All Risk Cover	**Restricted Cover**	**Basic Cover**
■ Fire of Explosion ■ Standing, Grounding, Sinking or Capsizing ■ Overturning or Derailment ■ Collision or contact of vessel craft or conveyance with any external object other than water ■ Discharge of cargo at point of distress ■ Earthquake, volcanic eruption or lightning and water damage by entry of sea/river water (excluding rainwater) ■ Total loss of package lost overboard ■ Total loss of package dropped during loading and unloading ■ Breakage ■ Scratching, Chipping, Denting & Bruising ■ Theft ■ Malicious Damage ■ Non Delivery ■ All water damage including rain damage	■ Fire or Explosion ■ Standing, Grounding, Sinking or Capsizing ■ Overturning or Deraliment ■ Collision or contact of vessel craft or conveyance with any external objects other than water ■ Discharge of cargo at point of distress ■ Earthquake, volcanic eruption or lightning and water damage by entry of sea/river water (excluding rainwater) ■ Total loss of package lost overboard ■ Total loss of package dropped during loading and unloading	■ Fire or Explosion ■ Standing, Grounding, Sinking or Capsizing ■ Overturning or Derailment ■ Collision or contact of vessel craft or conveyance with any external objects other than water. ■ Discharge of cargo at point of distress.

Inland Transit Clauses

Insurance of goods carried by Rail, Road, Inland waterways are covered as per coverage granted under Inland Transit (Rail/Road) Clauses A, B, C, Inland Transit (Inland Vessels Clauses).

Inland Transit (Rail/Road) B and C Clauses and Inland Transit (Inland vessels) Clauses are restrictive in nature. Where as Inland Transit (Rail/Road) A Clause provides all risk cover subject to certain specific exclusions.

Exclusions

At Reliance General Insurance, we would like things to be as transparent as possible. To ensure that you do not face any misunderstandings when you make a claim, we would like you to know some of the major exclusions under the Policy:

- Willful misconduct of the Insured
- Insufficiency or unsuitability of packing or preparation of the cargo insured;

SURVEY REQUEST FORM

To: Ian Short BEng CEng MRINA, 8 Queens Park Gardens, Seaford, East Sussex BN 25 2QE
Fax: +44 (0) 1323 896861 Tel: + 44 (0) 1323 873267 email : info@marine-surveys. org

I/we having obtained permission from the owners (if applicable) hereby request that you carry out a pre-purchase condition/insurance condition & valuation/partial survey (please delete as applicable), subject to your normal terms of survey as set out below, which I have received, read and understood, and to any special instructions listed below, on the vessel named:

Name of vessel					
Type or class of vessel					
Length		Beam		Draft	Year built
Builder				Construction material	
Vessel located at					
Arrangement for keys					
Owner/Brokers name				Telephone	
Please advise of any special instructions					

I/we hereby agree to pay any fees and expenses reasonably incurred and charged by the Surveyor and understand that I am/we are responsible for all charges for boat movements, slipping, docking, removals, replacement and reinstatement work arising in preparation for and process of the survey.

It is understood and agreed that the surveyor's report will be a factual statement of the examination carried out within stated limitations and with opinions given in good faith as far as seen and accessible at the time of survey. It carries with it no guarantee against faulty design or latent defects or suitability of the vessel for any particular purpose, nor any guarantee of compliance with any particular national or international rule, requirement, regulation, law, standard or code unless specifically requested on this form and confirmed in the text of the report. Liability for the report is solely to the instructing client and to no other third party unless otherwise specified and agreed. It is further agreed that no liability will arise for any consequential or economic loss, loss of profits, business interruption or loss of use.

I/we acknowledge that this survey contract shall be governed by and construed in accordance with English law and that any dispute arising hereunder shall be submitted to the exclusive jurisdiction of the courts of England and Wales.

Survey reports are normally released within 5 working days of the date of survey, subject to all outstanding accounts being settled.

Fee quoted	£	Date					
Name		Signed					
Address							
Tel day		Tel mobile					
Fax		email					
Where did you hear about Marine Surveys (tick box)		Internet		Magazine ad		other	

Cover Note Request Form

Thank you for selecting National Transport Insurance.

To ensure that your client's interests are fully protected we require the following information.

You acknowledge that completion and submission of this document represents that you act on behalf of your client.

You acknowledge that you have provided your client with advice in relation to the DUTY OF DISCLOSURE, AVERAGE/UNDER INSURANCE, THIRD PARTY INTERESTS AND SUBROGATION clauses.

You acknowledge that if requested by National Transport Insurance, your client agrees to obtain from the appropriate Commissioner of Motor Transport within 14 days of receiving notice thereof, a complete and up to date record of offences in respect of which your client has been reported and/or convicted.

You acknowledge that all particulars and statements contained in the original quote request are those of your client, and are true and correct, and that together with this declaration they shall form the basis of the contract between your client and National Transport Insurance and be incorporated therein.

You acknowledge that neither your client nor yourself have with held any information to our questions that is likely to affect our cover, in that we may reduce or refuse to pay a claim on this Cover Note.

You acknowledge that if your client answered our question fraudulently, we may refuse to pay a claim and treat the cover as not have been effected.

Please indicate your acceptance by ticking ☐ **I accept the terms of this declaration**

Cover Note Details

* Quotation Number : ______
* Cover Required From: ☐ ☐ ☐

Note: Cover will commence at 4pm local time on the above date unless specified by NTI Express.

Proposer Details

* Name of the Proposer: ______

ABN Number: ______

*Trading Name: ______

*Phone Number: ______ Mobile Phone Number : ______

*Street No & Name: ______

*Suburb: ______

*Postcode: ______

Email Address: ______

Trailers in Control

* If you have been quoted for Trailer in Control, do you require cover to be placed on the quoted Trailer in Control items: Select ▾

No Claim Bonus

* Are you entitled to a No Claim Bonus? Select ▾

*Name of Previous Insurer: ______

*Name of Policy Owner: ______

*Policy Number: ______ * Expiry Date: dd mm yy

*Vehicle Insured: ______

(or "As Above" if applicable)

Liability Cover

* If NTI Express has quoted you for Liability Cover, do you require Liability Cover? Select ▾

Marine Cargo Cover

* If NTI Express has quoted you for Marine Cargo Cover, do you require Marine Cargo Cover? Select ▾

Business Interruption Cover

* If NTI Express has quoted you for Business Interruption Cover, do you require Business Interruption Cover? Select ▾

Submit Cover

* Intermediary Email Address: ______

Print Form Send

RELIANCE General Insurance

Anil Dhirubhai Ambani Group

A Reliance Capital Company

1800 3002 8282 (toll free)
3989 8282 (local charges apply)
www.reliancegeneral.co.in

Proposal Form for Reliance Marine Cargo Policy

The policy does not commence until the proposal is accepted and premium paid

Specimen

Intermediary Details (To be filled in BLOCK LETTERS)

Intermediary Name ______ Code ______

Branch Name ______ Code ______

Sales Manager Name ______ Code ______

Personal Details

1. Name of the Proposer M/s ______
2. Address
   Flat Building ______
   Road/Street/Sector ______
   Area ______
   Taluka/Village/District City ______ Pin Code ______
   State ______ Country ______
3. Customer ID, if any ______
   Contact Person, if any ______ Phone ______
   Email ______

Cargo Details

In addition to questions i to ix, you are also required to answer questions x and xi only in case of specific policy and questions xii, xiii and xiv only in case of policies other than specific policy.

4. Goods proposed for insurance ______
5. Specify whether New or Secondhand ______
6. Packing used ______
7. Conveyance(s) ______
8. Containerization details ______
9. Terms of Sale ______
10. RR/GR/BL/AWB No. and date, if any ______
11. Details of the carrying vessel/vehicle such as name/no. and name of the transporter ______
12. Basis of valuation ______
13. Value of Cargo ______
14. Sum proposed for Insurance ______
15. Annual turnover ______
16. Limit per sending ______
17. Limit per location ______

Cover Details

18. Type of Policy required (Please tick whichever is applicable)
    1. Specific Policy/Open Policy ______
    2. Others (Please specify): ______

Reliance General Insurance Co. Ltd. Registere Office 19, Reliance Centre, Watchand Hirachand Marg, Ballard Estate, Mumbai 400 001

19. Voyage details [d|d|m|m|y|y|y|y] To [d|d|m|m|y|y|y|y]
20. Distance less than 100 kms ☐ Yes ☐ No
21. Policy period [| | | | | | |] To [| | | | | | |]
22. Multi transit involved ☐ Yes ☐ No
23. Is storage extension required? ____________________
24. Periodicity of Declaration (other than specific policy) ☐ Monthly ☐ Quarterly ☐ Others
25. Type of Cover (Please specify) ____________________
26. Do you wish to bear a protion of each and every loss (voluntary excess): ☐ Yes ☐ No
If YES, please specify the % of loss: ____________________

Claims Experience: (For last three years excluding current year)

Department	Year	Cover	Premium (Rs.)	Claims (Rs.) Paid	Outstanding
Marine					
Total					
Other than Marine					
Total					

Others

27. Has any other insurer refused to accept this insurance or imposed conditions to accept the same. If YES, give details, ____________________
28. Rate of premium charged by previous Insurer, if any. ____________________

Payment Details

☐ Cheque ☐ DD

Cheque or DD Amount [| | | | |] /- Amount in words (____________________)

Bank Name [| | | | | | | | | | | | | | | | | | | | | | | |]

Cheque/DD No. [| | | | | | | | | |] Cheque/DD Date [d|d|m|m|y|y|y|y]

Declaration

Duty of disclosure: The policy shall be void and all premium paid shall be forfeited to the Company in the event of misrepresentation, mis-description or non disclosure of any material fact.

I/We declare that the answers given by me/us are true and correct and that I/We have not with held any information, which might influence acceptance of this proposal. I/We agree that this declaration and the answers given by me/us shall be the basis of the insurance contract between me/us and Reliance General Insurance Company Limited and shall deemed to be incorporated in the policy.

I/We agree and undertake to covey to Reliance General Insurance Company Limited any additions/alterations carried out in the risk proposed for insurance after submission of this proposal form.

Place : ____________________

Date : ____________________

Signature of the Proposer

Prohibition of rebates-Section 41 of The Insurance Act 1938

1. No person shall allow or offer to allow, either directly or indirectly, as an inducement to any person to take out or renew or continue an insurance in respect of any kind or risk relating to lives or property in India, any rebate of the whole or part of the commission payable or any rebate of the premium shown on the policy, nor shall any person taking out or renewing or continuing a policy accept any rebate, except such rebate as may be allowed in accordance with the published prospectuses or tables of the insurer.

2. Any person making default in complying with the provisions of this section shall be punishable with fine which may extend to Rs. 500/-

Allianz

Marine
Commercial

Marine Hull/Liability Claim Form

The supply and acceptance of this form is not to be implied as as admission of liability on the part of Allianz.

Claim Number

Name of Insured
Contact Person
Home Phone No. Work Phone No. Mobile No.
Email
Postal Address
Post code
Broker/Agent Phone No.
Policy No. Excess $
Inception Date Expiry Date

Interested Parties : Is the vessel being claimed for under a Financial Agreement? Yes ☐ No ☐
Name of Financier

G.S.T. : Are you registered for GST purposes Yes ☐ No ☐ A.B.N.
To what extent are you entitled to claim an Input Tax Credit on the GST for this policy?
To what extent are you entitled to claim an Input Tax Credit on the GST for this vessel?

Details of Insured Vessel:
Vessel Name Registration No. Sail No.
Type of Vessel Motor Make Serial No.
Motor Type Inboard ☐ Outboard ☐ Petrol ☐ Diesel ☐
Is there any other Insurance Policy that would indemnify you in respect of this accident? Yes ☐ No ☐
If Yes, give details

Details of Damage to Insured Vessel:
Where can Vessel be inspected?
Name of Repairer
Address
Postcode
Telephone No. Estimate of Repair Costs $
Prior to this incident, was the Vessel in a fit condition to be used and seaworthy? Yes ☐ No ☐
Give Details

Details of Person in Charge of Vessel:
Name
Relationship to you Age Years
Address
Postcode
Phone No. (Home) Phone No. (work) Mobile No.
Boat Licence No. Expiry Date Place of Issue

Specimen

Marine

CLM008 01/04
Allianz Australia Insurance Limited AFS Licence No. 234708 ABN 15 000 122 850 Registered Office: 2 Market Street Sydney NSW 2000

Does the Person have any physical defect or infirmity in limbs, eyesight, or hearing, or have they ever suffered from a fit of any kind? Yes ☐ No ☐

If Yes, give details ____________________

Was the Person injured? ____________________

If Yes, give details ____________________

Particulars of Incident Date ________ Time ________ am/pm

Place of Incident ____________________

Estimated Speed at Time of Accident ________ Km/Hour

Estimated Speed of other Craft at time of Accident ________ Km/Hour

Speed Limit in area of the Accident ________ Km/Hour

Give a general description of the Accident with all the Circumstances and particulars

Diagram of Location of Accident/Loss (show direction of Vessels, Wind, Tide, etc.)

Personal Injury: Name of Injured Person ________ Occupation ________

Age ________ Years Sex Male ☐ Female ☐

Address ____________________

________ Postcode ________

Phone No. (Home) ________ Phone No. (work) ________ Mobile No. ________

Vessel Name ________ Registration No. ________ Sail No. ________

Describe where they were and how they were injured ____________________

Was treatment given at the scene of the incident? Yes ☐ No ☐

If Yes, by whom (if ambulance or doctor, give details) ____________________

Was transport provided to hospital Yes ☐ No ☐

Details of Other Vessel

Vessel Name ________ Registration No. ________ Sail No. ________

Type of Vessel ________ Motor Make ________ Serial No. ________

Motor Type Inboard ☐ Outboard ☐ Petrol ☐ Diesel ☐

Owner's Name ____________________

Address ____________________

________ Postcode ________

Name of the Insurer (if known) ____________________

Were there any passengers in the Other Vessel? Yes ☐ No ☐ How many? ________

Damage to Other Vessel or Property (Do Not Approach the Other Party to obtain this information)

Details of Damage ______________________________

____

Has a Claim been made to you by a Third Party? Yes ☐ No ☐

If Yes, give details ______________________________

____

Person(s) injured in other Vessel

Name ______________________________

Injury Details ______________________________

____

Name ______________________________

Injury Details ______________________________

____

If you have received any written communication, do not answer. Please attach it to this Form.

Witness: Were there any witnesses to the even? Yes☐ No☐ (if yes, please complete the following)

Name ______________________________

Address ______________________________

______________________________ Postcode ________

Phone No. (Home) ________ Phone No. (work) ________ Mobile No. ________

Where was the witness? ______________________________

Notifying Authority: Has the Accident or loss been reported to a Police or Maritime Services Officer? Yes ☐ No ☐

Name of Officer ________ Time reported ________ am/pm Date ________

Police Station ________ Police Report/MSB No. ________

In your opinion, who was at fault? ______________________________

Why? (Give details) ______________________________

____

Has the person responsible ever had their licence endorsed, suspended or cancelled?

Yes ☐ No ☐ If Yes, give details.

____

____

Was any liquor consumed by the person during the 12 hours before the accident?

Yes☐ No☐ If Yes, give details.

____

____

History:

Have you or the person in charge of the vessel had any insurance or renewal of insurance declined or cancelled or special conditions imposed in the last 5 years? Yes ☐ No ☐

Have you or the person in charge had an accident or made a claim on a marine insurance policy in the last 5 years? Yes ☐ No ☐

Have you or the person in charge been charged or convicted of any boating or marine offence in the last 5 years? Yes ☐ No ☐

Have you or the person in charge been charged or convicted of any criminal offence? Yes ☐ No ☐

If Yes to any history questions, please give details

____

____

____

Privacy: The Privacy Act 1988 requires us to tell you that as an insurer we collect your personal and sensitive information in order to calculate your loss and entitlements, determine our liability, compile data and handle claims.

When handling claims, we may have to disclose your personal and other information to third parties such as other insurers, reinsurers, loss adjusters, external claims data collectors, investigators and agents or other parties as required by law.

You have the right to seek access to your personal information and to correct it at any time. Please contact us on 1300 360 529 EST 9am-5pm Monday-Friday and advise us of the changes.

IDR Statement: Disputes are not an everyday occurrence at Allianz. However we do provide an internal dispute resolution process should any dispute arise. Please feel free to ask for details.

If You are not satisfied with the outcome of this process, we will advise you how to contact the insurance industry's external independent complaints scheme (subject to eligibility).

Declaration: I/We certify that the information given in this form is truthful, accurate and complete. No information likely to affect this claim has been with held. I/We understand that this claim may be refused if information is untrue, inaccurate or concealed.

I/We acknowledge that I/we have read and understood the Privacy Act 1988 information referred to above and consent to the collection, storage, use and disclosure of personal and sensitive information of all persons affected by this claim, with their approval. I/we acknowledge that if I/we do not agree to the collection of this personal and sensitive information then Allianz will be unable to process my/our claim.

Signature of Insured ____________________ Date ____________

Signature of Vessel Operator ____________________ Date ____________

42

INSURANCE INNOVATION

Innovation of Insurance business has taken accelerated development in India since 2000. It has been observed by international agencies, too. All the insurers in India are busy with New Product Development, Underwriting Simplification and Distribution strategies. The Government is cautious about fraud and misappropriation by insurers as well as insureds. Regulations are being framed by IRDA in India to safeguard the policyholders' interest and facilitate insurance development.

PRODUCT DEVELOPMENT

Different customers have different types of insurance needs for life, property and general interest. The product development has helped development of life insurance spectacularly as was never expected. There are abundant opportunities of development of property and general insurance, too. The Product Development has been analysed under Life Insurance and Non-Life Insurance.

LIFE INSURANCE

The premium income of life insurance has touched the highest ever level of Rs. 49,474 crore in 2005-2006 as compared to Rs. 25,316 crore in 2004-2005 and Rs. 17,716 crore in 2003–2004. The growth rate was 95.4 per cent in 2005-2006 and 34.4 per cent in 2004-2005. The main contribution for this phenomenal growth is because of individual insurance which was Rs. 23,528 crore in 2005-2006 and Rs. 6,332 crore in 2004-2005. Out of these, the non-single premium was Rs. 33,468 crore in 2005-2006 and Rs. 15,034 crore in 2004-2005. The linked policy explained Rs. 29,164 crore premium in 2005-2006 and Rs. 7981 crore in 2004-2005. It reveals the popularity of linked policies.

Link policy concept is expected to be more popular in future as it has the benefits of life-cum-investment cover. People are interested in investment mainly. On the other hand the potential market is waiting for cheap policies to cover risk only. Insurers are trying to develop life policies to cover the risk only.

Price: The potential buyers are looking for cheaper product. The risk cover policies are the cheapest. The premium is decided on the basis of mortality, interest and expenses. The mortality is natural factor wherein, the insurers can do nothing in this regard. The interest should be increased and expenses should be curtailed to minimise the premium rate. With the success of unit-linked insurance, the efficiency of the insurers count a lot in managing premium rate in the era of competition.

Process: Product development is outcome of opportunities available in the market. New products are introduced and developed to meet the competitive challenges and changes. Product development process involves analysis of environment, idea generation, market research, production concepts, process design, testing, product modification and launch. Insurers go through the process and adopt the product development promotion strategies for enhancing the business. In India, product development increased dramatically from various product line of whole life, endowment and term insurance. The market research and environment analysis explore the product mixed to be launched by the insurer. The legal framework, consumer demand and behaviour, competitive stage, economic and political conditions and social needs are the important factors to be considered under product innovation.

The product development is broadly divided into non-linked policies and linked policies which are further sold under individual business single premium, individual business non-single premium, group new business single premium and group new business non-single premium.

Table 42.1 Individual New Business Single Premium

(Rs. in Crores)

	Premium (Rs.)		Policies in Lakhs		Sum Assured (Rs.)	
Non-Linked	*2004-05*	*2005-06*	*2004-05*	*2005-06*	*2004-05*	*2005-06*
	1	*2*	*3*	*4*	*5*	*6*
1. Life						
(*a*) With Profit	396.99	242.34	0.44	0.32	534.24	367.53
(*b*) Without Profit	380.52	1,259.47	1.68	4.71	1,810.62	4,489.36
2. General Annuity						
(*a*) With Profit	0.27	0.40	—	—	0.44	0.78
(*b*) Without Profit	0.26	1.44	—	—	—	—
3. Pension						
(*a*) With Profit	129.32	62.13	0.75	0.12	4.49	1.46
(*b*) Without Profit	56.56	125.90	0.03	.03	0.39	1.81
4. Health						
(*a*) With Profit	—	—	—	—	—	—
(*b*) Without Profit	—	—	—	—	—	—
A. Sub Total	963.92	1,691.68	2.90	5.18	2,350.39	4,860.94
Linked						
1. Life						
(*a*) With Profit	0.71	0.05	—	—	0.72	0.04
(*b*) Without Profit	2,861.43	2,950.91	5.72	3.39	3,587.87	3,625.06
2. General Annuity						
(*a*) With Proifit	—	—	—	—	—	—
(*b*) Without Profit	—	0.63	—	—	—	—
3. Pension						
(*a*) With Profit	—	—	—	—	—	—
(*b*) Without Profit	2,078.06	6,355.33	9.45	18.39	10.73	5.17
4. Health						
(*a*) With Profit	—	—	—	—	—	—
(*b*) Without Profit	—	—	—	—	—	—
B. Sub Total	4,940.20	9,306.93	15.16	21.79	3,599.33	3,630.27
C. Total (A + B)	5,904.12	10,998.61	18.55	26.96	5,949.72	8,491.22

Source: IRDA Journal, Aug. 2006 / June 2007

First Year Premium of the Insurers for the Year Ended March 2007 (Provisional & Unaudited)

Individual Single Premium (Including Rural & Social)

(Rs. in Crore)

S. No.	Particulars	Premium Mar 2006	Premium Mar 2007	Policies Mar 2006	Policies Mar 2007	Sum Assured Mar 2006	Sum Assured Mar 2007
1.	**Non linked**						
	Life						
	with profit	242.34	291.20	31601	26200	367.53	386.87
	without profit	1259.47	784.28	470784	485730	4489.36	3987.38
2.	**General Annuity**						
	with profit	0.40	0.00	10	0	0.78	0.00
	without profit	1.44	12.55	145	642	0.00	0.68
3.	**Pension**						
	with profit	62.13	159.57	11567	10178	1.46	2.52
	without profit	125.90	2.26	3532	100	1.82	1.95
4.	**Health**						
	with profit	0.00	0.00	0	0	0.00	0.00
	without profit	0.00	0.00	0	0	0.00	0.00
A.	**Sub total**	1691.68	1249.85	517639	522850	4860.95	4379.40
	Linked						
1.	**Life**						
	with profit	0.05	0.00	5	1	0.05	0.00
	without profit	2950.91	4342.15	339740	764066	3625.06	7062.59
2.	**General Annuity**						
	with profit	0.00	0.00	0	0	0.00	0.00
	without profit	0.63	1.20	0	0	0.00	0.00
3.	**Pension**						
	with profit	0.00	0.00	0	0	0.00	0.00
	without profit	6355.33	17952.47	1839374	5430530	5.17	3.63
4.	**Health**						
	with profit	0.00	0.00	0	0	0.00	0.00
	without profit	0.00	0.00	0	0	0.00	0.00
B.	**Sub total**	9306.93	22295.83	2179119	6194597	3630.28	7066.22
C.	**Total (A + B)**	10998.61	23545.68	2696758	6717447	8491.23	11445.61
	Riders:						
	Non linked						
1.	Health	0.03	0.04	21	32	0.33	0.57
2.	Accident	0.18	0.06	1755	1050	12.47	7.07
3.	Term	0.03	0.01	135	33	0.82	0.25
4.	Others	0.00	0.00	0	0	0.00	0.00
D.	**Sub total**	0.24	0.10	1911	1115	13.63	7.90
	Linked						
1.	Health	0.04	0.04	59	89	0.78	1.04
2.	Accident	0.09	0.16	357	13043	8.10	84.56
3.	Term	0.00	0.00	4	8	0.05	0.12
4.	Others	0.00	0.00	0	0	0.00	0.00
E.	**Sub total**	0.14	0.20	420	13140	8.92	85.72
F.	**Total (D + E)**	0.38	0.31	2331	14255	22.55	93.62
G.	**Grand Total (C + F)**	**10998.99**	**23545.99**	**2696758**	**6717447**	**8513.77**	**11539.23**

Individual Non-Single Premium (Including rural & Social)

(*Rs. in Crore*)

S. No.	Particulars	Premium Mar 2006	Premium Mar 2007	Policies Mar 2006	Policies Mar 2007	Sum Assured Mar 2006	Sum Assured Mar 2007
	Non linked						
1.	**Life**						
	with profit	12819.57	16484.03	28409713	21169366	266239.86	201760.82
	without profit	702.42	1930.10	2087776	1048344	41343.05	24442.02
2.	**General Annuity**						
	with profit	0.86	0.23	845	242	15.54	4.13
	without profit	0.00	0.00	0	0	0.00	0.00
3.	**Pension**						
	with profit	70.87	48.61	52458	25323	294.28	187.93
	without profit	8.84	21.23	3649	6337	0.00	0.00
4.	**Health**						
	with profit	0.00	0.00	0	0	0.00	0.00
	without profit	7.37	27.88	34020	169703	1166.45	7604.73
A.	**Sub total**	13609.93	18512.07	30588461	22419315	309059.18	233999.62
	Linked						
1.	**Life**						
	with profit	0.97	0.18	330	87	6.71	1.96
	without profit	5676.56	16627.45	1950273	15704231	48030.97	215674.25
2.	**General Annuity**						
	with profit	0.00	0.00	0	0	0.00	0.00
	without profit	117.74	0.00	72527	0	224.42	0.00
3.	**Pension**						
	with profit	0.22	0.09	49	8	0.00	0.00
	without profit	452.80	2737.74	132032	1287337	51.32	1694.83
4.	**Health**						
	with profit	0.00	0.00	0	0	0.00	0.00
	without profit	0.00	0.00	0	0	0.00	0.00
B.	**Sub total**	6248.28	19365.45	2155211	16991663	48313.43	217371.03
C.	**Total (A + B)**	19858.22	37877.53	32743672	39410978	357372.60	451370.66
	Riders:						
	Non linked						
1.	Health	5.28	3.77	31807	20553	406.32	287.96
2.	Accident	9.31	6.79	417513	419127	8631.99	6969.34
3.	Term	1.37	0.53	24272	8884	221.00	95.09
4.	Others	5.53	17.65	10185	4814	434.84	2466.35
D.	**Sub total**	21.49	28.73	483777	453378	9694.15	9818.74
	Linked						
1.	Health	3.53	5.33	15119	18806	945.28	601.54
2.	Accident	3.78	7.96	87687	192737	1530.88	10907.00
3.	Term	0.87	1.70	8999	20881	189.19	585.88
4.	Others	1.16	1.27	22886	22573	25.09	1095.28
E.	**Sub total**	9.34	16.25	134691	254997	2690.43	13189.70
F.	**Total (D + E)**	30.83	44.99	618468	708375	12384.58	23008.44
G.	**Grand Total (C + F)**	**19889.04**	**37922.51**	**32743672**	**39410978**	**369757.18**	**474379.10**

Table 42.2 Individual New Business-Non Single Premium

(Rs. in Crores)

	Premium (Rs.)		*Policies in Lakhs*		*Sum Assured (Rs.)*	
	2004-05	*2005-06*	*2004-05*	*2005-06*	*2004-05*	*2005-06*
1	*2*	*3*	*4*	*5*	*6*	*7*
None-Linked						
(*a*) With profit	10,680.77	12,819.51	211.54	284.10	1,69,480.55	2,66,239.86
(*b*) Without Profit	740.55	702.42	14.05	20.88	27,122.63	41,343.05
General Annuity						
(*a*) With Profit	4.39	0.86	0.05	—	96.54	15.54
(*b*) Without Profit	—	—	—	—	—	—
Pension						
(*a*) With Profit	448.22	70.87	4.11	0.52	852.46	294.28
(*b*) Without Profit	—	8.84	—	0.03	—	—
Health						
(a) With Profit	115.79	—	2.32	—	2,739.00	—
(*b*) Without Profit	3.19	7.36	0.16	0.34	246.06	1166.45
A. Sub Total	11,992.92	13,609.93	232.23	305.88	2,00,537.26	3,09,059.18
Linked						
1. Life						
(*a*) With Profit	7.70	0.96	0.03	—	69.51	6.71
(*b*) Without Profit	2,599.84	5,676.56	8.02	19.50	21,454.06	48,030.96
2. General Annuity						
(*a*) With Profit						
(*b*) Without Profit	220.96	117.74	2.10	0.73	445.86	224.42
3. Pension						
(*a*) With Profit	2.35	0.22	—	—	—	—
(*b*) Without Profit	210.31	452.80	1.43	1.32	171.95	51.32
4. Health						
(*a*) With Profit	—	—	—	—	—	—
(*b*) Without Profit	—	—	—	—	—	—
Sub Total	3,041.16	6,248.28	11.58	21.55	22,141.38	48,313.42
Total (A + B)	15,034.08	19,858.22	243.81	327.44	2,22,678.64	3,57,372.60

Table 42.3 Group New Business-Single Premium

(Rs. in Crores)

Non-Linked	Premium (Rs.)		No. of Schemes		Lives Covered		Sum Assured (Rs.)	
	2004-05	2005-06	2004-05	2005-06	2004-05	2005-06	2004-05	2005-06
1	2	3	4	5	6	7	8	9
1. Life								
(a) **Group Gratuity Schemes**								
(i) With Profit	—	—	—	—	—	—	—	—
(ii) Without Profit	1042.83	1581.90	2203	2167	570718	766005	2848.61	3364.70
(b) **Group Savings Linked Schemes**								
(i) With Profit	—	—	—	—	—	—	—	—
(ii) Without Profit	18.75	58.25	675	1835	135101	502607	1266.79	4664.91
(c) **EDLI**								
(i) With Profit	—	—	—	—	—	—	—	—
(ii) Without Profit	2.73	5.47	990	1213	543330	718411	1595.44	3122.57
(d) **Others**								
(i) With Profit	—	—	—	—	—	—	—	—
(ii) Without Profit	529.78	574.51	14522	13051	7412858	10220727	36941.14	47257.92
2. General Annuity								
(i) With Profit	850.53	672.02	7	5	57.80	38.26	—	—
(ii) Without Profit	591.46	735.13	10	22	11284	7974	—	—
3. Pension								
(i) With Profit	—	—	—	—	—	—	—	—
(ii) Without Profit	964.93	678.70	214	113	25889	59599	—	—
4. Health (No pension)								
A. Sub Total	4001.02	4305.99	18621	18406	8704960	12279149	42651.99	58390.10
Linked								
1. Life								
(a) **Group Gratuity Schemes**								
(i) With Profit	—	—	—	—	—	—	—	—
(ii) Without Profit	4.91	86.85	12	24	1021	45962	0.08	4.60
(b) **Group Savings Linked Schemes**								
(i) With Profit	—	—	—	—	—	—	—	—
(ii) Without Profit	—	—	—	—	—	—	—	—
(c) **EDLI (No Business)**	—	—	—	—	—	—	—	—
(d) **Others**								
(i) With Profit	—	—	—	—	—	—	—	—
(ii) Without Profit	3.98	3.63	2	1	1623	352	0.17	0.03
2. General Annuity								
(i) With Profit	—	—	—	—	—	—	—	—
(ii) Without Profit	3.14	—	—	—	14	—	3.03	—
3. Pension								
(i) With Profit	—	—	—	—	—	—	—	—
(ii) Without Profit	1.82	8.66	1	3	10	3936	—	—
4. Health (No Business)	—	—	—	—	—	—	—	—
B. Sub Total	13.86	99.14	15	28	2668	50250	3.28	4.63
C. Total	4014.88	4405.13	18636	18434	8707628	12329399	42655.27	58394.73

Source: indicates no business.

First Year Premium of Life Insurance for the Year Ended March 2007 (Provisional & Unaudited)
Group Single Premium (Including Rural & Social)

(Rs. in Crore)

S. No.	*Particulars*	*Premium* *Mar 2006*	*Mar 2007*	*No. of Schemes* *Mar 2006*	*Mar 2007*	*Lives Covered* *Mar 2006*	*Mar 2007*	*Sum Assured* *Mar 2006*	*Mar 2007*
	Non linked*								
1.	Life								
a)	Group Gratuity Schemes								
	with profit	0.00	0.00	0	0	0	0	0.00	0.00
	without profit	1581.190	2473.23	2167	2287	766005	926223	3364.70	4086.88
b)	Group Savings Linked Schemes								
	with profit	0.00	0.00	0	0	0	0	0.00	0.00
	without profit	58.25	30.89	1835	1022	502607	281244	4644.91	2163.39
c)	EDLI								
	with profit	0.00	0.00	0	0	0	0	0.00	0.00
	without profit	5.47	5.69	1213	1047	718411	923126	3122.57	2585.38
d)	Others								
	with profit	0.00	0.00	0	0	0	0	0.00	0.00
	without profit	574.51	6477.96	13051	16296	10220727	12708409	47257.92	25847093
2.	General Annuity								
	with profit	672.02	1039.19	5	9	3826	3525	0.00	0.00
	without profit	735.13	883.32	22	61	7974	11275	0.00	0.00
3.	Pension								
	with profit	0.00	0.00	0	0	0	0	0.00	0.00
	without profit	678.70	1173.17	113	239	59599	101111	0.00	0.00
4.	Health								
	with profit	0.00	0.00	0	0	0	0	0.00	0.00
	without profit	0.00	0.00	0	0	0	0	0.00	0.00
A.	Sub total	4305.99	12083.45	18406	20961	12279149	14954913	58390.11	267306.58
	Linked*								
1.	Life								
a)	Group Gratuity Schemes								
	with profit	0.00	0.00	0	0	0	0	0.00	0.00
	without profit	86.85	233.14	24	88	45962	200027	4.60	629.76
b)	Group Savings Linked Schemes								
	with profit	0.00	0.00	0	0	0	0	0.00	0.00
	without profit	0.00	0.00	0	0	0	0	0.00	0.00
c)	EDLI								
	with profit	0.00	0.00	0	0	0	0	0.00	0.00
	without profit	0.00	0.00	0	0	0	0	0.00	0.00
d)	Others								
	with profit	0.00	0.00	0	0	0	0	0.00	0.00
	without profit	3.63	15.62	1	4	352	13225	0.04	1.32
2.	General Annuity								
	with profit	0.00	0.00	0	0	0	0	0.00	0.00
	without profit	0.00	0.00	0	0	0	0	0.00	0.00
3.	Pension								
	with profit	0.00	0.00	0	0	0	0	0.00	0.00
	without profit	8.66	89.15	3	18	3936	12448	0.00	0.00
4.	Health with profit	0.00	0.00	0	0	0	0	0.00	0.00
	without profit	0.00	0.00	0	0	0	0	0.00	0.00
B.	Sub total	99.14	337.90	28	110	50250	225700	4.63	631.09
C.	Total (A + B)	4405.13	12421.35	18434	21071	12329399	15180613	58394.74	267937.67
	Riders:								
	Non linked								
1.	Health#	0.37	0.40	25	19	18228	9237	344.21	0.00
2.	Accident##	0.75	0.28	21	39	37362	23415	1994.04	0.00
3.	Term	0.00	0.00	0	0	0	0	0.00	0.00
4.	Others	0.00	0.00	0	0	0	0	0.00	0.00
D.	Sub total	1.11	0.68	46	58	55590	32652	2338.25	0.00
	Linked								
1.	Health#	0.00	0.00	0	0	0	0	0.00	0.00
2.	Accident# #	0.00	0.00	0	0	0	0	0.00	0.00
3.	Term	0.00	0.00	0	0	0	0	0.00	0.00
4.	Others	0.00	0.00	0	0	0	0	0.00	0.00
E.	Sub total	0.00	0.00	0	0	0	0	0.00	0.00
F.	Total (D + E)	1.11	0.68	46	58	55590	32652	2338.25	0.00
G.	**Grand Total (C + F)	4406.24	12422.04	18434	21071	12329399	15180613	60732.99	267937.67

* Excluding rider figures : ** for no. of schemes & lives covered Ground Total is C. # All riders related to critical illness benefit, hospitalisation benefit and medical treatment. # # Disability related riders. The Premium is actual amount received and not annualised premium. Complied on the basis of data submitted by the Insurance companies

Group New Business – Non - Single Premium (Including Rural & Social)

(Rs. in Crore)

S. No.	Particulars	Premium		No. of Scheme		Lives Covered		Sum Assured	
		Mar 2006	Mar 2007	Mar 2006	Mar 2007	Mar 2006	Mar 2007	Mar 2006	Mar 2007
	Non linked*								
1.	Life								
a)	Group Gratuity Schemes								
	with profit	0.00	0.00	0	0	0	0	0.00	0.00
	without profit	126.60	247.96	56	59	58456	95517	370.57	346.49
b)	Group Savings Linked Schemes								
	with profit	0.00	0.00 .	0	0	0	0	0.00	0.00
	without profit	0.14	44.34	6	0	7543	446142	153.10	7221.68
c)	EDLI								
	with profit	0.00	0.00	0	0	0	0	0.00	0.00
	without profit	5.22	5.79	272	282	402135	420048	3330.62	3599.31
d)	Others								
	with profit	0.66	0.00	29	0	35994	0	408.24	0.00
	without profit	63.36	314.68	2539	1195	2075517	3348604	32364.88	61621.13
2.	General Annuity								
	with profit	0.00	0.00	0	0	0	0	0.00	0.00
	without profit	0.00	0.00	0	0	0	0	0.00	0.00
3.	Pension								
	with profit	0.00	0.00	0	0	0	0	0.00	0.00
	without profit	0.75	5.97	1	4	885	79	2.18	0.00
4.	Health								
	with profit	0.00	0.00	0	0	0	0	0.00	0.00
	without profit	0.00	0.00	0	0	0	0	0.00	0.00
A.	Sub total	196.73	618.74	2903	1540	2580530	4310390	36629.60	72788.61
	Linked*								
1.	Life								
a)	Group Gratuity Schemes								
	with profit	0.00	0.00	0	0	0	0	0.00	0.00
	without profit	222.17	473.52	253	369	257452	361554	705.32	2122.81
b)	Group Savings Linked Schemes								
	with profit	0.00	0.00	0	0	0	0	0.00	0.00
	without profit	0.00	0.00	0	0	0	0	0.00	0.00
c)	EDLI								
	with profit	0.00	0.00	0	0	0	0	0.00	0.00
	without profit	0.00	0.00	0	0	0	0	0.00	0.00
d)	Others								
	with profit	0.00	0.00	0	0	0	0	0.00	0.00
	without profit	4.24	11.39	13	14	249	167	1.79	1.97
2.	General Annuity								
	with profit	0.00	0.00	0	0	0	0	0.00	0.00
	without profit	15.59	38.26	11	12	906	2547	15.59	38.26
3.	Pension								
	with profit	0.00	0.00	0	0	0	0	0.00	0.00
	without profit	164.32	372.35	73	135	12549	62451	0.00	0.00
4.	Health								
	with profit	0.00	0.00	0	0	0	0	0.00	0.00
	without profit	0.00	0.00	0	0	0	0	0.00	0.00
B.	Sub total	406.32	895.52	350	530	271156	426719	722.69	2163.04
C.	Total (A + B)	603.05	1514.26	3253	2070	2851686	4737109	37352.29	74951.65
	Riders:								
	Non linked								
1.	Health #	0.15	0.34	7	21	1496	14141	124.08	601.01
2.	Accident # #	0.46	0.67	52	34	60348	46185	1807.32	1936.96
3.	Term	0.00	0.00	1	1	153	114	5.03	8.03
4.	Others	0.01	0.01	1	5	32	3987	20.67	216.56
D.	Sub total	0.63	1.02	61	61	62029	64427	1957.10	2762.55
	Linked								
1.	Health #	0.00	0.00	0	0	0	0	0.00	0.00
2.	Accident # #	0.00	0.70	0	47	0	48838	0.00	1635.54
3.	Term	0.00	0.00	0	0	0	0	0.00	0.00
4.	Others	0.00	0.00	0	0	0	0	0.00	0.00
E.	Sub total	0.00	0.70	0	47	0	48838	0.00	1635.54
F.	Total (D + E)	0.63	1.72	61	108	62029	113265	1957.10	4398.10
G.	** Grand total (C + F)	603.68	1515.98	3253	2070	2851686	4737109	39309.39	79349.75

Table 42.4 Group New Business — Non-Single Premium

(Rs. in Crores)

	Premium (Rs.)		*No. of Schemes*		*Lives Covered*		*Sum Assured (Rs.)*	
	2004-05	*2005-06*	*2004-05*	*2005-06*	*2004-05*	*2005-06*	*2004-05*	*2005-06*
1	*2*	*3*	*4*	*5*	*6*	*7*	*8*	*9*
Non-Linked								
1. Life								
(*a*) **Group Gratuity Schemes**								
(*i*) With Profit	—	—	—	—	—	—	—	—
(*ii*) Without Profit	25.78	126.60	26	56	13975	58456	40.76	370.57
(*b*) **Group Savings Linked Schemes**								
(*i*) With Profit	—	—	—	—	—	—	—	—
(*ii*) Without Profit	17.59	0.14	1	6	24240	7543	913.78	153.10
(*c*) **EDLI**								
(*i*) With Profit	0.74	—	57	—	29293	—	297.26	—
(*ii*) Without Profit	5.39	5.22	205	272	278770	402135	2256.31	3330.62
(*d*) **Others**								
(*i*) With Profit	0.41	0.66	25	29	29361	35994	302.52	408.24
(*ii*) Without Profit	58.66	63.36	4197	2539	1724647	2075517	18639.65	32364.88
2. General Annuity								
(*i*) With Profit	—	—	—	—	—	—	—	—
(*ii*) Without Profit	—	—	3	—	1766	—	8.54	—
3. Pension								
(*i*) With Profit	—	—	—	—	—	—	—	—
(*ii*) Without Profit	2.94	0.75	7	1	226	885	—	2.18
4. Health (No Business)	—	—	—	—	—	—	—	—
A. Sub Total	111.52	196.73	4521	2903	2102278	2580530	22458.83	36629.60
Linked								
1. Life								
(*a*) **Group Gratuity Schemes**								
(*i*) With Profit								
(*ii*) Without Profit	179.23	222.17	171	253	135115	257452	217.94	705.32
(*b*) **Group Savings Linked Schemes (No Business)**								
(*c*) **EDLI (No Business)**								
(*d*) **Others**								
(*i*) With Profit	—	—	—	—	—	—	—	—
(*ii*) Without Profit	3.55	4.24	10	13	179	249	12.75	1.79
2. General Annuity								
(*i*) With Profit (No Business)								
(*ii*) Without Profit	25.78	15.59	7	11	1994	906	25.78	15.59
3. Pension								
(*i*) With Profit	—	—	—	—	—	—	—	—
(*ii*) Without Profit	43.95	164.32	64	73	9964	12549	17.50	—
4. Health (No Business)	—	—	—	—	—	—	—	—
B. Sub Total	252.52	406.32	252	350	147252	271156	263.97	722.69
C. Total (A + B)	364.04	603.05	4773	3253	2249530	2851686	22722.80	37352.29

(–) Indicate No Business.

These four tables have revealed that life insurance is being diversified to meet different requirement of society. Health insurance is not becoming popular. The LIC has issued a large number of policies which are different degree mix of endowment and term insurance. On its anniversary, LIC issues some new policies in September of each year. Many of the policies are brand name starting with Jeevan *e.g.*, Jeevan Suraksha, Jeevan Kishore, Jeevan Sukanya, Jeevan Sneha, Jeevan Nidhi etc. Private sector insurers have been dependent on term insurance as it is the cheapest form of insurance.

NON-LIFE INSURANCE

Non-life insurance has invented new products to meet the different requirements of customers. The new products are Mediclaim Insurance, Terrorism cover, Janata Personal Accident, Insurance for plantations, cattle, pump sets, Hut Insurance, Social Security Scheme. Many insurers feel that it is prevalence of tariff coverage that prevented the growth of product innovation. The lack of market research, consumer behaviour, inability to identify customer needs and their buying habits and the lack of acturial talent in non-life insurance have inhibited promoting new products.

The future of market innovation lies mainly with the new players. The cost of operation will be reduced considerably. Bringing down transactional and distribution costs and adding value to current and future products are expected to popularise new products. Product innovation is bound to take off in a big way. It is another new game in the competitive arena, which would be more vigorously fought in the post-detariffication era. Insurers have to create need-based and differentiated products to suit various segments and within those segments, offer necessary choices and options to suit target customers. Design and pricing of products are based on certain basic requirements in the context of consumer choice, safety and competitions.

Role of NGO's and Self Help Groups

Insurance is expected to increase with the help of NGOs and Self Help Groups (SHGs). It is for the insurance to come forward to find out the SHGs who can undertake insurance business.

Risk Evaluation and Product Formation

The premium is fixed after proper evaluation of risk. Clear and transparent cover is valuable to the insured who get cover insurable risk. Standard clauses across policies should be used to help customer understanding. Products should be developed with the compliances of IRDA (Production of policyholders' Interests) Regulations 2002. Terms and conditions should be fair between the insurer and the insured. The product is innovated bases on the market needs and competitive position, The evaluation of risk bases on costs as stipulated by the acturial assessment. The product is sub-classified and segmented as per market requirements. Each product has operative clause, the schedule, exclusions, general conditions and warrantees. There are several other clauses such as cancellation, renewal, claim, settlement processes, dispute resolution and grievance redressal mechanisms.

Risk is insured on the basis of experience of rating or exposure rating based on circumstances, internal tariff rate, packaged products and insurance of large risks. In non-tariffed, rating is done on the basis of available data of industry, pricing decisions and policy terms, The acturial experience and rate components are evaluated to frame rate of the product. The pricing covers all costs and return on investment. The loss-calculation essential for determination of premium. The price cutting is resorted only in the hope of image-building which helps repositioning, repackaging of the product, used of temporary discounts, increased publicity and advertising.

Future of Product Development

The future of product development is very bright in the detariff era. Before pre-nationalisation period in 1972, the product development was not done as the insurers followed the practices of American and British insurers. After 1972, the entire conduct of insurance was vesting into the holding companies of the General Insurance Corporation of India. The GIC with the help of the Tariff Advisory Committee (TAC) regrouped the existing products in more than 130 products. It has introduced a lot of products. A Mediclaim Policy was introduced in 1980 with great success. During the post-liberalisation private companies brought new idea to the insurance industry and a lot of product has taken place.

The insurers have ample scope of designing new product and redesigning the old product to meet the individual requirements of the buyers. The future of non-life insurance exists in:

1. Combination of health and accident as well as life cover.
2. A first loss policy of households.
3. A multi-year policy for motor-vehicles.
4. Consequential loss policies.
5. Insurance of various products, property and business machines as well as industrial inputs and outputs.
6. Agricultural inputs, machine and outputs.
7. Work-in-progress of industrial and agro-bases industries.

UNDERWRITING

Underwriting is a process of accepting a risk, analysing the risks, framing terms and conditions and deciding the chargeable premium rate. It needs to know the risk features and factors of every risk offered for acceptance. Risk analysis determines the physical hazards and inherent moral hazards attacked to the cover of the products. Steps of risk management are adopted for underwriting purposes. Safety audit, staff drills, investigations and remedial steps are taken to prevent recurrence of risk. Moral hazard is minimised by staff-relations, compliance with legal enactments and affectiveness of corporate governance.

The acceptance of risks and pricing them has been the basic statutory function of the Tariff Advisory Committee (TAC) till detariffed market is governed by IRDA since January 1, 2007. The TAC has prescribed cover wordings and the minimum prices to be charged by insurers who breach them. The disciplinary standards are imposed by the TAC to safeguard the consumers' interest. The TAC has been working in India for more than 50 years. With liberalisation of market and entry of foreign players, the detariffication has started.

It has observed by the experience of 2005-2006 that only 6% claim has been reported in India as against 20 per cent losses in international markets. Only 1.2 lacks out of 32 lakhs insured persons reported for mediclaim. The claims paid as said by insurers are 120 per cent. Thus, the underwriting redesigning is needed for the purpose. The underwriting process is studied under life insurance, non-life insurance and detariffed era underwriting.

Life Insurance Underwriting

Life insurance underwriting is not merely selling of life insurance products. It is sold to those who qualify to be suitable person to buy insurance. It assesses proposers' needs, paying capacity and determining the price rate. Life insurance is embedded with an element of social responsibility with cooperative spirit. The risk qualifications and determination of price (premium-rate) for each class is essential function of underwriting. The insurer underwrites a policy to an insured by assessing his own experience of claims payment, expenses incurred and return on investment besides his ability to retain the risk and products.

In life insurance, underwriting is done by insurance agents or advisors. Based on the disclosures of the proposal forms, medical reports; the insurer may exercise his own investigation to insure the insurable risk. The underwriting takes two phases *i.e.,* financial underwriting and medical underwriting. The former deals with determining the eligible total amount of life assurance coverage. The latter deals with medical and diagnostic reports. There is need of close monitoring early death and should check the reasons of early death. The life insurance underwriting is based on mortality, expenses and interest.

Mortality: The cost of insurance depends on mortality insurers have to monitor whether the present tables of mortality and morbidity are in tune with the present rate of premium. Life Insurance Council and Acturial Society of India are working in this area. They will decide the extra premiums to be charged from the sub-standard lives and ensure fair premium rate to standard lives. Certified Life Underwriter is preparing professionals of underwriting life insurance.

Expenses: The life insurers incur certain expenses which are loaded on the net premium based on mortality and interest. Since there are different insurers having different expense rate, The premium rate may differ but under Tariff Advisors committee, the rates cannot vary significantly.

Interest: The interest or return on investment made of life fund. The post liberalisation has facilitated several insurers to earn varied rate of interest depending on the investment methodology.

The life insurance agents known as intermediates are playing significant role in underwriting of life insurance business. Medical development has reduced mortality and premium rate is expected to decline accordingly. On the other hand, pollution and crowd have created unexpected deaths. Occupation is considered as one of the key elements affecting the longevity of the insured. Stress and occupational hazards have added more risk.

NON-LIFE INSURANCE

Underwriting requires a kind of discipline which can exist on pure risk. Commercial considerations are adjusted for the purpose. The premium rate varies in non-tariff products like health, accident and so on. The clear examples of commercial consideration is Group Health policy which is renewed at 50-60% of average claims paid during last 3 years. It is below the underwriting principle. The insurer can adjust the loss experience in future premium calculation.

The premium calculation is based on individual risk and industry's experience, maximum potential loss attached to the proposed risk, estimate the customers capabilities for prevention and minimisation of losses, terms and conditions and expected moral hazard.

UNDERWRITING IN DETARIFFED ERA

The non-life insurers would go for detariffed era since January 1, 2007. Detariffing refers to freedom to the underwriters to conduct the business with their own individual experience. Underwriting had been understood as routine work of accepting the proposals to be operated under restricted and regulated market. Now underwriting is total management of product to be sold considering all factors influencing sale-decision *i.e.,* loss or profit related to underwriting, income generated through premium and investment and expenses of the company. The underwriting is designing the product to cover the risks price to be charged and claims management. In tariff regime, designing the product and pricing was done by Tariff Advisory Committee (TAC) and claim management was left to the insurance companies.

Detariff era is expected to make the insurer free to design the products and pricing them as per their insurance experience. The tariff will be deregulated with effect from January 1,2007. Thus, the current product *i.e.,* perils covered, exclusions, add-one terms and conditions etc. Will continue to be regulated by TAC till 31-3-2008. Now the insurers will be free to design their products as per their exposure to risk, expense management, premium rate and underwriting losses. The insurers assess the risk and fix the premium as per their experiences. But they will fix the price judiciously in the competitive market. The insured will be benefited with the lower price in the competitive situations. Detariffing refers to differential rates depending on the rate factors but unfair discrimination *i.e.,* differentiation not based on scientific and credible structure should not be practiced. It emphasises a higher regulatory role of IRDA.

Tele Underwriting

Underwriting is estimated to be more than USD 1500 billion world-wide. The IT industry is helping insurance business to grow. The process of modernisation and IT services has started gaining ground. In near future, the insurance will depend on tele-communication. The old system of underwriting was slow and expensive. The present system of computerisation, internetting, websites and satellite communication have accelerated growth of insurance business. The risk evaluation was slow process, issue of policy took long time and price fixation was manually done. Not only underwriting but serving the policyholders and payment of claims was time consuming. The IT facilitates faster, cheaper and better service. The processing and evaluating of risk will be done mechanically. Application of electronics gadgets make underwriting, price determination serving policyholders and claim-payment easy and faster.

Teleunderwriting starts with telephone interview with insurance applicants. It saves times and money. Similarly the policyholders ask for the services on telephone. Gradually it will extend to mail, fax, internetting and so on

DISTRIBUTION CHANNEL

Distribution Channel have become a useful components of insurance innovation. The banks have taken the responsibility of insurance-distribution. The *Bancassurances* have started in India. Its best example is Aviva which has developed link with more than 20 banks. It is spread in 378 town and cities in India. The two way flow is *easened* with Bancassurances *i.e.* Payment of premium of insured too insurers and payment of claims, health, pension, etc. by insurers to the insureds. Potentials of market have increased with the number deposits, consumer loans and housing finances, agricultural and industrial loans. The wide network of RRBs can be utilised for underwriting. Distribution and servicing the masses. Bancassurances have become cheaper than the agents for underwriting and servicing of insurance. Since banks' branches are available in rural areas, the rural insurance will extent with the help of banks.

Inspite of the growing needs of bancassurances, the personal approaches of agents are helpful to extend insurance business and serve the policyholders in a better manner. The distribution channel is analysed under life insurance, insurance intermediation and non-life insurance agents.

Insurance Intermediation

With the opening up of the insurance sector, one channel *i.e.,* broker is added as an effective intermediary. They are acting as consultant to the customer and agents of insurance company. Agents are very important for expansion of business, who provide personal services to the clients *i.e.,* the policyholders and the prospects of insurance. In the competitive atmosphere, the company will survive and grow, who can provide high level of services, back office and front office staff, consumer awareness and prompt and sensitive response to the clients' grievances.

Corporate agent may be allowed to tie up with more than one life or non-life insurer. This facilitates corporate agents to develop professionalism and competitiveness.

Life Insurance

Life insurance Agents are full of knowledge, compassion and sound people management. Life insurance agent of LIC have been gaining their role as club-members of Branch manager, Club Divisional Manager Club, Zonal Manager Club and Chairman's Club. The motivation of LIC has gone further to guide the agents become member of Million Dollar Round Table. Life Underwriters' Guild of India (LUGI) is also guiding the insurance agents to be professional. Life insurance agents quickly engage in their duties and contribute silently although discipline culture is not present there. There is competition amongst the agents to grow themselves higher and higher.

Technology in LIC

Innovation and technology have to go hand in hand so that some real and palpable results could be achieved. Innovation without technology is shapeless and technology without innovation is of no use. The relevance of technology in the insurance sector is of paramount importance today, because to-day's customer is more demanding than ever before, he has plenty of choices to shift his loyalty and finally the volume of work that can only be done through computers. Be it processing of proposals, the need for a standard practice of underwriting, the management of the records, valuation of surplus, preparation of Balance Sheets, keeping track of customers, reaching them in no time, you name the area — It is unthinkable and incomplete without a sound system of technology. Technology again is a vast subject. You need to make research for Productive Development. It is to be followed by product-Mix and Marketing, Obtaining feedback and finally Dissemination of Information. At every stage, the role of most advanced and modern technology comes to the fore. Consider the Case of LIC. It has established connectivity among all its officers, has opened Satellite officers, launched Websites (internet/intranet), Portals, Touch Screen Kiosks, IVRs, Corporate Messaging Service, Call Centres and the like. Its FEAP system has got several user-friendly modules. Its Touch Screen system works on a visual BASIC or C ++ front end and the like. Its internet site 'Jeevan Sanchar' is hosted on the most powerful operating system LINUX and designed by adapting the latest technologies of C, C++, Java, Perl, Oracle and COBOL. LIC has also embraced Online Data Sore and manages a Data Warehouse envied by many. It is pertinent to note that LIC has won the prestigious IT Excellence Award from NASSCOM for excellence in IT. Just imagine the plight of the corporation and the consumers under its 23 Crore policies without the advancement of these technologies. The entire purpose of the usage of these technologies, apart from managing its gigantic size of business, is ensuring consumer delight in an age what is called - digital. Can we say in a lighter vein, a person who does not know 'Windows' in this era of computers will be shown the door? But satisfaction of customers needs by launching new products and services through innovation and technology.

This life insurance agents have developed themselves as full-fledged persons maintaining work records, meeting clients and help them in calamity and serve them in a better way. They have great hopes and aspirations for a better standard of life, social acceptability and readiness to work hard although they are not highly educated, have less financial strength and inadequate skill, knowledge and experience. They have become financial advisors to the clients. Customer Relationship Management is present there. Many insurance agents have started selling shares and debentures of companies. They advise their clients in totality.

Non-Life Insurance

Non-Life insurance agents are less professional as the public sector organisations do not treat as business associates. They get scant training. Even the Agents Manuals and other knowledge tools such as product literature are not available to them as is available to life insurance agents.

MARKETING MANAGEMENT

Insurance innovation passes through transitional stages where at many problems are faced by the insurer. The marketing management is required for the purpose. The marketing management includes marketing audit and segmented approach.

Marketing Audit

In India, majority of the population have been unaware of the benefits of insurance although they need insurance. The psychological and emotional forces alongwith economic needs of the prospect should be completed, audited and forecasted by the management. The feelings of people are against insurance. It has to be averted. The insurer should develop marketing audit of the potentials and opportunities available for business and should be very clear of the weaknesses and threats of market. The saving and risk management has to be designed to meet the requirements of potential buyers of insurance. The role of marketing agents is generally doubted. They have to develop themselves in such a way as to make them helping agents of people.

The technique of recruiting, selecting, training and motivation of insurance agents should be modernised to train the insurance agents as social servers, economic adviser, friend and philosopher. The competition strategies are to be analysed and developed by them. Life Insurance is a need but not felt by people. Marketing manager should develop its force in such a way as to make people realise the need of insurance.

Segmented Approach

Insurance marketing needs segmented approach. The different needs of people are met differently by the insurer through its agents. Training and motivation of insurance agents are essential in this direction. They have to evaluate the present, guide the future and inspire people to come willingly for insurance products. Product development is a function of insurer and its distribution is the responsibility insurance agents.

REGULATORY MEASURES

Development of stable and strong insurance system is essential for economic development of the Country. Regulatory measures are required for instilling public confidence in insurance companies, deliver reliable and quality services. It has to secure the long-term stability of financial services through monitoring of their financial soundness and fair treatment of their customer. With the experience of failure of non-banking financial institutes and loss of depositors' money, regulatory measures have to very effective, considering the interests of insurers, government has changed its traditional regulatory role to control with facilitating investment and trade. Insurance Act 1938 is being modified as per the suggestions of IRDA. Globalisation of financial activity, innovations is financial instruments and practices have to be strictly controlled.

There is oftenly a conflict between strict regulation and development. Regulation is based on past experience whereas development is future oriented. Developing new products, processing and servicing is no easy matter. It is expected that regulations will work as driver for change to force players to do things in a better way. Regulations by IRDA in India is praireworthy as it is pro-development. It has emerged as prudential supervisor and developer of capacity in terms of risk pooling, reinsurance and skills. It has guide for insurance penetration and insurance density. It makes insurance available to poor in rural areas. Insurance companies have to provide risk cover as well as contribute to long term investment.

Self Regulatory Organisationn (SRO)

The key to effective market depends on public disclosure and consumer education. The role of self regulation is realised in the developing market. So Self Regulatory Organisation (SRO) is empowered to give greater rights and responsibilities to market participants. It anticipates and assists the industry to meet the needs of consumers, improves industry's image, promotes insurance awareness, encourages improvement of services and effectively manages the insurance resources.

SRO will develop link with Government, industry, public, consumer forum and technical researches. All the insurance companies will be the member of SRO. It will supply information to member companies, develop codes of conduct for member companies, develop compliance programmes, The SRO will have a separate secretariat headed by a secretary general and chairperson elected from the member. The international standards and practices will be adopted for the purpose.

Fraud

The possibilities of fraud exist in insurance business. The possibilities of fraud to agents are there if premium rates are not published. They may charge higher amount from the policyholder. The insured may inflate the value of the assets and get more amount than the assets in case of damage. The company can deduct some amount from the claim. Fraud may occur during underwriting by agents and brokers, surveyors and clients. The fraud is prevented by designing product step by step providing sufficient information to customers, customer identification and claim determination and direct contact with company by customers to prevent fraud created by agents. There have been a number of fraud cases which occur with connivance of claimant, lawyers and authorities. The insurer should develop fraud risk management.

Money Laundering

Money Laundering is the process through which criminals attempt to disguise the origin of the proceeds. International agencies are very much concerned with Money Laundering. RBI and SEBI have come out for anti money laundering guidelines for banking and capital market sectors. IDRA is planning to formulate such laws for insurance companies. If money laundering is not prevented, the company's reputation is at stake. The company may fail to comply the insurance contract due to risks involved in money-laundering. The IDRA has emphasised that insurer should know the customer. Agents if conscious of such movements can easily explore the money-laundering and anti-money laundering (AML) process may be adopted by them. IRDA has provided Anti money laundering in Aug. 2006.

1. Every insurer has to put in place an AML policy which should include following:
   (*i*) Internal policies, control and procedures for protection and detection of instances of money laundering.
   (*ii*) Appointment of a Principal Compliance Officer.
   (*iii*) Recruitment and Training.
   (*iv*) Internal control and audit of the AML framework.
2. Establish processes for carrying out 'Know Your Customer' (KYC) :
   (*i*) Identity the customers.
   (*ii*) Conduct detailed due diligence.
   (*iii*) Careful look at cash transactions.
   (*iv*) Conduct KYC also at payment stage.
3. Create a risk matrix for various classes of customers.
4. Defining suspicious transaction.
5. Internal Audit to deploy modules to list the efficacy of AML framework.

QUESTIONS

1. Discuss the present positions of insurance innovation.
2. What is product development ? How is it done in insurance industry? Explain.
3. Evaluate the various types of life insurance in India. Give the details of their progress.
4. Examine the product management of non-life insurance.

5. Forecast the future of product development in India.
6. What is underwriting ? Explain its role in insurance management.
7. What is detariffed Era ? What are its advantages ? Illustrate them.
8. Give the benefits and processes of telemarketing of insurance.
9. What is marketing audit of insurance ?
10. Explain the benefits of SRO.
11. Examine the role of Anti Money Laundering Act for developing insurance business in India.

(43)

RISK-MANAGEMENT

Risk Management is emerging an important area of insurance. The insurer succeeds if he is able to manage the risk properly. The risk may be insurance or uninsurable. Insurer transfers the risks to reinsurance companies. Risk is uncertainty or loss or profit. It may arise because of hazards routine business and dynamic functions. The risk may be financial and non-financial. Business risks and individual risks are also insured. Business risks include profit, price, credit and other risks. Personal risks include property risk and liability risk.

The risk management involves loss control, loss financing and risk reduction. Loss control is loss prevention method which reduces frequency of loss. Control devices to prevent loss are installed in property to prevent fire. Loss financing is done through retention, insurance hedging and risk transfers. Risk reduction is possible through better forecasts and diversification.

Risk is uncertainly of loss or profit. If business enterprises is not managing the potential risk, it may suffer incredible loss. The insurance industry ensuring risk has to be very particular about the risk management. The need and objectives of risk management, risk identification, principles of risk management, strategies of risk management and functions of important association of risk management will illustrate how to manage a risk effectively.

NEED AND OBJECTIVES

Risk management is essential to prevent financial disasters and achieve the objectives of capital management. The success must be sustainable, for which risk has to be prevented and managed. The aspirations of insurance customers can be easily met if the risk is properly managed. It helps right things performances and assists carrying out the duties of care, loyalty and good faith. The competition is beaten over by proper planning of risks. The shareholders' stake will remain intact if the risks are systematically managed. Many time policyholders and shareholders have competing interests. The insurer has to balance them. The development and solvency requirements are contradictory, sometimes. The disclosures, transparency and performance have become routine functions of insurance. The investor, suppliers of inputs and marketing management have credibility. Their interests should not be deluded in the organisation.

RISK IDENTIFICATION

Risk identification is a prime functions of underwriting and marketing management. The employees and agents of insurance companies are trained to identify the risk and also quantify the amount of risk. The risk is identified on the basis of economic and financial factors, accounting system, reputation, regulation and property and liability risk. The risks are managed by providing minimum interest rates, accounting guidance, premium calculation and knowing the unknown sources of risks.

Insurer uses rigorously technique to identify, monitor and manage the risks. Some of the techniques are stockastic modelling, value at risk, tail risk, economic capital calculations, stress tests and more and identify negative impact. The U.S. Enterprise, Risk Management (ERM) uses culture, currency, regulation, economic factors, geographical differences, Time Zone Language, distance from home office, credentials, loss of control etc. are used for identification of a risk.

Risk management involves identification, measurement and control of risk.

Identification of Risk

Identification of risk is determination of risk where does it lie. The risk may be relating to property, Life, Liability and Nature. Fire, theft, damage, natural calamities are the various hazards.

Property Loss: The factors responsible for loss are identified and evaluated for the purpose. The insured and uninsured perils are identified. Replacement possibilities and operational expenses of business, revenue loss, normal levels of production, pre-loss situation and post-loss situation are studied to identify the risk.

The book value is the minimum loss value of the property because it denotes the purchase price and depreciation of the property. But it is not economic value which is the real loss of the property. Market value is very near to economic value.If the firm does not get value of the property *i.e.*. no benefits of use of value, it will be equal to market value. Replacement cost is considered for insurance as it is the cost of replacemet of damaged property but it exceeds the market value as the new property value increases due to inflation, Firé insurance, marine insurance, motor insurance,machine insurance, profit insurance etc. are the methodologies of loss deduction due to risk.

Life Risk: Human life is exposed of several risks *e.g.,* old. age, death, health, accident and so on. Some responsibilities such as education and marriage of children, starting of their career, business responsibilities, key men employees, etc. are also attached with human life. Life insurance policies, health insurance, keyman insurance etc. are prevailing to minimise the loss of human life.

Liability: Liability mainly legal liabilities arise because of contractual relationship. Third party insurance of motor insurance, product liability and professional liability and many new liabilities are added in recent years.

Other Risks: There are several other risks which influence the cost and production. Profit insurance is taken for the purpose. Machine breakdown and crop insurance etc. are the recent examples of other risks which are separately insured to reduce the loss can used by such risks.

Risks are measured using probability methods. Last experiences and variance analysis with standard deviation are used for measuring risks. The probability is modified with the present situation and future expectation.

Control of Risk

The risks are controlled through insurance with the principle of pooling, cooperation and transfer of risks, Insurance of risks are becoming a gradual and continuous process. The Indian experience is very positive wherein insurance is expanding with more than 15 percent per annum.

PRINCIPLES OF RISK MANAGEMENT

The principles of risk management includes top level involvement, culture of accountability, risk prevention, appropriate control, discipline and forecasting negative events. Investment and accountability are important factors of risk management.

Investment

Risk management is embedded in insurance industry from the date of proposal to the final payment of claims. After sale services reveal the techniques of risk management. It reveals the investment process in Industry itself discovers the principles of risk management . The senior managers have knowledge of risk and risk management technique. There are a set procedure *e.g.,* LIC has agents manuals to guide them how to identify the risk and manage it properly. The L.I.C. provides oversight integration, coordination and consolidation of corporate functions, Many company has a separate department of risk management.

Accountability

The responsibility vested on the executive reduces the risk and forces them to manage risk. There are rating agencies (Tariff Advisory Committee) analysts, surveyors etc. who evaluate the risk. Management is responsible for identifying the risk setting the risk limits implementing process to back and identify new risks. Applying constant testing and monitoring. The agents, development officers and branch managers are responsible for risk evaluation and rate fixation. They sell right policy to right person.

STRATEGIES OF RISK MANAGEMENT

The risk management strategy is fully aligned with the company's overall strategy while ensuring a separation of duties between risk policy setting, monitoring and controls and business management. The strategies of minimise risk are formulated keeping into account the risk profile, reporting risk issues, implementation of risk management and so on. Corporate Risk Unit (CRU) is developed to assess and formulate risk management strategies. Risk model is developed with the help of actuaries, technical analysts, expertised consultancy pricing, financial management and capital management are analysed for the purposes. The strategies are formulated by imagination and identifying weaknesses.

Imagination

The insurer imagines control-devices. Regular dynamic reviews and current risk factors are adjusted. Liquidity, derivatives, rescuing credit exposure, counter-party exposure and reinsurer exposure are estipulated for the purpose. The depth study of previous losses due to epidemic mumps, meningitis etc. are conducted by the management.

Identifying Weaknesses

The risk management weaknesses are identified and remedied. The risk profiles, measure and metrics are thoroughly analysed for the purpose.

ASSOCIATIONS OF RISK MANAGEMENT

The risk management assoiations are formed for meeting the challenges of risk. There are two associations viz., International Federation of Risk and Insurance Management Association (IFRIMA) and Federation of European Risk Management Association in Europe (FERMA) which are guiding insurers to manage the potential risks.

INTERNATIONAL FEDERATION OF RISK AND INSURANCE MANAGEMENT ASSOCIATION (IFRIMA)

Risk management involves loss prevention and safety programmes. Insurers manage the risk in very effective manner so that policyholders may not suffer on account of higher premium. Reinsurance is practiced to avoid the loss. There is great pressure on the reinsurance companies as natural disasters are increasing. Catastrophe management is resorted to which insurance companies are financially helping for effective management of risks.

Risk management depends on good corporate governance. The insurance company increases its image through corporate governance. IFRIMA is motivating education of risk management. Insurers will have to manage hazards, operational risk, financial risk and so on.

Federation of European Risk Management Association in Europe (FERMA)

Every day people are coping with new types of risk. They have to manage them through insurance and insurers manage them through reinsurance. Insurance is needed for all those risks which could not actuarially be calculated by the insurers who have put them under exclusions. For example, storms were excluded previously, but now they need to be insured. Many insurers have started insuring those risks which were uninsurable. The resort risk management through risk transfer and risk financing.

FERMA having 14 members are looking into risk management issues. Many new companies are looking FERMA to help them. They have to comply the regulations of solvency, directives of intermediation and environmental issues. FERMA is providing education and training of risk management as well as global insurance learning.

RISK MANAGEMENT IN LIFE INSURANCE

Solvency Margin

The insurer makes assumptions into future for parameters such as mortality, morbidity, expenses, interest etc. Sub regulation (b) of Regulation 5 of IRDA Regulations (Assets, Liabilities and Solvency Margin of Insurers) 2000; specifies that the best estimate assumption shall be adjusted by an appropriate Margin for Adverse Deviation (MAD) which is dependent upon the degree confidence. The purpose of MAD is to build a buffer for mis-estimations of the best estimate or adverse fluctuations. But it does not cover for volatility and catastrophe risks for which a separate excess assets known as Solvency Margin should be provided by the insurer.

Risk Based Capital

Risks based capital includes asset default risk, mortality morbidity risk, volatility risk, catastrophe risk, margin risk and fund risk. Each company needs to develop implement and maintain appropriate and effective procedures to manage its capital position, i.e., on going minimum capital requirements, and future capital requirements. The capital management planning identifies the quantity, quality and sources of additional capital required, availability of any external sources, estimating the financial impact of raising additional capital, taking into account the plans and requirements of various business units of the company.

RISK MANAGEMENT IN GENERAL INSURANCE

Solvency Margin Formula

IRDA's relevant regulations prescribe required solvency margin (RSM) at 20% of the net premiums or 30% of net increased claims whichever in higher.

Risk Based Capital

Risk Based Capital (RBC) formula comprises asset risk, credit risk, underwriting loss, underwriting premium risk and off balance sheet risk.

Reserving

The importance of proper reserving cannot be over-emphasised. The failure to provide adequately for future claims is attributed to 'under reserving' or 'under provisioning'. Reserves can be classified as unearned premium reserves (UPR), Unexpired Risk Reserve (URR) outstanding Claims Reserve (OCR), Chain Ladder Method (CL), Average Cost Per Claim Method (ACPC) and Incurred but not reported Reserve (IBNR).

Alternate Risk Management

These are several alternate risk management strategies such as risk transfer (reinsurance), risk hedging through interest ratio etc. longevity bonds and managing financial market risks.

Solvency I

Solvency I is based on minimum solvency standards. The solvency I directive adopted in 2002 left the solvency calculation unchanged but only adjusted some other components. Solvency requirements should be fulfilled at all times rather than only at the time the financial statements are drawn up. All life insurers are required to Gold capital of at least the Solvency I minimum guarantee fund, or the Solvency I required solvency margin plus the resilience capital requirement. Solvency capital requirement will be calculation by applying either the standard approach or the insurer's won internal risk model.

Solvency I requires insurers to hold capital funds equal to the required solvency margin or the minimum guarantee fund, whichever is the higher. Solvency I for non-life insurance is defined as the higher of the premium and the claim index.

Premium Index = 18% of gross premium × retention rate

Claims Index = 26% of gross claim × retention rate

Retention = Net claims ÷ Gross claims (3 year average but not less than 50%)

Solvency I for Life Insurance is Required Solvency Margin

= 4% × gross mathematical provision × retention rate mathematical provision + 3% × capital at risk × retention rate capital at risk.

Solvency II

Solvency II requires adequate capital backing for the volatility of claims. The assess which lives of business may exhibit above-average volatility the loss rations of five non-life lives of business. European union (EU) adopted solvency I 2002 which was converted to solvency II in early 2003. EU commission is expected to adopt the solvency II directive in mid 2007. After its adoption by EU Parliament and the council of Ministers, the implementation is scheduled to be complete by 2010.

One of the objectives of Solvency II is to establish a solvency capital requirement which is better matched to the risks of an insurance company. The characteristic of solvency II are based on principles and not rules. These are two levels of capital requirements under solvency II, i.e., The Minimum Capital Requirement (MCR) and Solvency Capital Requirement. MCR is the minimum level below which ultimate supervisory action will be triggered. SCR should deliver a level of capital that enables an insurance undertaking to absolute significant unforeseen losses and gives reasonable assurance to policy holders that payment will be made as they fall due. Solvency II deals with quantitative requirements, supervisory review powers and for insurer's internal control and risk management and disclosure and transparency to reinforce market mechanism and risk based supervisors. It reinforces on risk/return fundamentals.

IRDA Role

The reporting framework for published accounts for insurance companies in prescribed by the IRDA and is mainly armed at demonstrating solvency and protecting the interest of policy holders. The IRDA reviews the functioning of the insurance company, from time to time, through inspections meetings with the CEO, CFO, the Appointed Actuary and other senior officials to form a view of compliance and how risk issuer are addressed by the company. The solvency requirements are related to mathematical reserves and sum at risk reflecting solvency I. The insurers are required to maintain, at all times, solvency margin at not less than 150% of the required level as per the regulators. As of now, the regulations allow only equity as the accepted form of capital.

Solvency framework in India is similar to some of the Asian countries which follow Solvency I. Although there is a move towards a risk based capital which is principles based and focuses on the specific risks to which the business is exposed. The IRDA is a number of International Association of Insurance Supervisors (IAIS) which is working towards a common structure and common standards for assessing insurer solvency as a new framework for insurance supervision. The risks faced by an insurer have been categorised under five heads viz., underwriting risk, credit risk, market risk, operational risk and liquidity risk.

De-tariffing

De-tariffing has provided significant opportunities in tapping more markets and will provide even more opportunities after product liberalisation. It has placed the onus of correct pricing on the players themselves. While this has resulted in players preparing to identify risk parameters and pricing products based on risks, the immediate response has been to drop the rates in hitherto non-profitable business. The price war will erose capital. The general insurances players are exposed to memerous such risks as financial and non-financial.

Financial risks include capital risks asset liability management risks insurance risks and credit risks. Capital risks relates to capital structure risks and capital adequacy risks. Asset Liability Management Risks takes into consideration of exchange rate risks, interest rate risks and investment management risks. Insurance risks are underwriting risks, catastrophic risks, reserves risks, pricing risks and claim and management risks. Credit risks include re-insurer's risks, policy holder premium, brokers, claim recoveries and other debtors.

Non Financial Risks are enterprise risks and operational risks. Enterprise risks include reputation risks parents risks and competitor behavior risks. Operational risks are regulators risks, business continuity risk, IT obgolescence risks, people and process risks, risks of frouds process-related risks regulatory compliance risks and outsourcing related risks.

Trained and devoted personnel as well as agents can manage these risks effectively.

QUESTIONS

1. What is risk ? Discuss the methods of its identification.
2. Explain the methods of evaluation of risk.
3. Illustrate the techniques of controlling various types of risk.
4. Discuss the risk management techniques in India.
5. Explain the International Risk Management Association.

44

HEALTH INSURNCE

Health Insurance has been realised as an instrument for the health of the economy. If the people of the country are healthy, they can contribute significantly in the economic development of the country. The health insurance industry would provide protection to social development. The insurance industry should come forward to provide health to the masses like life insurance and property insurance. The Government provisions for health have not succeeded for want of initiative on the part of government officers and beneficiaries. It is hoped that commercial bases of health insurance will be more suitable for health development of people. There is need of products, designs, structural facilities and sustainability of insurance products. Adequate environment is to be developed for the introduction and development of health insurance.

Environment

Health insurance requires sufficient information and data for development of a good product, proper pricing and health management. Many insurers are interested to provide health insurance provided consumers are properly educated in this area. Recently with the break of joint family system, the need of health insurance is more thrusting. Maintaining health responsibilities on commercial basis to insurance companies, economic growth, human resource development and prosperity will enhance in future.

Product Design

There is need of well designed health insurance product that may protect family savings in case of unexpected medical charges. People are interested in higher achievement than paid by them in the form of premium. Insurer, therefore is expected to invest the premium money in such a way as to earn sufficient money for meeting the expenses of insurance and insurance claims. Insurer has to meet the challenges of expenses and health services. The insurance cover should be reasonably comprehensive without counter productive gaps.

Mediclaim policies provide coverage of medical services rendered during hospitalisation. But, there is need of broader set of services. There is need of outpatient costs because a large number of persons are treated satisfactorily without being admitted in the hospital. Health insurance should cover all such types of expenses. The third need of health insurance is preventive measures by providing health education and quality life. Premium may be reduced on such types of proposals.

Additional incentives should be provided for purchasing health insurance. The tax exemption on health premium and medical saving accounts are few of the examples of financial incentives for health insurance. The alternative choices should be there for selecting a suitable hospitals nearby the insured persons. There is need of new products of non-patient services. The premium should be competitive and fair to the policy holders.

Educating to consumers about health consciousness is very essential in health insurance. It increases people's awareness of diseases, cost of treatments, alternative treatment options. People should know quality of health and health care services. Employers should be motivated to provide health cover to their employees. Like group insurance and group superannuation; employers should purchase policies for their employees and pay the premium. It enhances the images of the organisation.

Cost Effective Health Insurance: The product of Health Insurance should be designed in such a way as to reduce cost of premium. The insurer should design the product to attract more customers. People should get incentives to purchase health policies. Low premium rate attracts a larger number of persons to purchase health policies. The developed nations have popularised the health insurance as the insurers meet the most expensive treatments. People are ready to pay higher premium to meet the high cost of medical bill.

Investment cum Health Service Product: In India, people are interested mainly in investment. They went that health protection should be part of savings. While saving schemes are spreading Health Insurance should be linked with that. If people get health cover with a slight deduction of money from their saving rate, they would not mind as it becomes a regular feature after some time. They will fell that health cover is given free of cost.

Product of Causal and Usual Risks: Health product should cover the casual risks such as epidemics risk and claims uncertainty risks and usual risks *e.g.,* overhead expenses, interest and other business risks. With the past experience of claim payment, insurer should design a number of suitable policies to meet different requirements of the customers. Product design and pricing are key factors for enhancing insurance. High price reduces business and less price increases loss of insurer. Therefore, proper balance is established with the help of data analysis.

Trust and Confidence: The insured should have trust and confidence in the insurance company that premium rates are at the lowest possible and they will get the claim amount at the time of need. The insurer should influx the confidence of solvency, proper risk selection, reasonable cost of operation and timely payment of claims. Solvency plus financial and operational performance monitoring will be essential.

Structural Facilities

The structural facilities are provided by the government. Regulatory authority properly guide the insurer to design insurance for health care. The insurer should feel free to approach hospitals, doctors physicians and others for getting adequate information. International Classification of Diseases-10th Revision (ICD-10) and Procedure Classification System (PCS) are good guide for health care and developing structural facilities of health insurance.

The health insurance reduces the charges for health care. The structural facilities of health care are told to the insured on websites and electronic format. The insurer should assure that reimbursement for their services are fair and sufficient. It will cover all the costs of medical treatment. The possibilities of litigation are minimised to provide confidence to the insureds.

Sustainability of the Products

The insurance products should be sustained for developing the trust and confidence amongst the policyholder. The insurer has to adopt proper management of funds, pricing, product-designs and follow the regulatory features. Facilities of electronic data is crucial for long-term success of the insurance industry. It will improve efficiency of the employees who will provide quality services to the insureds. The insurers maintain risk capital for meeting the contingency of unexpected losses. The scope of insurance cover is expanded to include impatient, out patient facilities, physicians and pharmacy charges.

Health insurance as a class, is very young in the Indian insurance. But, it occupies the third place among the different non-life insurance classes. It has registered more than 50% rise in 2006-2007. While non-life insurance business increased only by 10%. However, health insurances has not received more attention because the customers awareness is very low. The insurers should make the classes very explicit and explain the exclusions in detail. The role of Third Party Administrators should be effectively ensured by them. They should take care of the customers' interests.

Retailing Health Insurance

Retailing health insurance requires products innovation channel innovation, risk based pricing and prevention.

Product Innovation

Individuals face a number of exposures driven by health and health-related events and costs, the risks of which they can bear to differing degrees. These risks range from low ticket-size expenses (e.g., for routine care) to higher ticket-size discretionary expenses (e.g., for elective surgery), catastrophic expenses (e.g., due to major illness, accident), end-of-life care expenses (e.g., due to life threatening illness), expenses related to chronic diseases and income risk (e.g., disability).

Channel Innovation

Health insurance products are likely to require additional distribution channels beyond the dominant agency force. Based of the U.S. experience, several innovations hold promise :

- **Direct-response channels.** These include a captive sales force, call centres, the Internet, direct mail, and television commercials. A leading U.S. player primarily uses the Internet, for example, to sell a product aimed at consumers aged 18 to 29 ("young invincibles") who think they do not need health insurance.
- **Retail stores.** Health insurers in the U.S. are now offering health benefit products through leading retail and pharmacy chains. One of the biggest success stories for payers has been selling Medicare-related products to the elderly through bricks-and-mortar retailers.
- **Affinity-marketing relationships.** Health insurance have entered successful affinity partnerships with diverse players.

Risk-based Pricing

Product and channel innovations alone are not enough, Health insurers need to understand the risk profile of individuals and their ability and willingness to pay, which often varies by sement and chennal.

Actuaries could determine now consumer behaviour would change *a priori* and build that into product pricing rather than wait for years to study observed behaviour, they could benefit from substantive gains. Insurers in the U.S. have leveraged detailed data to build sophisticated actuarial models, that are more powerful by a factor of over 1,000 relative to competitors.

Insurance Coverage Beyond Hospitalization Benefits

Private sector group and individual health insurance coverage in India today focuses on hospitalisation benefits with a limited sum assured. While this provides valuable coverage, preventive care techniques are important to improve medical outcomes and to provide cost-effective health insurance. In India, there remains a huge need for simple primary prevention that largely falls into the public domain. However, the private health insurance can make important contributions at the secondary and tertiary prevention levels.

Primary vs Advanced Prevention

In assessing the cost-benefit equation of a number of techniques and determining who is best positioned to provide these services it is helpful to distinguish between three levels of preventive care :

- **Primary prevention** entails reduction in the level of one or more identified macro risk factors to reduce the probability of the initial occurrence of a disease. Examples include road safety, clean water, food fortification and vaccinations, which are typically Government-led.
- **Secondary prevention** aims at detecting a disease at a very early stage to prevent or delay its progression. Examples include screening programme for cancer and diabetes, which could be provided for and funded by the private sector.
- **Tertiary prevention** consists of ongoing interventions aimed at decreasing or delaying the severity and frequency of recurrent events of chronic or episodic diseases. Example include family-oriented disease management therapies for cardio-vascular diseases, or disease

management programs for diabetes patients, where again the private sector can play an important role.

WHO statistics indicate that 8 million people die prematurely every year in India from diseases that are relatively easily preventable, if certain primary preventive measures were adopted by the public authorities.

HEALTH INSURANCE IN INDIA

The government has asked the public sector non-life insurance companies to devise an affordable health insurance scheme. Universal Health Insurance Policy is issued by them. It has failed to attract policy holders and people to get its benefits. The role of NGOs have been realised to benefit the poor by health insurance. There is urgent need of health insurance to product the masses against health hazards.

Government has subsidised the health insurance for the poor.

Health insurance in India is not gaining ground because people are skeptical about the payment of claims and services provided by insurance companies. Lack of health care services and infrastructure, illiteracy and lack of trust in health schemes and insurance companies have impeded the health insurance in India.

PROSPECTS OF HEALTH INSURANCE

The prospects of health insurance are very bright in future as the cost of medical treatment is escalating although it is not gaining at present. The underwriting practices have to be tightened. The health care utilisation increases with affluence of society. The socio-economic development in India is increasing fastly and need of insurance is realised gradually. Low premium is not always good because the coverage may be small. The medical inflation index provides the guidance for designing the product and pricing reasonably. In absence of medical inflation index, consumer price index is used for the purpose.

In India, medical claims and losses occur but they are not reported to any organisation. People suffer and get totally secret medicine inherent getting any receipts of purchases. Such types of activities are not useful for managing health insurance. Insurers have to anticipate such claims and manage in their total claims. It is observed that unhealthy lives would remain with insurer causes like in claims losses. They donot go to other insurers because they have to pay higher premium for new health policy. The insurer has to classify the healthy and unhealthy lives for proper insurance management and portfolio management. Information and data should be updated for future planning and product designing.

Health insurance is personal insurance that provides coverage for the cost of hospital and medical expenses arising from illness or injury. Benefits are paid as a fixed lump sum or as a proportion of actual treatment costs. It includes individually hospital cash, critical illness and disability benefits.

Indemnity mediclaim has covered only inpatient facility and professional claims along with some of the pre-admission and post admission expenses. Covering all outpatient expenses in additon to inpatient expenses would be a huge broadening of the scope of policy benefits and would represent a major shift in the philosophy of health insurance in India. Those companies in India that have experimented with such policy broadening have experienced huge increased in claim volumes and the associated administrative expenses. To this point, the focus has been on offering policies which protect the policyholder from costly care that might threaten a person's financial security. This has been done with an indemnity policy that has a sum insured cop on the insurer's ability.

Hospital Cash

In the case of hospital cash benefits, the actuary will need to tailor the pricing assumptions to the target popoulations being insured. Variables such as age, gender, geographic location, occupation and income level are known to correlate with hospital utilization and hence will be important considerations in pricing this benefit. The cash benefit usually makes a payment to a person that is hospitalized at some scheduled amount, typically on a per day basis and usually is limited to 60-90 days of cover per hospitalization. Certain types of hospitalization stays are excluded for specific surgeries and hospitalizations that commerce within 30 days of policy issuance.

As with all medical insurance policies, careful benefit design is crucial. Moral hazard is a concern. For example, an insurer will not want to offer a hospital cash benefit that covered more than the expected patient out-of-pocket expenses during a hospital stay; otherwise the patient would stay to gain financially by being in the hospital! The key here is not to create in incentive to such a degree that it encourages hospital admissions.

Critical Illness

Critical illness benefits are most commonly sold by life insurers as riders to life policies. They are usually structured in a way which pays a defined percentage of the policy amount in the event a policyholder is diagnosed with one of several designated critical illnesses. Some insurers are offering these policies on a stand alone basis.

A variation on the critical illness rider offers coverage for the treatment of the disease conditions as opposed to a cash payout if the diagnosis is present. Payment is made under the terms of these policies only to indemnify the insured for the cost of treatments. As with the Critical Illness benefit, adverse selection is always of great concern under these policies, and so offering these benefits requires skillful and expert underwriting.

Just as in the Critical Illness benefit, it is important to have some sense of the prevalence and incidence of the covered diseases. The Indian incidence rates, for these diseases, are not well known, particularly in an insured population. Public health officials have made estimates for the overall population of the prevalence of critical illness (see Table 1). Incidence of disease and the related treatment are of utmost interest to insurers. The mere existence of a disease in a population does not necessarily translate into incidence of treatment at any given point in time, given some people are asymptomatic and go from day to day without using the healthcare system.

Disability Benefits

Health Insurance products in India narrowly cover hospitalization benefits with a sum-assured limit. India's private health insurance sector could cover a number of secondary and tertiary preventive measures such as screening for cancer or diabetes, and preventive health check ups as well as disease management programs for specific conditions, which would be beneficial for insured and insurers alike.

QUESTIONS

1. What is health insurance?
2. Discuss the products of health insurance.
3. Explain the structural facilities needed for health insurance.
4. Examine the sustainability of the health products.
5. Project the future prospects of health insurance in India.

LIC'S HEALTH PLUS UNIT LINKED HEALTH INSURANCE PLAN

"In this policy, the Investment Risk in Investment Portfolio is Borne by the Policy-Holder"

Heal this a major concern on everybody's mind these days. With sky rocketing medical expenses, the possibility of any illness leading to hospitalization of surgery is a constant source of anxiety unless the family has actively provided for funds to meet such an eventuality. Most families rarely provide for healthcare, and even if they do, it is grossly inadequate. Given this scenario, LIC has launched LIC's Health Plus plan, a unique long term health insurance plan that combines health insurance covers for the entire family (husband, wife and the children) - Hospital Cash Benefit (HCB) and Major Surgical Benefit (MSB) along with a ULIP component (investment in the form of Units) that is specifically designed to meet domiciliary treatment related (DTB) expenses for the insured members.

1. Vital Information

1. Age	Principal Insured	Spouse Insured	Child Insured
Min Policy Entry Age -Age Last Birthday	18	18	3 months
Min Age -HCB Cover -Age Last Birthday	18	18	3 months
Min Age - MSB Cover -Age Last Birthday	18	18	18
Maximum Entry Age Age Nearest Birthday	55	55	17

2. Premium Payment

Mode of Payment

Yearly, Half-Yearly, & Monthly (ECS Mode only)

Minimum Annual Premium Conditions

Number of Lives covered	Higher of the two conditions in each category listed below:
Single Life	6 times the HCB of the Principal Insured OR Rs. 5000 p.a.
Two Lives	The arithmetic sum of 6 times the HBC of PI and 3 times the HCB of the second insured OR Rs. 7500 p.a.
More than two Lives	The arithmetic sum of 6 times the HCB of PI and 3 times the HCB of each of the others insured OR Rs. 10,000 p.a.

Annualized Premiums are payable in multiples of Rs. 500.

3. Sum Assured. The Principal Insured must first choose the respective levels of HCB for each member to be covered under the policy. The Sum assured for major surgical benefits will be 200 times of the HCB you choose.

Major Surgical Sum Assured	Principal Insured	Spouse Insured	Child Insured
	200 times the HCB applicable to each insured life under the policy		

4. Term of the Policy. The term of the policy is upto the policy anniversary on which the age nearer birthday of the principal insured in 65 years.

Age Nearest Birthday	Pincipal Insured	Spouse Insured	Child Insured
Max. Cover creasing age	65	65	25
Premium Ceasing Age	65 Years Nearest Birthday of the Principal Insured		

5. Addition of New Members. It is important for the principal Insured (the person taking the policy) to decide which of the existing family members are to be covered and include them at the beginning (proposal state) itself. Eligible existing family members cannot be added at a later stage. New members can however be added under the following three situations.

Situation	When to include?	The cover starts from
Marriage/remarriage of the Principal insured after taking the policy	Within one year from the date of marriage	The following policy anniversary
A Child born or Legally adopted child less than 3 months after taking the policy	Health Cover Starts from the policy anniversary falling immediately after the child completes 3 months	
Legally adopted child is more than 3 months old	From the policy anniversary falling after date of adoption	

- The new members will be eligible for the cover only if they satisfy the conditions of minimum premium and benefits.
- New members must be included by the Principal Insured only. No new members will be allowed after the death of the principal insured.

6. Increase/Decrease of Premiums. Increase or decrease of premiums is allowed during the term of the policy. Increase in premium must be in multiples of Rs. 500. In case of decrease, the minimum premium conditions must be satisfied. However, increase/decrease in premiums does not affect the level of health cover and HCB and MSB benefits.

Your Health is your most important Asset;

Take care of your Health

II. Benefits

1. Hospital Cash Benefit (HCB). A daily benefit is payable in case the insured is hospitalized due to either accidental body injury or sickness. The quantum of benefit depends upon the level of cover opted.

Insured	Initial Daily Benefit (IDB)* #	
	Minimum	Maximum
Principal Insured	Rs. 250	Rs. 2500
Spouse/Child	Rs. 250	Rs. 1500

* The Applicable Daily Benefit IDB is applicable during the first year of risk cover. The daily benefit will increase @5% p.a. simple of the IDB on each policy anniversary until it hits a cap of 1.5 times the initial benefit.

IDB of the spouse cannot exceed the Principal Insured's IDB; IDB of the children cannot exceed the spouse's IDB.

The initial HCB must be in multiples of Rs. 50. # Initial daily benefit that is payable in respect of stay in a non-ICU room or ward. In case the insured is required to stay in the ICU of a hospital, an enhanced rate of daily benefit is payable, which is twice the eligible daily cash benefit.

2. Major Surgical Benefit (MSB). In the event of the insured undergoing one of the major surgeries defined in the table in page 4, a lump sum benefit (regardless of the actual costs incurred) equivalent to the percentage of the sum assured mentioned against that surgery will be payable on providing proper proof of surgery to the satisfaction of the corporation.

3. Domiciliary Treatment Benefit (DTB). The Principal Insured can withdraw an amount equivalent to the actual expense he or she has incurred in respect of any domiciliary treatment or to meet the medical expenses incurred over and above the hospital cash/major surgical benefits in respect of either oneself or the others insured under the policy

Minimum domiciliary claimable	**Rs. 2500**
Maximum amount that can be claimed/payable*	Up to 50% of the policy fund at the date of payment

* Subject to a minimum balance of one annualized premium being left in the policy fund after making the payment.

Note: 1. A maximum of **two payments** will be allowed in a policy year subject to the above conditions - on production of supporting proof of treatment and bills of expenses **DTB is available only after at least 3 years premiums are paid.**

2. DTB is payable for the children covered until the health cover ceasing age.

4. Death Benefit. No death insurance cover is available under the plan. Following benefits/changes will take place on the happening of unfortunate death of Principal Insured (PI) and/or other insured member.

1. Where only a single life (Principal Insured) is insured under the policy:

Fund value of units held in the policy fund is payable to the nominee or legal heir(s) of the principal insured.

2. Where two or more are covered under the policy: Where the death of PI has occurred within 3 years from the commencement: The policy will terminate and the policy Fund Value will be payable to the nominee/legal heir.

Where death of PI has occurred after 3 years from the commencement. The premiums payment will cease but the health cover for the other insured, if any, will continue until the fund is sufficient to recover the charges or until the cover ceasing age, which ever is earlier.

3. On the death of insured members, other than the PI. Premium payment as well as the Risk cover will continue for the other members insured under the policy.

4. On the death of all the insured members. Fund value of units held in the policy fund is payable to the nominee or legal heir(s) of the principal insured.

5. On the death of the PI and the spouse (whether insured or not under the policy) after 3 years from the commencement. The benefits in respect of the insured children, if any, shall continue and can be claimed by the eldest major child covered under the policy it all children covered are minors, the legal guardian can claim the health cover benefits.

PROHIBITION OF REBATES SECTION 41 OF INSURANCE AT 1938

(1) No person shall allow or offer to allow, either directly or indirectly, as an inducement to any person to take out or renew or continue an insurance in respect of any kind of risk relating to lives or property in India, any rebate of the whole part of the commission payable or any rebate of the premium shown on the policy, nor shall any person taking out or renewing or continuing a policy accept any rebate, except such rebate as may be allowed in accordance with the published prospectus or tables of the insurer: provided that acceptance by an insurance agent of commission in connection with a policy of life insurance taken out by himself on his own life shall not be deemded to be acceptance of a rebate of premium within the meaning of this sub-section if at the time of such acceptance the

insurance agent satisfies the prescribed conditions establishing that he is a bona fide insurance agent employed by the insurer.

(2) Any person making default in complying with the provisions of this section shall be punishable with fine which may extend to five hundred rupees.

List of Surgical Procedures Covered	Sum Assured%
CARDIOVASCULAR SYSTEM	
Major Surgery of Aorta	100%
CABG (two or more coronary arteries must be bypassed) via open chest surgery	100%
Valve Replacement using mechanical prosthesis via open chest surgery	100%
Pericardiotomy/Pericardectomy done in chronic constrictive pericarditis	100%
Open chest surgery for repair of any of the heart valves	100%
Initial implantation of permanent pacemaker in the heart	[illegible]0%
Coronary Angioplasty with stent implantation (two or more corronary arteries must be stented)	40%
HAEMIC AND LYMPHATIC SYSTEM	
Bone Marrow transplant (as recipient)	60%
Splenectomy for hematological conditions	60%
NERVOUS SYSTEM	
Surgery to remove cerebral tumors (benign or malignant) and space occupying lesions requiring "Craniotomy"	100%
Repair of Cerebral or, Spinal Arterio-Venous Malformations and, Cerebral Aneurysms	100%
Other intra-cranial operations requiring craniotomy	100%
Excision of pineal gland	100%
Excision of the pituitary gland	100%
Operations of Surbaracahnoid space of brain	60%
Intracranial ransaction of Cranial nerve	60%
Drainge of Extradural space	40%
Drainge of Subdural space	40%
RESPIRATORY SYSTEM	
Lung Transplant or combined Heart-Lung Transplant	100%
Isolated Heart Transplant	100%
Pneumonectomy or Pleuro-pneumonecnomy -total lung of one side	100%
Pleurectomy or Pleural decortication	60%
Thoractoplasty	60%
Open Lobectomy of Lung	60%

Excision of begin medistinal, mediastinal lesions (evidence of thoracotomy needs to be ascertained	60%
Partial Extirpation of Bronchus	60%
Partial of Total Pharyngectomy	60%
Total Laryngectomy	60%
DIGESTIVE SYSTEM	
Resection and Anastomosis of any part of digestive tract	60%
Open Surgery for treatment of Peptic Ulcer	60%
Total excision of oesophagus	60%
Total excision of stomach	60%
Excision of oesophagus and stomach	100%
Artificial opening into stomach	40%
ENDOCRINE SYSTEM	
Complete excision of adrenal glands	60%
Partial excision of adrenal glands	40%
Complete excision of Thyroid gland	60%
Partial excision of Thyroid gland	40%
Complete excision of Parathyroid gland	60%
Partial excision of Parathyroid gland	40%
Thymectomy	60%
EYE	
Any eye surgery requiring corneal or retinal repair due to accident	40%
LIVER, GALL BLADDER & PANCREAS	
Partial Resection of Liver	60%
Partial Pancreatectomy	60%
MUSCULOSKELETAL SYSTEM	
Total Replacement of Hip or knee joint following accident	60%
Amputation of Arm or hand or Foot or Leg due to trauma or accident	60%
ORO-MAXILLOFACIAL SURGERY	
Major reconstructive oro-maxillafacial surgery due to trauma or burns and not for cosmetic purpose	60%
KIDNEY AND URINARY TRACT	
Renal transplant (recipient)	100%
Nephrectomy due to medical advice (not as a transplant donor)	60%

III. Conditions & Restrictions

1. Waiting Period. Both HCB and MSB covers are available subject to a waiting period from the commencement of the risk cover specified hereunder - in respect of each insured member:

Waiting Period from	Principal Insured	Spouse Insured	Child Insured
Dater of the cover	180 days	180 days	180 days
Date of revival/ reinstatement	90 days	90 days	90 days

No waiting period in respect of Accidental Bodily Injury. Also incase of children for MSB

2. Benefit Period Limits - Hospital Cash Benefit

HCB	Maximum Annual Benefit Period		Maximum Lifetime Benefit Period
	1st year	2n year & after	
Principal Insured Spouse Insured Child Insured*	18 days incl. 9 days for ICU	60 days incl. 30 days for ICU	365 days

*Maximum period of HCB for an insured child until he or she completes 5 years age is limited to 90 days

Important Note : HCB is available only in respect of hospitalization in a ward or ICU for continuous period of 24 hours of part there of over and above 48 hours, provided such part stay exceeds 4 hours.

3. Conditions for Availing Major Surgery Benefit

MSB	Principal Insured	Spouse Insured	Child Insured
Max. Annual benefit	100% of the Sum Assured applicable in respect of the each insured member		
Max. Lifetime Benefit	3 times the Sum Assured applicable in respect of the each insured member		

MSB is payable only if the surgery is performed in India

NOTE : Various HCB and MSB Benefit limits and restrictions applicable under this policy in respect of each insured shall solely and exclusively apply to that insured only and are not transferable to any other insured.

4. Limits on Availing Domiciliary Treatment Benefit

DTB Conditions	
Minimum domiciliary claimable	Rs. 2500
Maximum amount that can be payable during the policy term -for each payment	50% of the policy fund the date of payment
Maximum amount that can be claimed/ payable during the last policy anniversary by the Principal insured.	100% of the policy fund at the date of payment

*Equal to actual amount spent subject to a minimum balance of one annualized premium being left in the policy fund after making the payment.

5. Termination of HCB and MSB Benefits.

On attainment of the insured's maximum cover ceasing age 65 years n.b.d. for PI/spouse insured and 25 years n.b.d. for the children insured

One reaching the maximum lifetime benefit limits under HCB (365 days) and MSB (3 times the sum assured)

On the death of the insured; End of policy term or on the date of termination of the policy for any other reason

Insured spouse's cover terminates on the date of divorce/legal separation

On the date of lapsation: See 7 below.

6. Premium Discontinuance and Revival. The policy will lapse if the premiums are not paid within the days of grace. The Pl shall have the option to revive the policy any time within a period of two years from the due date of first unpaid premium.

If the Policy lapses before payment of 3 years premiums, the health cover will stop for all the insured. The policy can be revived anytime during a period of two years from the due date of first unpaid premium by payment of all the arrears of premium without interest but subject to proof of continued insurability.

If the policy is lapsed after payment of at least 3 years premiums, the policy can be revived with 2 years from due date of first unpaid premium by payment of arrears of premiums or by availing Premium Holidays. During the period of discontinuity, the charges for HCB and MSB covers will continue to be deducted from the policy fund till whichever of the following happens earlier.

i. the policy fund falls below one annualized premium, or

ii. the lives covered reach the benefit ceasing age, or

iii. the maximum lifetime benefits are exhausted, or

iv. the policy has reached the end of revival period/end of policy term.

v. the policy is terminated due to death or any other reason.

7. Premium Holidays. If the policy lapses after at least 3 years premiums have been paid the Principal Insured has the option of either paying all the due premiums in full or avail of premium holiday by just paying the latest instalment premium without any interest. The premium holidays can be availed only as long as the policy fund has a balance of at least one annualized premium at the time of revival.

8. Surrender. The surrender value, it any, is payable only on completion of the third policy anniversary. The policy can be surrendered by the Principal Insured. If the request for surrender is received with 3 years from the Date of Commencement (DOC), the monetary value of the fund as on the date of application is payable after 3 years from commencement date.

The Monetary Value of the fund is the NAV as on the date of application for surrender or the date when the revival period is over (in respect of compuslory surrender) as the case may be, multiplied by the number of units in the policyholder's fund as on that date. There will be no surrender charge.

9. Compulsory Surrender.

a. Where the premiums are paid for less than 3 years. In case the policy is not renewed and the fund value is not sufficient to cover relevant charges, the policy shall compulsorily be terminated and the balance amount, if any, will be refunded to the Pl immediately.

b. Where the premiums are paid for at least 3 years. The balance in the policy fund value is at all times, subject to a minimum balance of one annualized premium. In case the fund value falls below this limit, the policy shall compulsorily be terminated with a notice to the Pl and the balance amount in the policy fund, if any shall be refunded to the Pl.

10. Benefit Payable at the end of the term. At the end of the policy term, the balance in the policy fund, if any, will be payable to the principal insured.

11. Policy Loans. No policy loan will be available under this policy.

12. Assignment. No assignment will be allowed under this policy.

INCOME TAX BENEFIT AVAILABLE

"COOLING OFF" PERIOD

If you are not satisfied with the "Terms and Conditions" of the policy, you may return the policy to us within 15 days.

Important : If a person is covered under various policies of the corporation under this plan, then the maximum benefit available to such insured life shall not exceed the cap on benefits under this plan.

IV. Exclusions

1. Common Exclusions in respect of HCB & MSB Benefits:

No benefits are available hereunder and no payment will be made by the Corporation for any claim for Hospital Cash Benefit and Major Surgical Benefit under this Policy on account of Hospitalization directly or indirectly caused by, based on, arising out of or howsoever attributable to any of the following.

a. **"Pre-existing condition"**- any medical condition or any related condition (e.g. illnesses, symptoms, treatments, pains and surgery) that have arisen at some point prior to the commencement of this coverage, irrespective of whether any medical treatment or advice was sought. Any such condition or related condition about which the Pl or insured dependant know, knew or could reasonably have been assumed to have known, will be deemed to be pre-existing. The following conditions will also be deemed to be "pre-existing".

i. Conditions arising between signing the application form and confirmation of acceptance by the Corporation.

ii. Any **Sickness,** illness, complication or ailment arising out of or connected to the pre-existing illness.

b. Any **Sickness** that has been classified as an Epidemic by the Central or State Government.

c. Self afflicted injuries or conditions (attempted suicide), and/or the use of misuse of any drugs or alcohol.

d. Any sexually transmitted diseases or any condition directly or indirectly caused to or associated with Human immuno Deficiency (HV) Virus or any Syndrome or condition of a similar kind ommonly referred to as AIDS.

e. War, invasion, act of foreign enemy hostilities (whether war be declared or not), civit war rebellion revolution, insurrection military or usurped power of civil commotion or loot or pillage in connection herewith.

f. Naval or military operations (including duties of peace time) of the armed forces or air forces or air force and participation in operations requiring the use of arms or which are ordered by military authorities for combating terrorists, rebels and the like.

g. Any natural peril (including but not limited to avalanche, earthquake, volcanic eruptions or any kind of natural hazard).

h. Participation in any hazardous activity or sports including but not limited to racing scuba diving, aerial sports, bungee jumping and mountaineering or in any criminal or illegal activities.

i. Radioactive contamination.

j. Non-allopathic methods of surgery and treatment

2. Additional Exclusions in respect of Hospital Cash Benefit:

No benefits are available hereunder and no payment will be made by the Corporation for any claim for Hospital Cash Benefit under this Policy on account of Hospitalization directly or indirectly caused by, based on, arising out of or howsoever attributable to any of the following:

a. Hospitalization due to illness within the first 180 days from the Date of Cover commencement and 90 days from the date of revival/reinstatement after discontinuance of the cover.

b. Removal of any material that was implanted in a former surgery before Date of Cover commencement

c. Any diagnosis or treatment arising from or traceable to pregnancy (whether uterine or extra uterine), childbirth including caesarean section, medical termination of pregnancy and/or any treatment related to pre and post natal care of the mother or the new born.

d. Hospitalization for the sole purpose of physiotherapy or any ailment for which hospitalization is not warranted due to advancement in medical technology.

e. Any treatment not performed by a Physician or any treatment of a purely experimental nature.

f. Any routine or prescribed medical check up or examination.

g. Medical expenses relating to any hospitalization primarily for diagnostic, X-ray or laboratory examinations.

h. Circumcision, cosmetic or aesthetic treatments of any description, change of gender surgery, plastic surgery (unless such plastic surgery is necessary for the treatment of illness or Accidental Bodily Injury as a direct result of the insured event and performed with in 6 months of the same).

i. Hospitalization for donation of an organ.

j. Hospitalization for correction of birth defects or congenital aromalies.

k. Dental treatment of surgery of any kind unless necessitated by Accidental Bodily Injury.

l. Convalescence, general debility, nervous or other breakdown, rest cure, congenital diseases or defect or anomaly, sterilization or infertility (diagnosis and treatment), any sanatoriums, spa or rest cures or long term care or hospitalization undertaken as a preventive or recuperative measure.

3. Additional Exclusions in respect of Major Surgical Benefit:

No benefits are available hereunder and no payment will be made by the Corporation for any claim for Major Surgical Benefit under this Policy directly or indirectly caused by, based on, arising out of or howsoever attributable to any of the following:

a. Surgeries not listed in the "List of surgical procedures covered" under item II

b. Surgery triggered by health related causes (and not by Accident) within the first 180 days from the commencement date and 90 days from the date of revival/reinstatement after discontinuance of the cover.

c. Any Surgery for which claim has already been made and paid by the Corporation.

d. Any treatment not performed by a Physician/Surgeon

e. Any treatment including Surgery that is performed unconventionally under experimental conditions and purely experimental in nature.

f. Circumcision, cosmetic or aesthetic treatments of any description, change of life surgery or treatment, treatment (including surgery) for obesity, plastic surgery (unless necessary for the treatment of illnes or accidental Bodily Injury as a direct result of the insured event and performed within 6 months of the same).

g. Surgery for donation of an organ.

h. Removal or correction or replacement of any material that was implanted in a former surgery before date of cover commencement.

i. Surgery for correction of birth defects or congenital anomalies.

j. Any diagnosis or treatment or surgery arising from or traceable to pregnancy (whether uterine or extra uterine).

V. Investment of Funds

The premiums allocated to purchase units will be strictly invested in a Health Plus Fund (Income and Growth – Low Risk) as follows:

A. Government/Government guaranteed/ Corporate securities/debt	**Not Less Than 50%**
B. Short term investments: Money Market instruments including A above	Not more than 90%
C. Investment in listed equity shares	Not less than 10% & Not more than 50%

1. Method of Calculation of Unit Price: Unit will be allotted based on the Net Asset Value (NAV) on the date of allotment. There is no Bid-Offer spread. The NAV will be computed on daily basis and will be based on investment performance, Fund Management Charge and whether the fund is expanding or contracting.

a. Applicability of Net Asset Value (NAV) : The premiums received upto 3 p.m. (as per IRDA guidelines) by the servicing branch of the corporation by a local cheque or by a demand draft payable at par at the place where the premium is received, the closing NAV of the day on which premium is received shall be applicable. The premiums received after such time by the servicing branch of the corporation by a local cheque or by a demand draft payable at par at the place where the premium is received, the closing NAV of the next business day shall be applicable.

b. Redeeming of Units : In respect of valid applications received for reimbursement of medical expenses, death claim, etc up to such time by the servicing branch of the Corporation closing NAV of that day shall be applicable. For the valid applications received in respect of Domiciliary Treatment Benefit, death claim etc after 3 p.m. as per IRDA guidelines by the servicing branch of the Corporation the closing NAV of the next business day shall be applicable.

2. Charges Under the Plan :

a. Premium Allocation Charge: This is the percentage of the premium appropriated towards charges from the premium received. The balance known as allocation rate constitutes that part of the premium which is utilized to purchase (investment) units for the policy. The allocation charges are as below:

First year	Thereafter
30%	6%

The above allocation charges shall be applicable for all premiums including any additional premium paid in that particular policy year.

b. Health Insurance Charge: There will be two separate charges for the following benefits:

Hospital Cash Benefit **Major Surgical Benefit**

These charges will be taken every month in respect of all the members covered by canceling appropriate number of units out of the Policy Fund.

These charges, during a policy year, will be based on the age nearer birthday, of the each of the members covered, as at the Policy anniversary coinciding with or immediately preceding the due date of cancellation of units and hence may increase every year on each policy anniversary. The charges will also depend on whether the person covered is male or female and standard or sub-standard as per the underswriting decision.

If more than one member is covered under the policy then the total charges shall be based on the individual ages of all the members and the amount of cover for each such member.

In case of Hospital Cash Benefit, the charges will be applied on the Initial Daily Benefit as mentioned in the policy Schedule.

The charges for Hospital Cash Benefit and/or Major Surgical Benefit will not be deducted once the benefit terminates.

Specimen charges for Rs. 100/- per day for HCB & Rs. 1000/- SA for MSB for standard lives are given as under:

Age	HCB		MCB	
	M	F	M	F
5	24.43	24.43	0	0
15	20.71	20.71	0	0
25	31.39	24.34	1.02	1.38

35	33.59	29.96	1.58	1.75
45	49.29	53.20	3.54	2.64
55	76.08	72.53	7.28	5.16

Note: M & F stand for male & female lives.

Other Charges:

Policy Administration Charge	Rs. 75/- per month during the first policy year and Rs. 25/- per month during the subsequent year.
Fund Management Charge	Levived @ 1.25% per annum of the unit fund at the time of computation of NAV which will be done on daily basis.
Bid/Offer Spread	Nil
Surrender charges	Nil.

Service Tax Charge service tax charged at applicable rates. Currently the effective service rate is 12.36% which includes education cess @ 3%

Right to revise charges

The Corporation reserves the right to revise all or any of the above charges (subject to a maximum limit) except the Premium Allocation charge. The modification in charges will be done with prospective effect with the prior approval of IRDA.

SECTION 45 – INDISPUTABILITY CLAUSE

No policy of Life Insurance shall, after the expiry of two years from the date on which it was effected, be called in question by an insurer on the ground that a statement made in the proposal for insurance or in any report of a medical officer or referee or friend of the Insured or in any other document leading to the issue of the Policy, was inaccurate or false, unless the insurer shows such statement was on a material matter or suppressed facts which is it was material to disclose and that it was fraudulently made by the policy holder and that the policy holder knew at the time of making it that the statement was false or that it suppressed facts which it was material to disclose.

Note : "Material" shall mean and include all important, essential and relevant information in the context of underwriting the risk to be covered by the corporation.

BENEFIT ILLUSTRATION

Frequency of Premium Payment. Annual	Annual Premium Rs. 12,000
Number of Lives Covered. Single Male	Per Day Hospital Cash Benefit (HCB) Rs. 2000 Per Day Hospital Cash Benefit in ICU. Rs. 4000 Major Surgical Benefit (MSB). Rs. 4,00,000

Age at Entry: 35 years

End of Policy Year	Cumulative Premium Paid Till the Year	Maximum Guaranteed Benefit		Fund Value Available for Domiciliary Treatment Benefit	
		HCB	MSB	Variable SCENARIO 1	Variable SCENARIO 2
1	12000	54000	400000	6367	6649
2	24000	189000	400000	16600	17565
3	36000	198000	400000	27258	29369

4	48000	207000	400000	38350	42125
5	60000	216000	400000	49865	55883
6	72000	225000	400000	61787	70694
7	84000	234000	400000	74043	86555
8	96000	243000	400000	86739	103650
9	108000	252000	400000	99882	122068
10	120000	261000	400000	113464	141898
11	132000	270000	400000	127512	163265
12	144000	270000	400000	142005	186260
13	156000	270000	400000	156965	211024
14	168000	270000	400000	172410	237706
15	180000	270000	400000	188338	266447
16	192000	270000	400000	204790	297441
17	204000	270000	400000	221842	330938
18	216000	270000	400000	239442	367071
19	228000	270000	400000	257613	406066
20	240000	270000	400000	276346	448131
21	252000	270000	400000	295678	493544
22	264000	270000	400000	315609	542565
23	276000	270000	400000	336179	595518
24	288000	270000	400000	357406	652729
25	300000	270000	400000	379294	714541
26	312000	270000	400000	401870	781343
27	324000	270000	400000	425063	853464
28	336000	270000	400000	448692	931148
29	348000	270000	400000	472562	1014654
30	360000	270000	400000	496383	1104180

i. This illustration is applicable to a non-smoker male/female standard (from medical, life style and occupation point of view) life.

ii. The non-guaranteed benefits (1) and (2) in above illustration are calculated so that they are consistent with the Projected Investment Rate of Return assumption of 6% p.a. (Scenario I) and 10% p.a. (Scenario 2) respectively. In other words, in preparing this benefit illustration, it is assumed that the Projected Investment Rate of Return that LICI will be able to earn throughout the term of the policy will be 6% p.a. or 10% p.a., as the case may be. The Projected Investment Rate of Return is not guaranteed.

iii. The main objective of the illustration is that the clinet is able to appreciate the features of the product and the flow of benefits in different circumstances with some level of quantification.

iv. LIC does not authorise its agents/intermediaries, staff and officials to express their opinion on the future performance of the "ULIP" fund, excepting the above illustrative rate of 6% and 10% growth.

v. Domiciliary Treatment Benefit can be claimed from the 3rd year onwards after at least 3 years premiums have been paid.

1. For variable amounts in the benefit illustration, it is assumed that premiums have been paid as and when due and no domiciliary treatment benefit has been availed earlier.
2. Maximum HCB shown above is inclusive of 9 days stay in ICU in the first year and 30 days in subsequent years.

STATUTORY WARN : "Some benefits are guaranteed and some benefits are variable with returns based on the future performance of your life insurance company. If your policy offers guaranteed returns then these will be clearly marked "guaranteed" in the illustration table on this page. If your policy offers variable returns then the illustrations on this page will show two different rates of assumed investment returns. These assumed rates of return are not guaranteed and they are not upper or lower limits of what you might get back as the value of your policy is dependant on a number of factors including future investment performance."

RISKS BORNE BY THE POLICYHOLDER

i. LIC's Health Plus is a Unit Linked Health Insurance product which is different from the traditional insurance products and is subject to risk factors.

ii. The premium paid in Unit Linked Insurance policies are subject to investment risks associated with capital markets and the NAVs of the units may go up or down based on the performance of fund and factors influencing the capital market and the insured is responsible for his/her decisions.

iii. Life Insurance Corporation of India is only the name of the Insurance Company and LIC's Health Plus is only the name of the unit linked health insurance contract and does not in any way indicate the quality of the contract, its future prospects of returns.

iv. Please know the associated risks and the applicable charges, from your Insurance agent or the Intermediary or policy document of the insurer.

v. The fund offered under this contract is the name of the fund and do not in any way indicate the quality of these plans, their future prospects and returns.

vi. All benefits under the policy are also subject to the Tax Laws and other financial enactments as they exist from time to time.

45

CATASTROPHE INSURANCE

The tragic and unforeseen evenly of catastrophe causes multiple losses to society such as loss of life, destruction of property, loss of revenue, and additional expenses. Due to dislocation of such things, consequential losses occur such loss of business, non-availability of social facilities. The society expects that insurers should provide quick and effective indemnity of such losses. Insurance industry practively support the economic recovery process.

The insurers should manage the crises through insurance schemes by coordinating with the Insurance Councils, by quick survey and assessment of losses, develop response system and educate the policy-holders and general public against the catastrophe losses. The insurers should coordinate the loss compensation process through the General Council by taking the help of police, hospital and government machineries. The insurers after occurring of catastrophe should try to contract the beneficiaries at the earliest possible. They should through surveyors try to compensate the losses as quickly as possible on humanitarian grounds. The insurers and not the insured should take the responsibilities of verification and assessment of loss through photographs, newspaper, ratio and televisions. Insurers should waive documents other than essential ones in settlement of claims, work with other insurers and all other authorities in quick settlement of claims, allows disposal of salvage and settlements of other dues.

The catastrophe is unforeseen and unpredictable but it brings fury and ferocity to human life and property. The destruction is unimaginable. The resultant losses of life, property and other will take long time to recompensate. There is need of insuring and losses. The insurers have to be very careful in designing suitable product at a reasonable price. The insurers and government should educate people of the serious consequences of catastrophe e.g., floods, earth-quake and tsunamies. India is prone to serious socio-economic consequences and natural calamities. In India, Tariff Advisory Committee (TAC) is guiding fire insurance to protect catastrophe losses. Riot, strike and terrorism perils are the high profile social risks. The risks of flood, earthquake and convulsions are caused by nature. Therefore they are natural catastrophe. The catastrophe insurance covers social risks (such as, riots strikes, terrorism, perils) and natural risks (such as flood, earthquake and Tsunami etc.).

Riot

Generally property and generally insurance do not cover rit risks, but the increasing incidents of riots have compelled the insurer to consider its insurance. People in India, can get fire insurance policy plus coverage of riot at an additional premium payment. Since people have not purchased riot risk policies, they are denied of claims arising out riots. The Causa proxima is used to decide the riot risks and its payment. Government has been very particular about the purchase of riot policies. It motivates people to purchase fire policy wherein riots etc. are insured with payment of extra premium.

Riots have posed various problems in various parts of country. Even in U.S.A., riots killed 200 people and billions of dollars were destroyed in 1960. Insurers were unwilling to ensure riots risks because of his potential losses, inadequate premiums and moral hazard. Government provided reinsurance to insurance of riot-risks. Thus the riot insurance started since then.

Strikes

Strikes are also unforeseen and causing damage to property and life and also loss of revenue. Previously it was uninsured. But now it is insured under fire policy with payment of extra premium. The public sector companies have started insuring strike risks. The insurance act is amended accordingly.

Terrorism Risks

Terrorism is increasing fastly. Loss of life, property and revenue become unthinkable events. The extra-premium is paid under fire policy to cover terrorist risks. The devasting attack on the World Trade Centre and Pentagon on 11 September, 2001 forced insurers to confront the international terrorism. Companies have come forward for the protection against terrorism. They have started terrorism insurance policy covering terrorism risks.

Problems of terrorism insurance are non-availability of data for proper measurement of risks, absence of information of total loss exposure and high loss potential of terrorist actions. Insurance and reinsurance can contain terrorism risk. Insurers can insist on how to deal with terrorism and maintain minimum security standards and educate clients on best practices for protecting individuals and properties from attack. Government also help overcome the terrorist risk. Government can declare terrorism insurance mandatory. Terrorism premium surcharde is levied on all property policies. Spreading the risk throughout society expand the risk pool.

Besides terrorism insurance, fixed investment in risk securities is being practised. Multi-event securities may become a partial long-term solution for privately insuring terrorism risk.

Terrorism Risk Insurance Act was passed on 26th November, 2002. Now, all licensed/admitted primary insurers, surplus lives insurers, state workers' compensation funds and residual market will offer coverage for certified acts of terrorism. The federal government will pay upto 90 per cent of any insured losses arising from such acts but does not grant any backstop for "non-certified" terrorism.

Austria developed terrorism pool from January 1, 2003. The pool gives automatic protection against property damage and business interruption for industrial, commercial and private properties.

Floods

The cover of floods was excluded till March 2001 when it was offered on extra premium to fire policy. The fire policy covers the flood-risks today. If any one does not like to get cover of floods certain discounts will be made in the usual premium rate. Insurance cover for natural disasters have become socially oriented concept in India. The fire policy in this context reads as "Loss destruction or damage directly caused by storm, cyclone, typhoon, tempest, hurricane, tornado, flood or inundation excluding those resulting from earthquake, volcanic, eruption or other convulsion of nature" would be idemnified.

Heavy mansoon rains trigged landslides and floods in Mumbai of India in July 2005 and August 2006. All the losses were not insured although insured property was USD 0.8 billion. Insurers have received 20,000 incidents of claims ranging more than Rs. 2,000 crore.

In USA, National Flood Insurance Program (NFIP) has started to insure flood risks. The maximum limit was USD 2.50 lacs for buildings and USD 1.00 has for contents of buildings. Private insurers provide flood cover for large industrial risks as a part of comprehensive policies.

Building insurance in Switzerland covers fire and flood damage. It is compulsory to insure buildings.

Earthquake

Fire policy as social obligation has started providing cover for earthquake on an additional premium. It does not cover loss due to volcanic eruption or convulsions of nature. Fire policy, now, cover flood as well as losses due to an earthquake.

Pakistan, Afghanistan and India were hit by earthquake on 8th October, 2005 causing fatalities to 73,300 people. They were uninsured. Similarly the earthquake looses in China and Iran have also been uninsured. The life and property losses have been very high. Insurance has paid US USD 2068 million in 2004 out of total damage of USD 13442 in 2004. It reveals that there is need of insurance of earthquake losses.

Table 45.1 Earthquake losses

Date	*Country*	*Dead or missing*	*Injurd*	*Total Loss in USD in million*	*Insured Loss in USD in million*
07.01.2000	China	2,55,000	NA	19,222	0
26.01.2001	India, Pakistan Nepal	15,000	1,66,835	4,964	110
26.12.2003	Iran	26,271	30,000	2,018	0
26.12.2004	Indonesia, Thailand	2,20,000	1,25,000	13,442	2068
08.10.2005	Pakistan, India Afghanistan	73,300	74,000	5,000	0
27.05.2006	Indonesia, Sumatra	5778	37883 (1173742 homeless)	3,000	40

Hurricanes and Windstorms

The insured property damaged amounts to USD 48 billions due to hurricanes in Charley, Frances, Iran in 2005. The windstorm insured losses were to the extent of USD 69 billion in 2005. Katrina, Rita and Wilma have caused damage to property and life.

Winter storm in Europe caused damage totalling $ 1.9 billion in 2006. Insurance companies helped Denmark, Sweden, UK and Germany.

Japan was hit by 10 typhoons in 2004. The catastrophe losses particularly wind losses would increase in future as a result of global warming. It is for the insurance companies to come forward to insure wind losses exclusively over 26° c temperature of sea causes sea-storm which lashes the land. Property and life are endagered. Insurance is needed for the purpose. Since 2004, sea warming is common phenomena. So, the coastal areas of all the countries are facing the problems of wind losses, when wind speed is 150 km per hour, the sea surges with 1.7 metre and if the wind speed is more than 250 km per hour, the sea-tide taken more than 5 metre.

Tsunami

Tsunami has posed a great threat to the public for its survival and rehabilitation. It provides huge opportunity for insurance to enhance risk awareness of natural calamities. Insurance is most suitable financial protection to public in natural calamities. Underwriting natural catastrophe risk posses serious challenges to insurers. The immeasurability low frequency and high severity of catastrophe risks have made insurers to decide whether to sell or not catastrophe insurance decides the underwriting process and premium rate involving geology, engineering and economics Insurers refine their risk estimates by collecting and assessing additional data. Nanotechnology is an example of a new technology which is used by the insurers.

The Tsunami on 26th December 2004 hit 12 coastal states on the Indian Ocean and has been highest number of fatalities which ranged to more than 2,80,000. The scale of the catastrophe triggered worldwide sympathy. Wind storms and flood claimed 6,700 people in Haitti in 2004. Out of the total losses caused by catastrophes in 2004, USD 49 billion was covered by property insurance.

Insurance cover could be an effective way of minimising the tsunami damage, but it is very low in India.

Table 45.2 Insurance and Catastrophe Loss

Region	*Number*						*Victims*						*Insured Loss*					
	2004		*2005*		*2006*		*2004*		*2005*		*2006*		*2004*		*2005*		*2006*	
	No.	*%*	*No.*	*%*	*No.*	*%*	*No.*	*%*	*No.*	*%*	*No.*	*%*	*No.*	*%*	*No.*	*%*	*No.*	*%*
Nor. America	46	13.9	54	13.6	43	12.3	7342	2.4	3781	3.9	517	1.7	32911	67.7	72633	871	9658	60.8
Sou. America	16	4.8	21	5.3	11	3.2	718	0.2	943	1.0	485	1.6	2	0.0	47	0.1	587	3.7
Asia	169	50.9	208	52.4	169	48.4	290412	96.2	86633	92.4	19789	63.7	12094	24.9	2660	3.2	1814	11.4
Europe	46	13.9	59	14.9	45	12.9	1042	0.3	659	0.7	4166	13.4	1203	2.5	7039	8.4	2569	16.2
Africa	36	10.8	41	10.3	50	14.3	2666	0.9	1851	1.9	3569	11.5	577	1.2	49	0.1	68	0.4
Oceania/ Australia	5	1.5	6	1.5	2	0.6	39	0.0	26	0.0	14	0.0	1261	2.6	359	0.4	335	2.1
Ocean/Space	14	4.2	8	2.0	29	8.3	216	0.1	125	0.1	2531	8.1	578	1.2	609	0.7	850	5.4
World Total	332	100.0	397	100.0	349	100.0	302435	100.0	97018	100.0	31071	100.0	48626	100.0	83396	100.0	15881	100.0

Insured loss of total catastrophe has increased from USD 48626 mn in 2004 to USD 83396 mn in 2005. The maximum loss paid by insurance has been in North America followed by Asia and Europe. The catastrophe loss was 5 billion in 1987 which increased to 40 billion in 2005. It reveals rising trend of catastrophe loss which should be insured to the possible extent.

Atomic Risk Insurance

The Atomic Energy Commission in USA appointed insurance industry as a leader to study nuclear facilities and current state of the field. The commission concluded that the only solution was to creater risk pools. Share and Stock companies formed the Nuclear Energy Liability Insurance Association to write third party liability coverage and the Nuclear Energy property Insurance Association to write physical damage cover. Mutual insurers formed a combined reinsurance pool to write back types of coverage. The Price-Anderson Act in 1957 was passed to fix the maximum liability for any licensed nuclear facility at the amount of private liability insurance available. The Government was ready to pay to the extent of USD 500 million.

PROSPECTS OF CATASTROPHE INSURANCE

Catastrophe are unexpected occurrences and therefore, best protected through insurance pools. Catastrophes can be extremely large and destructive and hence uninsurable in the absence of the ability to create capacities. Its insurability requires coordinated action on the part of governments and insurers. There could be tie-up and coordination at regional and international levels for diversifying pools and lowering costs. The insurance facilitates risk taking and asset building across the economy and enables a virtuous cycle of wealth creation. Risk betterment is best possible in open underwriting one innovative approaches to rating or risks.

Insurance industry has been traditionally innovative inensuring insurability in all areas of the economy and has the capability to tailor insurance requirements. The sharing of the risk can be advantageously shared from the level of the policy holder to that of the insurer in catastrophe coverage.

The insurer, global reinsurer, capital markets and government should pool the funds for meeting catastrophic risks in such a way as occurrence of large magnitude do not prove a setback for the economy. There is need to make all economic losses as insured losses. Appropriate pricing and offering of terms require that the insured is motivated to reduce both physical and moral hazards. The insurer can use mathematical and technological tools and create maps and models to analyse and understand various risk profile across reforms and risk clusters. Mandatory insurance coverage may be experienced to couple people to join the pool High quality data is required by insurers to control exposures and determine risk premium as well as probable maximum losses.

Once the insurers and government come to take change of risk management in catastrophic area, many risk control measures will fall in place acrose the economy insurers have definite role in giving a dynamic impetus to an insured economy in hazard identification, risk assessment, risk, preventiors and mitigation in the area of catastrophic risks.

Mumbai flood has taken insurance companies by surprise. In 2006, all insurance companies had purchased more catastrophic reinsurance cover. With the increased reinsurance cover purchased.

Table 45.3

Major catastrophe in India *(Rs. in crore)*

Event	*Year*	*Market Loss*	*Equicted to 2006*	*Gross Premium*	*% to GDP*
Gujarat Cyclone	1998	1096	1591	8703	0.71
Orissa Cyclone	1999	170	215	9454	0.54
Gujarat Earth quabe	2001	431	500	9799	0.56
Mumbai Floods	2005	2500	2500	21337	0.61

Setting up of National Disaster Management Authority is a holistic approach to disaster prevention, mitigation and relief by Government Authority the role of Disaster and catastrophe insurance is very much realised in present age.

QUESTIONS

1. What is Catastrophe Insurance? Discuss its scope and feature.
2. "Catastrophe is natural or man made or both" Examine.
3. Explain the loss caused by strikes and riots.
4. Discuss how terrorism risks are insured. Explain its coverage.
5. Examine the progress of earthquake insurance.
6. Examine how hurricane and wind storms are insured.
7. Evaluate the total catastrophe insurance.
8. Illustrate the Atomic Risk Insurance.

46

LIABILITY INSURANCE

Liability insurance does not have direct policy-holder. Insurer does not deal with policy-holder but deals with third parties. Each liability policy has different nuances in its wording. The claim handling is largely dependent on policy wording. The right to defend exist on the insurer. Claims procedures are worded in the policy. The insured risks and excluded risks are properly given in the policy. Liability claims deserve more attention.

Doctors are liable for ill-treatment of their patients. Employers are liable for accident or death of employees during performance. There are several other examples which can cause liability to a party. Liability claims to be more complicated because of the sheer number of parties. The insurer is liable to pay the claims as per the contract of liability insurance and policy clause. The insured has to prove his liability to third party for which insurance is taken.

Liability policies may be assured either on claims. Made or an occurrence Based Wording Claims. Made Wording indicates that claim should have occurred during the period of insurance. The claim should be made during the policy period of 12 months during which the policy is inforce. In an occurrence Based Wording, the event giving risk to the clams must occur during the policy period. The insurer would respond whenever the claim is made.

Property and Casualty Risks

Liability insurance in USA deals with property and casualty insurance. Controlled Master Programs (CMF) are widely used by insurers. It aims to provide global risk managers with the ability to manage and control worldwide exposure. CMP is a group of linked insurance policies. The set of local policies is issued in conjunction with the master policy in any territories. Underwriters and intermediaries must assess, the local laws ana regulations. Certain laws require admitted liability policies. Non-admitted coverage is allowed.

CMP provides uniform coverage and uniform liability limits. Given the difference in the content of liability policies in different countries which is achieved through master policy. Difference in conditions allows the coverage provided by the master policy. CMP specifies worldwide jurisdiction and territory, so that the insurance company can respond to third party claims regardless of where they arise.

Local Insurance Requirements

The laws and regulations of local country govern the issue and operation of liability insurance. The business practices of the country also decide the procedure of insurance business. Warehousing, manufacturing, after sale services, maintenance or specific contract would call for an admitted policy of liability insurance. The local country's requirement of standard policy and compulsory provisions should be followed by the multinational insurance companies. For example, General liability policies are prevalent in Germany.

Local policies limit the clause of operation. For example, mandatory risk retention is imposed in Brazil. Insurers should issue all policies on economical and efficient bases.

Contracts' Liability Insurance

The contracts are given by the principal business house when the contractors give the proof of insurance for workmen's compensation, employers liability and general liability insurance.

American International Group Inc. (AIG) through its member companies around the world provides effective services to the contractors and business companies with its global experience and network. Multinational Companies admit to their membership only which have experienced claim professionals familiar with the legal requirements of the country to provide effective services and handling worldwide liability claims. CNP provides its services to membercountries with a true worldwide risk management tool.

Progress of Liability Insurance

The liability claims totalled $ 84 billion in 2002 worldwide. It one-sixth of all non-life claims. The costs of general liability claims grew faster than overall economic activity in developed nations. The most problematic lives of liability insurance are product liability, medical malpractices, directors and officers, errors, omissions and employment practices liability.

Insurers face the problems of premium calculation as the traditional methods of actuarial calculations are not suitable for it. So, they adopt risk prevention measures, limit accumulated risk. Insurers have to be vigilant in pricing and offering cover for liability risks. They pay more attention to wording and policy language. Insurers should cease underwriting if the limit may cross insurability and beyond imagination.

The growth of liability insurance depends upon economic factors, medical expenses, property value and wages, life spans, legal expenses and others. The severity of claims is affected by rising medical costs, property value and wages. Trust and compensation are also influencing liability claims.

The growth rate of liability insurance during 1998-2004 was 8.8% twice than the growth rate in non-life insurance Brazil, Chile and Colombia recorded the highest growth rates ranging from 13% to 15%.

Table 46.1 Liability Insurance Claims (2002)

Country	*General Liability*				*Motor Liability $ billions 2002*	*Total Non-Life $ billion 2002*
	$ Billion 1997	*Average Loss Ratio 2002*	*% of total Non-life*	*% of TDP*		
US	66.7	99.7	2.1	0.64	86.4	318.0
Canada	1.3	73.5	7.0	0.18	3.4	18.8
Germany	4.2	65.1	10.0	0.21	11.1	40.8
UK	3.1	99.0	12.0	0.20	15.2	25.9
France	2.8	113.2	9.0	0.19	6.5	30.6
Italy	2.3	102.0	10.0	0.19	13.0	22.3
Spain	0.5	N.A.	4.0	0.08	3.9	12.7
Netherland	0.4	N.A.	3.0	0.10	3.1	14.1
Japan	1.5	53.37	5.0	0.04	7.2	32.4
Australia	0.9	124.2	15.0	0.25	2.1	6.1
10 Countries	83.8	98.2	16.0	0.37	151.9	521.8

EMERGING MARKETS

Liability Insurance is growing in emerging markets. It has taken diversified forms of development *viz.*, commercial general liability, product liability, professional indemnity, directors and officers D & O liability, product recall, personal liability, motor liability, social security systems. The liability insurance has taken the form of third party risks, export financial protection. Liability insurance covers the financial consequences arising out of the insured's obligation to pay compensation for harm caused to third parties. There may be commercial as well as personal risks.

Liability insurance is called, "Long-tail" business where the claim picture will be fully developed long after the policy has expired Globalisation and burgeoning international trade stimulate demand for liability insurance. Ethical, moral, cultural, religious and social norms and standards play an important role for development of liability insurance.

Liability insurance penetration varies significantly even among industrialised economies. Technological and industrial development also contribute liability insurance. In many emerging markets, traditional principle of fault applies to liability insurance but recent changes have shifted the burden of proof onto defendant. The introduction of punitive damages and liability extension have destorted the economic functioning of liability insurance.

PROSPECTS OF LIABILITY INSURANCE

Indian mindset pertaining to happening, i.e., what is allotted cannot be blotted has hindered liability insurance in India. 'Liability and accidents are sure to happen and cannot be obviated, have been the main drawback of insurance. Liability insurance has taken a good start with the education and realization of one's responsibilities and duties. It keeps pace with global – business where ventures have crossed the domestic boundaries. It contemplates exporting of products and services to tough and unknown jurisdiction.

Liability insurance has become only source of financial recourse in the even of litigation compared with the normal course or business, if unfortunate entrepreneur is faced with litigation finds no help for expensing legal fees and compensation duty to defend claims handling also makes a compulsive case for buying liability insurance. Liability insurance makes it possible for the insured to outsource adverse litigation management. It provids definite value addition through the intervention in risk management and insurance buying. The coverage depends on interpretation and negotiation skills of product knowledge. Specialised brokers are required for liability programmes and insurance buyers.

The liability insurance claim is very low in India. It makes insurers to decide premium rate. Many of the anti-preneurs and professionals are encouraged to seek liability insurances. Liability insurance permits the insurer to heave a higher risk so that a large number of persons are willing to take this insurance. It keeps overall claim ratios within controllable limits. The insurers should keep adequate reserves to meet an unexpectedly large claim if ever it arises.

The Future

With the current growth, of the Indian economy, there is much hope of liability insurance. It requires Training, Expanding, Self reliance and Targeting (TEST) strategies for growth. Training is need to make the insurer-people expert in the line of liability procedures. The insurance players need intensive training 90 most classes of liability insurance demand intensive and sophisticated underwriting. The insurers have to find new avenues of insurance long term growth is possible through analysing the market, seeing the need for liability insurance. There is need of developing underwriting capability and expertise. In is must to set up a liability department within the company to gain experience of foreign underwriter, local adaptability and quick decision making. The industrial sectors and economic trends are helpful for developing liability insurance. Liability insurance has grown with IT sector. India has leap-frogged to the top of the heap in the provision of these services to the rest of the world.

With the explosion in internet usage and services together with hardware and software advances, it is surprising that insurance mechanisms to transfer risk have not been able to match these studies in equal measures. Legal liability led a rather blithe and low level existence in insurers' minds and consciousness in the form of compulsory third party motor insurance and workmen's compensation mandated by law. Public Liability Insurance ACT, 1991 has offered Indian insurer marketplace for premises, products and environmental pollution coverage, as a consequence of development tort and judicial reform. The technology insurance areas have physical assets, human assets liabilities, employee dishonesty and crime. The liabilities include premises, professional and management liabilities including directors and officers liability, employment practices liability, fiduciary liability, professional errors and omissions, intellectual property, internet liability and cyber crime. Physical assets included automobiles, equipment, property, catastrophes, terrorism and machinery Human assets include sickness and long term disability, workmen's compensation and employer's liability key man liability, kidnap and ransom.

Cross-border characteristics include the country's Political Risk arising out of confiscation, expropriations currency inconvertibility, mergers and acquisious risk, tax liability risk, investor management and professional liability risk, outside directorship liability and need for admitted insurance placements in different countries. Intellectual property, multi jurisdictional disputes, individual's identity, difficulty in assessing damages, technical exposures including mechanical faults, software errors, performance efficacy, programming errors. Exposures arising from errors, omissions, libel and trademark violations arising from the use of internet for a huge volume of transactions which could be laid waste by therefore, virus attacks.

Companies began to contractually require their vendors to obtains some form of insurance to protect them from accident or criminal losses. Litigation against the clinical trials industries has increased manifold-Clinical trails insurance can offer protection against some of the liabilities companies with inadequate risk management practices require insurance. The clinical trials insurance includes, liabilities arising from death or injury, properly damage, lack of care, improper disclosures, conflicts of interests.

The clinical trail insurance covers the trails carried out by the insured causing death physical injury and harm to health. The damage involves claimants' fees, cost, expenses etc. The maximum liability under this policy is limits to the indemnity chosen by the insured and stated in the policy. The deterioration of health occurred without participation in clinical trial is excluded. The clinical trial insurance does not cover claims arising out of war ionizory radiation, hepatitis AIDS deliberate disregard of the need to be taken reasonably to prevent claims and so on. If any event occurs that may affect this insurance, the insured must report it to the insurer without delay. Any death occurrence must be notified to the insurer early enough so that it to can arrange for a post mortem. The insured must help insurance company to ascertain the facts and reduce the damages.

The liability on the part of Directors and officers of the company has been increasing in recent times. The majority of these proceeding relate to wente collar crime like insider trading, fraud, tax liabilities, tax evasion or corporate man slaughter issues like the breath of health and safety offences statutes.

QUESTIONS

1. What is liability Insurance?
2. Explain the property and casualty risks.
3. Discuss the local insurance requirements for liability insurance.
4. Examine the contractor's, liability insurance.
5. Illustrate the progress of liability insurance.
6. Describe the emerging markets of liability insurance.

47

CREDIT INSURANCE AND SURETY

Credit insurance and surety is closely tied to the economic development. Credit insurance is a risk management tool the compensates policyholder when their clients fails to pay for goods and services. Credit insurance enables sellers to extend credit more liberally. Surety compensates the beneficiary if a contractual, legal or regularly obligation is not met. The legal need for surety is more important for the economic well-being of the country. Companies undertaking projects for government or semi-public institutions guarantee their work with surety bonds.

Credit insurance and surety are differently used in different countries according to their specific rules and regulations. The need for credit insurance is observed because of rising of international trade faster than GDP and growing specialisation. Export and domestic trade have opined emerging markets for credit insurance. The global surety insurance is expected to grow with rising GDP. It is oftenly demanded in Asian and European markets. The general insurers are the underwriters of credit insurance and surety. The credit insurance depends upon financial markets particularly banking products. The factoring companies in USA by company's receivable for immediate and discounted payment. Therefore, the factors often by credit insurance to cover the risk of not collecting then trade receivables.

Credit insurance companies control their exposures through limit management as they provide cover for 60 to 120 days. They gain better with the use of information technology for credit quality of policy-holder and risks accumulations. Reinsurance Companies cover 50% of the credit insurance. Similarly surety guarantees also increase. Credit insurance and surety bonds are guarantees insurance that the commitments will be fulfilled. Credit insurance assures payment and surety assures performances.

Suretyship is a bond and contract in which the insurer provides a guarantee to the policyholder or beneficiary that a third party *i.e.*, the principal will meet its contractual, legal or regulatory obligations. 'For example, a contractor is engaged to construct a building as per specification but the office room should be constructed first within 3 months. If the contractor fails to finish the work on some valid ground, the surety company undertakes the construction work. The contractor is known as principal and the building owner is beneficiary. The contract may be of any commercial nature. Suretyship includes performance bond, advance payment bond, labour and material payment bond and maintenance bond. Similarly commercial bonds includes customs bond, tax bonds, license and permit board and court bonds.

An surety bond increases the likelihood of a project being completed as initially agreed. It enhances the principal's credit worthiness. The surety company's expertise in pre-qualifying the principal. Surety involves disciplined underwriting, exposure management and use of reinsurance.

Background of Credit Insurance and Surety

The first credit insurance yook place in 1820 principally offer fire and life insurance by British Commercial Insurance Company. The surety market started in 1894 in USA which required the purchase of surety bonds on construction projects. The credit insurance and surety could not develop much. Credit insurance policies have covered commercial risks with the experience of last years. It has developed gradually since last 15 years. The political risks are covered only in combination of commercial risks coverage.

Short term credit covered provide for consumer goods, spare parts and raw materials. Medium term credit covers capital goods. Credit insurance is being helped.

The premium volume of credit insurance has increased from $ 4340 million in 1998 to $ 6591 million in 2004. Western Europe constitutes more than 70 per cent of share premium. 0.016 per cent of GDP is collected as premium credit insurance worldwide. The Suretyship premium has increased from $ 5391 million in 1998 to $ 7644 million in 2004. 0.019 per cent of GDP is collected as premiums for surety ship.

Functions of Credit Insurance

Credit insurance protects a seller from the risk of buyer nonpayment, which may occur due to commercial or political risks. The commercial risks cover buyer insolvency and extended late payment and, failure to pay within a fixed days of the due date. Extended late payment is protracted default. Political risks involves nonpayment on an export contract or project due to government's actions. It includes intervention to prevent the transfer of payment, cancellation of a license, acts of war or civil conflict or the government's enactment of laws or other measures.

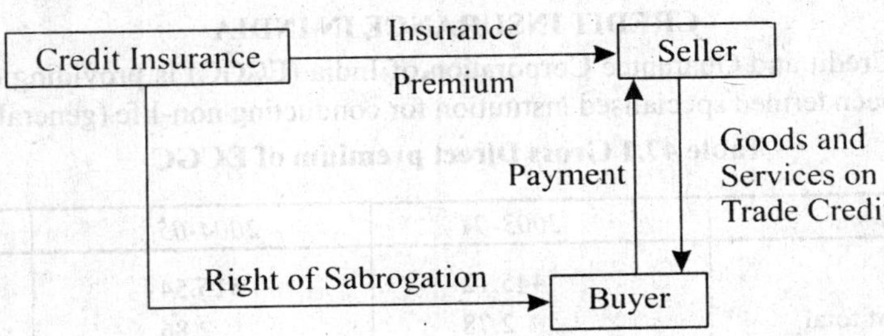

Fig. 47.1 Functions of credit Insurance.

The credit insurance gets the right of collection directly from buyer who failed to pay to seller. The credit insurer pays the amount of trade credit to seller if buyer fails to pay to the seller.

TYPES OF CREDIT INSURANCE

Credit insurance covers all the commercial trade receivable under 'Comprehensive Policy'. When the insurer finds that the individual buyer is not creditworthy, it does select the risk. Credit insurance policies are annually renewable. Premium rate is set at the inception of the policy. The insurer declares its turnover either monthly, quarterly or annually depending upon the policy. The renewal policy is issued at a discount of 10 to 20 percent, in non-claim. The insurer manages its trade credit relationship efficiently. There are specific account policies which cover only certain named accounts. Single Account Policies cover a single named account. The catastrophe credit policies insure risk from catastrophic trade credit default. It carries larger premium.

Credit insurers have started selling credit information to the sellers who will be cauthous in selling their creditworthy customers that is decided on the basis of capital character and capacity. Capital refers to the financial strength which is evaluated on the basis of 3–5 years of financial statements including balance sheet, income statement, statement of cash flows and statement of owners' equity. Cost records are used for contractors' jobs. Character refers to reputation for fair and business like dealings. Capacity refers to the ability to perform which is assessed by the buyers' capacity of operation and marketability.

Proper policy design is essential for credit insurance management. Self retention, coinsurance, limit setting, short term cover etc. are adopted for risk management. Reinsurance and risk scrutinisation are also done proper management of credit risks.

REINSURANCE

When credit insurers are confronted with default, reinsurance helps to smooth the loss impact. The loss ratio of an individual credit insurer tends to vary even more than that of overall market. It require transfer of risk through reinsurance. Reinsurance lowers the cost of capital of credit insures by reducing their earnings volatility.

Types of Reinsurance

There are two types of reinsurance *i.e.*, proportional and non-proportional. The insurer and the reinsurance share premiums and losses at a contractual defined ratio under proportional reinsurance. A treaty is set for an amount up to which the direct insurer will pay all losses and reinsurer pays all or predetermined percentage of losses above this amount upto a cover limit. The reinsurance is feasible through equity, debt and hybrid securities. Non-proportional reinsurance protects against exceptionally large losses. The advantage of reinsurance is that it is indemnity base and have no basis risk. Hedging tools leave the insurer exposed to the risk that the losses it incurs will not be covered.

CREDIT INSURANCE IN INDIA

In India, Export Credit and Guarantee Corporation of India (ECGC) is providing cover for credit insurance. It has been termed specialised institution for conducting non-life (general) insurance.

Table 47.1 Gross Direct premium of ECGC

Gross Direct Premium	*2003-04*	*2004-05*	*2005-06*
In Crore Rs.	445.12	515.54	578.46
Market share in % of total	2.78	2.86	—
Growth %	7.0	16.36	12.20

Source: Sigma various Issues

ECGC has done Rs. 445.12 crore in 2003-2004 as compare Rs. 374 crore in 2002-2003. It has increased to Rs. 578.46 crore in 2005-2006.

QUESTIONS

1. What is Credit Insurance and Surety? Discuss their salient features.
2. Examine the background of credit insurance and surety.
3. Explain the functions of Credit Insurance.
4. What are the types of Credit Insurance? Explain.
5. Illustrate the role of reinsurance in Credit Insurance and Surety.
6. Examine the progress of credit insurance in India.

48

CORPORATE GOVERNANCE

The insurance and consumer community is well protected by good corporate governance. There is need to involve consumers to express their responses through an effective method. The dominant shareholders should work for the interests of the consumers and not purely in their self interest. There is need to develop an effective mechanism to cheek corporate behaviour. Only market mechanism and regulatory frameworks cannot control their behaviour. Till market mechanism, the company has accumulated sufficient funds of policyholders and declare himself insolvent. Thus, the financial conditions of consumers are made unfavourable.

The management is made responsible for some failures towards consumers' interest whereas the shareholders are enjoying their supremacy. The healthy relationship between policyholders and shareholders should be developed for the economic and social development of country. The Board of shareholders and Management must see that the policyholders' interests are fully served by the company. The corporate Governance in Indian Insurance Companies have got momentum but its progress is very slow as the management is not very efficient. There are lack of experienced directors, inadequate information systems, inadequate system of control, individual and accountability is not developed. Ownership structure and lack of enforcement capabilities have caused poor governance.

COMPONENTS OF CORPORATE GOVERNANCE

The corporate governance is mainly concern with how ownership influence, promoting corporate fairness, transparency ana accountability Briefly, Corporate Governance means doing everything, to improve relationship between companies and their shareholders to improve the quality. If directors, to encourage people to think long-term, to ensure that information needs of all stakeholders. Corporate Governance becomes an organise system when companies are directed and controlled by the management in the best interest of the stakeholders and insuring greater transparency and financial reporting. The investors' confidence should be instilled and not shaken by the management practices. Corporate Governance in insurance companies makes corporate entities, institutional investment and business opportunity.

Insurance Companies are important constituent of Corporate Governance. Keeping an open mind, listening and learning from others, ready to share ideas and thoughts recognising and rewarding cooperation and franchise, development skill of employees. Concerned for delivering on promises inducing teamwork and inspiring management to their best are the various examples of corporate Governance.

TRANSPARENCY

The insurers should develop transparency of financial resources. The examples of transparency present in public sector *i.e.* LIC and GIC have been a guide line for the private insurers. The Board of Directors consists one Chairman (CMD). Two Executive Directors, three Nominee Directors and four independent Directors. The Board of Directors has set up *Audit Committees, Investment Committees, IT Committees and, Personnel and Administration Committees* apart from *policy-holders' Council* at divisional level and *Zonal Advisory Board* at Zonal Office.

The corporate performance is subject to public scrutiny. Insurance companies are directly and indirectly link with banking industry, financial markets and the industrial and agricultural development alongwith the protection of policyholders' interest. They are accountable to policy-holders and shareholders. The competitive atmosphere of insurance industry forces them to cut down their costs of operation.

Efficient and Indepenent—Directors

Directors are link between policyholders and share-holders. Their primary duty is to monitor management on behalf of the shareholders as well as for the interest of policyholders. There should be systems and mechanism to make management accountable to them. The directors must exercise due deligence in making decisions by collecting adequate information. They should supervise and approve financial objectives, major strategies and plans. They have to review the internal control system to mitigate risk exposures. The Board is responsible for the overall picture and not the daily business decisions. It has to create momentum, movement, improvement and direction. The Board should have information of financial statements, market intelligence, competitors role, regulations, measures, management, performance.

Management is dominant in day to day functionary. It has to enhance creativity and productivity. Management is accountable to Board of Directors which oversees whether management is effective and satisfying the consumers', policyholders and employees' interests. In this context Chief Executive Officer (CEO) is the main functioning body. His ability, expertise, resources, motivation and authority are sufficient for making the company grow alongwith servicing the interests of policyholders and shareholder. His decision should not invite conflicts. His accountable for within be should watch himself to make the appropriate decisions according to changing times and needs.

The most important aspects of Corporate Governance are Supervision of Management through proper discharge of its statutory responsibility, enforcement of effective internal control systems ensuring operation and monitoring of adequate and proper risk management and handling consumers grievances. The management should see that quality of the corporate Governance is very high. The insurance companies should follow the stricter norms of Corporate Governance formulate by SEBI.

The marketing systems have been self regulatory to monitor the activities of insurance companies apart from the IRDA regulations, SEBI guidelines and Insurance Acts. Insurers are an important class of institutional investors. It is needed to control the activities of management for investment system. They are required to observe the investment principles of safety, solvency and liquidity etc. RBI has Forex control. They have to develop public trust and confidence apart from strictly following the provisions of various rules and regulations for governing insurance companies.

The insurers should fairly deal with employees insured people and others avoiding manipulation, comcealment, abuse of priviledged information, misrepresentation of material facts and unfair dealings. There should be willing compliance with the law, refusal to take unfair advantages, concern and respect for others, prevention of harm, trustworthiness, benevolence and fairness.

NEED OF CORPORATE GOVERNANCE IN INSURANCE INDUSTRY

Insurance industry bears a fiduciary relationship with policyholders and has long term performances. The honesty and integrity of insurers are paramount important as the industry has financial functions. Officers and employees can break the regulatory measures and enjoy the money of policy-holder. No insurer will be successful unless his integrity is tested as sound and useful for the effective performances of the functions. The need of Corporate Governance is realised for confidence building change-management, investment and viability.

Confidence

Insurance is based on confidence. New insurance companies can develop only if the old insurance companies have demonstrated honestly and integrity. For example, LIC has proved the insurance has sorereign guarantee. Long-term contract is built only on confidence. Insurance particularly life insurance is long-term contract. There should be benchmark standards against which insurers should demonstrate public image.

Change Management

Insurance companies are facing several changes in the society. They have to cope with the changes and come forward to challenge the changes. It has been observed that insurance industry is growing faster than GDP. Specialised insurance companies are entering in the market. Many foreign companies have entered in India to conduct insurance business. Health insurance is becoming a need of the hour. The insurance companies have to manage themselves for maintaining safety and solvency. Non-insurers are growing in detarrified era challenging their fair play, policyholders servicing and transparency.

Investment

Insurance companies manage their funds through investment which involves safety solvency risk management and protection of policyholders' interest. The acturial experiences also help decide insurance expansion. It graples greater challenges such as increasing number of claims. There is need of good governance standard against which the companies conduct and performance would get measured against these backdrops. They have to live up with securities market and governing rules. SEBI has formulated several rules and regulation which have to be followed by the insurer.

Viability

The insurers have to prove their viability. Many new and existing companies now enter in the insurance business. Foreign, insurance companies have to prove their viability. Public Sector insurers have proved their viability and private sector insurers have to follow them. They have to operate in a safe and sound manner and in accordance with the applicable rules and regulations.

Social Responsibility

Approaches to Corporate Social Accounting & Reporting

Descriptive	Programme Management Corporate Rating
Quantitative	C.B. Analysis Se Statement Input Cost Index Cost
Others	Social Audit by Group Goal oriented Pictorial

Measurement of Social Benefits

Steps		***Particulars***	***Effect***
1. Input		Socially significant Action and cost	Installation of Equipment
2. Process	(*a*)	psychological changes in peoples effected	Clear Air, better Health, positive felling for the area
	(*b*)	Physical changes	More people try to move to the area.
3. Output		Behavioural change	
4. Economic		(Measured by Accounting)	

ANALYSIS OF BALANCE SHEET

Both the "Financial Balance Sheet" and "Social Balance Sheet" are analysed mainly to evaluate the following:

Four Major Aspects

Aspects	*Financial Balance Sheet*	*Social Balance Sheet*
1. Scale and Work of resources	Net-worth *i.e.*, Amount invested in business	Resources required and resources available for different projects.
2. Productivity	Earnings on capital employed	Degree of social impact per unit of resource invested.
3. Liquidity or flexibility of resources	Current nation (Current assets) (Current liabilities)	Capacity to adopt to social changes and disinvest.
4. Efficiency	Return on Assets	Benefits to be measured by alternatives.

Associates, Inc. of Social and Financial Balance Sheet

		Amount	*Amount*
1.	Staff Assets		
	Staff Available with one year	...	...
	Staff Available after one year	...	...
	Training Investment	...	...
	Less: Accumulated Training Obsolescence	...	...
	Total Staff Assets	...	...
	Total Organisational assets		...
2.	Use of public Goods		
	Public Services paid for through taxes (Net of Consumption)	...	...
3.	Financial Assets		
	Cash	...	...
	Accounts Receivable Net	...	...
	Untill add contract costs and fees	...	...
	Other current financial assets	...	...
	Other Long-Term Financial assets	...	...
	Total Financial Assets	...	...
4.	Physical Assets	...	...
	Land	...	...
	Buildings	...	...
	Improvements	...	...
	Equipment, Furniture & Fixtures	...	...
	Loss: Accumulated Appreciation	...	...
	Total physical Assets	...	...
	Total Assets	...	...

* Social Asset sand liabilities are identified in black types, and physical and financial assets and liabilities are indicated in lighter types.

I. Liabilities and Equity		
1. Staff Liabilities		
Staff wages payable	...	...
2. Organisational Liabilities		
Organisations Financing Requirements	...	
3. Public Liabilities		
Environmental Resources Used through pollution	...	
Electricity	...	
Commuting	...	
Other	...	
Total Public Liabilities		
4. Financial Liabilities		
Notes Payable (Short-term)	...	...
Accounts Expenses	...	...
Federal Income Taxes	...	
Reformed Federal Income Taxes	...	...
Household Interest in Property	...	...
Total Financial Liabilities	...	
5. Stockholder's Equity		
Common Stock	...	...
Additional paid-in Capital	...	...
Retained Earnings		
Total Stockholder's Equity	...	...
6. Society's Equity		
Society's Equity generated by increases ( ) in net social assets	...	...

Abt Associate, Inc. Social and Financial Income Statement

	Amount	*Amount*
(Income)		
1. to company / Stockholders		
Contract Revenue and other Income	...	...
Federal Services Consumed	...	...
State Service Consumed	...	
Local Services Consumed	...	
Developmental Resources Need through pollution		
Electricity		
Commuting		
Other	...	...
Total	...	...

*Net Social Income and expenditure are indicate in black type.

2. To Staff		
Salaries for time period	...	...
Current Advancement and Holidays	...	...
Health and Life Insurance	...	...

Sick Leave ... ...
Services ... ...
Facility of Space ... ...
Child care ... ...
Credit Union ... ...
Total ... ...

3. To Clients/General Public
Value of Contract work at cost ... ...
Staff Overtime Worked but not paid ... ...
Federal taxes paid by company ... ...
State and Federal tax with of net jobs created ... ...
State Taxes paid by Company ... ...
Contribution to knowledge (publications) ... ...
Total ... ...

4. To Community
Local taxes paid by company ... ...
Local Tax worth of net jobs created ... ...
Environment Improvements ... ...
Total ... ...

Costs (Expenditures)

1. No Company Stockholders
Salaries Paid (Exclusive of Training on Fringe Benefits) ... ...
Training Investment in Staff ... ...
Direct Contract Costs ... ...
Overhead/General and Administrative ... ...
Expenditure not Item ... ...
Vocation and Holidays ... ...
Improvements, Space and Environment ... ...
Federal Taxes paid ... ...
Health and Life Insurance ... ...
Sick Leave ... ...
State Taxes paid ... ...
Local Taxes paid ... ...
Services ... ...
Child Care ... ...
Company School and Tuition Reimbursement ... ...
Fiscal and Public offerings of Stock ... ...
Interest Payments ... ...
Income Foregone an paid-in Capital ... ...
Total ... ...

2. To Staff
Opportunity Costs of Total Time Worked ... ...
Absence of Retirement Income plan ... ...
Day-offs and involuntary termination ... ...
Inequality of Opportunity ... ...

Uncompensated losses through theft	...	...
Total	...	...
3. To Clients/General public	...	...
Cost of contracted work	...	...
Federal services consumed	...	...
State Services consumed	...	...
Environmental Resources used through pollution	...	...
Electricity	...	...
Commuting	...	...
Other	...	...
Total	...	...
4. To Community		
Local Services consumed	...	...
Total	...	...
NET INCOME	...	...
5. To Community/Shareholders		
Financial	...	...
Social	...	...
2. To Staff		
3. To Clients		
4. To Community	...	...
Total Net Social Income	...	...
Total Net Social and Financial Income Generated by Company Operations	...	...

II. SOCIO-ECONOMIC OPERATING MODEL—BY DAVID D.F. LINOWES

Statement Model – By David Lionwes Operating
Statement model presents the positive and negative aspects of its social activities. The positive aspects are broadly termed as, 'Social Benefits' and negative aspects as 'Social Costs'. The net social contribution of a firm is represented by the difference between social benefits and social costs. Under this model, social income statement and social balance sheet are not prepared. Instead, the firm presents, focusses the negative and positive aspects of social activities.

David Linowes concept of 'Social-economic Operating Statement' aims at focussing on 'what the corporation has done for the society on the one hand' and 'what it has failed to do on the other'. He suggested that a firm should prepares social statement periodically showing expenditure made for improvement in social areas, offset against the cost of programmes which were not undertaken but which would have resulted in improvement.

Linowes 'Socio-Economic Statement' contains the following sections:

— Section related with people;

— Section related with environment;

— Section product related with

and the net figure are reported within each section and a net total is also reported before the entity for the period.

The operating statement model has some advantages. These are: (*i*) it includes detriments in the statement (*ii*) it can be used for comparative analysis of firms within an industry and also for inter-industry comparability. But the main weakness of this model is the assumption that total cost measures the total benefits of the programme which is not true.

Socio-Economic Operating Statement for the year ended December 31, 19 ....

I. Relations with people:

A. Improvements:

1. Training programme for handicapped worked.
2. Contribution to black college.
3. Extra turnover costs because of minority hiring programme.
4. Cost of Nursery School for children of employees, voluntarily set up.

B. Less: Detriments

1. Postponed installing new safety devices on cutting machines (cost of the devices).

C. Net Improvement Deficit people actions for the year :

II. Relation with Environment:

A. Improvements:

1. Cost of reclaiming and landscaping old dump on company property.
2. Cost of installing pollution control devices on plant and smoketacks.
3. Cost of detoxifying waste from finishing process this year.

Total Improvements:

Less: Detriments:

1. Cost that would have been incurred to relendscape strip mining site used this year.
2. Estimated cost to have installed purification process to neutralise poisonous liquid being dupmed into stream.

Net Deficit/Improvement in Environment one for the year: Relations with Product:

Improvements:

1. Salary of V.P. while serving on Government Product Safety Commission.
2. Cost of substituting leave free pait for previously used poisonous lend paint.

Total Improvement:

Less: Detriments

1. Safety device recommended by safety Council but not added to product.

Net Improvements/Deficit in product actions for the year:

Total : Socio-Economic Deficit for the year.

Add : Net cumulative socio-economic Improvements as on January 1, 19....

Grand Total Net Socio-Economic Action to December 31, 19...

Source: David F. Linowes, Strategies for Survival (New York), The presidents Association, American Management Association, Inc.

III. COST BENEFIT STATEMENT MODEL—BY RALPH W. FASTES

Ralph W. Fastes has proposed an accounting model that systematically reflects the worth of all resources consumed, including those resources are values which are free to the consuming entity (non-internalised costs of external diseconomies), and then of all benefits produced, including those that provide no compensation to the producing entity (external economies). Estates defines the two terms, social benefits and social costs in the following way:

Social Benefits—any benefit to society (or to any element of society) whether economic or non-economic, internal or external. These social benefits include those benefits provided by an entity for which it is compensated as well as those external economies and bargains for which no compensated as well as those external economies and bargains for which no compensation (or inadequate compensation) is received.

Social Cost: Any cost, sacrifice or detriment to society (or to any element of society), whether economic or non-economic, internal or external. Social costs include sacrifices for which compensation is made (such as human services used and paid for an well detriments not paid for (such as air pollution); any payments are treated separately as benefit to society.

Allocation of resources at prewent depend heavily on information provided through the financial accounting model, which excludes certain benefits (external economies) and detriments (external diseconomies). Pastes notices that the financial accounting model generally reflects the view of entity looking out, towards society; benefits (products and services) provided to society are thus indicated by the surrogate of revenue received, whereas costs are measured only by the entity's expenditure. He proposed that improved resource allocations could result from a different view-point, that of society looking towards the entity. Benefits to society, in his proposal, would then be measured by the values or utilities actually received by society (which may differ from the amount paid to the entity); while costs would reflect the full detriments to society, and not only those for which the entity pays.[21] These opposing view-points are illustrated in Table given below:

Reporting View-Points

	Utility Produced	*(Social Benefits)*	
Entity			Society
	Utility Consumed	(Social Costs)	
	Financial Reporting view point	Social Reporting view point	

Source: Ralph W. Enstes, Corporate Social Accounting, New York, John Woley & Sons, 1976, p. 93.

Estates has argued that care must be taken in defining the reporting entity or system. The term reporting entity, according to Estates, includes the organisation or corporation itself, all activities of employees carried on behalf of the entity and while 'on duty', activities of a Board of Directors and of shareholders acting, collectively for the entity. The term 'reporting entity' for reporting purposes excludes personal activities of employees, including commenting: activity of customers, including use or misuse of the product; and all other secondary or indirect effects. Estates[22], in this regard, argues:

"The proposed model is a comprehensive report of the direct effects of a single entity or society. It is not designed to show that happens (how society would be better or worse off) if the entity has not existed during the reporting period; this would require the reporting of such indirect effects as a prorate share of pollution caused by suppliers and detriments produced by users of the entity's products. A model including such information would certainly be useful but would involve substantial double counting among entities."

The present model could, in fact, reflect indirect effect, but only if they were internalised (*i.e.*, built into entity's cost and reward structure.) This would occur if (*a*) each element of society accurately measured and reported all social benefits and costs created, (*b*) each element were periodically assessed or rewarded an amount equal to its net social surplus or deficit, and (*c*) each element then adjusted the prises of its goods and service upward in response to assessments or down-ward for rewards ofcourse, these condition do not presently obtain; consequently, the proposed model reflects significant indirect effects only in footnotes.

If all significant costs and benefits are reported 'gross' netting is avoided. For example, the cost to society of human services used by the reporting entity and the benefits to society in compensation paid might logically be netted against each other, but in the proposed report each would be separately disclosed. This approach permits the disclosure of total benefits and total-costs-useful information for evaluating the total impact of the organisation on society. It also focusses attention on value separate from exchange price; the latter may disguise bargain purchase, fraud, lack of information, and various market aberrations.

However, according to ebstes, this model is somewhat idealistic and may not be presently practical for all firms the objective is to suggest a standard, a goal, for social reporting. Nevertheless, much of the information is already available in every company, and a serious effort should produce adequate estimates for completion of the report in most companies.

Social Impact Statement for the year ending December 31st

	(Rs.)	*(Rs.)*	*(Rs.)*
Social benefits			
Products and services provided		×××	
Payments to other elements of society:			
Employment provided (salaries and wages)	×××		
Payment for goods and other services	×××		
Taxes paid	×××		
Contributios	×××		
Dividends and interest paid	×××		
Loans and other payments	×××	×××	
Additional direct employee benefits		×××	
Staff, equipment and facility services donated		×××	
Environmental improvement		×××	
Other benefits		×××	×××
Total social benefits			×××
Social costs:			
Goods and metals required		×××	
Buildings and equipments purchases		×××	
Labour and services used		×××	
Discrimination			
In hiring (External)		×××	
In placement and promotion (internal)		×××	×××
Work-related injuries and illness			×××
Public services and facilities			×××
Other resources used			×××
Environmental damage:			
Terrain damage		×××	
Air pollution		×××	
Water pollution		×××	
Noise pollution		×××	
Solid waste		×××	
Visual and aesthetic pollution		×××	
Other environmental damage		×××	×××
Payment from other elements of society:			
Payment for good and services provided		×××	

Additional capital investment loans	×××	
Other payment received	×××	×××
Other costs		×××
Total Social Costs		×××
Social surplus (Deficit) for the year		×××
Accumulate surplus (Deficit) current year		×××
Accumulated surplus (Deficit) precious year		×××

Standard Footnotes

1. Significant indirect effects associated with inputs.
2. Significant indirect effects associated with outputs.
3. Bases for measurement and estimates.
4. Progress in areas of current social concern (such as environmental protection outlays and activities, employment and promotion of minorities and women, and energy conservation efforts).

A. Environmental Concern:

I. Contributions

1. Installation of pollution abatement equipment required by Environmental Agencies.
2. Installation of pollution equipment on a voluntary basis.
3. Reclamation of land (Mandatory of Voluntary) .
5. Aesthetics.

II. Consumption:

1. Estimate of investment required for pollution abatement equipment.
2. The following environment pollution is unavoidable to the nature of the production process.
   - — Amount of Air pollution
   - — (*e.g.*, tons of surphur participants per unit time)
   - — Noise
   - — Scenic disturbance
   - — Amount of water Pollution
3. Utilisation of other physical and social environment (If quantification is not possible, a narrative description).

B. Product Concern:

I. Contributions

(*a*) Improvement in design.

(*b*) Improvement in packaging.

(*c*) Improvement in use of new material.

2. Reduction of pollution resulting from the product:

(*a*) Change in product to make it recyclable.

(*b*) Reduction in pollutive effects of using product.

II. Improvement Needed:

1. Estimated cost to fully meet the safety standards.
2. Complaints or legal cases pending resulting from the lack of product safety.

C. Human Resources:

Social Accounting and Reporting.

I. Contributions:

1. Hiring of employees from minority groups (Number of employees from each group).
2. Training programme for advancement of minorities
   (*a*) Training programme for all employees
   (*b*) Special programme for advancement of minorities.
3. Working Conditions:
   (*a*) Improvement in safety Conditions.
   (*b*) Other improvement in Working Environment.
4. Medical Plan for employees.
5. Leisure and recreation facilities for employees.

D. Community Investment:

I. Contribution.

1. Cash contributions to Educational Institutions.
2. Cash contributions to Social Institutions.
3. Cash contributions to Religious Institutions.
4. Other than cash contributions (man hours etc.).

PROSPECT OF CORPORATE GOVERNANCE IN L. I. C.

Corporate management has become an essential feature of any organisation. It involves corporation strategies particularly marketing strategy, financial strategy and human resources strategy. The Life Insurance Corporation has failed in corporate management although it has theoretically considered its importance.

Corporate Strategies

The LIC has formulated corporate objectives in 1974 to spread life insurance business much more widely particularly in rural areas, maximize insurance linked savings, investing insurance funds for the best advantage of investors, conduct business with utmost economy, act a business of the insured public, meet the various life insurance needs, involve people of the Corporation to the best of their capability, promote sense of participation and job satisfaction. The LIC has failed to achieve the objectives, as it has not formulated proper strategies to achieve them. It has not properly analysed the impacts of environmental factors. The economic, political, cultural, social and geographical factors have been accepted as constraints. The SWOT analysis has not been applied. The threats have been accepted as blocked barriers. No attempt has been made to convert the threats into opportunities. Similarly, the weakness of LIC has not been identified for its conversion into strength. It is smoothly sailing in the ocean of abundant market opportunities. Many untapped resources are lying idle. The poverty, need of insurance, political unawareness, demographic segments natural vagaries and competition have been taken as accepted parameters of non-development. Strategic audit is naive idea in the corporation although it is essential for success of a Corporation.

Marketing Strategy

The LIC has several attractive schemes of insurance but they are least utilized. Many field force personnel are unaware of the schemes. They do not have adequate knowledge of the insurance plans. The agent and development officers are working with routine knowledge. They have become merely sellers of insurance product from door to door; "Insurance is sold and not brought" has been accepted by them. The L.I.C. only pushing them to increase their sale from time to time through organizing seminars of Chairman's club, Zonal Manager's club, Divisional Manager's club and Branch Manager's club. The practice of organising such seminars has its utilities but many officers discourage such seminars and do not take deep interest for their success. This is the only strategy of pushing up business without caring the upgrading of their knowledge of the product, pricing, promotion and placement. There is only pushing strategy after patting their shoulders. There is no clear guidance to accomplish the objection, no positioning strategy, no customer research and no Lest marketing. After 15 years of establishment, the L.I.C. has been unknown of market penetration strategies, market development strategies, reformulation strategies and market extension strategies; product line strategies, concentric diversification strategies and so on.

Product Strategy

The LIC depends on market stretching by increasing usage of product among current users and not creating new users for the new product. The field force is more traditional and is unaware of the new insurance policies. New products are not adequately known to them. The agents who are the only business-procurers are not adopting psycho-graphic techniques of product-expansion, product modification change marketing strategy and product elimination and adoption strategy. The Central Office of LIC has done some jobs of market research but its findings have not been used by the field force.

Pricing Strategy

Pricing strategy' is rigid in the LIC. It has recently given some concessions in non-payment of regular premium. Pricing is not used for enhancing business. It believes that people have to purchase policies on the highest rate of premium because insurance is their needs. But the LIC has forgotten that insurance business has not reached to the level of being brought by purchasers. Only few policies and their rates of premium are known to the agents. The agent-manuals are not available to many agents who can understand the premium rates on their own. They totally depend on the development officer. The time lag between initiation of proposal talk and meeting with D.O. reduces the business prospects. Interest rate has been increasing till the end of the twentieth Century. Morality has declined and expenses have to be curtailed to reduce the premium rates for attracting potential prospects of insurance.

Promotion Strategy

The mass communication has been absent till 2000 in LIC Recently. It has started to educate people about its products, but it is merely half promoted. The terms and conditions of the policies are not advertised. They are left to be told by field force who do not oftenly know them. Market targets and position strategy, effective advertising, creative strategy and successful personal selling are absent in LIC. Publicity and public relations are inadequate and less appealing. Message, media and methods of promotion are not properly selected to make people aware, create desire, increase interest and behave for adopting insurance policies. Advertising effectiveness has not been measured.

Place Strategy

The objective of the LIC has been to increase insurance business to rural areas but the LIC has not adopted any dynamic place strategy. Unlike Regional Rural Bank, the LIC officers are present only in district headquarters or tehsil places. RRBs have benefited the masses at the maximum through their branches almost in every village of the country. The LIC has only theoretically decided to enhance business in rural and hitherto neglected areas. The link of people with LIC is only agents who are not properly trained. Many agents are totally unaware of LIC products and marketing techniques, channel strategy is inadequate and tardy.

Financial strategy

The cast benefits analysis is used in the LIC for launching new products but the income and outgo strategic management in inadequate. Premium income has increased significantly but its collection is incurring float cost and opportunity-cost. Premium collected by the agents are not received by the LIC the same day because of inadequate collection staff. It is a matter of pure mathematics that if crores of rupees are lined up in float persday, the interest thereon will be not less than the rate of bank deposit. The problems of salary saving scheme are more acute. It has been observed that the premium so collected by the employers is lying with them usually for six months. The LIC argues that the employer must submit its premium in time. If LIC is not very serious about collection of its own money, how the employer would be serious for remittances. It is the greatest fault of LIC corporate management. Similarly, premium are put in only in transit. More than a crore is lost per day in float and opportunity return; similarly, interest income is not promptly collected. The problem of float lies here too.

The expenses per policy in force continue to rise without any control and restrain. My study on LIC for 1957-1986 has revealed it. It has increased recently, too. No cost control is exercised similarly advances to agents have been rising rapidly. The financial management is very poor in LIC.

Human Resource Development

The specific strategy of HRD has been adopted by the LIC. The agents and the office staff are never trained on the corporate management. They are routinely motivated on money which is obsolete strategy. The recognition, learning and personality, perception and attitude development are totally absent in the LIC. The only traditional HRD is conferences of ZMs, DMs, BNs at some costly hotel. It is purely bureaucratic strategy of development. Unless the shop floor level employees are developed, HRD is impossible. Management must involve employees participation in development process. When employees are laggard and management is leader, the gap creates conflicts. The product and people oriented leadership cannot function effectively unless people are learnt about organisational belongingness. Employees are afraid of function and management is suppressed off under top management pressure. Job involvement is satisfaction that must be known by the employees. Agents do selling without developing their marketing attitudes, perception, learning and personality. Opening of only sales Training Centres and participation in insurance. Academy by few employees do not serve the purpose. Passing of examination by agents have become a difficult task for getting agency license. They are compelled to opt the classroom teaching, which is not efficient at functional level in office. Many officers who are unable to perform better in office are sent to train the agents in STC even if STC is telling about selling but is purely absence of actuating and motivating. The office staff and agents should be actuated to function on job satisfaction after proper attitude change, perception, formation, learning practices, personality development and self-motivation. The Life Insurance Corporation of India has to adopt dynamic strategies of marketing, finance and HRD to become successful Corporate Model in Insurance industry.

QUESTIONS

1. What is corporate Governance? Discuss its main features.
2. Explain the components of Corporate Governance.
3. What is transparency? Describe how is it maintained in insurance industry.
4. Explain the role of accountability in insurance industry.
5. Examine the investment and viability of Corporate Governance.
6. Explain Social Responsibility and Social Accounting with reference to Corporate Governance.
7. Project the future of corporate Governance in General Insurance and Life Insurance.

49

BANCASSURANCE

Insurance and Banking are coexisting financial institution while complementing and supplementing each other. The Insurance Regulatory and Development Authority Act, 1999 have created more opportunities to them for expansion of their markets. They can serve the society in a very effective manner. Banking Institutions have got the opportunities to enter in insurance business while insurance institutions have already under the autonomy of starting their banking business. Many non-banking institutions have been opened, acquired funds and dissolved with public money at their stakes. Since they were totally in the hands of private persons, the Government control became ineffective. Banking institutions in India are mainly under the control of Reserve Bank of India. People need insurance but they prefer investment over risk coverage although latter is more important. Indian mentally for insurance is very bleak people do not feel need of insurance although they have dire-necessity for that. Insurance institutions in India have not considered forced insurance. The voluntary-purchasing of insurance policies is rare phenomena. They prefer to go to bank-offices rather than going to insurance offices for getting risk coverage. The insurance institutions procure the business through their agents who are the main link between people and the company. Agents attitude and environment may work against the free will environment of insurance. The IRDA, Act is expected to mobiles insurance coverage and resources for investment in the economy. The Government has assured that there would not be any disinvestment in the LIC, GIC and their subsidiaries. Insurance Act, 1938, has not been sufficient to regulate the insurance business in India. Foreign companies would not be allowed to hike their equity in the country through their Indian subsidiaries. It has opened a great opportunities for the banking and insurance institutions. They can perform both the functions.

INSURANCE AS BANKING INSTITUTE

The life insurance and general insurance corporations are performing their respective functions with the help of banks. LIC and GIC have opened their accounts with banks. Policyholders have to approach the banks for realisation of cheques. Indirectly banks have to intervene in their business. If the insurance companies perform the business of banking institutions, they get benefits of business in financial transactions. Policyholders are also benefited as they have not to run from pillar to post. The claim amounts will be deposited in insurance banks. The account holders get all the benefits and facilities of banks. It can be analysed under premiurn Collection, claims, payment, pension plans, funds, investment consultant and employment opportunities.

Bancassurance is a strategy adopted by banks or insurance companies arming to operate in the financial market in a more or less integrated manner. It is inter-linkage of different financial services as well as the distribution of these products.

Premium Collection

Insurance as bank will facilitate deposits of premium. The burden on cash-counter is lessened or the cash transaction is shifted to insurance bank. The premiurn amount is regularly collected without any pressure on other activities of insurance. Insurance business is expanded with extra zeal and effort as people working in the marketing areas develop specialisation. They devote with additional knowledge and equipment for the expansion of insurance business on the other hand. Management of premium collection becomes easy as the insurance banks has diversified its activities. New bank customer get information about insurance. They collect, analyses and reinforce the available information at insurance-bank counter from the fellow depositor of premiums and receivers of claims-amount. Insurance policy is accepted by its realisation of actual benefits towards which Indian population is apathetic. The premium account is regularly collected as the customers visit often the insurance-bank for their daily transaction. They are reminded of premium-deposits. The premium collected are deposited in a commercial bank who use the money for their transactions and investment. If so much money is retained by insurance-bank, it would be utilised by them for getting some profit on the money.

Table 49.1 Premium Collected by (Rs. in Crores)

Years	*Life Insurance corporation of India*	*General Insurance*	*Total*
1990-91	5600	2742	8342
1991-92	6960	3450	10410
1992-93	7987	3868	11855
1993-94	9735	4427	14162
1994-95	11527	4879	16406
1995-96	14182	5956	20138
1996-97	16240	6734	22974
1997-98	19252	7357	26609
2000-01	34207.78		
2004-05	75083.37		

Table 49.1 reveals that the total premium collected by insurance industryes has gone from Rs. 8,342 crores in 1990-91 to Rs. 26,609 crores in 1997-98 by 3.18 times during the period of 7 years. If this much of money is retained by insurance industry they would earn enough profit margins. But, at present insurance industry operates its financial functions through a commercial banks. The functions of commercial banks should be performed by the insurance industry itself. There are many other income than the premium income which are also deposited in banks.

Table 49.2 Total Income

(Rs. in Crores)

Years	*Life Insurance*	*General Insurance*	*Total*
1990-91	8518	3308	11,826
1991-92	10691	4202	14,893
1992-93	12244	4727	16,971
1993-94	15212	5384	20,596
1994-95	18102	6029	24,131
1995-96	22047	7431	29,478
1996-97	25821	8431	34,252
1997-98	30732	8335	40,067
2000-01	53968.46		
2004-05	112346.24		

The public is accustomed to get insurance and banking services at a place. Insurance industry will work like a multiple shop store werein all the financial functions would be performed by them. The investor would also come to the insurance offices for getting all the information and services fulfilled. However the insurance-bank should not have to confine only on insurance-investment but should have widen its horizon to help all types of people seeking financial suggestions.

Payment of premium would be easy and prompt if the policyholder has opened account with the insurance-bank. It would be like salary saving scheme wherein no policyholder would bother for monthly remittance of premium. Merely accounting transaction in the insurance-bank facilitate the payments. The account holder would be reminded of the minimum balance in the account for payment of premiurn. The insurance bank becomes total bank of people as it takes cares of all financial transactions. Payment of electricity bill income tax and business-invoices would be easy by insurance-bank.

Total income received by insurance industries comes through banks. In other-words, banks maintain its total income which increased from Rs. 11,826 crore in 1990-91 to Rs. 40,067 crores in 1997-98 by 3.39 times during the period of seven years. If this amount is not deposited or transacted through commercial banks all these money is used by insurance industries as bank too. Therefore, it is advisable for the insurance industry to start its own bank wherein public is also invited to transact as bank-customer. Thus the deposit of insurance industry in a year would exceed Rs. 50 thousand crore at the minimum. Bank certainly gets some benefit on the amount deposited by insurance. They maintain their liquidity level and invest rest of the money received from insurance. This earning would be earned by insurance companies as commercial banks if they transact business of a commercial bank.

Claims Payment

The claims-amount paid by the insurance industry is not immediately used by the clients. It is deposited in the bank from whereby they withdraw their amount from time to time leaving a sufficient amount with the bank for their investment as per rules. If this amount is retained by the insurance-bank, the money would be utilised for further investment. The client's account in the insurance-bank is immediately credited With the amount of claim from which they withdraw amount from time to time. SUCH TYPES of facilities of premium-deposits and claim-settlement by bank motivate public to deal with the insurance, bank wherein they would prefer to deposit their other savings. Old-age people get monthly withdrawal of the amount. They would not suffer any more by making que commercial banks. The technological development wherein phone and computer facilities would serve their clients at their home. Employment opportunities would increase as expert people would have been appointed to meet the clients at the residence who would pay cash at the time of need. Only telephone facilities would do all the jobs as automatic-services would be completed on computers. If the client has personal computer it would be mere useful and efficient services to them. The claim amount of insurance industry reveals the bank or banking business based only on it.

Table 49.3 Claim-Amount

(Rs. in Crores)

Years	*Life Insurance*	*General Insurance*	*Total*
1990-91	1951	1898	3849
1991-92	2422	2303	4725
1992-93	3580	2839	6419
1993-94	3845	3050	6895
1994-95	4666	4289	8955
1995-96	5353	4427	9780
1996-97	6599	5105	11704
1997-98	7823	6525	13448
2000-01	11666.82		

The claim amount of insurance industry has increased from Rs. 3,849 crores in 1990-91 to Rs. 13,448 crore in 1997-98 by 3.49 times during seven years. It reveals that amount Rs. 13 thousand crore money would have been with the insurance-bank for a time-being as is put in commercial banks. The commercial bank collect to much of funds from insurance industry. They credit the amount with the accounts of their depositors who do not withdraw all the amount at a time. They gradually withdraw it leaving a major portion with the bank. Similarly a major portion of claim amount remain infloat *i.e.* date of writing the cheque to the date of realisation in account. This float would be abolished if the insurance-bank is Opened as it would do all the payments merely passing certain entries. It is thus clear that insurance bank would use a major portion of claims-payment for its transactions which are used by commercial banks. The insured can get the amount of claims in pension form which would again help insurance-expansion. The clients would get pension regularly from the insurance bank which can start door to door financial services. There exists a large potential of business of financial nature in adopting insurance-banking systems.

Pension Plans

People are investment-otiented. Risk of life is universal truth but people by their nature are least concerned with life insurance coverage. If insurance-bank is opened, people will enjoy the benefits of pension plans by depositing the saving, claim amount and purchasing pensionplans.

Table 49.4 Group Superannuation Schemes

Business in (Rs. in Crores)

Years	*Number of Members in lakhs*	*Amount of Annuities per annum*
1990-91	2.43	253.12
1991-92	2.54	301.77
1992-93	2.69	358.93
1993-94	3.14	403.51
1994-95	3.54	427.66
1995-96	4.19	483.05
1996-97	5.54	545.59
1997-98	6.71	682.84
2000-01	14.91	
2004-05	21.57	

The number of persons insured under group superannuation schemes has increased from 2.43 lakhs in 1990-91 to 6.71 lakhs in 1997-98 by two fold and the amount of annuities increased from Rs. 253.12 crores to Rs. 682.94 crores in the corresponding year by the same proportion. The rising trend reveals that LIC can manage a significant amount by its insurance bank. All the money is not immediately paid. A certain portion is paid as different interval. The rest of amount is managed as bank-money for credit and investing in the growing economy of India. Insurance-bank would perform better than the commercial bank. The claimamount would also be deposited with the insurance-bank from where a new pension-plan can be purchased. The total claimamount is usually converted into pension-plans. People would be benefited by such schemes. They are given option either to take all the money at the time of claim or convert some of them or all of them into pension-plan. This facility would benefit a large number of policyholder who would enjoy it and the LIC would get sufficient amount for financial transactions. The employment opportunities would increases and the contribution to economic development would be appreciable.

Funds

The insurance fund is significant contribution to national income as it is invested for economic development. The amount of fund available with LIC would increase further as saving in form premium income, claim amount and other out go would also enhance as a result of establishment of insurance bank.

Table 49.5 Life Insurance Fund (LIC)

(Rs. in Crores)

Years	*Total income*	*Outgo*	*Excess of Income cover outgo added to fund*	*Total Fund*
1990-91	8,517	3588	4929	28,400
1991-92	10,690	4400	6290	34,691
1992-93	12,244	5937	6306	40,998
1993-94	15,212	6544	8667	49,665
1994-95	18,102	7789	10313	59,978
1995-96	22,047	9245	12801	72,780
1996-97	25,821	10841	14979	87,760
1997-98	30,732	12659	18072	1,05,832
2000-01	53,968.96	21987.45	—	31,981.02
2004-05	1,12,346.24	48460.70	—	63,885.54

Table 49.6 Expected Investible Funds of LIC

(Rs. in Crores)

Years	*Total Life Insurance Funds*	*50% of the out go*	*50% of premium Income*	*Total Insurance Bank Funds for Investment*	*% Increase over life*
1990-91	28400	1794	2800	32994	116
1991-92	34691	2200	3480	40371	116
1992-93	40998	2968	3993	47959	116
1993-94	49665	3272	4867	57804	116
1994-95	59978	3894	9763	69635	116
1995-96	72780	4622	7091	84493	116
1996-97	87760	5420	8120	101300	(115)
1997-98	105832	6329	9626	121787	(115)
2000-01	175491.18				
2004-05	413800.95				

The investible funds for LIC has been Rs. 1,05,832 crore in 1997-98 as compared to Rs. 28,400 crore in 1990-91 an increase of 372.6 per cent. It is a welcome step. If LIC starts its banking business, the life insurance functions only will enhance the investible fund by more than 15 per cent of the total life fund. It is clear from table 49.6 that the investible bank fund would have been Rs. 14,787 crore in 1997-98 if insurance had started its banking business because about 50 per cent of outgo will remain in the bank for gradual withdrawal and the premium income would increase by 50 per cent as a result of banding operation. The total bank investible fund was expected to be Rs. 32,994 crore in 1990-91 an increase of 369 per cent over the period of seven years.

Table 49.7 Cash at Bank (Life Business)

(Rs. in Crore)

Years	*Deposit A/c*	*Call Short Notice Deposit A/c*	*Current A/c*	*Remittance in Transit*	*Total*
1990-91	31.67	631.35	174.93	51.42	889.39
1991-92	80.84	761.06	157.39	77.61	1,076.91
1992-93	88.70	314.28	416.61	118.91	938.50
1993-94	111.91	121.12	418.31	314.21	965.56
1994-95	38.71	653.59	519.27	258.46	1,570.04
1995-96	55.64	230.53	559.17	638.70	1,484.04
1996-97	284.97	272.84	563.76	539.88	1,661.47
1997-98	715.95	789.24	728.53	485.02	2,718.74

The deposits at banks have revealed that Rs. 2,718 crore was lying with commercial banks in 1997-98 which was Rs. 889 crore in 1990-91. The banks are not bothering for the remittance in transit which was Rs. 485 crore in 1997-98. On current account LIC is earning nothing which accounted Rs. 728 crore in 1997-98. The deposit account would have been properly utilised by LIC. Thus, it is clear that LIC would have earned sufficient income if it has opened its own bank.

Investment Consultant

The Life Insurance business as well as allied business would have been increased if LIC starts investment consultancy. People should approach to the offices of LIC for expert advises on investment. The present position is that LIC agents approach to people for procuring insurance business. But the people are investment-oriented. They go to take expert advises for investment to their relatives or private investment agents. The share-brokers and others are charging exhorbitant fees from the investors. Their money is not properly invested. If LIC starts consultancy services. It would benefit a large number of investors.

Employment Opportunities

Employment opportunities would increase if insurance bank starts functioning alongwith insurance-business. In foreign countries, insurance and banking business are co-existant. They perform better than pure insurance or banking business. Direct and indirect employment generation is possible if insurance-bank starts functioning. The LIC Act 1956 and GIC Act 1972 would have to be amended sufficiently to permit LIC and GIC to start their banking business.

Bank as Insurance Institution

The IRDA Act, 1999 has opened wide challenges to financial institutions. Now banks can also enter in insurance business. The insurance is the basic need of life. Uncertainty of life and death is reducing the working capacities of people because of tension involved. Once it is secured, person feels happy to perform life job effectively. In a bank where he has his bank account, if he gets facilities of insurance; he would certainly purchase insurance policies. Insurance link deposit would be more attractive to the account holders. With payment of slightly a higher amount at the time of deposit, he can secure term insurance. Term insurance would be the most appropriate form of life insurance to be sold by banks. Health schemes and accident-benefits can be lucrative business for a bank. The banks should chalk out at the earliest to start new business of life as well as general insurance. In canada, many banks have been successfully doing this job.

Coordination

The banking and insurance institutions would be working an competitive units but they are working in the same environment of India. Their coordination would strengthen their businesses. Plans formulation, strategies implementation socio-economic development and technological upgrading are coordinately achieved by both the institutions although Insurance Regulation, and Development Authority is there to guide them. Their own thinking and mutual discussion would benefit them. The age is competition but survival is possible with coordination. It is know that both institutions would interchange experienced employees for their development.

Market Expansion

People are aware of the product when there are a number of seller. They go to the market where selective bargaining is present for purchasing a desirable article. People want to purchase a insurance policy e.g. Health and accident which is not available. People do not want to purchase money back which are sold by LIC. These are mere examples. If people can find products of their choice in a market that is full of good sellers, they remain in the market. Ultimately insurance business would increase. A firm propagates his own product but at the same time propagates indirectly others product of the same line. If Banks are telling about insurance benefits, LIC and GIC are also benefited. If insurance industry is telling banking, facilities, the banks are also indirectly benefited. Market expansion is inevitable in insurance area.

MERGING OF WEAK BANKS WITH LIC OR GIC

Several banks are unable to maintain their profitability on account of non-performing assets and non-circulation of investible funds. They should merge with LIC or GIC who should be starting banking business, too for their development to achieve leadership. Competence in view of ecoming tough competition from outside country. Once banks have merged with LIC or GIC, they would perform better under their guidance who would need basis infrastructure for expansion of insurance banks. The banks would be performance a fresh. The employees would get a change of revival. They would get proper training and motivation. The productivity and performance would boost their morale. Highly motivated employees would share more responsibility of insurance and banks. The educated people would get opportunities to demonstrate their capabilities. Indian economy would get sufficient funds from insurance and banking institutions. Resource mobilisation would help development of people's health, economic conditions and entrepreneurship. India will emerge a powerful Nation.

PROSPECTS OF BANCASSURANCE

Bancassurance is more cost effective than traditional agency and broker channels. The primary advantage offered by bank distribution of insurance products is the customer relationship. Bancassurance margins were significantly higher than other traditional channels. The popularity of bancassurance has increased recently.

In India, bancassurance is contributing significantly in new business growth, specially among the private sector companies. Bancassurance is tied up with commercial banks, cooperative banks and regional rural banks. It is cost effective for insurers to top into rural communities. It is expected to account for 13% in life and 5% in non-life business during next five years. In India, more banks have come to realise the value of their distribution network and are reportedly trying to discard existing channels in favour of financial service sector including insurance companies.

The booming emerging equity markets have led to increasing interest in unit-linked and investment-linked products, which have become mainstay products sold through banks. The recent liberalisation of emerging insurance markets has brought with it a huge inflow of foreign companies. Many of the newly formed insurance companies resort to bancassurance to quickly penetrate the domestic markets although other channels are also used.

Aviva Life has tied up with ABN Amro Bank, American Express, Laxmi Vilas Bank, Punjab and Sindh Bank, Centurian Bank of Punjab, Induslnd Bank and many co-operative banks in Gujarat, Rajastan, J & K, Bihar, West Bengal and Maharashtra. They have 80% of their business coming through this channel.

ICICI Prudential Life Insurance Company has entered into agreement with ICICI bank, Lord Krishna Bank, Punjab and Maharashtra Co-operative Bank, Shamrao Vitthal Co-operative Bank, Federal Bank, Citi Bank etc. They have 20% of their business through bancassurance.

Bajaj Allianz Life Insurance Co. has tied up with standard Chartered Bank and syndicate Bank. With 22% of their business coming from this channel.

HDFC standard life has association with HDFC Bank and a few other banks with 45% of their business coming in.

Kotak OM Mahindra Life Insurance Co. has tied up with Dena Bank and Kotak Mahindra Bank.

Max New York Life Insurance Co. has tied up with Yes Bank, Kopol Co-operative Bank, Maratha Co-op. Bank and Thane Janata Co-op. Bank., 22% of their business comes from this channel.

SBI Life goes with their parent bank-State of India and 44% of their business comes through this.

LIC of India has tied up a few banks such as Corporation Bank, IOB, Andhra Bank, Central Bank of India, Oriental Bank of Commerce, Bank of Maharashtra, Vijaya Bank, Satara Bank, Centurian Bank, District Central Co-Op Banks, Pandyan Grama Bank etc.

ING Vysya Life Insurance Co. has doubled its new business premium income from alternate channels from Rs. 60 crores to Rs. 112 crores by sept. 2007 25% of this has come through bancassurance tie-ups with 120 co-operative banks and Vysya Bank.

Met Life Insurance Co. has tied up with J&K Bank, UTI Bank, Dhanlakshmi Bank and Karnataka Bank. 38% of their business comes from this channel.

Bancassurance - a global perspective

Bancassurance has been forecast to become the 2nd most important channel for insurance as per the Mckinsey Reports. Since this channel offers costs advantages, strategic placements and immense potential.

In Europe banks handle over 60% of life insurance business and also in France, Spain and Italy. In Asia this ranges from 5 - 40 % of new business in countries like Taiwan, Hongkong and Singapore.

Product Diversifications

Only standardised products are sold through bank channels specific products such as credit card or bank loans unit linked products are also being offered by bancassurers. Banks have developed more sophisticated investment products have more financial content. Accident and health products are being offered by bancassurers. The drive to diversify represents a key strategic challenge for bancassurers as these products, e.g., protection products rather than simply investment and savings products. Direct face to face contract is preferred which tends to favour bancassurance development.

Non-Life Bancassurance

Non-life bancassurance started early in 1990 when banks began to distribute mainly property insurance products. The operational model adopted by banks and insurers in non-life distribution ranges from full ownership to distribution agreements to joint ventures, with the latter being pursed so that bank can gain non-life products knowledge. Motor insurance being the biggest non-life business line in bancassurance is becoming popular.

Table 49.8

Share of Bancassurance Distribution in 2006 (%)

Selected Countries	*Non-Life*				*Life*			
	Bancassurers	*Agents*	*Brokers*	*Others*	*Bancassurers*	*Agents*	*Brokers*	*Others*
United State	N.A.	N.A.	N.A.	N.A.	2.0	N.A.	N.A.	N.A.
Canada	N.A.	18.0	74.0	8.0	1.0	60.0	34.0	5.0
Brazil	13.3	N.A.	71.6	N.A.	550	N.A.	30.0	N.A.
Chile	18.8	—	81.2	—	13.0	—	87.0	—
U.K.	10.0	4.0	54.0	32.0	20.3			
France	9.0	35.0	18.0	38.0	64.0	7.0	12.0	17.0
Germany	12.0	57.0	22.0	9.0	24.8	27.1	39.4	8.7
South Korea	4.0	49.7	0.9	45.4	8.5	—	91.5	—
India	13.0	—	—	—	5.0	—	—	—

Source : Re Sigma 5/2007

The table reveals that developing countries are depending more on bancassurance for distribution of their insurance products than other distribution channels.

QUESTIONS

1. What is Bank assurance? Explain its feature.
2. Discuss the role of insurance as Banking institution.
3. Discuss the role of Bank as Insurance Institution.
4. Examine the cohert and coordination of Bank and Insurance.
5. Project the future of Bank assurance in India.

50

INTERNATIONAL INSURANCE SCENE

The New Economic order of 1991 has brought several changes in insurance industry. The business of insurance has increased rapidly thereafter. Premium, profitability, financial strength, prospects catastrophe losses, solvency ratio, risk management and so on are the factors of analysis of international insurance scene. They are analysed under life insurance, non-life insurance and total insurance.

Life Insurance

The international life insurance scene has been analysed under premium, profitability, Solvency Ratio, Risk Management and prospects.

Premium

The life insurance premium in world market has increased rapidly upto 1986 but declined thereafter.

Table 50.1 Word premium Real Growth Rates (Approximately in percentage)

Year	*1980*	*1981*	*1982*	*1983*	*1984*	*1985*	*1986*	*1987*	*1988*	*1989*
% Increase (+) or Decrease (–)	2.5	3.5	5.1	4.0	12.0	13.5	21.0	12.5	12.7	5.0
Year	*1990*	*1991*	*1992*	*1993*	*1994*	*1995*	*1966*	*1977*	*1998*	*1999*
% Increase or Decrease	2.0	2.5	5.5	6.0	4.0	4.8	2.5	7.5	4.8	7.5
Year	2000	2001	2002	2003	2004	2005	2006	2007		
% Increase or Decrease	9.0	–1.5	2.5	–0.7	2.9	5.2	7.7	13.0		

Source: Sigma : February 2005, April and May 2006 issues. 4/2007

World Life Insurance premium increased by 3.9 per cent in real terms after inflation adjustment to US $/1974 on after 2.9 per cent growth in 2004. The world premium of life insurance business has been OSD 1973703 million in 2005. India has life premium only USD 20175 million in 2005 *i.e.*, 1.02 per cent. India's rank has improved from 18th to 17th in 2005.

The growth rate of life insurance premium in India has been 17.3 per cent in 2004 and 15.3 per cent in 2005 whereas world's growth rate has been 9.9 per cent and 5.7 per cent respectively. It reveals that India's growth more satisfactory than the world average. The real growth rate after adjustment of inflation has been 10.5 per cent which is more than all the highly ranked countries. The growth rate of life insurance premium has been constant in the worldmarket. European life business profited from the booming stock markets which favoured the sale of unit-linked policies. The flattering yield curve due to higher short-term interest rates made fixed annuities unattractive and the low-performing US stock markets did not support variable annuities. In Emerging markets, life insurance is mainly driven by the fastgrowing incomes of a relatively. Young population which needs savings as old age protection. The life insurance premium of unit-linked and pension products.

Table 50.2 Life premium Growth Rate by Region and Country

Continents	Rank		Premium Volume in Million of USD					Change in % Nominal USD				Inflation Adjusted change to %				Share of Total Business in % Life & Non-life				Share of world market (in%)			
	2004	2005	2003	2004	2005	2006	2007	2004	2005	2006	2007	2004	2005	2006	2007	2004	2005	2006	2007	2004	2005	2006	2007
North America			505400	531317	551530	572860	623950	3.7	3.8	7.5	9.2	0.7	0.0	3.8	5.8	44.9	45.1	45.5	46.9	28.36	27.94	25.93	26.07
Latin America & Caribean			16236	20116	23263	28923	35809	19.2	15.6	24.3	24.7	17.1	–2.1	14.1	11.4	41.0	39.7	40.5	41.0	1.05	1.18	1.31	1.50
Europe			597830	705096	769337	940586	1035942	16.2	9.1	15.8	17.5	3.8	7.1	12.4	5.6	58.0	69.7	63.3	61.6	37.57	38.98	2.57	43.29

Table 50.2A Selected Countries

	2004	2005	2003	2004	2005	2006	2007	2004	2005	2006	2007	2004	2005	2006	2007	2004	2005	2006	2007	2004	2005	2006	2007
Asia			518051	558334	573239	602266	623469	7.4	2.7	4.1	7.7	2.0	3.7	3.6	4.3	75.6	75.4	75.2	74.2	30.09	29.04	27.26	26.05
Africa			23269	25231	27795	35468	38111	12.8	10.2	19.5	6.8	–4.7	5.8	21.6	3.4	69.8	69.4	71.4	71.5	1.42	1.41	1.61	1.59
Oceania			21957	26543	28539	29214	35807	23.1	7.5	8.3	22,7	6.2	1.0	6.1	7.9	49.0	49.4	50.1	52.0	1.46	1.45	1.32	1.50
World			1682743	1866636	1973703	2209317	2393089	9.9	5.7	10.3	12.6	2.3	3.9	7.7	5.4	57.0	57.6	59.3	58.9	100.00	100.00	100.0	100.00

Table 50.2B Selected Countries

United States	1	1	481527	502303	517074	533649	578357	2.8	2.9	6.9	8.5	0.1	–0.4	3.6	5.5	45.1	45.2	45.6	47.0	26.77	26.20	24.15	25.17
Japan	2	2	371831	389846	375958	362766	330651	4.0	–3.6	–4.2	–3.7	–1.0	0.8	–2.0	–3.6	78.6	78.9	78.8	77.8	20.93	19.05	16.42	13.82
United Kingdom	3	3	161220	193196	199612	311691	349746	17.6	3.3	34.9	36.1	3.6	1.9	30.2	22.5	64.3	66.5	74.5	75.4	10.26	10.11	14.11	14.61
France	4	4	103947	133456	154058	177902	186993	23.9	15.4	18.2	5.9	10.6	13.5	15.1	–4.3	66.2	69.3	70.8	69.5	6.97	7.81	8.05	7.81
Germany	5	6	76246	84697	90225	94911	102419	10.9	6.5	5.2	10.2	–0.6	4.5	2.4	–1.3	44.3	45.7	46.4	46.0	4.57	4.57	4.30	4.28
Italy	6	5	71694	82083	91740	89576	88215	14.5	11.8	–4.6	–4.2	2.3	9.8	–7.5	–13.6	63.7	65.9	64.6	62.0	4.44	4.65	4.05	3.69
South Korea	7	7	42524	48485	58848	72298	81298	14.5	21.4	19.1	15.7	3.4	9.2	8.9	10.5	70.9	71.0	71.5	69.5	2.63	2.98	3.27	3.40
India	18	17	14425	17500	20175	37220	47132	17.3	15.3	64.8	36.3	10.5	8.9	60.1	14.2	79.6	80.6	86.5	86.7	0.92	1.02	1.68	1.97

Source: Sigma : 2/2005, 5/2006, 4/2007 and 3/2008

Per Capita Premium

Life insurance per capita premium in USD has been maximum in United Kingdom *i.e.*, USD 3287.1 in 2005 followed by USD 3078.1 of Switzerland. United States have been at twelfth rank in 2004 and also in 2005 having USD 1753.2 in 2005.

Table 50.3 Life Insurance Index

			Per Capita Premium in USD				*% of Premium to GDP*			
Continents & Countries	***Rank 2004***	***Rank 2005***	***Per Capita Premium 2004***	***2005***	***2006***	***2007***	***% to GDP 2004***	***2005***	***2006***	***2007***
North America			1617.2	1686.3	1731.8	1869.3	4.12	4.05	3.9	4.1
Latin Armerica and Caribbean			37.2	42.0	51.3	63.1	1.01	0.93	1.0	1.0
Europe			848.1	911.8	1119.6	1222.6	4.68	4.69	5.3	5.0
Asia			147.2	149.6	154.6	156.7	5.58	5.16	5.0	4.6
Africa			30.2	30.7	38.3	39.6	3.41	3.33	3.4	3.1
Oceania			851.0	885.0	896.3	1671.4	3.75	3.16	3.4	3.4
World			291.5	299.5	330.6	358.1	4.55	4.34	4.5	4.4

Selected Countries	***Rank 2004***	***2005***	***2006***	***Per Capita Premium 2004***	***2005***	***2006***	***2007***	***Selected Countries***	***Rank 2004***	***2005***	***2006***	***Percentage to GDP 2004***	***2005***	***2006***	***2007***
Switzerland	1	2	3	3275.1	3078.1	314.8	3159.1	South Africa	1	2	2	11.43	10.64	13.0	12.5
United Kingdom	2	1	1	3190.4	3287.1	5139.6	5730.5	Taiwan	2	1	3	11.06	11.17	11.6	12.9
Japan	3	4	9	3044.0	2956.3	2829.3	2583.9								
Ireland	4	5	2	2617.4	2759.7	4203.8	5715.1	U.K.	3	3	1	8.92	8.90	13.1	12.6
Finland	5	6	8	2461.0	2707.8	2903.1	3093.1	Japan	4	6	7	8.26	8.32	8.3	7.5
Denmark	6	7	4	2310.5	2489.9	2840.8	3381.0	Hong Kong	5	4	8	7.88	8.63	9.2	10.6
Belgium	7	3	10	2291.2	2988.7	2427.7	2972.6	South Korea	6	8	4	6.75	7.27	7.9	8.2
France	8	8	5	2150.2	2472.6	2922.5	2928.3	Switzerland	7	—	5	6.73	—	6.2	5.7
Hong Kong	9	9	14	1884.3	2213.2	2456.0	3031.9	Belgium	7	5	11	6.73	8.36	6.5	7.3
								Finland	8	7	12	6.89	7.33	7.2	6.7
Sweden	10	10	13	1764.3	2105.2	2214.6	2438.5	France	9	9	6	6.38	7.08	7.9	7.3
								Singapore	10	11	23	6.02	6.00	5.4	6.2
India	78	78	76	15.7	18.3	33.2	404	India	44	43	31	2.53	2.53	4.1	4.0
United States	12	12	6	1692.5	1753.2	1789.5	1922	United States	19	17	14	4.22	4.14	4.0	4.2

Source: Sigma : Various Issues

The per capita life premium has been more than 10 ranks in United Kingdom, Switzerland, Belgium, Japan, Ireland, Finland, Denmark, France, Hong Kong and Sweden. It reveals that almost all the developed nations have maximum life insurance cover. India stood at 78 rank having life insurance per capita merely 18.3 USD in 2005. She has enough scope of insurance development.

Percentage of Life premium to GDP

The percentage of premium to gross Domestic product of the country was maximum of 11.17 per cent in Taiwan in 2005 followed by 10.84 per cent in South Africa. The developed nation except United

States have more than 5 per cent of their GDP in the form of life insurance premium viz. 8.90 per cent in United States, 8.63 per cent in Hong Kong, 8.36 per cent in Belgium, 8.32 per cent in Japan, 7.33 per cent in Finland, 7.27 per cent in South Korea and 7.08 per cent in France.

The percentage of life premium to GDP was merely 4.14 per cent in United States and 2.53 per cent in India in 2005. It reveals that India has abundant scope of life insurance. The insurance companies should come forward to expand their business in India.

Profitability

The outlook for 2006 has been favourable for life insurance over 2005. There has been higher demand for old provisions in a situation in which the share of retirees in the population increases and the fact that government actively shift away frmm public old age provisions to private schemes. Changing taxation of life products plays an important role both for high growth. In Germany, premium drops in life business due to removal of tax advantages on life products. It is a good lesson for India that the life insurarce will decline, if Government removes the facilities of Income Taxes on the life insurance.

Profitability of life business has continued to improve in many countries as costs have been cut, guaranteed interest rates have been reduced and bonuses have been adjusted to reflect low interest rates.[1] Risks products a pension business are predicted to grow. The capital base will increased with rising retained earning in insurance companies. Many banks have started life insurance business Unit linked business of life insurance has also increased. The economic growth has been helpful for enhancing global insurance.

Solvency

Solvency is a challenge for life insurers as it involves different types of risk. The objective of solvency is to protect policyholers interest and reflect the risks to which an insurer is exposed. The solvency is decided on the bases of rules of financial resources, process of risk management and transparency. The market consistent valuation of assets and liabilities is the basis for provision for investment risks. Solvency should inforce insurers focus on risk/return fundamentals. It focusses on risk and capital management. European insurance industry has taken lead in solvency requirements.

European Union (EU) Solvency

Solvency in Europe was required by the Council Directive of 1973 and 1979 which necessitated to establish capital buffer to cope with the uncertainty of insurance business. In 1994, laws were enacted to detect the insolvency case in the early stage to better protect the policyholders.

Solvency I

The Solvency I Directives were passed in Feb. 2002. It ensured higher minimum guarantee fund increased threshold in solvency margin and composition of available capital. Solvency requirements should be fulfilled at all times and more power was given to insurance supervisory authorities. The life insurance solveney margin is calculated as:

Solvency = 4% × gross mathematical provision × retention rate mathematical provisions + 3% × capital at risk × retention rate capital at risk.

Retention Rate Mathematical provisions = net provisions ÷ gross provisions

Retention Rate capital at risk = net capital at risk ÷ gross capital at risk

The minimum guarantee fund was set up = one third of the required solveney margin.

The technical reserves will be invested by imposing restrictions on the asset classes. The available capital funds are calculated as the assets of the insurer free of any foreseeable liabilities less any intangible items.

1. Source: Swiss Re, Sigma No. 2/2005, 5/2006 and 4/2007

Criticisms

The valuation of assets and liabilities is not based on market consistent approach. Solvency requirements depend on mathematical reserves and capital at risk in life insurance Investment risk is not included in the required solveney margins.

Solvency II

The need for Solvency II was realised in 2001 by the EU Commission. Its Draft are being prepared is expected to be passed by EU parliament and the council of Ministers in 2007. The objectives are to protect policyholder, establish a solvency capital requirements, to reflect market developments and to avoid unnecessary over capitalisation. There is need of harmonisation of quantitative and qualitative supervisory methods, incorporation of international developments with the aim of promoting further convergence with International Association of Insurcance Supervisors, the International Association of Actuaries and the International Accounting Standards Board. Solvency II includes quantitative requirenents, qualitative requirements and market discipline Quantitative requirements includes basics for the calculation of technical provisions, minimum capital requirements, solvency capital requirements and investment rules. Quantitative requirements consist of principles of internal control and risk management and supervisory review process. Market discipline reveals disclosure and transparency.

Quantitative Requirements

Solvency II aims to harmonise methods for calculating technical provisions and to achieve congfuency with developments in the International Financial Reporting standards (IFRS). Valuation of insurance liabilities is based on the expected present value of cash flows together with risk margin. Solvency II envisages the Minimum Capital Requirement (MCR) and Solvency Capital Requirement (SCR).

The Minimum capital Requirement is the level of capital below which an insurance company present an unacceptable risk of policyholders. The Solvency capital requirement delivers a level of capital that enables an insurance company to absorb significant unforeseen losses and gives reasonable assurance to policyholders. All risks relating to underwriting, investment, credit, operation and liquidity are factored into its calculation. A risk measure is an amount of capital to a distribution of economic profit are loss. Appropriate risk and confidence level are also decided internally by the insurers.

Qualitative Requirements

Qualitative requirements envisage on rights and duties of the supervisory authorities and principles of transparency and accountability. Internal risk model uses the stress tests, governance process and quality of risk mitigation. Risk diversification is a key components of risk management. The risk diversification includes diversification with risk types, accross risk types, accross entities within territory and accross entities beyond territory. Capital mobility and risk transfer shall be recognised if financial resources are available to back policyholders and other creditors claim with sufficient value.

Market Discipline

The third factor for solvency II refers to disclosure and transparency to reinforce market mechanisms and riskbased supervision. The information of insurer's risk should have a discipline effect on policyholders, investors, rating agencies and any other interested parties. Certain supervisory information should be made public as it will be useful for the potential policyholders to select a sound insurer.

The US insurance supervisory authorities introduced the Risk Based Capital (RBC) system in 1994. It is to hold capital equal to atleast their RBC requirement. It slems stock, bond and real estate holdings, credit risk, underwriting risks *i.e.*, loss reserves and paid claims risks and risk from affiliates.

The biggest risk in life insurance is the other asset risk *i.e.*, stemming from investments in stock, bonds, mortgages and real estate.

Prospects

Life premium are expected to grow in future. Emerging markets are likely to benefit from their booming economies. Many governments have favoured private old age provision. So yough prospects for life insurance look very promising. When some governments have cut social security benefits, the individuals look for alternate protection-methods. The growth outlook for private risk insurance is very positive.

NON-LIFE INSURANCE

The non-life premium has slowed down after touching the highest growth rate of 13.50 per cent in 1986. It has continuously declining and increased slightly to 9.5 per cent in 2002. It came down to 0.6 per cent in 2005 although it was 2.4 per cent in 2004. The real non-life premium in us declined by 0.3 per cent and Western Europe increased by 0.6 per cent. The non-life premium in emerging markets increased by 6.0 per cent although it was less than 9.5 per cent of 2004.

Table 50.4 Growth of Non-Life Insurance Premium (in %)

Year	*1980*	*1981*	*1982*	*1983*	*1984*	*1985*	*1986*	*1987*	*1988*	*1989*
% Increase(+) or Decrease (–)	–4.0	0.0	1.0	4.0	4.5	9.5	13.5	4.8	5.2	2.0
Year	*1990*	*1991*	*1992*	*1993*	*1994*	*1995*	*1996*	*1997*	*1998*	*1999*
% Increase or Decrease (–)	2	4.5	3.5	4.0	2.5	1.5	1.0	1.0	0.0	2.5
Year	*2000*	*2001*	*2002*	*2003*	*2004*	*2005*	*2006*	*2007*		
% Increase or Decrease (–)	5.0	5.5	9.5	7.0	2.4	0.6	5.0	10.0		

Source: Sigma No. 2/2005 and 5/2006

Growth Rate of Non-Life Premium

The growth rate of non-life premium in real term has been very high *i.e.*, 10.1 per cent in 2004 and 11.5 per cent in 2005 in India. The real growth of non-life premium has been negative in USA, Germany, Canada and Australia in 2005. It reveals that the countries which have already reached to the level of higher rank are facing low growth rate. Countries which are having less business are getting higher growth rate.

Japan has faced negative growth rate (nominal base) in 2005. The share of non-life premium in world market has been 43.10 *i.e.*, the highest of all the countries. The life premium was also very high. United States of America have been very particular about insurance Germany has 7.37 per cent share in 2005. It has been observed that all countries above 10 ranks have growth rate more than two per cent. 6.93 per cent in United Kingdom, 6.92 per cent in Japan, 4.69 per cent in France, 3.27 per cent in Italy, 3.05 per cent in canada, 2.39 per cent in Spain and 2.01 per cent in Netherland have been the world-share in non-life premium.

The share of non-life premium to total business have been more than 50 per cent in United States, Germany, Canada and Spain. Japan has the lowest share in total business. It reveal that more life insurance business.

Table 50.5 Non-Life Premium Growth Rate by Region and Country

Continents	*Rank*			*Premium Volume in Millions of USD*					*Change in % Nominal*				*Inflation*				*Share of Total Business in % Life Non-Life*				*Share of world Market in %*			
	2004	*2005*	*2006*	*2003*	*2004*	*2005*	*2006*	*2007*	*2004*	*2005*	*2006*	*2007*	*2004*	*2005*	*2006*	*2007*	*2004*	*2005*	*2006*	*2007*	*2004*	*2005*	*2006*	*2007*
Table 50.5A Regions																								
North America				611498	647910	670105	685440	706116	5.2	3.4	4.6	2.2	2.0	–0.3	1.0	–1.0	55.1	54.9	54.5	53.1	46.10	46.15	45.27	42.34
Latin America & Carribean				25853	29197	3 5336	42505	51588	126.6	21.0	19.7	20.5	5.9	4.6	10.0	8.3	59.0	60.3	59.5	59.0	2.09	2.43	2.81	3.09
Europe				438008	501095	518583	544295	644751	15.0	3.5	4.1	12.4	2.5	0.7	0.5	0.7	42.0	40.3	36.7	38.4	36.10	35.71	35.95	38.66
Asia				166920	180584	186540	198553	217132	7.7	3.3	6.4	9.3	2.1	2.9	4.4	5.1	24.4	24.6	24.8	25.8	12.88	12.85	13.11	13.02
Africa				9192	11192	12230	14200	15183	23.7	9.3	8.9	7.0	10.1	10.7	6.2	0.6	30.2	30.6	28.6	28.5	0.81	0.84	0.94	0.91
Oceania				24145	27545	29217	29102	33011	16.6	6.1	–0.4	13.6	0.4	–0.7	–1.5	–0.2	51.0	50.6	49.9	48.0	2.02	2.01	1.92	1.98
World				1275616	1397522	1452011	1514094	1667780	9.4	3.9	5.0	7.7	2.3	0.6	1.5	0.7	43.0	42.4	46.7	41.1	100	10010.0		100.00
Table 50.5B Selected Countries																								
United States	1	1	1	575635	606988	625838	636452	651311	4.8	3.1	4.2	1.6	2.0	–0.3	1.0	–1.3	54.9	54.8	54.4	53.0	43.22	43.10	42.04	39.05
Japan	3	4	4	100989	104892	100523	97495	94182	4.6	–4.2	–2.0	–1.8	–0.5	0.2	0.3	–1.6	21.4	21.1	21.2	22.2	7.57	6.92	6.44	5.65
United Kingdom	4	3	3	93143	99003	100629	106676	113946	13.0	1.6	1.5	8.6	–0.5	0.2	–2.1	–2.3	35.7	33.5	25.5	24.6	7.54	6.93	7.05	6.83
France	5	5	5	57536	66407	68162	73262	81907	14.4	2.6	3.9	11.2	2.1	0.9	1.1	0.5	33.8	30.7	29.2	30.5	4.72	4.69	4.84	4.91
Germany	2	2	2	93891	106114	107026	109633	120407	13.2	0.9	1.8	10.0	1.5	–1.0	–1.0	–1.4	55.7	54.3	53.6	54.0	7.62	7.37	7.24	7.22
Italy	6	6	6	40716	46321	47453	49103	54112	19.2	2.4	3.9	11.2	2.5	0.7	1.1	0.1	36.3	34.1	29.2	38.0	3.35	3.27	4.84	3.24
Canada	7	7	7	35862	40922	44267	48988	54805	12.2	8.2	10.5	11.0	2.3	–1.5	1.5	2.9	57.7	56.2	55.5	54.6	2.88	3.05	3.24	3.29
Spain	8	8	8	27100	32410	34757	37528	43530	19.2	7.2	7.7	16.0	5.6	3.8	3.0	3.5	57.8	57.7	57.0	58.3	2.32	2.39	2.48	2.61
Netherland	9	9	10	24042	28857	29159	28762	66834	12.6	1.0	–1.1	12.1	N.A.	–0.6	–3.2	1.2	46.2	47.7	45.9	65.0	1.94	2.01	1.90	4.01
Australia	10	10	12	20345	23069	24300	24274	27508	16.6	5.3	–0.1	13.3	0.6	–1.0	–2.4	–0.3	48.0	46.8	46.2	44.2	1.70	1.67	1.60	1.65
India	27	27	26	3707	4108	4848	5812	7243	16.8	18.0	20.5	26.0	10.1	11.5	17.1	5.6	20.4	19.4	20.0	13.3	0.31	0.33	0.68	0.43

Source: Sigma 2/2005, 5/2006 and 4/2007

Table 50.6 Non-Life Insurance Index

Continents	*Rank*			*Per Capita Premium in USD*				*Continents*	*Rank*			*% of Premium to GDP*			
	2004	*2005*	*2006*	*2004*	*2005*	*2006*	*2007*		*2004*	*2005*	*2006*	*2004*	*2005*	*2006*	*2007*
North America				1984.0	2048.8	2072.2	2115.5					5.05	4.92	4.7	4.6
Latin Armerica % Caribbean				53.7	63.8	75.4	91.0					1.46	1.42	1.4	1.5
Europe				579.8	601.9	626.0	739.8					3.20	3.10	3.0	3.0
Asia				47.1	48.3	50.4	54.1					1.79	1.67	1.6	1.6
Africa				13.1	18.5	15.3	15.8					1.48	1.47	1.4	1.2
Oceamia				885.9	904.3	891.0	988.1					3.90	3.22	3.3	3.2
World				220.0	219.0	224.2	249.6					3.43	3.18	3.0	3.1
Countries															
Switzerland	1	1	1	2441.2	2480.3	2450.1	2581.7	U.S A	1	1	2	5.14	5.01	4.8	4.7
								Switzerland	2	2	1	5.02	4.99	4.9	4.6
United States	2	2	2	2062.6	2122.9	2134.2	2164.4	Netherland	3	3	9	4.67	4.67	2.5	8.7
Netherland	3	3	10	1663.1	1785.5	1152.9	4070.5	N. Zealand	4	4	6	4.42	4.39	3.3	4.3
Luxemburg	4	4	3	1555.8	1643.8	1817.9	2000.0	Canada	5	6	3	4.05	3.92	4.7	3.8
Ireland	5	5	6	1473.8	1417.4	1360.9	1456.4	Slovenia	6	5	8	3.96	3.96	3.1	3.8
United Kingdom	6	8	7	1318.0	1311.9	1327.1	1383.2	Germany	7	7	4	3.86	3.73	3.6	3.6
								Australia	8	10	7	3.85	3.09	3.2	3.0
Denmark	7	6	5	1309.9	1386.3	1430.6	1722.1	United Kingdom	9	8	5	3.68	3.55	3.4	3.0
Germany	8	9	8	1265.3	1268.4	1306.7	1427.9	France	10	9	8	3.14	3.13	3.1	3.0
Canada	9	7	4	1262.6	1377.1	1504.3	1667.0								
Austria	10	10	9	1204.4	1247.7	1292.1	1430.9	India	44	45	10	0.65	0.61	1.7	0.6
India	78	78	76	4.0	4.4	5.2	6.2								

Non-Life Insurance Index

Capita Premium

The per capita non-life premium in USD was maximum in switzerland *i.e.*, USD 2441.2 in 2004 and USD 2480.3 in 2005 followed by United States, Netherland, Luxumburg and Ireland. Their ranks have not changed. The other countries under ten ranks have been United Kingdom, Denmark, Germany, Canada and Austria. All the developed nations have maximum non-life per capita insurance. India is at 78th rank having per capita non-life premium USD 4.0 in 2004 and USD 4.4 in 2005. The non-life premium per capita is USD 1204.4 in 2004 and USD 1247.7 in 2005. India has to develop the non-life insurance.

Percentage of premium to Gross Domestic Premium

North America has 5.05 per cent premium to GDP in 2004 and 4.92 per cent of GDP in 2005. The lowest percentage was in Latin America *i.e.*, 1.46 per cent and 1.42 per cent in the respective years. United States has maximum share of non-life insurance to GDP *i.e.*, 5.14 per cent in 2004 and 5.01 per cent in 2005. Switzerland stood second, Netherland was third and Newzealand was fourth in this comparison in all the two years. Other countries within 10 ranks are Canada, Slovenia, Germany, Australia, United Kingdom and France. India stood at 44th rank in 2004 and 43th rank in 2005.

Table 50.7 Total Insurance
Total premium Growth Rate by Region and Country

Continents	***Rank***			***Premium Volume in Millions of USD***					***Change in % Nominal***				***Inflation Adjusted***				***Share of World Market in %***			
	2004	***2005***	***2006***	***2003***	***2004***	***2005***	***2006***	***2007***	***2004***	***2005***	***2006***	***2007***	***2004***	***2005***	***2006***	***2007***	***2004***	***2005***	***2006***	***2007***
North America				1116897	1179226	1221635	1258301	1330066	4.5	3.6	5.93	5.39	1.4	–0.2	2.24	2.10	35.99	35.66	33.79	32.75
Latin America and caribbean				42089	49313	58599	71428	87397	17.2	18.8	21.50	22.18	10.5	1.9	11.61	9.61	1.52	1.71	1.92	2.15
Europe				1035838	1206191	1287920	1484881	1680693	15.7	6.8	11.22	15.47	3.2	4.4	7.47	3.43	36.94	37.60	39.88	41.39
Asia				684970	738918	754779	800819	84060	7.5	2.8	4.65	8.09	2.1	3.5	3.83	4.52	22.69	22.18	21.51	20.70
Africa				32461	36422	40025	49667	53294	15.9	9.9	16.27	6.86	–1.3	7.1	17.55	2.80	1.16	1.17	1.33	1.30
Oceania				46103	54088	57756	58316	68818	19.7	6.8	3.78	18.17	3.2	0.1	2.17	3.89	1.70	1.69	1.57	1.69
World				2958359	3264158	3425714	3723412	4060870	9.7	4.9	8.06	10.50	2.3	2.5	4.97	3.22	100.00	100.00	100.00	100.0
Countries																				
United States	1	1	1	1057162	1109291	1142912	1170101	1229668	3.8	3.0	5.43	4.69	1.1	–0.3	2.13	1.78	33.84	33.36	31.43	30.28
Japan	2	2	2	472820	494735	476481	460261	424832	4.1	–3.7	–3.75	–3.31	–0·9	0.7	–1.49	–3.17	15.18	13·91	12.36	10.41
United Kingdom	3	3	3	254363	292199	300241	418366	463686	15.9	2.8	24.46	28.16	2.1	1.3	20.09	15.31	9.09	8.76	11.24	11.42
France	4	4	4	161483	199863	222220	251164	268900	0.5	11.2	13.65	10.09	7.6	9.3	10.61	–2.90	6.00	6.49	6.75	6.62
Germany	5	5	5	170137	190811	197251	204544	222825	12.1	3.4	3.32	7.47	0.6	1.4	0.55	–1.33	5.88	5.76	5.49	5.49
Italy	6	6	6	112410	128405	139194	138679	142328	14.6	8.4	–1.89	1.27	2.3	6.5	–4.90	–8.82	3.97	4.06	3.72	3.50
South Korea	8	7	7	60138	68806	82933	101179	116990	14.1	20.5	18.90	16.28	3.1	8.5	8.73	11.06	2.12	2.42	2.72	2.88
Canada	7	8	8	59735	69935	78723	88200	100398	16.8	3.6	12.99	14.74	6.5	–0.2	3.72	6.35	2.15	2.30	2.73	2.47
Netherlands	9	9	11	52037	59919	61073	62669	102831	12.6	1.9	5.19	11.98	N.A.	0.3	2.92	1.05	1.81	1.78	1.68	2.53
Spain	10	10	10	47282	56002	60275	65813	74696	18.2	7.6	8.92	13.50	4.6	4.2	4.11	1.25	1.72	1.76	1.77	1.84
India	19	19	15	18132	21608	25024	43032	54375	17.2	15.8	56.99	34.81	10.4	9.4	52.55	13.00	0.66	0.73	1.16	1.34

TOTAL INSURANCE

The total insurance has increased considerably. The growth rate of total insurance premium had –1.0 per cent in 1980 which increased to 17.0 per cent in 1986. The growth rate has declined to 2.0 per cent in 1990 and became 7.0 per cent in 2000. It remained constant at 2.5 per cent in 2005.

Growth Rate

The total premium growth rate has been highest *i.e.*, 20.5 per cent in 2004 in France and 20.5 per cent in 2005 in South Korea. The lowest growth rate has been 3.8 per cent in 2004 in United States and –3.7 per cent in 2005 in .Japan although the total premium volume in USD has been second highest in Japan. The total premium volume has been the highest in United States and the growth in 2005 was modest there. United Kingdom having third rank in total premium volume has been satisfactory in growth rate *i.e.*, 15.9 per cent in 2004 and 2.8 per cent in 2005. France has significantly high growth rate in premium volume and also has fourth rank in total premium volume. Germany and Italy have also maintained their ranks in total premium volume. After interchanging the growth rates with South Korea and Canada. Netherlands and Spain have maintained their ranks. India is 19th in total premium volume. It is good sign for India. The growth rate is moderately high *i.e.*, more than 15 per cent although its share in world's total insurance premium is merely 0.66 per cent in 2004 and 0.73 per cent in 2005. Inflation-adjusted growth rate is the highest in India *i.e.*, 10.4 per cent in 2004 and 9.4 per cent in 2005. United States have maximum share of world market *i.e.*, 33.84 per cent in 2004 and 33.36 per cent in 2005.

Table 50.8 Total Insurance Index

Continents	*Ranks*			*Per Capita Premium in USD*				*Continents*	*Rank*			*% of Premium to GDP*			
	2004	*2005*	*2006*	*2004*	*2005*	*2006*	*2007*		*2004*	*2005*	*2006*	*2004*	*2005*	*2006*	*2007*
North America				3601.1	3735.1	3804.0	3984.8					9.17	8.97	8.7	8.7
Latin America & Caribbean				90.9	105.7	126.7	154.1					2.47	2.35	2.4	2.5
Europe				1427.9	1513.8	1745.7	1962.4					7.89	7.78	8.3	8.0
Asia				194.3	197.9	205.0	210.7					7.37	6.83	6.6	6.2
Africa				43.4	44.2	53.6	55.3					4.89	4.80	4.8	4.3
Oceania				1736.9	1789.3	1787.3	2059.5					7.65	6.38	6.7	6.6
World				511.5	518.5	554.8	607.7					7.99	7.52	7.5	7.5
Countries															
Switzerland	1	1	3	5716.4	5558.4	5561.9	5740.7	South Africa	1	2	2	14.38	13.87	16.0	15.3
United Kingdom	2	2	1	4508.4	4599.0	6466.7	7113.7	Taiwan	2	1	3	14.13	14.11	14.5	15.7
Ireland	3	3	2	4091.2	4177.0	5564.7	7171.4	UK	3	3	1	12.60	12.45	16.5	15.7
Belgium	8	4	10	3275.6	3985.6	3681.2	4131.5	Switzerland	4	4	5	11.75	11.19	11.0	10.3
Denmark	6	5	4	3620.4	3876.2	4271.4	5103.1	Japan	5	6	7	10.51	10.54	10.5	9.6
United States	5	6	6	3755.1	3875.2	3923.7	4086.5	Netherland	6	10	10	10.10	9.79	10.4	13.4
Japan	4	7	9	3874.8	3746.7	3589.6	3319.9	Belgium	7	5	11	9.62	11.15	9.2	9.6
Netherlands	7	8	7	3599.6	3739.7	4075.4	6262.9	South Korea	8	7	4	9.52	10.25	11.1	11.8
France	9	9	5	3207.9	3568.5	4271.4	5103.1	France	9	8	6	9.52	10.21	11.0	10.3
Finland	10	10	8	3134.1	3389.3	3828.8	3905.8	USA	10	12	14	9.36	9.15	8.8	8.9
India	78	78	76	19.7	22.7	38.4	46.6	Hong Kong	11	9	8	9.27	9.93	10.5	11.8
								India	44	43	31	3.17	3.14	4.8	4.7

Total Insurance Index

The premium of total insurance has been analysed on the basis of per capita in USD and percentage share of Gross Domestic products (GDP).

Per Capita Premium

The per capita premium has been the highest in Switzerland *i.e.*, USD 5716.4 in 2004 and USD 5558.4 in 2005 followed by United Kingiom having per capita premium of USD 4508.4 in 2004 and USD 4599.0 in 2005 and Ireland USD 4091.2 in 2004 and USD 4177.0 in 2005. Belgium, Denmark, United States, Japan, Netherlands, France and Finland have been within 10 ranks. India has 78th rank so far per capita premium is concerned although it has 19th rank in total premium volume.

% of Premium to GDP

The highest percentage of premium to GDP has been South Africa *i.e.*, 14.38 per cent of GDP in 2004 and 13.87 per cent in 2005 followed by Taiwan, United Kingdom and Switzerland. Japan stood at 5th and 6th position in 2004 and 2005 respectively. Netherlands, Belgium, South Korea and France have been with 10 ranks. India has 44th rank covering 3.17 per cent of GDP in 2004 and 43th rank having 3.14 per cent of GDP.

QUESTIONS

1. Examine the International Insurance Scene.
2. Explain the progress of life Insurance in India and World.
3. Discuss the progress of non-life insurance in world.
4. What is solveney? How is it judged? Explain.
5. Examine the progress of total insurance in world.

PART SEVEN

INSURANCE LEGISLATION

51

INSURANCE LEGISLATION IN INDIA

History

From the writings of Manu, Yajnavalkya that the carrier in India was also an insurer in a restricted sense; yet is "not certain if the ancient Hindus also had a system of life insurance and practised it, though it seems highly problematical as legal codes do not reveal traces of any such system. Insurance against death was regarded till very recently, as want of belief in God which was not a very fertile soil for the growth of the insurance.

Up to the end of nineteenth century, the insurance was in its inceptional stage. Therefore, no legislation was required till that time. Usually the Indian Companies Act 1883 was applicable in business concerns, banking and insurance companies. New Indian Insurance companies and Provident Societies started at the time of national movement; but most of them were financial unsound. It was asserted that the Indian Companies Act, 1883 was inadequate for the purpose. *Therefore, two Acts were passed in 1912, namely, Provident Insurance Societies Act V of 1912 and Indian Life Insurance Companies Act VI of 1912.* These two Acts were in pursuit of the English Insurance Companies Act of 1909 with the difference that the Indian Life Insurance Companies related to Life insurance only and excluded the non-life business from its fold. The Act put the life insurance business in India on sounder footing and resulted in creating a healthier atmosphere than before. It was also instrumental in the dissolution of some unsound Indian as well as non-Indian life offices or in the merging of some of them with the others. The legislation in India was confining of some of them with the others. The legislation in India was confining to life business because there were very few general insurance companies and did not call for any legislation. To prevent financial weakness the insurers were required to keep certain stated deposits. The Indian insurers were required to submit returns giving particulars of their business. The foreign insurers were exempted from submitting separate particulars regarding the business done in India. Some English companies ceased to underwrite further business with a view to avoid submission of reports to the Government of India Insurance Legislation in India. Some Indian Companies which conducted business on assessments or on actuarially unsound basis, either dropped or mortgaged them to conform to actuarial requirements. The policies issued by these companies were not less than Rs. 1,000. The aim of the Provident Insurance Societies Act 1912 was to govern Provident Insurance Societies which were engaged in issuing life policies worth Rs. 1,000 or less and marriage and disease policies, of very nominal amount. This act was purely based on the Friendly Societies Act.

These two enactments were governing only life insurance. There were no control on general insurance since such businesses were not so developed. Besides, there were the following defects of these Acts:

Defects

1. There were no regulation pertaining to investment. The need for restriction on investments was felt in India because unenlightened public was not able to judge the position of a company. But simply because there was no restriction on investment in England, no restriction was placed in India.

2. The control and enquiry was slight. Non-compliance of rules and regulations was not strictly penalised.
3. The foreign companies were to submit report of their total business both in India and outside India. But separate particulars regarding business done in India were not demanded and the absence of these made it impossible to get any idea of the cost of procuring business in India for foreign companies and comparing them with similar data of the Indian companies.
4. The Government Actuary was not vested with the power to order investigation into the conduct of a company even when it appeared that the company was insolvent under the power of exemption, several new underwriters were granted exemption even from submitting reports to the Governments although the business transacted continued to be in force.
5. Any one can start life insurance business only with the sum of Rs. 25,000. It was too low to prevent the mushroom growth of companies. Foreign insurarer was not bound to deposit a certain sum of life policy issued in India. Thus, it was not sufficient to check the floatation of unhealthy concerns and provided discrimination in India.

These defects were compelling the above Acts to be replaced. Public was aware of the fact that the Indian companies in foreign countries or in England were directed to have a certain sum in the shape of reserve as contrary to above regulation. The law in India was not in line with the law in force in other countries. Persistent demands were made by various important public bodies in the country for statutory provisions which would provide for disclosure and publication of the business carried on in India by foreign companies. After a few years it was realised that there should be another efficient and adequate act.

Reasons of Replacement Act of 1912

(*i*) The above defects compel the replacement.

(*ii*) Persistent demands were made by various important public bodies and Swadeshi Movements.

(*iii*) The general insurance business should also be controlled.

(*iv*) The insurance companies particularly Fire, Marine and Accident insurance companies developed very fast during 1914-18 due to First World War. Therefore, it was essential to control such new companies and to provide them with some proper guidance.

(*v*) The important underwriters and business units demanded that there should be a full-fledged insurance Act.

(*vi*) The Foreign-underwriters should also be governed by the Indian Legislation.

(*vii*) Some guiding principles for starting new business or for completing the jobs were required.

So, the Government placed a bill for essential amendment of the Act, in 1924. The bill was containing a wide scope of insurance business. The bill came to the legislative assembly after a thorough comments by different bodies.

During the time, an important thing happened miraculously about the enactments of insurance business in England. The Government of India thought it fit to watch the course of new legislation on Insurance Law in England. Great Britain appointed Clauson (under the chairmanship of Mr. A. C. Clauson) Committee to report the possible and required changes in the Legislation. Therefore, the Government of India thought it wise to postpone the bill to include the reports of Clauson Committee. The Clauson Committee submitted its report in February, 1927, but no action was taken on its recommendations by the Government of England. The Government of India in 1928 passed a stop-gap legislation with the main object of collecting statistics regarding insurance matters so that the information collected would be of value when the time would come to pass a comprehensive Act. This act was not very comprehensive. The Government of India wanted to wait the English Legislation which was expected to be passed in 1929 or so and base the law for India on the British model but the legislation was not passed in Britain. The slow progress of events in Britain again revived the agitation for amendment of the law of Insurance in India.

Demand for another Act

Since the Act of 1928 was not very comprehensive, demand for another act was made. There were forceful and constant demand of such legislation which can control Indian as well as non-Indian insurance companies and can reduce the competition between these companies. The Government accepted the genuine demand and appointed one special officer for investigations the special and required reform of legislation in 1935. He was a well-known Calcutta Solicitor and was placed on special duty to report on the amendments necessary to modernise insurance legislation in India. His report was considered by the Advisory Committee appointed by the Government of India from representatives of all branches of insurance. The committee made several changes and the Government of India introduced the bill in the Legislative Assembly in 1937 and after much debate and several changes, it emerged as the Insurance Act of 1938.

Act of 1938

The Act does not follow the principle of minimum interference with maximum publicity and direct control. It was well balanced and was the first comprehensive piece of insurance legislation in this country governing both life and non-life branches of insurance. This Act provided to prevent the growth of mushroom companies, to enforce working on sound principles, to prevent misappropriation of funds and to protect the assets.

This Act of 1938 was wide and more comprehensive. There was strict control over the insurance business. This Act was amended from time to time. Since 1938, there were six amendments up to 1945. In 1945, it was deemed necessary to protect the interest of Insured Companies. Therefore in the Chairmanship of Sri Kavas Ji Jahangir, a meeting was appointed which was to investigate all the misconduct of the insurance business. The committee gave its reports after a thorough inquiry on which recommendation was made for amending many important sections and to introduce new sections. On this basis one amendment bill was made and was sent to different select committees and at last it was enacted on 18th April, 1950 by the Parliament. According to this amended Act, there are provisions pertaining to administration. The total right of control is with the Central Government. The Central Government controls the insurance business by appointing Controller of Insurance. The rules and regulations must be followed by the insurance companies, otherwise they will be penalised under this Act. The life insurance business was nationalised in 1956 and certain provisions of this Act apply to the Life Insurance Corporation of India. General Insurance Corporation of India Act was passed in 1972 to govern the business of general insurance which were nationalised in 1972.

THE INSURANCE ACT 1938

The Salient Features of Insurance Act 1938 have been discussed under the following headings:

1. Wide Scope
2. Requirements as to Capital
3. Deposits
4. Registration
5. Submission of Returns
6. Prohibition of Rebates, Restriction of Commission.
7. Licensing of Insurance Agents
8. Investment
9. Prohibition of loan
10. Investigation
11. Duties and Power of Controller of Insurance.

THE INSURANCE ACT 1938

The Salient Features of the Act

1. Wide Scope

(*a*) Application

The Act applies to all types of insurance business—life, fire, marine etc.—done by companies incorporated in India or elsewhere. It also governs the provident companies, mutual offices and cooperative-societies. Assessments in or dividing insurance business is Prohibited.

(*b*) Prohibition

According to Section 2-c of the .Act, there is prohibition of transaction of insurance business by certain persons.

"Save as hereinafter provided, no person shall, after the commencement of the Insurance Act, begin to carry on any class of insurance business in India and no insurer carrying on any class of insurance business in India shall after the expiry of one year, from such commencement, continue to carry on any such business unless he is

(*i*) a public company or,

(*ii*) a society registered under the Cooperative Societies. Act, 1912 or under any other law for any country outside India not being of the nature of a private company;

(*iii*) a body corporate incorporated under the law of any country outside India not being of the nature of a private company;

(*iv*) every notification issued under the Sub-section shall be laid before Parliament as soon as may be after it is issued.

2. Requirement as to Capital

(*a*) Section 6

No insurer incorporated after or who contained carrying on the business of life insurance in the States whether solely or in connection with any other business after the 26th day of January, 1937, shall be registered unless he has a working capital of a net sum of not less than fifty thousand rupees excluding of the deposit to be made before registration under sub-section (5) of Section 7 of this Act, and exclusive in the case of a company of any sums payable as preliminary expenses in the form of the company.

(*b*) Voting Powers

Notwithstanding anything to the contrary contained in any law for the time being in force or in the memorandum or articles of association but subject of the other provisions contained in this section, the voter's right of every shareholder of any public company as aforesaid in all cases be strictly proportionate to the paid up amount of the shares held by him.

(*d*) Maintenance of Registers of Members

A public company shall maintain in addition to the register of members to be maintained under the Indian Companies Act, a register of shares in which shall be inserted the name, occupation and address of the beneficial owner of each share and shall incorporate there any change of beneficial owner declared to it within 14 days from the receipt of such declaration.

3. Deposits

To prevent the growth of insurers of small financial resources or speculative concerns, the Act provided for registration of all insurers and a substantial deposit with the Reserve Bank.

Section 7

"Every insurer not being an insurer specified in sub-clause (*iii*) of clause (*i*) of Section 2 shall in respect of the insurance business carried on by him in India, deposit and keep deposited with the Reserve Bank of India in one of the offices in India of the bank for and on behalf of the Central Government. The amount hereafter specified, either in cash or in approved securities, estimated at the market value of the Securities on the day of deposit or partly in cash and partly in approved securities so estimated.

(*i*) Where the business done or to be done is life insurance only, two hundred thousand rupees.

(*ii*) Where the business done or to be done is fire insurance only, one hundred and fifty thousand rupees.

(*iii*) Where the business done or to be done is marine insurance only, one hundred and fifty thousand rupees.

(*iv*) Where the business done or to be done is miscellaneous insurance only, one hundred and fifty thousand rupees.

(*v*) Where the business done or to be done is life insurance and any one of the three classes specified in clauses (*ii*), (*iii*) and (*iv*), three hundred thousand rupees of which two hundred thousand rupees shall be the deposit for life insurance business.

(*vi*) Where the business done or to be done is life insurance and any two of the three classes specified in clauses (*ii*), (*iii*) and (*iv*), four hundred thousand rupees of which two hundred thousand shall be the deposit for life insurance business.

(*vii*) Where the business done or to be done is life insurance and all three classes specified in clauses (*ii*), (*iii*) and (*iv*) four hundred and fifty thousand rupees of which two hundred thousand rupees shall be the deposit for life insurance business:

(*viii*) Where the business done or to be done, does not include life insurance but is any two of the classes specified in clauses (*ii*), (*iii*) and (*iv*), two hundred and fifty thousand.

(*ix*) Where the business done or to be done does not include life insurance but is all three classes specified in clauses (*ii*) and (*iii*), Three hundred and fifty thousand rupees.

4. Registration

Section 3

1. No person shall, after the commencement of this Act, begin to carry on any class of insurance business in India and no insurer carrying on any class of insurance business in India shall after the expiry of three months from the commencement of this Act, continue of any or carry on any, such business, unless he has obtained from the controller a certificate of registration for the particular class of insurance business.

Provided that in the case of an insurer who was carrying on any class of insurance business in India at the commencement of this Act, failure to obtain a certificate of registration in accordance with the requirements of this Sub-clause shall not operate to invalidate any contract of insurance entered into by him if before such date as may be fixed in this behalf by the Central Government by notification in the Official Gazette, he has obtained that certificate.

Every application for registration shall be accompanied by:

(*i*) a certified copy of the memorandum and articles of association.

(*ii*) Name, address and occupation of directors.

(*iii*) a statement of the class or classes of insurance business done or to be done.

(*iv*) principal place of business or domicile outside India.

(*v*) a certified copy of the published prospectus.

(*vi*) the receipt showing payment in the prescribed manner of the prescribed fee which shall not be more than five hundred rupees.

2—A

On receipt of an application for registration and after making such inquiry as he deems fit the controller is satisfied that:

(*a*) The financial condition and the general character of management of the applicant are sound.

(*b*) The volume of business likely to be available to, and the capital structure and earning prospects of the applicant will be adequate.

(*c*) The interests of the general public will be served.

The controller may register the applicant as an insurer and grant him a certificate of registration.

The controller shall withhold registration or shall cancel a registration already made if any requirement is not satisfied.

2—4

The controller shall cancel the registration of an insurer either wholly or in so far as it related to a particular class of insurance business as the case may be:

(*a*) Insurer fails to apply Section 7 or 8 of deposits.

(*b*) Insurer is in liquidation or adjudged an insolvent.

(*c*) The business has been transferred to any other insured.

(*d*) Deposits have been returned to insurer.

(*e*) When clause 9 of Section 2 related to insurer's definition ceased or cancelled or suspended.

(*f*) Defaults in complying with any rules.

(*g*) Insurer has reason to cancel.

(*h*) Carry any business other than insurance business or any prescribed business.

Controller will give notice of his decision not more than two months before termination.

5. Submission of Returns

The Act provided for the creation of a past of Superintendent of Insurance and it was made obligatory on all companies–including the foreigner returns to submit all the quinquennial in the prescribed form within a stated period. The Superintendent had been given wide powers to reject all incomplete and inaccurate returns, etc.

Section 14

1. The audited accounts and balance sheet and actuarial report and abstract and four copies thereof shall be furnished as returns to the controller in the case of the accounts and balance sheet and the acturil report and abstract within nine months from the end of the period to which they refer. If the principal place is outside India, the period of submission may be extended by three months.
2. Of the four copies so furnished one shall be signed in the case of company by the Chairman and two directors and by the principal officer of the Company and if the Company has a managing director or managing agent, by that director or managing agent, in the case of a firm, by two partners of the firm, and in the case of an insurer being an individual by the insurer himself and one shall be signed by the auditor who made the audit or the actuary who made the valuation, as the case may be.
3. Where the insurer's principal place of business or domicile is outside India, he shall forward to the controller, along with the documents, a certified statement showing the total assets and liabilities of the insurer at the close of the period covered by the said documents.

16—2

The insurer, established outside India, shall, within the time specified in sub-section (1) of Section 15, furnish to the controller four certified copies in the English language of every balance-sheet, account abstract, report and statement supplied to the public authority and in addition thereto four certified copies in the English language of each of the following statement:

(*a*) a statement audited by an auditor or by a person duly qualified under the law of the insurer's country showing the assets held by the insurer in India at the date if any balance sheet so furnished;

(*b*) a separate account of receipts and payments and a revenue account for the period covered by any account so furnished;

(*c*) a separate abstract of the valuation report in respect of all business transacted in India in each class or sub-class of insurance business; and

(*d*) a declaration in the prescribed form stating that all amounts received by the insurer directly or indirectly whether from his head office or from any other source outside and have been shown in the revenue account.

6. Prohibition of Rebating, Restriction of Commission and Licensing of Agents

Section 40

"Prohibition of payment by was of commission of otherwise for procuring business."

1. No person shall, after the expiry of six months from the commencement of this Act, pay or contract to pay any remuneration or reward whether by way of commission or otherwise for soliciting or procuring insurance business in India to any person except an insurance agent or a principal, chief or special agent.
2. No Insurance agent shall be paid or contract to be paid by way of commission or as remuneration in any form an amount exceeding, in the case of life insurance business, 40% of the first year's premium payable on any policy or policies effected through him and 5% of a renewal premium, payable on such a policy, or, in the case of business of any other class 15%.

Provided that insurers, in respect of life insurance business only, may pay, during the first ten years of their business, to their insurance agents 55% of the first year's premium payable on any policy or policies effected through them and 6% of the renewal premium payable on such policies.

(40—A) Limitations of Expenditure on Commission

No person shall pay or contract to pay to an insurance agent, and no insurance agent shall receive or contract to receive by way of commission or remuneration in any form in respect of any policy of life insurance issued in India by an insurer after the 31st day of December 1950, and effected through an insurance agent, an amount exceeding.

(a) where the policy grants an immediate annuity or a deferred annuity in consideration of a single premium, or where only one premium is payable on the policy, 2% of that premium,

(*b*) where the policy grants a differed annuity in consideration of more than one premium, $7\frac{1}{2}$% of the first year's premium, and 2% of the each renewal premium payable on the policy, and

(*c*) in any other case, 35% of the first year's premium, $7\frac{1}{2}$ % of the second and third year's renewal premium and there after 5% of each renewal premium payable on the policy.

Provided that in a case referred to in clause (*c*), an insurer during the first 10 years of his business, may pay to an insurance agent, and an insurance agent may receive from such an insurer, 40% of the first year's premium payable on the policy.

2. No person shall pay or contract to pay to a special agent, and no special agent shall receive or contract to receive, by way of commission or as remuneration in any form, in respect of any policy of life insurance issued in India by an insurer of the 31st day of December, 1950 and effected through a special agent, an amount exceeding:
   (*a*) in a case referred to in clause (*a*) of Sub-section (1) one half per cent of the premium;
   (*b*) in a case referred to in clause (*b*) of Sub-section (1) two per cent of the first year's premium payable on the policies.
   (*c*) in a case referred to in clause (*c*) of Sub-section (1) fifteen per cent of the first-year's premium payable on the policies.

Section 41

Prohibition at rebates

1. No person shall allow or offer to allow either directly or in· directly as an inducement to any person to take out or renew or continue an insurance in respect of any kind of risk, relating to lives or property in India, any rebate of the whole or part of the commission payable or any rebate of the premium shown on the policy, nor shall any person taking out or renewing or continuing a policy accept any rebate, except such rebate as may be allowed in accordance with the published prospectuses or tables of the insurer.

   Provided that acceptance by an insurance agent of commission in connection with a policy of life insurance taken out by himself on his own life shall not be deemed to be acceptance of a rebate of premium within the meaning of this sub-section if at the time of such acceptance the insurance agent satisfies the prescribed conditions establishing that he is bona fide insurance agent employed by the insurer,
2. Any person making default in complying with the provisions of this section shall be punishable with fine which may extend to Rs. 500.

7. Licensing of Insurance Agents

Section 42

The controller or an officer authorised by him in this behalf shall, in the prescribed manner and on payment of the prescribed form which shall not be more than ten rupees, issue to any person making an application in the prescribed manner and a licence to act as an insurance agent for the purpose of soliciting or procuring insurance business:

Provided that:

(*a*) in the case of an individual, he does not suffer from any of the disqualification:
   (*i*) that the person is a minor;
   (*ii*) that he is found to be of unsound mind by a court of competent jurisdiction;
   (*iii*) that he has been found guilty of criminal misappropriation or criminal breach of trust or cheating or forgery or an abetment of or attempt to commit any such offence by a court of competent jurisdiction:

   Provided that, where at least five years have elapsed since the completion of sentence imposed on any person in respect of such person that his conviction shall cease to operate as a disqualification under this clause;

(*b*) in the case of a company or firm, any of its directors or partners does not suffer from any of the said disqualifications, and the company or firm was immediately before the 1st day or August 1957, holding a certificate issued under Section 42-A entitling, it to act as a principal agent for the purpose of procuring insurance business.

(42—2)

A licence issued under this section shall entitle the holder to act as an insurance agent for any insurer.

(42—3)

A licence issued under this section, after the commencement of the Insurance (Amendment) Act 1950, shall remain in force for a period of three years only from the date of issue, but shall, if the applicant does not suffer from any of the disqualification mentioned above and the application for renewal of the licence reaches the issuing authority at least thirty days before the date on which the licence ceases to remain in force, be renewed for a period of three years at any one time on payment of the prescribed fee which shall not be more than ten rupees, and an additional fee of a prescribed amount, not exceeding three rupees by way of penalty if the application for renewal of the licence does not reach the issuing authority at least thirty days before the date on which the licence ceases to remain in force.

8. Investments

It was laid down that 55% of net life liabilities of an Indian or a British insurer should be invested in India Government and Approved Securities with at least 25% in Indian Government Rupee Securities. All other companies had to invest 100% of their Indian liabilities in Indian Government and Approved Securities with at least one-third in Indian Government Rupee Securities. This provision had been made for the prevention of the misapplication of assets and for their preservation so that the funds of every insurer could not only be safely invested but they could also be so invested as to make them readily available and, if necessary, to be readily convertible into liquid funds.

5.27—A

1. No insurer shall invest or keep invested any part of his controlled fund otherwise than in any of the following approved investment, namely,
   (*a*) Approved securities.
   (*b*) Securities guaranteed by Government of U.K.
   (*c*) Debentures of Municipality in a State.
   (*d*) Debentures issued by a body constituted by any Central Act or Act of State Legislature.
   (*e*) First Mortgage on immovable property under any housing or building scheme.
   (*f*) Debentures secured on first charge on immovable property.
   (*g*) First debentures secured by a floating charge on all its assets.
   (*h*) Preference share of any company.
   (*i*) Shares of any company which is guaranteed by any company.
   (*j*) First Mortgage on immovable property.

Every insurer shall also submit to the controller a return in the prescribed form showing all the changes that occurred in the investments aforesaid during each of the quarters ending on the last day of March.

9. Prohibition of Loan

Section 29—1

No insurer shall grant loans or temporary advances either on hypothecation of property or on personal security or otherwise except loans on life Policies issued by him within their surrender value to any director, manager, managing agent, actuary auditor, or officer of the insurer if the company or where the insurer is a firm to any partner therein, or to any other company or firm in which any such director, manager, managing agent, actuary officer or partner holds such position.

10. Investigation

Section 33

The Central Government may, at any time, by order in writing direct the controller or any other person specified in the order to investigate the affairs of any insurer and to report to the Central Government on any investigation made by him.

11. Duties and Power of Controller of Insurance

The duties and power of controller are discussed under general duties, special duties and rights about investigation.

General Duties and Power

The controller is authorised to grant the certificate of registration, to inquire about deposit, and to receive reports and accounts from the insurers. He is empowered to issue licences to agents and to accept the amalgamations and reorganisation. He is also authorised to compose the dispute regarding claim of smaller amount, and may ask any report in this connection. He can delegate his Powers and duties to his subordinate.

Special Duties and Power

According to Section 21 (1), he is authorised to get completed the incomplete reports. He may require from the insurer such further information, certificate and documents as he may consider necessary. He may call upon the insurer to submit for his examination at the principal place of business of the insurer in the states any book of account, register, etc. He may examine any officer of the insurer on oath in relation to the return. He may decline to accept any such return unless the inaccuracy has been corrected or the deficiency has been supplied. He may examine the accounts and reports of past years. He is empowered to rectify the mistakes.

Rights about Investigation

The controller is authorised to investigate the organisational set-up and administration of the insurer. He may get special audit or actuarial or any reports by the auditors, actuaries or investigators appointed by him. He is authorised, after giving a short notice, to cancel the registration of an insurer and may order for liquidation or may take action for breach of law.

THE LIFE INSURANCE CORPORATION ACT, 1956

The essential features of the Act of 1956 have been discussed in the following headings:

(A) Termination of Personal Management.

(B) Termination of Private Ownership.

(C) Establishment of the Life Insurance Corporation of India:

1. Constitution.
2. Capital.
3. Functions of the Corporation.
4. Transfer of Services.
5. Set-up of the Corporation.
6. Committee of the Corporation.
7. Authorities.
8. Zonal Bodies.
9. Finance, Accounts and Audit.
10. Investment provisions.
11. Provisions pertaining to commission.
12. Provisions to Policy-holder's rights.

THE LIFE INSURANCE CORPORATION ACT, 1956

The process of nationalisation of Life Insurance is divided into two parts:

(A) Termination of Personal or Private Management; and

(B) Abolition of Private Ownership.

(A) Termination of Personal Management

The private management was eliminated on March 21, 1956 and was replaced by the Corporation management governed by the Life Insurance Corporation Act, 1956.

1. According to Section 3 of Life Insurance (Emergency Provisions) Act 1956, the management of controlled business were vested in Government on commencement of this Act (Emergency). On and from the 19th January, 1956 the appointed date, the management of the controlled business of all insurers shall vest in the Central Government, and pending the appointment of a custody for the controlled business immediately before the appointed day shall, on and from the appointed day, be in charge of the management of the business for and on behalf of the Central Government; and the controlled business of the insurer shall be carried on by them subject to the provisions contained in Sub-sections (3) and (5) and to such further directions, if any, as the Central Government may give to them by notice addressed and sent to the principal officer of the insurer.
2. Any contract, whether express or implied, providing for the management of the controlled business of an insurer made before the appointed day between the insurer and any person in charge of the management of the business immediately before the appointed date shall be deemed to have terminated on the appointed day.
3. No insurer shall, without the previous approval of the person specified by the Central Government in this behalf in respect of that insurer (hereinafter referred to as the authorised person):
   (*a*) make any payment or grant any loan in respect of a policy of life insurance otherwise than in accordance with the normal practice observed by him in respect of such matters immediately before the appointed day;
   (*b*) incur any expenditure from the assets appertaining to the controlled business otherwise than for the purpose of making routine payments of salaries or commission to employees, insurance, agents, special agents or chief agents or for the purpose of meeting the routine day-to-day expenditure;
   (*c*) transfer or otherwise dispose of any such assets or create any charges hypothecation in or other encumbrance thereon;
   (*d*) invest in any manner any money forming part of such assets;
   (*e*) acquire any immovable property out of any moneys forming part of such assets;
   (*f*) enter into any contract of service or agency, whether expressly or by implication, for purposes connected wholly or partly with the controlled business or vary the terms and conditions of any such contract subsisting on the appointed day; and
   (*g*) enter into any other transaction relating to controlled business other than a contract relating to the issue of a new policy of life insurance or vary the terms and conditions of any agreement relating to any such transaction subsisting at the commencement of this Act.

Appointment of Custodian

Section 4

The Central Government may, as soon as it is convenient administratively so to do, appoint any person as custodian for the purpose of taking over the management of the controlled business of an insurer.

On the appointment of a custodian all persons in charge of the management of the controlled business of the insurer for and on behalf of the Central Government immediately before such appointment shall cease to be in charge of such management and shall be bound to deliver to the custodian all books of account, registers or other documents in their custody relating to the controlled business of the insurer.

The custodian shall receive such remuneration as the Central Government may, by order, direct that the whole or any part of the deposit fix and the Central Government may at any time cancel the appointment of any person as custodian and appoint some other person in his stead.

Refund of Deposits Made under Insurance Act

The Central Government may, by order, direct that the whole or any part of the deposit appertaining to his controlled business made by an insurer under Section 7, 73 or 98 of the Insurance Act, as the case may be, shall be returned to the custodian who has been appointed to take over the management of the controlled business of the Insurer, and every such order shall have effect notwithstanding anything contained in the Insurance Act.

5.3 (6) Every insurer shall deliver forthwith at the place and to the person specified in this behalf by the Central Government in respect of that insurer the following documents:

(*i*) The minute book or any other book in India containing all resolution up to the appointed day of the persons in charge of the management of the controlled business before the appointed day.

(*ii*) The current cheque books relating to the controlled business which are at the head office of the principal office of the insurer;

(*iii*) All registers or other books containing particulars relating to the investments of any money appertaining to the controlled business including investment on mortgaged properties and all loans granted and advances made otherwise than on policies.

(*iv*) All brokers' notes, or certificates in the possession of the insurer in respect of any orders for the investment of any money appertaining to the controlled business.

Compensation for Acquiring Management

(*i*) Where the controlled business of an insurer has been transferred to and vested in the corporation under this Act, compensation shall be given by the corporation to that insurer in accordance with the principles contained in the first Schedule.

There the amount of compensation is determined as: One-twelfth of annual average of the Surplus determined according to the last two valuations of such surplus.

If the surplus cannot be determined, the basis of Income on premium is taken into account. Re. 1 on the income of Rs. 2,000/ or part there of is the basis of amount of compensation.

(B) Abolition of Private Ownership

The official management of Life Insurance continued for 6 months from January 19, 1956 to June 30, 1956. During this period the Act was passed. The Act commenced from July 1, 1956 and from this date the Act was implemented.

(C) Organisation, and Functions of Life Insurance Corporation

1. Constitution

Section 3

"Establishment and Incorporation of Life Insurance Corporation of India".

1. With effect from such date as the Central Government may, by notification in the official gazette, appoint there shall be established a corporation called the Life Insurance Corporation of India.

2. The corporation shall be a body corporate having perpetual succession and a common seal with power, subject to the provisions of this Act to acquire, hold and dispose of property and may by its name sue and be sued.

Section 4: "Constitution of the Corporation".

1. The corporation shall consist of such number of persons not exceeding fifteen as the Central Government may think fit to appoint thereto and one of them shall be appointed by the Central Government to be the Chairman thereof.
2. Before appointing a person to be a member the Central Government shall satisfy itself that the person has no such financial or other interest as is likely to affect prejudicially the exercise or performance by him of his functioning as a member, and the Central Government shall also satisfy itself from time to time with respect to every member that he has no such interest; and any person who is, or whom the Central Government proposes to appoint and who has consented to be a member shall, whenever required by the Central Government so to do, furnish to it such information as the Central Government considers necessary for the performance of its duties under this sub-section.
3. A member who is in any way directly or indirectly interested in a contract made or proposed to be made by the corporation shall as soon as possible report to the Corporation.

2. Capital

Section 5.

Capital of the Corporation:

1. The original capital of the corporation shall be five crores of rupees provided by the Central Government after due appropriation made by Parliament by law for the purpose and the terms and conditions relating to the provisions of such capital shall be such as may be determined by the Central Government.

3. Function of the Corporation

1. Subject to the rules, if any, made by the Central Government in this behalf it shall be the general duty of the Corporation to Carry on life insurance business, whether in or outside India, and the Corporation to carry on life insurance business, whether in or outside India, shall so exercise its powers under this Act as to secure that life insurance business is developed to the best advantage of the community.
2. Without prejudice to the generality of the provisions contained in Sub-section (1) but subject to the other provisions contained in this Act, the Corporation shall have power.
   (*a*) to carry on capital redemption business, annually certain business, or reinsurance business in so far as such reinsurance business appertains to life insurance business;
   (*b*) subject to the rules, if any, made by the Central Government in this behalf, to invest the funds of the Corporation in such manner as the Corporation may think fit and to take all such steps as may be necessary or expedient for the protection or realise of any investment, including the taking over of and administering any property offered as security for the investment until a suitable opportunity arises for its disposal;
   (*c*) to acquire, hold and dispose of any property for the purpose of its business;
   (*d*) to transfer the whole or any part of the life insurance business carried on outside India to any other person or persons, if in the interests of the Corporation it is expedient so to do;
   (*e*) to advance or lend money upon the security of any movable or immovable property or otherwise;

(*f*) to borrow or raise any money in such manner and upon such security as the Corporation may think fit;

(*g*) to carry on either by itself or through any subsidiary any other business in any case where such other business was being carried on by a subsidiary of an insurer whose controlled business has been transferred to and vested in the Corporation under this Act.

(*h*) to carry on any other business which may seem to the Corporation to be capable of being conveniently carried on in connection with its business and calculated directly or indirectly to render profitable the business of the Corporation; and

(*i*) to do also such thing as may be incidental or conducive to the proper exercise of any of the powers of the Corporation.

4. Transfer of Services

All the employees except chief agent will be vested into new life-business. The salary and terms of employment will remain the same unless insurance business think fit to change the terms of employment for the benefit of the policyholder.

If any term is not acceptable to an employee, he can be terminated by paying three months' salary as compensation.

Section 12

Subject to such rules as the Central Government may make in this behalf, every whole-time salaried employee of a Chief Agent of an insurer whose controlled business has been transferred to and vested in the Corporation and

(*a*) who was employed by the Chief Agent wholly or mainly in connection with the controlled business of the insurer;

(*b*) whose salary on the appointed day did not exceed five hundred rupees per mensem; and

(*c*) who was in the employment of the Chief Agent for a continues period of not less than one year immediately before the appointed day.

Shall, on and from the appointed day, become an employee of the Corporation and the provisions of Section 11 shall, so far as may be, apply in relation to such employee as they apply in relation to a whole-time employee of the insurer.

Provided that this section shall not apply except in cases where the Chief Agent of the insurer was required under the terms of his contract with the insurer to render the prescribed service top policy holders of the insurers.

Section 14

Power of Corporation to modify contracts of life insurance is given in certain cases.

Section 15

Right of Corporation to seek relief in respect of certain transaction of the insurer:

1. Where an insurer whose controlled business has been transferred to and vested in the corporation under this Act, has at any time within five years before the 19th day of January, 1956,

(*a*) made any payment to any person without consideration,

(*b*) sold or disposed of any property of the insurer without consideration or for an inadequate consideration,

(*c*) acquired any property or rights for an excessive consideration,

(*d*) entered into or varied any agreement so as to require an excess consideration and

(*e*) entered into any other transaction.

Section 18

(*i*) The Central Office of the Corporation shall be at such a place as the Central Government may, by notification in the Official Gazette, specify.

(*ii*) The Corporation shall establish a Zonal Office at each of the following places *i.e.* Bombay, Calcutta, Delhi, Kanpur and Madras and subject to the previous approval of the Central Government, may establish such other zonal offices as it thinks fit.

(*iii*) The territorial limits of each zone shall be such as may be specified by the corporations.

(*iv*) There may be established as many divisional offices and branches in each zone as the Zonal Manager thinks fit.

6. Committee of the Corporation

Section 19

1. The corporation may entrust the general superintendence and direction of its affairs and business to an executive committee consisting not more than five of its members and the executive committee may exercise all powers and do all such acts and things as may be delegated to it by the Corporation.
2. The Corporation may also constitute an Investment Committee for the purpose of advising it in matters relating to the investment of its funds, and the Investment amount shall consist of not more than seven members of whom not less than three shall be members of Corporations and the remaining members shall be person (whether members of the corporation or not) who have special knowledge and experience in financial matters, particularly matters relating to investment of funds.
3. The corporation may constitute such other committees as it may think fit for the purpose to discharge such of its functions as may be delegated to them.

7. Authorities

(*a*) Managing Director

The corporation may appoint, one or more persons to be the Managing Director or Directors of the Corporation and every Managing Director shall be a whole-time officer of the Corporation, and shall exercise such power and perform such duties as may be entrusted or delegated to him by the Executive Committee or the Corporation.

Corporation to be Guided by the Directions of Central Govt.

In the discharge of its function under this Act, the Corporation shall be guided by such directions in matters of policy involving public-interest as the Central Government may give to it in writing.

(*b*) Zonal Managers

1. The Corporation may entrust the superintendence and direction of the affairs and business of a zonal office to a person, whether a member or not, who shall be known as a Zonal Manager and the Zonal Manager shall perform all such functions of the Corporation as may be delegated to him with respect to the area within the jurisdiction of the Zonal Office.
2. The Corporation may constitute for each zone a Board consisting of such number, of persons as it thinks fit to appoint thereto for the-purpose of advising the zonal manager in respect of such matters as are referred to it under the regulations made by the Corporation.
3. The Corporation shall constitute in the prescribed manner for each zonal office an Employee and Agents Relations Committee consisting of such number of person as it thinks fit and every such committee shall consist of representatives of the Corporation.

8. Zonal Bodies

(a) Zonal Board

The Corporation will establish one board at every zone. The appointment of members and the numbers are determined according to corporation. These board suggests on the zonal management, on the rules and regulations of the Corporation.

(b) Employees of Agents Relations Committee

The Corporation shall constitute in the prescribed manner for each zonal office an Employees and Agents Relations Committee consisting of such number of the persons at it thinks fit and every such committee shall consist of representation of the Corporation and of its employees and agents, so that the number of representatives of the employees and agent on the Committee shall not be less than the number of representatives of the Corporation and it shall be the duty of the Committee to advise the Zonal Manager on matters which relate to the welfare of the employees and agents of the Corporation or which are likely to promote and secure amity and good relations between them and the Corporation.

9. Finance, Accounts and Audit

(a) Audit

The accounts of the Corporation shall be audited by auditors duly qualified to act as auditors of companies under the law for the time being in force relating to companies, and the auditors shall be appointed by the Corporation with the previous approval of the Central Government and shall receive such remuneration from the Corporation as the Central Government may fix.

1. Every auditor in the performance of his duties shall have at all reasonable time access to the books of accounts and other document of the Corporation.
2. The auditors shall submit their report to the Corporation and shall also forward a copy of their report to the Central Government.

(b) Actuarial Valuation

The Corporation shall, once at least in every two years, cause an investigation to be made of actuaries into the financial condition of the business of the Corporation, including a valuation of the liabilities of the Corporation and submit the report of the actuaries to the Central Government.

(c) Annual Report of activities of Corporation

The Corporation shall, as soon as may be, after the end of each financial year, prepare and submit to the Central Government in such form as may be prescribed a report giving an account of its activities during the previous financial year, and the report shall also give an account of the activities, if any, which are likely to be undertaken by the Corporation in the next financial year.

(d) Surplus how to be utilised

If as a regular of any investigation undertaken by the Corporation under Section 26 and surplus re-merges, not less than 95% of such surplus shall be allocated to or reserved for the policyholders, of the Corporation and the remainder may be utilised for such purposes and in such manners as the Central Government may determine.

(e) Reports to be laid before Parliament

The Central Government shall cause the report of the auditors under Section 25, the report of the actuaries under Section 26 and the report giving an account of the actuaries of the Corporation under Section 27 to be laid before both Houses of Parliament as soon as may be after each such report is received by the Central Government.

Section 30. Corporation to have the exclusive privilege of carrying on Life Insurance Business

Except to the extent otherwise expressly provided in this Act, on and from the appointed day the Corporation shall have the exclusive privilege of carrying on life insurance business in India; and on and from the said day any certificate of registration under the Insurance Act held by any insurer immediately before the said day shall cease to have effect in so far as it authorises him to carry on life insurance business in India.

Section 31. Exception in the case of Insurance business in respect of persons residing outside India

1. Notwithstanding anything contained in Section 30 or in the Insurance Act, the Central Government may, by order, permit any person who has made an application in that behalf, to carry on life insurance business in India in respect of the lives of persons ordinarily resident outside India, subject to such restrictions and conditions as may be specified in the order and any such order shall be deemed to have effect as if it were a certificate of registration issued by the Controller to such person under Section 3 of the Insurance Act in respect of that class of business.
2. Nothing in sub-section 1 shall authorise any person permitted to carry on life insurance business of the nature referred to in that sub-section, to insure the life of any person ordinarily resident outside India, during any period of his temporary residence in India.

Section 32. Power of Corporation to have official seal in certain cases

The Corporation may have for use in any zonal office, divisional office or in any office outside India an official seal which shall be a fascimile of the common seal of the Corporation, with the addition on its face of the name of the zonal office, divisional office other office where it is to be used and any such official seal may be affixed to any deed or document to which the Corporation is a party.

Section 33. Requirement of foreign laws to be complied with in certain cases

Where any property or rights appertaining to the controlled business of an insurer are transferred to and vested in the Corporation under this Act on would be so transferred and vested but for the fact that such transfer and vesting are governed otherwise than by the law of India, the insurer shall comply with such directions as may be given to him by the Corporation for the purpose of securing that the ownership of the property or, as the case may be, that the right is effectively transferred to the Corporation.

Section 34. Revesting of certain shares vested in the Administrator-General

Notwithstanding anything contained in the Insurance Act, all shares which have vested in the Administrator-General of any State under sub-section (8) of Section 6A of that Act and which have not been disposed of in accordance with the provision of that sub-section before the appointed day, shall, on payment of the amount of expenditure, if any, incurred by the Administrator-General in relation to such shares by the persons who would have been entitled to those shares if the said sub-section had not been enacted revest in such persons.

Section 35. Repatuation of assests and liabilities in the case of foreign insurers in certain cases

1. Any insurer incorporated outside India may, before the appointed day, make an application to the Central Government stating that among the assets appertaining to the controlled business of the insurer there are assets brought into India by the insurer for the purpose of building up his

life insurance business in India which, notwithstanding anything contained in Section 7, should not be transferred to and vested in the Corporation.

2. On receipt of an 'application under sub-section 1, the Central Government shall determine the value of the assets of the insurer appertaining to his controlled business in existence on the 31st day of December, 1955, computed as at that date in accordance with the provisions contained in paragraph 3 of part B of the First Schedule, and deduct therefrom the total amount of the liabilities of the insurer appertaining to this controlled business in existence on the 31st day of December, 1955, computed as at that date in accordance with the provisions contained in the Second Schedule and if there is any excess, the Central Government may, by order, direct that such assets equivalent in value to the excess as may be specified in the order shall not be transferred to or vested in the Corporation, or where the order is made after the appointed day, that the Corporation shall be divested of the said assets.

3. In the case of any insurer incorporated outside India, the Central Government may also, by order, direct that any such liabilities in respect of life insurance policies expressed in any foreign currency issued on the lives of persons who are not citizens of India as are specified in the order together with any such assets necessary to meet the liabilities, as may be so specified, shall not be transferred to or vested in the Corporation or, if the order is made after the appointed day, that the Corporation shall be divested of such liabilities and assets as aforesaid.

4. The amount of liabilities in respect of the policies referred to in an order made under sub-section 3. shall be computed as at the 31st day of December. 1955:

(*a*) in any case where in respect of the insurer concerned an order has been made under sub-section 2. in accordance with the provisions contained in clause of the Second Schedule; and

(*b*) in any other case, in accordance with method A specified in the Second Schedule.

Explanation—In computing the amount of labilities in respect of the policies referred to in this sub-section, allowance shall be made for receipts and payments in respect of such policies from the 31st day, of December, 1955, up to the date of the order.

5. Every order made by the Central Government under this section shall be carried out by the Corporation in such manner as the Central Government may direct.

Section 36. Contracts of chief agents and special agents to terminate

Notwithstanding anything contained in the Insurance Act or in any other law for the time being in force, every contract appertaining to controlled business subsisting immediately before the appointed day—

(*a*) between an insurer and his chief agent or between an insurer and special agent; or

(*b*) between the chief agent of an insurer and a special agent; shall as from the appointed day, cease to have effect and all rights accruing to the chief agent or the special agent under any such contract shall terminate on that day.

Provided that in every such case compensation shall be given by the Corporation to the chief agent or the special agent, as the case may be, in accordance with the principles contained in the Third Scheduled, and the provisions of sub-Section 2 of Section 16 shall, so far as may be, apply in every such case.

Section 37. Policies to be Guaranteed by Central Government

The sums assured by all policies issued by the Corporation including any bonuses declared in respect thereof and, subject to the provisions contained in Section 14 the amounts assured by all policies issued-by any insurer the labilities under which have vested in the Corporation under this Act, and all bonuses declared in respect thereof, whether before or after the appointed day, shall be guaranteed as to payment in cash by the Central Government.

Section 38. Liquidation of Corporation

No provision of law relating to the winding up of companies for corporations shall apply to the Corporation established under this Act, and the Corporation shall not be placed in liquidation save by order of the Central Government and in such manner as that Government may direct.

Section 39. Special provisions for winding up of certain insurers

Where any insurer being a company (other than a composite insurer) whose controlled business has been transferred to and vested in the Corporation under this Act has in accordance with the provisions of this Act collected and distributed any moneys paid to him by the Corporation by way of compensation or otherwise and has also complied with any direction given to him by the Corporation for the purpose of securing that the ownership, of any property or any right is effectively transferred to the Corporation, the Central Government may on application being made to it in this behalf by such insurer grant a certificate to the insurer that there is no reason for the continued existence of the insurer and where such a certificate has been granted shall cause the certificate to be published in the Official Gazette and upon the publication thereof the insurer shall be dissolved.

Section 40. Penalty for

If any person wilfully withholds or fails to deliver to the Corporation as required by Section 13, any property or any books, documents or other papers which may be in his possession or unlawfully retains Possession of any property of an insurer which has been transferred to and vested in the Corporation under this Act or wilfully applies any such property to purposes other than those expressed in or, authorised by this Act, he shall, on the Complaint of the Corporation, be punishable with imprisonment which may extend to one, year, or with fine which may extend to one thousand rupees, or with both.

Section 41. Tribunal to have exclusive jurisdiction in certain matters

No civil court shall have jurisdiction to entertain or adjudicate upon any matter which a Tribunal is empowered to decide or determine under this Act.

Section 42. Enforcement of Decisions of Tribunals

Any decision of a Tribunal may be enforced in any civil court within the local limits of whose jurisdiction the person against whome the decision is to be enforced actually and voluntarily resides or carries on business or personally works for gain or owns any property, as if it were a decree passed by that court.

Section 43. Application of the Insurance Act.

1. The following sections of the Insurance Act shall, so far as may be, apply to the Corporation as they apply to any other insurer, namely:

   Sections 2, 2B, 3, 18, 26, 33, 41, 46, 47 A, 50, 51, 52, 110A, 110B, 110C, 119, 121, 122 and 123.

2. The Central Government shall, as soon as may be after the commencement of this Act, by notification in the Official Gazette, direct that the following sections of the Insurance Act shall apply to the Corporation subject to such conditions and modifications as may be specified in the notification, namely:

   Sections 2D, 10, 11, 13, 14, 15, 20, 21, 22, 23, 25; 27A; 28 A; 35, 36, 37, 40, 40A, 40B, 43, 44, 102 to 106, 107 to 110, 111, 113, 114 and 116A.

   (2A) Section 42 of the Insurance Act shall have effect in relation to the issue to any individual of a licence to act as an agent for the purpose of soliciting or procuring life insurance business for the

Corporation as if the reference to an officer authorised by the Controller in this behalf in sub-section 1. thereof included a reference to an officer of the Corporation authorised by the Controller in this behalf.

3. The Central Government may, by notification in the official Gazette, direct that all or any of the provisions of the Insurance Act other than those specified in sub-section 1. or sub-section 2, shall apply to the Corporation subject to such conditions and modifications as may be specified in the notification.

4. Every notification issued under sub-section 2 or subsection 3 shall be laid for not less than 30 days before both Houses of Parliament as soon as possible after it is issued, and shall be subject to such modifications as Parliament may make during the session in which it is so laid or the session immediately following.

5. Save as provided in this section, nothing contained in the Insurance Act shall apply to the Corporation.

Section 44. Act not to apply in certain cases

Nothing contained in this Act shall apply in relation to:

(*a*) any, insurer whose business is being voluntarily wound up or is being wound up under the orders of the court;

(*b*) any insurer to whom the Insurance Act does not apply by reason of the provisions contained in Section 2E thereof;

(*c*) any composite insurer in respect of the management of whose affairs an Administrator has been appointed under Section 52A of the Insurance Act;

(*d*) the scheme run by the Central Government known as the Post Office Life Insurance Fund;

(*e*) any approved superannuation fund as defined in clause (*a*) of Section 58N of the Indian Income-tex Act 1922 which is in existence on the appointed day;

(*f*) any scheme in existence on the appointed day or any scheme framed after the appointed day with the approval of the Central Government whereby, in consideration of certain compulsory deductions made by Government from the salaries of its employees as part of the conditions of service, the payment of money is assured by Government on the death of the employee concerned or on the happening of any contingency dependent on his life.

Section 45. Special provisions regarding transfer of controlled business of certain composite insurers

Notwithstanding anything contained in clause (*c*) of section 44, the Central Government may, by notification in the Official Gazette, direct that on and with effect from such date as may be specified in the notification the assets and liabilities appertaining to the controlled business of a composite insurer in respect of the management of whose affairs an Administrator has been appointed under section 52A of the Insurance Act shall be transferred to and vested in the Corporation, and on the issue of such a notification the provisions of this Act shall so far as may be, apply in relation to such insurer and to the transfer and vesting of the assets and liabilities of his controlled business in the Corporation as they apply in relation to all other insurers and to the transfer and vesting of the assets and liabilities of their controlled business in the Corporation, subject to the modification that references in this Act to the appointed day shall be construed as references to the day specified in the notification.

Section 46. Defects in constitution of corporation or committees not to invalidate acts or proceedings

No act or proceeding of the Corporation or of any Committees of the Corporation shall be called in question on the ground merely of the existence on any vacancy or defect in the constitution of the Corporation or Committee, as the case may be.

Section 47. Protection of action taken under act

No suit, prosecution or other legal proceeding shall lie against any member or employee of the Corporation for anything which is in good faith done or intended to be done under this Act.

Section 48. Power to make rules

1. The Central Government may, by notification in the Official Gazette make rules to carry out the purposes of this Act.
2. In particular, and without prejudice to the, generality of the foregoing power, such rules may provide for all or any of the following matters, namely:
   (*a*) the term of office and the conditions of service of members.
   (*b*) the manner in which the moneys and other assets belonging to any such fund as is referred to in Section 8 shall be apportioned between the trustees of the fund and the Corporation;
   (*c*) the services which the chief agent should have rendered for the purpose of the proviso to Section 12;
   (*d*) the jurisdiction of the Tribuals constituted under Section 17;
   (*e*) the manner in which, and the persons to whom, any compensation under this Act may be paid;
   (*f*) the time within which any matter which may be referred to a Tribunal for decision under this Act may be so referred;
   (*g*) the manner in which and the conditions subject to which investments may be made by the Corporation;
   (*h*) the manner in which an Employees and Agents Relations Committee may be constituted for each zonal office;
   (*i*) the form in which the report giving an account of the activities of the Corporation shall be prepared.
   (*j*) the conditions subject to which the Corporation may appoint employees;
   (*k*) the fees payable under this Act and the manner in which they are to be collected;
   (*l*) any other matter which has to be or may be prescribed.
3. All rules made under this section shall be laid for not less than thirty days before both Houses of Parliament as soon as possible after they are made, and shall be subject to such modifications as Parliament may make during the session in which they are so laid or the session immediately following.

Section 49. Power to Make Regulations.

1. The Corporation may, with the previous approval of the Central Government, by notification in the Gazette of India, make regulations not Inconsistent with this Act and the rules made thereunder to provide for all matters for which provision is expendient for the purpose of giving effect to the provisions of this Act.
2. In particular, and without prejudice to the generality of the foregoing power, such regulations may provide for—

(*a*) the powers and functions of the Corporation which may be delegated to the Zonal Managers;

(*b*) the method of recruitment of employees and agents of the Corporation and the terms and conditions of service of such employees or agents;

(*bb*) the terms and conditions of service of persons who have become employees of the Corporation under sub-section (1) of Section 11;

(*c*) the number, term of office and conditions of service of members of Boards constituted under Section 22;

(*d*) the territorial limits of each zone established under this. Act and the business to be transacted in each zone;

(*e*) the manner in which the Fund of the Corporation shall be maintained;

(*f*) the maintenance of separate funds and accounts at each of the zonal office;

(*g*) the jurisdiction of each divisional office and the establishment of Councils representative of policy-holders in each area served by a divisional office for the purpose of advising the divisional office in respect or any matter which may be referred to it;

(*h*) the conduct of business at meetings of the Corporation;

(*i*) the formation of Committees of the Corporation and the delegation of powers and functions of the Corporation to such Committees, and the conduct of business to meetings of such Committees;

(*j*) the form and manner in which policies may be issued and contracts binding on the Corporation may be executed;

(*k*) the classification or by any insurer whose controlled business has been transferred to and vested in the Corporation for the purpose of declaring differential bonuses wherever necessary.

(*l*) the manner in which and the interval within which the accounts of the various zonal offices, divisional offices and branch offices may be inspected are their accounts audited;

(*m*) the conditions subject to which any payment may be made by the Corporation.

10. Investment Provisions

The Section 27-A of the Insurance Act, 1938 was made applicable to the Corporation with slight modifications. The investments of the Corporation were divided into three broad categories: (*i*) the government and approved securities which generally mean gilt-edged securities; (*ii*) investments approved under Section 27 A of the insurance Act; and (*iii*) other investments. The Corporation has to hold at least 50 per cent of the total funds in government and approved securities and the rest in approved investments. Not more than 15 per cent of the total funds may, however, be held in the form of other investments, provided that such investments is unanimously approved by the Investment Committee of the Corporation or by a resolution of the Corporation with a two-thirds majority.

11. Provisions Pertaining to Commission

The maximum amount of commission or remuneration in any form payable in respect of life insurance is 35 per cent of the first year's premium, 7½ per cent of the second and third years' renewal premium and 5 per cent of the renewal commission thereafter. In case of an immediate annually or a deferred annuity in consideration of a single premium or a single premium life policy, the maximum allowable rate is 2 per cent of the premium. In case of a defferred annuity, where consideration is payable in more than one Premium, the limit is $7\frac{1}{2}$ per cent for the first year and 2 per cent for other years.

The limit to the expenses of management can be prescribed by the controller. The controller may fix a further limit within which the actual expenses of an insurer may exceed the prescribed limit.

12. Provisions to Policyholders Rights

Section 37

The Central Government guarantees the payment in cash of the sums assured by all policies issued by the Corporation including any bonuses declared in respect thereof .

Section 38

A life insurance policy can be freely assigned to anybody.

Section 39

Similarly, the holder of a policy of life insurance may without any restriction nominate any person or persons to whom the money secured by the policy may be paid in the event of his death.

Section 45

After the expiry of two years from the date of the issue of a policy, the validity of it cannot be contested on grounds of breach of utmost good faith if the breach is unintentional.

Sections 51 and 52 made the payment of claims easier and smoother. Section 113 of the Insurance Act 1938 deals with the acquisition of surrender value.

THE MARINE INSURANCE ACT, 1963
(NO. 11 OF 1963)

An Act to codify the law relating to marine insurance.

[18th April, 1963.]

Be it enacted by Parliament in the Fourteenth Year of the Republic of India as follows:

1. Short title and commencement:

(*i*) This Act may be called the Marine Insurance Act, 1963.

(*ii*) It shall come into force on such date as the Central Government may, by notification in the Official Gazette, appoint.

2. Definitions. In this Act, unless the context otherwise requires

(*a*) "contract of marine insurance" means a contract of marine insurance as defined by Section 3;

(*b*) "freight" includes the profit derivable by a ship-owner from the employment of his ship to carry his own goods or other movables, as well as freight payable by a third party, but does not include passage money;

(*c*) "marine adventure" includes any adventure where:

(*i*) any insurable property is exposed to maritime perils;

(*ii*) the earnings or acquisition of any freight, passage money, commission, profit or other pecuniary benefit, or the security for any advances loans, or disbursements is endangered by the exposure of insurable property to maritime perils;

(*iii*) any liability to a third party may be incurred by the owner of, or other person interested in or responsible for, insurable property by reason of maritime perils;

(*e*) "maritime perils" means the perils consequent on, or in cidental to, the navigation of the sea, that is to say, perils of the seas, fire, war perils, pirates, rovers, thieves, captures, seizures restrains and detainments of princes and peoples, jettisons, barratry and any other perils which are either of the like kind or may be designated by the policy;

(*f*) "movables" means any movable tangible property, other than the ship, and includes money, valuable securities and other documents;

(*g*) "policy" means a marine policy;

(*h*) "ship" includes every description of vessel used in navigation;

(*i*) "suit" includes counter claim and set-off.

MARINE INSURANCE

3. Marine insurance defined. A contract of marine insurance is an agreement whereby the insurer undertakes to indemnify the assured, in the manner and to the extent thereby agreed, against marine losses, that is to say, the losses incidental to marine adventure.

4. Mixed sea and land risks;

(*i*) A contract of marine insurance may, by its express terms, or by usage of trade, be extended so as to protect the assured against losses on inland waters or on any land risk which may be incidental to any sea voyage.

(*ii*) Where a ship in course of building, or the launch of a ship, or any adventure analogous to a marine adventure, is covered by a policy in the form of a marine policy, the provisions of the Act, in so far as applicable, shall apply thereto, but, except as by this section provided, nothing in, this Act shall alter or affect any rule of law applicable to any contract of insurance other than a contract of marine insurance as by this Act defined.

Explanation—'An adventure analogous to a marine adventure' includes an adventure where any ship, goods or other movables are exposed to perils incidental to local or inland transit.

5. Lawful Marine Adventure. Subject to the provisions of this Act, every lawful marine adventure may be the subject of a contract of marine insurance.

INSURABLE INTEREST

6. Avoidance of wagering contracts.

(*i*) Every contract of marine insurance by way of wagering is void.

(*ii*) A contract of marine insurance is deemed to be a wagering contract—

(*a*) where the assured has not an insurable interest as defined by this Act, and the contract is entered into with no expectation of acquiring such an interest; or

(*b*) where the policy is made 'interest or no interest', or "without further proof of interest than the policy itself" or "without benefit of salvage to the insurer, or subject to any other like term.

Provided that, where there is no possibility of salvage, a policy may be effected without benefit of salvage to the insurer.

7. Insurable interest defined.

(*i*) Subject to the provisions or this, Act every person has an insurable interest who is interested in a marine adventure.

(*ii*) In particular a person is interested in a marine adventure where he stands in any legal or equitable relation to the adventure or to any insurable property at risk therein, in consequence of which he may benefit by the safety or due arrival of insurable property, or may be prejudiced by its loss, or by damage thereto or by the detention thereof, or may incur liability in respect thereof.

8. When interest must attach.

(*i*) The assured must be interested in the subject-matter insured at the time of the loss, though he need not be interested when the insurance is effected;

Provided that, where the subject-matter is insured "lost or not lost", the assured may recover although he may not have acquired his interest until after the loss, unless at the time of effecting the contract of insurance the assured was aware of the loss, and the insurer was not.

2. Where the assured has no interest at the time of the loss, he cannot acquire interest by any act or election after he is aware of the loss.

9. Defeasible or contingent interest

(*i*) A defeasible interest is insurable, as also is a contingent interest.

(*ii*) In particular, where the buyer of goods has insured them, he has an insurable interest, notwithstanding that he might, at his election, have rejected the goods, or have treated them as at the seller's risk, by reason of the latter's delay in making delivery or otherwise.

10. Partial interest—A partial interest of any nature is insurable.

11. Reinsurance.

(*i*) The insurer under a contract of maring insurance has an insurable interest in his risk, and may reinsure in respect of it.

(*ii*) Unless the policy otherwise provides, the original assured has no right or interest in respect of such reinsurance.

12. Bottomry. The lender of money on bottomry or respondentia has an insurable interest in respect of the loan.

13. Master's and Seamen's Wages. The master or any member of the crew of a ship has an insurable interest in respect of his wages.

14. Advance freight. In the case of advance freight, the person advancing the freight has an insurable interest, in so far as such freight is not repayable in case of loss.

15. Charges of insurance. The assured has an insurable interest in the charges of any insurance which he may effect.

16. Quantum of interest. Where the subject-matter insured is mortgaged the mortgagor has an insurable interest in the full value thereof, and the mortgagee has an insurable interest in respect of any sum due or to become due under the mortgage.

(*i*) A mortgagee, consignee, other person having an interest in the subject-matter insured may insure on behalf and for the benefit of other persons interested as well as for his own benefit.

(*ii*) The owner of insurable property has an insurable interest in respect of the full value thereof, notwithstanding that some third person may have agreed, or be liable to indemnify him in case of loss.

17. Assignment of interest. Where the assured assigns of otherwise parts with his interest in the subject-matter insured, he does not thereby transfer to the, assignee his rights under the contract of insurance, unless there be an express or implied agreement with the assignee to that effect.

But the provisions of this section do not affect transmission of interest by operation of law.

INSURABLE VALUE

18. Measure of insurable value. Subject to any express provision or valuation in the policy, the insurable value of the subject-matter insured must be ascertained as follows:

(*i*) In insurance on ship, the insurable value is the value, at the commencement of the risk, of the ship, including her outfit provisions, and stores for the officers and crew, money advanced for seamen's wages, and other disbursements (if any) incurred to make the ship fit for the voyage or adventure contemplated by the policy, plus the charges of insurance upon the whole:

The insurable value, in the case of a steamship, includes also the machinery, boilers and coals and engine stores if owned by the assured; in the case of a ship driven by power other than steam includes machinery and fuels and engine stores if owned by the assured; and in the case of a ship engaged in a special trade, includes also the ordinary fittings requisite for that trade;

(*ii*) In insurance on freight, whether paid in advance or otherwise, the insurable value is the gross amount of the freight, at the risk of the assured, plus the charges of insurance;

(*iii*) In insurance on goods or merchandise, the insurable value is the prime cost of the property insured, plus the expenses of and incidental to shipping and the charges of insurance upon the whole;

(*iv*) In insurance on any other subject-matter, the insurance value is the amount at the risk of the assured when the policy attaches, plus the charges of insurance.

DISCLOSURE AND REPRESENTATIONS

19. Insurance is uberrimae fidei. A contract of marine Insurance is a contract based upon the utmost good faith, and if the utmost good faith be not observed by either party, the contract can be avoided by the other party.

20. Disclosure by assured.

(*i*) Subject to the provisions of this section, the assured must disclose to the insurer, before the contract is concluded, every material circumstance which is known to the assured, and the assured is deemed to know every circumstance which, in the ordinary course of business, ought to be known to him. If the assured fails to make such disclosure, the insurer may avoid the contract.

(*ii*) Every circumstance is material which would influence the judgment of a prudent insurer in fixing the premium, or determining whether he will take the risk.

(*iii*) In the absence of inquiry the following circumstances need not be disclosed, namely:

(*a*) Any circumstance which diminishes the risk;

(*b*) any circumstance which is known or presumed to be known to the insurer. The insurer is presumed to know matters of common notoriety or knowledge and matters which an insurer in the ordinary course of his business as such, ought to know;

(*c*) any circumstance as to which information is waived by the insurer;

(*d*) any circumstance which it is superfluous to disclose by reason of any express or implied warranty.

(*iv*) Whether any particular circumstance, which is not disclosed, be material or not is, in each case, a question of fact.

(*v*). The term "circumstance" includes any communication made to, or information received by, the assured.

21. Disclosure by agent effecting insurance. Subject to the provisions of the preceding section as to circumstances which need not be disclosed, where an insurance is effected for the assured by an agent, the agent must disclose to the insurer:

(*a*) every material circumstance which is known to himself, and an agent to insure is deemed to know every circumstance which in the ordinary course of business ought to be known by, or to have been communicated to him; and

(*b*) every material circumstance which the assured is bound to disclose, unless it comes to his knowledge too late to communicate it to the agent.

22. Representations pending negotiation of contract.

1. Every material representation made by the assured or his agent to the insurer during the negotiations for the contract, and before the contract is concluded, must be true. If it be unture the insurer may avoid the contract.
2. A representation is material which would influence the judgment of a prudent insurer in fixing the premium, or determining whether he will take the risk.
3. A representation may be either as to a matter of fact, or as to a matter of expectation or belief.
4. A representation as to a matter of fact is true, if it be substantially correct, that is to say, if the difference between what is represented and what is actually correct would not be considered material by a prudent insurer.
5. A representation as to a matter of expectation or belief is true if it be made in good faith.
6. A representation may be withdrawn or corrected before the contract is concluded.
7. Whether a particular representation be material or not, is, in each case, a question of fact.

23. When contract is deemed to be concluded. A contract of marine insurance is deemed to be concluded when the proposal of the assured is accepted by the insurer, whether the policy be then issued or not; and for the purpose of showing when the proposal was accepted, reference may be made to the slip, covering note or other customary memorandum of the contract, although it be unstamped.

THE POLICY

24. Contract must be embodied in policy. A contract of marine insurance shall not be admitted in evidence unless it is embodied in a marine policy in accordance with this Act. The policy may be executed and issued either at the time when the contract is concluded, or afterwards.

25. What policy must specify. A marine policy must specify—

1. the name of the assured, or of some person who effects the insurance on his behalf;
2. the subject-matter insured and the risk insured against;
3. the voyage, or period of time, or both, as the case may be, covered by the insurance;
4. the sum or sums insured ;
5. the name or names of the insurer or insurers.

26. Signature of insurer.

1. A marine policy must be signed by or on behalf of the insurer.
2. Where a policy is subscribed by or on behalf of two or more insurers, each subscription, unless the contrary be expressed, constitutes a distinct contract with the assured.

27. Voyage and time policies.

1. Where the contract is to insure the subject-matter at and from, or from one place to another or others, the policy is called a 'voyage policy', and where the contract is to insure the subject-matter for a definite period of time, the policy is called a "time policy". A contract for both voyage and time may be included in the same policy.
2. A time policy which is made for any time exceeding twelve months is invalid.

28. Designation and subject-matter.

1. The subject-matter insured must be designated in a marine policy with reasonable certainty.
2. The nature and extent of the interest of the assured in the subject-matter insured need not be specified in the policy.
3. Where the policy designates the subject-matter insured in general terms, it shall be construed to apply to the interest intended by the assured to be covered.

4. In the application of this section regard shall be had to any usage regulating the designation of the subject-matter insured.

29. Valued policy.

1. A policy may be either valued or unvalued.
2. A valued policy is a policy which specifies the agreed value of the subject-matter insured.
3. Subject to the provisions of this Act, and in the absence of fraud, the value fixed by the policy is, as between the insurer and assured, conclusive of the insurable value of the subject intended to be insured, whether the loss be total or partial.
4. Unless the policy otherwise provides, the value fixed by the policy is not conclusive for the purpose of determining whether there has been a constructive total loss.

30. Unvalued policy. An unvalued policy is a policy which does not specify the value of the subject-matter insured, but subject to the limit of the sum insured, leaves the insurable value to be subsequently ascertained, in the manner herein-before explained.

31. Floating policy by ship or ships.

1. A floating policy is a policy which describes the insurance in general terms, and leaves the name or names of the ship or ships and other particulars to be defined by subsequent declaration.
2. The subsequent declaration or declarations may be made by endorsement on the policy, or in other customary manner.
3. Unless the policy otherwise provides, the declarations must be made in the order of dispatch or shipment. They must, in the case of goods, comprise all consignments within the terms of the policy, and the value of the goods or other property must be honestly stated, but an omission or erroneous declaration may be rectified even after loss or arrival, provided the omission or declaration was made in good faith.
4. Unless the policy otherwise provides, where a declaration of value is not made until after notice of loss or arrival, the policy must be treated as an unvalued policy as regards the subject-matter of that declaration.

32. Construction of terms in policy.

1. A policy may be in the form in the Schedule.
2. Subject to the provisions of this Act, and unless the context of the policy otherwise requires, the terms and expressions mentioned in the Schedule shall be construed as having the scope and meaning assigned to them in the Schedule.

33. Premium to be arranged.

1. Where an insurance is effected at a premium to be arranged, and no arrangement is made, a reasonable premium is payable.
2. Where an insurance is effected on the terms that an additional premium is to be arranged in a given event, and that event happens but no arrangement is made, then a reasonable additional premium is payable.

DOUBLE INSURANCE

34. Double insurance

1. Where two or more policies are effected by or on behalf of the assured on the same adventure and interest or any part thereof, and the sums insured exceed the indemnity allowed by this Act, the assured is said to be over-insured by double insurance.
2. Where the assured is over-insured by double insurance:

(*a*) the assured, unless the policy otherwise provides, may claim payment from the insurers in such order as he may think fit, provided that he is not entitled to receive any sum in excess of the indemnity allowed by this Act;

(*b*) where the policy under which the assured claims is a valued policy, the assured must give credit as against the valuation for any sum received by him under any other policy, without regard to the actual value of the subject-matter insured;

(*c*) where the policy under which the assured claims is an unvalued policy he must give credit, as against the full insurable value, for any sum received by him under any other policy;

(*d*) where the assured receives any sum in excess of the indemnity allowed by this Act, he is deemed to hold such sum in trust for the insurers, according to their right of contribution among themselves.

WARRANTIES, ETC.

35. Nature of warranty.

1. A warranty, in the following sections relating to warranties, means a promissory warranty, that is to say, a warranty by which the assured undertakes that some particular thing shall or shall not be done, or that some condition shall be fulfilled, or whereby he affirms or negatives the existence of a particular state of facts.
2. A warranty may be express or implied.
3. A warranty, as above defined, is a condition which must be exactly complied with, whether it be material to the risk or not. If it be not so complied with, then, subject to any express provision in the policy, the insurer is discharged from liability as from the date of the breach of warranty, but without prejudice to any liability incurred by him before that date.

36. When breach of warranty excused.

1. Non-compliance with a warranty is excused when, by reason of a change of circumstances, the warranty ceases to be applicable to the circumstances of the contract, or when compliance with the warranty is rendered unlawful by any subsequent law.
2. Where a warranty is broken, the assured cannot avail himself of the defence that the breach has been remedied, and the warranty complied with, before loss.
3. A breach of warranty may be waived by the insurer.

37. Express warranties.

1. An express warranty may be in any form of words from which the intention to warrant is to be inferred.
2. An express warranty must be included in, or written upon, the policy, or must be contained in some document incorporated by reference into the policy.
3. An express warranty does not exclude implied warranty unless it be inconsistent therewith.

38. Warranty of neutrality.

1. Where insurable property, whether ship or goods, is expressly warranted neutral, there is an implied condition that the property shall have a neutral character at the commencement of the risk, and that, so far as the assured can control the matter, its neutral character shall be preserved during the risk.
2. Where a ship is expressly warranted "neutral", there is also an implied condition that, so far as the assured can control the matter, she shall be properly documented, that is to say, that she shall carry the necessary papers to establish her neutrality, and that she shall not falsify or suppress her papers, or use simulated papers. If any loss occurs through breach of this condition, the **insurer may avoid the contract.**

39. No implied warranty of nationality. There is no implied warranty as to the nationality of a ship, or that her nationality shall not be changed during the risk.

40. Warranty of good safety. Where the Subject-matter insured is warranted "well" or "in good safety" on a particular day, it is sufficient if it be safe at any time during that day.

41. Warranty of sea-worthiness of ship.

1. In a voyage policy there is an implied warranty that at the commencement of the voyage the ship shall be seaworthy for the purpose of the particular adventure insured.
2. Where the policy attaches while the ship is in port, there is also an implied warranty that she shall, at the commencement of the risk, be reasonably fit to encounter the ordinary perils of the port.
3. Where the policy relates to a voyage which is performed in different stages, during which the ship requires different kinds of or further preparation or equipment, there is an implied warranty that at the commencement of each stage the ship is seaworthy in respect of such preparation or equipment for the purposes of that stage.
4. A ship is deemed to be seaworthy when she is reasonably fit in all respects to encounter the ordinary perils of the seas of the adventure insured.
5. In a time policy there is no implied warranty that the ship shall be seaworthy at any stage of the adventure, but where, with the privity of the assured, the ship is sent to sea in an unseaworthy state, the insurer is not liable for any loss attributable to unseaworthiness.

42. No implied warranty that goods are seaworthy.

1. In a policy on goods or other movables there is no implied warranty that the goods or movables are seaworthy.
2. In a voyage policy on goods or other movables there is an implied warranty that at the commencement of the voyage the ship is not only seaworthy as a ship but also that she is reasonably fit to carry the goods or other movables to the destination contemplated by the policy.

43. Warranty of legality. There is an implied warranty that the adventure insured is a lawful one, and that so far as the assured can control the matter, the adventure shall be carried out in a lawful manner.

44. Implied condition as to commencement of risk.

1. There the subject-matter is insured by a voyage policy "at and from" or "from" a particular place, it is not necessary that the ship should be at that place when the contract is concluded, but there is an implied condition that the adventure shall be commenced within a reasonable time, and that if the adventure be not so commenced the insurer may avoid the contract.
2. The implied condition may be negatived by showing that the delay was caused by circumstances known to the insurer before the contract was concluded, or by showing that he waived the condition.

45. Alteration of port of departure. Where the place of departure is specified by the policy, and the ship instead of sailing from that place sails from any other place, the risk does not attach.

46. Sailing for different destination. Where the destination is specified in the policy, and the ship, instead of sailing for that destination, sails for any other destination, the risk does not attach.

47. Change of voyage.

1. Where, after the commencement of the risk, the destination of the ship is voluntarily changed from the destination contemplated by the policy, there is said to be a change of voyage.
2. Unless the policy otherwise provides, where there is a change of voyage, the insurer is discharged from liability as from the time of change, that is to say, as from the time when the determination

to change is manifested; and it is immaterial that the ship may not in fact have left course of voyage contemplated by the policy when the loss occurs.

48. Deviation.

1. Where a ship, without lawful excuse deviates from the voyage contemplated by the policy, the insured is discharged from liability as from the time of deviation, and it is immaterial that the ship may have regained her route before any loss occurs.
2. There is a deviation from the voyage contemplated by the policy—
   (*a*) where the course of the voyage is specifically designated by the policy, and that course is departed from; or
   (*b*) where the course of the voyage is not specifically designated by the policy, but the usual and customary course is departed from.
3. The intention to deviate is immaterial; there must be a deviation in fact to discharge the insurer from his liability under the contract.

49. Several ports of discharge.

1. Where several ports of discharge are specified by the policy, the ship may proceed to all or any of them, but, in the absence of any usage or sufficient cause to the contrary, she must proceed to them, or such of them as she goes to, in the order designated by the policy. If she does not there is a deviation.
2. Where the policy is to "ports of discharge" within a given area, which are not named, the ship must, in the absence of any usage or sufficient cause to the contrary, proceed to them, or such of them as she goes to, in their geographical order. If she does not there is a deviation.

50. Delay in voyage. In the case of a voyage policy, the adventure insured must be prosecuted throughout its course with reasonable despatch, and if without lawful excuse it is not so prosecuted, the insurer is discharged from liability as from the time when the delay became unreasonable.

51. Excuse for deviation or delay.

1. Deviation or delay in prosecuting the voyage contemplated by the policy is excussed—
   (*a*) where authorised by any special term in the policy; or
   (*b*) where caused by circumstances beyond the control of the master and his employer; or
   (*c*) where reasonably necessary in order to comply with an express or implied warranty; or
   (*d*) where reasonably necessary for the safety of the ship or subject-matter insured; or
   (*e*) for the purpose of saying human life or aiding a ship in distress where human life may be in danger; or
   (*f*) where reasonably necessary for the purpose of obtaining medical or surgical aid for any person on board the ship; or
   (*g*) where caused by the barratrous conduct of the master or crew, if barratry be one of the perils insured against.
2. When the cause excusing the deviation or delay ceases to operate the ship must resume her course, and prosecute her voyage with reasonable despatch.

ASSIGNMENT OF POLICY

52. When and how policy, is assignable.

1. A marine policy may be transferred by assignment unless it contains terms expressly prohibiting assignment. It may be assigned either before or after loss.
2. Where a marine policy has been assigned so as to pass the beneficial interest in such policy, the assignee of the policy is entitled to sue thereon in his own name; and the defendant is entitled to

make any defence arising out of the contract which he would have been entitled to make if the suit had been brought in the name of the person by or on behalf of whom the policy was effected.

3. A marine policy may be assigned by endorsement thereon or in other customary manner.

53. Assured who has no interest cannot assign. Where the assured has parted with or lost his interest in the subject-matter insured, and has not, before or at the time of so doing expressly or impliedly agreed to assign the policy, any subsequent assignment of the policy is inoperative:

Provided that nothing in this section affects the assignment of a policy after loss.

THE PREMIUM

54. When premium payable. Unless otherwise agreed, the duty of the assured or his agent to pay the premium, and the duty of the insurer to issue the policy to the assured or his agent, are concurrent conditions, and the insurer is not bound to issue the policy until payment or tender of the premium.

LOSS AND ABANDONMENT

55. Included and excluded losses.

1. Subject to the provisions of this Act, and unless the policy otherwise provides, the insurer is liable for any loss proximately caused by a peril insured against, but, subject as aforesaid, he is not liable for any loss which is not proximately caused by a peril insured against.
2. In particular
   (*a*) the insurer is not liable for any loss attributable to the wilful misconduct of the assured, but, unless the policy otherwise provides, he is liable for any loss proximately caused by a peril insured against, even though the loss would not have happened but for the misconduct or negligence of the master or crew;
   (*b*) unless the policy otherwise provides, the insurer on ship or goods is not liable for any loss proximately caused by delay, although the delay be caused by a peril insured against;
   (*c*) unless the policy otherwise provides, the insurer is not liable for ordinary wear and tear, ordinary leakage and breakage, inherent vice or nature of the subject-matter insured, or for any loss proximately caused by rats or vermin, or for any injury to machinery not proximately caused by maritime perils.

56. Partial and total loss.

1. A loss be either total or partial. Any loss other than a total loss, as hereinafter defined, is a partial loss.
2. A total loss may be either an actual total loss, or a constructive total loss.
3. Unless a different intention appears from the terms of the policy, an insurance against total loss includes a constructive, as well as an actual, total loss.
4. Where the assured brings a suit for a total loss and the evidence proves only a partial loss, he may, unless the policy otherwise provides, recover for a partial loss.
5. Where goods reach their destination in specie, but by reason of obliteration of marks, or otherwise, they are incapable of identification, the loss, if any is partial and not total.

57. Actual total loss.

1. Where the subject-matter insured is destroyed, or so damaged as to cease to be a thing of the kind insured, or where the assured is irretrievably deprived thereof, there is an actual total loss.
2. In the case of an actual total loss no notice of abandonment need be given.

58. Missing ship. Where the ship concerned in the adventure is missing, and after the lapse of a reasonable time no news of her has been received, an actual total loss may be presumed.

59. Effect of transhipment, etc. Where, by a peril insured against, the voyage is interrupted at intermediate port or place, under such circumstances as apart from any special stipulation in the contract of affreightment; to justify the master in landing and reshipping the goods or other movables, or in transhipping them, and sending them on to their destination, the liability of the insurer continues, notwithstanding the landing or transhipment.

60. Constructive total loss defined.

1. Subject to any express provision in the policy, there is a constructive total loss where the subject matter insured is reasonably abandoned on account of its actual total loss appearing to be unavoidable, or because it could not be preserved from actual total loss without an expenditure which would exceed its value when the expenditure had been incurred.
2. In particular, there is a constructive total loss—

(*i*) where the assured is deprived of the possession of his ship or goods by a peril insured against, and

(*a*) it is unlikely that he can recover the ship or goods, as the case may be, or

(*b*) the cost of recovering the ship or goods, as the case may be

would exceed their value when recovered; or

(*ii*) in the case of damage to a ship; where she is damaged by a peril insured against that the cost of repairing the damage would exceed the value of the ship when repaired.

In estimating the cost of repairs, no deduction is to be made in respect of general average contributions to those repairs payable by other interest, but account is to be taken of the expense of future salvage operations and of any future general average contributions to which the ship would be liable if repaired; or

(*iii*) in the case of damage to goods, where the cost of repairing the damage and forwarding the goods to their destination would exceed their value on arrival.

61. Effect of constructive total loss. Where there is a constructive total loss the assured may either treat the loss as a partial loss, or abandon the subject-matter insured to the insurer and treat the loss as if it were an actual total loss.

62. Notice of abandonment.

1. Subject to the provisions of this section, where the assured elects to abandon the subject–matter insured to the insurer, he must give notice of abandonment. If he fails to do so the loss can only be treated as a partial loss.
2. Notice of abandonment may be given in writing, or by word of mouth, or partly in writing and partly by word of mouth, and may be given in any terms which indicate the intention of the assured to abandon his insured interest in the subject-matter insured unconditionally to the insurer.
3. Notice of abandonment must be given with reasonable diligence after the receipt of reliable information of the loss, but where the information is of a doubtful character the assured is entitled to a reasonable time to make enquiry.
4. Where notice of abandonment is properly given, the rights of the assured are not prejudiced by the fact that the insurer refuses to accept the abandonment.
5. The acceptance of an abandonment may be either express or implied from the conduct of the insurer. The mere silence of the insurer after notice is not an acceptance.
6. Where notice of abandonment is accepted the abandonment is irrevocable. The acceptance of the notice conclusively admits liability for the loss and the sufficiency of the notice.
7. Notice of abandonment is unnecessary where at the time when the assured receives information of the loss, there would be no possibility of benefit of the insurer if notice were given to him.

8. Notice of abandonment may be waived by the insurer.
9. Where an insurer has reinsured his risk, no notice of abandonment need be given by him.

63. Effect of abandonment.

1. Where there is a valid abandonment the insurer is entitled to take over the interest of the assured in whatever may remain of the subject-matter insured and all proprietary rights incidental thereto.
2. Upon the abandonment of a ship, the insurer thereof is entitled to any freight in course of being earned, and which is earned by her subsequent to the casualty causing the loss, less the expenses of earning it incurred after the casualty; and, where the ship is carrying the owner's goods, the insurer is entitled to a reasonable remuneration for the carriage of them subsequent to the casualty causing the loss.

PARTIAL LOSSES (INCLUDING SALVAGE AND GENERAL AVERAGE AND PARTICULAR CHARGES)

64. Particular average loss.

1. A particular average loss is a partial loss of the subject-matter insured, caused by a peril insured against, and which is not a general average loss.
2. Expenses incurred by or on behalf of the assured for the safety or preservation of the subject matter insured, other than general average and salvage charges are called particular charges. Particular charges are not included in particular average.

65. Salvage charges.

1. Subject to any express provision in the policy, salvage charges incurred preventing a loss by perils insured against may be covered as a loss by those perils.
2. "Salvage charges" means the charges recoverable under maritime law by a salver independently of contract. They do not include the expenses of services in the nature of salvage rendered by the assured or his agents, or any person employed for hire by them, for the purpose of averting a peril insured against. Such expenses, where properly incurred, may be recovered as particular charges or as a general average loss, according to the circumstances under which they were incurred.

66. General average loss.

1. A general average loss is a loss caused by or directly consequential on a general average act. It includes a general average expenditure as well as a general average sacrifice.
2. There is a general average act where any extraordinary sacrifice or expenditure is voluntarily and reasonably made or incurred in time of peril for the purpose of preserving the property imperilled in the common adventure.
3. Where there is a general average loss, the party on whom it falls is entitled, subject to the conditions imposed by maritime law, to a rateable contribution from the other parties interested, and such contribution is called a general average contribution.
4. Subject to any express provision in the policy, where the assured has incurred a general average of expenditure, he may recover from the insurer in respect of the proportion of the loss which falls upon him; and in the case of a general average sacrifice, he may recover from the insurer in respect of the whole loss without having enforced his right of contribution from the other parties liable to contribute.
5. Subject to any express provision in the policy, where the assured has paid, or is liable to pay, a general average contribution in respect of the interest insured, he may recover therefor from the insurer.
6. In the absence of express stipulation, the insurer is not liable for any general average loss or contribution where the loss was not incurred for the purpose of avoiding, or in connection with the avoidance of a peril insured against.

7. Where ship, freight, and cargo, or any two of those interests, are owned by the same assured, the liability of the insurer in respect of general average losses or contributions is to be determined as if those interests were owned by different persons.

67. Extent of liability of insurer for loss.

1. The sum which the assured can recover in respect of a loss on a policy by which he is insured. in the case of an unvalued policy to the full extent of the insurable value, or, in the case of a valued policy to the full extent of the value fixed by the policy, is called the measure of indemnity.
2. Where there is a loss recoverable under the policy, the insurer, or each insurer if there be more than one, is liable for such proportion of the measure of indemnity as the amount of his subscription bears to the value fixed by the policy in the case of a valued policy, or to the insurable value in the case of an unvalued policy.

68. Total loss. Subject to the provisions of this Act, and to any express provision in the policy, where there is a total loss of the subject-matter insured—

1. if the policy be a valued policy, the measure of indemnity is the sum fixed by the policy;
2. if the policy be an unvalued policy, the measure of indemnity is the insurable value of the subject-matter insured.

69. Partial loss of ship. Where a ship is damaged, but is not totally lost, the measure of indemnity subject to any express provision in the policy, is as follows—

1. where the ship has been repaired, the assured is entitled to the reasonable cost of the repairs, less the customary deductions, but more exceeding the sum insured in respect of any one casualty;
2. where the ship has been only partially repaired, the assured is entitled to the reasonable cost of such repairs, computed as above, and also to be indemnified for the reasonable depreciation, if any, arising from the unrepaired damage, provided that the aggregate amount shall not exceed the cost of repairing the whole damage, computed, as above;
3. where the ship has not been repaired, and has not been sold in her damaged state during the risk, the assured is entitled to be indemnified for the reasonable depreciation arising from the unrepaired damage, but not exceeding the reasonable cost of repairing such damage, computed as above;
4. where the ship has not been repaired and has been sold in her damaged state during the risk, the assured is entitled to be indemnified for the reasonable cost of repairing the damage, computed as above, but not exceeding the depreciation in value as ascertained by the sale.

70. Partial loss of freight. Subject to any express provision in the policy, where there is a partial loss of freight, the measure of indemnity is such proportion of the sum fixed by the policy in the case of a valued policy or of the insurable value in the case of an unvalued policy, as the proportion of freight lost by the assured bears to the whole freight at the risk of the assured under the policy.

71. Partial loss of goods, merchandise, etc. Where there is a partial loss of goods, merchandise, or other movables, the measure of indemnity, subject to any express provision in the policy, is as follows:—

1. where part of the goods, merchandise or other movables insured by a valued policy is totally lost, the measure of indemnity is such proportion of the sum fixed by the policy as the insurable value of the part lost bears to the insurable value of the whole, ascertained as in the case of an unvalued policy;

2. where part of the goods, merchandise or other movables insured by an unvalued policy is totally lost, the measure of indemnity is the insurable value of the part lost, ascertained as in case of total loss;
3. where the whole or any part of the goods or merchandise insured has been delivered at its destination, the measure of indemnity is such proportion of the sum fixed by the policy in the case of a valued policy, or of the insurable value in the case of an unvalued policy, as the difference between the gross sound and damaged values at the place of arrival bears to the gross sound value;
4. "Gross value" means the wholesale price, or, if there be no such price, the estimated value, with, in either case, freight, lending charges, and duty paid beforehand; provided that, in the case of goods or merchandise customarily sold in bond, the bonded price is deemed to be the gross value. "Gross proceeds" means the actual price obtained at a sale where all charges on sale paid by the sellers.

72. Apportionment of valuation.

1. Where different species of property are insured under a single valuation, the valuation must be apportioned over the different species in proportion to their respective insurable values, as in the case of an unvalued policy. The insured value of any part of a species is such proportion of the total insured value of the same as the insurable value of the part bears to the insurable value of the whole ascertained in both cases as provided by this Act.
2. Where a valuation has to be apportioned, and particulars of the prime cost of each separate species, quality, or description of goods cannot be ascertained, the division of the valuation may be made over the net arrived sound values of the different species, quality or descriptions of goods.

73. General average contributions and salvage charges.

1. Subject to any express provision in the policy, where the assured has paid, or is liable for, any general average contribution, the measure of indemnity is the full amount of such contribution if the subject-matter liable to contribution is insured for its full contributory value; but, if such subject-matter be not insured for its full contributory value, of if only part of it be insured, the indemnity payable by the insurer must be reduced in proportion to the under-insurance, and where there has been a particular average loss which constitutes a deduction from the contributory value, and for which the insurer is liable, that amount must be deducted from the insured value in order to acsertain what the insurer is liable to contribute.
2. Where the insurer is liable for salvage charges the extent of his liabilities must be determined on the like principle.

74. Liabilities to third parties. Where the assured has effected an insurance in express terms against any liability to a third party, the measure of indemnity subject to any express provision in the policy, is the amount paid or payable by him to such third party in respect of such liability.

75. General provisions as to measure of indemnity.

1. Where there has been a loss in respect of any subject-matter not expressly provided for in the foregoing, provisions of this Act, the measure of indemnity shall be ascertained as nearly as may be, in accordance with those provisions, in so far as applicable to the particular case.
2. Nothing in the provisions of this Act relating to the measure of indemnity shall affect the rules relating to double insurance, or prohibit the insurer from disproving interest wholly or in part, or from showing that at the time of the loss the whole or any part of the subject-matter insured was not at risk under the policy.

76. Particular average warranties.

1. Where the subject-matter insured is warranted free from particular average, the assured cannot recover for a loss of part, other than loss incurred by a general average sacrifice, unless the contract contained in the policy be apportionable; but, if the contract be apportionable, the assured may recover for a total loss of any apportionable part.
2. Where the subject-matter insured is warranted free from particular average, either wholly or under a certain percentage, the insurer is nevertheless liable for salvage charges, and for particular charges and other expenses properly incurred pursuant to the provisions of the suing and labouring clause in order to avert a loss insured against.
3. Unless the policy otherwise provides, where the subject matter insured is warranted free from particular average under a specified percentage, a general average loss cannot be added to a particular average loss to make up the specified percentage.
4. For the purpose of ascertaining whether the specified percentage has been reached, regard shall be had only to the actual loss suffered by the subject-matter insured. Particular charges and the expenses of and incidental to ascertaining and proving the loss must be excluded.

77. Successive losses.

1. Unless the policy otherwise provides, and subject to the provisions of this Act, the insurer is liable for successive losses, even though the total amount of such losses may exceed the sum insured.
2. Where, under the same policy, a partial loss, which has not been repaired or otherwise made good, is followed by a total loss the assured can only recover in respect of the total loss;

Provided that nothing in this section shall affect the liability of the insurer under the suing and labouring clause.

78. Suing and labouring clause.

1. Where the policy contains a suing and labouring clause, the engagement thereby entered into is deemed to be supplementary to the contract of insurance, and the assured may recover from the insurer any expenses properly incurred pursuant to the clause, notwithstanding that the insurer may have paid for a total loss, or that the subject-matter may have been warranted free from particular average, either wholly or wider a certain percentage.
2. General average losses and contributions and salvage charges, as defined by this Act, are not recoverable under the suing and labouring clause.
3. Expenses incurred for the purpose of averting or diminishing any loss not covered by the policy are not recoverable under the suing and labouring clause.
4. It is the duty of the assured and his agents, in all cases, to take such measures as may be reasonable for the purpose of averting or minimising a loss.

RIGHTS OF INSURER ON PAYMENTS

79. Right of subrogation.

1. Where the insurer pays for a total loss, either of the whole, or in the case of goods of any apportionable part, of the subject-matter insured, he there upon becomes entitled to take over the interest of the assured in what-ever may remain of the subject-matter so paid for, and he is thereby subrogated to all the rights and remedies of the assured in and in respect of that subject-matter as from the time of the casualty causing the loss.
2. Subject to the foregoing provisions, where the insurer pays for a partial loss, he acquires no title to the subject-matter insured, or such part of it as may remain, but he is thereupon subrogated to all rights and remedies of the assured in and in respect of the subject-matter insured as from, the time of the casualty causing the loss, in so far as the assured has been indemnified, according to this Act, by such payment for the loss.

80. Right of Contribution.

1. Where the assured is over-insured by double insurance, each insurer is bound, as between himself and the other insurers, to contribute rateably to the loss in proportion to the amount for which he is liable under his contract.

2. If any insurer pays more than his proportion of the loss, he is entitled to maintain a suit contribution against the other insurers, and is entitled to the like remedies as a surety who has paid more than his proportion of the debt.

81. Effect of under-insurance. Where the assured is insured for an amount less than the insurable value, or, in the case of a valued policy, for an amount less than the policy valuation, he is deemed to be his own insurer in respect of the uninsured balance.

RETURN OF PREMIUM

82. Enforcement of return. Where the premium, or a proportionate part thereof, is, by this Act, declared to be returnable—

(*a*) if already paid, it may be recovered by the assured from the insurer, and,

(*b*) if unpaid, it may be retained by the assured or his agent.

83. Return by agreement. Where the policy contains a stipulation for the return of the premium or a proportionate part thereof, on the happening of a certain event, and that event happens, the premium, or, as the case may be, the proportionate part thereof, is thereupon returnable to the assured.

84. Return for failure of consideration.

1. Where the consideration for the payment of the premium totally fails, and there has been no fraud or illegality on the part of the assured or his agents, the premium is thereupon returnable to the assured.

2. Where the consideration for the payment of the premium is apportionable and there is a total failure of any apportionable part of the consideration, a proportionate part of the premium is, under the like conditions, thereupon returnable to the assured.

3. In particular—

(*a*) where the policy is void, or is avoided by the insurer as from the commencement of the risk, the premium is returnable, provided there has been no fraud or illegality on the part of the assured, but if the risk is not apportionable, and has once attached, the premium is not returnable.

(*b*) where the subject-matter insured, or part thereof, has never been imperilled the premium, or, as the case may be, a proportionate part thereof, is returnable:

Provided that where the subject-matter has been;

(*c*) where the assured has no insured interest throughout insured "lost or not lost," and has arrived in safety at not returnable, unless, at such time, the insurer knew of the safe arrival;

the time when the contract is concluded, the premium is by way of wagering vided that this rule does not apply to a policy effected the currency of the risk the premium is returnable, pro-

(*d*) where the assured has a defeasible interest which is terminated during the currency of the risk, the premium is not returnable.

(*e*) where the assured has over-insured under an unvalued policy a proportionate part of the premium is returnable.

(*f*) subject to the foregoing provisions, where the assured has over-insured by double insurance, a proportionate part of the several premiums is returnable:

Provided that, if the policies are effected at different times, and any earlier policy has at any time borne the entire risk, or if a claim has been paid on the policy in respect of the full sum insured thereby, no premium is returnable in respect of that policy, and when the double insurance is effected knowingly by the assured no premium is returnable.

SUPPLEMENTAL

85. Ratification by assured. Where a contract of marine insurance is in good faith effected by one person on behalf of another, the person on whose behalf it is effected may ratify the contract even after he is aware of a loss.

86. Implied obligation varied by agreement or usage.

1. Where any right, duty, or liability would arise under a contract of marine insurance by implication of law, it may be negatived or varied by express agreement, or by usage, if the usage be such as to bind both parties to the contract.
2. The provisions of this section extend to any right, duty, or liability declared by this Act which may be lawfully modified by agreement.

87. Reasonable time, etc., a question of fact. Where by this Act any reference is made to reasonable time, reasonable premium, or reasonable diligence, the question what is reasonable is a question of fact.

88. Covering note as evidence. Where there is duly stamped policy, reference may be made, as heretofore, to the slip or covering note, in any legal proceeding.

89. Power to apply Act with modifications, etc., in certain cases. The Central Government may, by notification in the Official Gazette, direct that the provisions of this Act shall, in their application to contracts of marine insurance relating to any class of ships exclusively used in inland navigation, be subject to such conditions, exceptions and modifications as it may specify in the notification.

90. Centain provisions to override Transfer of Property Act 1882. Nothing in clause (*e*) of Section 6 of the Transfer of Property Act, 1882, shall affect the provisions of Sections 17, 52, 53 and 79.

91. Savings. The rules of law, including the law merchant, which applied to contracts of marine insurance immediately before the commencement of this Act, save in so far as they are inconsistent with the express provisions of this Act, shall continue to apply to contracts of marine insurance.

92. Repeals. Sub-sections (1), (2) and (3) of Section 7 of the Indian Stamp Act., 1899 and Sections 130A and 135A of the Transfer of Property Act, 1882 are hereby repealed.

SCHEDULE

FORM OF POLICY

(SEE SECTION 24)

BE IT KNOWN THAT .... as well in .... own name as for and in the name and names of all and every other person or persons to whom the same doth, may, or shall appertain, in part or in all doth make assurance and cause .... and them, and every of them, to be insured lost or not lost, at and from upon any kind of goods and merchandises, and also upon the body, tackle, apparel, ordnance, munition, artillery, boat and other furniture, of and in the good ship or vessel called the .... whereof is master for this present voyage .... or whosoever else go for master in the said ship or by whatsoever other name or names the said ship, or the master thereof, or shall be named or called; beginning the adventure upon the said goods and merchandises from the loading thereof aboard the said ship .... upon the said ship, etc .... and so shall continue and endure, during her abode there, upon the said ship, etc .... And further, until the said ship, with all her ordnance, tackle, apparel, etc., and goods and merchandises whatsoever shall be arrived at .... upon the said ship, etc., until she hath moored at anchor twenty-four hours in good safety; and upon the goods and merchandises, until the same be there discharged and safely landed. And it shall be lawful for the said ship, etc., in this voyage to proceed and sail to and touch and stay at any ports or places whatsoever without prejudice to this insurance. The said ship, etc., goods and merchandises, etc., for so much as concerned the assured by agreement between the assured and assurers in this policy, are and shall be .... valued at ....

Touching the adventures and perils which we the assurers are contented to bear and do take upon us in this voyage; they are of the seas, men of war, fire, enemies, pirates, roverbs, thieves, jettisons, letters of mart and countermart, surprisals, takings at sea, arrests, restraints, and detainments of all kings, princes, and people, of what nation, condition or quality so ever, barratry of the master and mariners, and of all other perils, losses, and misfortunes that have or shall come to the hurt, detriment, or damage of the said goods and merchandises, and ship, etc., or any part thereof.

And in case of any loss or misfortune it shall be lawful to the assured, their factors, servants and assigns, to sue, labour, and travel for, in and about the defence, safeguards and recovery of the said goods and merchandises and ship, etc., or any part thereof, without prejudice to this insurance; to the charges whereof we, the assurers, will contribute each one according to the rate and quantity of his sum herein assured.

And it is especially declared and agreed that no acts of the insurer or insured in recovering, saving, or preserving the property insured shall be considered as a waiver, or acceptance of abandonment. And so we, the assurers, are contented, and do hereby promise and bind ourselves, each one for his own part, our heirs, executors, and goods to the assured, their executors, administrators, and assigns, for the true performance of the premises, confessing ourselves paid the consideration due unto us for this assurance by the assured, at and after the rate of ....

In witness whereof we, the assurers, have subscribed our names and sums assured in ....

MEMORANDUM N.B. Corn, fish, salt, fruit, flour, and seed are warranted free from average, unless general or the ship be stranded—sugar, tobacco, hemp, flax, hides and skins are warranted free from average, under five per cent, and all other goods, also the ship and freight, are warranted free from average, under three per cent, unless general, or the ship be stranded.

RULES FOR CONSTRUCTION OF POLICY

The following are the rules referred to by this Act for the construction of a policy in the above or other like form, where the context does not otherwise require:—

1. Lost or not lost. Where the subject-matter is insured "lost or not lost" and the loss has occurred before the contract is concluded, the risk attaches unless, at such time the assured was aware of the loss, and the insurer was not.

2. From. Where the subject-matter is insured "from" a particular place, the risk does not attach until the ship starts on the voyage insured.

3. At and from.

(*a*) Where a ship is insured "at and from" a particular place, and she is at that place in good safety when the contract is concluded, the risk attaches immediately.

(*b*) If she be not at that place when the contract is concluded, the risk attaches as soon as she arrives there in good safety, and, unless the policy otherwise provides, it is immaterial that she is covered by another policy for a specified time after arrival.

(*c*) Where chartered freight is inured "at and from" a particular place, and the ship is at that place in good safety when the contract is concluded, the risk attaches immediately. If she be not there when the contract is concluded, the risk attaches as soon as she arrives there in good safety.

(*d*) Where freight, other than chartered freight, is payable without special conditions and is insured "at and from" a particular place, the risk attaches pro rata as the goods or merchandise are shipped; provided that if there be cargo in readiness which belongs to the ship-owner, or which some other person has contracted with him to ship, the risk attaches as soon as the ship is ready to receive such cargo.

4. From the loading thereof. Where goods or other movables are insured "from the loading thereof", the risk does not attach until such goods or movables are actually on board, and the insurer is not liable for them while in transit from the shore to the ship.

5. Safety landed. Where the risk on goods or other movables continues until they are "safely landed", they must be landed in the customary manner and within a reasonable time after arrival at the port of discharge, and if they are not so landed the rise ceases.

6. Touch and stay. In the absence of any further licence or usage, the liberty to touch and stay "at any port or place whatsoever" does not authorise the ship to depart from the course of her voyage from the port of departure to the port of destination.

7. Perils of the Seas. The term "perils of the seas" refers only to fortuitous accidents or casualties of the seas. It does not include the ordinary action of the winds and waves.

8. Pirates. The term "pirates" includes passengers who mutiny and rioters who attack the ship from the shore.

9. Thieves. The term "thieves" does not cover clandestine theft or a theft committed by any one of the ship's company, whether crew or passengers.

10. Restraint of princes. The term "arrests, etc., of kings, princes, and people" refers to political or executive acts, and does not include a loss caused by riot or by ordinary judicial process.

11. Barratry. The term "barratry" includes every wrongful act wilfully committed by the master or crew to the prejudice of the owner, or, as the case may be, the charterer.

12. All other perils. The term "all other perils' , includes only perils similar in kind to the perils specifically mentioned in the policy.

13. Average unless General. The term "average unless general" means a partial loss of the subject-matter insured other than a general average loss, and does not include "particular charges".

14. Stranded. Where the ship has stranded, the insurer is liable for the excepted losses although the loss is not attributable to the stranding, provided that when the stranding takes place the risk has attached and, if the policy be on goods, that the damaged goods are on board.

15. Ship. The term "ship" includes the hull, material and outfit, stores and provisions for the officers and crew, and in the case of vessels engaged in a special trade, the ordinary fittings requisite for the trade, and also, in the case of a steamship, the machinery, boilers, and coals and engine stores, if owned by the assured and also in the case of a ship driven by power other than steam, the machinery and fuels and engine stores, if owned by the assured.

16. Freight. The term "freight" includes the profit derivable by a ship-owner from the employment of his ship to carry his own goods or movables as well as freight payable by a third party, but does not include passage money.

17. Goods. The term "goods" means goods in the nature of merchandise, and does not include personal effects or provisions and stores for use on board.

In the absence of any usage to the contrary, deck cargo and living animals must be insured specifically, and not under the general denomination of goods.

THE GENERAL INSURANCE BUSINESS (NATIONALISATION) ACT, 1972

(57 OF 1972)

An Act provide for the acquisition and transfer of shares of Indian insurance companies and undertaking of other existing insurers in order to serve better the needs of the economy by securing the development of general insurance business in the best interests of the community and to ensure that the operation of the economic system does not result in the concentration of wealth to the common detriment, for the regulation and control of such business and for matters connected therewith or incidental thereto.

(20th September, 1972.)

Be it enacted by Parliament in the Twenty-third Year of the Republic of India as follows:—

CHAPTER 1

PRELIMINARY

1. Short title. This Act may be called the General Insurance Business (Nationalisation) Act, 1972.

2. Declaration as to the policy of the State. It is hereby declared that this Act is for giving effect to the policy of the State towards securing the principles specified in clause (c) of Article 39 of the Constitution.

Explanation. In this section, "State" has the same meaning as in article 12 of the Constitution.

3. Definitions. In this Act, unless the context otherwise requires,

(*a*) "Acquiring company" means any Indian insurance company and, where a scheme has been framed involving the merger of one Indian insurance company in another or the amalgamation of two or more such companies, means the Indian insurance company in which any other company has been merged or the company which has been formed as a result of the amalgamation;

(*b*) "Appointed day" means such day, not being a day later than the 2nd day of January, 1973, as the Central Government may, by notification, appoint;

(*c*) "Companies Act" means the Companies Act, 1956;

(*d*) "Corporation" means the General Insurance Corporation of India formed under Section 9;

(*e*) "Existing insurer" means every insurer the management of whose undertaking has vested in the Central Government under Section 3 of the General Insurance (Emergency Provisions) Act, 1971, and includes the undertaking of the Life Insurance Corporation in so far as it relates to the general insurance business carried on by it;

(*f*) "Foreign insurer" means an existing insurer incorporated under the law of any country outside India;

(*g*) "General insurance business" means fire, marine or miscellaneous insurance business, whether carried on singly or in combination with one or more of them, but does not include capital redemption business and annuity certain business;

(*h*) "Government company" means a Government company as defined in Section 617 of the Companies Act;

(*i*) "Indian insurance company" means an existing insurer having a share capital who is a company within the meaning of the Companies Act;

(*j*) "Insurance Act" means the Insurance Act, 1938;

(*k*) "Life Insurance Corporation" means the Life Insurance Corporation of India established under the Life Insurance Corporation Act, 1956;

(*l*) "Notification" means a notification published in the Official Gazette;

(*m*) "Prescribed" means prescribed by rules made under this Act;

(*n*) "Schedule" means the Schedule to this Act;

(*o*) "Scheme" means the scheme framed under Section 16;

(*p*) "Words and expressions used in this Act but not defined herein or in the Insurance Act and defined in the companies Act, shall have the meanings respectively assigned to them in the Companies Act.

CHAPTER II

TRANSFER TO PUBLIC OWNERSHIP OF GENERAL INSURANCE BUSINESS

4. Transfer of shares of Indian insurance companies.

1. On the appointed day all the shares in the capital of every Indian insurance company shall, by virtue of this Act, stand transferred to and vested in the Central Government free of all trusts, liabilities and encumbrances affecting them.
2. Out of the shares of transferred and vested, the Central Government shall, immediately thereafter, by notification, provide for the transfer of not less than ten shares of every such company to such persons as may be specified in the notification to enable the Indian insurance company to function as a Government company.
3. Every notification made under sub-section (2) shall specify the names and description of the persons to whom the shares are transferred and the particulars of the shares which are transferred to each such person.
4. A copy of every notification made under sub-section (2) shall, as soon as may be after it is made, be sent by the Central Government to the concerned Indian insurance company, who shall, on receipt of such copy, and notwithstanding anything contained in the Companies Act or in its articles of association, forthwith rectify its register of members by including therein the persons mentioned in the notification as the holders of the shares specified therein.
5. For the removal of doubts it is hereby declared that the transfer and vesting of shares effected under sub-section (1) shall not be deemed to affect any right of the Indian insurance company subsisting immediately before the appointed day against any shareholder to recover from him any sum of money on the ground that shareholder has not paid or credited to the insurer the whole or any part of the value of the shares held by him or on any other ground whatsoever.

5. Transfer of undertakings of other existing insurers.

1. On the appointed day, the undertaking of every existing insurer who is not an Indian insurance company shall stand transferred to and vested in the Central Government and the Central Government shall immediately thereafter provide, by notification, for the transfer to and vesting in such Indian insurance company, as it may specify in the notification, of that undertaking.
2. Any notification made under sub-section (1) may provide that any of the undertakings aforesaid may be transferred to and vested in more than one Indian insurance company in such manner and subject to such conditions as may be specified in the notification.

6. Effect of transfer of undertakings.

1. The undertaking of every such existing insurer as is referred to in Section 5 shall be deemed to include all assets, rights, powers, authorities and privileges and all property, movable and immovable, cash balances, reserve funds, investments and all other rights and interests in, or arising out of, such property as were immediately before the appointed day in the ownership, possession, power or control of such existing insurer in relation to the undertaking whether within or without India, and all books of accounts, records and all other documents of whatever nature relating thereto, and shall also be deemed to include all borrowings, liabilities and obligations of whatever kind then subsisting of the existing insurer in relation to the undertaking.

2. Unless otherwise expressly provided by this Act, all deeds, bonds, agreements, powers of attorney, grants of legal representation and other instruments of whatever nature subsisting or having effect immediately before the appointed day and to which any such insurer as is referred to in Section 5 is a party or which are in favour of such existing insurer shall be of as full force and effect against or in favour of the Indian insurance company in which the undertaking or the part to which the instrument relates, has vested and may be enforced or acted upon as fully and effectually as if, in the place of the existing insurer referred to in Section 5, the Indian insurance company in which the undertaking or any part thereof has vested had been a party thereto, or as if they had been issued in its favour.
3. If, on the appointed day any suit appeal or other proceeding of whatever nature in relation to any business of the undertaking which has been transferred under Section 5 is pending by or against any such existing insurer as is referred to in that section, the same shall not abate, be discontinued or be in any way prejudicially affected by reason of the transfer of the undertaking or of anything contained in this Act but the suit appeal or other proceeding may be continued, prosecuted and enforced by or against the Indian insurance company in which the undertaking or the part to which the proceeding relates has vested.
4. For the removal of doubts it is hereby declared that in the case of foreign insurer or as the cas may be, the Life Insurance Corporation the provisions of Section 5 and the preceding subsections shall only apply to the extent to which any property appertains in the former case to the general insurance business carried on in India and in the latter case to the general insurance business carried on whether within or without India and to rights and powers acquired and to debts, liabilities and obligations incurred and to contracts agreements and other instruments made by the foreign insurer of the Life Insurance Corporation as the case may be for the purpose of such general insurance business and to legal proceeding relating to those purposes and the said provisions shall be construed accordingly.
5. If any question arise as to whether any property appertains to any such general insurance business as is referred to in this section or whether any rights, powers, liabilities or obligations were acquired or incurred or any contract, agreement or other instrument was made by the foreign insurer or the Life Insurance Corporation, as the case may be, for the purposes of any such business or whether any documents relate to those purposes, the question shall be referred to the Central Government which shall, after giving an opportunity of being heard to the persons interested in the matter, decide it in such manner as it thinks fit.

7. Transfer of service employees in certain cases.

1. Every whole-time officer or other employee of an existing insurer other than an Indian insurance company who was employed by that insurer wholly or mainly in connection with his general insurance business immediately before the appointed day shall, on the appointed day, become an officer or other employee as the case may be, of the Indian insurance company in which the undertaking of that insurer or that part of the undertaking to which the service of the officer or other employee relates has vested, and shall hold his office or service under the Indian insurance company on the terms and same conditions and with the same rights to pension, gratuity and other matter as would have been admissible to him if there had been no such vesting and shall continue to do so unless and until his employment in the Indian insurance company in which the undertaking or part has vested is terminated or until his remuneration, terms and conditions are duly altered by that Indian Insurance company:

   Provided that nothing in this sub-section shall apply to any such officer or other employee who has given, in writing, notice to the Central Government or to any person nominated in this behalf by that Government before the appointed day intimating his intention of not becoming an officer or employee of the Indian insurance company in whom the undertaking or part thereof to which his service relates has vested.

2. If any question arises as to whether any person was a wholetime officer or employee, or as to whether any officer or employee was employed wholly or mainly in connection with the general insurance business of the existing insurer referred to in sub-section (1), immediately before the appointed day, the question shall be referred within a period of two years from the appointed day and not thereafter, the Central Government which shall, after giving an opportunity of being heard to the person concerned in the matter, decide it in such manner as it thinks fit and such decision shall be final.
3. Notwithstanding anything contained in the Industrial Disputes Act, 1947 or in any other law for the time being in force the transfer of the services of any officer or other employee under subsection (1) shall not entitle any such officer or other employee to any compensation under that Act or such other law and no such claim shall be entertained by any court, tribunal or other authority.

8. Provident, Superannuation, welfare and other funds.

1. Where an existing insurer has established a provident, superannuation, welfare or any other fund for the benefit of his employees and constituted a trust in respect thereof (hereafter in this section referred to as an existing trust), the moneys standing to the credit of such fund on the appointed day, together with any other assets belonging to such fund, shall stand transferred to and vested in the Indian insurance company on the appointed day free from any such trust.
2. Where all the employees of the Life Insurance Corporation or any other existing insurer do not become employees of an Indian insurance company, the moneys and other assets belonging to any such fund as is referred to in sub-section (1), shall be apportioned between the trustees of the fund and the Indian insurance company in the prescribed manner; and in case of any dispute about such apportionment the decision of the Central Government thereon shall be final.
3. Where the undertaking of an existing insurer has vested in more than one Indian insurance company, the Central Government may, by order, provide for the apportionment among such Indian insurance companies of moneys and other assets belonging to any existing trust relating to that undertaking in such manner as in its opinion may be appropriate.
4. The Indian insurance company shall as soon as may be after the appointed day constitute in response of the moneys and other assets which are transferred to and vested in it under this section one or more trusts having objects as similar to the objects of the existing trusts as in the circumstances may be practicable.
5. Where all the moneys and other assets belonging to an existing trust are transferred to and vested in an Indian insurance company under this section, the trustees of such trust shall, as from the appointed day, stand discharged from the trust, except as respects things done or omitted to be done before the appointed day.

CHAPTER III

GENERAL INSURANCE CORPORATION OF INDIA

9. Formation of General Insurance Corporation of India.

1. As soon as may be after the commencement of this Act, the Central Government shall form a Government company in accordance with the provisions of the Companies Act, to be known as the General Insurance Corporation of India for the purpose of superintending, controlling and carrying on the business of general insurance.

2. The authorised capital of the Corporation shall be rupees seventy-five crores, divided into seventy-five lakhs fully paid-up shares of one hundred rupees each, out of which rupees five crores shall be the initial subscribed capital of the Corporation.
3. Notwithstanding anything contained in the Companies Act, 1956, it shall not be necessary to add the word "Limited" as the last word of the name of the Corporation.

10. Transfer to Corporation of shares vested in Central Government. All the shares in the capital of every Indian insurance company which stand transferred to and vested in the Central Government by virtue of Section 4 [with the exception of the shares transferred to any person under sub-section (2) of that section] shall, immediately after such vesting, stand transferred to and vested in the Corporation and every Indian insurance company shall forthwith give effect to such transfer of shares and rectify its register of members by including therein the Corporation as the holder of such shares.

CHAPTER IV

AMOUNTS TO BE PAID ACQUISITIONS

11. Amounts to be paid for transfer and vesting of share or undertakings.

1. For the transfer of the shares of each Indian insurance company to, and vesting in, the Central Government, under Section 4, there shall be paid by the Central Government to the Corporation, for distribution to the shareholders of each such company, the amount specified against such company in the corresponding entry under column (3) of Part A of the Schedule.
2. For the transfer to, and vesting in, the Central Government, under Section 5, of the undertaking of each existing insurer who is not an Indian insurance company, there shall be paid by the Central Government to the Corporation, for payment to each such existing insurer, the amount specified against such insurer in the corresponding entry under column (3) of Part B of the Schedule.

12. Disbursement of amounts by Corporation.

1. The total amount Paid by the Central Government under Section 11 shall be treated as additional contribution to the subscribed capital of the Corporation and such additional subscribed capital shall stand allotted to, and vested in, the Central Government.
2. The Corporation shall distribute the amount paid to it under Section 11, to the shareholders of each Indian insurance company and to each existing insurer, who is not an Indian insurance company, in accordance with their rights and interests, and, if there is any doubt or dispute as to the right, or extent of the right, of any person to receive the whole or any part of such amount, refer such doubt or dispute to the Central Government for determination and thereafter act in accordance with the determination made by that Government.
3. Save as otherwise provided in sub-section (2), the amount referred to in Section 11 shall be given in accordance with the provisions of Section 13, Section 14 or Section 15, as the case may be.

13. Mode of Payment.

1. Where the amount referred to in Section 11 is to be given—

(*a*) to the members of an Indian insurance company, the amount due to each such member shall be paid in full, where it does not exceed twenty-five thousand rupees, and where it execeeds twenty-five thousand rupees, each such member shall be paid twenty-five thousand rupees and the balance of the amount due to such members shall be paid to him in three equal installments, the first of which shall fall due on the appointed day;

(*b*) to a foreign insurer, it shall be given to him in cash within three months from the appointed day;

(*c*) to the Life Insurance Corporation, it shall be given to it in three equal annual instalments, the first of which within three months from the appointed day;

(*d*) to an existing insurer who is a co-operative society, it shall be distributed as soon as may be after the appointed day in accordance with the rules of the society which will apply in case of dissolution of the society;

(*e*) to an existing insurer not falling within any of the foregoing provisions, it shall be apportioned by the acquiring company among the individual policy-holders of the insurer whose policies with that insurer were in force on the appointed day and were comprised in the undertaking of such insurer in proportion to the premiums paid by the policy-holder such policies and every such payment shall be made either—

(*i*) in cash, to be sent by postal money order, or

(*ii*) at the option of the policy-holder, as a deduction in the premium due at the time of the renewal of the policy and such option shall be exercised by the policy holder before the expiry of three months from the appointed day (or within such further time not exceeding three months as the Central Government may, on the application of the policy-holder, allow) and the option so exercised shall be final and shall not be altered or rescinded after it has been exercised;

Provided that if any policy-holder fails to exercise his option within the time allowed, he shall be deemed to have exercised his option in favour of payment in cash by postal money orders;

2. Where any amount is payable whether in instalments or otherwise under the provision of this section, the unpaid amount, where its payment has become due, shall carry interest at the rate of four per cent, per annum from the appointed day.

14. Amount payable to share-holders may be paid to named persons instead in certain cases.

1. Notwithstanding anything contained elsewhere in this Act, if a majority in number of the persons, who, immediately before the appointed day, were registered in the books of an Indian insurance company as the members thereof, and representing two-thirds in value of the amount payable to the Indian insurance-company, agree either in person or by proxy at a meeting specially convened for the purpose that the amount so payable instead of being distributed among the members shall be given to any such person or body of persons as the members may nominate either at that meeting or subsequently for the purpose of carrying on any business, and the Central Government is satisfied that due provision has been or will be made for the payment of the value of their respective shares to persons who have dissented from the resolution, the amount may be given to the person or body of persons so nominated in such manner and subject to such conditions as the Central Government may think fit.
2. No resolution passed at any such meeting as is referred to in sub-section (1) held after the appointed day shall have any effect unless the meeting has been convened after obtaining the approval of the Central Government.

15. Payment into court in case of rival claims. Where a claim to the amount payable under Section 11 is made by two or more persons adversely to one another, the Corporation may cause the amount to be deposited in any civil court having jurisdiction in that behalf and the court shall decide as to whom the payment shall be made.

CHAPTER V

SCHEME FOR REORGANISATION OF GENERAL INSURANCE BUSINESS

16. Schemes for mergers of companies, etc.

1. If the Central Government is of opinion that for the more efficient carrying on of general insurance business it is necessary so to do, it may, by notification, from one or more schemes providing for all or any of the following matters:—

(*a*) the merger in one Indian insurance company of any other Indian insurance company, or the formation of a new company by the amalganation of two or more Indian insurance companies;

(*b*) the transfer to and vesting in the acquiring company of the undertaking (including all its business, properties assets and liabilities) of any Indian insurance company which ceases to exist by reason of the scheme;

(*c*) the constitution name and registered office and the capital structure of the acquiring company and the issue and allotment of shares;

(*d*) the constitution of a board of management by whatever namecalled for the management of the acquiring company;

(*e*) the alteration of the memorandum and articles of association of the acquiring company for such purposes as may be necessary to give effect to the scheme;

(*f*) the continuance in the acquiring company of the services of all officers and other employees of the Indian insurance company which has ceased to exist by reason of the scheme, on the same terms and conditions which they were getting or, as the case may be, which they were governed immediately before the commencement of the scheme;

(*g*) the rationalisation or revision of pay scales and other terms and conditions of service of officers and other employees wherever necessary;

(*h*) the transfer to the acquiring company of the provident superannuation, welfare and other funds relating to the officers and other employees of the Indian insurance company which has ceased to exist by reason of the scheme;

(*i*) the continuance by or against the acquiring company of legal proceedings pending by or against any Indian insurance company which has ceased to exist by reason of the scheme, and the initiation of such legal proceedings, civil or criminal, as the Indian insurance company might have initiated if it had not ceased to exist;

(*j*) such incidental, consequential and supplemental matters as are necessary to give full effect to the scheme;

2. In framing schemes under sub-section (1); the object of Central Government shall he to ensure that ultimately there are only four companies (excluding the Corporation) in existence and that they are so situate as to render their combined services effective in all parts of India.
3. Where a scheme under sub-section (1) provides for the transfer of any property or liabilities, then, by virtue of the scheme, the property shall stand transferred to and vested in, and those liabilities shall be transferred to and become the liabilities of, the acquiring company.
4. If the rationalisaton or revision of any pay scale or other terms and conditions of service under any scheme is not acceptable to any officer or other employee, the acquiring company may terminate his employment by giving him compensation equivalent to three months' remuneration, unless the contract of service with such employee provides for a shorter notice of termination.

   Explanation—The compensation payable to an officer or other employee under this sub-section shall be in addition to, and shall not affect, any pension, gratuity, provident fund or other benefit to which employee may be entitled under his contract of service.
5. Notwithstanding anything contained in the Industrial Disputes Act, 1947 or in any other law for the time being in force, the transfer of the services of any officer or other employee of an Indian insurance company to the acquiring company shall not entitle any such officer or other employee to any compensation under that Act or other law, and no such claim shall be entertained by any court, tribunal or other authority.
6. The Central Government may, by notification, add to, amend or vary any scheme framed under this section.

7. The provisions of this section and of any scheme framed under it shall have effect notwithstanding anything to the contrary contained in any other law or any agreement, award or other instrument for the time being in force.

17. Schemes to be laid before Parliament. A copy of every scheme and every amendment thereto framed under Section 16 shall be laid, as soon as may be after it is made, before each House of Parliament.

CHAPTER VI

FUNCTIONS OF CORPORATION, AND ACQUIRING COMPANIES AND THEIR MANAGEMENT

18. Functions of Corporation.

1. The functions of the Corporation shall include—
   (*a*) the carrying on of any part of the general insurance business, if it thinks it desirable to do so;
   (*b*) aiding, assisting and advising the acquiring companies in the matter of setting up of standards of conduct and sound practice in general insurance business and in the matter of rendering efficient service to holders of policies of general insurance;
   (*c*) advising the acquiring companies in the matter of controlling their expenses including the payment of commission and other expenses;
   (*d*) advising the acquiring companies in the matter of the investment of their funds;
   (*e*) issuing directions to acquiring companies in relation to the conduct of general insurance business.
2. In issuing any directions under sub-section (1) the Corporation shall keep in mind the desirability of encourageing competition amongst the acquiring companies as far as possible in order to render their services more efficiently.

19. Functions of acquiring companies.

1. Subject to the rules, if any, made by the Central Government in this behalf and to as memorandum and articles of association, it shall be the duty of every aquiring company to carry on generate insurance business.
2. Each acquiring company shall so function under this Act as to secure that general-insurance business is developed to the best advantage of the community.
3. In the discharge of any of its functions each acquiring company shall act so far as may be on business principles and where any directions have been issued by the Corporation, shall be guided by such directions.
4. For the removal of doubts it is hereby declared that the corporation and any acquiring company may, subject to the rules, if any; made by the Central Government in this behalf, enter into such contracts of reinsurance or reinsurance treaties as it—may think fit for the protection of its' interests.

20. Balance of profit how to be utilised.

1. After making provision for bad and doubtful debts, depreciation in assets, provident, superannuation, welfare and other funds; debts due to Government and all other matters for which provision is necessary under any law or which are usually provided for by insurance companies, every acquiring company shall distribute the balance of profit as dividends.
2. Any profit made by the Corporation and any sums received by the Corporation by way of dividends or otherwise shall be dealt, with by it in such manner as may be prescribed.

21. Interim provisions for management of Indian insurance companies.

1. Notwithstanding anything contained in the Companies Act, or in the memorandum and articles of association of any Indian insurance company, on and from the appointed day and until a new board of directors of the Indian insurance company is duly constituted the management of the company shall continue to vest in the Custodian in charge of the management of the undertaking of that company immediately before the appointed day by virtue of the provisions contained in the General Insurance (Emergency Provisions) Act, 1911, and the Custodian shall be entitled, subject to such directions as the Central Government may in this behalf, to exercise all the powers and do all acts and things as may be exercised or done by the company or by its board of directors:
2. Nothing contained in sub-section. (1) shall be deemed to prevent the Central Government from appointing any other person to take charge of the management of the undertaking of any Indian insurance company during period referred to in that sub-section if for any reason it becomes necessary so to do, and any person so appointed may exercise all the powers and do all acts and things which a Custodian may exercise or do under sub-section (1).
3. The Custodian referred to in sub-section (1) and the persons appointed under sub-section (2) shall be entitled to such salaries and other allowances as the Central Government may specify in this behalf and shall hold office during the pleasure of the Central Government.

22. Power of Central Government to transfer employees. The Corporation may at any time transfer any officer or employee from an acquiring company or the Corporation to any other acquiring company or the Corporation, as the case may be, and the officer or employee so transferred, shall continue to have the same terms and conditions of service as were applicable to him immediately before such transfer.

23. Power of Central Government to issue directions. The Corporation and every acquiring company shall, in the discharge of its functions, be guided by such directions in regard to matters of policy involving public interest as the Central Government may give.

CHAPTER VII

MISCELLANEOUS

24. Acquiring companies to have the exclusive privilege of carrying on general insurance business.

1. Except to the extent expressly provided in this Act, on and from the appointed day the Corporation and the acquiring companies shall have exclusive privilege of carrying on general insurance business in India.
2. Subject to the provisions of Section 36, any certificate of registration granted under the Insurance Act to any insurer other than an insurer referred to in sub-section (1) shall, on and from the appointed day, cease to have effect:

Provided that nothing in this sub-section shall apply to the carrying on by the Life Insurance Corporation of life insurance business and capital redemption and annuity certain business.

25. Properties in India not to be with foreign insurers except with permission of Central Government.

1. No person shall take out or renew any policy of insurance in respect of any property in India or any ship or other vessel or aircraft registered in India with an insurer whose principal place of business is outside India save with the prior permission of the Central Government.
2. If any person contravenes any provision of sub-section (I), he shall be punishable with imprisonment for a term which may extend to one year, or with fine which may extend to one thousand rupees or with both.

26. Acquiring companies and income-tax. For the purposes of the Income-tax Act, 1961, every acquiring company shall be deemed to be an Indian company and a company in which the public are substantially interested.

27. Power to reduce amounts of insurance in certain cases. An acquiring company may, having regard to its financial condition on the 13th day of May, 1971, or the financial condition on the said date of any existing insurer whose undertaking have been transferred to and vested in it under this Act reduce the liabilities which have arisen under contracts of general insurance entered in to before the said date in such manner and subject io such conditions as it thinks fit:

Provided that no such reduction shall be made except in accordance with specific proposals made by the acquiring company in this behalf and approved by the Central Government.

28. Right of acquiring company to seek relief in respect of certain transactions.

1. Where an existing insurer has at any time within five years before the 13th day of May, 1971—
   (*a*) made any payment to any person without consideration,
   (*b*) sold or disposed of any property of the insurer without consideration or for an inadequate consideration,
   (*c*) acquired any property or rights for an excessive consideration,
   (*d*) entered into or varied any agreement so as to require an excessive consideration to be paid or given by the insurer,
   (*e*) entered into any other transaction of such an onerous nature as to cause a loss to, or impose a liability, on the insurer exceeding any benefit accruing to the insurer and the payment, sale, disposal, acquisition, agreement or variation thereof or there transaction was not reasonably necessary for the purpose of the general insurance business of the insurer or was made with an unreasonable lack of prudence on the part of the insurer, regard being had in either case to the circumstances at the time, the acquiring company may apply for relief to the circumstances at the time, the acquiring company may apply for relief to the court in respect of such transaction, and all parties to the transaction shall, unless the court otherwise directs, be made parties to the application.
2. The court may make such order against any of the parties to the application as it thinks just having regard to the extent to which those parties were respectively responsible for the transaction or benefited from it and all the circumstances of the case.
3. Where an application is made to the court under this section in respect of any transaction and the application is determined in favour of the acquiring company, the court shall have exclusive jurisdiction to determine any claim outstanding in respect of the transaction.

29. Duty to deliver possession of property and documents relating thereto.

1. Where any property appertaining to an existing insurer has been transferred to and vested in an Indian insurance company under Section 5—
   (*a*) every person in whose possession, custody or control any such property may be, shall deliver the property to the Indian insurance company forthwith,
   (*b*) any person who immediately before such vesting has in his possession, custody or control any books, documents or other papers relating to an existing insurer shall be liable to account for the said books, documents and papers to the Indian insurance company, and shall deliver them to that company or to such person as that company may direct.
2. In particular, all the assets of an existing insurer appertaining to the undertaking held in deposit, by the Reserve Bank of India under the Insurance Act or by trustees in trust shall be delivered to the Indian insurance company.

3. Without prejudice to the other provisions contained in this section, it shall be lawful for each Indian insurance company to take all necessary steps for taking possession of all properties which have been transferred to and vested in it under this Act.

31. Penalty for withholding property, etc. If any person wilfully withholds or fails to deliver to an Indian insurance company as required by Section 29 any property or any books, documents or other papers which may be in his possession or unlawfully retains possession of any property of an existing insurer which has been transferred to and vested in an Indian insurance company under Section 5 or wilfully applies any such property to purposes other than those expressed in or authorised by this Act, he shall, on the complaint of the Indian insurance company, be punishable with imprisonment for a term which may extend to one year, or with fine may extend to one thousand rupees, or with both.

31. Officers and employees of Corporation or of acquiring companies to be public servants. Every officer or other employee of the Corporation or of an acquiring company shall be deemed to be a public servant for the purposes of Chapter IX of the Indian Penal Code.

32. Indemnity. Every officer of the Central Government and every officer or other employee of the Corporation and of any acquiring company shall be indemnified by the Central Government or the Corporation of the acquiring company, as the case may be, against all losses and expenses incurred by him in, or in relation to, the discharge of his duties under this Act except such as have been caused by his own wilful act or default.

33. Dissolution of Corporation and acquiring companies. No provision of law relating to the winding up of companies shall apply to the Corporation or to an acquiring company, and neither the Corporation nor any such company shall be placed in liquidation save by order of the Central Government and in such manner as it may direct.

34. Reference to existing insurer in other laws. Any reference to an existing insurer in any law other than this Act or any contract or other instrument shall, in so far as it relates to an acquiring company, be construed as a reference to that company.

35. Application of Insurance Act. Subject to such exceptions, restrictions and limitations, if any, as the Central Government may, by notification, specify in this behalf, the Insurance Act shall apply to or in relation to the Corporation and every acquiring company as if the Corporation or the acquiring company, as the case may be, were a insurer carrying on general insurance business within the meaning of that Act.

36. Exemptions.

1. Nothing contained in this Act shall apply in relation to—

(*a*) any general insurance business carried on by a State Government, to the extent to which such insurance relates to properties belonging to it or undertakings owned wholly or mainly by the State Government; or to properties belonging to semi-government bodies, or any Board or body corporate established by the State Government under any statute or any industrial or commercial undertaking in which the State Government has substantial financial interest, whether as shareholder, lender or guarantor;

(*b*) any general insurance business not falling within clause (*a*) which has been carried on by a state Government before the commencement of this Act, to the extent to which it is necessary to allow such business to run off :

Provided that nothing contained in this clause shall be deemed to authorise the State Government to issue any new policies or renew any existing policies;

(*c*) any insurer whose business is being voluntarily wound up or is being wound up by a court;

(*d*) the insurance business carried on by the Calcutta Hospital and Nursing Home Benefits Association. Limited;

(*e*) the insurance business carried on by the Export Credit and Guarantee Corporation Limited and the Deposit Insurance Corporation established under Section 3 of the Deposit Insurance Corporation Act, 1961;

(*f*) any scheme in existence immediately before the 14th day of May, 1971, or an scheme framed after the said day with the approval of the Central Government for the insurance of crops or of cattle or of flood risks or of war or emergency risks.

2. If the Central Government is satisfied that an insurer, whether established before or after the appointed day, carries on only such general insurance business as is not carried on ordinarily by insurers, it may, by notification, direct that nothing contained in this Act shall apply to such insurer.

37. Vacancies, etc., not to invalidate proceedings. No act or proceeding of the Corporation or of an acquiring company shall be called in question merely on the ground of the existence of any vacancy in or defect in the constitution of the Corporation or the company.

38. Protection of action taken in good faith. No suit, prosecution or other legal proceeding shall lie against any officer of the Central Government or officer or other employee of the Corporation or of the acquiring company for anything which is in good faith done or intended to be done under this Act.

39. Power to make rules.

1. The Central Government may, by notification, make rules to carry out the provisions of this Act.
2. In particular, and without prejudice to the generality of the foregoing power, rules made under this section may provide for—

(*a*) the manner in which the profits, if any, and other moneys received by the Corporation may be dealt with;

(*b*) the conditions, if any, subject to which the Corporation and the acquiring companies shall Carry on general insurance business;

(*c*) the terms and conditions subject to which any reinsurance contracts or treaties may be entered into;

(*d*) the form and manner in which any notice or application may he given or made to the Central Government;

(*e*) the reports which may be called for by the Central Government from the Corporation and the acquiring companies;

(*f*) any other matter which is required to be, or may be, prescribed.

3. Every rule made under this section and every notification issued under Section 35 shall be laid, as soon as may be after it is made, before each House of Parliament, while it is in session, for a total period of thirty days which may be comprised in one session or in two or more successive sessions, and if, before the expiry of the session immediately following the session or the successive sessions aforesaid, both houses agree in making any modification in the rule or notification or both Houses agree that the rule or notification should not be made, the rule or notification shall thereafter have effect only in such modified form or be of no effect, as the case may be; so, however, that any such modification or annulment shall be without prejudice to the validity of anything previously done under that rule or notification.

APPENDIX—B

Whereas the Insured named in the Schedule below, carrying on the business mentioned therein and no other for the purpose of this Insurance has, by a Proposal and Declaration dated as stated in the said Schedule, which Proposal and Declaration it is hereby agreed shall be the basis of this Contract and be considered as in corporated herein, applied to the ORIENTAL FIRE AND GENERAL INSURANCE COMPANY LIMITED (hereinafter called the "Company") for the Insurance hereinafter contained for the period stated in the Schedule hereto and in consideration of the Insured having paid or agreed to pay to the Company the sum shown as the first premium for or on account of such Insurance.

Now this policy Witnesseth that if during the period stated in the Schedule hereto or during any subsequent period in respect of which the Insured shall have paid and the Company accepted a renewal premium this property or any part thereof described in the Schedule below, whilst contained within the premises (which expression shall not include any garden, yard or outbuilding or other appartenances) mentioned in the said Schedule and whilst the premises are occupied by the Insured as stated in the proposal above referred to shall be lost or damaged by.

HOUSE BREAKING OR BURGLARY

or any attempt, thereat or if there shall arise any damage to the said premises by the risks insured against falling to be made good by the Insured then the company shall pay or make good to the Insured such loss or damage to the extent of the intrinsic value of the property so lost or to the amount of the damage so sustained, but not exceeding, in respect of each or any of the several items specified, the sum set opposite thereto respectively, nor in the whole of any one year of insurance the total sum insured by this Policy.

Provided always that this Policy shall not cover

(*a*) loss or damage where any member of the Insured's household or of his business staff is concerned as principal or accessory, or resulting from any act committed by any other person lawfully on the premises wherein the property insured may happen to be;

(*b*) loss or damage upon the occasion of or consequent upon, fire or explosion within such premises or any loss or damage which can be insured against by a Fire or Glass Insurance Policy.

(*c*) Unless specially mentioned, deeds, bonds, bills of exchange, promissory notes, cash, treasury notes and bank notes, cheques, securities for money stamps, stamp collections, books of account, documents of any kind, manuscripts, medals and coins, motor vehicles and accessories or livestock;

(*d*) (*i*) any accident or any loss or destruction of or damage to any property whatsoever or any loss or expense whatsoever resulting or arising therefrom or any consequential loss.

(*ii*) any legal liability of whatsover nature,

directly or indirectly cause by or contributed to by or arising from ionising radiations or contaminations by radioactivity from any nuclear fuel or from any nuclear waste from the combustion of nuclear fuel. Solely for the purpose of this exclusion, combustion shall include any self-sustaining process of nuclear fission.

The indemnity or compensation provided by this Policy shall not apply to nor include any accident, loss, destruction, damage or legal liability directly or indirectly caused why or contributed to by or arising from nuclear weapons material.

(*e*) loss, destruction or damage directly or indirectly proximately or remotely occasioned by contributed to by or traceable to or arising out or in connection with Hurricane, Volcanic Eruption, Earthquake or other convulsions of nature, Invasion act or Foreign Enemies, Hostilities or Warlike Operations (whether before or after Declaration of War), Civil War, Strike, Riot, Civil Commotion, Mutiny, Rebellion Military or Usurped Power or by any direct or indirect consequences of any of the said occurrences and in the event of any claim hereunder the Insured shall prove that the loss, destruction or damage arose independently of and was in no way connected with or occasioned by or contributed to by or traceable to any of the said occurrences or any consequence thereof and in default of such proof the Company shall not be liable to make any payment in respect of such a claim.

Provided always that the due observance and fulfilment of the conditions contained herein or endorsed hereon shall so far as the nature of them respectively will permit be deemed to be conditions precedent to the right of the Insured to recover hereunder.

The Agents of the Company shall in no case be made personally responsible on account of any legal or other investigation which they may find it necessary to institute for the satisfaction of the Company; nor can their personal property be attached on account of any Claim by the Insured. If the insured should commence such proceedings against the Agents it is hereby declared and stipulated that the Insured shall foreit thereby all Claims upon the Company under this Policy and shall moreover be responsible for all expenses which shall accrue in consequence of such proceedings.

1. For the purposes of this Policy the term "Housebreaking or Burglary" shall mean:—
   (*a*) Theft of property from the premises described in the Schedule, to this Policy following upon felonious entry of the said premises by violent and forcible means or
   (*b*) Theft by a person in the premises who subsequently breaks out by violent and forcible means, PROVIDED there shall be visible marks made upon the premises at the plate of such entry or exit by tools, explosives, electricity or chemicals.
2. Each and every item specified in the Schedule to this Policy is separately but similarly subject to Average, that is to say, if the property insured. Shall at the time of no loss or damage be collectively of greater value than the sum insured thereon then the insured shall be considered to be his own Insurer for the different and shall bear rateable share of the loss or damage accordingly.
3. Every notice or communication to be given or made under this Policy shall be delivered in writing at the Registered Office or any Branch Office or Agency of the Company with which the Insured has been in communication
4. This Policy shall be void if there be any misstatement in or if a material fact be omitted from the proposal.
5. If any claim under this Policy shall be in any respect fraudulent or if any fraudulent means or devices are used by the insured or anyone acting on his behalf to obtain any benefit under this Policy or if books showing an purchases of goods or stock, particulars of articles or goods manufactured, and of goods or stock sold or otherwise disposed of shall not have been duly and correctly kept during the time the insured has carried on the business, then this Policy shall be void and all benefit thereunder shall be forfeited.
6. The Insured shall exercise reasonable care in the selection and suppervision of employees and shall take all reasonable precautions to safeguard the property insured and to secure all doors, windows and other openings.
7. Upon the happening of any event giving rise or likely to give rise to a claim under this Policy coming to the knowledge of the Jnsured, or of the Insured's representative for the time being, the Insured or the representative shall:
   (*a*) Give immediate notice to the Police and take all practicable steps to discover the guilty person or persons and to recover the property lost and shall also give immediate notice to the Company siating the circumstances of the case.
   (*b*) Within seven days after such notice deliver to the Company a detailed statement in writing of the loss or damage, with an estimate of the intrinsic value of each article lost and the amount of the damage sustained.

(*c*) Furnish to the Company all such particulars and evidence, documentary or otherwise and execute and do all such assurances and things and give all such access as the Company may reasonably require to substantiate the claim, to discover and punish the guilty person or persons, to trace and recover the property lost, and to recoup the Company, so far as may be in respect of the amount they shall pay, or be liable to pay under this Policy. The Company shall bear the expense of all such particulars, evidence, assurances and things as they may require with the above objects or any of them other than those required to substantiate the claim.

Unless notice as required in paragraph (*a*) of this condition be receivel by the Company within six weeks after the happening of such event, the Company will be under no liability for any loss or damage in connection therewith.

8. The Company may reinstate, replace, or repair the property or premises as the case may be or any part thereof, instead of paying the amount of the loss or damage, and may join with other Insurers in so doing. If the Company elect to reinstate or replace, the Insured shall furnish to them when required all such specifications, and information as may be deemed necessary or expedient for the purpose. Upon payment of any claim for loss under this Policy, the property in respect of which the payment is made shall belong to the Company.

9. If at the time of the happening of any loss or damage covered by the Policy there shall be any other insurance covering the same risk, whether effected by the Insured or not, then the Company shall not be liable to contribute more than its rateable proportion of any payment in respect of such loss or damage.

10. This Policy ceases to be in force as to any property which shall pass from the Insured to any other person otherwise than by Will or Operation of Law, unless notice thereof be given to the Company, and the subsistence of the Insurance in favour of such other person be declared by a memorandum endorsed thereon by or on behalf of the Company.

11. The Company may by notice in writing to the Insured to his last known address cancel this Policy at any time paying on demand a proportion of the premium corresponding to the unexpired period of the Policy.

12. This Policy does not cover loss of cash and or other property abstracted from safe is following the use of the key to the said after or any duplicate thereof belonging to the Insured unless such key has been obtained by threats or violence.

A complete list of the amount of cash and or other property in the safe shall be kept secure in some place other than the said safe, and the liability of the Company shall be limited to the amount actually shown by such record to be in the safe at the time of Burglary not exceeding in all the sum insured.

13. If any difference arises as to the amount of any loss or damage such difference shall independently of all other questions be referred to the decision of an Arbitrator, to be appointed in writing by the parties in difference, or if they cannot agree upon a single Arbitrator, to the decision of two disinterested persons as arbitrators, of whom one shall be appointed in writing by each of the parties within two calendar months after having been required so to do in writing by the other party. In case either party shall refuse or fail to appoint an arbitrator within two calendar months after receipt of notice in writing requiring an appointment, the other party shall be at liberty to appoint a sole arbitrator; and in case of disagreement between the arbitrators, the difference shall be referred to the decision of an umpire who shall have been appointed by them in writing before entering on the reference and who shall sit with the arbitrators and preside at their

meetings. The death of any party shall not revoke or affect the authority or powers of the arbitrator, arbitrators or umpire respectively; and in the event of the death of an arbitrator or umpire, another shall in each case be appointed in his stead by the party or arbitrators (as the case may be) by whom the arbitrator or umpire so dying was appointed. The costs of the reference and of the award shall be in the discretion of the arbitrator, arbitrators or umpire making the award. And it is hereby expressly stipulated and declared that it shall be a condition precedent to any right of action or suit upon this Policy that the award by such arbitrator, arbitrators or umpire of the amount of the loss or damage if disputed shall be first obtained.

QUESTIONS

1. Describe the main features of the Insurance Act, 1938.
2. What are the duties and liabilities of the Controller of Insurance?
3. Discuss the main functions of Life Insurance Corporation of India.
4. Detail the set-up and organisation of Life Insurance Corporation of India.
5. Discuss the main Proviso of the Marine Insurance Act.
6. Discuss the functions of the General Insurance Corporation of India.

THE INSURANCE REGULATORY AND DEVELOPMENT AUTHORITY ACT, 1999[1]

(NO. 41 OF 1999)

(*December* 29, 1999)

CONTENTS

CHAPTER 1

PRELIMINARY

CHAPTER II

INSURANCE REGULATORY AND DEVELOPMENT AUTHORITY

CHAPTER III

TRANSFER OF ASSETS, LIABILITIES, ETC. OF INTERIM INSURANCE REGULATORY AUTHORITY

An Act to provide for the establishment of an Authority to protect the interests of holders of insurance policies, to regulate, promote and ensure orderly growth of the insurance industry and for matters connected therewith or incidental thereto and for there to amend the Insurance Act, 1938, the Life insurance Corporation Act, 1956 and the General Insurance Business (Nationalisation) Act, 1972.

Be it enacted by Parliament in the Fiftieth Year of the Republic of India as follows:

Prefatory Note—Statement of Objects and Reasons—The insurance industry requires a high degree of regulation. The Insurance Act, 1938 provides for the institution of the Controller of Insurance to act as strong and powerful supervisory and regulatory authority with powers to direct, advise, caution, prohibit, investigate, inspect, prosecute, search, seize, fine, amalgamate, authorise, register and liquidate insurance companies. However, after the nationalisation of the life insurance

1. Received the assent of the President on December 29, 1999 and published in the Gazette of India, Extra., Part II, Section I, dated December 29, 1999, pp. 1-29, No, 54.

industry in 1956 and the general insurance industry in 1972, the role of the Controller of Insurance diminished in significance over a period of time.

2. In April 1993, the Government set up a high-powered committee headed by Shri R.N. Malhotra, former Governor, Reserve Bank of India, to examine the structure of the insurance industry and recommend changes to make it more efficient and competitive keeping in view the structural changes in other part of the financial system of the economy. The Committee which submitted its report on the 7th January, 1994 felt that the insurance regulatory apparatus should be activated even in the present set up of nationalised insurance sector and recommended, inter alia, the establishment of a strong and effective Insurance Regulatory Authority in the form of a statutory autonomous board on the lines of the Securities and Exchange Board of India.
3. The recommendations of the Committee were discussed at different forums including the Consultative Committee of the Parliament attached to the Ministry of Finance, managements of the Life Insurance Corporation, the General Insurance Corporation and its subsidiary companies, trade unions, chambers of commerce and consumer interest groups. The recommendation to set up an autonomous Insurance Regulatory Authority found wide support. In view of the general support received, the then Government decided to bring in a legislation to establish an independent Regulatory Authority for the insurance industry. Since enacting legislation for creating the Insurance Regulatory Authority was to take time, the then Government constituted through a Government resolution an Interim Insurance Regulatory Authority pending the enactment of a comprehensive legislation. The Chairman, Insurance Regulatory Authority has been notified as Controller of Insurance under the Insurance Act, 1938. The said Interim Insurance Regulatory Authority at present is discharging certain functions and exercising powers of the Controller.
4. In pursuance of the Budget Speech in July 1996, the then Government introduced on the 20th December, 1996, the Insurance Regulatory Authority Bill, 1996 for establishment of an authority to protect the interest of holders of insurance policies and to regulate, promote and ensure orderly growth of the insurance industry and for matters connected therewith or incidental thereto. The Bill was referred to the Department related Standing Committee on the Ministry of Finance. The Committee submitted its report on 9th May, 1997. However, the said Bill incorporating therein the recommendations of the said Standing Committee was taken for consideration but could not be passed and the Bill was withdrawn by the then Government.
5. In order to provide better insurance coverage to our citizens and also to augment the flow of long-term resources for financing infrastructure, in the Budget Speech, 1998, the policy of the Government was announced to open up the insurance sector and also to establish a Statutory Regulatory Authority. Accordingly, the Insurance Regulatory Authority Bill, 1998 was introduced in the previous Lock Sabha on the 15th December, 1998 providing for setting a Statutory Insurance Regulatory Authority and containing three Schedules incorporating amendments to the Insurance act, 1938, the Life Insurance Corporation Act, 1956 and the General Insurance Business (Nationalisation) Act, 1972 to permit the entry of private Indian companies into the insurance sector and to make certain consequential amendments to the Insurance Act, 1938. The Bill was referred to the Standing Committee on Finance on the 4th January, 1999 for examination and report. The Standing Committee while recommending the Bill suggested some amendments. These were accepted by the Government and amendments to the Bill were circulated on the 18th March, 1999. However, the Bill could not be taken up for consideration consequent on the dissolution of the Lock Sabha.
6. It is now proposed to re-introduce a fresh Bill by incorporating the provisions of the Insurance Regulatory Authority Bill, 1998 and the amendments suggested by the Standing Committee on Finance. The Bill will be titled Insurance Regulatory and Development Authority Bill on the

basis of the recommendation of the Standing Committee. In the main text of the Bill, provisions are incorporated to give a Statutory character to the Interim Insurance Regulatory Authority and the Three Schedules contain amendments to the Insurance Act, 1938, amendment to the Life Insurance Corporation Act, 1956 and the General Insurance Business (Nationalisation) Act, 1972.

7. The proposed Authority shall be a body corporate having perpetual succession and a common seal with power to acquire, hold and dispose of property and to contract. It will consist of a Chairperson and other members not exceeding nine in number, of whom not more than five shall serve full time, to be appointed by the Central Government from amongst persons of ability, integrity and standing who have knowledge or experience of life insurance, general insurance, actuarial science, finance, economics, law, accountancy, administration or any other discipline which in the opinion of the Central Government shall be useful to the Authority. The Chairperson and other whole-time members, shall hold office for a term of 5 years or until the age of 65 years in the case of Chairperson and 62 years in the case of other whole-time members whichever is earlier and they shall be eligible for reappointment subject to age consideration. A part-time member shall hold office for a term not exceeding 5 years.

8. The duties, powers and functions of Authority, inter alia, shall include:

(*a*) Issue to the applicant a certificate of registration, renew, modify, withdraw, suspend or cancel such registration;

(*b*) Protection of the interests of the policyholders in matters concerning assigning of policy, nomination by policyholders, insurable interest, settlement of insurance claim, surrender value of policy, and other terms and conditions of contracts of insurance;

(*c*) Specifying requisite qualifications, code of conduct and practical training for intermediary or insurance intermediaries and agents;

(*d*) Specifying the code of conduct for surveyors and loss assessors;

(*e*) Promoting efficiency in the conduct of insurance business;

(*f*) Promoting and regulating professional organisations connected with the insurance and reinsurance business;

(*g*) Levying fees and other charges for carrying out the purposes of this Act;

(*h*) Calling for information from, undertaking inspection of, conducting enquiries and investigations including audit of insurers, intermediaries, insurance intermediaries and other organisations connected with the insurance business;

(*i*) Control and regulation of the rates, advantages, term and conditions that may be offered by insurers in respect of general insurance business not so controlled and regulated by the Tariff Advisory Committee under Section 64-U of the Insurance Act, 1938;

(*j*) Specifying the form and manner in which books of account shall be maintained and statement of accounts will be rendered by insurers and other insurance intermediaries;

(*k*) Regulating investment of funds by insurance companies;

(*l*) Regulating maintenance of margin of solvency;

(*m*) Adjudication of disputes between insurers and intermediaries or insurance intermediaries;

(*n*) Supervising the functioning of the Tariff Advisory Committee;

(*O*) Specifying the percentage of premium income of the insurer to finance schemes for promoting and regulating professional organisations referred to in clause(f).

(*p*) Specifying percentage of life insurance business and general insurance business to be undertaken by the insurer in the rural or social sector; and

(*q*) Exercising such other powers as may be prescribed.

9. The powers and functions mentioned above would enable the Authority to perform the role of all effective watchdog and a regulator for the insurance sector in India. To enable the Authority to function in a truly independent manner and discharge its assigned responsibilities effectively, it is proposed to vest the Authority with statutory status.
10. The First Schedule contains consequential provisions relating to amendments to the Insurance Act, 1938 to update certain outdated provisions and for smooth and efficient regulation of the opened up sector. The Second and Third Schedules contain amendment to the Life Insurance Corporation Act, 1956 and the General Insurance Business (Nationalisation) Act, 1972 respectively to remove the exclusive privilege of the nationalised companies to transact insurance business.
11. The Bill seeks to achieve the above objects.

CHAPTER I

PRELIMINARY

1. **Short title, extent and commencement:** (1) This Act may be called the Insurance Regulatory and Development Authority Act, 1999.
2. It extends to the whole of India.
3. It shall come into force on such date as the Central Government may, by notification in the Official Gazette, appoint:

Provided that different dates may be appointed for different provisions of this Act and any reference in any such provision to the commencement of this Act shall be construed as a reference to the coming into force of that provision.

Notes

Commencement of Act. There are two ways of the laws coming into operation. One way that in the law itself it is laid down that it shall come into force on a particular day. If that is not provided in the Act, then the Act comes into operation on the date of assent. *Chandrasekhar Singh v. State of Orissa,* (1967) 33 Cut LT 263.

2. Definitions.

1. In this Act, unless the context otherwise requires:
   (*a*) "Appointed day" means the date on which the Authority is established under sub-section (1) of Section 3;
   (*b*) "Authority" means the Insurance Regulatory and Development Authority established under sub-section (1) of Section 3;
   (*c*) "Chairperson" means the Chairperson of the Authority;
   (*d*) "Fund" means the Insurance Regulatory and Development Authority Fund constituted under sub-section (1) of Section 16;
   (*e*) "Interim Insurance Regulatory Authority" means the Insurance Regulatory Authority set up by the Central Government through Resolution No. 17(2)/94-Ins.-V, dated the 23rd January, 1996;
   (*f*) "Intermediary or insurance intermediary" includes insurance brokers, reinsurance brokers, insurance consultants, surveyors and loss assessors;
   (*g*) "Member" means a whole-time or a part-time member of the Authority and includes the Chairperson;
   (*h*) "Notification" means a notification published in the Official Gazette;

(*i*) "Prescribed" means prescribed by rules made under this Act;

(*j*) "Regulations" means the regulations made by the Authority.

2. Words and expressions used and not defined in this Act but defined in the Insurance Act, 1938 (4 of 1938) or the Life Insurance Corporation Act, 1972 (57 of 1972) shall have the meanings respectively assigned to them in those Acts.

Chapter II
Insurance Regulatory and Development Authority

3. Establishment and incorporation of Authority.

1. With effect from such date as the Central Government may, by notification, appoint, there shall be established, for the purposes of this Act, an Authority to be called "the Insurance Regulatory and Development Authority".
2. The Authority shall be a body corporate by the name aforesaid having perpetual succession and a common seal with power, subject to the provisions of this Act, to acquire, hold and dispose of property, both movable and immovable, and to contract and shall, by the said name, sue or be sued.
3. The head office of the Authority shall be at such place as the Central Government may decide from time to time.
4. The Authority may establish offices at other places in India.

4. Composition of Authority. The Authority shall consist of the following members, namely:

(*a*) a Chairperson;

(*b*) not more than five whole-time members;

(*c*) not more than four part-time members;

to be appointed by the Central Government from amongst persons of ability, integrity and standing who have knowledge or experience in life insurance, general insurance, actuarial science, finance, economics, law, accountancy, administration or any other discipline which would, in the opinion of the Central Government, be useful to the Authority;

Provided that the Central Government shall, while appointing the Chairperson and the whole-time members, ensure that at least one person each is a person having knowledge or experience in life insurance, general insurance or actuarial science, respectively.

5. Tenure of office of Chairperson and other members.

1. The Chairperson and every other whole-time member shall hold office for a term of—five years from the date on which he enters upon his office and shall be eligible for reappointment:
   Provided that no person shall hold office as a Chairperson after he has attained the age of sixty-five years:
   Provided further that no person shall hold office as a whole-time member after he has attained the age of sixty-two years.
2. A part-time member shall hold office for a term not exceeding five years from the date on which he enters upon his office.

6. Removal from office

7. Salary and allowances of Chairperson and members

8. Bar on future employment of members

9. Administrative power's of Chairperson

10. Meetings of Authority

11. Vacancies, etc., not to invalidate proceedings of Authority

12. Officers and employees of Authority
13. Transfer of assets, liabilities etc. of Interim Insurance Regulatory Authority
14. Duties, powers and functions of Authority
15. Grants by Central Government
16. Constitution of Fund
17. Accounts and audit
18. Power of Central Government to issue directions
19. Power of Central Government to supersede Authority
20. Furnishing of returns, etc. to Central Government
21. Chairperson, members, officers and other employees of Authority to be public servants
22. Protection of action taken in good faith
23. Delegation of powers
24. Power to make rules
25. Establishment of Insurance Advisory Committee
26. Power to make regulations

27. Rules and regulations to be laid before Parliament. Every rule and every regulation made under this Act shall be laid, as soon as may be after it is made, before each House of Parliament, while it is in session, for a total period of thirty days which may be comprised in one session or in two or more successive sessions, and if, before the expiry of the session immediately following the session or the successive sessions aforesaid, both Houses agree in making any modification in the rule or regulation or both Houses agree that the rule or regulation should not be made, the rule or regulation shall thereafter have effect only in such modified form or be of no effect, as the case may be; so, however, that any such modification or annulment shall be without prejudice to the validity of anything previously done under that rule or regulation.

28. Application of other laws not barred. The provisions of this Act shall be in addition to, and not in derogation of, the provisions of any other law for the time being in force.

29. Power to remove difficulties.

1. If any difficulty arises in giving effect to the provisions of this Act, the Central Government may, by order published in the Official Gazette, make such provisions not inconsistent with the provisions of this Act as may appear to be necessary for removing the difficulty:
   Provided that no order shall be made under this section after the expiry of two years from the appointed day.
2. Every order made under this section shall be laid as soon as may be after it is made, before each House of Parliament.

30. Amendment of Act 4 or 1938. The Insurance Act, 1938 shall be amended in the manner specified in the First Schedule to this Act.

31. Amendment of Act 31 of 1956. The Life Insurance Corporation Act, 1956 shall be amended in the manner specified in the Second Schedule to this Act.

32. Amendment of Act 57 of 1972. The General Insurance Business (Nationalisation) Act, 1972 shall be amended in the manner specified in the Third Schedule to this Act.

The First Schedule

(See Section 30)

Amendments to the Insurance Act, 1938

(4 of 1938)

1. In the Act, except in clause (5-B) of Section 2 and Section 2-B, for "Controller" wherever it occurs, substitute "Authority" and such consequential changes as the rules of grammar may require shall also be made.

2. In Sections 27, 27-A, 27-B, 31, 32-A, 40-A, 48-B, 64-F, 64-G, 64-1, 64-J, 64-L, 64-R, 64-UC, 64-UM, 113 and 115, for "Central Government" wherever they occur, substitute "Authority".

3. Section 2

(*a*) after clause (1), *insert* the following:

'(1-A) "Authority" means the Insurance-Regulatory and Development authority established under sub-section (1) of Section 3 of the Insurance Regulatory and Development Authority Act, 1999;';

(*b*) for clause (5-B), *substitute* the following:

(5-B) "Controller of Insurance" means the officer appointed by the Central Government under Section 2-B to exercise all the powers, discharge the functions and perform the duties of the Authority under this Act or the Life Insurance Corporation Act, 1956 (31 of 1956), or the General Insurance Business (Nationalisation) Act, 1972 (57 of 1972), or the Insurance Regulatory and Development Authority Act, 1999;' ;

(*c*) after clause (7), *insert* the following:

'(7-A) "Indian Insurance Company" means any insurer being a company

(*a*) which is formed and registered under the Companies Act, 1956;

(*b*) in which the aggregate holdings of equity shares by a foreign company, either by itself or through its subsidiary companies or its nominees, do not exceed twenty-six per cent paid-up equity capital of such Indian insurance company;

(*c*) whose sole purpose is to carry on life insurance business or general insurance business or re-insurance business.

Explanation—For the purposes of this clause, the expression "foreign company" shall have the meaning assigned to it under clause (23-A) of Section 2 of the Income Tax Act, 1961 (43 of 1961).

(*d*) in clause (14), for "*Section 114" substitute* "this Act".

4. After Section 2, insert the following:

"2-A. *Interpretation of certain words and expressions.* Words and expressions used and not defined in this Act but defined in the Life Insurance Corporation Act, 1956 (31 of 1956), the General Insurance Business (Nationalisation) Act, 1972 (57 of 1972) and the Insurance Regulatory and Development Authority Act, 1999 shall have the meanings respectively assigned to them in those Acts".

5. Section 2-B, for sub-section (1), *substitute* the following:

"(1) If at any time, the Authority is superseded under sub-section (l) of Section 19 of the Insurance Regulatory and Development Authority Act, 1999, the Central Government may, by notification in the official Gazette, appoint a person to be the Controller of Insurance till such time the Authority is reconstituted under sub-section (3) of Section 19 of that Act."

6. Section 2-C, in sub-section (1), after the second proviso, *insert* the following:

"Provided also that no insurer other than an Indian insurance company shall begin to carry on any class of insurance business in India under this Act on or after the commencement of the Insurance Regulatory and Development Authority Act, 1999."

7. Section 3

(*a*) in sub-section (1), after the first proviso, *insert* the following:

"Provided further that a person or insurer, as the case may be, carrying on any class of insurance business in India, on or before the commencement of the Insurance Regulatory and Development Authority Act, 1999, for which no registration certificate was necessary prior to such commencement, may continue to do so for a period of three months from such commencement or, if he had made an application for such registration within the said period of three months, till the disposal of such application:

Provided also that any certificate of registration, obtained immediately before the commencement of the Insurance Regulatory and Development Authority Act, 1999, shall be deemed to have been obtained from the Authority in accordance with the provisions of this Act.";

(*b*) in sub-section (2),

(*i*) in the opening portion, for "Every application for registration shall be accompanied by—", *substitute* the following:

"Every application for registration shall be made in such manner as may be determined by the regulations made by the Authority and shall be accompanied by—";

(*ii*) in clause (*d*), for "working capital", *substitute* "paid-up equity capital or working capital or working capital";

(*iii*) in clause (*f*), in the proviso, *omit* "and" occurring at the end;

(*iv*) for clause (*g*), *substitute* the following:

"(*g*) the receipt showing payment of fee as may be determined by the regulations which shall not exceed fifty thousand rupees for each class of business as may be specified by the regulations made by the Authority;

(*h*) such other documents as may be specified by the regulations made by the Authority;";

(*c*) after sub-section (2-A), *insert*—

"(2-AA) The Authority shall give preference to register the applicant and grant him a certificate of registration if such applicant agrees, in the form and manner as may be specified by the regulations made by the Authority, to carry on the life insurance business or general insurance business for providing health cover to individuals or group of individuals." ;

(*d*) in sub-section (4),—

(*i*) in clause (*f*), for "of any rule or order made thereunder, or" *substitute* the following: of any rule or any regulation or order made or, any direction issued thereunder, or;

(*ii*) in clause (*h*), *insert* "or" at the end;

(*iii*) after clause (*h*), *insert* the following:

"(*i*) if the insurer makes a default in complying with any direction issued or order made, as the case may be, by the Authority under the Insurance Regulatory and Development Authority Act, 1999, or

(*j*) if the insurer makes a default in complying with, or acts in contravention of, any requirement of the Companies Act, 1956 (1 or 1956) or the Life Insurance Corporation Act, 1956 (31 of 1956) or the General Insurance Business (Nationalisation) Act, 1972 (57 of 1972) or the Foreign Exchange Regulation Act, 1973 (46 of 1973),

(*e*) in sub-section (5-C),

(*i*) for "clause (*h*)", *substitute* "clause (*h*) or clause (*i*) or clause (*j*)";

(*ii*) for "any requirement of this Act or of any rule or order made thereunder" substitute the following

(*iii*) "any requirement of this Act or the Insurance Regulatory and Development Authority Act, 1999, or of any rule or any regulation, or any order made thereunder or any direction issued under those Acts";

(*f*) after sub-section (5-D), *insert* the following:

'(5-E) The Authority may, by order, suspend or cancel any registration in .such manner as may be determined by the regulations made by it:

Provided that no order under this sub-section shall be made unless the person concerned has been given a reasonable opportunity of being heard."

(*g*) for sub-section (7), *substitute* the following:

"(7) The authority may, on payment of such fee, not exceeding five thousand rupees, as may be determined by the regulations, issue a duplicate certificate of registration to replace a certificate lost, destroyed or mutilated, or in any other case where the Authority is of the opinion that the issue of duplicate certificate is necessary.".

8. Section 3-A,—

(*a*) in sub-section (1), for "the 31st day of December, 1941.", *substitute* the following:

"the 31st day of March, after the commencement of the Insurance Regulatory and Development Authority Act, 1999.";

(*b*) in sub-section (2),

(*i*) for "prescribed fee", *substitute* "fee as determined by the regulations made by the Authority";

(*ii*) for clause (*i*), *substitute* the following:

(*i*) exceed one-fourth of one per cent of such premium income or rupees five crores, whichever is less,";

(*iii*) for clause (*ii*), *substitute* the following:

"(*ii*) be less, in any case, then fifty thousand rupees for each class of insurance business:";

(*c*) in sub-section (3), for "prescribed fee", substitute "fee as determined by the regulations made by the Authority";

(*d*) in sub-section (4), for "prescribed fee", substitute "fee as determined by the regulations made by the Authority, and".

9. For Section 6, *substitute* the following:

"6. *Requirement as to capital.* No insurer carrying on the business of life insurance, general insurance or re-insurance in India on or after the commencement of the Insurance Regulatory and Development Authority Act, 1999, shall be registered unless he has,—

(*i*) a paid-up equity capital of rupees one hundred crores, in case of a person carrying on the business of life insurance or general insurance; or

(*ii*) a paid-up equity capital of rupees two hundred crores, in case of a person carrying on exclusively the business as are insurer:

Provided that in determining the paid-up equity capital specified under clause (*i*) or clause (*ii*), the deposit to be made under Section 7 and any preliminary expenses incurred in the formation and registration of the company shall be excluded:

Provided further that an insurer carrying on business of life insurance, general insurance or re-insurance in India before the commencement of the Insurance Regulatory and Development Authority Act, 1999 and who is required to be registered under this Act, shall have a paid-up equity capital in accordance with clause (*i*) and clause (*ii*), as the case may be, within six months of the commencement of that Act.".

10. Section 6-A,

(*a*) in sub-section (4), in clause (b),—

(I) in sub-clause (*i*), *omit* "and" occurring at the end;

(II) in sub-clause (*ii*), for "sanction of the Central Government has been obtained to the transfer.", *substitute* "approval of the Authority has been obtained to the transfer;";

(III) after sub-clause (*ii*), *insert* the following:

'(*iii*) where, the nominal value of the shares intended to be transferred by any individual, firm, group, constituents of a group, or body corporate under the same management, jointly or severally exceeds one per cent of the paid up equity capital of the insurer, unless the previous approval of the Authority has been obtained for the transfer.

Explanation. For the purposes of this sub-clause, the expressions "group" and "same management" shall have the same meanings respectively assigned to them in the Monopolies and Restrictive Trade Practices Act, 1969 (54 of 1969).';

(*b*) in sub-section (II),—

(*i*) for "Explanation 1", substitute "Explanation";

(*ii*) omit Explanation 2.

11. After Section 6-A, *insert* the following:

"6-AA. *Manner of divesting excess shareholding by promoter in certain cases.* 1. No promoter shall at any time hold more than twenty-six per cent or such other percentage as may be prescribed, of the paid-up equity capital in an Indian insurance company:

Provided that in a case where an Indian insurance company beings the business of life insurance, general insurance or re-insurance in which the promoters hold more than twenty-six per cent of the paid-up equity capital or such other excess percentage as may be prescribed, the promoters shall divest in a phased manner the share capital in excess of the twenty-six per cent of the paid-up equity capital or such excess paid-up equity capital as may be prescribed, after a period of ten years from the date of the commencement of the said business by such Indian insurance company or within such period as may be prescribed by the Central Government.

Explanation. For the removal of doubts, it is hereby declared that nothing contained in the proviso shall apply to the promoters being foreign company, referred to in sub-clause (*b*) of clause (7-A) of Section 2.

2. The manner and procedure for divesting the excess share capital under sub-section (1) shall be specified by the regulations made by the Authority.".

12. Section 7,—

(*a*) in sub-section (1),

(*i*) *omit* "not being an insurer specified in sub-clause (*c*) of clause (9) of Section 2";

(*ii*) for clauses (*a*) and (*b*), substitute the following:

"(*a*) in the case of life insurance business, a sum equivalent to one per cent of his total gross premium written in India in any financial year commencing after the 31 st day of March, 2000, not exceeding rupees ten crores;

(*b*) in the case of general insurance business, a sum equivalent to three per cent of his total gross premium written in India, in any financial year commencing after the 31 st day of March, 2000, not exceeding rupees ten crores;

(*c*) in the case of re-insurance business, a sum of rupees twenty crores:";

(*b*) *omit* sub-section (1-A), (I-B), (1-C), (1-D) and (1-E).

13. Section 11

(*a*) in sub-section (1), for "calendar year", *substitute* "financial year";

(*b*) after sub-section (1), *insert* the following:

"(I-A) Notwithstanding anything contained in sub-section (1), every insurer, on or after the commencement of the Insurance Regulatory and Development Authority Act, 1999, in respect of insurance business transacted by him and in respect of his shareholders' funds, shall, at the expiration of each financial year, prepare with reference to that year, a balance sheet, a profit and loss account, a separate account of receipts and payments, a revenue account in accordance with the regulations made by the Authority.

(I-B) Every insurer shall keep separate accounts relating to funds of shareholders and policyholders.".

14. Section 13,

(*a*) in sub-section (1),

(*i*) for "once at least in every three years", substitute "every year";

(*ii*) in the first proviso, for "not later than four years", substitute "not later than two years";

(*iii*) after the second proviso, *insert* the following:

"Provided also that for an insurer carrying on life insurance business in India immediately before the commencement of the Insurance Regulatory and Development Authority Act, 1999, the last date as at which the first investigation after such commencement should be caused by an actuary, shall be the 31st day of March, 2001:";

(*iv*) after the third proviso, *insert* the following:

"Provided also that every insurer on or after the commencement of the Insurance Regulatory and Development Authority Act, 1999, shall cause an abstract of the report of the actuary to be made in the manner specified by the regulations made by the Authority.";

(*b*) in sub-section (4), after the proviso, insert the following:

"Provided further that the statement referred to in sub-section (4) shall be appended in the form and in the manner specified by the regulations made by the Authority .".

15. After Section 27-B, *insert* the following:

"27-C. *Prohibition for investment of funds outside India.* No insurer shall directly or indirectly invest outside India the funds of the policyholders.

27-D. *Manner and conditions of investment.*

1. Without prejudice to anything contained in Sections 27, 27-A and 27-B, the Authority may, in the interests of the policy-holders, specify by the regulations made by it, the time, manner and other conditions of investment of assets to be held by an insurer for the purposes of this Act.
2. The Authority may give specific directions for the time, manner and other conditions subject to which the funds of policyholders shall be invested in the infrastructure and social sector as may be specified by regulations made by the Authority and such regulations shall apply uniformly to all the insurers carrying on the business of life insurance, general insurance, or re-insurance in India on or after the commencement of the insurance Regulatory and Development Authority Act, 1999.
3. The Authority may, after taking into account the nature of business and to protect the interests of the policy-holders, issue to an insurer the directions relating to the time, manner and other conditions of investment of assets to be held by him:

   Provided that no direction under this sub-section shall be issued unless the insurer concerned has been given a reasonable opportunity of being heard.".

16. Section 28-A, in sub-section (1), for "31st day of December", *substitute* "31st day of March".

17. Section 28-B, in sub-section (1), for "31st day of December", *substitute* "31st day of March".

18. Section 31-B,

(*a*) in sub-section (1), for ''Central Government" at both the places where they occur, substitute "Authority";

(*b*) in sub-section (2), for "a statement in the prescribed form", *substitute* "a statement, in the form specified by the regulations made by the Authority,";

(*c*) after sub-section (3), *insert* the following:

"(4) Every direction under this section shall be issued by an order made by the Authority:

Provided that no order under this section shall be made unless the person concerned has been given an opportunity of being heard .".

19. After Section 32-A, *insert* the following:

"32-B. *Insurance business in rural or social sector.* Every insurer shall, after the commencement of the Insurance Regulatory and Development Authority Act, 1999, undertake such percentages of life insurance business and general insurance business in the rural or social sector, as may be specified, in the Official Gazette by the Authority, in this behalf.

32-C. *Obligations of insurer in respect of rural or unorganised sector and backward classes.* Every insurer shall, after the commencement of the Insurance Regulatory and Development Authority Act, 1999, discharge the obligations specified under Section 32-B to provide life insurance or general insurance policies to the persons residing in the rural sector, workers in the unorganised or informal sector or for economically vulnerable or backward classes of the society and other categories of persons as may specified by regulations made by the Authority and such insurance policies shall include insurance for crops.".

20. For Section 33, *substitute* the following:

INVESTIGATION

33. *Power of investigation and inspection by Authority.*

1. The Authority may, at any time, by order in writing, direct any person (thereafter in this section referred to as "Investigating Authority") specified in the order to investigate the affairs of any insurer and to report to the Authority on any investigation made by such Investigating Authority:
   Provided that the Investigating Authority may, wherever necessary, employ any auditor or actuary or both for the purpose of assisting him in any investigation under this section.
2. Notwithstanding anything to the contrary contained in Section 235 of the Companies Act, 1956 (1 of 1956), the Investigating Authority may, at any time, and shall, on being directed so to do by the Authority, cause an inspection to be made by one or more of his officers of any insurer and his books of account; and the Investigating Authority shall supply to the insurer a Copy of his report on such inspection.
3. It shall be the duty of every manager, managing director or other officer of the insurer to produce before the Investigating Authority directed to make the investigation under sub-section (I), or inspection under sub-section (2), all such books of account, registers and other documents in his custody or power and to furnish him with any statement and information relating to the affairs of the insurer as the said Investigating Authority may require of him within such time as the said Investigating Authority may specify.
4. Any Investigating Authority, directed to make an investigation under sub-section (1), or inspection under sub-section (2), may examine on oath, any manager, managing director or other officer of the insurer in relation to his business and may administer oaths accordingly.
5. The Investigating Authority shall, if he has been directed by the Authority to cause an inspection to be made, and may, in any other case, report to the Authority on any inspection made under this section.
6. On receipt of any report under sub-section (1), or sub-section (5), the Authority may, after giving such opportunity to the insurer to make a representation in connection with the report as, in the opinion of the Authority, seems reasonable, by order in writing,

(*a*) require the insurer, to take such action in respect of any matter arising out of the report as the Authority may think fit; or

(*b*) cancel the registration of the insurer; or

(*c*) direct any person to apply to the court for the winding up of the insurer, if a company, whether the registration of the insurer has been cancelled under clause (*b*) or not.

7. The Authority may, after giving reasonable notice to the insurer, publish the report submitted by the Investigating Authority under sub-section (5) or such portion thereof as may appear to it to be necessary.

8. The Authority may by the regulations made by it specify the minimum information to be maintained by insurers in their books, the manner in which such information shall be maintained, the checks and other verifications to be adopted by insurers in that connection and all other matters incidental thereto as are in its opinion, necessary to enable the Investigating Authority to discharge satisfactorily his functions under this section.

Explanation. For the purposes of this section, the expression "insurer" shall include in the case of an insurer incorporated in India

(*a*) all its subsidiaries formed for the purpose of carrying on the business of insurance exclusively outside India; and

(*b*) all its branches whether situated in India or outside India.

9. No order made under this section other than an order made under (*b*) of sub-section clause (6) shall be capable of being called in question in any court.

10. All expenses of 'and incidental to any investigation made under this shall be defrayed by the insurer, shall have priority over that debts due from the insurer and shall be recoverable as an arrear of land revenue.'

21. Section 33-A, *omit* "Central Government or the".

22. Section 34-H,

(*a*) in sub-section (1),

(*i*) for "Controller", *substitute* "Chairperson of the Authority";

(*ii*) for "an Assistant Controller of Insurance", substitute "an officer thorised by the Authority";

(*b*) in sub-section 5. and 7. for "Controller" wherever it occurs, *substitute* "Chairperson of the Authority".

23. Section 35,

(*a*) sub-section (1) for "sanctioned by the Controller", *substitute* "approved by the Authority";

(*b*) in sub-section (3),

(*i*) in the first paragraph for "to sanction any such scheme", substitute "to approve any such scheme";

(*ii*) in the second paragraph, for "the amalgamation or transfer if sanctioned", substitute "the amalgamation or transfer if approved".

24. Section 36,

(*a*) in sub-section (1) for "may sanction the arrangement", *substitute* "may approve the arrangement";

(*b*) in sub-section (2),

(*i*) for "the insurers concerned in the amalgamation, the Controller may sanction", *substitute* "the insurers concerned in the amalgamation, the Authority may approve";

(*ii*) for "contracts as sanctioned by the Controller", *substitute* "contracts as approved by the Authority".

25. Section 37, in clause (*c*), for "scheme sanctioned", *substitute* "scheme approved".

26. In Section 40-A, in sub-section (3), for the portion beginning with the words "an amount exceeding" and ending with the words "ten per cent of the premium payable on the policy", substitute "an amount not exceeding fifteen per cent of the premium payable on the policy where the policy relates to fire or marine insurance or miscellaneous insurance."

27. Section 42,

(*a*) for sub-section (1), *substitute* the following :-

"(1) The Authority or an officer authorised by it in this behalf shall, in the manner determined by the regulations made by it and on payment of the fee determined by the regulations, which shall not be more than two hundred and fifty rupees, issue to any person making an application in the manner determined by the regulations, a licence to act as an insurance agent for the purpose of soliciting or procuring insurance business:

Provided that,

(*i*) in the case of an individual, he does not suffer from any of the disqualifications mentioned in sub-section (4); and

(*ii*) in the case of a company or firm, any of its directors or partners does not suffer from any of the said disqualifications:

Provided further that any licence issued immediately before the commencement of the Insurance Regulatory and Development Authority Act, 1999 shall be deemed to have been issued in accordance with the regulations which provide for such licence.";

(*b*) for sub-section (3), *substitute* the following:

"(3) A licence issued under this section, after the date of the commencement of the Insurance Regulatory and Development Authority Act, 1999, shall remain in force for a period of three years only from the date of issue, but shall, if the applicant, being an individual does not, or being a company or firm any of its directors or partners does not, suffer from any of the disqualifications mentioned in clauses (*b*), (*c*), (*d*), (*e*) and (*f*) of sub-section (4) and the application of renewal of licence reaches the issuing authority at least thirty days before the date on which the licence ceases to remain in force be renewed for a period of three years at anyone time on payment of the fee determined by the regulations made by the Authority which shall not be more than rupees two hundred and fifty, and additional fee of an amount determined by the regulations not exceeding rupees one hundred by way of penalty, if the application for renewal to the licence does not reach the issuing authority at least thirty days before the date on which the licence ceases to remain in force.";

(*c*) in sub-section (3-A), for the proviso, *substitute* the following:

"Provided that the Authority may, if satisfied that undue hardship would be caused otherwise, accept any application in contravention of this sub-section on payment by the applicant of a penalty of seven hundred and fifty rupees.";

(*d*) in sub-section (4), after clause (*d*), insert the following:

"(*e*) that he does not possess the requisite qualifications and practical training for a period not exceeding twelve months, as may be specified by the regulations made by the Authority in this behalf;

(*f*) that he has not passed such examination as may be specified by the regulations made by the Authority in this behalf:

Provided that a person who had been issued a licence under sub-section (1) of this section or sub-section (1) of Section 64-UM shall not be required to possess the requisite qualifications, practical training and pass such examination as required by clauses (*e*) and (*f*);

(*g*) that he violates the code of conduct as may be specified by the regulations made by the Authority.";

(*e*) for sub-section (6), *substitute* the following:

"(6) The Authority may issue a duplicate licence to replace a licence lost, destroyed or mutilated, on payment of such fee not exceeding fifty rupees as may be determined by regulations.";

(*f*) in sub-section (7),

(*i*) for "fifty rupees", *substitute* "five hundred rupees";

(*ii*) for "one hundred rupees", *substitute* "one thousand rupees";

(*g*) in sub-section (8), for "fifty rupees", substitute "five thousand rupees".

28. Section 42-A, in sub-section (1)

(*a*) for "Controller or an officer authorised by him", *substitute* "Authority or an officer authorised by it";

(*b*) for "an application to him", *substitute* "an application to it".

29. After Section 42-C, insert the following:

"42-D. *Issue of licence to intermediary or insurance intermediary.* (1) The Authority or an officer authorised by it in this behalf shall, in the manner determined by the regulations made by the Authority, and on payment of the fees determined by the regulations made by the Authority, issue to any person making an application in the manner determined by the regulations, and not suffering from any of the disqualifications herein mentioned, a licence to act as an intermediary or an insurance intermediary under this Act:

Provided that,

(*a*) in the case of an individual, he does not suffer from any of the disqualifications mentioned in sub-section (4) of Section 42, or

(*b*) in the case of a company or firm, any of its directors or partners does not suffer from any of the said disqualifications.

2. A licence issued under this section shall entitle the holder thereof to act as an intermediary or insurance intermediary.

3. A licence issued under this section shall remain of force for a period of three years only from the date of issue, but shall, if the applicant, being an individual does not, or being a company or firm any of its directors or partners does not suffer from any of the disqualifications mentioned in clauses (*b*), (*c*), (*d*), (*e*) and (*f*) of sub-section (4) of Section 42 and the application for renewal of licence reaches the issuing authority at least thirty days before the date on which the licence ceases to remain in force, be renewed for a period of three years at anyone time on payment of the fee, determined by the regulations made by the Authority and additional fee for an amount determined by the regulations, not exceeding one hundred rupees by way of penalty, if the application for renewal of the licence does not reach the issuing authority at least thirty days before the date on which the licence ceases to remain in force.

4. No application for the renewal of a licence under this section shall be entertained if the application does not reach the issuing authority before the licence ceases to remain in force:

Provided that the Authority may, if satisfied that undue hardship would be caused otherwise, accept any application in contravention of this sub-section on payment by the applicant of a penalty of seven hundred and fifty rupees.

5. The disqualifications above referred to shall be the following:

(*a*) that the person is a minor;

(*b*) that he is found to be of unsound mind by a court of competent jurisdiction;

(*c*) that he has been found guilty of criminaless appropriation or criminal breach of trust or cheating or forgery or an abetment of or attempt to commit any such offence by a court of competent jurisdiction:

Provided that, where at least five years have elapsed since the completion of the sentence imposed do any person in respect of any such offence, the Authority shall ordinarily declare in respect of such person that his conviction shall cease to operate as a disqualification under this clause;

(*d*) that in the course of any judicial proceeding relating to any policy of insurance of the winding up of an insurance company or in the course of an investigation of the affairs of an insurer it has been found that he has been guilty of or has knowingly participated in or connived at any fraud dishonestly or misrepresentation against an Insurer or an insured;

(*e*) that he does not possess the requisite qualifications and practical training for a period not exceeding twelve months, as may be specified by the regulations made by the Authority in this behalf;

(*f*) that he has not passed such examinations as may be specified by the regulations made by the Authority in this behalf;

(*g*) that he violates the code of conduct as may be specified by the regulations made by the Authority.

6. If it be found that an intermediary or an insurance intermediary suffers from any of the foregoing disqualifications, without prejudice to any other penalty to which be may be liable, the Authority shall, and if the intermediary or an insurance intermediary has knowingly contravened any provision of this Act may cancel the licence issued to the intermediary or insurance intermediary under this section.

7. The Authority may issue a duplicate licence to replace a licence lost, destroyed or mutilated, on payment of such fee, as may be determined by the regulations made by the Authority.

8. Any person who acts as an intermediary or an insurance intermediary without holding a licence issued under this section to act as such, shall be punishable with fine, and my insurer or any person not licensed to act as such or transacts any insurance business in India through any such person, shall be punishable with fine.

9. Where the person contravening sub-section 8 is a company or a firm, then without prejudice to any other proceedings which may be taken against the company or firm, every director, manager, secretary or other officer of the company, and every partner of the firm who is knowingly a party to such contravention shall be punishable with fine.".

30. Section 64-UA, in sub-section (1), in sub-clause (*a*), for "Controller of Insurance", *substitute* "Chairperson of the *Authority*".

31. Section 64-UB

(*a*) for sub-section (1) *substitute* the following:

"(1) The Authority may, by notification in the Official Gazette, make regulations to carry out the purposes of this part.";

(*b*) in sub-section (2), for "*rules*", *substitute* "regulations";

(*c*) in sub-section (3), for "Central Government" at both the places where it occur, *substitute* "Authority';

(*d*) in sub-section (5), for "Controller of Insurance", *substitute* "Chairperson of the Authority".

32. Section. 64-UC, in sub-section (1), in proviso, for "the Controller may, with the previous approval of the Central Government", *substitute* "the Authority may".

33. Section 64-UD, after sub-section (1), *insert* the following:

"Provided that the Chairperson of the Authority shall become the Chairman of the Advisory Committee with effect from the commencement of the Insurance Regulatory and Development Authority Act, 1999 and function as such, and any Chairman of the Tariff Committee holding office immediately before such commencement shall cease to be the Chairman."

34. Section 64-UJ, in sub-section (5), for "Central Government", wherever it occurs, *substitute* "Authority".

35. Section 64-UM

(*a*) in sub-section (1),

(*i*) in paragraph (B), after "the Insurance (Amendment) Act, 1968", *insert* "but before the commencement of the Insurance Regulatory and Development Authority Act, 1999";

(*ii*) after paragraph (B), insert the following:

"(B-A) Every person who intends to act as a surveyor or loss assessor after the expiry of a period of one year from the commencement of the Insurance Regulatory and Development Authority Act, 1999, shall make an application to the Authority within such time, in such manner and on payment of such fee as may be determined by the regulations made by the Authority:

Provided that any licence issued immediately before the commencement of the Insurance Regulatory and Development Authority Act, 1999 shall be deemed to have been issued in accordance with the regulations providing for such licence.";

(*iii*) in paragraph (C), for "as may be prescribed", *substitute* "as may be determined by the regulations";

(*iv*) in paragraph (D), in clause (*i*),

(A) for item (*a*), *substitute* the following:

"(*a*) has been in practice as a surveyor or loss assessor on the date of commencement of the Insurance Regulatory and Development Authority Act, 1999, or";

(B) in item (*f*), for "prescribed", *substitute* "specified by the regulations made by the Authority";

(*b*) after sub-section (l), *insert*

"(I-A) Every surveyor and loss assessor shall comply with the code of conduct in respect of their duties, responsibilities and other professional requirements as may be specified by the regulations made by the Authority:".

36. Section 64-V,

(*a*) in sub-section (1),

(*i*) in clause (*i*), after sub-clause (*g*), insert the following:

"(*h*) such other asset or assets as may be specified by the regulations made in this behalf;";

(*ii*) in clause (*ii*),

(A) in sub-clause (*b*), in items (*i*) and (*ii*), for "40 per cent", *substitute* "50 per cent";

(B) after sub-clause (*t*), insert the following:

"(*g*) such other liability which may be made in this behalf to be included for the purpose of clause (*ii*).";

(*b*) for sub-section (2), *substitute* the following:

2. Every insurer shall furnish to the Authority with his returns under Section 15 or Section 16, as the case may be, a statement certified by an auditor approved by the Authority in respect of general insurance business, or an actuary approved by the Authority in respect of life insurance business, as the case may be, of his assets and liabilities assessed in the manner required by this section as on the 31st day of March of the preceding year.

3. Every insurer shall value his assets and liabilities in the manner required by this section and in accordance with the regulations which may be made by the Authority in this behalf.".

37. Section 64-VA,

(*a*) in sub-section (1), for "at all times", *substitute* "at all times before the commencement of the Insurance Regulatory and Development Authority Act, 1999";

(*b*) after sub-section (1), *insert* the following:

'(I-A) Every insurer shall, at all times, on or after the commencement of the Insurance Regulatory and Development Authority Act, 1999, maintain an excess of the value of his assets over the amount of his liabilities of not less than the amount arrived at as follows (hereinafter referred to in this section referred to as the "required solvency margin"), namely:

(*i*) in the case of an insurer carrying on life insurance business, the required solvency margin shall be the higher of the following amounts

(*a*) fifty crores of rupees (one hundred crores of rupees in case of re-insurers); or

(*b*) the aggregate sums of the results arrived at in items (I) and (II) stated below:

(I) the aggregate of the results arrived at by applying the calculation described in item (A) below (Step I) and the calculation described in item (B) below (Step II):

(A) for Step 1

(A.1) there shall be taken, a sum equal to a percentage determined by the regulations not exceeding five per cent of the mathematical reserves for direct business and reinsurance acceptances without any deduction for re-insurance cessions;

(A.2) the amount of mathematical reserves at the end of the preceding financial year after the deduction of reinsurance cessions shall be expressed as a percentage of the amount of those mathematical reserves before any such deduction; and

(A.3) the sum mentioned in item (A.1) above shall be multiplied;

(A.3.l) where the percentage arrived at under item (A.2) above is greater then eighty-five per cent (or in the case of a reinsurer carrying on exclusive re-insurance business, fifty per cent), by that greater percentage; and

(A.3.2) in any other case, by eighty-five per cent (or in the case of a re-insurer carrying on exclusive reinsurance business, by fifty per cent);

(B) for Step II

(B. 1) there shall be taken, a sum equal to a percentage determined by the regulations made by the Authority not exceeding one per cent of the sum at risk for the policies on which the sum at risk is not a negative figure, and

(B.2) the amount of sum at risk at the end of the preceding financial year for policies on which the sum at risk is not a negative figure after the deduction of reinsurance cession shall be expressed as a percentage of the amount of that sum at risk before any such deduction, and

(B.3) the sum arrived at under item (B.I) above shall be multiplied

(B.3.1) where the percentage arrived at under item (B.2) above is greater than fifty Per cent, by that greater percentage; and

(B.3.2) in any other case, by fifty per cent.

(II) a percentage determined by the regulations made by the Authority of the value of assets determined in accordance with the provisions of Section 64- V;

(*ii*) in the case of an insurer carrying on general insurance business, the required solvency margin, shall be the highest of the following amounts:

(*a*) fifty crores of rupees (one hundred crores of rupees in case of reinsurer); or

(*b*) a sum equivalent to twenty per cent of net premium income; or

(*c*) a sum equivalent to thirty per cent of net incurred claims, subject to credit for re-insurance in computing net premiums and net incurred claims being actual but a percentage, determined by the regulation, not exceeding fifty per cent:

Provided that if in respect of any insurer, the Authority is satisfied that either by reason of an unfavourable claim experience or because of sharp increase in the volume of the business, or for any other reason, compliance with the provisions of this sub-section would cause undue hardship to the insurer, the Authority may direct, for such period and subject to such conditions, such solvancy margin not being less than the lower of the amount mentioned in sub-clause (*i*) or sub-clause (*ii*) above, as the case may be.

Explanation. For the purposes of this sub-section, the expressions

(*i*) "mathematical reserves" means the provision made by an insurer to cover liabilities (excluding liabilities which have fallen due and liabilities arising from deposit back arrangement in relation to any policy whereby an amount is deposited by re-insurer with the cedant) arising under or in connection with the policies or contracts for life insurance business. Mathematical reserves also include specific provision for adverse deviations of the bases, such as mortality and morbidity rates, interest rates, and expense rates, and any explicit provisions made, in the valuation of liabilities, in accordance with the regulations made by the Authority for this purpose;

(*ii*) "net incurred claims" means the average of the net incurred claims during the specified period of not exceeding three preceding financial years;

(*iii*) "sum at risk", in relation to a life insurance policy, means a sum which is

(*a*) in any case in which an amount is payable in consequence of death other than a case falling within sub-clause (*b*) below, the amount payable on death, and

(*b*) in any case in which the benefit under the policy in question consists of the making, in consequence of death, of the payments of annuity, payment of a sum by installments or any other kind of periodic payments, the present value of that benefit, less in either case the mathematical reserve in respect of the relevant policies.";

(*c*) after sub-section (2), *insert* the following:

"(2-A) If, at any time an insurer does not maintain the required solvency margin in accordance with the provisions of this section, he shall, in accordance with the directions issued by the Authority, submit a financial plan, indicating a plan of action to correct the deficiency to the Authority within a specified period not exceeding three months.

(2-B) An insurer who has submitted a plan under sub-section (2-A) to the Authority shall propose modifications to the plan if the Authority considers it inadequate, and shall give effect to any plan accepted by the Authority as adequate.

(2-C) An insurer who does not comply with the provisions of sub-section (2-A) shall be deemed to be insolvent and may be wound up by the court.";

(*d*) after sub-section (6), *insert* the following:

7. Every insurer shall furnish to the Authority his returns under Section 15 or Section 16, as the case may be, in case of life insurance business a statement certified by an actuary approved by the Authority, and in case of general insurance business a statement certified by an auditor approved by the Authority, of the required solvency margin maintained by the insurer in the manner required by sub-section (I-A).".

38. Section 70, in sub-section (1), for "the Controller a certificate of registration", *substitute* "the Authority, before the date of commencement of the Insurance Regulatory and Development Authority Act, 1999, a certificate of registration".

39. Section 95, in sub-section (1), for "In this Part-", *substitute*, "In this Part, before the date of commencement of the Insurance Regulatory and Development Authority Act, 1999."

40. Section 101-A,

(*a*) in sub-section (1), for "the Central Government", substitute "the Authority, with the previous approval of the Central Government,";

(*b*) in sub-section (2), for "the Central Government", substitute "the Authority".

41. Section 101-B,

(*a*) in sub-section (1), for "the Central Government", *substitute* "the Authority with the previous approval of the Central Government.';

(*b*) in sub-section (2), for "prescribed"; substitute "determined by the regulations made by the Authority".

42. For Sections 102 to 105, *substitute* the following:

102. *Penalty for default in complying with, or act in contravention of, this Act*. If any person, who is required under this Act, or rules or regulations made thereunder,

(*a*) to furnish any document, statement, account, return or report to the Authority, fails to furnish the same; or

(*b*) to comply with the directions, fails to comply with such directions;

(*c*) to maintain solvency margin, fails to maintain such solvency margin;

(*d*) to comply with the directions on the insurance treaties, fails to comply with such directions on the insurance treaties, he shall be liable to a penalty not exceeding five lakh rupees for each such failure and punishable with fine.

103. *Penalty for carrying on insurance business in contravention of Sections* 3, 7 and 98. If a person makes a statement, or furnishes any document, statement, account, return or report which is false and which he either knows or believes to be false or does not belief to be true,

(*a*) he shall be liable to a penalty not exceeding five lakh rupees for each such failure; and

(*b*) he shall be punishable with imprisonment which may extend to three years or with fine for each such failure.

104. *Penalty for false statement in document.* If a person falls to comply with the provisions of Section 27 or Section 27-A or Section 27-B or Section 27-C or Section 27-D, he shall be liable to a penalty not exceeding five lakh rupees for each such failure.

105. *Wrongfully obtaining or withholding property.* If any director, managing director, manager or other officer or employee of an insurer wrongfully obtains possession of any property or wrongfully applies to any purpose of the Act, he shall be liable to a penalty not exceeding two lakh rupees for each such failure.

105-A. *Offences by companies.* (l) Where any offence under this Act has been committed by a company, every person who, at the time the offence was committed, was in charge of, and was responsible to, the company for the conduct of the business of the company as well as the company shall be deemed to be guilty of the offence and shall liable to be proceeded against and punished accordingly:

Provided that nothing contained in this sub-section shall render any such person liable to any punishment, if he proves that the offence was committed without his knowledge or that he had exercised all due diligence to prevent the commission of such offence.

2. Notwithstanding anything contained in sub-section (1) where any offence under this Act has been committed by a company and it is proved that the offence has been committed with the consent or connivance of, or is attributable to any neglect on the part of, any director, manager, secretary or other officer of the company, such director, manager, secretary or other officer shall be deemed to be guilty of that offence and shall be liable to be proceeded against and punished accordingly.

Explanation. For the purposes of this Section,

(*a*) "company". means any body corporate, and includes

(*i*) a firm; and

(*ii*) association of persons or a body of individuals whether incorporated or not; and

(*b*) "director", in relation to

(*i*) a firm, means a partner in the firm;

(*ii*) an association of persons or a body of individuals, means any member controlling the affairs thereof.

105-B. *Penalty for failure to comply with Section-32-B.* If an insurer fails to comply with the provisions of Section 32-B, he shall be liable to a penalty not exceeding five lakh rupees for each such failure and shall be punishable with imprisonment which may extend to three years or with fine for each such failure.

105-C. *Penalty for failure to comply with Section 32-G.* If an insurer fails to comply with the provisions of Section 32-C, he shall be liable to a penalty not exceeding twenty-five lakh rupees for each such failure and in the case of subsequent and continuing failure, the registration granted to such insurer under Section 3 shall be cancelled by the Authority.".

43. In Sections 110-A, 110-B and 110-C, for "Controller" wherever it occurs, *substitute* "Chairperson of the Authority".

44. In Sections 110-G, for "Controller" at both the places where it occurs, *substitute* "Chairperson of the Authority".

45. Section 100-H, in sub-section (l), for "under sections", *substitute* "under sections 27-D.".

46. Section 114, in sub-section (2).

(*a*) after clause (*a*), *insert* the following:

"(aa) such other percentage of paid-up equity capital in excess of twenty-six per cent of the paid-up equity capital and the period within which such excess paid-up equity capital shall be divested under sub-section (1) of Section 6-AA.";

(*b*) omit clauses (*g*) and (II).

47. After Section 114, *insert* the following:

114-A. *Power of Authority to make regulations.* (l) Authority may, by notification in the Official Gazette, make regulations consistent with this Act and the rules made thereunder, to carry out the purposes of this Act.

2. In particular, and without prejudice to the generality of the foregoing power, such regulations may provide for all or any of the following matters, namely:—

(*a*) the matters including fee relating to the registration of insurers under Section 3;

(*b*) the manner of suspension or cancellation of registration under sub-section (5-E) of Section 3;

(*c*) such fee, not exceeding five thousand rupees, as may be determined by the regulations for issue of a duplicate certificate of registration under sub-section (7) of Section 3;

(*d*) the matters relating to the renewal of registration and fee therefor under Section 3-A;

(*e*) the manner and procedure for divesting excess share capital under sub-section (2) of Section 6-AA;

(*f*) the preparation of balance sheet, profit and loss account and a separate account of receipts and payments and revenue account under sub-section (1-A) of Section 11;

(*g*) the manner in which an abstract of the report of the actuary to be specified under the fourth proviso to sub-section (1) of Section 13;

(*h*) the form and manner in which the statement referred to in subsection (4) of Section 13 shall be appended;

(*i*) the time, manner and other conditions of investment of assets held by an insurer under sub-section (1), (2) and (3) of Section 27-D;

(*j*) the minimum information to be maintained by insurer in their books the manner in which such information should be maintained, the checks and other verifications to be adopted by insurers in that connection and all other matters incidental thereto under sub-section (8) of Section 33;

(*k*) the manner for making an application, the manner and the fee for issue of a licence to, act as an insurance agent under sub-section (1) of Section 42;

(*l*) the fee and the additional fee to be determined for renewal of licence of insurance agent under sub-section (3) of Section 42;

(*m*) the requisite qualifications and practical training to act as an insurance agent under clause (*e*) of sub-section (4) of Section 42;

(*n*) the passing of examination to act as an insurance agent under clause (f) of sub-section (4) of Section 42;

(*o*) the code of conduct under Clause (*g*) of sub-section (4) of Section 42;

(*p*) the fee not exceeding rupees fifty for issue of duplicate licence under sub-section (6) of Section 42;

(*q*) the manner and the fees for issue of a licence to an intermediary or an insurance intermediary under sub-section (1) of Section 42-D;

(*r*) the fee and the additional fee to be determined for renewal of licence of intermediaries or insurance intermediaries under subsection (3) of Section 42-D;

(*s*) the requisite qualifications and practical training of intermediaries or insurance intermediaries under clause (*e*) of sub-section (5) of Section 42-D;

(*t*) the examination to be passed to act as an intermediary or insurance intermediary under clause (*f*) of sub-section (5) of Section 42-D;

(*u*) the code of conduct under clause(*g*) of sub-section (5) of Section 42-D;

(*v*) the fee for issue of duplicate licence under sub-section (7) of Section 42-D;

(*w*) such matters as specified under sub-section (2) of Section 64-UB relating to the Tariff Advisory Committee;

(*x*) the matters relating to licensing of surveyors and loss assessors, their duties, responsibilities and other professional requirements under Section 64-UM;

(*y*) such other asset or assets as may be specified under clause (*h*) of sub-section (1) of Section 64-V for the purposes of ascertaining sufficiency of assets under Section 64-V A;

(*z*) the valuation of assets and liabilities under sub-section (3) of Section 64-V;

(*za*) the matters specified under sub-section (1-A) of Section 64-VA relating to sufficiency of assets;

(*zb*) the matters relating to re-insurance under Sections 101-A and 101-B;

(*zc*) the matters relating to redressal of grievances of policy-holders to protect their interest and to regulate, promote and ensure orderly growth of insurance industry; and

(*zd*) any other matter which is to be, or may be, specified by the regulations made of the Authority or in respect of which provision is to be made or may be made by the regulations.

3. Every regulation made under this Act shall be laid, as soon as may be after it is made, before each House of Parliament, while it is in session, for a total period of thirty days which may be comprised in one session or in two or more successive sessions, and if, before the expiry of the session immediately following the session or the successive sessions aforesaid, both Houses agree in making any modification in the regulation or both Houses agree that the regulation should not be made, the regulation shall thereafter, have effect only in such modified form or be of no effect, as the case may be; so, however, that any such modification or annulment shall be without prejudice to the validity of anything previously done under that regulation."

48. Section I 16-A, for "Central Government", at both places where they occur, *substitute* "Central Government, before the date of commencement of the Insurance Regulatory and Development Authority Act, 1999".

The Second Schedule

(*See Section 31*)

Amendments to the Life Insurance Corporation Act, 1956 (31 of 1956)

1. In the Act, for "Controller" wherever it occurs, *substitute* "Authority".
2. After Section 30, insert the following:—

"30-A. *Exclusive privilege of Corporation to cease*—Notwithstanding anything contained in this Act, the exclusive privilege of carrying on life insurance business in India by the Corporation shall cease on and from the commencement of the Insurance Regulatory and Development Authority Act, 1999 and the Corporation shall, thereafter, carry on life insurance business in India in accordance with the provisions of the Insurance Act, 1938 (4 of 1938).".

The Third Schedule

(*See Section 32*)

Amendment to the General Insurance Business (Nationalisation) Act, 1972 (57 of 1972)

After Section 24, *insert* the following:—

"24-A. *Exclusive privilege of Corporation and acquiring companies to cease.*—Notwithstanding anything contained in this Act, the exclusive privilege of the Corporation and the acquiring companies of carrying on general insurance business in India shall cease on and from the commencement of the Insurance Regulatory and Development Authority Act, 1999 and the Corporation and the acquiring companies shall, thereafter, carry on general insurance business in India in accordance with the provisions of the Insurance Act, 1938 (4 of 1938)."

Insurance Regulatory and Development Authority (obligations of insurers to rural or social sectors) Regulations, 2000.

(In exercise of the powers conferred by section 32C read with section 32B of the Insurance Act, 1938 (4 of 1938), the Authority in consultation with the Insurance Advisory Committee, hereby, markes the following regulation, namely:—

Short title and Commencement

1. 1. These regulations may be called the Insurance Regulatory and Development Authority (obligation of Insurers to Rural or Social Sectors) Regulations, 2000.
   2. They shall come into force from the date of their publications in the official gazette.

Definitions:

2. In these regulations, unless the context otherwise requires:
   (*a*) "Act" means the Insurance Act, 1938 (4 of 1938);
   (*b*) "Authority" means the Insurance Regulatory and Development Authority Act, 1999 (41 of 1999),
   (*c*) Rural Sector shall mean any place as per the latest census which has—
   (*i*) a population of not more than five thousand
   (*ii*) a density of population of not more than four hundred per square kilometer, and
   (*iii*) at least seventy five per cent of the male working population is engaged in agriculture.
   (*d*) "Social Sector" includes unorganised sector, informal sector, economically vulnerable or backward classes and other categories of persons, both in rural and urban areas.
   (*e*) "unorganised sector" includes self employed workers such as agricultural labourers, bill wokers, brick kiln workers, carpenters, cobblers, construction workers, fisherman, hamals, handicraft, artisans, handloom and khadi workers, lady tailors, leather and tannery workers, papad makers, powerloom workers, physically handicapped self employed persons, primary milk producers rickshaw puller, safai karmacharis, salt growers, sericulture workers, sugarcane cutters, tendu leaf colectors, toddy tappers, vegetable vendors, washer women, workilg women in hills, or such other categories of persons.
   (*f*) "economically vulnerable or backward classes" means persons who live below the poverty line.
   (*g*) "other categories of persons" includes person with disability as defined in the persons with Disabilities (equal opportunities protection of Right and full Participation) Act, 1995 ,and who may not be gainfully employed and also includes guardians who need insurance to protect spastic persons or persons with disability.
   (*h*) All words and expressions used herein and not defined herein but defined in the Insurance Act, 1938 (4 of 1938) or in the Insurance Regulatory and Development Authority Act, 1999 (41 of 1999) shall have the meanings respectively assigned them in those Acts.

Obligations:

3. Every insurer who begins to carryon insurance business after the commencement of Insurance Regulatory and Development Authority Act, 1999 (41 of 1999), shall for the purposes of Section 32B and 32C of the Act, ensure that he undertakes the following obligations, during the first five financial years, pertaining to the persons in—

(*a*) Rural Sector

(*i*) in respect of a life insurer:

(I) five per cent in the first financial year;

(II) seven per cent in the second financial year;
(III) ten per cent in the third financial year;
(IV) twelve per cent in the fourth financial year;
(V) fifteen per cent in the fifth year;
of total policies, written direct in that year;

(*ii*) in respect of a general insurer:
(I) two per cent in the first financial year;
(II) three per cent in the second financial year;
(III) five per cent thereafter;
of total gross premium income written direct in that year;

(*b*) Social sector, in respect of all insurers;
(I) five thousand lives in the first financial year;
(II) seven thousand five hundred lives in the second financial year;
(III) ten thousand lives in the third financial year;
(IV) fifteen thousand lives in the fourth financial year;
(V) twenty thousand lives in the fifth year.

Provided that in the first financial year where the period of operation is less than twelve months, proportionate percentage or number of lives as the case may be, shall be undertaken.

Provided further that in case of a general insurers, the obligations specified shall include insurance for crops.

Provided further that the Authority may normally, once in every five years, prescribe or revise the obligations as specified in Regulations 3.

Obligations of Existing Insurers

4. 1. The obligations of existing insurers as on the date of commencement of IRDA Act shall be decided by the Authority after consultation with them and the quantum of insurance business to be done shall not be less than what has been recorded by them for the accounting year ended 31st Marct 2000.
2. The Authority shall review such quantum of insurance business periodically and give directions to the insurers for achieving the specified targets.

INSURANCE REGULATORY AND DEVELOPMENT AUTHORITY (OBLIGATIONS OF INSURERS TO RURAL OR SOCIAL SECTORS) REGULATIONS, 2000

In exercise of the powers conferred by section 32C, read with section 32B of the Insurance Act, 1938 (4 of 1938) the Authority, in consultation with the Insurance Advisory Committee, hereby makes the following regulations, namely:—

Short title and commencement

1. 1. These regulations may be called the Insurance Regulatory and Development Authority (Obligations of Insurers to Rural or Social Sectors) Regulations, 2000.
2. They shall come into force from the date of their publication in the Official Gazette.

Definitions

2. In these regulations, unless the context otherwise requires.

Gazette No. 102, Extra ordinary dated 19-7-2000.

(*a*) "Act" means the Insurance Act, 1938 (4 of 1938);

(*b*) "Authority" means the Insurance Regulatory and Development Authority established under the provisions of section 3 of the Insurance Regulatory and Development Authority Act, 1999 (41 of 1999);

(*c*) "Rural sector" shall mean any place as per the latest census which has:—

(*i*) a population of not more than five thousand;

(*ii*) a density of populatin of not more than four hundred per square kilometer; and

(*iii*) at least seventy-five per cent of the male working population is engaged in agriculture.

(*d*) "Social sector" includes unorganised sector, informal sector, economically vulnerable or backward classes and other categories of persons, both in rural and urban areas;

(*e*) "Unorganised sector" includes self-employed workers such as agricultutral labourers, bidi workers, brick kiln workers, carpenters, cobblers, construction workers, fishermen, hamals, handicraft artisans, handloom and khadi workers, physically handicapped selfemployed persons, primary milk producers, rickshaw pullers, safaikarmacharis, salt growers, seri-culture workers, sugarcane cutters, tendu leaf collectors, toddy tappets, vegetable vendors, washerwomen, working women in hills, or such other categories of persons:

(*f*) "economically vulnerable or backward classes" means persons who live below the poverty line;

(*g*) "other categories of person" includes persons with disability as defined in the Persons with Disabilities (Equal Opportunities, Protection of Rights and Full Participation) Act, 1995 and who may not be gainfully employed; and also includes guardians who need insurance to protect spastic persons or person with disabifity;

(*h*) All words and expressions used herein and not defined herein but defined in the Insurance Act, 1938 (4 of 1938), or in the Insurance Regulatory and Development Authority Act, 1999 (41 of 1999), shall have the meanings respectively assigned to them in those Acts.

Obligations.

3. Every insurer, who begins to carry on insurance business after the commencement of the Insurance Regulatory and Development Authority Act, 1999 (41 of 1999), shall, for the purposes of section 32B and 32C of the Act, insure that he undertakes the following obligations, during the first five financial years, pertaining to the persons in.

(*a*) Rural sector,

(*i*) in respect of a life insurer,

(I) five per cent in the first financial year;

(II) seven per cent in the second financial year;

(III) ten percent in the third financial year;

(IV) twelve percent in the fourth financial year;

(V) fifteen percent in the fifth year;

of total policIes written direct in that year;

(*ii*) in respect of a general insurer;

(I) two per cent in the first financial year;

(II) three per cent in the second financial year;

(III) five per cent thereafter,

of total gross premium income written direct in that year.

(*b*) social sector, in respect of all insurers,

(I) five thousand Fives in the first financial year;

(II) seven thousand five hundred lives in the second financial year;

(III) ten thousand lives in the third financial year;

(IV) fifteen thousand lives in the fourth financial year;

(V) twenty thousand lives in the fifth year;

Provided that in the first financial year, where the period of operation is less than twelve months, proportionate percentage or number of lives, as the case may be, shall be undertaken, Provided further that, in case of a general insurer, the obligations specified shall include insurance for crops.

Provided further that the Authority may normally, once in every five years, prescribe or revise the obligations as specified in Regulation 3.

Obligations of existing insurers

4. 1. The obligations of existing insurers as on the date of commencement of IRDA Act shall be decided by the Authority after consultation with them and the quantum of insurance business to be done shall not be less than what has been recorded by them for the accounting year ended 31st March, 2000.

2. The Authority shall review such quantum of insurance business periodically and give directions to the insurers for achieving the specified targets.

INSURANCE REGULATORY AND DEVELOPMENT AUTHORITY (INSURANCE ADVERTISEMENTS AND DISCLOSURE) REGULATIONS, 2000

In exercise of the powers conferred by section 26 of the Insurance Regulatory and Development Authority Act, 1999 (41 of 1999), the Authority in consultation with the Insurance Advisory Comittee, hereby makes the following regulations, namely:—

1. Short title and commencement.

1. These regulations may be called the Insurance Regulatory and Development Atithority (Insurance Advertisements and Disclosure) Regulations, 2000.

2. Definitions. Unless the context otherwise requires:

(*a*) "Authority" means the Insurance Regulatory and Development Authority established under sub-section (1) of section 3 of the Insurance Regulatory and Development Authority Act, 1999 (41 of 1999);

(*b*) "Insurance advertisement" means and includes any communication directly or indirectly related to a policy and intended to result in the eventual sale or solicitation of a policy from the members of the public, and shall include all forms of printed and published materials or any material using the print and or electronic medium for public communication such as:

(*i*) newspapers, magazines and sales talks;

(*ii*) billboards, hoardings, panels;

(*iii*) radio, television, website, e-mail, portals;

(*iv*) representations by intermediaries;

(*v*) leaflets;

(*vi*) descriptive literature/circulars;

(*vii*) sales aids flyers;

Gazette No. 102, Extra ordinary dated 19-7-2000.

(*viii*) illustration form letters;

(*ix*) telephone solicitations;

(*x*) business cards;

(*xi*) videos;

(*xii*) faxes; or

(*xiii*) any other communication with a prospect or a policyholder that urges him to purchase, renew, increase, retain or modify a policy of insurance.

Explanation. The following materials shall not be considered to be an advertisement provided they are not used to induce the purchase, increase, modification or retention of a policy of insurance:—

(*i*) materials used by an insurance company within its own organisation and not meant for distribution to the public;

(*ii*) communications with policyholders other than materials urging them to purchase, increase, modify,

(*iii*) materials used solely for the training, recruitment and education of an insurer's personnel, intermediaries, counselors and solicitors, provided they are not used to induce the public to prrchase, increase, modify or retain a policy of insurance;

(*iv*) any general announcement sent by a group policyholder to members of the eligible group that a policy has been written or arranged.

(c) "intermediary or insurance intermediary" includes insurance brokers, reinsurance brokers, insurance consultants, surveyors and loss assessors, or any other person representing or assisting an insurer in one or more of the following:

(*i*) soliciting, negotiating, procuring or effectuating an insurance contract or a renewal of an insurance contnct;

(*ii*) disseminating information relating to coverage or rates;

(*iii*) forwarding an insurance application;

(*iv*) servicing and delivering an insurance policy or contract;

(*v*) inspecting a risk;

(*vi*) setting a rate;

(*vii*) investigating or assessing a claim or loss;

(*viii*) transacting a matter after the effectuation of a contract; or

(*ix*) representing or assisting an insurance or other person in any other manner in the transaction of insurance with respect to a subject of insurance resident, located or to be performed in India;

(*x*) servicing a policy or contract;

(*d*) "unfair or misleading advertisement" will mean and include any advertisement:

(*i*) that fails to clearly identify the product as hsurance;

(*ii*) makes claims beyond the ability of the policy to deliver or beyond the reasonable expectation of performance;

(*iii*) describes benefits that do not match the poley provisions;

uses words or phrases in a way which hides or minimizes the costs of the hazard insured against or the risks inherent in the policy;

omits to disclose or discloses insufficiently, important exclusions, limitations and conditions of the contract;

gives information in a misleading way;

illustrates future benefits or assumptions which are not realistic nor realisable in the light of the insurer's current performance.

where the benefits are not guaranteed, does not explicitly say so as prominently as the benefits are stated or says so in a manner or form that it could remain unnoticed;

implies a group or other relationship like sponsorship, affiliation or approval, that does not exist;

makes unfair or incomplete comparisons with products which are not comparable or disparages competitors.

(*e*) "prospect" means any party that enters or proposes to enter into an insurance contract directly, or through an insurance intermediary.

Words and expressions used and not defined in these regulations but defined in the Insurance Act, 1938 (4 of 1938), or the Life Insurance Corporation Act, 1956 (31 of 1956) or the General Insurance Business Nationalisation Act, 1972 (57 of 1972), or Insurance Regulatory and Development Authority Act, 1999 (41 of 1999) shall have the meanings respectively assigned to them in those Acts or the rules as the case may be.

3. Compliance and control

1. Every insurer or intermediary or insurance agent shall—

(*i*) have a compliance officer, whose name and official position in the organisation shall be communicated to the Authority, and he shall be responsible to oversee the advertising programme;

(*ii*) establish and maintain a system of control over the content, form, and method of dissemination of all advertisements concerning its policies;

(*iii*) maintain an advertising register at its corporate office which much include;

(*a*) a specimen of every advertisement disseminated, or issued or a record of any broadcast or telecast, etc.;

(*b*) a notation attached to each advertisement indicating the manner, extent of distribution and form number of any policy advertised; and

(*iv*) maintain a specimen of all advertisements for a minimum period of three years;

(*v*) file a copy of each advertisement with the Authority as soon as it is first issued, together with information:

(*a*) an identifying number for the advertisement;

(*b*) the form number (s) of the policy(ies) advertised and when the product/s were approved by the Authority;

(*c*) a description of the advertisement and how it is used;

(*d*) the method or media used for dissemination of the advertisement;

(*vi*) file a certificate of compliance with their annual statement stating that, to the best of its knowledge, advertisement disseminated by the insurer or by its intermediaries during the preceding year have complied with the provisions of these regulations an the advertisement code as stated in regulation 12.

2. The advertisement register shall be subject to inspection and review by the Authority for content, context, prominance and position of required disclosure, omissions of required information, etc.

4. Changes in advertisement.

1. Any change in an advertisement would be considered a new advertisement.

2. All the provisions of regulation 3 shall apply mutatis mutandis to an advertisement referred to in sub-regulations (1).
3. The Authority shall be informed at the time of filing the advertisement the extent of change the original advertisement.

5. Insurance company advertisement.

1. Every insurance company shall be required to prominently disclose in the advertisement and that part of the advertisement that is required to be returned to the company or insurance intermediary or insurance agent by a prospect or an insured the full particulars of the insurance company, and not merely any trade name or monogram or logo.
2. Where benefits are more that briefly described, the form number of the policy and the type of coverage shall be disclosed fully.

6. Advertisement by insurance agents.

1. Every advertisement by an insurance agent that affects an insurer must be approved by the insurer in writing prior to its issue.
2. It shall be the responsibility of the insurer while granting such approval to ensure that all advertisements that pertain to the company or its products or performance comply with these regulations and are not deceptive or misleading.

Explanation: An agent shall not be required to obtain written approval of the company prior to issue for:

(*i*) those advertisements developed by the insurer and provided to the agents;
(*ii*) generic advertisements limited to information like the agent's name, logo, address and phone number; and
(*iii*) advertisements that consist only of simple and correct statements describing the availability of lines of insurance, references to experience, service and qualifications of agents; but making no reference to specific policies, benefits, costs of insurers.

7. Advertising by insurance intermediaries. Only properly licensed intermediaries may advertise or solicit insurance through advertisements .

8. Advertisement on the Internet.

1. Every insurer or intermediary's website or portal shall
   (*i*) include disclosure statements which outline the site's specific policies vis-a-vis the privacy of personal information for the protection of both their own businesses and the consumers they serve;
   (*ii*) display their registration/license numbers on their websites.
2. For the purposes of these regulations, except where otherwise specifically excluded or restricted, no form or policy otherwise permissible for use shall be deemed invalid or impermissible if such form or policy accurately reflects the intentions of the parties in such form or policy as published electronically or transmitted electronically between parties.

9. Identity of advertiser. Every advertisement for insurance shall

(*i*) State clearly and unequivocally that insurance is the subject matter of the solicitation; and
(*ii*) State the full registered name of the insurer/intermediary/insurance agent.

10. Endorsements and other third-party involvement.

1. A third party, group or association shall not:
   (*i*) distribute information about an insurance policy, intermediary or insurer on its letterhead;
   (*ii*) allow an insurance intermediary or insurer to distribute information about an insurance policy, insurance or insurance company on its letterhead;

(*iii*) distribute information about an individual insurance policy, or about an intermediary or insurer in its envelopes, unless

(*a*) the third party is providing only a distribution service for the insurance advertisement and is not itself soliciting the coverage, and

(*b*) the insurance information is a piece separate from any other information distributed by the third party and clearly indicates its origin;

(*iv*) recommend that its members purchase specific insurance products;

(*v*) imply that a person must become a member of its organization in order to purchase the policy;

(*vi*) imply that a purchaser of a policy by becoming a member of a limited group of persons shall receive special advantages from the insurer not provided for in the policy;

Provided that a third party, group or association may:

(*i*) endorse an insurance company or insurance intermediary's product and provide truthful statements, quotes and testimonials endorsing the insurance products to the insurance company for use in the company's advertisements, so long as the language does not convey directly or indirectly a recommendation that members of the organisation purchase the products;

(*ii*) provide an insurance company with information about its membership and collect compensation based upon sales for that information.

11. Procedure for action in case of complaint.

1. If an advertisement is not in accordance with these regulations the Authority may take action in one or more of the following ways:

(*i*) issue a letter to the advertiser seeking information within a specific time, not being more than ten days from the date of issue of the letter;

(*ii*) direct the advertiser to correct or modify the advertisement already issued in a manner suggested by the Authority with a stipulation that the corrected or modified advertisement shall receive the same type of publicity as the one sought to be corrected or modified;

(*iii*) direct the advertiser to discontinue the advertisement forthwith;

(*iv*) any other action deemed fit by the Authority, keeping in view the circumstances of the case, to ensure that the interests of the public are protected.

The advertiser may seek additional time from the Authority to comply with the directions justifying the reasons therefore. The Authority, may, however, refuse to grant extension of time if it feels that the advertiser is seeking time only to delay the matters.

Any failure on the part of the advertiser to comply with the directions of the Authority may entail the Authority to take such action as deemed necessary including levy of penalty.

12. Adherence to advertisement code. Every insurer or intermediary shall follow recognised standards of professional conduct as prescribed by the Advertisement Standards Council of India (ASCI) and discharge its functions in the interest of the policyholders.

13. Statutory warning.

1. Every proposal for an insurance product shall carry the following stipulation, as prescribed in section 41 of the Insurance Act, 1938 (4 of the 1938):

"No person shall allow or offer to allow, either directly or indirectly, as an inducement to any person to take out or renew or continue an insurance in respect of any kind of risk relating to lives or property in India, any rebate of the whole or part of the commission payable or any rebate of the premium shown on the policy, nor shall any person taking out or renewing or continuing a policy accept any rebate, except such rebate as may be allowed in accordance with the published prospectus or tables of the insurer."

2. If any person fails to comply with sub-regulation (1) above, he shall be liable to payment of a fine which may extend to rupees five hundred.

INSURANCE REGULATORY AND DEVELOPMENT AUTHORITY (LICENSING OF INSURANCE AGENTS) REGULATIONS, 2000

F.No. IRDA/Reg./7/2000.

In exercise of the powers conferred by sub-section (6) of section 42 and clauses (k), (1), (m), (n), (0) and (p) of sub-section (2) of section 114A of the Insurance Act, 1938 (4 of 1938), the Authority, in consultation with the Insurance Advisory Committee, hereby makes the following regulations, namely:

1. Short title and commencement.

1. These regulations may be called Insurance Regulatory and Development Authority (Licensing of Insurance Agents) Regulations, 2000.
2. They shall come into force on tlhe date of their publication in the Official Gazette.

2. Definitions. In these regulations, unless the context otherwise requires:

(*a*) "Act" means the insurance, Act,1938 (4 of 1938);

(*b*) "Approved Institution' means an Institution engaged in education and/or training particularly in the area of insurance sales, service and marketing, approved and notified by the Authority;

(*c*) "Authority" means the Insurance Regulatory and Development Authority established under the provisions of Section 3 of the Insurance Regulatory and Development Authority Act, 1999 (41 of 1999);

(*d*) "Composite insurance agent" means an insurance agent who holds a licence to act as an insurance agent for a life insurer and a general insurer;

(*e*) "Corporate Agent" means a person other than an individual as specified in clause (*i*);

(*f*) "Designated person" means an officer normally in charge of marketing operations, as specified by an insurer, and authorised by the Authority to issue or renew licences under these regulations;

(*g*) "Examination Body" means an Institution, which conducts pre-recruitment tests for insurance agents and which is duly recognised by the Authority;

(*h*) "Licence" means a certificate of licence to act as an insurance agent issued under these regulations;

(*i*) "Person" means:

(i) an individual;

(*ii*) a firm' or

(*iii*) a company formed under the Companies Act, 1956 (1 of 1956), and includes a banking company as defined in clause (4A) of section 2 of the Act;

(j) "Practical Training" includes orientation, particularly in the area of insurance sales, service and marketing, through training modules as approved by the Authority;

(*k*) "Proposal form" means an application for purchase of an insurance product which shall be the basis of insurance contract;

(*l*) "Prospect" means a potential purchaser of an insurance product;

(*m*) "Recognised Board or Institution" means such board or institution as may be recognised by any State Government or the Central Government.

2. All words and expressions used herein and not defined but defined in the Insurance Act, 1938 (4 of 1938), or in the Insurance Regulatory and Development Authority Act, 1999 (41 of 1999), shall have the meanings respectively assigned to them in those Acts.

3. Issue or renewal of licence.

1. A person desiring to obtain or renew a licence (hereinafter referred to as "the applicant") to act as an insurance agent or a composite insurance agent shall proceed as follows:
   (*a*) the applicant shall make an application to a designated person:
   (*i*) in Form IRDA-Agents-VA, if the applicant is an individual;
   (*ii*) in Form IRDA-Agents-VC, if the applicant is a firm or a company;
   Provided that the applicant, who desires to be a composite insurance agent, shall make two separate applications.
   (*b*) The fees payable by the applicant to the Authority shall be as specified in Regulation 7.
2. The designated person may, on receipt of the application along with the evidence of payment of fees to the Authority, and on being satisfied that the applicant—
   (*i*) possesses the qualifications as specified-under Regulation 4;
   (*ii*) possesses the practical training as specified under Regulation 5;
   (*iii*) has passed the examination as specified under Regulation 6;
   (*iv*) has furnished the application complete in all respects;
   (*v*) has the requisite knowledge to solicit and procure insurance business; and
   (*vi*) is capable of providing the necessary service to the policyholders;
   grant or renew, as the case may be, a licence in Form IRDA-Agents-VB, along with identity card in Form IRDA-Agents-VZ:

   Provided that in the case of a corporate agent, the identity card shall be in Form IRDA-Agent -VY.

   Provided further that such identity card from one life insurer and such identity card from one general insurer shall be provided to the applicant seeking licence to act as a composite insurance agent.

   Provided further that in the case of a firm or a company, all of its partners or directors, as the case may be, shall fulfil the requirements of sub-clauses (*i*) to (*iii*).

   Provided further a licence issued in accordance with this regulation shall entitle the applicant to act as insurance agent for one life insurer or one general insurer or both, as the case may be.
3. If the designated person refuses to grant or renew a licence under this regulation, he shall give the reasons therefor to the applicant.

4. Qualifications of the applicant. The applicant shall possess the minimum qualification of a pass in 12th Standard or equivalent examination conducted by any recognised Board/Institution, where the applicant resides in a place wtth a population of five thousand or more as per the last census, and a pass in 10th Standard or equivalent examination from a recognised Board/Institution if the applicant resides in any other place.

5. Practical Training.

1. The applicant shall have completed from an approved institution, at least, one hundred hours practical training in life or general insurance business, as the case may be, which may be spread over three to four weeks, where such applicant is seeking licence for the first time to act as insurance agent.

   Provided that the applicant shall have completed from an approved institution, at least, one hundred fifty hours' practical training in life and general insurance business, which may be spread over six to eight weeks, where such applicant is seeking licence for the first time to act as a composite insurance agent.

2. Where the applicant, referred to under sub-regulation (I), is
   (*a*) an Associate/Fellow of the Insurance Institute of India, Mumbai;
   (*b*) an Associate/Fellow of the Institute of Chartered Accountants of India, New Delhi;
   (*c*) an Associate/Fellow of the Institute of Costs and Works Accountants of India, Calcutta;
   (*d*) an Associate/Fellow of the Institute of Company Secretaries of India, New Delhi;
   (*e*) an Associate/Fellow of the Actuarial Society of India, Mumbai;
   (*f*) a Master of Business Administration of any Institution/University recognised by any State Government or the Central Government; or
   (*g*) possessing any professional qualification in marketing from any Institution/University recognised by any State Government or the Central Govemment

   he shall have completed, at least, fifty hours practical training from an approved institution.

   Provided that such applicant shall have completed from an approved institution, at least, seventy hours practical training in life and general insurance business, where such applicant is seeking licence for the first time to act as a composite insurance agent.

3. An applicant, who has been granted a licence after the commencement of these regulations, before seeking renewal of licence to act as an insurance agent, shall have completed, at least twenty-five hours' practical training in life or general insurance business, as the case may be, from an approved institution.

   Provided that such applicant before seeking renewal of licence to act as a composite insurance agent shall have completed from an approved institution, at least, fifty hours' practical training in life and general insurance business.

6. Examination. The Applicant shall have passed the pre-recruitment examination in life or general insurance business, or both, as the case may be, conducted by the Insurance Institute of India, Mumbai, or any other examination body.

7. Fees payable.

1. The fees payable to the Authority for issue or renewal of licence to act as insurance agent or a composite insurance agent shall be rupee two hundred and fifty.
2. The additional fees payable to the Authority, under the circumstances mentioned in sub-section (3) of section 42 of the Act, shall be rupees one hundred.

8. Code of Conduct.

1. Every person holding a licence, shall adhere to the code of conduct specified below:
   (*i*) **Every insurance agent shall:**
      (*a*) identify himself and the insurance company of whom he is an insurance agent;
      (*b*) disclose his licence to the prospect on demand;
      (*c*) disseminate the requisite information in respect of insurance products offered for sale by his insurer and take into account the needs of the prospect while recommending a specific insurance plan;
      (*d*) disclose the scales of commission in respect of the insurance product offered for sale, if asked by the prospect;
      (*e*) indicate the premium to be charged by the insurer for the insurance product offered for sale;
      (*f*) explain to the prospect the nature of information required in the proposal form by the insurer, and also the importance of disclosure of material information in the purchase of an insurance contract;

(*g*) bring to the notice of the insurer any adverse habits or income inconsistency of the prospect, in the form of a report (called "Insurance Agent's Confidential Report") along with every proposal submitted to the insurer, and any material fact that may adversely affect the underwriting decision of the insurer as regards acceptance of the proposal, by making all reasonable enquiries about the prospect;

(*h*) inform promptly the prospect about the acceptance or rejection of the proposal by the insurer;

(*i*) obtain the requisite documents at, the time of filing the proposal form with the insurer; and other documents subsequently asked for by the insurer for completion of the proposal;

(*j*) render necessary assistance to the policyholders or claimants or beneficiaries in complying with the requirements for settlement of claims by the insurer;

(*k*) advise every individual policyholder to effect nomination or assignment or change of address or exercise of options, as the case may be, and offer necessary assistance in this behalf, wherever necessary;

(*ii*) **No insurance agent shall:**

(*a*) solicit or procure insurance business without holding a valid licence;

(*b*) induce the prospect to omit any material information in the proposal form;

(*c*) induce the prospect to submit wrong information in the proposal form or documents submitted to the insurer for acceptance of the proposal;

(*d*) behave in a discourteous manner with the prospect;

(*e*) interfere with any proposal inttoduced by any other insurance agent;

(*f*) offer different rates, advantages, terms and conditions other than those offered by his insurer;

(*g*) demand or receive a share of proceeds from the beneficiary under an insurance contract;

(*h*) force a policyholder to terminate the existing policy and to effect a new proposal from him within three years from the date of such termination;

(*i*) have, in case of corporate agent, a portfolio of insurance business under which the premium is in excess of fifty percent of total premium procured, in any year, from one person (who is not an individual) or one organisation or one group of organisations;

(*j*) apply for fresh licence to act as an insurance agent, if his licence was earlier cancelled by the designated person, and a period of five years has not elapsed from the date of such cancellation;

(*k*) become or remain a director of any insurance company;

(*iii*) Every insurance agent shall, with a view to conserve the insurance business already procured through him, make every attempt to ensure remittance of the premiums by the policyholders within the stipulated time, by giving notice to the policyholder orally and in writing;

9. Cancellation of Licence. The designated person may cancel a licence of an insurance agent, if the insurance agent suffers, at any time during the currency of the licence, from any of the disqualifications mentioned in sub-section (4) of section 42 of the Act, and recover from him the licence and the identity card issued earlier.

10. Issue of duplicate Licence. The Authority may issue a duplicate licence replace a licence lost, destroyed, or mutilated on payment a fee of rupees fifty.

11. Non-application to existing insurance agents. Nothing contained in Regulations 4 to 6 of these Regulations shall apply to the existing agents before the commencement of these Regulations.

FORM IRDA-AGENTS-VA
(SEE REGULATION 3)

Insurance Regulatory and Development Authority
(Licensing of Insurance Agents) Regulations, 2000

APPLICATION FOR A LICENCE /RENEWAL OF LICENCE TO ACT AS AN INSURANCE AGENT

TO
THE INSURANCE REGULATORY
AND DEVELOPMENT AUTHORITY
DEPARTMENT OF LICENSING,
NEW DELHI

DEAR SIRS,

I request that -------

(*a*) a licence to act as an insurance agent*/a composite insurance agent* may be granted to me.

(*b*) *my licence bearing number ______________ and expiry date ______________ may be renewed for a further period of three years.

2. I hereby declare that particulars given below are true and that the licence for which I apply will be used only by myself for soliciting or procuring insurance business for one life insurance's */one general insurer*/both*.

(1) Name: [ ][ ][ ][ ][ ][ ][ ][ ][ ][ ][ ][ ][ ][ ][ ][ ][ ]

(2) Father's, Husband's
Name: [ ][ ][ ][ ][ ][ ][ ][ ][ ][ ][ ][ ][ ][ ][ ][ ]

(3) Full Address:
House No.: [ ][ ][ ][ ][ ][ ][ ][ ][ ][ ][ ][ ][ ][ ][ ][ ]
Street: [ ][ ][ ][ ][ ][ ][ ][ ][ ][ ][ ][ ][ ][ ][ ][ ][ ]
Town: [ ][ ][ ][ ][ ][ ][ ][ ][ ][ ][ ][ ][ ][ ][ ][ ][ ]
District: [ ][ ][ ][ ][ ][ ][ ][ ][ ][ ][ ][ ][ ][ ][ ][ ][ ]
State: [ ][ ][ ][ ][ ][ ][ ][ ][ ][ ][ ][ ][ ][ ][ ][ ][ ]
Pin Code:[ ][ ][ ][ ][ ]
Tel No. [ ][ ][ ][ ][ ][ ][ ][ ][ ][ ][ ][ ][ ][ ][ ][ ]
(STD Code — Number)

(4) Date of Birth: [ ][ ]—[ ][ ]—[ ][ ]
Day Month Year

(5) Title: State 1 if are Mr., 2 Mrs., 3 Miss:

(6) If you ever held a Licence, state No. and date of expiry, otherwise say "Nil".

(*a*) Licence Number: [ ][ ][ ][ ][ ][ ][ ][ ][ ][ ][ ][ ][ ][ ]

(*b*) Date of Expiry: [ ][ ][ ][ ][ ][ ][ ][ ]
Day Month Year

(7) If you apply for licence to work for a life insurer, state 1, for a general insurer, state 2, for both state 3 in the box. [ ]

(8) If your are an applicant from a rural place, State 1, in the box . [ ]

(9) Education Qualifications:

State 1, if you passed Class X; 2: Class XII; 3: Graduate; 4: Post-graduate; 5: if you hold a professional qualification such as ACA, FASI, AICWA.): [ ]

(10) Give particulars of pass in pre-recruitment test conducted by the Insurance Institute of India or any examination body:

(*a*) Name of Examination Body: [ ][ ][ ][ ][ ][ ][ ][ ][ ][ ][ ][ ][ ]
[ ][ ][ ][ ][ ][ ][ ][ ][ ][ ]

(*b*) Candidate's Number: [ ][ ][ ][ ][ ][ ][ ][ ][ ][ ][ ][ ][ ][ ]

(*c*) Centre of Examination: [ ][ ][ ][ ][ ][ ][ ][ ][ ][ ][ ][ ][ ]
[ ][ ][ ][ ][ ][ ][ ][ ][ ][ ]

(*d*) Date of Passing: [ ][ ]—[ ][ ]—[ ][ ][ ][ ]
Day Month Year

(11) Give particulars of Practical raining completed from an approved institution.

(*a*) Training Hours completed: [ ][ ]

(*b*) Name of Training Institute: [ ][ ][ ][ ][ ][ ][ ][ ][ ][ ][ ][ ]
[ ][ ][ ][ ][ ][ ][ ][ ][ ][ ]

(*c*) Candidate's Number: [ ][ ][ ][ ][ ][ ][ ][ ][ ][ ][ ][ ][ ][ ]

(*d*) Centre (Place) of Training:[ ][ ][ ][ ][ ][ ][ ][ ][ ][ ][ ][ ]
[ ][ ][ ][ ][ ][ ][ ][ ][ ][ ]

(*e*) Starting Date of Training : [ ][ ]—[ ][ ]—[ ][ ][ ][ ]
Day Month Year

3. I further declare that:

(*a*) I have not been found to be of unsound mind by a court of competent jurisdiction;

(*b*) I have not been found guilty of criminal misappropriation or criminal breach of trust or cheating or forgery or an abetment of or attempt to commit any such offence by a court of competent jurisdiction;

(*c*) I have not been found guilty of or to have knowingly participated in or connived at any fraud, dishonestly or mis-representation against an insurer or an insured in the course of any judicial proceeding relating to any policy of insurance or the winding up of an insurance company or in the course of an investigation of the affairs of an insurer; and

(*d*) # have not violated the code of conduct specified under Regulation 8 of Insurance Regulatory and Development Authority (Licensing of Insurance Agents) Regulations, 2000.

4. I have made the payment of licence fee of rupees two hundred and fifty and for which I enclose the documentary evidence.

5. I enclose the following documents in supports of the educational qualification, pre-recruitment test, and the practical training.

(a) ____________________

(b) ____________________

Place: Yours faithfully,

Date:

Signature of applicant

(*Strike out portion not required).

(# not applicable to the applicants seeking licence for the first time.)

Notes and Instructions

1. An individual can apply for only one licence which will entitle him to solicit or procure insurance business of any class and to act as an insurance agent for one life insurer, one general insurer, or both.
2. The application should be filled in, as far as possible, in Hindi language or English language.
3. Any correction or alteration made many answer to the questions in the application should be initialled by the applicant.
4. An applicant must be at, least 18 years of age on the date of the application. If required the applicant shall furnish proof of age.
5. An applicant shall furnish the proof of educational qualification, pass in the pre-recruitment test conducted by the Insurance Institute of India, Mumbai or an examination body approved by the Insurance Regulatory and Development Authority, and completion of practical training from a training institution approved by the Insurance Regulatory and Development Authority, along with the application. This is not applicable where the applicant is an absorbed agent.
6. The fees payable by an applicant is rupees two hundred and fifty.
7. The name and licence No. given in the application are identical with those shown in the last licence held. If there is any subsequent change in the name, the reasons for the same should be stated furnishing documentary evidence for the name.
8. The application should reach the designated person before the expiry of licence held by the applicant but not more than three months before such expiry. If the application does not reach the designated person at least 30 days before the date on which the last licence ceases to be in force, an additional fee of one hundred rupees should be payable. In this connection please also refer to the provisions of subsections (3) and (3A) of section 42 of the Insurance Act, 1938.
9. If the applicant desires to work for a life insurer or a general insurer or both, as the case may be, he should enclose the documentary evidence of the relevant pass in the pre-recruitment test and the completion of the relevant practical training.

FORM IRDA-AGENTS- VB

(SEE REGULATION 3)

INSURANCE REGULATORY AND DEVELOPMENT AUTHORITY (LICENSING OF INSURANCE AGENTS) REGULATIONS, 2000.

INSURANCE REGULATORY AND DEVELOPMENT AUTHORITY, NEW DELHI

LICENCE NO. [ ][ ][ ][ ][ ][ ][ ][ ][ ][ ][ ]

LICENCE TO ACT AS AN INSURANCE AGENT UNDER PART II OF THE INSURANCE ACT, 1938

NAME OF INSURANCE AGENT*/
COMPOSITE INSURANCE
AGENT*: ____________________

ADDRESS:

Having paid the prescribed fee and having made the necessary declaration is hereby authorised to act an insurance agent for three years from ____________________ for procuring or soliciting insurance business of one life insurer*/ one general insurer*/both*.

(*strike out portion not required)

Place:

Date:

For Insurance Regulatory and Development Authority

Designated Person:

Signature of Licence holder:

This licence is not valid unless it bears a fascimile of the signature of the chairperson of the insurance and Regulatory and Development Authority and the initials of a person authorised by him in this behalf, the signature of the licence holder and the identity card (s). The licence holder should put his signature as soon as licence is received.

(See Notes on the reverse)

Notes

1. **If it is desired to renew this licence for a further period the procedure laid down in Regulation 3 of INSURANCE REGULATORY AND DEVELOPMENT AUTHORITY (LICENSING OF INSURANCE AGENTS) REGULATIONS, 2000, SHALL BE FOLLOWED, AND APPLICATION for renewal should reach the Designated Person before the licence expires. In this connection attention is also invited to the provisions of sub-sections (3) and 3(A) of section 42 of the Insurance Act, 1938.**
2. **This licence authorises the licence holder to act as an agent for the insurance business specified thereunder, and therefore no identifying mark or note of any description by which the identity of an insurer might be established should be placed on the licence.**
3. **No correction in this licence will be valid unless initialled by the Insurance Regulatory and Development Authority or a person authorised by in this behalf.**
4. **The attention of the licence holder is drawn to the code of conduct specified under Regulation 8 of INSURANCE REGULATORY AND DEVELOPMENT AUTHORITY (LICENSING OF INSURANCE AGENTS) REGULATIONS, 2000, and any violation of code of conduct may result is cancellation of licence.**

FORM IRDA-AGENTS-VC
(SEE REGULATION 3)

Insurance Regulatory and Development Authority
(Licensing of Insurance Agents) Regulations, 2000.

APPLICATION FORM A FIRM OR COMPANY FOR A LICENCE/ RENEWAL OF LICENCE TO ACT AS AN INSURANCE AGENT

TO

THE INSURANCE REGULATORY
AND DEVELOPMENT AUTHORITY
DEPARTMENT OF LICENSING,
NEW DELHI.

DEAR SIRS,

I request that —

(*a*) *a licence to act as an insurance agent*/a composite insurance agent* may be granted to our Firm/Company;

(*b*) *our licence bearing number ____________ and expiry date ____________ may be renewed for a further period of three years.

2. It hereby declared that particulars given below are true and that the licence for which our Firm/ Company apply will be used only by our Firm/Company for soliciting or procuring insurance business.

(1) Name: [ ][ ][ ][ ][ ][ ][ ][ ][ ][ ][ ][ ][ ][ ][ ][ ][ ]

(2) Full Address: [ ][ ][ ][ ][ ][ ][ ][ ][ ][ ][ ][ ][ ][ ][ ][ ]

House No: [ ][ ][ ][ ][ ][ ][ ][ ][ ][ ][ ][ ][ ][ ][ ][ ]

Street: [ ][ ][ ][ ][ ][ ][ ][ ][ ][ ][ ][ ][ ][ ][ ][ ][ ]

Town: [ ][ ][ ][ ][ ][ ][ ][ ][ ][ ][ ][ ][ ][ ][ ][ ][ ]

District: [ ][ ][ ][ ][ ][ ][ ][ ][ ][ ][ ][ ][ ][ ][ ][ ][ ]

State: [ ][ ][ ][ ][ ][ ][ ][ ][ ][ ][ ][ ][ ][ ][ ][ ][ ]

Pin Code:[ ][ ][ ][ ][ ][ ]

Telephone No.: [ ][ ][ ][ ][ ][ ][ ][ ]—[ ][ ][ ][ ][ ][ ][ ]

(STD Code — Number)

(3) (*i*) (In the case of a Firm) the names of all the partners therein:

(*ii*) (In the case of Company) the names of the Directors:

(4) Whether the Partnership Deed*/Memorandum of Association* contains as main objects the carrying on of soliciling or procuring insurance business as an insurance agent. (Please enclose a certified copy of the Partnership Deed*/Memorandum of Association*).

(5) The date from when the licence should be effective:

(6) If you apply for licence to work for a life insurer, state 1, a general insurer, state 2, for both, state 3 in the box. [ ]

3. It is further declared that —

(*a*) any partner of our Firm*/any Director of our Company* has not been found to be of unsound mind by a court of competent jurisdiction;

(*b*) any partner of our Firm*/any Director of our Company* has not been found guilty of criminal misappropriation or criminal breach of trust or cheating or forgery or an abetment of or attempt to commit any such offence by a court of competent jurisdiction;

(*c*) any partner of our Firm*/any Director of our Company* has not been found guilty of or to have knowingly participated in or connived at any fraud, dishonestly or mis-representation against an insurer or an insured in the course of any judicial proceeding relating to any policy of insurance or the winding up of an insurance company or in the course of an investigation of the affairs of an insurer;

(*d*) any partner of our Firm*/any Director of our Company* has not violated the code of conduct specified under Regulation 8 of Insurance Regulatory and Development Authority (Licensing of Insurance Agents) Regulations, 2000;

(*e*) the application in Form IRDA-Agents-V for each partner of our Firm*/each Director of our Company* has been enclosed along with this form;

(*f*) any partner of our Firm*/any Director of our Company* is not a minor.

4. The payment of licence fee of rupees two hundred and fifty has been made and for which the receipt is enclosed.
5. The documents in support of the educational qualification, pre-recruitment test, and the practical training, in respect of all partners of our Firm*/all Directors of our Company* have been enclosed along with this form.

(* Strike out portion not required.)

Place: Yours faithfully,

Date:

Signature of applicant

Notes

1. The application should be filled in, as far as possible, in Hindi language or English language.
2. Any correction or alteration made in any answer to the questions in the application should be initialled by the applicant.
3. The fees payable by an applicant is rupees two hundred and fifty.
4. The name and the licence No. given in the application are identical with those shown in the last licence held. If there is any subsequent change in the name, the reasons for the same should be stated furnishing documentary evidence for the same.
5. The application should reach the designated person before the expiry of licence held by the application but not more than three months before such expiry. If the application does not reach the designated person at least 30 days before the date on which the last licence ceases to be in force, an additional fee of one hundred rupees should be payable. In this connection please also refer to the provisions of sub-sections (3) and (3A) of section 42 of the Insurance Act, 1938.
6. If the, Firm or Company desires to act as an insurance agent or a composite insurance agent, as the case may be, the documentary evidence of the relevant pass in the pre-recruitment test and the completion of the relevant practical training of partners of the Firm or directors of the Company should be enclosed.
7. In case of a Firm, the signatory to the application (being a partner) should enclose a certified copy of the resolution of all the partners authorising him to make the application. In the case of a Company, the signatory to the application (being a director) should enclose a certified copy of the resolution of Board of Directors authorising him to make the application.

FORM IRDA-AGENTS-VZ
(SEE REGULATION 3)

INSURANCE REGULATORY AND DEVELOPMENT AUTHORITY (LICENSING OF INSURANCE AGENTS) REGULATIONS, 2000)

Individual Insurance Agent's identity card

Photo

Agent's Licence No.:

Name of the Agent:

Father's/Husband's Name:

Office of the Insurer with whom the agent is attached:

Agent's signature

The holder of this card is authorised to sell our insurance products, as per our terms and conditions.

Male/Female

Issued on:

[ ][ ]-[ ][ ]-[ ][ ]

Signature of Designated Person

Valid upto:

Name of Insurer (With Seal)

[ ][ ]-[ ][ ]-[ ][ ]

born on:

[ ][ ]-[ ][ ]-[ ][ ]

(Please see on the reverse)

Address and telephone number of the Insurer: (If required to be contacted by any one in connection with the holder of this card):

Address and telephone Numbers of the Agent:

IRDA (Protection of Policyholders' Interests) Regulations 2002

The Insurance Regulatory and Development Authority in exercise of the powers conferred by Section 114A of the Insurance Act, 1938 read with Sections 14 & 26 of the IRDA Act, 1999 and in consultation with the Insurance Advisory Council has made the IRDA (Protection of Policyholder's Interests) Regulations, 2002. These regulations have been notified on 26th April, 2002 and here we reproduce these regulations in full. These regulations establish the benchmarks in the quality of sales as well as service in life insurance and it is necessary that every employee and agent in the organisation is fully aware of regulations as well as their implications.

1. Short title and commencement

1.(1) These regulations may be called the Insurance Regulatory and Development Authority (Protection of Policyholder's Interests) Regulations, 2002.

(2) They shall come into force on the date of their publication in the Official Gazette and shall apply to all contracts of insurance effected thereafter, except regulation 4(1) which shall come into force on 1st October, 2002.

(3) These Regulations are in addition to any other regulations made by Authority, which may, inter alia, provide for protection of the interest of policyholders.

(4) These Regulations apply to all insurers, insurance agents, insurance intermediaries and policyholders.

2. Definitions

2.(1) in these regulations, unless the context otherwise requires:

(*a*) "Act" means the Insurance Act, 1938 (4 of 1938);

(*b*) "Authority" means the Insurance Regulatory and Development Authority established under the provisions of section 3 of the Insurance Regulatory and Development Authority Act, 1999 (41 of 1999);

(*c*) "Cover" means an insurance contract whether in the form of a policy or a cover note or a Certificate of Insurance or any other form prevalent in the industry of evidence the existence of an insurance contract;

(*d*) "Proposal form" means a form to be filled in by the proposer for insurance, for furnishing all material information required by the insurer in respect of a risk, in order to enable the insurer to decide whether to accept or decline, to undertake the risk, and in the event of acceptance of the risk, to determine the rates, terms and conditions of a cover to be granted.

Explanation: "Material" for the purpose of these regulations shall mean and include all important, essential and relevant information in the context of underwriting the risk to be covered by the insurer.

(*e*) "Prospectus" means a document issued by the insurer or in its behalf to the prospective buyers of insurance, and should contain such particulars as are mentioned in Rule, 11 of Insurance Rules, 1939 and includes a brochure or leaflet serving the purpose. Such a document should also specify the type and character of riders on the main product indicating the nature of benefits flowing thereupon;

(*f*) Words and expressions used and not defined in these regulations, but defined in the Act, or the Life Insurance Corporation Act, 1956, (31 of 1956) or the General Insurance Business (Nationalisation) Act, 1972 (57 of 1972), or the Insurance Regulatory and Development Authority Act, 1999 (41 of 1999) or the Insurance Rules, 1939 shall have the meanings respectively assigned to them in those Acts of the Rules.

3. Point of Sale

1. Notwithstanding anything mentioned in regulations 2(e) above, a prospectus of any insurance product shall clearly state the scope of benefits, the extent of insurance cover and in an explicit manner explain the warranties, exceptions and conditions of the insurance cover and, in case of life insurance, whether the product is participating (with-profits) or non-participating (without-profits). The allowable rider or riders on the product shall be clearly spelt out with regard to their scope of benefits, and in no case, the premium relatable to all the riders put together shall exceed 30% of the premium of the main product.

   Explanation: The rider or riders attached to a life policy shall bear the nature and character of the main policy, *viz.* participating or non-participating and accordingly the life insurer shall make provisions, etc., in its books.

2. An insurer or its agent or other intermediary shall provide all material information in respect of a proposed cover to the prospect to enable the prospect to decide on the best cover that would be in his or her interest.

3. Where the prospect depends upon the advice of the insurer or his agent or an insurance intermediary, such a person must advise the prospect dispassionately.

4. Where, for any reason, the proposal and other connected papers are not filled by the prospect, a certificate may be incorporated at the end of proposal form from the prospect that the contents of the form and documents have been fully explained to him and that he has fully understood the significant of the proposed contract.
5. In the process of sale, the insurer or its agent or any intermediary shall act according to the code of conduct prescribed by:
   (*i*) the Authority
   (*ii*) the Councils that have been established under section 64C of the Act and
   (*iii*) the recognised professional body or association of which the agent or intermediary or insurance intermediary is a member.

4. Proposal for Insurance

1. Except in cases of a marine insurance cover, where current market practices do not insist on a written proposal form, in all cases, a proposal for grant of a cover, either for life business or for general business, must be evidenced by a written document. It is the duty of an insurer to furnish to the insured free of charge, within 30 days, of the acceptance of a proposal, a copy of the proposal form.
2. Forms and documents used in the grant of cover may, depending upon the circumstances of each case, be made available in languages recognised under the Constitution of India.
3. In filling the form of proposal, the prospect is to be guided by the provisions of Section 45 of the Act. Any proposal form seeking information for grant of life cover may prominently state therein the requirements of Section 45 of the Act.
4. Where a proposal form is not used, the insurer shall record the information obtained orally or in writing, and confirm it within a period of 15 days thereof with the proposer and incorporate the information in its cover note or policy. The onus of proof shall rest with the insurer in respect of any information not so recorded, where the insurer claims that the proposer suppressed any material information or provided misleading or false Information on any matter material to the grant of a cover.
5. Where the benefit of nomination is available to the proposer, in terms of the Act or the conditions of policy, the insurer shall draw the attention of the proposer to it an encourage the prospect to avail the facility.
6. Proposals shall be processed by the insurer with speed and efficiency and all decisions thereof shall be communicated by it in writing within a reasonable period not exceeding 15 days from receipt of proposals by the insurer.

5. Grievance Redressal Procedure

Every insurer shall have in place proper procedures and effective mechanism to address complaints and grievances of policyholders efficiently and with speed and the same along with the information in respect of Insurance Ombudsman shall be communicated to the policyholder along with the policy document and as may be found necessary.

6. Matters to be Stated in Life Insurance Policy

1. A life insurance policy shall clearly state:
   (*a*) the name of the plan governing the policy, its terms and conditions;
   (*b*) whether it is participating in profits or not;
   (*c*) the basis of participation in profits such as cash bonus, deferred bonus, simple or compound reversionary bonus;

(*d*) the benefits payable and the contingencies upon which these are payable and the other terms and conditions of the insurance contract;

(*e*) the details of the riders attaching to the main policy;

(*f*) the date of commencement of risk and the date of maturity or date(s) on which the benefits are payable;

(*g*) the premiums payable, periodicity of payment, grace period allowed for payment of the premium, the date of the last instalment of Premium, the implication of discontinuing the payment of an instalment(s) of premium and also the provisions of a guaranteed surrender value.

(*h*) the age at entry and whether the same has been admitted;

(*i*) the policy requirements for (*a*) conversion of the policy into paid up policy, (*b*) surrender (*c*) non-forfeiture, and (*d*) revival of lapsed policies;

(*j*) contingencies excluded from the scope of the cover, both in respect of the main policy and the riders;

(*k*) the provisions for nomination, assignment, and loans on security of the policy and a statement that the rate of interest payable on such loan amount shall be as prescribed by the insurer at the time of taking the loan;

(*l*) any special clauses or conditions, such as, first pregnancy clause, suicide clause etc.;

(*m*) the address of the insurer to which all communications in respect of the policy shall be sent.

(*n*) the documents that are normally required to be submitted by a claimant in support of a claim under the policy.

2. While acting under regulation 6(1) in forwarding the policy to the insured, the insurer shall inform by the letter forwarding the policy that he has a period of 15 days from the date of receipt of the policy document to review the terms and conditions of the policy and where the insured disagrees to any of those terms or conditions, he has the option to return the policy stating the reasons for his objection, when he shall be entitled to a refund of the premium paid, subject only to a deduction of a proportionate risk premium for the period on cover and the expenses incurred by the insurer on medical examination of the proposer and stamp duty charges.

3. In respect of a unit linked policy, in addition to the deductions under sub-regulation (2) of this regulation, the insurer shall also be entitled to repurchase the unit at the price of the units on the date of cancellation .

4. In respect of a cover, where premium charged is dependent on age, the insurer shall ensure that the age is admitted as far as possible before insurance of the policy document. In case where age has not been admitted by the time the policy is issued, the insurer shall make efforts to obtain proof of age and admit the same as soon as possible.

7. Matters to be stated in general insurance policy

1. A general insurance policy shall clearly state:

(*a*) the name(s) and address(es) of the insured and of any bank(s) or any other person having financial interest in the subject matter of insurance;

(*b*) full description of the property or interest insured;

(*c*) the location or locations of the property or interest insured under the policy and where appropriate, with respective insured values;

(*d*) period of Insurance;

(*e*) sums insured;

(*f*) perils covered and not covered;

(*h*) any franchise or deductible applicable;

(*i*) premium payable and where the premium is provisional subject to adjustment, the basis of adjustment of premium be stated;

(*j*) policy terms, conditions and warranties;

(*k*) action to be taken by the insured upon occurrence of a contingency likely to give rise to a claim under the policy;

(*l*) the obligations of the insured in relation to the subject matter of insurance upon occurrence of an event giving rising to a claim and the rights of the insurer in the circumstances;

(*m*) any special conditions attaching to the policy;

(*n*) provision for cancellation of the policy on grounds of misrepresentation, fraud, non-disclosure or material facts or noncooperation of the insured;

(*o*) the address of the insurer to which all communications in respect of the insurance contract should be sent;

(*p*) the details of the riders attaching to the main policy;

(*q*) proforma of any communication the insurer may seek from the policyholders to service the policy.

2. Every insurer shall inform and keep informed periodically the insured on the requirements to be fulfilled by the insured regarding lodging of a claim arising in terms of the policy and the procedures to be followed by him to enable the insurer to settle a claim early.

8. Claims procedure in respect of a life insurance policy

1. A life insurance policy shall state the primary documents which are normally required to be submitted by a claimant in support of a claim.
2. A life insurance company, upon receiving a claim, shall process the claim without delay. Any queries or requirement of additional documents, to the extent possible, shall be raised all at once and not in a piece-meal manner, within a period of 15 days of the receipt of the claim.
3. A claim under a life policy shall be paid or be disputed giving all the relevant reasons, within 30 days from the date of receipt of all relevant papers and clarifications required. However, where the circumstances of a claim warrant an investigation in the opinion of the insurance company, it shall initiate and complete such investigation at the earliest. Where in the opinion of the insurance company the circumstances of a claim warrant an investigation, it shall initiate and complete such investigation at the earliest, in any case not later than 6 months from the time of lodging the claim.
4. Subject to the provisions of section 47 of the Act, where a claim is ready for payment but the payment cannot be made due to any reasons of a proper identification of the payee, the life insurer shall hold the amount for the benefit of the payee and such an amount shall earn interest at the rate applicable to a savings bank account with a scheduled bank (effective from 30 days following the submission of all papers and information).
5. Where there is a delay on the part of the insurer in processing a claim for a reason other than one covered by sub-regulation (4), the life insurance company shall pay interest on the claim amount at a rate which is 2% above the bank rate prevalent at the beginning of the financial year in which the claim is reviewed by it.

9. Claim procedure in respect of a general insurance policy

1. An insured or the claimant shall give notice to the insurer of any loss arising under contract of insurance at the earliest or within such extended time as may be allowed by the insurer. On receipt of such a communication, a general insurer shall respond immediately and give clear indication to the insured on the procedures that he should follow. In cases where a surveyor has to be appointed for assessing a loss/claim, it shall be so done within 72 hours of the receipt of intimation from the insured.
2. Where the insured is unable to furnish all the particulars required by the surveyor or where the surveyor does not receive the full cooperation of the insured, the insurer or the surveyor as the case may be, shall inform in writing the insured about the delay that may result in the assessment of the claim. The surveyor shall be subjected to the code of conduct laid down by the Authority while assessing the loss, and shall communicate his findings to the insurer within 30 days of his appointment with a copy of the report being furnished to the insured, if he so desires. Where, in special circumstances of the case, either due to its special and complicated nature, the surveyor shall under intimation to the insured, seek an extension from the insurer for submission of his report. In no case shall a surveyor take more than six months from the date of his appointment of furnish his report.
3. If an insurer, on the receipt of a survey report, finds that it is incomplete in any respect, he shall require the surveyor under intimation to the insured, to furnish an additional report on certain specific issues as may be required by the insurer. Such a request may be made by the insurer within 15 days of the receipt of the original survey report.
   Provided that the facility of calling for an additional report by the insurer shall not be resorted to more than once in the case of a claim.
4. The surveyor on receipt of this communication shall furnish an additional report within three weeks of the date of receipt of communication from the insurer.
5. On receipt of the survey report or the additional survey report, as the case may be, an insurer shall within a period of 30 days offers a settlement of the claim to the insured. If the insurer, for any reasons to be recorded in writing and communicated to the insured, decides to reject a claim under the policy, it shall do so within a period of 30 days from the receipt of the survey report or the additional survey report, as the case may be.
6. Upon acceptance of an offer of settlement as stated in sub-regulation (5) by the insured, the payment of the amount due shall be made within 7 days from the date of acceptance of the offer by the insured. In the cases of delay in the payment, the insurer shall be liable to pay interest at a rate which is 2% above the bank rate prevalent at the beginning of the financial year in which the claim is reviewed by it.

10. Policyholders' Servicing

1. An insurer carrying on life or general business, as the case may be, shall at all times, respond within 10 days of the receipt of any communication from its policyholders in all matters, such as:
   (*a*) recording change of address;
   (*b*) noting a new nomination or change of nomination under a policy;
   (*c*) nothing an assignment on the policy;
   (*d*) providing information on the current status of a policy indicating matters, such as, accrued, bonus, surrender value and entitlement to a loan;
   (*e*) processing papers and disbursal of a loan on security of policy;
   (*f*) issuance of duplicate policy;

(*g*) issuance of an endorsement under the policy, nothing a change of interest or sum assured or perils insured, financial interest of a bank and other interests; and

(*h*) guidance on the procedure for registering a claim and early settlement thereof.

11. General

1. The requirements of disclosure of "material information" regarding a proposal or policy apply, under these regulations, both to the insurer and the insured.
2. The policyholder shall assist the insurer, if the latter so requires, the prosecution of a proceeding or in the matter of recovery of claims which the insurer has against third parties.
3. The policyholder shall furnish all information that is sought from him by the insurer and also any other information which the insurer considers as having a bearing on other risk to enable the latter to assess properly the risk sought to be covered by a policy.
4. Any breaches of the obligations cast on an insurer or insurance agent or insurance intermediary in terms of these regulations may enable the Authority to initiate action against each or all of them, jointly or severally, under the Act and/or the Insurance Regulatory and Development Authority Act, 1999.

NOTES

NOTES

NOTES

NOTES